CHILTON'S
CHEVROLET
REPAIR MANUAL
1980-1987

President	Lawrence A. Fornasieri
Vice President & General Manager	John P. Kushnerick
Editor-In-Chief	Kerry A. Freeman
Managing Editor	Dean F. Morgantini
Senior Editor	Richard J. Rivele

CHILTON BOOK COMPANY
Chilton Way, Radnor, PA 19089

Manufactured in USA

© 1987 Chilton Book Company

ISBN 0–8019–7772–X
Library of Congress Card Catalog No. 86-47792
34567890   654321098

SAFETY NOTICE

Proper service and repair procedures are vital to the safe, reliable operation of all motor vehicles, as well as the personal safety of those performing repairs. This manual outlines procedures for servicing and repairing vehicles using safe effective methods. The procedures contain many NOTES, CAUTIONS and WARNINGS which should be followed along with standard safety procedures to eliminate the possibility of personal injury or improper service which could damage the vehicle or compromise its safety.

It is important to note that repair procedures and techniques, tools and parts for servicing motor vehicles, as well as the skill and experience of the individual performing the work vary widely. It is not possible to anticipate all of the conceivable ways or conditions under which vehicles may be serviced, or to provide cautions as to all of th epossible hazards that may result. Standard and accepted safety precautions and equipment should be used when handling toxic or flammable fluids, and safety goggles or other protection should be used during cutting, grinding chiseling, prying, or any other process that can cause material removal or projectiles.

Some procedures require the use of tools specially designed for a specific purpose. Before substituting another tool or procedure, you must be completely satisfied that neither your personal safety, nor the performance of the vehicle will be endangered.

PART NUMBERS

Part numbers listed in this reference are not recommendations by Chilton for any product by brand name. They are references that can be used with interchange manuals and aftermarket supplier catalogs to locate each brand supplier's discrete part number.

Although information in this manual is based on industry sources and is as complete as possible at the time of publication, the possibility exists that some car manufacturers made later changes which could not be included here. While striving for total accuracy, Chilton Book Company cannot assume responsibility for any errors, changes, or omissions that may occur in the compilation of this data.

CONTENTS

Specifications 1

INDEX

CORVETTE

VEHICLE IDENTIFICATION NUMBER (VIN)

It is important for servicing and ordering parts to be certain of the vehicle and engine identification. The (VIN) (vehicle identification number) is a 13 or 17 digit number visible through the windshield on the driver's side of the dash and contains the vehicle and engine identification codes. It can be interpreted as follows:

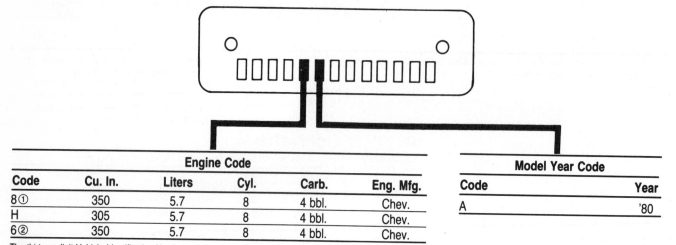

Engine Code						Model Year Code	
Code	Cu. In.	Liters	Cyl.	Carb.	Eng. Mfg.	Code	Year
8①	350	5.7	8	4 bbl.	Chev.	A	'80
H	305	5.7	8	4 bbl.	Chev.		
6②	350	5.7	8	4 bbl.	Chev.		

The thirteen digit Vehicle Identification Number can be used to determine engine application and model year. The 6th digit indicates the model year, and the 5th digit identifies the factory installed engine.
① Standard performance L48 engine
② High performance L82 engine

VEHICLE IDENTIFICATION NUMBER (VIN)

It is important for servicing and ordering parts to be certain of the vehicle and engine identification. The VIN (vehicle identification number) is a 13 or 17 digit number visible through the windshield on the driver's side of the dash and contains the vehicle and engine identification codes. It can be interpreted as follows:

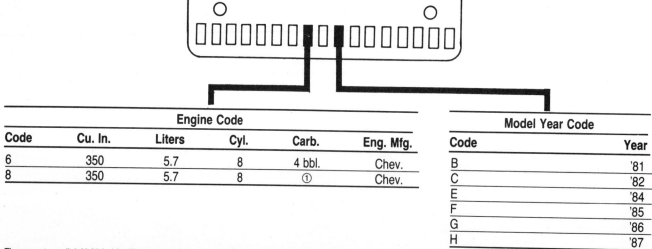

Engine Code						Model Year Code	
Code	Cu. In.	Liters	Cyl.	Carb.	Eng. Mfg.	Code	Year
6	350	5.7	8	4 bbl.	Chev.	B	'81
8	350	5.7	8	①	Chev.	C	'82
						E	'84
						F	'85
						G	'86
						H	'87

The seventeen digit Vehicle Identification Number can be used to determine engine application and model year. The 10th digit indicates the model year, and the 8th digit identifies the factory installed engine. There is no 1983 Corvette model.
① Throttle body fuel injection (TBI) on 1984 models; port fuel injection (PFI) on 1985 and later.

GENERAL ENGINE SPECIFICATIONS

Year	Engine No. of Cyl. Displacement (cu. in.)	Engine VIN Code	Fuel Delivery	Horsepower @ rpm①	Torque @ rpm (ft. lbs.)①	Bore × Stroke (in.)	Compression Ratio	Oil Pressure @ 2000 rpm
'80	8-305	H	4 bbl.	180 @ 4200	255 @ 2000	3.736 × 3.480	8.6:1	45
	8-350	8	4 bbl.	190 @ 4400	280 @ 2400	4.000 × 3.480	8.2:1	45
	8-350	6	4 bbl.	230 @ 5200	275 @ 3600	4.000 × 3.480	9.0:1	45
'81	8-350	6	4 bbl.	190 @ 4200	280 @ 1600	4.000 × 3.480	8.2:1	45
'82	8-350	8	TBI	200 @ 4200	285 @ 2800	4.000 × 3.480	9.0:1	45
'84	8-350	8	TBI	205 @ 4300	290 @ 2800	4.000 × 3.480	9.0:1	50–65
'85	8-350	8	PFI	230 @ 4300	330 @ 2900	4.000 × 3.480	9.0:1	50–65
'86–'87	8-350	8	PFI	230 @ 4000	330 @ 3200	4.000 × 3.480	9.5:1	50–65

NOTE: All engines used in the Corvette are manufactured by Chevrolet Motor Division, G.M. Corp.
TBI—Throttle body fuel injection system
PFI—Port fuel injection system

① Horsepower and torque are SAE net figures. They are measured at the rear of the transmission with all accessories installed and operating. Since the figures vary when a given engine is installed in different models, some are representative rather than exact.

TUNE UP SPECIFICATIONS

(When analyzing compression test results, look for uniformity among cylinders rather than specific pressures.)

Year	Engine No. of Cyl. Displacement (cu. in.)	VIN Code	Option Code	hp	Spark Plugs Type (A.C.)	Spark Plugs Gap (in.)	Ignition Timing (deg.)④ Man. Trans.	Ignition Timing (deg.)④ Auto. Trans.	Valves Intake Opens ⑤(deg.)	Fuel Pump Pressure (psi)	Idle Speed (rpm)④ Man. Trans.	Idle Speed (rpm)④ Auto. Trans.
'80	8-305	H	LG4	180	R45TS	0.045	4B	4B	28	7½–9	②	②
	8-350	8	L48	190	R45TS	0.045	6B③	6B	28	7½–9	②	②
	8-350	6	L82	230	R45TS	0.045	12B	12B	52	7½–9	②	②
'81	8-350	6	L81	190	R45TS	0.045	6B	6B	38	7½–9	②	②
'82	8-350	8	L83	200	R45TS	0.045	①	②	32	9–13	①	②
'84	8-350	8	L83	205	R45TS	0.045	②	②	32	9–13	②	②
'85–'86	8-350	8	L98	230	R45TS	0.045	②	②	NA	NA	②	②
'87	See Underhood Specifications Sticker											

NOTE: All models use electronic ignition systems. No adjustments are necessary. The underhood specifications sticker often reflects tuneup specification changes made in production. Sticker figures must be used if they disagree with those in this chart. Part numbers in this chart are not recommendations by Chilton for any product by brand name.
B—Before Top Dead Center
① Manual transmission not available
② See Underhood Sticker

③ Except Calif. and High Altitude: 6B Calif. and High Altitude: 8B
④ See text for procedure
⑤ All figures Before Top Dead Center

FIRING ORDER
NOTE: To avoid confusion, always replace spark plug wires one at a time.

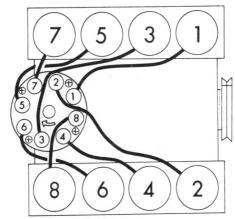

GM (Chevrolet) V8
Engine firing order: 1-8-4-3-6-5-7-2
Distributor rotation: clockwise

CAPACITIES

| Year | Engine No. of Cyl. Displacement (cu. in.) | Engine Crankcase Add 1 qt. for New Filter | Transmission (Pts. to Refill After Draining) | | | Gasoline Tank (gals.) | Cooling System (qts.) | |
			Manual 4-Speed	Automatic ①	Drive Axle (pts.)		With Heater	With A/C
'80–'81	8-305, 350	4	3	8	4	24	21	22
'82	8-350	4	—	10	4	24	21	22
'84–'87	8-350	4	3.5②	10	3.75	20	14	14

① For pan removal and filter change only
— Not applicable
② Four speed overdrive uses Dexron® II in the overdrive section and 80W GL 5 Lube in the trans. section

VALVE SPECIFICATIONS

| Year | Engine No. of Cyl. Displacement (cu. in.) | Seat Angle (deg.) | Face Angle (deg.) | Spring Test Pressure (lbs. @ in.) | Spring Installed Height (in.) | Stem-to-Guide Clearance (in.) | | Stem Diameter (in.) | |
						Intake	Exhaust	Intake	Exhaust
'80	8-305, 350 (std. perf.)	46	45	180–188 @ 1.25	1²³⁄₃₂	0.0010–0.0027	0.0010–0.0027	0.3410–0.3417	0.3410–0.3417
'80	8-350 (high perf.)	46	45	196–204 @ 1.25	1²³⁄₃₂①	0.0010–0.0027	0.0010–0.0027	0.3410–0.3417	0.3410–0.3417
'81–'82	All	46	45	196–204 @ 1.25	1²³⁄₃₂①	0.0010–0.0027	0.0010–0.0027	0.3410–0.3417	0.3410–0.3417
'84–'87	8-350	46	45	194–206 @ 1.25②	1²³⁄₃₂①	0.0010–0.0027	0.0010–0.0027	0.3410–0.3417	0.3410–0.3417

① 1¹⁹⁄₃₂ for the exhaust valve spring
② 1.16 exhaust valve

CRANKSHAFT AND CONNECTING ROD SPECIFICATIONS

(All measurements are given in inches)

| Year | Engine No. of Cyl. Displacement (cu. in.) | Crankshaft | | | | Connecting Rod | | |
		Main Brg. Journal Dia.	Main Brg. Oil Clearance	Shaft End-Play	Thrust on No.	Journal Diameter	Oil Clearance	Side Clearance
'80–'87	8-305, 350	2.4484–2.4493①	0.0008–0.0020②	0.002–0.006	5	2.0988–2.0998	0.0013–0.0035	0.008–0.014

① Nos. 2, 3, 4—2.4481–2.4490; No. 5—2.4479–2.4488
② Nos. 2, 3, 4—.0011–.0023; No. 5—.0017–.0033
③ 1986 and later: .006–.014

TORQUE SPECIFICATIONS

(All readings in ft. lbs.)

| Year | Engine No. of Cyl. Displacement (cu. in.) | Cylinder Head Bolts | Rod Bearing Bolts | Main Bearing Bolts | Crankshaft Balancer Bolt | Flywheel-to-Crankshaft Bolts | Manifold | |
							Intake	Exhaust
'80–'83	8-305, 350	65	45	75①	60	60	30③	②
'84–'87	8-350	65	45	80	60	60	35	20

① Engines with 4-bolt mains—Outer bolts: 70 ft. lbs.
② Center bolts—30, end bolts 20
③ Also torque the throttle body plate bolts to 20–34 ft. lbs. on 1982 models.

PISTON AND RING SPECIFICATIONS

(All measurements are given in inches)

Year	Engine No. of Cyl. Displacement (cu. in.)	Ring Gap			Ring Side Clearance			Piston-to-Bore Clearance (in.)
		Top Compression	Bottom Compression	Oil Control	Top Compression	Bottom Compression	Oil Control	
'80	8-305, 350 (exc. L82)	.010–.020	.010–.023①	.015–.065	.0012–.0032	.0012–.0032	.0020–.0080	.0007–.0027
'80	8-350 (L82)	.010–.020	.010–.023	.015–.065	.0012–.0032	.0012–.0032	.0020–.0080	.0036–.0061
'81	8-350	.010–.020	.010–.023	.015–.065	.0012–.0032	.0012–.0032	.0020–.0080	.0046–.0061
'82	8-350	.010–.020	.010–.023	.015–.065	.0012–.0032	.0012–.0032	.0020–.0080	.0025–.0045
'84–'87	8-350	.010–.020	.010–.025	.015–.055	.0012–.0032	.0012–.0032	.002–.007	.0025–.0035

① 185 and 195 horsepower engines—.010–.025

WHEEL ALIGNMENT SPECIFICATIONS

(All measurements stated in degrees, unless noted.)

Year	Front Wheel Caster		Front Wheel Camber		Rear Wheel Camber		Toe (in.)	
	Range	Preferred	Range	Preferred	Range	Preferred	Front Wheel	Rear Wheel
'80	2P–2½P	2¼P	¼P–1P	¾P	½N ± ½	—	3/32–5/32	3/32 ± 1/32
'81–'82	1¾P–2¾P	2¼P	¼P–1¼P	¾P	0 ± ½	—	¼ ± 1/16	1/16 ± 1/16
'84	2½P–3½P	3P	5/16P–1 5/16P	13/16P	½N–½	0	0–¼P	3/32P–7/13P
'85–'86	2½P–3½P	3P	5/16P–1 5/16P	13/16P	1/32N–29/52P	13/32	0–¼P	3/32P–7/32P

N—Negative
P—Positive

CAPRICE, IMPALA, MALIBU AND MONTE CARLO

VEHICLE IDENTIFICATION NUMBER (VIN)

It is important for servicing and ordering parts to be certain of the vehicle and engine identification. The VIN (vehicle identification number) is a 13 or 17 digit number visible though the windshield on the driver's side of the dash and contains the vehicle and engine identification codes. It can be interpreted as follows:

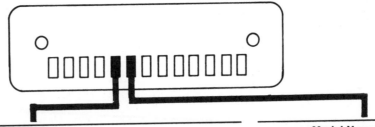

Engine Code						Model Year Code	
Code	Cu. In.	Liters	Cyl.	Carb.	Eng. Mfg.	Code	Year
K	229	3.8	6	2	Chev.	A	1980
A	231	3.8	6	2	Buick		
J	267	4.4	8	2	Chev.		
H	305	5.0	8	4	Chev.		
N	350	5.7	8	Diesel	Olds.		

The thirteen digit Vehicle Identification Number can be used to determine engine application and model year. The sixth digit indicates the model year, and the fifth digit identifies the factory installed engine.

VEHICLE IDENTIFICATION NUMBER (VIN)

It is important for servicing and ordering parts to be certain of the vehicle and engine identification. The VIN (vehicle identification number) is a 13 or 17 digit number visible though the windshield on the driver's side of the dash and contains the vehicle and engine identification codes. It can be interpreted as follows:

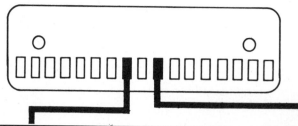

Engine Code						Model Year Code	
Code	Cu. In.	Liters	Cyl.	Carb.	Eng. Mfg.	Code	Year
K	229	3.8	6	2	Chev.	B	1981
9	229	3.8	6	2	Chev.	C	1982
A	231	3.8	6	2	Buick	D	1983
3	231	3.8	6	Turbo	Buick	E	1984
Z	262	4.3	6	TBI	Chev.	F	1985
V	263	4.3	6	Diesel	Olds.	G	1986
J	267	4.4	8	2	Chev.	H	1987
G	305	5.0	8	4	Chev.		
H	305	5.0	8	4	Chev.		
7	305	5.0	8	4	Chev.		
Y	307	5.0	8	4	Olds.		
N	350	5.7	8	Diesel	Chev.		

The seventeen digit Vehicle Identification Number can be used to determine engine application and model year. The tenth digit indicates the model year, and the eighth digit identifies the factory installed engine.

GENERAL ENGINE SPECIFICATIONS

Year	VIN Code	Engine No. Cyl. Displ. (cu. in.)	Eng. Mfg.	Fuel Delivery System	Horsepower @ rpm	Torque @ rpm ft. lb.	Bore × Stroke	Compression Ratio	Oil Pressure 2000 rpm
'80–81	K	6-229	Chev.	2 bbl	110 @ 4200	170 @ 2000	3.736 × 3.480	8.2:1	37
'82	K	6-229	Chev.	2 bbl	115 @ 4000	170 @ 2000	3.736 × 3.480	8.6:1	45
'83–'84	9	6-229	Chev.	2 bbl	115 @ 4000	170 @ 2000	3.736 × 3.480	8.6:1	45
'80–'81	3	6-231	Buick	Turbo	170 @ 4000	275 @ 2400	3.800 × 3.400	8.0:1	37
'80–'84	A	6-231	Buick	2 bbl	110 @ 3800	190 @ 1600	3.800 × 3.400	8.0:1	45
'85	Z	6-262	Chev.	TBI	130 @ 3600	218 @ 2000	4.000 × 3.480	9.3:1	45
'86–'87	Z	6-262	Chev.	TBI	140 @ 3800	225 @ 2200	4.000 × 3.480	9.3:1	45
'82–'83	V	6-263	Olds.	Diesel	85 @ 3200	165 @ 1600	4.057 × 3.385	21.6:1	45①
'80–'82	J	8-267	Chev.	2 bbl	115 @ 4000	200 @ 2400	3.500 × 3.480	8.3:1	45
'80–'87	H	8-305	Chev.	4 bbl	150 @ 3800	240 @ 2400	3.736 × 3.480	8.6:1	45
'85–'87	H	8-305	Chev.	4 bbl②	165 @ 4200	245 @ 2400	3.736 × 3.480	9.5:1	45
'84	G	8-305	Chev.	4 bbl	134 @ 4800	319 @ 3200	3.736 × 3.480	9.5:1	45
'85–'87	G	8-305	Chev.	4 bbl	180 @ 4800	235 @ 3200	3.736 × 3.480	9.5:1	45
'86–'87	Y	8-307	Olds.	4 bbl	148 @ 3800	250 @ 2400	3.800 × 3.385	8.0:1	40①
'80–'86	N	8-350	Olds.	Diesel	105 @ 3200	205 @ 1600	4.057 × 3.385	22.5:1	30–45①

The seventeen digit Vehicle Identification Number can be used to determine engine application and model year. The tenth digit indicates the model year, and the eighth digit identifies the factory installed engine.

■ Horsepower and torque are SAE net figures. They are measured at the rear of the transmission with all accessories in stalled and operating. Since the figures vary when a given engine is installed in different models, some are representative rather than exact.

① @ 1500
① Caprice only

TUNE-UP SPECIFICATIONS

(When analyzing compression test results, look for uniformity among cylinders rather then specific pressures.)

| Year | V.I.N. Code | Eng. No. Cyl. Displ. Cu. In. | Eng. Mfg. | Spark Plugs | | Ignition Timing (deg)▲● | | Intake Valve Opens ■(deg)● | Fuel Pump Pressure (psi) | Idle Speed (rpm)▲* | |
				Orig Type	Gap (in.)	Man. Trans	Auto. Trans			Man.● Trans	Auto. Trans
'80–'81	K	6-229	Chev.	R-45TS	0.045	8B	12B	42	4.5–6.0	700	600
	A	6-231	Buick	R-45TSX	0.060	①	15B	16	4.25–5.75	①	560(600)
	3	6-231	Buick	R-45TSX	0.060	①	15B	16	4.25–5.75	①	550(600)
	J	8-267	Chev.	R-45TS	0.045	①	4B	28	7.5–9.0	①	500
	H	8-305	Chev.	R-45TS	0.045	4B	4B	28	7.5–9.0	700	500(550)
	N	8-350	Olds. Diesel	—	—	①	①	16	5.5–6.5	①	①
'82	K	6-229	Chev.	R-45TS	0.045	—	6B	42	4.5–6.0	—	600
'82–'83	A	6-231	Buick	R-45TS	0.045	—	15B	16	4.25–5.75	—	500
	V	6-263	Olds. Diesel	—	—	—	①	16	5.5–6.5	—	①
'82	J	8-267	Chev.	R-45TS	0.045	—	6B	44	5.5–7.0	—	500
'82–'83	H	8-305	Chev.	R-45TS	0.045	—	6B	44	5.5–7.0	—	500
'82–'84	N	8-350	Olds. Diesel	—	—	—	①	16	5.5–6.5	—	①
'83–'84	9	6-229	Chev.	R-45TS	0.045	—	6B	42	4.5–6.0	—	600
'84	A	6-231	Buick	R-45TS	0.045	—	①	16	4.25–5.75	—	①
'84–'86	G	8-305	Chev.	R-45TS③	0.045③	—	①	—	7.5–9.0	—	①
	H	8-305	Chev.	R-45TS③	0.045③	—	①	44	5.5–7.0	—	①
'86–'87	Z	6-262	Chev.	R-43CTS②	0.035	—	①	—	—	—	①
'86	Y	8-307	Olds.	FR3LS6	0.060	—	①	—	6–7.5	—	①
'87	All			See Underhood Specifications Sticker							

NOTE: The underhood specifications sticker often reflects tune-up specifications changes made in production. Sticker figures must be used if they disagree with those in this chart.

▲ See text for procedure
● Figure in parentheses indicates California engine
■ All figures Before Top Dead Center
* When two idle speed figures are spearated by a slash, the lower figure is with the idle speed solenoid disconnected
B Before Top Dead Center

TDC Top Dead Center
— Not available
① Refer to underhood specifications sticker
② '86 Monte Carlo: R-43TS w/.035 gap
③ '86 Caprice: R-44TS w/.035 gap

FIRING ORDERS

NOTE: To avoid confusion, always replace spark plug wires one at a time.

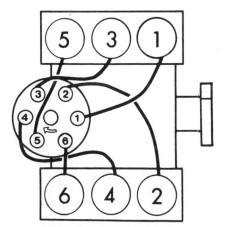

Chevrolet-built V6 engine
Engine firing order: 1-6-5-4-3-2
Distributor rotation: clockwise

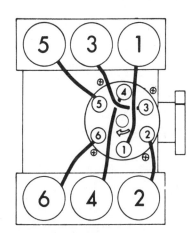

GM (Buick) 231 V6
Engine firing order: 1-6-5-4-3-2
Distributor rotation: clockwise

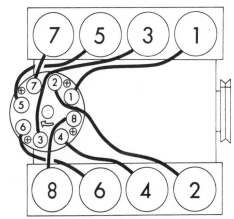

GM (Chevrolet) V8
Engine firing order: 1-8-4-3-6-5-7-2
Distributor rotation: clockwise

CAPACITIES
Monte Carlo, Malibu

Year	Engine No. Cyl. Displacement (cu. in.)	Engine Crankcase Add 1 qt For New Filter ■	Transmission (Pts to Refill After Draining) Manual 3-Speed	4-Speed	Automatic ●	Drive Axle (pts.)	Gasoline Tank (gals.)	Cooling System (qts.) With Heater	With A/C
'80–'81	6-229 Chev.	4	3.0	3.4	②	3.25	18.1	18.8⑦	18.8⑦
	6-231 Buick	4	3.0	3.4	②	3.25	18.1	15.4④	15.4④
	8-267 Chev.	4	3.0	3.4	②	3.25	18.1	20.6	20.6
	8-305 Chev.	4	3.0	3.4	②	⑤	18.1	①	①
	8-350 Chev.	4	3.0	3.4	②	4.25	18.1	16.4	16.4
'82	6-229 Chev.	4	—	—	②	3.5	18.1	15.0	15.0
	6-231 Buick	4	—	—	②	3.5	18.1	12.5	12.2
	6-263 Diesel	6③	—	—	②	3.5	18.1	15.0	15.0
	8-267 Chev.	4	—	—	6.0	3.5	18.1	18.9	18.0
	8-305 Chev.	4	—	—	6.0	3.5	18.1	16.5	16.5
	8-350 Diesel	7③	—	—	6.0	3.5	18.1	18.0	18.0
'83	6-229 Chev.	4	—	—	6.0	3.5	18.1	15.0	15.0
	6-231 Buick	4	—	—	6.0	3.5	18.1	15.0	15.0
	6-263 Diesel	6③	—	—	6.0	3.5	18.1	15.0	15.0
	8-305 Chev.	4	—	—	6.0	3.5	18.1	15.0	15.0
	8-350 Diesel	7③	—	—	6.0	3.5	18.1	18.0	18.0
'84	6-229 Chev.	4	—	—	6.0	3.5	18.1	15.0	15.0
	6-231 Buick	4	—	—	6.0	3.5	18.1	15.0	15.0
	8-305 Chev.⑧	4	—	—	6.0	3.5	18.1	16.6	16.6
	8-305 Chev.	4	—	—	6.0	3.5	18.1	16.3	16.3
	8-350 Diesel	7③	—	—	6.0	3.5	19.8	17.3	17.3
'85–'87	6-262 Chev.	4③	—	—	7.0	⑤	17.6	12.0	12.0
	8-305 Chev.	4③	—	—	7.0	⑤	18.1	16.3	16.3
	8-305 Chev.⑧	4③	—	—	7.0	⑤	18.1	16.6	16.6

● Specifications do not include torque converter Add just enough fluid to fill the transmission to the proper level. It takes only one pint to raise the level from the "ADD" to "FULL" with a hot transmission. Do not overfill.

■ On models with micro oil filters, capacity is the same with or without new filter

① 19.2 (thru 1980), 16.5 (1981)

② 1981–82: 7.0 pts. w/200, 200C, 200-4R; 8.0 pts w/250, 250C; 6.3 pts w/350, 350C

③ Includes mandatory filter change

④ 1981: 12.5 w/heater, 12.2 w/A/C

⑤ With 7.5 inch ring gear: 3.5
With 8.75 inch ring gear: 5.4

⑥ 1981: 15.2 w/heater, 15 w/A/C

⑦ 1981: 16.61 w/heater, 16.63 w/A/C—Not applicable

⑧ Eng. Code G

CAPACITIES
Impala, Caprice

Year	Engine No. Cyl. Displacement (cu. in.)	Engine Crankcase Add 1 qt. For New Filter	Transmission Pts to Refill After Draining Manual 3-Speed	4-Speed	Automatic ●	Drive Axle (pts.)	Gasoline Tank (gals.)	Cooling System (qts.) With Heater	With A/C
'80–'82	6-229	4③	—	—	7.0	4.0	18.5⑨	—	14¼④
	6-231	4③	—	—	7.0	4.0①	18.5⑨	—	11¾④
	8-267	4	—	—	6.0②	4.0①	18.5⑨	—	16¾
	8-305	4	—	—	6.0	4.0①	18.5⑨	—	15½
	8-350⑤	4	—	—	6.0	4.0①	18.5⑨	—	16¼
	8-350 Diesel	7	—	—	6.0	4.0①	18.5⑨	—	16¼

CAPACITIES
Impala, Caprice

Year	Engine No. Cyl. (cu. in.) Displacement	Engine Crankcase Add 1 qt. For New Filter	Transmission Pts to Refill After Draining			Drive Axle (pts.)	Gasoline Tank (gals.)	Cooling System (qts.)	
			Manual		Automatic ●			With Heater	With A/C
			3-Speed	4-Speed					
'83	6-229	4	—	—	6.0	⑥	⑦	—	14¼④
	6-231	4	—	—	6.0	⑥	⑦	—	11¾④
	8-305	4	—	—	6.0⑧	⑥	⑦	—	15½
	8-350 Diesel	6	—	—	6.0	⑥	⑦	—	18.3
'84	6-229	4	—	—	6.0	⑥	⑦	—	14¼
	6-231	4	—	—	6.0	⑥	⑦	—	11¾
	8-305	4	—	—	6.0⑧	⑥	⑦	—	15½
	8-350 Diesel	6	—	—	6.0⑧	⑥	⑦	—	18.3
'85	6-262	4③	—	—	7.0⑧	⑥	⑦	—	14.0⑩
	8-305	4	—	—	7.0⑧	⑥	⑦	—	15.3⑪
	8-350 Diesel	6	—	—	7.0⑧	⑥	⑦	—	18.3
'86–'87	6-262	4③	—	—	7.0⑧	⑥	⑦	12.2	12.5
	8-305	4	—	—	7.0⑧	⑥	⑦	16.8	17.5
	8-307	4	—	—	7.0⑧	⑥	⑦	17.1	17.6

● Specifications do not include torque converter
Add just enough fluid to fill the transmission to the proper level. It takes only one pint to raise the level from "ADD" to "FULL" with a hot transmission. Do not overfill.
—Not applicable
① with 7.5 inch ring gear: 3.25

② 7.5 pt. w/200 T.H. Trans.
③ 4 qt. with filter change
④ Cooling system capacity, Station wagon heavy duty capacity 16¾ qts.
⑤ Not available after 1980.
⑥ 7.5" ring gear: 3.5 pts
   8.5" ring gear: 4.25 pts
   8.75" ring gear: 5.0 pts

⑦ Gasoline coupe and sedan—25 gal;
   Diesel coupe and sedan—26 gal
   All station wagons—22 gal.
⑧ Automatic Overdrive; 10 pts
⑨ Station wagons: 22 gal.
⑩ With H.D. cooling: 14.6
⑪ With H.D. cooling: 16.1

VALVE SPECIFICATIONS

Year	VIN Code	Engine No. Cyl. Displacement (cu. in.)	Seat Angle (deg.)	Face Angle (deg.)	Spring Test Pressure (lbs. @ in.)	Spring Installed Height (in.)	Stem-to-Guide Clearance (in.)		Stem Diameter (in.)	
							Intake	Exhaust	Intake	Exhaust
'80–'82	K	6-229	46	45	200 @ 1.25	1.70	0.0010–0.0027	0.0010–0.0027	0.3414	0.3414
'80–'84	A	6-231	45	45	168 @ 1.32	1.72	0.0015–0.0032	0.0015–0.0032	0.3407	0.3409
'83–'84	9	6-229	46	45	200 @ 1.25	1.70	0.0010–0.0027	0.0010–0.0027	0.3414	0.3414
'80–'81	3	6-231	45	45	168 @ 1.32	1.72	0.0015–0.0032	0.0015–0.0032	0.3407	0.3409
'82–'83	V	6-263 Diesel	45③	44③	210 @ 1.22	1.67	0.0010–0.0027	0.0010–0.0027	0.3414	0.3414
'80–'82	J	8-267	46	45	200 @ 1.25	1.70	0.0010–0.0027	0.0010–0.0027	0.3414	0.3414
'80–'87	H	8-305	46	45	200 @ 1.25	1.70	0.0010–0.0027	0.0010–0.0027	0.3414	0.3414
'84–'87	G	8-305	46	45	200 @ 1.25	1.70	0.0010–0.0027	0.0010–0.0027	0.3414	0.3414
'85–'87	Z	6-262	46	45	200 @ 1.25	1.70	0.0010–0.0027	0.0010–0.0027	0.3414	0.3414
'86–'87	Y	8-307	45	44	187 @ 1.27	1.67	0.0010–0.0027	0.0015–0.0032	0.3429	0.3429
'80–'85	N	8-350 Diesel	45①	44②	205 @ 1.300	1.67	0.0010–0.0027	0.0015–0.0032	0.3429	0.3424

① Exhaust: 31°
② Exhaust: 30°
③ Exhaust: Face 30°; Seat 31°

CRANKSHAFT AND CONNECTING ROD SPECIFICATIONS

(All measurements are given in inches.)

Year	VIN Code	Engine No. Cyl. Displacement (cu. in.)	Crankshaft				Connecting Rod		
			Main Brg. Journal Dia.	Main Brg. Oil Clearance	Shaft End-Play	Thrust on No.	Diameter Journal	Clearance Oil	Clearance Side
'84–'87	G	8-305	2.4484–2.4493⑤	.0008–.0020④	.002–.006	5	2.0986–2.0998	.0013–.0035	.006–.014
'80–'81	3	6-231	2.4995	.0004–.0015	.004–.008	2	2.2495–2.2487	.0005–.0026	.006–.027
'83–'84	9	6-229	2.4484–2.4493④	.0008–.0020③	.002–.006	4	2.0986–2.0998	.0013–.0035	.006–.014
'85–'87	Z	6-262	2.4484–2.4493④	.0008–.0020③	.002–.006	4	2.0986–2.0998	.0013–.0035	.006–.014
'80–'82	K	6-229	2.4484–2.4493④	.0008–.0020③	.002–.006	4	2.0986–2.0998	.0013–.0035	.006–.014
'80–'84	A	6-231	2.4995	.0004–.0015	.004–.008	2	2.2495–2.2487	.0005–.0026	.006–.027
'82–'83	V	6-263 Diesel	2.9993–3.0003	.0005–.0021①	.0035–.0135	3	2.2490–2.2510	.0005–.0026	.006–.020
'80–'82	J	8-267	2.4484–2.4493④	.0008–.0020③	.002–.006	5	2.0986–2.0998	.0013–.0035	.006–.014
'80–'87	H	8-305	2.4484–2.4493④	.0008–.0020③	.002–.006	5	2.0986–2.0998	.0013–.0035	.006–.014
'86–'87	Y	8-307	2.4990–2.4995⑤	.0005–.0021②	.0035–.0135	3	2.1238–2.1248	.0004–.0033	.006–.020
'80–'85	N	8-350 Diesel	2.9993–3.0003	.0005–.0021②	.0035–.0135	3	2.1238–2.1248	.0005–.0026	.006–.020

① No. 4: .0020–.0034
② No. 5: .0015–.0031
③ Intermediate—.0011–.0023
　 Rear—.0017–.0032
④ Intermediate—2.4481–2.4490
　 Rear—2.4479–2.4488
⑤ No. 1: 2.4993–2.4998

PISTON AND RING SPECIFICATIONS

(All measurements are given in inches.)

Year	V.I.N. Code	Engine Type/ Disp. cu. in.	Piston-to-Bore Clearance	Ring Gap			Ring Side Clearance		
				Top Compression	Bottom Compression	Oil Control	Top Compression	Bottom Compression	Oil Control
'80–'82	A	6-231	0.0008–0.0012	0.010–0.020	0.010–0.020	0.015–0.035	0.003–0.005	0.003–0.005	0.0035 Max.
'80–'82	K	6-229	0.0012	0.010–0.020	0.010–0.025	0.010–0.035	0.0012–0.0032	0.0012–0.0032	0.0020–0.0070
'80–'81	3	6-231	0.0008–0.0012	0.010–0.020	0.010–0.020	0.015–0.035	0.003–0.005	0.003–0.005	0.0035 Max.
'80–'82	J	8-267	0.0012	0.010–0.020	0.010–0.025	0.015–0.055	0.0012–0.0032	0.0012–0.0032	0.0020–0.0070
'83–'84	9	6-229	0.0012	0.010–0.020	0.010–0.025	0.010–0.055	0.0012–0.0032	0.0012–0.0032	0.0020–0.0070
'85–'87	Z	6-262	0.0012	0.010–0.020	0.010–0.025	0.015–0.055	0.0012–0.0032	0.0012–0.0032	0.0020–0.0070
'82–'83	V	6-263	0.0030–0.0040	0.015–0.025	0.015–0.025	0.015–0.035	0.005–0.007	0.003–0.005	0.001–0.005
'80–'87	H	8-305	0.0012	0.010–0.020	0.010–0.025	0.015–0.055	0.0012–0.0032	0.0012–0.0032	0.0020–0.0070
'84–'87	G	8-305	0.0012	0.010–0.020	0.010–0.025	0.015–0.055	0.0012–0.0032	0.0012–0.0032	0.0020–0.0070
'86–'87	Y	8-307	0.0008–0.0018	0.009–0.019	0.009–0.019	0.015–0.055	0.0020–0.0040	0.0020–0.0040	0.000–0.0035
'80–'85	N	8-350	0.0050–0.0060	0.015–0.025	0.015–0.025	0.015–0.055	0.005–0.007	0.003–0.005	0.0010–0.0050
'83–'84	A	6-231	0.0012	0.010–0.020	0.010–0.025	0.015–0.055	0.0012–0.0032	0.0012–0.0032	0.0020–0.0070

TORQUE SPECIFICATIONS

(All readings in ft. lbs.)

Year	Engine No. Cyl. Displacement (cu. in.)	Cylinder Head Bolts	Rod Bearing Bolts	Main Bearing Bolts	Crankshaft Bolt	Flywheel to Crankshaft Bolts	Manifold	
							Intake	Exhaust
'80–'87	6-200, 6-229, 8-267, 8-305	65	45	70⑥	60	60	30	20④
'80–'84	6-231	80	40	100	175②	60	45	25
'85–'87	6-262	60–75	45	80	70	70	45	20
'86–'87	8-307	125①	42	⑤	200–310	46	40①	25
'82–'85	8-350 Diesel	130①	42	120	310	60	40①	25
'82–'83	6-263 Diesel	142③	42	107	160–350	48	41	29

① Dip bolt in oil before tightening
② '83–'85: 225 ft. lbs.
③ Bolts No. 5, 6, 11, 12, 13, 14: 59 ft. lbs.
④ 8-305 inside bolts: 25 ft. lbs.
⑤ No. 1 thru 4: 80 ft. lbs., No. 5: 120 ft. lbs.
⑥ '85–'87: 70–85

WHEEL ALIGNMENT SPECIFICATIONS

Year	Model	Caster		Camber		Toe In (in.)	Steering Axis (deg.) Inclination
		Range (deg.)	Pref. Setting (deg.)	Range (deg.)	Pref. Setting (deg.)		
'80–'87	Malibu, Monte Carlo, Man. Steer.	0 to 2P	1P	³⁄₁₀N to 1³⁄₁₀P	½P	¹⁄₁₆ to ¼	7⅞
	Malibu, Monte Carlo, Pow. Steer.	2P to 4P	3P	³⁄₁₀N to 1³⁄₁₀P	½P	¹⁄₁₆ to ¼	7⅞
'80–'87	Impala, Caprice	2P to 4P	3P	0 to 1⅗P	⅘P	¹⁄₁₆ to ¼	—

N Negative   P Positive

CELEBRITY AND CITATION

VEHICLE IDENTIFICATION NUMBER (VIN)

It is important for servicing and ordering parts to be certain of the vehicle and engine identification. The VIN (vehicle identification number) is a 13 or 17 digit number visible through the windshield on the driver's side of the dash and contains the vehicle and engine identification codes. It can be interpreted as follows:

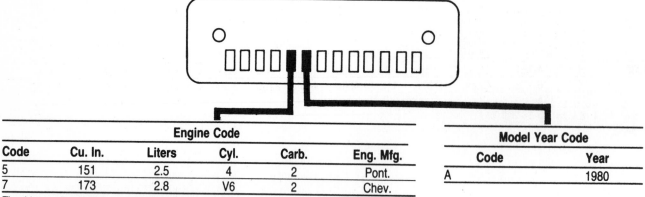

	Engine Code					Model Year Code	
Code	Cu. In.	Liters	Cyl.	Carb.	Eng. Mfg.	Code	Year
5	151	2.5	4	2	Pont.	A	1980
7	173	2.8	V6	2	Chev.		

The thirteen digit Vehicle Identification Number can be used to determine engine application and model year. The 6th digit indicates the model year, and the 5th digit identifies the factory installed engine.

VEHICLE IDENTIFICATION NUMBER (VIN)

It is important for servicing and ordering parts to be certain of the vehicle and engine identification. The VIN (vehicle identification number) is a 13 or 17 digit number visible through the windshield on the driver's side of the dash and contains the vehicle and engine identification codes. It can be interpreted as follows:

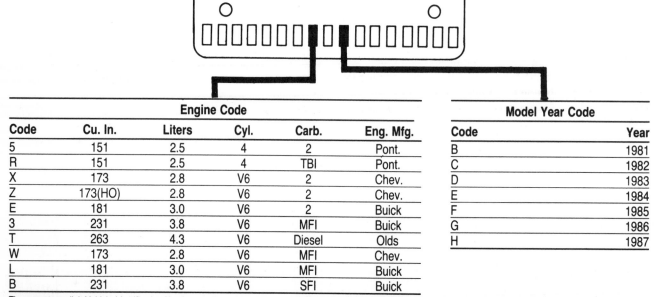

	Engine Code					Model Year Code	
Code	Cu. In.	Liters	Cyl.	Carb.	Eng. Mfg.	Code	Year
5	151	2.5	4	2	Pont.	B	1981
R	151	2.5	4	TBI	Pont.	C	1982
X	173	2.8	V6	2	Chev.	D	1983
Z	173(HO)	2.8	V6	2	Chev.	E	1984
E	181	3.0	V6	2	Buick	F	1985
3	231	3.8	V6	MFI	Buick	G	1986
T	263	4.3	V6	Diesel	Olds	H	1987
W	173	2.8	V6	MFI	Chev.		
L	181	3.0	V6	MFI	Buick		
B	231	3.8	V6	SFI	Buick		

The seventeen digit Vehicle Identification Number can be used to determine engine application and model year. The 10th digit indicates the model year and the 8th digit identifies the factory installed engine.
TBI: Throttle Body Injection
MFI: Multi-Point Fuel Injection

GENERAL ENGINE SPECIFICATIONS

Year	VIN Code	Engine No. Cyl. Displ. (cu. in.)	Eng. Mfg.	Fuel Delivery System	Horsepower @ rpm	Torque ft. lb. @ rpm	Bore × Stroke	Compression Ratio	Oil Pressure @ 2000 rpm
1980–81	5	4-151	Pont.	2-bbl	90 @ 4000	135 @ 2400	4.000 × 3.000	8.2:1	37.5
	5	4-151 Calif.	Pont.	2-bbl	90 @ 4400	128 @ 2400	4.000 × 3.000	8.2:1	37.5
	X	6-173	Chev.	2-bbl	115 @ 4800	150 @ 2000	3.500 × 3.000	8.5:1	30–45
	X	6-173 Calif.	Chev.	2-bbl	110 @ 4800	140 @ 2000	3.500 × 3.000	8.5:1	30–45
	Z	6-173 HO	Chev.	2-bbl	135 @ 4800	165 @ 2400	3.500 × 3.000	8.9:1	30–45
1982	R	4-151	Pont.	TBI	90 @ 4000	134 @ 2400	4.000 × 3.000	8.2:1	37.5
	X	6-173	Chev.	2-bbl	112 @ 5100	148 @ 2400	3.500 × 3.000	8.42:1	30–45
	Z	6-173 HO	Chev.	2-bbl	135 @ 5400	142 @ 2400	3.500 × 3.000	8.94:1	30–45
1983	R	4-151	Pont.	TBI	92 @ 4000	134 @ 2800	4.000 × 3.000	8.2:1	37.5
	X	6-173	Chev.	2-bbl	112 @ 4800	145 @ 2100	3.500 × 3.000	8.5:1	50–65
	Z	6-173 HO	Chev.	2-bbl	135 @ 5400	145 @ 2400	3.500 × 3.000	8.9:1	①
	E	6-181	Buick	2-bbl	110 @ 4800	145 @ 2600	3.800 × 2.660	8.45:1	35–42
1984	R	4-151	Pont.	TBI	92 @ 4000	134 @ 2800	4.000 × 3.000	9.0:1	37.5
	X	6-173	Chev.	2-bbl	112 @ 4800	145 @ 2100	3.500 × 2.990	8.5:1	①
	Z	6-173 HO	Chev.	2-bbl	130 @ 5400	145 @ 2400	3.500 × 2.900	8.9:1	①
	E	6-181	Buick	2-bbl	110 @ 4800	145 @ 2600	3.800 × 2.660	8.45:1	35–42
1985	R	4-151	Pont.	TBI	92 @ 4400	134 @ 2800	4.000 × 3.000	9.0:1	37.5
	X	6-173	Chev.	2-bbl	112 @ 4800	145 @ 2100	3.500 × 2.990	8.5:1	50–65
	W	6-173	Chev.	MFI	130 @ 4800	155 @ 3600	3.500 × 2.990	8.9:1	50–65
	Z	6-173 HO	Chev.	MFI	125 @ 4500	165 @ 3600	3.500 × 2.990	8.9:1	50–65
	E	6-181	Buick	2-bbl	110 @ 4800	145 @ 2600	3.800 × 2.660	8.45:1	35–42
	3	6-231	Buick	MFI	125 @ 4400	195 @ 2000	3.800 × 3.400	8.0:1	35–42
1986–87	R	4-151	Pont.	TBI	92 @ 4400	134 @ 2800	4.000 × 3.000	9.0:1	37.5
	X	6-173	Chev.	2-bbl	112 @ 4800	145 @ 2100	3.500 × 2.990	8.0:1	①
	W	6-173	Chev.	MFI	125 @ 4800	160 @ 3600	3.500 × 2.990	8.5:1	①
	L,E	6-181	Buick	MFI	125 @ 4900	150 @ 2400	3.800 × 2.660	8.45:1	②
	B,3	6-231	Buick	SFI	125 @ 4400	195 @ 2000	3.800 × 3.400	8.0:1	②

① 50–65 psi @ 1200 rpm
② 37 psi @ 2400 rpm

DIESEL ENGINE SPECIFICATIONS

Year	VIN Code	Engine No. Cyl. (cu. in.)	Eng. Mfg.	Fuel Delivery System	Horsepower @ rpm	Torque ft. lb. @ rpm	Bore × Stroke	Compression Ratio	Oil Pressure @ 2000 rpm
1983–85	T	6-263	Olds.	Diesel	85 @ 3600	165 @ 1600	4.057 × 3.385	21.6:1	40–45

TUNE-UP SPECIFICATIONS

When analyzing compression test results, look for uniformity among cylinders rather than specific pressures.

Year	VIN Code	Eng. No. Cyl. Displ. (cu. in.)	Eng. Mfg.	hp	Spark Plugs Orig. Type	Spark Plugs Gap (in.)	Ignition Timing (deg) ▲ Man. Trans.	Ignition Timing (deg) ▲ Auto. Trans.	Intake Valve Opens (deg)■	Fuel Pump Pressure (psi)	Idle Speed (rpm) ▲ Man. Trans.	Idle Speed (rpm) ▲ Auto. Trans.
'80	5	4-151	Pont.	90	R-43TSX	0.060	10B③	10B	33	6.5–8.0	1000	650
	X	6-173	Chev.	110	R-44TS	0.045	2B④	6B⑤	25	6.0–7.5	750⑥	750⑥
'81	5	4-151	Pont.	90	R-44TSX	0.060	4B	4B	33	6.5–8.0	1000	675
	X	6-173	Chev.	110	R-43TS	0.045	6B	10B	25	6.0–7.5	850	850⑦
	Z	6-173 HO	Chev.	135	R-42TS	0.045	10B	10B	31	6.0–7.5	700	700

1 SPECIFICATIONS

TUNE-UP SPECIFICATIONS

When analyzing compression test results, look for uniformity among cylinders rather than specific pressures.

Year	VIN Code	Eng. No. Cyl. Displ. (cu. in.)	Eng. Mfg.	hp	Spark Plugs Orig. Type	Gap (in.)	Ignition Timing (deg) ▲ Man. Trans.	Ignition Timing (deg) ▲ Auto. Trans.	Intake Valve Opens (deg) ■	Fuel Pump Pressure (psi)	Idle Speed (rpm) ▲ Man. Trans.	Idle Speed (rpm) ▲ Auto. Trans.
'82–'84	5,R	4-151	Pont.	90	R-44TSX	0.060	8B	8B	33	6.0–8.0	950①	750②
	X	6-173	Chev.	112	R-43CTS	0.045	10B	10B	25	6.0–7.5	800	600
	Z,W	6-173 HO	Chev.	135⑩	R-42CTS	0.045	6B	10B	31	6.0–7.5	850⑧	750
	E	6-181	Buick	110	R-44TS8	0.080	—	15B	16	6.0–8.0	—	see text
	3	6-231	Buick	125	R-44TS8	0.080	⑨	⑨		4.0–6.5	⑨	⑨
	T	6-263	Olds.	85	—	—	—	6A	N.A.	5.8–8.7	—	650
'85–'86	5	4-151	Pont.	92	R-43TXS	0.045	⑨	⑨	33	6.0–7.0	⑨	⑨
	R	4-151	Pont.	92	R-43TXS	0.60	⑨	⑨	33	12.0	⑨	⑨
	X	6-173	Chev.	112	R-43CTS	.045	⑨	⑨	25	6.0–7.5	⑨	⑨
	Z	6-173 HO	Chev.	—	R-42CTS	.045	⑨	⑨	—	—	⑨	⑨
	W	6-173	Chev.	125	R-42CTS	.045	⑨	⑨	—	24.0–37.0	⑨	⑨
	B,3	6-231	Buick	125	R-44TS8	.080	⑨	⑨	—	—	⑨	⑨
	T	6-263	Diesel Olds	—	—	—	⑨	⑨	—	5.5–6.5	⑨	⑨
	L,E	6-181	Buick	110	R-44TS	.060	⑨	⑨	—	3.9–6.5	⑨	⑨
'87	See Underhood Specifications Sticker											

NOTE: The underhood specifications sticker often reflects tune-up specification changes made in production. Sticker figures must be used if they disagree with those in this chart.

▲ See text for procedure
■ All figures Before Top Dead Center
B: Before Top Dead Center
A: After Top Dead Center
Part numbers in this chart are not recommendations by Chilton for any product by brand name.
N.A.: Information not available
① Without air conditioning: 850
② Without air conditioning: 680
③ Calif.: 12B
④ Calif.: 6B
⑤ Calif.: 10B
⑥ Calif.: 700
⑦ With A/C: 900
⑧ Calif.: 750
⑨ See underhood specifications sticker
⑩ 130 on code W engine, 1982–84 only

FIRING ORDERS

NOTE: To avoid confusion, always replace sparkplug wires one at a time.

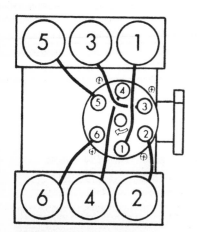

GM (Buick) 181 V6 (3.0L)
GM (Buick) 231 V6 (3.8 L)
Engine firing order: 1-6-5-4-3-2
Distributor rotation: clockwise

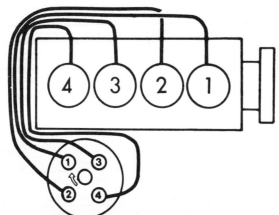

GM (Pontiac) 151-4
Engine firing order: 1-3-4-2
Distributor rotation: clockwise

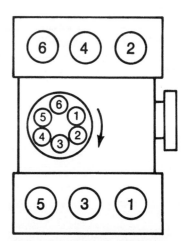

GM (Chevrolet) 173 V6 (2.8 L)
Engine firing order: 1-2-3-4-5-6
Distributor rotation: clockwise

CAPACITIES
A-Body

Year	VIN Code	Engine Displacement (cu. in.)	Eng. Mfg.	Crankcase (qts)		Transaxle Pints		Gas Tank (gals)	Cooling System (qts)	
				w/filter	wo/filter	Manual	Auto		w/heater	w/AC
'82–'85	R	4-151	Pont.	3.0	2.8	6.0	10.0	16.0	9.5	9.75
	X,W	6-173	Chev.	4.0	3.0	6.0	10.0	16.0	11.5	11.75
	E	6-181	Buick	4.0	3.0	—	10.0②	16.0	13.5	14.25
	3	6-231	Buick	4.0①	4.0	—	13.0	16.0	12.25	12.75
	T	6-263	Olds.	6.0	5.5	—	10.0②	16.0	13.25	13.75
'86–'87	R	4-151	Pont.	3.0	3.0	6.0	18	15.7	9.8	9.6
	X,W	6-173	Chev.	4.0	4.0	6.0	18	16.4	12.5	12.6
	L,E	6-181	Buick	4.0	4.0	6.0	18	16.0	14.4	14.0
	B,3	6-231	Buick	4.0	4.0	6.0	18	16.0	11.4	12.0
	T	6-263	Olds.	6.0	6.0	6.0	18	16.6	13.2	13.9

① Add as necessary to bring to appropriate level.
② 13.0 pts w/440T4 transaxle.

CAPACITIES
X-Body

Year	VIN Code	Engine No. Cyl. Displacement (cu. in.)	Engine Crankcase Add 1 qt For New Filter	Transmission (Pts-to-Refill After Draining)		Drive Axle (pts)	Gasoline Tank (gals)	Cooling System (qts)	
				Manual	Automatic			w/Heater	w/AC
'80–'81	5,R	4-151	3	5.9	10.5	①	14	8.3	8.6
	7	6-173	4	5.9	10.5	①	14	10.2	10.6
'82	5,R	4-151	3	5.9	10.5	①	14	8.3	8.6
	X	6-173	4	5.9	10.5	①	14	10.6	10.8
'83–'85	5,R	4-151	3	5.9	10.5	①	14.6	8.3	8.6
	X	6-173	4	5.9	10.5	①	15.1	10.6	10.8
	Z,W	6-173 HO	4	5.9	10.5	①	15.5	10.6	10.8

① Transaxle refill given with transmission capacity

CRANKSHAFT AND CONNECTING ROD SPECIFICATIONS

All measurements are given in inches

Year	VIN Code	Engine No. Cyl. Displacement (cu. in.)	Eng. Mfg.	Crankshaft				Connecting Rod		
				Main Brg. Journal Diameter	Main Brg. Oil Clearance	Shaft End-Play	Thrust on No.	Journal Diameter	Oil Clearance	Side Clearance
'80–'87	R,5	4-151	Pont.	2.2995–2.3005	0.0005–0.0022	0.0035–0.0085	5	1.9995–2.0005	0.0005–0.0026	0.006–0.022
	W,X,Z	6-173	Chev.	2.4937–2.4946	0.0017–0.0030	0.0020–② 0.0067③	3	1.9984–1.9994	0.0014–0.0036	0.006–0.017
	L,E	6-181	Buick	2.4990–2.5000	0.0003–0.0018	0.0030–0.0090	2	2.2487–2.2495	0.0005–0.0026	0.006–0.023
	B,3	6-231	Buick	2.4995	0.0003–0.0018	0.003–0.011	2	2.2487–2.2495	0.0005–0.0026	0.006–0.023
	T	6-263	Olds.	2.9993–3.0003	①	0.0035–0.0135	4	2.2490–2.2510	0.0003–0.0025	0.008–0.021

① No. 1, 2, 3: 0.0005–0.0021
   No. 4: 0.0020–0.0034
② 1980: 0.0020–0.0079
③ 1986–87: 0.0020–0.0033

VALVE SPECIFICATIONS

Year	VIN Code	Engine No. Cyl. Displacement (cu. in.)	Eng. Mfg.	Seat Angle (deg)	Face Angle (deg)	Spring Test Pressure (lbs. @ In.)	Spring Installed Height (in.)	Stem-to-Guide Clearance (in.)		Stem Diameter (in.)	
								Intake	Exhaust	Intake	Exhaust
'80–'85	R,5	4-151	Pont.	46	45	176 @ 1.254	1.660	0.0010–0.0027	0.0010–0.0027	0.3418–0.3425	0.3418–0.3425
	W,X,Z	6-173	Chev.	46	45	155 @ 1.160	1.610	0.0010–0.0027	0.0010–0.0027	0.3410–0.3416	0.3410–0.3416
	E	6-181	Buick	45	45	220 @ 1.340	1.727	0.0015–0.0035	0.0015–0.0032	0.3401–0.3412	0.3402–0.3415
	3	6-231	Buick	45	45	220 @ 1.340	1.727	0.0015–0.0035	0.0015–0.0032	0.3401–0.3412	0.3405–0.3412
	T	6-263	Olds.	①	②	210 @ 1.220	1.670	0.0010–0.0027	0.0015–0.0032	0.3425–0.3432	0.3420–0.3427
'86–'87	R	4-151	Pont.	46	45	170–180 @ 1.260	1.690	—	—	0.3420–0.3430	0.3420–0.3430
	W,X	6-173	Chev.	46	45	155 @ 1.160	1.610	0.0260–0.0268	0.0260–0.0268	—	—
	L,E	6-181	Buick	45	45	220 @ 1.340	1.727	0.0015–0.0032	0.0015–0.0032	0.3405–0.3412	0.3405–0.3412
	B,3	6-231	Buick	45	45	220 @ 1.340	1.727	0.0015–0.0032	0.3405–0.3412	0.3405–0.3412	
	T	6-263	Olds.	①	②	210 @ 1.220	1.670	0.0010–0.0027	0.0015–0.0027	0.3425–0.3432	0.3420–0.3427

① Intake: 45
  Exhaust: 32
② Intake: 44
  Exhaust: 30

CAMSHAFT SPECIFICATIONS

All measurements are given in inches

Year	VIN Code	Engine	Eng. Mfg.	Journal Diameter					Bearing Clearance	Lobe Lift		Camshaft End Play
				1	2	3	4	5		Intake	Exhaust	
'80–'85	R,5	4-151	Pont.	1.869	1.869	1.869	—	—	0.0007–0.0027	0.398	0.398	0.0015–0.0050
	W,X,Z	6-173	Chev.	1.869	1.869	1.869	1.869	—	0.0010–0.0040	0.231	0.263	—
	E	6-181	Buick	1.786	1.786	1.786	1.786	1.786	①	0.406	0.406	—
	3	6-231	Buick	1.786	1.786	1.786	1.786	1.786	①	N.A.	N.A.	—
	T	6-263	Olds.	②	2.205	2.185	2.165	—	0.0020–0.0059	N.A.	N.A.	0.0008–0.0228
'86–'87	R	4-151	Pont.	1.869	1.869	1.869	—	—	0.0007–0.0027	0.398	0.398	0.0015–0.0050
	W	6-173	Chev.	1.8678	1.8678	1.8678	1.8678	—	.001–.004	.2626	.2732	—
	X	6-173	Chev.	1.8678	1.8678	1.8678	—	.001–.004	.231	.2626	—	
	L,E	6-181	Buick	1.786	1.786	1.786	1.786		①	.358	.384	—
	B	6-231	Buick	1.786	1.786	1.786	1.786		①	.392	.392	—
	T	6-263	Olds.	②	2.205	2.185	2.165	—	0.0020–0.0059	N.A.	N.A.	0.0008–0.0228
	3	6-231	Buick	1.786	1.786	1.786	1.786		①	.368	.384	—

① No. 1: 0.0005–0.0025
  No. 2–5: 0.0005–0.0035
② No. 1 bearing is not borable, but must be
  replaced separately.
N.A. Not available.

PISTON AND RING SPECIFICATIONS

All measurements are given in inches.

Year	VIN Code	Engine Type/ Disp. (cu. in.)	Eng. Mfg.	Piston-to-Bore Clearance	Ring Gap			Ring Side Clearance		
					Top Compression	Bottom Compression	Oil Control	Top Compression	Bottom Compression	Oil Control
'80–'85	R,5	4-151	Pont.	0.0025–0.0033	0.010–① 0.022	0.020–② 0.027	0.015–0.055	0.0015–0.0030	0.0015–0.0030	snug
	W,X,Z	6-173	Chev.	0.0017–0.0027	0.0098–0.0197	0.0098–0.0197	0.020–③ 0.055	0.0012–④ 0.0028	0.0016–④ 0.0037	0.008 max.
	L,E	6-181	Buick	0.0008–0.0020	0.013–0.023	0.013–0.023	0.015–0.035	0.0030–0.0050	0.0030–0.0050	0.0035 max.
	B,3	6-231	Buick	0.0008–0.0020	0.010–0.020	0.010–0.020	0.015–0.055	0.0030–0.0050	0.0030–0.0050	0.0035 max.
	T	6-263	Olds.	0.0030–0.0040	0.015–0.025	0.015–0.025	0.015–0.055	0.0050–0.0070	0.0030–0.0070	0.001–0.005
'86–'87	R	4-151	Pont.	0.0014–0.0022	0.010–0.020	0.010–0.020	0.020–0.060–	0.002–0.003	0.001–0.003	0.015–0.055
	W	6-173	Chev.	0.001–0.002	0.0012–0.0027	0.0016–0.0037	0.020–0.055	0.0098–0.0197	0.0098–0.0197	0.020–0.055
	L,E	6-181	Buick	0.0008–0.0020	0.010–0.020	0.010–0.020	0.015–0.055	0.0030–0.0050	0.0030–0.0050	0.0035 max
	B,3	6-231	Buick	0.0008–0.0020	0.010–0.020	0.010–0.020	0.015–0.055	0.0030–0.0050	0.0030–0.0050	0.0035 max
	X	6-173	Chev.	0.0007–0.0017	0.0012–0.0027	0.0016–0.0037	0.020–0.055	0.0098–0.0197	0.0098–0.0197	0.020–0.055

① 1980: 0.015–0.025
② 1980: 0.009–0.019
③ 1980: 0.015–0.055
④ 1980: 0.012–0.032

TORQUE SPECIFICATIONS

All readings in ft. lbs.

Year	VIN Code	Engine No. Cyl. Displacement (cu. in.)	Eng. Mfg.	Cylinder Head Bolts	Rod Bearing Bolts	Main Bearing Bolts	Crankshaft Bolt	Flywheel-to-Crankshaft Bolts	Manifold	
									Intake	Exhaust
'80–'87	R,5	4-151	Pont.	85③	32	70	200	44④	29	44
	W,X,Z	6-173	Chev.	70⑤	37	68	75	50	23	25
	L,E	6-181	Buick	80	40–45	100	225	60	32	25–37
	B,3	6-231	Buick	80	40–45	100	225	60	32	25–37
	T	6-263	Olds.	①	42	107	255②	76	41	29

① All exc. No. 5, 6, 11, 12, 13, 14: 142
   No. 5, 6, 11, 12, 13, 14: 59
② Range: 160–350 ft. lb.
③ 1980–81: 75
   1984–87: 92
④ 1986–87: 55
⑤ 1986–87: 65–90

WHEEL ALIGNMENT SPECIFICATIONS

Year	Model	Caster*		Camber		Toe-In (in.)	Steering Axis (deg) Inclination
		Range (deg)	Pref. Setting (deg)	Range (deg)	Pref. Setting (deg)		
'80–'81	All	2N–2P	0	0–1P	½P	0–³⁄₁₆	14.5
'82–'87	All	0–4P	2P	½N–½P	0	¹³⁄₆₄–¹³⁄₆₄	14.5

* Caster is not adjustable

GENERAL ENGINE SPECIFICATIONS

Year	Engine No. Cyl. Displ. Cu. in.	Engine VIN Code	Fuel Delivery System	Engine Mfg.	Horsepower @ rpm	Torque @ rpm (ft. lb.)	Bore × Stroke	Compression Ratio	Oil Pressure 2400 rpm
'82	4-110	G	2-bbl	Chev.	88 @ 5100	100 @ 2800	3.50 × 2.91	9.0:1	45
'83–'87	4-110	O	TBI	Pont.	84 @ 5200	102 @ 2800	3.34 × 3.13	8.8:1	45
	4-110	J	MFI②	Pont.	150 @ 5600	150 @ 2800	3.34 × 3.13	8.0:1	65④
	4-122	P	TBI	Chev.	86 @ 4900	100 @ 3000	3.50 × 3.15	9.3:1	68③
	4-122	B	①	Chev.	90 @ 5100	111 @ 2800	3.50 × 3.15	9.0:1	45
	6-173	W	MFI	Chev.	120 @ 4800	155 @ 3600	3.50 × 2.99	8.9:1	50

① 1982: 2 bbl
  1983 and later: TBI

② Turbocharged
③ @ 1200 rpm
④ @ 2500 rpm

TUNE-UP SPECIFICATIONS

When analyzing compression test results, look for uniformity among cylinders rather than specific pressures.

Year	Eng. VIN Code	Engine No. Cyl. Displacement (cu. in.)	Eng. Mfg.	hp	Spark Plugs Orig Type	Spark Plugs Gap (in.)	Ignition Timing (deg) Man. Trans.	Ignition Timing (deg) Auto. Trans.	Intake Valve Opens (deg)■	Fuel Pump Pressure (psi)	Idle Speed (rpm) Man. Trans.	Idle Speed (rpm) Auto. Trans.
'82	G	4-110	Chev.	88	R-42TS	0.045①	12B	12B	30	4.5–6.0	②	②
'83–'86	O	4-110	Pont.	84	R-42XLS6④	0.060	8B	8B	N.A.	9–13	②	②
	B	4-122	Chev.	90	R-42CTS	0.035	—	12B	30	4.5–6.0③	②	②
	P	4-122	Chev	86	R-42CTS	0.035	②	②	N.A.	12	②	②
	J	4-110	Pont.	150	R-42CXLS	0.035	②	②	N.A.	12	②	②
	W	6-173	Chev.	130	R42CTS	0.045	②	②	31	9–13	②	②
'87	All				See Underhood Specifications Stickers							

NOTE: The underhood specifications sticker often reflects tune-up specification changes made in production. Sticker figures must be used if they disagree with those in this chart.

■ All figures Before Top Dead Center
B Before Top Dead Center
Part numbers in this chart are not recommendations

by Chilton for any product by brand name.
① Certain models may use 0.035 in. Gap—see underhood specifications sticker to be sure

② See underhood specifications sticker
③ 1983–84 w/TBI—12 psi
④ 1984–85—R44XLS
N.A.: Not Available

FIRING ORDERS

NOTE: To avoid confusion, always replace spark plug wires one at a time.

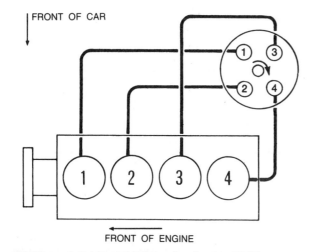

GM (Chevrolet) 110 and 122 overhead valve (OHV)
Engine firing order: 1-3-4-2
Distributor rotation: clockwise

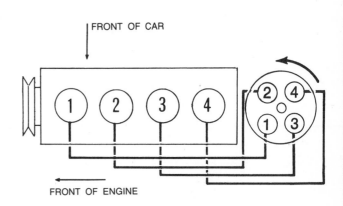

GM (Pontiac) 110 overhead camshaft (OHC)
Engine firing order: 1-3-4-2
Distributor rotation: counterclockwise

1 SPECIFICATIONS

CAPACITIES

Year	Eng. VIN Code	Engine Displacement (Cu. In.)	Eng. Mfg.	Crankcase Quarts (Liters) w/filter	Crankcase Quarts (Liters) wo/filter	Transaxle Pints (L) 4 speed	Transaxle Pints (L) 5 speed	Auto.	Gas Tank Gal (L)	Cooling System Qts (L) w/heater	Cooling System Qts (L) w/AC
'82	G	110	Chev.	4.0 (3.8)	4.0 (3.8)	5.9 (2.8)	—	10.5 (5.0)	14 (53)	8.0 (7.57)	8.0 (7.57)
'82–'87	0, J	110	Pont.	①	①	—	2.5 (5.3)	10.5 (5.0)	14 (53)	7.8 (7.4)	7.9 (7.5)
	B, P	122	Chev.	4.0 (3.8)	4.0 (3.8)	5.9 (2.8)	—	10.5 (5.0)	14 (53)	8.3 (7.7)	8.3 (7.7)
	W	173	Chev.	4.0 (3.8)	4.0 (3.8)	6 (2.8)	—	8 (3.8)	14 (53)	12.4 (11.7)	12.4 (11.7)

① Add 3 qts, check oil level at dipstick and add as necessary.

VALVE SPECIFICATIONS

Year	Eng. VIN Code	Engine No. Cyl. Displacement (cu. in.)	Eng. Mfg.	Seat Angle (deg)	Face Angle (deg)	Spring Test Pressure (lbs. @ In.)	Spring Installed Height (in.)	Stem-to-Guide Clearance (in.) Intake	Stem-to-Guide Clearance (in.) Exhaust	Stem Diameter (in.) Intake	Stem Diameter (in.) Exhaust
'82	G	4-110	Chev.	46	45	183 @ 1.33	1.60	0.0011–0.0026	0.0014–0.0031	0.3139–0.3144	0.3129–0.3136
'83–'87	0, J	4-110	Pont.	46	46	N.A.	N.A.	0.0006–0.0016	0.0012–0.0024	N.A.	N.A.
	B, P	4-122	Chev.	46	45	183 @ 1.33	1.60	0.0011–0.0026	0.0014–0.0031	0.3139–0.3144	0.3129–0.3136
	W	6-173	Chev.	46	45	195 @ 1.18	1.57	0.0010–0.0027	0.0010–0.0027	N.A.	N.A.

N.A.: Not Available

CAMSHAFT SPECIFICATIONS

All measurements in inches

Year	Eng. VIN Code	Engine	Eng. Mfg.	Journal Diameter 1	Journal Diameter 2	Journal Diameter 3	Journal Diameter 4	Journal Diameter 5	Bearing Clearance	Lobe Lift Intake	Lobe Lift Exhaust	Camshaft End Play
'82	G	4-110	Chev.	1.8677–1.8696	1.8677–1.8696	1.8677–1.8696	1.8677–1.8696	1.8677–1.8696	0.0010–0.0039	0.2625	0.2625	N.A.
'82–'87	0, J	4-110	Pont.	1.6714–1.6720	1.6812–1.6816	1.6911–1.6917	1.7009–1.7015	1.7108–1.7114	N.A.	0.2409	0.2409	0.016–① 0.064
	B, P	4-122	Chev.	1.8677–1.8696	1.8677–1.8696	1.8677–1.8696	1.8677–1.8696	1.8677–1.8696	0.0010–0.0039	0.2600	0.2600	N.A.
	W	6-173	Chev.	1.8678–1.8815	1.8678–1.8815	1.8678–1.8815	1.8678–1.8815	1.8678–1.8815	N.A.	0.2626	0.2732	N.A.

N.A.: Not Available
① 1986–87: 0.04–0.16

CRANKSHAFT AND CONNECTING ROD SPECIFICATIONS

All measurements are given in inches

Year	Eng. VIN Code	Engine No. Cyl Displacement (cu in.)	Eng. Mfg.	Crankshaft Main Brg Journal Dia	Crankshaft Main Brg Oil Clearance	Crankshaft Shaft End-Play	Thrust on No.	Connecting Rod Journal Diameter	Connecting Rod Oil Clearance	Connecting Rod Side Clearance
'82	G	4-110	Chev.	2.4944–2.4954②	0.0006–0.0018③	0.0019–0.0071	4	1.9983–1.9993	0.0009–0.0031	0.0039–0.0240

28

CRANKSHAFT AND CONNECTING ROD SPECIFICATIONS

All measurements are given in inches

Year	Eng. VIN Code	Engine No. Cyl Displacement (cu in.)	Eng. Mfg.	Crankshaft			Thrust on No.	Connecting Rod		
				Main Brg Journal Dia	Main Brg Oil Clearance	Shaft End-Play		Journal Diameter	Oil Clearance	Side Clearance
'83–'87	O, J	4-110	Pont.	①	0.0006– 0.0016	0.0118– 0.0027	3	1.9278– 1.9286	0.0007– 0.0024	0.0027– 0.0095
	B, P	4-122	Chev.	2.4944– 2.4954②	0.0006– 0.0018③	0.0019– 0.0071	4	1.9983– 1.9993	0.0009– 0.0031	0.0039– 0.0240④
	W	6-173	Chev.	2.6473– 2.6482	.0016– .0033	.0024– .0083	3	1.9983– 1.9994	0.0014– 0.0037	0.0063– 0.0173

① Bearings are identified by color: Green 2.2827–2.2830   ③ No. 5: 0.0014–0.0027
Brown 2.2830–2.2832   ② No. 5: 2.4936–2.4946   ④ '84–'85: .004–.015

PISTON AND RING SPECIFICATIONS

All measurements are given in inches.

Year	Eng. VIN Code	Engine No. Cyl. Disp. (cu in.)	Eng. Mfg.	Piston-to-Bore Clearance	Ring Gap			Ring Side Clearance		
					Top Compression	Bottom Compression	Oil Control	Top Compression	Bottom Compression	Oil Control
'82	G	4-110	Chev.	0.0008– 0.0018	0.0098– 0.0197	0.0098– 0.0197	snug	0.0012– 0.0027	0.0012– 0.0034	0.0078
'83–'87	O, J	4-110	Pont.	0.0008①	0.0010– 0.0020	0.0010– 0.0020	0.0010– 0.0020	0.0020– 0.0030	0.0010– 0.0024	snug
	B, P	4-122	Chev.	0.0008– 0.0018②	0.0098– 0.0197	0.0098– 0.0197	snug	0.0012– 0.0027	0.0012– 0.0034	0.0078
	W	6-173	Chev.	0.0007– 0.0017	0.0098– 0.0197	0.0098– 0.0197	0.020– 0.055	0.0012– 0.0027	0.0016– 0.0037	0.0078 max

① Code J: 0.0004–0.0012
② 1984–85: 0.0007–0.0017

TORQUE SPECIFICATIONS

All readings in ft. lbs.

Year	Eng. VIN Code	Engine No. Cyl Displacement (cu in.)	Liters	Eng. Mfg.	Cylinder Head Bolts	Rod Bearing Bolt	Main Bearing Bolt	Crankshaft Pulley Bolt	Flywheel to Crankshaft Bolts	Manifold	
										Intake	Exhaust
'80–'87	G	4-110	1.8	Chev.	65–75	34–40	63–74	66–84	45	20–25	22–28
	O, J	4-110	1.8	Pont.	①	39	57	115	45	25	15
	B, P	4-122	2.0	Chev.	65–75	34–43	63–77	66–89	②45–63	18–25	20–30
	W	6-173	2.8	Chev.	70	37	68	75	45	23	25

CAUTION: Verify the correct original equipment engine is in the vehicle by referring to the VIN engine code before torquing any bolts.
① Torque bolts to 18 ft. lb., then turn each bolt 60°, in sequence, 3 times for a 180° rotation, then run the engine to normal operating temperature and turn each bolt, in sequence, an additional 30°– 50°.
② Auto. trans.: 45–59.

WHEEL ALIGNMENT SPECIFICATIONS

Year	Camber (positive)		Toe	
	Range (degrees)	Preferred (degrees)	Range (degrees)	Preferred (degrees)
'82	1/16 to 1 1/16	9/16	1/4 to 0	1/8①
'83	7/32 to 1 7/32	23/32	5/16 to 1/16	1/8①
'84–'87	3/16 to 1 3/16	11/16	1/4 to 0	1/8①

① Out

CHEVETTE

VEHICLE IDENTIFICATION NUMBER (VIN)

It is important for servicing and ordering parts to be certain of the vehicle and engine identification. The VIN (vehicle identification number) is a 13 or 17 digit number visible through the windshield on the driver's side of the dash and contains the vehicle and engine identification codes. It can be interpreted as follows:

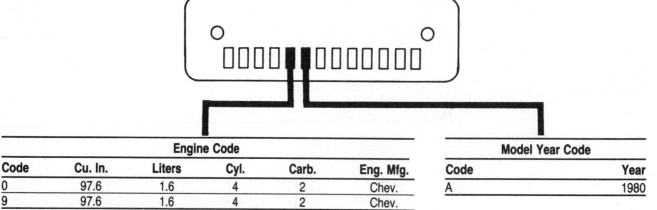

Engine Code						Model Year Code	
Code	Cu. In.	Liters	Cyl.	Carb.	Eng. Mfg.	Code	Year
0	97.6	1.6	4	2	Chev.	A	1980
9	97.6	1.6	4	2	Chev.		

The thirteen digit Vehicle Identification Number can be used to determine engine application and model year. The 6th digit indicates the model year, and the 5th digit identifies the factory installed engine.

VEHICLE IDENTIFICATION NUMBER (VIN)

It is important for servicing and ordering parts to be certain of the vehicle and engine identification. The VIN (vehicle identification number) is a 13 or 17 digit number visible through the windshield on the driver's side of the dash and contains the vehicle and engine identification codes. It can be interpreted as follows:

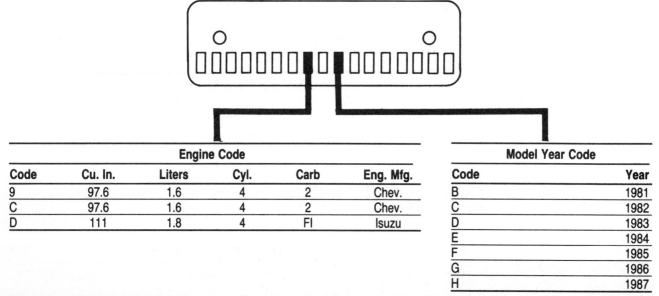

Engine Code						Model Year Code	
Code	Cu. In.	Liters	Cyl.	Carb	Eng. Mfg.	Code	Year
9	97.6	1.6	4	2	Chev.	B	1981
C	97.6	1.6	4	2	Chev.	C	1982
D	111	1.8	4	FI	Isuzu	D	1983
						E	1984
						F	1985
						G	1986
						H	1987

The seventeen digit Vehicle Identification Number can be used to determine engine application and model year. The 10th digit indicates the model year, and the 8th digit identifies the factory installed engine.

GENERAL ENGINE SPECIFICATIONS

Year	Eng. VIN Code	No. Cyl. Displacement liters (cu in.)	Mfg.	Carburetor Type	Horsepower @ rpm	Torque @ rpm (ft lbs)	Bore × Stroke (in.)	Compression Ratio	Oil Pressure @ 2000 rpm
'80	9	4-1.6 (97.6)	Chev.	6510C	70 @ 5200	82 @ 2400	3.228 × 2.980	8.5:1	55
'80	0	4-1.6 (97.6)	Chev.	6510C	74 @ 5200	88 @ 2800	3.228 × 2.980	8.5:1	55
'81–'87	C	4-1.6 (98)	Chev.	6510C	65 @ 5200③	80 @ 2400④	3.228 × 2.980	9.0:1①	55
'81–'87 Diesel	D	4-1.8 (111)	Isuzu	Fuel Injection	51 @ 5000	72 @ 2000	3.310 × 3.230	22.0:1	64②

NOTE: Horsepower and torque are SAE net figures. They are measured at the rear of the transmission with all accessories installed and operating. Since the figures vary when a given engine is installed in different models, some are representative rather than exact.

① '81—8.5:1
② @ 5000
③ '81—70 @ 5200
④ '81—82 @ 2400

FIRING ORDER

NOTE: To avoid confusion, replace spark plugs and wires one at a time.

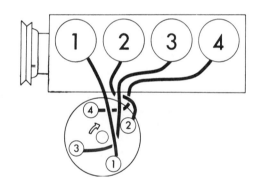

Chevrolet 98 cu. in. (1.6 liter) 4 cyl.
Engine firing order: 1-3-4-2
Distributor rotation: clockwise

TUNE-UP SPECIFICATIONS

When analyzing compression test results, look for uniformity among cylinders rather than specific pressures.

Year	Eng. V.I.N. Code	No. Cyl. Displace- ment (liters)	Mfg.	Spark Plugs Orig. Type	Spark Plugs Gap (in.)	Distributor Point Dwell (deg)	Distributor Point Gap (in.)	Ignition Timing (deg) Man Trans	Ignition Timing (deg) Auto Trans	Valves Intake Opens (deg)	Fuel Pump Pressure (psi)	Idle Speed (rpm) Man Trans	Idle Speed (rpm) Auto Trans.
'80	9	4-1.6	Chev.	R42TS	.035	Electronic		12B	18B	28B	5–6.5	800	750①
	0	4-1.6 HO	Chev.	R42TS	.035	Electronic		12B	18B	31B	5–6.5	800	750
'81	9	4-1.6	Chev.	R42TS	.035	Electronic		18B	18B	28B	2.5–6.5	800	700
'82–'87	C	4-1.6	Chev.	R42CTS	.035	Electronic		8B	8B	—	5.5–6.5	800	700
'87	All			See Underhood Specifications Sticker									

NOTE: The underhood specifications sticker often reflects tune-up specification changes made in production. Sticker figures must be used if they disagree with those in this chart. Product numbers in this chart are not recommendations by Chilton for any product by brand name.
B Before Top Dead Center
HO High Output
① California: 800 rpm

DIESEL TUNE-UP SPECIFICATIONS

Year	No. Cyl.–Displacement (liters)	Static Injection Timing	Fuel Injection Order	Compression (lbs)	Injection Nozzle Opening Pressure (psi)	Intake Valve Opens (deg)	Idle Speed ▲ (rpm) Man.	Idle Speed ▲ (rpm) Auto.
'81–'82	L-4 (1.8)	18 BTDC	1-3-4-2	441①	1707	32	625	725
'83–'84	L-4 (1.8)	11BTDC	1-3-4-2	441①	1707	32	620	720
'85–'86	L-4 (1.8)	18 BTDC	1-3-4-2	441①	1706–1848	32	625	—
'87	L-4 (1.8)	See Underhood Specifications Sticker						

NOTE: The underhood specifications sticker often reflects changes made in production. Sticker figures must be used if they disagree with those in the above chart.
▲ See underhood sticker for fast idle speed.
BTDC Before Top Dead Center
① At 200 rpm

CAPACITIES

Year	Engine No. Cyl. Displacement (liters)	Engine Crankcase	Transmission Pts. to Refill After Draining Manual 4-Speed	Manual 5-Speed	Automatic ●	Drive Axle (pts)	Gasoline Tank (gals)	Cooling System (qts) With Heater	Cooling System (qts) With A/C
'80–'87	4-1.6	4①	3½	4	6	1¾	12.5	9	9¼
'81–'87	4-1.8 Diesel	6①	3½	3¼	6	1¾	12.5	8.5	9.0

● Specifications do not include torque converter
① With filter change

VALVE SPECIFICATIONS

Year	Engine No. Cyl. Displacement (liters)	Seat Angle (deg)	Face Angle (deg)	Spring Test Pressure (lbs @ in.)	Spring Installed Height (in.)	Stem-to-Guide Clearance (in.) Intake	Stem-to-Guide Clearance (in.) Exhaust	Stem Diameter (in.) Intake	Stem Diameter (in.) Exhaust
'80–'87	4-1.6	45	46	173 @ .886	1.25	.0006–.0017	.0014–.0025	.3141	.3133
'81–'87	4-1.8 Diesel	45	45	108 @ 1.24①	1.61	.0015–.0028	.0018–.0030	.3128–.3134	.3126–.3132

① Exhaust 112 @ 1.22; Inner spring test
   pressures—intake 58 @ 1.14
       exhaust 60 @ 1.12

CRANKSHAFT AND CONNECTING ROD SPECIFICATIONS

All measurements are given in inches

Year	Engine No. Cyl. Displacement (liters)	Crankshaft Main Brg. Journal Dia	Main Brg. Oil Clearance	Shaft End-Play	Thrust on No.	Connecting Rod Journal Diameter	Oil Clearance	Side Clearance
'80–'87	4-1.6	2.0078–2.0088	①	.004–.008	4	1.809–1.810	.0014–.0031	.004–.012
'81–'87	4-1.8 Diesel	2.2010–2.2020	.0015–.0027	.0024–.0094	3	1.927–1.928	.0016–.0032	N.A.

N.A.—Not Applicable
① No. 5—.0009–.0026
  All others—.0005–.0018

CAMSHAFT SPECIFICATIONS

All measurements in inches. To convert inches to metric units, refer to Metric Information section.

Year	Engine Type/ Disp. L(cu in.)	Journal Diameter					Bearing Clearance	Lobe Lift		Camshaft End Play
		1	2	3	4	5		Intake	Exhaust	
'80–'87	4-1.6(98)	1.7682–1.7697	1.7584–1.7598	1.7485–1.7500	1.7387–1.7402	1.1816 1.1837	.0020–.0044	.2410	.2410	.0067–.0169
'81–'87	4-1.8(111)	NA					.0008–.0035	6.1163	6.1163	.17–.43

NA—Not Available

TORQUE SPECIFICATIONS

All readings in ft. lbs.

Year	Engine No. Cyl. Displacement (liters)	Cylinder Head Bolts	Rod Bearing Bolts	Main Bearing Bolts	Crankshaft Pulley Bolt	Flywheel to Crankshaft Bolts	Manifold	
							Intake	Exhaust
'80–'87	1.6	75	40	40	100	40	18	①
'81–'87	4-1.8 Diesel	②	65	75	N/A	N/A	30	N/A

N/A Not available
① Center bolts—13-18; end bolts—19-25
② First tighten to 21-36 ft. lbs. then retighten to 83-98 (new bolt), 90-105 (reused bolt)

PISTON AND RING SPECIFICATIONS

All measurements are given in inches.

Year	Engine Type/ Disp. L(cu in.)	Piston-to-Bore Clearance	Ring Gap			Ring Side Clearance		
			Top Compression	Bottom Compression	Oil Control	Top Compression	Bottom Compression	Oil Control
'80–'87	4-1.6	.0008–.0016	.009–.019	.008–.018	.015–.055	.0012–.0027	.0012–.0032	.0000–.0050
'81–'82	4-1.8 Diesel	.0006–.0014	.0078–.0157	.0078–.0157	.0078–.0157	.0035–.0049	.0014–.0020	.0012–.0028
'83–'87	4-1.8 Diesel	.0002–.0017	.0078–.0157	.0078–.0157	.0078–.0157	.0035–.0049	.0019–.0033	.0012–.0028

WHEEL ALIGNMENT SPECIFICATIONS

Year	Model	Caster		Camber		Toe-in (in.)
		Range (deg)	Pref. Setting (deg)	Range (deg)	Pref. Setting (deg)	
'80–'81	All	3½P–5½P	4½P	¼P–½P	¼P	1/16P
'82–'87	All	4P–6P	5P	¼P–½P	¼P	1/16P

N Negative
P Positive

SPECTRUM

VEHICLE IDENTIFICATION NUMBER (VIN)

It is important for servicing and ordering parts to be certain of the vehicle and engine identification. The VIN (vehicle identification number) is a 13 or 17 digit number visible through the windshield on the driver's side of the dash and contains the vehicle and engine indentification codes. It can be interpreted as follows:

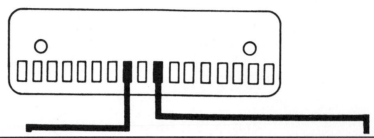

	Engine Code						Model Year Code	
Code	Cu. In.	Liters	Cyl.	Carb.	Eng. Mfg.		Code	Year
K	94	1.5	4	2bbl	Isuzu		F	1985
							G	1986
							H	1987

GENERAL ENGINE SPECIFICATIONS

Year	Engine No. Cyl. Displ. (cu. in.)	Engine VIN Code	Fuel Delivery System	Engine Mfg.	Horsepower @ rmp	Torque @ rpm (ft. lb.)	Bore × Stroke	Compression Ratio	Oil Pressure @ 3800 rpm
'85–'87	4–94	K	2bbl	Isuzu	70 @ 5400	87 @ 3400	3.031 × 3.110	9.6:1	57–85

TUNE-UP SPECIFICATIONS

When analyzing compression test results, look for uniformity among cylinders rather than specific pressures.

Year	Eng. VIN Code	Engine No. Cyl. Displacement (cu. in.)	Eng. Mfg.	hp	Spark Plugs Orig. Type	Gap (in.)	Ignition Timing (deg BTDC) Man. Trans.	Auto. Trans.	Valves Intake Opens (deg)	Fuel Pump Pressure (psi)	Idle Speed (rpm) Man. Trans.	Auto. Trans.
'85–'86	K	4–94	Isuzu	70	BPR6ES-11	.040	15	10	17B	6–8	700	950
'87	All				See Underhood Specifications Sticker							

NOTE: The underhood specifications sticker often reflects tune-up specification changes made in production. Sticker figures must be used if they disagree with those in this chart.

CAPACITIES

Year	Eng. VIN Code	Engine Displacement (cu. in.)	Eng. Mfg.	Crankcase Quarts w/filter	wo/filter	Transaxle Pints Manual	Auto.	Gas Tank Gal	Cooling System Quarts w/heater	w/AC
'85–'87	K	94	Isuzu	3.4	3.0	5.6	12.6	11	6.7	6.7

FIRING ORDER

NOTE: To avoid confusion, replace spark plugs and wires one at a time.

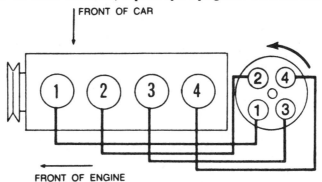

GM (ISUZU) 94–4 (1.5L)
Engine firing order: 1–3–4–2
Distributor rotation: counterclockwise

CRANKSHAFT AND CONNECTING ROD SPECIFICATIONS

All measurements are given in inches

Year	Eng. VIN Code	Engine No. Cyl Displacement (cu. in.)	Eng. Mfg.	Crankshaft				Connecting Rod		
				Main Brg. Journal Diameter	Main Brg. Oil Clearance	Shaft End-Play	Thrust on No.	Journal Diameter	Oil Clearance	Side Clearance
'85–'87	K	4-94	Isuzu	1.8865–1.8873	.00079–.00199	.0024–.0095	2	1.5720–1.5726	.00098–.00229	.0079–.0138

VALVE SPECIFICATIONS

Year	Eng. VIN Code	Engine No. Cyl. Displacement (cu. in.)	Eng. Mfg.	Seat Angle (deg)	Face Angle (deg)	Spring Test Pressure (lbs. @ In.)	Spring Installed Height (in.)	Stem-to-Guide Clearance (in.)		Stem Diameter (in.)	
								Intake	Exhaust	Intake	Exhaust
'85–'87	K	4-94	Isuzu	45	45	47 @ 1.57	1.57	.0009–.0022	.00118–.00248	.2740–.2750	.2740–.2744

CAMSHAFT SPECIFICATIONS

All measurements in inches

Year	Eng. VIN Code	Engine (cu. in.)	Eng. Mfg.	Journal Diameter					Bearing Clearance	Lobe Life		Camshaft End Play
				1	2	3	4	5		Intake	Exhaust	
'85–'87	K	94	Isuzu	—1.021—					.00236–.00437	—1.426—		.00394–.00710

TORQUE SPECIFICATIONS

All readings in ft. lbs.

Year	Eng. V.I.N. Code	Engine No. Cyl. Displacement (cu. in.)	Eng. Mfg.	Cylinder Head Bolts	Rod Bearing Bolt	Main Bearing Bolt	Crankshaft Pulley Bolt	Flywheel-to-Crankshaft Bolts	Manifold	
									Intake	Exhaust
'85–'87	K	4-94	Isuzu	②	25	65	108	22①	17	17

① Tighten an additional 45° after torquing
② 1st step: 29 ft. lbs., 2nd step: 58 ft. lbs.

PISTON AND RING SPECIFICATIONS

All measurements are given in inches

Year	Eng. VIN Code	Engine No. Cyl. Disp. (cu. in.)	Eng. Mfg.	Piston-to-Bore Clearance	Ring Gap			Ring Side Clearance		
					Top Compression	Bottom Compression	Oil Control	Top Compression	Bottom Compression	Oil Control
'85–'87	K	4–94	Isuzu	.0012–.0020	.0098–.0137	—	.0039–.0236	.00098–.00256	—	—

WHEEL ALIGNMENT

Year	Model	Caster		Camber		Toe-in (in.)
		Range (deg)	Pref Setting (deg)	Range (deg)	Pref Setting (deg)	
'85–'87	Spectrum	1¾P–2¾P	2¼P	¼N–1½P	⅜P	0 ± .08

SPRINT

VEHICLE IDENTIFICATION NUMBER (VIN)

It is important for servicing and ordering parts to be certain of the vehicle and engine identification. The VIN (vehicle identification number) is a 17 digit number visible through the windshield on the driver's side of the dash and contains the vehicle and engine identification codes. It can be interpreted as follows:

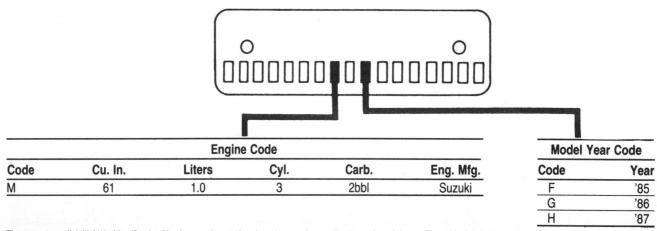

Engine Code						Model Year Code	
Code	Cu. In.	Liters	Cyl.	Carb.	Eng. Mfg.	Code	Year
M	61	1.0	3	2bbl	Suzuki	F	'85
						G	'86
						H	'87

The seventeen digit Vehicle Identification Number can be used to determine engine application and model year. The 10th digit indicates the model year, and the 8th digit identifies the factory installed engine.

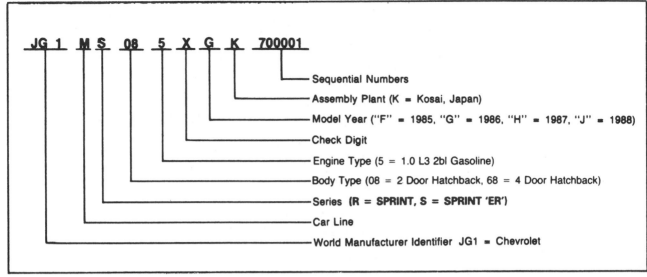

Vehicle Identificaton Number

VEHICLE IDENTIFICATION NUMBER (VIN)

It is important for servicing and ordering parts to be certain of the vehicle and engine identification. The VIN (vehicle identification number) is a 17 digit number visible through the windshield on the driver's side of the dash and contains the vehicle and engine identification codes. It can be interpreted as follows.

GENERAL ENGINE SPECIFICATIONS

Year	Engine No. Cyl. Displ. (cu. in.)	Engine VIN Code	Fuel Delivery System	Engine Mfg.	Horsepower @ rpm	Torque @ rpm (ft. lb.)	Bore × Stroke	Compression Ratio	Oil Pressure 2400 rpm
'85–'87	3-61	M	2bbl	Suzuki	48 @ 5100	57 @ 3200	2.91 × 3.03	9.5:1	48 psi

TUNE-UP SPECIFICATIONS

When analyzing compression test results, look for uniformity among cylinders rather than specific pressures

Year	Eng. VIN Code	Engine No. Cyl. Displacement (cu. in.)	Eng. Mfg.	hp	Spark Plugs Orig. Type	Gap (in.)	Ignition Timing (deg) Man. Trans.	Auto. Trans.	Valves Intake Opens (deg)	Fuel Pump Pressure (psi)	Idle Speed (rpm) Man. Trans.	Auto. Trans.
'85–'86	M	3-61	Suzuki	48	①	③	③	③	N.A.	3.5②	③	③
'87					See Underhood Specifications Sticker							

① NGK:BPRGES-11 or Nippondenso WIGEXR-U11
② @ 5,000 rpm
③ Refer to underhood specifications sticker

CAPACITIES

Year	VIN Code	Engine Displacement cu. in.	Eng. Mfg.	Crankcase (qts)	Manual Transaxle (pts)	Gas Tank (gals)	Cooling System (qts)
'85–'87	M	61	Suzuki	3.7	4.8	8.3	4.5

FIRING ORDERS

NOTE: To avoid confusion, replace spark plugs and wires one at a time.

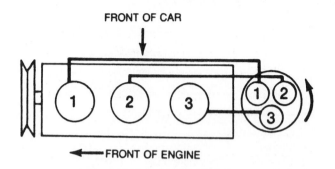

FRONT OF CAR

FRONT OF ENGINE

GM (SUZUKI) 63–3 (1.0L)
Engine firing order: 1–3–2
Distributor rotation: counterclockwise

CHAMSHAFT SPECIFICATIONS

Year	Engine Displacement (cu. in.)	Journal Diameter 1	2	3	4	Journal Clearance	Lobe Life Intake	Exhaust
'85–'87	61	1.7372–1.7381	1.7451–1.7460	1.7530–1.7539	1.7609–1.7618	0.0029	1.5012	1.5012

PISTON AND RING SPECIFICATIONS

All measurements are given in inches.

Year	VIN Code	Engine No. Cyl. Disp. (cu. in.)	Eng. Mfg.	Piston-to-Bore Clearance	Ring Gap Top Compression	Bottom Compression	Oil Control	Ring Side Clearance Top Compression	Bottom Compression	Oil Control
'85–'87	M	3-61	Suzuki	0.0008–0.0015	0.0079–0.0129	0.0079–0.0137	0.0079–0.0275	0.0012–0.0027	0.0008–0.0023	—
'86–'87	M	3-61	Suzuki ER Model	0.0008–0.0023	0.0079–0.0157	—	0.0079–0.0275	0.0012–0.0027	—	—

VALVE SPECIFICATIONS

Year	Engine Displacement (cu. in.)	Seat Angle (deg.)	Face Angle (deg.)	Spring Test Pressure (lbs. @ in.)	Spring Installed Height (in.)	Stem-to-Guide Clearance (in.) Intake	Exhaust	Stem Diameter (in.) Intake	Exhaust
'85–'87	61	45°	45°	60	1.63	0.0014	0.0020	0.2745	0.2740

CRANKSHAFT AND CONNECTING ROD SPECIFICATIONS

(All specifications in inches)

Year	Engine Displacement (cu. in.)	Main Brg. Journal Dia.	Main Brg. Oil Clearance	Crankshaft End Play	Thrust on No.	Connecting Rod Journal Dia.	Rod Bearing Oil Clearance	Rod Bearing Side Clearance
'85–'87	61	1.7714	0.0012	0.0083	3	1.6532	0.0015	0.0058

TORQUE SPECIFICATIONS

(ft. lbs.)

Year	Engine Displacement (cu. in.)	Cylinder Head Bolts	Connecting Rod Bearing Bolts	Main Bearing Bolts	Crankshaft Bolt	Flywheel to Crankshaft Bolts	Camshaft Cap Bolts
'85–'87	61	48	35	38	50	44	—

NOVA

ENGINE IDENTIFICATION

Code	Cu. In.	Liters	Cyl.	Carb.	Eng. Mfg.
4A-C	97	1.5	4	2 bbl	Toyota
4A-LC	97	1.5	4	2 bbl	Toyota

GENERAL ENGINE SPECIFICATIONS

Year	Eng. No. Cyl. Displ. Cu. In.	Engine Code	Fuel Delivery System	Engine Mfg.	Horsepower @ rpm	Torque @ rpm (ft lbs)	Bore × Stroke	Compression Ratio	Oil Pressure @ rpm
'85	4-97	4A-C	2 bbl	Toyota	70 @ 4800	85 @ 2800	3.19 × 3.03	9.0:1	34 @ 2000
'86–'87	4-97	4A-LC	2 bbl	Toyota	74 @ 4800	85 @ 2800	3.19 × 3.03	9.0:1	34 @ 2000

TUNE-UP SPECIFICATIONS

When analyzing compression test results, look for uniformity among cylinders rather than specific pressures

Year	Engine Code	Engine No. Cyl. Displacement (cu. in.)	Eng. Mfg.	hp	Spark Plugs		Ignition Timing (deg)		Fuel Pump Pressure (psi)	Idle Speed (rpm)	
					Orig. Type	Gap (in.)	Man. Trans.	Auto. Trans.		Man. Trans.	Auto. Trans.
'85	4A-C	4-97	Toyota	70	BPR5EY11	.043	5B	5B	2.5–3.5	650	800
'86	4A-LC	4-97	Toyota	74	BPR5E11	.043	5B	5B	2.5–3.5	650	750
'87	4A-LC	See Underhood Specifications Sticker									

NOTE: The underhood specifications sticker often reflects tune-up specification changes made in production. Sticker figures must be used if they disagree with those in this chart.

FIRING ORDER

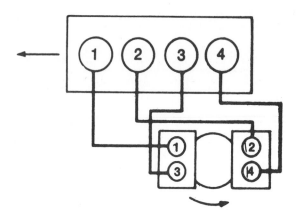

Firing order: 1–3–4–2

CAPACITIES

Year	Eng. Code	Engine Displacement (Cu. In.)	Eng. Mfg.	Crankcase Quarts		Transaxle Pints		Gas Tank Gals.	Cooling System Quarts	
				w/filter	wo/filter	Manual	Auto.		w/heater	w/AC
'85	4A-C	97	Toyota	3.2	3.0	5.4	11.6	13.3	6.2	6.2
'86–'87	4A-LC	97	Toyota	3.5	3.2	5.4	11.6	13.2	6.3	6.3

VALVE SPECIFICATIONS

Year	Engine No. Cyl. Displacement (cu. in.)	Seat Angle (deg)	Face Angle (deg)	Outer Spring Test Pressure (lbs. @ in.)	Spring Installed Height (in.)	Stem-to-Guide Clearance (in.)		Stem Diameter (in.)	
						Intake	Exhaust	Intake	Exhaust
'85	4-97	45	45.5	52 @ 1.52	1.52	0.0010–0.0024	0.0012–0.0026	0.2744–0.2750	0.2742–0.2748
'86–'87	4-97	45	45.5	46.3 @ 1.52	1.52	0.0010–0.0024	0.0012–0.0026	0.2744–0.2750	0.2742–0.2748

CRANKSHAFT AND CONNECTING ROD SPECIFICATIONS

All measurements are given in inches

Year	Eng. Code	Engine No. Cyl. Displacement (cu. in.)	Crankshaft				Connecting Rod		
			Main Brg. Journal Dia.	Main Brg. Oil Clearance	Shaft End-Play	Thrust on No.	Journal Diameter	Oil Clearance	Side Clearance
'85	4A-C	4-97	1.8892– 1.8898	0.0005–① 0.0019	0.0008– 0.0073	3	1.5742– 1.5748	0.0008– 0.0020	0.0059– 0.0098
'86–'87	4A-LC	4-97	1.8892– 1.8898	0.0005–② 0.0015	0.0008– 0.0073	3	1.5742– 1.5748	0.0008 0.0020	0.12

① Maximum clearance—0.0031
② Maximum clearance is .0039 for 1986 engines, .0031 for 1985 engines

CAMSHAFT SPECIFICATIONS

All measurements are given in inches

Year	Eng. Code	Engine No. Cyl. Displacement (cu. in.)	Journal Diameter					Bearing Clearance	Lobe Lift		Camshaft End Play
			1	2	3	4	5		Intake	Exhaust	
'85	4A-C	4-97			1.1015–1.1022			0.0015– 0.0029	1.5528– 1.5531	1.5528– 1.5531	0.0031– 0.0071
'86–'87	4A-LC	4-97			1.1015–1.1022			0.0015– 0.0029	1.5409①	1.5409①	0.0031– 0.0071

① Minimum lobe height

PISTON AND RING SPECIFICATIONS

All measurements are given in inches.

Year	Eng. Code	Engine No. Cyl. Disp. (cu. in.)	Piston-to-Bore Clearance	Ring Gap			Ring Side Clearance		
				Top Compression	Bottom Compression	Oil Control	Top Compression	Bottom Compression	Oil Control
'85	4A-C	4-97	0.0039– 0.0047	0.0079– 0.0157	0.0059– 0.0138	0.0039– 0.0236	0.0016– 0.0031	0.0012– 0.0028	snug
'86–'87	4A-LC	4-97	0.0035– 0.0043	0.0098– 0.0185	0.0059– 0.0165	0.0018– 0.0402	0.0016– 0.0031	0.0012– 0.0028	snug

TORQUE SPECIFICATIONS

All readings in ft. lbs.

Year	Eng. Code	Engine No. Cyl. Displacement (cu. in.)	Cylinder Head Bolts	Rod Bearing Bolts	Main Bearing Bolts	Crankshaft Bolt	Flywheel-to-Crankshaft Bolts	Manifold	
								Intake	Exhaust
'85	4A-C	4-97	40–47	34–39	40–47	80–94	55–61	15–21	15–21
'86–'87	4A-LC	4-97	43	29	43	80–94	55–61	15–21	15–21

WHEEL ALIGNMENT SPECIFICATIONS

Year		Caster Range (deg)	Caster Pref. Setting (deg)	Camber Range (deg)	Camber Pref. Setting (deg)	Toe (in.)	Steering Axis (deg) Inclination
'85	Front	¼–1¾P	1P	1¼N–¼P	½N	0 ± 0.16	11¾–13¼
	Rear	—	—	1¼N–¼P	½N	0.150 ± 0.16	—
'86–'87	Front	⅙P–1⅔P	⅚P	¾N–¼P	¼P	0 ± 0.078	—
	Rear	—	—	1¼N–¼P	¾N	.075–.233	—

CORSICA AND BERETTA

VEHICLE IDENTIFICATION CHART

It is important for servicing and ordering parts to be certain of the vehicle and engine identification. The VIN (vehicle identification number) is a 17 digit number visible through the windshield on the driver's side of the dash and contains the vehicle and engine identification codes. It can be interpreted as follows:

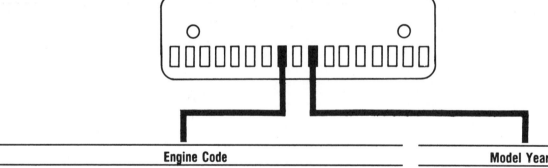

		Engine Code					Model Year	
Code	Cu. In.	Liters	Cyl.	Fuel Sys.	Eng. Mfg.		Code	Year
1	121	2.0	4	TBI	Chevrolet		H	1987
W	173	2.8	6	MFI	Chevrolet		J	1988

The seventeen digit Vehicle Identification Number can be used to determine engine identification and model year. The tenth digit indicates model year, and the fourth digit indicates engine code.

GENERAL ENGINE SPECIFICATIONS

Year	VIN	No. Cylinder Displacement cu. in. (liter)	Fuel System Type	Net Horsepower @ rpm	Net Torque @ rpm (ft.lbs.)	Bore × Stroke (in.)	Compression Ratio	Oil Pressure @ rpm
1987-88	1	4-121 (2.0)	TBI	90 @ 5600	108 @ 3200	3.500 × 3.150	9.0:1	63-77 @ 1200
	W	6-173 (2.8)	MFI	125 @ 4500	160 @ 3600	3.500 × 2.990	8.9:1	50-65 @ 1200

GASOLINE ENGINE TUNE-UP SPECIFICATIONS

Year	VIN	No. Cylinder Displacement cu. in. (liter)	Spark Plugs Type	Spark Plugs Gap (in.)	Ignition Timing (deg.) MT	Ignition Timing (deg.) AT	Compression Pressure (psi)	Fuel Pump (psi)	Idle Speed (rpm) MT	Idle Speed (rpm) AT	Valve Clearance In.	Valve Clearance Ex.
1987-88	1	4-121 (2.0)	FR3LM	.035	①	①	②	10-12	①	①	Hyd.	Hyd.
	W	6-173 (2.8)	R43CTLSE	.045	①	①	②	10-12	①	①	Hyd.	Hyd.

① Ignition timing and idle speed is controlled by the electronic control module. No adjustments are possible

② When analyzing compression test results, look for uniformity among cylinders rather than specific pressures

CAPACITIES

Year	Model	No. Cylinder Displacement cu. in. (liter)	Engine Crankcase with Filter	Engine Crankcase without Filter	Transmission (pts.) 4-Spd	Transmission (pts.) 5-Spd	Transmission (pts.) Auto.	Drive Axle (pts.)	Fuel Tank (gal.)	Cooling System (qts.)
1987-88	Beretta	4-121 (2.0)	4.5	4.0	—	5.36 ①	8.0 ②	—	13.6	8.8
		6-173 (2.8)	4.5	4.0	—	5.36 ①	8.0 ②	—	13.6	11.4
	Corsica	4-121 (2.0)	4.5	4.0	—	5.36 ①	8.0 ①	—	13.6	8.8
		6-173 (2.8)	4.5	4.0	—	5.36 ①	8.0 ①	—	13.6	11.4

① This figure applies to both available 5 speed transaxles.

② This figure is for drain and refill. After a complete overhaul, use 16.0 pts. If the torque converter is replaced, use 18.0 pts.

CAMSHAFT SPECIFICATIONS
All measurements given in inches.

Year	VIN	No. Cylinder Displacement cu. in. (liter)	Journal Diameter 1	Journal Diameter 2	Journal Diameter 3	Journal Diameter 4	Journal Diameter 5	Lobe Lift In.	Lobe Lift Ex.	Bearing Clearance	Camshaft End Play
1987-88	1	4-121 (2.0)	1.867–1.869	1.867–1.869	1.867–1.869	1.867–1.869	1.867–1.869	.260	.260	.001–.004	NA
	W	6-173 (2.8)	1.867–1.881	.1.867–1.881	1.867–1.881	1.867–1.881	1.867–1.881	.262	.273	.001–.004	NA

CRANKSHAFT AND CONNECTING ROD SPECIFICATIONS
All measurements are given in inches.

Year	VIN	No. Cylinder Displacement cu. in. (liter)	Crankshaft Main Brg. Journal Dia.	Crankshaft Main Brg. Oil Clearance	Crankshaft Shaft End-play	Crankshaft Thrust on No.	Connecting Rod Journal Diameter	Connecting Rod Oil Clearance	Connecting Rod Side Clearance
1987-88	1	4-121 (2.0)	2.4945–2.454	.006–.0019	.002–.008	4	1.9983–1.9994	.001–.0031	.004–.015
	W	6-173 (2.8)	2.6473–2.6483	.0016–.0033	.002–.008	3	1.9983–1.9993	.0013–.0026	.006–.017

1 SPECIFICATIONS

VALVE SPECIFICATIONS

Year	VIN	No. Cylinder Displacement cu. in. (liter)	Seat Angle (deg.)	Face Angle (deg.)	Spring Test Pressure (lbs.)	Spring Installed Height (in.)	Stem-to-Guide Clearance (in.)		Stem Diameter (in.)	
							Intake	Exhaust	Intake	Exhaust
1987-88	1	4-121 (2.0)	45	45	105 ①	1.60	.0011–.0023	.0014–.0028	NA	NA
	W	6-173 (2.8)	46	45	90 ①	1.70	.0010–.0027	.0010–.0027	NA	NA

① With valve closed

PISTON AND RING SPECIFICATIONS
All measurments are given in inches.

Year	VIN	No. Cylinder Displacement cu. in. (liter)	Piston Clearance	Ring Gap			Ring Side Clearance		
				Top Compression	Bottom Compression	Oil Control	Top Compression	Bottom Compression	Oil Control
1987-88	1	4-121 (2.0)	.00098–.0022	.010–.020	.010–.020	.010–.050	.001–.003	.001–.003	.008
	W	6-173 (2.8)	.002–.003	.010–.020	.010–.020	.020–.055	.001–.003	.001–.003	.008

TORQUE SPECIFICATIONS
All readings in ft. lbs.

Year	VIN	No. Cylinder Displacement cu. in. (liter)	Cylinder Head Bolts	Main Bearing Bolts	Rod Bearing Bolts	Crankshaft Pulley Bolts	Flywheel Bolts	Manifold		Spark Plugs
								Intake	Exhaust	
1987-88	1	4-121 (2.0)	62-70 ①	63-77	34-43	66-89	45-59 ②	15-22	6-13	7-20
	W	6-173 (2.8)	③	63-83	34-44	67-85	45-59 ②	18	15-23	10-25

① Specification is for the shorter bolts. Torque the longer bolts to 73-83 ft.lbs.
② Specification is for automatic transaxle. Torque the manual transaxle bolts to 47-63 ft.lbs.
③ 2.8 Liter engine cylinder head bolts should first be torqued to 33 ft.lbs. Then tighten the bolts by rotating the torque wrench an additional 90°

BRAKE SPECIFICATIONS
All measurements in inches unless noted

Year	Model	Lug Nut Torque (ft. lbs.)	Master Cylinder Bore	Brake Disc		Standard Brake Drum Diameter	Minimum Lining Thickness	
				Minimum Thickness	Maximum Runout		Front	Rear
1987-88	Beretta	100	.945	.830	.004	7.899	$^3/_{32}$	$^3/_{32}$
	Corsica	100	.945	.830	.004	7.899	$^3/_{32}$	$^3/_{32}$

WHEEL ALIGNMENT

Year	Model	Caster Range (deg.)	Caster Preferred Setting (deg.)	Camber Range (deg.)	Camber Preferred Setting (deg.)	Toe-in (in.)	Steering Axis Inclination (deg.)
1987-88	Beretta, Corsica	1P-1.7P	1.2P	.5P-.8P	.8P	0-.1P	14

LIGHT TRUCKS AND VANS
BLAZER/JIMMY — FULL SIZE, BLAZER/JIMMY — S-SERIES
PICK-UPS — FULL SIZE, PICK-UPS — S-SERIES, SUBURBAN,
VANS — FULL SIZE AND ASTRO

GENERAL ENGINE SPECIFICATIONS

Year	Engine No. Cyl Displacement (cu. in.)	Carburetor Type	Horsepower @ rpm ■	Torque @ rpm (ft lbs) ■	Bore and Stroke (in.)	Compression Ratio	Oil Pressure @ 2000 rpm
'79	6-250 LD	2 bbl	130 @ 3800	210 @ 2400	3.870 × 3.530	8.3:1	40–60
	6-250 Calif	2 bbl	125 @ 4000	205 @ 2000	3.870 × 3.530	8.3:1	40–60
	6-250 HD	2 bbl	130 @ 4000	205 @ 2000	3.870 × 3.530	8.3:1	40–60
	6-292	1 bbl	115 @ 3400	215 @ 1600	3.870 × 4.120	7.8:1	40–60
	8-305	2 bbl	140 @ 4000	240 @ 2000	3.740 × 3.480	8.4:1	45
	8-350 LD	4 bbl	165 @ 3600	270 @ 2000	4.000 × 3.480	8.2:1	45
	8-350 Hi Alt	4 bbl	155 @ 3600	260 @ 2000	4.000 × 3.480	8.2:1	45
	8-350 HD	4 bbl	165 @ 3800	255 @ 2800	4.000 × 3.480	8.3:1	45
	8-350	Diesel	120 @ 3600	220 @ 1600	4.057 × 3.385	22.5:1	35
	8-400 HD	4 bbl	180 @ 3600	310 @ 2400	4.125 × 3.750	8.2:1	40
	8-454 LD	4 bbl	205 @ 3600	335 @ 2800	4.250 × 4.000	8.0:1	40
	8-454 HD	4 bbl	210 @ 3800	340 @ 2800	4.250 × 4.000	7.9:1	40
'80	6-250	2 bbl	130 @ 4000	210 @ 2000	3.870 × 3.530	8.3:1	40–60
	6-250 Calif.	2 bbl	130 @ 4000	205 @ 2000	3.870 × 3.530	8.3:1	40–60
	6-292	1 bbl	115 @ 3400	215 @ 1600	3.870 × 4.120	7.8:1	40–60
	8-305	2 bbl	135 @ 4200	235 @ 2400	3.740 × 3.480	8.5:1	45
	8-350 LD	4 bbl	175 @ 4000	275 @ 2400	4.000 × 3.480	8.2:1	45
	8-350 LD Calif	4 bbl	170 @ 4000	275 @ 2000	4.000 × 3.480	8.2:1	45
	8-350 HD	4 bbl	165 @ 3800	255 @ 2800	4.000 × 3.480	8.3:1	45
	8-350	Diesel	125 @ 3600	225 @ 1600	4.057 × 3.385	22.5:1	35
	8-400 HD	4 bbl	180 @ 3600	310 @ 2400	4.125 × 3.750	8.3:1	40
	8-454 HD	4 bbl	210 @ 3800	340 @ 2800	4.250 × 4.000	7.9:1	40
'81	6-250	2 bbl	130 @ 4000	210 @ 2000	3.870 × 3.530	8.3:1	40–60
	6-250 Calif	2 bbl	130 @ 4000	205 @ 2000	3.870 × 3.530	8.3:1	40–60
	6-292	1 bbl	115 @ 3400	215 @ 1600	3.870 × 4.120	7.8:1	40–60
	8-305	2 bbl	135 @ 4200	235 @ 2400	3.740 × 3.480	8.5:1	45
	8-305	4 bbl	155 @ 4400	252 @ 2400	3.740 × 3.480	9.2:1	45
	8-350 LD	4 bbl	175 @ 4000	275 @ 2000	4.000 × 3.480	8.2:1	45
	8-350 HD	4 bbl	165 @ 3800	255 @ 2800	4.000 × 3.480	8.3:1	45
	8-350	Diesel	125 @ 3600	225 @ 1600	4.057 × 3.385	22.5:1	35
	8-454	4 bbl	210 @ 3800	340 @ 2800	4.250 × 4.000	7.9:1	40

1 SPECIFICATIONS

GENERAL ENGINE SPECIFICATIONS

Year	Engine No. Cyl Displacement (cu. in.)	Carburetor Type	Horsepower @ rpm ■	Torque @ rpm (ft lbs) ■	Bore and Stroke (in.)	Compression Ratio	Oil Pressure @ 2000 rpm
'82	4-119	2 bbl	84 @ 4600	101 @ 3000	3.43 × 3.23	8.4:1	57
	4-121	2 bbl	83 @ 4600	108 @ 2400	3.50 × 3.15	9.3:1	45
	4-137	Diesel	58 @ 4300	93 @ 2200	3.46 × 3.62	21.0:1	55
	6-173	2 bbl	110 @ 4800	148 @ 2000	3.50 × 2.99	8.5:1	45
	6-250	2 bbl	130 @ 4000	210 @ 2000	3.870 × 3.530	8.3:1	40–60
	6-292	1 bbl	115 @ 3400	215 @ 1600	3.870 × 4.120	7.8:1	40–60
	8-305	4 bbl	140 @ 4200	240 @ 2400	3.740 × 3.480	8.5:1	45
	8-305	4 bbl	155 @ 4400	252 @ 2100	3.740 × 3.480	9.2:1	45
	8-350 LD	4 bbl	175 @ 4000	275 @ 2000	4.000 × 3.480	8.2:1	45
	8-350 HD	4 bbl	165 @ 3800	255 @ 2800	4.000 × 3.480	8.3:1	45
	8-379	Diesel	130 @ 3600	240 @ 2000	3.900 × 3.800	21.5:1	45
	8-454	4 bbl	210 @ 3800	340 @ 2800	4.250 × 4.000	7.9:1	40
'83	4-119	2 bbl	84 @ 4600	101 @ 3000	3.43 × 3.23	8.4:1	57
	4-121	2 bbl	83 @ 4600	108 @ 2400	3.50 × 3.15	9.3:1	45
	4-137	Diesel	58 @ 4300	93 @ 2200	3.46 × 3.62	21.0:1	55
	6-173	2 bbl	110 @ 4800	148 @ 2000	3.50 × 2.99	8.5:1	45
	6-250	2 bbl	130 @ 4000	210 @ 2000	3.870 × 3.530	8.3:1	40–60
	6-292	1 bbl	115 @ 3400	215 @ 1600	3.870 × 4.120	7.6:1	40–60
	8-305	4 bbl	140 @ 4200	240 @ 2400	3.740 × 3.480	8.5:1	45
	8-305	4 bbl	155 @ 4400	252 @ 2100	3.740 × 3.480	9.2:1	45
	8-350 LD	4 bbl	175 @ 4000	275 @ 2000	4.000 × 3.480	8.2:1	45
	8-350 HD	4 bbl	165 @ 3800	255 @ 2800	4.000 × 3.480	8.3:1	45
	8-379	Diesel	130 @ 3600	240 @ 2000	3.980 × 3.800	21.5:1	45
	8-454 HD	4 bbl	210 @ 3800	340 @ 2800	4.250 × 4.000	7.9:1	40
'84	4-119	2 bbl	84 @ 4600	101 @ 3000	3.43 × 3.23	8.4:1	57
	4-121	2 bbl	83 @ 4600	108 @ 2400	3.50 × 3.15	9.3:1	45
	4-137	Diesel	58 @ 4300	93 @ 2200	3.46 × 3.62	21.0:1	55
	6-173	2 bbl	110 @ 4800	148 @ 2000	3.50 × 2.99	8.5:1	45
	6-250	2 bbl	130 @ 4000	210 @ 2000	3.870 × 3.530	8.3:1	40–60
	6-292	1 bbl	115 @ 3400	215 @ 1600	3.870 × 4.120	7.8:1	40–60
	8-305	4 bbl	140 @ 4200	240 @ 2400	3.740 × 3.480	8.5:1	45
	8-305	4 bbl	155 @ 4400	252 @ 2100	3.740 × 3.480	9.2:1	45
	8-350 LD	4 bbl	175 @ 4000	275 @ 2000	4.000 × 3.480	8.2:1	45
	8-350 HD	4 bbl	165 @ 3800	255 @ 2800	4.000 × 3.480	8.3:1	45
	8-379	Diesel	130 @ 3600	240 @ 2000	3.980 × 3.800	21.5:1	45
	8-454 HD	4 bbl	210 @ 3800	340 @ 2800	4.250 × 4.000	7.9:1	40
'85	4-119	2bbl	82 @ 4600	101 @ 3000	3.43 × 3.23	8.4:1	57
	4-137	Diesel	62 @ 4300	96 @ 2200	3.46 × 3.26	21.0:1	55
	4-151	TBI	92 @ 4400	132 @ 2800	4.00 × 3.00	9.0:1	40–60
	6-173	2 bbl	110 @ 4800	145 @ 2100	3.50 × 2.99	8.5:1	45
	6-262	4 bbl	150 @ 4000	225 @ 2400	4.00 × 3.480	9.3:1	40–60
	8-305	4 bbl	155 @ 4000	245 @ 1600	3.740 × 3.480	8.6:1	45
	8-305	4 bbl	160 @ 4400	235 @ 2000	3.740 × 3.480	9.2:1	45
	8-350	4 bbl	165 @ 3800	275 @ 1600	4.00 × 3.480	8.2:1	45
	8-379	Diesel	130 @ 3600	240 @ 2000	3.980 × 3.800	21.5:1	45
	8-454	4 bbl	210 @ 3800	340 @ 2800	4.250 × 4.000	8.0:1	40

GENERAL ENGINE SPECIFICATIONS

Year	Engine No. Cyl Displacement (cu. in.)	Carburetor Type	Horsepower @ rpm ■	Torque @ rpm (ft lbs) ■	Bore and Stroke (in.)	Compression Ratio	Oil Pressure @ 2000 rpm
'86	4-119	2 bbl	82 @ 4600	101 @ 3000	3.43 × 3.23	8.4:1	57
	4-137	Diesel	62 @ 4300	96 @ 2200	3.46 × 3.62	21.0:1	55
	4-151	TBI	92 @ 4400	134 @ 2800	4.00 × 3.00	9.0:1	40-60
	6-173	2 bbl	110 @ 4800	145 @ 2100	3.50 × 2.99	8.5:1	45
	6-262	4 bbl	150 @ 4000	225 @ 2400	4.00 × 3.480	9.3:1	40-60
	8-305	4 bbl	155 @ 4400	245 @ 1600	4.00 × 3.480	8.6:1	45
	8-305	4 bbl	160 @ 4400	235 @ 2000	4.00 × 3.480	9.2:1	45
	8-350 LD	4 bbl	165 @ 3800	275 @ 1600	4.00 × 3.480	8.2:1	45
	8-350 HD	4 bbl	155 @ 4000	240 @ 2800	4.00 × 3.480	8.3:1	45
	8-379	Diesel	130 @ 3600	240 @ 2600	3.980 × 3.800	21.5:1	45
	8-454	4 bbl	230 @ 3800	360 @ 2800	4.250 × 4.000	8.0:1	40

■ Horsepower and torque are SAE net figures. They are measured at the rear of the transmission with all accessories installed and operating. Since the figures vary when a given engine is installed in different models, some are representative rather than exact.
FI—Fuel Injection
TBI—Throttle body injection

CAPACITIES
Blazer and Jimmy

Year	Engine No. Cyl. Displacement (cu in.)	Engine Crankcase (qts) incl. Filter	Transmission Pts To Refill After Draining Manual 3-Speed	4-Speed	Automatic	Transfer Case (Pts)	Drive Axle (pts) Front/Rear	Gasoline Tank (gals) Std/Opt	Cooling System ■ (qts) With Heater	A/C	With HD Cooling
'79	6-250	5	3.0	8.0	5.0	5.0 ④	5/3.5 ⑤	25/31	15	15.5	15.5
	8-305	5	3.0	8.0	5.0	5.0 ④	5/3.5 ⑤	25/31	17.5	17.5	17.5
	8-350	5	3.0	8.0	5.0	5.0 ④	5/3.5 ⑤	25/31	17.5	18	18
	8-400	5	—	—	5.0	5.0 ④	5/3.5 ⑤	25/31	18	19	19
'80-'81	6-250	5	3.0	8.0	5.0	5.0	5/3.5 ⑤	25/31	15	15.5	15.5
	8-305	5	3.0	8.0	5.0	5.0	5/3.5 ⑤	25/31	17.5	17.5	17.5
	8-350	5	3.0	8.0	5.0	5.0	5/3.5 ⑥	25/31	17.5	18	18
'82	6-250	5	2.0	8.0	6.0	5.0	5/ ⑦	25/31	15.0	15.5	—
	8-305	5	2.0	8.0	6.0	5.0	5/ ⑦	25/31	17.5	18.0	—
	8-350	5	2.0	8.0	6.0 ⑥	5.0	5/ ⑦	25/31	17.5	18.0	—
	8-379	7	—	8.0	6.0 ⑥	5.0	5/ ⑦	27/32	24.8	24.8	—
'83	6-250	5	3.0	8.0	6.0	5.0	5/ ⑦	25/31	15.0	15.5	—
	8-305	5	3.0	8.0	6.0	5.0	5/ ⑦	25/31	17.5	18.0	—
	8-350	5	3.0	8.0	6.0 ⑥	5.0	5/ ⑦	25/31	17.5	18.0	—
	8-379	7	—	8.0	6.0 ⑥	5.0	5/ ⑦	27/32	24.5	24.5	—
	8-454	7 ③	—	8.0	6.0 ⑥	5.0	5/ ⑦	25/31	23	24.5	—
'84	6-250	5	3.0	8.0	6.0	5.0	5/ ⑦	25/31	15.0	15.5	—
	8-305	5	3.0	8.0	6.0	5.0	5/ ⑦	25/31	17.5	18.0	—
	8-350	5	3.0	8.0	6.0 ⑥	5.0	5/ ⑦	25/31	17.5	18.0	—
	8-379	8	—	8.0	6.0 ⑥	5.0	5/ ⑦	27/32	24.5	24.5	—
	8-454	7 ③	—	8.0	6.0 ⑥	5.0	5/ ⑦	25/31	23	24.5	—

CAPACITIES
Blazer and Jimmy

Year	Engine No. Cyl. Displacement (cu in.)	Engine Crankcase (qts) incl. Filter	Transmission Pts To Refill After Draining Manual 3-Speed	4-Speed	Automatic	Transfer Case (Pts)	Drive Axle (pts) Front/ Rear	Gasoline Tank (gals) Std/ Opt	Cooling System ■ (qts) With Heater	A/C	With HD Cooling
'85–'86	8-305, 350	5	3.0	8.0	①	5.0	②③	25/31	17.5	18	—
	8-379	7	3.0	8.0	①	5.0	②③	27/32/41	23	24.5	—
	8-454	6	3.0	8.0	①	5.0	②③	25/31/40	23	24.5	—

■ Automatic transmission models have either the A/C or HD radiator; capacity may be increased on trucks with 4.11:1 axle ratios; when two figures are separated by a slash, the first is for 2 wheel drive
① Auto Trans capacities are:
  TH350—6.3
  TH400—9.0
  700R4—10
② Front Axle Capacities are:
  10–20 Series—4
  30 Series—6
③ Rear Axle Capacities are:
  8½"—4¼

  8⅞"—3½
  9¾"—6.0
  10½" (Chev)—6½
  10½" (Dana)—7.2
  12¼"—26.8
④ 8¼ with full-time 4 wheel drive
⑤ 8.5 ring gear—4.2
⑥ with TH-M 400:7.0
  with TH-M 700-R4: 10.0
⑦ 8½" ring gear: 4.25
  8⅞" ring gear: 3.5
  9¾" ring gear (Dana): 6.0
  10½" ring gear (Dana): 7.2
          (Chev.): 6.5

CAPACITIES
Pick-Ups and Suburban

Year	Engine (No. Cyl.) Displacement (cu. in.)	Engine Crankcase (qts) With Filter	Transmission (pts) Manual 3-spd	4-spd	Auto (Refill)	Drive Axle (pts) Front	Rear	Transfer Case (pts)	Fuel Tank (gals)	Cooling System (qts) w/o A/C	w/ A/C	HD
'79–'81	6-250	5	3.2 ⑦	8.0	②	5 ⑧	⑥	5 ⑤	20 ⑩	15.0	15.6	15.0
	6-292	6	3.2 ⑦	8.0	②	5 ⑧	⑥	5 ⑤	20 ⑩	14.8	15.4	14.8
	8-305	5	3.2 ⑦	8.0	②	5 ⑧	⑥	5 ⑤	20 ⑩	17.6	18.0	18.0
	8-350	5	3.2 ⑦	8.0	②	5 ⑧	⑥	5 ⑤	20 ⑩	17.6	18.0	18.0
	8-350 Diesel	7	—	—	5.0	—	⑥	—	20 ⑩	18.0	18.0	18.0
	8-400	5	3.2 ⑦	8.0	②	5 ⑧	⑥	5 ⑤	20 ⑩	20.4	20.4	20.4
	8-454	5 ⑪	3.2 ⑦	8.0	②	5 ⑧	⑥	5 ⑤	20 ⑩	24.4 ⑨	24.7	24.7
'82	6-250	5	3.0	8.0	6.0	5.0	⑯	5.0 ⑬	⑭	15.0	15.5	—
	6-292	6	3.0	8.0	6.0	5.0	⑯	5.0 ⑬	⑭	15.0	15.5	—
	8-305	5	3.0	8.0	6.0	5.0	⑯	5.0 ⑬	⑭	17.5	18.0	—
	8-350	5	3.0	8.0	⑮	5.0	⑯	5.0 ⑬	⑭	17.5	18.0	—
'83	6-250	5	3.0	8.0	6.0	5.0	⑯	10 ①	⑭	15	15.5	—
	8-305	5	3.0	8.0	6.0	5.0	⑯	10 ①	⑭	17.5	18	—
	8-350	5	3.0	8.0	6.0 ⑥	5.0	⑯	10 ①	⑭	17.5	18	—
	8-379	7	—	8.0	6.0 ⑥	5.0	⑯	10 ①	⑭	23	24.5	—
	8-454	5	—	8.0	6.0 ⑥	5.0	⑯	10 ①	⑭	23	24.5	—
'84	6-250	5	3.0	8.0	6.0	5.0	⑯	10 ①	⑭	15	15.5	—
	8-305	5	3.0	8.0	6.0	5.0	⑯	10 ①	⑭	17.5	18	—
	8-350	5	3.0	8.0	6.0 ⑥	5.0	⑯	10 ①	⑭	17.5	18	—
	8-379	7	—	8.0	6.0 ⑥	5.0	⑯	10 ①	⑭	23	24.5	—
	8-454	5	—	8.0	6.0 ⑥	5.0	⑯	10 ①	⑭	23	24.5	—

CAPACITIES
Pick-Ups and Suburban

Year	Engine (No. Cyl.) Displacement (cu. in.)	Engine Crankcase (qts) With Filter	Transmission (pts) Manual 3-spd	Manual 4-spd	Auto (Refill)	Drive Axle (pts) Front	Rear	Transfer Case (pts)	Fuel Tank (gals)	Cooling System (qts) w/o A/C	w/ A/C	HD
'85–'86	6-262	5	3.0	8.0	6.3	⑰	⑯	4.0	⑭	10.9	10.9	—
	6-292	6	3.0	8.0	6.3	⑰	⑯	4.0	⑭	15.5	16	—
	8-305	5	3.0	8.0	6.3	⑰	⑯	4.0	⑭	17.5	18	—
	8-350	5	3.0	8.0	9.0	⑰	⑯	4.0	⑭	17.5	18	—
	8-379	7	3.0	8.0	9.0	⑰	⑯	6.0	⑭	23	24.5	—

① Heavy-duty 3-speed—3.5 pts
② Turbo Hydra-Matic 350—5.0 pts
Turbo Hydra-Matic 400—7.5 pts
③ 3,300 and 3,500 lb Chevrolet axles—4.5 pts
5,200 and 7,200 lb Chevrolet axles—6.5 pts
5,500 lb Dana axles—6.0 pts
11,000 lb Chevrolet axles—14.0 pts
④ 20 Series—21.0 gals
⑤ Full-time 4 wd—8.25 pts
⑥ 8½ in. ring gear—4.2 pts
8⅞ in. ring gear (Chevrolet)—4.5 pts (3.5 pts '77–'78)
10½ in. ring gear (Chevrolet)—5.4 pts
10½ in. ring gear (Dana)—7.2 pts

12½ in. ring gear (Chevrolet)—26.8 pts
⑦ Tremec 3-spd—4.0 pts
Muncie 3-spd—3.0 pts
⑧ 8½ in. ring gear—4.25 pts ('77–'81)
⑨ 22.8—'79–'81
⑩ 16.0 gal—short wheelbase models
⑪ 6 qts with filter, 5 qts without filter, '78–'81
⑫ OPT.: 20 gal
⑬ All 1-ton models: 10.0
⑭ Short bed w/single tank: 16 gal.
Short bed w/dual tanks: 32 gal.
Longbed w/single tank: 20 gal.
Long bed gasoline models w/dual tanks, under 8600 lb GVWR: 32 gal

Long bed gasoline models with dual tanks over 8600 lb GVWR, and all diesel models w/dual tanks: 40 gal.
⑮ TH-M 350: 6.0
TH-M 400: 7.0
TH-M 700-R4:10.0
⑯ Ring gear   Capacity
8½″   4.25
8⅞″   3.5
9¾″ (Dana)   6.0
10½″ (Dana)   7.2
10½″ (Chev)   6.5
12¼″ (Dana)   26.8
⑰ Front Axle Capacities are:
10–20 Series—4
30 Series—6

CAPACITIES
S-Series, Blazer and Jimmy

Year	Engine (No. Cyl.) Displacement cu. in.	Crankcase (qts.)	Transmission (pts) 4 sp	5 sp	Auto.	Transfer Case (pts)	Rear Drive Axle (pts)	Front Drive Axle (pts)	Gas Tank (gal)	Cooling System (qts) Manual	Auto.
'82	4-119	4.0	2.7	2.7	7.0 ②	5.2	3.5	1.7	13.0 ①	9.6	9.6
	4-121	4.0	2.7	2.7	7.0 ②	5.2	3.5	1.7	13.0 ①	9.6	9.6
	4-137 Diesel	5.0	2.7	2.7	7.0 ②	5.2	3.5	1.7	13.0 ①	10.0	10.0
	6-173	4.5 ③	2.7	2.7	7.0 ②	5.2	3.5	1.7	13.0 ①	12.4	12.4
'83	4-119	4	2.7	2.7	7	10	3.5	3	13 ①	9.4	9.5
	4-121	4	2.7	2.7	7	10	3.5	3	13 ①	9.6	9.7
	4-137 Diesel	4	2.7	2.7	7	10	3.5	3	13 ①	10	10
	6-173	4.5 ③	2.7	2.7	7	10	3.5	3	13 ①	12	12
'84	4-119	4	2.7	2.7	7	10	3.5	3	13 ①	9.4	9.5
	4-121	4	2.7	2.7	7	10	3.5	3	13 ①	9.6	9.7
	4-137 Diesel	4	2.7	2.7	7	10	3.5	3	13 ①	10	10
	6-173	4.5 ③	2.7	2.7	7	10	3.5	3	13 ①	12	12
'85–'86	4-119	4	2.7	2.7	7	5.2	3.5	2.6	13 ①	9.5	—
	4-137	5.5	2.7	2.7	7	5.2	3.5	2.6	14 ①	11.5	12 ④
	4-151	3	2.7	2.7	7	5.2	3.5	2.6	13 ①	12	12
	6-173	4	2.7	2.7	7	5.2	3.5	2.6	13 ①	12	12

① Optional: 20.0 gal.
② Figure shown is for pan removal only. Total overhaul capacity is 19.0 pts.
③ 4 qts. without filter
④ Automatic and manual transmission figures are the same for heavy duty cooling or cooling with air conditioning

CAPACITIES
Vans (Except Astro)

Year	Model	Engine (No. Cyl.) Displacement (cu. in.)	Engine Crankcase (qts) With Filter	Transmission (pts) Manual 3-spd	4-spd	Automatic	Drive Axle (pts)	Gasoline Tank (gals)	Cooling System (qts) wo/AC	w/AC
'79–'82	All	6-250	5	3.2	—	5③	3.5④	22/33	17	18.5
	All	8-305	5	3.2①	—	5③	3.5④	22/33	19.5	21.0
	10, 20, 1500, 2500	8-350	5	3.2①	—	5③	3.5④	22/33	20	21.5
	30, 3500	8-350	5	3.2①	—	5③	3.5④	22/33	20	21.5
	All	8-400	5	3.2①	—	5③	3.5④	22/33	20	21.5
'83	All	6-250	5	3	8	③	④	22/33	17	—
	All	8-305	5	3	8	③	④	22/33	19	20
	All	8-350	5	3	8	③	④	22/33	19	20
	All	8-379	7	3	8	③	④	22/33	24	24
'84	All	6-250	5	3	8	③	④	22/33	17	—
	All	8-305	5	3	8	③	④	22/33	19	20
	All	8-350	5	3	8	③	④	22/33	19	20
	All	8-379	7	3	8	③	④	22/33	24	24
'85–'86	All	6-252	5	3	8	6.3	④	22/23	11.1	11.1
	All	8-305	5	3	8	6.3	④	22/23	17	17
	All	8-350	5	3	8	⑤	④	22/23	17	17
	All	8-379	7	3	8	⑤	④	22/23	24⑥	24⑥

① 4 pts with top-cover Tremec three-speed and Saginaw three-speed
② 7 pts with 10,000 lb or higher GVW.
③ '82 TH-M 350: 6.0

TH-M 400: 7.0
TH-M 700-R4: 10.0
④ 9¾" ring gear: 6.0
   10½" ring gear (Dana): 7.2
   10½" ring gear (Chev): 6.5

12½" ring gear (Dana): 26.8
⑤ TH350—6.3
   TH400—9.0
⑥ 25.6 w/HD cooling

CAPACITIES
Astro Vans

Year	Engine (No. Cyl.) Displacement (cu. in.)	Engine Crankcase (qts) With Filter	Transmission (pts) Manual 3-spd	4-spd	Automatic	Drive Axle (pts)	Gasoline Tank (gals)	Cooling System (qts) wo/AC	w/AC
'85–'86	4-151	3	3.0	8.0	6.3	①	17/27	10	10
	6-262	5	3.0	8.0	6.3	①	17/27	13.5	13.5

① Capacities vary according to ring gear:
8½"—4.5
8⅞"—3.5
9¾"—6.0
10½" (Chev)—6.5
10½" (Dana)—7.2

TUNE-UP SPECIFICATIONS
Pick-ups and Suburban

Year	Engine Displacement (cu in.)	Spark Plugs Type	Gap (in.)	Distributor	Ignition Timing (deg) MT	AT	Fuel Pump Pressure (psi)	Compression Pressure (psi) ●	Idle Speed (rpm)* MT	AT
'79	6-250 (LD Fed)	R46TS	0.035	Electronic	10B	10B	4.5–6.0	130	750	600
	6-250 ③	R46TS	0.035	Electronic	6B	8B	4.5–6.0	130	750	600
	6-292	R44T	0.035	Electronic	8B	8B	4.5–6.0	130	700	700
	8-305	R45TS	0.045	Electronic	6B	6B	7.5–9.0	150	600	500
	8-350 (LD)	R45TS	0.045	Electronic	8B	8B	7.5–9.0	150	700	500
	8-350 (HD)	R44T	0.045	Electronic	4B	4B	7.5–9.0	150	700	700(N)
	8-400	R45TS	0.045	Electronic	—	4B	7.5–9.0	150	—	500
	8-454 (LD)	R45TS	0.045	Electronic	8B	8B	7.5–9.0②	150	700	500
	8-454 (HD)	R44T	0.045	Electronic	—	4B	7.5–9.0②	150	—	700(N)

TUNE-UP SPECIFICATIONS
Pick-ups and Suburban

Year	Engine Displacement (cu in.)	Spark Plugs Type	Gap (in.)	Distributor	Ignition Timing (deg) MT	AT	Fuel Pump Pressure (psi)	Compression Pressure (psi) ●	Idle Speed (rpm)* MT	AT
'80	6-250 (LD Fed)	R46TS	0.035	Electronic	10B	10B	4.5–6.0	130	750	650
	6-250 (LD Calif)	R46TS	0.035	Electronic	10B	10B	4.5–6.0	130	750	600
	6-250 ③	R46TS	0.035	Electronic	—	8B	4.5–6.0	130	—	600
	6-292	R44T	0.035	Electronic	8B	8B	4.5–6.0	130	700	700(N)
	8-305	R45TS	0.045	Electronic	8B	8B	7.5–9.0	150	600	500
	8-350 (LD)	R45TS	0.045	Electronic	8B	8B	7.5–9.0	150	700	500
	8-350 (HD Fed)	R44T	0.045	Electronic	4B	4B	7.5–9.0	150	700	700(N)
	8-350 (HD Calif)	R44T	0.045	Electronic	6B	6B	7.5–9.0	150	700	700(N)
	8-400 (HD Fed)	R44T	0.045	Electronic	—	4B	7.5–9.0	150	—	700(N)
	8-400 (HD Calif)	R44T	0.045	Electronic	—	6B	7.5–9.0	150	—	700(N)
	8-454	R44T	0.045	Electronic	4B	4B	7.5–9.0 ②	150	700	700(N)
'81	6-250 (Fed)	R45TS	0.035	Electronic	10B	10B	4.5–6.0	130	750	650(D)
	6-250 (Calif)	R46TS	0.035	Electronic	10B	10B	4.5–6.0	130	750	650(D)
	6-292	R44T	0.035	Electronic	8B	8B	4.5–6.0	130	700	700(N)
	8-305 2 bbl	R45TS	0.045	Electronic	8B	8B	7.5–9.0	150	600	500(D)
	8-305 4 bbl	R45TS	0.045	Electronic	4B	4B ④	7.5–9.0	150	700	500(D)
	8-350 (LD)	R45TS	0.045	Electronic	8B	8B ⑤	7.5–9.0	150	700	500(D)
	8-350 (HD Fed)	R44T	0.045	Electronic	4B	4B	7.5–9.0	150	700	700(N)
	8-350 (HD Calif)	R44T	0.045	Electronic	6B	6B	7.5–9.0	150	700	700(N)
	8-350 Diesel	—	—	Electronic	—	8B ⑥		450	—	575(D) ⑦
	8-454	R44T	0.045	Electronic	4B	4B	7.5–9.0	150	700	700(N)
'82	6-250	R45TS	⑧	Electronic	⑧	⑧	4.5–6	—	⑧	⑧
	6-292	R44T	.035	Electronic	8	8	4–5	—	700	700
	8-305	R45TS	.045	Electronic	⑧	⑧	⑧	—	⑧	⑧
	8-350 LD	R45TS	.045	Electronic	⑧	⑧	⑧	—	⑧	⑧
	8-350 HD	R44T	.045	Electronic	⑧	⑧	⑧	—	⑧	⑧
	8-379	Diesel	—	—	⑧	⑧	⑧	—	⑧	⑧
	8-454	R44T	.045	Electronic	⑧	⑧	⑧	—	⑧	⑧
'83	6-250	R45TS	⑧	Electronic	⑧	⑧	4.5–6	—	⑧	⑧
	6-292	R44T	.035	Electronic	8	8	4–6	—	700	700
	8-305	R45TS	.045	Electronic	⑧	⑧	⑧	—	⑧	⑧
	8-350 LD	R45TS	.045	Electronic	⑧	⑧	⑧	—	⑧	⑧
	8-350 HD	R44T	.045	Electronic	⑧	⑧	⑧	—	⑧	⑧
	8-379	Diesel	—	—	⑧	⑧	⑧	—	⑧	⑧
	8-454	R44T	.045	Electronic	⑧	⑧	⑧	—	⑧	⑧
'84	6-250	R45TS	⑧	Electronic	⑧	⑧	4.5–6	—	⑧	⑧
	6-292	R44T	.035	Electronic	8	8	4.5–6	—	700	700
	8-305	R45TS	.045	Electronic	⑧	⑧	⑧	—	⑧	⑧
	8-350 LD	R45TS	.045	Electronic	⑧	⑧	⑧	—	⑧	⑧
	8-350 HD	R44T	.045	Electronic	⑧	⑧	⑧	—	⑧	⑧
	8-379	Diesel	—	—	⑧	⑧	⑧	—	⑧	⑧
	8-454	R44T	.045	Electronic	⑧	⑧	⑧	—	⑧	⑧
'85–'86	6-292	R43CTS	⑧	Electronic	⑧	⑧	4–6.5	—	⑧	⑧
	6-292	R44T	⑧	Electronic	⑧	⑧	4–6.5	—	⑧	⑧
	8-305	R45TS	⑧	Electronic	⑧	⑧	4–6.5	—	⑧	⑧
	8-350	R45TS	⑧	Electronic	⑧	⑧	4–6.5	—	⑧	⑧
	8-454	R44T	⑧	Electronic	⑧	⑧	4–6.5	—	⑧	⑧

NOTE: All engines use hydraulic valve lifters
NOTE: Part numbers in this chart are not recommendations by Chilton for any product by brand name.
NOTE: The underhood sticker often reflects tune-up changes made in production. Sticker figures must be used if they disagree with those in this chart.
● Maximum variation among cylinders—20 psi
B Before Top Dead Center
LD Light-duty
HD Heavy-duty

1 SPECIFICATIONS

TUNE-UP SPECIFICATIONS
Pick-ups and Suburban

Year	Engine Displacement (cu in.)	Spark Plugs Type	Gap (in.)	Distributor	Ignition Timing (deg) MT	AT	Fuel Pump Pressure (psi)	Compression Pressure (psi) ●	Idle Speed (rpm)* MT	AT

Fed Federal (49 states)
Calif California only
MT Manual transmission
AT Automatic transmission
N Neutral
* Automatic transmission idle speed set in
  Drive unless otherwise indicated
NA Not available
— Not applicable
Hyd Hydraulic
① 700 rpm—California
② 5.5–7.0 with vapor return line
③ California C-20, C-2500 only
④ Calif.: 8B
  High Alt.: 2B
  Emission Label Code AAN: 6B
⑤ Calif.: 6B
  Calif. w/Emission Label Code
  AAD: 8B
⑥ Calif.: 5B
⑦ Calif.: 600(D)
⑧ See underhood sticker

TUNE-UP SPECIFICATIONS
Vans (Except Astro)

When analyzing compression results, look for uniformity among cylinders rather than specific pressures.

Year	Engine Cu In. Displacement	Spark Plugs Orig Type	Gap (in.)	Distributor	Ignition Timing ● (deg)▲ MT	AT	Fuel Pump Pressure (psi)	Curb Idle Speed (rpm)● MT	AT
'79	6-250	R46TS	.035	Electronic	10B ⑥	10B ⑦	4.5–6	750	600
	8-305	R45TS	.045	Electronic	6B	6B	7.5–9	700	600
	8-350 ⑧	R45TS	.045	Electronic	8B	8B	7.5–9	700	500
	8-400 ⑧	R45TS	.045	Electronic	—	4B	7.5–9	—	500
'80–'81	6-250	R46TS	.035	Electronic	10B	8B ⑨	4–6	750	650(D)
	8-305 (2-bbl)	R45TS	.045	Electronic	8B	8B	7–9	700	600(D)
	8-305 (4-bbl)	R45TS	.045	Electronic	6B	4B	7–9	700	500(D)
	8-350	R45TS	.045	Electronic	8B ⑩	8B ⑪	7–9	700	500(D) ⑫
'82	6-250	R45TS	.045	Electronic	①	①	4–6	①	①
	8-305	R45TS	.045	Electronic	①	①	7–9	①	①
	8-350	R45TS	.045	Electronic	①	①	7–9	①	①
'83	6-250	R45TS	.045	Electronic	①	①	4–6	①	①
	8-305	R45TS	.045	Electronic	①	①	7–9	①	①
	8-350	R45TS	.045	Electronic	①	①	7–9	①	①
	8-379	Diesel	—	—	①	①	—	①	①

TUNE-UP SPECIFICATIONS
Vans (Except Astro)

When analyzing compression results, look for uniformity among cylinders rather than specific pressures.

Year	Engine Cu In. Displacement	Spark Plugs Orig Type	Gap (in.)	Distributor	Ignition Timing ● (deg)▲ MT	AT	Fuel Pump Pressure (psi)	Curb Idle Speed (rpm) ● MT	AT
'84	6-250	R45TS	.045	Electronic	①	①	4–6	①	①
	8-305	R45TS	.045	Electronic	①	①	7–9	①	①
	8-350	R45TS	.045	Electronic	①	①	7–9	①	①
	8-379	Diesel	—	—	①	①	—	①	①
'85–'86	6-252	R43CTS	①	Electronic	①	①	4–6.5	③	③
	8-305	R45TS	①	Electronic	①	①	4–6.5	③	③
	8-350	R45TS	②	Electronic	①	①	4–6.5	③	③
	8-379	—	—	Diesel	—	—	6.5–9	650	650 ④

NOTE: The underhood specifications sticker often reflects tune-up changes made in production. Sticker figures must be used if they disagree with those in this chart.
NOTE: Part numbers in this chart are not recommendations by Chilton for any product by brand name.
NOTE: All engines use hydraulic valve lifters.

● Figures in parentheses are for California, and are given only if they differ from the 49 state specification. Automatic transmission idle speeds are set in Drive, unless specified otherwise.
▲ At idle speed with vacuum advance hose disconnected and plugged, unless specified otherwise in the text.
N—Transmission in Neutral
D—Transmission in Drive
HD Heavy Duty
LD Light Duty
① See the underhood specifications sticker
② Vehicles w/HD emissions use R44T
③ If equipped w/ECM, no adjustment required
④ Adjust w/AT in Park
⑤ California only
⑥ G-20, G-30, 2500, 3500 series in Calif.—6B
⑦ G-20, G-30, 2500, 3500 series in Calif.—8B

⑧ Some G-30/3500 series vans differ. Check the underhood emission sticker.
⑨ High Alt.—10B
⑩ Fed 1 ton models—4B
   Calif ¾ and 1 ton models—6B
⑪ 1 ton models—6B
⑫ 1 ton models—700(N)
   Calif. ½ and ⅓ ton models—550 (D)

TUNE-UP SPECIFICATIONS
Astro Vans

When analyzing compression results, look for uniformity among cylinders rather than specific pressures.

Year	Engine Cu In. Displacement	Spark Plugs Orig Type	Gap (in.)	Distributor	Ignition Timing ● (deg)▲ MT	AT	Fuel Pump Pressure (psi)	Curb Idle Speed (rpm) ● MT	AT
'85–'86	4-151	R43TSX	①	Electronic	①	①	4–6.5	②	②
	6-262	R43CTS	①	Electronic	①	①	4–6.5	②	②

① Refer to underhood sticker
② Controlled by ECM and non-adjustable

TUNE-UP SPECIFICATIONS
Blazer/Jimmy

When analyzing compression test results, look for uniformity among cylinders rather than specific pressures.

Year	Engine No. Cyl Displacement	Spark Plugs Orig Type	Gap (in.)	Distributor	Ignition Timing (deg) Man Trans	Auto Trans	Fuel Pump Pressure (psi)	Idle Speed (rpm) Man Trans	Auto Trans ▲
'79	6-250	R46TS	.035	Electronic	10B	10B	4½-6	750	600
	8-305	R45TS	.045	Electronic	6B	6B	7-9	600	500
	8-350	R45TS	.045	Electronic	8B	8B	7-9	700	500
	8-400	R45TS	.060	Electronic	—	4B	7-9	—	500
'80-'81	6-250	R46TS	.035	Electronic	10B	10B	3.5-4.5	750	650(D)
	8-305	R45TS	.045	Electronic	4B	2B	7.0-8.5	700	500(D)
	8-350	R45TS	.045	Electronic	8B	8B	7.0-8.5	700	500(D)
'82	6-250	R45TS	.045	Electronic	①	①	4-6	①	①
	8-305	R45TS	.045	Electronic	①	①	7-9	①	①
	8-350	R45TS	.045	Electronic	①	①	7-9	①	①
	8-379	Diesel	—	—	①	①	—	①	①
'83	6-250	R45TS	.045	Electronic	①	①	4-6	①	①
	8-305	R45TS	.045	Electronic	①	①	7-9	①	①
	8-350	R45TS	.045	Electronic	①	①	7-9	①	①
	8-379	Diesel	—	—	①	①	—	①	①
	8-454	R44T	.045	Electronic	①	①	—	①	①
'84	6-250	R45TS	.045	Electronic	①	①	4-6	①	①
	8-305	R45TS	.045	Electronic	①	①	7-9	①	①
	8-350	R45TS	.045	Electronic	①	①	7-9	①	①
	8-379	Diesel	—	—	①	①	—	①	①
	8-454	R44T	.045	Electronic	①	①	—	①	①
'85-'86	8-305	R45TS	①	Electronic	①	①	4-6.5	①②	①②
	8-350 LD	R45TS	①	Electronic	①	①	4-6.5	①②	①②
	8-350 HD	R45TS	①	Electronic	①	①	4-6.5	①②	①②
	8-379	—	—	Diesel	—	—	6.5-9	①	①
	8-454	R44T	①	Electronic	①	①	4-6.5	①②	①②

NOTE: The underhood specifications sticker often reflects tuneup specification changes made in production. Sticker figures must be used if they disagree with those in this chart. Part numbers in this chart are not recommendations by Chilton for any product name.

NOTE: All engines use hydraulic valve lifters.

● Figures in parentheses are for California, and are given only when they differ from the 49 State models. When two idle speeds separated by a slash are given, the lower figure is with the solenoid disconnected.

▲ Automatic transmission idle speed set in Drive unless otherwise indicated

B Before Top Dead Center

N Neutral

TDC Top Dead Center

2WD Two wheel drive

4WD 4 wheel drive

① See under hood sticker

② Computer controlled on some models

TUNE-UP SPECIFICATIONS
S-Series Blazer/Jimmy

When analyzing compression results, look for uniformity among cylinders rather than specific pressures.

Year	Engine Cu In. Displacement	Spark Plugs Orig Type	Gap (in.)	Distributor	Ignition Timing ● (deg)▲ MT	AT	Fuel Pump Pressure (psi)	Idle Speed (rpm) MT	AT
'82	4-119	R-42XLS	.040	Electronic	6B	6B	3.0	800	900
	4-121	R-42CTS	.035	Electronic	12B	12B	5.0	750	700
	6-173	R-42TS	.040	Electronic	6B	10B	7.0	1000	750
'83	4-119	R-42XLS	.040	Electronic	①	①	3.0	①	①
	4-121	R-42CTS	.035	Electronic	①	①	5.0	①	①
	6-173	R-42TS	.040	Electronic	①	①	7.0	①	①
'84	4-119	R-42XLS	.040	Electronic	①	①	3.0	①	①
	4-121	R-42CTS	.035	Electronic	①	①	5.0	①	①
	6-173	R-42TS	.040	Electronic	①	①	7.0	①	①
'85–'86	4-119	R42XLS	①	Electronic	①	①	4-6.5	③	③
	4-137	—	—	Diesel	—	—	—	①	①
	4-151	R43TSX	①	Electronic	①	①	4-6.5	③	③
	4-173	R43CTS ②	①	Electronic	①	①	4-6.5	③	③

Note: The under hood specifications sticker often reflects tune-up specification changes made in production. Sticker figures must be used if they disagree with those in this chart.
① See under hood sticker
② Use R42TCS if vehicle is subjected to hard usage
③ Controlled by ECM, does not require adjustment

FIRING ORDERS

NOTE: Always replace spark plug wires one at a time.

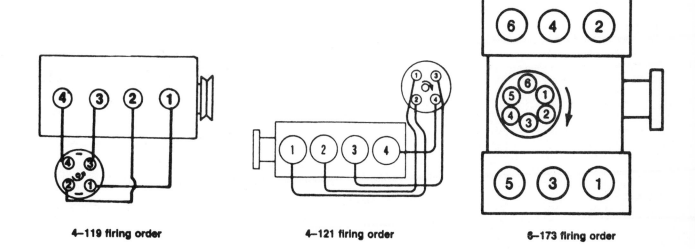

4–119 firing order   4–121 firing order   6–173 firing order

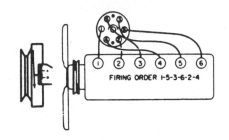

Six cylinder

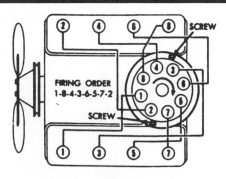

V8

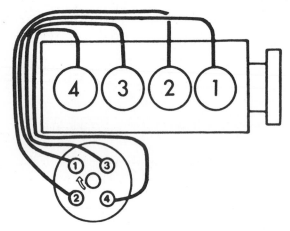

2.5 L-4 firing order

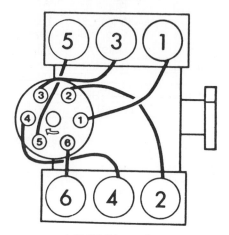

4.3 L V6 firing order

VALVE SPECIFICATIONS

Engine No. Cyl Displacement (cu in.)	Seat Angle (deg)	Face Angle (deg)	Spring Test Pressure (lbs @ in.)	Spring Installed Height (in.) ①	Stem-to-Guide Clearance (in.)		Stem Diameter (in.)	
					Intake	Exhaust	Intake	Exhaust
4-119	45	45	35 @ 1.614	20 @ 1.515	.0009–.0022	.0015–.0031	.3102 min.	.3091 min.
4-121	46	45	182 @ 1.330	—	.0011–.0026	.0014–.0031	.3410–.3416	.3410–.3416
4-137	45	45	145 @ 1.535	44 @ 1.457	.0015–.0027	.0025–.0037	.3150	.3150
4-151	46	45	122–180 @ 1.254	1.66	0.0010–0.0027 ④	0.0010–0.0027 ④	0.3418–0.3425	0.3418–0.3425
6-173	46	45	195 @ 1.180	—	.0010–.0027	.0010–.0027	.3410–.3416	.3410–.3416
6-250	46	45	175 @ 1.26	1.66	0.0010–0.0027	0.0015–0.0032	0.3414	0.3414
6-262	46	45	194–206 @ 1.25	1.70	0.0010–0.0027	0.0010–0.0027	—	—
6-292	46	45	175 @ 1.26	1.66	0.0010–0.0027	0.0015–0.0032	0.3414	0.3414
8-305	46	45	200 @ 1.25	1 23/32	0.0010–0.0027	0.0010–0.0027	0.3414	0.3414
8-350	46	45	200 @ 1.25	1 23/32	0.0010–0.0027	0.0010–0.0027	0.3414	0.3414
8-379 Diesel	46	45	230 @ 1.40	1 13/15	0.0010–0.0027	0.0010–0.0027	0.3414	0.3414
8-400	46	45	200 @ 1.25	—	0.0010–0.0027	0.0012–0.0029	0.3414	0.3414
8-454	46	45	220 @ 1.40	1 51/64	0.0010–0.0027	0.0012–0.0029	0.3719	0.3719
8-350 Diesel	②	③	205 @ 1.00	—	0.0010–0.0027	0.0015–0.0032	0.3429	0.3424

① ± 1/32 in.
② Intake—45° Exhaust—31°
③ Intake—44° Exhaust—30°
④ As measured at top. At bottom, clearance is 0.0020–0.0037
⑤ Face angle is 46° on 1984 and later models

CRANKSHAFT AND CONNECTING ROD SPECIFICATIONS

(All measurements are given in in.)

Year	Engine No. Cyl. Displacement (cu in.)	Crankshaft				Connecting Rod		
		Main Brg Journal Dia	Main Brg Oil Clearance	Shaft End-Play	Thrust on No.	Journal Diameter	Oil Clearance	Side Clearance
'82–'84	4-119	2.2050	0.008–0.0025	0.0117 max.	3	1.9290	0.0007–0.0030	0.0137 max.
	4-121	⑪	⑫	0.0020–0.0071	3	1.9990	0.0010–0.0031	0.0039–0.0240
	4-837	2.3590	0.0011–0.0033	0.0018	3	2.0837	0.0016–0.0047	0.0024
	6-173	2.4940	0.0017–0.0030	0.0020–0.0067	3	1.9980	0.0014–0.0032	0.0063–0.0173
'79–'81	6-250	2.2979–2.2994	Nos. 1–6 .0010–.0024 No. 7 .0016–.0035	.002–.006	7	1.999–2.000	.0010–.0026	.006–.017
	6-292	2.2979–2.2994	Nos. 1–6 .0010–.0024 No. 7 .0016–.0035	.002–.006	7	2.099–2.100	.0010–.0026	.006–.017
	8-305, 350, 400	⑤	.0008–.0020 ②	.002–.006	5	2.199–2.200 ⑫	.0013–.0035	.008–.014
	8-454	③	④	.006–.010	5	2.1985–2.1995	.0009–.0025	.013–.023
	8-350 Diesel	2.9993–3.0003	Nos. 1–4 .0005–.0021 No. 5 .0015–.0031	.0035–.0135	5	2.1238–2.1248	.0005–.0026	.006–.020
'82–'84	6-250	2.2979–2.2994	Nos. 1–6 0.0010–0.0024 No. 7 0.0016–0.0025 ⑩	0.002–0.006	7	1.999–2.000	0.0010–0.0026	0.006–0.017
	6-292	2.2979–2.2994	Nos. 1–6 0.0010–0.0024 No. 7 0.0016–0.0025 ⑩	0.002–0.006	7	2.099–2.100	0.0010–0.0026	0.006–0.017
	8-305	⑤	0.008–0.0020 ②	0.002–0.006	5	2.0988–2.0998	0.0013–0.0035	0.008–0.014
	8-350	⑤	0.008–0.0020 ②	0.002–0.006	5	2.0988–2.0998	0.0013–0.0035	0.008–0.014
	8-379 Diesel	⑧	⑨	0.002–0.007	5	2.3981–2.3991	0.0018–0.0039	0.007–0.025
'82–'86	8-454	⑦	④	0.006–0.010	5	2.2000–2.1990	0.0009–0.0025	0.013–0.023
'85–'86	4-151	2.300	0.0005–0.0022	0.0035–0.0085	5	2.000	0.0005–0.0026	0.005–0.022
	6-263	⑬	⑭	0.002–0.006	Rear	2.2497–2,2487	0.010–0.0032	0.007–0.015
	6-292	2.2979–2.2994	Nos. 1–6 0.0010–0.0024 No. 7 0.0016–0.0025	0.002–0.006	7	2.099–2.100	0.0010–0.0026	0.006–0.017
	8-305, 350	⑤	③	0.002–0.006	5	2.0988–2.0998	0.0013–0.0035	0.008–0.014
	8-379 Diesel	⑧	⑨	0.0039–0.0098	5	2.3981–2.3992	0.0018–0.0039	0.007–0.025

① No. 5—2.4479–2.4488
② Nos. 2–4—.0011–.0023
 No. 5—.0017–.0033
③ No. 1—2.7485–2.7494
 Nos. 2–4—2.7481–2.7490
 No. 5—2.7478–2.7488
④ Nos. 1–4—.0013–.0025
 No. 5—.0024–.0040
⑤ '79–'84 only: 305,
 350—No. 1—2.4484–2.4493
 Nos. 2–4—2.4481–2.4490

 No. 5—2.4479–2.4488
 400—Nos. 1–4—2.6484–2.6493
 No. 5—2.6479–2.6488
⑥ '79–'81: 2.0988–2.0998
⑦ Nos. 1–4—2.7481–2.7490
 No. 5—2.7476–2,7486
⑧ Nos. 1–4—2.9495–2.9504
 No. 5—2.9492–2.9502
⑨ Nos. 1–4—0.0018–0.0033
 No. 5—0.0022–0.0037
⑩ '83–'84 .0016–.0035

⑪ Nos. 1–4—2.4940–2.4950
 No. 5—2.4930–2.4950
⑫ Nos. 1–4—.0006–.0019
 No. 5—.0014–.0027
⑬ Front—2.4484–2.4493
 Int.—2.4481–2.4990
 Rear—2.4479–2.4488
⑭ Front—.0008–.0020
 Int.—.0011–.0023
 Rear—.0017–.0032

PISTON AND RING SPECIFICATIONS

Engine	Year	Piston to Bore Clearance	Ring Side Clearance			Ring Gap		
			Top Compression	Bottom Compression	Oil Control	Top Compression	Bottom Compression	Oil Control
4-119	'82–'84	.0018–.0026	.0059 Max	.0059 Max	.0059 Max	.012–.020	.008–.016	.008–.035
4-121	'82–'84	.0008–.0018	.0012–.0027	.0012–.0038	.0078 Max	.010–.020	.010–.020	.020–.055
4-137	'82–'84	.0062–.0070	.0018–.0028	.0012–.0021	.0008–.0021	.008–.016	.008–.016	.008–.016
4-151	'85–'86	0.0017–0.0041	0.0015–0.0030	0.0015–0.0030	Snug	0.010–0.022	0.010–0.020	0.015–0.055
6-173	'82–'84	.0017–.0027	.0012–.0028	.0016–.0037	.0078 Max	.010–.020	.010–.020	.020–.055
6-250	'77–'84	0.0005–0.0015 ②	0.0012–0.0027	0.0012–0.0032	.005 Max	0.010–0.020	0.010–0.020	0.015–0.055
6-263	'85–'86	0.0007–0.0017	0.0012–0.0032	0.0012–0.0032	0.002–0.007	0.010–0.020	0.010–0.025	0.015–0.055
6-292	'77–'84	0.0026–0.0036	0.0020–0.0040	0.0020–0.0040	.005 Max	0.010–0.020	0.010–0.020	0.015–0.055
6-292	'85–'86	0.0026–0.0036	0.0020–0.0040	0.0020–0.0040	0.005–0.0055	0.010–0.020	0.010–0.020	0.015–0.055
8-305	'79–'86	0.0007–0.0017	0.0012–0.0032	0.0012–0.0032	0.002–0.007	0.010–0.020	0.010–0.025	0.015–0.055
8-350	'79–'86	0.0007–0.0017	0.0012–0.0032	0.0012–0.0032	0.002–0.007	0.010–0.020	0.010–0.025	0.015–0.055
8-350 Diesel	'79–'81	0.0050–0.0060	0.0040–0.0060	0.0018–0.0038	0.001–0.005	0.015–0.025	0.015–0.025	0.015–0.055
8-379 Diesel	'82–'84	0.0040–0.0050	0.0030–0.0070	0.0015–0.0031	0.0016–0.0038	0.012–0.021	0.030–0.039	0.0098–0.020
8-379 Diesel	'85–'86	0.0035–0.0045 ⑤	0.0030–0.0070	0.0015–0.0031	0.0016–0.0037	0.0118–0.0216	0.0295–0.0393	0.0098–0.020
8-400	'79–'81	0.0014–0.0024	0.0012–0.0032	0.0012–0.0032	0.002–0.007	0.010–0.020	0.010–0.025	0.010–0.055
8-454	'79–'84	0.0014–0.0024 ③	0.0017–0.0032	0.0017–0.0032	0.002–0.007 ④	0.010–0.020	0.010–0.020	0.010–0.055
8-454	'85–'86	0.0030–0.0040	0.0017–0.0032	0.0017–0.0032	0.005–0.0065	0.010–0.020	0.010–0.020	0.015–0.055

① '78–'82: 0.0010–0.0020
② '83–'84: .0010–.0020
③ '83–'84: .0030–.0040
④ '83–'84: .005–.0065
⑤ Applies to Bohn pistons. Zollner— 0.0044–0.0054. Bore 7 & 8 must fit .0005" looser

TORQUE SPECIFICATIONS
(ft. lb.)

Engine	Cylinder Head Bolts	Rod Bearing Bolts	Main Bearing Bolts	Crankshaft Damper Bolt	Flywheel Bolts	Manifold	
						Intake	Exhaust
119	72	43	75	87	76	17	16
121	70	37	70	75	50	23	25
137 Diesel	60	65	116–130	125–150	70	15	15
4-151	92	32	70	160	60–75	29	44
173	70	37	70	75	50	23	25
6-250	95	35	65	—	60	—	30 ①
6-263	65	45	70	60	55–75	30	20
6-292	95	35 ⑥	65	60	110 ⑧	35 ⑨	30
8-305	65	45	70	60	60	30	20
8-350	65	45	70	60	60	30	30 ①
8-350 Diesel	130 ②	42	120	200–310	60	40 ②	25
8-379 Diesel	88–103 ⑤	44–52	④	140–162	60	25–37	18–25
8-400	65	45	70	60	60	30	30
8-454	80	50 ③	110	65 ⑦	65	30	20

① End bolts only are torqued to 20 ft. lbs through 1984: on later models torque all bolts to 20 ft. lbs.
② Dip in oil
③ 7/16 in. bolts: 70
④ Inner: 105–117
   Outer: 94–105

⑤ Applies to models through 1984: 1985 and later; torque in sequence to 20 ft. lbs, then again in sequence torque to 50 ft. lbs and finally to ¼ turn more—in sequence

⑥ 40: on 1985 and later models
⑦ 85: on 1985 and later models
⑧ 100: on 1985 and later models
⑨ 40: on 1985 and later models— exhaust-to-intake: 45 ft. lbs

BATTERY AND STARTER SPECIFICATIONS

	Battery			Starter ③			
						No Load Test	
	Amp Hour		Ground			Amps	
Year	Capacity	Volts	Terminal	Identification	Volts	①	rpm
'79–'82	60	12	Neg	1108778 ②	9	50–80	5500–10,500
	80	12	Neg	1187780 ②	9	50–80	3500–6000
				1109056 ②	9	50–80	5500–10,500
				1109052 ②	9	65–95	7500–10,500
				1108776 ②	9	65–95	7500–10,500
	125	12	Neg	1108776 ②	9	65–95	7500–10,500
'83–'84	—	12	Neg	1109561	9	50–75	6000–11,900
	—	12	Neg	1109535	9	45–70	7000–11,900
	—	12	Neg	1998241	10	65–95	7500–10,500
	—	12	Neg	1998244	10	60–85	6800–10,500
	—	12	Neg	1998211	10	65–95	7500–10,500
	—	12	Neg	1998396	10	70–110	6500–10,700
	—	12	Neg	1998397	10	70–110	6500–10,700
	—	12	Neg	1109563	10	120–210	9000–13,400

① Solenoid included
② "R" terminal removed
③ Brush spring tension is 35 oz.
   for all starters. Lock test is not
   recommended.

BATTERY AND STARTER SPECIFICATIONS

	Battery ①			Starter			
		Test Load				No Load Test	
Year	Identification	(Amps)		Identification	Volts	Amps	rpm
'85–'86	1981103	200		1998427	10	50–75	6000–11,900
	1981110	190		1998437	10	60–90	6500–10,500
	1981200	230		1998438	10	70–110	6500–10,700
	1981109	150		1998439	10	70–110	6500–10,700
	1981102	170		1998441	10	70–110	6500–10,700
	1981104	250		1998443	10	70–110	6500–10,700
	1981108	370		1998444	10	—	—

① All batteries are 12 bolt, negative
   ground

ALTERNATOR AND REGULATOR SPECIFICATIONS

	Alternator			
	Part No. or	Field Current	Output	
Year	Manufacturer	@ 12 V	(amps)	Regulator
'79–'82	1102394	4.0–4.5	37	①
	1102491			
	1102889			
	1102485	4.0–4.5	42	①
	1102841, 87			
	1102480, 86	4.0–4.5	61	①
	1102886, 88			
	1101016, 28	4.0–4.5	80	①

1 SPECIFICATIONS

ALTERNATOR AND REGULATOR SPECIFICATIONS

Year	Alternator Part No. or Manufacturer	Field Current @ 12 V	Output (amps)	Regulator
'83–'84	1105185	4.0–4.5	37	①
	1100227	4.0–4.5	37	①
	1100204	4.0–4.5	37	①
	1100203	4.0–4.5	37	①
	1100207	4.0–4.5	66	①
	1100249	4.0–4.5	66	①
	1100275	4.0–4.5	66	①
	1100242	4.0–4.5	66	①
	1100208	4.0–4.5	66	①
	1100241	4.0–4.5	66	①
	1100209	4.0–4.5	78	①
	1100273	4.0–4.5	78	①
	1100276	4.0–4.5	78	①
	1100217	4.0–4.5	78	①
	1100259	4.0–4.5	78	①
'85–'86	1100203	4.0–4.5	37	①
	1100209	4.0–4.5	66	①
	1100217	4.0–4.5	78	①
	1100225	4.0–4.5	37	①
	1100241	4.0–4.5	66	①
	1100242	4.0–4.5	66	①
	1100207	4.0–4.5	66	①
	1100204	4.0–4.5	37	①
	1100208	4.0–4.5	66	①
	1101063	4.0–4.5	80	①
	1101064	4.0–4.5	80	①
	1100259	4.0–4.5	78	①
	1100229	4.0–4.5	42	①
	1100231	4.0–4.5	42	①
	1100293	4.0–4.5	85	①

—Not available
NA Not applicable
① All alternators use integral regulators

Routine Maintenance 2

INDEX

TOOLS AND EQUIPMENT

Naturally, without the proper tools and equipment, it is impossible to properly service your vehicle. It would be impossible to catalog each tool that you would need to perform each or any operation in this manual. It would also be unwise for the amateur to rush out and buy an expensive set of tools on the theory that he may need one or more of them at sometime.

The best approach is to proceed slowly, gathering a good quality set of tools that are used most frequently. Don't be misled by the low cost of bargain tools. It is far better to spend a little more for better quality. Forged wrenches, 6 or 12 point sockets and fine tooth ratchets are by far preferable to their less expensive counterparts. As any good mechanic can tell you, there are few worse experiences than trying to work on a vehicle with bad tools. Your monetary savings will be far outweighed by frustration and mangled knuckles.

Begin accumulating tools that are used most frequently; those associated with routine maintenance and tune-up.

In addition to the normal assortment of screwdrivers and pliers you should have the following tools for routine maintenance jobs:

1. SAE (or Metric) or SAE/Metric wrenches—sockets and combination open end/box end wrenches in sizes from ⅛–¾" (6–19mm) and a spark plug socket ($^{13}/_{16}$" or ⅝" depending on plug type).

NOTE: If possible, buy various length socket drive extensions. One break in this department is that the metric sockets available in the U.S. will all fit the ratchet handles and extensions you may already have (¼", ⅜" and ½" drive).

2. Jackstands, for support
3. Oil filter wrench
4. Oil filler spout, for pouring oil
5. Grease gun, for chassis lubrication
6. Hydrometer, for checking the battery
7. A container for draining oil
8. Many rags for wiping up the inevitable mess.

In addition to the above items there are several others that are not absolutely necessary but handy to have around. These include oil dry, a transmission funnel and an usual supply of lubricants, antifreeze and fluids, although these can be purchased as needed. This is a basic list for routine maintenance but only your personal needs and desires can accurately de-

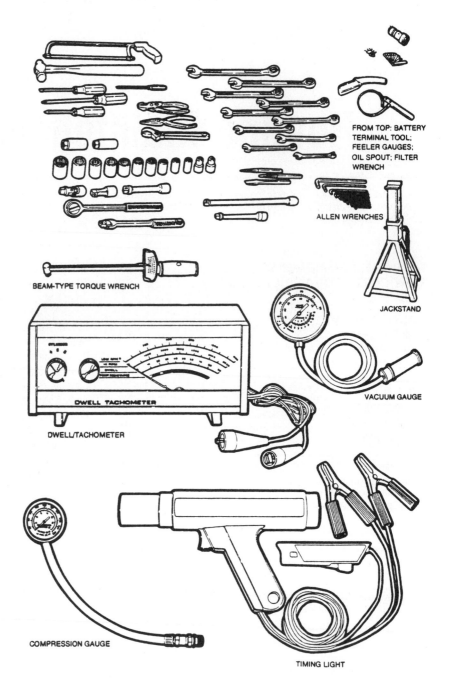

FROM TOP: BATTERY TERMINAL TOOL; FEELER GAUGES; OIL SPOUT; FILTER WRENCH

ALLEN WRENCHES

JACKSTAND

BEAM-TYPE TORQUE WRENCH

DWELL/TACHOMETER

VACUUM GAUGE

COMPRESSION GAUGE

TIMING LIGHT

You need only a basic assortment of hand tools and test instruments for most maintenance and repair jobs

termine your list of tools. If you are serious about maintaining your own vehicle, then a floor jack is as necessary as a spark plug socket. The greatly increased utility, strength and safety of a hydraulic floor jack makes it pay for itself many times over throughout the years.

The second list of tools is for tune-ups. While the tools involved here are

slightly more sophisticated, they need not be outrageously expensive. There are several inexpensive tach/dwell meters on the market that are every bit as good for the average mechanic as an expensive professional model. Just be sure that it goes to at least 1,200–1,500 rpm on the tach scale and that it works on 4 or 6 cylinder engines. A basic list of tune-up equipment could include:

1. Tach/dwell meter.
2. Spark plug wrench.
3. Timing light (a DC light that works from the vehicle's battery is best, although an AC light that plugs into 110V house current will suffice at some sacrifice in brightness).
4. Wire spark plug gauge/adjusting tools.
5. Set of feeler gauges.

Here again, be guided by your own needs. A feeler gauge will set the points as easily as a dwell meter will read dwell but slightly less accurately. Since you will need a tachometer anyway ... well, make your own decision.

In addition to these basic tools, there are several other tools and gauges you may find useful. These include:
1. A compression gauge. The screw-in type is slower to use but eliminates the possibility of a faulty reading due to escaping pressure.
2. A manifold vacuum gauge.
3. A test light, volt/ohm meter.
4. An induction meter. This is used for determining whether or not there is current in a wire. These are handy for use if a wire is broken somewhere in a wiring harness.

As a final note, you will probably find a torque wrench necessary for all but the most basic work. The beam type models are perfectly adequate, although the newer click type are more precise.

NOTE: Special tools are occasionally necessary to perform a specific job or are recommended to make a job easier. Their use has been kept to a minimum. When a special tool is indicated, it will be referred to by manufacturer's part number, and, where possible, an illustration of the tool will be provided so that an equivalent tool may be used. A list of tool manufacturers and their addresses follows:

In the United States, contact:

**Service Tool Division
Kent-Moore Corporation
29784 Little Mack
Roseville, MI 48066-2298**

In Canada, contact:

**Kent-Moore of Canada, Ltd.
2395 Cawthra Mississauga
Ontario, Canada L5A 3P2.**

SERVICING YOUR VEHICLE SAFELY

It is virtually impossible to anticipate all of the hazards involved with automotive maintenance and service but care and common sense will prevent most accidents.

The rules of safety for mechanics range from "don't smoke around gasoline," to "use the proper tool for the job." The trick to avoiding injuries is to develop safe work habits and take every possible precaution.

Do's

• Do keep a fire extinguisher and first aid kit within easy reach.

• Do wear safety glasses or goggles when cutting, drilling, grinding or prying, even if you have 20/20 vision. If you wear glasses for the sake of vision, then they should be made of hardened glass that can serve also as safety glasses or wear safety goggles over your regular glasses.

• Do shield your eyes whenever you work around the battery. Batteries contain sulphuric acid. In case of contact with the eyes or skin, flush the area with water or a mixture of water and baking soda, then get medical attention immediately.

• Do use safety stands for any under vehicle service. Jacks are for raising the vehicle. Safety stands are for making sure the vehicle stays raised until you want it to come down. Whenever the vehicle is raised, block the wheels remaining on the ground and set the parking brake.

• Do use adequate ventilation when working with any chemicals. Like carbon monoxide, the asbestos dust resulting from brake lining wear can be poisonous in sufficient quantities.

• Do disconnect the negative battery cable when working on the electrical system. The primary ignition system can contain up to 40,000 volts.

• Do follow the manufacturer's directions whenever working with potentially hazardous materials. Both brake fluid and antifreeze are poisonous if taken internally.

• Do properly maintain your tools. Loose hammer heads, mushroomed punches/chisels, frayed or poorly grounded electrical cords, excessively worn screwdrivers, spread wrenches (open end), cracked sockets, slipping ratchets and/or faulty droplight sockets cause accidents.

• Do use the proper size and type of tool for the job being done.

• Do when possible, pull on a wrench handle rather than push on it and adjust your stance to prevent a fall.

• Do be sure that adjustable wrenches are tightly adjusted on the nut or bolt and pulled so that the face is on the side of the fixed jaw.

• Do select a wrench or socket that fits the nut or bolt. The wrench or socket should sit straight, not cocked.

• Do strike squarely with a hammer – avoid glancing blows.

• Do set the parking brake and block the drive wheels if the work requires that the engine be running.

Dont's

• Don't run an engine in a garage or anywhere else without proper ventila-

Always use jackstands when working under the vehicle

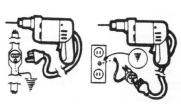

When using electrical tools, make sure they are properly grounded

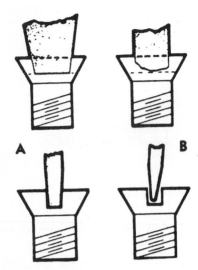

Keep screwdriver tips in good shape. They should fit the slot as in "A". If they look like those in "B", they need grinding or replacing

tion—EVER! Carbon monoxide is poisonous. It takes a long time to leave the body and can build up a deadly supply of it in your system by simply breathing in a little every day. You may not realize you are slowly poisoning yourself. Always use power vents, windows, fans or open the garage doors.

• Don't work around moving parts while wearing a necktie or other loose clothing. Short sleeves are much safer than long, loose sleeves and hard-toed shoes with neoprene soles protect your toes and give a better grip on slippery surfaces. Jewelry such as watches, fancy belt buckles, beads or body adornment or any kind is not safe working around a vehicle. Long hair should be hidden under a hat or cap.

• Don't use pockets for tool boxes. A fall or bump can drive a screwdriver deep into your body. Even a wiping cloth hanging from the back pocket can wrap around a spinning shaft or fan.

• Don't smoke when working

around gasoline, cleaning solvent or other flammable material.

• Don't smoke when working around the battery. When the battery is being charged, it gives off explosive hydrogen gas.

• Don't use gasoline to wash your hands. There are excellent soaps available. Gasoline may contain lead, and lead can enter the body through a cut, accumulating in the body until you are very ill. Gasoline also removes all the natural oils from the skin so that bone dry hands will suck up oil and grease.

• Don't service the air conditioning system unless you are equipped with the necessary tools and training. The refrigerant, R-12, is extremely cold and when exposed to the air, will instantly freeze any surface it comes in contact with, including your eyes. Although the refrigerant is normally non-toxic, R-12 becomes a deadly poisonous gas in the presence of an open flame. One good whiff of the vapors from burning refrigerant can be fatal.

ROUTINE MAINTENANCE

Air Cleaner

The air cleaner element is a paper cartridge type, it should be replaced every year or 30,000 miles; if the vehicle is operated in heavy traffic or under dusty conditions, replace the element at more frequent intervals.

REMOVAL & INSTALLATION

1. Remove the top of the air cleaner.
2. Remove and discard the paper element.
3. Using a new element, reverse the removal procedures.

Gasoline Fuel Filter

The fuel filter should be serviced every 15,000 miles; if operated under severe conditions, change it more often. Three types of fuel filters are used, a pleated-paper element type (with a internal check valve), an in-line type and an in-tank type.

NOTE: If an in-line fuel filter is used on an engine which has a filter installed in the carburetor body, be sure to change both at the same time.

——— CAUTION ———
Filter replacement should not be attempted when the engine is HOT. Additionally, it is

a good idea to place some absorbent rags under the fuel fittings to catch the gasoline which will spill out when the lines are loosened.

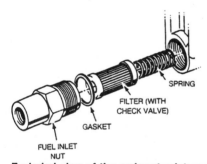

Exploded view of the carburetor internal fuel filter; check valve facing the fuel inlet nut

REMOVAL & INSTALLATION

There are three types of fuel filters: Internal (in the carburetor fitting), inline (in the fuel line) and in-tank (the sock on the fuel pickup tube).

Internal Filter

1. Disconnect the fuel line connection at the fuel inlet filter nut on the carburetor.
2. Remove the fuel inlet filter nut from the carburetor.
3. Remove the filter and the spring.

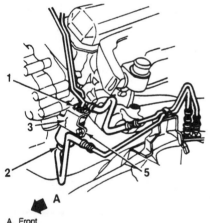

A. Front
1. Upper fuel line fitting
2. Lower fuel line fitting
3. Bracket
5. Bolt

View of the in-line fuel filter—2.8L TBI engine

View of the in-line fuel filter

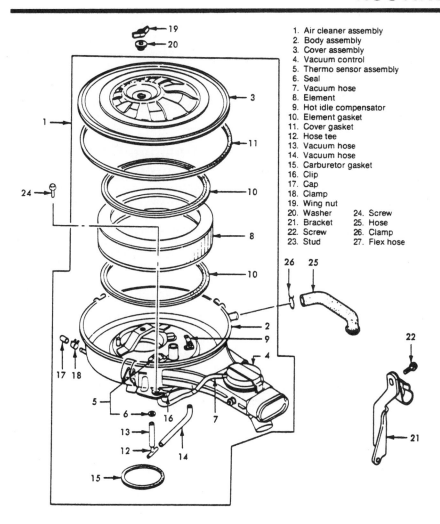

1. Air cleaner assembly
2. Body assembly
3. Cover assembly
4. Vacuum control
5. Thermo sensor assembly
6. Seal
7. Vacuum hose
8. Element
9. Hot idle compensator
10. Element gasket
11. Cover gasket
12. Hose tee
13. Vacuum hose
14. Vacuum hose
15. Carburetor gasket
16. Clip
17. Cap
18. Clamp
19. Wing nut
20. Washer
21. Bracket
22. Screw
23. Stud
24. Screw
25. Hose
26. Clamp
27. Flex hose

Typical air cleaner

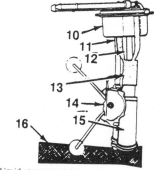

10. Liquid-vapor separator
11. Return tube
12. Fuel tube
13. Coupler and sound insulator
14. Fuel level sender
15. Electric fuel pump
16. Filter strainer

View of the in-tank fuel filter — electric fuel pump ONLY

NOTE: If a check valve is not present with the filter, one must be installed when the filter is replaced.

4. Install the spring, filter and check valve (must face the fuel line), then reverse the removal procedures. Torque the filter nut-to-carburetor to 25 ft.lb. and the fuel line-to-connector to 18 ft.lb.; DO NOT overtighten.

5. Start the engine and check for leaks.

In-Line Filter

——————— **CAUTION** ———————

Before disconnecting any component of the fuel system (2.5L engine), refer to the "Fuel Pressure Release" procedures in this section and release the fuel pressure.

1. Remove the fuel filler cap to relieve the pressure in the fuel tank.
2. Disconnect the fuel lines from the filter.
3. Remove the fuel filter from the retainer or mounting bolt.

4. To install, reverse the removal procedures. Start the engine and check for leaks.

NOTE: The filter has an arrow (fuel flow direction) on the side of the case, be sure to install it correctly in the system, with the arrow facing away from the fuel tank.

In-Tank Filter

To service the in-tank fuel filter, refer to the "Electric Fuel Pump" section.

Diesel Fuel Filter

REMOVAL & INSTALLATION

Filter Element

1. Disconnect the negative battery terminal.
2. Disconnect the water sensor wire connector from the filter assembly.

3. Disconnect the water sensor-to-main body hose.

4. Using a filter band wrench, remove the fuel filter element by turning the cartridge counterclockwise, while being careful not to spill diesel fuel from the element.

5. Drain the fuel from the element into a container and discard it. Take precautions to avoid the risk of fire during replacement procedures.

6. Remove the water and heater sensor from the bottom of the used filter element.

7. Apply a thin coat of diesel fuel to the water sensor O-ring, then install the water and heater sensor on the bottom of the replacement filter element and tighten.

8. Wipe all filter sealing surfaces clean before installing the new filter and apply a thin coat of diesel fuel to the gasket on the new fuel filter element.

9. Install the new filter element by turning it clockwise until the gasket contacts the sealing surfaces on the main filter body. Hand tighten another ⅔ of a turn after the gasket contacts the sealing surface; DO NOT overtighten.

10. Reconnect the water sensor wiring connector, then disconnect the fuel outlet hose from the injection pump and place the end in a clean container.

11. Operate the priming pump handle on the injection pump several times to fill the new filter with fuel, until fuel flows from the outlet hose. Reconnect the outlet hose to the injection pump when priming is complete.

12. Start the engine and check for leaks.

NOTE: It is very important to prime the new filter element before starting the engine, as the shock of the diesel engine's high

operating fuel pressure hitting a dry element can tear small pieces of debris away and allow them to pass into the injection pump and injectors, possibly causing injection pump or injector damage.

Filter Assembly

1. Disconnect the negative battery terminal.
2. Disconnect the water sensor electrical connector.
3. Disconnect the fuel hoses from the filter assembly.
4. Remove the filter assembly-to-bracket screws and the filter main body, element and sensors as an assembly.
5. To install, reverse the removal procedures. Refer to the "Draining the Water Separator" procedures in this section and prime the fuel system.

Draining the Water Separator

1. Turn the engine Off and allow it to cool.
2. Open the hood and place a 2 quart container under the end of the drain hose attached to the separator.

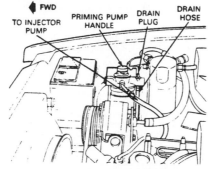

Typical diesel fuel filter assembly

3. Turn the wing nut about four turns **counterclockwise** to open the drain plug, then operate the priming pump lever until all of the water is drained and ONLY clean diesel fuel flows from the water separator.
4. Tighten the drain plug wing nut **clockwise** until securely closed; DO NOT overtighten. Again operate the priming pump handle until resistance is felt, indicating that the fuel filter is properly primed.
5. Start the engine and check for fuel leaks from the separator and fuel lines. Make sure the "Water In Fuel" light is Off; if the light remains On, the fuel tank must be purged of water with a siphon hose and hand pump fed into the tank through the fuel filter.

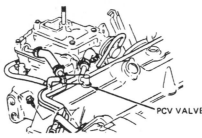

Typical PCV valve

Positive Crankcase Ventilation (PCV)

The PCV valve is attached to the valve cover by a rubber grommet and connected to the intake manifold through a ventilation hose. Replace the PCV valve and the PCV filter (located in the air cleaner) every 30,000 miles.

REMOVAL & INSTALLATION

1. Pull the PCV from the valve cover grommet and disconnect it from the ventilation hose(s).
2. Inspect the valve for operation: (1) Shake it to see if the valve is free; (2) Blow through it (air will pass in one direction only).

NOTE: When replacing the PCV valve, it is recommended to use a new one.

3. To install, reverse the removal procedures.

Evaporative Canister

To limit gasoline vapor discharge into the air, this system is designed to trap fuel vapors, which normally escape from the fuel tank and the intake manifold. Vapor arrest is accomplished through the use of the charcoal canister. This canister absorbs fuel vapors and stores them until they can be re-

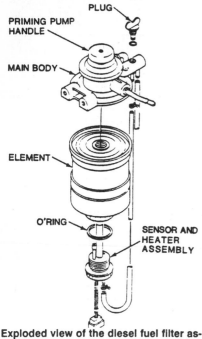

Exploded view of the diesel fuel filter assembly

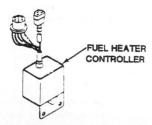

View of the diesel fuel heater controller

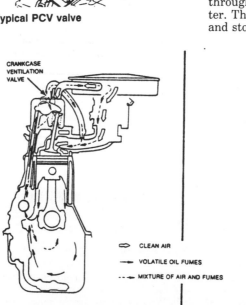

⇨ CLEAN AIR
→ VOLATILE OIL FUMES
--→ MIXTURE OF AIR AND FUMES

Typical PCV flow

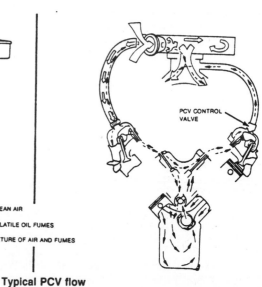

moved to be burned in the engine. Removal of the vapors from the canister to the engine is accomplished by a canister mounted purge valve, the throttle valve position, a thermostatic vacuum (TVS) switch or a computer controlled canister purge solenoid.

In addition to the modifications and the canister, the fuel tank requires a non-vented gas cap. The domed fuel tank positions a vent high enough above the fuel to keep the vent pipe in the vapor at all times. The single vent pipe is routed directly to the canister. From the canister, the vapors are routed to the intake system, where they will be burned during normal combustion.

SERVICING

Every 30,000 miles or 24 months, check all fuel, vapor lines and hoses for proper hookup, routing and condition. If equipped, check that the bowl vent and purge valves work properly. Remove the canister and check for cracks or damage, then replace (if necessary).

REMOVAL & INSTALLATION

1. Disconnect and mark the charcoal canister vent hoses.
2. Remove the canister-to-bracket bolt.
3. Lift the canister from the bracket.
4. To install, reverse the removal procedures.

CHARCOAL CANISTER SOLENOID REPLACEMENT

1. Disconnect the negative battery cable.
2. Remove the solenoid retaining bolt, the cover and the solenoid.
3. Disconnect the electrical connector and the hoses from the solenoid.
4. To install, reverse the removal procedures.

Battery

All models have a Maintenance Free battery as standard equipment, eliminating the need for fluid level checks and the possibility of specific gravity tests. Never-the-less, the battery does require some attention.

Once a year, the battery terminals and the cable clamps should be cleaned. Remove the side terminal bolts and the cables, negative cable first. Clean the cable clamps and the battery terminals with a wire brush until all corrosion, grease, etc. is removed and the metal is shiny. It is especially important to clean the inside

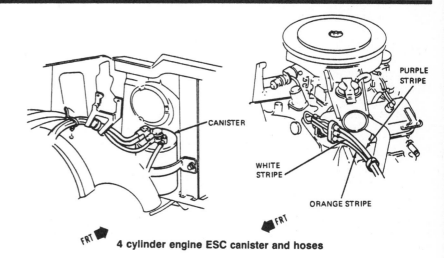

4 cylinder engine ESC canister and hoses

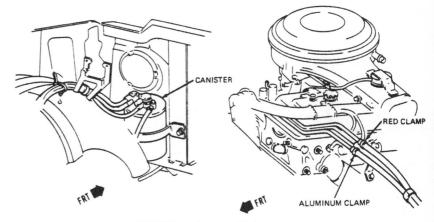

V6 ESC canister and hoses

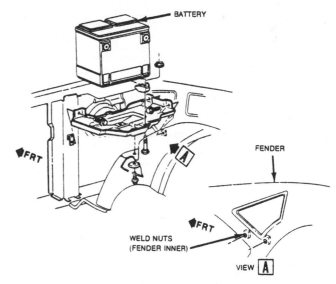

Typical battery tray installation

of the clamp thoroughly, since a small deposit of foreign material or oxidation there will prevent a sound electrical connection and inhibit either starting or charging. Special tools are available for cleaning the side terminal clamps and terminals.

Before installing the cables, loosen the battery holddown clamp, remove the battery and check the battery tray. Clear it of any debris and check it for soundness. Rust should be wire brushed away and the metal given a coat of anti-rust paint. Replace the battery and tighten the holddown clamp securely but be careful not to overtighten, which will crack the battery case.

NOTE: Batteries can be cleaned using a solution of baking soda and water. Surface coatings on battery cases can actually conduct electricity which will cause a slight voltage drain, so make sure the battery case is clean.

After the clamps and terminals are clean, reinstall the cables, negative cable last. Give the clamps and terminals a thin external coat of nonmetallic grease after installation, to retard corrosion.

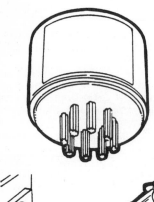

Special tools are also available for cleaning the posts and clamps on side terminal batteries

Check the cables at the same time that the terminals are cleaned. If the cable insulation is cracked, broken or the ends are frayed, the cable should be replaced with a new one of the same length and gauge.

─────── CAUTION ───────
Keep flames or sparks away from the battery. It gives off explosive hydrogen gas. The battery electrolyte contains sulphuric acid. If you should get any on your skin or in your eyes, flush the affected areas with plenty of clear water. If it lands in your eyes, seek medical help immediately.

Testing the Maintenance Free Battery

Maintenance free batteries, do not require normal attention as far as fluid level checks are concerned. However, the terminals require periodic cleaning, which should be performed at least once a year.

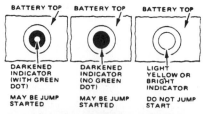

Maintenance-free batteries contain their own built-in hydrometer

The sealed top battery cannot be checked for charge in the normal manner, since there is no provision for access to the electrolyte. To check the condition of the battery:

1. If the indicator eye on top of the battery is dark, the battery has enough fluid. If the eye is lit, the electrolyte fluid is too low and the battery must be replaced.

2. If a green dot appears in the middle of the eye, the battery is sufficiently charged. Proceed to Step 4. If no green dot is visible, charge the battery as in Step 3.

3. Charge the battery at this rate:

NOTE: DO NOT charge the battery for more than 50 amp-hours. If the green dot appears or if the electrolyte squirts out of the vent hole, stop the charge and proceed to Step 4.

It may be necessary to tip the battery from side-to-side to get the green dot to appear after charging.

─────── CAUTION ───────
When charging the battery, the electrical system and control unit can be quickly damaged by improper connections, high output battery chargers or incorrect service procedures.

Battery	Test Load (Amps)
83–50	150
83–60	180
85A-60	170
87A-60	230
89A-60	270
1981103	200
1981104	250
1981105	270
1981577	260

Temperature (°F)	Minimum Voltage
70 or above	9.6
60	9.5
50	9.4
40	9.3
30	9.1
20	8.9
10	8.7
0	8.5

Charging Rate Amps	Time
75	40 min
50	1 hr
25	2 hr
10	5 hr

4. Connect a battery load tester and a voltmeter across the battery terminals (the battery cables should be disconnected from the battery). Apply a 300 amp load to the battery for 15 seconds to remove the surface charge. Remove the load.

5. Wait 15 seconds to allow the battery to recover. Apply the appropriate test load, as specified in the following chart:

Apply the load for 15 seconds while reading the voltage. Disconnect the load.

6. Check the results against the following chart. If the battery voltage is at or above the specified voltage for the temperature listed, the battery is good. It the voltage falls below what's listed, the battery should be replaced.

Early Fuel Evaporation (EFE) Heater

The EFE heating system is used on all carbureted engines. The purpose of the heating unit is to further vaporize the fuel droplets as they enter the intake manifold; vaporization of the air/fuel mixture ensures complete combustion which provides the maximum power output of the fuel used.

REMOVAL & INSTALLATION

Heater Unit

The EFE heater unit is located directly under the carburetor and is electrically operated.

1. Disconnect the negative battery terminal. Remove the air cleaner.

2. From the carburetor, disconnect the vacuum hoses, electrical connectors and fuel hoses. Disconnect the EFE Heater electrical connector from the wiring harness.

3. Remove the carburetor-to-intake manifold nuts and the carburetor from the manifold. Lift the EFE Heater from the intake manifold.

4. Using a putty knife, clean the gasket mounting surfaces.

5. To install, use new gaskets and reverse the removal procedures. Torque the carburetor-to-intake manifold nuts to 13 ft.lb.

Heater Switch

The heater switch is located near the thermostat housing (2.8L carbureted engine), on the bottom rear-side of the intake manifold (2.0L carbureted engine) or on the top right-side of the engine (1.9L carbureted engine).

1. Using a drain pan, position it under the radiator, then open the drain cock and drain the coolant to a level below the heater switch.

—————— CAUTION ——————

When draining the coolant, keep in mind that cats and dogs are attracted by the ethylene glycol antifreeze, and are quite likely to drink any that is left in an uncovered container or in puddles on the ground. This will prove fatal in sufficient quantity. Always drain the coolant into a sealable container. Coolant should be reused unless it is contaminated or several years old.

2. Disconnect the wiring harness connector from the EFE heater switch.

3. Remove the EFE heater switch (turn it counterclockwise) from the intake manifold.

4. To install the new EFE heater switch, coat the threads with a soft setting sealant and torque it to 10 ft.lb. Reconnect the wiring harness connector to the EFE heater switch. Refill the cooling system.

NOTE: When applying sealant to the EFE heater, be careful not to coat the sensor and/or the switch.

Heater Switch Relay

The heater switch relay is located on the left-fender.

1. Disconnect the negative battery terminal.

2. Disconnect the wiring harness connector(s) from the heater switch relay.

3. Remove the heater switch relay-to-bracket screw and the relay from the vehicle.

4. To install, use a new relay and reverse the removal procedures.

TESTING

1. Disconnect the wiring harness connector from the EFE heater switch, located near the thermostat housing (2.8L carbureted engine), on the bottom rear-side of the intake manifold (2.0L carbureted engine) or on the top right-side of the engine (1.9L carbureted engine).

NOTE: To perform the following inspection, the engine temperature must be below 140°F (60°C).

2. Using a 12V test lamp, connect it across the EFE wiring harness connector terminals. Turn the ignition switch On (the engine is Off), the lamp

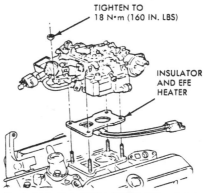

Exploded view of the EFE heater assembly—2.8L carbureted engine

Exploded view of the EFE heater switch assembly—2.8L carbureted engine

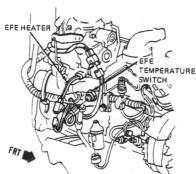

View of the EFE heater and heater switch assembly—1.9L engine

should glow; if the lamp glows, the EFE heater is good.

3. If the lamp does not glow, reconnect the wiring harness connector to the EFE heater switch.

4. Using a DC voltmeter, place it on the 0–15V scale, insert the test probes into the rear of the wiring harness connector body (the black wire is to be grounded) and measure the voltage; it should read 11–13V.

5. If the voltage is not 11–13V, insure that the black wire is grounded; if the voltage is not 0V, the black (grounded) wire is an Open circuit, repair it.

6. If the voltage is 0V, check for voltage-to-ground at each heater switch terminal—the voltage at each switch terminal should be 11–13V.

7. If one terminal measures 11–13V and the other is low or 0V, check the

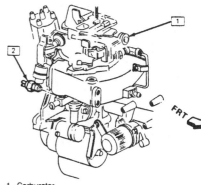

1. Carburetor
2. EFE heater switch

Exploded view of the EFE heater switch—2.0L engine

connector for deformed terminals and repair, as necessary.

8. If the electrical connector is making proper contact, replace the EFE heater switch.

9. If the voltage is not 11–13V at each switch terminal, check the wiring harness circuit between the heater switch and the ignition switch, then repair as necessary.

10. Start the engine, allow it to warm to 170°F (76.7°C), then check the voltage across the EFE heater terminals; it should be 0V. If the voltage is not 0V, replace the EFE heater switch.

Drive Belts

INSPECTION

Check the drive belt(s) every 15,000 miles/12 months (heavy usage) or 30,000 miles/24 months (light usage) for evidence of wear such as cracking, fraying and incorrect tension. Determine the belt tension at a point halfway between the pulleys by pressing on the belt with moderate thumb pressure. The belt should deflect about ¼" (6mm) over a 7–10" (178–254mm) span, or ½" (12.7mm) over a 13–16" (330–406mm) span, at this point. If the deflection is found to be too much or too little, perform the tension adjustments.

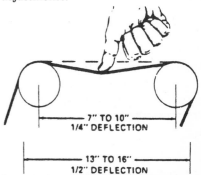

A gauge is recommended, but you can check the belt tension with thumb pressure

HOW TO SPOT WORN V-BELTS

V-Belts are vital to efficient engine operation—they drive the fan, water pump and other accessories. They require little maintenance (occasional tightening) but they will not last forever. Slipping or failure of the V-belt will lead to overheating. If your V-belt looks like any of these, it should be replaced.

Cracking or weathering

This belt has deep cracks, which cause it to flex. Too much flexing leads to heat build-up and premature failure. These cracks can be caused by using the belt on a pulley that is too small. Notched belts are available for small diameter pulleys.

Softening (grease and oil)

Oil and grease on a belt can cause the belt's rubber compounds to soften and separate from the reinforcing cords that hold the belt together. The belt will first slip, then finally fail altogether.

Glazing

Glazing is caused by a belt that is slipping. A slipping belt can cause a run-down battery, erratic power steering, overheating or poor accessory performance. The more the belt slips, the more glazing will be built up on the surface of the belt. The more the belt is glazed, the more it will slip. If the glazing is light, tighten the belt.

Worn cover

The cover of this belt is worn off and is peeling away. The reinforcing cords will begin to wear and the belt will shortly break. When the belt cover wears in spots or has a rough jagged appearance, check the pulley grooves for roughness.

Separation

This belt is on the verge of breaking and leaving you stranded. The layers of the belt are separating and the reinforcing cords are exposed. It's just a matter of time before it breaks completely.

HOW TO SPOT BAD HOSES

Both the upper and lower radiator hoses are called upon to perform difficult jobs in an inhospitable environment. They are subject to nearly 18 psi at under hood temperatures often over 280°F., and must circulate nearly 7500 gallons of coolant an hour—3 good reasons to have good hoses.

Swollen hose

A good test for any hose is to feel it for soft or spongy spots. Frequently these will appear as swollen areas of the hose. The most likely cause is oil soaking. This hose could burst at any time, when hot or under pressure.

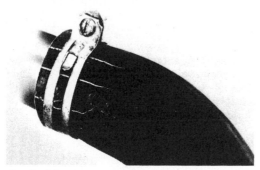

Cracked hose

Cracked hoses can usually be seen but feel the hoses to be sure they have not hardened; a prime cause of cracking. This hose has cracked down to the reinforcing cords and could split at any of the cracks.

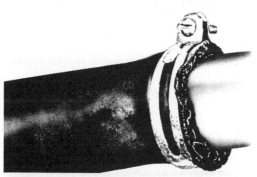

Frayed hose end (due to weak clamp)

Weakened clamps frequently are the cause of hose and cooling system failure. The connection between the pipe and hose has deteriorated enough to allow coolant to escape when the engine is hot.

Debris in cooling system

Debris, rust and scale in the cooling system can cause the inside of a hose to weaken. This can usually be felt on the outside of the hose as soft or thinner areas.

ADJUSTING TENSION

NOTE: The following procedures require the use of GM Belt Tension Gauge No. BT-33-95-ACBN (regular V-belts), BT-33-97M (poly V-belts) or equivalent.

1. If the belt is cold, operate the engine (at idle speed) for 15 minutes; the belt will seat itself in the pulleys allowing the belt fibers to relax or stretch. If the belt is hot, allow it to cool, until it is warm to the touch.

NOTE: A used belt is one that has been rotated at least one complete revolution on the pulleys. This begins the belt seating process and it must never be tensioned to the new belt specifications.

2. Loosen the component-to-mounting bracket bolts.
3. Using a GM Belt Tension Gauge No. BT-33-95-ACBN (standard V-belts), BT-33-97M (poly V-belts) or equivalent, place the tension gauge at the center of the belt between the longest span.
4. Applying belt tension pressure on the component, adjust the drive belt tension to the correct specifications.
5. While holding the correct tension on the component, tighten the component-to-mounting bracket bolt.
6. When the belt tension is correct, remove the tension gauge.

NOTE: It is better to have belts too loose than too tight, because overtight belts will lead to bearing failure, particularly in the water pump and alternator. However, loose belts place an extremely high impact load on the driven components due to the whipping action of the belt.

REMOVAL & INSTALLATION

1. Loosen the component-to-mounting bracket bolts.
2. Rotate the component to relieve the tension on the drive belt.
3. Slip the drive belt from the component pulley and remove it from the engine.

NOTE: If the engine uses more than one belt, it may be necessary to remove other belts that are in front of the one being removed.

4. To install, reverse the removal procedures. Adjust the component drive belt tension to specifications.

Hoses

The upper/lower radiator hoses and all heater hoses should be checked for deterioration, leaks and loose hose clamps every 15,000 miles or 12 months.

REMOVAL & INSTALLATION

1. Drain the cooling system.

——————— CAUTION ———————

When draining the coolant, keep in mind that cats and dogs are attracted by the ethylene glycol antifreeze, and are quite likely to drink any that is left in an uncovered container or in puddles on the ground. This will prove fatal in sufficient quantity. Always drain the coolant into a sealable container. Coolant should be reused unless it is contaminated or several years old.

2. Loosen the hose clamps at each end of the hose.
3. Working the hose back and forth, slide it off it's connection and then install a new hose, if necessary.

NOTE: When replacing the heater hoses, maintain a 1½" (38mm) clearance between the hose clip-to-upper control arm and between the rear overhead heater core lines-to-exhaust pipe.

4. To install, reverse the removal procedures. Refill the cooling system.

NOTE: Draw the hoses tight to prevent sagging or rubbing against other components; route the hoses through the clamps as installed originally. Always make sure that the hose clamps are beyond the component bead and placed in the center of the clamping surface before tightening them.

Air Conditioning

NOTE: This section contains simple testing procedures for your car or trucks's air conditioning system. More comprehensive testing, diagnosis and service procedures may be found in CHILTON'S GUIDE TO AIR CONDITIONING SERVICE AND REPAIR, book part number 7580, available at your local retailer.

SAFETY WARNINGS

Because of the importance of the necessary safety precautions that must be exercised when working with air conditioning systems and R-12 refrigerant, a recap of the safety precautions are outlined.

• Avoid contact with a charged refrigeration system, even when working on another part of the air conditioning system or vehicle. If a heavy tool comes into contact with a section of copper tubing or a heat exchanger, it can easily cause the relatively soft material to rupture.

• When it is necessary to apply force to a fitting which contains refrigerant, as when checking that all system couplings are securely tightened, use a wrench on both parts of the fitting involved, if possible. This will avoid putting torque on the refrigerant tubing. It is advisable, when possible, to use tube or line wrenches when tightening these flare nut fittings.

• DO NOT attempt to discharge the system by merely loosening a fitting or removing the service valve caps and cracking these valves. Precise control is possible only when using the service gauges. Place a rag under the open end of the center charging hose while discharging the system to catch any drops of liquid that might escape. Wear protective gloves when connecting or disconnecting service gauge hoses.

• Discharge the system only in a well ventilated area, as high concentrations of the gas can exclude oxygen and act as an anaesthetic. When leak testing or soldering, this is particularly important, as toxic gas is formed when R-12 contacts any flame.

• Never start a system without first verifying that both service valves are back-seated (if equipped) and that all fittings throughout the system are snugly connected.

• Avoid applying heat to any refrigerant line or storage vessel. Charging may be aided by using water heated to less than 125° to warm the refrigerant container. Never allow a refrigerant storage container to sit out in the sun or near any other heat source, such as a radiator.

• Always wear goggles when working on a system to protect the eyes. If refrigerant contacts the eyes, it is advisable in all cases to see a physician as soon as possible.

• Frostbite from liquid refrigerant should be treated by first gradually warming the area with cool water and then gently applying petroleum jelly. A physician should be consulted.

• Always keep the refrigerant drum fittings capped when not in use. Avoid any sudden shock to the drum, which might occur from dropping it or from banging a heavy tool against it. Never carry a drum in the passenger compartment of a vehicle.

• Always completely discharge the system before painting the vehicle (if the paint is to be baked on), or before welding anywhere near the refrigerant lines.

NOTE: Any repair work to an air conditioning system should be left to a professional. DO NOT, under any circumstances, attempt to loosen or tighten any fittings or perform any work other than that outlined here.

SYSTEM INSPECTIONS

NOTE: The Cycling Clutch Orfice Tube (CCOT) A/C system does not use a sight glass.

Checking For Oil Leaks

Refrigerant leaks show up as oily areas on the various components because the compressor oil is transported around the entire system along with the refrigerant. Look for oily spots on all the hoses and lines, especially on the hose and tubing connections. If there are oily deposits, the system may have a leak, have it checked by a qualified repairman.

NOTE: A small area of oil on the front of the compressor is normal and no cause for alarm.

Checking The Compressor Belt

Refer to the Drive Belts section.

Keep The Condenser Clear

Periodically inspect the front of the condenser for bent fins or foreign material (dirt, buts, leaves, etc.). If any cooling fins are bent, straighten them carefully with needlenose pliers. You can remove any debris with a stiff bristle brush or hose.

Operate The A/C System Periodically

A lot of A/C problems can be avoided by simply running the air conditioner at least once a week regardless of the

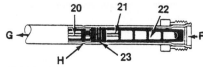

F. Inlet
G. Outlet (to evaporator)
H. Dent on tube (retains the expansion tube)
20. Outlet Screen
21. Expansion tube
22. Inlet screen

Sectional view of the oriface tube — A/C system

season. Simply let the system run for at least 5 minutes a week (even in the winter) and you'll keep the internal parts lubricated as well as preventing the hoses from hardening.

Leak Testing the System

There are several methods of detecting

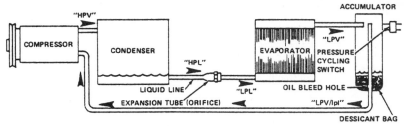

PRESSURE CYCLING SYSTEM

"HPV" — HIGH PRESSURE VAPOR LEAVING COMPRESSOR.
"HPL" — VAPOR IS COOLED DOWN BY CONDENSER AIR FLOW AND LEAVES AS HIGH PRESSURE LIQUID.
"LPL" — ORIFICE METERS THE LIQUID R-12 INTO EVAPORATOR, REDUCING ITS PRESSURE, AND WARM BLOWER AIR ACROSS EVAPORATOR CORE CAUSES BOILING OFF OF LIQUID INTO VAPOR.
"LPV" — LEAVES EVAPORATOR AS LOW PRESSURE VAPOR AND RETURNS WITH THE SMALL AMOUNT OF ...
"lpl" — ... LOW PRESSURE LIQUID THAT DIDN'T BOIL OFF COMPLETELY BACK TO THE COMPRESSOR TO BE COMPRESSED AGAIN.

Typical air conditioning system layout

leaks in an air conditioning system; among them, the two most popular are (1) halide leak detection or the open flame method and (2) electronic leak detector.

The Halide Leak Detection tool No. J-6084 or equivalent, is a torch like device which produces a yellow-green color when refrigerant is introduced into the flame at the burner. A purple or violet color indicates the presence of large amounts of refrigerant at the burner.

An Autobalance Refrigerant Leak Detector tool No. J-29547 or equivalent, is a small portable electronic device with an extended probe. With the unit activated, the probe is passed along those components of the system which contain refrigerant. If a leak is detected, the unit will sound an alarm signal or activate a display signal depending on the manufacturer's design.

It is advisable to follow the manufacturer's instructions as the design and function of the detection may vary significantly.

------ CAUTION ------

Caution should be taken to operate either type of detector in well ventilated areas, so as to reduce the chance of personal injury, which may result from coming in contact with poisonous gases produced when R-12 is exposed to flame or electric spark.

GAUGE SETS (USE)

Most of the service work performed in air conditioning requires the use of a set of two gauges, one for the high (head) pressure side of the system, the other for the low (suction) side.

The low side gauge records both pressure and vacuum. Vacuum read-

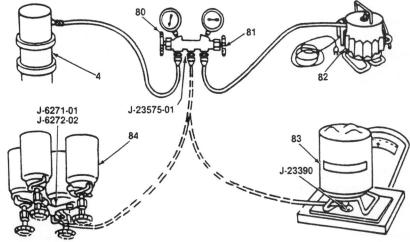

80. Low side valve
81. High side valve
82. Vacuum pump
83. 12 or 30 Lb. drum
84. Disposable cans
4. Accumulator

View of the A/C charging gauges

ings are calibrated from 0–30 in. Hg, and the pressure graduations read from 0–60 psi.

The high side gauge measures pressure from 0–600 psi.

Both gauges are threaded into a manifold that contains two hand shut-off valves. Proper manipulation of these valves and the use of the attached test hoses allow the user to perform the following services:

1. Test high and low side pressures.
2. Remove air, moisture and/or contaminated refrigerant.
3. Purge the system of refrigerant.
4. Charge the system with refrigerant.

The manifold valves are designed so they have no direct effect on the gauge readings but serve only to provide for or cut off the flow of refrigerant through the manifold. During all testing and hook-up operations, the valves are kept in a Closed position to avoid disturbing the refrigeration system. The valves are Opened ONLY to purge the system of refrigerant or to charge it.

When purging the system, the center hose is uncapped at the lower end and both valves are cracked (Opened) slightly. This allows the refrigerant pressure to force the entire contents of the system out through the center hose. During charging, the valve on the high side of the manifold is Closed and the valve on the low side is cracked (Opened). Under these conditions, the low pressure in the evaporator will draw refrigerant from the relatively warm refrigerant storage container into the system.

Service Valves

For the user to diagnose an air conditioning system he or she must gain entrance to the system in order to observe the pressures; the type of terminal for this purpose is the familiar Schrader valve.

The Schrader valve is similar to a tire valve stem and the process of connecting the test hoses is the same as threading a hand pump outlet hose to a bicycle tire. As the test hose is

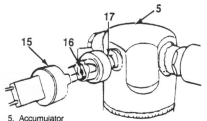

5. Accumulator
15. Electrical connector
16. Pressure cycling switch adjusting screw
17. "Schrader" type valve

View of the A/C accumulator with the Schraeder valve

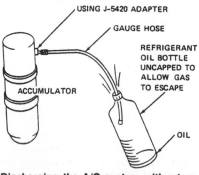

USING J-5420 ADAPTER
GAUGE HOSE
REFRIGERANT OIL BOTTLE UNCAPPED TO ALLOW GAS TO ESCAPE
ACCUMULATOR
OIL

Discharging the A/C system without using a charging station

threaded to the service port the valve core is depressed, allowing the refrigerant to enter the test hose outlet. Removal of the test hose automatically closes the system.

Extreme caution must be observed when removing test hoses from the Schrader valves as some refrigerant will normally escape, usually under high pressure; observe safety precautions.

Using The Manifold Gauges

The following are step-by-step procedures to guide the user to the correct gauge usage.

───── CAUTION ─────

Wear goggles or face shield during all testing operations. Backseat hand shut-off type service valves.

1. Remove the caps from the high and low side service ports. Make sure both gauge valves are closed.
2. Connect the low side test hose to the service valve that leads to the evaporator (located between the evaporator outlet and the compressor).
3. Attach the high side test hose to the service valve that leads to the condenser.
4. Mid-position the hand shutoff type service valves.
5. Start the engine and allow it to warm-up. All testing and charging of the system should be done after the engine and system has reached normal operating temperatures (except when using certain the charging stations).
6. Adjust the air conditioner controls to Max. cold.
7. Observe the gauge readings.

When the gauges are not being used it is a good idea to:

a. Keep both hand valves in the closed position.

b. Attach both ends of the high and low service hoses to the manifold, if extra outlets are present on the manifold or plug them (if not).

c. Keep the center charging hose attached to an empty refrigerant can. This extra precaution will re-

duce the possibility of moisture entering the gauges. If the air and moisture have gotten into the gauges, purge the hoses by supplying refrigerant under pressure to the center hose with both gauge valves open and all openings unplugged.

DISCHARGING THE SYSTEM

───── CAUTION ─────

Be sure to perform operation in a well ventilated area.

When it is necessary to remove (purge) the refrigerant pressurized in the system, follow this procedure:

1. Operate the air conditioner for at least 10 minutes.
2. Attach the gauges, turn Off the engine and the air conditioner.
3. Place a container or rag at the outlet of the center charging hose on the gauge. The refrigerant will be discharged there and this precaution will avoid its uncontrolled exposure.
4. Open the low side hand valve on gauge slightly.
5. Open the high side hand valve slightly.

NOTE: Too rapid a purging process will be identified by the appearance of an oily foam. If this occurs, close the hand valves a little more until this condition stops.

6. Close both hand valves on the gauge set when the pressures read 0 and all the refrigerant has left the system.

Evacuating the System

Before charging any system it is necessary to purge the refrigerant and draw out the trapped moisture with a suitable vacuum pump. Failure to do so will result in ineffective charging and possible damage to the system.

Use this hook-up for the proper evacuation procedure:

1. Connect both service gauge hoses to the high and low service outlets.
2. Open the high and low side hand valves on the gauge manifold.
3. Open both service valves a slight amount (from the back seated position), then allow the refrigerant to discharge from the system.
4. Install the center charging hose of the gauge set to the vacuum pump.
5. Operate the vacuum pump for at least one hour. If the system has been subjected to open conditions for a prolonged period of time, it may be necessary to "pump the system down" overnight. Refer to the System Sweep procedure.

NOTE: If the low pressure gauge does not show at least 28 in. Hg within 5 minutes, check the system for a leak or loose gauge connectors.

6. Close the hand valves on the gauge manifold.

7. Turn Off the pump.

8. Observe the low pressure gauge to determine if the vacuum is holding. A vacuum drop may indicate a leak.

System Sweep

An efficient vacuum pump can remove all the air contained in a contaminated air conditioning system very quickly, because of its vapor state. Moisture, however, is far more difficult to remove because the vacuum must force the liquid to evaporate before it will be able to be removed from the system. If the system has become severely contaminated, as it might become after all the charge was lost in conjunction with vehicle accident damage, moisture removal is extremely time consuming. A vacuum pump could remove all of the moisture only if it were operated for 12 hours or more.

Under these conditions, sweeping the system with refrigerant will speed the process of moisture removal considerably. To sweep, follow the following procedure:

1. Connect the vacuum pump to the gauges, operate it until the vacuum ceases to increase, then continue the operation for ten more minutes.

2. Charge the system with 50% of its rated refrigerant capacity.

3. Operate the system at fast idle for ten minutes.

4. Discharge the system.

5. Repeat (twice) the process of charging to 50% capacity, running the system for ten minutes, then discharging it for a total of three sweeps.

6. Replace the drier.

7. Pump the system down as in Step 1.

8. Charge the system.

CHARGING

—————— CAUTION ——————

Never attempt to charge the system by opening the high pressure gauge control while the compressor is operating. The compressor accumulating pressure can burst the refrigerant container, causing sever personal injuries.

1. Start the engine, operate it with the choke Open and normal idle speed, then position the A/C control lever on the Off.

2. Using drum or 14 oz. cans of refrigerant, in the inverted position, allow about 1 lb. of refrigerant to enter

the system through the low side service fitting on the accumulator.

3. After 1 lb. of refrigerant enters the system, position the control lever on Norm (the compressor will engage) and the blower motor on Hi speed; this operation will draw the remainder of the refrigerant into the system.

NOTE: To speed up the operation, position a fan in front of the condenser; the lowering of the condenser temperature will allow refrigerant to enter the system faster.

4. When the system is charged, turn Off the refrigerant source and allow the engine to run for 30 seconds to clear the lines and gauges.

5. With the engine running, remove the hose adapter from the accumulator service fitting (unscrew the hose quickly to prevent refrigerant from escaping).

—————— CAUTION ——————

Never remove the gauge line from the adapter when the line is connected to the system; always remove the line adapter from the service fitting first.

6. Replace the accumulator protective caps and turn the engine Off.

7. Using a leak detector, inspect the A/C system for leaks. If a leak is present, repair it.

Windshield Wipers

For maximum effectiveness and longest element life, the windshield and wiper blades should be kept clean. Dirt, tree sap, road tar and so on will cause streaking, smearing and blade deterioration if left on the glass. It is advisable to wash the windshield carefully with a commercial glass cleaner at least once a month. Wipe off the rubber blades with the wet rag, afterwards.

If the blades are found to be cracked, broken or torn, they should be replaced immediately. Replacement intervals will vary with usage, although ozone deterioration usually limits blade life to about one year. If the wiper pattern is smeared, streaked or if the blade chatters across the glass, the elements should be replaced. It is easi-

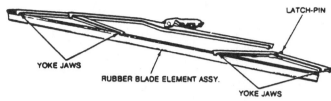

View of the windshield wiper assembly

est and most sensible to replace the elements in pairs.

BLADE REPLACEMENT

1. Lift the wiper arm assembly from the windshield.

2. Depress the wiper arm-to-blade assembly pin to disconnect the blade assembly from the wiper arm.

3. To install, use new blade assemblies and reverse the removal procedures.

Tires and Wheels

TIRE ROTATION

Tire wear can be equalized by switching the position of the tire about every 6,000 miles. Including a conventional spare in the rotation pattern can give up to 20% more tire life.

—————— CAUTION ——————

DO NOT include the new Space Saver® or temporary spare tires in the rotation pattern.

There are certain exceptions to tire rotation, however. Studded snow tires should not be rotated and radials should be kept on the same side of the vehicle (maintain the same direction of rotation). The belts on radial tires get set in a pattern. If the direction of rotation is reversed, it can cause rough ride and vibration.

NOTE: When radials or studded snows are taken off the vehicle, mark them, so you can maintain the same direction of rotation.

TIRE TYPES

For maximum satisfaction, tires should be used in sets of five. Mixing of different types (radial, bias-belted, fiberglass belted) should be avoided. Conventional bias tires are constructed so that the cords run bead-to-bead at an angle. This type of construction gives rigidity to both tread and sidewall. Bias-belted tires are similar in construction to conventional bias ply tires. Belts run at an angle and also at a 90° angle to the bead, as in the radial tire. Tread life is improved considera-

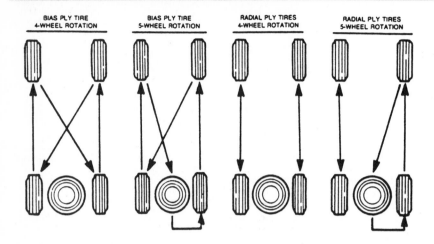

| BIAS PLY TIRE 4-WHEEL ROTATION | BIAS PLY TIRE 5-WHEEL ROTATION | RADIAL PLY TIRES 4-WHEEL ROTATION | RADIAL PLY TIRES 5-WHEEL ROTATION |

Tire rotation patterns

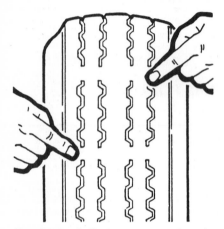

Tread wear indicators appear when the tire is worn out

Tread depth can be checked with an inexpensive gauge

If all of Lincoln's head is visible in two or more adjacent grooves, the tire should be replaced

bly over the conventional bias tire. The radial tire differs in construction, but instead of the carcass plies running are an angle of 90° to each other, they run at an angle of 90° to the bead. This gives the tread a great deal of rigidity and the sidewall a great deal of flexibility and accounts for the characteristic bulge associated with radial tires.

Chevrolet cars and trucks are capable of using radial tires and they are recommended. If they are used, tire sizes and wheel diameters should be selected to maintain ground clearance and tire load capacity equivalent to the minimum specified tire. Radial tires should always be used in sets of five, but in an emergency, radial tires can be used with caution on the rear axle only. If this is done, both tires on the rear should be of radial design.

— CAUTION —

Radial tires should never be used on only the front axle.

Snow tires should not be operated at sustained speeds over 70 mph.

On four wheel drive trucks, all tires must be of the same size, type, and tread pattern, to provide even traction on loose surfaces, to prevent driveline bind when conventional four wheel drive is used, and to prevent excessive wear on the center differential with full time four wheel drive.

TREAD DEPTH

All tires have 8 built-in tread wear indicator bars that show up as ½" (12.7mm) wide smooth bands across the tire when $\frac{1}{16}$" (1.5mm) of tread remains. The appearance of tread wear indicators means that the tires should be replaced. In fact, many states have laws prohibiting the use of tires with less than $\frac{1}{16}$" (1.5mm) tread.

You can check your own tread depth with an inexpensive gauge or by using a Lincoln head penny. Slip the Lincoln penny into several into several tread grooves. If you can see the top of Lincoln's head in 2 adjacent grooves, the tires have less than $\frac{1}{16}$" (1.5mm) tread left and should be replaced. You can measure snow tires in the same manner by using the tails side of the Lincoln penny. If you can see the top of the Lincoln memorial, it's time to replace the snow tires.

TIRE STORAGE

Store the tires at proper inflation pressures if they are mounted on wheels. All tires should be kept in a cool, dry place. If they are stored in the garage or basement, DO NOT let them stand on a concrete floor, set them on strips of wood.

ALUMINUM WHEELS

— CAUTION —

If your vehicle has aluminum wheels, be very careful when using any type of cleaner on either the wheels or the tires. Read the label on the package of the cleaner to make sure that it will not damage aluminum.

TIRE INFLATION

The inflation is the most ignored item of auto maintenance. Gasoline mileage can drop as much as 0.8% for every 1 pound/square inch (psi) of under inflation.

Two items should be a permanent fixture in every glove compartment: a tire pressure gauge and a tread depth gauge. Check the tire air pressure (including the spare) regularly with a pocket type gauge. Kicking the tires won't tell you a thing and the gauge on the service station air hose is notoriously inaccurate.

The tire pressures recommended for your vehicle are usually found on the glove box door or in the owner's manual. Ideally, inflation pressure should be checked when the tires are cool. When the air becomes heated it expands and the pressure increases. Every 10° rise (or drop) in temperature means a difference of 1 psi, which also explains why the tire appears to lose air on a very cold night. When it is impossible to check the tires cold, allow for pressure build-up due to heat. If the hot pressure exceeds the cold pressure by more than 15 psi, reduce your speed, load or both. Otherwise internal heat is created in the tire. When the heat approaches the temperature at which the tire was cured, during manufacture, the tread can separate from the body.

— **CAUTION** —

Never counteract excessive pressure build-up by bleeding off air pressure (letting some air out). This will only further raise the tire operating temperature.

Before starting a long trip with lots of luggage, you can add about 2–4 psi to the tires to make them run cooler but never exceed the maximum inflation pressure on the side of the tire.

Factory installed wheels and tires are designed to handle loads up to and including their rated load capacity when inflated to the recommended inflation pressures. Correct tire pressures and driving techniques have an important influence on tire life. Heavy cornering, excessively rapid acceleration and unnecessary braking increase tire wear. Underinflated tires can cause handling problems, poor fuel economy, shortened tire life and tire overloading.

Maximum axle load must never exceed the value shown on the side of the tire. The inflation pressure should never exceed 35 psi (standard tires) or 60 psi (compact tire).

Tire Size Comparison Chart

"Letter" sizes			Inch Sizes	Metric-inch Sizes		
"60 Series"	"70 Series"	"78 Series"	1965–77	"60 Series"	"70 Series"	"80 Series"
			5.50-12, 5.60-12	165/60-12	165/70-12	155-12
		Y78-12	6.00-12			
		W78-13	5.20-13	165/60-13	145/70-13	135-13
		Y78-13	5.60-13	175/60-13	155/70-13	145-13
			6.15-13	185/60-13	165/70-13	155-13, P155/80-13
A60-13	A70-13	A78-13	6.40-13	195/60-13	175/70-13	165-13
B60-13	B70-13	B78-13	6.70-13	205/60-13	185/70-13	175-13
			6.90-13			
C60-13	C70-13	C78-13	7.00-13	215/60-13	195/70-13	185-13
D60-13	D70-13	D78-13	7.25-13			
E60-13	E70-13	E78-13	7.75-13			195-13
			5.20-14	165/60-14	145/70-14	135-14
			5.60-14	175/60-14	155/70-14	145-14
			5.90-14			
A60-14	A70-14	A78-14	6.15-14	185/60-14	165/70-14	155-14
	B70-14	B78-14	6.45-14	195/60-14	175/70-14	165-14
	C70-14	C78-14	6.95-14	205/60-14	185/70-14	175-14
D60-14	D70-14	D78-14				
E60-14	E70-14	E78-14	7.35-14	215/60-14	195/70-14	185-14
F60-14	F70-14	F78-14, F83-14	7.75-14	225/60-14	200/70-14	195-14
G60-14	G70-14	G77-14, G78-14	8.25-14	235/60-14	205/70-14	205-14
H60-14	H70-14	H78-14	8.55-14	245/60-14	215/70-14	215-14
J60-14	J70-14	J78-14	8.85-14	255/60-14	225/70-14	225-14
L60-14	L70-14		9.15-14	265/60-14	235/70-14	
	A70-15	A78-15	5.60-15	185/60-15	165/70-15	155-15
B60-15	B70-15	B78-15	6.35-15	195/60-15	175/70-15	165-15
C60-15	C70-15	C78-15	6.85-15	205/60-15	185/70-15	175-15
	D70-15	D78-15				
E60-15	E70-15	E78-15	7.35-15	215/60-15	195/70-15	185-15
F60-15	F70-15	F78-15	7.75-15	225/60-15	205/70-15	195-15
G60-15	G70-15	G78-15	8.15-15/8.25-15	235/60-15	215/70-15	205-15
H60-15	H70-15	H78-15	8.45-15/8.55-15	245/60-15	225/70-15	215-15
J60-15	J70-15	J78-15	8.85-15/8.90-15	255/60-15	235/70-15	225-15
	K70-15		9.00-15	265/60-15	245/70-15	230-15
L60-15	L70-15	L78-15, L84-15	9.15-15			235-15
	M70-15	M78-15				255-15
		N78-15				

Note: Every size tire is not listed and many size comparisons are approximate, based on load ratings. Wider tires than those supplied new with the vehicle, should always be checked for clearance.

FLUID AND LUBRICANTS

Engine Oil and Fuel Recommendations

ENGINE OIL

Use ONLY SF/CC or SF/CD rated oils of the recommended viscosity. Under the classification system developed by the American Petroleum Institute, the SF rating designates the highest quality oil for use in passenger vehicles. In addition, Chevrolet recommends the use of an SF/Energy Conserving oil. Oils labeled Energy Conserving (or Saving), Fuel (Gas or Gasoline) Saving, etc. are recommended due to their superior lubricating qualities (less friction—easier engine operation) and fuel saving characteristics. Pick your oil viscosity with regard to the anticipated temperatures during the period before your next oil change. Using the accompanying chart, choose the oil viscosity for the lowest expected temperature. You will be assured of easy cold starting and sufficient engine protection.

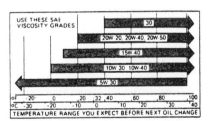

Gasoline engine oil selection chart

FUEL

Gasoline

NOTE: **Some fuel additives contain chemicals that can damage the catalytic converter and/or oxygen sensor. Read all of the labels carefully before using any additive in the engine or fuel system.**

Fuel should be selected for the brand and octane which performs best with your engine. Judge a gasoline by its ability to prevent pinging, it's engine starting capabilities (cold and hot) and general all weather performance.

If the compression ratio is 9.0:1 or lower, in most cases a regular unleaded grade of gasoline can be used. If the compression ratio is 9.0:1–9.3:1, use a premium grade of unleaded fuel.

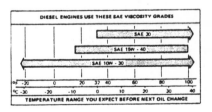

Diesel engine oil selection chart

NOTE: **Your car or truck's engine fuel requirement can change with time, due to carbon buildup, which changes the compression ratio. If your car or truck's engine knocks, pings or runs on, switch to a higher grade of fuel (if possible) and check the ignition timing. Sometimes changing brands of gasoline will cure the problem. If it is necessary to retard the tim-**

ing from specifications, don't change it more than a few degrees. Retarded timing will reduce the power output and the fuel mileage, plus it will increase the engine temperature.

Diesel

Diesel-engined models require the use of diesel fuel. Two grades are manufactured, #1 and #2, although #2 grade is generally the only grade available. Better fuel economy results from the use of #2 grade fuel. In some northern parts of the USA, and in most parts of Canada, #1 grade fuel is available in winter, or a winterized blend of #2 grade is supplied in winter months. If #1 grade is available, it should be used whenever temperatures fall below 20°F (−7°C). Winterized #2 grade may also be used at these temperatures. However, unwinterized #2 grade should not be used below 20°F (−7°C). Cold temperatures cause unwinterized #2 grade to thicken (it actually gels), blocking the fuel lines and preventing the engine from running.

DO NOT use home heating oil or gasoline in the diesel engine. DO NOT attempt to "thin" unwinterized #2 diesel fuel with gasoline. Gasoline or home heating oil will damage the engine and void the manufacturer's warranty.

—————— CAUTION ——————
A mixture of gasoline and diesel fuel produces an extremely potent explosive that is more volatile than gasoline alone.

Engine

OIL CHECK LEVEL

The engine oil should be checked on a regular basis, ideally at each fuel stop. If the car or truck is used for trailer towing or for heavy-duty use, it would be safer to check more often.

When checking the oil level it is best that the oil be at operating temperature, although checking the level immediately after stopping will give a false reading because all of the oil will not have drained back into the crankcase. Be sure that the vehicle is resting on a level surface, allowing time for the oil to drain back into the crankcase.

1. Open the hood and locate the dipstick. Remove it from the tube. The oil dipstick is located on the driver's side.
2. Wipe the dipstick with a clean rag.
3. Insert the dipstick fully into the tube and remove it again. Hold the dipstick horizontally and read the oil lev-

The oil level is checked with the dipstick

The oil level should be between the 'ADD' and 'FULL' marks on the dipstick

el. The level should be between the FULL and ADD marks. If the oil level is at or below the ADD mark, oil should be added as necessary. Oil is added through the capped opening on the valve cover(s) on gasoline engines. Diesel engines have a capped oil full tube at the front of the engine. Refer to the "Engine Oil and Fuel Recommendations" in this section for the proper viscosity oil to use.

4. Replace the dipstick and check the level after adding oil. Be careful not to overfill the crankcase. Approximately one quart of oil will raise the level from ADD to FULL.

OIL AND FILTER CHANGE

Engine oil should be changed every 6,000 miles on gasoline engines and every 3,000 miles on diesel engines. The oil change and filter replacement interval should be cut in half under conditions such as:

• Driving in dusty conditions.
• Continuous trailer pulling or RV use.
• Extensive or prolonged idling.
• Extensive short trip operation in freezing temperatures (when the engine is not thoroughly warmed-up).
• Frequent long runs at high speed and high ambient temperatures.
• Stop-and-go service.

Operation of the engine in severe conditions such as a dust storm may require an immediate oil and filter change.

Chevrolet recommends changing both the oil and filter during the first oil change and the filter every other oil change thereafter. For the small price of an oil filter, it's cheap insurance to replace the filter at every oil change. One of the larger filter manufacturers points out in its advertisements that not changing the filter leaves one

quart of dirty oil in the engine. This claim is true and should be kept in mind when changing your oil.

NOTE: The oil filter on the diesel engine must be changed every oil change.

To change the oil, the vehicle should be on a level surface and the engine should be at operating temperature. This is to ensure that the foreign matter will be drained away along with the oil and not left in the engine to form sludge. You should have available a container that will hold a minimum of 8 quarts of liquid, a wrench to fit the old drain plug, a spout for pouring in new oil and a rag or two, which you will always need. If the filter is being replaced, you will also need a band wrench or filter wrench to fit the end of the filter.

NOTE: If the engine is equipped with an oil cooler, this will also have to be drained, using the drain plug. Be sure to add enough oil to fill the cooler in addition to the engine.

1. Position the vehicle on a level surface and set the parking brake or block the wheels. Slide a drain pan under the oil drain plug.
2. From under the vehicle, loosen, but do not remove the oil drain plug. Cover your hand with a rag or glove and slowly unscrew the drain plug.

—————— CAUTION ——————
The engine oil will be HOT. Keep your arms, face and hands clear of the oil as it drains out.

3. Remove the plug and let the oil drain into the pan. Do not drop the plug into the drain pan.
4. When all of the oil has drained, clean off the drain plug and reinstall it into pan. Torque the drain plug to 20 ft.lb. (gasoline) or 30 ft.lb. (diesel) engines.
5. Using an oil filter wrench, loosen the oil filter. On most Chevrolet engines, especially the V6s, the oil filter is next to the exhaust pipes. Stay clear of these, since even a passing contact will result in a painful burn.

NOTE: On models equipped with catalytic converters stay clear of the converter. The outside temperature of a hot catalytic converter can approach 1200°F.

6. Cover your hand with a rag and spin the filter off by hand; turn it slowly.
7. Coat the rubber gasket on a new filter with a light film of clean engine oil. Screw the filter onto the mounting stud and tighten it according to the di-

rections on the filter (usually hand-tight one turn past the point where the gasket contacts the mounting base); DO NOT overtighten the filter.

8. Refill the engine with the specified amount of clean engine oil.

9. Run the engine for several minutes, checking for leaks. Check the level of the oil and add oil if necessary.

When you have finished this job, you will notice that you now possess four or five quarts of dirty oil. The best thing to do with it is to pour it into plastic jugs, such as milk or antifreeze containers. Then, locate a service station where you can pour it into their used oil tank for recycling.

—————— **CAUTION** ——————

Pouring used motor oil into a storm drain not only pollutes the environment, it violates Federal law. Dispose of waste oil properly.

Manual Transmission

FLUID RECOMMENDATIONS

All manual transmissions use Dexron® II automatic transmission fluid.

LEVEL CHECK

Remove the filler plug from the passenger's-side of the transmission (the upper plug if the transmission has two

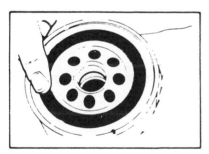

1. *Warm the car up before changing your oil. Raise the front end of the car and support it on drive-on ramps or jackstands.*

BLOCKS   DRIVE-UP RAMP

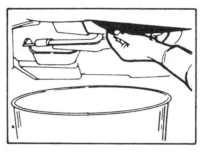

2. *Locate the drain plug on the bottom of the oil pan and slide a low flat pan of sufficient capacity under the engine to catch the oil. Loosen the plug with a wrench and turn it out the last few turns by hand. Keep a steady inward pressure on the plug to avoid hot oil from running down your arm.*

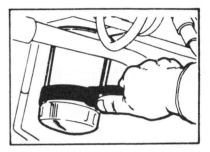

3. *Remove the oil filter with a filter wrench. The filter can hold more than a quart of oil, which will be hot. Be sure the gasket comes off with the filter and clean the mounting base on the engine.*

4. *Lubricate the gasket on the new filter with clean engine oil. A dry gasket may not make a good seal and will allow the filter to leak.*

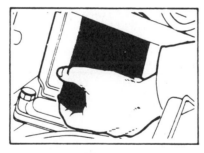

5. *Position a new filter on the mounting base and spin it on by hand. Do not use a wrench. When the gasket contacts the engine, tighten it another ½–1 turn by hand.*

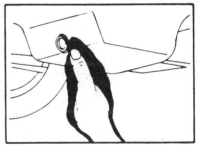

6. *Using a rag, clean the drain plug and the area around the drain hole in the oil pan.*

7. *Install the drain plug and tighten it finger-tight. If you feel resistance, stop and be sure you are not cross-threading the plug. Finally, tighten the plug with a wrench.*

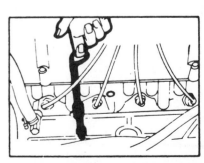

8. *Locate the oil cap on the valve cover. An oil spout is the easiest way to add oil, but a funnel will do just as well.*

9. *Start the engine and check for leaks. The oil pressure warning light will remain on for a few seconds; when it goes out, stop the engine and check the level on the dipstick.*

plugs). The oil should be level with the bottom edge of the filler hole. This should be checked at least once every 6,000 miles or more often if any leakage or seepage is observed.

DRAIN AND REFILL

Under normal conditions, the transmission fluid should not be changed. However, if the vehicle is driven in deep water, replace the fluid.

1. Raise and support the vehicle on jackstands.
2. Place a fluid catch pan under the transmission.
3. Remove the bottom plug and drain the fluid.
4. Install the bottom plug and refill the transmission housing.

Automatic Transmission

FLUID RECOMMENDATIONS

When adding fluid or refilling the transmission, use Dexron® II automatic transmission fluid.

LEVEL CHECK

Before checking the fluid level of the transmission, drive the vehicle for at least 15 miles to warm the fluid.

1. Place the vehicle on a level surface, apply the parking brake and block the front wheels.
2. Start the engine and move the selector through each range, then place it in Park.

NOTE: When moving the selector through each range, DO NOT race the engine.

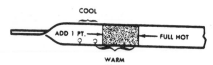

Automatic transmission fluid dipstick

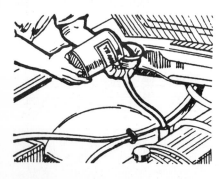

Adding automatic transmission fluid

3. With the engine running at a low idle, remove the transmission's dipstick to check the fluid level.
4. The level should be at the Full Hot mark of the dipstick. If not, add fluid.

————— CAUTION —————
DO NOT overfill the transmission, damage to the seals could occur. Use Dexron® II automatic transmission fluid. One pint raises the level from Add to Full.

DRAIN AND REFILL

The vehicle should be driven 15 miles to warm the transmission fluid before the pan is removed.

NOTE: The fluid should be drained while the transmission is warm.

1. Raise and support the front of vehicle on jackstands.
2. Place a drain pan under the transmission pan.
3. Remove the pan bolts from the front and the sides, then loosen the rear bolts 4 turns.
4. Using a small pry bar, pry the pan from the transmission. This will allow the pan to partially drain. Remove the remaining pan bolts and lower the pan from the transmission.

NOTE: If the transmission fluid is dark or has a burnt smell, transmission damage is indicated. Have the transmission checked professionally.

5. Empty the pan, remove the gasket material and clean with a solvent.
6. Using a putty knife, clean gasket mounting surfaces.
7. To install the oil pan, use a new gasket and sealant, then reverse the removal procedures. Torque the pan bolts to 8 ft.lb. in a criss-cross pattern.
8. Using Dexron® II automatic transmission fluid, add it through the filler tube. See the Capacities Chart to determine the proper amount of fluid to be added.

————— CAUTION —————
DO NOT OVERFILL the transmission. Foaming of the fluid and subsequent transmission damage due to slippage will result.

9. With the gearshift lever in PARK, start the engine and let it idle. DO NOT race the engine.
10. Apply the parking brake and move the gearshift lever through each position. Return the lever to Park and check the fluid level with the engine idling. The level should be between the two dimples on the dipstick, about ¼″ (6mm) below the ADD mark. Add fluid, if necessary.

11. Check the fluid level after the vehicle has been driven enough to thoroughly warm the transmission.

PAN AND FILTER SERVICE

1. Refer to the Drain and Refill procedures in this section and remove the oil pan.
2. Remove the screen and the filter from the valve body.
3. Install a new filter using a new gasket or O-ring.

NOTE: If the transmission uses a filter having a fully exposed screen, it may be cleaned and reused.

4. To install the oil pan, use a new gasket and sealant, then reverse the removal procedures. Torque the pan bolts to 8 ft.lb. in a criss-cross pattern. Refill the transmission.

Transfer Case

FLUID RECOMMENDATIONS

When adding fluid or refilling the transfer case, use Dexron® II automatic transmission fluid.

LEVEL CHECK

1. Raise and support the vehicle (level) on jackstands.
2. At the rear-side of the transfer case, remove the filler plug.
3. Using your finger, check the fluid level, it should be level with the bottom of the filler hole.
4. If the fluid level is low, use Dexron® II automatic transmission fluid to bring the fluid up to the proper level.
5. Install the filler plug and torque it to 30–40 ft.lb.

DRAIN AND REFILL

1. Raise and support the front of the vehicle on jackstands.
2. Position drain pan under transfer case.
3. Remove drain and fill plugs, then drain the lubricant into the drain pan.
4. Install drain plug. Torque the plug to 30–40 ft.lb.
5. Remove the drain pan and dump the fluid into a used oil storage tank, for recycling purposes.
6. Using Dexron® II automatic transmission fluid, fill transfer case to edge of fill plug opening.
7. Install fill plug and torque it to 30–40 ft.lb.
8. Lower vehicle and check the operation of the transfer case.

Drive Axles

If the vehicle is equipped with a front drive axle, perform the same procedures as for the standard rear drive axle. No draining of the axle fluid is recommended; be sure to maintain a Full fluid level of ⅜″ below the filler plug hole.

FLUID RECOMMENDATIONS

Standard Axle

Always use SAE-80W or SAE 80W-90 GL5. Drain and refill the differential at first oil fill, then at every other oil fill.

Locking Axle

——————— CAUTION ———————

Never use standard differential lubricant in a positraction differential.

Always use GM Rear Axle Fluid No. 1052271. Before refilling the rear axle, add 4 ounces of GM Fluid No. 1052358. Drain and refill the differential at first oil fill, then at every other oil fill.

LEVEL CHECK

The lubricant level should be checked at each chassis lubrication and maintained at ⅜″ below the bottom of the filler plug hole.
1. Raise and support the vehicle on jackstands; be sure that the vehicle is level.
2. Remove the filler plug, located at the side of the differential carrier.
3. Check the fluid level, it should be ⅜″ below the bottom of the filler plug hole, add fluid (if necessary).
4. Replace the filler plug.

DRAIN AND REFILL

Refer to Fluid Recommendations in this section for information on when to change the fluid.
1. Run the vehicle until the lubricant reaches operating temperature.
2. Raise and support the vehicle on jackstands; be sure that the vehicle is level.
3. Using a floor jack, support the drive axle. Position a drain pan under the rear axle.
4. Remove the cover from the rear of the drive axle and drain the lubricant.
5. Using a putty knife, clean the gasket mounting surfaces.
6. To install, use a new gasket, sealant and reverse the removal procedures.
7. Torque the cover-to-rear axle

bolts in a criss-cross pattern to 20 ft.lb. Using a suction gun or a squeeze bulb, install the fluid through the filler plug hole. Install the filler plug.

Cooling System

At least once every 2 years or 30,000 miles, the engine cooling system should be inspected, flushed and refilled with fresh coolant. If the coolant is left in the system too long, it loses its ability to prevent rust and corrosion. If the coolant has too much water, it won't protect against freezing.

FLUID RECOMMENDATIONS

Using a good quality of ethylene glycol antifreeze (one that will not effect aluminum), mix it with water until a 50–50 antifreeze solution is attained.

LEVEL CHECK

NOTE: When checking the coolant level, the radiator need not be removed, simply check the coolant tank.

Check the coolant recovery bottle (see through plastic bottle). With the engine Cold, the coolant should be at the ADD mark (recovery tank ¼ full). With the engine warm, the coolant should be at the FULL mark (recovery tank ½ full). If necessary, add fluid to the recovery bottle.

View of the (see though) coolant recovery tank – cooling system

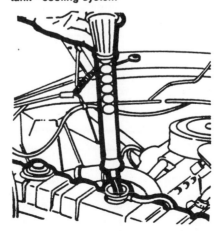

Coolant protection can be checked with a simple, float-type tester

DRAIN AND REFILL

——————— CAUTION ———————

To avoid injuries from scalding fluid and steam, DO NOT remove the radiator cap while the engine and radiator are still HOT.

1. When the engine is cool, remove the radiator cap using the following procedures.
  a. Slowly rotate the cap counterclockwise to the detent.
  b. If any residual pressure is present, WAIT until the hissing noise stops.
  c. After the hissing noise has ceased, press down on the cap and continue rotating it counterclockwise to remove it.
2. Place a fluid catch pan under the radiator, open the radiator drain valve and the engine drain plugs, then drain the coolant.

——————— CAUTION ———————

When draining the coolant, keep in mind that cats and dogs are attracted by the ethylene glycol antifreeze, and are quite likely to drink any that is left in an uncovered container or in puddles on the ground. This will prove fatal in sufficient quantity. Always drain the coolant into a sealable container. Coolant should be reused unless it is contaminated or several years old.

3. Close the drain valve and install the engine drain plugs.
4. Empty the coolant reservoir and flush it.
5. Using the correct mixture of antifreeze, fill the radiator to the bottom of the filler neck and the coolant tank to the FULL mark.
6. Install the radiator cap (make sure that the arrows align with the overflow tube).
7. Run the engine until it reaches the operating temperatures, allow it to cool, then check the fluid level and add fluid (if necessary).

The system should be pressure tested at least once a year

FLUSHING AND CLEANING THE SYSTEM

1. Refer to the Drain and Refill procedures in this section, then drain the cooling system.

---- CAUTION ----

When draining the coolant, keep in mind that cats and dogs are attracted by the ethylene glycol antifreeze, and are quite likely to drink any that is left in an uncovered container or in puddles on the ground. This will prove fatal in sufficient quantity. Always drain the coolant into a sealable container. Coolant should be reused unless it is contaminated or several years old.

---

2. Close the drain valve and install the engine drain plugs, then add sufficient water to the cooling system.
3. Run the engine, then drain and refill the system. Perform this procedure several times, until the fluid (drained from the system) is clear.
4. Empty the coolant reservoir and flush it.
5. Using the correct mixture of antifreeze, fill the radiator to the bottom of the filler neck and the coolant tank to the FULL mark.
6. Install the radiator cap (make sure that the arrows align with the overflow tube).

Master Cylinder

Chevrolets are equipped with a dual braking system, allowing a vehicle to be brought to a safe stop in the event of failure in either the front or rear brakes. The dual master cylinder has two entirely separate reservoirs, one connected to the front brakes and the other connected to the rear brakes. In the event of failure in either portion, the remaining part is not affected.

FLUID RECOMMENDATIONS

Use only heavy-duty Delco Supreme 11 or DOT-3 brake fluid.

---- CAUTION ----

Brake fluid damages paint. It also absorbs moisture from the air; never leave a container or the master cylinder uncovered any longer than necessary. All parts in contact with the brake fluid (master cylinder, hoses, plunger assemblies and etc.) must be kept clean, since any contamination of the brake fluid will adversely affect braking performance.

LEVEL CHECK

The brake fluid level should be inspected every 6 months.
1. Remove the master cylinder reservoir cap.

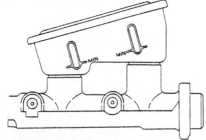

View of the master cylinder reservoir

NOTE: If equipped with a see through reservoir, it is not necessary to remove the reservoir cap unless you are adding fluid.

2. The fluid should be ¼" (6mm) from top of the reservoir, if necessary, add fluid.
3. Replace the reservoir caps.

Hydraulic Clutch

NOTE: The clutch master cylinder is mounted on the firewall next to the brake master cylinder.

FLUID RECOMMENDATIONS

Use only heavy duty Delco Supreme 11 or DOT-3 brake fluid.

LEVEL CHECK

The hydraulic clutch reservoir should be checked at least every 6 months. Fill to the line on the reservoir.

Power Steering Pump

The power steering pump reservoir is located at the front left-side of the engine.

FLUID RECOMMENDATIONS

Use GM Power Steering Fluid No. 1050017 or equivalent.

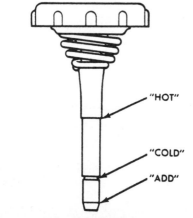

Power steering fluid dipstick

NOTE: Avoid using automatic transmission fluid in the power steering unit, except in an emergency.

LEVEL CHECK

The power steering fluid should be checked at least every 6 months. There is a Cold and a Hot mark on the dipstick. The fluid should be checked when the engine is warm and turned OFF. If necessary, add fluid to the power steering pump reservoir.

NOTE: On models equipped with a remote reservoir, the fluid level should be ½–1" (25.4mm) from the top when the wheels are turned to the extreme left position.

Manual Steering Gear

The steering gear is factory-filled with a lubricant which does not require seasonal change. The housing should not be drained; no lubrication is required for the life of the gear.

FLUID RECOMMENDATIONS

Use GM steering gear lubricant No. 1052182 or equivalent.

LEVEL CHECK

The steering lubricant should be checked every 6 months or 7,500 miles.

The gear should be inspected for seal leakage when specified in the "Maintenance" chart. Look for solid grease, not an oily film. If a seal is replaced or the gear overhauled, it should be refilled with lubricant.

Chassis Greasing

Chassis greasing should be performed every 6 months or 7,500 miles, it can be performed with a commercial pressurized grease gun or at home by using a hand operated grease gun. Wipe the grease fittings clean before greasing in order to prevent the possibility of forcing any dirt into the component.

The four wheel drive front driveshaft requires special attention for lubrication. The large constant velocity joint at the front of the transfer case has a special grease fitting in the centering ball; a special needle nose adapter for a flush type fitting is required, as well as a special lubricant, GM part No. 1050679. You can only get at this fitting when it is facing up toward the floorboard, so you need a flexible hose, too.

Water resistant EP chassis lubricant (grease) conforming to GM specification 6031-M should be used for all chassis grease points.

Body Lubrication

HOOD LATCH AND HINGES

Clean the latch surfaces and apply clean engine oil to the latch pilot bolts and the spring anchor. Use the engine oil to lubricate the hood hinges as well. Use a chassis grease to lubricate all the pivot points in the latch release mechanism.

DOOR HINGES

The gas tank filler door, the front doors and rear door hinges should be wiped clean and lubricated with clean engine oil. Silicone spray also works well on these parts but must be applied more often. The door lock cylinders can be lubricated easily with a shot of GM silicone spray No. 1052276 or one of the many dry penetrating lubricants commercially available.

PARKING BRAKE LINKAGE

Use chassis grease on the parking brake cable where it contacts the guides, links, levers and pulleys. The grease should be a water resistant one for durability under the vehicle.

ACCELERATOR LINKAGE

Lubricate the throttle body lever, the cable and the accelerator pedal lever (at the support inside the vehicle) with clean engine oil.

TRANSMISSION SHIFT LINKAGE

Lubricate the shift linkage with water resistant chassis grease which meets

GM specification No. 6031M or equivalent.

Front Wheel Bearings—2WD Only

Once every 30,000 miles, clean and re-pack wheel bearings with a GM Wheel Bearing Grease No. 1051344 or equivalent. Use only enough grease to completely coat the rollers. Remove any excess grease from the exposed surface of the hub and seal.

REMOVAL, PACKING AND INSTALLATION

NOTE: The following procedures require the use of GM tools No. J-29117, J-8092, J-8850, J-8457, J-9746-02 or equivalent.

1. Raise and support the front of the vehicle on jackstands.
2. Remove the tire/wheel assembly.
3. Remove the caliper-to-steering knuckle bolts and the caliper from the steering knuckle. Using a wire, support the caliper from the vehicle; DO NOT disconnect the brake line.
4. From the hub/disc assembly, remove the dust cap, the cotter pin, the spindle nut, the thrust washer and the outer bearing.
5. Grasping the hub/disc assembly firmly, pull the assembly from the axle spindle.
6. Using a small pry bar, pry the grease seal from the rear of the hub/disc assembly, then remove the inner bearing.

NOTE: DO NOT remove the bearing races from the hub, unless they show signs of damage.

7. If it is necessary to remove the wheel bearing races, use the GM front bearing race removal tool No. J-29117 or equivalent, to drive the races from the hub/disc assembly.
8. Using solvent, clean the grease from all of the parts, then blow them

dry with compressed air.
9. Inspect all of the parts for scoring, pitting or cracking, replace the parts (if necessary).
10. If the bearing races were removed, perform the following procedures to the install the them:
    a. Using grease, lightly lubricate the inside of the hub/disc assembly.
    b. Using the GM seal installation tools No. J-8092 and J-8850 or equivalent, drive the inner bearing race into the hub/disc assembly until it seats.

NOTE: When installing the bearing races, be sure to support the hub/disc assembly with GM tool No. J-9746-02 or equivalent.

    c. Using the GM seal installation tools No. J-8092 and J-8457 or equivalent, drive the outer race into the hub/disc assembly until it seats.
11. Using wheel bearing grease, lubricate the bearings, the races and the spindle; be sure to place a gob of grease (inside the hub/disc assembly) between the races to provide an ample supply of lubricant.

NOTE: To lubricate each bearing, place a gob of grease in the palm of the hand, then roll the bearing through the grease until it is well lubricated.

12. Place the inner wheel bearing into the hub/disc assembly. Using a flat plate, drive the new grease seal into the rear of the hub/disc assembly until it is flush with the outer surface.
13. Onto the spindle, install the hub/disc assembly, the thrust washer and the hub nut. While turning the wheel, torque the hub nut to 16 ft.lb. until the bearings seat. Loosen the nut, retighten it and back it off until the nearest nut slot aligns with a spindle hole (not more than a ½ turn).
14. Install a new cotter pin through the nut and the spindle, then bend the ends and cut off the excess pin. Install the grease cap.

TRAILER TOWING

General Recommendations

Wiring

Trucks are popular as trailer towing vehicles. Their strong construction and variety of power train combinations make them ideal for towing campers, boat trailers and utility trailers.

Factory trailer towing packages are available on many models. However, if you are installing a trailer hitch and wiring on your vehicle, there are a few things you ought to know.

Wiring the vehicle for towing is fairly easy. There are a number of good wiring kits available and these should be used, rather than trying to design your own. All trailers will need brake lights, turn signals, tail lights and side marker lights. Most states require extra marker lights for overwide trailers. Also, most states have recently required back-up lights for trailers, and most trailer manufacturers have been building trailers with back-up lights for several years.

Additionally, some Class I, most Class II and just about all Class III trailers will have electric brakes.

Add to this number an accessories

wire, to operate the trailer internal equipment or to charge the trailer's battery, and you can have as many as seven wires in the harness.

Determine the equipment on your trailer and buy the wiring kit necessary. The kit will contain all the wires needed, plus a plug adapter set which included the female plug, mounted on the bumper or hitch, and the male plug, wired into, or plugged into the trailer harness.

When installing the kit, follow the manufacturer's instructions. The color coding of the wires is standard throughout the industry.

One point to note: some domestic vehicles and most imported vehicles, have separate turn signals. On most domestic vehicles, the brake lights and rear turn signals operate with the same bulb. For those vehicles with separate turn signals, you can purchase an isolation unit so that the brake lights won't blink whenever the turn signals are operated, or, you can go to your local electronics supply house and buy four diodes to wire in series with the brake and turn signal bulbs. Diodes will isolate the brake and turn signals. The choice is yours. The isolation units are simple and quick to install, but far more expensive than the diodes. The diodes, however, require more work to install properly, since they require the cutting of each bulb's wire and soldering in place of the diode.

One, final point, the best kits are those with a spring loaded cover on the vehicle mounted socket. This cover prevents dirt and moisture from corroding the terminals. Never let the vehicle socket hang loosely; always mount it securely to the bumper or hitch.

Cooling
ENGINE

One of the most common, if not the most common, problems associated with trailer towing is engine overheating.

With factory installed trailer towing packages, a heavy duty cooling system is usually included. Heavy duty cooling systems are available as optional equipment on most models, with or without a trailer package. If you have one of these extra capacity systems, you shouldn't have overheating problems.

If you have a standard cooling system, without an expansion tank, you'll definitely need to get an aftermarket expansion tank kit, preferably one with at least a 2 quart capacity. These kits are easily installed on the radiator's overflow hose, and come with a

pressure cap designed for expansion tanks.

Another helpful accessory is a Flex Fan. These fan are large diameter units are designed to provide more air flow at low speeds, with blades that have deeply cupped surfaces. The blades then flex, or flatten out, at high speed, when less cooling air is needed. These fans are far lighter in weight than stock fans, requiring less horsepower to drive them. Also, they are far quieter than stock fans.

If you do decide to replace your stock fan with a flex fan, note that if your vehicle has a fan clutch, a spacer between the flex fan and water pump hub will be needed.

Aftermarket engine oil coolers are helpful for prolonging engine oil life and reducing overall engine temperatures. Both of these factors increase engine life.

While not absolutely necessary in towing Class I and some Class II trailers, they are recommended for heavier Class II and all Class III towing.

Engine oil cooler systems consist of an adapter, screwed on in place of the oil filter, a remote filter mounting and a multi-tube, a finned heat exchanger, which is mounted in front of the radiator or air conditioning condenser.

TRANSMISSION

An automatic transmission is usually recommended for trailer towing. Modern automatics have proven reliable and, of course, easy to operate, in trailer towing.

The increased load of a trailer, however, causes an increase in the temperature of the automatic transmission fluid. Heat is the worst enemy of an automatic transmission. As the temperature of the fluid increases, the life of the fluid decreases.

It is essential, therefore, that you install an automatic transmission cooler.

The cooler, which consists of a multi-tube, finned heat exchanger, is usually installed in front of the radiator or air conditioning compressor, and hooked inline with the transmission cooler tank inlet line. Follow the cooler manufacturer's installation instructions.

Select a cooler of at least adequate capacity, based upon the combined gross weights of the vehicle and trailer.

Cooler manufacturers recommend that you use an aftermarket cooler in addition to, and not instead of, the present cooling tank in your vehicle's radiator. If you do want to use it in place of the radiator cooling tank, get a cooler at least two sizes larger than normally necessary.

One note: transmission cooler can, sometimes, cause slow or harsh shifting in the transmission during cold weather, until the fluid has a chance to come up to normal operating temperature. Some coolers can be purchased with or retrofitted with a temperature bypass valve which will allow fluid flow through the cooler only when the fluid has reached operating temperature, or above.

Trailer and Hitch Weight Limits

Trailer Weight

Trailer weight is the first, and most important, factor in determining whether or not your vehicle is suitable for towing the trailer you have in mind. The horsepower-to-weight ratio should be calculated. The basic standard is a ratio of 35:1. That is, 35 lbs. of GVW for every horsepower.

To calculate this ratio, multiply you engine's rated horsepower by 35, then subtract the weight of the vehicle, including passengers and luggage. The resulting figure is the ideal maximum trailer weight that you can tow. One point to consider: a numerically higher axle ratio can offset what appears to be a low trailer weight. If the weight of the trailer that you have in mind is somewhat higher than the weight you just calculated, you might consider changing your rear axle ratio to compensate.

Hitch Weight

There are three kinds of hitches: bumper mounted, frame mounted and load equalizing.

Bumper mounted hitches are those which attach solely to the vehicle's bumper. Many states prohibit towing with this type of hitch, when it attaches to the vehicle's stock bumper, since it subjects the bumper to stresses for which it was not designed. Aftermarket rear step bumpers, designed for trailer towing, are acceptable for use with bumper mounted hitches.

Frame mounted hitches can be of the type which bolts to two or more points on the frame, plus the bumper, or just to several points on the frame. Frame mounted hitches can also be of the tongue type, for Class I towing, or, of the receiver type, for classes II and III.

Load equalizing hitches are usually used for large trailers. Most equalizing hitches are welded in place, they use equalizing bars and chains to level the vehicle after the trailer is connected.

The bolt-on hitches are the most common, since they are relatively easy to install.

Check the gross weight rating of your trailer. Tongue weight is usually figured as 10% of gross trailer weight. Therefore, a trailer with a maximum gross weight of 2,000 lbs. will have a maximum tongue weight of 200 lbs. Class I trailers fall into this category.

Class II trailers are those with a gross weight rating of 2,000–3,500 lbs., while Class III trailers fall into the 3,500–6,000 lbs. category. Class IV trailers are those over 6,000 lbs. and are for use with fifth wheel trucks, only.

When you've determined the hitch that you'll need, follow the manufacturer's installation instructions, exactly, especially when it comes to fastener torques. The hitch will subjected to a lot of stress and good hitches come with hardened bolts. Never substitute an inferior bolt for a hardened bolt.

PUSHING AND TOWING

———— CAUTION ————

Pushing or tow your vehicle to start it may result in unusually high catalytic converter and exhaust system temperatures, which under extreme conditions may ignite the interior floor covering material above the converter.

Pushing

Chevrolets with manual transmissions can be push started.

To push start, make sure that both bumpers are in reasonable alignment. Turn the ignition switch ON and engage High gear. Depress the clutch pedal. When a speed of about 10 mph is reached, slightly depress the gas pedal and slowly release the clutch. The engine should start.

NOTE: Automatic transmission equipped vehicles cannot be started by pushing.

Towing

Chevrolets can be towed on all four wheels (flat towed) at speeds of less than 35 mph for distances less than 50 miles, providing that the axle, driveline and engine/transmission are operable. The transmission should be in Neutral, the engine should be Off, the steering column unlocked, and the parking brake released.

Do not attach chains to the bumpers or bracketing. All attachments must be made to the structural members. Safety chains should be used. it should also be remembered that power steering and brake assists will not be working with the engine off.

The rear wheels must be raised off the ground or the driveshaft disconnected when the transmission is not operating properly, or when speeds or over 35 mph will be used or when towing more than 50 miles.

———— CAUTION ————

If a vehicle is towed on its front wheels only, the steering wheel must be secured with the wheels in a straight ahead position.

JUMP STARTING

The following procedure is recommended by the manufacturer. Be sure that the booster battery is 12 volt with negative ground. Follow this procedure exactly to avoid possible damage to the electrical system, especially on models equipped with computerized engine controls.

———— CAUTION ————

DO NOT attempt this procedure on a frozen battery; it will probably explode. DO NOT attempt it on a sealed Delco Freedom battery showing a light color in the charge indicator. Be certain to observe correct polarity connections. Failure to do so will result in almost immediate computer, alternator and regulator destruction. Never allow the jumper cable ends to touch each other.

1. Position the vehicles so that they are not touching. Set the parking brake and place automatic transmission in Park and manual transmission in Neutral. Turn Off the lights, heater and other electrical loads. Turn both ignition switches Off.
2. Remove the vent caps from both the booster and discharged battery.

Lay a cloth over the open vent cells of each battery. This isn't necessary on batteries equipped with sponge type flame arrestor caps, and it isn't possible on sealed batteries.

3. Attach one cable to the positive terminal of the booster battery and the other end to the positive terminal of the discharged battery.

NOTE: If you are attempting to start a Chevrolet with the diesel engine, it is suggested that this connection be made to the battery on the driver's side of the vehicle, because this battery is closer to the starter, and thus the resistance of the electrical cables is lower. From this point on, ignore the other battery in the vehicle.

———— CAUTION ————

DO NOT attempt to jump start the vehicle with a 24 volt power source.

4. Attach one end of the remaining cable to the negative terminal of the booster battery and the other end to a good ground. Do not attach to the negative terminal of discharged batteries. Do not lean over the battery when making this last connection.

5. Start the engine with the booster battery. Start the engine with the discharged battery. If the engine will not start, disconnect the batteries as soon as possible. If this is not done, the two batteries will soon reach a state of equilibrium, with both too weak to start an engine. This will not be a problem of the engine of the booster vehicle is kept running fast enough. Lengthy cranking can also overheat and damage the starter.

6. Reverse the above steps to disconnect the booster and discharge batteries. Be certain to remove negative connections first.

7. Reinstall the vent caps. Dispose of the cloths; they may have battery acid on them.

———— CAUTION ————

The use of any "hot shot" type of jumper system in excess of 12 volts can damage the electronic control units or cause the discharged battery to explode.

2 ROUTINE MAINTENANCE

JUMP STARTING A DEAD BATTERY

Jump Starting Precautions

1. Be sure both batteries are of the same voltage.
2. Be sure both batteries are of the same polarity (have the same grounded terminal).
3. Be sure the vehicles are not touching.
4. Be sure the vent cap holes are not obstructed.
5. Do not smoke or allow sparks around the battery.
6. In cold weather, check for frozen electrolyte in the battery.
7. Do not allow electrolyte on your skin or clothing.
8. Be sure the electrolyte is not frozen.

Jump Starting Procedure

1. Determine voltages of the two batteries; they must be the same.
2. Bring the starting vehicle close (they must not touch) so that the batteries can be reached easily.
3. Turn off all accessories and both engines. Put both cars in Neutral or Park and set the handbrake.
4. Cover the cell caps with a rag—do not cover terminals.
5. If the terminals on the run-down battery are heavily corroded, clean them.
6. Identify the positive and negative posts on both batteries and connect the cables in the order shown.
7. Start the engine of the starting vehicle and run it at fast idle. Try to start the car with the dead battery. Crank it for no more than 10 seconds at a time and let it cool off for 20 seconds in between tries.
8. If it doesn't start in 3 tries, there is something else wrong.
9. Disconnect the cables in the reverse order.
10. Replace the cell covers and dispose of the rags.

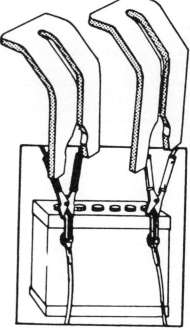

Side terminal batteries occasionally pose a problem when connecting jumper cables. There frequently isn't enough room to clamp the cables without touching sheet metal. Side terminal adaptors are available to alleviate this problem and should be removed after use.

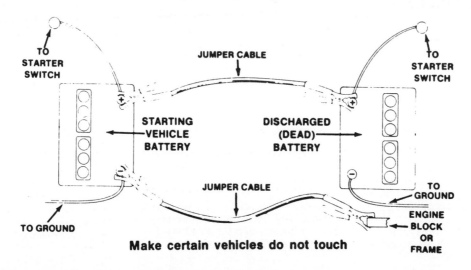

Make certain vehicles do not touch

JACKING AND HOISTING

The jack supplied with the vehicle is meant for changing tires. It was not meant to support the vehicle while you crawl under it and work. Whenever it is necessary to get under a vehicle to perform service operations, always be sure that it is adequately supported, by jackstands at the proper points. Always block the wheels when changing tires.

If your vehicle is equipped with a Positraction rear axle, do not run the engine for any reason with one rear wheel off the ground. Power will be transmitted through the rear wheel remaining on the ground, possibly causing the vehicle to drive itself off the jack.

Some of the service operations in this manual require that one or both ends of the vehicle be raised and supported safely. The best arrangement for this, of course, is a grease pit or a vehicle lift, but these items are seldom found in the home garage. However, small hydraulic, screw, or scissors jacks are satisfactory for raising the vehicle.

Heavy wooden blocks or adjustable jackstands should be used to support the vehicle while it is being worked on. Drive-on trestles or ramps are also a handy and a safe way to raise the vehicle, assuming their capacity is adequate. These can be bought or constructed from suitable heavy timbers or steel.

In any case, it is always best to spend a little extra time to make sure that your vehicle is lifted and supported safely.

——— **CAUTION** ———

Concrete blocks are not recommended. They may crumble if the load is not evenly distributed. Boxes and milk crates of any description must not be used. Shake the vehicle a few times to make sure the jackstands are securely supporting the weight before crawling under.

HOW TO BUY A USED CAR OR TRUCK

Many people believe that a 2–3 year old used vehicle is a better buy than a new one. This may be true. The new vehicle suffers the heaviest depreciation in the first two years but is not old enough to present a lot of costly repair problems. Whatever the age of the used vehicle you might want to buy, this section and a little patience will help you select one that should be safe and dependable.

TIPS

1. First decide what model you want and how much you want to spend.
2. Check the used car lots and your local newspaper ads. Privately owned vehicles are usually less expensive, however you will not get a warranty that, in most cases, comes with a used vehicle purchased from a lot.
3. Never shop at night. The glare of the lights make is easy to miss faults on the body caused by accident or rust repair.
4. Try to get the name and phone number of the previous owner. Contact him/her and ask about the vehicle. If the owner of the lot refuses this information, look for a vehicle somewhere else.

NOTE: A private seller can tell you about the vehicle and maintenance. Remember, however, there's no law requiring honesty from private citizens selling used vehicles. There is a law that forbids the tampering with or turning back the odometer mileage. This includes both the private citizen and the lot owner. The law also requires that the seller or anyone transferring ownership of the vehicle must provide the buyer with a signed statement indicating the mileage on the odometer at the time of transfer.

5. Write down the year, model and serial number before you buy any used vehicle. Then dial 1-800-424-9393, the toll free number of the National Highway Traffic Safety Administration, and ask if the vehicle has ever been included on any manufacturer's recall list. If so, make sure the needed repairs were made.
6. Use the Used Car Or Truck Checklist in this section and check all the items on the used vehicle you are considering. Some items are more important than others. You know how much money you can afford for repairs, and, depending on the price of the vehicle, may consider doing any needed work yourself. Beware, however, of trouble in areas that will affect operation, safety or emission. Problems in the Used Car Or Truck Checklist break down as follows:

1–8: Two or more problems in these areas indicate a lack of maintenance. You should beware.

9–13: Indicates a lack of proper care, however, these can usually be corrected with a tune-up or relatively simple parts replacement.

14–17: Problems in the engine or transmission can be very expensive. Walk away from any vehicle with problems in both of these areas.

7. If you are satisfied with the apparent condition of the vehicle, take it to an independent diagnostic center or mechanic for a complete check. If you have a state inspection program, have it inspected immediately before purchase or specify on the bill of sale that the sale is conditional on passing the state inspection.

8. Road test the vehicle—refer to the Road Test Checklist in this section. If your original evaluation and the road test agree—the rest is up to you.

USED CAR OR TRUCK CHECKLIST

1. **Mileage:** Average mileage is about 12,000 miles per year. More than average mileage may indicate hard usage. The catalytic converter may need converter service at 50,000 miles.
2. **Paint:** Check around the tail pipe, molding and windows for overspray indicating that the vehicle has been repainted.
3. **Rust:** Check the fenders, doors, rocker panels, window molding, wheelwells, floorboards, under the floormats and in the truck bed for any signs of rust. Any rust at all will be a problem. There is no way to check the spread of rust, except to replace the part of panel.
4. **Body Appearance:** Check the moldings, the bumpers, grille, vinyl roof, glass, doors, tail gate and body panels for general overall condition.

with manual transaxles and 850 rpm on models with automatic transaxles.

NOTE: To adjust the idle speed, turn the throttle adjustment screw on the carburetor.

4. With the engine at the proper idle speed, direct the timing light to the crankshaft pulley. The "V" timing mark of the pulley should be at the 10 degrees BTDC mark on the timing plate.

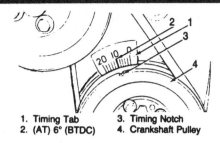

1. Timing Tab
2. (AT) 6° (BTDC)
3. Timing Notch
4. Crankshaft Pulley

View of the timing mark and notch

NOTE: To adjust the timing, loosen the distributor hold down bolt and turn the distributor. When the timing marks are aligned, tighten the hold down bolt.

5. With the timing adjusted, stop the engine and remove the testing equipment.

NOVA

Ignition Timing Adjustment

1. Install a timing light to the No. 1 (crankshaft pulley end) spark plug wire and to the battery according to the manufacturer's instructions. On inductive timing lights, the induction clip can simply be installed over the plug wire; on most lights, the wire will have to be disconnected by pulling on the boot at the end of the wire and connecting the timing light pickup between the plug and the end of the wire. Connect a tachometer according to the manufacturer's instructions.

2. Note the routing of the two vacuum lines going to the distributor vacuum advance/retard unit or mark their locations. Disconnect the two vacuum lines and plug both. Then start the engine and run it until it reaches normal operating temperature. Check the engine rpm; it should be 950 or less with either type of transmission in neutral. If it is too high, adjust it as described later in this section.

3. Aim the timing light at the scale on the front cover near the front pulley. Timing is 5 degrees BTDC. If the timing is not correct, loosen the distributor hold-down bolt until it is just finger tight and turn the distributor slightly to correct it. Once the reading is correct, tighten the hold-down bolt and recheck the timing. Correct it if necessary. Stop the engine, remove the

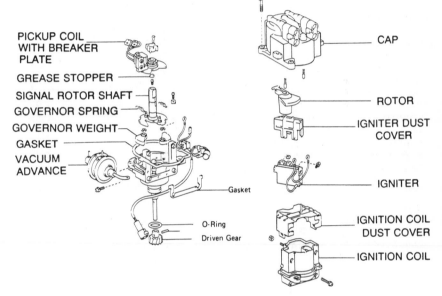

PICKUP COIL WITH BREAKER PLATE
GREASE STOPPER
SIGNAL ROTOR SHAFT
GOVERNOR SPRING
GOVERNOR WEIGHT
GASKET
VACUUM ADVANCE

Gasket
O-Ring
Driven Gear

CAP
ROTOR
IGNITER DUST COVER
IGNITER
IGNITION COIL DUST COVER
IGNITION COIL

Exploded view of distributor assembly

timing light, and unplug and reconnect the hoses.

TACHOMETER HOOKUP

The ignition system is equipped with a service connector plug that shares a common wiring harness with the primary wiring connector leading to the distributor assembly. One lead of the tachometer is connected to that plug. Connect the tachometer leads according to the instruction manual for the instrument. Since not all types of tachometers are compatible with this ignition system, you should consult the instruction book that came with your instrument to make sure it will work with electronic ignition systems, and will not damage the system. Never ground the TACH terminal of the distributor assembly or damage to the ignition system will result.

BERETTA AND CORSICA

Ignition Timing Adjustment

Ignition timing is controlled by the Electronic Control Module (ECM). No adjustments are possible.

BLAZER/JIMMY — FULL SIZE, BLAZER/JIMMY — S-SERIES, PICK-UPS — FULL SIZE, PICK-UPS — S-SERIES, SUBURBAN, VANS — FULL SIZE AND ASTRO

Ignition Timing Adjustment

Timing should be checked at each tuneup. It isn't likely to change much with HEI. The timing marks consist of a notch on the rim of the crankshaft pulley or vibration damper and a graduated scale attached to the engine front (timing) cover. A stroboscopic flash (dynamic) timing light must be used, as a static light is too inaccurate for emission controlled engines.

There are three basic types of timing light available. The first is a simple neon bulb with two wire connections. One wire connects to the spark plug terminal and the other plugs into the end of the spark plug wire for the No.1 cylinder, thus connecting the light in series with the spark plug. This type of light is pretty dim and must be held very closely to the timing marks to be seen. Sometimes a dark corner has to be sought out to see the flash at all. This type of light is very inexpensive. The second type operates from the vehicle battery: two alligator clips connect to the battery terminals, while an adapter enables a third clip to be connected between the No.1 spark plug and wire. This type is a bit more expensive, but it provides a nice bright flash that you can see even in bright sunlight. It is the type most often seen in professional shops. The third type replaces the battery power source with 110 volt current.

1. To check and adjust the timing: Warm up the engine to normal operating temperature. Stop the engine and connect the timing light to the No.1 (left front on V8, front on six and four cylinder) spark plug wire, either at the plug or at the distributor cap. Consult the engine compartment sticker for specific instructions for the particular

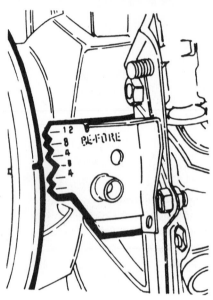

Typical timing marks

vehicle/engine combination in question. On vehicles with Electronic Spark Timing, disconnect the four prong EST connector at the distributor so the engine will operate in the bypass timing mode. Otherwise, you will not be able to set the timing as the EST system will continuously attempt to compensate for changes in the position of the distributor.

——— **CAUTION** ———

Do not pierce the plug wire insulation with HEI; it will cause a miss. Use an inductive pickup timing light.

2. Clean off the timing marks and mark the pulley or damper notch and timing scale with white chalk. Disconnect and plug the vacuum line at the distributor. This is done to prevent any distributor vacuum advance.

Check the underhood emission sticker for any other hoses or wires which may need to be disconnected.

3. Start the engine and adjust the idle speed to that specified in the "Tune-Up Specifications" chart. With automatic transmission, set the specified idle speed in Park. It will be too high, since it is normally (in most cases) adjusted in Drive. You can disconnect the idle solenoid, if any, to get the speed down. Otherwise, adjust the idle speed screw. This is done to prevent any centrifugal (mechanical) advance. The tachometer connects to the TACH terminal on the distributor and to a ground. Some tachometers must connect to the TACH terminal and to the positive battery terminal. Some tachometers won't work with HEI.

——— **CAUTION** ———

Never ground the HEI TACH terminal; serious system damage will result.

4. Aim the timing light at the pointer marks. Be careful not to touch the fan, because it may appear to be standing still. If the pulley or damper notch isn't aligned with the proper timing mark the timing will have to be adjusted.

5. Loosen the distributor base clamp locknut. You can buy trick wrenches which make this task a lot easier on V8s. Turn the distributor slowly to adjust the timing, holding it by the body and not the cap. Turn the distributor in the direction of rotor rotation to retard, and against the direction of rotation to advance.

6. Tighten the locknut. Check the timing again, in case the distributor moved slightly as you tightened it.

7. Replace the distributor vacuum line. Correct the idle speed.

8. Stop the engine and disconnect the timing light.

IDLE SPEED AND MIXTURE ADJUSTMENTS

CORVETTE

When adjusting a carburetor with two idle mixture screws, adjust them alternately and evenly, unless otherwise stated. In the following adjustment procedures the term ''lean roll'' means turning the mixture adjusting screws in (clockwise) from optimum setting to obtain an obvious drop in engine speed (usually 20 rpm).

For all adjustments and specifications not detailed below, please refer to the Fuel System section.

Idle Speed Adjustments

Refer to the underhood tune-up decal for specific procedures concerning your vehicle.

IDLE MIXTURE ADJUSTMENTS

1980

Changes in the idle systems of these models make it impossible to adjust the mixture without the aid of a propane enrichment system, not available to the general public. Blacking out the mixture screw, of itself, will have little or no effect. All carburetors have mixture screws concealed under staked-in plugs. Mixture adjustments are possible only during carburetor overhaul.

1981-87

The previously used propane enrichment or lean drop methods should not be used when adjusting carburetors used on Computer Command Control equipped vehicles. Because of the sensitivity of the CCC system any adjustments to the carburetor can impair the ability of the system to maintain correct control of the air/fuel mixture. The only time adjustments should be made is when the carburetor is being overhauled.

CAPRICE, IMPALA, MALIBU AND MONTE CARLO

Idle Speed Adjustment

GASOLINE ENGINES— CARBURETED

1980

NOTE: An idle speed control system is used on some engines to control the idle speed. No adjustments are necessary with this system.

V6–229, V6–231, V8–267 AND V8–305

1. Run the engine to normal operating temperature.
2. Make sure that the choke is fully opened, turn the A/C off, set the parking brake, block the drive wheels and connect a tachometer to the engine according to the manufacturer's instructions.
3. Disconnect and plug the vacuum hoses at the EGR valve and the vapor canister.
4. Place the transmission in Park (A/T) or Neutral (M/T).
5. Disconnect and plug the vacuum advance hose at the distributor. Check and adjust the timing.
6. Connect the distributor vacuum line.
7. If the vehicle is equipped with a M/T and NOT equipped with A/C or a solenoid, place the idle speed screw on the low step of the fast idle cam and turn the screw to achieve the specified idle speed.

NOTE: If equipped with A/C, turn the idle speed screw to the specified rpm, disconnect the compressor clutch wire, turn the A/C On. Open the throttle momentarily to extend the solenoid plunger, then adjust the solenoid screw to obtain the specified rpm. If NOT equipped with A/C, momentarily open the throttle to extend the solenoid plunger, turn the solenoid screw to obtain the specified rpm, disconnect the solenoid wire and turn the idle speed screw to obtain the slow engine idle speed.

1981-87

ROCHESTER E2ME OR E4ME MODELS

NOTE: No idle speed adjustment is necessary; the idle speed is controlled by the ECM.

GASOLINE ENGINES—FUEL INJECTED

NOTE: The throttle body injection (TBI) unit is set at the factory and no further adjustment is necessary. Only if the TBI unit has been replaced should an idle speed adjustment be performed.

1985-87

1. Run the engine until it reaches normal operating temperatures.
2. Remove the air cleaner and the gasket.
3. Using an awl, puncture idle stop screw cover plug and pry the plug from the TBI.
4. Connect a jumper lead from the Idle Air Control (IAC) motor diagnostic lead to ground.
5. Connect a tachometer to the engine.
6. Turn the ignition ON (DO NOT start the engine) and wait 30 seconds.
7. Disconnect the IAC electrical connector from the TBI unit and remove the diagnostic lead jumper wire.
8. Start the engine, engage the parking brake, place the Automatic Transmission in Drive and allow the engine speed to stabilize.
9. Adjust the idle speed screw to 475–625 rpm.
10. Stop the engine and reconnect the IAC motor electrical connector.
11. Using a voltmeter, adjust the Throttle Position Sensor (TPS) to 0.450–0.600 volts.
12. Recheck the setting.
13. Start the engine and check for proper idle operation.
14. To install, seal the throttle stop screw with silicone sealant and reverse the removal procedures.

3 TUNE-UP AND ENGINE PERFORMANCE

DIESEL ENGINES

1. Run the engine until it reaches operating temperature.
2. Insert the probe of a magnetic pickup tachometer into the timing indicator hole.
3. Set the parking brake and block the drive wheels.
4. Put the transmission in Drive and, if necessary, turn the A/C off.
5. Turn the slow idle screw on the injection pump to obtain the idle speed specified on the emisson control label.

Fast Idle Solenoid Adjustment

1. With the ignition off, disconnect the single green wire from the fast idle relay located on the front of the firewall. This will energize the solenoid so the adjustment you will be making will effect fast idle speed only.
2. Set the parking brake and block the drive wheels.
3. Start the engine and adjust the solenoid to the specifications on the emission control label.
4. Turn the ignition switch off and reconnect the green wire to the fast idle relay.

Fast Idle Solenoid Adjustment

1. With the ignition OFF, disconnect the single green wire from the fast idle relay located on the front of the firewall.
2. Set the parking brake and block the drive wheels.
3. Start the engine and adjust the solenoid (energized) to the specifications on the underhood emission control label.
4. Turn the ignition switch OFF and reconnect the green wire.

Idle Mixture Adjustment

1980

Rochester M2ME/M2MC Models

1. Set the parking brake and block the drive wheels.

NOTE: If the vehicle is equipped with a vacuum parking brake release system, disconnect and plug the vacuum hose at the brake.

2. Refer to the "Emission Control Label" in the engine compartment, then disconnect and plug the necessary hoses.

3. Connect a tachometer to the engine, disconnect and plug the vacuum advance hose at the distributor, then set the timing.
4. Operate the engine to normal operating temperatures; make sure that the choke is open and the A/C is turned OFF.

NOTE: If the vehicle is equipped with Electronic Spark Timing (EST), check and/or adjust the timing and the idle speed according to the "Emission Control Label."

5. Disconnect the crankcase ventilation tube from the air cleaner.
6. Using tool J-26911, connect a hose from a propane tank to the crankcase tube opening at the air cleaner.

─── CAUTION ───
When using a propane tank, make sure it is secured in a safe place in the vertical position.

7. Place the transmission in Drive (A/T) or Neutral (M/T).
8. Slowly OPEN the propane valve until the maximum engine speed is reached.

NOTE: The addition of too much propane will cause the engine speed to drop.

9. If the idle mixture speed does not meet specifications, remove the idle mixture screw plug covers.
10. Turn the idle mixture screws clockwise until lightly seated, then back them OUT (equally) until the lean best idle point at the enriched idle speed is reached.
11. Turn the propane tank OFF and turn the idle mixture screws clockwise (equally) until the curb idle speed is reached.
12. Turn ON the propane tank and recheck the engine speed, if not within specifications, repeat the propane setting.
13. To complete the adjustment, turn OFF the engine, remove the propane tank, reconnect the crankcase ventilation tube to the air cleaner and install new idle mixture screw plugs.

1980-87

Rochester E2ME And E4ME

1. Remove the carburetor from the engine and invert it. Using a hacksaw, make 2 parallel cuts (1/8 in. deep) in the throttle body on either side of the idle mixture screws locator points; the cuts should reach to the steel plug.
2. Using a flat center punch, hold it at a 45° angle to the cut segiments, drive the segiments into the throttle

body. Using a center punch, drive the steel plugs from the housing.
3. Using tool J-29030, turn the idle mixture screws inward until they seat, then back them out 2 turns.
4. Reinstall the carburetor to the engine but NOT the gasket and air cleaner.
5. Set the parking brake, block the drive wheels, start the engine and run it to normal operating temperatures.
6. Disconnect and plug the vacuum hoses according to the Emission Control Label in the engine compartment.
7. Connect a dwell meter, a tachometer and a timing light to the engine, then check and/or adjust the timing.
8. Place the transmission in Drive (A/T) or in Neutral (M/T), then check and/or adjust the idle speed.

NOTE: If equipped with an Idle Speed Control (ISC) or an Idle Load Compensator (ILC), DO NOT adjust the curb idle speed.

9. The dwell should be within the 10°–50° range, if NOT, perform the following procedures:
   a. Turn the engine OFF. Cover the internal bowl vents and the Air Bleed Valve inlets with masking tape, then the primary and the secondary carburetor air intakes with a shop cloth.
   b. Using a No. 35 (0.110 in.) drill bit, drill the rivet heads from the Idle Air Bleed Valve cover. Using a small drift punch, drive the remaining rivets from the air horn tower.
   c. Remove and discard the cover. Using compressed air, blow the metal chips from the air horn.
   d. Remove the cloth and the masking tape from the carburetor, start the engine and allow it to idle with the A/T in Drive or the M/T in Neutral. Slowly turn the Idle Air Bleed Valve until the dwell reading varies between 25°–35°; adjust it as close to 30° as possible.

NOTE: The Idle Air Bleed Valve is very sensitive and should ONLY be turned in 1/8 in. increments. If the dwell remains below 25°, turn the idle mixture screws OUT one full turn. If the dwell is above 35°, turn the idle mixture screws IN one full turn. Readjust the Idle Air Bleed Valve to obtain the dwell limits.

10. After adjusting the idle mixture, fill the idle mixture screw holes with silicone sealant.
11. Check and/or adjust the Fast Idle Speed according the Emissions Control Label.
12. Remove the test equipment, unplug and reconnect the vacuum hoses, then install the air cleaner and gasket.

Fast Idle Adjustment

1980

Rochester M2ME

1. Refer to the emission label and prepare the vehicle for adjustment.
2. Place the transmission in Park (A/T) or Neutral (M/T).
3. Place the fast idle screw on the highest step of the fast idle cam.
4. Turn the fast idle screw to obtain the fast idle speed.

1980-87

Rochester E2ME

1. Refer to the emission label and prepare the vehicle for adjustment.
2. Place the transmission in Park (A/T) or Neutral (M/T).
3. Place the fast idle screw on the highest step of the fast idle cam.
4. Turn the fast idle screw to obtain the fast idle speed.

1982-87

Rochester E4ME

NOTE: The fast idle speed adjustment must be performed according to the emission control label instructions. See the underhood sticker.

1982-87 Idle Mixture Adjustment (All Models)

All models have sealed idle mixture screws; in most cases these are concealed under staked-in plugs. Idle mixture is adjustable only during carburetor overhaul and requires the addition of propane as an artificial enrichener, along with the use of an emissions tester or infrared analyzer.

CELEBRITY AND CITATION

Idle Speed And Mixture Adjustments

GASOLINE ENGINES— CARBURETED MODELS

1980

1. Run the engine to normal operating temperature.
2. Make sure that the choke is fully opened, turn the A/C Off, set the parking brake, block the drive wheels and connect a tachometer to the engine according to the manufacturer's instructions.
3. Disconnect and plug the vacuum hoses at the EGR valve and the vapor canister.
4. Place the transmission in Park (AT) or Neutral (MT).
5. Disconnect and plug the vacuum advance hose at the distributor. Check and adjust the timing.
6. Connect the distributor vacuum line.
7. Manual transmission cars with A/C and without solenoid; place the idle speed screw on the low step of the fast idle cam and turn the screw to achieve the specified idle speed.
Cars with A/C: set the idle speed screw to the specified rpm. Disconnect the compressor clutch A/C On. Open the throttle momentarily to extend the solenoid plunger. Turn the solenoid screw to obtain the specified rpm.
Automatic transmission cars without A/C; manual transmission cars without A/C, solenoid-equipped carburetor: momentarily open the throttle to extend the solenoid plunger. Turn the solenoid screw to obtain the specified rpm. Disconnect the solenoid wire

① PREPARE VEHICLE FOR ADJUSTMENTS— SEE EMISSION LABEL ON VEHICLE. NOTE: IGNITION TIMING SET PER LABEL

③ SOLENOID ENERGIZED—A/C COMPRESSOR LEAD DISCONNECTED AT A/C COMPRESSOR, A/C ON, A/T IN DRIVE, M/T IN NEUTRAL

⑤ TURN SOLENOID SCREW TO ADJUST TO SPECIFIED RPM. (RECONNECT A/C COMPRESSOR LEAD AFTER ADJUSTMENT)

② TURN IDLE SPEED SCREW TO SET CURB IDLE SPEED TO SPECIFICATIONS— A/C OFF (SEE EMISSION LABEL)

④ OPEN THROTTLE SLIGHTLY TO ALLOW SOLENOID PLUNGER TO FULLY EXTEND

ELECTRICAL CONNECTION

1980 idle speed adjustment w A/C

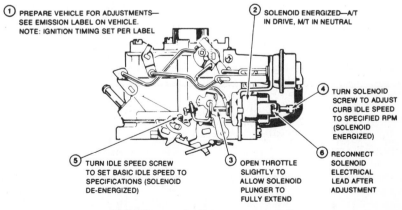

① PREPARE VEHICLE FOR ADJUSTMENTS— SEE EMISSION LABEL ON VEHICLE. NOTE: IGNITION TIMING SET PER LABEL

② SOLENOID ENERGIZED—A/T IN DRIVE, M/T IN NEUTRAL

④ TURN SOLENOID SCREW TO ADJUST CURB IDLE SPEED TO SPECIFIED RPM (SOLENOID ENERGIZED)

⑥ RECONNECT SOLENOID ELECTRICAL LEAD AFTER ADJUSTMENT

⑤ TURN IDLE SPEED SCREW TO SET BASIC IDLE SPEED TO SPECIFICATIONS (SOLENOID DE-ENERGIZED)

③ OPEN THROTTLE SLIGHTLY TO ALLOW SOLENOID PLUNGER TO FULLY EXTEND

1980 Idle speed adjustment—w/o A/C

and turn the idle speed screw to obtain the slow engine idle speed.

1981–87

Mixture adjustments are a function of the Computer Command Control (CCC) system. The idle speed on models equipped with an Idle Speed Control (ISC) motor is also automatically adjusted by the Computer Command Control System, making manual adjustment unnecessary. The underhood specifications sticker will indicate ISC motor use.

On non-A/C models not equipped with the ISC, the idle speed is adjusted at the idle speed screw on the carburetor. Before adjusting, check the underhood sticker for any preparations required. On A/C equipped models which do not have an ISC motor, an idle speed solenoid similar to the ones on earlier models is used. This solenoid is adjusted at the solenoid screw, using the same procedures as on earlier models. Consult the underhood specifications sticker for special instructions.

GASOLINE ENGINES—FUEL INJECTED MODELS

No idle speed or mixture adjustments

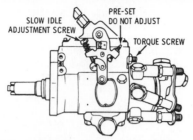

Idle speed adjustment points, CAV pump shown

are possible on 1982-87 fuel injected engines.

DIESEL ENGINES

1. Apply the parking brake, place the transmission selector lever in Park and block the drive wheels.
2. Start engine and allow it to run until warm, usually 10–15 minutes.
3. Shut off the engine, remove the air cleaner assembly.
4. Clean the front cover rpm counter (probe holder) and the crankshaft balancer rim.
5. Install the magnetic pick-up probe of tool J-26925 fully into the rpm counter. Connect the battery leads; red to positive (+) and black to negative (–).

6. Disconnect the two-lead connector at the generator.
7. Turn off all electrical accessories.
8. Allow no one to touch either the steering wheel or service brake pedal.
9. Start the engine and place the transmission selector lever in Drive.
10. Check the slow idle speed reading against the one given on the underhood emission control sticker. Reset if required.
11. Unplug the connector from the fast idle cold advance (engine temp.) switch and install a jumper between the connector terminals. Do not allow the jumper to touch ground.
12. Check the fast idle solenoid speed against the one given on the underhood sticker and reset if required.
13. Remove the jumper and reconnect the connector to the temperature switch.
14. Recheck and reset the slow idle speed if necessary.
15. Shut off the engine.
16. Reconnect the lead at the generator.
17. Disconnect and remove the tachometer.
18. If equipped with cruise control adjust the servo throttle cable to minimum slack then install the clip on the servo stud.

CAMARO

Idle Speed Adjustments

CARBURETED ENGINES

1980-81

All models have sealed idle mixture screws; in most cases these are concealed under staked-in plugs. Idle mixture is adjustable only during carburetor overhaul and requires the addition of propane as an artificial mixture enricher.

NOTE: See the emission control label in the engine compartment for procedures and specifications not supplied here. To prepare the engine for adjustment, warm the engine, open the choke and move the fast idle screw off the fast idle cam.

1 BBL

1. Run the engine to normal operating temperature.
2. Make sure that the choke is fully open.

3. Turn the A/C off and disconnect the vacuum line at the vapor canister. Plug the line.
4. Set the parking brake, block the drive wheels and place the transmission in Drive (A/T) or Neutral (M/T). Connect a tachometer to the engine according to the manufacturer's instructions.
5. Turn the solenoid assembly to achieve the solenoid-on speed.
6. Disconnect the solenoid wire and turn the $\frac{1}{8}$ in. hex screw in the solenoid end, to adjust the solenoid-off speed.
7. Remove the tachometer, connect the canister vacuum line and turn the engine OFF.

2 BBL AND 4 BBL (EXCEPT 350 V8)

1. Run the engine to normal operating temperature.
2. Make sure that the choke is fully open, turn the A/C off, set the parking brake, block the drive wheels and connect a tachometer to the engine according to the manufacturer's instructions.

3. Disconnect and plug the vacuum hoses at the EGR valve and the vapor canister.
4. Place the transmission in Park (A/T) or Neutral (M/T).
5. Disconnect and plug the vacuum advance hose at the distributor. Check and adjust the timing.
6. Connect the distributor vacuum line.
7. On vehicles without A/C or a solenoid, place the idle speed screw on the low step of the fast idle cam and turn the screw to the specified idle speed.
8. On vehicles with A/C, set the idle speed screw to the specified rpm. Disconnect the compressor clutch wire and turn the A/C "ON." Open the throttle momentarily to extend the solenoid plunger. Turn the solenoid screw to obtain the specified rpm.
9. On vehicles without A/C but with a solenoid, momentarily open the throttle to extend the solenoid plunger. Turn the solenoid screw to obtain the specified rpm. Disconnect the solenoid wire and turn the idle speed screw to the correct curb idle speed.

350 V8 ONLY

1. Run the engine to normal operating temperature.
2. Set the parking brake and block the drive wheels.
3. Connect a tachometer to the engine according to the manufacturer's instructions.
4. Disconnect and plug the purge hose at the vapor canister. Disconnect and plug the EGR vacuum hose at the EGR valve.
5. Turn the A/C off.
6. Place the transmission in Park (A/T) or Neutral (M/T).
7. Disconnect and plug the vacuum advance line at the distributor. Check and adjust the timing.
8. Connect the vacuum advance line. Place the automatic transmission in Drive.
9. On manual transmission vehicles without A/C, adjust the idle stop screw to obtain the specified rpm.
10. On vehicles with A/C, turn the A/C off, adjust the idle stop screw to obtain the specified rpm. Disconnect the compressor clutch wire and turn the A/C on. Open the throttle sightly to allow the solenoid plunger to extend. Turn the solenoid screw to obtain the solenoid rpm listed on the underhood emission sticker.
11. Connect all hoses and remove the tachometer.

1982-84

ROCHESTER E2SE MODELS

For all overhaul and service adjustment procedures, refer to "Carburetors" in the Unit Repair section.

——————— CAUTION ———————
Before performing the idle adjustments, block the drive wheels and set the parking brake.

WITH A/C
1. Refer to the emission label in the engine compartment and follow the instructions to prepare the vehicle for adjustment.
2. Place the A/T in Drive or the M/T in Neutral and turn the throttle slightly to allow the solenoid plunger to fully extend.
3. Turn the solenoid screw to adjust the curb idle rpm, then disconnect the solenoid lead.
4. Turn the idle speed screw to set the basic idle speed. Reconnect the solenoid electrical leak after adjustment.

WITHOUT A/C
1. Refer to the emission label in the engine compartment and follow the instructions to prepare the vehicle for adjustment.

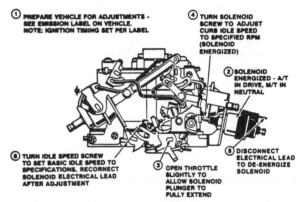

Idle speed adjustment—E2SE model (with A/C)

Idle speed adjustment—E2SE model (without A/C)

2. With the A/C off, turn the idle speed screw to set the curb idle speed.
3. Turn the A/C on, disconnect the A/C compressor lead at the A/C compressor and place the A/T in Drive or the M/T in Neutral.
4. Open the throttle slightly to allow the solenoid plunger to extend.
5. Turn the solenoid screw to adjust to the specified rpm. After adjustment, reconnect the A/C compressor lead.
6. Turn the A/C off. Set the curb idle speed by turning the idle speed screw.

1982-87

ROCHESTER E4ME MODELS

NOTE: No idle speed adjustment is necessary; the idle speed is controlled by the ECM.

FUEL INJECTED ENGINES

NOTE: The TBI unit is adjusted at the factory and no further ad-
justment is necessary. Only if the TBI unit has been replaced should an adjustment be performed.

1982-87

Model 300 (TBI)

1. Remove the air cleaner and the gasket.
2. Disconnect and plug the THERMAC vacuum port on the TBI unit.
3. Remove the TV cable from the throttle control bracket to provide access to the minimum air adjustment screw.
4. Connect a tachometer to the engine.
5. Remove the Idle Air Control (IAC) connector from the TBI unit.
6. Start the engine, place the transmission in Park (A/T) or Neutral (M/T) and allow the engine speed to stabilize.
7. Install tool J-33047 into the idle air passage of the TBI unit. Make sure

that the tool is seated and no air leaks exist.

8. Using a No. 20 Torx Bit tool, turn the idle stop screw until the engine speed is 475–525 rpm (A/T) or 750–800 rpm (M/T).

9. Stop the engine and remove the tool from the TBI unit.

10. To install, seal the throttle stop screw with silicone sealant and reverse the removal procedures.

Model 400 (CFI)

1. Remove the air cleaner and the gasket.

2. Disconnect and plug the THERMAC vacuum port at the rear TBI unit.

3. If necessary, remove the plug covering the minimum air adjusting screw.

4. Block the wheels, set the parking brake, connect a tachometer to the engine, start the engine and allow the engine speed to stabilize.

5. Place the automatic transmission in Drive.

6. Using 2 tools J-33047, plug the idle air passages of each throttle body. Make sure that the tools are seated and no air leaks exist.

NOTE: When the plugs are installed, the rpm should drop below the curb idle speed. If the speed does not drop, check for an air leak.

7. At the rear TBI unit, remove the cap from the ported tube and connect a water manometer J-23951.

8. Adjust the minimum air adjustment screw to obtain 6 inches of water on the manometer. Remove the manometer and install the cap on the ported tube.

9. At the front TBI unit, remove the cap from the ported tube and connect the water manometer J-23951. The reading should be 6 inches of water on the manometer.

NOTE: If the manometer reading is not correct, locate the idle balance screw on the throttle linkage. If the screw is welded, break the weld and install a new screw with thread sealing compound. Adjust the screw to obtain 6 inches of water on the manometer.

10. Remove the manometer and install the cap on the ported tube.

11. At the rear TBI unit, adjust the minimum air adjustment screw to obtain 475 rpm.

12. Stop the engine and remove the idle air passage plugs.

13. Place the transmission in Neutral and start the engine.

NOTE: The engine will run at a high rpm but will decrease when the IAC motors close the air passages. When the rpm drops, stop the engine.

14. Check the Throttle Position Sensor (TPS) voltage and adjust, if necessary.

15. To install, reverse the removal procedures. Reset the IAC motors.

NOTE: To reset the IAC motors, drive the vehicle at 30 mph or if equipped with cruise control, disconnect the speedometer cable at the transducer, turn the key ON and rotate the cable to 30 mph.

TUNED PORT INJECTION (TPI)—V6 AND V8

NOTE: The idle stop screw of the throttle body, used to regulate

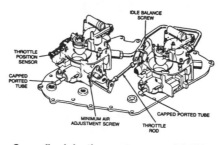

Throttle body—model 300

Cross fire injection system—model 400

the minimum idle speed, is adjusted and sealed at the factory. If it is necessary to adjust the idle speed, perform the following procedures.

1. Using an awl, pierce the idle stop screw plug and pry it from the throttle body housing.

2. With Idle Air Control (IAC) valve connected to the throttle body, ground the diagnostic lead.

3. Turn the ignition ON (DO NOT start the engine), wait 30 seconds, disconnect the IAC electrical connector, remove the IAC grounded lead and start the engine.

4. If equipped with an automatic transmission, place it in Drive and adjust the idle speed to 450–550 rpm by turning the idle stop screw. If equipped with a manual transmission, place it in Neutral and adjust the idle speed to 550–650 rpm (V6).

5. Turn the ignition OFF and reinstall the electrical connector to the IAC valve.

6. At the Throttle Position Sensor (TPS), install 3 jumper wires between the TPS and the harness connector.

7. Connect a digital voltmeter to terminals "A" and "B" of the TPS. Turn the ignition ON and check for voltages of 0.50–0.60 volts (V6) or 0.465–0.615 volts (V8).

NOTE: If the voltages of the TPS are not correct, loosen the mounting screws and adjust the TPS. When the voltages meet specifications, tighten the mounting screws.

8. If adjustment of the TPS has been performed, recheck the readings.

9. Turn the ignition OFF, remove the jumper wires and reconnect the electrical connector to the TPS.

10. Start the engine and check for proper idle operation. Seal the idle stop screw housing with silicone sealant.

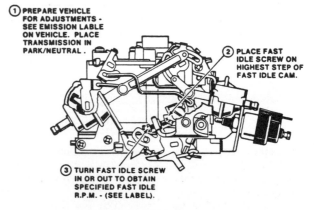

Fast idle speed adjustment

Idle Mixture Adjustment

ALL MODELS

All models have sealed idle mixture screws; in most cases these are concealed under staked-in plugs. Idle mixture is adjustable only during carburetor overhaul and requires the addition of propane as an artificial enrichener.

Fast Idle Adjustment

1982-84

Rochester E2SE Models

1. Refer to the emission label and prepare the vehicle for adjustment.
2. Place the transmission in Park (A/T) or Neutral (M/T).
3. Place the fast idle screw on the highest step of the fast idle cam.

4. Turn the fast idle screw to obtain the fast idle speed.

1982-87

Rochester E4ME Models

NOTE: The fast idle speed adjustment must be performed according to the emission control label instructions. See the underhood sticker.

CAVALIER

IDLE SPEED AND MIXTURE ADJUSTMENTS

CARBURETED MODELS

Idle Mixture

A E2SE carburetor is used with a Computer Command Control system (CCC), the carburetor is equipped with a mixture control solenoid.

——————— CAUTION ———————

Idle mixture screws have been preset at the factory and sealed. Idle mixture should be adjusted only in the case of major carburetor overhaul, throttle body replacement or high emissions as determined by official inspections. Adjusting mixture by other than the following method may violate Federal and/or California or other state or Provincial laws. Because of the sealed idle mixture screws, the idle mixture checking procedure requires artificial enrichment by adding propane.

NOTE: Before checking or resetting the carburetor as the cause of poor engine performance or rough idle, check ignition system including distributor, timing, spark plugs and wires. Check air cleaner, evaporative emission system, EFE system, PCV system, EGR valve and engine compression. Also inspect intake manifold vacuum hose gaskets and connections for leaks and check torques of carburetor mounting bolts/ nuts.

1. Remove the carburetor.
2. Remove the idle mixture screw plugs, then lightly seat the screws.
3. Back out the screws 5 turns each for the four cylinder engine.
4. Remove the idle air bleed screw plug from the air horn. Lightly seat

the air bleed screw, then back it out 3 turns for the four cylinder engine.
5. Remove the vent stack and screen assembly in order to gain access to the lean mixture screw. Lightly seat the lean mixture screw, then back it out 2 ½ turns.
6. Reinstall the carburetor on the engine, but DO NOT install the air cleaner and gasket.
7. Disconnect the bowl vent line at the carburetor.
8. Disconnect and plug the vacuum hose at the tee in the bowl vent line (if so equipped).
9. Disconnect the canister purge and EGR lie at the carburetor, then plug the carburetor fitting.
10. Connect a dwell meter to the mixture control solenoid test lead (green connector) and set the dwell meter to the 6 cylinder position.
11. Connect a tachometer to the distributor TACH lead (brown connector).
12. Block the drive wheels, place the transmission in Park (auto. trans.) or Neutral (man. trans.), and apply the parking brake.
13. Start the engine and let it idle until the cooling fan starts to cycle, indicating that the engine is warm and operating in the closed loop mode.
14. Run the engine at 3000 rpm and adjust the lean mixture screw in small increments (allowing the dwell to stabilize after each adjustment) until the average dwell is 35°. If you are unable to adjust to this specification, check the carburetor main metering circuit for leaks, restrictions, etc.

NOTE: It is normal for the dwell to vary about 2 ½ below and above 35°. The dwell reading may also read 10–15° momentarily due to temporary mixture changes.

15. Allow the engine to return to idle and adjust the idle speed to 700 rpm, with the cooling fan in the Off cycle.

16. Adjust the idle mixture screw (in the same manner as in Step 14.) until a dwell (average) of 25° is obtained. The adjustment is very sensitive-the final check must be made with the adjusting tool removed. If you are unable to set the dwell to specification, check the carburetor idle system for leaks, restrictions, etc.
17. Raise the engine rpm to 3000, and make sure that the dwell stabilizes and averages 35° at this rpm. Repeat Steps 14–17 if required.
18. Remove the tachometer and dwell meter, reattach the hoses as they were originally, and reinstall the items previously removed.
19. Set the idle speed to the figure given on the underhood emissions label.

Idle Speed Control (ISC)

The idle speed control (ISC) is controlled by the electronic control module (ECM), which has the desired idle speed programmed in its memory. The ECM compares the actual idle speeder is moved in or out. This automatically adjusts the throttle to hold an idle rpm independent of the engine loads.

An integral part of the ISC is the throttle contact switch. The position of the switch determines whether or not the ISC should control idle speed. When the throttle lever is resting against the ISC plunger, the switch contacts are closed, at which time the ECM moves the ISC to the programmed idle speed. When the throttle lever is not contacting the ISC plunger, the switch contacts are open; the ECM stops sending idle speed commands and the driver controls engine speed.

NOTE: Before starting engine, place transmission selector lever in park or neutral, set parking brake, and block drive wheels.

When a new ISC assembly is installed, a base (minimum authority) and high (minimum authority) rpm speed check must be performed and adjustment made as required. These adjustment limit the low and high rpm speeds to the ECM. When making a low and high speed adjustment, the low speed adjustment is always made first. DO NOT use the ISC plunger to adjust curb idle speed as the idle speed is controlled by the ECM.

NOTE: Do not disconnect or connect ISC connector with ignition on as damage to the ECM may occur.

1. Connect tachometer (distributor side of tach filter, if used).
2. Connect dwell meter to mixture control (M/C) solenoid dwell lead. Remember to set dwell meter on the six cylinder scale, regardless of the engine being tested.
3. Turn A/C off.
4. Start engine and run until stabilized by entering "closed loop" (dwell meter needle starts to vary).
5. Turn ignition off.
6. Unplug connector from ISC motor.
7. Fully retract ISC plunger by applying 12 volts DC (battery voltage) to terminal "C" of the ISC motor connection and ground lead to terminal "D" of the ISC motor connection. It may be necessary to install jumper leads from the ISC motor in order to make proper connections.

NOTE: Do not apply battery voltage to motor longer than necessary to retract ISC plunger. Prolonged contact will damage motor. Also, never connect voltage source across terminals "A" and "B" as damage to the internal throttle contact switch will result.

8. Start engine and wait until dwell meter needle starts to vary, indicating "closed loop" operation.
9. With parking brake applied and drive wheels blocked, place transmission in Drive (Neutral, manual transmission models).
10. With ISC plunger fully retracted, adjust carburetor base (slow) idle stop screw to the specified rpm (see specifications). ISC plunger should not be left in full retracted position.
11. Place transmission in Park or Neutral and fully extend ISC plunger by applying 12 volts DC to terminal "D" of the ISC motor connection and ground lead to terminal "C" of the ISC motor connection.

NOTE: Never connect voltage source across terminal "A" and "B" as damage to the internal throttle contact switch will result.

12. With ISC plunger fully extended, using Tool J-29831 or equivalent, turn ISC plunger to obtain ISC adjustment rpm. Verify ISC adjustment rpm

with voltage applied to motor will ratchet in and out.
   Auto trans. only; place transmission in Drive and readjust ISC plunger to ISC adjustment rpm.
13. Place transmission in Park or Neutral and turn ignition off. Disconnect 12 volt DC power source, jumper leads, ground lead, tachometer, and dwell meter.
14. Reconnect four terminal harness connector to ISC motor.
15. "Tricking" the ISC motor as described will cause the "Check Engine" light to come on and an ISC motor trouble code to be set. By restoring the system to normal operation, the light will go out, but the trouble code will continue to be stored as an intermittent problem. In this case, it will be necessary to clear the diagnostic trouble code.

FAST IDLE

1. Prepare the car for adjustment as specified on the underhood emission label. Place the transmission in Park or Neutral.
2. Place the fast idle screw on the highest step of the fast idle cam.
3. Turn the fast idle screw in or out to obtain the specified fast idle speed.

FUEL INJECTED MODELS

The idle speed and mixture are electronically controlled by the electronic control module (ECM), no adjustments are necessary.

CHEVETTE

Idle Speed Adjustment

GASOLINE ENGINES

Two idle speeds are controlled by a solenoid on models without both automatic transmission and air conditioning. One is normal curb idle speed (solenoid energized). The second is low idle speed (solenoid de-energized) which prevents dieseling when the ignition is turned off. On cars with both automatic transmission and air conditioning the solenoid is energized when air conditioning is on to maintain curb idle speed.

1980

MODELS WITH 6510-C CARBURETOR

1. Adjust the ignition timing as previously outlined.

2. On non-air conditioned models, connect the PCV and the vacuum advance hoses and adjust the idle speed to specification using the idle speed adjusting screw on the carburetor.
3. If the car is equipped with air conditioning:
   a. Disconnect the electrical connection at the A/C compressor.
   b. Disconnect and plug the EGR and PCV hoses.
   c. Turn the air conditioning On and start the engine.
   d. Open the throttle slightly to extend the throttle solenoid on the carburetor. If the speed is incorrect, turn off the engine and turn the solenoid screw to adjust. Start the engine and check the speed. Repeat this until the correct idle speed is obtained.
   e. Connect the wiring at the compressor and unplug and connect the hoses.

1981-87

On these models, the carburetor mixture and idle speed are adjusted by the Computer Command Control (CCC) System. It is possible to adjust the basic idle speed; however, this procedure requires special knowledge and tools.

DIESEL ENGINES

1. Set the parking brake and block the wheels.
2. Place the transmission in Neutral. Connect a diesel tachometer as per the manufacturer's instructions.

NOTE: A standard gasoline engine tachometer will not work on a diesel engine.

3. Start the engine and allow it to reach normal operating temperature.
4. Loosen the lock nut on the idle speed adjusting screw and turn the

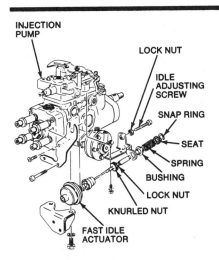

Exploded view of diesel injection pump linkage showing idle adjusting screw and fast idle adjuster (knurled nut)

screw to obtain the correct idle speed (see underhood specifications sticker).

5. Tighten the lock nut, turn the engine off and disconnect the tachometer.

Fast Idle Speed

1. Set the parking brake and block the wheels.
2. Place the transmission in Neutral.
3. Connect a diesel tachometer.
4. Start the engine and allow it to run until it reaches normal operating temperature.
5. Apply vacuum to the fast idle actuator.
6. Loosen the lock nut on the fast idle adjusting screw and adjust the

knurled nut to obtain the fast idle speed specified on the emission label. After adjusting, retighten the lock nut.

Idle Mixture Adjustment

Turning the mixture screw on these carburetors will have no appreciable effect. The factory-recommended idle mixture adjustment procedure on many 1980 models requires special apparatus to artificially enrich the mixture with propane gas. On 1981-87 models, the idle mixture is adjusted by the CCC system and requires no manual adjustment.

SPECTRUM

Idle Speed Adjustment

1. Set the parking brake and block the wheels.
2. Place the manual transmission in Neutral or the automatic transmission in Park. Check the float level. Establish a normal operating temperature and make sure that the choke plate is open.
3. Turn off all of the accessories and wait until the cooling fan is not operating.
4. If equipped with power steering, place the wheels in the straight forward position. Remove the air filter.
5. Disconnect and plug the distributor vacuum line, canister purge line, EGR vacuum line and ITC valve vacuum line.
6. Connect a tachometer to the coil tachometer connector and a timing light to the No. 1 spark plug wire. Check the timing and idle speed.
7. If the idle speed needs adjusting, turn the idle speed adjusting screw.
8. If equipped with A/C, adjust the system to Max. Cold and place the blower on "High" position. Set the fast idle speed by turning the Fast Idle Adjusting Screw.
9. When adjustment is completed, turn the engine off, remove the test equipment, install the air filter and vacuum lines.

Idle Mixture Adjustments

NOTE: The idle mixture screw

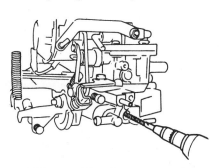

Adjusting the idle speed screw

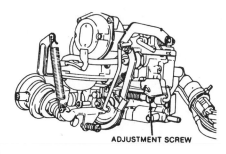

Drilling the idle mixture screw plug

is adjusted and sealed at the factory and no adjustment is required.

1. Remove the carburetor from the engine.
2. Using a center punch, make a punch mark on the idle mixture sealing plug. Drill a hole through the plug, insert a threaded screw and pull the plug from the throttle body.

NOTE: If the idle mixture screw is damaged from the drilling process, replace the screw.

3. Lightly seat the idle mixture screw, then back out 3 turns (M/T) or 2 turns (A/T). DO NOT overtighten the idle mixture screw.
4. Reinstall the carburetor and the air cleaner.
5. Adjust the idle speed.
6. Using a dwell meter, connect the positive lead to the duty monitor and the negative lead to ground. Place the meter dial on the 4 or 6 cylinder scale. Turn the idle mixture screw until the dwell meter reads 36 degrees (4 cylinder scale) or 24 degrees (6 cylinder scale).
7. Adjust the throttle adjusting screw to 750 rpm (M/T) or 1000 (A/T), then stop the engine and remove the tachometer.
8. Drive a new idle mixture plug into the throttle body, flush with the throttle body.

Idle Speed Adjustment (With A/C)

1. With the engine running, turn the A/C control to MAX COLD and the blower on high.
2. Turn the FIDC adjusting screw, on the tip of the throttle lever, to set the idle speed to 850 rpm (M/T) or 980 rpm (A/T).
3. Check the fast idle speed.

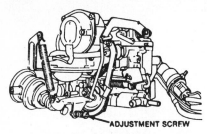

Adjusting the fast idle screw

Fast Idle Speed Adjustment

1. Remove the air cleaner.
2. Open the throttle valve slightly, close the choke valve and release the throttle; set on the 1st stage of the fast idle cam.
3. Start the engine. DO NOT touch the accelerator pedal.

4. Connect a tachometer to the engine and check the fast idle speed; 850 rpm (M/T) or 980 rpm (A/T).

NOTE: Adjust the fast idle speed by turning the FIDC screw, located on the tip of the throttle lever.

5. Stop the engine, remove the tachometer and install the air cleaner.

SPRINT

Idle Speed AdjustmenT

Check and/or adjust the accelerator cable play, the timing, the valve lash, the emission control wiring and hoses. Make sure that the headlights, the heater fan, the engine cooling fan and any other electrical equipment is turned OFF. If any of the current drawing systems are operating, the idle up system will operate, causing the idle speed to be higher than normal.
1. Connect a tachometer to the primary negative terminal of the ignition coil and refer to the underhood sticker.
2. Place the transaxle in Neutral, set the parking brake and block the wheels.
3. Start the engine and bring it to normal operating temperatures.
4. Check and/or adjust the idle speed, it should be 700–800 rpm with manual transaxles, 800–900 rpm with automatic transaxles.

NOTE: To adjust the idle speed, turn the throttle adjustment screw on the carburetor.

5. With the engine at the proper idle speed, check and/or adjust the idle up speed.
6. Stop the engine and remove the tachometer.

Idle Mixture Adjustments

The carburetor is adjusted at the factory and no further adjustment should be necessary. However, if the engine performance is poor, the emission test fails, or the carburetor has been replaced or overhauled, an idle mixture adjustment is necessary. Before adjusting the idle mixture, check the timing/idle speed, the valve lash and make sure that all electrical accessories are turned OFF.

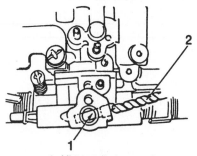

1. Mixture adjust screw pin
2. Drill

Removing the idle mixture pin

1. Refer to the "Carburetor Removal & Installation" procedures in this section and remove the carburetor from the intake manifold.
2. Using an $^{11}/_{64}$ inch bit, drill through the idle mixture screw housing, in line with the retaining pin. Use a punch to drive the pin from the housing.
3. Install the carburetor to the intake manifold by reversing the removal procedures.
4. Place the transaxle in Neutral, set the parking brake and block the wheels.
5. Start the engine and bring it to normal operating temperatures.
6. Disconnect the Duty Cycle Check connector, located near the water reservoir tank. Connect the positive terminal of a dwell meter to the blue/red wire and the negative terminal to the black/green wire.
7. Set the dwell meter to the 6 cylinder position, make sure that the indicator moves.
8. Check and/or adjust the idle speed.
9. Operate the engine at idle speed and adjust the idle mixture screw, allow the engine to stabilize between adjustments. Adjust the dwell to 21°–27°; recheck the idle speed and adjust, if necessary.
10. After completing the adjustment,

stop the engine, disconnect the dwell meter and connect the Duty Cycle Check connector to the coupler.
11. Install a new idle mixture adjust screw pin in the throttle housing, drive it in place.

Idle-Up Adjustment

Make sure that the headlights, the heater fan, the engine cooling fan and any other equipment is turned OFF. If any of the current drawing systems are operating, the idle up system will operate, causing the idle speed to be higher than normal.
1. Connect a tachometer to the engine.
2. Place the transaxle in Neutral, apply the parking brake and block the wheels.
3. Start and warm the engine to normal operating temperatures. Check the idle speed.
4. Turn the headlights ON and make sure that the screw on the idle up actuator, moves down.

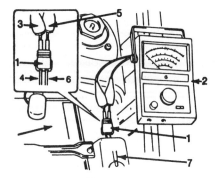

1. Duty Check Connector
2. Dwell Meter
3. Positive (+) Terminal
4. "Blue/Red" Wire
5. Negative (−) Terminal
6. "Black/Green" Wire
7. Water Reservoir Tank
8. Battery

Connecting the dwell meter to the duty check connector

cable and remove the valve cover(s).

2. Remove the rocker arm nut and rocker arm ball.

3. Lift the rocker arm off the rocker arm stud. Always keep the rocker arm assemblies together and assemble them on the same stud.

4. Remove the pushrod from its bore. Make sure the rods are returned to their original bores, with the same end in the block.

5. To install, reverse the removal procedures. Adjust the valves.

V8 Diesel Engine

NOTE: When the diesel engine rocker arms are removed or loosened, the lifters must be bled down to prevent oil pressure buildup inside each lifter, which could cause it to raise up higher than normal and bring the valves within striking distance of the pistons.

1. Remove the valve cover.

2. Remove the rocker arm pivot bolts, the bridged pivot and rocker arms.

3. Remove each rocker set as a unit.

4. To install, lubricate the pivot wear points and position each set of rocker arms in its proper location. Do not tighten the pivot bolts, to prevent bending the valves when the engine is turned.

5. The lifters can be bled down for six cylinders at once with the crankshaft in either of the following two positions:

a. For cylinders number 3, 5, 7, 2, 4 and 8, turn the crankshaft so the saw slot on the harmonic balancer is at 0° on the timing indicator.

b. For cylinders 1, 3, 7, 2, 4 and 6, turn the crankshaft so the saw slot on the harmonic balancer is at 4 O'clock.

6. Tighten the rocker arm pivot bolts to 28 ft. lbs. It will take 45 minutes to completely bleed down the lifters in this position. If additional lifters must be bled, rotate the engine to the other position, tighten the rocker arm pivot bolts, and again wait 45 minutes before rotating the crankshaft.

7. Assemble the remaining components in the reverse order of disassembly. The rocker covers do not use gaskets, but instead are sealed with a bead of RTV (room temperature vulcanizing) silicone sealer.

V6 Diesel Engines

NOTE: When the diesel engine rocker arms are removed or loosened, the lifters must be bled down to prevent oil pressure buildup inside each lifter, which could cause it to raise up higher

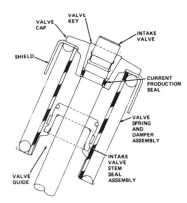

INTAKE VALVE DETAIL
CHEVROLET BUILT
V-8 & V-6

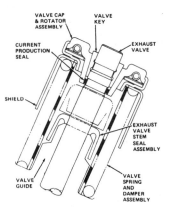

EXHAUST VALVE DETAIL
CHEVROLET BUILT
V-8 & V-6

Valve seal and retainer details for Chevrolet V6 and V8 engines.

than normal and bring the valves within striking distance of the pistons.

1. Remove the valve cover.

2. Remove the rocker arm pivot bolts, the bridged pivot and rocker arms.

3. Remove each rocker set as a unit.

4. Before installing any removed rocker arms, rotate the engine crankshaft so that No. 1 cylinder is 32° before top dead center. This is 2 in. counterclockwise from the 0° pointer. To verify that No. 1 cylinder TDC is coming up, if only the right valve cover was removed, remove the No. 1 cylinder glow plug, then turn the engine: compression pressure will force air out the glow plug hole. If the left valve cover was removed, rotate the crankshaft until the No. 5 cylinder intake valve pushrod ball is 0.28 in. above the No. 5 cylinder exhaust valve pushrod ball.

NOTE: Use only hand wrenches to torque the rocker arm pivot bolts to avoid engine damage.

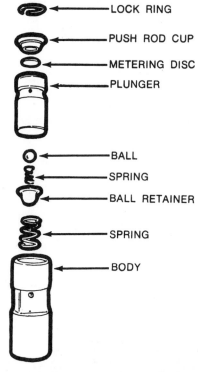

Hydraulic lifter plunger and body are fitted pairs and must not be mismated

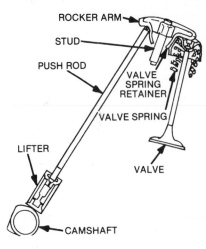

V8 engine valve system

5. If removed, install the No. 5 cylinder pivot and rocker arms, then torque the bolts alternately between the intake and exhaust valves until the intake valve begins to open, then stop.

6. Install the remaining rocker arms, except No. 3 exhaust (if this rocker was removed).

7. If removed, install the No. 3 cylinder exhaust valve pivot, but do not torque beyond the point that the valve would be fully open. This is indicated by strong resistance while still turning the pivot retaining bolts. Going beyond this point will bend the pushrod. Torque the bolts SLOWLY, allowing the lifter to bleed down.

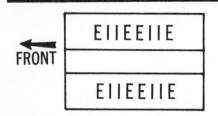

Chevrolet intake(I) and exhaust(E) valve arrangements (except the V6 engine)

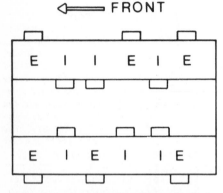

Valve arrangement of the Chevrolet-built V6 engines (E-exhaust; I-intake)

8. Finish torquing No. 5 cylinder rocker arm pivot bolt slowly. Do not go beyond the point that the valve would be fully open, as in Step 7.

9. Do not turn the engine for at least 45 minutes.

10. Finish assembling the engine as the lifters are being bled.

Valve Clearance Adjustment

Corvette

Engines equipped with hydraulic lifters VERY RARELY need adjustment of the valve lash. If the vehicle runs well and there is no audible "clicking" in the valve train, leave it alone. This is because removal of the valve covers on vehicles equipped with air conditioning, various emission controls, cruise control, etc., can be a major project in itself.

On air conditioned models, the A/C compressor must be moved out of the way to gain access to one of the valve covers. Do not disconnect the refrigerant lines to move the compressor.

Caprice, Impala, Malibu and Monte Carlo

GASOLINE ENGINES

1. Disconnect the negative battery cable and remove the valve covers.

2. Turn the crankshaft until the mark on the damper pulley aligns with the 0° mark on the timing plate at the

front of the engine and the No. 1 cylinder is at the TDC of the compression stroke.

NOTE: If the valves of the No. 1 cylinder DO NOT move when checked, the engine is at the TDC of the compression stroke. If the valves DO move when checked, the engine is at the TDC of the No. 6 cyl. (V8) or No. 4 cyl. (V6); turn the crankshaft one complete revolution.

3. With the engine at the No. 1 firing position, adjust the exhaust valves of No. 1, 3, 4 & 8 on the V8 or No. 1, 5 & 6 on the V6 and the intake valves of No. 1, 2, 5 & 7 on the V8 or No. 1, 2 & 3 on the V6.

NOTE: To adjust the valves, back out the adjusting nut until lash is felt at the pushrod, then turn the nut in until the lash disappears. Once the play has be removed, turn the adjusting IN one full turn (to center the lifter plunger).

4. After adjusting the indicated valves, turn the crankshaft one full rotation and align the mark on the damper pulley with the 0° mark on the timing plate.

5. With the engine at the No. 6 (V8) or No. 4 (V6) firing position, adjust the exhaust valves of No. 2, 5, 6 & 7 on the V8 or No. 2, 3 & 4 on the V6 and the intake valves of No. 3, 4, 6 & 8 on the V8 or No. 4, 5 & 6 on the V6.

6. To install, reverse the removal procedures. Start the engine, then check and/or adjust the idle speed.

DIESEL ENGINES

These valves cannot be adjusted. If there is excessive clearance in the valve train, look for worn pushrods, rocker arms, valve springs, or collapsed or stuck valve lifters.

Cylinder Head

REMOVAL & INSTALLATION

NOTE: The engine should be "overnight" cold before the cylinder head is removed to prevent warpage.

——— CAUTION ———
DO NOT discharge the compressor or disconnect the A/C lines. Personal injury could result.

All Gasoline Engines

1. Refer to the "Intake Manifold Removal & Installation" procedures in this section and remove the intake manifold.

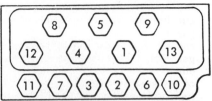

Cylinder head torque sequence-200, 229, and 262 V6 engines

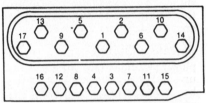

Cylinder head torque sequence for the Chevrolet V8 engines

2. Remove the alternator's lower mounting bolt and move the unit aside.

3. Remove the exhaust manifold(s), the rocker arm cover(s) and the rocker arm assemblies.

4. Drain the cooling system.

5. Remove the diverter valve, the cylinder head bolts and the cylinder head(s).

6. Using a putty knife, clean the gasket mounting surfaces.

7. To install, use new gaskets and reverse the removal procedures. Torque the cylinder head bolts in sequence to specifications. Check and/or adjust the valve clearances, the timing and the idle speed.

Diesel Engines

1. Remove the intake manifold, using the procedure outlined above.

2. Remove the rocker arm cover(s), after removing any accessory brackets which interfere with cover removal.

3. Disconnect and label the glow plug wiring.

4. If the right cylinder head is being removed, remove the ground strap from the head.

5. Remove the rocker arm bolts, the bridged pivots, the rocker arms, and the pushrods, keeping all the parts in order so that they can be returned to their original locations. It is a good practice to number or mark the parts to avoid interchanging them.

6. Remove the fuel return lines from the nozzles.

7. Remove the exhaust manifold(s), using the procedure outlined above.

8. Remove the engine block drain plug on the side of the engine from which the cylinder head is being removed. On V6s, remove the pipe-thread plugs covering the upper cylinder head bolts.

9. Remove the head bolts. Remove the cylinder head.

10. To install, first clean the mating surfaces thoroughly. Install new head gaskets on the engine block. Do not coat the gaskets with any sealer. The gaskets have a special coating that eliminates the need for sealer. The use of sealer will interfere with this coating and cause leaks. Install the cylinder head onto the block.

11. Clean the head bolts (and pipe-thread plugs — V6s) thoroughly. On the V8, dip the bolts in clean engine oil and install into the cylinder block until the heads of the bolts lightly contact the cylinder head. On V6s, coat the plug threads, bolt threads and the area under the bolt threads with sealer/lubricant part No. 1052080 or equivalent.

NOTE: The correct sealer must be used or coolant leaks and bolt torque loss will result.

12. On the V8, tighten the bolts, in the sequence illustrated, to 100 ft. lbs. When all bolts have been tightened to this figure, begin the tightening sequence again, and torque all bolts to 130 ft. lbs.

13. On V6s, tighten all head bolts in sequence to the following torques: all except bolts 5, 6, 11, 12, 13 and 14—100 ft. lbs.; bolts 5, 6, 11, 12, 13 and 14—41 ft. lbs. Finally, tighten all bolts except 5, 6, 11, 12, 13 and 14 to 142 ft. lbs., and bolts 5, 6, 11, 12, 13 and 14 to 59 ft. lbs. in the proper sequence. Install the pipe thread plugs.

14. Install the engine block drain plug(s), the exhaust manifold(s), the fuel return lines, the glow plug wiring, and the ground strap for the right cylinder head.

15. Install the valve train assembly. Refer to "Diesel Engine, Rocker Arm Replacement," above, for valve lifter bleeding procedures.

16. Install the intake manifold.

17. Install the rocker cover(s). The valve covers are sealed with RTV (room temperature vulcanizing) silicone sealer instead of a gasket. Use GM No.1052434 or its equivalent. Install the cover to the head within 10 minutes (while the sealer is still wet).

Timing Chain Cover

REMOVAL & INSTALLATION

Gasoline Engines

1. Disconnect the negative battery cable and drain the cooling system.
2. Remove the fan assembly, the drive belts and the fan pulley.
3. Raise and support the vehicle on jackstands.
4. Remove the crankshaft pulley and the damper pulley bolt.

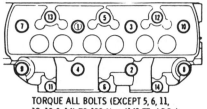

TORQUE ALL BOLTS (EXCEPT 5, 6, 11, 12, 13 & 14) TO 193 N·m (142 FT. LBS.). NUMBERS 5, 6, 11, 12, 13 & 14 TORQUE TO 80 N·m (59 FT. LBS.).

V6 diesel engine cylinder head torque sequence

5. Using tool J-23523, remove the damper pulley.
6. Remove the alternator and the brackets. If equipped with power steering, remove the lower pump bracket and swing aside.
7. Remove the heater and the lower radiator hoses from the water pump.
8. Remove the water pump bolts and the pump from the engine.
9. Remove the timing cover bolts and the timing cover.
10. Using a putty knife, clean the gasket mounting surfaces.
11. To install, use new gaskets, sealant and reverse the removal procedures. Torque the timing cover bolts to 8 ft. lbs., the damper bolts to 65–75 ft. lbs. and the water pump bolts to 25–35 ft. lbs.

Diesel Engines

NOTE: To perform this operation on the V–8, you'll need a set of special tools designed to pull the crankshaft pulley off the crankshaft without damaging the rubber insert separating inner and outer pulley halves. Use tools equivalent to GM No. J-8614-3, J-8614-2, J-8614-1, and J-7583-3.

1. Drain the cooling system and disconnect the radiator hoses.
2. Remove all belts, fan and pulley. Remove the crankshaft pulley and balancer, utilizing the special tools described in the note above on the V–8. See the illustration for proper assembly of these tools. On the V6, make sure you use a puller that will bolt to the outside of the balancer and pull it off by applying pressure to a pilot inserted into the center of the crankshaft.

CAUTION

The use of any other type of puller, such as a universal claw type which pulls on the outside of the hub, can destroy the balancer. The outside ring of the balancer is bonded in rubber to the hub. Pulling on the outside will break the bond. The timing mark is on the outside ring. If it is suspected that the bond is broken, check that the center of the keyway is 16° from the center of the timing slot. In addition, there are chiseled aligning marks between the weight and the hub.

3. Unbolt and remove the cover, timing indicator and water pump.
4. It may be necessary to grind a flat on the cover for gripping purposes.
5. Grind a chamfer on one end of each dowel pin.
6. Cut the excess material from the front end of the oil pan gasket on each side of the block.
7. Clean the block, oil pan and front cover mating surfaces with solvent.
8. Trim about $\frac{1}{8}$ in. off each end of a new front pan seal.
9. Install a new front cover gasket on the block and a new seal in the front cover.
10. Apply sealer to the gasket around the coolant holes.
11. Apply sealer to the block at the junction of the pan and front cover. On

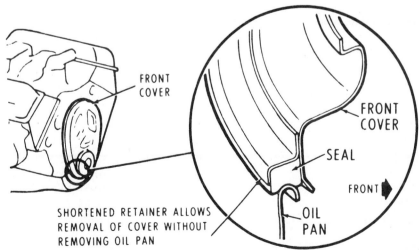

FRONT COVER

SHORTENED RETAINER ALLOWS REMOVAL OF COVER WITHOUT REMOVING OIL PAN

FRONT COVER

SEAL

FRONT

OIL PAN

On Chevrolet V6 and V8 engines, it is not necessary to lower or remove the oil pan in order to remove the timing cover. The seal retainer is short enough to clear the pan

V6, apply RTV sealer on the front cover oil pan seal retainer.

12. Place the cover on the block and press down to compress the seal. Rotate the cover left and right and guide the pan seal into the cavity using a small screwdriver. Oil bolt threads and heads, install two to hold the cover in place, then install both dowel pins (chamfered end first). Install remaining front cover bolts.

13. Apply a lubricant, compatible with rubber, on the balancer seal surface.

14. Install the balancer and bolt. Torque the bolt to 200–300 ft. lbs. on V8, 160–350 ft. lbs. on V6.

15. Install all other parts in the reverse order of removal.

Timing Chain Cover Oil Seal

REMOVAL & INSTALLATION

All Engines

COVER REMOVED

1. Refer to the "Timing Cover Removal & Installation" procedures in this section and remove the timing cover.

2. Using a small pry bar, pry the oil seal from the timing cover.

3. Using tool J-23042, drive the new oil seal into the timing cover.

NOTE: When installing the new oil seal, be sure to support the rear side of the timing cover.

4. To complete the installation, reverse the removal procedures.

COVER INSTALLED

1. Refer to the "Timing Cover Removal & Installation" procedures in this section and remove the balancer from the crankshaft.

2. Using a small pry bar, pry the oil seal from the timing cover.

3. Place the new seal (open end toward the engine) on the timing cover and drive it into the cover using tool J-23042.

4. To complete the installation, reverse the removal procedures. Torque the balancer bolt to 65–75 ft. lbs.

Timing Chain And Sprocket

REMOVAL & INSTALLATION

All Gasoline Engines and V8 Diesel Engines

1. Remove the timing case cover, turn crankshaft to line up timing

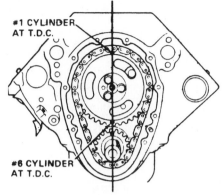

Timing mark alignment on 1980 and later Chevrolet V6 and V8 engines

marks, and take off the camshaft sprocket.

NOTE: The fuel pump operating cam is bolted to the front of the camshaft sprocket and the sprocket is mounted on the camshaft by means of a dowel.

2. Remove the oil slinger, timing chain, and the camshaft sprocket. If the crankshaft sprocket is to be replaced, remove it also at this time. Remove the crankshaft key before using the puller. If the key cannot be removed, align the puller so it does not overlap the end of the key, as the keyway is only machined part of the way into the crankshaft gear.

3. Reinstall the crankshaft sprocket being careful to start it with the keyway in perfect alignment since it is rather difficult to correct for misalignment after the gear has been started on the shaft. Turn the timing mark on the crankshaft gear until it points directly toward the center of the camshaft. Mount the timing chain over the camshaft gear and start the camshaft gear onto its shaft with the timing marks as close as possible to each other and in line between the shaft centers. Rotate the camshaft to align the shaft with the new gear.

NOTE: To set crankshaft and camshaft gear marks for timing chain installation; position the engine with the No. 6 piston at top dead center. Slowly rotate the crankshaft one revolution until the camshaft gear mark is at 12 o'clock. No. 1 piston will now be at TDC on the compression stroke.

4. Install the fuel pump eccentric with the flat side toward the rear.

5. Drive the key in with a brass hammer until it bottoms.

6. Install the oil slinger.

NOTE: Whenever the timing chain and gears are replaced on

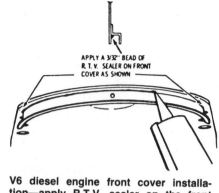

APPLY A 3/32" BEAD OF R.T.V. SEALER ON FRONT COVER AS SHOWN

V6 diesel engine front cover installation—apply R.T.V. sealer on the front cover oil pan seal retainer as shown

the diesel engine it will be necessary to retime the engine. Refer to the paragraph on "Diesel Engine Injection Timing" in the Fuel System section.

V6 Diesel Engines

1. Remove the front cover. See above for procedure. Remove the valve covers.

2. Loosen all rocker arm pivot bolts evenly so that lash exists between the rocker arms and valves. It is not necessary to completely remove the rocker arms unless related service is being performed.

3. Remove the crankshaft oil slinger and the camshaft sprocket bolt and washer.

4. Remove the timing chain, camshaft and crankshaft sprockets. If the crankshaft sprocket is a tight fit on the crankshaft use an appropriate puller to remove it.

5. If the camshaft sprocket-to-cam key comes out with the camshaft sprocket, remove the front camshaft bearing retainer and install the key into the injection pump drive gear. Install the bearing retainer.

6. Install the key in the crankshaft, if removed.

7. Install the camshaft sprocket, crankshaft sprocket and the timing chain together, align the timing marks on the camshaft and the crankshaft. Tighten the camshaft sprocket bolt to 70 ft. lbs.

8. Install the oil slinger and the remaining parts of the front cover assembly.

9. After installing the front cover, bleed down the valve lifters as instructed in "Diesel Engine Rocker Arm Replacement", above.

10. Remaining installation is in the reverse order of removal. Sealant is used in place of valve cover gaskets.

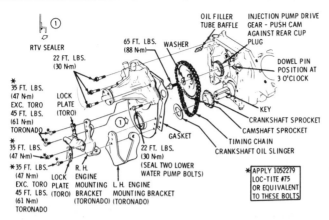

V8 diesel engine front cover and timing chain assembly

Camshaft

REMOVAL & INSTALLATION

Gasoline Engines

1. Refer to the "Timing Chain Removal & Installation" procedures in this section and remove the camshaft sprocket and the timing chain.

NOTE: If the camshaft sprocket is tight on the camshaft, use a plastic hammer to bump it loose.

2. On the V8, remove the oil cooler lines and the hoses from the radiator, then the radiator.

3. Remove the intake manifold and the rocker arm covers.

4. On the V8, remove the AIR pump bracket and disconnect the fuel lines at the fuel pump, then remove the fuel pump.

5. If equipped with A/C on the V8, remove the compressor and the condenser, then move them aside.

6. Remove the rocker arm assemblies, the push rods and the valve lifters.

7. Install two $^5/_{16}$ x 18 x 4 in. bolts in the camshaft and carefully pull the it from the front of the engine.

NOTE: When removing or replacing the camshaft, be careful not to damage the camshaft bearings.

8. To install, reverse the removal procedures. Torque the camshaft mounting bolts to 13–23 ft. lbs. Check and/or adjust the engine timing. Refill the cooling system.

Diesel Engines

NOTE: If the camshaft is to be removed the air conditioning system must be discharged by a professional and the condenser removed. Removal of the camshaft also requires removal of the injec- tion pump drive and driven gears, removal of the intake manifold, disassembly of the valve lifters, and re-timing of the injection pump.

1. Disconnect the negative battery cables. Drain the coolant. Remove the radiator.

2. Remove the intake manifold and gasket and the front and rear intake manifold seals. Refer to the intake manifold removal and installation procedure. Remove the oil pump drive assembly on the V6.

3. Remove the balancer pulley and the balancer. See "Caution" under V8 diesel engine front cover removal and installation, above, for V8 engine. Remove the engine front cover using the appropriate procedure. Rotate the engine so that the timing marks align on V6s.

4. Remove the valve covers. Remove the rocker arms, pushrods and valve lifters; see the procedure earlier in this section. Be sure to keep the parts in order so that they may be returned to their original locations.

5. On V8s, if equipped with air conditioning, the condenser must be discharged and removed from the car.

─────── **CAUTION** ───────

Compressed refrigerant expands (boils) into the atmosphere at a temperature of -26°F. It will freeze any surface it contacts, including your skin or eyes.

6. Remove the camshaft sprocket retaining bolt, and remove the timing chain and sprockets, using the procedure outlined earlier.

7. On V6s, remove the front camshaft bearing retainer bolt and the retainer, then remove the camshaft sprocket key and the injection pump drive gear.

8. Position the camshaft dowel pin at the 3 o'clock position on the V8.

9. On V8s, push the camshaft rearward and hold it there, being careful not to dislodge the oil plug at the rear of the engine. Remove the fuel injection pump drive gear by sliding it from the camshaft while rocking the pump driven gear.

10. To remove the fuel injection pump driven gear, remove the injection pump intermediate pump adapter (V6s) and the pump adapter (All), remove the snap ring, and remove the selective washer. Remove the driven gear and spring.

11. Remove the camshaft by sliding it out the front of the engine. Be extremely careful not to allow the cam lobes to contact any of the bearings, or the journals to dislodge the bearings during camshaft removal. Do not force the camshaft, or bearing damage will result.

12. If either the injection pump drive or driven gears are to be replaced, replace both gears. Make certain the marks are in alignment on both gears before inserting the cam gear key on the V6.

13. Coat the camshaft and the cam bearings with GM lubricant No.1052365 or the equivalent.

14. Carefully slide the camshaft into position in the engine.

15. Fit the crankshaft and camshaft sprockets, aligning the timing marks as shown in the timing chain removal and installation procedure, above. Remove the sprockets without disturbing the timing.

16. Install the injection pump driven gear, spring, shim, and snap ring. Check the gear end play. If the end play is not within 0.002–0.015 in. on V8s, or 0.002–0.006 on V6s, replace the shim to obtain the specified clearance. Shims are available in 0.003 in. increments, from 0.080–0.115 in.

17. On V8s, bring the camshaft dowel pin to the 3 o'clock position. Align the zero marks on the pump drive gear and pump driven gear. Hold the camshaft in the rearward position and slide the pump drive gear onto the camshaft. On the V6, align the zero marks on the injection pump drive and driven gears, then install the camshaft sprocket key. Install the camshaft bearing retainer.

18. Install the timing chain and sprockets, making sure the timing marks are aligned.

19. Install the lifters, pushrods and rocker arms. See "Rocker Arm Replacement, Diesel Engine" for lifter bleed down procedures. Failure to bleed down the lifters could bend valves when the engine is turned over.

20. Install the injection pump adapter and injection pump. See the appropriate procedures in the Fuel System section.

21. Install the remaining components in the reverse order of removal.

Piston and Connecting Rod Positioning

The pistons have a machined hole, the letter "F" or a notch on the top of the piston, which should face the front of the engine when installed.

NOTE: Before removing the pistons from the cylinders, use a silver pencil or quick drying paint to mark their positions. The piston pins are offset toward the thrust side (right hand side).

On the inline 6 cyl. engine, make sure that the bearing tang slots of the connecting rods are positioned on the opposite side of the camshaft, with the numbers of the connecting rod and the bearing cap on the same side.

On the V6 and V8 engines, the connecting rods on have bosses on one side of the rod and chamfered corners on the connecting rod cap. The bosses must face rearward on the left bank

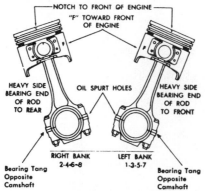

Piston-to-rod relationship—small block V8 and all V6

Piston-to-rod relationship for Chevrolet V8 engines

and to the forward on the right bank. The chamfered corners of the rod caps must face forward on the left bank and

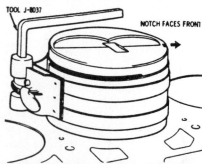

Piston installation of V6 and V8 diesel engines

rearward on the right bank. Some V6 engines have oil squirt holes on the connecting rods; these holes must face the camshaft.

NOTE: If replacing a piston or connecting rod, be sure to mark the position of the new part and replace the connecting rod bearing with a new one.

CELEBRITY AND CITATION

Engine

REMOVAL & INSTALLATION

4-151 with Manual Transaxle

NOTE: Before attempting this procedure, relieve the pressure in the fuel system as described under "Fuel Pump" in the Fuel System section.

1. Disconnect battery cables at battery.
2. Raise the car and support it safely.
3. Remove front mount-to-cradle nuts.
4. Remove forward exhaust pipe.
5. Remove starter assembly (wires attached and swing to side).
6. Remove flywheel inspection cover.
7. Lower the car.
8. Remove air cleaner.
9. Remove all bellhousing bolts.
10. Remove forward torque reaction rod from engine and core support.
11. If equipped with A/C, remove A/C belt and compressor and swing to side.
12. Remove emission hoses at canister.
13. Remove power steering hose (if so equipped).
14. Remove vacuum hoses and electrical connectors at solenoid.
15. Remove heater blower motor.
16. Disconnect throttle cable.

17. Drain cooling system.
18. Disconnect heater hose.
20. Disconnect engine harness at bulkhead connector.
21. With engine lifting tool, hoist engine (remove heater hose at intake manifold and disconnect fuel line).
22. Installation is the reverse of removal.

4-151 with Automatic Transaxle

NOTE: Relieve the pressure in the fuel system as described under "Fuel Pump" in the Fuel System section.

1. Disconnect battery cables at battery.
2. Drain cooling system.
3. Remove air cleaner and preheat tube.
4. Disconnect engine harness connector.
5. Disconnect all external vacuum hose connections.
6. Remove throttle and transaxle linkage at EFI assembly and intake manifold.
7. Remove upper radiator hose.
8. If equipped with air conditioning, remove A/C compressor from mounting brackets and set aside. Do not disconnect hoses.
9. Remove front engine strut assembly.
10. Disconnect heater hose at intake manifold.

11. Remove transaxle to engine bolts leaving the upper two bolts in place.
12. Remove front mount-to-cradle nuts.
13. Remove forward exhaust pipe.
14. Remove flywheel inspection cover and remove starter motor.
15. Remove torque converter to flywheel bolts.
16. Remove power steering pump and bracket and move to one side.
17. Remove heater hose and lower radiator hose.
18. Remove two rear transaxle support bracket bolts.
19. Remove fuel supply line at fuel filter.
20. Using a floor jack and a block of wood placed under the transaxle, raise engine and transaxle until engine front mount studs clear cradle.
21. Connect engine lift equipment and put tension on engine.
22. Remove two remaining transaxle bolts.
23. Slide engine forward and left from car. Install engine on stand.
24. Installation is the reverse of removal. Do not completely lower the engine with a jack supporting the transaxle.

6-173 with Manual Transaxle

1. Disconnect cables from battery.
2. Remove air cleaner.
3. Drain cooling system.
4. Disconnect vacuum hosing to all nonengine mounted components.

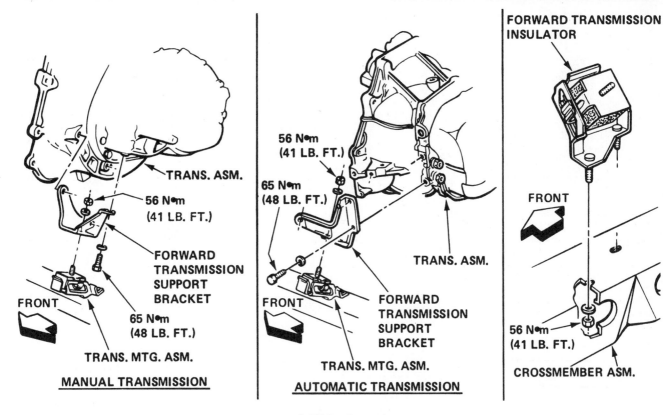

MANUAL TRANSMISSION

TRANS. ASM.

56 N•m
(41 LB. FT.)

FORWARD
TRANSMISSION
SUPPORT
BRACKET

FRONT

65 N•m
(48 LB. FT.)

TRANS. MTG. ASM.

AUTOMATIC TRANSMISSION

56 N•m
(41 LB. FT.)

65 N•m
(48 LB. FT.)

TRANS. ASM.

FRONT

FORWARD
TRANSMISSION
SUPPORT
BRACKET

TRANS. MTG. ASM.

FORWARD TRANSMISSION
INSULATOR

FRONT

56 N•m
(41 LB. FT.)

CROSSMEMBER ASM.

4-151 front mounts

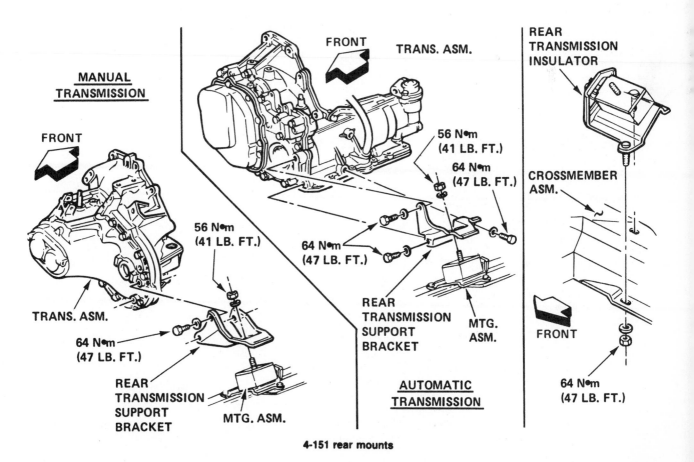

**MANUAL
TRANSMISSION**

FRONT

FRONT   TRANS. ASM.

REAR
TRANSMISSION
INSULATOR

56 N•m
(41 LB. FT.)

64 N•m
(47 LB. FT.)

56 N•m
(41 LB. FT.)

CROSSMEMBER
ASM.

64 N•m
(47 LB. FT.)

TRANS. ASM.

64 N•m
(47 LB. FT.)

REAR
TRANSMISSION
SUPPORT
BRACKET

MTG. ASM.

REAR
TRANSMISSION
SUPPORT
BRACKET

MTG.
ASM.

FRONT

**AUTOMATIC
TRANSMISSION**

64 N•m
(47 LB. FT.)

4-151 rear mounts

6. Remove the timing chain and camshaft sprocket as described earlier.

7. Installation is the reverse of removal.

6-263 Engine

NOTE: This procedure requires the removal, disassembly, cleaning, reassembly and bleed-down of all the valve lifters. Read that procedure, described earlier, before proceeding.

1. Remove the engine as described earlier.

2. Remove the intake manifold.

3. Remove the oil pump drive assembly.

4. Remove the timing chain cover.

5. Align the timing marks.

6. Remove the rocker arms, pushrods and lifters, keeping them in order for reassembly.

7. Remove the timing chain and camshaft sprocket as described earlier.

8. Remove the camshaft bearing retainer.

9. Remove the cam sprocket key.

10. Remove the injection pump drive gear.

11. Remove the injection pump driven gear, intermediate pump adapter and pump adapter. Remove the snap ring and selective washer. Remove the driven gear and spring.

12. Carefully slide the camshaft out of the block.

13. If the camshaft bearings are being replaced, you'll have to remove the oil pan.

14. Installation is the reverse of removal. Perform the complete valve lifter bleed-down procedure mentioned earlier.

Piston and Connecting Rod Positioning

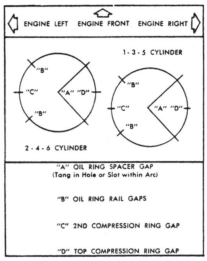

Arrange the piston rings on all V6 engines as shown

On all engines, the piston assemblies are installed with the notch facing forward

CAMARO

Engine

REMOVAL & INSTALLATION

NOTE: In the middle of the 1986 model year, General Motors introduced a limited addition (1000) Camaro IROC, equipped with the 350 5.7L engine similar to the Corvette engine. There is no information on that particular vehicle at the time of publication. If information is needed on the that particular engine, please refer to the Corvette section in this book.

Four Cylinder Engine

1. Disconnect the negative battery cable.

2. Mark the location of the hood on the hood hinges and remove the hood.

3. Drain the cooling system.

4. Remove the A/C compressor and any necessary brackets to gain working clearance.

---- CAUTION ----

DO NOT disconnect any air conditioning refrigerant lines unless you are familiar with discharge procedures. Escaping refrigerant can freeze any surface it contacts, including skin and eyes.

5. Remove the radiator hoses from the engine. Remove the fan assembly. Remove the radiator shroud and radiator.

6. If the vehicle is equipped with power steering, remove the power steering pump.

7. Tag and disconnect the electrical connector at the bulkhead connector.

8. Disconnect the fuel lines at the carburetor.

9. Remove the brake hoses from the filter and the ground strap from the rear of the cylinder head.

10. Working from inside the vehicle, remove the right-hand hush panel and the ECM harness at the main ECM connector. Remove the right-hand splash shield from the right fender and feed the ECM harness out from inside the vehicle.

11. Disconnect the heater hoses from the heater core. Remove the canister hose and the throttle cable from the electronic fuel injection if equipped.

12. Raise the vehicle and support safely. Disconnect the electrical connections from the transmission.

13. Remove the flywheel dustcover. If the vehicle is an automatic, remove the torque converter to flywheel holding bolts.

14. Remove the bolts holding the bellhousing to the engine. Remove the bellhousing to engine exhaust pipe support.

15. Remove the exhaust pipe at the manifold. Remove the catalytic converter assembly.

16. Remove the starter assembly.

17. Remove the clutch fork return spring if vehicle is equipped with a manual transmission.

18. Remove the motor mount bolts.

19. Lower the vehicle and install a suitable engine lifting device.

20. Position a floor jack under the transmission to support the transmission.

21. Lift the engine from the vehicle and place in a suitable engine holding fixture.

22. Installation is the reverse of the removal procedures.

V6 and V8 Engines

1. Disconnect the negative battery cable.

2. Mark the location of the hood and remove the hood from the vehicle.

3. Drain the cooling system. Remove the lower raditor hose and the upper fan shroud. Remove the fan assembly.

4. Remove the upper radiator hose and the coolant recovery hose. Remove the radiator.

5. Remove the transmission cooler lines.

6. Remove the heater hoses.

7. Disconnect the carburetor linkage. If the vehicle is equipped with cruise control, disconnect the detent cable.

8. Remove the vacuum brake booster line.

9. Remove the distributor cap and lay aside with the wiring to gain working clearance.

10. Disconnect all necessary wires and hoses.

11. Remove the power steering pump and lay aside.

12. Raise the vehicle support safely.

13. Remove the exhaust pipes from the manifold. Remove the dust cover from the vehicle. Remove the converter bolts.

14. Disconnect the starter wires and remove the starter assembly.

15. Remove the bellhousing bolts. Remove the motor mount through bolts.

16. Disconnect the fuel lines at the fuel pump.

17. Lower the vehicle and support the transmission using a suitable fixture.

18. Remove the air injection reaction system if equipped.

19. Attach a suitable engine lifting device and remove the engine from the vehicle.

20. Installation is the reverse of the removal procedure.

Exhaust Manifold

REMOVAL & INSTALLATION

1980-81 Models

V6 and V8 ENGINES

1. If equipped with the AIR system, remove the air injector manifold assembly.

NOTE: The ¼ in. pipe threads in the manifold are straight threads.

2. Disconnect the negative battery cable.

3. If equipped, remove the air cleaner pre-heater shroud.

4. Remove the spark plug wire heat shields.

5. At the left exhaust manifold, disconnect and remove the alternator.

6. Disconnect the exhaust pipe from the manifold and allow it to hang.

7. Bend the locktabs. Remove the end bolts, the center bolts and the exhaust manifold.

NOTE: A $9/16$ in. thin wall 6-point socket, sharpened at the leading edge and tapped onto the head of the bolt, simplifies bending the locktabs. If installing a new manifold on the right side of the 1980–81 V8, transfer the heat stove from the old manifold to the new one.

8. Clean the gasket mounting surfaces.

9. To install, use new gaskets and reverse the removal procedures. Torque the bolts to specifications from the inside working outwards.

1982-87 Models

4 CYL ENGINE

1. Disconnect the negative battery cable.

2. Remove the air cleaner assembly, mark the hoses for proper identification.

3. Remove the EFI preheat tube.

4. Remove the oxygen sensor and disconnect the exhaust pipe from the exhaust manifold.

5. Remove the engine oil level dipstick and tube.

6. Remove the exhaust manifold attaching bolts and the manifold.

7. To install, use a new gasket and reverse the removal procedures. Torque the bolts to 44 ft. lbs.

V6 ENGINE – LEFT SIDE

1. Disconnect the negative battery cable.

2. Raise and support the vehicle on jackstands.

3. Disconnect the exhaust pipe from the exhaust manifold.

4. Remove the 4 rear manifold bolts and the nut, then lower the vehicle.

5. Disconnect the air management hoses and wires.

6. If equipped, remove the power steering bracket and move aside.

7. Remove the manifold attaching bolts and the manifold.

8. To install, use a new gasket and reverse the removal procedures.

Torque the manifold bolts to 25 ft. lbs., from the inside working outwards.

V6 ENGINE – RIGHT SIDE

1. Disconnect the negative battery cable.

2. Raise and support the vehicle on jackstands.

3. Disconnect the exhaust pipe from the exhaust manifold.

4. Lower the vehicle and remove the exhaust manifold bolts.

5. Disconnect the air management hose and remove the manifold.

6. To install, reverse the removal procedures. Torque the manifold bolts, from the inside working outwards.

V8 ENGINE – LEFT SIDE

1. Disconnect the negative battery cable.

2. Mark and disconnect the spark plug wires.

3. Disconnect the air injection system hoses.

4. If equipped with A/C, unbolt the A/C compressor (DO NOT disconnect the refrigerant hoses) and move aside.

5. If equipped with power steering, remove the power steering pump (DO NOT disconnect the hydraulic lines) and move aside.

6. Remove the rear A/C and power steering adjusting brackets.

7. Raise and support the vehicle on jackstands.

8. Disconnect the exhaust pipe from the exhaust manifold, then lower the vehicle.

9. Remove the manifold attaching bolts and the manifold.

10. Clean the gasket mounting surfaces.

11. To install, use a new gasket and reverse the removal procedures. Torque the manifold bolts to 20 ft. lbs. from the inside working outwards.

V8 ENGINE – RIGHT SIDE

1. Disconnect the negative battery cable.

2. Mark and disconnect the spark plug wires.

3. Disconnect the air injection system hoses and remove the air management valve.

4. Raise and support the vehicle on jackstands.

5. Disconnect the exhaust pipe from the exhaust manifold, then lower the vehicle.

6. Remove the manifold attaching bolts and the manifold.

7. Clean the gasket mounting surfaces.

8. To install, use a new gaskets and reverse the removal procedures.

Intake Manifold

REMOVAL & INSTALLATION

NOTE: **When servicing late model vehicles, be absolutely sure to mark the vacuum hoses and wiring, so that these items may be properly reconnected during installation. Also, when disconnecting fittings or metal lines (fuel, power brake vacuum), always use two flare nut wrenches. Hold the wrench as if tightening the fitting (clockwise), THEN loosen and disconnect the smaller fitting from the larger fitting. If this is not done, damage to the line will result.**

1980-81 Models

231 V6

1. Disconnect the negative battery cable.
2. Drain the cooling system. Remove the air cleaner.
3. Remove the upper radiator and the coolant bypass hoses from the intake manifold.
4. Disconnect the throttle linkage and bracket from the carburetor-to-manifold assembly.

NOTE: **If equipped with an automatic transmission, remove the downshift linkage.**

5. Disconnect the fuel line from the carburetor. If equipped, disconnect the power brake vacuum line from the manifold.
6. Disconnect the choke pipe, the vacuum lines and the anti-dieseling solenoid wire.
7. Remove the manifold bolts.

NOTE: **It will be necessary to remove the distributor cap and the rotor, to gain access to the left front manifold bolt. The bolt is a special Torx® type.**

8. Remove the manifold and clean the gasket mounting surfaces.
9. To install, use new gaskets and

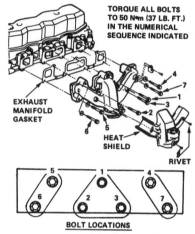

Exhaust manifold bolt tightening sequence—151 4 cylinder engine through 1984

seals, coat the seals with non-hardening silicone sealer and reverse the removal procedures. Torque the head bolts in sequence, starting in the center and working outwards. Refill the cooling system, start the engine and check for leaks.

V6 AND V8 MODELS (EXCEPT 231 V6)

1. Remove the air cleaner. Drain the cooling system.
2. Disconnect the negative battery cable.
3. Remove the upper radiator, the heater and the PCV hoses.
4. Remove the fuel line(s), the accelerator linkage and the electrical wiring connectors.
5. If equipped, remove the distributor vacuum and the power brake hoses.
6. Remove the distributor cap and the distributor.

NOTE: **Before removing the distributor, mark the rotor's position, relative to the distributor housing and the engine.**

7. If necessary, remove the alternator upper bracket, the air cleaner bracket and the accelerator bellcrank.
8. If equipped, remove the A/C compressor and bracket, set the compressor aside.
9. If equipped, remove the crusie control servo and bracket.
10. Remove the manifold-to-head attaching bolts, then remove the manifold and carburetor assembly.

NOTE: **If the mainfold is to be replaced, transfer the manifold equipment to the new manifold.**

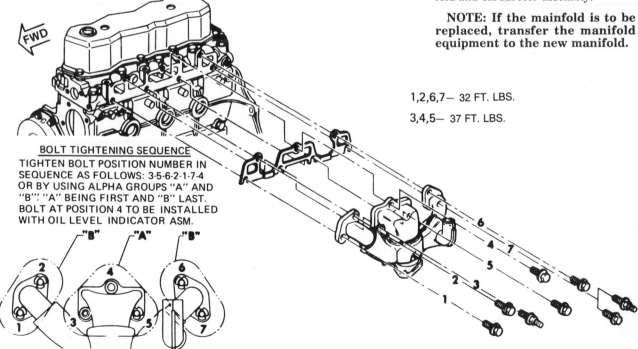

1,2,6,7 – 32 FT. LBS.

3,4,5 – 37 FT. LBS.

Exhaust manifold bolt tightening sequence—1985 and later 151 4 cylinder engine

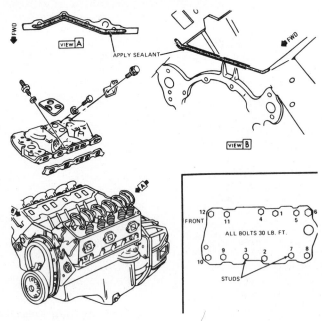

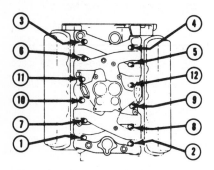

Intake manifold bolt tightening sequence for the Chevrolet-built 229 V6 engine

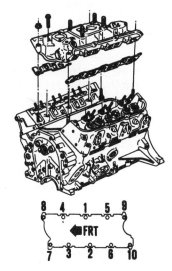

Intake manifold bolt tightening sequence for the Oldsmobile-built V8 engines

11. Clean the gasket mounting surfaces.

12. To install, use new gaskets and sealant, then reverse the removal procedures. Torque the manifold bolts to 25–45 ft. lbs. Refill the cooling system, then start the engine and check for leaks. Check the ignition timing.

1982-87 Carbureted Engines

173 V6 ENGINE

1. Disconnect the negative battery cable.

2. Remove the air cleaner assembly.

3. Drain the cooling system.

4. Mark and disconnect the wiring and hoses from the carburetor.

5. Disconnect the fuel line at the carburetor.

6. Disconnect the throttle, the transmission downshift and the cruise control (if equipped) cables from the carburetor.

7. Mark and disconnect the wiring from the ignition coil.

Intake manifold bolt tightening sequence for the 173 V6 engine

8. Remove the distributor cap and the distributor.

NOTE: Before removing the distributor, mark the rotor position relative to the distributor housing and the engine.

9. Remove the air management hose.

10. Mark and disconnect the hoses from the emission canister. Remove the pipe bracket from the left valve cover.

11. Remove the left valve cover.

12. Remove the air management bracket from the right valve cover.

13. Remove the right valve cover.

14. Remove the upper radiator hose and the heater hose from the intake manifold.

15. Disconnect the wiring from the coolant switches.

16. Remove the manifold attaching bolts and lift the manifold from the engine.

17. Clean the gasket mounting surfaces.

18. To install, use new gaskets, sealant and reverse the removal procedures. Torque the manifold bolts to 23 ft. lbs. in sequence. Refill the cooling system, start the engine and check for leaks. Check the idle speed.

NOTE: The manifold gaskets are marked for the right and left sides of the engine.

V8 ENGINES

1. Disconnect the negative battery cable.

2. Remove the air cleaner assembly.

3. Drain the cooling system.

4. Disconnect the upper radiator and the heater hoses from the intake manifold.

5. Disconnect the throttle, the transmission downshift and the cruise control (if equipped) linkages from the carburetor.

6. Disconnect the fuel line at the carburetor.

7. Disconnect the spark plug wires from the right side of the engine.

8. Mark and disconnect the wiring and hoses from the intake manifold and carburetor.

9. Remove the distributor as previously outlined.

NOTE: Before removing the distributor, mark the rotor's position, relative to the distributor housing and the engine.

10. If equipped, remove the A/C compressor from the brackets and move aside. DO NOT disconnect the refrigerant hoses.

11. If equipped, remove the A/C compressor brackets and the cruise control servo and bracket, then move aside.

12. Remove the upper alternator mounting bracket.

13. Remove the EGR solenoid and the bracket.

14. Remove the power brake booster vacuum line from the intake manifold-to-carburetor connection.

15. Remove the manifold mounting bolts and lift the manifold from the engine.

16. Clean the gasket mounting surfaces.

17. To install, use new gaskets, sealant and reverse the removal procedures. Refill the cooling system, start the engine and check for leaks. Check the engine speed.

TBI Equipped Engines

151 4 CYL

1. Disconnect the negative battery cable.
2. Remove the air cleaner assembly and the heat stove pipe.
3. Remove the PCV valve and hose.
4. Drain the cooling system.
5. Disconnect the fuel lines from the Throttle Body Injection (TBI) unit.

--------- CAUTION ---------

Before removing any component of the fuel system, relieve the fuel pressure.

6. Mark and disconnect the vacuum lines and the electrical connections from the TBI unit.
7. Disconnect the throttle and the bell crank linkages from the TBI unit, then move aside.
8. Disconnect the transaxle downshift and the cruise control (if equipped).
9. Remove the ignition coil and the alternator brace.
10. Disconnect the heater hose from the intake manifold.
11. Remove the A/C compressor support brackets and the compressor, move aside. DO NOT disconnect the refrigerant lines from the compressor.
12. Remove the manifold attaching bolts and the manifold.
13. Clean the gasket mounting surfaces.
14. To install, use new gaskets and sealant, then reverse the removal procedures. Torque the manifold bolts to 29 ft. lbs. Refill the cooling system, start the engine and check for leaks. Adjust the idle speed.

305 V8 TBI

1. Disconnect the negative battery cable.
2. Remove the air cleaner assembly. Drain the cooling system.
3. Disconnect the fuel inlet line at the front Throttle Body Injection (TBI) unit.

--------- CAUTION ---------

Before removing any component of the fuel system, relieve the fuel pressure.

4. Remove the exhaust gas recirculation (EGR) solenoid.
5. Remove the alternator adjusting bracket.
6. Disconnect the wiring from the idle air motors, the injectors and the throttle position sensor (TPS).
7. Disconnect the fuel return line at the rear TBI unit.
8. Remove the power brake booster line.
9. Disconnect the accelerator and cruise control cables, tie the cable and bracket assembly aside.

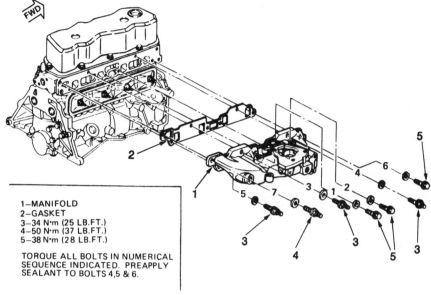

1—MANIFOLD
2—GASKET
3—34 N·m (25 LB.FT.)
4—50 N·m (37 LB.FT.)
5—38 N·m (28 LB.FT.)

TORQUE ALL BOLTS IN NUMERICAL SEQUENCE INDICATED. PREAPPLY SEALANT TO BOLTS 4,5 & 6.

Intake manifold bolt tightening sequence—1986 and later 151 4 cylinder engine

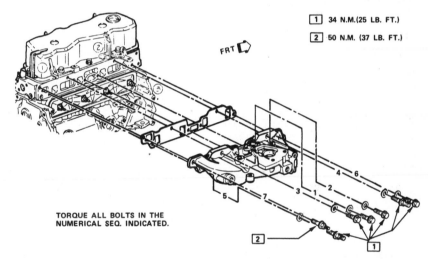

[1] 34 N.M. (25 LB. FT.)

[2] 50 N.M. (37 LB. FT.)

TORQUE ALL BOLTS IN THE NUMERICAL SEQ. INDICATED.

Intake manifold bolt tightening sequence—1982–85 151 4 cylinder engine

NOTE: If equipped with A/C, remove the A/C strut.

10. Disconnect the positive crankcase ventilation (PCV) hose at the manifold and move the hose aside.
11. Mark and disconnect any vacuum hoses which will interfere with the removal of the manifold.
12. If you plan on removing the TBI units from the upper manifold plate, remove the fuel balance tube (connecting the units).
13. Remove the TBI plate-to-intake manifold bolts, then lift the TBI and plate assembly from the intake manifold.
14. Remove the distributor cap and the distributor.

NOTE: Before removing the distributor, mark the rotor's position, relative to the distributor housing and the engine.

15. Disconnect the upper radiator hose from the thermostat housing.
16. Disconnect the heater hose from the intake manifold.
17. Remove the intake manifold-to-cylinder head bolts and lift the intake manifold assembly from the engine.
18. Clean the gasket mounting surfaces.
19. To install, use new gaskets and sealant, then reverse the removal procedures. Torque the intake manifold bolts to 25–45 ft. lbs., the TBI and plate assembly bolts to 20–34 ft. lbs. Refill the cooling system. Adjust the

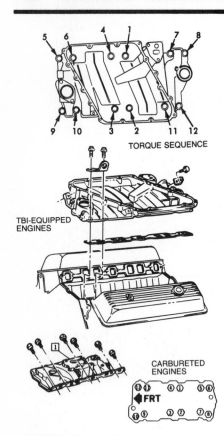

TORQUE SEQUENCE

TBI-EQUIPPED ENGINES

CARBURETED ENGINES

◀ FRT

Intake manifold bolt tightening sequence of all Chevrolet-built V8 engines. Note that the lower sequence is used for all carbureted engines, whereas the upper sequence is used for all TBI-equipped engines

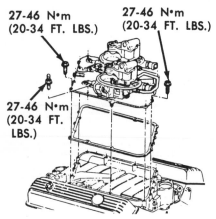

27-46 N•m (20-34 FT. LBS.)

27-46 N•m (20-34 FT. LBS.)

27-46 N•m (20-34 FT. LBS.)

TBI plate and gasket installation on V8 engines, if equipped

throttle body linkages. Check the idle speed.

173 V6 MFI

1. Disconnect the negative battery cable.
2. Remove the air cleaner and drain the cooling system.
3. Remove the air intake plenum and the fuel rail assembly.

———— **CAUTION** ————

Before removing any component of the fuel system, relieve the fuel pressure.

4. Disconnect the wires from the spark plugs and the coil.
5. Remove the distributor cap and the spark plug wires.

NOTE: Mark the rotor's position, relative to the distributor housing and the engine.

6. Remove the distributor.
7. If equipped with a manual transmission, remove the air management hose and bracket.
8. Disconnect the emission canister hoses.
9. Remove the pipe bracket from the left valve cover and the left valve cover.
10. Remove the right valve cover, the upper radiator hose and the heater hose.
11. Disconnect the coolant switches.
12. Remove the bolts and the manifold.
13. Clean the gasket mounting surfaces.
14. To install, use new gaskets and sealant, then reverse the removal procedures. Torque the manifold bolts to 13–25 ft. lbs. Refill the cooling system. Start the engine and check for leaks. Check the timing.

305 V8 PFI

1. Disconnect the negative battery cable.
2. Drain the cooling system.
3. Disconnect the accelerator T.V. and the cruise control cables.
4. Remove the air intake duct.
5. Disconnect the coolant hoses and the electrical wiring connectors from the throttle body.
6. Disconnect the vacuum and the breather hoses from the throttle body.
7. Remove the throttle body from the plenum.
8. Remove the shield from the distributor and the distributor.

NOTE: Before removing the distributor, mark the rotor's position, relative to the distributor housing and the engine.

9. Remove the power brake and the vacuum hoses from the plenum.
10. Remove the plenum, the fuel rail, the cold start injector and the runners.

———— **CAUTION** ————

Before removing any component of the fuel system, relieve the fuel pressure.

11. Disconnect the EGR solenoid.
12. Remove the bolts and the intake manifold.
13. Clean the gasket mounting surfaces.

NOTE APPLY A SMOOTH CONTINUOUS BEAD APPROX 2.0-3.0 WIDE AND 3.0-5.0 THICK ON BOTH SURFACES BEAD CONFIGURATION MUST INSURE COMPLETE SEALING OF WATER AND OIL. SURFACE MUST BE FREE OF OIL AND DIRT TO INSURE ADEQUATE SEAL.

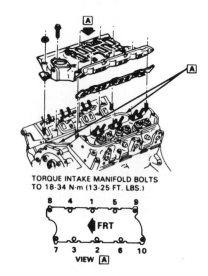

TORQUE INTAKE MANIFOLD BOLTS TO 18-34 N•m (13-25 FT. LBS.)

8 4 1 5 9
◀ FRT
7 3 2 6 10
VIEW A

View of the PFI intake manifold

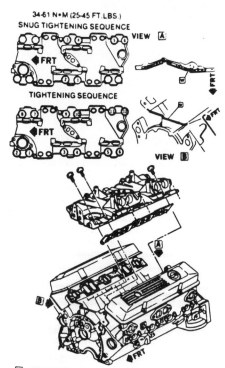

34-61 N•M (25-45 FT.LBS.)
SNUG TIGHTENING SEQUENCE

VIEW A
◀ FRT

TIGHTENING SEQUENCE
◀ FRT

VIEW B

W AT TIME OF INSTALLATION SURFACE AREA MUST BE FREE OF OIL AND SEALING COMPOUND MUST BE WET TO TOUCH WHEN BOLT/SCREWS ARE TORQUED. APPLY SEALING COMPOUND .12 THICK.

View of the MFI intake manifold

14. To install, use new gaskets and sealant, then reverse the removal procedures. Torque the manifold bolts to 25–45 ft. lbs. Refill the cooling system, then start the engine and check for leaks. Check the timing.

Rocker Arm and Pushrod

REMOVAL & INSTALLATION

4 Cyl Engine

1. Remove the air cleaner, the spark plug wires and clips.
2. Disconnect the PCV valve and the hose.
3. Remove the EGR valve.
4. Remove the cylinder head cover bolts and the cover, by tapping it with a rubber mallet.
5. Remove the rocker arm bolt, the ball washer and the rocker arm.

NOTE: If removing the push rod ONLY, loosen the rocker arm bolt, swing it aside and remove the push rod. If removing all of the push rods, mark them for reinstallation purposes.

6. Clean the gasket mounting surfaces.
7. To install, use a new head gasket and reverse the removal procedures. Torque the rocker arm bolt to 20 ft. lbs. Start the engine, check the timing and the idle speed.

V6 Engine

1. Disconnect the negative battery cable.
2. Disconnect the air management hose, the vacuum hoses, the electrical wiring, the coil and the pipe brackets.
3. If equipped with a carburetor, remove the fuel lines, the throttle controls and the bracket from the carburetor.
4. Remove the cylinder head cover nuts and the covers, by tapping on them with a rubber mallet.
5. Remove the rocker arm nuts, the ball washers, the rocker arms and the push rods.

NOTE: If removing the push rod ONLY, loosen the rocker arm nut, swing it aside and remove the push rod. If removing all of the push rods, mark them for reinstallation purposes.

6. Clean the gasket mounting surfaces.
7. To install, use new cylinder head cover gaskets and sealant, then reverse the removal procedures. Torque the rocker arms nuts to 10–15 ft. lbs. and the cylinder head cover nuts to 7–15 ft. lbs. Adjust the valves. Start the engine, check the timing and the idle speed.

V8 Engine

1. Disconnect the negative battery cable.

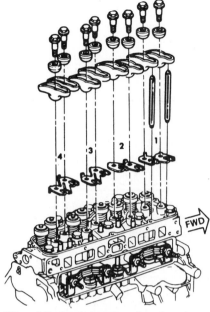

View of the rocker arm and push rod assembly—151 4 cylinder engine

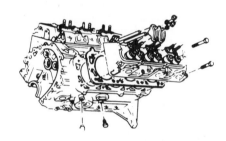

View of the rocker arm and pushrod assembly—V6 shown, V8 is similiar

2. Remove the air cleaner.
3. Disconnect the AIR, the EGR solenoid, the air management, the power brake booster hoses and/or tubes.
4. Remove the EGR solenoid.
5. Remove the PCV valve and the air management valve bracket, then move aside.
6. Move the air management bracket and the wiring harness aside.
7. Disconnect the alternator wiring.
8. Remove the cylinder head cover nuts and the covers, by tapping on them with a rubber mallet.
9. Remove the rocker arm nuts, the ball washers, the rocker arms and the push rods.

NOTE: If removing the push rod ONLY, loosen the rocker arm nut, swing it aside and remove the push rod. If removing all of the push rods, mark them for reinstallation purposes.

10. Clean the gasket mounting surfaces.
11. To install, lubricate the parts, use new cylinder head cover gaskets and sealant, then reverse the removal procedures. Torque the rocker arm nuts to 5–11 ft. lbs. and the cylinder head cover nuts to 4–6 ft. lbs. Adjust the valves. Start the engine, check the timing and the idle speed.

Valve Clearance Adjustment

4 Cyl Engine

All engines use hydraulic valve lifters, which eliminate the need for periodic valve adjustments. If the rocker arms and/or cylinder heads have been removed or replaced, the rocker arms must be adjusted for zero lash.

V6 Engine

1. Refer to the "Rocker Arm and Pushrod Removal & Installation" procedures in this section and remove the cylinder head covers.
2. Turn the crankshaft, so that the No. 1 cyl. is at TDC of the compression stroke and the timing mark of the crankshaft pulley is on "0" of the timing plate.

NOTE: With the No. 1 cyl. on TDC, adjust the intake valves of cylinders No. 1, 5 and 6 and the exhaust valves of cylinders No. 1, 2 and 3.

3. Loosen the rocker arm nut until valve lash is felt. Tighten the nut until the lash disappears, then tighten the nut down 1½ more turns.
4. Turn the crankshaft 1 revolution, so that the No. 4 cyl. is at TDC and the crankshaft pulley is on the "0" mark of the timing plate.

NOTE: With the No. 4 cyl. on TDC, adjust the intake valves of cylinders No. 2, 3 and 4 and the exhaust valves of cylinders No. 4, 5 and 6.

5. Adjust the remaining valves in a similar manner.
6. Clean the gasket mounting surfaces.
7. To install, use new cylinder head cover gaskets and sealant, then reverse the removal procedures. Torque the cylinder head cover nuts to 7–15 ft. lbs. Start the engine, check the timing and the idle speed.

V8 Engine

1. Refer to the "Rocker Arm and Pushrod Removal & Installation" procedures in this section and remove the cylinder head covers.
2. Turn the crankshaft, so that the No. 1 cyl. is at TDC of the compression stroke and the timing mark of the

crankshaft pulley is on "0" of the timing plate.

NOTE: With the No. 1 cyl. on TDC, adjust the intake valves of cylinders No. 1, 2, 5 and 7 and the exhaust valves of cylinders No. 1, 3, 4 and 8.

3. Loosen the rocker arm nut until valve lash is felt. Tighten the nut until the lash disappears, then turn the nut down 1 full rotation.

4. Turn the crankshaft 1 revolution, so that the No. 6 cyl. is at TDC and the crankshaft pulley is on the "0" mark of the timing plate.

NOTE: With the No. 6 cyl. on TDC, adjust the intake valves of cylinders No. 3, 4, 6 and 8 and the exhaust valves of cylinders No. 2, 5, 6 and 7.

5. Adjust the remaining valves in the similar manner.

6. Clean the gasket mounting surfaces.

7. To install, use new cylinder head cover gaskets and sealant, then reverse the removal procedures. Torque the cylinder head cover nuts to 4–6 ft. lbs. Start the engine, check the timing and the idle speed.

Cylinder Head

REMOVAL & INSTALLATION

NOTE: When servicing late model vehicles, be absolutely sure to mark vacuum hoses and wiring so that these items may be properly reconnected during installation. Also, when disconnecting fittings of metal lines (fuel, power brake vacuum), always use two flare nut (or line) wrenches. Hold the wrench on the large fitting with pressure on the wrench as if you were tightening the fitting (clockwise), THEN loosen and disconnect the smaller fitting from the larger fitting. If this is not done, damage to the line will result.

1. Refer to the "Intake Manifold Removal & Installation" procedures in this section and remove the intake manifold.

2. Remove the alternator and lay the unit aside. If necessary, remove the alternator brackets.

3. Disconnect the exhaust pipe(s) and remove the exhaust manifold(s). If equipped with A/C, dismount the A/C compressor and position it aside.

NOTE: On the 4 cyl. engine, remove the power steering pump, if it is top mounted. On the V6 engine, it may be necessary to re-

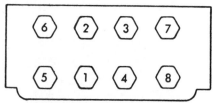

173 V6 cylinder head torque sequence

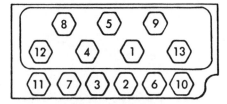

Chevrolet-built 229-V6 cylinder head bolt torque sequence

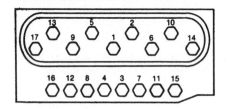

Chevrolet-built V8 engine cylinder head bolt torque sequence

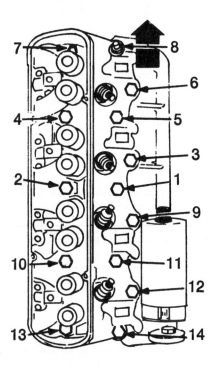

Pontiac-built V8 engine cylinder head bolt torque sequence

move the dipstick tube. On the V8 engine, remove the diverter valve, if equipped.

4. Remove the cylinder head cover(s).

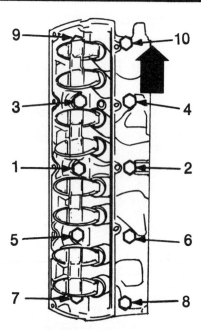

Oldsmobile-built V8 engine cylinder head bolt torque sequence

5. Back off the rocker arm nuts and pivot the rocker arms so that the pushrods can be removed. Identify the pushrods so that they can be reinstalled in their original locations.

6. Remove the cylinder head bolts and the cylinder head(s).

7. Clean the gasket mounting surfaces.

8. To install, use new gaskets and reverse the removal procedures. The head gasket is installed with the bead up. Torque the head bolts to 60–75 ft. lbs. (V8), 65–90 ft. lbs. (V6), and 92 ft. lbs. (4 cyl.) a little at a time, in sequence, starting in the center and working towards both ends. Adjust the valves. Refill the cooling system, start the engine and check for leaks. Check the idle speed.

NOTE: On engines using a steel gasket, thinly and evenly, coat both sides with sealer. If a steel asbestos gasket is used, DO NOT apply sealer. Clean the bolt threads, apply sealing compound and install the bolts finger tight.

Timing Cover and Oil Seal

REMOVAL & INSTALLATION

4 Cyl Engine

1. Remove the drive belts from the crankshaft pulley.

2. Remove the damper pulley bolt and the pulley from the crankshaft.

3. Remove the oil pan-to-timing

cover and the timing cover-to-engine bolts.

4. Remove the timing cover.

5. Clean the gasket mounting surfaces.

6. Using a small pry bar, pry the oil seal from the timing cover.

NOTE: The oil seal may be removed from the timing cover without removing the cover. To do this, remove the damper pulley and pry the oil seal from the timing cover, using a small pry bar.

7. To install, use a new oil seal, a new cover gasket and sealant, then reverse the removal procedures. Torque the timing cover bolts to 7 ft. lbs. and the damper pulley bolt to 160 ft. lbs.

NOTE: Place a Seal Installation Tool J-34995 on the crankshaft (to prevent damaging the seal) when installing the new oil seal or the front cover. To install the new oil seal, place the seal's open end toward the inside of the cover and drive it into the cover.

V6 and V8 Engines

1. Refer to the "Water Pump Removal & Installation" procedures under Engine Cooling in this section and remove the water pump.

2. If equipped with A/C, remove the compressor and the mounting bracket, then move the compressor aside.

3. Remove the crankshaft center bolt. Using the wheel puller tool J-23523, pull the damper pulley from the crankshaft.

NOTE: On the V6 engine, disconnect the lower radiator hose from the timing cover and the heater hose from the water pump.

4. Remove the timing cover bolts and the cover.

5. Using a small pry bar, pry the oil seal from the timing cover.

NOTE: The oil seal may be removed from the timing cover without removing the cover. To do this, remove the damper pulley and pry the oil seal from the timing cover, using a small pry bar.

6. Clean the gasket mounting surfaces.

7. To install, use a new oil seal, a new timing cover gasket and sealant, then reverse the removal procedures. Torque the timing cover bolts to 20 (V6) or 6–8 (V8) ft. lbs., the water pump bolts to 22 (V6) or 25–35 (V8) ft. lbs. and the damper pulley bolt to 67–85 ft. lbs.

NOTE: To install the new oil seal, place the seal's open end to-

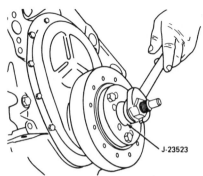

Removing and installing the damper pulley—V8, V6 is similiar

Removing the camshaft thrust plate screws—151 4 cylinder engine

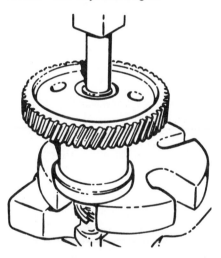

Removing the timing gear from the camshaft—151 4 cylinder engine

ward the inside of the cover and drive it into the cover using tool J-23042. To install the damper pulley, lubricate with engine oil and use tool J-29113 (V6) or J-23523 (V8) to press it onto the crankshaft.

Timing Gear

REMOVAL & INSTALLATION

4 Cyl Engine

NOTE: The timing gear is pressed onto the camshaft. To re-

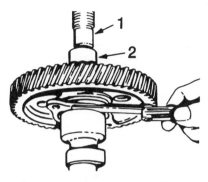

1—ARBOR PRESS
2—J-21474-13 OR J-21795-1

Checking the thrust plate end clearance —151 4 cylinder engine

move or install the timing gear an arbor must be used.

1. Refer to the "Camshaft Removal & Installation" procedures in this section and remove the camshaft from the engine.

2. Using an arbor press, a press plate and a gear removal tool J-971, press the timing gear from the camshaft.

NOTE: When pressing the timing gear from the camshaft, be certain that the position of the press plate does not contact the woodruff key.

3. To assemble, position the press plate to support the camshaft at the back of the front journal. Place the gear spacer ring and the thrust plate over the end of the camshaft, then install the woodruff key. Press the timing gear onto the camshaft, until it bottoms against the gear spacer ring.

NOTE: The end clearance of the thrust plate should be 0.0015– 0.005 in. If less than 0.0015 in., replace the spacer ring; if more than 0.005 in., replace the thrust plate.

4. To complete the installation, align the marks on the timing gears and reverse the removal procedures.

Timing Chain and Sprocket

REMOVAL & INSTALLATION

V6 and V8 Engines

1. Refer to the "Timing Cover Removal & Installation" procedures in this section and remove the timing cover.

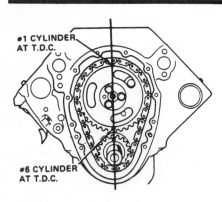

Installing the timing chain and sprocket —V8 engine

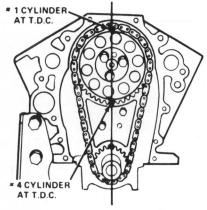

Installing the timing chain and sprocket —V6 engine

2. Turn the crankshaft to place the No. 1 cylinder on TDC and so that the camshaft sprocket the No. 4 cyl (V6) or the No. 6 cyl (V8) TDC mark aligns with the crankshaft sprocket mark.

3. Remove the camshaft sprocket bolts, the sprocket and the timing chain.

NOTE: If the camshaft sprocket does not come off easily, lightly strike the edge of it with a plastic hammer.

4. To install, lubricate the timing chain, align the timing sprocket marks, the camshaft dowel pin with the sprocket and insert the bolts. Torque the camshaft sprocket bolts to 15–20 ft. lbs.

5. To complete the installation, reverse the removal procedures.

Camshaft

REMOVAL & INSTALLATION

4 Cyl Engine

1. Disconnect the negative battery cable.

2. Drain the cooling system and the crankcase.

3. Remove the upper and lower radiator hoses. Remove the radiator.

NOTE: If equipped with A/C, remove the compressor and move aside.

4. Remove the fan and the water pump pulley.

5. Remove the cylinder head cover. Loosen the valve rocker bolts and pivot the rockers out of the way.

6. Remove the spark plugs. Turn the crankshaft to place the No. 4 cyl on TDC.

NOTE: To determine TDC, place a finger over No. 4 cyl spark plug hole. Turn the crankshaft until the pressure blows your finger from the hole; also check the position of the distributor rotor.

7. Remove the oil pump drive shaft and gear assembly.

8. Mark the position of the distributor rotor-to-housing and the distributor housing-to-engine. Remove the distributor.

9. Remove the push rod cover, the push rods and the valve lifters.

NOTE: When removing the push rods and the valve lifters, keep them in order for reinstallation purposes.

10. Remove the damper pulley and the timing gear cover.

11. Working through the holes in the camshaft gear, remove the 2 thrust plate bolts.

12. Pull the camshaft and gear assembly out through the front of the engine, be careful not to damage the camshaft lobes or the bearing surfaces.

13. Clean the gasket mounting surfaces.

14. To install, align the timing marks of the timing gears and reverse the re-

moval procedures. Use new gaskets and sealant where necessary. Torque the camshaft thrust plate bolts to 7 ft. lbs., the timing cover bolts to 8 ft. lbs., the rocker arm bolts to 20 ft. lbs. and the damper pulley bolt to 160 ft. lbs. Adjust the valve clearances. Replace the cooling fluid and the engine oil. Check and/or adjust the timing.

V6 and V8 Engines

1. Refer to the "Intake Manifold Removal & Installation" and the "Timing Chain and Sprockets Removal & Installation" procedures in this section, then remove the intake manifold and the timing cover.

2. Remove the grille and the radiator. Remove the valve covers.

3. Remove the rocker arm nuts, the ball washers, the rocker arms, the push rods and the lifters.

NOTE: When removing the rocker arms, the push rods and the lifters, store them in order for installation purposes.

4. Remove the fuel pump and the push rod.

5. Install two bolts into the camshaft bolt holes and carefully pull the camshaft from the engine block, be careful not to damage the camshaft lobes or the bearings.

6. Clean the gasket mounting surfaces.

7. To install, use new gaskets and sealant, then reverse the removal procedures. Refill the cooling system. Adjust the valves and check the timing.

Piston and Connecting Rod Positioning

The pistons have a machined hole or a cast notch in the top of the piston, which should face the front of the en-

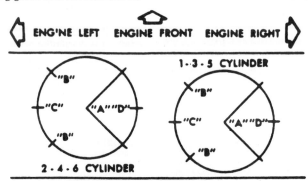

"A" OIL RING SPACER GAP
(Tang in Hole or Slot within Arc)

"B" OIL RING RAIL GAPS

"C" 2ND COMPRESSION RING GAP

"D" TOP COMPRESSION RING GAP

Ring gap location for a V6 engine—V8 is similiar

gine when installed. Before removing the pistons from the cylinders, use a silver pencil or quick drying paint to mark their positions. The piston pins are offset toward the thrust side (right hand side).

NOTE: On the 4 cylinder engine, make sure that the raised notch side of the connecting rod (at the bearing end) is installed opposite the notch on the piston head.

Make sure that the bearing tang

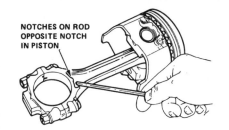

Connecting rod identification—4 cylinder engine

slots of the connecting rods are positioned on the opposite side of the camshaft, with the numbers of the connecting rod and the bearing cap on the same side. When installing the piston rings make sure that the marked side of the ring faces upwards. Position the rings according to the illustration.

NOTE: If replacing a piston or connecting rod, be sure to mark the position of the new part and replace the connecting rod bearing with a new one.

CAVALIER

NOTE: J-Cars use three different four cylinder engines. Two are built by Chevrolet, a 1.8L (112 cu.in.) and a 2.0L (122 cu. in.). Both of these Chevrolet-built engines are of the overhead valve configuration (OHV). That means that the camshaft is in the block and the rest of the valve train is on top of the head. The other engine is a Pontiac-built 1.8L (112 cu. in.) overhead cam engine (OHC). This means that the camshaft and valve components are all located in the engine head. The two Chevrolet-built engines are virtually identical in all aspects except cubic inch displacement. The Pontiac-built engine is quite different in most respects. Beginning in 1985, a Chevrolet-built 2.8L (173 cu. in.) V6 is available as an option. The V6 is equipped with multiport fuel injection.

Engine

REMOVAL & INSTALLATION

OHV 4 Cyl Engines

NOTE: This procedure will require the use of a special powertrain alignment tool No. M6XIX65.

1. Disconnect the battery cables at the battery, negative cable first.
2. Remove the air cleaner. Drain the cooling system.
3. Remove the power steering pump (if so equipped) and position it out of the way. Leave the lines connected. Remove the windshield washer bottle.
4. If the car is equipped with A/C, remove the relay bracket at the bulkhead connector. Remove the bulk-

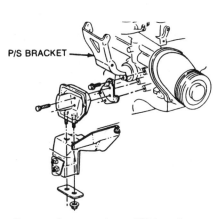

Rear engine mounts on OHV engines

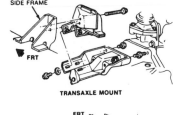

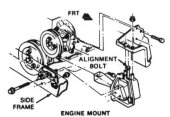

Front engine mounts on OHV engines

connector and then separate the wiring harness connections.
5. If equipped with cruise control, remove the servo bracket and position it out of the way.
6. Tag and disconnect all vacuum hoses and wires.
7. Remove the master cylinder at the vacuum booster.
8. Remove all heater and radiator

hoses and position them out of the way.
9. Remove the fan assembly. Remove the horn.
10. Disconnect the carburetor linkage. Raise the front of the car and support it with jackstands.
11. Disconnect the fuel line at the intake manifold.
12. Remove the air conditioning brace (if so equipped).
13. Remove the exhaust shield. Remove the starter.
14. Disconnect the exhaust pipe at the manifold. Remove the wheels.
15. Disconnect the stabilizer bar from the lower control arms. Remove the ball joints from the steering knuckle.
16. Remove the drive axles at the transaxle and then remove the transaxle strut.
17. If equipped with A/C, remove the inner fender shield. Remove the drive belt, tag and disconnect the wires and then remove the compressor. Do not disconnect any of the refrigerant lines.
18. Remove the rear engine mount nuts and plate.
19. If equipped with an automatic transaxle, remove the oil filter.
20. Disconnect the speedometer cable and lower the vehicle.
21. If equipped with an automatic transaxle, remove the oil cooler at the transaxle.
22. Remove the front engine mount nuts.
23. Disconnect the clutch cable on the manual transaxle. Disconnect the detent cable on the automatic transaxle.
24. Install an engine lifting device, remove the transaxle mount and bracket. Lift the engine out of the car.
25. Install the engine mount alignment bolt (M6XIX65) to ensure proper power train alignment.

1. Distributor Assembly
2. Oil Filter
3. Vacuum Pump
4. Dipstick
5. Cam Sprocket
6. Thrust Plate
7. Camshaft and Bearings
8. Cylinder Block

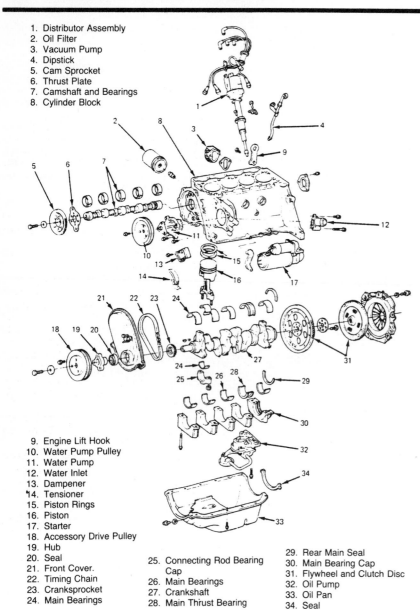

9. Engine Lift Hook
10. Water Pump Pulley
11. Water Pump
12. Water Inlet
13. Dampener
14. Tensioner
15. Piston Rings
16. Piston
17. Starter
18. Accessory Drive Pulley
19. Hub
20. Seal
21. Front Cover.
22. Timing Chain
23. Cranksprocket
24. Main Bearings

25. Connecting Rod Bearing Cap
26. Main Bearings
27. Crankshaft
28. Main Thrust Bearing

29. Rear Main Seal
30. Main Bearing Cap
31. Flywheel and Clutch Disc
32. Oil Pump
33. Oil Pan
34. Seal

Exploded view of the cylinder block—2.0L

26. Lower the engine into the car, leaving the lifting device attached.
27. Install the transaxle bracket. Install the mount to the side frame and secure with NEW mount bolts.
28. With the weight not yet on the mounts, tighten the transaxle bolts. Tighten the right front mount nuts.
29. Lower the engine fully onto the mounts, remove the lifting device and then raise the front of the car.
30. Installation of the remaining components is in the reverse order of removal. Check the powertrain alignment bolt; if excessive force is required to remove the bolt, loosen the transaxle adjusting bolts and realign the powertrain. Adjust the drive belts and the clutch cable (if equipped with manual transaxle).

2.8L V6 Engine

1. Disconnect the negative battery cable. Drain the cooling system and remove the air cleaner assembly.
2. Remove the air flow sensor. Remove the exhaust crossover heat shield, then remove the crossover pipe.
3. Remove the serpentine belt tensioner and the serpentine belt.
4. Remove the power steering pump mounting bracket. Disconnect the heater pipe at the power steering pump mounting bracket.
5. Disconnect the radiator hoses from the engine.
6. Disconnect the accelerator and throttle valve cable at the throttle valve.
7. Remove the alternator. Tag and

disconnect the wiring harness at the engine.
8. Disconnect the fuel hose. Disconnect the coolant bypass and the overflow hoses at the engine.
9. Tag and remove the vacuum hoses to the engine.
10. Raise the vehicle and support it safely.
11. Remove the inner fender splash shield, then remove the harmonic balancer.
12. Remove the flywheel cover. Remove the starter bolts, then tag and disconnect the electrical connections to the starter. Remove the starter.
13. Disconnect the wires at the oil sending unit.
14. Remove the A/C compressor and related brackets.
15. Disconnect the exhaust pipe at the rear of the exhaust manifold.
16. Remove the flex plate-to-torque converter bolts.
17. Remove the transaxle-to-engine bolts. Remove the engine-to-rear mount frame nuts.
18. Disconnect the shift cable bracket at the transaxle. Remove the lower bell housing bolts.
19. Lower the vehicle and disconnect the heater hoses at the engine.
20. Install a suitable engine lifting device and, while supporting the engine and transaxle, remove the upper bell housing bolts.
21. Remove the front mounting bolts.
22. Remove the master cylinder.
23. Remove the engine.
24. Installation is the reverse of removal.

OHC Engines

NOTE: This procedure requires the use of a special tool.

1. Remove battery cables.
2. Drain cooling system.
3. Remove air cleaner.
4. Disconnect engine electrical harness at bulkhead.
5. Disconnect electrical connector at brake cylinder.
6. Remove throttle cable from bracket and EFI assembly.
7. Remove vacuum hoses from EFI assembly.
8. Remove power steering high pressure hose at cut-off switch.
9. Remove vacuum hoses at map sensor and canister.
10. Disconnect air conditioning relay cluster switches.
11. Remove power steering return hose at pump.
12. Disconnect ECM wire connections, feed harness through bulkhead and lay harness over engine.
13. Remove upper and lower radiator hoses from engine.

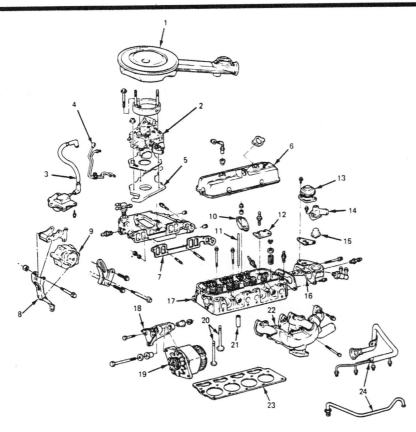

1. Air Cleaner
2. TBI Unit
3. Coil And Coil Wire
4. Fuel Line
5. E.F.E. Grid
6. Rocker Arm Cover
7. Intake Manifold And Gasket
8. A.I.R. Mounting Bracket
9. A.I.R. Pump
10. Rocker Arm
11. Push Rod
12. Push Rod Guide
13. E.G.R. Valve
14. Thermostat Outlet
15. Thermostat
16. Adapter
17. Cylinder Head
18. Generator Bracket
19. Generator
20. Valves ⇐
21. Lifter
22. Exhaust Manifold
23. Cylinder Head Gasket
24. Air or Pulsair Pipe

Exploded view of the cylinder head—2.0L

14. Remove electrical connections from temperature switch at thermostat housing.

15. Disconnect transmission shift cable at transmission.

16. Raise the car.

17. Remove speedometer cable at transmission and bracket.

18. Disconnect exhaust pipe at exhaust manifold.

19. Remove exhaust pipe from converter.

20. Remove heater hoses from heater core.

21. Remove fuel lines at flex hoses.

22. Remove transmission cooler lines at flex hoses.

23. Remove left and right front wheels.

24. Remove right hand spoiler section and splash shield.

25. Remove right and left brake calipers and support with wire.

26. Remove right and left tie rod ends.

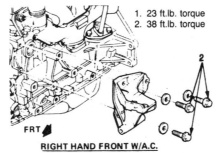

1. 23 ft.lb. torque
2. 38 ft.lb. torque

FRT

RIGHT HAND FRONT W/A.C.

Front right engine mount on OHC engines with air conditioning

27. Disconnect electrical connections at A/C compressor.

28. Remove A/C compressor and mounting brackets, support A/C compressor with wire in wheel opening.

29. Remove front suspension support attachment bolts (6 bolts each side).

30. Lower the car.

31. Support front of vehicle by plac-

ing two short jack stands under core support.

32. Position front post hoist to the rear of cowl.

33. Position a 4 x 4 x 6 timber on front post hoist.

34. Raise vehicle enough to remove jack stands.

35. Position a 4-wheel dolly under engine and transaxle assembly.

36. Position three (3) 4 x 4 x 12 blocks under engine and transaxle assembly only, letting support rails hang free.

37. Lower vehicle onto 4-wheel dolly slightly.

38. Remove rear transaxle mount attachment bolts (2).

39. Remove left front engine mount attachment bolts (3).

40. Remove two (2) engine support to body attachment bolts behind right hand inner axle U-joint.

41. Remove one (1) attaching bolt and nut from right hand chassis side rail to engine mount bracket.

42. Remove six (6) strut attachment nuts.

43. Raise vehicle letting engine, transaxle and suspension resting on 4-wheel dolly.

Reverse removal procedure for engine installation with the following exceptions:

1. With one man's assistance, position engine and transaxle assembly in chassis.

2. Install transaxle and left front mounts to side rail bolts loosely.

3. Install M6 x I x 65 alignment bolt in left front mount to prevent powertrain misalignment.

4. Torque transaxle mount bolts to 42 ft. lbs. and left front mount bolts to 18 ft. lbs.

5. Install right rear mount to body bolts and torque to 38 ft. lbs.

6. Install right rear mount to chassis side rail bolt and nut torque to 38 ft. lbs.

7. Place a floor jack under control arms, jack struts into position and install retaining nuts.

8. Raise vehicle.

9. Using a transmission jack or suitable lifting equipment, raise control arms and attach tie rod ends.

Intake Manifold

REMOVAL & INSTALLATION

OHV 4 Cyl Engines

1. Disconnect the negative battery cable.

2. Remove the air cleaner. Drain the cooling system.

3. Tag and disconnect all necessary vacuum lines and wires. Remove the idler pulley.

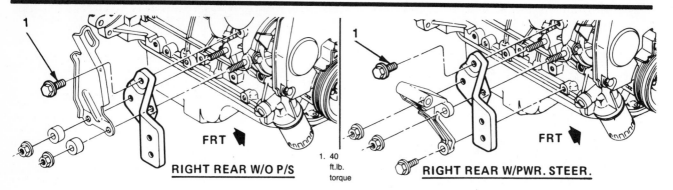

Rear engine mounts on OHC engines

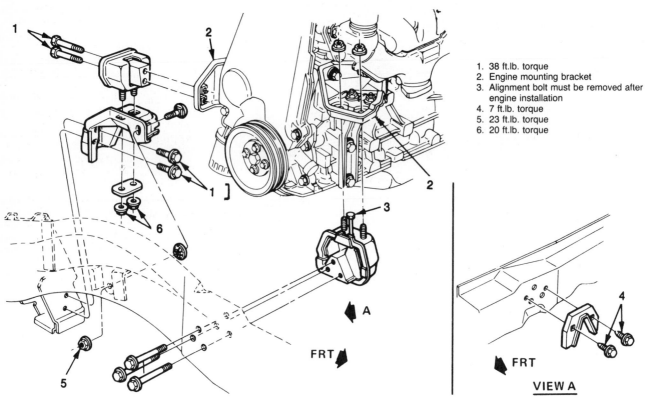

1. 40 ft.lb. torque

RIGHT REAR W/O P/S

RIGHT REAR W/PWR. STEER.

FRT

1. 38 ft.lb. torque
2. Engine mounting bracket
3. Alignment bolt must be removed after engine installation
4. 7 ft.lb. torque
5. 23 ft.lb. torque
6. 20 ft.lb. torque

FRT

VIEW A

Front engine mounts on OHC engines. The right mount is for cars without air conditioning

4. Remove the A.I.R. drive belt. If equipped with power steering, remove the drive belt and then remove the pump with the lines attached. Position the pump out of the way.

5. Remove the A.I.R. bracket-to-intake manifold bolt. Remove the air pump pulley.

6. If equipped with power steering, remove the A.I.R. thru-bolt and then the power steering adjusting bracket.

7. Loosen the lower bolt on the air pump mounting bracket so that the bracket will rotate.

8. Disconnect the fuel line at the carburetor. Disconnect the carburetor linkage and then remove the carburetor.

9. Lift off the Early Fuel Evaporation (EFE) heater grid.

10. Remove the distributor.

11. Remove the mounting bolts and nuts and remove the intake manifold. Make sure to disconnect the heater hose and condenser from the bottom of the intake manifold before you lift it all the way out.

12. Using a new gasket, replace the manifold, tightening the nuts and bolts to specification.

13. Installation of the remaining components is in the reverse order of removal. Adjust all necessary drive belts and check the ignition timing.

2.8L V6 Engine

1. Disconnect the negative battery cable.

2. Disconnect the accelerator cable bracket at the plenum.

3. Disconnect the throttle body and the EGR pipe from the EGR valve. Remove the plenum assembly.

4. Disconnect the fuel line along the fuel rail.

5. Disconnect the serpentine drive belt. Remove the power steering pump mounting bracket.

6. Remove the heater pipe at the power steering pump bracket.

7. Tag and disconnect the wiring at the alternator and remove the alternator.

8. Disconnect the wires from the cold start injector assembly. Remove the injector assembly from the intake manifold.

9. Disconnect the idle air vacuum hose at the throttle body. Disconnect the wires at the injectors.

10. Remove the fuel rail, breather

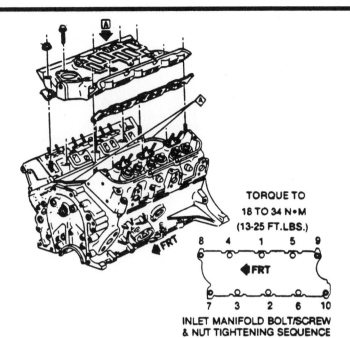

TORQUE TO
18 TO 34 N•M
(13-25 FT.LBS.)

```
  8   4   1   5   9
 ┌─────────────────┐
 │  ◄ FRT          │
 └─────────────────┘
  7   3   2   6   10
```

**INLET MANIFOLD BOLT/SCREW
& NUT TIGHTENING SEQUENCE**

A NOTE APPLY A SMOOTH CONTINUOUS BEAD
APPROX. 2.0-3.0 WIDE AND 3.0-5.0 THICK
ON BOTH SURFACES. BEAD CONFIGURATION
MUST INSURE COMPLETE SEALING OF WATER
AND OIL. SURFACE MUST BE FREE OF OIL
AND DIRT TO INSURE ADEQUATE SEAL.

2.8L V6 intake manifold installation

tube and the fuel runners from the engine.

11. Tag and disconnect the coil wires.

12. Remove the rocker arm covers. Drain the cooling system, the disconnect the radiator hose at the thermostat housing. Disconnec the heater hose from the thermostat housing and the thermostat wiring.

13. Remove the distributor.

14. Remove the thermostat assembly housing.

15. Remove the intake manifold bolts, then remove the intake manifold from the engine.

16. Installation is the reverse of removal. Upon installation, note that the gaskets are marked for right and left sides. Torque the intake manifold bolts to specifications in the sequence shown.

OHC Engines

1. Remove air cleaner.

2. Drain cooling system.

3. Remove generator and generator bracket at camshaft carrier.

4. Remove power steering pump and lay to one side.

5. Remove power steering bracket at intake manifold.

6. Remove ignition coil.

7. Remove throttle cable from bracket at intake manifold.

Installing intake manifold gasket on 2.8L V6 engine

8. Disconnect throttle, downshift and TV cables from EFI assembly.

9. Disconnect wire harness connectors from TBI assembly.

10. Remove vacuum brake hose at filter.

11. Disconnect inlet and return fuel lines at flex joints.

12. Remove preheat water hose at water pump and intake manifold.

13. Remove "S" hose from inlet tube to water pump.

14. Disconnect necessary ECM harness connectors and move ECM harness assembly for access to lower intake manifold retaining nuts.

15. Remove four (4) lower intake manifold retaining nuts and washers.

16. Remove five (5) upper intake manifold retaining nuts and washers and remove intake manifold.

17. Installation is the reverse of removal. Torque the bolts to 16 ft. lbs.

Exhaust Manifold

REMOVAL & INSTALLATION

OHV 4 Cyl Engines

1. Disconnect the negative battery cable.

2. Remove the air cleaner. Remove the exhaust manifold shield. Raise and support the front of the vehicle.

3. Disconnect the exhaust pipe at the manifold and then lower the vehicle.

4. Disconnect the air management-to-check valve hose and remove the bracket. Disconnect the oxygen sensor lead wire.

5. Remove the alternator belt. Remove the alternator adjusting bolts, loosen the pivot bolt and pivot the alternator upward.

6. Remove the alternator brace and the A.I.R. pipes bracket bolt.

7. Unscrew the mounting bolts and remove the exhaust manifold. The manifold should be removed with the A.I.R. plumbing as an assembly. If the manifold is to be replaced, transfer the plumbing to the new one.

8. Clean the mating surfaces on the manifold and the head, position the manifold and tighten the bolts to the proper specifications.

9. Installation of the remaining components is in the reverse order of removal.

2.8L V6 Engine

LEFT SIDE

1. Disconnect the negative battery cable.

2. Remove the air cleaner assembly.

3. Remove the air flow sensor. Remove the engine heat shield.

4. Disconnect the crossover pipe at the manifold.

5. Remove the exhaust manifold bolts.

6. Remove the exhaust manifold.

7. Installation is the reverse of removal.

RIGHT SIDE

1. Disconnect the negative battery cable.

2. Remove the air cleaner assembly.

3. Remove the air flow sensor. Remove the engine heat shield.

4. Disconnect the crossover pipe at the manifold.

5. Disconnect the accelerator and throttle valve cable at the throttle lever and the plenum. Move aside to gain working clearance.

6. Disconnect the power steering line at the power steering pump.

7. Remove the EGR valve assembly.

8. Raise the vehicle and support it safely.

9. Disconnect the exhaust pipe at the exhaust manifold.

10. Lower the vehicle.

11. Remove the manifold bolts, then remove the exhaust manifold.

12. Installation is the reverse of removal.

OHC Engines

1. Remove air cleaner.

2. Remove spark plug wires and retainers.

3. Remove oil dipstick tube and breather assembly.

4. Disconnect oxygen sensor wire.

5. Disconnect exhaust pipe from manifold flange.

6. Remove exhaust manifold to cylinder head attaching nuts and remove manifold and gasket.

7. Installation is the reverse of removal. Torque the bolts to 16–19 ft. lbs.

NOTE: Before installing a new gasket on the 1.8L MFI Turbo engine (code J), check for the location of the stamped part number on the surface. This gasket should be installed with this number toward the manifold. The gasket appears to be the same in either direction but it is not. Installing the gasket backwards will result in a leak.

Rocker Arms and Push Rods

REMOVAL, INSTALLATION AND ADJUSTMENT

OHV Engines

1. Remove the air cleaner. Remove the cylinder head cover.

2. Remove the rocker arm nut and ball. Lift the rocker arm off the stud. Always keep the rocker arm assemblies together and install them on the same stud. Remove the push rods.

3. To install, coat the bearing surfaces of the rocker arms and the rocker arm balls with Molykote® or its equivalent.

4. Install the push rods making sure that they seat properly in the lifter.

5. Install the rocker arms, balls and nuts. Tighten the rocker arm nuts until all lash is eliminated.

6. Adjust the valves when the lifter is on the base circle of a camshaft lobe:

    a. Crank the engine until the mark on the crankshaft pulley lines up with the '0' mark on the timing tab. Make sure that the engine is in the No. 1 firing position. Place your fingers on the No. 1 rocker arms as the mark on the crank pulley comes

near the "0" mark. If the valves are not moving, the engine is in the No. 1 firing position. If the valves move, the engine is in the No. 4 firing position; rotate the engine one complete revolution and it will be in the No. 1 position.

    b. When the engine is in the No. 1 firing position, on all 4 cylinder engines, adjust the EXHAUST valves of cylinders 1 and 3 and the INTAKE valves of cylinders 1 and 2. On V6 engines, adjust the INTAKE valves of cylinders 1, 5 and 6 and the EXHAUST valves of cylinders 1, 2 and 3.

    c. Back the adjusting nut out until lash can be felt at the push rod, then turn the nut until all lash is removed (this can be determined by rotating the push rod while turning the adjusting nut). When all lash has been removed, turn the nut in $1\frac{1}{2}$ additional turns, this will center the lifter plunger.

    d. Crank the engine one complete revolution until the timing tab and the '0' mark are again in alignment. Now the engine is in the No. 4 firing position. On all 4 cylinder engines, adjust the EXHAUST valves of cylinders 2 and 4 and the INTAKE valves of cylinders 3 and 4. On the V6, adjust the INTAKE valves of cylinders 2, 3 and 4 and the EXHAUST valves of cylinders 4, 5 and 6.

7. Installation of the remaining components is in the reverse order of removal.

OHC Engines

NOTE: A special tool is required for this procedure.

1. Remove the camshaft carrier cover.

2. Using a valve train compressing fixture, tool J-33302, depress all the lifters at once.

3. Remove the rocker arms, placing them on the workbench in the same order that they were removed.

4. Remove the hydraulic valve lash compensators keeping them in the order in which they were removed.

5. Installation is in the reverse of removal. Rocker arms and compensators must be replaced in the exact same position as when they were removed.

Cylinder Head

REMOVAL & INSTALLATION
OHV 4 Cyl Engines

NOTE: The engine should be "overnight" cold before removing the cylinder head.

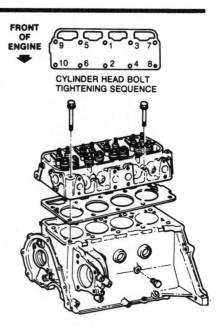

OHV engine cylinder head bolt torque sequence

1. Disconnect the negative battery cable.

2. Drain the cooling system into a clean container; the coolant can be reused if it is still good.

3. Remove the air cleaner. Raise and support the front of the vehicle.

4. Remove the exhaust shield. Disconnect the exhaust pipe.

5. Remove the heater hose from the intake manifold an then lower the car.

6. Unscrew the mounting bolts and remove the engine lift bracket (includes air management).

7. Remove the distributor. Disconnect the vacuum manifold at the alternator bracket.

8. Tag and disconnect the remaining vacuum lines at the intake manifold and thermostat.

9. Remove the air management pipe at the exhaust check valve.

10. Disconnect the accelerator linkage at the carburetor or TBI unit and then remove the linkage bracket.

11. Tag and disconnect all necessary wires. Remove the upper radiator hose at the thermostat.

12. Remove the bolt attaching the dipstick tube and hot water bracket.

13. Remove the idler pulley. Remove the A.I.R. and power steering pump drive belts.

14. Remove the A.I.R. bracket-to-intake manifold bolt. If equipped with power steering, remove the air pump pulley, the A.I.R. thru-bolt and the power steering adjusting bracket.

15. Loosen the A.I.R. mounting bracket lower bolt so that the bracket will rotate.

16. Disconnect and plug the fuel line at the carburetor.

17. Remove the alternator. Remove the alternator brace from the head and then remove the upper mounting bracket.

18. Remove the cylinder head cover. Remove the rocker arms and push rods.

19. Remove the cylinder head bolts in the order given in the illustration. Remove the cylinder head with the carburetor or TBI unit, intake and exhaust manifolds still attached. To install, the gasket surfaces on both the head and the block must be clean of any foreign matter and free of any nicks or heavy scratches. Cylinder bolt threads in the block and the bolt must be clean.

20. Place a new cylinder head gasket in position over the dowel pins on the block. Carefully guide the cylinder head into position.

21. Coat the cylinder bolts with sealing compound and install them finger tight.

22. Using a torque wrench, gradually tighten the bolts in the sequence shown in the illustration to the proper specifications.

23. Installation of the remaining components is in the reverse order of removal.

2.8L V6 Engine

1. Disconnect the negative battery cable.

2. Remove the intake manifold.

3. Remove the exhaust manifold.

4. Tag and disconnect the spark plug wires.

5. Remove the pushrods.

6. Remove the cylinder head bolts in the reverse of the tightening sequence, then remove the cylinder head from the engine.

7. Installation is the reverse of the removal procedure. Install the head gasket with the note "This Side Up" showing. Use sealer No. 1052080 or equivalent on the cylinder head bolt threads, and tighten the head bolts to specifications in the sequence shown.

OHC Engine

1. Remove air cleaner.

2. Drain cooling system.

3. Remove generator and pivot bracket at camshaft carrier housing.

4. Disconnect power steering pump and bracket and lay to one side.

5. Disconnect ignition coil electrical connections and remove coil.

6. Disconnect spark plug wires and distributor cap and remove.

7. Remove throttle cable from bracket at intake manifold.

8. Disconnect throttle cable, downshift cable and T.V. cable from EFI assembly.

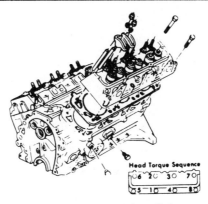

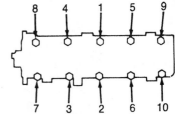

2.8L V6 cylinder head installation

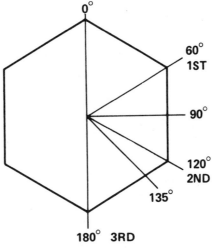

OHC engine cylinder head bolt torque degree sequence

9. Disconnect the ECM connectors from the EFI assembly.

10. Remove vacuum brake hose at filter.

11. Disconnect inlet and return fuel lines at flex joints.

12. Remove water pump bypass hose at intake manifold and water pump.

13. Disconnect ECM harness connectors at intake manifold.

14. Disconnect heater hose from intake manifold.

15. Disconnect exhaust pipe at exhaust manifold.

16. Disconnect breather hose at camshaft carrier.

17. Remove upper radiator hose.

18. Disconnect engine electrical harness and wires from thermostat housing.

19. Remove timing cover.

20. Remove timing probe holder.

21. Loosen water pump retaining bolts and remove timing belt.

22. Loosen camshaft carrier and cylinder head attaching bolts a little at a time in sequence shown.

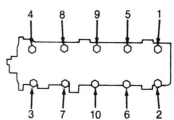

OHC engine camshaft carrier and head bolt tightening sequence

OHC engine camshaft carrier and head bolt loosening sequence

NOTE: Camshaft carrier and cylinder head bolts should only be removed when engine is cold.

23. Remove camshaft carrier assembly.

24. Remove cylinder head, intake manifold and exhaust manifold as an assembly.

25. Installation is the reverse of removal. Torque head bolts in the sequence shown. Make sure that you follow the note on torquing, at the bottom of the Torque Chart.

Crankcase Front Cover

REMOVAL & INSTALLATION

OHV 4 Cyl Engines Only

NOTE: The following procedure requires the use of a special tool.

1. Remove the engine drive belts.

2. Although not absolutely necessary, removal of the right front inner fender splash shield will facilitate access to the front cover.

3. Unscrew the center bolt from the crankshaft pulley and slide the pulley and hub from the crankshaft.

4. Remove the alternator lower bracket.

5. Remove the oil pan-to-front cover bolts.

6. Remove the front cover-to-block bolts and then remove the front cover. If the front cover is difficult to remove, use a plastic mallet.

7. The surfaces of the block and front cover must be clean and free of oil. Apply a $\frac{1}{8}$ in. bead of RTV sealant to the cover. The sealant must be wet

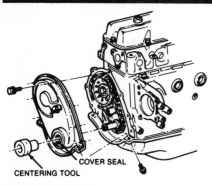

Front cover installation on OHV engines; a centering tool will aid in positioning

to the touch when the bolts are torqued down.

NOTE: When applying RTV sealant to the front cover, be sure to keep it out of the bolt holes.

8. Position the front cover on the block using a centering tool (J-23042) and tighten the screws.

9. Installation of the remaining components is in the reverse order of removal.

2.8L V6 Engine

1. Disconnect the negative battery cable.

2. Drain the cooling system and remove the coolant recovery tank from the vehicle.

3. Disconnect the manifold and EGR sensor solenoids.

4. Remove the serpentine belt and adjusting pulley.

5. Tag and disconnect the heater hose at the power steering bracket.

6. Tag and disconnect the alternator wiring and remove the alternator.

7. Raise the vehicle and support it safely.

8. Remove the inner fender splash shield. Remove the air conditioner compressor belt.

9. Remove the harmonic balancer if necessary to gain working clearance.

10. Remove the pan to block bolts. Remove the lower cover bolts.

11. Lower the vehicle and disconnect the radiator hoses at the water pump.

12. Remove the heater hose from the thermostat housing.

13. Disconnect the overflow hoses and the canister purge hose.

14. Remove the front cover.

15. Installation is the reverse of removal. Upon installation, apply a 3mm coninuous bead of RTV sealant to the oil pan surface and make sure all mating surfaces are clean of old gasket material.

TIMING COVER OIL SEAL
OHV Engines Only

The oil seal can be replaced with the

cover either on or off the engine. If the cover is on the engine, remove the crankshaft pulley and hub first. Pry out the seal using a large screwdriver, being careful not to distort the seal mating surface. Install the new seal so that the open side or helical side is towards the engine. Press it into place with a seal driver made for the purpose. Install the hub if removed.

Timing Chain and Sprockets

REMOVAL & INSTALLATION

OHV 4 Cyl Engines Only

1. Remove the front cover as previously detailed.

2. Place the No. 1 piston at TDC of the compression stroke so that the marks on the camshaft and crankshaft sprockets are in alignment (see illustration).

3. Loosen the timing chain tensioner nut as far as possible without actually removing it.

4. Remove the camshaft sprocket bolts and remove the sprocket and chain together. If the sprocket does not slide from the camshaft easily, a light blow with a soft mallet at the lower edge of the sprocket will dislodge it.

5. Use a gear puller (J-2288-8-20) and remove the crankshaft sprocket.

6. Press the crankshaft sprocket back onto the crankshaft.

7. Install the timing chain over the camshaft sprocket and then around the crankshaft sprocket. Make sure that the marks on the two sprockets are in alignment (see illustration). Lubricate the thrust surface with Molykote® or its equivalent.

8. Align the dowel in the camshaft with the dowel hole in the sprocket and then install the sprocket onto the camshaft. Use the mounting bolts to draw the sprocket onto the camshaft and then tighten them to 27–33 ft. lbs.

9. Lubricate the timing chain with clean engine oil. Tighten the chain tensioner.

10. Installation of the remaining components is in the reverse order of removal.

2.8L V6 Engine

1. Disconnect the negative battery cable.

2. Remove the crankcase cover as described earlier.

3. Position the No. 1 piston at Top Dead Center with the marks on the crankshaft and camshaft sprockets aligned.

4. Remove the camshaft sprocket bolts.

5. Remove the camshaft sprocket and chain from the front of the engine.

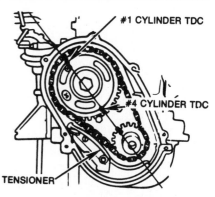

Timing mark alignment on OHV engines

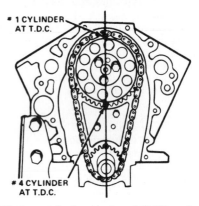

Timing mark alignment on 2.8L V6 engine

NOTE: If the sprocket does not move freely from the camshaft, a light blow using a plastic hammer on the lower edge of the sprocket should dislodge it.

6. Installation is the reverse of removal. Draw the camshaft sprocket onto the camshaft using the mounting bolts. Lubricate the timing chain with engine oil prior to installation.

Timing Belt

REMOVAL & INSTALLATION

OHC Engine Only

NOTE: The following procedure requires the use of a special tool.

1. Remove the timing belt front cover.

2. Rotate the crankshaft so that the timing mark on the crankshaft pulley lines up with the 10° BTDC mark on the indicator scale. The mark on the camshaft sprocket must line up with mark on the camshaft carrier.

3. Remove the crankshaft pulley as previously described.

4. Remove timing probe holder.

5. Loosen the water pump retaining bolts and rotate the water pump to loosen the timing belt.

6. Remove the timing belt.
7. Install timing belt on sprockets.
8. Install the crankshaft pulley.
9. Check if the mark on the camshaft sprocket lines up with mark on the camshaft carrier. The timing mark on the crankshaft pulley should line up at 10° BTDC on the indicator scale.
10. Rotate the water pump clockwise using Tool J-33039 until all slack is removed from the belt. Slightly tighten the water pump retaining bolts.
11. Install Tool J-26486 between the water pump and camshaft sprockets so that the pointer is midway between the sprockets.

NOTE: Whenever a timing belt is replaced on a 1.8L OHC (code 0,J) engine it must be adjusted when the engine is at normal operating temperature (Thermostat Open).

12. If the tension is incorrect, loosen the water pump and rotate it using Tool J-33039 until the proper tension is obtained.
13. Fully torque the water pump retaining bolts to 19 ft. lbs. taking care not to further rotate the water pump.
14. Install timing probe holder. Torque nuts to 19 ft. lbs.
15. Install the timing belt front cover and torque the attaching bolts to 5 ft. lbs.
16. Install and adjust the generator and power steering belt. Refill the cooling system, if necessary.

Timing Belt Rear Cover

REMOVAL & INSTALLATION

OHC Engines Only

1. Remove the timing belt from the crankshaft sprocket as previously outlined.
2. Remove the timing belt rear covers attaching bolts and the rear covers.
3. Install the rear covers and torque the attaching bolts to 19 ft. lbs.
4. Install the timing belt and adjust as previously outlined.

Camshaft

REMOVAL & INSTALLATION

OHV 4 Cyl Engines

1. Remove the engine.
2. Remove the intake manifold.
3. Remove the cylinder head cover, pivot the rocker arms to the sides, and remove the pushrods, keeping them in order. Remove the valve lifters, keeping them in order. There are special

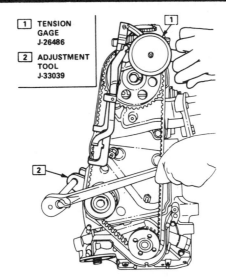

| 1 | TENSION GAGE J-26486 |
| 2 | ADJUSTMENT TOOL J-33039 |

Timing belt tension adjustment on OHC engines

tools which make lifter removal easier.
4. Remove the front cover.
5. Remove the distributor.
6. Remove the fuel pump and its pushrod.
7. Remove the timing chain and sprocket as described earlier in this chapter.
8. Carefully pull the camshaft from the block, being sure that the camshaft lobes do not contact the bearings.
9. To install, lubricate the camshaft journals with clean engine oil. Lubricate the lobes with Molykote or the equivalent. Install the camshaft into the engine, being extremely careful not to contact the bearings with the cam lobes.
10. Install the timing chain and sprocket. Install the fuel pump and pushrod. Install the timing cover. Install the distributor.
11. Install the valve lifters. If a new camshaft has been installed, new lifters should be used to ensure durability of the cam lobes.
12. Install the pushrods and rocker arms and the intake manifold. Adjust the valve lash after installing the engine. Install the cylinder head cover.

2.8L V6 Engine

1. Disconnect the negative battery cable. Remove the engine assembly from the vehicle.
2. Remove the intake manifold as described earlier.
3. Remove the rocker arm covers. Remove the rocker arm nuts, balls, rocker arms and pushrods.
4. Remove the upper front cover bolts. Remove the lower cover bolts and the front cover.
5. Remove the camshaft sprocket

bolts, camshaft sprocket and timing chain.
6. Remove the camshaft by carefully sliding it out the front of the engine. Measure the camshaft bearing journals using a micrometer and replace the camshaft if the journals exceed 0.0009 in. (0.025mm) out of round.
7. Installation is the reverse of removal. When installing a new camshaft, lubricate the camshaft lobes with GM E.O.S. or equivalent.

OHC Engines

NOTE: The following procedure requires the use of a special tool.

1. Remove camshaft carrier cover.
2. Using valve train compressing Fixture J-33302, compress valve springs and remove rocker arms.
3. Remove timing belt front cover.
4. Remove timing belt as previously outlined.
5. Remove camshaft sprocket as previously outlined.
6. Remove distributor.
7. Remove camshaft thrust plate from rear of camshaft carrier.
8. Slide camshaft rearward and remove it from the carrier.
9. Install a new camshaft carrier front oil seal using Tool J-33085.
10. Place camshaft in the carrier.

NOTE: Take care not to damage the carrier front oil seal when installing the camshaft.

11. Install camshaft thrust plate retaining bolts. Torque bolts to 70 inch lbs.
12. Check camshaft end play, which should be within 0.04–0.16 in. (0.016–0.064mm).
13. Install distributor.
14. Install camshaft sprocket as previously described.
15. Install timing belt as previously described.
16. Install timing belt front cover.
17. Using valve train compressing fixture J-33302, compress valve springs and replace rocker arms.
18. Install camshaft carrier cover as previously described.

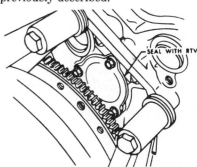

Camshaft rear cover on 2.8L V6

Camshaft Carrier

REMOVAL & INSTALLATION

OHC Engines Only

NOTE: Whenever the camshaft carrier bolts are loosened, it is necessary to replace the cylinder head gasket. To do this, see the previous instructions under "Cylinder Head Removal & Installation."

1. Disconnect the positive crankcase ventilation hose from the camshaft carrier.
2. Remove the distributor.
3. Remove the camshaft sprocket as previously outlined.
4. Loosen the camshaft carrier and cylinder head attaching bolts a little at a time in the sequence shown in the "Cylinder Head Removal & Installation" procedure.

NOTE: Camshaft carrier and cylinder head bolts should be loosened only when the engine is cold.

5. Remove the camshaft carrier.
6. Remove the camshaft thrust plate from the rear of the camshaft carrier.
7. Slide the camshaft rearward and remove it from the carrier.
8. Remove the carrier front oil seal.
9. Install a new carrier front oil seal using Tool J-33085.
10. Place the camshaft in the carrier.

NOTE: Take care not to damage the carrier front oil seal when installing the camshaft.

11. Install the camshaft thrust plate and the retaining bolts. Torque the bolts to 70 inch lbs.
12. Check the camshaft end-play which should be within 0.016–0.064 in. (0.04–0.16mm).
13. Clean the sealing surfaces on cylinder head and carrier. Apply a continuous 3mm bead of RTV sealer.
14. Install the camshaft carrier on the cylinder head.
15. Install the camshaft carrier and cylinder head attaching bolts.
16. Torque the bolts a little at a time in the proper sequence, to 18 ft. lbs. Then turn each bolt 60° clockwise in the proper sequence for three times until a 180° rotation is obtained, or equivalent to ½ turn. After remainder of installation is completed (with the exception of brackets that attach to carrier), start engine and let it run until thermostat opens. Torque all bolts

an additional 30° to 50° in the proper sequence.
17. Install the camshaft sprocket as outlined below.
18. Install the distributor.
19. Connect the positive crankcase ventilation hose to the camshaft carrier.

Camshaft Sprocket

REMOVAL & INSTALLATION

OHC Engines Only

1. Remove the timing belt front cover.
2. Align the mark on camshaft sprocket with mark on camshaft carrier.
3. Remove timing probe holder.
4. Loosen the water pump retaining bolts and remove the timing belt from the camshaft sprocket.
5. Remove the camshaft carrier cover as previously outlined.
6. Hold the camshaft with an open-end wrench. For this purpose a hexagonal is provided in the camshaft. Remove the camshaft sprocket retaining bolt and washer and then the sprocket.
7. Install the camshaft sprocket and align marks on camshaft sprocket and camshaft carrier.
8. Hold the camshaft with a hexagonal open-end wrench. Install the sprocket washer and retaining bolt. Torque to 34 ft. lbs.
9. Install the camshaft carrier cover as previously outlined.
10. Install the timing belt on sprockets and adjust as previously outlined.
11. Install timing probe holder. Torque nuts to 19 ft. lbs.
12. Install timing belt front cover.

Crankshaft Sprocket

REMOVAL & INSTALLATION

OHC Engines Only

1. Remove the timing belt from the crankshaft sprocket as previously described.
2. Remove the crankshaft sprocket to crankshaft attaching bolt and the thrust washer.
3. Remove the sprocket.
4. Position the sprocket over the key on end of crankshaft.
5. Install the thrust washer and the attaching bolt. Torque to 115 ft. lbs.
6. Install the timing belt and adjust as previously described.

Piston and Ring Installation

Pistons are installed with the notch in the top of the piston facing the front end of the engine. See the accompanying illustration for ring positioning.

Camshaft sprocket removal on OHC engines

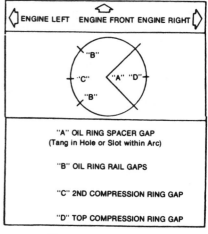

| | ENGINE LEFT | ENGINE FRONT | ENGINE RIGHT | |

"A" OIL RING SPACER GAP
(Tang in Hole or Slot within Arc)

"B" OIL RING RAIL GAPS

"C" 2ND COMPRESSION RING GAP

"D" TOP COMPRESSION RING GAP

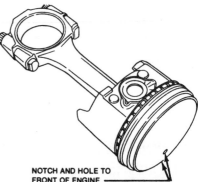

NOTCH AND HOLE TO FRONT OF ENGINE

Install the piston and rod with the notch and/or hole facing front (engine's front end)

CHEVETTE

Engine

REMOVAL & INSTALLATION

——— **CAUTION** ———

Do not discharge the air conditioning compressor or disconnect any of the refrigerant lines unless you have the skill and experience necessary to do so. Personal injury from the freon gas may result.

1. Remove the hood.
2. Disconnect the battery cables.
3. Remove the battery cable clips from the frame rail.
4. Drain the cooling system. Disconnect the radiator hoses from the engine and the heater hoses at the heater.
5. Tag and disconnect any wires leading from the engine.
6. Remove the radiator upper support and remove the radiator and engine fan. On the diesel, you must also remove the oil cooler.
7. Remove the air cleaner assembly.
8. Disconnect the following items:
    a. Fuel line at the rubber hose along the left frame rail. On the diesel, disconnect and plug the fuel lines at the injector pump and position them out of the way.
    b. Automatic transmission throttle valve linkage.
    c. Accelerator cable.
9. On air conditioned cars, remove the compressor from its mount and lay it aside. If equipped with power steering, remove the power steering pump and bracket and lay it aside.
10. Raise the car and support it with jackstands.
11. Remove the engine strut (shock-type) on the diesel.
12. Disconnect the exhaust pipe at the exhaust manifold.
13. Remove the flywheel dust cover on manual transmission cars or the torque converter underpan on automatic transmission cars.
14. On automatic transmission cars, remove the torque converter-to-flywheel bolts.
15. Remove the converter housing or flywheel housing-to-engine retaining bolts and lower the car.
16. Position a floor jack or other suitable support under the transmission.
17. Remove the safety straps from the front engine mounts and remove the mount nuts.
18. Remove the oil filter on the diesel.
19. Install the engine lifting apparatus.

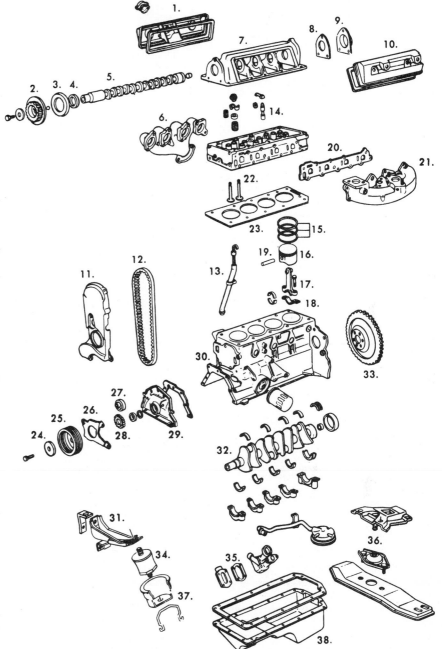

1. Camshaft Cover and Gasket
2. Camshaft Sprocket
3. Camshaft Sprocket Guide
4. Camshaft Oil Seal
5. Camshaft
6. Exhaust Manifold
7. Camshaft Housing
8. Camshaft Rear Cover Gasket
9. Camshaft Rear Cover
10. Camshaft Housing Cover and Gasket
11. Timing Belt Cover
12. Timing Belt
13. Oil Dipstick and Tube
14. Rocker Arm, Adjuster, Valve Springs, Valve Spring Cap, and Keys
15. Piston Rings
16. Piston
17. Connecting Rod
18. Connecting Rod Bearing and Cap
19. Piston Pin
20. Intake Manifold Gasket
21. Intake Manifold
22. Valves
23. Cylinder Head Gasket
24. Washer
25. Crankshaft Pulley
26. Lower Cover
27. Idler
28. Crankshaft Sprocket
29. Crankcase Front Cover
30. Cylinder Block
31. Engine Mounting Bracket
32. Crankshaft and Bearings
33. Flywheel
34. Engine Mount
35. Oil Pump Assembly
36. Transmission Mounting and Support
37. Engine Mounting Plate and Spring
38. Oil Pan and Gasket

Exploded view of the gasoline engine

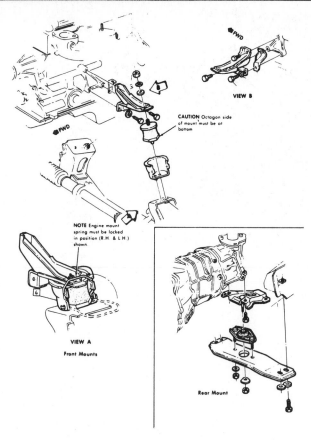

CAUTION Octagon side of mount must be at bottom

NOTE Engine mount spring must be locked in position (R.H. & L.H.) shown.

VIEW B

@FWD

VIEW A
Front Mounts

Rear Mount

Engine mounts—gasoline engine

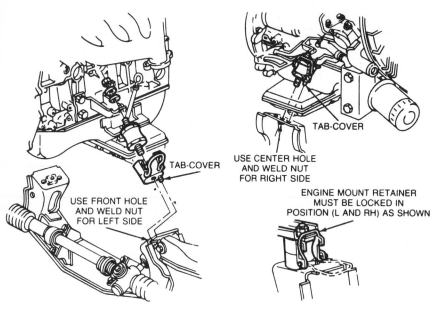

TAB-COVER

TAB-COVER

USE CENTER HOLE AND WELD NUT FOR RIGHT SIDE

USE FRONT HOLE AND WELD NUT FOR LEFT SIDE

ENGINE MOUNT RETAINER MUST BE LOCKED IN POSITION (L AND RH) AS SHOWN

Engine mounts—diesel engine

20. Remove the engine by pulling forward to clear the transmission while lifting slowly. Check to make sure that all necessary disconnections have been made and that proper clearance exists with surrounding components. Remove the lifting apparatus.

To install the engine:

21. Install the engine lifting apparatus and install guide pins in the engine block.

22. Install the engine in the car by aligning the engine with the transmission housing.

23. Install the front engine mount nuts and safety straps.

24. Raise the car and support it with jackstands.

25. Install the engine-to-transmission housing bolts. Tighten to 25 ft. lbs.

26. On automatic transmission cars, install the torque converter to the flywheel. Torque the bolts to 35 ft. lbs.

27. Install the flywheel dust cover or torque converter underpan as applicable.

28. Install the engine strut on the diesel.

29. Install the exhaust pipe to the exhaust manifold and lower the car.

30. Install the air conditioning compressor or the power steering pump if necessary, and adjust drive belt tension.

31. Connect the fuel lines, automatic transmission throttle valve linkage and accelerator cable.

32. Install the air cleaner.

33. Install the engine fan, radiator, and radiator upper support. Install the oil cooler if so equipped.

34. Connect all wires previously disconnected.

35. Connect the radiator and heater hoses and fill the cooling system.

36. Install the battery cable clips along the frame rail.

37. Install the engine hood.

38. Connect the battery cables, start the engine and check for leaks.

Intake Manifold

REMOVAL & INSTALLATION

Gasoline Engine

1. Disconnect the battery ground.
2. Drain the cooling system.
3. Remove the air cleaner.
4. Disconnect the upper radiator and heater hoses.
5. Remove the EGR valve.
6. Disconnect all electrical wiring, vacuum hoses and the accelerator linkage from the carburetor.
7. Disconnect the fuel line from the carburetor.
8. Remove the coil.
9. Remove the manifold.
10. If installing a new manifold, transfer all good parts. Always use a new gasket. Installation is the reverse of removal. Torque all bracket bolts to 30 ft. lbs. and intake manifold bolts to 15 ft. lbs.

Diesel Engine

1. Disconnect the negative battery cable.
2. Disconnect the fresh air hose and the vent hose. Remove the fuel separator.

3. Tag and disconnect all electrical connectors, the accelerator linkage and the glow plug wires.

4. Disconnect the injector lines at the injection pump and at the injector nozzles. Remove the injector lines and the hold-down clamps.

5. Remove the glow plug line at the cylinder head.

6. If equipped with power steering, remove the drive belt, the idler pulley and the bracket.

7. Remove the upper half of the front cover and the bracket.

8. Unscrew the mounting bolts and remove the intake manifold.

9. Places a new gasket over the mounting studs on the cylinder head and install the manifold. Tighten the bolts to 30 ft. lbs.

10. Installation of the remaining components is in the reverse order of removal.

Exhaust Manifold

REMOVAL & INSTALLATION

1. Disconnect the battery ground.
2. Raise the vehicle and support it on stands.
3. Disconnect the exhaust pipe from the flange.
4. Lower the vehicle.
5. On the diesel, remove the power steering belt, the flex hose and the power steering pump (if so equipped).
6. Remove the carburetor heat tube (gasoline engine only).
7. Remove the pulse air tubing, if so equipped.
8. Remove the manifold.
9. Installation is the reverse of removal. Install the two upper inner bolts first, to properly position the manifold. Tighten the bolts to the specified torque.

Valve Adjustment

Gasoline Engines

Adjustment of the hydraulic valve lash adjusters is not possible. Cleanliness should be exercised when handling the valve lash adjusters. Before installation of lash adjusters, fill them with oil and check the lash adjuster oil hole in the cylinder head to make sure that it is free of foreign matter.

Diesel Engines

NOTE: The rocker arm shaft bracket bolts and nuts should be tightened to 20 ft. lbs. before adjusting the valves.

1. Unscrew the retaining bolts and remove the cylinder head cover.
2. Rotate the crankshaft until the

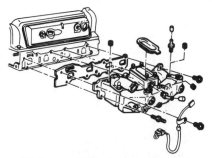

Intake manifold—gasoline engine

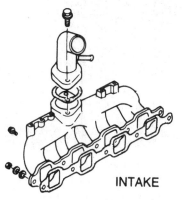

INTAKE

Intake manifold—diesel engine

Exhaust manifold—gasoline engine

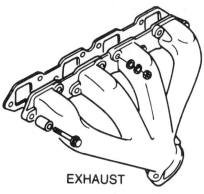

EXHAUST

Exhaust manifold—diesel engine

No. 1 or No. 4 piston is at TDC of the compression stroke.

3. Start with the intake valve on the No. 1 cylinder and insert a feeler gauge of the correct thickness (intake—0.01

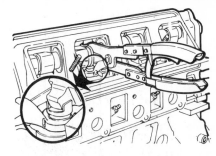

Depressing the valve spring using the special tool—gasoline engine

CYLINDER NO.	1		2		3		4	
VALVES	I	E	I	E	I	E	I	E
STEP. 1	○	○	○			○		
STEP. 2				○	○		○	○

I : INTAKE VALVE
E : EXHAUST VALVE

Valve adjustment sequence for the diesel engine

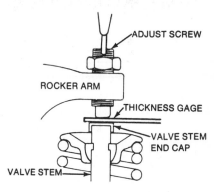

Valve adjustment—diesel engine

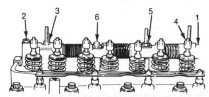

Loosening and tightening sequence for the rocker arm shaft bracket bolts and nuts—Diesel engine

in.; exhaust—0.014 in.) into the gap between the valve stem cap and the rocker arm. If adjustment is required, loosen the lock nut on top of the rocker arm and turn the adjusting screw clockwise to decrease the gap and counterclockwise to increase it. When the proper clearance is reached, tighten the lock nut and then recheck the gap. Adjust the remaining three valves in this step (see illustration) in the same manner.

4. Rotate the crankshaft one complete revolution and then adjust the remaining valves accordingly (see illustration).

Rocker Arm

REMOVAL & INSTALLATION

Gasoline Engine

NOTE: A special valve spring compressor is necessary for this procedure. (Tool-J-25477) Also prelubricate new rocker arms with Molykote® or its equivalent.

1. Remove the camshaft cover.
2. Using the special valve spring compressor, compress the valve springs and remove the rocker arms. Keep the rocker arms and guides in order so that they can be installed in their original locations.
3. To install the rocker arms, compress the valve springs and install the rocker arm guides.
4. Position the rocker arms in the guides and on the valve lash adjusters.
5. Install the camshaft cover.

Diesel Engines

1. Disconnect the negative battery cable.
2. Remove the cylinder head cover.
3. Remove the rocker arm shaft bracket bolts and nuts in sequence (see illustration). Remove the rocker arm shaft bracket and the rocker arm assembly.
4. Remove the rocker arms.
5. Apply a generous amount of clean engine oil to the rocker arm shaft, rocker arms and the valve stem end caps.
6. Install the rocker arm shaft assembly and then tighten the bolts to 20 ft. lbs. in the same sequence as removal.
7. Adjust the valves as previously detailed and reinstall the cylinder head cover.

Cylinder Head

REMOVAL & INSTALLATION

Gasoline Engines

1. Disconnect the negative battery cable.
2. Remove all accessory drive belts.
3. Remove the engine fan, timing belt cover and the timing belt, as outlined later in this section.
4. Remove the air cleaner and snorkel (silencer) assembly.
5. Drain the cooling system and disconnect the upper radiator hose and heater hose at the intake manifold.
6. Remove the accelerator cable support bracket.
7. Disconnect and label the spark plug wires.
8. Disconnect and label the wires

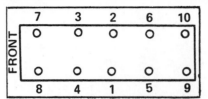

Cylinder head torque sequence—gasoline engine

from the idle solenoid, choke, temperature sender, and alternator.
9. Disconnect the exhaust pipe from the exhaust manifold.
10. Remove the dipstick tube bracket-to-manifold attaching bolt.
11. Disconnect the fuel line at the carburetor.
12. Take off the coil cover. Remove the coil bracket bolts and lay the coil aside.
13. Remove the camshaft cover.
14. Remove the camshaft cover-to-camshaft housing attaching stubs.
15. Remove the rocker arms, rocker arm guides, and valve lash adjusters. Keep the parts in order so that they can be installed in their original locations.
16. Remove the camshaft carrier bolts and remove the camshaft carrier. A sharp wedge may be necessary to separate the camshaft carrier from the cylinder head. Be very cautious not to damage the mating surfaces.
17. Remove the manifold and cylinder head assembly.
18. Install a new cylinder head gasket with the words "This Side Up" facing up over dowel pins in the block. Make sure that the gasket is absolutely clean.
19. Install the manifold and cylinder head assembly.
20. Apply a light, thin continuous bead of sealant to the jointing surfaces of the cylinder head and the camshaft carrier and install the camshaft carrier. Clean any excess sealer from the cylinder head. Apply sealing compound to the camshaft carrier/cylinder head bolts and install the bolts finger-tight. Tighten the bolts a little at a time and in the proper sequence until the final specified torque figure is reached.
21. Install the camshaft cover-to-camshaft housing attaching studs.
22. Install the valve lash adjusters and rocker arm guides. Prelube the rocker arms with engine assembly lubricant and install the rocker arms.
23. Using new gaskets, install the camshaft covers.
24. Install the coil bracket mounting bolt.
25. Connect the fuel line to the carburetor.
26. Install the dipstick tube bracket-to-manifold attaching bolt.

27. Attach the exhaust pipe to the exhaust manifold.
28. Connect the wires to the idle solenoid, choke, temperature sender, and alternator.
29. Connect the spark plug wires.
30. Apply Teflon® tape or its equivalent to the threads of the accelerator cable support bracket attaching bolts and install the bracket.
31. Install the air cleaner and snorkel (silencer) assembly.
32. Connect the upper radiator hose and heater hose to the intake manifold.
33. Fill the cooling system.
34. Install the timing belt, timing belt cover, engine fan, drive belts and connect the negative battery cable.

Diesel Engines

1. Disconnect the negative battery cable.
2. Drain the cooling system.
3. Remove the cylinder head cover.
4. Disconnect the bypass hose. Remove the upper half of the front cover.
5. Loosen the tension pulley bolts and then remove the camshaft as detailed later in this section.
7. Tag and disconnect the glow plug resistor wire.
8. Disconnect the injector lines at the injector pump and at the injector nozzles and then remove the injector lines. Disconnect and plug the fuel leak-off hose.
9. Disconnect the exhaust pipe at the manifold.
10. Remove the oil feed pipe from the rear of the cylinder head.
11. Disconnect the upper radiator hose and position it out of the way.
12. Remove the head bolts in the sequence shown and then remove the cylinder head with the intake and exhaust manifolds installed.

NOTE: The gasket surfaces on both the head and the block must be clean of any foreign matter and free of nicks or heavy scratches. Cylinder bolt threads in the block and on the bolt must also be clean.

13. Place a new gasket over the dowel pins with the word "TOP" facing up.
14. Apply engine oil to the threads and the seating face of the cylinder head bolts, install them and then tighten them in the proper sequence.
15. Install the camshaft and rocker arm assembly. Loosen the adjusting screws so that the entire rocker arm assembly is held in a free state.
16. Reinstall the timing belt as outlined later in this section.
17. Connect the upper radiator hose and the oil feed pipe.

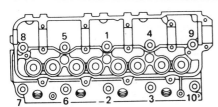

Cylinder head torque sequence—diesel engine

18. Connect the exhaust pipe to the manifold.
19. Install the fuel leak-off hose. Connect the injector lines.
20. Connect the glow plug resistor wire.
21. Adjust the valve clearance as previously detailed. Install the cylinder head cover.
22. Refill the cooling system.

Timing Belt Cover

REMOVAL & INSTALLATION

Upper Front Cover

1. Disconnect the negative battery cable. Remove the radiator upper mounting panel on models without A/C or fan shroud on models with A/C.
2. Remove engine accessory drive belts on the gasoline engine. Remove the bypass hose on the diesel engine.
3. Remove the engine fan.
4. Remove the cover retaining screws and nuts and remove the cover.
5. To install; align the screw slots on the upper and lower parts of the cover.
6. Install the cover retaining screws and nuts.
7. Install the engine fan.
8. Install the engine accessory drive belts or the bypass hose.
9. Connect the negative battery cable.

Lower Front Cover

1. Disconnect the negative battery cable.
2. Loosen the alternator and the A/C compressor bolts, if so equipped. Remove the drive belt.
3. Remove the damper pulley-to-crankshaft bolt and washer and remove the pulley.
4. Remove the upper front timing belt cover as outlined previously.
5. Remove the lower cover retaining nut (gasoline) or bolts (diesel). Remove the lower cover.
6. To install the cover, align the cover with the studs on the engine block.
7. Install the lower front cover retaining nut or bolts.
8. Install the upper front timing belt cover.
9. Install the crankshaft damper

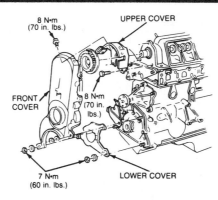

Timing belt front cover fasteners—gasoline engine

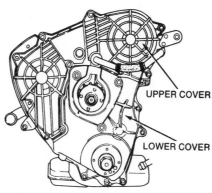

Timing belt covers—diesel engine

pulley. Torque the retaining bolt to the specified torque.
10. Install the drive belt and tighten the alternator and compressor mounting bolts.
11. Connect the negative battery cable.

Upper Rear Cover—Gasoline Engines

1. Crank the engine so that No. 1 cylinder is at TDC of the compression stroke.
2. Disconnect the negative battery cable.
3. Remove the upper and lower front cover, the timing belt, and the camshaft timing sprocket.
4. Remove the three screws retaining the camshaft sprocket cover to the camshaft carrier.
5. Inspect the condition of the cam seal
6. Position and align a new gasket over the end of the camshaft and against the camshaft carrier.
7. Install the three camshaft sprocket cover retaining screws.
8. Install the camshaft sprocket, timing belt, and the upper and lower front covers.
9. Connect the negative battery cable.

Timing Belt & Sprockets

REMOVAL & INSTALLATION

Gasoline Engines

—— **CAUTION** ——
Do not discharge the air conditioning compressor or disconnect the air conditioning lines. Personal injury could result.

NOTE: Rotate the engine to bring No. 1 cylinder to TDC. The timing mark should be at the 0° mark on the timing scale. With No. 1 cylinder at TDC, a ⅛ in. drill bit may be inserted through a hole in the timing belt upper rear cover into a hole in the camshaft drive sprocket. These holes are provided to facilitate and verify camshaft timing. Aligning these holes now will make installation of the new belt much easier.

1. Disconnect the negative battery cable.
2. Remove the alternator and air conditioning compressor drive belts.
3. Remove the engine fan and pulley.
4. Remove the engine upper and lower front timing belt covers.

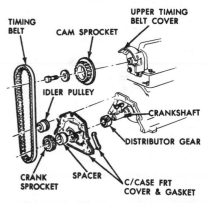

Timing belt and gears—gasoline engine

5. Remove the timing belt idler pulley.
6. Remove the timing belt from the camshaft and crankshaft timing sprockets.
7. With the distributor cap off, mark the location of the rotor in the No. 1 spark plug firing position on the distributor housing. On air conditioned cars, remove the compressor and lower its mounting bracket.
8. Remove the camshaft timing sprocket bolt and washer and remove the camshaft sprocket.
9. Remove the crankshaft sprocket.
10. To install; place the crankshaft sprocket on the crankshaft making

sure that the locating tabs face outward.

11. Install the crankshaft sprocket.

12. Align the camshaft sprocket dowel with the hole in the end of the camshaft and install the sprocket on the camshaft.

13. Apply thread locking compound to the camshaft sprocket retaining bolt and washer and torque to 65–85 ft. lbs.

14. Position the timing belt over the crankshaft sprocket.

15. Install the crankshaft pulley.

16. Align the crankshaft pulley timing mark with the "0" mark on the timing scale and the distributor rotor with the scribed mark on the distributor housing.

17. Align the hole in the camshaft sprocket with the hole in the upper rear timing belt cover. Insert a $\frac{1}{8}$ in. drill bit to hold the sprocket in alignment.

18. Install the timing belt on the camshaft and crankshaft sprockets.

19. To adjust timing belt tension see "Timing Belt Adjustment."

20. Install the distributor cap. On air conditioned cars, install the lower compressor bracket and the compressor.

21. Install the upper and lower front timing belt covers.

22. Install the engine fan and pulley.

23. Install the alternator and, if necessary, the air conditioning compressor drive belts.

24. Connect the negative battery cable.

Diesel Engines

NOTE: In order to complete this procedure you will need three special tools. A gear puller (J-22888), a fixing plate (J-29761) and a belt tension gauge (J-26484).

1. Disconnect the negative battery cable.

2. Drain the cooling system.

3. Remove the fan shroud, cooling fan and the pulley.

4. Disconnect the bypass hose and then remove the upper half of the front cover.

5. With the No. 1 piston at TDC of the compression stroke, make sure that the notch mark on the injection pump gear is aligned with the index mark on the front plate. If so, thread a lock bolt (8mm x 1.25) through the gear and into the front plate.

6. Remove the cylinder head cover and install a fixing plate (J-29761) in the slot at the rear of the cam. This will prevent the cam from rotating during the procedure.

7. Remove the crankshaft damper

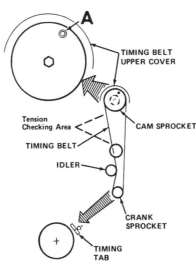

Timing belt Installation—1.6 L Chevette. When camshaft Is aligned at No. 1 cylinder TDC compression stroke, a 1/8 in. drill bit should fit through rear timing belt cover and Into quick check hole In sprocket.

Correct distributor rotor alignment for timing belt installation

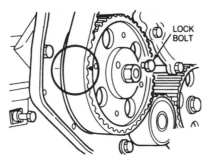

Injection gear setting mark—diesel engine

pulley and check to make sure that the No. 1 piston is still at TDC.

8. Remove the lower half of the front cover and then remove the timing belt holder from the bottom of the front plate.

9. Remove the tension spring be-

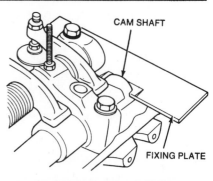

Camshaft fixing plate—diesel engine

hind the front plate, next to the injection pump.

10. Loosen the tension pulley and slide the timing belt off the pulleys.

11. Remove the camshaft gear retaining bolt, install a gear puller and remove the gear.

12. When assembling, reinstall the cam gear loosely so that it can be turned smoothly by hand.

13. Slide the timing belt back over the gears and note the following: the belt should be properly tensioned between the pulleys, the cogs on the belt and the gears should be properly engaged, the crankshaft should not be turned and the belt slack should be concentrated at the two tension pulleys. Push the tension pulley in with your finger and install the tension spring.

14. Partially tighten the tension pulley bolts in sequence (top first, bottom second) so as to prevent any movement of the pulley.

15. Tighten the camshaft gear retaining bolt to 45 ft. lbs. Remove the injection pump gear lock bolt.

16. Remove the fixing plate from the end of the cam.

17. Install the crankshaft damper pulley and then check that the No. 1 piston is still at TDC. Do not try to adjust it by moving the crankshaft.

18. Check that the marks on the injection pump gear and the front plate are still aligned and that the fixing plate still fits properly into the slot on the camshaft.

19. Loosen the tensioner pulley and plate bolts, concentrate the looseness of the timing belt around the tensioner and then tighten the bolts.

20. Belt tension should be 46–63 lbs., checked at a point midway between the upper two pulleys.

21. Remove the damper pulley again and install the belt holder in position away from the timing belt.

22. Installation of the remaining components is in the reverse order of removal.

TIMING BELT ADJUSTMENT

1. Remove the fan, fan belt, water

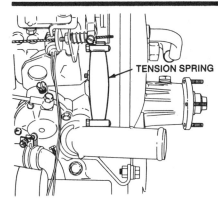

Tension spring—diesel engine

Tighten the tension pulley bolts in sequence—diesel engin

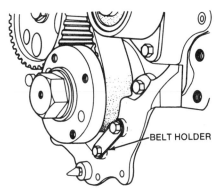

Diesel engine: the timing belt holder must be removed before the timing belt can be taken off

pump pulley and upper cam belt cover.

2. Rotate the crankshaft clockwise a minimum of one revolution. Stop with No. 1 piston at TDC. DO NOT TURN THE ENGINE BACKWARD!

3. Install a belt tension gauge on the same side as the idler pulley (injection pump pulley on diesel), midway between the cam sprocket and the idler pulley (injection pump pulley on diesel). Be sure that the center finger of the gauge extension fits in a notch between the teeth on the belt. Correct belt tension is 70 lbs. (46–63 lbs. for the diesel).

4. If the tension is incorrect, loosen the idler pulley attaching bolt and using a ¼ in. Allen wrench, rotate the

pulley counterclockwise on its attaching bolt until the proper tension is obtained. Torque the bolt to 15 ft. lbs.

5. The remainder of the installation is the reverse of the removal procedure.

Camshaft

REMOVAL & INSTALLATION

Gasoline Engines

NOTE: A special valve spring compressor (tool No. J-25477) is necessary for this procedure. If replacing the camshaft or rocker arms, prelube new parts with engine assembly lubricant.

1. Disconnect the negative battery cable.

2. Remove engine accessory drive belts.

3. Remove the engine fan and pulley.

4. Remove the upper and lower front timing belt covers.

5. Loosen the idler pulley and remove the timing belt from the camshaft sprocket.

6. Remove the camshaft sprocket attaching bolt and washer and remove the camshaft sprocket.

7. Remove the camshaft cover. Using the special valve spring compressor, remove the rocker arms and guides. Keep the rocker arms and guides in order so that they can be installed in their original locations.

8. Remove any components necessary to gain working clearance.

NOTE: The heater assembly will probably have to be removed from the firewall.

9. Remove the camshaft carrier rear cover.

10. Remove the camshaft thrust plate bolts. Slide the camshaft slightly to the rear and remove the thrust plate.

11. Remove the engine mount nuts and wire retainers.

12. Using a floor jack, raise the front of the engine.

13. Remove the camshaft from the camshaft carrier. Heavy pressure will be needed to pull the camshaft and seal forward.

14. Install the camshaft into the camshaft carrier.

15. Lower the engine.

16. Install the engine mount nuts and attach the retaining wires.

17. Slide the camshaft slightly to the rear and install the thrust plate. Slide the camshaft forward and install the carrier rear cover.

18. Position and align a new gasket

over the end of the camshaft, against the camshaft carrier.

19. Install any components which were removed to gain working clearance.

20. Install the valve rocker arms and guides in their original locations using the special valve spring compressor. Install the camshaft covers.

21. Align the dowel in the camshaft sprocket with the hole in the end of the camshaft and install the sprocket.

22. Apply thread locking compound to the sprocket retaining bolt threads and install the bolt and washer. Torque the sprocket retaining bolt to 65–85 ft. lbs.

23. Turn the crankshaft clockwise to bring the No. 1 cylinder to top dead center. Make sure that the distributor rotor is in position to fire the No. 1 spark plug. Align the hole in the camshaft sprocket with the hole in the upper rear timing belt cover and install the timing belt on the camshaft sprocket.

24. Adjust timing belt tension as previously outlined.

25. Install the upper and lower front timing belt covers.

26. Install the engine fan and pulley.

27. Install the engine accessory drive belts.

28. Connect the negative battery cable.

Diesel Engines

NOTE: In order to complete this procedure you will need a gear puller (J-22888) and a fixing plate (J-29761).

1. Remove the cylinder head cover.

2. Remove the timing belt as previously detailed. Remove the plug.

3. Install the fixing plate into the slot at the rear of the camshaft.

4. Remove the camshaft gear retaining bolt and then use a puller to remove the cam gear.

5. Remove the rocker arms and shaft as previously detailed.

6. Unscrew the bolts attaching the front head plate and then remove the plate.

7. Unscrew the camshaft bearing cap retaining bolts and remove the bearing caps with the cap side bearings.

8. Lift out the camshaft oil seal and then remove the camshaft.

9. Coat the cam and cylinder head journals with clean engine oil.

10. Position the camshaft back in the cylinder head with a new oil seal.

11. Apply a suitable liquid gasket to the cylinder head face of the No. 1 camshaft bearing cap.

12. Install the remaining bearing caps. Install the rocker arm shaft assembly, leaving the adjusting screws loose.

13. Install the front head plate.

14. Install the timing belt as previously detailed.

15. Adjust the valve clearance to specifications and then install the cylinder head cover.

Piston and Connecting Rod Positioning

Install piston and connecting rod assemblies into their original cylinders. Install the piston and rod assemblies with the notch (arrow-diesel) on the piston crown facing to the front of the engine. The numbers on the connecting rods and bearing caps must be on the same side when installing pistons and connecting rods.

SPECTRUM

The Spectrum uses an Isuzu 1.5L (94 cu. in.) overhead cam (OHC) engine. The 4-cylinder, in-line engine utilizes one compression and one oil control ring on each piston. The overhead camshaft, which is driven by the crankshaft through a timing belt, directly drives the rocker arms.

Engine

REMOVAL & INSTALLATION

1. Remove the hood and disconnect the negative battery cable.
2. Drain the cooling system.

3. Remove the air cleaner and the throttle cable at the carburetor.
4. Disconnect the heater hoses at the intake manifold, the coolant hose at the thermostat housing and the thermostat housing at the cylinder head.

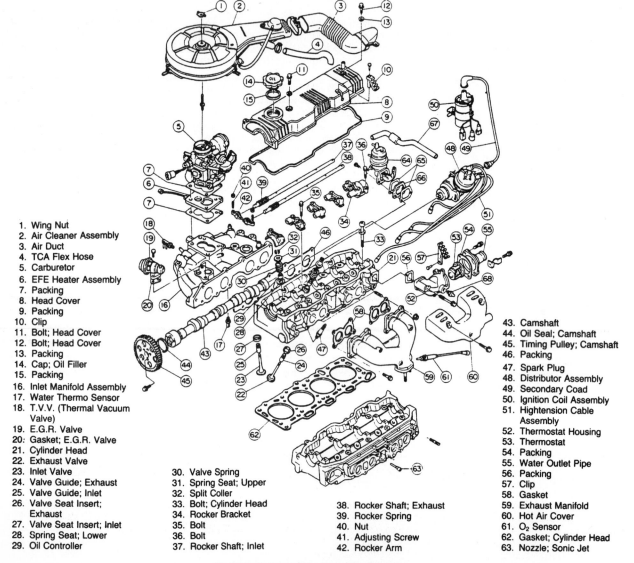

1. Wing Nut
2. Air Cleaner Assembly
3. Air Duct
4. TCA Flex Hose
5. Carburetor
6. EFE Heater Assembly
7. Packing
8. Head Cover
9. Packing
10. Clip
11. Bolt; Head Cover
12. Bolt; Head Cover
13. Packing
14. Cap; Oil Filler
15. Packing
16. Inlet Manifold Assembly
17. Water Thermo Sensor
18. T.V.V. (Thermal Vacuum Valve)
19. E.G.R. Valve
20. Gasket; E.G.R. Valve
21. Cylinder Head
22. Exhaust Valve
23. Inlet Valve
24. Valve Guide; Exhaust
25. Valve Guide; Inlet
26. Valve Seat Insert; Exhaust
27. Valve Seat Insert; Inlet
28. Spring Seat; Lower
29. Oil Controller

30. Valve Spring
31. Spring Seat; Upper
32. Split Coller
33. Bolt; Cylinder Head
34. Rocker Bracket
35. Bolt
36. Bolt
37. Rocker Shaft; Inlet

38. Rocker Shaft; Exhaust
39. Rocker Spring
40. Nut
41. Adjusting Screw
42. Rocker Arm

43. Camshaft
44. Oil Seal; Camshaft
45. Timing Pulley; Camshaft
46. Packing
47. Spark Plug
48. Distributor Assembly
49. Secondary Coad
50. Ignition Coil Assembly
51. Hightension Cable Assembly
52. Thermostat Housing
53. Thermostat
54. Packing
55. Water Outlet Pipe
56. Packing
57. Clip
58. Gasket
59. Exhaust Manifold
60. Hot Air Cover
61. O2 Sensor
62. Gasket; Cylinder Head
63. Nozzle; Sonic Jet

Exploded view of the top of the engine

5. Remove the distributor from the cylinder head.

6. Disconnect the oxygen sensor electrical connector.

7. Support the engine using a vertical lift and remove the right motor mount.

8. Disconnect the necessary electrical connectors and vacuum hoses.

9. Disconnect the flex hose at the exhaust manifold and the lower radiator hose at the block.

10. Remove the upper A/C compressor bolt and remove the belt.

11. Disconnect the power steering bracket at the block and remove the belt.

12. Disconnect the fuel lines from the fuel pump and the electrical connectors from under the carburetor.

13. Remove the upper starter bolt and raise the vehicle.

14. Drain the oil from the crankcase and remove the oil filter.

15. Disconnect the oil temperature switch connector.

16. Disconnect the exhaust pipe bracket at the block and the exhaust pipe at the manifold.

17. Remove the A/C compressor and move to one side. Do not disconnect the A/C refrigerant lines. Remove the alternator wires.

18. Remove the flywheel cover and the converter bolts, then install the flywheel holding tool (J-35271).

19. Disconnect the starter wires and remove the starter.

20. Remove the front right wheel and inner splash shield.

21. Lower the engine by lowering the crossmember enough to gain access to the crankshaft pulley bolts, then remove the pulley.

22. Raise the engine and crossmember. Remove the engine support.

23. Lower the vehicle and support the transmission.

24. Remove the transmission to engine bolts. Remove the engine.

25. To install, reverse the removal procedure, adjust the drive belts and refill the fluids.

Exhaust Manifold

REMOVAL & INSTALLATION

1. Disconnect the negative battery cable and the oxygen sensor wiring connector.

2. Disconnect the thermostatic air cleaner (TAC) flex hose.

3. Remove the hot air cover and raise the vehicle.

4. Disconnect the exhaust pipe from the exhaust manifold and lower the vehicle.

5. Remove the nuts and bolts securing the exhaust manifold to the cylinder head. Clean the gasket mounting surfaces.

6. To install, use new gaskets and reverse the removal procedures. Torque the exhaust manifold to 17 ft. lbs. and the exhaust pipe to 42 ft. lbs., then start the engine and check for leaks.

Intake Manifold

REMOVAL & INSTALLATION

1. Disconnect the negative battery cable. Drain the engine coolant.

2. Remove the bolt securing the alternator adjusting plate to the engine.

3. Disconnect and label all of the hoses attached to the air cleaner and remove the air cleaner.

4. Disconnect the air inlet temperature switch wiring connector.

5. Disconnect and label the hoses, electrical connectors, and control cable attached to the carburetor.

6. If equipped with A/C, disconnect the FIDC vacuum hose, the pressure tank control valve hose, the distributor/3-way connector hose and the VSV wiring connector.

7. Remove the carburetor attaching bolts (located beneath the intake manifold), then remove the carburetor and the EFE heater.

8. At the intake manifold, remove the PCV hose, the water bypass hose, the heater hoses, the EGR valve/canister hose, the distributor vacuum advance hose and the ground wires.

9. Disconnect the thermometer unit switch wiring connector.

10. Remove the intake manifold attaching nuts/bolts and the intake manifold.

11. Clean the sealing surfaces of the intake manifold and cylinder head.

12. To install, use new gaskets and reverse the removal procedure. Torque the intake manifold to 17 ft. lbs.; then adjust the engine control cable and the alternator belt tension. Refill the engine with coolant and check for leaks.

Rocker Arm Shafts and Rocker Arms

REMOVAL & INSTALLATION

1. Refer to the "Cylinder Head Cover Removal and Installation" procedure in this section and remove the cylinder head cover.

2. Remove the rocker arm bracket bolts in sequence (work from both ends equally, toward the middle).

3. Remove the rocker arm shafts and then the rocker arms from the shafts.

4. To install, reverse the removal procedure.

NOTE: The rocker arm shafts are different from each other, make sure they are installed in the same position that they were removed. Install the rocker arms with the identification marks toward the front of the engine. Apply sealant to the bracket and cylinder head mating surfaces of the front and rear rocker brackets.

5. Mount the rocker assemblies securely to the dowel pins on the cylinder head. Torque the rocker arm bolts to 16 ft. lbs.

Valve Spring and Seal

REMOVAL & INSTALLATION

Cylinder Head On Engine

1. Refer to the "Rocker Arm Shafts and Rocker Arms Removal and Installation" procedure in this section and remove the rocker arm shaft assemblies.

2. Remove the spark plugs.

3. Rotate the engine to close the valves of the cylinder being worked on.

4. Pressurize the cylinder with compressed air to hold the valves in place.

5. Use the valve spring compression tool (J-26513-A), to compress the valve springs.

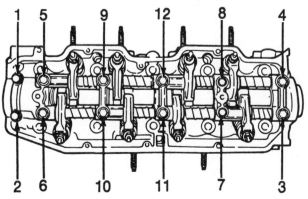

Rocker arm/shaft assembly removal sequence

6. Remove the split collars, valve springs and valve seals.

7. To install, use new valve seals and reverse the removal procedure.

Cylinder Head Removed

1. Remove the rocker arm bracket bolts, rocker arm assemblies, camshaft and oil seals.

2. Using valve spring compression tool (J-8062), compress the valve springs.

3. Remove the split collars, valve springs and seals.

4. To install, use new oil seals and reverse the removal procedure.

VALVE CLEARANCE ADJUSTMENT

1. Refer to the "Cylinder Head Cover Removal and Installation" procedure in this section and remove the cylinder head cover.

2. Rotate the engine until the notched line on the crankshaft pulley aligns with the "O" degree mark on the timing gear case. The position of the No. 1 piston should be at TDC of the compression stroke.

3. Set the intake valve to 0.006 in. (cold) for No. 1 and 2 cylinders; exhaust valves to 0.010 in. (cold) for No. 1 and 3 cylinders.

4. Rotate the crankshaft one complete revolution. Set the intake valves to 0.006 in. (cold) for No. 3 and 4 cylinders; exhaust valves to 0.010 in. (cold) for No. 2 and 4 cylinders.

5. After the adjustment has been completed, replace the head cover.

Cylinder Head

REMOVAL & INSTALLATION

1. Disconnect the negative battery cable.

2. Drain the cooling system.

3. Remove the air cleaner.

4. Disconnect the flex hose and oxygen sensor at the exhaust manifold.

5. Disconnect the exhaust pipe bracket at the block and the exhaust pipe at the manifold.

6. Disconnect the spark plug wires.

7. Remove the thermostat housing, the distributor, the vacuum advance hoses and the ground cable at the cylinder head.

8. Disconnect the fuel hoses at the fuel pump.

9. At the carburetor, remove the necessary hoses and the throttle cable.

10. Disconnect the vacuum switching valve electrical connector and the heater hoses.

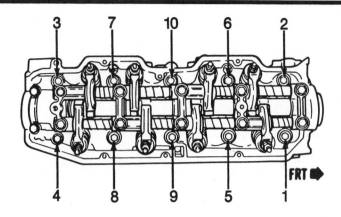

Cylinder head bolt removal sequence

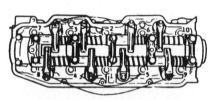

Cylinder head bolt torque sequence

11. Remove the alternator, P/S and A/C adjusting bolts, brackets and drive belts.

12. Support the engine using a vertical hoist. Remove the right hand motor mount and the bracket at the front cover.

13. Rotate the engine to align the timing marks, then remove the timing gear cover.

14. Loosen the tension pulley and remove the timing belt from the camshaft timing pulley.

15. Disconnect the carburetor fuel line at the fuel pump and remove the fuel pump.

16. Disconnect the intake manifold coolant hoses.

17. Remove the cylinder head bolts (remove the bolts from both ends at the same time, working toward the middle) and the cylinder head. Clean all of the mounting surfaces.

18. Compress the valves; then remove the keepers, springs, seals and valves.

19. To install, use new seals and gaskets, apply oil to the bolt threads and torque the head bolts.

NOTE: When torquing the cylinder head bolts, work from the middle toward both ends at the same time. First, torque the bolts to 29 ft. lbs. and then final torque them to 58 ft. lbs.

20. After torquing, adjust the valve clearance and complete the installation procedure, by reversing the removal procedure.

Timing Cover

REMOVAL & INSTALLATION

1. Refer to the "Engine Removal and Installation" procedure in this section. Remove the engine and support it on an engine stand.

2. Remove the accessory drive belts.

3. Remove the engine mounting bracket from the timing cover.

4. Remove the starter and install the flywheel holding tool (J-35271).

5. Remove the crankshaft bolt, boss and crankshaft pulley.

6. Remove the timing cover.

7. To install, reverse the removal procedure.

Front Oil Seal

REMOVAL & INSTALLATION

The oil seal is part of the oil pump assembly; to replace the oil seal, refer to the "Oil Pump Removal and Installation" procedure in this section.

1. With the oil pump removed from the engine, pry the oil seal from the oil pump housing with a small pry bar.

2. To install the new oil seal, drive it into the housing using the seal installing tool (J-35269).

Timing Belt

REMOVAL

1. Remove the engine by referring to the "Engine Removal and Installation" procedure in this section. Mount the engine to an engine stand.

2. Remove the accessory drive belts.

3. Remove the engine mounting bracket from the timing cover.

4. Rotate the crankshaft until the notch on the crankshaft pulley aligns with the "O" degree mark on the tim-

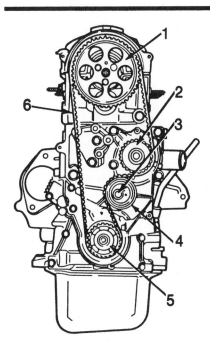

1. Camshaft timing pulley
2. Water pump timing pulley
3. Bolt
4. Tension pulley
5. Crankshaft timing pulley
6. Timing belt

Timing belt assembly

ing cover and the No. 4 cylinder is on TDC of the compression stroke.

5. Remove the starter and install the flywheel holding tool (J-35271).

6. Remove the crankshaft bolt, boss and pulley.

7. Remove the timing cover bolts and the timing cover.

8. Loosen the tension pulley bolt.

9. Insert an allen wrench into the tension pulley hexagonal hole and loosen the timing belt by turning the tension pulley clockwise.

10. Remove the timing belt.

NOTE: Inspect the timing belt for signs of cracking, abnormal wear and hardening. Never expose the belt to oil, sunlight or heat. Avoid excessive bending, twisting or stretching.

INSTALLATION

1. Position the woodruff key on the crankshaft followed by the crankshaft

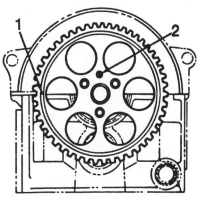

| 1 ALIGNMENT MARK | 2 DOWEL |

Alignment of the camshaft pulley

timing gear. Align the groove on the timing gear with the mark on the oil pump.

2. Align the camshaft timing gear mark with the upper surface of the cylinder head and the dowel pin in its uppermost position.

3. Place the timing belt arrow in the direction of the engine rotation and install the timing belt. Tighten the tension pulley bolt.

4. Turn the crankshaft two complete revolutions and realign the crankshaft timing gear groove with the mark on the oil pump.

5. Loosen the tension pulley bolt and apply tension to the belt with an allen wrench. Torque the pulley bolt to 37 ft. lbs. while holding the pulley stationary.

6. Adjust the valve clearances.

7. To complete the installation, reverse the removal procedure.

Cylinder Head Cover

REMOVAL & INSTALLATION

1. Disconnect the negative battery cable and remove the PCV hoses.

2. Remove the spark plug wires from the mounting clip.

3. Remove the ground wire from the right rear side of the head cover.

4. Support the engine and remove the right side engine mounting rubber, bolts and plate.

5. Remove the mounting bracket on the timing cover.

6. Remove the four bolts holding the timing cover and the two bolts holding the cylinder head cover.

7. Loosen the timing cover and remove the cylinder head cover.

NOTE: If the cylinder head cover sticks, strike the end of the cover with a rubber mallet or pry it from the cylinder head.

8. With the cover removed, clean the sealing surfaces of the cover and the cylinder head.

9. To install, apply sealer to the sealing surfaces and reverse the removal procedures.

10. Start the engine and check for leaks.

Camshaft

REMOVAL & INSTALLATION

1. Disconnect the negative battery cable.

2. Align the crankshaft pulley notch with the "O" degree mark on the timing cover.

3. Remove the cylinder head cover.

4. Remove the timing cover.

5. Loosen the camshaft timing gear bolts (DO NOT rotate the engine).

6. Loosen the timing belt tensioner and remove the timing belt from the camshaft timing gear.

7. Remove the rocker arm shaft/rocker arm assembly.

8. Remove the distributor bolt and the distributor.

9. Remove the camshaft and the camshaft seal.

10. To install, drive a new camshaft seal on the camshaft using the seal installation tool (J-35268), reverse the removal procedure, adjust the valves and the timing belt.

Piston & Rod Positioning

Install the piston and rod assemblies into the same cylinder bore, facing the same direction from which they were removed. Each piston has a front directional mark stamped on the top surface.

SPRINT

Engine

REMOVAL & INSTALLATION

1. Remove the battery cables.
2. Remove the hood, the battery, the battery tray, the air cleaner and the outside air duct.
3. Drain the cooling system, the engine and the transaxle.
4. Remove the radiator, heater and vacuum hoses from the engine.
5. Disconnect the cooling fan wires.
6. Remove the cooling fan, the shroud and the radiator as an assembly.
7. Remove the fuel hoses from the fuel pump.
8. Remove the brake booster hose from the intake manifold, the accelerator cable from the carburetor and the speed control cable from the transaxle.
9. Remove the clutch cable and the bracket from the transaxle.
10. Remove the necessary wiring from the engine and transaxle.
11. Remove the A/C adjusting bolt and the drive belt splash shield.
12. Raise and support the vehicle on jackstands.
13. Disconnect the exhaust pipe from the exhaust manifold.
14. Remove the A/C pivot bolt, the drive belt and the mounting bracket.
15. Disconnect the gearshift control shaft and extension rod at the transaxle.
16. Disconnect the ball joints.
17. Remove the axle shafts from the transaxle.
18. Remove the engine torque rods and the transaxle mount nut.
19. Lower the vehicle.
20. Remove the engine side mount and the mount nuts.
21. Connect a vertical hoist to the engine, then lift the engine and transaxle assembly from the vehicle.
22. To install, reverse the removal procedures. Refill the engine, the transaxle and the cooling system.

Intake Manifold

REMOVAL & INSTALLATION

1. Disconnect the negative battery cable.
2. Drain the cooling system.
3. Disconnect the air cleaner element, the EGR modulator, the warm air, the cool air, the 2nd air and the vacuum hoses from the air cleaner case.
4. Remove the air cleaner case, the

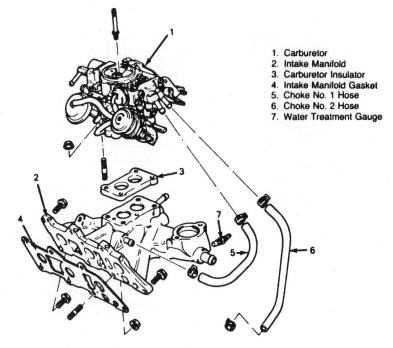

1. Carburetor
2. Intake Manifold
3. Carburetor Insulator
4. Intake Manifold Gasket
5. Choke No. 1 Hose
6. Choke No. 2 Hose
7. Water Treatment Gauge

Exploded view of the intake mainfold and carburetor assembly

electrical lead wires and the accelerator cable from the carburetor.
5. Disconnect the emission control and the fuel hoses from the carburetor.
6. Remove the water hoses from the choke housing.
7. Remove the electrical lead wires, the emission control, the coolant and the brake vacuum hoses from the intake manifold.
8. Remove the intake manifold from the cylinder head.
9. Clean the mating gasket surfaces.
10. To install, use new gaskets and reverse the removal procedures. Torque the intake manifold-to-cylinder head bolts to 14–20 ft. lbs. Refill the cooling system.

Exhaust Manifold

REMOVAL & INSTALLATION

1. Disconnect the negative battery cable.
2. Raise and support the vehicle on jackstands.
3. Remove the exhaust pipe at the exhaust manifold.
4. Remove the lower heat shield bolt and the 2nd air pipe at the exhaust manifold.
5. If equipped, remove the A/C drive belt and the lower adjusting bracket.
6. Lower the vehicle.

7. Remove the spark plug and the oxygen sensor wires.
8. Remove the hot air shroud from the exhaust manifold.
9. Remove the 2nd air valve hoses, the valve and the pipe from the exhaust manifold.
10. Remove the mounting bolts and the exhaust manifold.
11. Clean the gasket mating surfaces.
12. To install, use a new gasket and reverse the removal procedures. Torque the exhaust manifold fasteners to 14–20 ft. lbs. and the exhaust pipe to 30–43 ft. lbs.

Rocker Arms/Shafts

REMOVAL & INSTALLATION

1. Disconnect the negative battery cable.
2. Remove the air cleaner and the cylinder head cover.
3. Remove the distributor cap, then mark the position of the rotor and the distributor housing with the cylinder head. Remove the distributor and the case from the cylinder head.
4. Loosen the rocker arm valve adjusters, turn back the adjusting screws so that the rocker arms move freely.
5. Remove the rocker arm shaft retaining screws and pull out the shafts. Remove the rocker arms and springs from the cylinder head.

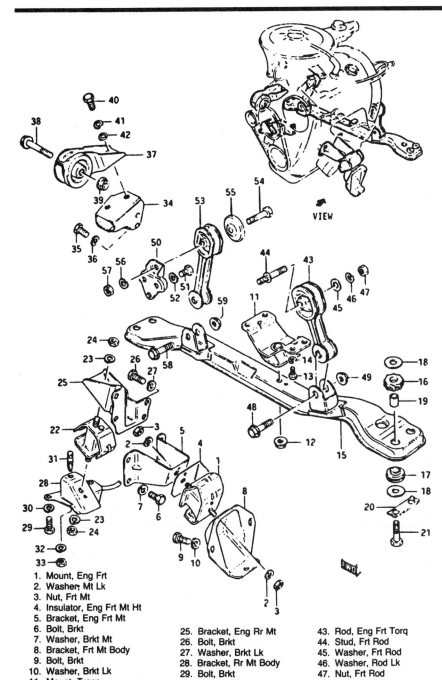

1. Mount, Eng Frt
2. Washer, Mt Lk
3. Nut, Frt Mt
4. Insulator, Eng Frt Mt Ht
5. Bracket, Eng Frt Mt
6. Bolt, Brkt
7. Washer, Brkt Mt
8. Bracket, Frt Mt Body
9. Bolt, Brkt
10. Washer, Brkt Lk
11. Mount, Trans
12. Nut, Trans Mt
13. Bolt (M8 × 1.25 × 20)
14. Washer
15. Member, Trans Mt
16. Cushion, Mt Mbr Upr
17. Cushion, Mt Mbr Lwr
18. Washer, Mt Mbr
19. Spacer, Mbr
21. Bolt, Mbr
22. Mount, Eng Rr
23. Washer, Mt
24. Nut (M10 × 1.25 × 8)

25. Bracket, Eng Rr Mt
26. Bolt, Brkt
27. Washer, Brkt Lk
28. Bracket, Rr Mt Body
29. Bolt, Brkt
30. Washer, Brkt Lk
31. Stud, Brkt
32. Washer, Brkt Lk
33. Nut, Brkt
34. Bracket, Eng Si Mt
35. Bolt, Si Brkt
36. Washer, Brkt Lk
37. Bushing, Eng Si Mt
38. Bolt, Mt Bush
39. Nut, Mt Bush
41. Washer, Lk
42. Washer, Bush

43. Rod, Eng Frt Torq
44. Stud, Frt Rod
45. Washer, Frt Rod
46. Washer, Rod Lk
47. Nut, Frt Rod
48. Bolt, Frt Rod
49. Nut, Frt Rod
50. Bracket, Rr Torq Rod
51. Bolt, Rod Brkt
52. Washer, Brkt Lk
53. Rod, Eng Rr Torq
54. Bolt, Rr Rod
55. Plate, Rr Torq Stopper
56. Washer, Rr Rod Lk
57. Nut, Rr Rod
58. Bolt, Rr Rod
59. Nut, Rr Rod

Engine mounting

NOTE: Make a note of the differences between the rocker arm shafts. The intake shaft's stepped end is 0.55 inch, which faces the camshaft pulley; the exhaust shaft's stepped end is 0.59 inch, which faces the distributor.

6. To install, use new gaskets and reverse the removal procedures. Torque the rocker arm shaft screws to

7–9 ft. lbs. Adjust the valve clearances. Check and/or adjust the ignition timing.

Valve Clearance

ADJUSTMENT

1. Remove the air cleaner and the cylinder head cover.
2. Rotate the crankshaft clockwise and align the "V" mark on the crankshaft pulley with the "0" mark on the timing plate.
3. Remove the distributor cap and to make sure that the rotor is facing the fuel pump, if not, rotate the crankshaft 860°.
4. Check and/or adjust the valves of the No. 1 cylinder.

NOTE: On a COLD engine, adjust the valves to 0.006 in. (intake) and 0.008 in. (exhaust). On a HOT engine, adjust the valves to 0.010 in. (intake) and 0.012 in. (exhaust).

5. After adjusting the valves of the No. 1 cylinder, rotate the crankshaft pulley 240° (the "V" mark should align with the lower left oil pump mounting bolt, when facing the crankshaft pulley) and adjust the valves of the No. 3 cylinder.
6. After adjusting the valves of the No. 3 cylinder, rotate the crankshaft pulley 240° (the "V" mark should align with the lower right oil pump mounting bolt, when facing the crankshaft pulley) and adjust the valves of the No. 2 cylinder.
7. After the valves have been adjusted, install the removed items by reversing the removal procedures. Torque the valve adjustment locknuts to 11–13 ft. lbs.

Cylinder Head

REMOVAL & INSTALLATION

1. Disconnect the negative battery cable.
2. Drain the cooling system.
3. Remove the air cleaner and the cylinder head cover.
4. Remove the distributor cap, then mark the position of the rotor and the distributor housing with the cylinder head. Remove the distributor and the case from the cylinder head.
5. Remove the accelerator cable from the carburetor. Remove the emission control and the coolant hoses from the carburetor/intake manifold.
6. Remove the electrical lead connectors from the carburetor/intake manifold and the lead wire from the oxygen sensor.

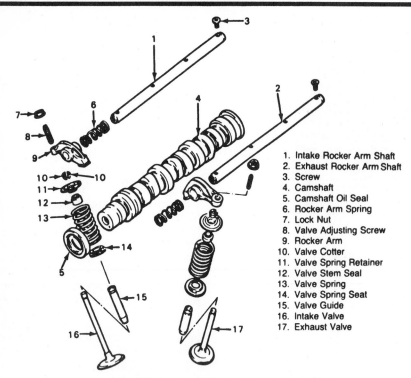

1.	Intake Rocker Arm Shaft
2.	Exhaust Rocker Arm Shaft
3.	Screw
4.	Camshaft
5.	Camshaft Oil Seal
6.	Rocker Arm Spring
7.	Lock Nut
8.	Valve Adjusting Screw
9.	Rocker Arm
10.	Valve Cotter
11.	Valve Spring Retainer
12.	Valve Stem Seal
13.	Valve Spring
14.	Valve Spring Seat
15.	Valve Guide
16.	Intake Valve
17.	Exhaust Valve

Exploded view of the rocker arm assembly

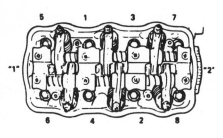

"1" Camshaft Pulley Side
"2" Distributor Side

Cylinder head torque sequence

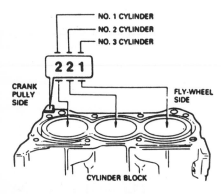

Cylinder Identification

7. Remove the fuel hoses from the fuel pump and the pump from the cylinder head.

8. Remove the brake vacuum hose from the intake manifold.

9. Remove the crankshaft pulley, the outside cover, the timing belt and

the tensioner from the front of the engine.

10. Remove the exhaust and the 2nd air pipes from the exhaust manifold.

11. Remove the exhaust/intake manifolds and the engine side mount from the cylinder head.

12. Loosen the rocker arm valve adjusters, turn back the adjusting screws so that the rocker arms move freely. Remove the rocker arm shaft retaining screws and pull out the shafts. Remove the rocker arms and springs from the cylinder head.

NOTE: Make a note of the differences between the rocker arm shafts. The intake shaft's stepped end is 0.55 inch, which faces the camshaft pulley; the exhaust shaft's stepped end is 0.59 inch, which faces the distributor.

13. Remove the mounting bolts and the cylinder head from the engine.

14. To install, use new gaskets and reverse the removal procedures. Torque the cylinder head bolts to 46–50.5 ft. lbs. and the rocker arm shaft screws to 7–9 ft. lbs. Adjust the valve clearances. Refill the cooling system. Check and/or adjust the ignition timing.

Timing Cover, Timing Belt And Tensioner

REMOVAL

1. Disconnect the negative battery cable.

2. Loosen the water pump pulley bolts and the alternator adjusting bolt.

3. If equipped, remove the A/C compressor adjusting bolt.

4. Raise and support the vehicle on jackstands.

5. Remove the drive belt splash shield, the right fender plug and the drive belts.

6. Remove the crankshaft and the water pump pulleys.

7. Remove the bolts from the bottom of the belt cover.

8. Lower the vehicle.

9. Remove the bolts from the top of the belt cover and the cover.

10. Remove the cylinder head cover and loosen the rocker arm adjusting bolts.

11. Remove the distributor cap.

12. Loosen the tensioner pulley and adjusting stud bolt.

13. Remove the timing belt, the tensioner, the tensioner plate and spring.

INSTALLATION

1. Install the tensioner assembly but DO NOT tighten the bolts.

2. Turn the camshaft pulley clockwise and align the mark on the pulley with the "V" mark on the inside cover.

3. Using a 17mm wrench, turn the crankshaft clockwise and align the punch mark on the crankshaft pulley with the arrow mark on the oil pump.

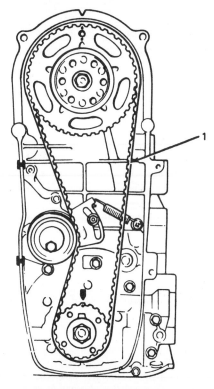

1. DRIVE SIDE OF BELT
View of the timing belt assembly

4. With the timing marks aligned, install the timing belt so that there is no belt slack on the right side (facing the engine) of the engine, apply belt tension with the tensioner pulley.

5. Turn the crankshaft 1 rotation clockwise to remove the belt slack. Torque the tensioner stud, first, and then the tensioner bolt to 17–21 ft. lbs.

6. To complete the installation, use new gaskets and reverse the removal procedures. Torque the crankshaft pulley to 7–9 ft. lbs. Adjust the valve clearances.

Camshaft

REMOVAL & INSTALLATION

1. Refer to "Timing Cover, Timing Belt and Tensioner Removal & Installation" procedures in this section and remove the timing belt.

2. Remove the air cleaner, the cylinder head cover, the distributor and the distributor case. Remove the rocker arm shafts and the rocker arms.

3. Remove the fuel pump and the push rod from the cylinder head.

4. Using a spanner wrench tool J–34836 to hold the camshaft pulley, remove the camshaft pulley bolt, the pulley, the alignment pin and the inside cover.

5. Carefully slide the camshaft from the rear of the cylinder head.

6. Clean the gasket mounting surfaces. Check for wear and/or damage, replace the parts as necessary.

7. To install, use new gaskets/seals and reverse the removal procedures. Torque the camshaft pulley bolt to 41–46 ft. lbs. Adjust the valve clearances and check the timing.

Piston And Connecting Rod Positioning

There are two sizes of pistons available: a No. 1 and a No. 2 (indicating the outside diameter of the piston), the numbers are stamped on top of each piston. An arrow is also stamped on

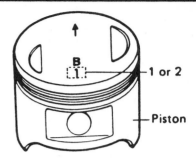

Piston identification

top of each piston, indicating the front of the engine.

A number is stamped at the front right of the engine block, on the cylinder head gasket surface. The number indicates of the pistons sizes, in order, ranging from the front-to-rear cylinders. Install the correct diameter piston (with the arrow facing the front of the engine) and the connecting rod (with the oil hole facing the intake manifold) into the correct cylinder bore.

NOVA

Engine
REMOVAL & INSTALLATION

1. Remove the battery cover and battery. Drain coolant into a clean container from both radiator and block drain cocks.

2. Drain the engine crankcase and transaxle fluid.

3. Remove the hood (use an assistant).

4. Remove the air cleaner and associated ducting.

5. Drain and remove the coolant reservoir tank.

6. Remove the radiator and shroud as described earlier in this section.

7. Disconnect the throttle and automatic transaxle linkages at the carburetor.

8. Disconnect the following wires:
   a. Vacuum Control Valve connector
   b. Oxygen sensor connector
   c. Back-up light switch connector on manual transaxle-equipped cars
   d. Neutral safety switch connector on automatic transaxle-equipped cars
   e. Water temperature switch connector
   f. Distributor connector
   g. Starter wiring
   h. Ground cables at the engine and transmission

   i. Oil pressure switch connector
   j. A/C compressor clutch connector (if A/C equipped)
   k. Alternator wiring
   l. Water temperature sending unit connector
   m. Electric (carburetor) bowl vent control valve
   n. CMH relay connector (located in the air cleaner)
   o. Fuel cut solenoid connector

9. Label and then disconnect all vacuum hoses running between the engine and firewall or fender well mounted accessories.

10. Disconnect both fuel hoses at the pump.

11. Disconnect the heater hose at the water pump inlet housing and the cooling water hose at the rear plate of the cylinder head.

12. Loosen the adjusting and mounting bolts for the power steering pump (if equipped) and then remove the belt. Then, remove these bolts, pull the air pump out of the way and suspend it.

13. Loosen the A/C compressor belt tension adjusting bolt (on cars so-equipped) and remove the belt. Then, remove the four mounting bolts and remove the compressor, suspending it out of the way with hoses still connected.

14. Disconnect the speedometer cable at the transaxle.

15. Working on the clutch slave cylinder:
   a. Remove the clip from the hydraulic line bracket
   b. Disconnect the mounting bracket at the transaxle
   c. Remove the two mounting bolts for the slave cylinder and then move it out of the way, suspending it with the hydraulic line still connected.

16. Disconnect the shift cable by removing the clip and washers and then disconnecting the cable at the outer shift lever or outer selector lever.

17. Raise the vehicle and support it securely.

18. Disconnect the exhaust pipe at the manifold. Then, disconnect the front and rear mounts at the crossmember by first removing the two bolt covers and then removing the two bolts from each mounting. Then, remove the center crossmember (supporting the engine).

19. To disconnect the driveshafts from the transaxle, remove the nuts and bolts. Have someone depress the brake pedal while you loosen the nuts.

20. Lower the vehicle to the ground. Attach a chain hoist to the lift bracket on the engine keeping the wiring harness in front of the chain. Put enough tension on the chain to support the engine.

21. Remove the right hand mount through bolt; then remove the left hand mount through bolt; remove the left hand mount from the transaxle by removing the two bolts. Remove the mounting bracket from the transaxle.

22. Lift the engine/transaxle assembly out of the engine compartment, proceeding slowly in order to clear the right side mount, the power steering housing and neutral safety switch. Make sure wiring, hoses, and cables are clear of the engine.

23. Mount the engine/transaxle assembly on a stand. Then, remove the starter, and engine rear plate. On automatic transmission-equipped cars, remove the six torque converter mounting bolts by turning the crankshaft to gain access to each bolt from underneath. Hold the crankshaft pulley bolt with a wrench to remove these bolts without turning the crankshaft. Then, remove the transaxle.

24. Install the engine in reverse order. After reinstalling the transaxle, starter, and rear plate, position the engine carefully in place. Lower the engine into position with the transaxle tilted downward, making sure to clear the left side mounting.

25. Align the mounts as well as possible; then precisely align the right side mount and bracket and install the through-bolt without installing the nut. Then, install the left hand mounting bracket onto the transaxle. Install the left hand mount onto the bracket, align the left hand bracket with the body bracket and install the mounting bolt and nut hand tight. Disconnect the lifting chain from the engine.

26. Support the vehicle up in the air in a secure manner. Reverse the remaining removal procedures to install. Observe the following torque figures:
  a. Driveshaft bolts — 27 ft. lbs.
  b. Engine mount center crossmember — 29 ft. lbs.
  c. Exhaust pipe-to-manifold — 46 ft. lbs.
  d. Power steering pump mounting bolts — 29 ft. lbs.
  e. Power steering pump adjusting bolt — 32 ft. lbs.
Make sure the power steering pump belt runs in all three pulley grooves. Replenish all fluids with approved type at the proper level. Then start the engine and correct any leaks.

Combination Manifold

REMOVAL & INSTALLATION

1. Remove the air cleaner assembly and hoses.
2. Disconnect the accelerator and choke linkages from the carburetor. If

Intake and Exhaust Manifold

Combination manifold and gasket

necessary, label and then disconnect all vacuum lines going to the carburetor. Disconnect the fuel lines, draining any fuel into a metal container. Disconnect the fuel line from the fuel pump at the pump, as well. Disconnect the electric lines.

3. Disconnect or remove any emission control hardware that is in the way; then, remove the mounting bolts, and remove the carburetor from the manifold.

4. Remove the EFE gasket. Remove the vacuum line and the dashpot bracket. Remove the carburetor heat shield.

5. Raise the vehicle and support it securely. Then, disconnect the exhaust pipe at the manifold, the pipe bracket at the engine, and the hose at the converter pipe. Lower the vehicle.

6. Disconnect the brake vacuum hose. Remove the accelerator and throttle cable brackets.

7. Working from the center outward, remove the manifold retaining nuts in several stages so tension is gradually released.

8. Remove the intake/exhaust manifold from the head as a unit.

9. To install, make sure both gasket surfaces are clean and position a new gasket on the head. Then, position the manifold and install retaining nuts just hand tight. Tighten them alternately is several stages to the specification shown in the Torque Specifications Chart. Reverse the remaining removal procedures. When installing the carburetor, clean both gasket surfaces, use a new gasket and tighten bolts alternately and evenly. When the installation is complete, start the engine and check for leaks.

Rocker Arm and Shaft Assembly

REMOVAL & INSTALLATION

1. Remove the air cleaner and valve cover.

2. Remove the five rocker shaft assembly retaining bolts in several stages — note that they MUST be loosened in the correct sequence. That is: front bolt first; rear bolt second; forward-center bolt third; rearward-center bolt fourth; and center bolt fifth.

3. Remove the rocker arm and shaft assembly.

4. Inspect for wear by attempting to rock the rocker levers on the shaft. If negligible motion is felt, wear is acceptable. If there is noticeable wear, note order of assembly and the fact that there are two types of rockers, and then remove bolts and slide rockers, springs and pedestals off the shaft.

5. Measure the inside diameter of each rocker lever with a dial indicator; measure the shaft diameter at rocker wear areas with a micrometer. Subtract the shaft diameter from the rocker inside diameter; the difference must not exceed 0.0024 in. Replace rockers and, if necessary, the shaft to correct clearance problems.

6. Also inspect the rocker camshaft follower pads. If the surfaces are worn irregularly or are rough replace the parts or grind them smooth.

7. Assemble the pedestals, rockers, springs and bolts in exact reverse order. Oil all wear surfaces thoroughly with clean engine oil. Note that rocker shaft oil holes MUST face downward. Install the assembly on the head and start the bolts, tightening them finger tight. Torque in three stages going in this sequence each pass: center bolt first, center/rearward bolt second, center/forward bolt third, rear bolt fourth, and front bolt fifth. Final torque figure is 18 ft. lbs. Adjust the valves as described below. Install the valve cover using new gaskets and seals and the air cleaner.

Valve Clearance Adjustment

1. The valve clearances must be set with the engine hot. If clearances are being set because parts have been disassembled and clearances changed, you should set the valves cold and then reset them with the engine hot. The best procedure is to drive the car a few miles (well past the point where the temperature gauge reaches normal readings) in order to have the engine as warm as possible throughout the procedure. Then, remove the air cleaner and valve cover.

2. Turn the engine over by using a socket wrench on the pulley retaining bolt until the timing marks on the front pulley indicate TDC and both No. 1 (front) cylinder rocker arms are loose. Note that you must adjust the intake valves to one clearance and ex-

haust valves to another. Half the valves are adjusted with the crankshaft in one position; then the other half are adjusted with the crankshaft tuned 360 degrees. It's best to adjust all the intake valves for the first adjustment sequence, then switch feeler gauges and adjust all the exhaust valves. Proceed in the same way for the next sequence. Intake valves are adjusted to 0.008 in. and exhaust to 0.012 in.

4. To adjust each valve, first slide the feeler gauge straight between the rocker and valve tip. The surfaces will just touch, giving a VERY slight pull on the gauge. If the gauge is tight or won't fit, or if the gauge slides with no pull at all, loosen the adjusting nut. Tighten the adjusting stud with a screwdriver to reduce the clearance or loosen it to increase the clearance. Don't tighten the stud past the point where you can feel it start to touch the gauge. Once clearance is correct (gauge has a very slight pull), hold the stud position while you tighten the nut. Then, recheck the clearance and readjust if necessary. On the first sequence, you can adjust the No. 1 and 2 cylinder intakes and No. 1 and 3 cylinder exhaust valves. You can determine whether valves are intakes or exhausts by aligning them with manifold intake or exhaust tubes. The sequence from front to rear is: intake, exhaust; exhaust, intake; intake, exhaust; exhaust, intake.

5. Once the first adjustment sequence has been completed, proceed with the second. Turn the engine crankshaft just 360 degrees until the TDC marks again align. Then, proceed with the adjustment for the intakes on No. 3 and 4 cylinders and the exhausts on No. 2 and 4.

6. Install the valve cover using new gaskets and seals. Install the air cleaner.

Cylinder Head

REMOVAL & INSTALLATION

1. Disconnect the negative battery connector.

2. Drain the coolant into a clean container, opening both the radiator and cylinder block drain cocks.

3. Remove the air cleaner and all connecting hoses. First label and then disconnect all vacuum hoses.

4. Raise the vehicle and support it securely. Drain the engine oil. Disconnnect the exhaust pipe at the manifold. Remove the exhaust pipe bracket at the engine. Remove the hose at the converter pipe.

5. If the car has power steering, loosen the power steering pump pivot

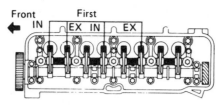

Valve adjustment sequence—step one

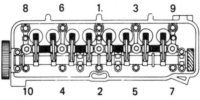

Valve adjustment sequence—step two

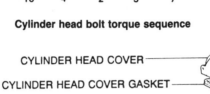

Cylinder head bolt torque sequence

bolt. Then, lower the vehicle to the ground.

5. Disconnect the accelerator and throttle cables at the carburetor and at the cable bracket.

6. Disconnect wiring at the cowl, oxygen sensor, and distributor.

7. Disconnect the fuel hoses at the fuel pump.

8. Disconnect the upper radiator hose at the water outlet. Then, remove the water outlet from the head. Remove the heater hose.

9. Remove the power steering pump adjusting bracket, if the car has power steering.

10. Turn the engine over with a socket wrench on the crankshaft so it is at Top Dead Center and both No. 1 cylinder rocker arms are loose. Label the spark plug wires as to their location in the distributor cap. Disconnect the vacuum hoses, electrical connections and spark plug wires at the distributor and remove the distributor.

11. Remove the PCV valve. Remove the wiring harness that passes over the valve cover.

12. Remove the upper timing belt cover bolts. Remove the cylinder head

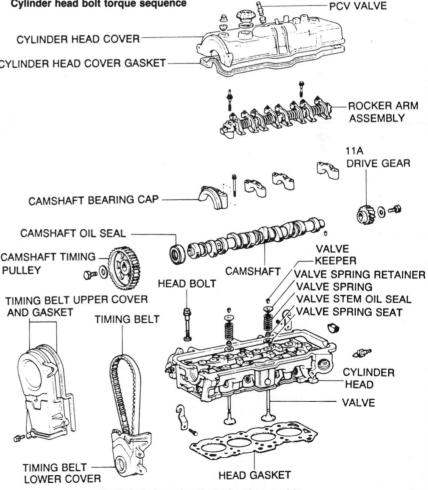

Exploded view of cylinder head assembly

cover and gasket. Remove the alternator belt.

13. Remove the water pump pulley bolts and remove the pulley. Then, remove the upper timing cover and its gasket.

14. Remove both remaining timing covers. Then, matchmark the timing belt and both sprockets for reassembly in the same position; mark an arrow on the belt for rotation in the same direction, also.

15. Loosen the idler pulley bolt. Move it so as to release the timing belt tension, and then snug the idler pulley bolt back up. Then, remove the timing belt. Avoid twisting or bending it.

16. Loosen the head bolts in reverse of the torque sequence shown, in three stages, and then remove them. Then, lift the head directly off the block. If it is necessary to pry the head off the block, use a bar between the head and the projection provided on top of the block.

NOTE: Do not pry except at the projection provided. Be careful not to damage the block deck or cylinder head sealing surface.

17. To install the cylinder head, reverse the removal procedure, referring to the "Timing Belt Removal & Installation" procedure. Install and torque the head bolts in the order shown. Observe the following torque figures:
   a. Timing gear idler bolt – 22–32 ft. lbs.
   b. Head bolts – 43 ft. lbs.
Adjust the valves with the engine cold, then replace the valve cover. Run the engine until it is hot and then readjust the valves.

Timing Belt Covers

REMOVAL & INSTALLATION

1. Disconnect the negative battery cable.

2. Loosen the water pump pulley bolts and then remove the alternator/ water pump drive belt. If the car has power steering, remove the steering pump drive belt.

3. Remove the bolts and then remove the water pump pulley. Drain the cooling system.

4. Disconnect the upper radiator hose at the water pump outlet. Then, label and disconnect all vacuum hoses that are in the way.

5. If the car has air conditioning, loosen the idler pulley mounting bolt. Loosen the adjusting nut and then remove the A/C drive belt. Then, remove the idler pulley and its adjusting bolt. Remove the alternator.

6. Remove the crankshaft pulley mounting bolt and remove the pulley with a puller.

7. Remove the bolts from the upper timing cover that are accessible from above. Then, raise and support the car securely and remove the lower bolts from this cover and remove the upper cover.

8. Remove the mounting bolts from the lower timing belt cover and then remove that cover and gasket.

9. Lower the vehicle back to its normal position. Finally, remove the center cover bolts, the cover, and gasket.

10. Install in reverse order, torquing the crankshaft pulley bolt to 80–94 ft. lbs. and the center engine mount bolts to 29 ft. lbs.

Front Crankshaft Oil Seal

REMOVAL & INSTALLATION

1. Remove the No. 1 (top) timing belt cover as described earlier. Remove the air conditioning belt if the car has A/C.

2. Turn the crankshaft clockwise until No. 1 cylinder is at Top Center firing position (air is expelled from the spark plug hole as the piston approaches Top Center).

3. Remove the right side under cover. Remove the flywheel cover.

4. Remove the crankshaft pulley with a puller.

5. Remove the No. 2 (lower) timing cover and its gasket. Mark the locations of both timing pulleys and the rotating direction of the belt.

6. Loosen the idler pulley bolt, move the idler so as to release belt tension, and then retighten the bolt to retain the tensioner in the released position.

7. Remove the timing belt guide and then remove the belt from the crankshaft timing pulley. Then, slide the pulley off the crankshaft.

8. Pry out the oil seal from the front using a flat bladed screwdriver.

9. Tap a new seal into the recess using an installer such as GM special tool No. J-35403 or equivalent and a hammer. Make sure the seal sits squarely in the bore; it must not be cocked. Coat the sealing surfaces with Multipurpose grease.

10. Reassemble all parts removed in reverse order. Make sure to properly adjust the timing belt as described in the next procedure.

Timing Belt and Sprockets

REMOVAL & INSTALLATION

1. Remove the timing belt covers as described above. Set the engine to TDC No. 1 firing position as described in the procedure for removing the covers above.

2. If you may be reusing the timing belt, mark an arrow showing direction of rotation and then matchmark the belt and both pulleys.

3. Loosen the idler pulley mounting bolt and push the idler pulley to the left as far as it will go and hold it; then, retighten the mounting bolt.

4. Remove the timing belt. Then, you may remove the idler pulley mounting bolt and the pulley and return spring if they require service. If the sprockets must be removed, simply pull the crankshaft sprocket and key off. Loosen the camshaft pulley bolt with a socket wrench, using an open

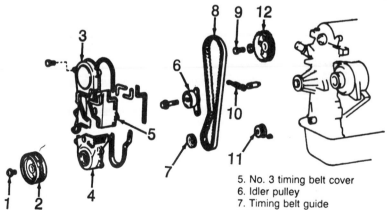

1. 87 ft. lbs.
2. Crankshaft pulley
3. No. 1 timing belt cover
4. NO. 2 timing belt cover

5. No. 3 timing belt cover
6. Idler pulley
7. Timing belt guide
8. Timing belt
9. 34 ft. lbs.
10. Tensioner spring
11. Crankshaft timing belt pulley
12. Camshaft timing belt pulley

Exploded view of timing belt assembly

end wrench on the camshaft portion with flats to keep the camshaft from turning. Install these sprockets in reverse order, torquing the camshaft pulley retaining bolt to 34 ft. lbs.

5. Be careful not to bend, twist, or turn the belt inside out. Keep grease or water from contacting it as you handle it. Inspect the belt for cracks or missing teeth, or general wear, and replace it if necessary.

6. Install the idler pulley, return spring and bolt, with the pulley in the retracted position. Install the belt. Align timing marks earlier if the belt is being reused. Point the directional arrow in the right direction. Otherwise, make sure timing marks on both pulleys align with the timing marks on the engine.

7. Loosen the bolt mounting the idler pulley so the spring tensions the belt, then install the crankshaft pulley bolt and turn it with a wrench so the crankshaft turns just two revolutions forward. Recheck the valve timing. If it is incorrect, adjust the position of the belt and then repeat this step.

8. Torque the idler pulley mounting bolt to 27 ft. lbs.

9. Measure the belt deflection with about 4.5 lbs. pressure; it must be 0.24–0.28 in. If necessary, reposition the idler pulley to correct the tension.

10. Install the timing covers and front crankshaft pulley as described above.

Camshaft

REMOVAL & INSTALLATION

1. Follow the procedure for cylinder head removal above up to the point where the valve covers and timing covers have been removed, but leave the timing belt in position (through Step 14).

2. Remove the distributor.

3. Remove the fuel pump.

4. Remove the distributor gear bolt.

5. Unbolt and remove the rocker shaft assembly.

6. Loosen the idler pulley mount bolt and push the pulley as far to the left as it will go. Then, retightn the bolt to hold the pulley there. Now, gently pull the belt off the camshaft timing gear, holding it up so it will not come out of mesh with the crankshaft pulley. Support the belt securely so it will remain in mesh as you work. Also, be careful not to get oil on the belt or drop anything down inside the valve cover.

7. Use a large open-end wrench to

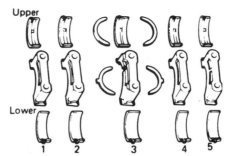

Correct positioning of crankshaft bearing shells. Note that the grooved shells must be at the top to lubricate the connecting rods

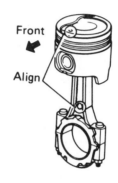

Piston alignment marks

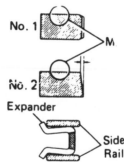

Piston ring installation. Note that the No. 2 compression ring taper faces up and that both compression rings are marked on top. Proper installation of the oil ring and side rail are also shown

hold the camshaft while you remove the sprocket bolt. The flats for the wrench are located between the first and second cam lobes. Remove the sprocket. Then, loosen the distributor drive gear bolt, keeping the camshaft from turning in the same way.

8. Loosen the camshaft bearing cap bolts a little at a time and alternately, using the proper sequence: front cap first, rear cap second, foreward-center cap third, and rearward-center cap

last. Once bolt tension is gone, remove the bolts and then the caps, keeping the caps in proper order and in the same direction (you may want to number and arrow them).

9. Remove the camshaft oil seal and the camshaft from the head. Remove the distributor drive gear.

10. To install the camshaft, first install the distributor drive gear and plate washer and bolt.

11. Coat all bearing surfaces with clean engine oil, and then put the camshaft into position. Install bearing caps Nos. 2, 3 and 4 in proper positions and direction.

12. Grease the inside surface of the oil seal and liquid sealer to the outside edge and then slip the seal onto the camshaft. Make sure it is on straight, as a crooked seal will leak.

13. Apply liquid sealer to the bottom surfaces of the No. 1 bearing cap and then put it into position. Install all cap bolts finger tight.

14. Torque the bearing cap bolts alternately and evenly. Repeat the basic sequence, which is the reverse of the removal sequence, until the torque of 9 ft. lbs. is reached. The torquing sequence is: front-center first, rear-center second, front third, and rear last.

15. Recheck the camshaft thrust clearance at the front of the camshaft with a dial indicator. Normal range is 0.0031–0.0071 in. with a limit of 0.0098 in. Then, torque the distributor drive gear bolt to 22 ft. lbs. Install the remaining components in the reverse of the "Cylinder Head Removal & Installation" procedure above.

Piston and Connecting Rod Positioning

Note the locations of main bearings. Upper bearings are all grooved for distribution of oil to the connecting rods, while the lower mains are all plain. Thrust is taken by washers on either side of the center (No. 3) bearing cap, with tabs on the lower washers which fit into notches in the lower cap. Note that both the piston crowns and rod sides have marks that must both face forward when the engine is finally assembled. Note also the sequence of ring installation; in fact the upper outside diameter of the No. 2 compression ring is smaller than the lower O.D., while the No. 1 compression ring has an even, barrel face. Note also the positioning of the oil ring expander and side rail.

CORSICA AND BERETTA

Engine

REMOVAL & INSTALLATION

2.0 Liter Engines

1. Disconnect the battery cables; negative first. Remove the battery from the vehicle.
2. Drain the cooling system. Remove the air intake hose.
3. Disconnect the T.V. and accelerator cables at the throttle body. Disconnect the ECM harness at the engine.
4. Remove the exhaust manifold shield. Disconnect and tag the engine wiring harness at the firewall.
5. Remove the windshield washer bottle. Remove the serpentine belt.
6. Disconnect and plug the fuel hoses. Raise and safely support the vehicle.
7. Remove the right side inner fender splash shield.
8. Remove the A/C compressor but do not disconnect the refrigerant lines. Support the compressor so it will not interfere with the engine.
9. Remove the flywheel splash shield. Disconnect and tag the starter wires.
10. Remove the front starter brace and remove the starter.
11. On automatic transaxle vehicles, remove the torque converter bolts and push the converter back into the transaxle.
12. Remove the crankshaft pulley using tool J–24420, or equivalent.
13. Remove the oil filter. Remove the engine to transaxle support bracket.
14. Disconnect the right rear engine mount. Disconnect the exhaust pipe at the manifold.
15. Disconnect the exhaust pipe at the center hanger and loosen the muffler hanger.
16. Remove the T.V. and shift cable bracket. Remove the two lower engine to transaxle bolts.
17. Lower the vehicle. Disconnect the T.V. and accelerator cable bracket on the intake manifold.
18. Remove the right front engine mount nuts. Remove the alternator.
19. Disconnect and plug the brake lines at the master cylinder and remove and support the master cylinder.
20. Install an engine lift on the engine.
21. Remove the right front engine mount bracket. Remove the remaining engine to transaxle mounting bolts.
22. Lift the engine slightly and disconnect the power steering pump.
23. Remove the engine from the vehicle.

24. Installation is the reverse of the removal. Install the power steering pump while lowering the engine into the vehicle.
25. To insure proper engine alignment, loosely install the engine mounts and raise the engine slightly. Then, torque the engine to engine mount bolts to 40 ft. lbs. and the mount nuts to 20 ft. lbs. Torque the engine to transaxle bolts to 55 ft. lbs.

2.8 Liter Engines

1. Disconnect the battery cables; negative first. Remove the battery from the vehicle.
2. Remove the air cleaner, air inlet hose and mass air flow sensor.
3. Drain the cooling system. Remove the exhaust manifold-crossover assembly.
4. Remove the serpentine belt and tensioner. Remove the power steering pump.
5. Disconnect the radiator hose at the engine.
6. Disconnect the T.V. and accelerator cables from the bracket at the plenum.
7. Remove the alternator. Disconnect and tag the wiring harness at the engine.
8. Disconnect and plug the fuel hoses. Remove the coolant overflow and bypass hoses at the engine.
9. Disconnect the canister purge hose at the canister. Disconnect and tag all necessary vacuum hoses.
10. Support the engine with engine holding fixture J–28467, or equivalent.
11. Raise and safely support the vehicle.
12. Remove the right inner fender splash shield. Remove the harmonic balancer.
13. Remove the flywheel cover. Disconnect and tag the starter wires and remove the starter.
14. Disconnect the wires at the oil pressure sending unit.
15. Remove the A/C compressor mounting bolts and support the compressor so it will not interfere with the engine. Do not disconnect the refrigerant lines.
16. Disconnect the exhaust pipe at the rear of the manifold.
17. On automatic transaxle vehicles, remove the flywheel to torque converter bolts and push the converter into the transaxle.
18. Remove the front and rear engine mount bolts and remove the mounts.
19. Remove the intermediate shaft bracket at the engine.

20. Disconnect the shifter cable at the transaxle.
21. Remove the lower engine to transaxle bolts and lower the vehicle.
22. Disconnect the heater hoses at the engine. Install an engine lift.
23. Remove the engine holding fixture. Support the transaxle with a floor jack.
24. Remove the upper engine to transaxle bolts. Remove the front mount bolts and transaxle mounting bracket.
25. Remove the engine from the vehicle.
26. Installation is the reverse of the removal.
25. To insure proper engine alignment, loosely install the engine mounts and raise the engine slightly. Then, torque the engine mounting bolts to 65 ft. lbs. Torque the engine to transaxle bolts to 55 ft. lbs.

Cylinder Head

REMOVAL & INSTALLATION

2.0 Liter Engines

1. Disconnect the negative battery cable.
2. Drain the cooling system. Remove the TBI cover.
3. Raise and safely support the vehicle.
4. Disconnect the exhaust pipe from the exhaust manifold.
5. Lower the vehicle. Disconnect the heater hose at the intake manifold.
6. Disconnect the T.V. and accelerator cable bracket.
7. Disconnect and tag the vacuum lines at the intake manifold and thermostat.
8. Disconnect the accelerator linkage at the TBI.
9. Disconnect and tag the engine wiring.
10. Disconnect the upper radiator hose at the thermostat. Remove the serpentine belt.
11. Remove the power steering pump and support it out of the way.
12. Disconnect and plug the fuel lines. Remove the alternator with the wires attached and support it out of the way.
13. Remove the alternator rear brace.
14. Remove the rocker arm cover. Remove the rocker arms and push rods. Keep all valve train parts in the order that they were removed.
15. Starting with the outer bolts, remove the cylinder head attaching bolts.

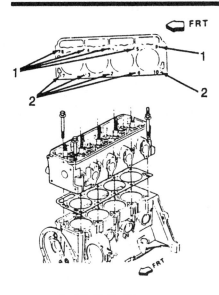

1. 73–83 ft. lbs.
2. 62–70 ft. lbs.

Cylinder head bolt torque sequence-2.0 Liter engine

16. Inspect and clean the surfaces of the cylinder head and block carefully. Make sure that the threads on the cylinder head bolts and the threads in the block are clean.

17. Coat the new head gasket with a proper sealer and install the gasket on the dowl pins on the block.

18. Install the cylinder head and tighten the head bolts hand tight.

19. Following the correct sequence, torque the head bolts to the proper specifications.

20. Install the push rods and rocker arms in the same order they were removed. Torque the rocker arm nuts to 7–11 ft. lbs. The remainder of the installation is the reverse of the removal.

2.8 Liter Engines

LEFT SIDE

1. Drain the cooling system. Remove the rocker cover.

2. Remove the intake manifold. Disconnect the exhaust crossover at the right exhaust manifold.

3. Disconnect the oil level indicator tube bracket.

4. Loosen the rocker arms nuts enough to remove the push rods.

5. Starting with the outer bolts, remove the cylinder head bolts. Remove the cylinder head with the exhaust manifold.

6. Clean and inspect the surfaces of the cylinder head, block and intake manifold. Clean the threads in the block and the threads on the bolts.

7. Align the new gasket over the dowels on the block with the note "This Side Up" facing the cylinder head.

HEAD TORQUE SEQUENCE

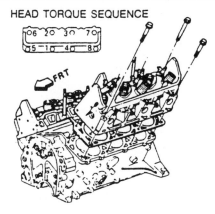

Cylinder head bolt torque sequence-2.8 Liter engine

8. Install the cylinder head and exhaust manifold crossover assembly on the engine.

9. Coat the cylinder head bolts with a proper sealer and install the bolts hand tight.

10. Following the correct sequence, torque the bolts to 33 ft. lbs. After all bolts are torqued to 33 ft. lbs., rotate the torque wrench another 90° or ¼ turn. This will apply the correct torque to the bolts.

11. Install the push rods in the same order that they were removed in. Torque the rocker arm nuts to 14–20 ft. lbs.

12. Install the intake manifold using a new gasket and following the correct sequence, torque the bolts to the correct specification.

13. The remainder of the installation is the reverse of the removal.

RIGHT SIDE

1. Disconnect the negative battery cable. Drain the cooling system.

2. Raise and safely support the vehicle. Disconnect the exhaust manifold from the exhaust pipe.

3. Lower the vehicle. Disconnect the exhaust manifold from the cylinder head and remove the manifold.

4. Remove the rocker cover. Remove the intake manifold.

5. Loosen the rocker arms enough so that the push rods can be removed. Note the position of the push rods for assembly.

6. Starting with the outer bolts, remove the cylinder head bolts and remove the cylinder head.

7. Inspect and clean the surfaces of the cylinder head, engine block and intake manifold.

8. Clean the threads in the engine block and the threads on the cylinder head bolts.

9. Align the new gasket on the dowels on the engine block with the note "This Side Up" facing the cylinder head.

10. Install the cylinder head on the engine. Coat the head bolts with a proper sealer. Install and tighten the bolts hand tight.

11. Using the correct sequence, torque the bolts to 33 ft. lbs. After all bolts are toqued to 33 ft. lbs., rotate the torque wrench another 90° or ¼ turn. This will apply the correct torque to the bolts.

12. Install the push rods in the same order as they were removed. Torque the rocker arm nuts to 14–20 ft. lbs.

13. Install the intake manifold using a new gasket. Following the correct sequence, torque the bolts to the proper specification.

14. The remainder of the installation is the reverse of the removal.

Rocker Arms

REMOVAL & INSTALLATION

2.0 Liter Engines

1. Disconnect the negative battery cable. Remove the air hose at the TBI and the air cleaner.

2. Remove the hose from the intake manifold to the rocker cover.

3. Remove the rocker arm cover bolts and remove the cover.

4. Remove the rocker arm nuts and

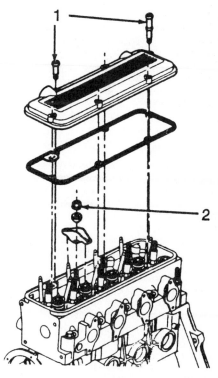

1. 6–9 ft. lbs.
2. 11–18 ft. lbs.

Rocker arm and cover installation-2.0 Liter engine

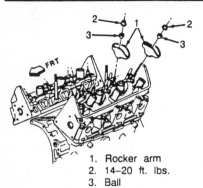

1. Rocker arm
2. 14–20 ft. lbs.
3. Ball

Rocker arm installation-2.8 Liter engine

remove the rocker arms. Note the order that the rocker arms are in for installation.

5. Install the rocker arms in the correct order. Torque the rocker arm nuts to 7–11 ft. lbs.

6. The remainder of the installation is the reverse of the removal. Use a new gasket on the rocker arm cover.

2.8 Liter Engines

LEFT SIDE

1. Disconnect the negative battery cable. Disconnect the bracket tube at the rocker cover.

2. Remove the spark plug wire cover. Drain the cooling system and remove the heater hose at the filler neck.

3. Remove the rocker arm cover bolts and remove the rocker cover.

4. Remove the rocker arm nuts and remove the rocker arms. Note the order of removal for installation.

5. Install the rocker arms in the correct order. Torque the rocker arm nuts to 14–20 ft. lbs.

6. The remainder of the installation is the reverse of the removal. Use a new gasket on the rocker arm cover.

RIGHT SIDE

1. Disconnect the negative battery cable. Disconnect the brake booster vacuum line at the bracket.

2. Disconnect the cable bracket at the plenum.

3. Disconnect the vacuum line bracket at the cable bracket.

4. Disconnect the lines at the alternator brace stud.

5. Remove the rear alternator brace.

6. Remove the serpentine belt.

7. Remove the alternator and support it out of the way.

8. Remove the PCV valve.

9. Loosen the alternator bracket.

10. Disconnect the spark plug wires at the spark plugs. Remove the rocker cover bolts and remove the rocker cover.

11. Remove the rocker arm nuts and remove the rocker arms. Note the order of removal for installation.

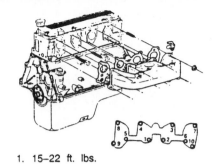

1. 15–22 ft. lbs.

Intake manifold bolt torque sequence-2.0 Liter engine

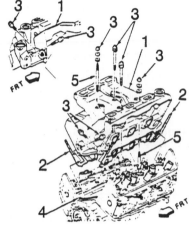

1. Intake manifold
2. Gasket
3. 18 ft. lbs.
4. Sealer
5. 24 ft. lbs

Intake manifold installation-2.8 Liter engine

12. Install the rocker arms in the correct order. Torque the rocker arm nuts to 14–20 ft. lbs.

13. The remainder of the installation is the reverse of the removal. Use a new gasket on the rocker arm cover.

Intake Manifold

REMOVAL & INSTALLATION

2.0 Liter Engines

1. Disconnect the negative battery cable. Remove the TBI cover.

2. Drain the cooling system. Disconnect and tag the vacuum lines and wires on the intake manifold.

3. Disconnect and plug the fuel line.

4. Disconnect the TBI linkage. Remove the TBI assembly.

5. Remove the power steering pump mounting bolts and support the pump out of the way.

6. Raise and safely support the vehicle.

7. Disconnect the T.V. and accelerator cables and brackets.

8. Disconnect the heater hose at the bottom of the intake manifold.

9. Remove the intake manifold mounting bolts and remove the manifold.

10. Inspect and clean the mounting surfaces of the intake manifold and cylinder head.

11. Using a new gasket, install the intake manifold on the engine. Torque the bolts in the proper sequence to 15–22 ft. lbs.

12. The remainder of the installation is the reverse of the removal.

2.8 Liter Engines

1. Disconnect the negative battery cable. Drain the cooling system.

2. Disconnect the T.V. and accelerator cables at the plenum.

3. Disconnect the throttle body at the plenum. Remove the EGR valve.

4. Remove the plenum. Disconnect and plug the fuel lines and return pipes at the fuel rail.

5. Remove the serpentine belt. Remove the power steering pump mounting bolts and support the pump out of the way.

6. Disconnect the alternator mounting bolts and support the alternator out of the way.

7. Loosen the alternator bracket. Disconnect the idle air vacuum hose at the throttle body.

8. Disconnect and tag the wires at the fuel injectors. Remove the fuel rail.

9. Remove the breather tube. Disconnect the runners.

10. Using the correct procedure, remove both rocker arm covers. Remove the radiator hose at the thermostat housing.

11. Disconnect and tag the wires at the coolant temperature sensor and oil pressure sending unit.

12. Remove the bypass hose at the filler neck and cylinder head.

13. Remove the intake manifold mounting bolts and remove the manifold.

14. Clean and inspect the surfaces of the manifold and cylinder head.

15. Place a 5mm bead of silicone sealer on the ridges of the manifold and using a new gasket, install the manifold on the engine.

16. Following the correct sequence, torque the manifold bolts to 24 ft. lbs. and the manifold nuts to 18 ft. lbs.

17. The remainder of the installation is the reverse of the removal.

Exhaust Manifold

REMOVAL & INSTALLATION

2.0 Liter Engines

1. Disconnect the negative battery cable.

2. Disconnect the oxygen sensor wire.

3. Remove the serpentine belt.

4. Remove the alternator with the wires attached and support it out of the way.

5. Raise and safely support the vehicle.

6. Disconnect the exhaust pipe from the manifold and lower the vehicle.

7. Remove the exhaust manifold to cylinder head mounting bolts.

8. Lift the exhaust manifold from the exhaust pipe and remove the manifold from the vehicle.

9. Clean and inspect the mating surfaces of the manifold and cylinder head.

10. Using a new gasket, install the manifold. Torque the manifold nuts to 3–11 ft. lbs. and the bolts to 6–13 ft. lbs.

11. The remainder of the installation is the reverse of the removal.

12. Check for exhaust leaks when finished.

2.8 Liter Engines

LEFT SIDE

1. Disconnect the negative battery cable. Drain the cooling system.

2. Remove the air cleaner, air inlet hose and the mass air flow sensor.

3. Remove the coolant bypass pipe.

4. Remove the manifold heat shield.

5. Disconnect the exhaust manifold crossover assembly at the right manifold.

6. Remove the exhaust manifold to cylinder head attaching bolts.

7. Remove the exhaust manifold with the crossover assembly from the vehicle.

8. Clean and inspect the mating surfaces of the manifold and cylinder head.

9. Using a new gasket, loosely install the manifold on the engine.

10. Loosely connect the crossover assembly on to the right manifold. Torque the exhaust manifold to cylinder head bolts to 19 ft. lbs. Torque the crossover bolts to 25 ft. lbs.

11. The remainder of the installation is the reverse of the removal.

12. Check for exhaust leaks when finished.

RIGHT SIDE

1. Disconnect the negative battery cable.

2. Raise and safely support the vehicle.

3. Remove the heat shield.

4. Disconnect the exhaust pipe from the exhaust manifold.

5. Disconnect the crossover pipe from the exhaust manifold.

6. Disconnect the EGR pipe from the exhaust manifold.

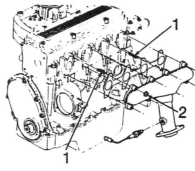

1. 3–11 ft. lbs.
2. 6–13 ft. lbs.

Exhaust manifold Installation-2.0 Liter engine

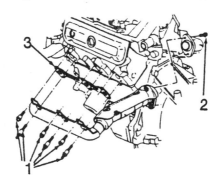

1. 14–22 ft. lbs.
2. 22–30 ft. lbs.
3. Gasket

Left side exhaust manifold installation-2.8 Liter engine

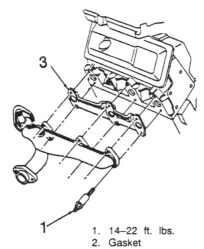

1. 14–22 ft. lbs.
2. Gasket

Right side exhaust manifold installation-2.8 Liter engine

7. Disconnect the oxygen sensor wire.

8. Remove the exhaust manifold to cylinder head attaching bolts and remove the exhaust manifold from the vehicle.

9. Clean and inspect the mating surfaces of the exhaust manifold and cylinder head.

10. Using a new gasket, install the exhaust manifold on the engine. Torque the exhaust manifold to cylinder head bolts to 19 ft. lbs. Torque the crossover bolts to 25 ft. lbs.

11. The remainder of the installation is the reverse of the removal.

12. Check for exhaust leaks when finished.

Front Cover

REMOVAL & INSTALLATION

2.0 Liter Engines

1. Disconnect the negative battery cable.

2. Raise and safely support the vehicle.

3. Drain the engine oil and remove the oil pan.

4. Lower the vehicle.

5. Remove the serpentine belt and the belt tensioner.

6. Remove the crankshaft pulley retaining bolt and using a suitable puller, remove the crankshaft pulley.

7. Remove the front cover bolts. Tap the cover with a rubber mallet and remove the cover.

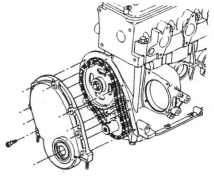

Front cover installation-2.0 Liter engine

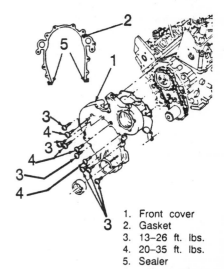

1. Front cover
2. Gasket
3. 13–26 ft. lbs.
4. 20–35 ft. lbs.
5. Sealer

Front cover installation-2.8 Liter engine

8. Clean and inspect the sealing surfaces of the engine and the front cover.

9. Using a new gasket, install the front cover over the dowels on the block.

10. Install the front cover retaining bolts and torque the bolts to 6–9 ft. lbs.

11. Install the crankshaft pulley on the crankshaft using tool J–29113, or equivalent.

12. Torque the pulley retaining bolt to 66–88 ft. lbs.

13. The remainder of the installation is the reverse of the removal.

14. Check for oil leaks when finished.

2.8 Liter Engines

1. Disconnect the negative battery cable. Drain the cooling system.

2. Remove the serpentine belt and the belt tensioner.

3. Remove the alternator and mounting bracket with the wires attached and support out of the way.

4. Remove the power steering pump and support it out of the way.

5. Raise and safely support the vehicle.

6. Remove the right side inner fender splash shield. Remove the flywheel dust cover.

7. Remove the crankshaft damper using tool J–24420, or equivalent.

8. Disconnect and tag the starter wires and remove the starter.

9. Loosen the front five oil pan bolts on both sides enough to lower the oil pan ½ in.

10. Lower the vehicle. Disconnect the radiator hose at the water pump.

11. Disconnect the heater coolant hose at the cooling system fill pipe.

12. Remove the bypass and overflow hoses.

13. Remove the water pump pulley. Disconnect the canister purge hose.

14. Remove the spark plug wire shield at the water pump.

15. Remove the upper front cover retaining bolts and remove the front cover.

16. Clean and inspect the sealing surfaces of the front cover and the engine.

17. Apply a thin bead of silicone sealer on the front cover mating surface and using a new gasket, install the front cover on the engine. Apply silicone sealer to the sections of the oil pan rails that were lowered and install the mounting bolts.

18. Install the damper on the engine using tool J–29113, or equivalent.

19. The remainder of the installation is the reverse of the removal.

20. Check for oil leaks when finished.

OIL SEAL REPLACEMENT
2.0 Liter Engines

1. Disconnect the negative battery

cable. Remove the serpentine belt.

2. Raise and safely support the vehicle. Remove the wheel and tire assembly.

3. Remove the inner fender splash shield.

4. Remove the crankshaft pulley bolt.

5. Install tool J–24420, or equivalent on the pulley and remove the crankshaft pulley.

6. Using a suitable tool, pry out the seal in the front cover.

NOTE: Use care not to damage the seal seat or the crankshaft while removing or installing the seal. Inspect the sealing surface of the crankshaft for grooves or other wear.

7. Using a suitable seal driver, install the new seal in the cover with the lip facing towards the engine.

8. Install tool J–29113, or equivalent on the crankshaft pulley and install the pulley on the engine.

9. Torque the pulley bolt to 66–88 ft. lbs. The remainder of the installation is the reverse of the removal.

2.8 Liter Engines

1. Disconnect the negative battery cable. Remove the serpentine belt.

2. Raise and safely the vehicle. Remove the right side inner fender splash shield.

3. Remove the damper retaining bolt.

4. Install tool J–24420, or equivalent on the damper and pull the damper off of the crankshaft.

5. Using a suitable tool, pry out the seal in the front cover.

NOTE: Use care not to damage the seal seat or the crankshaft while removing or installing the seal. Inspect the crankshaft seal surface for signs of grooves or wear.

6. Using a suitable seal driver, install the new seal in the cover with the lip facing towards the engine.

7. Install tool J–29113, or equivalent on the crankshaft pulley and install the pulley on the engine.

8. Torque the damper bolt to 67–85 ft. lbs. The remainder of the installation is the reverse of the removal.

Timing Chain and Sprockets
REMOVAL & INSTALLATION
2.0 Liter Engines

1. Using the correct procedure, remove the front cover.

2. Rotate the engine and align the

NOTE— ALIGN TABS ON TENSIONER WITH MARKS ON CAMSHAFT & CRANKSHAFT SPROCKETS.

1. 66–88 ft. lbs.
2. Tensioner
3. Camshaft sprocket
4. Crankshaft sprocket

Timing chain and sprockets installation- 2.0 Liter engine

marks on the crankshaft and camshaft sprockets.

3. Remove the timing chain tensioner upper bolt.

4. Loosen the timing chain tensioner nut as far as possible but do not remove the nut.

5. Remove the timing chain and sprocket.

6. Using a suitable puller, remove the crankshaft sprocket.

7. Lubricate the thrust side of the crankshaft sprocket with Molykote® and install the sprocket on the crankshaft using tool J–5590, or equivalent.

8. Align the marks on the camshaft sprocket with the marks on the crankshaft sprocket and install the timing chain and camshaft sprocket.

9. Pull the camshaft sprocket on the camshaft using the camshaft sprocket bolt. Torque the camshaft sprocket bolt to 66–88 ft. lbs.

10. Align the tabs on the tensioner with the marks on the camshaft and crankshaft sprockets and tighten the tensioner.

11. The remainder of the installation is the reverse of the removal.

12. Check for leaks when finished.

2.8 Liter Engines

1. Using the correct procedure, remove the front cover.

2. Rotate the engine so that the No. 1 piston is at top dead center with the marks on the camshaft and crankshaft sprockets aligned. This is the No. 4 firing position.

3. Remove the camshaft sprocket and timing chain.

4. Using a suitable puller, remove the crankshaft sprocket.

5. Apply Molykote®, or equivalent to the thrust face of the crankshaft sprocket.

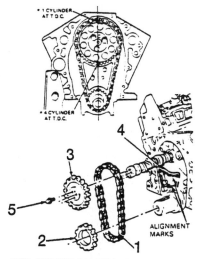

NOTE—ALIGN TIMING MARKS ON CAM & CRANK SPROCKETS USING ALIGNMENT MARKS ON DAMPER STAMPING OR CAST ALIGNMENT MARKS ON CYL & CASE.

1. Timing chain
2. Crankshaft sprocket
3. Camshaft sprocket
4. Damper
5. 15–20 ft. lbs.

Timing chain and sprockets installation- 2.8 Liter engine

6. Install the sprocket on the crankshaft.

7. Hold the camshaft sprocket with the chain hanging down. Align the marks on the camshaft and crankshaft sprockets.

8. Align the dowel in the camshaft with the sprocket and install the sprocket and timing chain using a camshaft bolt to pull the sprocket into position.

9. Torque the camshaft bolts to 15–20 ft. lbs.

10. Lubricate the new timing chain with clean engine oil. Using the correct procedure, install the front cover.

11. Check for oil leaks when finished.

Camshaft

REMOVAL & INSTALLATION

2.0 Liter Engines

1. Using the correct procedure, remove the engine from the vehicle.

2. Drain the engine oil. Remove the oil filter.

3. Using the correct procedures, remove the intake manifold, rocker cover, pushrods and lifters. Note the posi-

tion of the valve train parts for assembly.

4. Using the correct procedure, remove the front cover.

5. Remove the oil pump drive. Remove the timing chain and sprockets.

6. Remove the camshaft from the engine.

NOTE: Use care when removing and installing the camshaft. Do not damage the camshaft bearings or the bearing surfaces on the camshaft.

7. Clean and inspect the timing chain, sprockets, valve train and mating surfaces of the front cover and rocker cover.

8. Lubricate the lobes of the new camshaft with GM E.O.S. 1051396, or equivalent and insert the camshaft in the engine.

NOTE: If a new camshaft is being used replace all of the lifters. Used lifters can only be used on the camshaft that they were originally installed with; provided that they are replaced in the exact same position that they were removed.

9. Using the correct procedure, align the marks on the camshaft and crankshaft sprockets and install the timing chain and sprocket.

10. Following the correct procedures, install the front cover and valve train parts. Torque the rocker arm nuts to 11–18 ft. lbs.

11. Install the intake manifold and rocker cover using the correct procedures.

12. Install the engine in the vehicle following the correct procedure.

2.8 Liter Engines

1. Using the correct procedure, remove the engine from the vehicle.

2. Using the correct procedures, remove the intake manifold, rocker covers, pushrods and lifters. Note the position of the valve train parts for assembly.

3. Using the correct procedure, remove the front cover.

4. Using the correct procedure, remove the timing chain and sprocket.

5. Remove the camshaft from the engine.

NOTE: The camshaft journals are the all the same size. Use extreme care when removing or in-

stalling the camshaft not to damage the camshaft bearings or the bearing journals on the camshaft.

6. Clean and inspect the timing chain, sprockets, valve train and mating surfaces of the front cover and rocker covers.

7. Lubricate the lobes of the new camshaft with GM E.O.S. 1051396, or equivalent and insert the camshaft in the engine.

NOTE: If a new camshaft is being used replace all of the lifters. Used lifters can only be used on the camshaft that they were originally installed with; provided that they are replaced in the exact same position that they were removed.

8. Using the correct procedure, align the marks on the camshaft and crankshaft sprockets and install the timing chain and sprocket.

9. Following the correct procedures, install the front cover and valve train parts. Torque the rocker arm nuts to 14–20 ft. lbs.

10. Install the intake manifold and rocker covers using the correct procedures.

11. Install the engine in the vehicle following the correct procedure.

Piston and Connecting Rod

POSITIONING

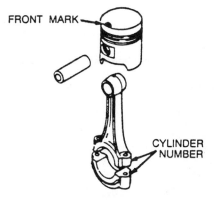

Piston and connecting rod position-2.0 and 2.8 Liter engine

TRUCKS

Engine

REMOVAL & INSTALLATION

Vans (Except Astro)

1. Disconnect the negative battery cable, then the positive battery cable, at the battery.
2. Drain the cooling system.
3. Remove the engine cover.
4. Remove the air cleaner. On V8s remove the air stove pipe.
5. Remove the grille. On the six cylinder, remove the grille cross brace. On V8s, remove the upper radiator support and the lower grille valance.
6. Disconnect the radiator hoses at the radiator.
7. On V8s, remove the radiator coolant reservoir bottle.
8. If the van is equipped with an automatic transmission, remove the fluid cooler lines from the radiator.

------ CAUTION ------

Discharging the air conditioning refrigerant should only be attempted by those who have the proper tools and training to do so, as serious personal injury may result. The refrigerant will instantly freeze any surface it comes in contact with, including your eyes.

9. Discharge the air conditioning system and remove the A/C vacuum reservoir. On the V8, remove the A/C condenser from in front of the radiator. On the six cylinder, remove the A/C compressor.
10. Remove the windshield washer jar and bracket.
11. Disconnect the accelerator linkage at the carburetor and remove the carburetor.
12. Remove the radiator support bracket and remove the radiator and the shroud.
13. On the six cylinder, remove the A/C compressor mounting bracket and position the compressor out of the way.
14. On V8s, disconnect the engine wiring harness from the firewall connection. On the six cylinder, disconnect the wiring at the alternator, distributor, oil pressure and temperature sending switches and the starter motor.
15. On V8s:
   a. Disconnect the heater hoses at the engine.
   b. Remove the thermostat housing.
   c. Remove the oil filler pipe.
   d. Remove the cruise control servo, servo bracket and transducer.

16. Raise the vehicle and drain the engine oil.
17. Remove the fuel line from the fuel tank at the fuel pump.
18. Disconnect the exhaust pipe at the manifold.
19. Remove the driveshaft and plug the end of the transmission.
20. Disconnect the transmission shift linkage and the speedometer cable.
21. Remove the transmission mounting bolts.
22. On the six cylinder with manual transmission, disconnect the clutch linkage and remove the clutch cross shaft.
23. On the V8, remove the engine mount bracket-to-frame bolts.
24. Remove the engine mount through bolts.
25. On the six cylinder:
   a. Lower the van and attach a lifting device to the engine.
   b. Raise the engine slightly and remove the right hand mount from the engine.
26. On the V8:
   a. Raise the engine slightly and remove the engine mounts. Support the engine with wood between the oil pan and the crossmember.
27. Remove the engine and transmission as one unit.
28. Reverse the removal procedure to install.

Astro w/2.5L (4 Cyl)

1. Disconnect the battery ground cable at both the battery and the cylinder head.
2. Open the radiator drain cock and then remove the cap. Drain coolant into a clean container.
3. Remove the engine cover.
4. Remove the headlight bezel. Then, remove the grille.
5. Remove the lower radiator closeout panel. Then, remove the radiator support brace.
6. Remove the lower tie bar. Remove the cross brace.
7. Remove the hood latch mechanism. Remove the radiator upper core support.
8. Disconnect the hoses at the radiator. Remove the radiator filler panels. Then, remove the radiator and fan shroud as an assembly.
9. Disconnect the engine harness at the bulkhead connector. Disconnect the harness at the ECM and pull it through the bulkhead.
10. Disconnect the heater hoses at the core.

11. Disconnect the accelerator cable. Disconnect the canister purge hose.
12. Remove the air cleaner and air cleaner adapter.
13. Remove the oil filler neck and the thermostat outlet.
14. Raise the vehicle and support it securely at approved jacking points.
15. Disconnect the exhaust pipe at the manifold.
16. Disconnect the wiring harness at both the transmission and the frame.
17. Label and then disconnect all starter wiring. Remove the starter as described above.
18. Remove the flywheel splash shield.
19. Disconnect the fuel hoses, being careful to collect any fuel that drains out in a metal container.
20. Remove the motor mount through bolts.
21. Remove the bell housing bolts.
22. Lower the vehicle.
23. Install a lifting crane to the engine lifting hooks. Support the transmission from underneath with a floorjack. Make sure weight is spread so the transmission pan will not be damaged.
24. Lift the engine out of the vehicle.
25. Installation is the reverse of the removal procedure. Replenish all fluids. Operate the engine and check for leaks.

Astro w/4.3L V6

1. Disconnect the battery ground cable. Drain the cooling system.
2. Raise the vehicle and support it securely at approved jacking points.
3. Disconnect both exhaust pipes at the manifolds.
4. Disconnect the strut rods at the flywheel inspection cover. Then, remove the inspection cover. Remove the torque converter-to-flywheel bolts by turning the engine over to gain access to the bolts one by one.
5. Label and disconnect all starter wiring. Remove the starter as described above.
6. Place a drain pan below the oil filter and remove it. Cover the oil filter connection on the block to keep dirt out of the lubrication system.
7. Disconnect the wiring harness at both the transmission and the frame.
8. Disconnect the fuel hoses at the frame.
9. Disconnect the lower transmission and engine oil cooler lines at the radiator.
10. Remove the lower fan shroud mounting bolts.
11. Remove the bell housing bolts.

Remove the engine mount through bolts.

12. Lower the vehicle to the ground.

13. Remove the headlight bezels and the grille.

14. Remove the lower radiator close-out panel.

15. Remove the radiator support brace and core support cross brace.

16. Remove the lower tie bar.

17. Remove the hood latch mechanism.

18. Disconnect the master cylinder, plug all openings, and lay the master cylinder aside.

19. Remove the upper fan shroud. Remove the upper core support.

18. Disconnect the radiator hoses at the radiator. Disconnect the upper transmission cooler line and upper engine oil cooler line. Remove the radiator.

19. Have a mechanic who does air conditioning work discharge the refrigerant from the air conditioning (A/C) system, if the vehicle has one. Unless you are trained in air conditioning work and have proper equipment, you should not attempt such a procedure.

20. Remove the radiator filler panels.

21. Remove the engine cover and remove the A/C brace at the back of the compressor.

22. Disconnect the A/C compressor hoses leading to the accumulator and condenser and seal open ends.

23. Remove the air conditioning compressor and mounting bracket.

24. Remove the power steering pump as described later in this section.

25. Label and then disconnect all vacuum hoses leading from the engine to components mounted in the engine compartment.

26. Disconnect the engine wiring harness at the bulkhead.

27. Remove the right side kick panel. Then, disconnect the wiring harness at the ESC module and then push it through the bulkhead.

28. Disconnect the two refrigerant lines leading to the A/C accumulator and plug the openings. Disconnect the electrical connections for the pressure cycling switch. Then, remove the accumulator.

29. Disconnect the fuel line at the carburetor and collect any fuel that drains in a metal container.

30. Remove the diverter valve.

31. Remove the (automatic) transmission dipstick tube.

32. Disconnect the heater hoses at the heater core.

33. Disconnect and remove the horn.

34. Remove the Air Injection Reactor system check valves.

35. Install a lifting crane to the engine lifting hooks. Support the transmission from underneath with a floorjack. Make sure weight is spread

so the transmission pan will not be damaged.

36. Lift the engine out of the vehicle.

37. Installation is the reverse of the removal procedure. Refill the master cylinder and bleed the brakes. Have the A/C system charged with oil and refrigerant by a mechanic trained in this work. (Unless you are trained in air conditioning work and have proper equipment, you should not attempt such a procedure). Replenish all fluids. Operate the engine and check for leaks.

Pickups & Suburban

The factory recommended procedure for engine removal is to remove the engine/transmission as a unit on two wheel drive models, except for the diesel. Only the engine should be removed on diesels and four wheel drive models.

1. Disconnect and remove the battery, negative cable first. On diesels, disconnect the negative cables at the batteries and ground wires at the inner fender panel.

2. Drain the cooling system.

3. Drain the engine oil.

4. Remove the air cleaner and ducts.

5. Scribe alignment marks around the hood hinges, and remove the hood.

6. Remove the radiator and hoses, and the fan shroud if so equipped.

7. Disconnect and label the wires at:

a. Starter solenoid.

b. Alternator.

c. Temperature switch.

d. Oil pressure switch.

e. Transmission controlled spark solenoid.

f. CEC solenoid.

g. Coil.

h. Neutral safety switch.

8. Disconnect:

a. Accelerator linkage (hairpin at bellcrank, throttle and T.V. cables at intake manifold brackets on diesels. Position away from the engine).

b. Choke cable at carburetor (if so equipped).

c. Fuel line to fuel pump.

d. Heater hoses at engine.

e. Air conditioning compressor with hoses attached. Do not remove the hoses from the air conditioning compressor. Remove it as a unit and set it aside. Its contents are under pressure, and can freeze body tissue on contact.

f. Transmission dipstick and tube on automatic transmission models, except for diesel. Plug the tube hole.

g. Oil dipstick and tube. Plug the hole.

h. Vacuum lines.

i. Oil pressure line to gauge, if so equipped.

j. Parking brake cable.

k. Power steering pump. This can be removed as a unit and set aside, without removing any of the hoses.

l. Engine ground straps.

m. Exhaust pipe (support if necessary).

9. Loosen and remove the fan belt, remove the fan blades and pulley. If you have the finned aluminum viscous drive fan clutch, keep it upright in its normal position. If the fluid leaks out, the unit will have to be replaced.

10. Remove the clutch cross-shaft.

11. Attach a chain or lifting device to the engine. If your engine doesn't have any lifting eyes, the usual locations are under the intake manifold bolts on V8s, or under the cylinder head bolts at either end on the sixes. You may have to remove the carburetor. Take the engine weight off the engine mounts, and unbolt the mounts. On all models except the gas engined C10, 1500, C20, and 2500, support and disconnect the transmission. With automatic transmission, remove the torque converter underpan and starter, unbolt the converter from the flywheel, detach the throttle linkage and vacuum modulator line, and unbolt the engine from the transmission. Be certain that the converter does not fall out. With manual transmission, unbolt the clutch housing from the engine.

12. On two wheel drive models, remove the driveshaft. Either drain the transmission or plug the driveshaft opening. Disconnect the speedometer cable at the transmission. Disconnect the shift linkage or lever, or the clutch linkage. Disconnect the transmission cooler lines, if so equipped. If you have an automatic or a four speed transmission, the rear crossmember must be removed. With the three speed, unbolt the transmission from the crossmember. Raise the engine/transmission assembly and pull it forward.

13. On diesels, remove the three bolts, transmission, right side; disconnect the wires to the starter and remove the starter.

14. On four wheel drive, raise and pull the engine forward until it is free of the transmission. On diesels, slightly raise the transmission, remove the three left transmission to engine bolts, and remove the engine.

15. On all trucks, lift the engine out slowly, making certain as you go that all lines between the engine and the truck have been disconnected.

16. Installation is as follows: On four wheel drive and diesels, lower the engine into place and align it with the transmission. Push the engine back gently and turn the crankshaft until the manual transmission shaft and

clutch engage. Bolt the transmission to the engine. With automatic transmission, align the converter with the flywheel, bolt the transmission to the engine, bolt the converter to the flywheel, replace the underpan and starter, and connect the throttle linkage and vacuum modulator line.

17. On two wheel drive, lower the engine/transmission unit into place. Replace the rear crossmember if removed. Bolt the three speed transmission back to the crossmember. Replace the driveshaft.

18. Install the engine mounts.

19. Replace all transmission connections and the clutch cross-shaft. Replace the fan, pulley, and belts.

20. Replace all the items removed from the engine earlier. Connect all the wires which were detached.

21. Replace the radiator and fan shroud, air cleaner, and battery or battery cables. Fill the cooling system and check the automatic transmission fuel level. Fill the crankcase with oil. Check for leaks.

Blazer & Jimmy

1. Disconnect the negative battery cable, then the positive battery cable.

2. Drain the cooling system.

3. Remove the air cleaner.

4. Scribe matchmarks on the hood hinges for reassembly and remove the hood.

5. Remove the radiator and fan shroud as outlined later in this chapter.

6. Disconnect and label (to avoid confusion) the wires at the following locations:

　a. Starter solenoid.

　b. Alternator.

　c. Temperature sending switch.

　d. Oil pressure sending switch.

　e. Coil.

　f. Vacuum advance solenoid and/or the CEC solenoid.

　g. TCS solenoid (V8, if so equipped).

7. Disconnect the:

　a. Accelerator linkage at the manifold.

　b. Fuel line from the tank at the fuel pump.

　c. Heater hoses at the engine block.

　d. Oil pressure gauge and the vacuum lines at the engine.

　e. Evaporative emission system lines at the carburetor and later the hose at the fuel vapor storage canister.

　f. Power steering pump at the mounting bracket (lay the pump aside without disconnecting any of the lines).

　g. Ground straps at the engine block.

　h. Exhaust pipe at the manifold (hang the pipe from the frame with a wire).

　i. TCS switch at the transmission (V8, if so equipped).

　j. Vacuum line to the power brake unit at the manifold.

8. If equipped with air conditioning, unbolt the compressor at the bracket and lay it aside.

———— CAUTION ————

Do not disconnect any of the refrigerant lines. Evacuation of the air conditioning system should only be performed by someone who has the proper skill and training to do so, as the refrigerant will instantly freeze anything it contacts, including your eyes.

9. Raise the vehicle and drain the engine oil.

10. Disconnect the exhaust pipe at the manifold.

11. Remove the flywheel splash shield or the converter housing cover, as applicable.

12. Remove the starter motor.

13. On automatic transmission models remove the converter-to-flywheel attaching bolts.

14. Remove the engine mount through bolts.

15. On four wheel drive models, remove the strut rods at the engine mount.

16. Remove the engine-to-bellhousing attaching bolts.

17. Lower the vehicle.

18. Using a floor jack, raise the transmission slightly.

19. Attach a lifting device to the engine and raise it slightly, taking the weight off the engine mounts.

20. Remove the engine mount-to-engine brackets.

21. Remove the engine.

22. Reverse the removal procedure to install.

S-Series

GASOLINE ENGINES

1. Raise the hood and disconnect the battery cables.

2. Remove the skid plate and drain both the cooling system and the oil pan.

3. Remove the air cleaner assembly and vacuum hoses. Mark the vacuum hoses for reinstallation.

4. Disconnect all hoses, tubing and electrical leads from the engine and mark them for reinstallation.

5. Remove the radiator and fan blade assembly.

6. Disconnect the exhaust pipe from the exhaust manifold.

7. Raise the vehicle and, if equipped with a manual transmission, remove the clutch return spring and cable.

8. Remove the starter motor and fasten it to the frame rail with a piece of wire.

9. Remove the flywheel cover pan.

10. Remove the bell housing bolts and support the transmission.

11. Lift the engine slightly and remove the engine mount nuts.

12. Make certain that all lines, hoses, wires and cables have been disconnected from the engine and the frame.

13. Remove the engine from the vehicle with the front of the engine raised slightly.

14. Installation is the reverse of removal.

DIESEL ENGINES (2WD)

1. Raise engine hood.

2. Disconnect the battery ground cable.

3. Remove the hood.

4. Remove the battery assembly.

5. Remove under cover and drain the cooling system by opening the drain plugs on the radiator and on the cylinder block.

6. Remove the air cleaner assembly as follows:

　a. Remove the intake silencer.

　b. Remove the bolts fixing the air cleaner and loosen the clamp bolt.

　c. Lift the air cleaner slightly and disconnect the breather hose, then remove the air cleaner assembly.

7. Disconnect the upper water hose at the engine side.

8. Loosen the compressor drive belts by moving the power steering pump or idler (if so equipped).

9. Remove the cooling fan and fan shroud.

10. Disconnect the lower water hose at the engine side.

11. Remove the radiator grille.

12. Remove the radiator attaching bolts and remove the radiator.

13. Disconnect the accelerator control cable from the injection pump side.

14. Disconnect the air conditioner compressor control cable (if so equipped).

15. Disconnect the fuel hoses from the injection pump.

16. Disconnect the battery cable from the cylinder body.

17. Disconnect the transmission wiring.

18. Disconnect the vacuum hose from the fast idle actuator.

19. Disconnect the connector at fuel cut solenoid.

20. Disconnect the A/C compressor wiring.

21. Disconnect the heater hoses extending from the heater unit from the dash panel side.

22. Disconnect the hose for mastervac from the vacuum pump.

23. Disconnect vacuum hose from the vacuum pump.

24. Disconnect the generator wiring at the connector.

25. Disconnect the exhaust pipe from the exhaust manifold at the flange.

26. Remove the exhaust pipe mounting brake from the engine back plate.

27. Disconnect the starter motor wiring.

28. Disconnect the battery cable from starter motor.

29. Slide the gearshift lever boot upwards on the lever. Remove 2 gearshift lever attaching bolts and remove lever.

30. Place a pan under transmission to receive oil, disconnect speedometer cable at the transmission then disconnect the ground cable.

31. Disconnect the driveshaft at differential side.

32. Remove the driveshaft.

33. Remove return spring from clutch fork.

34. Disconnect clutch cable from hooked portion of clutch fork and pull it out forward through stiffener bracket.

35. Remove two bracket to transmission rear mount bolts and nuts.

36. Raise engine and transmission as required and remove (4) crossmember to frame bracket bolts.

37. Remove the rear mounting nuts from the transmission rear extension.

38. Disconnect electrical connectors at CRS switch and back-up lamp switch.

39. Remove the engine mounting bolt and nuts. Check that the engine is slightly lifted before removing the engine mounting bolt and nuts.

40. Check to make certain all the parts have been removed or disconnected from the engine that are fastened to the frame side. Remove the engine toward front of the vehicle by maneuvering the hoist, so that front part of the engine is lifted slightly. Install in the reverse order.

4WD

1. Raise engine hood.
2. Disconnect the battery ground cable.
3. Remove the engine hood.
4. Remove the battery assembly.
5. Remove under cover and drain the cooling system by opening the drain plugs on the radiator and on the cylinder block.
6. Remove the air cleaner as follows:
   a. Remove the intake silencer.
   b. Remove the bolts fixing the air cleaner and loosen the clamp bolt.
   c. Lift the air cleaner slightly and disconnect the breather hose, then remove the air cleaner assembly.
7. Disconnect the upper water hose at the engine side.
8. Loosen the compressor drive

belts by moving the power steering oil pump or idler (if so equipped).

9. Remove the cooling fan and fan shroud.

10. Disconnect the lower water hose at the engine side.

11. Remove the radiator grille.

12. Remove the radiator attaching bolts and remove the radiator.

13. Disconnect the accelerator control cable from the injection pump side.

14. Disconnect the air conditioner compressor control cable (if so equipped).

15. Disconnect the fuel hoses from the injection pump.

16. Disconnect the battery cable from the cylinder body.

17. Disconnect the transmission wiring.

18. Disconnect the vacuum hose from the fast idle actuator.

19. Disconnect the connector at fuel cut solenoid.

20. Disconnect the A/C compressor wiring.

21. Disconnect the heater hoses extending from the heater unit from the dash panel side.

22. Disconnect the hose for master-vac from the vacuum pump.

23. Disconnect the vacuum hose from the vacuum pump.

24. Disconnect the generator wiring at the connector.

25. Disconnect the exhaust pipe from the exhaust manifold at the flange.

26. Remove the exhaust pipe mounting brake from the engine back plate.

27. Disconnect the starter motor wiring.

28. Disconnect the battery cable from starter motor.

29. Slide the transmission and transfer gearshift lever boot upwards on each lever, remove gearshift lever attaching bolts.

30. Remove return spring from transfer gear shift lever then remove levers.

31. Remove the transmission.

32. Remove the engine mounting bolts and nuts. Check that the engine is slightly lifted before removing the engine mounting bolts and nuts.

33. Check to make certain all the parts have been removed or disconnected from the engine that are fastened to the frame side. Remove the engine toward front of the vehicle by maneuvering the hoist, so that front part of the engine is lifted slightly. Install in the reverse order.

Cylinder Head
REMOVAL & INSTALLATION
4-119

1. Remove cam cover.

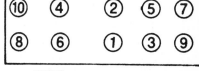

FRONT ———————→

4-119 head bolt torque sequence

2. Remove EGR pipe clamp bolt at rear of cylinder head.

3. Raise vehicle and support the vehicle.

4. Disconnect exhaust pipe at exhaust manifold.

5. Lower the vehicle.

6. Drain cooling system.

7. Disconnect heater hoses at intake manifold and at front of cylinder head.

8. Remove A/C and/or P/S compressor or pump and lay them aside.

9. Disconnect accelerator linkage at carburetor, fuel line at carburetor, all necessary electrical connections, spark plug wires and necessary vacuum lines.

10. Rotate camshaft until No.4 cylinder is in firing position. Remove distributor cap and mark rotor to housing relationship. Remove the distributor.

11. Remove the fuel pump.

12. Lock the shoe on automatic adjuster in fully retracted position by depressing the adjuster lock lever with a screwdriver or equivalent in direction as indicated in the drawing.

13. Remove timing sprocket to camshaft bolt and remove the sprocket and the fuel pump drive cam from the camshaft. Keep the sprocket on the chain damper and tensioner—do not remove the sprocket from the chain.

14. Disconnect AIR hose and check valve at air manifold.

15. Remove cylinder head to timing cover bolts.

16. Remove cylinder head bolts using Extension Bar Wrench J-24239-01; remove bolts in progressal sequence, beginning with the outer bolts.

17. Remove the cylinder head, intake and exhaust manifold as an assembly.

18. Clean all gasket material from cylinder head and block surfaces.

NOTE: The gasket surfaces on both the head and block must be clean of any foreign matter and free of nicks or heavy scratches. Cylinder bolt threads in the block and threads on the bolts must be cleaned (dirt will affect bolt torque).

19. Place new gasket over dowel pins with "TOP" side of gasket up. Install the cylinder head in the reverse order. Tighten cylinder head bolts a little at a

time in the proper sequence. Torque to 60 ft. lbs. and then retighten to specified torque of 72 ft. lb.

4-121

NOTE: The engine should be "overnight" cold before removing the cylinder head.

1. Disconnect the negative battery cable.
2. Drain the cooling system into a clean container; the coolant can be reused if it is still good.
3. Remove the air cleaner. Raise and support the front of the vehicle.
4. Remove the exhaust shield. Disconnect the exhaust pipe.
5. Remove the heater hose from the intake manifold and then lower the car.
6. Unscrew the mounting bolts and remove the engine lift bracket (includes air management).
7. Remove the distributor. Disconnect the vacuum manifold at the alternator bracket.
8. Tag and disconnect the remaining vacuum lines at the intake manifold and thermostat.
9. Remove the air management pipe at the exhaust check valve.
10. Disconnect the accelerator linkage at the carburetor and then remove the linkage bracket.
11. Tag and disconnect all necessary wires. Remove the upper radiator hose at the thermostat.
12. Remove the bolt attaching the dipstick tube and hot water bracket.
13. Remove the idler pulley. Remove the A.I.R. and power steering pump drive belts.
14. Remove the A.I.R. bracket-to-intake manifold bolt. If equipped with power steering, remove the air pump pulley, The A.I.R. thru-bolt and the power steering adjusting bracket.
15. Loosen the A.I.R. mounting bracket lower bolt so that the bracket will rotate.
16. Disconnect and plug the fuel line at the carburetor.
17. Remove the alternator. Remove the alternator brace from the head and then remove the upper mounting bracket.
18. Remove the cylinder head cover. Remove the rocker arms and push rods.
19. Remove the cylinder head bolts in the order given in the illustration. Remove the cylinder head with the carburetor, intake and exhaust manifolds still attached. To install, the gasket surfaces on both the head and the block must be clean of any foreign matter and free of any nicks or heavy scratches. Cylinder bolt threads in the block and the bolt must be clean.
20. Place a new cylinder head gasket

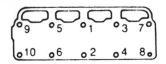

CYLINDER HEAD BOLT
TIGHTENING SEQUENCE

4–121 head bolt torque sequence

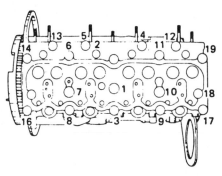

4–137 diesel head bolt torque sequence

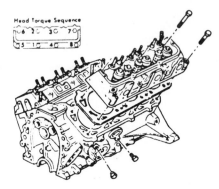

6–173 head bolt torque sequence

in position over the dowel pins on the block. Carefully guide the cylinder head into position.
21. Coat the cylinder bolts with sealing compound and install them finger tight.
22. Using a torque wrench, gradually tighten the bolts in the proper sequence.
23. Installation of the remaining components is in the reverse order of removal.

4-137 Diesel

1. Remove the intake and exhaust manifolds.
2. Remove the intake and exhaust manifold gasket.
3. Drain the cooling system by opening the drain plugs on the radiator and on the cylinder block.
4. Disconnect the upper water hose at the engine side.
5. Remove the cooling fan and fan shroud.
6. Remove the sleeve nuts and disconnect the injection pipes.

7. Remove the nozzle holder fixing nuts and remove the nozzle holder assembly.
8. Follow the rocker arm, bracket and shaft assembly removal steps.
9. Remove the pushrods.
10. Remove the joint bolt and disconnect the leak-off pipe.
11. Remove the 19 bolts fixing the cylinder head, then remove the cylinder head and gasket.
12. Install the cylinder head gasket with the TOP mark side up on the cylinder body by aligning the holes with the dowels.
13. Install the cylinder head. Tighten the mounting bolts in proper sequence.
14. Install the pushrod in position on the cylinder head.
15. Install the rocker arm assembly on the cylinder head. Tighten the bracket fixing bolts evenly in sequence commencing with the inner ones.
16. Follow the intake and exhaust manifold installation steps.
17. Install the cooling fan and fan shroud.
18. Connect the upper water hose to engine side.
19. Fill the engine cooling system.

6-173

LEFT SIDE

1. Raise and support the truck.
2. Drain the coolant from the block and lower the truck.
3. Remove the intake manifold.
4. Remove the crossover.
5. Remove the alternator and AIR pump brackets.
6. Remove the dipstick tube.
7. Loosen the rocker arm bolts and remove the pushrods. Keep the pushrods in the same order as removed.
8. Remove the cylinder head bolts in stages and in the reverse order of the tightening sequence.
9. Remove the cylinder head. Do not pry on the head to loosen it.
10. Installation is the reverse of removal. The words "This side Up" on the new cylinder head gasket should face upward. Coat the cylinder head bolts with sealer and torque to specifications in the sequence shown. Make sure the pushrods seat in the lifter seats and adjust the valves.

RIGHT SIDE

1. Raise and support the vehicle. Drain the coolant from the block.
2. Disconnect the exhaust pipe and lower the vehicle.
3. If equipped, remove the cruise control servo bracket.
4. Remove the air management valve and hose.
5. Remove the intake manifold.
6. Remove the exhaust crossover.

7. Loosen the rocker arm nuts and remove the pushrods. Keep the pushrods in the order in which they were removed.

8. Remove the cylinder head bolts in stages and in the reverse order of the tightening sequence.

9. Remove the cylinder head, do not pry on the cylinder head to loosen it.

10. Installation is the reverse of removal. The words "This Side Up" on the new cylinder head gasket should face upwards. Coat the cylinder head bolts with sealer and tighten them to specifications in the sequence shown. Make sure the lower ends of the pushrods seat in the lifter seats and adjust the valves.

2.5L (4 Cyl)

1. Disconnect the negative battery cable at the battery and at the cylinder head and remove it. Remove the rocker cover as described later in this section.

2. Drain the cooling system. Disconnect the upper radiator hose at the intake manifold and thermostat housing, and remove the housing and thermostat. Disconnect or shift aside the heater hoses, if they might interfere with head removal.

3. Disconnect the accelerator cable.

4. Disconnect the alternator brace at the intake manifold. Then, remove the rear alternator bracket and move the alternator aside.

5. Remove the air conditioner compressor mounting bolts and brackets and place the compressor aside. Do not disconnect, disturb or stress the air conditioner hoses!

6. Carefully survey the cylinder head assembly and determine which vacuum lines will have to be disconnected. Then label and disconnect them.

7. Disconnect the fuel lines, collecting fuel that drains in a metal container.

8. Disconnect and remove the ignition coil. Disconnect the spark plug wires at the plugs.

9. Support the vehicle securely at approved jacking points. Disconnect the exhaust pipe at the manifold.

10. Disconnect the oxygen sensor.

11. Lower the vehicle to the ground.

12. Remove the rocker arms and associated parts as described later in this section. Then, remove the pushrods, keeping them in order for reinstallation in the same positions.

13. Loosen the head bolts in several stages, going from bolt to bolt, and turning each a fraction of a turn until tension is lost. Then, remove the bolts. Install a lifting crane and lift the head off the block. Rock the head, if necessary, to break the seal, don't pry it.

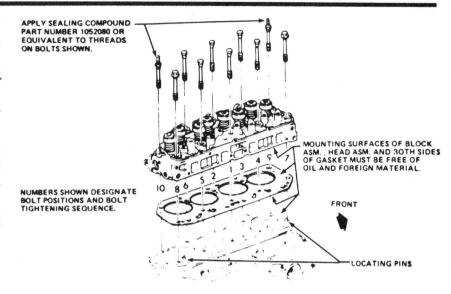

APPLY SEALING COMPOUND PART NUMBER 1052080 OR EQUIVALENT TO THREADS ON BOLTS SHOWN.

MOUNTING SURFACES OF BLOCK ASM., HEAD ASM. AND 30TH SIDES OF GASKET MUST BE FREE OF OIL AND FOREIGN MATERIAL.

NUMBERS SHOWN DESIGNATE BOLT POSITIONS AND BOLT TIGHTENING SEQUENCE.

FRONT

LOCATING PINS

Torque the head bolts in the sequence shown in several stages (2.5 L engine)

14. Carefully remove any dirt or gasket pieces that cling to the block deck or cylinder head gasket surface with a dull scraper. Clean the threads on the cylinder head bolts and those in the head must be clean and dry or the bolts will not torque properly.

15. Install a new gasket in position, right side up, over the dowel pins in the block deck. Note that the gasket will not align with the corners of the block if it is installed upside down.

16. Guide the head precisely into position.

17. Coat both the heads and the threads of the head bolts with sealer, and install them finger tight.

18. Torque the bolts in at least 3 equal stages, using the sequence shown in the illustration, to 92 ft. lbs. final torque.

19. Reverse the remaining removal procedures. Install the pushrods, rockers, balls, and nuts in original positions. Torque the nuts to 20 ft. lbs. Refill the cooling system, run the engine until it reaches operating temperature, and then recheck the coolant level and replenish coolant as necessary. Operate the engine and check for leaks.

4.3L V6

LEFT SIDE

1. Remove the intake manifold.

2. Disconnect the electrical harness at the rocker cover. Then remove the rocker cover.

3. Remove the rocker arms and associated parts as described later in this section. Then, remove the pushrods, keeping them in order for reinstallation in the same positions.

4. Raise the vehicle and then support it securely at approved jacking points. Disconnect the left side of the exhaust Y-pipe at the manifold.

5. Disconnect the air pump at the left side head.

6. Remove the exhaust manifold for this head as described later in this section.

7. Lower the vehicle to the ground. Remove the power steering pump as described later in this section.

8. Remove the A/C idler pulley. Remove the A/C compressor mounting bracket.

9. Note the routing and firing order and then disconnect the spark plug wires at the cylinder head. Remove the spark plugs.

10. Loosen the head bolts in several stages, going from bolt to bolt, and turning each a fraction of a turn until tension is lost. Then remove the bolts. Install a lifting crane and lift the head off the block. Rock the head, if necessary, to break the seal, don't pry it.

11. Carefully remove any dirt or gasket pieces that cling to the block deck or cylinder head gasket surface with a dull scraper. Clean the threads on the cylinder head bolts and those in the head. Threads must be clean and dry or the bolts will not torque properly.

12. If the gasket is made of steel, coat both sides of the new gasket with sealer, making sure the coating is THIN and regular. You can use a paint roller very effectively to do this. If the gasket is steel/asbestos, USE NO SEALER.

13. Position the gasket on the block deck with the bead up and so that is is located by the dowel pins.

14. Guide the cylinder head into position over the dowel pins and position it squarely over them and the gasket. Install the bolts finger tight.

15. Torque the bolts in at least 3 equal stages, using the sequence shown in the illustration, to 67 ft. lbs. final torque.

16. Install the remaining parts in reverse of the installation procedure. Note that the pushrods must be installed in the same positions as before. Adjust the valves as described below. Refill the cooling system, run the engine until it reaches operating temperature, and then recheck the coolant level and replenish coolant as necessary. Operate the engine and check for leaks.

RIGHT SIDE

1. Remove the intake manifold as described later in this section.

2. Raise and support the vehicle at approved jacking points. Disconnect the exhaust Y-pipe at the exhaust manifold. Then, lower the vehicle.

3. Remove the exhaust manifold for this head as described later in this section.

4. Label and then disconnect the plug wires.

5. Remove the PCV hose and the oil filler tube.

6. Disconnect the Air Injection Reactor pipe and the wiring harness at the back of the right head. Remove the engine ground wire also located there.

7. Remove the rocker cover.

8. Remove the spark plugs.

9. Remove the alternator lower mounting bolt; then, remove the alternator as described earlier in this section and set it aside.

10. Remove the rocker arms and associated parts as described later in this section. Then, remove the pushrods, keeping them in order for reinstallation in the same positions.

11. Loosen the head bolts in several stages, going from bolt to bolt, and turning each a fraction of a turn until tension is lost. Then remove the bolts. Install a lifting crane and lift the head off the block. Rock the head, if necessary, to break the seal, don't pry it.

12. Carefully remove any dirt or gasket pieces that cling to the block deck or cylinder head gasket surface with a dull scraper. Clean the threads on the cylinder head bolts and those in the head must be clean and dry or the bolts will not torque properly.

13. Follow Steps 12–16 of the precedure for the left side cylinder head directly above.

Inline Six Cylinder

1. Drain the cooling system and remove the air cleaner. Disconnect the PCV hose. If equipped, disconnect the air injection hose.

2. Disconnect the accelerator pedal rod at the bellcrank on the manifold,

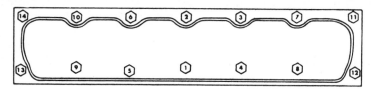

6-250, 292 head bolt torque sequence

and the fuel and vacuum lines at the carburetor.

3. Disconnect the exhaust pipe at the manifold flange, then remove the manifold bolts and clamps and remove the manifolds and carburetor as an assembly.

4. Remove the fuel and vacuum line retaining clip from the water outlet. Then disconnect the wire harness from the heat sending unit and coil, leaving the harness clear of clips on the rocker arm cover.

5. Disconnect the radiator hose at the water outlet housing and the battery ground strap at the cylinder head.

6. Disconnect the wires and remove the spark plugs. Disconnect the coil-to-distributor primary wire lead at the coil and remove the coil on models without HEI.

7. Remove the rocker arm cover. Back off the rocker arm nuts, pivot the rocker arms to clear the pushrods and remove the pushrods.

8. Remove the cylinder head bolts, cylinder head and gasket.

9. To install: Place a new cylinder head gasket over the dowel pins in the cylinder block with the head up. Do not use sealer on composition steel/asbestos gaskets.

10. Guide and lower the cylinder head into place over the dowels and gasket.

11. Use sealant on the cylinder head bolts, install and tighten them down snugly.

12. Tighten the cylinder head bolts a little at aa time with a torque wrench in the correct sequence. Final torque should be as specified.

13. Install the valve pushrods down through the cylinder head openings and seat them in their lifter sockets.

14. Install the rocker arms, balls and nuts and tighten the rocker arm nuts until all pushrod play is taken up.

15. Install the thermostat, the thermostat housing and the water outlet using new gaskets. Then connect the radiator hose.

16. Install the temperature sending switch.

17. Install the spark plugs.

18. Use new plug gaskets (if required) and torque to specifications.

19. Install the coil, then connect the heat sending unit and coil primary wires, and the battery ground cable at the cylinder head.

20. Clean the surfaces and install a new gasket over the manifold studs. Install the manifold. Install the bolts and clamps and torque as specified.

21. Connect the throttle linkage.

22. Connect the PCV fuel and vacuum lines and secure the lines in the clip at the water outlet. Connect the air injection line.

23. Fill the cooling system and check for leaks.

24. Adjust the valve lash as explained later.

25. Install the rocker arm cover and position the wiring harness in the clips.

26. Clean and install the air cleaner.

V8 Gas Engines

1. Remove the intake manifold.

2. Remove the exhaust manifolds.

3. If the truck is equipped with air conditioning, remove the A/C compressor and the forward mounting bracket and lay the compressor aside. Do not disconnect any of the refrigerant lines.

4. Remove the rocker covers. Back off the rocker arm nuts and pivot the rocker arms out of the way so that the pushrods can be removed. Identify the pushrods so that they can be installed in their original positions.

5. Remove the cylinder head bolts and remove the heads.

6. Install the cylinder heads using new gaskets. Coat a steel gasket on both sides with sealer. If a composition gasket is used, do not use sealer.

7. Clean the bolts, apply sealer to the threads, and install them hand tight.

8. Tighten the head bolts a little at a time in the proper sequence. Head bolt torque is listed in the Torque Specifications chart.

9. Install the intake and exhaust manifolds and components in the reverse order of removal. Adjust the rocker arms aand check ignition timing.

Diesel

1. Remove the intake manifold.

2. Remove the rocker arm cover(s), after removing any accessory brackets which interfere with cover removal.

3. Disconnect and label the glow plug wiring.

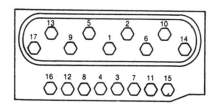

8-454 head bolt torque sequence

Small block V8 head bolt tightening sequence

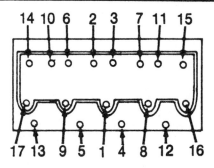

8-379 (6.2L) diesel head bolt torque sequence

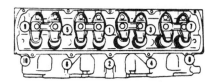

8-350 (5.7L) diesel head bolt torque sequence

4. On the right cylinder head, remove the ground strap from the head.

5. Remove the rocker arm bolts, the bridge pivots, the rocker arms, and the pushrods, keeping all the parts in order so that they can be returned to their original positions. It is a good practice to number or mark the parts to avoid interchanging them.

6. Remove the fuel return lines from the nozzles.

7. Remove the exhaust manifold(s).

8. Remove the engine block drain plug on the side of the engine from which the cylinder head is being removed.

9. Remove the head bolts. On the 379 cid (6.2L), the rear left head bolt may have to remain in the head. Remove the cylinder head.

10. To install, first clean the mating surfaces thoroughly. Install new head gaskets on the engine block. Do NOT coat the gaskets with any sealer. The gaskets have a special coating that eliminates the need for sealer. The use of sealer will interfere with this coating and cause leaks. Install the cylinder head onto the block. On the 379 cid, install the left rear head bolt before installing the head.

11. Clean the head bolts thoroughly. On the 350 (5.7L), dip the bolts in clean engine oil and install into the cylinder block until the heads of the bolts lightly contact the cylinder head. On the 379 cid, coat the bolt threads with G sealer.

12. Tighten the bolts, in the proper sequence, to 100 ft. lbs. for the 350, and 60 ft. lbs. for the 379 (6.2L). When all bolts have been tightened to this figure, begin the tightening sequence again, and torque all bolts to 130 ft. lbs. for the 350, and 96 ft. lbs. for the 379 (6.2L).

13. Install the engine block drain plug(s), the exhaust manifold(s), the

fuel return lines, the glow plug wiring, and the ground strap for the right cylinder head.

14. After disassembling, cleaning, and reassembling the valve lifters, bleed them down and install them into the engine. Install the pushrods, rocker arms, and pivots into their original locations.

15. Install the intake manifold.

16. Install the rocker cover(s). The covers do not use gaskets, but are sealed with a bead of RTV (room temperature vulcanizing) silicone sealer instead. Apply a $\frac{3}{32}$ inch bead of RTV sealer, G.M. #1052289 or the equivalent, to the clean and dry mating surface of the rocker arm cover. Run the bead of sealer to the inside of the bolt holes. Install the cover to the head within 10 minutes (while the sealer is still wet).

Rocker Arm Cover

REMOVAL & INSTALLATION

Except Astro 4.3L

1. Disconnect the negative battery cable.

2. Remove the air cleaner.

3. Disconnect the crankcase ventilation hose at the rocker arm cover.

4. Disconnect the wiring from the rocker cover clips. If so equipped, disconnect the Air Injection Reactor hoses at the diverter valve. Then, disconnect the diverter valve bracket at the intake manifold.

5. Remove the carburetor heat stove pipe, on models so equipped. On diesels, remove the injection lines.

6. If the truck is equipped with A/C,

remove the compressor rear brace. Do not disconnect any of the refrigerant lines.

7. Remove the rocker arm attaching bolts and remove the cover. If the cover is difficult to remove, gently tap the front of the cover rearward with your hand or a rubber mallet. If this still does not work, CAREFULLY pry the cover off. Be very careful not to distort the sealing surface.

8. On installation, apply a $\frac{3}{16}$ in. bead of sealer to the mating surface after removing all the old loose sealer.

9. Reverse the removal procedure to install.

Astro 4.3L V6

RIGHT SIDE

1. Disconnect the battery negative cable and remove the engine cover.

2. Remove the air cleaner.

3. Disconnect the Air Injection Reactor hoses at the diverter valve. Then, disconnect the diverter valve bracket at the intake manifold.

4. Disconnect the engine oil filler tube and the transmission fluid filler tube at the alternator bracket.

5. Remove the PCV valve at the valve cover.

6. Remove the bolts retaining the Air Injection Reactor pipes at the back of the cylinder head and move the hose out of the way.

7. Remove the distributor cap and wires. Then, remove the rocker cover bolts and remove the rocker cover.

8. Scrape all remaining pieces of gasket off both sealing surfaces with a dull scraper. Coat both sides of a new gasket with sealer, and install it and the cover with all boltholes aligned.

9. Install the bolts and torque alternately in several stages to 4 ft. lbs.

10. Reverse the remaining removal procedures to complete the installation.

LEFT SIDE

1. Disconnect the battery negative cable and remove the engine cover.

2. Remove the air cleaner.

3. Disconnect the vacuum pipe at the carburetor.

4. Disconnect the electrical harness at the rocker cover.

5. Disconnect the detent and accelerator cables at the carburetor. Then, remove the bracket for the detent and accelerator cables at the intake manifold.

6. Remove the rocker arm cover bolts. Remove the rocker cover.

7. Scrape all remaining pieces of gasket off both sealing surfaces with a dull scraper. Coat both sides of a new gasket with sealer, and install it and the cover with all boltholes aligned.

9. Install the bolts and torque alternately in several stages to 4 ft. lbs.

10. Reverse the remaining removal procedures to complete the installation. Adjust the detent and accelerator cables.

Valve System

VALVE LASH ADJUSTMENT

4-119 and 4-137 Diesel

NOTE: The valves are adjusted with the engine cold.

1. Make sure that the cylinder head and camshaft retaining bolts are tightened to the proper torque.

2. Remove the camshaft carrier side cover.

3. Turn the crankshaft with a wrench on the front pulley attaching bolt or by bumping the engine with the starter or remote starter button until the No.1 piston is at TDC of the compression stroke. You can tell when the piston is coming up on the compression stroke by removing the spark plug and placing your thumb over the hole and you will feel air being forced out of the spark plug hole past your thumb. Stop turning the crankshaft when the TDC timing mark on the crankshaft pulley is directly aligned with the timing pointer.

4. With the No.1 piston at TDC of the compression stroke, check the clearance between the rocker arm an the camshaft with the proper thickness feeler gauge on Nos.1 and 2 intake valves and Nos.1 and 3 exhaust valves.

5. Adjust the clearance by loosening the locknut with an open-end wrench, turning the adjuster screw with a phillips head screwdriver and retightening the locknut. The proper thickness feeler gauge should pass between the camshaft and the rocker with a slight drag when the clearance is correct.

6. Turn the crankshaft one full turn to position the No.4 piston at TDC of its compression stroke. Adjust the remaining valves: Nos.2 and 4 exhaust and Nos.3 and 4 intake in the same manner as outlined in Step 5.

7. Install the camshaft carrier sidecover.

Gas Engines Except 4.3L

1. Remove the rocker covers and gaskets.

2. Adjust the valves on inline six cylinder engines as follows:

   a. Mark the distributor housing with a piece of chalk at Nos.1 and 6 plug wire positions. Remove the distributor cap with the plug wires attached.

   b. Crank the engine until the distributor rotor points to No.1 cylinder (piston on compression stroke at TDC). At this point, adjust the following valves: No.1 Exhaust and Intake; No.2 Intake; No.3 Exhaust; No.4 Intake; No.5 Exhaust

   c. Back out the adjusting nut until lash is felt at the pushrod, then turn the adjusting nut in until all lash is removed. This can be determined by checking pushrod end-play while turning the adjusting nut. When all play has been removed, turn the adjusting nut in 1 full turn.

   d. Crank the engine until the distributor rotor points to No.6 cylinder (on compression stroke at TDC). The following valves can be adjusted: No.2 Exhaust; No.3 Intake; No.4 Exhaust; No.5 Intake; No.6 Intake and Exhaust.

3. Adjust the valves on V8 engines as follows:

   a. Crank the engine until the mark on the damper aligns with the TDC or 0° mark on the timing tab and the engine is in No.1 firing position. This can be determined by placing the fingers on the No.1 cylinder valves as the marks align. If the valves do not move, it is in No.1 firing position. If the valves move, it is in No.6 firing position and the crankshaft should be rotated one more revolution to the No.1 firing position.

   b. The adjustment is made in the same manner as 6 cylinder engines.

   c. With the engine in No.1 firing position, the following valves can be adjusted: Exhaust Nos.1,3,4,8; Intake Nos.1,2,5,7

   d. Crank the engine 1 full revolution until the marks are again in alignment. This is No.6 firing position. The following valves can now be adjusted: Exhaust Nos.2,5,6,7; Intake Nos.3,4,6,8

4. Reinstall the rocker arm covers using new gaskets.

5. Install the distributor cap and wire assembly.

4.3L V6

1. Remove the valve covers. If you have just completed reassembly of the valve train after parts have been replaced, it is wise to check that all the pushrods are properly seated in the lifter sockets. Crank the engine until it reaches the center or "0" mark on the timing tab on the front cover. Put your fingers in contact with both No.1 cylinder rocker arms and feel for motion while cranking the engine. If, as the crankshaft comes up on the "0" mark there is no motion in the rockers, the engine is in proper position (at TDC of the compression stroke). If there is

motion, turn the engine another 360°, following the same procedure, to get No.1 cylinder to firing position.

2. In this position adjust: Exhaust valves Nos.1, 5 and 6; Intake valves Nos.1, 2, 3. Back out the adjusting nut until lash is felt at the pushrod. Then tighten the nut down very gradually until lash just disappears. A precise way to do this is to rotate the pushrod with your fingers. When valve lash is lost, the effort required to turn the pushrod abruptly increases a great deal. Note the position of the adjusting nut precisely at this point. Then turn it downward (clockwise) exactly one more turn (360°). Repeat the adjustment procedure for each of the valves listed with the engine in this position.

3. Turn the engine one full turn (360°) until the timing mark again reaches the "0" mark. The engine will now be in No.4 firing position. Adjust the remaining valves: Exhaust: Nos.2, 3 and 4; Intake: Nos.4, 5, 6.

4. Reinstall the valve covers with new gaskets as described above.

VALVE GUIDES

Valve guides are integral with the cylinder head on all engines. Valve guide bores may be reamed to accommodate oversize valves. If wear permits, valve guides can be knurled to allow the retention of standard valves. Maximum allowable valve stem-to-guide bore clearances are listed on the Valve Specifications Chart.

Rocker Arms

REMOVAL & INSTALLATION

4-119

1. Remove the camshaft carrier as outlined under Cylinder Head Removal.

2. Remove the rocker spring from the pivot and lift the rocker from the cylinder head. Be careful not to lose the rocker guide resting on the top of each of the valves.

3. Install in the reverse order of removal.

4-137 Diesel

1. Remove the rocker cover.

2. Remove the 8 bolts fixing the rocker arm brackets in sequence commencing with the outer ones.

3. Remove the rocker arm, bracket and shaft assembly.

4. To install, follow the removal procedure in reverse order.

5. Tighten the bracket fixing bolts evenly in sequence commencing with the inner ones to 15 ft. lbs.

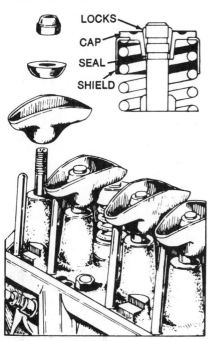

LOCKS
CAP
SEAL
SHIELD

Rocker arm components

4-121

1. Remove the air cleaner. Remove the cylinder head cover.

2. Remove the rocker arm nut and ball. Lift the rocker arm off the stud. Always keep the rocker arm assemblies together and install them on the same stud. Remove the push rods.

3. To install: Coat the bearing surfaces of the rocker arms and the rocker arm balls with "Molykote" or its equivalent.

4. Install the push rods making sure that they seat properly in the lifter.

5. Install the rocker arms, balls and nuts. Tighten the rocker arm nuts until all lash is eliminated.

6. Adjust the valves when the lifter is on the base circle of a camshaft lobe: Crank the engine until the mark on the crankshaft pulley lines up with the '0' mark on the timing tab. Make sure that the engine is in the No.1 firing position. Place your fingers on the No.1 rocker arms as the mark on the crank pulley comes near the '0' mark. If the valves are not moving, the engine is in the No.1 firing position. If the valves move, the engine is in the No.4 firing position; rotate the engine one complete revolution and it will be in the No.1 position.

7. When the engine is in the No.1 firing position, adjust the following valves: Exhaust Nos.1, 3; Intake Nos.1, 2.

8. Back the adjusting nut out until lash can be felt at the push rod, then turn the nut until all lash is removed (this can be determined by rotating the push rod while turning the adjusting nut). When all lash has been removed, turn the nut in 1½ additional turns, this will center the lifter plunger.

9. Crank the engine one complete revolution until the timing tab and the '0' mark are again in alignment. Now the engine is in the No.4 firing position. Adjust the following valves: Exhaust Nos.2, 4; Intake Nos.3, 4.

10. Installation of the remaining components is in the reverse order of removal.

6-173

NOTE: Some engines are assembled using RTV (Room Temperature Vulcanizing silicone sealant in place of rocker arm cover gasket. If the engine was assembled using RTV, never use a gasket when reassembling. Conversely, if the engine was assembled using a rocker arm cover gasket, never replace it with RTV. When using RTV, an ⅛ in. bead is sufficient. Always run the bead on the inside of the bolt holes.

Rocker arms are removed by removing the adjusting nut. Be sure to adjust valve lash after replacing rocker arms.

NOTE: When replacing an exhaust rocker, move an old intake rocker arm to the exhaust rocker arm stud and install the new rocker arm on the intake stud.

Cylinder heads use threaded rocker arm studs. If the threads in the head are damaged or stripped, the head can be retapped and a helical type insert installed.

NOTE: If engine is equipped with the A.I.R. exhaust emission control system, the interfering components of the system must be removed. Disconnect the lines at the air injection nozzles in the exhaust manifolds.

Gasoline Engines Except 4-119, 2.5L & 4.3L

Rocker arms are removed by removing the adjusting nut. Be sure to adjust the valve lash after replacing the rocker arms. Coat the replacement rocker arm and ball with engine assembly lube before installation.

Rocker arm studs that have damaged threads or are loose in the cylinder heads may be replaced by reaming the bore and installing oversize studs. Oversizes available are .003 and .013 in. The bores may also be tapped and screw-in studs installed. Several aftermarket companies produce complete rocker arm stud kits with installation tools.

2.5L (4 cyl)

1. Remove the rocker cover as described above.

2. Remove the rocker bolt, ball, and then the rocker arm. Keep them in order for installation in the same positions if they might be reused. Note that if you are replacing the pushrod only, you can loosen the nut until it is nearly to the top of the sutd and then swing the rocker out of the way without removing it. The pushrod may now be removed and replaced.

3. If replacing the pushrod, install it and make sure it seats in the lifter. Then, coat the wear surfaces of any new rocker, ball, or pushrod parts with a lubricant designed for engine rebuilding purposes (an example is Molykote™).

4. Install the parts in proper order, making sure the top of the pushrod engages with the end of the rocker where it is recessed. Install the bolt and torque it to 20 ft. lbs. The bolt must not be overtorqued!

5. Install the rocker cover.

4.3L V6

1. Remove the rocker covers.

2. Remove the rocker arm nuts, and then the rocker arm balls, rocker arms, and pushrods (if necessary). Keep them in order for installation in the same positions if they might be reused.

3. If replacing the pushrod, install it and make sure it seats in the lifter. Then, coat the wear surfaces of any new rocker, ball, or pushrod parts with a lubricant designed for engine rebuilding purposes (an example is Molykote™).

4. Install the parts in proper order, making sure the top of the pushrod engages with the end of the rocker where it is recessed. Just start the nut onto the stud, its final position will be reached in the next step.

5. Adjust the valves (see the valve adjustment procedure).

6. Install the rocker cover as described above.

Diesel Engines Except 4-137

1. Remove the air cleaner, high pressure fuel lines to the injectors, and the rocker arm cover.

2. Remove the arm pivot bolts and the pivot(s). Remove the rocker arms. The use of bridged pivots require that the rocker arms be removed in pairs.

3. To install, position the set of rocker arms in the original locations.

4. Lubricate the pivot contact surfaces and install the pivot(s).

5. Install the pivot bolts. Tighten the bolts alternately and evenly to 25 ft. lbs., following the bleed down proce-

dure outlined previously under Valve Lash Adjustment for diesel engines.

6. Install the rocker arm cover as outlined in Step 16 of the diesel engine cylinder head removal and installation procedure. Install the fuel lines and the air cleaner.

VALVE LIFTER SERVICE

Diesel Engines Except 4-137

Whenever the rocker arms and the intake manifold have been removed, the valve lifters must be removed, disassembled, assembled while submerged in diesel fuel or kerosene and bled down using a specially weighted press. The lifters also must be disassembled, reassembled while submerged and bled down on the press whenever they are removed. Note that if the rocker arms have been removed but the intake manifold has not been disturbed, the lifters can be bled down as outlined in the "Valve Lash Adjustment" procedure for diesel engines. The following procedure is to be used for lifter removal and installation, or whenever both the rocker arms and the intake manifold have been disturbed.

1. Remove the intake manifold.
2. Remove the rocker covers, the rocker arms, and the pushrods. Keep all the parts in order so that they may be installed in their original locations.
3. Remove the valve lifters.
4. To disassemble the lifters: Remove the retainer ring with a small screwdriver.
5. Remove the pushrod seat. Remove the oil metering valve. Remove the plunger and plunger spring. Remove the check valve retainer from the plunger, and remove the valve and its spring.
6. Clean all parts in a safe solvent. Check for burrs, nicks, scoring, or excessive wear, and replace as necessary.
7. Check the lifter foot for excessive wear: Place a straightedge across the lifter foot. Hold the lifter at eye level. Check for light appearing between the lifter foot and the straightedge. If light is visible, indicating a concave surface, the lifter should be replaced and the camshaft inspected. If the cam lobe is worn across the full width of the cam base circle (opposite the high lobe of the cam), the camshaft should be replaced. Wear at the center of the cam base circle is normal. Wear across the full width of the nose of the lobe is also normal.
8. After the lifter parts have been cleaned, assemble the valve disc spring and retainer into the plunger. Be sure the retainer flange is pressed tightly against the bottom of the recess in the plunger.

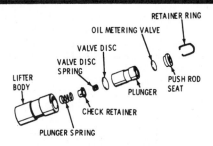

Exploded view of the 5.7L diesel valve lifter

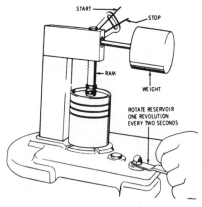

A specially weighted hand press must be used to assemble the diesel valve lifters

9. Install the plunger spring over the check retainer.
10. Hold the plunger with the spring up. Insert into the lifter body. Hold the plunger vertically while doing this to avoid cocking the spring.
11. Fill the reservoir of G.M. tool J–5790 with kerosene to within ½ inch of the top of the reservoir. This tool is a specially weighted press with provision for reservoir rotation.
12. Place the valve lifter assembly into the reservoir. Position the oil control valve and the pushrod seat onto the plunger.
13. Install a ¼ inch steel ball onto the pushrod seat. Lower the tester ram until it contacts the steel ball. Do not press on the ram. Allow the ram to move downward by its own weight, until the air bubbles expelled from the lifter assembly disappear.
14. Raise the ram, then allow it to lower by its own weight. Repeat this operation until all air is expelled from the lifter. Do not attempt to hasten the process by pumping the ram up and down.
15. After all air has been expelled, allow the ram to descend, bleeding the lifter, until the retaining ring groove is exposed. Install the retaining ring.
16. Adjust the ram screw so that it contacts the steel ball in the pushrod seat at the same time as the pointer is at the start line.
17. Raise the arm of the tester, then

start the bleed down test by resting the ram on the steel ball and starting a timer. Rotate the reservoir one revolution every two seconds, and time the indicator from the start line to the stop line. Acceptable leak down time is 6 seconds minimum for used lifters, and from 9–60 seconds for a new lifter.
18. If the lifter leak down rate falls within the specified limit, the lifter may be reused. If not, new lifters should be installed in the engine.
19. If new lifters are to be installed, they must first be filled with kerosene or diesel fuel. Install the lifter in the tester. Fill the reservoir to within ½ inch of the top, and fill the lifter as outlined in Steps 13–15.
20. To install the lifters: Coat the foot of the lifter with G.M. lubricant #562458 or the equivalent.
21. Install the lifters into their original positions. Install the pushrods into their original positions.
22. Install the intake manifold.
23. Install the rocker arms and pivots.
24. Bleed down the lifters as outlined under Valve Lash Adjustment for the diesel engine.
25. Install the rocker covers.

Intake Manifold

REMOVAL & INSTALLATION

4-119

1. Disconnect the battery ground cable and remove the air cleaner assembly.
2. Remove the EGR pipe clamp bolt at the rear of the cylinder head.
3. Raise the vehicle and remove the EGR pipe from the intake and exhaust manifolds.
4. Remove the EGR valve and bracket assembly from the intake manifold.
5. Lower the vehicle and drain the cooling system.
6. Remove the upper coolant hoses from the manifold.
7. Disconnect the accelerator linkage, vacuum lines, electrical wiring and fuel line from the intake manifold.
8. Remove the retaining nuts and remove the manifold from the cylinder head.
9. Remove the lower heater hose while holding the manifold away from the engine. Remove the manifold from the vehicle.
10. Installation is the reverse of removal.

4-137 Diesel

1. Raise engine hood.
2. Remove the bolts fixing the air cleaner and loosen the clamp bolt.

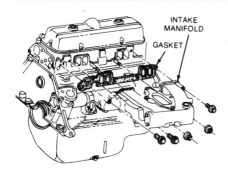

4–119 intake manifold

3. Lift the air cleaner slightly and disconnect the breather hose, then remove the air cleaner assembly.

4. Remove the 2 bolts and 4 nuts mounting the intake manifold.

5. Remove the intake manifold.

6. Installation is the reverse of removal. Torque the bolts to 15 ft. lbs.

4-121

1. Disconnect the negative battery cable.

2. Remove the air cleaner. Drain the cooling system.

3. Tag and disconnect all necessary vacuum lines and wires. Remove the idler pulley.

4. Remove the A.I.R. drive belt. If equipped with power steering, remove the drive belt and then remove the pump with the lines attached. Position the pump out of the way.

5. Remove the A.I.R. bracket-to-intake manifold bolt. Remove the air pump pulley.

6. If equipped with power steering, remove the A.I.R. thru-bolt and then the power steering adjusting bracket.

7. Loosen the lower bolt on the air pump mounting bracket so that the bracket will rotate.

8. Disconnect the fuel line at the carburetor. Disconnect the carburetor linkage and then remove the carburetor.

9. Lift off the Early Fuel Evaporation (EFE) heater grid.

10. Remove the distributor.

11. Remove the mounting bolts and nuts and remove the intake manifold. Make sure to disconnect the heater hose and condenser from the bottom of the intake manifold before you lift it all the way out.

12. Using a new gasket, replace the manifold, tightening the nuts and bolts to specification.

13. Installation of the remaining components is in the reverse order of removal. Adjust all necessary drive belts and check the ignition timing.

2.5L (4 cyl)

1. Disconnect the negative battery cable. On the Astro van, remove the glovebox assembly and the engine cover.

2. Remove the air cleaner assembly. Drain the cooling system.

3. Disconnect the rail that mounts the vacuum pipes at both the thermostat housing and the exhaust manifold.

4. Go around the engine and label (if necessary) and then disconnect all vacuum and electrical connectors that would interfere with manifold removal. Where these lines are routed so as to be mounted on or near the manifold, disconnect mounts or harnesses also.

5. Disconnect the accelerator cable at the TBI throttle body. Disconnect fuel lines at the TBI throttle body and anywhere they are fastened down to the manifold, catching any fuel that spills in a metal cup.

6. Disconnect the coolant hoses at the intake manifold.

7. Disconnect the alternator wiring, remove the belt, and then remove the alternator mounting bolts and move the alternator aside.

8. Unplug the coil electrical connector at the top. The coil is attached via its mount to the two rear studs mounting the intake manifold. Remove the ignition coil attacting nuts at the intake manifold, and remove the coil assembly.

9. Note locations of the two different types of studs and the bolts (you can refer to the illustration. Then, remove studs and bolts and the washers. Remove the manifold and gasket.

10. Scrape both gasket surfaces with a dull scraper. If the manifold is suspected of leaking, check the flatness of the manifold gasket surface with a straightedge. Replace the manifold if it is significantly distorted.

11. Install a new gasket with all holes lined up and then position the manifold against it. Install all the studs and then install finger tight.

12. First torque the studs numbered 1 (in the illustration) to 25 ft. lbs.; then torque those numbered 2 to 37 ft. lbs.; finally torque those numbered 3 to 28 ft. lbs. Reverse the remaining removal procedures to complete the installation.

4.3L V6

1. Disconnect the negative battery cable. Remove the engine cover.

2. Remove the air cleaner. Drain the cooling system.

3. Mark and then remove the dis-

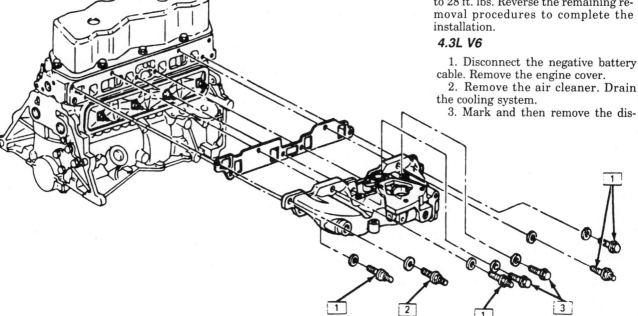

2.5 L four Cylinder engine intake manifold mounting. Bolts 1 are torqued to 25 ft.-lbs.; 2 to 37 fts.-lbs.; and 3 to 28 ft.-lbs.

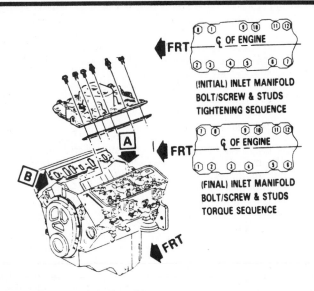

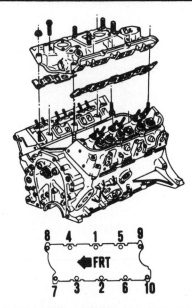

Torque the manifold bolts in the sequence shown on the 4.3 L V-6

6-173 intake manifold torque sequence

tributor cap and plug wires. Disconnect the Electronic Spark Control connector. Then, remove the distributor (you can refer to the removal procedure located earlier in this section, if necessary).

4. Disconnect the transmission and accelerator cables at the throttle linkage.

5. Remove the air conditioning compressor rear brace, leaving the compressor and lines in position.

6. Disconnect both the transmission and engine oil filler tubes at the alternator brace.

7. Remove the air conditioner compressor idler pulley at the alternator brace. Then, remove the alternator brace.

8. Disconnect the fuel line at the carburetor, catching any fuel that spills in a metal cup.

9. Label and then remove any vacuum hoses and electrical connectors at the carburetor which will interfere with carburetor and manifold removal.

10. Remove Air Injection Reactor hoses and their brackets.

11. Disconnect the heater hose at the manifold.

12. Remove the manifold bolts and remove the manifold.

14. Clean all RTV sealant and any other foreign material from the gasket and seal surfaces on the manifold, block and heads with a degreaser.

15. Install the gaskets on the heads and then run a $^{3}/_{16}$ in. bead of RTV sealer #1052917 or equivalent on the front and rear ridges of the cylinder case. The bead must also be extended $^{1}/_{2}$ in. up each cylinder head to seal the manifold side gaskets and retain them during manifold installation. Apply an appropriate sealer at the water passages as well.

16. Carefully put the manifold in position precisely, with all thread holes and passages precisely lined up. Install the studs and bolts finger tight. Torque them to 30 ft. lbs. first in the order shown at the top of the illustration. Then, repeat the torquing operation at 30 ft. lbs. in the second sequence.

17. Perform the remaining steps in the reverse of the removal procedure. Operate the engine and check for leaks.

6-173

1. Remove the rocker covers.
2. Drain the cooling system.
3. If equipped, remove the AIR pump and bracket.
4. Remove the distributor cap. Mark the position of the ignition rotor in relation to the distributor body, and remove the distributor. Do not crank the engine with the distributor removed.
5. Remove the heater and radiator hoses from the intake manifold.
6. Remove the power brake vacuum hose.
7. Disconnect and label the vacuum hoses. Remove the EFE pipe from the rear of the manifold.
8. Remove the carburetor linkage. Disconnect and plug the fuel line.
9. Remove the manifold retaining bolts and nuts.
10. Remove the intake manifold. Remove and discard the gaskets, and scrape off the old silicone seal from the front and rear ridges.
11. To install: The gaskets are marked for right and left side installation; do not interchange them. Clean the sealing surface of the engine block, and apply a $^{3}/_{16}$ in. bead of silicone sealer to each ridge.

12. Install the new gaskets onto the heads. The gaskets will have to be cut slightly to fit past the center pushrods. Do not cut any more material than necessary. Hold the gaskets in place by extending the ridge bead of sealer $^{1}/_{4}$ in. onto the gasket ends.

13. Install the intake manifold. The area between the ridges and the manifold should be completely sealed.

14. Install the retaining bolts and nuts, and tighten in sequence to 23 ft. lbs. Do not overtighten; the manifold is made from aluminum, and can be warped or cracked with excessive force.

15. The rest of installation is the reverse of removal. Adjust the ignition timing after installation, and check the coolant level after the engine has warmed up.

Six Cylinder With Combination Manifold

1. The intake and exhaust manifolds are removed as an assembly. Remove the air cleaner.
2. Disconnect the throttle rods at the bellcrank and remove the throttle return spring.
3. Disconnect the fuel and vacuum lines at the carburetor. Plug the fuel line. Disconnect the choke cable at the carburetor.
4. Disconnect the crankcase ventilation hose at the carburetor. Disconnect the vapor hose at the evaporativ canister, if so equipped.
5. Disconnect the exhaust pipe at the manifold flange and discard the packing.
6. Disconnect the EGR valve hose (if equipped).
7. Remove the manifold attaching

bolts and clamps and remove the manifold assembly. Discard the gaskets.

8. The manifold assembly can be separated by removing 1 bolt and 2 nuts at the center. Don't tighten these down all the way until the manifold assembly is installed on the engine.

9. Check the manifold for straightness along the exhaust port faces. If it is distorted more than 0.015 in. it should be replaced. Clean all mounting faces.

10. Installation is the reverse of removal. Use all new gaskets. Bolt torques are given in the Torque Specifications.

V8 Except Diesel

1. Remove the air cleaner.
2. Drain the radiator.
3. Disconnect:
   a. Battery cables at the battery.
   b. Upper radiator and heater hoses·at the manifolds.
   c. Crankcase ventilation hoses as required.
   d. Fuel line and choke cable at the carburetor.
   e. Accelerator linkage at the carburetor.
   f. Vacuum hose at the distributor.
   g. Power brake hose at the carburetor base or manifold, if applicable.
   h. Temperature sending switch wires.
   i. Water pump by-pass at the water pump (Mark IV only).

4. Remove the distributor cap and scribe the rotor position relative to the distributor body.

5. Remove the distributor.

6. As required, remove the oil filler bracket, air cleaner bracket, air compressor and bracket and accelerator bellcrank.

7. Remove the manifold-to-head attaching bolts then remove the manifold and carburetor as an assembly.

8. If the manifold is to be replaced, transfer the carburetor (and mounting studs), water outlet and thermostat (use a new gasket) heater hose adapter, EGR valve (use new gasket) and, if applicable, TVS switch and the choke coil. All engines use a carburetor heat choke tube which must be transferred to a new manifold.

9. Before installing the manifold, thoroughly clean the gasket and seal surfaces of the cylinder heads and manifold.

10. Install the manifold end seals, folding the tabs if applicable, and the manifold/head gaskets, using a sealing compound around the water passages, 1980-87 models use RTV (Room Temperature Vulcanizing) silicone seal at the front and rear ridges of the cylinder block, instead of seals. On these

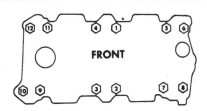

Small block V8 intake manifold torque sequence

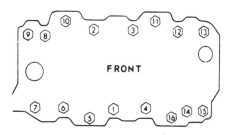

8-454 intake manifold torque sequence

models, remove any loose RTV from the sealing surfaces. Apply a $\frac{3}{16}$ in. bead of RTV sealer, G.M. #1052366 or the equivalent, on the front and rear ridges, extending the bead up $\frac{1}{2}$ in. on the cylinder heads to seal and retain the intake manifold side gaskets.

11. When installing the manifold, care should be taken not to dislocate the end seals. It is helpful to use a pilot in the distributor opening. Tighten the manifold bolts to 30 ft. lbs. in the sequence illustrated.

12. Install the distributor with the rotor in its original location as indicated by the scribe line. If the engine has been disturbed, refer to Distributor Removal and Installation.

13. If applicable, install the alternator upper bracket and adjust the belt tension.

14. Connect all components disconnected in Steps 3 and 6.

15. Fill the cooling system, start the engine, check for leaks and adjust the ignition timing and carburetor idle speed and mixture.

Diesel

1. Remove the air cleaner.

2. Drain the radiator. Loosen the upper bypass hose clamp, remove the thermostat housing bolts, and remove the housing and the thermostat from the intake manifold.

3. Remove the breather pipes from the rocker covers and the air crossover. Remove the air crossover. It is a good idea to cover the air intakes in the manifold to prevent nuts and bolts from falling down into the engine, if dropped. The intake passages can simply be taped over.

4. Disconnect the throttle rod and the return spring. If equipped with cruise control, remove the servo.

5. Remove the hairpin clip at the bellcrank and disconnect the cables. Remove the throttle cable from the bracket on the manifold; position the cable away from the engine. Disconnect and label any wiring as necessary.

6. Remove the alternator bracket as necessary. If the truck is equipped with air conditioning, remove the compressor mounting bolts and move the compressor aside, without disconnecting any of the hoses. Remove the compressor mounting bracket from the intake manifold.

7. Disconnect the fuel line from the pump and the fuel filter. Remove the fuel filter and bracket.

8. Disconnect the fuel return line from the injection pump. Using two wrenches to prevent the lines from being twisted, disconnect the injection pump lines at the nozzles.

— **CAUTION** —
Do not bend the injection pump lines!

9. Remove the three nuts retaining the injection pump, using G.M. special tool No. J26987 or the equivalent. Remove the pump and cap all open lines and nozzles.

10. Disconnect the vacuum lines at the vacuum pump. Remove the bolt and the bracket holding the pump to the block and remove the pump.

11. Remove the intake manifold drain tube clamp and remove the drain tube.

12. Remove the intake manifold bolts and remove the manifold. Remove the adapter seal. Remove the injection pump adapter.

13. Clean the mating surfaces of the cylinder heads and the intake manifold using a putty knife. Be extremely careful not to scratch or gouge the surfaces. Clean and dry the surfaces with solvent.

NOTE: If the rocker arms have been removed, the valve lifters must be removed, disassembled, then reassembled while submerged in kerosene or diesel fuel, then bled down using the specially weighted press (see the procedure earlier in this section). Do not install the manifold until the affected lifters have been serviced.

14. To install the manifold: Coat both sides of the gasket surface that seal the intake manifold to the cylinder heads with G.M. sealer 1050805 or the equivalent. Position the intake manifold gaskets on the cylinder heads. Install the end seals, making sure that the ends are positioned under the cylinder heads.

15. Carefully lower the intake manifold into place on the engine.

16. Clean the intake manifold bolts thoroughly, then dip them in clean engine oil. Install the bolts and tighten to 15 ft. lbs. in the sequence shown. Next, tighten all the bolts to 30 ft. lbs., in sequence, and finally tighten to 40 ft. lbs. in sequence.

17. Install the intake manifold drain tube and clamp.

18. File the mark from the injection pump adapter.

—————— CAUTION ——————

Do not file the mark from the injection pump.

19. Place the engine on TDC for the No.1 cylinder. The mark on the harmonic balancer on the crankshaft will be aligned with the zero mark on the timing tab, and both valves for No.1 cylinder will be closed. The index mark on the injection pump driven gear should be offset to the right when No.1 is at TDC. Check that all these conditions are met before continuing.

20. Apply chassis grease to the seal area on the adapter, the tapered edge and the seal area on the intake manifold. Install the adapter but leave the bolts loose.

21. Apply chassis grease to the inside and outside diameters of the adapter seal, and to the seal installing tool, G.M. J28425. Install the seal onto the tool.

22. Push the seal onto the injection pump adapter, using the tool (J-28425 or the equivalent). Remove the tool and inspect the seal to see if it is properly positioned.

23. Tighten the adapter bolts to 25 ft. lbs.

24. Install a timing tool, G.M. J26896 or the equivalent, into the injection pump adapter. Tighten the tool toward No.1 cylinder to 50 ft. lbs. While holding the tool and adapter at this torque, mark the injection pump adapter by striking the marking pin with a hammer. Remove the tool.

25. Remove the protective caps from the lines. Line up the offset tang on the injection pump driveshaft with the pump driven gear. Install the pump.

26. Install the three retaining nuts and lockwashers for the injection pump but do not tighten the nuts. Connect the injection pump lines to the nozzles. Use two wrenches to tighten the lines (25 ft. lbs.).

—————— CAUTION ——————

Do not bend or twist the injection pump lines.

27. Connect the fuel return lines to the pump.

28. Align the injection pump mark with the adapter mark and tighten the nuts. Use a ¾ in. open end wrench on the boss at the front of the injection

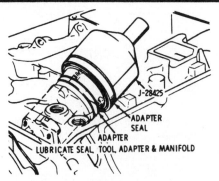

Adapter seal installation

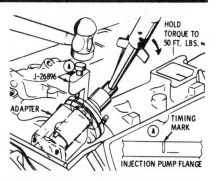

Injection pump timing mark application

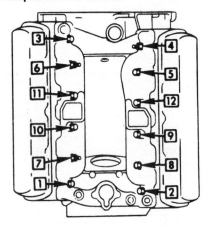

8-350 diesel intake manifold torque sequence

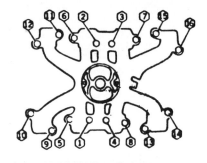

8-379 diesel intake manifold torque sequence

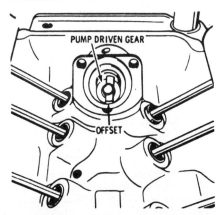

The index mark on the injection pump driven gear will be offset to the right when the no. 1 cylinder is at TDC

pump to aid in rotating the pump to align the marks. Tighten the nuts to 18 ft. lbs.

29. Adjust the throttle rod and return spring.

30. Install the fuel filter and bracket and install the fuel line to the pump and the filter.

31. Install the vacuum pump and the vacuum lines. Do not operate the engine without the vacuum pump installed, it is the drive for the engine oil pump.

32. Connect the wiring.

33. Install the alternator and air conditioning compressor brackets.

34. Install the cable in the bracket and bellcrank, then install the bellcrank.

35. Connect the throttle rod and the return spring.

36. Remove the tape from the air intakes and install the air crossover. Install the breather tubes and the flow control valve at the air crossover. Connect the upper radiator hose and the heater hose, install the thermostat and thermostat housing, fill the cooling system, start the engine and check for leaks.

Exhaust Manifold

REMOVAL & INSTALLATION

4-119

1. Disconnect the battery ground cable and remove the air cleaner assembly.

2. Remove the EGR pipe clamp bolt at the rear of the cylinder head.

3. Raise the vehicle and remove the EGR pipe from the intake and exhaust manifolds.

4. Separate the exhaust pipe from the manifold.

5. Remove the manifold shield and remove the heat stove.

6. Remove the manifold retaining nuts and remove the manifold from the engine.

7. Installation is the reverse of removal.

4-137 Diesel

1. Raise engine hood.
2. Remove the bolts fixing the air cleaner and loosen the clamp bolt.
3. Lift the air cleaner slightly and disconnect the breather hose, then remove the air cleaner assembly.
4. Disconnect the exhaust pipe from the exhaust manifold at the flange.
5. Remove the 3 nuts fixing the exhaust manifold, then remove the engine hanger and exhaust manifold.
6. Installation is the reverse of removal. Torque the bolts to 15 ft. lbs.

4-121

1. Disconnect the negative battery cable.
2. Remove the air cleaner. Remove the exhaust manifold shield. Raise and support the front of the vehicle.
3. Disconnect the exhaust pipe at the manifold and then lower the vehicle.
4. Disconnect the air management-to-check valve hose and remove the bracket. Disconnect the oxygen sensor lead wire.
5. Remove the alternator belt. Remove the alternator adjusting bolts, loosen the pivot bolt and pivot the alternator upward.
6. Remove the alternator brace and the A.I.R. pipes bracket bolt.
7. Unscrew the mounting bolts and remove the exhaust manifold. The manifold should be removed with the A.I.R. plumbing as an assembly. If the manifold is to be replaced, transfer the plumbing to the new one.
8. Clean the mating surface on the manifold and the head, position the manifold and tighten the bolts to the proper specifications.
9. Installation of the remaining components is in the reverse order of removal.

2.5L (4 cyl)

1. Disconnect the negative battery cable. On the Astro van, remove the glove box and the engine cover.
2. Remove the exhaust heat stove pipe at the manifold. Disconnect the oxygen sensor wire at the oxygen sensor.
3. Raise the vehicle and support it securely at approved locations. Disconnect the exhaust pipe at the manifold.
4. Lower the vehicle again and remove the rear air conditioner compressor bracket, leaving the front compressor bracket and compressor in place.
5. Remove the bolts and remove the manifold.
6. Use a dull-edged scraper and scrape any carbon or gasket pieces from the gasket surfaces. If you suspect the manifold may have been leak-

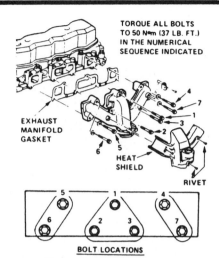

TORQUE ALL BOLTS TO 50 N•m (37 LB. FT.) IN THE NUMERICAL SEQUENCE INDICATED

EXHAUST MANIFOLD GASKET

HEAT SHIELD

RIVET

BOLT LOCATIONS

Torque sequence for torquing the exhaust manifold bolts on the 2.5 L four cylinder engine

ing due to distortion, check the flatness of its gasket surface with a straightedge; replace it if a significant distortion is found.
7. Install a new gasket as shown in the illustration. Install the manifold and all bolts, just finger tight.
8. Torque the bolts to 44 ft. lbs. in the sequence shown in the illustration.
9. Reverse the remaining removal procedures to complete the installation. Operate the engine and check carefully for leaks, repairing any problems as necessary.

6-173

LEFT SIDE

1. Remove the air cleaner. Remove the carburetor heat stove pipe.
2. Remove the air supply plumbing from the exhaust manifold.
3. Raise and support the car. Unbolt and remove the exhaust pipe at the manifold.
4. Unbolt and remove the manifold.
5. To install: Clean the mating surfaces of the cylinder head and manifold. Install the manifold onto the head, and install the retaining bolts finger tight.
6. Tighten the manifold bolts in a circular pattern, working from the center to the ends, to 25 ft. lbs. in two stages.
7. Connect the exhaust pipe to the manifold.
8. The remainder of installation is the reverse of removal.

RIGHT SIDE

1. Raise and support the vehicle.
2. Tighten the exhaust pipe-to-manifold flange bolts until they break off. Remove the pipe from the manifold. Later models are equipped with flange bolts.

3. Lower the vehicle. Remove the spark plug wires from the plugs. Number them first if they are not already labeled.
4. Remove the air supply pipes from the manifold. Remove the PULSAIR bracket bolt from the rocker cover, on models so equipped, then remove the pipe assembly.
5. Remove the manifold retaining bolts and remove the manifold.
6. To install: Clean the mating surfaces of the cylinder head and manifold. Position the manifold against the head and install the retaining bolts finger tight.
7. Tighten the bolts in a circular pattern, working from the center to the ends, to 25 ft. lbs. in two stages.
8. Install the air supply system.
9. Install the spark plug wires. Raise and support the car. Connect the exhaust pipe to the manifold and install new flange bolts.

Six Cylinder With Integral Head

1. Remove the air cleaner. Disconnect negative battery terminal.
2. Remove the power steering pump and, if equipped, the AIR pump.
3. Remove the EFE (early fuel evaporation) valve bracket.
4. Disconnect the throttle controls and the throttle return spring.
5. Disconnect the exhaust pipe at the manifold flange. Disconnect the converter bracket at the transmission mount, if so equipped. If equipped with manifold converter, disconnect the exhaust pipe from the converter, and remove the converter.
6. Remove the manifold attaching bolts and remove the manifold. Discard the gasket.

Six cylinder integral manifold torque sequence

7. Check for cracks in the manifold before it is replaced.
8. Install a new gasket on the exhaust manifold.
9. Clean and oil the bolts and install the bolts, torquing them to specifications.
10. Connect the exhaust pipe, throttle controls, and return spring. Install the air cleaner, start the engine, and check for leaks.

4.3L V6

RIGHT SIDE

1. Disconnect the negative battery

cable. Raise the vehicle and support it at approved locations.

2. Disconnect the exhaust pipe at the manifold. Then, lower the vehicle back to the floor.

3. Remove the engine cover. Disconnect the Air Injection Reactor hose at the check valve.

4. Remove the exhaust manifold bolts. Then, disconnect the AIR pipe bracket at the head.

5. Remove the manifold.

6. Using a dull-edged scraper, scrape any carbon or gasket pieces from the gasket surfaces. If you suspect the manifold may have been leaking due to distortion, check the flatness of its gasket surface with a straightedge; replace it if a significant distortion is found.

7. Install a new gasket in the proper position and then install the manifold in position over it. Install the bolts finger tight.

8. Refer to the applicable part of the illustration and torque the bolts to the specification given for each bolt according to its numbered location. Complete the remaining steps of the installation procedure in reverse of removal.

LEFT SIDE

1. Disconnect the negative battery cable. Raise the vehicle and support it securely at approved positions.

2. Disconnect the exhaust pipe at the manifold.

3. Disconnect the Air Injection Reactor pipe at the head.

4. Remove the manifold bolts and remove the manifold.

5. Using a dull-edged scraper, scrape any carbon or gasket pieces from the gasket surfaces. If you suspect the manifold may have been leaking due to distortion, check the flatness of its gasket surface with a straightedge; replace it if a significant distortion is found.

6. Install a new gasket in the proper position and then install the manifold in position over it. Install the bolts finger tight.

7. Refer to the applicable part of the illustration and torque the bolts to the specification given for each bolt according to its numbered location. Complete the remaining steps of the installation procedure in reverse of removal.

V8 Except Diesel

1. If equipped with AIR, remove the air injector assembly. The $\frac{1}{4}$ in. pipe threads in the manifold are straight cut threads. Do not use a $\frac{1}{4}$ in. tapered pipe tap to clean the threads.

2. Disconnect the battery.

3. If equipped, remove the carburetor heat stove pipe.

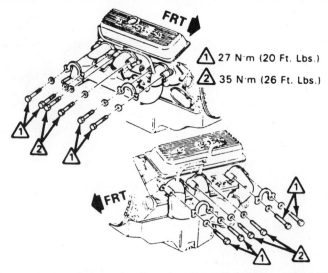

Torque sequence for torquing the exhaust manifold bolts on the 4.3 L V-6

4. Remove the spark plug wire heat shields. On Mark IV, remove spark plugs.

5. On the left exhaust manifold, disconnect and remove the alternator.

6. Disconnect the exhaust pipe from the manifold and hang it from the frame out of the way.

7. Bend the locktabs and remove the end bolts, then the center bolts. Remove the manifold.

NOTE: A $\frac{9}{16}$ in. thin wall 6-point socket, sharpened at the leading edge and tapped onto the head of the bolt, simplifies bending the locktabs.

8. Installation is the reverse of removal. Clean all mating surfaces and use new gaskets. Torque all bolts to specifications from the inside working out.

Diesel

LEFT SIDE

1. Remove the air cleaner.

2. Remove the lower alternator bracket.

3. Raise the truck and remove the exhaust pipe from the manifold flange.

4. Lower the truck. Bend the locktabs away from the manifold mounting bolts. Remove the bolts and remove the manifold from above. Do not lose the locktabs, and do not use the washers for the bolts, which go under the locktabs.

5. Installation is the reverse. Tighten the manifold bolts to 25 ft. lbs. in two stages, working in a circular pattern from the center to the ends. Then tighten the front bolt to 30 ft. lbs.

RIGHT SIDE

1. Raise and support the truck. Re-

move the bolts retaining the exhaust pipe to the manifold flange.

2. Bend the locktabs away from the manifold mounting bolts. Remove the bolts and remove the manifold. Do not lose the locktabs and the washers for the bolts, which go under the locktabs.

3. Installation is the reverse. Tighten the bolts to 25 ft. lbs. in two progressive steps, working in a circular pattern from the center to the ends.

Timing Cover

REMOVAL & INSTALLATION

4-119

1. Remove the cylinder head.

2. Remove the oil pan.

3. Remove the oil pickup tube from the oil pump.

4. Remove the harmonic balancer.

5. Remove the AIR pump drive belt.

6. On air conditioned vehicles: Remove the compressor, with lines still connected, and lay it to one side. Remove the compressor mounting brackets. If equipped with power steering, remove the pump, with hoses attached, and bracket and lay aside.

7. Remove the distributor cap and then remove the distributor.

8. Remove the front cover attaching bolts and remove the front cover.

9. Remove and discard the front cover to block gasket.

10. Install a new gasket onto cylinder block.

11. Align the oil pump drive gear punch mark with the oil filter side of cover; then align the center of dowel pin with alignment mark on oil pump case.

12. Rotate the crankcase until Nos. 1 and 4 cylinders are at top dead center.

13. Install the front cover by engaging the pinion gear with the oil pump drive gear on the crankshaft.

14. Check that the punch mark on the oil pump drive gear is turned to the rear side as viewed through clearance between front cover and cylinder block.

15. Check that the slit at the end of oil pump shaft is parallel with front face of cylinder block and that it is off-set forward.

16. With all parts correctly installed, install and tighten front cover bolts.

17. Reverse Steps 1–7 of Removal procedure.

18. Check engine timing.

19. Check for leaks.

4-121

NOTE: The following procedure requires the use of a special tool.

1. Remove the engine drive belts.

2. Although not absolutely necessary, removal of the right front inner fender splash shield will facilitate access to the front cover.

3. Unscrew the center bolt from the crankshaft pulley and slide the pulley and hub from the crankshaft.

4. Remove the alternator lower bracket.

5. Remove the oil pan-to-front cover bolts.

6. Remove the front cover-to-block bolts and then remove the front cover. If the front cover is difficult to remove, use a plastic mallet.

7. The surfaces of the block and front cover must be clean and free of oil. Apply a $1/8$ in. bead of RTV sealant to the cover. The sealant must be wet to the touch when the bolts are torqued down.

NOTE: When applying RTV sealant to the front cover, be sure to keep it out of the bolt holes.

8. Position the front cover on the block using a centering tool (J23042) and tighten the screws.

9. Installation of the remaining components is in the reverse order of removal. The oil seal can be replaced with the cover either on or off the engine. If the cover is on the engine, remove the crankshaft pulley and hub first. Pry out the seal using a large screwdriver, being careful not to distort the seal mating surface. Install the new seal so that the open side or helical side is towards the engine. Press it into place with a seal driver made for the purpose. Install the hub if removed.

4-137 Diesel

1. Remove the radiator.

2. Remove the compressor drive belt by moving the power steering oil or idler (if so equipped).

3. Loosen the alternator adjusting plate bolt and fixed bolt, then remove the fan belt.

4. Remove the 4 bolts mounting the crankshaft pulley and remove the crankshaft pulley.

5. Remove the bolts mounting the timing pulley housing covers, then remove the covers.

6. Installation is the reverse of removal.

2.5L (4 cyl)

1. Disconnect the negative battery cable.

2. Disconnect the power steering pump reservoir fan shroud at the timing cover. Remove the upper radiator fan shroud.

3. Loosen the bolts on the fan and pulley. Loosen the drive belts. Then remove the fan and pulley.

4. Remove the alternator as described earlier in this section. Then, remove the alternator brace and front and rear brackets.

5. Remove the front crankshaft pulley. Then, remove the hub bolt.

6. Remove the crankshaft hub with a puller.

7. Drain the cooling system. Disconnect the lower radiator hose at the water pump.

8. Remove the front cover bolts (including the two that also attach the oil pan) and remove the front cover.

9. Clean the gasket surfaces on the block, cover and oil pan. Then, apply a continuous bead of RTV sealer on the block and pan side of the cover. Keep the sealer out of the boltholes.

NOTE: The cover must be installed using a centering tool J34995 or equivalent; otherwise the installation of the hub after the cover is back in place will damage the seal, or at least result in seal leakage due to imperfect alignment.

10. Install the centering tool into the front seal. Then, install the cover as you install the centering tool over the front of the crankshaft. Install the two cover-to-oil pan bolts finger tight. Then, install the remaining cover bolts finger tight.

11. Torque all the bolts to 90 inch lbs.

12. Remove the centering tool.

13. Coat the front cover oil seal contact area of the hub with engine oil. Then, position the hub on the crankshaft with the keyway aligned with the key on the shaft and slide it into position until it bottoms on the crank-

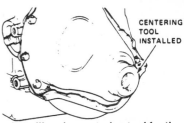

Installing the centering tool for the timing gear cover on the 2.5 L four

shaft. Install the center bolt and torque it to 160 ft. lbs.

14. Complete the installation in reverse of the removal procedure.

6-173

1. Remove the water pump.

2. Remove the compressor without disconnecting any A/C lines and lay it aside.

3. Remove harmonic balancer, using a puller.

NOTE: The outer ring (weight) of the harmonic balancer is bonded to the hub with rubber. The balancer must be removed with a puller which acts on the inner hub only. Pulling on the outer portion of the balancer will break the rubber bond or destroy the tuning of the torsional damper.

4. Disconnect the lower radiator hose and heater hose.

5. Remove timing gear cover attaching screws, and cover and gasket.

6. Clean all the gasket mounting surfaces on the front cover and block. Apply a continuous $3/32$ in. bead of sealer (1052357 or equivalent) to front cover sealing surface and around coolant passage ports and central bolt holes.

7. Apply a bead of silicone sealer to the oil pan-to-cylinder block joint.

8. Install a centering tool in the crankcase snout hole in the front cover and install the cover.

9. Install the front cover bolts finger tight, remove the centering tool and tighten the cover bolts. Install the harmonic balancer, pulley, water pump, belts, radiator, and all other parts.

Inline Six Cylinder

1. Remove the radiator after draining it.

2. Remove the fan, pulley, and belt. Remove any power steering and/or AIR pump drive belts. Remove any braces for the above pumps which will interfere with cover removal and position the pumps out of the way.

3. Remove the crankshaft pulley and damper. Use a puller to remove the damper. Do not attempt to pry or

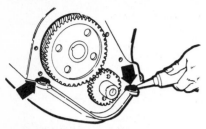

Apply sealer to the six cylinder timing cover at the areas shown

hammer the damper off, or it will be damaged.

4. Remove the mounting bolts. Remove the cover. These engines use RTV (room temperature vulcanizing) silicone seal at the oil pan to front cover junction; no front rubber seal is used.

5. Apply a $^3/_{16}$ in. bead of RTV silicone seal on the cover sealing surface.

6. Coat the front cover gasket with sealer and use a $^1/_8$ in. bead of silicone sealer at the oil pan to cylinder block joint. Replace the damper before tightening the cover bolts down, so that the cover seal will align. The damper must be drawn into place. Hammering it will destroy it.

7. Replace the oil pan if it was removed, and fill the crankcase with oil.

4.3L V6

1. Disconnect the negative battery cable.

2. Remove the drive belts and front pulley.

3. Raise and support the vehicle at approved jacking points for access. Then install a threaded puller such as J23523-1 or equivalent to the front hub. Turn the puller screw to remove the hub from the crankshaft.

4. Drain the cooling system. Remove the water pump.

5. Remove the front cover attaching screws and remove the front cover. Remove the gasket and discard it. Scrape the gasket surfaces with a dull scraper to remove any remaining gasket material. Cut any remaining gasket material protruding from the joint between the oil pan gasket and the block with a sharp knife.

6. Apply a $^1/_8$ in. bead of RTV sealer such as 1052917 or equivalent to the joint formed between the oil pan and block, keeping the sealer out of bolt holes. Coat a new gasket with gasket sealer and apply it to the cover with all holes lined up.

7. Install the timing cover-to-oil pan seal. Coat the bottom of this seal with clean engine oil and then position the timing cover over the end of the crankshaft. Loosely install the upper cover attaching screws to hold the cover in place.

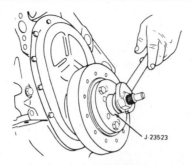

Installing the torsional damper on the 4.3 L V-6 after the timing cover is in place

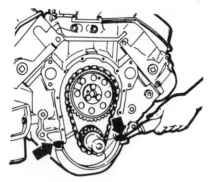

Apply sealer to the V8 cover pads at the areas shown

8. Press downward on the cover so the dowels on the block enter the holes in the cover without binding and without distortion in the cover. Tighten the attaching screws alternately and evenly to hold the cover in this position. Then, install the remaining cover screws just finger tight.

9. Torque all the front cover attaching screws to 7 ft. lbs.

10. Coat the front cover seal contact area on the front hub with clean engine oil. Place the hub in position over the crankshaft and key.

NOTE: The front hub and damper must be installed with a tool designed especially for this purpose. This is because the intertial weight section of the damper is attached to the hub with a rubber material that cannot tolerate any end thrust.

11. Use a damper installing tool such as J23523 or equivalent to pull the hub into position. When installing the threaded end of the tool into the center of the crankshaft, make sure that at least $^1/_2$ in. of thread enagement is obtained. Then, install the plate, thrust bearing and nut and turn the nut to force the hub onto the crankshaft. When the hub bottoms out, remove the tool and install the hub retaining bolt into the center of the crankshaft. Torque it to 60 ft. lbs.

12. Perform the remaining steps of

the installation procedure in reverse order.

Small Block V8

1. Drain the oil.

2. Drain and remove the radiator.

3. Remove the fan, pulley and belt. Remove any power steering and/or AIR pump drive belts. Remove any braces for these pumps which will interfere with cover removal and position the pumps out of the way.

4. Remove the water pump.

5. Remove the crankshaft pulley and damper. Use a puller on the damper. Do not attempt to pry or hammer the damper off.

6. Rotate the retaining bolts, and remove the timing cover.

7. Clean the gasket surfaces on the block and the front cover.

8. Use a sharp knife to trim any excess oil pan gasket material which protrudes from the oil pan-to-engine block junction.

9. Apply a $^1/_8$ in. bead of RTV silicone sealer, G.M. 1052366 or the equivalent, to the joint of the oil pan and cylinder block.

10. Coat the front cover gasket with sealer and install the gasket onto the cover.

11. Install the front cover-to-oil pan seal. Lightly coat the bottom of the seal with clean engine oil and position over the crankshaft end.

12. Loosely install the front cover upper attaching bolts.

13. Press downward on the cover so that the dowels in the block are aligned with the holes in the cover. While holding the cover in position, tighten the upper attaching bolts alternately and evenly.

14. Install the remaining bolts and tighten all the bolts to specification.

15. Install the torsional damper and the water pump.

Mark IV V8

1. Remove the torsional damper and water pump.

2. Remove the two oil pan-to-front cover attaching screws.

3. Remove the front cover-to-block attaching screws.

4. Pull the cover slightly forward to permit cutting the oil pan front seal.

5. Using a sharp knife, cut the oil pan front seal flush with the cylinder block at both sides of the cover.

6. Remove the front cover and the portion of the oil pan front seal. Remove the front cover gasket.

7. Clean the gasket mating surfaces.

8. Cut the tabs from a new oil pan front seal, using a sharp knife to get a clean cut.

9. Install the seal on the front cover

pressing the tips into the holes in the front cover.

10. Coat a new gasket with gasket sealer and install the gasket on the cover.

11. Apply a $\frac{1}{8}$ in. bead of RTV sealant to the joint formed at the junction of the oil pan and cylinder block.

12. Place the front cover in position.

13. Align the cover over the dowel pins in the block.

14. Further installation is the reverse of removal.

Diesel

1. Drain cooling system. Disconnect radiator hoses and bypass hose.

2. Remove all belts, fan and fan pulley, crankshaft pulley and harmonic balancer, and accessory brackets. The harmonic balancer must be removed with a puller which pulls from the rear center of the balancer. Any other type of puller, such as a universal claw type which pulls on the outside of the hub, can destroy the balancer. The outside ring of the balancer is bonded in rubber to the hub; by pulling on the outside, it is possible to break that bond.

3. Remove cover-to-block attaching bolts and remove the cover, timing indicator and water pump assembly.

4. Remove the front cover and dowel pins. It may be necessary to grind a flat on the pins to get a rough surface for gripping.

5. To install: Grind a chamfer on one end of each dowel pin.

6. Cut excess material from front end of oil pan gasket on each side of engine block.

7. Clean block, oil pan, and front cover mating surfaces with solvent.

8. Trim about $\frac{1}{8}$ in. from each end of a new front pan seal, using a sharp knife to insure a straight cut.

9. Install the new front cover gasket on engine block and new front seal on front cover. Apply sealer to gasket around coolant holes and place on block.

10. Apply silicone sealer at junction of block, pan, and front cover.

11. Place the cover on block and press downward to compress the seal. Rotate cover left and right and guide pan seal into cavity using a small screwdriver.

12. Apply engine oil to bolts (threads and heads). Install two bolts finger tight to hold cover in place.

13. Install two dowel pins chamfered end first.

14. Install timing indicator and water pump assembly. Torque bolts evenly to 13 ft. lbs. for the water pump bolts, and 35 ft. lbs. for cover bolts.

15. Apply lubricant to balancer seal surface. Install balancer, and balancer

bolt. Torque to approximately 250 ft. lbs.

16. Install brackets. Connect bypass hose and radiator hoses. Install crankshaft pulley and four attaching bolts. Torque to 20 ft. lbs.

17. Install fan pulley, fan, and four attaching bolts. Torque to 20 ft. lbs. Install belts and adjust tension. Fill radiator. Road test and check for leaks.

Timing Gear Cover Oil Seal

REPLACEMENT

All Engines

The seal may be replaced with the cover either on or off the engine.

1. With the cover removed: Pry the old seal from the cover using a wooden or plastic pick to prevent damage to the sealing lip. A plastic knitting needle makes a good removal tool.

2. Oil the lip of the new seal. Place a support under the cover so that it is not damaged when the seal is installed.

3. Install the seal so that the open side of the seal is toward the inside of the cover. Drive the seal into place with a tool made for the purpose (G.M. tool J23042 or the equivalent).

4. The seal can also be replaced with the cover in place on the engine: Remove the torsional damper. Pry the old seal from the cover, as outlined in Step 1.

5. Oil the lip of the new seal and place it into position, with the open side of the seal toward the engine. Drive the seal into position with a tool designed for the purpose (G.M. tool J23042 or the equivalent).

6. Install the damper.

Timing Chain, Gear or Belt

REMOVAL & INSTALLATION

4-119

1. Remove front cover assembly.

2. Lock the shoe on automatic adjuster in fully retracted position by depressing the adjuster lock lever in direction as shown.

3. Remove timing chain from crankshaft sprocket.

4. Check timing sprockets for wear or damage. If crankshaft sprocket must be replaced, remove sprocket and pinion gear from crankshaft using puller J25031.

5. Check timing chain for wear or damage; replace as necessary. Measure distance (L) with chain stretched

with a pull of approximately 22 lbs (98 N). Standard (L) value is 15 in, (381mm); replace chain if (L) is greater than 15.1 in. (385mm).

6. Remove attaching bolt and remove automatic chain adjuster.

7. Check that the shoe becomes locked when shoe is pushed in with the lock lever released.

8. Check that lock is released when the shoe is pushed in. The adjuster assembly must be replaced if rack teeth are found to be worn excessively.

9. Remove "E" clip and remove chain tensioner. Check tensioner for wear or damage; replace as necessary.

10. Inspect tensioner pin for wear or damage. If replacement is necessary, remove pin from cylinder block using locking pliers. Lubricate NEW pin tensioner with clean engine oil. Start new pin in block, place tensioner over appropriate pin. Place "E" clip on pin and then tap pin into block, using a hammer, until clip just clear tensioner. Check tensioner and adjuster for freedom of rotation on pins.

11. Inspect guide for wear or damage and plugged lower oil jet. If replacement or cleaning is necessary, remove guide bolts, guide and oil jet. Install new guide and upper attaching bolt. Install lower oil jet and bolt so that oil port is pointed toward crankshaft as shown.

12. Install timing sprocket and pinion gear (groove side toward front cover). Align key grooves with key on crankshaft, then drive into position using Installating Tool J26587.

13. Turn crankshaft so that key is turned toward cylinder head side (Nos. 1 and 4 pistons at top dead center).

14. Install the timing chain by aligning mark plate on chain with mark on crankshaft timing sprocket. The side of the chain with the mark plate is on the front side and the side of chain with the most links between mark plates is on the chain guide side. Keep the timing chain engaged with the camshaft timing sprocket until the camshaft timing sprocket is installed on camshaft.

15. Install the camshaft timing sprocket so that marked side of sprocket faces forward and so that the triangular mark aligns with the chain mark plate.

16. Install the automatic chain adjuster.

17. Release lock by depressing the shoe on adjuster by hand, and check to make certain the chain is properly tensioned when lock is released.

18. Install front cover assembly.

4-121

1. Remove the front cover as previously detailed.

nel to prevent damaging the seal during installation.

NOTE: The seal lip must be positioned inboard of the engine and the small dust lip to the flywheel side.

6. Apply sealing compound to the other half of the new seal as described in Step 4.

7. Apply approximately $1/32$ in. of RTV sealant GM 1052357, or equivalent, to the cap between the rear main seal and the oil pan rear seal groove.

NOTE: Keep the sealant off of the rear main seal, bearing, and out of the drain slot.

8. Just prior to assembly, apply a light coat of engine oil on the crankshaft surface that will contact the seal.

9. Install the rear main bearing cap and torque to 70 ft. lbs.

3.8L V6 Engine

1. Refer to the "Oil Pan Removal & Installation" procedures in this section and remove the oil pan.

2. Remove the rear main bearing cap from the engine.

3. Using the packing tool J-21526-2, gently drive one end of the old seal into the engine block until it is lightly packed. Repeat the procedure on the other side.

4. Measure the amount the seal was driven up on 1 side and add $1/16$ in.

5. Using a single edge razor blade, cut the measured amount from the old seal of the lower half (use the rear main bearing cap as a holding fixture). Repeat the procedure for the other side.

6. Bolt the guide tool J-21526-1 to the upper half of the rear main bearing.

7. Using the packing and the guide tools, drive the short pieces of cut seal into the cylinder block until they are equal with the parting line. Perform this procedure on both sides.

NOTE: The guide and the packing tools have been machined to

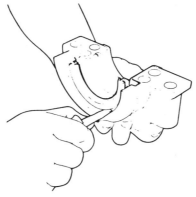

Removing the oil seal from the lower half—V8 engine

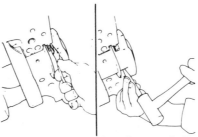

Removing the oil seal from the upper half—V8 engine

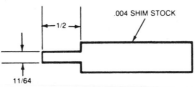

Oil seal installation tool

provide built in stops. Apply oil to the short pieces of seal before driving them into the engine block.

8. Install a new fabric seal to the rear main bearing cap and trim the ends flush the parting line.

9. To complete the installation, reverse the removal procedures. Torque the rear main bearing cap to 100 ft. lbs.

V8 Engine

1. Refer to the "Oil Pan Removal &

Installation" procedures in this section and remove the oil pan.

2. Remove the oil pump and the rear main bearing cap.

3. Using a small pry bar, pry the oil seal from the rear main bearing cap.

4. Using a small hammer and a brass pin punch, drive the top half of the oil seal from the rear main bearing. Drive it out far enough, so it may be removed with a pair of pliers.

5. Using a non-abrasive cleaner, clean the rear main bearing cap and the crankshaft.

6. Fabricate an oil seal installation tool from 0.004 in. shim stock, shape the end to $1/2$ in. long by $11/64$ in. wide.

7. Coat the new oil seal with engine oil; DO NOT coat the ends of the seal.

8. Position the fabricated tool between the crankshaft and the seal seat in the cylinder case.

9. Position the new half seal between the crankshaft and the tip of the tool, so that the seal bead contacts the tip of the tool.

NOTE: Make sure that the seal lip is positioned toward the front of the engine.

10. Using the fabricated tool as a shoe horn, to protect the seal's bead from the sharp edge of the seal seat surface in the cylinder case, roll the seal around the crankshaft. When the seal's ends are flush with the engine block, remove the installation.

11. Using the same manner of installation, install the lower half onto the lower half of the rear main bearing cap.

12. Apply sealant to the cap-to-case mating surfaces and install the lower rear main bearing half to the engine; keep the sealant off of the seal's mating line.

13. Install the rear main bearing cap bolts and torque to 10–12 ft. lbs. Using a lead hammer, tap the crankshaft forward and rearward, to line up the thrust surfaces. Torque the main bearing bolts to 70–85 ft. lbs. and reverse the removal procedures. Refill the crankcase.

CAVALIER

Oil Pan

REMOVAL & INSTALLATION

OHV 4 Cyl Engines

1. Disconnect the negative battery cable.

2. Drain the crankcase. Raise and support the front of the vehicle.

3. Remove the A/C brace if so equipped.

4. Remove the exhaust shield and disconnect the exhaust pipe at the manifold.

5. Remove the starter motor and

position it out of the way.

6. Remove the flywheel cover. Remove the oil pan.

NOTE: Prior to oil pan installation, check that the sealing surfaces on the pan, cylinder block and front cover are clean and free

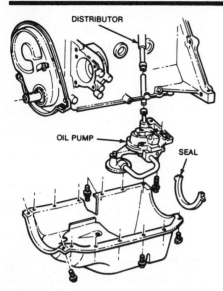

OHV engine oil pan and pump mounting

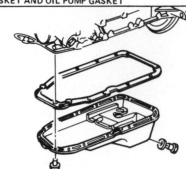

APPLY RTV SEALER BETWEEN OIL PAN GASKET AND OIL PUMP GASKET

OHC engine oil pan mounting

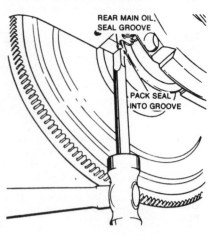

On OHV engines, pack the upper seal into its groove, ¼ inch on each side

of oil. If installing the old pan, be sure that all old RTV has been removed.

7. Apply a ⅛ in. bead of RTV sealant to the oil pan sealing surface. Use a new oil pan rear seal and install the pan in place. Tighten the bolts to 9–13 ft. lbs.

8. Installation of the remaining components is in the reverse order of removal.

2.8L V6 Engine

1. Disconnect the negative battery cable.
2. Raise the vehicle and support it safely.
3. Drain the oil from the crankcase.
4. Remove the flywheel dust cover.
5. Tag and disconnect the electrical connections at the starter motor.
6. Remove the starter retainer bolts and remove the starter.
7. Remove the oil pan bolts and remove the oil pan.
8. Installation is the reverse of removal. Start the engine and check for leaks.

OHC Engines

1. Raise the vehicle and support it safely.
2. If a twin-post hoist is being used, position jack stands at jacking points and lower hoist.
3. Remove right front wheel.
4. Remove right hand splash shield.
5. Remove lower A/C bracket strut rod attachment bolt and swing aside.
6. Remove flywheel dust cover.
7. Remove exhaust pipe to manifold attachment bolts.
8. Drain engine oil.
9. Remove oil pan.
10. Installation is the reverse of removal. Torque the pan bolts to 4 ft. lbs.

Rear Main Oil Seal

REMOVAL & INSTALLATION

OHV 4 Cyl Engines

1. Remove the oil pan and pump.
2. Remove the rear main bearing cap.
3. Gently pack the upper seal into the groove approximately ¼ inch on each side.
4. Measure the amount the seal was driven in on one side and add ⅟₁₆ in. Cut this length from the old lower cap seal. Be sure to get a sharp cut. Repeat for the other side.
5. Place the piece of cut seal into the groove and pack the seal into the block. Do this for each side.
6. Install a piece of Plastigage or the equivalent on the bearing journal. Install the rear cap and tighten to 75 ft. lbs. Remove the cap and check the gauge for bearing clearance. If out of specification, the ends of the seal may be frayed or not flush, preventing the cap from proper seating. Correct as required.
7. Clean the journal, and apply a thin film of sealer to the mating surfaces of the cap and tighten to 70 ft. lbs. Install the pan and pump.

2.8L V6 Engine

1. Disconnect the negative battery cable.
2. Support the engine and remove the transaxle assembly as described later in this section.
3. Remove the flywheel and verify that the leak is originating from the rear main seal.
4. Remove the seal from the dust lip.

NOTE: Care must be exercised during removal so as not to damage the crankshaft outside diameter area.

5. Clean the cylinder block and crankshaft sealing surface.
6. Inspect the crankshaft for nicks, burrs, scratches, etc.
7. Coat the seal and the engine mating surface with engine oil.
8. Install the new seal using seal installation tool J-34686 or equivalent. Follow the manufacturers instructions supplied with the seal installation tool.
9. For the remainder of the installation, reverse Steps 3 through 1 of the removal procedure.

NOTE: Some 1982 1.8L engines (Code G), experience a rear main seal oil leak. To correct this condition a new crankshaft part No. 14086053 and a one piece rear main seal kit part No. 14081761 has been released for service. The one piece seal kit contains an installation tool, rear main seal, and an instruction sheet.

OHC Engines

NOTE: The following requires the use of special tools.

1. Remove engine as previously outlined.
2. Remove flywheel dust cover.
3. Remove flexplate to torque converter attachment bolts on automatic vehicles.
4. Remove bellhousing bolts and separate engine from transaxle assembly.
5. Remove flexplate on automatic transaxle vehicles.
6. Remove pressure plate, clutch disc and flywheel on manual transaxle vehicles.
7. Using a screwdriver or suitable tool, remove rear main oil seal.
8. Clean cylinder block and crankshaft sealing surface.
9. Inspect crankshaft for nicks, scratches, etc.

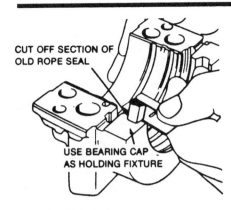

CUT OFF SECTION OF OLD ROPE SEAL

USE BEARING CAP AS HOLDING FIXTURE

On OHV engines, use the bearing cap to hold the lower seal while you cut it

COATED AREA INDICATED WITH #1052357 SEALER OR EQUIVALENT.

SEALER

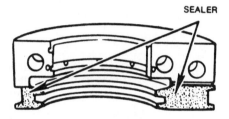

Applying sealer to the rear cap on OHV engines

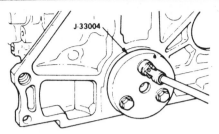

J-33004

Rear main seal installation on OHC engines

10. Coat seal and engine mating surfaces with engine oil.
11. Position seal on Protector (J-33084-2) and place onto crankshaft flywheel flange.
12. Install Seal Installer (J-33084) on crankshaft flywheel flange, starting the three (3) bolts EVENLY in a rotational sequence until the seal bottoms in the block.
13. Installation is in the reverse order of removal.

Oil Pump

REMOVAL & INSTALLATION

OHV 4 Cyl Engines

1. Remove the engine oil pan.
2. Remove the pump attaching bolts and carefully lower the pump.

3. Install in reverse order. To ensure immediate oil pressure on start-up, the oil pump gear cavity should be packed with petroleum jelly. Installation torque is 26–35 ft. lbs.

2.8L V6 Engine

1. Disconnect the negative battery cable.
2. Remove the oil pan as described earlier.
3. Remove the bolt holding the rear main bearing cap.
4. Remove the oil pump and extension shaft.
5. Installation is the reverse of removal.

OHC Engines

1. Remove the crankshaft sprocket.
2. Remove the timing belt rear covers.
3. Disconnect the oil pressure switch wires.
4. Remove the oil pan.
5. Remove the oil filter.
6. Unbolt and remove the oil pick-up tube.
7. Unbolt and remove the oil pump.
8. Installation is the reverse of removal. Use new gaskets in all instances. Torque the oil pump bolts to 5 ft. lbs. Torque the oil pan bolts to 4 ft. lbs., and the oil pickup tube bolts to 5 ft. lbs.

CHEVETTE

Oil Pan

REMOVAL & INSTALLATION

Gasoline Engine

1. Disconnect the negative battery cable.
2. Drain the cooling system.
3. Remove the heater housing assembly from the firewall and rest it on top of the engine.
4. Remove the upper radiator support. On cars with A/C, remove the upper half of the fan shroud.
5. Remove the radiator hoses and on cars with automatic transmission, disconnect and plug the cooler lines from the radiator.
6. Remove the radiator.
7. On cars equipped with A/C, remove the condenser from its supporting bracket. Lay the condenser on top of the engine. Do not disconnect any of the refrigerant lines.
8. Remove the motor mount nuts and clips.

9. Raise the car and drain the engine oil.
10. Remove the flywheel splash shield.
11. On all models with the 200 automatic transmission, loosen the catalytic converter-to-exhaust pipe clamp bolts. On other models, disconnect the exhaust pipe at the manifold.
12. Remove the body-to-crossmember braces, if so equipped.
13. Remove the rack and pinion unit from the crossmember and the steering shaft. Pull the unit down and out of the way.
14. With a floor jack and a lifting adapter, raise the front of the engine.
15. Remove the oil pan bolts.
16. Pull the oil pan down and remove the oil pump suction pipe and the screen.
17. Remove the oil pan.
18. Clean all of the old sealer that is loose off the oil pan mating surface. It is not necessary to clean all of the sealer material off. Reverse the above procedure to install. Tighten the oil pan attaching bolts to 5 ft. lbs.

Diesel Engine

1. Remove the engine as detailed earlier in this section.
2. Support the engine in a stand.
3. Unscrew the nuts and bolts attaching the oil pan to the crankcase and then remove the pan.
4. Clean the mating surfaces of the oil pan and the block. Apply a suitable liquid gasket to the front and rear mating surfaces and then install a new gasket.
5. Install the oil pan retaining bolts and tighten them to 5 ft. lbs.
6. Reinstall the engine.

Oil Pump

REMOVAL & INSTALLATION

Gasoline Engine

1. Remove the ignition coil attaching bolts and lay the coil aside.
2. Raise the car and remove the fuel pump, pushrod, and gasket.
3. Lower the car and remove the distributor. On air conditioned cars,

remove the compressor mounting bolts and lay it aside. Do not disconnect any refrigerant lines.

4. Raise the car and remove the oil pan as previously outlined.

5. Remove the oil pump pipe and screen assembly clamp and remove the bolts attaching the pipe and screen assembly.

6. Remove the pipe and screen assembly from the oil pump.

7. Remove the pick-up tube seal from the oil pump.

8. Remove the oil pump attaching bolts and remove the oil pump.

9. Installation is the reverse of removal. Torque the oil pump bolts to 15 ft. lbs.

NOTE: Make certain that the pilot on the oil pump engages the case.

10. Install the pick-up tube seal in the oil pump.

11. Install the pick-up pipe and screen assembly in the oil pump and install the pick-up pipe and screen clamp. Torque the clamp bolt to 6–8 ft. lbs. Torque the pick-up tube and screen mounting bolt to 19–25 ft. lbs.

12. Install the oil pan.

13. Install the fuel pump with gasket and pushrod.

14. Lower the car and install the distributor and the ignition coil.

Diesel Engine

1. Remove the timing belt as previously detailed.

2. Unscrew the four allen bolts attaching the oil pump to the front plate and remove the pump complete with the pulley.

3. Coat the vane with clean engine

Removing the allen bolts attaching the oil pump to the front pate—diesel engine

oil and then install it with the taper side toward the cylinder body.

4. Install a new O-ring, coated with engine oil, into the pump housing.

5. Position the rotor in the vane and then install the pump body together with the pulley. Tighten the Allen bolts to 15 ft. lbs.

6. Install the timing belt as previously detailed.

Rear Main Oil Seal

REPLACEMENT

Gasoline Engine

1. Remove the engine from the car and place it in a stand.

2. Remove the flywheel or flexplate.

3. Remove the oil pan.

4. Remove the rear main bearing cap.

5. Clean the bearing cap and case.

6. Check the crankshaft seal for excessive wear, etc.

7. Install a new crankshaft seal. Make sure that it is properly seated

against the rear main bearing seal bulkhead.

8. Apply RTV sealer or its equivalent to the bearing cap horizontal split line.

9. With the sealer still wet, install the rear main baring cap. Tighten the bearing bolts to 10–12 ft. lbs. Tap the crankshaft toward the rear, then toward the front to be sure everything is properly seated. Tighten the cap bolts to the specified torque.

10. Apply RTV sealer or its equivalent in the vertical grooves of the rear main bearing cap.

11. Remove any excess sealer and install the oil pan. Torque the oil pan bolts to 4–5 ft. lbs.

12. Install the engine.

Diesel Engine

1. Remove the transmission as detailed later in this section. If equipped with a manual transmission, remove the clutch.

2. Loosen the flywheel retaining bolts in a diagonal pattern and then remove the flywheel.

3. Pry off the old oil seal.

4. Coat the lipped portion and the fitting face of the new oil seal with engine oil and install it into the crankshaft bearing. Make sure that the seal is properly seated.

5. Coat the threads of the new mounting bolts with Loctite® and install the flywheel. Tighten the bolts to 40 ft. lbs. in a diagonal sequence. Do not reuse the old bolts, they must be new.

6. Installation of the remaining components is in the reverse order of removal.

SPECTRUM

Oil Pan

REMOVAL & INSTALLATION

1. Disconnect the negative battery cable.

2. Raise the vehicle, place it on jack stands and drain the crankcase.

3. Disconnect the exhaust pipe bracket from the block and the exhaust pipe at the manifold.

4. Disconnect the right hand tension rod located under the front bumper.

5. Remove the oil pan bolts and oil pan, then clean the sealing surfaces.

6. To install, use a new gasket, ap-

ply sealant to the oil pump housing and the rear retainer housing, reverse the removal procedure.

Oil Pump

REMOVAL & INSTALLATION

1. Refer to the "Engine Removal and Installation" procedure in this section and remove the engine.

2. Drain the crankcase.

3. Remove the alternator belt and the starter.

4. Install the flywheel holding tool (J-35271) to secure the flywheel.

5. Remove the crankshaft pulley and boss.

6. Remove the timing cover bolts and the timing cover.

7. Loosen the tension pulley and remove the timing belt.

8. Remove the crankshaft timing gear and the tension pulley.

9. Remove the oil pan bolts, oil pan, oil strainer fixing bolt and the oil strainer assembly.

10. Remove the oil pump bolts and the oil pump assembly.

11. Remove the sealing material from the oil pump and engine block sealing surfaces.

12. To install, lubricate the oil pump, use new gaskets, apply sealant to the

sealing surfaces and reverse the removal procedure.

Rear Main Seal

REMOVAL & INSTALLATION

1. Remove the transaxle.
2. Remove the oil pan.

3. Remove the pressure plate and clutch for M/T or torque converter for A/T, the flywheel bolts and the flywheel from the crankshaft.

4. Remove the rear oil seal retainer and remove the oil seal from the retainer. Clean the sealing surfaces.

5. Using a new oil seal, install the new seal in the oil seal retainer.

6. To install, use new gaskets, apply sealer to the mounting surfaces, apply oil to the seal lips, align the dowel pins of the retainer with the engine block and reverse the removal procedure.

SPRINT

Oil Pan

REMOVAL & INSTALLATION

1. Remove the negative battery cable.
2. Raise and support the vehicle on jackstands.
3. Drain the engine oil.
4. Remove the flywheel dust cover.
5. Remove the exhaust pipe at the exhaust manifold.
6. Remove the oil pan bolts, the pan and the oil pump strainer.
7. Clean the gasket mating surfaces.
8. To install, use new gaskets and reverse the removal procedures. Torque the oil pan bolts to 9–12 ft. lbs. Refill the engine oil.

Rear Main Seal

REMOVAL & INSTALLATION

1. Remove the transaxle.
2. Raise and support the vehicle. Remove the oil pan.

3. Remove the pressure plate, the clutch plate and the flywheel.

4. Remove the mounting bolts and the rear seal housing.

5. Pry the oil seal from the oil seal housing.

6. To install, use new gaskets/seals and reverse the removal procedures. Torque the oil seal housing to 7–9 ft. lbs. and the flywheel to 57–65 ft. lbs.

NOTE: After installing the oil seal housing, trim the gasket flush with the bottom of the case.

Oil Pump And Front Seal

REMOVAL & INSTALLATION

1. Refer to the "Timing Cover, Timing Belt and Tensioner Removal & Installation" procedures in this section and remove the timing belt.

2. Raise and support the vehicle. Remove the oil pan.

3. Use a screwdriver to hold the crankshaft timing belt pulley, remove the crankshaft bolt and pull the timing pulley from the shaft.

4. Remove the alternator mounting bracket and the A/C compressor bracket, if equipped.

5. Remove the alternator adjusting bolt and the upper cover bolt.

6. Remove the oil pump mounting bolts and the oil pump.

7. Pry the crankshaft oil seal from the oil pump.

8. Clean the gasket mounting surfaces. Remove the gear plate from the back of the oil pump and pack the oil pump gears with petroleum jelley.

9. To install, use new gaskets/seals and reverse the removal procedures. Torque the oil pump bolts to 7–9 ft. lbs. and the crankshaft timing pulley bolt to 47–54 ft. lbs. Adjust the valve clearances and check the timing.

NOTE: To install the oil pump to the engine, place the Oil Seal Guide tool J–34853 on the crankshaft and slide the oil pump onto the alignment pins. After installing the oil seal housing, trim the gasket flush with the bottom of the case.

NOVA

Oil Pan

REMOVAL & INSTALLATION

1. Disconnect the negative battery cable. Raise the vehicle and support it on axle stands.

2. Drain the oil pan. Remove the stabilizer bar. On some models, it may be necessary to remove other steering linkage parts; do this now if it appears other parts will interfere with pan removal.

3. Remove the right side undercover.

4. Disconnect the exhaust pipe at the manifold.

5. Support the engine securely using a floor jack with a wooden block to cushion the impact of the jack on engine parts. Then, remove various engine mount parts as described in the "Timing Belt Covers Removal & Installation" procedure above. Also, remove the engine shock absorber.

6. Raise the engine far enough to provide clearance for removal of the pan. Then, remove the pan bolts and the pan and gasket.

7. Install the oil pan in reverse order. Make sure to scrape both gasket surfaces, and use a new gasket, and an appropriate type of liquid sealer. Torque oil pan bolts to 4 ft. lbs. Refer

again to procedures elsewhere to reassemble engine mounts and suspension components.

Oil Pump

REMOVAL & INSTALLATION

1. Remove the engine under cover. Drain the oil pan. Matchmark and then remove the hood.

2. Unbolt the engine right hand under cover and flywheel cover.

3. Remove the oil pan as described above.

4. Remove the two oil pickup brace bolts (at the block) and the two mounting bolts and remove the oil pickup.

5. Attach a lifting sling to the engine lift points and securely suspend the engine.

6. Loosen the water pump pulley mounting bolts and then remove the alternator/water pump drive belt. Remove the power steering pump drive belt. Then, remove the water pump pulley.

7. If the car has air conditioning, remove the compressor drive belt and idler pulley.

8. Remove the crankshaft pulley with a puller.

9. Remove the center and lower timing belt covers as described above. Mark the relationship between the timing belt and the crankshaft sprocket. Set the engine at TDC with No. 1 cylinder in firing position and then release the tension from the belt tensioner as described under Timing Belt Removal & Installation, above. Remove the timing belt from the crankshaft sprocket, keeping it engaged with the upper sprocket.

10. Remove the lower timing belt sprocket. Remove the timing belt idler pulley.

11. Remove the dipstick and dipstick tube.

12. Remove the seven oil pump mounting bolts and remove the oil pump. You can tap lightly on the lower surface of the pump from the rear to loosen it.

13. To install the pump, first install a new gasket and then engage the teeth of the oil pump drive (smaller) gear with the crankshaft gear. There are both small and large spline teeth, so make sure the teeth correspond properly. Then, put the pump in position, and install the seven mounting bolts, torquing to 15 ft. lbs.

14. Perform the remaining steps of installation in reverse of the removal procedure, referring to the "Oil Pan Removal & Installation" and "Timing Belt Removal & Installation" procedures as necessary.

Rear Main Seal

REMOVAL & INSTALLATION

1. Remove the transmission as described below.

2. On manual transmission cars, remove the clutch and then remove the flywheel. On cars with automatic transmissions, remove the torque converter drive plate.

3. Remove the rear end plate. Unbolt and then remove the oil seal retainer.

4. Support the oil seal retainer edges rear side downward on blocks so the entire area below the seal is open. Then, use a screwdriver at various points around the outer edge of the seal to tap the seal downward and out of the retainer.

5. Support the seal in a similar way but with the front (or engine) side downward. Coat the outer diameter with Multipurpose grease and then use a seal installer (such as GM Tool J–35388 or equivalent) or large wood block to tap the seal straight into the bore in the retainer.

6. Coat the seal inside diameter with Multipurpose grease and carefully install the seal and retainer straight over the crankshaft rear sealing surface. Use a new gasket under the retainer. Install the remaining parts in reverse order. The flywheel mounting bolts should be torqued in several stages, going back and forth and around the center of the flywheel to get even tightening. Torque them to 58 ft. lbs. Torque the drive plate for automatic transaxle equipped cars in the same way, but use a figure of 61 ft. lbs.

CORSICA AND BERETTA

Oil Pan

REMOVAL & INSTALLATION

2.0 Liter Engine

1. Disconnect the negative battery cable. Remove the exhaust pipe shield.

2. Raise and safely support the vehicle. Drain the engine oil.

3. Disconnect the A/C brace at the starter and at the A/C bracket.

4. Disconnect the starter brace at the block. Disconnect and tag the starter wires and remove the starter.

5. Remove the flywheel dust cover. Remove the A/C brace.

6. Remove the four (4) right support bolts and lower the support for clearance to remove the oil pan. Remove the oil filter and extension on automatic transaxle vehicles.

7. Remove the oil pan bolts and remove the oil pan.

8. Clean and inspect the sealing surfaces of the engine block, oil pan and front cover. Remove any old sealer.

9. Place a small bead of RTV sealer on the oil pan to engine block sealing surface.

10. Using a new oil pan rear seal, Apply a thin layer of RTV sealer to the ends of the seal and install the oil pan and attaching bolts.

11. Torque the oil pan bolts to 6 ft. lbs.

12. The remainder of the installation is the reverse of the removal.

13. Install a new oil filter. Fill the engine with the correct engine oil. Run the engine and check for leaks when finished.

2.8 Liter Engine

1. Disconnect the negative battery cable.

2. Raise and safely support the vehicle. Drain the engine oil.

3. Remove the flywheel dust cover.

4. Disconnect and tag the starter wires and remove the starter.

5. Remove the oil pan attaching nuts and bolts and remove the oil pan.

6. Clean and inspect the sealing surfaces of the engine block and oil pan.

7. Using a new gasket, install the oil pan and attaching nuts and bolts.

8. Torque the oil pan nuts to 6–9 ft. lbs. and the bolts to 15–22 ft. lbs.

9. The remainder of the installation is the reverse of the removal.

10. Install a new oil filter. Fill the engine with the correct engine oil. Run the engine and check for leaks when finished.

Rear Main Bearing Oil Seal

REMOVAL & INSTALLATION

2.0 and 2.8 Liter Engines

NOTE: This procedure should only be performed if tool J-34686, or equivalent is available. This is a special tool designed for this application.

1. Disconnect the negative battery cable.

2. Raise and safely support the vehicle.

3. Using the correct procedure, support the engine and remove the transaxle.

4. On manual transaxle vehicles, matchmark and remove the clutch assembly and flywheel. On automatic

transaxle vehicles, remove the flywheel.

5. Remove the rear main seal by inserting a suitable tool into the dust lip and pulling the seal outwards.

NOTE: Use care when removing or installing the seal to avoid damage to the crankshaft sealing surface. Inspect the condition of the clutch on manual transaxle vehicles to insure that the clutch was not damaged by oil loss from the rear main seal.

6. Lubricate the seal bore and seal surface with engine oil.

7. Install the new seal using tool J–34686, or equivalent. The seal must fit squarely against the back of the tool.

8. Line the dowel pin of the tool with the dowel pin in the crankshaft and tighten the attaching screws on the tool to 2–5 ft. lbs.

9. Tighten the "T" handle of the tool to push the seal into the seal bore.

10. Loosen the "T" handle and remove the attaching screws and tool.

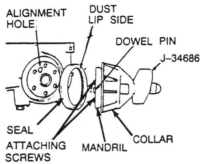

Rear main bearing oil seal installation- 2.0 and 2.8 Liter engine

11. Check the seal to make sure it is seated squarely in the bore.

12. Install the flywheel. Torque the flywheel bolts to 45–59 ft. lbs. for automatic transaxles, or to 47–63 ft. lbs. for manual transaxles.

13. The remainder of the installation is the reverse of the removal.

14. Check for any leaks when finished.

Oil Pump

REMOVAL & INSTALLATION

2.0 and 2.8 Liter Engines

1. Raise and safely support the vehicle. Drain the engine oil.

2. Using the correct procedure, remove the oil pan.

3. Remove the oil pump to rear main bearing cap bolt and remove the oil pump and extension shaft.

4. Place the new oil pump and extension shaft into position engaging the pump drive. Install the oil pump to bearing cap bolt.

5. Torque the oil pump to bearing cap bolt to 25–38 ft. lbs. Torque the oil pump drive upper retaining bolt on the 2.0 Liter engine to 14–22 ft. lbs. and to 25–38 ft. lbs. on the 2.8 Liter engine, if removed.

6. Using the correct procedure, install the oil pan.

7. Fill the engine with oil. Check for oil pressure and leaks when finished.

TRUCKS

Oil Pan

REMOVAL & INSTALLATION

Pickups and Suburban

INLINE SIX CYLINDER

1. Disconnect the battery ground cable.

2. Raise and support the vehicle. Disconnect the starter leaving the wires attached and swing it out of the way.

3. If there is not enough clearance, remove the bolts securing the engine mounts to the crossmember and raise the engine high enough to insert a 2 in. × 4 in. piece of wood between the engine mounts and the crossmember brackets.

4. Drain the engine oil.

5. Remove the flywheel or converter cover.

6. Remove the oil pan.

7. Clean all gasket surfaces and install a new seal in the rear main bearing groove and a new seal in the crankcase front cover. Installation is the reverse of removal. Install new side gaskets on the block, but do not use sealer. Fill the engine with oil and run the engine, checking for leaks.

V8 EXCEPT DIESEL

1. Drain the engine oil.

2. Remove the oil dipstick and tube.

3. If necessary, remove the exhaust crossover. On 454s, remove the air cleaner, fan shroud, and distributor cap.

4. Remove the flywheel or converter cover. Remove the starter. On 454s, remove the oil pressure line from the block. On four wheel drive models with automatic transmission, remove the strut rods at the motor mounts.

5. On 454s only, remove the engine mount through bolts and raise the engine.

6. Remove the oil pan and discard the gaskets.

7. Installation is the reverse of removal. Clean all gasket surfaces and use new gaskets to assemble. Use gasket sealer to retain the side gaskets to the cylinder block. Install a new oil pan rear seal in the rear main bearing cap slot with the ends butting the side gaskets. Install a new front seal in the crankcase front cover with the ends butting the side gaskets. Fill the engine with oil and check for leaks.

DIESEL

1. Remove the drive and vacuum pump.

2. Disconnect the battery cables.

3. Remove the fan shroud attaching screws and pull the shroud up from the clips.

4. Block the rear wheels and jack up the front of the truck. Drain the oil.

5. Remove the flywheel cover.

6. Remove the starter and solenoid.

7. Remove both of the engine mount through bolts and raise the engine. Loosen the right hand mount and remove the left hand mount.

8. Unbolt and remove the oil pan.

NOTE: If extended work is to be done, the mounts should be reinstalled and the engine lowered to the frame brackets.

9. To install: After cleaning the mounting surfaces thoroughly, apply sealer to both sides of the pan gaskets and install the gaskets on the block.

10. Install the front and rear rubber seals.

11. Apply a thin coat of all purpose grease on the seals, and install the oil pan. Torque the bolts to 10 ft. lbs. in a circular sequence, starting in the middle and working out.

12. Further installation is the reverse of removal. Fill the engine with oil and check for leaks.

Vans Except Astro

INLINE SIX CYLINDER

1. Disconnect the negative battery cable and remove the engine cover.

2. Remove the air cleaner and studs.

3. Remove the fan finger guard.

4. Remove the radiator upper supporting brackets.

5. Raise and safely support the van.

6. On vans with manual transmissions: Disconnect the clutch cross shaft from the left front mounting bracket. Remove the transmission-tobellhousing upper bolt. Remove the transmission rear mounting bolts and install two $7/16 \times 3$ in. bolts. Raise the transmission and place a small piece of 2×4 wood in between the mount and the crossmember.

7. Remove the starter motor.

8. Drain the engine oil.

9. Remove the engine mount through bolts.

10. Raise the engine slightly and place small 2×4 wooden blocks in between the mount and the block.

11. Remove the flywheel splash shield or the converter cover, as applicable.

12. Remove the oil pan attaching bolts and remove the oil pan.

13. Clean the gasket surface thoroughly and use a new gasket on installation.

14. Reverse to install.

V8

1. Drain the engine oil.

2. Remove the oil dipstick and tube.

3. If necessary, remove the exhaust pipe crossover.

4. If equipped with automatic transmission, remove the converter housing pan.

5. Remove the starter brace and bolt and swing the starter aside.

6. Remove the oil pan and discard the gaskets.

7. Installation is the reverse of removal. Clean all gasket surfaces and use new gaskets to assemble. Use gasket sealer to retain the side gaskets to the cylinder block. Install a new oil pan rear seal in the rear main bearing cap slot with the ends butting the side gaskets. Install a new front seal in the crankcase front cover with the ends butting the side gaskets. Fill the engine with oil and check for leaks.

Blazer and Jimmy

INLINE SIX CYLINDER

1. Disconnect the battery ground cable.

2. Raise and support the vehicle. Disconnect the starter leaving the wires attached and swing it out of the way.

3. Remove the flywheel or converter cover.

4. Drain the engine oil.

5. On some models, there may be enough clearance to remove the oil pan without raising the engine. If there isn't, remove the through bolts securing the engine mounts to the brackets

and raise the engine high enough to insert a 2 in. × 4 in. piece of wood between the engine mounts and brackets.

6. Lower the engine so it rests on the blocks, in a slightly raised position. This should provide enough clearance.

7. Remove the oil pan attaching screws.

8. Remove the oil pan.

9. Clean all gasket surfaces and install a new seal in the rear main bearing groove and a new seal in the crankcase front cover. Installation is the reverse of removal. Install new side gaskets on the block, but do not use sealer. Fill the engine with oil and run the engine, checking for leaks.

V8 EXCEPT DIESEL

NOTE: For diesel engine procedures, follow the previous Pickup Truck instructions.

1. Drain the engine oil.

2. If necessary, remove the exhaust pipe crossover.

3. If equipped with automatic transmission, remove the converter housing pan.

4. On four wheel drive models equipped with automatic transmission, remove the strut rods at the engine mounts.

5. Remove the oil pan and discard the gaskets.

6. Installation is the reverse of removal. Clean all gasket surfaces and use new gaskets to assemble. Use gasket sealer to retain the side gaskets to the cylinder block. Install a new oil pan rear seal in the rear main bearing cap slot with the ends butting the side gaskets. Install a new front seal in the crankcase front cover with the ends butting the side gaskets. Reassemble, fill the engine with oil and check for leaks.

S-Series

4-119

NOTE: On 4-wheel drive the engine must be removed before removing the oil pan.

1. Disconnect the negative battery terminal.

2. Jack up your vehicle and support it with jackstands.

3. Drain the oil.

4. Remove the front splash shield.

5. Remove the front crossmember, if necessary.

6. Disconnect the relay rod at the idler arm and lower the relay rod.

7. Remove the left side bellhousing bracket.

8. Remove the vacuum line at the oil pan.

9. Remove the oil pan bolts and the pan.

NOTE: It may be necessary to remove the motor mounts and jack up the engine in order to remove the oil pan.

10. Installation is the reverse of removal. Tighten the retaining bolts to 43 inch lbs.

4-121

1. Disconnect the negative battery cable.

2. Drain the crankcase. Raise and support the front of the vehicle.

3. Remove the A/C brace if so equipped.

4. Remove the exhaust shield and disconnect the exhaust pipe at the manifold.

5. Remove the starter motor and position it out of the way.

6. Remove the flywheel cover. Remove the oil pan.

NOTE: Prior to oil pan installation, check that the sealing surfaces on the pan, cylinder block and front cover are clean and free of oil. If installing the old pan, be sure that all old RTV has been removed.

7. Apply a $1/8$ in. bead of RTV sealant to the oil pan sealing surface. Use a new oil pan rear seal and install the pan in place. Tighten the bolts to 9–13 ft. lbs.

8. Installation of the remaining components is in the reverse order of removal.

4-137 Diesel

The engine must be removed from the truck.

1. With the engine on a work stand, unbolt and remove the oil pan from the crankcase.

2. Discard the gasket and clean the gasket surfaces.

3. At this time, the crankcase may also be removed from the block. Discard the gasket and seals and clean the gasket surfaces.

4. Install the oil pan and/or crankcase using new gaskets coated with sealer. Torque the oil pan bolts to 5–9 ft. lb.; the crankcase bolts to 15 ft. lb.

6-173

The engine must be removed from the truck.

1. With the engine on a work stand, unbolt and remove the pan.

2. Discard the gasket and clean the gasket surfaces.

3. The oil pan does not use a preformed gasket. Rather it is sealed with RTV gasket material. Make sure that the sealing surfaces are free of oil and old RTV material.

4. Run a $1/8$ in. bead of sealer along the entire sealing surface of the pan.

5. Place the pan on the engine and finger tighten the bolts. Torque the smaller bolts to 6–9 ft. lb.; the larger bolts to 15–22.ft. lb.

Astro

2.5L (4 Cyl)

1. Disconnect the negative battery cable. Raise the vehicle and support it at approved jacking points. Drain the engine oil.
2. Label and then disconnect the starter wiring. Remove the flywheel splash shield. Unbolt and remove the starter.
3. Disconnect the exhaust pipe at the manifold. Disconnect all exhaust hangers.
4. Remove the oil pan bolts and remove the oil pan.
5. Remove all RTV sealant and oil from the sealing surfaces on the pan, cylinder case and front cover. Make sure RTV sealant is removed from blind attaching holes.
6. Squeeze a ⅛ in. bead of RTV sealer over the entire sealing flange of the oil pan. Install the pan square in position, and then install all bolts finger tight. Torque alternately and evenly to 75 inch lbs.
7. Reverse the remaining removal procedures to install. Refill the oil pan, operate the engine and check for leaks.

4.3L V6

1. Disconnect the negative battery cable. Raise the vehicle and support it at approved jacking points. Drain the engine oil.
2. Disconnect the exhaust pipes at the manifolds.
3. Remove the engine strut rods at the inspection cover and then remove the inspection cover.
4. Label and then disconnect the starter wiring. Then, remove the starter mounting bolts, and remove the starter.
5. Install a suitable jack under the engine and support it. Then, remove the bolts attaching both engine mounts to the block. Raise the engine until there is adequate clearance to remove the oil pan.
6. Remove the oil pan mounting bolts and remove the pan.
7. Clean all gasket surfaces thoroughly. Install the pan in reverse order, using all new gaskets and seals. Torque the ⁵⁄₁₆-18 mounting bolts to 14 ft. lbs. and the ½-20 mounting bolts to 7 ft. lbs.
8. Complete the installation in reverse order, torquing the engine mount-to-block bolts to 35 ft. lbs. Make sure the crankcase is refilled to the proper level with clean oil. Operate the engine and check for leaks.

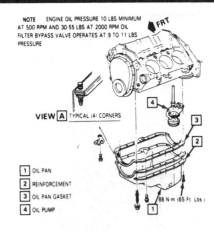

NOTE ENGINE OIL PRESSURE 10 LBS MINIMUM AT 500 RPM AND 30-55 LBS AT 2000 RPM OIL FILTER BYPASS VALVE OPERATES AT 9 TO 11 LBS PRESSURE

FRT

VIEW A TYPICAL (4) CORNERS

1 OIL PAN
2 REINFORCEMENT
3 OIL PAN GASKET
4 OIL PUMP

88 N·m (65 Ft. Lbs.)

Mounting the oil pan on the 2.5 L V6

Oil Pump

REMOVAL & INSTALLATION

4-119

1. Drain and remove the oil pan.
2. Disconnect the oil feed pipe.
3. Remove the two bolts securing the oil pump to the cylinder block and remove the oil pump.
4. Install in the reverse order of removal.

4-121

1. Remove the engine oil pan.
2. Remove the pump attaching bolts and carefully lower the pump.
3. Install in reverse order. To ensure immediate oil pressure on start-up, the oil pump gear cavity should be packed with petroleum jelly. Installation torque is 26–35 ft. lbs.

4-137 Diesel

1. Remove the engine assembly from the vehicle.
2. Remove the 20 bolts mounting the crankcase and remove the crankcase together with the oil pan.

NOTE: Pry off the crankcase by fitting a suitable pry bar into the slots in the crankcase.

3. Remove the oil pipe sleeve nut.
4. Remove the 2 bolts fixing the oil pump and remove the oil pump with oil pipe.
5. Install the oil pipe and leave the joints semi-tight.
6. Fully tighten the oil pump fixing screws, then tighten the oil pipe joints.
7. Reverse the removal procedure for the remaining parts.

6-173

1. Remove the oil pan.
2. Unbolt and remove the oil pump and pickup.

3. Installation is the reverse of removal. Torque the pump bolts to 26–35 ft. lb. Before installing an oil pump, fill it with clean oil.

2.5L (4 Cyl)

1. Remove the oil pan.
2. Remove the bolt that retains the pickup to the block. Then, remove the bolts retaining the oil pump-to-block positioning flange to the block, and remove that flange and the oil pump.
3. If the pump has been disassembled, is being replaced, or for any reason oil has been removed from it, it must be primed. It can either be filled with oil before installing the cover plate (and oil kept within the pump during handling), or the entire pump cavity can be filled with petroleum jelly. IF THE PUMP IS NOT PRIMED, THE ENGINE COULD BE DAMAGED BEFORE IT RECEIVES ADEQUATE LUBRICATION WHEN YOU START IT.
4. To install the pump, first align the slot in the oil pump shaft with the tang on the oil pump driveshaft in the block. Then, slide the pump into place (it should slide easily); the pump positioning flange will fit over the lower driveshaft bushing (note that no gasket is required). Install the mounting bolts and torque to 22 ft. lbs.
5. Install the oil pan.

Inline Six Cylinder

1. Drain the oil and remove the oil pan.
2. Remove the 2 flanged mounting bolts and remove the pickup pipe bolt.
3. Remove the pump and screen as an assembly.
4. To install, align the oil pump driveshafts with the distributor tang and install the oil pump. Position the flange over the distributor lower bushing, using no gasket. The oil pump should slide easily into place. If not, remove it and reposition the slot to align with the distributor tang.
5. Reinstall the oil pan and fill the engine with oil.

4.3L V6

1. Remove the oil pan.
2. Remove the bolt attaching the pump to the rear main bearing cap. Remove the pump and the extension shaft, which will come out behind it.
3. If the pump has been disassembled, is being replaced, or for any reason oil has been removed from it, it must be primed. It can either be filled with oil before installing the cover plate (and oil kept within the pump during handling), or the entire pump cavity can be filled with petroleum jelly. IF THE PUMP IS NOT PRIMED,

THE ENGINE COULD BE DAMAGED BEFORE IT RECEIVES ADEQUATE LUBRICATION WHEN YOU START IT.

4. Engage the extension shaft with the oil pump shaft. Align the slot on the top of the extension shaft with the drive tang on the lower end of the distributor drive shaft, and then position the pump at the rear maing bearing cap so the mounting bolt can be installed. Install the bolt, torquing to 65 ft. lbs.

5. Install the oil pan.

V8 and Diesel

1. Drain the oil and remove the oil pan.

2. Remove the bolt (two bolts on diesels) holding the pump to the rear main bearing cap. Remove the pump and extension shaft.

3. To install, assemble the pump and extension shaft to the rear main bearing cap aligning the slot on the top of the extension shaft with the drive tang on the distributor driveshaft. The installed position of the oil pump screen is with the bottom edge parallel to the oil pan rails. Further installation is the reverse of removal.

Oil Cooler

REMOVAL & INSTALLATION

4-137 Diesel

1. Place a suitable size tray under the oil filter to receive oil and water flowing out from the filter.

2. Drain the cooling system by opening the drain plugs on the radiator and on the cylinder block.

3. Remove the oil cooler water drain plug and drain the water.

4. Disconnect the oil cooler hoses at the cooler side.

5. Remove the oil filter cartridge using filter wrench.

6. Remove the nut fixing the oil cooler, then remove the oil cooler assembly.

7. Install the cooler using a new O-ring. Torque to 55–60 ft. lbs.

Rear Main Oil Seal

REPLACEMENT

All Engines Except Below

Both halves of the rear main oil seal can be replaced without removing the crankshaft. Always replace the upper and lower seal together. The lip should face the front of the engine. Be very careful that you do not break the sealing bead in the channel on the outside portion of the seal while installing it.

An installation tool can be fabricated to protect the seal bead.

1. Remove the oil pan, oil pump and rear main bearing cap.

2. Remove the oil seal from the bearing cap by prying it out with a suitable tool.

3. Remove the upper half of the seal with a small punch. Drive it around far enough to be gripped with pliers.

4. Clean the crankshaft and bearing cap.

5. Coat the lips and bead of the seal with light engine oil, keeping oil from the ends of the seal.

6. Position the fabricated tool between the crankshaft and seal seat.

7. Position the seal between crankshaft and tip of the tool so that the seal bead contacts the tip of the tool. The oil seal lip should face forward.

8. Roll the seal around the crankshaft using the tool to protect the seal bead from the sharp corners of the crankcase.

9. The installation tool should be left installed until the seal is properly positioned with both ends flush with the block.

10. Remove the tool.

11. Install the other half of the seal in the bearing cap using the tool in the same manner as before. Light thumb pressure should install the seal.

12. Install the bearing cap with sealant applied to the mating areas of the cap and block. Keep sealant from the ends of the seal.

13. Torque the main bearing cap retaining bolts to 10–12 ft. lbs. Tap the end of the crankshaft first rearward, then forward with a lead hammer. This will line up the rear main bearing and the crankshaft thrust surfaces. Tighten the main bearing cap to specification.

14. Further installation is the reverse of removal.

Diesel

It is not necessary to remove the crankshaft to correct seal leaks at the rear main bearing.

1. Drain oil and remove oil pan. Remove rear main bearing cap.

2. Insert a packing tool such as a screwdriver or a punch against one end of the seal in the cylinder block and drive the old seal gently into the groove until it is packed tight. This varies from $\frac{1}{4}$–$\frac{3}{4}$ in., depending on the pack required. Be careful not to nick the main bearing when packing the seal.

3. Repeat this procedure on the other end of the cylinder block seal.

4. Measure the amount the seal was driven up on one side. Add $\frac{1}{16}$ in., then use a razor blade to cut this length

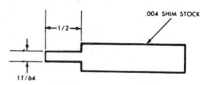

Fabricated oil seal installation tool

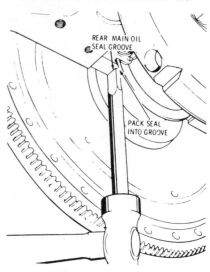

Pack the old seal into the groove

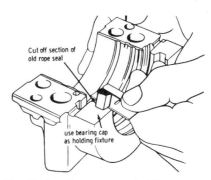

Use the bearing cap as a holding fixture for cutting the old rope seal

from the old seal removed from the bearing cap. Repeat for the other side.

5. Place a drop of sealer on each end of the cut pieces of seal.

6. Work these two pieces of seal into the cylinder block with two small screwdrivers. Pack them into the block firmly. Trim the ends of the seal flush with the block.

NOTE: Place a piece of shim stock or strip of metal between the seal and the crankshaft to protect the bearing surface before trimming.

7. Clean the bearing cap and seal grooves.

8. Install a new seal into the bearing cap, packing by hand.

9. Using a seal installer, pack the seal firmly into the groove. These tools

are generally available in automotive parts stores.

10. Cut the seal flush with the mating surface of the bearing cap. Pack the seal end fibers away from the edges, toward the center with a screwdriver.

11. Clean the bearing insert and install in the bearing cap.

12. Clean the crankshaft bearing journal, and the mating surface of the bearing cap. Place a dab of sealer, such as Loctite® 496, on the mating surface of the cap. Lay a piece of Plastigage® on the bearing surface.

13. Install the bearing cap, lubricate the bolt threads with engine oil, and install. Torque the bolts to 120 ft. lbs. on the 350 and 70 ft. lbs. on the 379. Check the bearing clearance. If clearance is excessive, check for frayed seal edges. When the clearance is correct, retorque the cap.

14. Install the oil pan.

4–119

1. Disconnect the negative battery terminal.
2. Remove the oil pan.
3. Remove the transmission.

NOTE: On manual transmissions, remove the clutch assembly.

4. Unbolt the starter and tie it out of the way.
5. Remove the flywheel.
6. Remove the rear main seal retainer.
7. Remove the oil seal and discard it.
8. Install the new oil seal.
9. Installation is the reverse of removal. Fill the space between the seal lips with grease and lubricate the seal lips with engine oil.

4-121

1. Remove the oil pan and pump.
2. Remove the rear main bearing cap.
3. Gently pack the upper seal into the groove approximately $\frac{1}{4}$ in. on each side.
4. Measure the amount the seal was driven in on one side and add $\frac{1}{16}$ in. Cut this length from the old lower cap seal. Be sure to get a sharp cut. Repeat for the other side.
5. Place the piece of cut seal into the groove and pack the seal into the block. Do this for each side.
6. Install a piece of Plastigage or the equivalent on the bearing journal. Install the rear cap and tighten to 75 ft. lbs. Remove the cap and check the gauge for bearing clearance. If out of specification, the ends of the seal may be frayed or not flush, preventing the cap from proper seating. Correct as required.

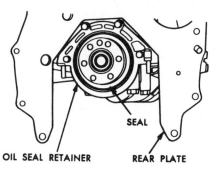

OIL SEAL RETAINER   SEAL   REAR PLATE

4–119 rear main seal

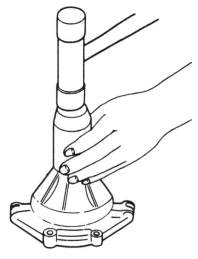

4–119 rear main seal installation

7. Clean the journal, and apply a thin film of sealer to the mating surfaces of the cap and tighten to 70 ft. lbs. Install the pan and pump.

4-137 Diesel

1. Remove the engine.
2. Remove the 6 bolts mounting the flywheel and remove the flywheel assembly. When loosening the flywheel bolts, hold the crankshaft front bolt with a wrench to prevent turning of the crankshaft.
3. Remove the crankshaft rear seal.
4. Install the new seal with seal installer, J22928 or equivalent. Reverse removal procedures for all other parts.

2.5L (4 Cyl)

1. Raise and support the vehicle safely at approved jacking points. Remove the transmission.
2. If the truck has a manual transmission, see the applicable procedures later in this section and remove the pressure plate and clutch disc. Then remove tha flywheel with either manual or automatic transmssion.
3. Using a flat-bladed screwdriver or similar tool, pry the seal out of the rear of the block.
4. Clean the block-to-seal mating surface carefully. Then, apply a light

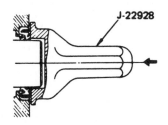

J-22928

4–137 diesel rear main seal installation

coating of engine oil to the outer surface of a new seal.

5. Use a seal installer (J–34924 or equivalent) to tap a new seal into position. Make sure the seal seats squarely.
6. Install the flywheel, torquing the mounting bolts alternately and evenly to 44 ft. lbs.
7. On manual transmission cars, install the clutch disc and pressure plate.
8. Install the transmission.

6-173

1. Remove the oil pan and pump.
2. Remove the rear main bearing cap.
3. Gently pack the upper seal into the groove approximately $\frac{1}{4}$ in. on each side.
4. Measure the amount the seal was driven in on one side and add $\frac{1}{16}$ in. Cut this length from the old lower cap seal. Be sure to get a sharp cut. Repeat for the other side.
5. Place the piece of cut seal into the groove and pack the seal into the block. Do this for each side.

NOTE: G.M. makes a guide tool (J–29114–1) which bolts to the block via on oil pan bolt hole, and a packing tool (J–29114–2) which are machined to provide a built-in stop for the installation of the short cut pieces. Using the packing tool, work the short pieces of seal onto the guide tool, then pack them into the block with the packing tool.

6. Install a new lower seal in the rear main cap.
7. Install a piece of Plastigage or the equivalent on the bearing journal. Install the rear cap and tighten to 70 ft. lbs. Remove the cap and check the gauge for bearing clearance. If out of specification, the ends of the seal may be frayed or not flush, preventing the cap from proper sealing. Correct as required.
8. Clean the journal, and apply a thin film of sealer to the mating surfaces of the cap and block. Do not allow any sealer to get onto the journal or bearing. Install the bearing cap and tighten to 70 ft. lbs. Install the pan and pump.

ENGINE COOLING

CORVETTE

Most 1980-82 Corvettes equipped with the heavy duty cooling system option use an auxiliary electric cooling fan. The auxiliary fan is used to supplement the engine-mounted fan during conditions of very high engine temperatures. The auxiliary fan circuit is energized anytime the ignition switch is in the RUN position, though the fan itself will not operate until the engine coolant temperature reaches 238°F, as sensed by the cylinder head-mounted coolant temperature sensor. When the coolant temperature decreases to approximately 201°F, the fan will turn off.

——— **CAUTION** ———

Keep hands, tools, clothing, etc. clear of the auxiliary fan. The fan can come on automatically even when the engine is not running.

1984-87 models use an electric, single-speed cooling fan mounted directly to the radiator shroud. Fan operation is determined by coolant temperature, operating only enough to maintain engine coolant at or below a preset maximum temperature. The cooling fan is energized through a relay controlled by a sending unit located in the right cylinder bank. The fan only operates when road speed is below 35 mph.

Radiator

REMOVAL & INSTALLATION
1980-82

1. Disconnect the negative battery cable at the battery.
2. Drain the cooling system.
3. Remove the air cleaner snorkel.
4. Raise the front of the vehicle and support it with jack stands.
5. Disconnect the fan shroud from the radiator support bracket.
6. If so equipped, disconnect the automatic transmission cooler lines from the radiator.
7. Remove the radiator support brackets.
8. Disconnect the radiator upper and lower hoses and the overflow tube from the radiator.
9. Remove the radiator.
10. Installation is the reverse of removal. When installing the radiator make sure it is seated in the mounting pads. When replacing the radiator cap make sure the arrows line up with the overflow tube.

NOTE: It may be necessary to remove the fan shroud when removing the radiator.

1984-87

1. Disconnect the negative battery cable.
2. Drain the cooling system.
3. Remove the upper and lower radiator hoses.
4. Remove overflow hose at radiator.
5. Remove A/C accumulator and move aside.
6. Remove transmission cooler line.
7. Remove fan wires from fan and shroud.
8. Remove fan to gain access to lower cooler line.
9. Remove transmission cooler line at fitting.
10. Remove upper shroud bolts.
11. Remove upper shroud.
12. Remove radiator.
13. Installation is the reverse of removal.

Water Pump

REMOVAL & INSTALLATION
1980-82

1. Drain the radiator and loosen the fan pulley bolts.
2. Disconnect the heater hose, lower radiator hose and, if applicable, the bypass hose at the water pump.
3. Remove the alternator upper brace. Loosen the swivel bolt and remove the fan belt.
4. Remove the fan blade and pulley. Replace a bent or damaged fan.

NOTE: Thermostatic fan clutches must be kept in an "in-car" position. When removed from the car the assembly should be supported so that the clutch disc remains in a vertical plane to prevent silicone fluid leakage.

5. Remove the water pump attaching bolts and, if applicable, the power steering-to-pump bolts and remove the pump and gasket.
6. Install the pump assembly using a new gasket. Coat the gasket on both sides with sealer. Tighten the $\frac{3}{8}$ in. bolts to 30 ft. lbs.
7. Install the pulley and fan.
8. Connect the hoses and fill the cooling system.
9. Install the alternator upper brace

and fan belt. Install the power steering pump bolt.
10. Adjust the belts, then start the engine and check for leaks.

1984-87

NOTE: If the compressor lines do not have enough slack to move the compressor out of the way without disconnecting the refrigerant lines, the air conditioning system must be evacuated (using the required tools) before the refrigerant lines can be disconnected.

——— **CAUTION** ———

Do not disconnect any refrigerant lines unless experienced with air conditioning systems. Escaping refrigerant will freeze any surface it contacts, including skin and eyes.

1. Disconnect the negative battery cable.
2. Drain cooling system.
3. Remove serpentine drive belt.
4. Remove water pump pulley.
5. Remove AIR pump pulley.
6. Remove air management valve adapter.
7. Remove AIR pump.
8. Disconnect fuel inlet and return lines.
9. Remove rear A/C compressor braces.
10. Remove lower A/C compressor mounting bolt.
11. Remove A/C compressor and idler pulley bracket nuts.
12. Disconnect A/C compressor wires.
13. Slide mounting bracket forward and rear A/C compressor bolt.
14. Remove A/C compressor.
15. Remove right and left AIR hoses at check valve.
16. Remove AIR pipe at intake and power steering reservoir bracket.
17. Remove power steering reservoir bracket including top alternator bolt.
18. Remove lower AIR bracket on water pump.
19. Remove lower radiator and heater hose at water pump.
20. Remove water pump.
21. Installation is the reverse of removal. Tighten the water pump bolts 100–125 inch lbs.

Thermostat
REMOVAL & INSTALLATION

The thermostat is located on the front

of the intake manifold directly in the center. It is not necessary to remove the top radiator hose to remove the thermostat.

1. Drain the cooling system about halfway.
2. Remove the two retaining bolts from the thermostat housing and lift

up the housing with the hose attached. Remove the thermostat.
3. Insert the new thermostat, spring end down, and install the housing with a new gasket.

CAPRICE, IMPALA, MALIBU AND MONTE CARLO

Radiator

REMOVAL & INSTALLATION

1. Disconnect the negative battery cable and drain cooling system.
2. If necessary, remove the fan, the upper fan shroud or the upper support.
3. Disconnect upper and lower hoses.
4. Disconnect and plug the oil cooler lines, if equipped with an A/T.
5. Lift radiator and shroud straight up and out of vehicle.

NOTE: If equipped with a clutch type fan, keep it in an upright position to prevent the fluid from leaking.

6. To install, reverse the removal procedures. Make sure the lower cradles are properly located and A/T is full.

Water Pump

The water pump is a die cast, centrifugal-type with sealed bearings. Since it is pressed together, it must be serviced as a unit.

REMOVAL & INSTALLATION

All Engines Except Diesel

1. Disconnect the negative battery cable and drain the cooling system.
2. If necessary, remove the fan shroud or the upper radiator support.

3. Remove the necessary drive belts.
4. Remove the fan and water pump pulley.
5. Remove the alternator and the power steering pump (if equipped) brackets, then move the units aside.
6. Remove the heater hose and the lower radiator hose from the pump.
7. Remove the water pump retaining bolts and the pump. Clean the gasket mounting surfaces.

NOTE: Use an anti-seize compound on the water pump bolt threads.

8. To install, use new gaskets and reverse the removal procedures. Torque the water pump, the alternator and the power steering (if equipped) mounting bolts to 30 ft. lbs. Adjust the drive belts and fill the cooling system.

NOTE: If a belt tensioning gauge is available, adjust the belts to 100–130 lbs. of tension on new belts or to 70 lbs. on used belts. If the gauge is not available, adjust the belts so that a $1/4$–$1/2$ inch deflection can be made on the longest span of the belt under moderate thumb pressure.

Diesel Engine Only

1. Disconnect the negative battery cable and drain the cooling system.
2. Disconnect the lower radiator hose, the heater hose and the by-pass hose from the water pump.

3. Remove the fan assembly, the drive belts and the water pump pulley.
4. Remove the alternator, the power steering pump and the A/C compressor (if equipped) brackets, then move the units aside.
5. Remove the water pump mounting bolts and the pump. Clean the gasket mounting surfaces.
6. To install, use new gaskets, sealant and reverse the removal procedures. Torque the water pump bolts to 22 ft. lbs. Adjust the belts and refill the cooling system.

NOTE: Apply sealer to the lower water pump bolts.

Thermostat

REMOVAL & INSTALLATION

1. Disconnect the negative battery cable and drain cooling system to below thermostat level.
2. Remove the air cleaner. Disconnect upper radiator hose.
3. Remove the thermostat housing bolts, the housing and the thermostat.
4. Clean the gasket mounting surfaces.

NOTE: When installing the thermostat, place the pin side facing upwards.

5. To install, use new gaskets, sealant and reverse the removal procedures. Torque the thermostat housing mounting bolts to 30 ft. lbs. Refill the cooling system.

CELEBRITY AND CITATION

Radiator

REMOVAL & INSTALLATION

1. Disconnect the negative battery cable.
2. Drain the cooling system.
3. Remove the forward strut brack-

et for the engine at the radiator. Loosen the bolt to prevent shearing the rubber bushing, then swing the strut rearward.
4. Disconnect the headlamp wiring harness from the fan frame. Unplug the fan electrical connector.
5. Remove the attaching bolts for the fan.

6. Scribe the hood latch location on the radiator support, then remove the latch.
7. Disconnect the coolant hoses from the radiator. Remove the coolant recover tank hose from the radiator neck. Disconnect and plug the automatic transmission fluid cooler lines from the radiator, if so equipped.

8. Remove the radiator attaching bolts and remove the radiator. If the car has air conditioning, it first may be necessary to raise the left side of the radiator so that the radiator neck will clear the compressor.

To install:

1. Install the radiator in the car, tightening the mounting bolts to 7 in. lbs. Connect the transmission cooler lines and hoses. Install the coolant recovery hose.

2. Install the hood latch. Tighten to 6 ft. lbs.

3. Install the fan, making sure the bottom leg of the frame fits into the rubber grommet at the lower support. Install the fan wires and the headlamp wiring harness. Swing the strut and brace forward, tightening to 11 ft. lbs. Connect the engine ground strap to the strut brace. Install the negative battery cable, fill the cooling system, and check for leaks.

Water Pump

REMOVAL & INSTALLATION

4 Cyl Engine

1. Disconnect battery negative cable.

2. Remove accessory drive belts.

3. Remove water pump attaching bolts and remove pump.

4. If installing a new water pump, transfer pulley from old unit. With sealing surfaces cleaned, place a $\frac{1}{8}$ in. (3mm) bead of sealant No. 1052289 or equivalent on the water pump sealing surface. While sealer is still wet, install pump and torque bolts to 6 ft. lbs.

5. Install accessory drive belts.

6. Connect battery negative cable.

V6–173 Engine

1. Disconnect battery negative cable.

2. Drain cooling system and remove heater hose.

3. Remove water pump attaching bolts and nut and remove pump.

4. With the sealant surfaces cleaned, place a $\frac{3}{32}$ in. (2mm) bead of sealant No. 1052357 or equivalent on the water pump sealing surface.

5. Clean old sealant from pump.

6. Coat bolt threads with pipe sealant No. 1052080 or equivalent.

7. Install pump and torque bolts to 10 ft. lbs.

8. Connect battery negative battery cable.

NOTE: When replacing the water pump on a car equipped with the V6 engine, the timing cover must be clamped to the cylinder block prior to removing the water

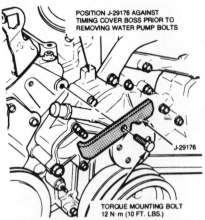

POSITION J-29176 AGAINST TIMING COVER BOSS PRIOR TO REMOVING WATER PUMP BOLTS

J-29176

TORQUE MOUNTING BOLT 12 N·m (10 FT. LBS.)

Install the special tool on the 6-173 to insure that the front cover does not separate from the crankcase when the pump is removed

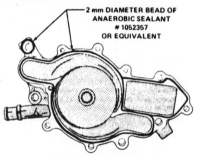

2 mm DIAMETER BEAD OF ANAEROBIC SEALANT # 1052357 OR EQUIVALENT

Applying sealer to the 6-173 water pump

pump bolts. Certain bolts holding the water pump pass through the front cover, and when removed, may allow the front cover to pull away from the cylinder block, breaking the seal. This may or may not be readily apparent and if left undetected, could allow coolant to enter the crankcase. To prevent this possible separation during water pump removal, Special Tool No. J29176 will have to be installed.

1982-83 V6–181 Engine

1. Disconnect the negative battery cable.

2. Remove accessory drive belts.

3. Remove water pump attaching bolts.

4. Remove the engine support strut.

5. Place a floor jack under the front crossmember of the cradle and raise the jack until the jack just starts to raise the car.

6. Remove the front two body mount bolts with the lower cushions and retainers.

7. Thread the body mount bolts with retainers a minimum of three turns into the cage so that the bolts restrain cradle movement.

8. Release the floor jack slowly until the crossmember contacts the body

mount bolt retainers. As the jack is being lowered watch and correct any interference with hoses, lines, pipes and cables.

NOTE: Do not lower the cradle without its being restrained as possible damage can occur to the body and underhood items.

9. Remove water pump from engine.

10. Reverse removal procedure.

11. Install pump and torque to 25 ft. lbs.

12. Connect negative battery cable.

13. Fill with coolant and check for leaks.

1984-87 V6–181, 231 Engines

1. Disconnect the negative cable at the battery.

2. Drain the cooling system.

3. Remove the accessory drive belts.

4. Disconnect the radiator and heater hoses at the water pump.

5. Remove the water pump pulley bolts (long bolt removed through access hole provided in the body side rail), then remove the pulley.

6. Remove the water pump attaching bolts, then remove the water pump.

7. Clean all gasket mating surfaces.

8. Using a new gasket, install the water pump on the engine. Torque the bolts to specifications.

9. Install the water pump pulley, then torque the bolts to specifications. (See illustration).

10. The remainder of the installation is the reverse of removal.

V6–263 Engine

1. Drain radiator.

2. Disconnect lower radiator hose at water pump.

3. Disconnect the heater return hose at the water pump, remove the bolt retaining the heater water return pipe to the intake manifold and position the pipe out of the way.

4. If equipped with A/C, remove the vacuum pump drive belt.

5. Remove the serpentine drive belt.

6. Remove the generator. A/C compressor or vacuum pump brackets.

7. Remove the water pump attaching bolts and remove the water pump assembly.

8. Remove the water pump pulley.

9. Clean gasket material from engine block.

10. Apply a thin coat of 1050026 sealer or equivalent to the water pump housing to retain the gasket, then position new gasket on the housing. Also apply sealer to water pump mounting bolts. Torque bolts to 12–15 ft. lbs.

Thermostat

REMOVAL & INSTALLATION

1. Disconnect the negative battery cable.
2. Drain the cooling system.
3. Some models with cruise control have a vacuum modulator attached to the thermostat housing with a brack-et. If equipped, remove the bracket from the housing.
4. On the four cylinder engine, unbolt the water outlet from the thermostat housing, remove the outlet and lift the thermostat out of the housing. On all other models, unbolt the water outlet from the intake manifold, remove the outlet and lift the thermostat out of the manifold.
5. Clean both of the mating surfaces and run a $\frac{1}{8}$ in. bead of RTV sealer in the groove of the water outlet.
6. Install the thermostat with the spring toward the engine and bolt the water outlet into place while the sealer is still wet. Torque the bolts to 21 ft. lbs. The remainder of the installation is in the reverse of the removal procedures. Check for leaks after the car is started and correct as required.

CAMARO

Radiator

REMOVAL & INSTALLATION

1980-81 Models

1. Disconnect the negative battery cable.
2. Drain the cooling system.
3. Disconnect the upper and lower hoses.
4. If equipped with an automatic transmission, disconnect and plug the oil cooler lines.
5. Remove the upper fan shield (6 cyl.) or the upper shroud bracket (V8).
6. Remove the radiator hold-down bolts, the radiator and shroud assembly from the vehicle.
7. To install, reverse the removal procedures. Torque the hold-down bolts to 12 ft. lbs. Refill the cooling system. If equipped with an automatic transmission, make sure that the fluid level is correct.

1982-87 Models

1. Disconnect the negative battery cable.
2. Drain the cooling system.
3. Remove the engine cooling fan. If equipped with a fan clutch, the clutch MUST be set aside in an upright position to prevent seal leakage.
4. Disconnect the radiator hoses from the radiator.
5. If equipped with an automatic transmission, disconnect and plug the transmission cooler lines at the radiator.
6. If equipped, remove the fan shield assembly.
7. Remove the radiator and shroud assembly, then lift the assembly straight up.

NOTE: The radiator assembly is held at the bottom by 2 cradles which are secured to the radiator support. If installing a new radiator, transfer the fittings from the old radiator to the new one.

8. To install, reverse the removal procedures. Refill the cooling system, operate the engine to normal operating temperatures and check for leaks. If equipped with an automatic transmission, check the transmission fluid level and adjust the level as required.

Water Pump

REMOVAL & INSTALLATION

NOTE: When servicing the V6 or V8 engines, disconnect the negative battery cable.

1. Drain the cooling system.
2. If equipped, remove the fan shroud and the upper radiator support.
3. Remove the drive belts.
4. Remove the fan and the pulley from the water pump.

NOTE: Viscous drive fans should not be stored horizontally. The silicone fluid can leak out of the fan assemble if it is not kept upright.

5. On the V6 and V8 engines, remove the upper and lower brackets, the air brace, the bracket and the lower power steering pump bracket (if equipped), swing the bracket aside.
6. Disconnect the heater and lower radiator hoses, from the water pump.
7. Remove the water pump-to-cylinder block bolts and the water pump.

NOTE: On the 4 cyl. engines, remove the pump by pulling it straight out of the block.

8. Clean the gasket mounting surfaces.
9. To install, use a new gasket and reverse the removal procedures. Torque the water pump bolts to 15 ft. lbs. and the accessories mounting bolts to 30 ft. lbs. Adjust the drive belt deflection to $\frac{1}{2}$ in. between the longest span of two pulleys. Refill the cooling system. Start the engine and check for leaks.

Thermostat

REMOVAL & INSTALLATION

1. Drain the cooling system until the coolant level is below the thermostat.
2. Remove the air cleaner assembly (except on 4 cyl).
3. Remove the upper radiator hose.
4. Remove the thermostat housing bolts, the thermostat housing and the thermostat.
5. Clean the gasket mounting surfaces.
6. To install, use a new gasket(s) and RTV sealant, the thermostat and reverse the removal procedures. Torque the housing bolts to 20 ft. lbs. (4 cyl.) or 30 ft. lbs. (all others). Fill the cooling system. Start the engine and check for leaks.

NOTE: Make sure that the thermostat spring is installed towards the engine; NOT the radiator.

— CAUTION —
DO NOT use RTV sealant with the gasket on 4 cylinder engines.

CAVALIER

Radiator

REMOVAL & INSTALLATION

1. Disconnect the negative battery cable.
2. Drain the cooling system.
3. Disconnect the electrical lead at the fan motor.
4. Remove the fan frame-to-radiator support attaching bolts and then remove the fan assembly.
5. Disconnect the upper and lower radiator hoses and the coolant recovery hose from the radiator.
6. Disconnect the transmission oil cooler lines from the radiator and wire them out of the way.
7. Remove the radiator-to-radiator support attaching bolts and clamps. Remove the radiator.
8. Place the radiator in the vehicle so that the bottom is located in the lower mounting pads. Tighten the attaching bolts and clamps.
9. Connect the transmission oil cooler lines and tighten the bolts to 20 ft. lbs.
10. Installation of the remaining components is in the reverse order of removal.

Water Pump

REMOVAL & INSTALLATION

OHV Engines

1. Disconnect the negative battery cable.
2. Drain the cooling system.
3. Remove all accessory drive belts.
4. Remove the alternator.
5. Unscrew the water pump pulley mounting bolts and then pull off the pulley.
6. Remove the mounting bolts and remove the water pump.
7. Place a $1/8$ in. bead of RTV sealant on the water pump sealing surface. While the sealer is still wet, install the pump and tighten the bolts to 13–18 ft. lbs.

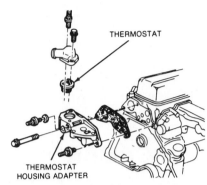

THERMOSTAT

THERMOSTAT HOUSING ADAPTER

OHV engine thermostat mounting

1. Thermostat housing cap
2. Thermostat
3. Thermostat housing assembly
4. Cylinder head

OHC engine thermostat mounting

8. Installation of the remaining components is in the reverse order of removal.

OHC Engines

1. Remove the timing belt as described later.
2. Remove the timing belt rear protective covers.
3. Remove the hose from the pump.
4. Unbolt and remove the pump.
5. Installation is in the reverse of removal. Torque the bolts to 19 ft. lbs.

Thermostat

REMOVAL & INSTALLATION

OHV Engines

The thermostat is located inside a housing on the back of the cylinder head. It is not necessary to remove the radiator hose from the thermostat housing when removing the thermostat.

1. Disconnect the negative battery cable.
2. Drain the cooling system and remove the air cleaner.
3. Disconnect the A.I.R. pipe at the upper check valve and the bracket at the water outlet.
4. Disconnect the electrical lead.
5. Remove the two retaining bolts from the thermostat housing and lift up the housing with the hose attached. Lift out the thermostat.
6. Insert the new thermostat, spring end down. Apply a thin bead of silicone sealer to the housing mating surface and install the housing while the sealer is still wet. Tighten the housing retaining bolts to 6 ft. lbs.

NOTE: Poor heater output and slow warmup is often caused by a thermostat stuck in the open position; occasionally one sticks shut causing immediate over-heating. Do not attempt to correct a chronic overheating condition by permanently removing the thermostat. Thermostat flow restriction is designed into the system; without it, localized overheating (due to coolant turbulence) may occur, causing expensive troubles.

7. Installation of the remaining components is in the reverse order of removal.

OHC Engines

1. Remove the thermostat housing.
2. Grasp the handle of the thermostat and pull it from the housing.
3. Install the thermostat in the housing, pushing it down as far as it will go to make sure it's seated.
4. Install the housing on the engine, using a new gasket coated with sealer.

CHEVETTE

A standard pressurized cooling system is used. A permanently lubricated impeller-type water pump forces coolant through engine and cylinder head water jackets and into a cross-flow radiator. Some models use a heavy-duty radiator with a fan shroud. The pressure-type radiator cap pressurizes the cooling system to 15 psi. A 190°F

(180°F on Diesel) thermostat in the coolant outlet passage is used to control coolant flow. A translucent plastic coolant recover reservoir is used to provide for coolant expansion. Coolant level is checked by observing the amount present in the reservoir with the engine at normal operating temperature. Add coolant to the reservoir, not the radiator. A 50/50 mixture of ethylene glycol antifreeze and water yielding freeze protection to −20°F should be used as coolant.

Radiator

REMOVAL & INSTALLATION

1. Disconnect the negative battery cable.
2. Drain the cooling system.
3. Remove the upper radiator support or the upper fan shroud, as necessary.
4. Disconnect the coolant hoses and the automatic transmission cooler lines from the radiator.
5. Remove the radiator.
6. Reverse to install.

Water Pump

REMOVAL & INSTALLATION
Gasoline Engine

1. Disconnect the battery negative cable and remove the alternator, and A/C compressor drive belts.
2. Remove the engine fan, spacer (air conditioned models), and the pulley.
3. Remove the timing belt front cover by removing the two upper bolts, center bolt, and two lower nuts. Remove the timing belt lower cover retaining nut and remove the cover.

4. Drain the coolant from the engine.
5. Remove the lower radiator hose and the heater hose at the water pump.
6. Turn the crankshaft pulley so that the mark on the pulley is aligned with the "O" mark on the timing scale and that a 1/8 in. drill bit can be inserted through the timing belt upper rear cover and camshaft sprocket.
7. Remove the idler pulley and pull the timing belt off the sprocket. Don't disturb crankshaft position.
8. Remove the water pump retaining bolts and remove the pump and gasket from the engine.
9. Clean all the old gasket material from the cylinder case.
10. With a new gasket in place on the water pump, position the water pump in place on the cylinder case and install the water pump retaining bolts.
11. Install the timing belt onto the cam sprocket.
12. Apply sealer to the idler pulley attaching bolt and install the bolt and the idler pulley. Turn the idler pulley counterclockwise on its mounting bolt to remove the slack in the timing belt.
13. Use a tension gauge to adjust timing belt tension. Check belt tension midway between the tensioner and the cam sprocket on the idler pulley side. Correct belt tension is 70 lbs. Torque the idler pulley mounting bolt to 13–18 ft. lbs.
14. Remove the 1/8 in. drill bit from the upper rear timing belt cover and cam sprocket.
15. Install the lower radiator hose and the heater hose to the water pump.
16. Install the timing belt front covers.

17. Install the water pump pulley, spacer (if equipped), and engine fan.
18. Install the engine drive belt(s).
19. Refill the cooling system.
20. Connect the battery negative cable.
21. Start the engine and check for leaks. Run the engine with the heater on until the thermostat opens, then recheck the coolant level.

Diesel Engines

1. Disconnect the negative battery cable and drain the cooling system.
2. Remove the fan shroud, fan assembly and the accessory drive belt.
3. Unscrew the retaining bolts and remove the damper pulley.
4. Remove the upper and lower halves of the front cover and then remove the bypass hose at the pump.
5. Unscrew the pump retaining bolts and remove the pump assembly.
6. Installation is in the reverse order of removal.

Thermostat

REMOVAL & INSTALLATION

1. Drain the radiator and remove the radiator hose at the water outlet.
2. Remove the thermostat housing bolts and remove the housing, gasket, and thermostat.
3. Install the thermostat. Use a new gasket on the thermostat housing and install the thermostat housing bolts.
4. Install the radiator hose at the water outlet.
5. Fill the cooling system. Run the engine with the heater on until the thermostat opens, then recheck the coolant level.

SPECTRUM

Radiator

REMOVAL & INSTALLATION

1. Disconnect the negative battery cable.
2. Drain the cooling system.
3. Remove the air intake duct.
4. Remove the fan motor cable from the fan motor socket.
5. Disconnect the thermo switch cable.
6. Remove the fan motor assembly.
7. Remove the radiator hoses at the radiator, the coolant recovery hose at the filler neck and the Auto. Trans. oil cooler lines.
8. Remove the radiator mounting bolts and the radiator.

9. To install, reverse the removal procedures.

Water Pump

REMOVAL & INSTALLATION

1. Drain the cooling system.
2. Loosen the power steering pump adjustment bolts and remove the belt.
3. Remove the timing belt.
4. Remove the tension pulley and spring.
5. Remove the water pump mounting bolts, the water pump and gasket. Clean the mounting surfaces of all gasket material.
6. To install, reverse the removal procedures. Torque the water pump to

17 ft. lbs. and the tension pulley to 30 ft. lbs.

Thermostat

REMOVAL & INSTALLATION

1. Remove the negative battery cable. Drain the cooling system.
2. Remove the top radiator hose from the outlet pipe.
3. Remove the outlet pipe bolts, the outlet pipe, gasket and thermostat from the thermostat housing.
4. To install, reverse the removal procedure. Use 17 ft. lbs. of torque when installing the outlet pipe.

SPRINT

Radiator

REMOVAL & INSTALLATION

1. Disconnect the negative battery cable.
2. Drain the cooling system.
3. Disconnect the cooling fan motor wire and the air inlet hose.
4. Remove the inlet, the outlet and the reservoir tank hoses from the radiator.
5. Remove the mounting bolts, the cooling fan motor, the shroud and the radiator.
6. To install, reverse the removal procedures and fill the cooling system.

Water Pump

REMOVAL & INSTALLATION

1. Disconnect the negative battery cable.

2. Drain the cooling system.
3. Remove the water pump belt and pulley.
4. Remove the crankshaft pulley, the timing belt outside cover, the timing belt and the tensioner.
5. Remove the mounting bolts and the water pump.
6. Clean the gasket mating surfaces.
7. To install, use a new gasket/sealer and reverse the removal procedures. Torque the water pump bolts to 7.5–9 ft. lbs. Adjust the water pump belt deflection to $1/4-3/8$ inch between the water pump and the crankshaft pulleys.

Thermostat

REMOVAL & INSTALLATION

1. Disconnect the negative battery cable.

2. Drain the cooling system to a level below the thermostat.
3. Remove the air cleaner.
4. Disconnect the electrical connector at the thermostat cap.
5. Remove the inlet hose, the cap mounting bolts and the thermostat from the thermostat housing.
6. Clean the gasket mounting surfaces.

NOTE: Make sure that the thermostat air bleed hole is clear.

7. To install, use a new gasket, place the thermostat spring side down and reverse the removal procedures. Fill the cooling system, run the engine to normal operating temperatures and check for leaks.

NOVA

Radiator

REMOVAL & INSTALLATION

1. Open the drain cock in the lower radiator tank and drain the coolant into a clean container.
2. Disconnect the engine and A/C fan motor electrical connectors. On cars with air conditioning, remove the four bolts going into the top tank and two going into the bottom tank and remove the fan shroud.
3. On cars with automatic transmissions, place a clean pan underneath where you are working and then disconnect the two oil cooler hoses at the radiator and plug the open ends.
4. Disconnect the hose to the coolant reservoir and fasten it in a position that is high enough to keep the coolant in the reservoir from draining.
5. Loosen the clamps, pull them well back from the ends of the hoses, and disconnect the top and bottom hoses at the radiator.
6. Unbolt the two radiator supports at the top, remove the two supports, and remove the radiator.
7. Install the radiator in reverse order. Make sure the radiator fits properly at the bottom so the rubber cushions under the two supports are only slightly compressed.
8. Refill both the automatic transmission and cooling system with ap-

proved fluids. Bring the engine to operating temperature, recheck fluid levels, and operate the engine while checking for leaks.

Water Pump

REMOVAL & INSTALLATION

1. Remove the mounting bolts and remove the upper timing cover and gasket. Drain the coolant into a clean container through both the radiator and engine block drain cocks. Once one drain cock is opened and pressure relieved, remove the radiator cap to vent the system and aid draining.
2. Just begin loosening each of the four water pump pulley mounting bolts,. Then loosen the alternator adjusting and mounting bolts, move the alternator toward the engine to remove belt tension, and remove the alternator/water pump drive belt.
3. Remove the water pump pulley mounting bolts and remove the pulley.
4. Remove the water pump inlet mounting bolt from the side of the block, then remove the two nuts attaching the inlet pipe to the rear of the water pump and remove the pipe.
5. Remove the mounting bracket bolt and then remove the dipstick tube. Plug the hole in the block with a clean rag. Remove the right hand under cover. If the car has power steer-

ing, remove the power steering adjusting bracket.
6. Remove the three bolts and remove the water pump. Keep engine coolant off the timing belt! Remove the O-ring from the block.
7. To install the pump, first replace the O-ring in the block with a new one. Then, reverse the remaining removal procedures, torquing the three water pump mounting bolts to 11 ft. lbs. When installing the oil dipstick tube, install a new O-ring there also, coating it with oil prior to installation. Refill the cooling system, if necessary adding clean anti-freeze and water in a 50–50 mixture. Operate the engine until it has reached operating temperature and air has bled out, then add coolant until the system is full and replace the cap. Check for leaks.

Thermostat

REMOVAL & INSTALLATION

1. Drain coolant from the radiator drain cock until the level is well below the top tank. After the drain cock is opened and pressure relieved, remove the radiator cap to aid draining.
2. Loosen clamps and disconnect the small and large hoses at the thermostat housing. Then, remove the two bolts and pull the water inlet off the

housing base. Remove the thermostat and O-ring.

3. Install a new thermostat with the bellows inward. Make sure the thermostat fits squarely in the indented portion of the housing. Install a new O-ring into the water inlet.

4. Install the water inlet and two bolts, tightening the bolts alternately in small increments.

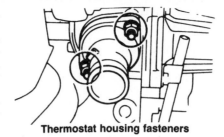

Thermostat housing fasteners

5. Reconnect hoses and position and tighten the clamps. Refill the cooling system, if necessary adding clean anti-freeze and water in a 50–50 mixture. Operate the engine until it has reached operating temperature and air has bled out, then add coolant until the system is full and replace the cap. Check for leaks.

CORSICA AND BERETTA

Radiator

REMOVAL & INSTALLATION

1. Disconnect the battery cables, negative first. Remove the battery.

2. Drain the cooling system. Remove the air cleaner housing and bracket.

3. Remove the upper radiator air baffle. On some models, remove the right and left air baffles.

4. Remove the air intake duct. Disconnect the cooling fan wire.

5. Remove the cooling fan.

6. Disconnect the radiator hoses at the radiator.

7. Remove the upper radiator retainers.

8. Remove the headlight attaching bolts and retainers and position them out of the way.

9. Remove the radiator attaching bolts and remove the radiator.

10. Installation is the reverse of the removal. Fill and bleed the cooling system when finished.

Water Pump

REMOVAL & INSTALLATION

2.0 and 2.8 Liter Engines

1. Disconnect the negative battery cable. Drain the cooling system.

2. Remove the serpentine belt.

3. On the 2.0 Liter engine, remove the alternator and bracket with the wires attached and position it out of the way.

4. Remove the water pump pulley bolts and remove the pulley.

5. Remove the water pump attaching bolts and remove the water pump.

6. Clean the water pump mounting surface on the engine.

7. Using a new gasket, install the water pump and bolts.

8. Torque the water pump mounting bolts to 14–22 ft. lbs. for the 2.0 Liter engine and to 6–9 ft. lbs. for the 2.8 Liter engine.

9. Make sure that the pump rotates freely. The remainder of the installation is the reverse of the removal.

Thermostat

REMOVAL & INSTALLATION

2.0 and 2.8 Liter Engines

1. Drain the coolant level below the level of the thermostat.

2. Remove the thermostat housing mounting bolts and remove the housing.

3. Clean the mating surfaces of the housing and engine.

4. Install a new thermostat and the housing.

5. Torque the bolts to 6–9 ft. lbs. for the 2.0 Liter engine and to 15–22 ft. lbs. for the 2.8 Liter engine.

COOLING SYSTEM BLEEDING

After working on the cooling system, even to replace the thermostat, it must be bled. Air trapped in the system will, otherwise, prevent proper filling, leaving the radiator coolant level low and causing risk of overheating.

To bleed the system, start with the system cool, the radiator cap off, and the radiator filled to about an inch below the filler neck. Start the engine and run it at slightly above normal idle speed, to ensure adequate circulation. If air bubbles appear and the coolant level drops, fill the system with a 50% antifreeze/water mixture to bring the level back to the proper level. Run the engine until the thermostat opens. When this happens, coolant will move abruptly across the top of the radiator and the temperature of the radiator will suddenly rise. At this point, air is often expelled and the level may drop quite a bit. Keep refilling the system until the level is near the top of the radiator and remains constant. If the car has an overflow tank, fill the radiator right up to the filler neck. Replace the radiator filler cap.

TRUCKS

Radiator

REMOVAL & INSTALLATION

All Except Astro

1. Drain the coolant.

2. Disconnect the hoses and automatic transmission cooler lines (if equipped). Plug the cooler lines. Diesels have transmission cooler and oil cooler lines.

3. Disconnect the coolant recovery system hose.

4. If the vehicle is equipped with a fan shroud, detach the shroud and hang it over the fan to provide clearance.

5. On six cylinder engines, remove the finger guard.

6. Remove the mounting panel from the radiator support and remove the upper mounting pads.

7. Lift the radiator up and out of the truck. Lift the shroud out if necessary.

8. Installation is the reverse of re-

moval. Fill the cooling system and check the automatic transmission fluid level, and run the engine, checking for leaks.

Astro

1. Disconnect the negative battery cable. Loosen the radiator drain cock and drain the cooling system into a clean container.
2. Disconnect the master cylinder, unbolt it, and lay it aside. Plug all openings.
3. Remove the upper fan shroud. Disconnect the radiator hoses.
4. Disconnect the upper transmission cooler lines and engine oil cooler lines.
5. Raise the vehicle and support it securely at approved jacking points. Disconnect the lower transmission cooler and engine oil cooler lines. Remove the lower fan shroud.
6. Disconnect the overflow tube.
7. Lift the radiator upward above the lower fan shroud and remove it.
8. Install the radiator in reverse order, making sure the upper shroud and insulator fit properly over the top of the radiator. After refilling the brake system, bleed the system thoroughly. Refill the cooling system with a 50/50 antifreeze and water mix and then start and run the engine until the thermostat opens. Refill the radiator as necessary, install the cap, and run the engine, checking for leaks.

Water Pump

REMOVAL & INSTALLATION

Except Below

1. Drain the radiator and loosen the fan pulley bolts.
2. Disconnect the heater hose and radiator. Disconnect the lower radiator hose at the water pump.
3. Loosen the alternator swivel bolt and remove the fan belt. Remove the fan bolts, fan and pulley.
4. Remove the water pump attaching bolts and remove the pump and gasket from the engine. On inline engines, remove the water pump straight out of the block to avoid damaging the impeller.

NOTE: Do not store viscous drive (thermostatic) fan clutches in any other position than the normal installed position. They should be supported so that the clutch disc remains vertical; otherwise, silicone fluid may leak out.

5. Installation is the reverse of removal. Clean the gasket surfaces and install new gaskets. Coat the gasket with sealer. On the 2.5L, coat the water pump bolts with a sealer such as GM part 1052080 or the equivalent. A $5/16$ in. × 24 × 1 in. guide stud installed in one hole of the fan will make installing the fan onto the hub easier. It can be removed after the other 3 bolts are started. Fill the cooling system and adjust the fan belt tension.

4-119 and 4-137 Diesel

1. Disconnect the battery ground. Drain the cooling system.
2. Remove the front cover. Disconnect the hoses at the pump.
3. On models without air conditioning, remove the fan.
4. On models with air conditioning, remove the fan belt, fan pulley, fan, air pump pulley and fan set plate.
5. Unbolt and remove the pump.
6. Clean the gasket surfaces thoroughly.
7. Installation is the reverse of removal. Always use a new gasket.

4-121

1. Disconnect the battery ground.
2. Drain the cooling system.
3. Remove all drive belts. Disconnect the hoses at the pump.
4. Remove the alternator.
5. Unbolt and remove the pump.
6. Thoroughly clean the gasket surfaces. Discard the old gasket.
7. Using a new gasket, install the pump and assemble all other components in reverse order of removal.

6-173

1. Disconnect the battery ground.
2. Drain the cooling system.
3. Disconnect the hoses at the pump.

4. Unbolt and remove the pump.
5. Thoroughly clean the sealing surfaces of old gasket material. This engine uses RTV sealant in place of a gasket.
6. Place a $3/32$ in. bead of sealer on the water pump mating surface. Coat the bolt threads with pipe compound and mount the pump on the engine.
7. Assemble all other components in reverse order of removal.

Thermostat

The factory installed thermostat is a 195°F unit.

NOTE: Poor heater output and slow warmup is often caused by a thermostat stuck in the open position; occasionally one sticks shut causing immediate overheating. Do not attempt to correct a chronic overheating condition by permanently removing the thermostat. Thermostat flow restriction is designed into the system; without it, localized overheating due to turbulence may occur.

REMOVAL & INSTALLATION

1. Drain approximately $1/3$ the coolant. This will reduce the coolant level to below the level of the thermostat housing.
2. It is not necessary to remove the upper radiator hose from the thermostat housing. Remove the 2 retaining bolts from the thermostat housing (located on the front top of V8 intake manifolds and directly in front of the valve cover on six cylinder engines) and remove the thermostat.
3. To test the thermostat, place it in hot water or a solution of 33% glycol, 25° above the temperature stamped on the valve. Submerge the valve and agitate the solution. The valve should open fully. Remove the thermostat and place it in the same solution 10° below the temperature stamped on the valve. The valve should close completely.
4. Installation is the reverse of removal. Use a new gasket and sealer. Refill the cooling system and run the engine, checking for leaks.

Fuel System 5

INDEX

CORVETTE

Mechanical Fuel Pump

The 1980-81 Corvette fuel pump is a mechanically operated diaphragm-type pump. The camshaft of the engine has an eccentric (similar to a cam lobe, but more rounded) cast as part of the camshaft. As the camshaft rotates, the eccentric actuates a pushrod which pushes the fuel pump rocker arm to activate the pump. The fuel pump is attached to the right front of the cylinder block. A fuel pump mounting plate is used, with two gaskets; one between the pump and the plate; the other between the plate and the block.

The inlet, or suction line of the pump, draws fuel from the tank. The outlet, or pressure line of the pump, supplies pressurized fuel to the carburetor. Some models use a third line, which is a vapor return. The purpose of the vapor return is to route the hot fuel and fuel vapor from the pump back to the fuel tank, which considerably reduces the chance of vapor lock.

NOTE: The fuel pump is not rebuildable—if defective, it must be replaced.

REMOVAL & INSTALLATION

1. Disconnect the fuel inlet, outlet, and vapor return (if equipped) lines from the pump.
2. Remove the bolt from the front right face of the engine block which is almost opposite the forward pump mounting bolt. Insert a longer bolt ($^3/_8$ x 16 x 2 in.) in this hole and snug down the bolt. This will hold the fuel pump pushrod in place.
3. Remove the fuel pump mounting bolts and remove the fuel pump.
4. Installation of the pump is the revere of the previous steps. Replace the fuel pump gasket(s) during installation. Start the engine and check the pump for proper operation, and check for leaks.

TESTING

If the engine exhibits a tendency to "starve-out", never assume that the fuel pump is defective until you test the pump. In most cases, a "starve-out" condition is caused by a weak ignition system, plugged fuel filter, or restricted fuel line.

1. Disconnect the fuel line from the carburetor. While this line is disconnected, check the fuel filter.
2. Run a piece of fuel-resistant rub-

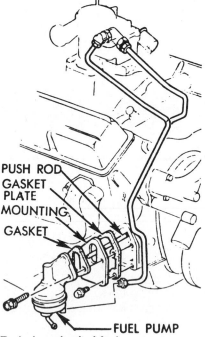

PUSH ROD
GASKET
PLATE
MOUNTING
GASKET

FUEL PUMP
Typical mechanical fuel pump mounting

ber hose from the line to a graduated container.
3. Disconnect the BAT connector from the coil terminal.
4. Crank the engine. Fuel should be pumped into the container at a rate of 1 pint in 30 seconds.
5. Remove the added hose and container and connect a fuel pressure gauge to the fuel line. Crank the engine and read the highest pressure obtained on the gauge. See the Tune-Up Specifications Chart.
6. If the pump failed the tests of either Step 4 or 5, replace the pump as previously outlined. If the pump checked okay, remove the pressure gauge and reconnect the fuel line to the carburetor. Reconnect the ignition wiring as originally connected.

Electric Fuel Pump

An electric, impeller-type fuel pump is used on all 1982-87 Corvettes. The pump is designed to deliver a constant flow of fuel to the fuel injectors. The fuel pressure is regulated at the pressure regulator and/or compensator units. The pump is mounted inside the fuel tank as part of the fuel gauge sending unit. The pump can be replaced independently of the sending unit.

FUEL SYSTEM BLEEDING

—— CAUTION ——
This procedure must be performed to relieve the fuel system pressure before ANY work is done to the fuel system which requires that a fuel line be disconnected.

1982-84 TBI (Throttle Body Injection) System

With the engine OFF, remove the fuse from the fuse block designated "F.P." (fuel pump). Start the engine and allow it to run until it dies due to fuel starvation. Turn the ignition OFF, replace the fuel pump fuse, and service the fuel system as required.

1985-87 PFI (Port Fuel Injection) System

Connect fuel gauge J34730-1 or equivalent to the fuel pressure tap. Wrap a shop towel around the fitting while connecting the gauge to catch any fuel spray. Install a bleed hose into a suitable container, then open the valve to bleed the fuel system pressure.

REMOVAL & INSTALLATION

1982-87

1. Disconnect the battery cables at the battery.
2. Remove the fuel filler door and bezel.
3. Remove the fuel filler neck seal and drain hose.
4. Disconnect the lines and electrical connectors from the sending unit/pump assembly, and remove the screws which retain the assembly.
5. Remove the sending unit/pump assembly and the gasket.
6. Separate the pump from the sending unit.
7. Installation is the reveres of the previous steps. DO NOT connect the battery until all other steps have been completed.

TESTING

NOTE: A special fuel pressure gauge is required to safely perform this test. On engines equipped with TBI, use gauge J-29658; on engines equipped with PFI, use gauge J-34730-1.

TBI System

1. Remove the air cleaner assembly and plug the vacuum connection(s) at the TBI unit.

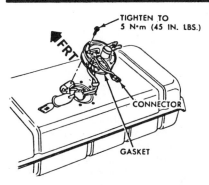

Electric fuel pump and gauge sender assembly, used with T.B.I.-equipped models

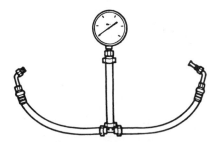

Fuel pressure gauge used to test the fuel pressure on T.B.I.-equipped models

2. Remove the fuel tube which connects between both TBI units.

NOTE: Use two line wrenches of the appropriate sizes to disconnect each fitting, one wrench to hold the large fitting, the other to loosen the smaller fitting.

———— CAUTION ————

A small amount of fuel will be released from the connections.

3. Install the fuel pressure guage between the two TBI units.

4. Turn the ignition switch On and check for fuel leakage at the gauge arrangement. If leakage is noted, turn the ignition switch OFF and correct the leak.

5. Start the engine and read the fuel pressure on the gauge. Fuel pressure should be 9–13 psi. Turn the engine

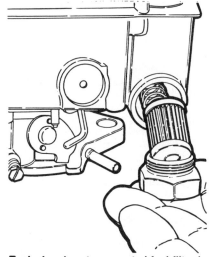

Typical carburetor-mounted fuel filter installation

OFF. Replace the fuel pump if the pressure is not within this range.

6. Remove the fuel pressure gauge, install the fuel tube assembly, and check for leaks.

7. Reinstall the air cleaner and connect the vacuum lines as originally connected.

PFI System

Attach fuel pressure gauge J-34730-1 to the fuel pressure tap on the fuel rail. Wrap a shop towel around the connection to catch any fuel spray. Turn the ignition ON and read the fuel pressure on the gauge. It should be 34–39 psi.

Fuel Filter

REMOVAL & INSTALLATION

1980-81

Fuel filters are integral with the carburetor body. The filter element can be replaced as follows:
1. Disconnect the fuel line.
2. Remove the fuel filter nut from the carburetor.
3. Remove the filter element and spring. Blow through the filter end. If

the air does not flow freely, replace the element. Do not attempt to clean the filter element.

4. Install the spring, then the element.

5. Install the inlet fitting using a new gasket.

6. Install the fuel line.

NOTE: A check valve is installed in the fuel filter to meet roll over safety standards. New service replacement filters (paper) include the check valve. Install the check valve end of the filter toward the fuel line.

1982-87

On these models, an inline fuel filter is used. The filter is mounted on the passenger-side frame rail, beneath the vehicle. Replacement is a simple matter of bleeding the system (as previously outlined), disconnecting the hoses, and dismounting the filter. Check for leaks after installing the new filter

NOTE: A woven plastic filter is located on the lower end of the fuel pick-up tube in the tank. This filter is self cleaning and normally requires no maintenance.

Carburetor

REMOVAL & INSTALLATION

1. Remove the air cleaner.
2. Disconnect the fuel line.
3. Disconnect the throttle linkage.
4. Disconnect and label all vacuum hoses.
5. Remove the retaining bolts.
6. Remove the carburetor.
7. Installation is the reverse of removal.

Fuel Injection

For further information on fuel injection, please refer to *Chilton's Guide To Fuel Injection And Feedback Carburetors.*

CAPRICE, IMPALA, MALIBU AND MONTE CARLO

GASOLINE ENGINES

The fuel pump is the single action AC

diaphragm type. The pump is actuated by an eccentric located on the engine camshaft. On inline engines, the eccentric actuates the pump rocker arm. On V6 and V8 engines, a pushrod between the camshaft eccentric and the fuel pump actuates the pump rocker arm.

Fuel Pump

REMOVAL & INSTALLATION

Mechanical Pump

The mechanical fuel pumps are diaphragm operated and are located on either side of the engine. The fuel pressure should be 4–6.5 psi.

NOTE: Some vehicles have a special fuel pump, which has a metering outlet, for vapor return; this system reduces the possibility of vapor lock. Before working on the fuel system, release the fuel pressure. Remove and replace the fuel tank cap.

1. Disconnect the fuel inlet, outlet and return (if equipped) hoses from the fuel pump.
2. Remove the retaining bolts.
3. Remove the fuel pump, pushrod, gasket and mounting plate (if equipped).

NOTE: On the Chevrolet engines (V6 and V8), if the pushrod is not to be removed, remove the upper bolt from the right front mounting boss. Insert a longer bolt ($\frac{3}{8}$ x 16 x 2 in.) in this hole to hold the fuel pump pushrod.

4. Clean the gasket mounting surfaces.
5. To install, use new gasket(s) and reverse the removal procedures.

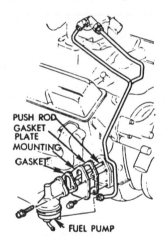

Typical small block V8 fuel pump

Torque the mounting plate bolts to 3 ft. lbs. and the fuel pump bolts to 27 ft. lbs. Start the engine and check for fuel leaks.

Electric Pump

The electric fuel pump is part of the fuel sending unit and is located in the fuel tank. The fuel pressure is 3 psi (carbureted) or 4–13 psi (throttle body).

────── CAUTION ──────

Before removing any component of the fuel system, refer to the "Fuel Pressure Release" procedures in this section and release the fuel pressure.

1. Disconnect the negative battery cable.
2. Remove the fuel tank.
3. Disconnect the fuel tubes and the electrical connectors from the sending unit of the fuel tank.
4. Using a brass drift and a hammer, loosen the sending unit and pump assembly retaining ring.
5. Lift the sending unit and pump assembly from the fuel tank.
6. Remove the fuel pump from the sending unit.
7. To install, use a new sealing O-ring and reverse the removal procedures.

FUEL PRESSURE RELEASE

Carbureted Engine

To release the fuel pressure on the carbureted system, simply remove the fuel tank cap. All tank pressure will vent out the fuel filler pipe.

Throttle Body Fuel Injection (TBI)

To release the fuel pressure on the TBI system, remove the fuel pump fuse from the fuse panel, then start and operate the engine until it stalls. Crank the engine for three seconds to make sure all fuel pressure is removed from the fuel lines, then replace the fuel pump fuse.

Fuel Filter

There are three types of fuel filters; internal (in the carburetor fitting), inline (in the fuel line) and in-tank (the sock on the fuel pick-up tube).

Before removing any component of the fuel system, refer to the "Fuel Pressure Release" procedures in this section and release the fuel pressure.

REMOVAL & INSTALLATION

Internal Filter

1. Disconnect the fuel line connection at the fuel inlet filter nut on the carburetor.
2. Remove the fuel inlet filter nut from the carburetor.
3. Remove the filter and the spring.

NOTE: If a check valve is not present with the filter, one must be installed when the filter is replaced.

4. Install the spring, filter and check valve (must face the fuel line), then reverse the removal procedures.
5. Start the engine and check for leaks.

Inline Filter

1. Disconnect the fuel lines.
2. Remove the fuel filter from the retainer or mounting bolt.
3. To install, reverse the removal procedures. Start the engine and check for leaks.

NOTE: The filter has an arrow (fuel flow direction) on the side of the case, be sure to install it correctly in the system, with the arrow facing away from the fuel tank.

In-Tank Filter

To service the in-tank fuel filter, refer to the "Electric Fuel Pump Removal & Installation" procedures in this section.

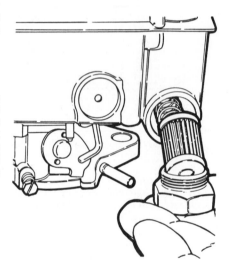

Fuel filter—typical

Fuel Tank
────── CAUTION ──────

Before removing any component of the fuel system, refer to the "Fuel Pressure Release" procedures in this section and release the fuel pressure.

REMOVAL & INSTALLATION

1. Release the pressure from the fuel system.
2. Raise and support the vehicle on jackstands.
3. Remove the fuel tank cap and drain the fuel.
4. Disconnect the fuel pump and the sending unit electrical connector at the body electrical harness connector.

────── CAUTION ──────

DO NOT pry up on the cover connector. The pump and the sending unit wiring harness are an integral part of the sending unit.

5. Disconnect the flexible fuel lines from the metal fuel pipes at the tank.

6. Remove the fuel tank strap bolts and lower the fuel tank from the vehicle.

7. To install, reverse the removal procedures.

Carburetors

──── CAUTION ────

Fuel system is under pressure. Before removing any component of the fuel system, refer to the "Fuel Pressure Release" procedures in this section and relieve the fuel pressure.

REMOVAL & INSTALLATION

1. Disconnect the negative battery cable.

2. Remove the air cleaner and gasket.

3. Disconnect the fuel and vacuum lines.

4. Disconnect the choke electrical connector.

5. Disconnect the throttle linkage.

6. If equipped with an automatic transmission, disconnect the throttle valve linkage.

7. Remove the carburetor attaching nuts or bolts, gasket and the carburetor.

8. If equipped, remove the electric EFE heater and the insulator.

9. Clean the gasket mounting surfaces.

10. To install, use a new gasket and reverse the removal procedures. Torque the short bolts to 7 ft. lbs. and the long bolts or nuts to 12 ft. lbs. Check the idle and the fast idle speeds.

Electronic Fuel Injection

Before removing any component of the fuel injection system, refer to the "Fuel Pressure Release" procedures in this section and release the fuel pressure. For all fuel injection information, removal and service procedures, please refer to *Chilton's Guide To Fuel Injection And Feedback Carburetors*.

DIESEL ENGINES

The fuel system is the heart of the diesel engine. The main components are the injection pump, injection lines and fuel injectors. The fuel injection pump is a small, high pressure rotary pump which delivers a small, metered amount of fuel to the injection nozzles at the proper time. The high pressure lines are all of equal length to avoid differences in timing. The nozzles project into the combustion chambers and inject the fuel into the chambers in a finely atomized, precisely controlled spray. A small, low pressure transfer pump is employed in the inlet line to the injection pump to keep the injection pump supplied. Engine rpm is controlled by a rotary fuel metering valve operated by the accelerator linkage. A fuel filter is located between the transfer pump and the injection pump. On all engines, the fuel pump is of the mechanical diaphragm type, mounted on the engine.

Fuel Pump

REMOVAL & INSTALLATION

V8 Models

The fuel supply pump on the V8 diesel engine is serviced in the same manner as the fuel pump on the gasoline engine. See the procedure above under "Gasoline Fuel System."

V6 MODELS

NOTE: The fuel pump used on the V6 diesel engine is located at the front of the engine, next to the fuel heater.

1. Disconnect negative battery cable, remove the air cleaner, and unplug all electrical connectors from the pump.

2. Place a rag under the pump inlet and outlet fittings, and carefully unscrew the inlet and the outlet fittings. Cap all fittings to keep dirt out.

3. Remove the pump mounting bracket nut, then the fuel pump.

4. To install fuel pump, reverse above procedure, and tighten the nut of the pump mounting bracket to 18 ft. lbs. Then torque inlet and outlet line fittings to 19 ft. lbs.

NOTE: In some cases you may have to adjust pump position slightly to align pump fittings with the fuel lines.

5. After installing the fuel pump, position a catch basin and disconnect the fuel line at the filter and turn on the ignition switch to prime and bleed the lines. If after torquing the fuel line, the pump runs with a click-like sound, or the fuel bubbles, check for leaks in the fuel lines. When the pump quiets down, tighten the fuel line at the filter.

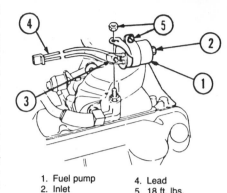

1. Fuel pump
2. Inlet
3. Outlet
4. Lead
5. 18 ft. lbs.

V6 diesel fuel pump

Diesel Fuel Filter

REMOVAL & INSTALLATION

The fuel filter is a square assembly located at the back of the engine above the intake manifold. Disconnect the fuel lines and remove the filter. Install the lines to the new filter. Start the engine and check for leaks.

Tachometer Hook-Up – Diesel Engine

A magnetic pickup tachometer is necessary because of the lack of an ignition system. The tachometer probe is inserted into the hole in the timing indicator.

Cruise Control Servo Relay Rod

ADJUSTMENT

1. Turn the engine OFF.

2. Adjust the rod to minimum slack then put the clip in the first free hole closest to the bellcrank, but within the servo ball.

Diesel Injection Pump and Lines

REMOVAL & INSTALLATION

NOTE: This procedure contains throttle rod and transmission cable adjustments.

1. Remove the air cleaner.

2. Remove the filters and pipes from the valve covers and air crossover.

3. Remove the air crossover and cap the intake manifold with screened covers (J-26996-1 on V8's or 29657 V6), or tape.

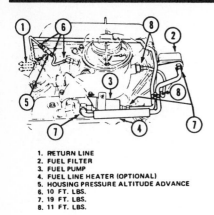

1. RETURN LINE
2. FUEL FILTER
3. FUEL PUMP
4. FUEL LINE HEATER (OPTIONAL)
5. HOUSING PRESSURE ALTITUDE ADVANCE
6. 10 FT. LBS.
7. 19 FT. LBS.
8. 11 FT. LBS.

V6 diesel fuel lines

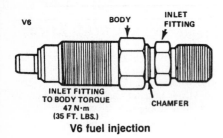

V6 fuel injection

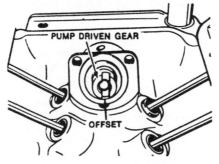

Offset on pump driven gear

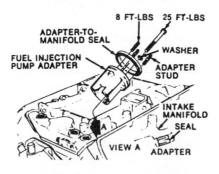

Injection pump adapter bolts

4. Disconnect the throttle rod and return spring.

5. Remove the bellcrank.

6. Remove the throttle and transmission cables from the intake manifold brackets.

7. Disconnect the fuel lines from the filter and remove the filter.

8. Disconnect the fuel inlet line at the pump.

9. Remove the rear A/C compressor brace and remove the fuel line.

10. Disconnect the fuel return line from the injection pump.

11. Remove the clamps and pull the fuel return lines from each injection nozzle.

12. Using two wrenches, disconnect the high pressure lines at the nozzles.

13. Remove the three injection pump retaining nuts with tool J-26987 or its equivalent.

14. Remove the pump and cap all lines and nozzles.

To install:

15. Remove the protective caps from all lines and nozzles. Place the engine on TDC for the No. 1 cylinder. The mark on the harmonic balancer on the crankshaft will be aligned with the zero mark on the timing tab, and both valves for No. 1 cylinder will be closed. The index mark on the injection pump driven gear should be offset to the right when No. 1 is at TDC. Check that all of these conditions are met before continuing.

16. Line up the offset tang on the pump driveshaft with the pump driven gear and install the pump.

17. Install, but do not tighten the pump retaining nuts.

18. Connect the high pressure lines at the nozzles.

19. Using two wrenches, torque the high pressure line nuts to 25 ft. lbs.

20. Connect the fuel return lines to the nozzles and pump.

21. Align the timing mark on the injection pump with the line on the timing mark adapter and torque the mounting nuts to 35 ft. lbs. V6, 18 ft. lbs. V8.

NOTE: A 3/4 in. open end wrench on the boss at the front of the injection pump will aid in rotating the pump to align the marks.

22. Adjust the throttle rod:

a. remove the clip from the cruise control rod and remove the rod from the bellcrank.

b. loosen the locknut on the throttle rod a few turns, then shorten the rod several turns.

c. rotate the bellcrank to the full throttle stop, then lengthen the throttle rod until the injection pump lever contacts the injection pump full throttle stop, then release the bellcrank.

d. tighten the throttle rod locknut.

23. Install the fuel inlet line between the transfer pump and the filter.

24. Install the rear A/C compressor brace.

25. Install the bellcrank and clip.

26. Connect the throttle rod and return spring.

27. Adjust the transmission cable:

a. push the snap-lock to the disengaged position.

b. rotate the injection pump lever to the full throttle stop and hold it there.

c. push in the snap-lock until it is flush.

d. release the injection pump lever.

28. Start the engine and check for fuel leaks.

29. Remove the screened covers or tape and install the air crossover.

30. Install the tubes in the air flow control valve in the air crossover and install the ventilation filters in the valve covers.

31. Install the air cleaner.

32. Start the engine and allow it to run for two minutes. Stop the engine, let it stand for two minutes, then restart. This permits the air to bleed off within the pump.

Injection Timing

ADJUSTMENT

For the engine to be properly timed, the lines on the top of the injection pump adapter and the flange of the injection pump must be aligned.

1. The engine must be off for resetting the timing.

2. Loosen the three pump retaining nuts with J-26987 on V8's or J-25304 on V6's, an injection pump intake manifold wrench, or its equivalent.

3. Align the timing marks and torque the pump retaining nuts to 35 ft. lbs.

NOTE: The use of a 3/4 in. open end wrench on the boss at the front of the pump will aid in rotating the pump to align the marks.

4. Adjust the throttle rod. See "Fuel Injection Pump Removal and Installation," Step 22.

Injection Nozzle

REMOVAL & INSTALLATION

The injection nozzles on these engines are simply unbolted from the cylinder head, after the fuel lines are removed, in similar fashion to a spark plug. Be careful not to damage the nozzle end and make sure you remove the copper nozzle gasket from the cylinder head if it does not come off with the nozzle.

Clean the carbon off the tip of the nozzle with a soft brass wire brush and install the nozzles, with gaskets.

NOVA

Mechanical Fuel Pump

REMOVAL & INSTALLATION

1. Note the routing of fuel lines and mark if necessary. Then, use a pair of pliers to slide the retaining clips for the fuel lines well off the fuel pump connections. Disconnect the fuel lines, using a twisting motion to break them loose if they are hard to disconnect.

2. Remove the two bolts from the cylinder head, and remove the pump, gasket, and heat shield, noting the position of the shield. Reseal the surface of the block to prevent loss of oil.

3. Scrape the gasket surfaces of the block (and pump, if it's being reused) with a scraper that will not scratch the aluminum surface of the head.

4. Install in reverse order. When reconnecting the fuel lines, make sure the clips are installed to the inside of the bulged sections of the fuel pump connections, and are not right at the ends of the fuel lines. Start the engine and check for leaks.

Fuel Filter
REMOVAL & INSTALLATION

1. Note the routing of inlet and outlet lines and the direction of flow as marked on the filter. The arrow points toward the carburetor. Then, with a pair of pliers, shift the clips on the inlet and outlet hoses back and well away from the connections on the filter.

2. Disconnect the fuel lines, using a twisting motion to break them loose. Immediately plug the openings to prevent the spillage of fuel and entry of dirt. Pull the filter out of its retaining clip.

3. Install the filter in reverse order. When reconnecting the fuel lines, make sure the clips are installed to the inside of the bulged sections of the fuel filter connections, and are not right at the ends of the fuel lines. Start the engine and check for leaks.

Carburetor

REMOVAL & INSTALLATION

1. Disconnect the emission control hoses from the air cleaner, labeling them or noting their routing as necessary. Remove the wingnut and mounting bolts and remove the air cleaner.

2. Disconnect the accelerator cable at the carburetor. If the car has an automatic transmission, disconnect the transmission cable at the throttle linkage.

3. Disconnect the wiring connector for the carburetor solenoid valves.

4. Label and then disconnect the carburetor emission control hoses. Disconnect the fuel line, draining any fuel into a metal or ceramic container (not a styrofoam cup). Disconnect the evaporative emissions canister hose.

5. Remove the carburetor mounting nuts. Then, remove the cold mixture heater wire clamp and the EGR vacuum control bracket. Remove the carburetor.

6. Remove the insulating gasket from the manifold. Use a clean rag to seal off the intake manifold opening.

7. Clean the sealing surfaces of the carburetor and manifold and install a new insulating gasket. Put the carburetor in position and install the mounting nuts, torquing them alternately and evenly.

8. Reverse the remaining removal procedures to reconnect linkages and hoses. Install and adjust the throttle and transmission linkages. Install the air cleaner. Start the engine and run it while checking for leaks.

CORSICA AND BERETTA

Fuel Filter

REMOVAL & INSTALLATION

The fuel filter is mounted on the rear crossmember of the vehicle directly behind the fuel tank.

————— CAUTION —————
The fuel pressure must be relieved before working on any part of the fuel system. Fuel systems that are under constant pressure will spray a small amount of fuel when opened. On the TBI injection, cover all fuel fittings with a shop towel while loosening them to collect the excess fuel. Place the shop towel in an approved container and discard it properly. On the MFI injection, install pressure gauge J–34730–1, or equivalent on the pressure fitting located on the front of the fuel rail. Place a shop towel around the fitting to collect the excess fuel. Dispose of the shop towel correctly. Place a

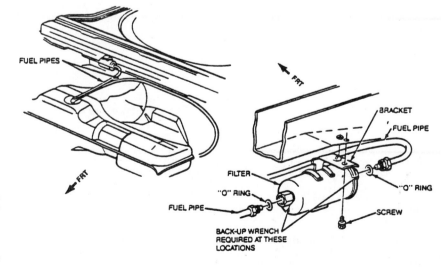

Fuel filter location and mounting

bleed hose into an approved container and bleed off the system pressure. Dispose of the fuel properly. After servicing either system, check all connections, run the engine and check for leaks.

1. Using the correct procedure, relieve the fuel pressure.
2. Use a back-up wrench to hold the fittings on the filter and loosen the fuel line fittings.
3. Using care not to damage or loose the O-rings, remove the fuel lines from the filter.
4. Remove the filter from the mounting clamp.
5. Install the new filter and O-rings. Torque the fittings to 22 ft. lbs.
6. Run the engine and check for leaks.

Electric Fuel Pump

PRESSURE TESTING

TBI Injection

1. Turn the engine OFF.
2. Remove the TBI cover bonnet and gasket.
3. Disconnect the fuel supply hose in the engine compartment.
4. Install and tighten a pressure gauge between the steel line and flexible hose.
5. Start the engine and check the reading.
6. Correct reading should be 62–90 kPa.
7. Turn the engine off, relieve the fuel pressure and disconnect the gauge. Reconnect the fuel lines.
8. Run the engine and check for leaks.

MFI Injection

1. Using the correct procedure, relieve the fuel pressure.
2. Install a pressure gauge on the connection on the fuel rail.

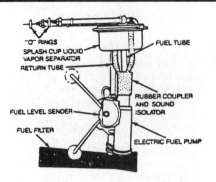

"O" RINGS
SPLASH CUP LIQUID VAPOR SEPARATOR
RETURN TUBE
FUEL LEVEL SENDER
FUEL FILTER
FUEL TUBE
RUBBER COUPLER AND SOUND ISOLATOR
ELECTRIC FUEL PUMP

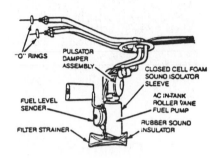

"O" RINGS
PULSATOR DAMPER ASSEMBLY
FUEL LEVEL SENDER
FILTER STRAINER
CLOSED CELL FOAM SOUND ISOLATOR SLEEVE
AC IN-TANK ROLLER VANE FUEL PUMP
RUBBER SOUND INSULATOR

Fuel pump and sending unit assemblies

3. With the ignition ON, the pressure should be 280–325 kPa (40–47 Psi).
4. Starting and idling the engine will result in a lower pressure since the manifold pressure will be lower and applied to the regulator diaphragm.
5. Relieve the fuel pressure and remove the gauge.

ADJUSTMENT

No adjustments are possible on either system. If the pressure is not within specifications, problems could be caused by a faulty fuel pump, clogged fuel filter, a leaking coupling or hose, a faulty regulator, or an injector sticking open.

REMOVAL & INSTALLATION

The fuel pump is located inside the fuel tank. Removal and installation requires that the fuel tank be removed from the vehicle.

1. Disconnect the negative battery cable.
2. Using the correct procedure, relieve the fuel pressure.
3. Raise and safely support the vehicle.
4. Remove the lower fuel line on the tank and drain the fuel tank into an approved container.
5. Support the fuel tank and disconnect the fuel tank retaining straps.
6. Lower the tank enough to disconnect the wires, ground strap and hoses.
7. Remove the fuel tank from the vehicle.
8. Remove the sending unit and pump assembly by turning the locking ring counterclockwise.
9. Lift the assembly from the tank and disconnect the pump from the sending unit.
10. Install the new fuel pump onto the sending unit. Use care not to damage any hoses.
11. The remainder of the installation is the reverse of the removal.
12. Check for any leaks when finished.

Fuel Injection

Due to the complex nature of modern fuel injection systems, comprehensive diagnosis and testing procedures fall outside the confines of this repair manual. For complete information on fuel injection diagnosis, testing and repair procedures, please refer to *"Chilton's Guide to Fuel Injection and Feedback Carburetors".*

TRUCKS

GASOLINE ENGINES

Fuel Pump

TESTING THE FUEL PUMP

Fuel pumps should always be tested on the vehicle. The larger line between the pump and tank is the suction side of the system and the smaller line, between the pump and carburetor, is the pressure side. A leak in the pressure side would be apparent because of dripping fuel. A leak in the suction side is usually only apparent because of a reduced volume of fuel delivered to the pressure side.

1. Tighten any loose line connections and look for any kinks or restrictions.
2. Disconnect the fuel line at the carburetor. Disconnect the distributor-to-coil primary wire. Place a container at the end of the fuel line and crank the engine a few revolutions. If little or no gasoline flows from the line, either the fuel pump is not working or the line is plugged. Disconnect the line at the pump and the tank;

blow through the line with compressed air and try again. Reconnect the line. If the problem is traced to the tank, the tank and gauge unit must be removed to check the condition of the inlet filter screen.

3. If fuel flows in good volume, check the fuel pump pressure to be sure.

4. Attach a pressure gauge to the pressure side of the fuel line.

5. Run the engine and note the reading on the gauge. Stop the engine and compare the reading with the specifications listed in the Tune-Up Specifications. If the pump is operating properly, the pressure will be as specified and will be constant at idle speed. If pressure varies or is too high or low, the pump should be replaced.

6. Remove the pressure gauge.

REMOVAL & INSTALLATION

Except Below

NOTE: When you connect the fuel pump outlet fitting, always use 2 wrenches to avoid damaging the pump.

1. Disconnect the fuel intake and outlet lines at the pump and plug the pump intake line.

2. On V8 engines, you can remove the upper bolt from the right front engine mounting boss (on the front of the block) and insert a long bolt $3/8$-16 × 2 in.) to hold the fuel pump pushrod.

3. Remove the two pump mounting bolts and lockwashers; remove the pump and its gasket.

4. If the rocker arm pushrod is to be removed from V8s, remove the two adapter bolts and lockwashers and remove the adapter and its gasket.

5. Install the fuel pump with a new gasket reversing the removal procedure. Heavy grease can be used to hold the fuel pump pushrod up while installing the pump, if you didn't install the long bolt in Step 2. Coat the mating surfaces with sealer.

6. Connect the fuel lines and check for leaks.

4-119

1. Disconnect the battery ground.
2. Remove the distributor.
3. Disconnect the fuel hoses at the pump.
4. Remove the engine lifting hook.
5. Unbolt and remove the fuel pump. Discard the gasket.
6. Installation is the reverse of removal. It will be easier if you rotate the engine so the cam lobe is on a down stroke. Use sealer on the new gasket. Set the timing.

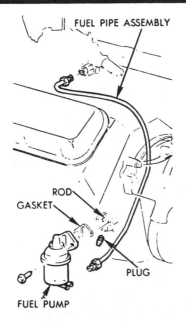

Typical gasoline fuel pump

4-121

1. Disconnect the negative cable at the battery. Raise and support the vehicle.
2. Disconnect the inlet hose from the pump. Disconnect the vapor return hose, if equipped.
3. Loosen the fuel line at the carburetor, then disconnect the outlet pipe from the pump.
4. Remove the two mounting bolts and remove the pump from the engine.
5. To install, place a new gasket on the pump and install the pump on the engine. Tighten the two mounting bolts alternately and evenly.
6. Install the pump outlet pipe. This is easier if the pipe is disconnected from the carburetor. Tighten the fitting while backing up the pump nut with another wrench. Install the pipe at the carburetor.
7. Install the inlet and vapor hoses. Lower the car, connect the negative battery cable, start the engine, and check for leaks.

6-173

1. Disconnect the battery ground.
2. Disconnect the fuel hoses at the pump.
3. Unbolt and remove the pump. Discard the gasket.
4. Installation is the reverse of removal. Use sealer on the new gasket. It will be easier if you rotate the engine so that the cam lobe is on a down stroke.

Carburetor

REMOVAL & INSTALLATION

NOTE: This procedure is a general one that covers all models. Remember that each carburetor application may differ slightly.

1. Remove the air cleaner and its gasket.
2. Disconnect the fuel and vacuum lines from the carburetor.
3. Disconnect the choke coil rod or heated air line tube.
4. Disconnect the throttle linkage.
5. On automatic transmission trucks, disconnect the throttle valve linkage.
6. Remove the CEC valve vacuum hose and electrical connector.
7. Remove the idle stop electrical wiring from the idle stop solenoid, if so equipped.
8. Remove the carburetor attaching nuts and/or bolts, gasket or insulator, and remove the carburetor.
9. Install the carburetor using a reverse of the removal procedure. Use a new gasket and fill the float bowl with gasoline to ease starting the engine.

Fuel Tank

REMOVAL & INSTALLATION

1. Drain the tank.
2. Raise and support the truck on jackstands.
3. Disconnect the wiring and ground strap at the tank.
4. Disconnect the filler neck hose and vent hose at the tank.
5. Disconnect the fuel feed line and vapor line at the tank.
6. Place a floor jack under the tank to take up its weight.
7. Remove the fuel tank support bolts and lower the tank.
8. Installation is the reverse of removal.

DIESEL ENGINES

Fuel Supply Pump

REMOVAL & INSTALLATION

The fuel supply pump is serviced in the same manner as the fuel pump on the gasoline engine.

Fuel Filter

REMOVAL & INSTALLATION

The fuel filter is a square assembly located at the back of the engine above the intake manifold. Disconnect the fuel lines and remove the filter. Install the lines to the new filter. Start the engine and check for leaks.

Fuel Injection Pump and Lines

REMOVAL & INSTALLATION

Except 4-137

NOTE: **This procedure contains throttle rod and transmission cable adjustments.**

1. Remove the air cleaner.
2. Remove the filters and pipes from the valve covers and air crossover.
3. Remove the air crossover and cap the intake manifold with screened covers (tool J–26996–1) or tape.
4. Disconnect the throttle rod and return spring.
5. Remove the ballcrank.
6. Remove the throttle and transmission cables from the intake manifold brackets.
7. Disconnect the fuel lines from the filter and remove the filter.
8. Disconnect the fuel inlet line at the pump.
9. Remove the rear A/C compressor brace and remove the fuel line.
10. Disconnect the fuel return line from the injection pump.
11. Remove the clamps and pull the fuel return lines from each injection nozzle.
12. Using two wrenches, disconnect the high pressure lines at the nozzles.
13. Remove the three injection pump retaining nuts with tool J–26987 or its equivalent.
14. Remove the pump and cap all lines and nozzles.
15. To install: Remove the protective caps from all lines and nozzles. Place the engine on TDC for the No. 1 cylinder. The mark on the harmonic balancer on the crankshaft will be aligned with the zero mark on the timing tab, and both valves for No.1 cylinder will be closed. The index mark on the injection pump driven gear should be offset to the right when No. 1 is at TDC. Check that all of these conditions are met before continuing.
16. Line up the offset tang on the pump driveshaft with the pump driven gear and install the pump.
17. Install, but do not tighten the pump retaining nuts.
18. Connect the high pressure lines at the nozzles.
19. Using two wrenches, torque the high pressure line nuts to 25 ft. lbs.

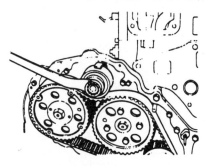

Loosening tension pulley

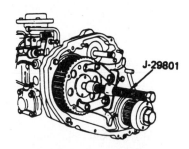

J-29801

Removing timing pulley

20. Connect the fuel return lines to the nozzles and pump.
21. Align the timing mark on the injection pump with the line on the timing mark adapter and torque the mounting nuts to 35 ft. lbs. A $\frac{3}{4}$ in. open end wrench on the boss at the front of the injection pump will aid in rotating the pump to align the marks.
22. To adjust the throttle rod: Remove the clip from the cruise control rod and remove the rod from the bellcrank. Loosen the locknut on the throttle rod a few turns, then shorten the rod several turns. Rotate the bellcrank to the full throttle stop, then lengthen the throttle rod until the injection pump lever contacts the injection pump full throttle stop, then release the bellcrank. Tighten the throttle rod locknut.
23. Install the fuel inlet line between the transfer pump and the filter.
24. Install the rear A/C compressor brace.
25. Install the bellcrank and clip.
26. Connect the throttle rod and return spring.
27. To adjust the transmission cable: Push the snap-lock to the disengaged position. Rotate the injection pump lever to the full throttle stop and hold it there. Push in the snap-lock until it is flush. Release the injection pump lever.
28. Start the engine and check for fuel leaks.
29. Remove the screened covers or tape and install the air crossover.
30. Install the tubes in the air flow control valve in the air crossover and

install the ventilation filters in the valve covers.
31. Install the air cleaner.
32. Start the engine and allow it to run for two minutes. Stop the engine, let it stand for two minutes, then restart. This permits the air to bleed off within the pump.

4-137

1. Raise engine hood.
2. Disconnect the battery ground cable.
3. Remove the battery.
4. Remove the under cover.
5. Drain the cooling system by opening the drain plugs on the radiator and on the cylinder block.
6. Disconnect the upper water hose at the engine side.
7. Loosen the compressor drive belt by moving the power steering oil pump or idler. (If so equipped.)
8. Remove the cooling fan and fan shroud.
9. Disconnect the lower water hose at the engine side.
10. Remove the air conditioner compressor (If so equipped.)
11. Remove the fan belt.
12. Remove the crankshaft pulley.
13. Remove the timing pulley housing covers.
14. Remove the tension spring and fixing bolt, then remove the tension center and pulley.
15. Remove the timing belt.
16. Remove the engine control cable and wiring harness of the fuel cut solenoid.
17. Remove the fuel hoses and injection pipes. Use a wrench to hold the delivery holder when loosening the sleeve nuts on the injection pump side.
18. Install a 6mm bolt (with pitch of 1.25) into threaded hole in the timing pulley housing through the hole in pulley to prevent turning of the pulley. Remove the bolts fixing the injection pump timing pulley, then remove the pulley using pulley puller.
19. Remove injection pump flange fixing nuts and rear bracket bolts, then remove the injection pump.
20. Install the injection pump by aligning notched line on the flange with the line on the front bracket.
21. Install the injection pump timing pulley by aligning it with the key groove. Torque to 42–52 ft. lbs.
22. Bring the piston in No. 1 cylinder to top dead center on compression stroke and align marks on the timing pulleys.
23. Follow the timing belt installation steps.
24. Check the injection timing.
25. To install remaining parts, follow the removal steps in reverse order.

SLOW IDLE SPEED ADJUSTMENT

Except 4–137 and 8–379

1. Run the engine to normal operating temperature.
2. Insert the probe of a magnetic pickup tachometer into the timing indicator hole.
3. Set the parking brake and block the drive wheels.
4. Place the transmission in Drive and turn the A/C Off.
5. Turn the slow idle screw on the injection pump to obtain the idle specification on the emission control label.

4–137

1. Set parking brake and block drive wheels.
2. Place transmission in neutral.
3. Start and normalize the engine. Engine coolant temperature: above 80°C (176°F).
4. Set the engine tachometer.
5. If the idle speed deviates from the specified range of 700–800 rpm, loosen the idle speed adjusting screw lock nut.
6. Turn the adjusting screw in or out until the idle speed is in the correct range. After tightening the lock nut lock it in place.

Cruise Control Servo Relay Rod

ADJUSTMENT

1. Turn the engine Off.
2. Adjust the rod to minimum slack then put the clip in the first free hole closest to the bellcrank, but within the servo ball.

Injection Timing

ADJUSTMENT

Except 4–137 and 8–379

For the engine to be properly timed, the lines on the top of the injection pump adapter and the flange of the injection pump must be aligned.

1. The engine must be off for resetting the timing.
2. Loosen the three pump retaining nuts with J–26987, an injection pump intake manifold wrench, or its equivalent.
3. Align the timing marks and torque the pump retaining nuts to 35 ft. lbs.

NOTE: The use of a ³⁄₄ in. open end wrench on the boss at the front of the pump will aid in rotating the pump to align the marks.

#1 piston at TDC

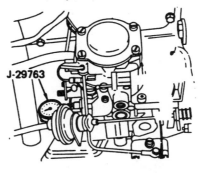

Static timing gauge installed

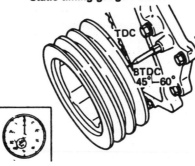

#1 piston 45–60 degrees before TDC

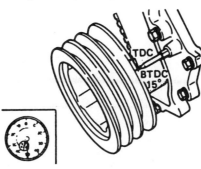

#1 piston 15 degrees before TDC

4. Adjust the throttle rod. (See Fuel Injection Pump Removal and Installation, Step 22.)

4–137

1. Check that notched line on the injection pump flange is in alignment with notched line on the injection pump front bracket.
2. Bring the piston in No. 1 cylinder to top dead center on compression

stroke by turning the crankshaft as necessary.
3. With the timing pulley housing cover removed, check that timing belt is properly tensioned, and that timing marks are aligned.
4. Disconnect the injection pipe from the injection pump and remove the distributor head screw, then install static timing gauge. Set the lift approximately 1mm (0.04 in.) from the plunger.
5. Use a wrench to hold the delivery holder when loosening the sleeve nuts on the injection pump side.
6. Bring the piston in No. 1 cylinder to a point 45–60 degrees before top dead center by turning the crankshaft, then calibrate the dial indicator to zero.
7. Turn the crankshaft pulley slightly in both directions and check that gauge indication is stable.
8. Turn the crankshaft in normal direction of rotation, and take the reading of the dial indicator when the timing mark (15 degrees) on the crankshaft pulley is in alignment with the pointer. Reading should be 0.020 in.
9. If the reading of dial indicator deviates from the specified range, hold crankshaft in position 15 degrees before top dead center and loosen two nuts on injection pump flange.
10. Move the injection pump to a point where dial indicator gives reading of 0.020 in., then tighten the pump flange nuts.

8–379

For the engine to be properly timed, the marks on the top of the engine front cover and the injection pump flange must be aligned. The engine must be off when the timing is reset. On Federal models, align scribe marks. On California models, align half circles. If the marks are not aligned, adjustment is necessary.

1. Loosen the three pump retaining nuts.
2. Align mark on injection pump with mark on front cover and tighten nuts to 40 Nm (30 ft. lbs.).
3. Adjust throttle rod.
4. Set engine to TDC No. 1 cylinder (firing).
5. Install timing fixing J–33042 or equivalent in F.I. pump location. Do not use gasket.
6. Slot of F.I. pump gear to be in vertical 6 o'clock position. (If not, remove fixture and rotate engine crankshaft 360°). The timing marks on gears will be aligned.
7. Fasten gear to fixture, and tighten.
8. Install on 10mm nut to housing upper stud to hold fixture flange nut to be "finger" tight.

9. Torque large bolt (18mm head) counterclockwise (toward left bank) to 50 ft. lbs. Tighten 10mm nut.

10. Insure crankshaft has not rotated (and fixture did not bind on 10mm nut).

11. Strike scriber with mallet to mark "TDC" on front housing.

12. Remove timing fixture.

13. Install fuel injection pump with gasket.

14. Install one 8mm bolt to attach gear to pump hub and tighten to specification.

15. Align timing marks on F.I. pump to front housing mark. Tighten to specification (3) 10mm attachment nuts.

16. Rotate engine and install remaining (2) pump gear attaching bolts and tighten to specification.

Injection Nozzle

REMOVAL & INSTALLATION

350 Diesel

The injection nozzles on these engines are simply unbolted from the cylinder head, after the fuel lines are removed, in similar fashion to a spark plug. Be careful not to damage the nozzle end and make sure you remove the copper nozzle gasket from the cylinder head if it does not come off with the nozzle.

Clean the carbon off the tip of the nozzle with a soft brass wire brush and install the nozzles, with gaskets.

NOTE: 1981-87 models use two type of injectors, CAV Lucas and Diesel Equipment. When installing the inlet fittings, torque the Diesel Equipment injector fitting to 45 ft. lbs. and the CAV Lucas to 25 ft. lbs.

8-379

NOTE: Nozzles used in Pickups and Blazers are different than those used in Vans and are not interchangeable.

1. Disconnect batteries.
2. Disconnect fuel line clip.
3. Remove fuel return hose.
4. Remove fuel injection line as previously outlined.
5. Remove injection nozzle using tool J-29873 or equivalent whenever possible.

NOTE: When removing an injection nozzle, use tool J-29873 or equivalent. Be sure to remove the nozzle using the 30mm hex. Failure to do so will result in damage to the injection nozzle. Always cap the nozzle and lines to prevent damage and contamination.

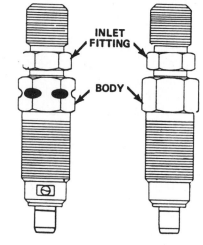

DIESEL EQUIPMENT   **C.A.V. LUCAS**

Diesel injector identification—1980 and later

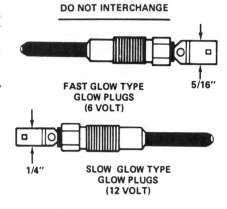

Glow plug identification

Injection Pump Adapter, Adapter Seal, and New Adapter Timing Mark

REMOVAL & INSTALLATION

NOTE: Skip Steps 4 and 9 if a new adapter is not being installed.

1. Remove injection pump and lines.
2. Remove the injection pump adapter.
3. Remove the seal from the adapter.
4. File the timing mark from the adapter. Do not file the mark off the pump.
5. Position the engine at TDC of No.1 cylinder. Align the mark on the

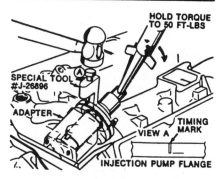

Marking the injection pump adapter

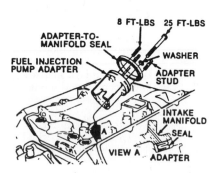

Injection pump adapter bolts

NOTE: LUBRICATE SEAL, TOOL, ADAPTER & MANIFOLD

Installing the adapter seal

balancer with the zero mark on the indicator. The index is offset to the right when No.1 is at TDC.

6. Apply chassis lube to the seal areas. Install, but do not tighten the injection pump.

7. Install the new seal on the adapter using tool J-28425, or its equivalent.

8. Torque the adapter bolts to 25 ft. lbs.

9. Install timing tool J-26896 into the injection pump adapter. Torque the tool, toward No.1 cylinder, to 50 ft. lbs. Mark the injection pump adapter. Remove the tool and install the injection pump.

Injection Pump

REMOVAL & INSTALLATION

8-379 — Pickup and Blazer

1. Disconnect batteries.

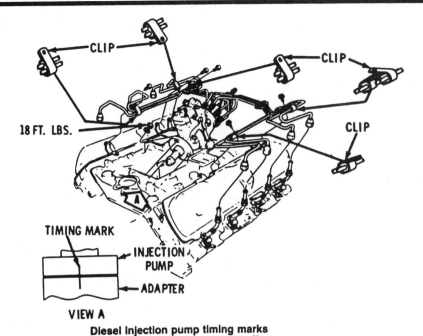

VIEW A

Diesel injection pump timing marks

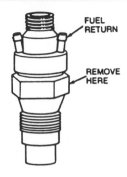

8–379 injection nozzle

29. Install fan shroud and fan.
30. Connect batteries. Start engine and check for leaks.

Vans

1. Remove intake manifold.
2. Remove air cleaner inlet hose (rotate snorkel up).
3. Remove hood latch, disconnect cable and move aside.
4. Remove windshield washer bottle.
5. Remove fan shroud bolts.
6. Remove upper shroud.
7. Disconnect rubber hose from oil fill tube.
8. Disconnect oil fill tube attaching nuts and remove oil fill tube.
9. Remove oil fill tube grommet.
10. Rotate engine as necessary and remove drive gear to pump bolts.
11. Remove fuel filter and bracket—includes line to injection pump.
12. Disconnect wire looms from injection lines.
13. Disconnect injection lines at brackets. Also disconnect oil pan dipstick tube at left cylinder head.
14. Disconnect electrical connections at injection pump.
15. If equipped with automatic transmission, disconnect T.V. cable.
16. Disconnect accelerator cable.
17. Disconnect injection lines at nozzles Numbers 2, 4, 5, 6, 7, 8.
18. Raise vehicle.
19. Disconnect Number 1 and 3 injection lines at nozzles.
20. Cover nozzles Numbers 1, 3, 5, 7.
21. Lower vehicle.
22. Cover nozzles Number 2, 4, 6, 8.
23. Disconnect injection lines at pump and remove lines. Tag lines for reinstallation.
24. Cap all lines.
25. Disconnect fuel return line.
26. Scribe a mark on front cover and pump flange for reinstallation.
27. Remove pump to front cover attaching nuts.
28. Remove injection pump and cap all open discharge fittings.
29. Install using the following sequence; Replace gasket. Align locating

2. Remove fan.
3. Remove fan shroud.
4. Remove intake manifold.
5. Remove fuel lines.
6. Disconnect accelerator cable at injection pump, and detent cable where applicable.
7. Disconnect necessary wires and hoses at injection pump.
8. Disconnect fuel return line at top of injection pump.
9. Disconnect fuel feed line at injection pump.
10. Remove A/C hose retainer bracket if equipped with A/C.
11. Remove oil fill tube, includes C.D.R.V. vent hose assembly.
12. Remove grommet.
13. Scribe or paint a mark on front cover and injection pump flange.
14. It will be necessary to rotate engine in order to gain access to driven gear to injection pump retaining bolts through the oil filler neck hole.
15. Remove injection pump to front cover attaching nuts.
16. Remove pump and cap all open lines and nozzles.
17. Install pump per the following: Replace gasket and align locating pin on pump hub with slot in injection pump driven gear. At the same time, align timing marks.
18. Attach injection pump to front cover, torque nuts to 30 ft. lbs. Align timing marks before fully torquing nuts.
19. Install drive gear to injection pump bolts, torque bolts to 20 ft. lbs.
20. Install oil fill tube, includes C.D.R.V. vent hose assembly.
21. Install grommet.

Offset on the diesel fuel pump driven gear

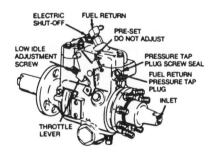

Injection pump

22. Install A/C hose retainer bracket if equipped.
23. Install fuel feed line at injection pump, torque to 20 ft. lbs..
24. Install fuel return line at top of injection pump.
25. Connect necessary wires and hoses.
26. Connect accelerator cable.
27. Connect injection lines.
28. Install intake manifold.

pin on pump hub with slot in injection pump gear. At the same time, align timing marks.

30. Attach injection pump to front cover, torque nuts to 30 ft. lbs.. Align timing marks before fully torquing nuts.

31. Attach pump to drive gear, torque bolts to 20 ft. lbs..

32.. For the remainder of installation procedures, reverse removal steps.

Fuel Injection Line

REMOVAL & INSTALLATION

Pick-Up and Blazer

1. Disconnect batteries.
2. Disconnect air cleaner bracket at valve cover.
3. Remove crankcase ventilator bracket and move aside.
4. Disconnect secondary filter lines.
5. Remove secondary filter adapter.
6. Loosen vacuum pump hold-down clamp and rotate pump in order to gain access to intake manifold bolt.
7. Remove intake manifold bolts. Injection line clips are retained by the same bolts.
8. Remove intake manifold.
9. Install protective covers J–29664–1 or equivalent.
10. Remove injection line clips at loom brackets.
11. Remove injection lines at nozzles and cover nozzles with protective caps.
12. Remove injection lines at pump and tag lines for reinstallation.
13. Remove fuel line from injection pump.
14. Installation is the reverse of removal.

Vans

1. Disconnect batteries.
2. Remove engine cover.
3. Remove intake manifold.
4. Install protective covers J–29664–1 or equivalent.
5. Remove injection line clips at loom brackets.
6. Raise vehicle (left bank only).
7. Remove injection lines at nozzles and cover nozzles with protective caps.
8. Lower vehicle (left bank only).
9. Remove injection lines at pump and tag lines for reinstallation.
10. Installation is the reverse of removal.

GLOW PLUGS

There are two types of glow plugs used on General Motors diesels: the "fast glow" type and the "slow glow" type. The fast glow type use pulsing current applied to 6 volt glow plugs while the slow glow type use continuous current applied to 12 volt glow plugs.

An easy way to tell the plugs apart is that the fast glow (6 volt) plugs have a $5/16$ in. wide electrical connector plug while the slow glow (12 volt) connector plug is $1/4$ in. wide. Do not attempt to interchange any parts of these two glow plug systems.

Chassis Electrical

INDEX

CORVETTE

Headlight Switch

REMOVAL & INSTALLATION

1. Disconnect the negative battery terminal.
2. Remove the left air distribution duct.
3. Remove the instrument cluster attaching screws and pull the cluster rearward.
4. Disconnect the speedometer cable, electrical connectors and remove the cluster.
5. Remove the instrument panel to left door pillar attaching screws and pull the left side of the instrument panel slightly forward for access.
6. Depress the shaft retainer, pull the knob and shaft assembly out and remove the switch bezel.
7. Disconnect the vacuum hoses from the switch, tagging them for installation.
8. Pry the connector from the switch and remove the switch from the panel.
9. Installation is the reverse of removal.

Instrument Cluster

REMOVAL & INSTALLATION

1980-82

1. Disconnect negative battery cable.
2. Remove left air distribution duct.
3. Remove lens to bezel attaching screws and remove lens.
4. Remove cluster to instrument panel attaching screws.
5. Pull cluster assembly slightly forward to obtain clearance for removal of speedometer cable housing, headlamp switch connectors and panel illuminating lamps.
6. Install by reversing removal procedure, being careful not to kink the speedometer cable casing.

1984-87

1. Disconnect battery ground cable.
2. Remove light switch knob (spring loaded), and light switch nut.
3. Remove steering column trim cover.
4. Remove 2 steering column attaching bolts and lower steering column for access.
5. Remove cluster bezel front and left side attaching screws.
6. Remove cluster bezel from instrument panel.

7. Remove 4 cluster to instrument panel attaching screws.
8. Pull cluster rearward for access to disconnect cluster electrical connectors. Metal retaining clips are located at back side of connectors.
9. Remove cluster from instrument panel. Odometer may be removed for service or replacement.
10. Reverse above procedure to install.

Speedometer Cable

REMOVAL & INSTALLATION

Reach behind the speedometer and depress the retaining clip. Pull the cable from the casing. If the cable is broken, raise the car and disconnect the cable at the transmission. Lubricate only the bottom $\frac{3}{4}$ of the cable with speedometer cable lubricant. Reconnect all parts.

NOTE: This procedure is easier to complete if the instrument panel cluster has previously been removed.

Windshield Wiper Motor

REMOVAL & INSTALLATION

1980-82

1. With wiper motor in park position and hood open, disconnect the washer hoses and all wiring from the motor assembly.
2. Remove the plenum chamber grill.
3. Remove the nut which retains the crank arm to the motor assembly.
4. Remove the ignition shield, if used, and distributor cap. Remove and identify the left bank spark plug leads.
5. Remove the motor mounting screws or nuts and remove the motor.
6. To install, reverse the above procedure.

1984-87

1. Open hood and install fender covers.
2. Remove wiper arms.
3. Remove air inlet leaf screen.
4. Turn ignition ON, and activate motor with wiper switch. Allow motor crank arm to rotate to point to a position between 4 and 5 o'clock as viewed from passenger compartment. Stop crank arm in this position by turning off ignition switch.
5. Disconnect battery ground cable.

6. Disconnect upper motor electrical connectors.
7. Remove motor mounting bolts.
8. With crank arm in position described in Step 4 above, motor may now be removed from vehicle. Lower electrical connector may be disconnected as motor is partially removed.
9. To install, reverse the above procedure.

Wiper Transmission

REMOVAL & INSTALLATION

1. Make sure the wiper is in the park position.
2. Disconnect the battery ground cable.
3. Open the hood and remove the plenum chamber screen.
4. Loosen the nuts retaining the ball sockets to the crank arm and detach the drive rod from the crank arm.
5. Remove the transmission nuts, then lift the rod assemblies from the plenum chamber.
6. Remove the transmission linkage from the plenum chamber.
7. To install, reverse the removal procedure. Make sure the wipers are in the park position.

Radio

REMOVAL & INSTALLATION

1. Disconnect the battery ground cable.
2. Remove the console tunnel side panels.
3. Pull the radio control knobs from the shaft.
4. Remove the two screws that secure the console trim plate to the instrument cluster.
5. Remove the rear defogger switch if so equipped.
6. Remove the five screws from around the upper perimeter of the instrument cluster.
7. Pull the instrument cluster enough to disconnect the electrical connector from the rear of the cluster.

NOTE: The center instrument cluster trim panel is designed to collapse under impact. Do not deflect the panel to gain access to the radio.

8. Remove the screw holding the radio bracket reinforcement to the floor pan.
9. Pull the radio outward and disconnect the wiring from the back.
10. Installation is the reverse of re-

moval. If a new radio is being installed, save the mounting bracket from the rear of the old one.

NOTE: The radio heat sink must be removed when radio service is required. It is located behind the passenger side dash panel.

Fuses

The fuse block is located beneath the instrument panel above the headlight dimmer floor switch. Fuse holders are labeled as to their service and the correct amperage. Always replace blown fuses with new ones of the correct amperage. Otherwise electrical overloads and possible wiring damage will result.

The fuse block on some models is a swing-down unit located in the underside of the instrument panel adjacent to the steering column. Access to the fuse block on some models is gained through the glove box opening. The Convenience Center on some models is a swing-down unit located on the underside of the instrument panel. The swing-down feature provides center location and easy access to buzzers, relays and flasher units. All units are serviced by plug-in replacement. Location of Convenience Center on specific models may vary.

Circuit Breaker

A circuit breaker is an electrical switch which breaks the circuit during an electrical overload. The circuit breaker will remain open until the short or overload condition in the circuit is corrected.

Fusible Links

Fusible links are sections of wire, with special insulation, designed to melt under electrical overload. Replacements are simply spliced into the wire. There may be as many as five of these in the engine compartment wiring harnesses. These are:
1. Horn relay to fuse panel circuit—one link.
2. Charging circuit, from the starter solenoid to the horn relay—two links.
3. Starter solenoid to ammeter circuit—one link.
4. Horn relay to rear window defroster circuit—one link.
5. Connect the new fusible link to the harness wire using a crimp on connector. Solder the connection using rosin core solder.
6. Tape all exposed wires with plastic electrical tape.
7. Connect the fusible link to the

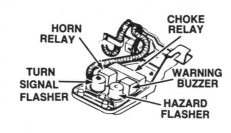

Swing–down convenience center—typical

junction block or starter solenoid and reconnect the battery ground cable.

Heater Blower

REMOVAL & INSTALLATION

1980-82

1. Disconnect the negative battery cable at the battery.
2. On 1981-82 models, unbolt the A/C compressor and move the compressor out of the way. DO NOT disconnect the refrigerant lines from the compressor.
3. Remove the coolant recover jar, if so equipped.
4. Disconnect the wiring from the motor and the cooling tube from the motor case, if so equipped.
5. Remove the mounting screws from the blower motor and remove the motor. If the motor sticks to the case due to the sealer, pry the motor GENTLY away from the case.
6. Installation is the reverse of the previous steps.

1984-87

1. Open the hood and disconnect the battery ground cable.
2. Remove the front wheel house rear panel and move wheel house seal aside.
3. Remove the motor cooling tube.
4. Remove the relay.
5. Remove the blower motor assembly to case attaching screws.
6. Remove the motor and impeller.
7. To install, reverse the replacement procedure and check the operation.

Heater Core

REMOVAL & INSTALLATION

1980

1. Disconnect the battery ground cable.
2. Drain the cooling system. It is not necessary to evacuate the A/C refrigerant.
3. Disconnect the heater hoses at the firewall and plug the pipes.

4. Remove the nuts from the distributor studs protruding through the firewall.
5. Remove the right side dash pad and center dash cluster.
6. Disconnect the right dash outlet from the center duct.
7. Remove the center duct from the selector duct.
8. Remove the selector duct to the dash panel and pull it to the right and to the rear.
9. Remove the cables and wiring connectors from the selector and remove it from the car.
10. Remove the temperature door cam plate from the selector duct.
11. Remove the heater core and housing from the selector.
12. Reverse the removal procedure to install.

1981-82

1. Disconnect the negative cable at the battery.
2. Drain the coolant from the radiator.
3. Raise the right front of the vehicle and support it safely.
4. Disconnect the heater hoses at the heater core connections.
5. Remove the heater case retaining nut which is located on the top of the blower case.
6. Remove the glove box.
7. Remove the console side panels.
8. Remove the knobs and nuts from the radio shafts.
9. Remove the two screws which secure the console trim plate to the instrument cluster.
10. Remove the instrument cluster attaching screws.
11. Pull the cluster out slightly and disconnect the electrical connector from the rear of the cluster.
12. Remove the radio as previously outlined.
13. Remove the right side windshield pillar trim panel.
14. Remove the right side dash panel retaining screws and pull the panel rearward to release the upper retaining clip.
15. Remove the following ducts.
    a. Right side vent
    b. Main vent distribution
    c. Lower heater deflector
    d. Heater-defroster distribution duct assembly (Disconnect the vacuum line).
16. Disconnect both the temperature cable and the vacuum line at the heater housing.
17. Remove the heater core from the housing.
18. Installation is the reverse of the previous steps.

6 CHASSIS ELECTRICAL

1984-87

1. Disconnect the negative battery cable. Drain the cooling system.
2. Remove the instrument cluster bezel including the tilt wheel lever and instrument panel pad.
3. Remove the A/C distributor duct and disconnect the flex hose.
4. Remove the right side hush panel.
5. Remove the side window defroster flex hose.
6. Remove the side window defrost-

er to heater cover screws and disconnect the extension.
7. Remove the temperature control cable and bracket assembly at heater cover including disconnecting heater door control shaft.
8. Remove the ECM (Electric Control Module) and disconnect the electrical connectors.

—————— CAUTION ——————
Make sure the ignition switch is OFF when disconnecting ECM.

9. Remove the tubular support brace from the door pillar to aluminum, instrument panel reinforcement brace.
10. Remove heater core cover attaching screws.
11. Remove heater pipe and heater water control bracket attaching screws.
12. Remove heater hose at heater core pipes.
13. Remove the heater core.
14. Installation is the reverse of removal.

CAPRICE, IMPALA, MALIBU AND MONTE CARLO

Headlight Switch

REMOVAL & INSTALLATION

1980-84 Caprice And Impala

1. Disconnect the negative battery cable.
2. Pull the knob out to ON position.
3. Reach under the instrument panel and depress the switch shaft retainer. Remove the knob and shaft assembly, then the windshield wiper switch.
4. Remove the retaining ferrule nut.
5. Remove the switch from instrument panel.
6. Disconnect the multi-plug connector from the switch.
7. To install, reverse the removal reverse the removal procedure.

1985-87 Caprice And Impala

1. Disconnect the negative battery cable.
2. Remove the steering column trim cover.
3. Remove the headlight switch mounting screws.
4. Pull the switch and disconnect the lighting connector.
5. To install, reverse the removal procedures.

Malibu and Monte Carlo

1. Disconnect negative battery cable.
2. Remove the screws and the instrument panel pad.
3. Remove the three windshield wiper/light switch mounting screws.
4. Pull the knob to the ON position.
5. Reach behind the instrument panel and depress the switch shaft retainer, then remove the knob and shaft assembly.
6. Remove the ferrule nut and the

switch assembly from the instrument panel.
7. To install, reverse the removal procedures.

Speedometer Cable

REMOVAL & INSTALLATION

Caprice And Impala

1. Disconnect the negative battery cable.
2. Remove the attaching screws and lower the steering column bottom cover.
3. Disconnect the shift lever indicator from the steering column.
4. Unbolt the column from the instrument panel.
5. Remove the screws and the plastic snap retainers, then lift off the lens.
6. Remove the screws from the upper surface of the grey sheet metal trim plate.
7. Remove the nuts from two studs in the lower corner of the cluster.
8. Reach behind the cluster and depress the cable retaining clip, then remove the speedometer cable.
9. Pull the core from the casing.

NOTE: If the core is broken, raise the vehicle and disconnect the cable from the transmission.

10. To install, lubricate the new cable core with speedometer cable lubricant and reverse the removal procedures.

Malibu And Monte Carlo

1. Disconnect the negative battery cable.
2. Remove the radio knobs and the clock stem.

3. Remove the instrument bezel retaining screws.
4. Disconnect the tailgate release or defogger switch.
5. Remove the instrument cluster bezel.
6. Remove the speedometer head.
7. Disconnect the cable from the head by depressing the clip.
8. Pull the core from the casing. If the core is broken, raise the vehicle and remove the lower cable end from the transmission.
9. To install, lubricate the core with cable lubricant and reverse the removal procedures.

Instrument Cluster

REMOVAL & INSTALLATION

1. Disconnect the negative battery cable.
2. Remove the screws securing the steering column lower cover and remove the cover.
3. Disconnect the shift indicator cable from the steering column.
4. Remove the screws securing the steering column to the instrument panel and lower the steering column.
5. Remove the screws and the snap-in-plastic fasteners from the perimeter of the instrument cluster lens.
6. Remove the 2 screws from the upper surface of the grey sheet metal trim plate.
7. Remove the nuts from the two studs in the lower corner of the cluster.
8. Reach behind the instrument cluster and disconnect the speedometer cable, then remove the cluster by pulling outward.
9. To install, reverse the removal procedure.

Wiper Motor

REMOVAL & INSTALLATION

All Models

1. Disconnect the negative battery cable.
2. Remove the cowl vent screen.
3. Remove the transmission drive link(s) from the motor crank arm.
4. Disconnect the electrical connectors and the washer hoses.
5. Remove the 3 motor mounting screws and the motor.

NOTE: When removing the motor, guide the crank arm through the hole.

6. To install, reverse the removal procedures. The motor must be in the "Park" position before assembling the crank arm to the transmission drive link(s).

Wiper Arms And Blades

REMOVAL & INSTALLATION

If the wiper assembly has a press type release tab at the center, simply depress the tab and remove the blade. If the blade had no release tab, use a screwdriver to depress the spring at the center. This will release the assembly. To install, position the blade over the pin at the tip of the arm and press until the spring retainer engages the groove in the pin. To remove the element, either depress the release button or squeeze the spring type retainer clip at the outer end together and slide the blade element out. Just slide the new element in until it latches.

1. Insert tool J-8966 or equivalent under the wiper arm and lever the arm off the shaft.
2. If equipped, disconnect the washer hose from the arm. Remove the arm.
3. To install, reverse the removal procedures.

NOTE: Be sure that the motor is in the "Park" position before installing the wiper arms.

Blower Motor

REMOVAL & INSTALLATION

Caprice And Impala

1. Disconnect the negative battery cable.
2. Disonnect the blower lead wire.

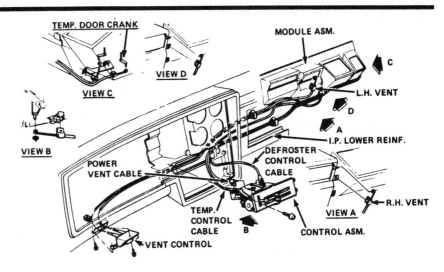

Chevrolet heater control cable adjustments

3. Remove the attaching screws and gently pry the blower from the case.

NOTE: When removing the blower motor, the sealer may act as an adhesive.

4. To install, reverse the removal procedures. Replace the sealer if it was damaged.

Malibu And Monte Carlo

1. Disconnect the negative battery cable.
2. Disconnect the motor lead wire.

NOTE: If equipped with A/C, disconnect the cooling tube.

3. Remove the blower-to-case screws.
4. Remove the retaining nut, then separate the motor from the wheel.
5. To install, place the open end of the blower away from the motor and reverse the removal procedures.

Heater Core

REMOVAL & INSTALLATION

Caprice And Impala
WITHOUT A/C

1. Disconnect the negative battery cable.
2. Drain the cooling system.
3. Disconnect and plug the heater hoses at the core and the core tubes.

NOTE: It may be necessary to remove the inner fender to remove the heater hoses.

4. Remove the screws from the perimeter of the core cover on the engine side of the cowl.
5. Pull the core cover from the cowl mounting.

6. Pull the core assembly from the module.
7. To install, reverse the removal procedures.

WITH A/C

1. Disconnect the negative battery cable and drain the cooling system.
2. Disconnect and plug the heater hoses at the core tubes.

NOTE: It may be necessary to remove the inner fender to remove the heater hoses.

3. Remove the module retaining bracket and the ground strap.
4. Remove the module rubber seal and the screen.
5. Remove the right windshield wiper arm.
6. Remove the diagnostic connector, the high blower relay and the thermal switch mounting screws.
7. Remove the electrical connectors from the top of the module.
8. Remove the module top cover and lift out the core.
9. To install, reverse the removal procedures.

Malibu And Monte Carlo
WITHOUT A/C

1. Disconnect the negative battery cable and drain the cooling system.
2. Disconnect and plug the heater hoses from the core tubes.
3. Disconnect the electrical connectors from the module case.
4. Unbolt and remove the module's front cover and lift out the core.
5. To install, use sealant and reverse the removal procedures.

WITH A/C

1. Disconnect the negative battery cable and drain the cooling system.

2. Disconnect and plug the heater hoses at the core tubes.

3. Remove the retaining bracket and the ground strap.

4. Remove the module's rubber seal and screen.

5. Remove the right windshield wiper arm.

6. Remove the diagnostic connector, the high blower relay and the thermostatic switch.

7. Disconnect the electrical connectors from the module.

8, Remove the module's top cover and the screen.

9. To install, use sealant and reverse the removal procedures.

Radio

REMOVAL & INSTALLATION

1980-84 Caprice And Impala

1. Disconnect the negative battery cable.

2. Pull the control knobs off of the radio.

3. Remove the 3 mounting screws and the trim plate.

4. Remove the 2 receiver bracket-to-instrument panel screws and bottom nut.

5. Detach the wiring and the antenna from the rear of the receiver.

6. Remove the radio and the mounting bracket.

7. To install, reverse the removal procedures.

NOTE: To prevent damage to the radio, always connect the speaker wiring harness before applying power to the radio.

1980-83 Malibu
1980-84 Monte Carlo

1. Disconnect the negative battery cable.

2. Pull the control knobs from the shafts.

3. Remove the trim plate screws and the trim plate.

4. Remove the wiring and antenna cable from the rear of the radio.

5. Remove the receiver stud nut at the right side bracket.

6. Remove the control knob nuts.

7. Remove the instrument panel bracket screws and the bracket.

8. Remove the radio through the panel opening.

9. To install, reverse the removal procedures.

NOTE: To prevent damage to the radio, always connect the speaker wiring harness before applying power to the radio.

1985-87 Models

1. Disconnect the negative battery cable.

2. Remove the glove box, then remove the temperature control cable from the temperature door.

3. Remove the radio, heater and A/C assembly control panel-to-dash fasteners.

4. Pull the panel from the dash, then remove the vacuum and the electrical connectors.

5. Remove the A/C control trim plate and knobs.

6. Remove the radio from the bracket.

7. To install, reverse the removal procedures.

NOTE: To prevent damage to the radio, always connect the speaker wiring harness before applying power to the radio.

Fuses

The fuse block is located on a swing down unit beneath the instrument panel next to the steering column or through the glove box opening (on some models). Fuse holders are labeled as to their service and the correct amperage. Always replace blown fuses with new ones of the correct amperage. Otherwise electrical overloads and possible wiring damage will result.

Fusible Links

Fusible links are sections of wire, with the special insulation, designed to melt under electrical overload. Replacements are simply spliced into the wires. There may be as many as five of these in the engine compartment wiring harness. These are:

1. Horn relay-to-fuse panel circuit — 1 link.

2. Charging circuit, from the starter solenoid-to-horn relay — 2 links.

3. Starter solenoid-to-ammeter circuit — 1 link.

4. Horn relay-to-rear window defroster circuit — 1 link.

NOTE: The fusible links are all two wire gauge sizes smaller than the wires they protect.

REPLACEMENT

1. Disconnect the negative battery cable.

2. Disconnect the fusible link from the junction block or the starter solenoid.

3. Cut the harness directly behind the connector to remove the damaged fusible link.

4. Strip the harness wire approximately $1/2$ in.

5. Connect the new fusible link to the harness wire using a crimp on connector. Solder the connection using rosin core solder.

6. Tape all of the exposed wires with plastic electrical tape.

7. To complete the installation, reverse the removal procedures.

CELEBRITY AND CITATION

Heater Blower

REMOVAL & INSTALLATION

This procedure is for all cars, with or without air conditioning.

1. Disconnect the negative cable at the battery.

2. Working inside the engine compartment, disconnect the blower motor electrical leads.

3. Remove the motor retaining screws, and remove the blower motor.

4. Reverse to install.

Heater Core

REMOVAL & INSTALLATION

Cars Without Air Conditioning

1. Drain the cooling system.

2. Remove the heater inlet and outlet hoses at the firewall, inside the engine compartment.

3. Remove the radio noise suppression strap.

4. Remove the heater core cover retaining screws. Remove the cover.

5. Remove the core. Reverse to install.

Cars With Air Conditioning
CELEBRITY

1. Drain the·cooling system.
2. On the diesel, raise and support the car on jackstands.
3. Disconnect the hoses at the core.
4. On the diesel, remove the instrument panel lower sound absorber.
5. Remove the heater duct and lower side covers.
6. Remove the lower heater outlet.
7. Remove the two housing cover-to-air valve housing clips.
8. Remove the housing cover.
9. Remove the core restraining straps.
10. Remove the core tubing retainers and lift out the core.
11. Installation is the reverse of removal.

CITATION

1. Drain the cooling system.
2. Remove the heater hoses from the core tubes at the firewall.
3. Remove the heater duct and heater case side cover from under the instrument panel.
4. Remove the core retaining clamps. Remove the inlet and outlet tube support clamps.
5. Remove the core. Reverse to install.

Radio

REMOVAL & INSTALLATION

Celebrity

1. Disconnect the battery ground.
2. Remove the steering column trim panel including hush panel.
3. Remove the ashtray and ashtray assembly fuse block, seperate ashtray assembly from fuse block. Move both for access.
4. Disconnect the cigarette lighter and rear defogger switch connectors.
5. Remove the cigarette lighter.
6. Remove the glove box.
7. Remove the instrument panel center trim panel attaching nuts.
8. Pull the trim panel away from the instrument panel (enough to remove the radio).
9. Remove the radio.
10. Installation is the reverse of removal.

Citation

1. Disconnect the negative battery cable.
2. Remove the radio knobs, the shaft nuts, and the clock knob, if equipped.
3. Remove the instrument cluster trim bezel attaching screws and pull the bezel rearward.

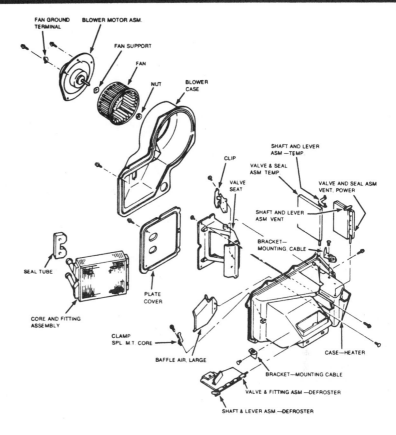

Heater assembly, without air conditioning

4. Remove the headlamp shaft and knob. Reach behind the instrument panel bezel with a long screwdriver and push the headlamp shaft release button to release the knob.
5. Disconnect the wiring and remove the bezel.
6. Remove the two screws attaching the radio bracket to the instrument panel. Pull the radio rearward while at the same time twisting it slightly to the left, and disconnect the electrical connectors and antenna lead. Remove the lamp socket.
8. Remove the radio.
9. Installation is the reverse of removal.

Windshield Wiper Switch

REMOVAL & INSTALLATION

1. Disconnect the negative battery cable.
2. Remove the steering wheel, the cover and the lock plate assembly.
3. Remove the turn signal actuator arm, the lever and the hazard flasher button.
4. Remove the turn signal switch

screws, the lower steering column trim panel and the steering column bracket bolts.
5. Disconnect the the turn signal switch and the wiper switch connectors.
6. Pull the turn signal switch rearward 6-8 inches, then remove the key buzzer switch and cylinder lock.
7. Remove and pull the steering column housing rearward, then remove the housing cover screw.
8. Remove the wiper switch pivot and the switch.
9. To install, reverse the removal procedure.

Windshield Wiper Motor

REMOVAL & INSTALLATION

Celebrity

1. Raise the hood.
2. Remove the grille.
3. Loosen the wiper linkage to drive arm attaching nuts.
4. Remove the transmission link from the drive arm.
5. Disconnect the wiring and hoses from the motor.
6. Unbolt and remove the motor.

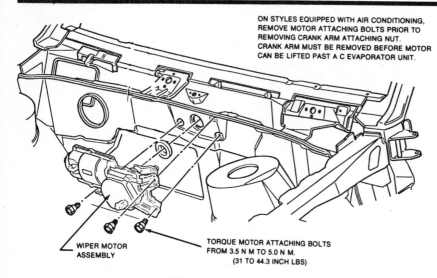

ON STYLES EQUIPPED WITH AIR CONDITIONING, REMOVE MOTOR ATTACHING BOLTS PRIOR TO REMOVING CRANK ARM ATTACHING NUT. CRANK ARM MUST BE REMOVED BEFORE MOTOR CAN BE LIFTED PAST A C EVAPORATOR UNIT.

WIPER MOTOR ASSEMBLY

TORQUE MOTOR ATTACHING BOLTS FROM 3.5 N M TO 5.0 N M. (31 TO 44.3 INCH LBS)

Wiper motor removal

7. Installation is the reverse of removal.

Citation

1. Remove the wiper arms.
2. Remove the lower windshield reveal molding, the front cowl panel and the cowl screen. Disconnect the washer hose under the screen.
3. Disconnect the motor electrical leads.
4. Loosen, but do not remove, the transmission drive link attaching nuts to the motor crank arm.
5. Disconnect the drive link from the motor crank arm.
6. Remove the three motor attaching bolts. On models with air conditioning, remove the bolts and while supporting the motor, remove the motor crank arm nut using lock-ring type pliers and a closed end wrench. The motor attaching bolts must be removed first to avoid damage to the nylon gear inside the motor. On all models, rotate the motor up and out to remove.
7. Reverse the procedure to install.

Headlight Switch

REPLACEMENT

1980 Citation

1. Disconnect the negative battery cable.
2. Pull the knob out to the ON position.
3. Remove the instrument cluster trim bezel attaching screws.
4. Remove the radio knobs and shaft nuts, and clock knob, if so equipped.
5. Pull the bezel rearward slightly and depress the shaft retaining button. Pull the knob and shaft from the switch.
6. Disconnect the accessory electrical connectors.
7. Remove the bezel.
8. Remove the switch retaining nut and push the switch out from its mounting hole.
9. Disconnect the electrical connector and remove the switch.

1981-85 Citation

1. Disconnect the negative battery cable.
2. Pull the headlamp switch knob out to the last detent.
3. Remove the spring clip retainer on the knob shaft and remove the shaft.
4. Disconnect all accessory switch connectors.
5. Remove the headlamp switch ferrule nut and push switch forward out of the mounting hole.
6. Lift the switch up and out through the opening above the switch mounting and disconnect the switch electrical connector.
7. Remove the switch from the instrument panel.

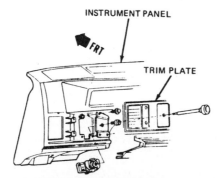

INSTRUMENT PANEL

FRT

TRIM PLATE

Celebrity headlight switch

8. Installation is the reverse of removal.

Celebrity

1. Disconnect the battery ground.
2. Remove the headlamp switch knob.
3. Remove the instrument panel trim pad.
4. Unbolt the switch mounting plate from the instrument panel carrier.
5. Disconnect the wiring from the switch.
6. Remove the switch.
7. Installation is the reverse of removal.

Instrument Cluster

REMOVAL & INSTALLATION

Citation

1. Disconnect the negative battery cable.
2. Remove the radio knobs (pull off), the shaft nuts, and the clock knob.
3. Remove the instrument cluster bezel (trim plate) attaching screws; there are three at the top and one each in the two lower corners. Pull the bezel slightly rearward.
4. Remove the headlamp shaft and knob.
5. Disconnect the accessory switch wiring.
6. Remove the bezel.
7. Remove the four screws holding the instrument cluster to the instrument panel.
8. Disconnect the shift indicator cable from the steering column shift bowl on models with automatic transaxle.
9. Pull the cluster towards you and disconnect the speedometer cable and instrument electrical connections.
10. Remove the instrument cluster. Installation is the reverse of removal.

Celebrity

1. Disconnect battery ground cable.
2. Remove instrument panel hush panel.
3. Remove vent control housing (heater only vehicles).
4. On non A/C cars remove steering column trim cover screws and lower cover with vent cables attached. On A/C equipped vehicles, remove trim cover attaching screws (6) and remove cover.
5. Remove instrument cluster trim pad as outlined in this section.
6. Remove ash try, retainer and fuse block, disconnect wires as necessary.
7. Remove headlamp switch knob

and instrument panel trim plate and disconnect electrical connectors of any accessory switches in trim plate.

8. Remove cluster assembly and disconnect speedometer cable. PRNDL and cluster electrical connectors.

9. Installation is the reverse of removal.

Speedometer Cable

REPLACEMENT

1. Remove the instrument cluster.
2. Slide the cable out from the casing. If the cable is broken, the casing will have to be unscrewed from the transaxle and the broken piece removed from that end.
3. Before installing a new cable, slip a piece of cable into the speedometer and spin it between your fingers in the direction of normal rotation. If the mechanism sticks or binds, the speedometer should be repaired or replaced.
4. Inspect the casing; if it is cracked, kinked, or broken, the casing should be replaced.

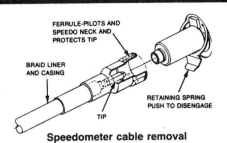

FERRULE-PILOTS AND SPEEDO NECK AND PROTECTS TIP

BRAID LINER AND CASING

RETAINING SPRING PUSH TO DISENGAGE

TIP

Speedometer cable removal

5. Slide a new cable into the casing, engaging the transaxle end securely. Sometimes it is easier to unscrew the casing at the transaxle end, install the cable into the transaxle fitting, and screw the casing back into place. Install the instrument cluster.

Fuses, Fusible Links & Circuit Breakers

On some models, the fuse block is a swingdown unit located in the underside of the instrument panel, adjacent to the steering column. On other models, access to the fuse block is gained through the glove box. All models use miniaturized plug type fuses which are color-coded and stamped with the amperage rating.

Fusible links are provided in all circuits and fed directly from the battery. Fusible links are lengths of copper wire, about 4 in. long and four gauge sizes smaller than the wire that they protect. Burned out fusible links should be replaced with the same gauge wire for continued circuit protection.

The head lights are protected by a circuit breaker in the headlamp switch. If the circuit breaker trips, the headlights will either flash on and off, or stay off all toeghter. The circuit breaker resets automatically after the overload is removed.

The windshield wipers are also protected by a circuit breaker. If the motor overheats, the circuit breaker will trip, remaining off until the motor cools and the overload is removed.

The circuit breakers for the power door locks and power windows are located in the fuse box.

CAMARO

Headlamp Switch

REMOVAL & INSTALLATION

1980-81

1. Disconnect negative battery cable and pull the light switch to the ON position.
2. Remove steering column lower cover (6 screws).
3. Reach up under cluster on the left side and depress the light switch shaft retainer (located on the switch), while pulling gently on the switch knob.
4. Remove the nut that secures the switch to the instrument cluster.
5. Remove four cluster carrier screws in front and two from the rear,

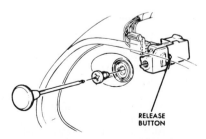

RELEASE BUTTON

Typical headlamp switch. Note the position of the knob and shaft release button

3. Remove the instrument panel cluster trim plate.
4. Remove the two screws retaining the switch assembly.
5. Depress the side tangs and pull out the switch assembly.
6. Disconnect the wiring harness then tilt the right side of the cluster out.
6. Disconnect the wiring harness connector and remove the switch.
7. To install, reverse the removal procedures.

1982-87

1. Disconnect the negative battery cable.
2. Remove the right and left lower trim plates; DO NOT remove the lower instrument panel cover.
connector and remove the headlight switch from the assembly.
7. Reverse the removal procedures to install.

Speedometer Cable

REMOVAL & INSTALLATION

1980–81

1. Disconnect the battery ground cable.

2. Reach up behind the speedometer and depress the retaining tab while pushing in, then out on the cable end.
3. Remove the firewall panel sealing plug to allow movement of the cable.
4. Pull the speedometer cable core from the casing. If the core is broken, it will be necessary to raise the car and disconnect the cable from the transmission to remove the other end.
5. To install, lubricate the core with cable lubricant and reverse the removal procedures. Make sure the core engages the transmission drive unit.

1982-87

1. Disconnect the negative battery cable.
2. If equipped with cruise control, disconnect the speedometer cable at the cruise control transducer. If NOT equipped with cruise control, disconnect the speedometer cable strap at the power brake booster.
3. Remove the instrument cluster bezel.
4. Remove the six instrument cluster screws and pull the cluster out far enough to gain access to the rear of the speedometer head.
5. Reach beneath the cable connection at the speedometer head, push in

on the cable retaining spring and disconnect the cable from the speedometer.

6. Slide the old cable out of the speedometer cable case. If the cable is broken, remove the cable from both ends of the casing.

NOTE: Using a short piece of the old cable to fit the speedometer connection, turn the speedometer to increase the speed indicated on the dial and check for any binding during rotation. If binding is noted, the speedometer must be removed for repair or replacement. Check the entire cable casing for extreme bends, chafing, breaks, etc. and replace if necessary.

7. To install, wipe the cable clean using a lint-free cloth. Flush the casing with petroleum spirits and blow dry with compressed air, then lubricate the speedometer cable with an appropriate lubricant (be sure to cover the lower $2/3$ of the cable). Insert the cable into the case and reverse the removal procedures.

Instrument Cluster

REMOVAL & INSTALLATION

1980-81

1. Disconnect the negative battery cable.
2. Remove the six cluster bezel screws.
3. Reach behind the left cluster and press on the retainer button of the headlamp switch shaft while pulling on the switch knob.

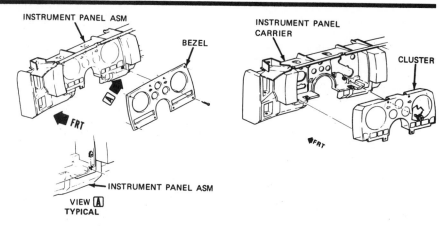

Typical instrument panel cluster and bezel—1982 and later

4. Remove the retaining nut from the switch.
5. Disconnect the electrical connectors from the headlight and the windshield wiper switches.
6. Remove the headlight switch from the bezel mounting hole.
7. Remove the two wiper switch screws and the switch from the bezel.
8. Disconnect the cigarette lighter electrical connector and unscrew the retainer from the bezel.
9. Pull the bezel rearward and remove the cluster retaining screws.
10. Pull the cluster rearward and disconnect the printed circuit connector.
11. Disconnect the speedometer cable and the wiring harness clips, then remove the cluster.
12. To install, reverse the removal procedures.

Optional Instrument Cluster

To remove all bulbs, instruments (except speedometer) and printed circuits, it is not necessary (unless air-conditioned) to remove the cluster. The instruments are installed and removed from the rear of the cluster. On vehicles with air conditioning, it will be necessary to remove the cluster to remove the ammeter, fuel and temperature gauges.

NOTE: When performing any operation behind the cluster, disconnect the battery ground cable.

1982-87

SPORT COUPE MODEL

1. Disconnect the negative battery cable.
2. Remove the instrument cluster bezel.
3. Remove the six cluster attachment screws.
4. Pull the cluster out, then disconnect the speedometer cable and electrical connections.
5. Remove the cluster lens.
6. To install, reverse the removal procedures.

BERLINETTA MODEL

1. Disconnect the negative battery cable.
2. Remove the instrument cluster bezel.
3. Remove the eight steering column trim cover screws and the trim cover.
4. Remove the right and the left hand pod attaching screws at the bottom front of each pod. Pull the pods rearward and disconnect the electrical connection.
5. Remove the five cluster lens screws and the lens.
6. Remove the two steering column bolts and lower the column.
7. Pull the instrument cluster rearward and disconnect the electrical connection. Remove the instrument cluster.

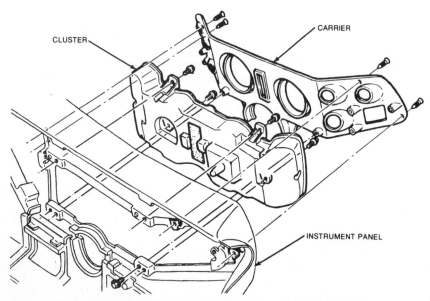

Typical instrument cluster mounting—models through 1981

8. To install, reverse the removal procedures.

Emissions Indicator

An emissions indicator flag may appear in the odometer window of the speedometer. The flag could say "Sensor" "Emissions" or "Catalyst" depending on the part or assembly that is scheduled for regular emissions maintenance replacement. The word "Sensor" indicates a need for oxygen sensor replacement and the words "Emissions" or "Catalyst" indicate the need for catalytic converter replacement.

Reset Procedure

1. Remove the instrument panel trim plate.
2. Remove the instrument cluster lens.
3. Locate the flag indicator reset notches at the driver's side of the odometer.
4. Use a pointed tool to apply light downward pressure on the notches, until the indicator is reset.

NOTE: When the indicator is reset an alignment mark will appear in the left center of the odometer window.

Wiper Motor

REMOVAL & INSTALLATION

1. Disconnect the negative battery cable.

2. Remove the cowl vent screen.
3. Remove the transmission drive link(s) from the motor crank arm.
4. Disconnect the electrical connectors and the washer hoses.
5. Remove the motor mounting screws and the motor.

NOTE: When removing the motor, guide the crank arm through the hole.

6. To install, reverse the removal procedures. The motor must be in the "Park" position before assembling the crank arm to the transmission drive link(s).

Wiper Arms and Blades

REMOVAL & INSTALLATION

If the wiper assembly has a press type release tab at the center, simply depress the tab and remove the blade. If the blade had no release tab, use a screwdriver to depress the spring at the center. This will release the assembly. To install the assembly, position the blade over the pin at the tip of the arm and press until the spring retainer engages the groove in the pin. To remove the element, either depress the release button or squeeze the spring type retainer clip at the outer end together and slide the blade element out. Just slide the new element in until it latches.

1. Insert tool J-8966 or equivalent

under the wiper arm and lever the arm off the shaft.
2. If equipped, disconnect the washer hose from the arm. Remove the arm.
3. To install, reverse the removal procedures.

NOTE: Be sure that the motor is in the "Park" position before installing the wiper arms.

Radio

REMOVAL & INSTALLATION

1980-81

1. Disconnect the battery ground cable.
2. Pull off the knobs and bezels.
3. Remove the control shaft nuts and washers, using a deep well socket. If equipped, remove the center air duct and hose.
4. Remove the mounting bracket screws or nuts.
5. Move the radio back until the shafts clear the instrument panel. Lower it and disconnect the antenna, speaker and power wires.
6. Remove the radio.
7. To install, reverse the removal procedures.

NOTE: Make sure to connect the speaker leads before turning the radio ON. Operating the radio without a speaker will damage the transistors.

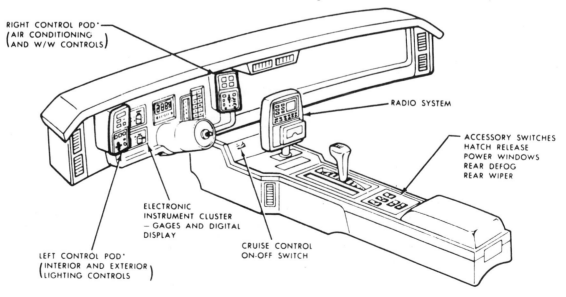

View of the Berlinetta style dash and console

1982-87
SPORT COUPE MODEL

1. Disconnect the negative battery cable.
2. Remove the console bezel screws and the console bezel.
3. Remove the radio-to-console mounting screws.
4. Remove the radio and disconnect the electrical connector.
5. To install, reverse the removal procedures.

——————— CAUTION ———————

Never apply power to the radio until the speaker wiring is connected; radio damage could result.

BERLINETTA MODEL

1. Disconnect the negative battery cable. Remove the four screws at the console trim plate.
2. Lift the receiver, with the connector attached and turn to one side.
3. Remove the four control head mounting bracket screws. Remove the control head by pulling back on the pawl spring and pulling up on the control head.
4. Disconnect the electrical connectors from the control head.
5. Remove the four screws at the receiver bracket and the slotted screw at the receiver.
6. Disconnect the electrical connector and remove the receiver.
7. To install, reverse the removal procedures.

Blower Motor

REMOVAL & INSTALLATION

1980-81

1. Disconnect the negative battery cable.
2. Tag and disconnect any electrical connections at the motor.
3. Remove the heater front module screws and nuts.
4. Lift off the front module and the motor.
5. Installation is in the reverse order of removal. Replace all sealer.

1982-87

1. Disconnect the negative battery cable.
2. Tag and disconnect the electrical connectors from the blower motor.
3. Remove the blower motor cooling tube.
4. Remove the blower motor retaining screws.
5. Remove the blower motor and fan assembly from the case.
6. To install, reverse the removal procedures.

Heater Core

REMOVAL & INSTALLATION

1980-81

1. Disconnect the negative battery cable. Drain the radiator and disconnect the heater hoses.
2. Remove the nuts retaining the heater case-to-firewall and then the screws from inside the vehicle.
3. Remove the glovebox and door. Remove the heater outlet duct-to-heater case mounting screws and the duct.
4. Remove the defroster screw and pull the heater case out. The core may now be pulled from the case.
5. To install, reverse the removal procedures.

NOTE: Use new seals between the heater case and the firewall.

1982-87

1. Disconnect the negative battery cable.
2. Drain the cooling system.
3. Disconnect the heater hoses from the heater core.
4. Remove the right side lower hush panel.
5. Remove the right side lower instrument panel trim panel and the electronic spark control (ESC) module, if necessary.
6. Remove the right side lower instrument panel carrier-to-cowl screw.
7. Remove the four heater case cover screws.

NOTE: The upper left heater case cover screw may be reached with a long socket extension. Carefully lift the lower right corner of the instrument panel to align the extension.

8. Remove the heater case cover.
9. Remove the heater core support plate and the baffle screws.
10. Remove the heater core, the support plate and the baffle from the heater case.
11. To install, reverse the removal procedures. Refill the cooling system and check for leaks after the engine has been started.

Circuit Breakers

A circuit breaker in the light switch protects the headlight circuit. A separate 30 amp breaker mounted on the firewall protects the power window, seat and power top circuits. On the 1982-87 vehicles, this is located in the fuse box. Circuit breakers open and close rapidly to protect the circuit if current is excessive.

Fuses and Flashers

The fuse box is located under the instrument panel on the left side. The turn signal flasher is under the dash to the right of the steering column. The hazard flasher is under the dash, to the left of the steering column. On the 1980-81 models, both the turn signal flasher and the hazard flasher are located at the lower left hand and the upper right hand corners of the fuse box respectively. On 1982-87 vehicles, the hazard flasher is located in the convenience center which is on the underside of the instrument panel to the right of the steering column. The turn signal flasher is located in a clip behind the instrument panel to the right of the steering column. There is an inline fuse for the underhood and spotlamp circuit. The fuse box is marked to indicate fuse size and the circuit(s) protected.

Fusible Links

In addition to circuit breakers and fuses, the wiring harness incorporates fusible links to protect the wiring. Links are used rather than a fuse, in wiring circuits that are not normally fused, such as the ignition circuit. Fusible links are color coded red in the charging and load circuits they protect. Each link is 4 gauges smaller than the cable it protects and is marked on the insulation with the gauge size because the insulation makes it appear heavier than it really is.

The engine compartment wiring harness has several fusible links. The same size wire with a special hypalon insulation must be used when replacing a fusible link. The links are typically located in the following areas:

1. A molded splice at the starter solenoid "Bat" terminal, a 14 gauge red wire.
2. A 16 gauge red fusible link at the junction block to protect the unfused wiring of 12 gauge or larger wire. This link stops at the bulkhead connector.
3. The alternator warning light and field circuitry is protected by a 20 gauge red wire fusible link used in the "battery feed-to-voltage regulator No. 3 terminal." The link is installed as a molded splice in the circuit at the junction block.
4. The ammeter circuit is protected by two 20 gauge fusible links installed as molded splices in the circuit at the junction block and battery to starter circuit.

CAVALIER

Heater Blower Motor

REMOVAL & INSTALLATION

1. Disconnect the negative battery cable.

2. Disconnect the electrical connections at the blower motor and blower resistor.

3. Remove the plastic water shield from the right side of the cowl.

4. Remove the blower motor retaining screws and then pull the blower motor and cage out.

5. Hold the blower motor cage and remove the cage retaining nut from the blower motor shaft.

6. Remove the blower motor and cage.

7. Installation is in the reverse order of removal.

Heater Core

REMOVAL & INSTALLATION

Cars Without Air Conditioning

1. Disconnect the negative battery cable and drain the cooling system.

2. Remove the heater inlet and outlet hoses from the heater core.

3. Remove the heater outlet deflector.

4. Remove the retaining screws and then remove the heater core cover.

5. Remove the heater core retaining straps and then remove the heater core.

6. Installation is in the reverse order of removal.

Cars With Air Conditioning

1. Disconnect the negative battery cable and drain the cooling system.

2. Raise and support the front of the vehicle.

3. Disconnect the drain tube from the heater case.

4. Remove the heater hoses from the heater core.

5. Lower the car. Remove the right and left hush panels, the steering column trim cover, the heater outlet duct and the glove box.

6. Remove the heater core cover. Be sure to pull the cover straight to the rear so as not to damage the drain tube.

7. Remove the heater core clamps and then remove the core.

8. Installation is in the reverse order of removal.

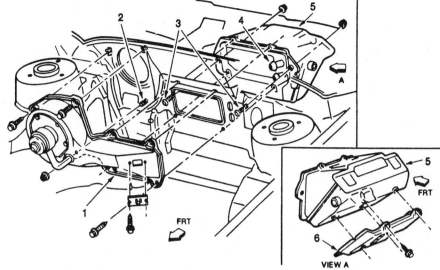

1. Heater case
2. Stud dash panel
3. Locating studs dash panel
4. Heater core
5. Heater module
6. Module cover

Heater assembly on models without air conditioning

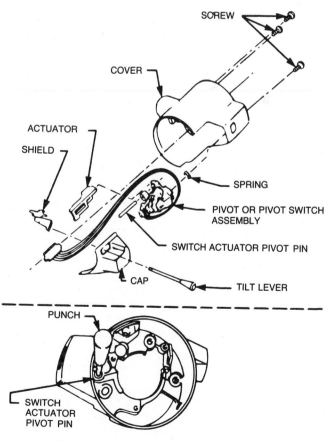

REMOVE AND INSTALL PIVOT AND SWITCH ASSEMBLY

Removal and installation of the washer switch

Radio

REMOVAL & INSTALLATION

NOTE: Do not operate the radio with the speaker leads disconnected. Operating the radio without an electrical load will damage the output transistors.

1. Disconnect the negative battery cable.
2. Remove the instrument panel trim plate.
3. Check the right side of the radio to determine whether a nut or a stud is used for side retention.
4. If a nut is used, remove the hush panel and then loosen the nut from below on cars without air conditioning. On cars with air conditioning, remove the hush panel, the A/C duct and the A/C control head for access to the nut. Do not remove the nut; loosen it just enough to pull the radio out. If a rubber stud is used, go on to Step 5.
5. Remove the two radio bracket-to-instrument panel attaching screws. Pull the radio forward far enough to disconnect the wiring and antenna and then remove the radio.
6. Installation is in the reverse order of removal.

Windshield Wiper Switch

REMOVAL & INSTALLATION

1. Remove the steering wheel and directional signal switch, It may be necessary to loosen the two column mounting nuts and remove the four bracket-to-mast jacket to allow the connector clip on the ignition switch to be pulled out of the column assembly.
2. Disconnect the washer/wiper switch lower connector.
3. Remove the screws attaching the column housing to the mast jacket. Be sure to note the position of the dimmer switch actuator rod for reassembly in the same position. Remove the column

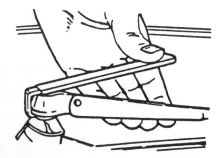

Removing the wiper arm with a special tool

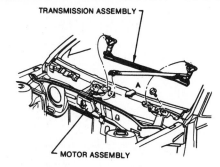
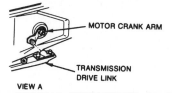

Wiper motor and linkage

housing-and-switch as an assembly.

NOTE: The tilt and travel columns have a removable plastic cover on the column housing. This provides access to the wiper switch without removing the entire column housing.

4. Turn upside down and use a drift to remove the pivot pin from the washer/ wiper switch. Remove the switch.
5. Place the switch into the position in the housing, then install the pivot pin.
6. Position the housing onto the mast jacket and attach by installing the screws. Install the dimmer switch actuator rod in the same position as noted earlier. Check switch operation.
7. Reconnect lower end of the switch assembly.
8. Install the remaining components in reverse order of removal. Be sure to attach column mounting bracket in original position.

Blade and Arm

REPLACEMENT

Removal of the wiper arms requires the use of a special tool, GM J8966 or its equivalent. Versions of this tool are generally available in auto parts stores.

1. Insert the tool under the wiper arm and lever the arm off the shaft.
2. Disconnect the washer hose from the arm (if so equipped). Remove the arm.
3. Installation is in the reverse order of removal. The proper park position is at the top of the blackout line on the glass. If the wiper arms and blades were in the proper position prior to re-

moval, adjustment should not be required.

ADJUSTMENT

The only adjustment for the wiper arms is to remove an arm from the transmission shaft, rotate the arm the required distance and direction and then install the arm back in position so it is in line with the blackout line on the glass. The wiper motor must be in the Park position.

The correct blade-out wipe position on the driver's side is $1\frac{3}{32}$ in. (28mm) from the tip of the blade to the left windshield pillar moulding. The correct blade-down wipe position on the passenger side of the car is in line with the blackout line at the bottom of the glass.

Linkage

REMOVAL & INSTALLATION

1. Remove the wiper arms.
2. Remove the shroud top vent grille.
3. Loosen (but do not remove) the drive link-to-crank arm attaching nuts.
4. Unscrew the linkage-to-cowl panel retaining screws and remove the linkage.
5. Installation is in the reverse order of removal.

Wiper Motor

REMOVAL & INSTALLATION

1. Loosen (but do not remove) the drive link-to-crank arm attaching nuts and detach the drive link from the motor crank arm.
2. Tag and disconnect all electrical leads from the wiper motor.
3. Unscrew the mounting bolts, rotate the motor up and outward and remove it.
4. Guide the crank arm through the opening in the body and then tighten the mounting bolts to 4–6 ft. lbs.
5. Install the drive link to the crank arm with the motor in the park position.
6. Installation of the remaining components is in the reverse order of removal.

Instrument Cluster

REMOVAL & INSTALLATION

1. Disconnect the negative battery cable.
2. Remove the right and left hush

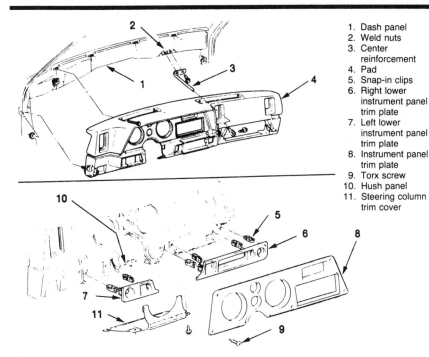

1. Dash panel
2. Weld nuts
3. Center reinforcement
4. Pad
5. Snap-in clips
6. Right lower instrument panel trim plate
7. Left lower instrument panel trim plate
8. Instrument panel trim plate
9. Torx screw
10. Hush panel
11. Steering column trim cover

Instrument panel and trim plate mounting

panels and the steering column trim cover. Disconnect the vent panels from the bottom of the panel (if so equipped).

3. Remove the glove box. Disconnect the temperature and mode control cables on cars without air conditioning. On cars with air conditioning, remove the lower A/C duct.

4. Remove the three steering column retaining bolts (two at the instrument panel pad and one at the cowl) and lower the steering column.

5. Remove the lower right hand trim plate. Disconnect the cigar lighter and accessory switches.

6. Pull the heater or A/C control head out far enough to disconnect any wiring or vacuum harnesses, then remove the head.

7. Disconnect the front end and engine harnesses from the bulkhead connector in the engine compartment and then remove the bulkhead connector from the cowl (2) screws.

8. Loosen the set screw and remove the hood release handle. Unscrew the retaining nut and pull the hood release cable loose.

9. Unscrew the four upper instrument panel retaining screws (in the defroster duct openings).

10. Unscrew the two lower corner instrument panel retaining nuts. Remove the screw to the instrument panel brace from the left side of the glove box opening.

11. Pull the instrument panel out far enough to disconnect the ignition, the headlight dimmer switch and the turn

signal switch. Tag and disconnect all other wiring and vacuum lines.

12. Remove the instrument panel with the wiring harness intact.

13. Installation is in the reverse order of removal.

Center Console

REMOVAL & INSTALLATION

Manual Transmission

1. Place the gear selector in Neutral and apply the parking brake.

2. Lift the ashtray out of the console and then remove the two screws in the opening.

3. Loosen the set screw underneath the shifter knob and remove the knob.

4. Remove the screw under the parking brake handle. Remove the two screws at the rear of the console and lift it off.

5. Installation is in the reverse order of removal.

Automatic Transmission

1. Place the gear selector in Neutral and apply the parking brake.

2. Lift out the ashtray from the front of the console and remove the two screws from the opening.

3. Gently pry the emblem out of the center of the shift knob and remove the snap ring that secures the knob. Remove the knob.

4. Lift the trim plate assembly out

by pulling the front end up first. Disconnect the wiring harness.

5. Remove the three screws under the trim plate and then lift out the rear ashtray and remove the screw under it. Remove the console.

6. Installation is in the reverse order of removal.

Speedometer Cable

REPLACEMENT

1. Reach behind the instrument cluster and push the speedometer cable casing toward the speedometer while depressing the retaining spring on the back of the instrument cluster case. Once the retaining spring has released, hold it in while pulling outward on the casing to disconnect the casing from the speedometer.

NOTE: Removal of the steering column trim plate and/or the speedo cluster may provide better access to the cable.

2. Remove the cable casing sealing plug from the dash panel. Then, pull the casing down from behind the dash and remove the cable.

3. If the cable is broken and cannot be entirely removed from the top, support the car securely, and then unscrew the cable casing connector at the transmission. Pull the bottom part of the cable out, and then screw the connector back onto the transmission.

4. Lubricate the new cable. Insert it into the casing until it bottoms. Push inward while rotating it until the square portion at the bottom engages with the coupling in the transmission, permitting the cable to move in another inch or so. Then, reconnect the cable casing to the speedometer and install the sealing plug into the dash panel.

Fuses

All major electrical systems are protected by fuses. In the event of an overload, the fuse melts, protecting the component. If a fuse blows, the cause should be investigated before replacing the fuse. The fuse box is located under the left side of the instrument panel. The amperage of each fuse and the circuit it protects is stamped on the fuse box.

Fusible Links

A fusible link is a length (usually about 4 inches) of wire located in the circuit it protects. The wire is usually 4 gauge sizes smaller than the circuit wire it protects. In the event of a short or overload, the fusible link melts and stops the flow of current. Components fed directly from the battery are protected by a fusible link. Use only a fusible link of the correct gauge size when replacing a melted link.

Circuit Breakers

The headlights, windshield wipers, power door locks and power windows are protected by circuit breakers. The CB for the headlights is located in the headlight switch; the one for the wipers is located in the wiper switch; the ones for the power door locks and power windows are located in the fuse box. Breakers reset themselves automatically when the problem is relieved. A convenience center is located on the underside of the instrument panel on later models, providing a central location for various relays, hazard flasher unit and buzzer. All units are plug-in modules. The turn signal flasher is locted directly under the steering column of the vehicle. In order to gain access, it may be necessary to remove the under dash padding panel.

CHEVETTE

Instrument Cluster and Speedometer Cable

REMOVAL & INSTALLATION

The instrument cluster must be removed to replace light bulbs, gauges, and printed circuit board.
1. Disconnect the negative battery cable.
2. Remove the clock stem knob (if equipped).
3. Remove the four screws and remove the instrument cluster bezel and lens.
4. Remove the two nuts securing the instrument cluster to the instrument panel and pull the cluster slightly forward.
5. Disconnect the electrical connector and speedometer cable from the cluster and remove it.
6. Pull the core from the speedometer cable housing. If the core is broken in the middle, it will be necessary to disconnect the speedometer cable at the transmission and remove the rest of the core through the bottom of the cable housing.
7. Attach the cable housing to the transmission and insert the new core through the top of the housing.
8. Attach the speedometer cable to the rear of the speedometer.
9. Installation is the reverse of removal procedures.

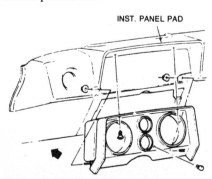

Instrument cluster mounting

Headlight Switch

REMOVAL & INSTALLATION

1. Disconnect the negative battery cable.
2. Pull the headlight switch control knob to the On position.
3. Reach up under the instrument panel and depress the switch shaft retainer button while pulling on the switch control shaft knob.
4. Remove the three screws and remove the headlight switch trim plate.
5. Remove the light switch ferrule nut from the front of the instrument panel.
6. Disconnect the multi-contact connector from the bottom of the headlight switch.
7. Installation is the reverse of removal.

Windshield Wiper Motor

REMOVAL & INSTALLATION

1. Working inside the car, reach up under the instrument panel above the steering column and loosen, but do not remove, the transmission drive link-to-motor crank arm attaching nuts.
2. Disconnect the transmission drive link from the wiper rotor crank arm.
3. Raise the hood and disconnect the wiper motor wiring.
4. Remove the three motor attaching bolts.
5. Remove the motor while guiding the crank arm through the hole.
6. To install, align the sealing gasket to the base of the motor and reverse the rest of the removal procedure.

NOTE: If the wiper motor-to-firewall sealing gasket is damaged during removal, it should be replaced with a new gasket to prevent possible water leaks.

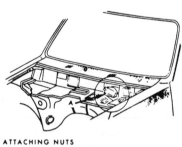

Headlight switch mounting

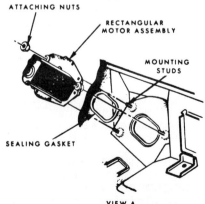

Wiper motor mounting

Drive Train 7

INDEX

CLUTCH AND MANUAL & AUTOMATIC TRANSMISSIONS/TRANSAXLES

CORVETTE

Clutch

——— CAUTION ———

When servicing clutch parts, do not create dust by grinding or sanding clutch disc or by cleaning parts with a dry brush or with compressed air. A water dampened cloth — NOT SOAKED — should be used. The clutch disc contains asbestos fibers which can become airborne if dust is created during servicing. Breathing dust containing asbestos fibers may cause serious bodily harm.

Clutches on 1980-82 models are of the diaphragm spring type. The throwout bearing is a ball bearing with no provision for lubrication. The throwout fork pivots on a ball stud which is mounted in the rear face of the bellhousing.

1984-87 models use a hydraulic clutch system. The hydraulic system consists of a master cylinder and a slave cylinder. When pressure is applied to the clutch pedal (pedal depressed), the push rod contacts the plunger and pushes it up the bore of the master cylinder. In the first $\frac{1}{32}$ in. of movement, the center valve seal closes the port to the fluid reservoir tank and as the plunger continues to move up the bore of the cylinder, the fluid is forced through the outlet line to the slave cylinder mounted on the clutch housing. As fluid is pushed down the pipe from the master cylinder, this in turn forces the piston in the slave cylinder outward. A push rod is connected to the slave cylinder and rides in the pocket of the clutch fork. As the slave cylinder piston moves rearward the push rod forces the clutch fork and release bearing to disengage the pressure plate from the clutch disc. On the return stroke (pedal released), the plunger moves back as a result of the return pressure of the clutch. Fluid returns to the master cylinder and the final movement of the plunger lifts the valve seal off the seat, allowing an unrestricted flow of fluid between system and reservoir. A piston return spring in the slave cylinder preloads the clutch linkage and assures contact of the release bearing with the clutch release fingers at all

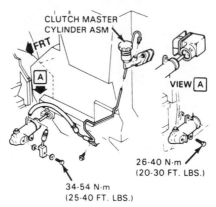

Exploded view of hydraulic clutch components

26-40 N·m (20-30 FT. LBS.)

34-54 N·m (25-40 FT. LBS.)

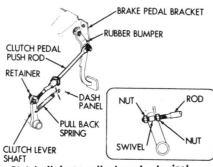

Clutch linkage adjustment—typical

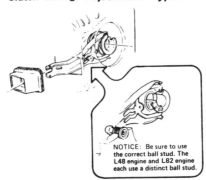

NOTICE: Be sure to use the correct ball stud. The L48 engine and L82 engine each use a distinct ball stud.

Ball stud attachment

times. As the driven disc wears, the diaphragm spring fingers move rearward forcing the release bearing, fork and push rod to move. This movement forces the slave cylinder piston forward in its bore, displacing hydraulic fluid up into the mast cylinder reser-

voir, thereby proving the "self-adjusting" feature of the hydraulic clutch linkage system.

REMOVAL & INSTALLATION

1. Support the engine and remove the transmission.
2. Disconnect the clutch fork pushrod and spring. On 1984-87 models, remove the slave cylinder attaching bolts.
3. Remove the flywheel housing.
4. Slide the clutch fork from the ball stud and remove the fork from the dust boot. The ball stud is threaded into the clutch housing and is easily replaced, if necessary.
5. Install a clutch pilot tool.

NOTE: Look for the assembly markings "X" on the flywheel and the clutch cover (pressure plate assembly). If there are none, scribe marks to identify the position of the clutch cover relative to the flywheel.

6. Loosen the clutch cover bolts evenly until the spring pressure is relieved, then remove the bolts and clutch assembly.
7. Before installing, clean the pressure plate and the flywheel face.
8. Position the disc and pressure plate assembly on the flywheel and install a pilot tool.

NOTE: On single-disc models, the clutch disc is installed with the damper springs and slinger toward the transmission. On dual disc models, the discs are installed with the springs away from the flywheel.

9. Install the pressure plate assembly bolts. Make sure the mark on the cover is aligned with the mark on the flywheel. Tighten the bolts alternately and evenly to 35 ft. lbs.
10. Remove the pilot tool.
11. Remove the release fork and lubricate the ball socket and the fork fingers at the throwout bearing with graphite or Moly Grease. Reinstall the release fork.

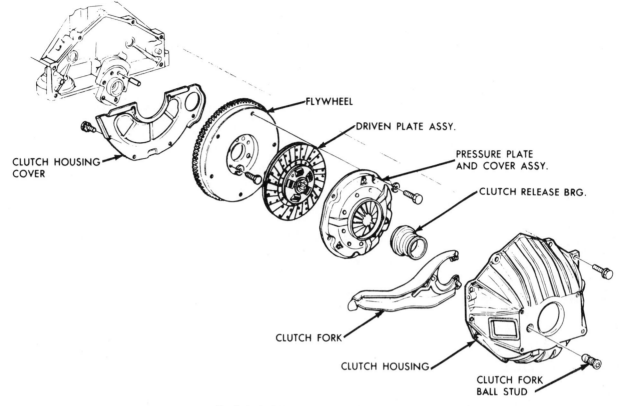

Exploded view of the clutch assembly

12. Lubricate the inside recess and the fork groove of the throwout bearing with a light coat of graphite or moly grease.

13. Install the clutch release fork and dust boot in the clutch housing and the throwout bearing on the fork, then install the flywheel housing. Tighten flywheel housing bolts to 30 ft. lbs. Reinstall the slave cylinder.

14. Connect the fork pushrod and spring.

15. Adjust the shift linkage.

16. Adjust the clutch pedal free play. Bleed the hydraulic clutch system on 1984-87 models.

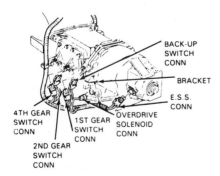

Electrical connectors on 4–speed overdrive transmission

ADJUSTMENT

1. Disconnect the return spring between the floor and the cross shaft.

2. Push the clutch lever and shaft assembly until the clutch pedal is tightly against the rubber stop under the dash.

3. Loosen the two locknuts on the shaft.

4. Push the shaft until the throwout bearing just touches the pressure plate spring.

5. Tighten the top locknut towards the swivel until the distance between it and the swivel is 0.4 in.

6. Tighten the bottom locknut against the swivel.

7. Check pedal free travel. It should be 1–1½ in.

BLEEDING HYDRAULIC CLUTCH

1984-87 Models

Bleeding air from the hydraulic clutch system is necessary whenever any part of the system has been disconnected, or level of fluid in the reservoir has been allowed to fall so low that air has been drawn into the master cylinder. Fill master cylinder reservoir with new brake fluid conforming to Dot 3 or Dot 4 specifications.

CAUTION
Never, under any circumstances, use fluid which has been bled from a system to fill the reservoir as it may be aerated (have too much moisture content) and possibly be contaminated.

1. Raise the vehicle and support it safely.

2. Remove the slave cylinder attaching bolts.

3. Hold slave cylinder at approximately 45° with the bleeder at highest point. Fully depress clutch pedal and open bleeder.

4. Close bleeder valve and release clutch pedal.

5. Repeat Steps 3 and 4 until all air is evacuated from the system. Check and refill master cylinder reservoir as required to prevent air from being drawn through the master cylinder.

Clutch Master Cylinder

REMOVAL & INSTALLATION

1984-87 Models

1. Disconnect negative battery cable.

2. Remove hush panel from under dash.

3. Disconnect push rod from clutch pedal.

4. Disconnect hydraulic line at the clutch master cylinder.

5. Remove the mounting bolts for the master cylinder at the front of dash assembly. Remove master cylinder and overhaul, if necessary, as described later.

6. Install mounting bolts for master cylinder at front of dash. Torque bolts to 15–22 ft. lbs. (20–30 Nm).

7. Connect hydraulic line at master cylinder.

8. Connect push rod at clutch pedal. Lubricate pivot point.

9. Install hush panel.

10. Fill master cylinder with new hydraulic fluid conforming to Dot 3 or Dot 4 specifications.

11. Raise vehicle and bleed hydraulic clutch system as previously described. Check all hydraulic lines and fittings for damage or leaks.

Clutch Slave Cylinder

REMOVAL & INSTALLATION

1. Disconnect negative battery cable.

2. Raise the vehicle and support it safely.

3. Disconnect hydraulic line at slave cylinder.

4. Remove mounting bolts for the slave cylinder at clutch housing.

5. Remove the push rod and slave cylinder from the vehicle. Overhaul, if necessary, as described later.

6. Install the hydraulic line to the slave cylinder.

7. Fill master cylinder with new brake fluid conforming to Dot 3 or Dot 4 specifications.

8. Bleed the hydraulic system as previously outlined.

9. Install slave cylinder to clutch housing. Lubricate leading end of cylinder with Girling Rubber Lube or equivalent. Torque mounting bolts to 20–30 ft. lbs. (26–40 Nm).

Manual Transmission

Transmission refill capacities are in the Capacities table of this section. The Warner is used on all 1980-82 models. Identification is determined by side cover design and linkage. The Warner 4-speeds have the reverse fork mounted in the tailshaft.

1984-87 models use a computer-controlled 4-speed overdrive manual transmission which is essentially a combination of two separate transmissions. The first is a conventional 4-speed (83mm) manual system. The second is a three-speed overdrive system that is electronically controlled by the Electronic Control Module (ECM).

By combining these two transmissions, the complete unit is actually capable of operating with seven separate gear ratios. The overdrive unit performs its function using a planetary gear system in combination with two sets of clutch packs controlled by hydraulic pressure just like the automatic transmission. The ECM is programmed to control the entire overdrive unit by monitoring both road speed and throttle position. Overdrive is locked out when the transmission is in first gear and automatically engages at road speeds above 110 mph. The overdrive can be locked out by a switch on the console or shifter knob.

Shift Linkage

ADJUSTMENT

1980-81

1. Place the shift lever in the Neutral position.

2. Raise the vehicle and support it safely with jackstands.

3. Disconnect the shift rods from the transmission levers.

4. Perform this step for each of the transmission levers individually: Rotate the transmission lever counterclockwise (forward detent position) then turn it back until the first detent is felt (Neutral position). This is done to verify that each transmission lever is in its Neutral position.

5. Fabricate a locating gauge according to the accompanying illustration. Insert the locating gauge into the notch of the shifter housing and through the shift levers to properly align the levers. It may be necessary to move the shift lever(s) to install the locating gauge completely.

6. Loosen the locknuts of the 3–4 shift rod swivel (front of transmission side cover) and turn the swivel as necessary to allow the swivel to easily enter the hole of the 3–4 transmission lever. Apply a slight rearward pressure to the transmission lever and tighten the swivel locknuts. Attach the shift rod to the transmission lever with the retaining clip (and washer, if used).

7. Repeat Step 6 for the 1–2 and reverse shift rods.

8. Remove the locating gauge and lower the vehicle.

NOTE: After the adjustments have been made, the centerlines of the shifter levers must be aligned to prevent rubbing.

1984-87

1. Disconnect the negative battery cable.

2. Remove the left seat from the vehicle. If equipped with power seats, disconnect the electrical leads.

3. Remove the shift knob.

4. Remove the console cover.

5. Remove the glove box lock.

6. Remove the left side panel from the console.

7. Remove the shifter cover.

8. Loosen the adjusting nuts on the shifter rods.

9. With the transmission and shifter in neutral, install the alignment pin in shifter as illustrated.

10. Equalize the swivels on all three shift levers. Hand tighten the forward and rear adjusting nuts at the same time with equal force. Do this for all three shifter rods and then torque the forward and rear adjusting nuts at the same time to specifications.

11. Reintall the components removed by reversing Steps 1-7. Lubricate all linkage pivot points. If, after adjusting the linkage, it is found that high shift effort still exists, an anti-chatter lubricant (positraction additive) may be used. The lubricant is available in a small plastic bottle and can be squirted into the transmission through the filler plug.

REMOVAL & INSTALLATION

1980-82

1. Disconnect the battery ground cable.

2. Remove the shifter ball and "T" handle.

3. Remove the console trim plate.

4. Raise the vehicle on a hoist.

5. Remove the right and left exhaust pipes. It may be necessary to remove the catalytic converter and its mounting bracket to gain sufficient clearance to remove the transmission.

6. Disconnect the driveshaft at the transmission, lower the driveshaft and remove the slip yoke from the transmission.

7. Remove the rear mount to bracket bolts, then jack the engine enough to raise the transmission from the mount.

8. Remove the transmission linkage mounting to frame bolts.

9. Disconnect the shift levers at the transmission.

10. Remove the bolts attaching the gearshift assembly to mounting bracket and remove the mounting bracket. Remove the shifter mechanism with the rods and levers attached.

11. Disconnect the speedometer cable.

12. Remove the transmission mount bracket.

13. Remove the transmission to clutch housing retaining bolts and the lower left extension bolt.

14. Pull the transmission rearward

until it is clear of the clutch housing, then rotate it clockwise while pulling to the rear.

15. To allow room for the transmission removal slowly lower the rear of the engine until the distributor gently touches the fire wall.

NOTE: Do not allow the engine to rest against the distributor as damage may result. Place two blocks of wood directly behind the heads to keep the engine weight off the distributor.

16. Installation is the reverse of removal. Adjust the shift linkage. Torque the transmission-to-clutch housing bolts to 52 ft. lbs. Torque the crossmember bolts to 25 ft. lbs.

1984-87

1. Disconnect the negative battery cable.
2. Remove the air cleaner assembly.
3. Disconnect the throttle valve (T.V.) cable at the left TBI unit.
4. Remove the distributor cap and lay aside.

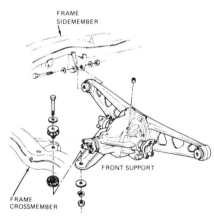

Differential carrier installation—1980 and later

5. Raise the vehicle and support it safely.
6. Remove the complete exhaust system assembly as follows:
   a. Disconnect A.I.R. pipe at the catalytic converter.
   b. Disconnect A.I.R. pipe clamps at exhaust manifold.
   c. Disconnect oxygen sensor electrical lead.
   d. Remove the bolts attaching the mufflers to the hangers.
   e. Remove hanger bracket at the converter.
   f. Disconnect the exhaust pipes from the exhaust manifolds and remove the exhaust system.
7. Remove the exhaust hanger at the transmission.
8. Support the transmission with a jack.

9. Remove the bolts attaching the driveline beam at the axle and transmission. Remove the driveline beam from the vehicle.
10. Mark the relationship of the propeller shaft to the axle companion flange. Remove the trunnion bearing straps and disengage the rear universal joint from the axle. Slide the propeller shaft slip yoke out from the overdrive unit and remove shaft from the vehicle.
11. Disconnect the cooler lines at the overdrive unit.
12. Disconnect the T.V. cable at the overdrive unit.
13. Disconnect the shift linkage at the side cover.
14. Disconnect the electrical connectors at the side cover switches, backup light switch, overdrive unit and speedometer sensor.
15. Lower the transmission and support the engine.
16. Remove the bolts attaching the transmission to the bellhousing. Slide the transmission rearward to disengage the input shaft from the clutch. Remove the transmission from the vehicle.
17. Inspect the clutch components for signs of wear or heat damage. See the Clutch Section, if necessary.
18. Installation is the reverse of removal. Clean and repack the clutch release bearing.
19. Refer to the Rear Suspension Section for installation and specifications for the driveline beam.
20. Torque all fasteners to specifications. Do not overtighten.
21. Adjust the throttle valve (T.V.) cable.
22. Refill the transmission with fluid (4 Speed) SAE-80W or SAE-80W-90 GL-5 gear lube (Overdrive Unit) Dexron® II Automatic Transmission Fluid.

——— **CAUTION** ———

Do not overtorque the bolts attaching the driveline beam to the transmission. Overtorqueing can damage the bushing and seal in the overdrive unit and result in fluid leakage. Inadequate fluid level will damage the transmission.

Automatic Transmission

Two Turbo HydraMatics have been available. The 700R-4 is the only automatic available in 1982-87 models. Identification can be made by the shape of the pan.

REMOVAL & INSTALLATION

1. Disconnect the negative battery

cable at the battery.
2. If so equipped, disconnect the detent/downshift cable at its upper end (accelerator pedal or carburetor).
3. Raise the vehicle and support it safely with jackstands. Preferably, the front AND rear of the vehicle should be raised to provide adequate clearance for transmission removal.
4. Disconnect the exhaust crossover pipe at the manifolds, if exhaust system-to-transmission interference is obvious. It may be necessary to remove the catalytic convertor, exhaust pipe, or just the brackets in order to clear the transmission.

——— **CAUTION** ———

Exhaust system services must be performed while all components are COLD.

5. Remove the transmission inspection cover.
6. Remove the torque convertor-to-flywheel bolts. The relationship between the flywheel and convertor must be marked so that proper balance is maintained after installation.
7. Matchmark the drive shaft and the rear yoke (for reinstallation purposes). With a drain pan positioned under the front yoke, unbolt and remove the drive shaft.
8. Mark and disconnect vacuum lines, wiring, and the speedometer cable from the transmission as required.
9. Place a transmission jack (carefully) up against the transmission oil pan, then secure the transmission to the jack.
10. Remove the transmission mounting pad bolt(s), then carefully raise the transmission just enough to take the weight of the transmission off of the supporting crossmember. Remove the transmission mounting pad.

——— **CAUTION** ———

Exercise extreme care to avoid damage to underhood components while raising or lowering the transmission.

11. Remove the transmission dipstick, then unbolt and remove the filler tube.
12. Disconnect the shift linkage (or cable on floor shift-equipped models) and oil cooler lines from the transmission.
13. Support the engine using a jack placed beneath the engine oil pan. Be sure to put a block of wood between the jack and the oil pan, to prevent damage to the pan.
14. Securely wire the torque convertor to the transmission case.
15. Remove the transmission-to-engine mounting bolts, then carefully move the transmission rearward, downward, and out from beneath the vehicle.

7 DRIVE TRAIN

— CAUTION —

If interference is encountered with the cable(s), cooler lines, etc., remove the component(s) before finally lowering the transmission.

16. Installation is basically the reverse of the previous steps. Note the following points during and after installation:

a. Torque the transmission-to-

engine mounting bolts to 30–40 ft. lbs.

b. Align the matchmarks of the drive shaft with the marks of the rear yoke before installing the joint straps and bolts.

c. Align the converter and flywheel markings before installing the converter bolts.

d. Add the proper type and quantity of transmission fluid. If the converter was replaced, an additional 4

pints (approx.) should be added. NEVER overfill the transmission.

e. Adjust the shift linkage (or cable) and the detent/downshift cable.

f. Make sure that all vacuum lines, electrical connections, and oil cooler line connections are secure before driving the vehicle.

g. Check for fluid leakage, then after the transmission is hot, recheck the fluid level.

CAPRICE, IMPALA, MALIBU AND MONTE CARLO

Clutch

The only service adjustment necessary on the clutch is to maintain the correct pedal free play. The clutch pedal free play or throwout bearing lash decreases with disc wear.

REMOVAL & INSTALLATION

1. Support the engine and remove the transmission.
2. Disconnect the clutch fork push rod and the spring.
3. Remove the flywheel housing.
4. Slide the clutch fork from the ball stud and remove the fork from the dust boot. The ball stud is threaded into the clutch housing and may be replaced, if necessary.
5. Install a clutch alignment tool J-5824 to support the clutch assembly during removal. Mark the relationship between the flywheel and the clutch cover for reinstallation, if they do not already have X marks.
6. Loosen the clutch-to-flywheel bolts evenly, one turn at a time, until the spring pressure is released, then remove bolts and the clutch assembly.
7. To install, reverse the removal procedures. Adjust the shift linkage and the clutch pedal free-play.

FREE PLAY ADJUSTMENT

This adjustment must be made under

the vehicle on the clutch operating linkage. Free play is measured at the clutch pedal.

1. Disconnect the return spring at the clutch operating fork.
2. Rotate the clutch lever until the pedal is firmly against the bumper.
3. Push the outer end of the clutch operating fork to the rear until the release bearing can just be felt to contact the pressure plate fingers.
4. Detach the front end of the operating rod from the clutch pivot shaft arm and place it in the gauge hole on the arm.
5. Loosen the locknut and lengthen the rod just enough to take all the play out of the linkage, then tighten the locknut.
6. Replace the operating rod in its original location.
7. Replace the return spring and check the free play at the pedal pad, it should be about $3/4–1\frac{1}{4}$ inches.

Manual Transmission

REMOVAL & INSTALLATION

1. On the 3 speed floorshift models, remove the shift knob; on the 4 speed floorshift models, remove the spring and the "T" handle.
2. Raise and support the vehicle on jackstands.
3. Disconnect the speedometer cable at the transmission.
4. Remove the driveshaft.
5. Support the rear of the engine and remove the crossmember.
6. Detach the shift rods from the transmission levers.

NOTE: On the floorshift models, disconnect the back drive rod at the bell crank (if equipped).

7. On floorshift models, remove the shift control assembly from the transmission; pull down until the shift lever clears the rubber boot.
8. Remove the upper transmission-

to-clutch housing bolts and replace them with headless guide pins, then remove the lower bolts.

9. Slide the transmission back along the guide pins until the input shaft clears the clutch and remove the transmission.

10. To install, reverse the removal procedures. If the input shaft won't engage the clutch splines, put the transmission in gear and turn the output shaft slightly. Torque the transmission-to-clutch housing bolts to 52 ft. lbs. (4 speed–83mm) or 75 ft. lbs. (all others).

SHIFT LINKAGE ADJUSTMENT

Floorshift

1. Turn the ignition switch OFF.
2. Raise and support the vehicle on jackstands.
3. Loosen the locknuts on the shift rods; the rods should pass freely through the swivels.
4. Set the transmission levers in the Neutral position.
5. Set the floorshift lever in the Neutral position. Install a locating gauge (3.0 x $\frac{1}{8}$ in. dia.) into the alignment slot of the control lever bracket assembly.
6. Adjust the length of the shift rods at the swivels and tighten the locknuts, then remove the locating gauge.
7. Shift the control lever into Reverse and LOCK the ignition switch.

NOTE: If equipped with a back drive rod, pull down slightly on the rod at the steering column, to remove any slack and tighten the locknut. The ignition switch must move freely to the LOCK position and it must not be possible to turn the key to LOCK when in any other position. If the interlock binds, leave the switch in the Lock position and readjust the back drive rod.

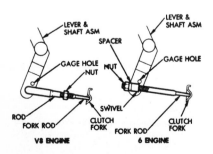

Clutch pedal free-play adjustment

8. Check shifting operation and re-adjust (if necessary).

Automatic Transmission

REMOVAL & INSTALLATION

1. Disconnect the negative battery cable.
2. Remove the air cleaner, the T.V. cable at the upper end and the transmission fluid level indicator.
3. Raise and support the vehicle on jackstands.
4. Remove the drive shaft and the floor pan reinforcement (if necessary).
5. At the transmission, disconnect the speedometer cable, the shift link-age, the electrical leads and retainers.
6. Remove the torque converter cover and the torque converter-to-flexplate nuts.

NOTE: Before removing the torque converter from the flex plate, mark the flex plate to the torque converter.

7. If equipped with a gas engine, re-move the catalytic converter bracket.
8. Remove the transmission sup-port mounting bolts at the transmission mount and at the frame, then raise the transmission slightly and slide the support rearward.
9. Lower the transmission, then re-move the oil cooler lines and the T.V. cable from the transmission.

NOTE: After removing the oil cooler lines, be sure to cap them to prevent dirt from entering the system.

10. Support the engine and remove the transmission-to-engine bolts.
11. Install the torque converter hold-ing tool J-21366 to support the torque converter, then remove the transmission from the vehicle.
12. To install, reverse the removal procedures. Torque the transmission-to-engine bolts to 35 ft. lbs., the torque converter-to-flex plate to 46 ft. lbs., the transmission support-to-frame bolts to 40 ft. lbs., the transmission support-to-transmission mount to 25 ft. lbs. and the drive shaft bolts to 16 ft. lbs. Adjust the shift linkage and the T.V. cable.

CELEBRITY AND CITATION

Clutch

The only service adjustment necessary on the clutch is to maintain the correct pedal free play. Clutch pedal free play, or throwout bearing lash, decreases with driven disc wear.

REMOVAL & INSTALLATION

1. Remove the transaxle.
2. Mark the pressure plate assembly and the flywheel so that they can be assembled in the same position. They were balanced as an assembly at the factory.
3. Loosen the attaching bolts one turn at a time until spring tension is relieved.
4. Support the pressure plate and remove the bolts. Remove the pressure plate and clutch disc. Do not disassemble the pressure plate assembly; re-place it if defective.
5. Inspect the flywheel, clutch disc, pressure plate, throwout bearing and the clutch fork and pivot shaft assembly for wear. Replace the parts as re-quired. If the flywheel shows any signs of overheating, or if it is badly grooved or scored, it should be replaced.
6. Clean the pressure plate and fly-wheel mating surfaces thoroughly. Po-sition the clutch disc and pressure plate into the installed position, and support with a dummy shaft or clutch aligning tool. The clutch plate is as-sembled with the damper springs off-set toward the transaxle. One side of the factory-supplied clutch disc is stamped ''Flywheel side''.
7. Install the pressure plate-to-fly-wheel bolts. Tighten them gradually in a crisscross pattern.
8. Lubricate the outside groove and the inside recess of the release bearing with high temperature grease. Wipe off any excess. Install the release bearing.
9. Install the transaxle.

CLUTCH LINKAGE AND PEDAL HEIGHT/FREE-PLAY ADJUSTMENT

All cars use a self-adjusting clutch mechanism which may be checked as follows. As the clutch friction material wears, the cable must be lengthened. This is accomplished by simply pulling the clutch pedal up to its rubber bumper. This action forces the pawl against its stop and rotates it out of mesh with the quadrant teeth, allow-ing the cable to play out until the quadrant spring load is balanced against the load applied by the release bearing. This adjustment procedure is required every 5000 miles or less.

1. With engine running and brake on, hold the clutch pedal approximate-ly ½ in. from floor mat and move shift lever between first and reverse several times. If this can be done smoothly without clashing into reverse, the clutch is fully releasing. If shift is not smooth, clutch is not fully releasing and linkage should be inspected and corrected as necessary.
2. Check clutch pedal bushings for sticking or excessive wear.
3. Have an assistant sit in the driv-er's seat and fully apply the clutch ped-al to the floor. Observe the clutch fork level travel at the transaxle. The end

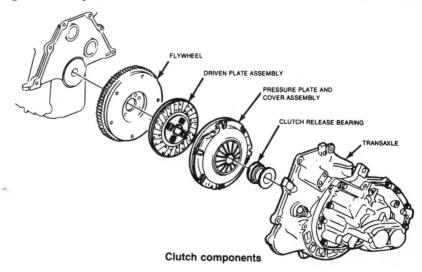

FLYWHEEL

DRIVEN PLATE ASSEMBLY

PRESSURE PLATE AND COVER ASSEMBLY

CLUTCH RELEASE BEARING

TRANSAXLE

Clutch components

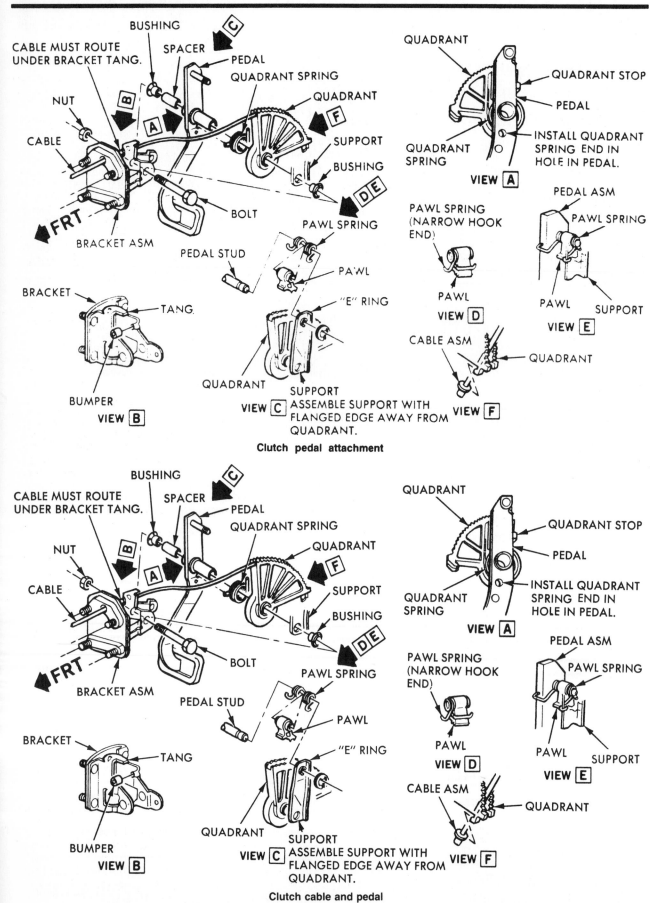

Clutch pedal attachment

Clutch cable and pedal

CABLE MUST ROUTE UNDER BRACKET TANG.

BUSHING
SPACER
PEDAL
QUADRANT SPRING
QUADRANT
SUPPORT
BUSHING
NUT
CABLE
BOLT
PAWL SPRING
PEDAL STUD
BRACKET ASM
FRT

QUADRANT
QUADRANT STOP
PEDAL
INSTALL QUADRANT SPRING END IN HOLE IN PEDAL.
QUADRANT SPRING
VIEW A

PAWL SPRING (NARROW HOOK END)
PAWL
VIEW D

PEDAL ASM
PAWL SPRING
PAWL
SUPPORT
VIEW E

CABLE ASM
QUADRANT
VIEW F

BRACKET
TANG
BUMPER
VIEW B

QUADRANT
"E" RING
SUPPORT
ASSEMBLE SUPPORT WITH FLANGED EDGE AWAY FROM QUADRANT.
VIEW C
PAWL

of the clutch fork lever should have a total travel of approximately 1.5–1.7 in.

4. If fork lever is not correct, check the adjusting mechanism by depressing the clutch pedal and looking for pawl to firmly engage with the teeth in the quadrant.

Clutch Cable

REMOVAL

1. Support the clutch pedal upward against the bumper stop to release the pawl from the quadrant. Disconnect the end of the cable from the clutch release lever at the transaxle. Be careful to prevent the cable from snapping rapidly toward the rear of the car. The quadrant in the adjusting mechanism can be damaged by allowing the cable to snap back.

2. Disconnect the clutch cable from the quadrant. Lift the locking pawl away from the quadrant, then slide the cable out on the right side of the quadrant.

3. From the engine side of the cowl disconnect the two upper nuts holding the cable retainer to the upper studs. Disconnect the cable from the bracket mounted to the transaxle, and remove the cable.

4. Inspect the clutch cable for frayed wires, kinks, worn ends and excessive friction. If any of these conditions exist, replace the cable.

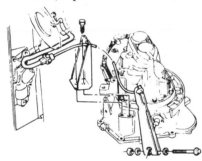

Clutch cable routing

INSTALLATION

1. With the gasket in position on the two upper studs, position a new cable with the retaining flange against the bracket.

2. Attach the end of the cable to the quadrant, being sure to route the cable underneath the pawl.

3. Attach the two upper nuts to the retainer mounting studs, and torque to specifications.

4. Attach the cable to the bracket mounted to the transaxle.

5. Support the clutch pedal upward against the bumper stop to release the pawl from the quadrant. Attach the outter end of the cable to the clutch release lever. Be sure not to yank on the cable, since overloading the cable could damage the quadrant.

6. Check clutch operation and adjust by lifting the clutch pedal up to allow the mechanism to adjust the cable length. Depress the pedal slowly several times to set the pawl into mesh with the quadrant teeth.

Manual Transaxle

All models use a Muncie model MT-125 four speed transaxle. Shifting is controlled by a two-cable push-pull arrangement. Final drive is an integral part of the transaxle assembly.

REMOVAL & INSTALLATION

1. Disconnect the negative battery cable from the transaxle case.

2. Remove the two transaxle strut bracket bolts on the left side of the engine compartment, if equipped.

3. On some models equipped with a V6 engine, disconnect the fuel lines and fuel line clamps at the clutch cable bracket.

4. Remove the top four engine-to-transaxle bolts, and the one at the rear near the firewall. The one at the rear is installed from the engine side.

5. Loosen the engine-to-transaxle bolt near the starter, but do not remove.

6. Disconnect the speedometer cable at the transaxle, or at the speed control transducer on cars so equipped.

7. Remove the retaining clip and washer from the shift linkage at the transaxle. Remove the clips holding the cables to the mounting bosses on the case.

8. Support the engine with a lifting chain.

9. Unlock the steering column and raise and support the car. Drain the transaxle. Remove the two nuts attaching the stabilizer bar to the left lower control arm. Remove the four bolts which attach the left retaining plate to the engine cradle. The retaining plate covers and holds the stabilizer bar.

10. Loosen the four bolts holding the right stabilizer bracket.

11. Disconnect and remove the exhaust pipe and crossover if necessary.

12. Pull the stabilizer bar down on the left side.

13. Remove the four nuts and disconnect the front and rear transaxle mounts from the engine cradle. Remove the two rear center crossmember bolts.

14. Remove the three right side front cradle attaching bolts. They are accessible under the splash shield.

15. Remove the top bolt from the lower front transaxle shock absorber if equipped.

16. Remove the left front wheel. Remove the front cradle-to-body bolts on the left side, and the rear cradle-to-body bolts.

17. Pull the left side drive shaft from the transaxle using G.M. special tool J-28468 or the equivalent. The right side axle shaft will simply disconnect from the case. When the transaxle is removed, the right shaft can be swung out of the way. A boot protector should be used when disconnecting the driveshafts.

18. Swing the cradle to the left side. Secure out of the way, outboard of the fender well.

19. Remove the flywheel and starter shield bolts, and remove the shields.

20. Remove the two transaxle extension bolts from the engine-to-transaxle bracket, if equipped.

21. Place a jack under the transaxle case. Remove the last engine-to-transaxle bolt. Pull the transaxle to the left, away from the engine, then down and out from under the car.

22. Installation is the reverse of removal. Position the right axle shaft into its bore as the transaxle is being installed. When the transaxle is bolted to the engine, swing the cradle into position and install the cradle-to-body bolts immediately. Be sure to guide the left axle shaft into place as the cradle is moved back into position.

SHIFT LINKAGE ADJUSTMENT

1. Remove the shifter boot and retainer inside the car. Shift into first gear.

2. Install two No. 22 drill bits, or two $5/32$ in. rods, into the two alignment holes in the shifter assembly to hold it in first gear.

3. Place the transaxle into first gear by pushing the rail selector shaft down just to the point of feeling the resistance of the inhibitor spring. Then rotate the shift lever all the way counterclockwise.

4. Install the stud, with the cable attached, into the slotted area of the select lever, while gently pulling on the lever to remove all lash.

5. Remove the two drill bits or pins from the shifter.

6. Check the shifter for proper operation. It may be necessary to fine tune the adjustment after road testing.

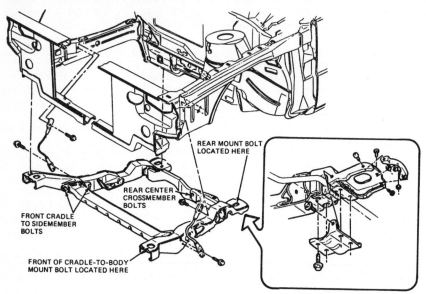

Typical engine/transaxle cradle

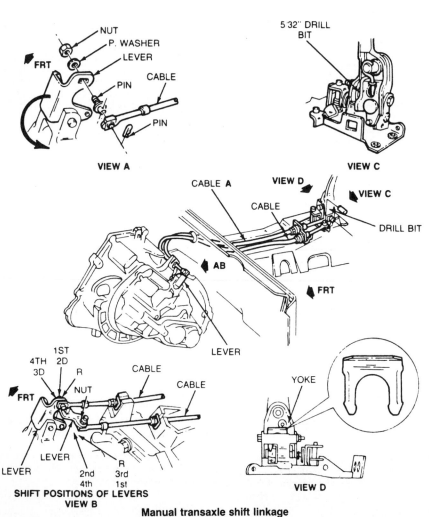

VIEW A

VIEW C

Manual transaxle shift linkage

SHIFT POSITIONS OF LEVERS
VIEW B

VIEW D

Automatic Transmission

All models use a Turbo Hydro-Matic 125 or 125C automatic transmission. The 125C is equipped with a torque converter clutch (TCC) which under certain conditions mechanically couples the engine to the transaxle for greater power transfer efficiency and increased fuel mileage. A cable operated throttle valve linkage is used. Automatic transaxle operation is provided through a conventional three element torque converter, a compound planetary gear set, and a dual sprocket and drive link assembly.

SHIFT LINKAGE ADJUSTMENT, BAND ADJUSTMENT, FLUID AND FILTER CHANGE

——————— CAUTION ———————

Any inaccuracies in shift linkage adjustments may result in premature failure of the transmission due to operation without the controls in full detent. Such operation results in reduced fluid pressure and in turn, partial engagement of the affected clutches. Partial engagement of the clutches, with sufficient pressure to permit apparently normal vehicle operation will result in failure of the clutches and/or other internal parts after only a few miles of operation.

REMOVAL & INSTALLATION

1. Disconnect the negative battery cable from the transaxle. Tape the wire to the upper radiator hose to keep it out of the way.
2. Remove the air cleaner and disconnect the detent cable. Slide the detent cable in the opposite direction of the cable to remove it from the carburetor.
3. Unbolt the detent cable attaching bracket at the transaxles.
4. Pull up on the detent cable cover at the transaxle until the cable is exposed. Disconnect the cable from the rod.
5. Remove the two transaxle strut bracket bolts at the transaxle, if equipped.
6. Remove all the engine-to-transaxle bolts except the one near the starter. The one nearest the firewall is installed from the engine side; you will need a short handled box wrench or ratchet to reach it.
7. Loosen, but do not remove the engine-to-transaxle bolt near the starter.
8. Disconnect the speedometer cable at the upper and lower coupling.

On cars with cruise control, remove the speedometer cable at the transducer.

9. Remove the retaining clip and washer from the shift linkage at the transaxle. Remove the two shift linkage at the transaxle. Remove the two shift linkage bracket bolts.

10. Disconnect and plug the two fluid cooler lines at the transaxle. These are inch-size fittings ($\frac{1}{2}$ and $\frac{11}{16}$); use a back-up wrench to avoid twisting the lines.

11. Install an engine holding chain or hoist. Raise the engine enough to take its weight off the mounts.

12. Unlock the steering column and raise the car.

13. Remove the two nuts holding the anti-sway (stabilizer) bar to the left lower control arm (driver's side).

14. Remove the four bolts attaching the covering plate over the stabilizer bar to the engine cradle on the left side (driver's side).

15. Loosen but do not remove the four bolts holding the stabilizer bar bracket to the right side (passenger's side) of the engine cradle. Pull the bar down on the driver's side.

16. Disconnect the front and rear transaxle mounts at the engine cradle.

17. Remove the two rear center crossmember bolts.

18. Remove the three right (passenger) side front engine cradle attaching bolts. The nuts are accessible under the splash shield next to the frame rail.

19. Remove the top bolt from the lower front transaxle shock absorber, if equipped (V6 engine only).

20. Remove the left (driver) side front and rear cradle-to-body bolts.

21. Remove the left front wheel. Attach an axle shaft removing tool (GM No. J-28468 or equivalent) to a slide hammer. Place the tool behind the axle shaft cones and pull the cones out away from the transaxle. Remove the right shaft in the same manner. Set the shafts out of the way. Plug the openings in the transaxle to prevent fluid leakage and the entry of dirt.

22. Swing the partial engine cradle to the left (driver) side and wire it out of the way outboard of the fender well.

23. Remove the four torque converter and starter shield bolts. Remove the two transaxle extension bolts from the engine-to-transaxle bracket.

24. Attach a transaxle jack to the case.

25. Use a felt pen to matchmark the torque converter and flywheel. Remove the three torque converter-to-flywheel bolts.

26. Remove the transaxle-to-engine bolt near the starter. Remove the transaxle by sliding it to the left, away from the engine.

27. Installation is the reverse of removal. As the transaxle is installed, slide the right axle shaft into the case. Install the cradle-to-body bolts before the stabilizer bar is installed. To aid in stabilizer bar installation, a pry hole has been provided in the engine cradle.

CAMARO

Clutch

REMOVAL & INSTALLATION

CAUTION

If equipped with a hydraulic clutch system, disconnect the master cylinder from the clutch pedal BEFORE removing the slave cylinder from the clutch lever. This procedure is to prevent any possible damage to the slave cylinder.

---

1. Refer to the "Transmission Removal & Installation" procedures in this section and remove the transmission.

NOTE: On 1984-87 vehicles, a hydraulic operated clutch is used. When removing the clutch, remove the slave cylinder heat shield and the cylinder from the clutch housing.

2. Disconnect the clutch fork push rod and spring.

3. Remove the clutch housing.

4. Slide the clutch fork from the ball stud and remove the fork from the dust boot. The ball stud is threaded into the clutch housing and may be replaced, if necessary.

5. Install an alignment tool J-5824 (4-speed) or J-33169 (5-speed) to support the clutch assembly during removal. Mark the flywheel and the pressure plate for reinstallation, if they do not already have "X" marks.

6. Loosen the pressure plate-to-flywheel attaching bolts evenly, 1 turn at a time, until spring pressure is released. Remove the bolts and clutch assembly.

7. To install, place the clutch disc with the damper springs toward the transmission and reverse the removal

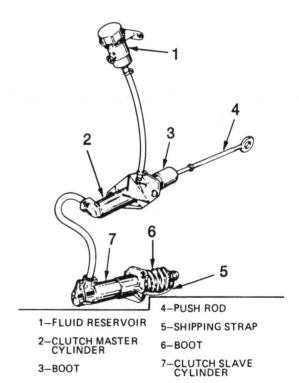

1—FLUID RESERVOIR
2—CLUTCH MASTER CYLINDER
3—BOOT
4—PUSH ROD
5—SHIPPING STRAP
6—BOOT
7—CLUTCH SLAVE CYLINDER

Hydraulic clutch assembly

procedures. Torque the clutch housing-to-engine to 55 ft. lbs., the slave cylinder-to-clutch housing to 15 ft. lbs. and the heat shield-to-clutch housing to 15 ft. lbs.

Clutch Hydraulic System

The clutch hydraulic system was introduced in 1984 and is to be serviced as a complete unit.

REMOVAL & INSTALLATION

——— CAUTION ———

Disconnect the master cylinder from the clutch pedal BEFORE removing the slave cylinder from the clutch lever; this procedure is to prevent any possible damage to the slave cylinder.

1. Disconnect the negative battery cable.
2. Remove the hush panel and the steering column trim cover.
3. Disconnect the master cylinder push rod from the clutch pedal.
4. Remove the clutch master cylinder-to-cowl nuts, the brake booster-to-cowl nuts and the clutch fluid reservoir from the bracket.
5. Pull the brake master cylinder forward to gain access to the clutch master cylinder.
6. Raise and support the vehicle on jackstands.
7. Remove the slave cylinder heat shield and the slave cylinder from the clutch housing.
8. Lower the vehicle and remove the clutch hydraulic system from the vehicle.
9. To install, reverse the removal procedures. Torque the clutch reservoir assembly-to-bracket to 30 inch lbs., the clutch master cylinder-to-cowl to 10 ft. lbs., the slave cylinder-to-clutch housing to 15 ft. lbs., the heat shield-to-clutch housing to 15 ft. lbs.

BLEEDING

——— CAUTION ———

When adding fluid to the hydraulic system, NEVER use fluid that has been bled from the system.

1. Clean the dirt and grease from around the cap.
2. Remove the cap and the diaphragm from the master cylinder. Fill the reservoir to the top with DOT 3 brake fluid.
3. Loosen the bleed screw at the slave cylinder body next to the inlet connection.
4. Allow the system to bleed until

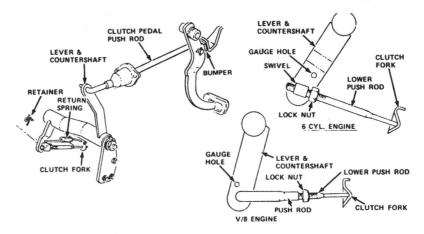

Typical clutch linkage and adjustment points

the air bubbles disappear from the fluid, then tighten the bleeder screw.
5. Refill the reservoir, then install the diaphragm and the cap.
6. To expell any air trapped in the system, exert 20 lbs. of force on the clutch release lever and open the bleeder screw. Maintain pressure until a steady stream of fluid flows from the bleeder screw, then tighten the screw.

NOTE: It may be necessary to repeat the bleeding procedure several times, until all of the air is bleed from the system.

7. Refill the reservoir.
8. Check the system, by starting the engine, operating the clutch and shifting the transmission into several gears; there should be no grinding of the gears.

FREE-PLAY ADJUSTMENT— 1980-83

1. Disconnect the return spring at the clutch fork.
2. Hold the pedal against the rubber bumper on the dash brace.
3. Push the clutch fork so that the throwout bearing lightly contacts the pressure plate fingers.
4. Loosen the locknut and adjust the length of the rod so that the swivel or rod can slip freely into the gauge hole of the lever. Increase the length of the rod until the free-play is removed.
5. Remove the rod or swivel from the gauge hole and insert it in the other (original) hole on the lever. Install the retainer and tighten the locknut.
6. Install the return spring and check free-play measurement from the floor mat to top of the pedal pad. It should measure: $7/8$ to $1\,1/2$ in. (1980-81) or $7/8$ to $1\,1/8$ in. (1982-87).

Manual Transmission

REMOVAL & INSTALLATION

1980-81 Models

1. On the floor-shift models, remove the shift knob and console trim plate.
2. Raise and support the vehicle on jackstands.
3. Disconnect the speedometer cable and the TCS switch wiring, if equipped.
4. Remove the driveshaft.
5. Remove the transmission mounts-to-crossmember bolts, the crossmember-to-frame bolts and the crossmember.
6. Remove the shift levers from the transmission.
7. Disconnect the back drive rod from the bellcrank.
8. Remove the shift control assembly bolts and lower the assembly until the shift lever clears the rubber shift boot. Remove the assembly from the vehicle.
9. Remove the transmission-to-clutch housing bolts and lower the transmission from the vehicle.
10. To install, reverse the removal procedures. Refill the transmission and adjust the shift linkage.

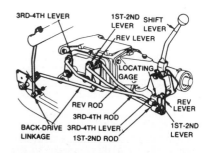

Typical 4 speed transmission shift linkage—through 1981

1982-84 4-Speed

1. Disconnect the negative battery cable.
2. Raise and support the vehicle on jackstands.
3. Drain the lubricant from the transmission.
4. Remove the torque arm from the vehicle.
5. Mark the driveshaft and the rear axle pinion flange to indicate their relationship. Remove the rear universal joint straps, lower the rear of the driveshaft, withdraw the it from the transmission and remove it from the vehicle.

NOTE: When removing the driveshaft, be careful to keep the universal joint caps in place.

6. Disconnect the speedometer cable and the electrical connectors from the transmission.
7. Remove the exhaust pipe brace.
8. Remove the transmission shifter support-to-transmission bolts.
9. Disconnect the shift linkage at the shifter.
10. Raise the transmission and remove the crossmember attaching bolts.
11. Remove the transmission mount bolts, the mount and the crossmember from the vehicle.
12. Remove the transmission bolts and the transmission from the vehicle.
13. To install, reverse the removal procedures. Torque the transmission-to-clutch housing bolts to 55 ft. lbs., the crossmember-to-body bolts to 35 ft. lbs., the transmission-to-crossmember bolts to 35 ft. lbs., the mount-to-transmission bolts to 35 ft. lbs. and the shifter bracket-to-extension housing to 25 ft. lbs. Adjust the shift linkage and refill the transmission with lubricant.

NOTE: Apply a light coating of high temperature grease to the main drive gear bearing retainer and to the splined portion of the main drive gear. This will assure free movement of the clutch and transmission components during assembly.

1982-87 5-Speed

1. Disconnect the negative battery.
2. Remove the shift lever boot screws and slide the boot up the shift lever.
3. Remove the shift lever from the transmission.
4. Raise and support the vehicle on jackstands.
5. Drain the lubricant from the transmission.
6. Remove the torque arm from the vehicle.
7. Mark the driveshaft and the rear axle pinion flange to indicate their relationship. Remove the rear universal joint straps, lower the rear of the driveshaft, withdraw the driveshaft from the transmission and remove it from the vehicle.

NOTE: When removing the driveshaft, be careful to keep the universal joint caps in place.

8. Disconnect the speedometer cable and the electrical connectors from the transmission.
9. Remove the catalytic converter hanger.
10. Raise the transmission and remove the crossmember bolts.
11. Remove the transmission mount bolts, the mount and crossmember from the vehicle.
12. Remove the dust cover-to-transmission bolts.
13. Remove the transmission-to-engine bolts and the transmission from the vehicle.
14. To install, reverse the removal procedures. Torque the transmission-to-clutch housing bolts to 55 ft. lbs., the crossmember-to-body bolts to 35 ft. lbs., the mount-to-crossmember bolts to 35 ft. lbs. and the mount-to-transmission bolts to 35 ft. lbs. Adjust the shift linkage and refill the transmission with lubricant.

NOTE: Apply a light coating of high temperature grease to the main drive gear bearing retainer and to the splined portion of the main drive gear. This will assure free movement of the clutch and transmission components during assembly.

SHIFT LINKAGE ADJUSTMENT

4-Speed

NOTE: The 5-speed transmission gearshift lever is floor-mounted and is located on top of the extension housing. The shift mechanism does not require adjustment.

1980-81

1. Turn the ignition switch OFF, raise the vehicle and support it on jackstands.
2. Loosen the swivel locknuts on all shift rods and on the back drive control rod.
3. Place the transmission shift levers (on the side of transmission) in Neutral (centered).
4. Place the floor shift lever in Neutral and lock it in this position by installing a pin into the lever bracket assembly directly below the shift lever.
5. Move the shift rod nut up against the swivel on each shift rod and hold it in place by tightening the locknuts.
6. Remove the locating pin from the control bracket assembly and shift the

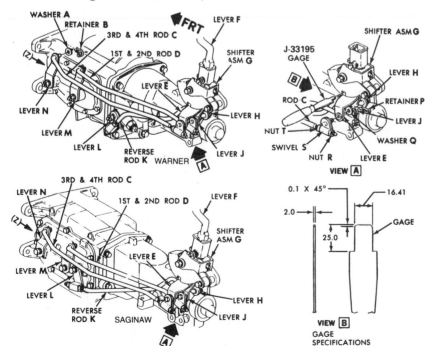

Transmission shift linkage adjustment on 1982–84 models. Note that all component references in the illustration match those in the text and that the dimensions are expressed in millimeters.

transmission into Reverse. Place the ignition key in LOCK. To remove any slack in the steering column mechanism, pull down on the back drive rod and tighten the nut. When in reverse, it must be possible to easily turn the ignition key in and out of the LOCK position. If any binding exists, leave the key in LOCK and readjust the back drive control rod.

7. Check the shifting operation and readjust if necessary.

1982-84

NOTE: All terms used in the following procedure match those which are used in the accompanying illustration.

1. Disconnect the negative battery cable.
2. Place the shift control lever (F) in Neutral.
3. Raise and support the vehicle on jackstands.
4. Remove the swivel retainers (P) from the levers (E, H and J).
5. Remove the swivels (S) from the the shifter assembly (G) and loosen the swivel locknuts (R and T).
6. Make sure that levers L, M and N are in their Neutral positions (center detents).
7. Align the holes of levers E, H and J with the notch in the shifter assembly (G). Insert an alignment gauge (J-33195) to hold the levers in this position.
8. Insert swivel S into lever E and install washer Q. Secure with retainer P.
9. Apply rearward pressure (Z) to lever N. Tighten locknuts R and T (at the same time) against swivel S to 25 ft. lbs.
10. Repeat Steps 8 and 9 for rod D and levers J and M.
11. Repeat Steps 8 and 9 for rod K and levers H and L.
12. Remove the alignment gauge, lower the vehicle and check the operation of the shifting mechanism.
13. Reconnect the negative battery cable.

Automatic Transmission

REMOVAL & INSTALLATION

1. Disconnect the negative battery cable.
2. Remove the air cleaner assembly.
3. Disconnect the throttle valve (TV) control cable at the carburetor.
4. Remove the transmission dipstick and the tube.
5. Raise and support the vehicle on jackstands.

NOTE: In order to provide adequate clearance for transmission removal, it may be necessary to raise both the front and the rear of the vehicle.

6. Mark the relationship between the driveshaft and the rear pinion flange, so that the driveshaft may be reinstalled in its original position.
7. Unbolt the universal joint straps from the pinion flange (use care to keep the universal joint caps in place), lower and remove the driveshaft from the vehicle.
8. Disconnect the catalytic convertor support bracket at the transmission.

NOTE: If equipped with a PM generator, instead of a speedometer cable, disconnect the electrical connector at the generator.

9. Disconnect the speedometer cable, electrical connectors and the shift control cable from the transmission.

--- CAUTION ---

During the next step, rear spring force will cause the torque arm to move toward the floor pan. When disconnecting the arm from the transmission, carefully place a piece of wood between the floor pan and the torque arm. This will prevent possible personal injury and/or floor pan damage.

10. Remove the torque arm-to-transmission bolts.

11. Remove the flywheel cover, then mark the relationship between the torque convertor and the flywheel, so that these parts may be reassembled in the same relationship.

NOTE: On the 1980-81 models, remove the tunnel strap.

12. Remove the torque convertor-to-flywheel bolts.
13. Support the transmission with a jack and remove the transmission mount bolt.
14. Unbolt and remove the transmission crossmember.
15. Lower the transmission slightly. Disconnect the TV cable and oil cooler lines from the transmission.
16. Fasten the support tool BT-6424 to the engine, then remove the transmission-to-engine mounting bolts.

--- CAUTION ---

The transmission must be secured to the transmission jack.

17. Remove the transmission from the vehicle. Be careful not to damage the oil cooler lines, TV cable or the shift control cable.

NOTE: When removing the transmission, install the torque converter holding tool J-21366 to keep the torque convertor from falling out of the transmission.

18. To install, reverse the removal procedures. Torque the transmission-to-engine bolts to 35 ft. lbs., the torque converter-to-flywheel to 35 ft. lbs., the transmission-to-frame bolts to 40 ft. lbs. and the transmission-to-mount to 25 ft. lbs. Adjust the shift linkages, the TV cable and add fluid to the transmission (if necessary).

NOTE: Before installing the convertor-to-flywheel bolts, be sure that the weld nuts on the convertor are flush with the flywheel and that the convertor rotates freely by hand in this position. Install a O-ring to the dipstick tube.

CAVALIER

Clutch

ADJUSTMENT

The J-cars have a self-adjusting clutch mechanism located on the clutch pedal, eliminating the need for periodic free play adjustments. The self-adjust-

ing mechanism should be inspected periodically as follows:

1. Depress the clutch pedal and look for the pawl on the self-adjusting mechanism to firmly engage the teeth on the ratchet.
2. Release the clutch. The pawl should be lifted off of the teeth by the metal stop on the bracket.

CLUTCH REMOVAL & INSTALLATION

1. Remove the transaxle.
2. Mark the pressure plate assembly and the flywheel so that they can be assembled in the same position. They were balanced as an assembly at

the factory.

3. Loosen the attaching bolts one turn at a time until spring tension is relieved.

4. Support the pressure plate and remove the bolts. Remove the pressure plate and clutch disc. Do not disassemble the pressure plate assembly; replace it if defective.

5. Inspect the flywheel, clutch disc, pressure plate, throwout bearing and the clutch fork and pivot shaft assembly for wear. Replace the parts as required. If the flywheel shows any signs of overheating, or if it is badly grooved or scored, it should be refaced or replaced.

6. Clean the pressure plate and flywheel mating surfaces thoroughly. Position the clutch disc and pressure plate into the installed position, and support with a dummy shaft or clutch aligning tool. The clutch plate is assembled with the damper springs offset toward the transaxle. One side of the factory-supplied clutch disc is stamped "Flywheel Side."

7. Install the pressure plate-to-flywheel bolts. Tighten them gradually in a criss-cross pattern.

8. Lubricate the outside groove and the inside recess of the release bearing with high temperature grease. Wipe off any excess. Install the release bearing.

9. Install the transaxle.

Neutral Start Switch

A neutral start switch is located on the clutch pedal assembly; the switch prevents the engine from starting unless the clutch is depressed. If the switch is faulty, it can be unbolted and replaced without removing the pedal assembly from the car. No adjustments for the switch are provided.

Clutch Cable

REPLACEMENT

1. Press the clutch pedal up against the bumper stop so as to release the pawl from the detent. Disconnect the clutch cable from the release lever at the transaxle assembly. Be careful that the cable does not snap back toward the rear of the car as this could damage the detent in the adjusting mechanism.

2. Remove the hush panel from inside the car.

3. Disconnect the clutch cable from the detent end tangs. Lift the locking pawl away from the detent and then pull the cable forward between the detent and the pawl.

4. Remove the windshield washer bottle.

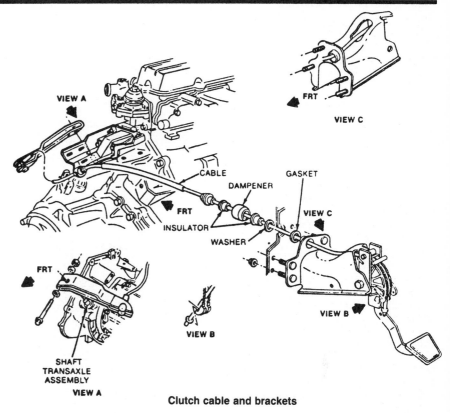

Clutch cable and brackets

5. From the engine side of the cowl, pull the clutch cable out to disengage it from the clutch pedal mounting bracket. The insulators, dampener and washers may separate from the cable in the process.

6. Disconnect the cable from the transaxle mounting bracket and remove it.

7. Install the cable into both insulators, damper and washer. Lubricate the rear insulator with tire mounting lube or the like to ease installation into the pedal mounting bracket.

8. From inside the car, attach the end of the cable to the detent. Be sure to route the cable underneath the pawl and into the detent cable groove.

9. Press the clutch pedal up against the bumper stop to release the pawl from the detent. Install the other end of the cable at the release lever and the transaxle mount bracket.

10. Install the hush panel and the windshield washer bottle.

11. Check the clutch operation.

Manual Transaxle

REMOVAL & INSTALLATION

1. Disconnect the negative battery cable.

2. Install an engine holding bar so that one end is supported on the cowl tray over the wiper motor and the other end rests on the radiator support. Use padding and be careful not to damage the paint or body work with the bar. Attach a lifting hook to the engine lift ring and to the bar and raise the engine enough to take the pressure off the motor mounts.

NOTE: If a lifting bar and hook is not available, a chain hoist can

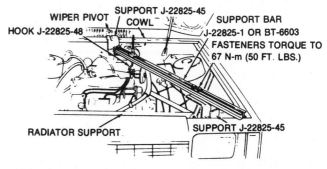

Install an engine holding bar when removing the manual transmission

be used, however, during the procedure the vehicle must be raised, at which time the chain hoist must be adjusted to keep tension on the engine/transaxle assembly.

3. Remove the heater hose clamp at the transaxle mount bracket. Disconnect the electrical connector and remove the horn assembly.

4. Remove the transaxle mount attaching bolts. Discard the bolts attaching the mount to the side frame; new bolts must be used at installation.

5. Disconnect the clutch cable from the clutch release lever. Remove the transaxle mount bracket attaching bolts and nuts.

6. Disconnect the shift cables and retaining clips at the transaxle. Disconnect the ground cables at the transaxle mounting stud.

7. Remove the four upper transaxle-to-engine mounting bolts.

8. Raise the vehicle and support it on stands. Remove the left front wheel.

9. Remove the left front inner splash shield. Remove the transaxle strut and bracket.

10. Remove the clutch housing cover bolts.

11. Disconnect the speedometer cable at the transaxle.

12. Disconnect the stabilizer bar at the left suspension support and control arm.

13. Disconnect the ball joint from the steering knuckle.

14. Remove the left suspension support attaching bolts and remove the support and control arm as an assembly.

15. Install boot protectors and disengage the drive axles at the transaxle. Remove the left side shaft from the transaxle.

16. Position a jack under the transaxle case, remove the lower two transaxle-to-engine mounting bolts and remove the transaxle by sliding it towards the driver's side, away from the engine. Carefully lower the jack, guiding the right shaft out the transaxle.

17. When installing the transaxle, guide the right drive axle into its bore as the transaxle is being raised. The right drive axle CANNOT be readily installed after the transaxle is connected to the engine. Installation of the remaining components is in the reverse order of removal with the following notes. Tighten the transaxle-to-engine mounting bolts to 55 ft. lbs. Tighten the suspension support-to-body attaching bolts to 75 ft. lbs. and the clutch housing cover bolts to 10 ft. lbs. Using new bolts, install and tighten the transaxle mount-to-side frame to 40 ft. lbs. When installing the bolts

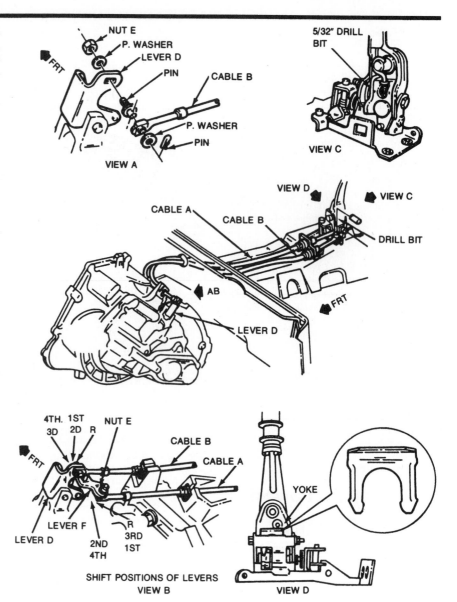

Shift linkage adjustment

attaching the mount-to-transaxle bracket, check the alignment bolt at the engine mount. If excessive effort is required to remove the alignment bolt, realign the powertrain components and tighten the bolts to 40 ft. lbs., and then remove the alignment bolt.

SHIFT LINKAGE ADJUSTMENT

1. Disconnect the negative battery cable.

2. Place the transaxle in first gear, then loosen the shift cable attaching pins at the transaxle levers on the transaxle case.

3. Remove the shifter boot and retainer.

4. Install a No. 22 ($5/32$ in.) drill bit into the alignment hole at the side of the shifter assembly. Install a yoke clip between the shifter tower and carrier.

5. Remove the lash from the transaxle by rotating the upright select lever (lever D) while tightening the cable attaching pin nut.

6. Remove the drill bit and yoke at the shifter assembly, install the shifter boot and retainer and connect the negative battery cable.

7. Road test the vehicle to check for good gate feel during shifting. Fine tune the adjustment as necessary.

Automatic Transaxle

REMOVAL & INSTALLATION

1. Disconnect the negative battery cable where it attaches to the transaxle.

2. Insert a $\frac{1}{4}$ x 2 in. bolt into the hole in the right front motor mount to prevent any mislocation during the transaxle removal.

3. Remove the air cleaner. Disconnect the T.V. cable at the carburetor.

4. Unscrew the bolt securing the T.V. cable to the transaxle. Pull up on the cable cover at the transaxle until the cable can be seen. Disconnect the cable from the transaxle rod.

5. Remove the wiring harness retaining bolt at the top of the transaxle.

6. Remove the hose from the air management valve and then pull the wiring harness up and out of the way.

7. Install an engine support bar as shown in the illustration. Raise the engine just enough to take the pressure off the motor mounts.

—————— **CAUTION** ——————

The engine support bar must be located in the center of the cowl and the bolts must be tightened before attempting to support the engine.

8. Remove the transaxle mount and bracket assembly. It may be necessary to raise the engine slightly to aid in removal.

9. Disconnect the shift control linkage from the transaxle.

10. Remove the top transaxle-to-engine mounting bolts. Loosen, but do not remove, the transaxle-to-engine bolt nearest to the starter.

11. Unlock the steering column.

Raise and support the front of the car. Remove the front wheels.

12. Pull out the cotter pin and loosen the castellated ball joint nut until the ball joint separates from the control arm. Repeat on the other side of the car.

13. Disconnect the stabilizer bar from the left lower control arm.

14. Remove the six bolts that secure the left front suspension support assembly.

15. Connect an axle shaft removal tool (J-28468) to a slide hammer (J-23907).

16. Position the tool behind the axle shaft cones and then pull the cones out and away from the transaxle. Remove the axle shafts and plug the transaxle bores to reduce fluid leakage.

17. Remove the nut that secures the transaxle control cable bracket to the transaxle, then remove the engine-to-transaxle stud.

18. Disconnect the speedometer cable at the transaxle.

19. Disconnect the transaxle strut (stabilizer) at the transaxle.

20. Remove the four retaining screws and remove the torque converter shield.

21. Remove the three bolts securing the torque converter to the flex plate.

22. Disconnect and plug the oil cooler lines at the transaxle. Remove the starter.

23. Remove the screws that hold the brake and fuel line brackets to the left

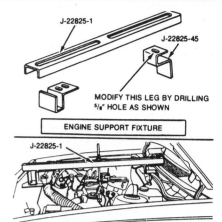

Supporting the engine with a holding bar when removing the automatic transmission

side of the underbody. This will allow the lines to be moved slightly for clearance during transaxle removal.

24. Remove the bolt that was loosened in Step 10.

25. Remove the transaxle to the left. Installation is in the reverse order of removal. Please note the following:

a. Reinstall both axle shafts AFTER the transaxle is in position.

b. When installing the front suspension support assembly you must follow the tightening sequence shown in the illustration.

CHEVETTE

Clutch

All manual transmission models use a cable-operated diaphragm spring-type clutch. The clutch cable is attached to the clutch pedal at its upper end and is threaded at its lower end where it attaches to the clutch fork. The clutch release fork pivots on a ball stud located opposite the clutch cable attaching point. The pressure plate, clutch disc, and throwout bearing are of conventional design.

REMOVAL & INSTALLATION

1. Raise the car on a hoist.
2. Remove the transmission.
3. Remove the throwout bearing from the clutch fork by sliding the fork off the ball stud against spring tension. If the ball stud is to be replaced, remove the locknut and stud from the bellhousing.

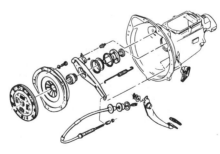

Clutch assembly

4. If the balance marks on the pressure plate and the flywheel are not easily seen, mark them with paint or a centerpunch.

5. Alternately loosen the pressure plate-to-flywheel attaching bolts one turn at a time until spring tension is released.

6. Support the pressure plate and cover assembly, then remove the bolts and the clutch assembly.

—————— **CAUTION** ——————

Do not disassemble the clutch cover and pressure plate for repair. If defective, replace the assembly.

7. Check the pressure plate, clutch plate and flywheel for wear. If the flywheel is scored, worn or discolored from overheating, it should be either refaced or replaced. Replace the clutch plate as necessary.

8. Align the balance marks on the clutch disc on the pressure plate with the long end of the splined hub facing forward and the damper springs inside the pressure plate. Insert a dummy shaft through the cover and clutch disc.

9. Position the assembly against the flywheel and insert the dummy shaft into the pilot bearing in the crankshaft.

10. Align the balance marks and install the pressure plate-to-flywheel bolts finger tight.

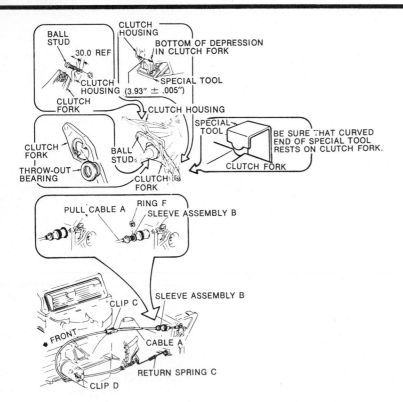

Clutch cable and ball stud adjustment details

─────── **CAUTION** ───────

Tighten all bolts evenly and gradually until tight to avoid possible clutch distortion. Torque the bolts to 18 ft. lbs. (14 ft. lbs. on diesel engine) and remove the dummy shaft.

11. Pack the groove on the inside of the throwout bearing with graphite grease. Also coat the fork groove and ball stud depression with the lubricant.

12. Install the throwout bearing and release fork assembly in the bellhousing with the fork spring hooked under the ball stud and the fork spring fingers inside the bearing groove.

13. Position the transmission and clutch housing and install the clutch housing attaching bolts and lockwashers. Torque the bolts to 25 ft. lbs.

14. Complete the transmission installation.

NOTE: Check the position of the engine in the front mounts and realign as necessary. A special gauge (J-23644) is necessary to adjust ball stud position if it has been removed.

15. Adjust clutch pedal free-play if necessary.

16. Lower the car and check operation of the clutch and transmission.

CLUTCH PEDAL FREE-PLAY ADJUSTMENT

Adjustment is made at the firewall end of the outer clutch cable. Pedal free-play should be ½ to 1 in. at the pedal.

1. Pull the adjusting ring clip from the cable at the firewall.

2. To increase free-play, move the cable into the firewall, one notch at a time, and replace the clip.

3. To decrease free-play, pull the cable out, one notch at a time, and replace the clip.

4. If, after the adjustment, the pedal won't return tight against the bumper, the ball stud will have to be adjusted. Use the special gauge mentioned in the clutch replacement procedure.

Manual Transmission

Chevettes use either a four or five speed fully synchronized transmission. Gear shifting is accomplished by an internal shifter shaft. No adjustment of the shift mechanism is possible.

REMOVAL & INSTALLATION

Gasoline Engine

1. Remove the floor console and the boot retainer.

2. Lift up the boot in order to gain access to the locknut on the shift lever. Loosen the locknut and unscrew the upper portion of the shift lever with the knob attached.

3. Remove the foam insulator.

4. Remove the three bolts on the extension and remove the control assembly.

5. Carefully remove the retaining clip.

6. Remove the locknut, the boot retainer and the seat from the threaded end of the control lever.

7. Remove the spring and the guide from the forked end of the control lever.

8. Raise the car on a hoist and drain the lubricant from the transmission.

9. Remove the driveshaft.

10. Disconnect the speedometer cable and back-up light switch.

11. Disconnect the return spring and clutch cable at the clutch release fork.

12. Remove the crossmember-to-transmission mount bolts.

13. Remove the exhaust manifold nuts and converter-to-tailpipe bolts and nuts. Remove the converter-to-transmission bracket bolts and remove the converter.

14. Remove the crossmember-to-frame bolts and remove the crossmember.

15. Remove the dust cover.

16. Remove the clutch housing-to-engine retaining bolts, slide the transmission and clutch housing to the rear, and remove the transmission.

17. To install, place the transmission in gear, position the transmission and clutch housing, and slide forward. Turn the output shaft to align the input shaft splines with the clutch hub.

18. Install the clutch housing retaining bolts and lockwashers. Torque the bolts to 25 ft. lbs.

19. Install the dust cover.

20. Position the crossmember to the frame and loosely install the retaining bolts. Install the crossmember-to-transmission mounting bolts. Torque the center nuts to 33 ft. lbs.; the end nuts to 21 ft. lbs. Torque the crossmember-to-frame bolts to 40 ft. lbs.

21. Install the exhaust pipe to the manifold and the converter bracket on the transmission.

22. Connect the clutch cable. Adjust clutch pedal free-play.

23. Connect the speedometer cable and back-up light switch.

24. Install the driveshaft.

25. Fill the transmission to the correct level with SAE 80W or SAE 80W–90 GL-5 gear lubricant. Lower the car.

26. Install the shift lever and check operation of the transmission.

Diesel Engine

1. Disconnect the negative battery cable.

2. Unscrew the retaining screws and then remove the shift lever console.

3. Remove the mounting screws and remove the shift lever assembly.

4. Unscrew and remove the upper starter mounting bolts.

5. Raise the front of the car and drain the lubricant from the transmission.

6. Remove the drive shaft as detailed later in this section.

7. Disconnect the speedometer and the back-up light switch wires.

8. Disconnect the return spring and clutch cable at the clutch release fork.

9. Remove the starter lower bolt and support the starter.

10. Unscrew the retaining bolts and disconnect the exhaust pipe from the manifold.

11. Remove the flywheel inspection cover.

12. Unscrew the rear transmission support mounting bolt. Support the transmission underneath the case and then remove the rear support from the frame.

13. Lower the transmission approximately four inches.

14. Remove the transmission housing-to-engine block bolts. Pull the transmission straight back and away from the engine.

15. Installation of the remaining components is in the reverse order of removal. Please note the following:

a. Be sure to lubricate the drive gear shaft with a light coat of grease before installing the transmission.

b. After installation, fill the transmission to the level of the filler hole with 5W-30SF engine oil.

Automatic Transmission

All Chevettes use either the Turbo Hydra-Matic 180 or 200 transmission.

REMOVAL & INSTALLATION

1. Before raising the car, disconnect the negative battery cable and the T.V./detent cable at the bracket and carburetor or pump.

2. Remove the air cleaner and dipstick.

3. On vehicles with air conditioning, remove the heater core cover screws from the heater assembly. Disconnect the wire connector and with hoses attached, place the heater core cover out of the way.

4. Raise vehicle on hoist and remove propeller shaft.

5. Disconnect speedometer cable, electrical lead to case connector and oil cooler pipes.

6. Disconnect shift control linkage.

7. Support transmission with suitable transmission jack and remove the rear transmission support bolts.

8. Remove the nuts holding the converter bracket to the support.

9. Disconnect exhaust pipe at the rear of the catalytic converter.

10. Disconnect exhaust pipe at manifold and remove the exhaust pipe, catalytic converter and converter bracket as an assembly.

11. Remove the torque converter under pan.

12. Remove converter to flexplate bolts.

13. Lower transmission until jack is barely supporting it and remove transmission to engine mounting bolts.

14. Raise transmission to its normal position, then place a block of wood between the rack-and-pinion housing and the engine oil pan, then support engine with jack and slide transmission rearward from engine and lower it away from vehicle.

NOTE: The use of a converter holding tool J-5384 is necessary when lowering the transmission or keep the rear of the transmission lower than the front so not to lose the converter.

15. Installation is the reverse of removal. Before installing the flex plate to converter bolts, make certain that the weld nuts on the converter are flush with the flex plate and the converter rotates freely by hand in this position. Hand start the three bolts and tighten finger tight, then torque to specifications. This will insure proper converter alignment. Install new oil seal on oil filler tube before installing tube.

SPECTRUM

Clutch

REMOVAL & INSTALLATION

1. Refer to the "Manual Transaxle Removal and Installation" procedure in this section and remove the transaxle.

2. Install a pilot shaft tool (J-35282) into the pilot bearing to support the clutch assembly during the removal procedure.

NOTE: Observe the alignment marks on the clutch and the clutch cover and pressure plate assembly. If the markings are not present, be sure to add them.

3. Loosen the clutch cover and pressure plate assembly retaining bolts evenly (one at a time) until the spring pressure is released.

4. Remove the clutch cover and pressure plate assembly and clutch plate.

NOTE: Check the clutch disc, flywheel and pressure plate for wear, damage or heat cracks. Replace all damaged parts.

5. Before installation, lightly lubricate the pilot shaft splines, pilot bearing and pilot release bearing surface with grease.

6. To install, reverse the removal procedure. Tighten the clutch cover and pressure plate evenly (torque to 13 ft. lbs.) to avoid distortion.

Clutch Cable

ADJUSTMENT

1. Disconnect the negative battery cable.

2. Loosen the adjusting nut and pull the cable to the rear until it turns freely.

3. Adjust the cable length by turning the adjusting nut.

4. When the clutch pedal free play travel reaches 0.39–0.79 in. release the cable.

5. When the adjustment has been completed, tighten the lock nut.

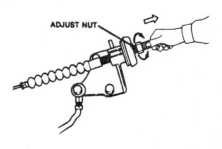

Adjustment of the clutch cable

REMOVAL & INSTALLATION

1. Disconnect the negative battery cable.
2. Loosen the clutch cable adjusting nuts. Disconnect the cable from the release arm and cable bracket.
3. At the clutch pedal, remove the cable retaining bolt.
4. Disconnect the cable from the front of the dash.
5. Remove the clutch cable from the vehicle.
6. To install, grease the clutch cable pin and reverse the removal procedure.
7. Adjust the clutch cable.

Clutch Start Switch

REMOVAL & INSTALLATION

The clutch switch is mounted above the clutch pedal. It is connected to the electrical circuit of the starter motor and operates in accordance to the movement of the clutch pedal. To operate the starter, the clutch pedal must be depressed all the way.

1. Disconnect the negative battery cable.
2. Remove the lead wire at the switch.
3. At the clutch pedal stop bracket, remove the switch mounting screw.
4. Remove the switch from the clutch pedal.
5. To install, reverse the removal procedure.

Clutch Release Bearing

REMOVAL & INSTALLATION

1. Refer to the "Manual Transaxle Removal and Installation" procedure in this section and remove the transaxle.
2. Disconnect the return spring from the shaft fork.
3. Remove the clutch release bearing from the pilot shaft bearing retainer.

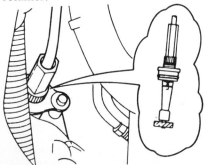

Checking the fluid level of the transaxle

NOTE: Inspect the bearing for wear, damage or rough rotation. DO NOT place the bearing in solvent or damage may occur to the seals.

4. Lightly lubricate the bearing with grease.
5. To install, reverse the removal procedure.

Manual Transaxle

REMOVAL & INSTALLATION

1. Drain the oil from the transaxle.
2. Disconnect the negative battery cable at the battery and the transaxle.
3. Disconnect the wiring connectors, speedometer cable, clutch cable and shift cables from the transaxle.
4. Remove the air cleaner heat tube.
5. Remove the upper transaxle to engine retaining bolts.
6. Raise the vehicle. Remove the left-front wheel assembly and splash shield.
7. Disconnect the left tie rod at the steering knuckle and the left tension rod.
8. Disconnect the drive axles and remove the shafts by pulling them straight out from the transaxle (avoid damaging the oil seals).
9. Remove the dust cover at the clutch housing.
10. Support the transaxle with a floor jack and remove the transaxle-to-engine retaining bolts.
11. While sliding the transaxle away from the engine, carefully lower the jack, guiding the right axle shaft out of the transaxle.

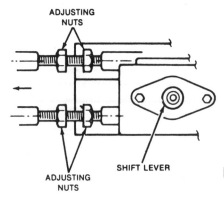

SHIFT AND SELECT CABLE ADJUSTMENT PROCEDURE

1. Place transaxle and shift lever in the neutral position.
2. Turn adjusting nuts until shift lever is in a vertical position.
3. After adjustment, tighten adjusting nuts securely

Adjusting the shift linkage of the transaxle

NOTE: The right axle shaft MUST be installed to the transaxle when the transaxle is being installed to the engine.

12. To install, reverse the removal procedure.

Shift Control Assembly

REMOVAL & INSTALLATION

1. Disconnect the negative battery cable.
2. Remove the shifter boot and console.
3. Disconnect the shift cables at the control assembly.
4. Remove the shift control assembly.
5. To install, reverse the removal procedure.

Shift Cables

REMOVAL & INSTALLATION

1. Disconnect the negative battery cable.
2. Disconnect the retaining clips and the shift cables at the transaxle.
3. Remove the shifter boot and console.
4. Disconnect the shift cables at the control assembly.
5. Pull the carpet back and remove the front left sill plate.
6. Remove the shift cable plate screws.
7. To install, reverse the removal procedure and adjust the shift cables.

Shift Linkage

ADJUSTMENT

1. Loosen the adjusting nuts.
2. Place the transaxle and the shift lever in the Neutral position.
3. Turn the adjusting nuts until the shift lever is in the vertical position.
4. Tighten the adjusting nuts.

Automatic Transaxle

REMOVAL & INSTALLATION

1. Disconnect the negative battery cable.
2. Remove the air duct tube from the air cleaner.
3. At the transaxle, disconnect the shift cable, speedometer cable, vacuum diaphragm hose, engine wiring harness clamp and the ground cable.
4. At the left fender, disconnect the inhibitor switch and the kickdown solenoid wiring connectors.
5. Disconnect the oil cooler lines

from the transaxle.

6. Remove the three upper transaxle-to-engine mounting bolts and raise the vehicle.

7. Remove both front wheels and the left front fender splash shield.

8. Disconnect both tie rod ends at the steering knuckles.

9. Remove both front tension rod brackets and disconnect the rods from the control arms.

10. Disengage the axle shafts from the transaxle.

11. Remove the flywheel dust cover and the converter-to-flywheel attaching bolts.

12. Remove the transaxle rear mount through bolt.

13. Disconnect the starter wiring and the starter. Support the transaxle.

14. Remove the lower transaxle-to-engine mounting bolts and remove the transaxle.

15. To install, reverse the removal procedure, torque the converter-to-flywheel at 30 ft. lbs., transaxle-to-engine at 56 ft. lbs., adjust the shift linkage and fill the transaxle with Dexron® II automatic transmission fluid.

SPRINT

Clutch

REMOVAL & INSTALLATION

1. Refer to the "Manual Transaxle Removal & Installation" procedures in this section and remove the transaxle.

2. Install tool J–34860 into the pilot bearing to support the clutch assembly.

NOTE: Look for the "X" mark or white painted number on the clutch cover and the "X" mark on the flywheel. If there are no markings, mark the clutch cover and the flywheel for reassembly purposes.

3. Loosen the clutch cover-to-flywheel bolts, one turn at a time (evenly) until the spring pressure is released.

4. Remove the clutch cover and clutch disc.

5. Inspect the parts for wear, if necessary, replace the parts.

6. To install, reverse the removal procedures. Torque the clutch cover bolts to 14–20 ft. lbs.

FREE PLAY ADJUSTMENT

1. At the transaxle, move the clutch release arm to check the free play, it should be 0.08–0.16 in.

2. If necessary, turn the clutch cable joint nut to adjust the cable length.

Manual Transaxle

REMOVAL & INSTALLATION

1. Disconnect the negative battery cable and the ground strap at the transaxle.

2. Remove the air cleaner and the air pipe.

3. Remove the clutch cable from the clutch release lever.

4. Remove the starter, the speedometer cable, the electrical wires and

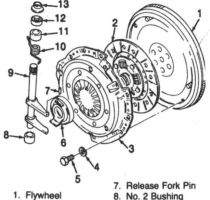

1. Flywheel
2. Disc
3. Clutch Cover
4. Lock Washer
5. Bolt
6. Release Bearing
7. Release Fork Pin
8. No. 2 Bushing
9. Release Shaft
10. Return Spring
11. No. 1 Bushing
12. Shaft Seal
13. Shaft Cover

Exploded view of the clutch assembly

the wiring harness from the transaxle.

5. Remove the front and rear torque rod bolts at the transaxle.

6. Raise and support the vehicle on jackstands.

7. Drain the transaxle fluid.

8. Remove the exhaust pipe at the exhaust manifold and at the 1st exhaust hanger.

9. Remove the clutch housing lower plate.

10. Disconnect the gear shift control shaft and the extension rod at the transaxle.

11. Remove the left front wheel.

12. Using a pry bar, pry on the inboard joints of the right and left hand axle shafts, to detach the axle shafts from the snap rings of the differential side gears.

13. On the left side, remove the stabilizer bar mounting bolts and the ball joint stud bolt. Push down on the stabilizer bar and remove the ball joint stud from the steering knuckle.

14. Pull the left axle shaft out of the transaxle.

15. Remove the front torque rod.

16. Secure and support the transaxle

case with a floor jack.

17. Remove the transaxle-to-body mounting bolts and the mounts.

18. Remove the transaxle-to-engine mounting bolts.

19. Disconnect the transaxle from the engine by sliding it to the left side and lower the jack.

NOTE: When removing the transaxle, support the right axle shaft, so it does not become damaged.

20. To install, guide the right axle shaft into the transaxle and reverse the removal procedures. Torque the transaxle-to-engine bolts to 35 ft. lbs.; the transaxle-to-mount bolts to 34 ft. lbs.; the mounting member bolts to 40 ft. lbs.; the stabilizer bar bolts to 30 ft. lbs. and the ball joint stud bolt to 44 ft. lbs. Adjust the clutch cable and refill the transaxle.

SHIFT LINKAGE ADJUSTMENT

1. At the console, loosen the gear shift control housing nuts and the guide plate bolts.

2. Adjust the guide plate, so that the shift lever is centered and at a right angle to the plate.

3. When the guide plate is positioned correctly, torque the guide plate bolts to 7 ft. lbs. and the housing nuts to 4 ft. lbs.

Automatic Transmission/ Transaxle

REMOVAL & INSTALLATION

1. Disconnect the air suction guide from the air cleaner.

2. Disconnect the negative and the positive battery cables.

3. Remove the battery and the battery bracket tray.

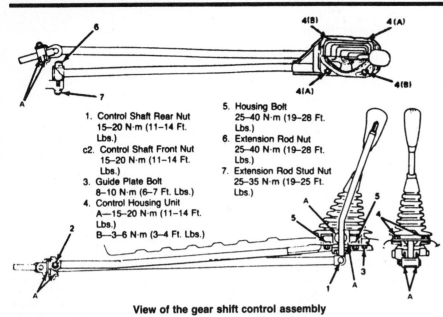

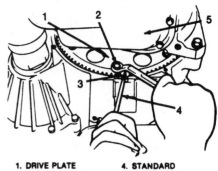

1. DRIVE PLATE   4. STANDARD
2. DRIVE PLATE BOLT   SCREWDRIVER
3. NOTCH   5. ENGINE OIL PAN

Removing drive plate bolts

1. Control Shaft Rear Nut 15–20 N·m (11–14 Ft. Lbs.)
c2. Control Shaft Front Nut 15–20 N·m (11–14 Ft. Lbs.)
3. Guide Plate Bolt 8–10 N·m (6–7 Ft. Lbs.)
4. Control Housing Unit A—15–20 N·m (11–14 Ft. Lbs.) B—3–6 N·m (3–4 Ft. Lbs.)
5. Housing Bolt 25–40 N·m (19–28 Ft. Lbs.)
6. Extension Rod Nut 25–40 N·m (19–28 Ft. Lbs.)
7. Extension Rod Stud Nut 25–35 N·m (19–25 Ft. Lbs.)

View of the gear shift control assembly

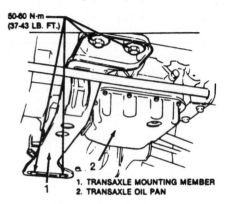

1. TRANSAXLE MOUNTING MEMBER
2. TRANSAXLE OIL PAN

Transaxle mounting member and oil pan

4. Remove the negative cable from the transaxle.

5. Disconnect the solenoid wire coupler and the shift lever switch wire couplers.

6. Remove the wiring harness from the transaxle.

7. Remove the speedometer cable from the transaxle.

8. Disconnect the oil pressure control cable from the accelerator cable, and then the accelerator cable from the transaxle.

9. Remove the select cable from the transaxle.

10. Remove the starter motor.

11. Drain the transaxle fluid.

12. Disconnect the oil outlet and inlet hoses from the oil pipes. After disconnecting, plug the two oil hoses to prevent fluid in the hoses and oil cooler from draining.

13. Raise the vehicle and support it safely.

14. Remove the exhaust No. 1 pipe.

15. Remove the clutch housing lower plate.

16. Remove the six drive plate bolts. To lock the drive plate, engage a screwdriver with the drive plate gear through the notch provided at the under side of the transmission case.

17. Remove the left hand front drive axle. See drive axle section for removal procedures.

18. Detach the inboard joint of the right hand drive axle from the differential.

19. Disconnect the transaxle mounting member.

20. Securely support the transaxle with a suitable jack for removal.

21. Remove the transaxle left mounting.

22. Remove the bolts fastening the engine and the transaxle.

23. Disconnect the transaxle from the engine by sliding towards the left side, and then, carefully lower the jack.

NOTE: When removing the transaxle assembly from the engine, move it in parallel with the crankshaft and use care so as not to apply excessive force to the drive plate and torque converter. After removing the transaxle assembly, be sure to keep it so that the oil pan is at the bottom. If the transaxle is tilted, fluid in it may flow out.

24. To install the transaxle, reverse the removal procedure noting the following important steps.

25. Before installing the transaxle assembly apply grease around the cup at the center of the torque converter.

Then measure the distance between the torque converter flange nut and the transaxle case housing. The distance should be more than 0.85 in. (21.4 mm). If the distance is less than 0.85 in. (21.4 mm), the torque converter has been installed incorrectly and must be removed and reinstalled correctly.

26. When installing the transaxle, guide the right drive axle into the differential side gear as the transaxle is being raised.

27. After inserting the inboard joints of the right hand and left hand drive axles into the differential side gears, push the inboard joints into the side gears until the snap rings on the drive axles engage the side gears.

28. After connecting the oil pressure control cable to the accelerator cable, check the oil pressure control cable play and adjust if necessary.

29. Install the select cable.

30. Refill the transaxle and check the fluid level.

31. Tighten the following bolts and nuts to specifications.

   a. Drive Plate Bolts—14 ft. lbs. (19 Nm).

   b. Mounting Member Bolts—40 ft. lbs. (55 Nm).

   c. Transaxle Mounting Nuts—33 ft. lbs. (45 Nm).

   d. Transaxle Mounting Bolts (8mm)—40 ft. lbs. (55 Nm).

   e. Transaxle Mounting Nuts—40 ft. lbs. (55 Nm).

   f. Stabilizer Shaft Mounting Bolts—31 ft. lbs. (42 Nm).

   g. Ball Stud Bolt—44 ft. lbs. (60 Nm).

   h. Wheel Nuts—40 ft. lbs. (55 Nm).

NOVA

Clutch

REMOVAL & INSTALLATION

NOTE: Do not allow grease or oil to contaminate any of the disc, pressure plate, or flywheel friction surfaces.

1. Remove the transmission from the car as described below.
2. Remove the clutch cover and disc from the bellhousing.
3. Unfasten the clips that retain the release fork bearing, then withdraw the release bearing hub complete with the release bearing.
4. Remove the tension spring from the clutch linkage. Remove the release fork and support.
5. Punch matchmarks on the clutch cover and pressure plate so the pressure plate can be returned to its original position when you reinstall it. This is important to maintain the balance of the flywheel/pressure plate assembly.
6. Loosen the mounting bolts for the pressure plate, turning each only about a half-turn at a time and alternating back and forth across the plate so pressure will be released gradually and evenly all around. If the tension is not released in this way, the tremendous spring pressure behind the plate could be released suddenly and violently! When the spring pressure has been fully released, remove the bolts and remove the pressure plate and clutch disc.
7. To install, insert a clutch alignment tool or an old transmission mainshaft through the clutch disc and then insert the tool or shaft into the pilot bearing. Note that the the disc is installed with the concave side toward the flywheel.
8. Install the pressure plate over the disc with matchmarks aligned and install the bolts, tightening alternately and evenly to apply even pressure all around. Final torque the bolts to 14 ft. lbs. Remove the centering tool or input shaft.
9. The remaining steps of installation are the reverse of the removal procedure, except that you must lubricate the release bearing hub and release fork contact points with a light coating of Multipurpose grease.

FREE-PLAY ADJUSTMENT

1. Check pedal height as measured from the insulating sheet on the floor

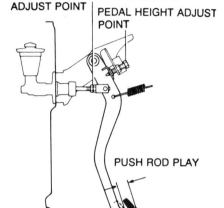

Clutch pedal free play adjustment

to the center of the pedal. It should be 5.65–6.043 in. If height is correct, go to Step 2. If not, remove the instrument lower finish panel and air duct. Then, Loosen the locknut located high and on your side of the pedal lever. Turn the bolt in to decrease or out to increase it until it is within specifications. Tighten the locknut, recheck, and readjust if necessary.

2. Measure the position of the clutch pedal. Now, push in the pedal until you feel increased resistance as the clutch pressure plate springs begin being compressed. Measure the position of the pedal at this point and then subtract the smaller figure from the larger one. This will give the freeplay dimension. The dimension should be 0.51–0.91 in. on cars built before l986, and 0.20–0.59 in. on 1986-87 models. If not, loosen the pushrod locknut, located below the pedal height adjustment locknut and on the cowl side of the pedal lever. Turn the clutch master cylinder pushrod clockwise to decrease the freeplay dimension or counter-clockwise to increase it until the dimension is within specification. Tighten the locknut, recheck, and readjust if necessary.

Manual Transaxle

REMOVAL & INSTALLATION

1. Disconnect the negative battery cable. Drain the cooling system, and

then remove the upper radiator hose.
2. Remove the air cleaner and inlet duct.
3. Disconnect the backup lamp switch connector at the switch on the transaxle. Disconnect the speedometer cable and tie it out of the way.
4. Remove the clip and washers from the select and shift control cables, remove the retainers from the cables, and disconnect the cables.
5. Remove the two mounting bolts and remove the thermostat housing from the top of the transaxle.
6. Raise the vehicle and support it securely by approved points on the body. Disconnect the hydraulic line to the clutch slave cylinder and plug it. Then, remove the two bolts and remove the slave cylinder from the transaxle.
7. Remove the left wheel. Remove all three of the engine covers from underneath. Remove the mounting bolts and the front and rear mounting crossmember.
8. Unbolt and remove the center member to which the engine is mounted.

9. Remove the protective cover and then remove the nuts attaching the right side driveshaft to the transaxle.
10. Disconnect the steering knuckle from the lower control arm as described later in this section. Remove the left side driveshaft attaching nuts. Pull the steering knuckle outward and remove the left side driveshaft from the transaxle. Repeat both procedures on the opposite side.
11. Disconnect the battery cable and ignition switch wire at the starter. Remove the two bolts and remove the starter.
12. Disconnect the ground cable at the transaxle. Unbolt and remove the plate that covers the lower section of the bell housing.
13. Using a wooden block atop a floor jack, raise the engine slightly with pressure on the bottom of the oil pan. Support the transaxle underneath with another floorjack and wooden block. Then, unbolt the left side engine-transmission mount at the body.
14. Remove the transaxle mounting bolts where it attaches to the engine. Then, lower the left side of the engine and remove the transaxle.
15. Installation is the reverse of the removal procedure. When installing the transaxle, make sure the input shaft aligns with the splines in the center of the clutch disc and then position the transaxle against the engine

with bolt holes lined up. Torque the 12mm transmission attaching (bell housing) bolts to 47 ft. lbs. and the 10mm bolts to 34 ft. lbs. Torque the driveshaft attaching nuts/bolts to 27 ft. lbs. Torque the front and rear cross-member and center crossmember mounting bolts to 29 ft. lbs. Torque the left side engine mount bolts to 38 ft. lbs. Make sure to refill the transmission with approved fluid. Refill the cooling system with 50/50 antifreeze-water mix. Make sure to bleed and re-fill the clutch hydraulic system.

Automatic Transaxle

REMOVAL & INSTALLATION

1. Disconnect the negative battery cable.
2. Remove the air cleaner. Disconnect the Throttle Valve cable at the carburetor.
3. Disconnect the neutral safety switch. Disconnect the speedometer cable at the transmission.
4. Disconnect the shift control cable at the transmission.
5. Disconnect the oil cooler lines at the transmission and plug them.
6. Remove the thermostat housing assembly from the top of the transmission.
7. Remove the single upper mount-to-bracket bolt. Remove the two upper bellhousing bolts.
8. Raise and support the vehicle at approved locations on jackstands.

9. Drain the transmission fluid.
10. Remove the left wheel. Remove all three of the engine covers from underneath. Remove the mounting bolts and the front and rear mounting crossmember.
11. Unbolt and remove the center member to which the engine is mounted.
12. Remove the nuts attaching the right side driveshaft to the transaxle. Do the same on the opposite side.
13. Disconnect the steering knuckle from the lower control. Remove the left side driveshaft attaching nuts. Pull the steering knuckle outward and remove the left side driveshaft from the transaxle.
14. Disconnect the battery cable and ignition switch wire at the starter. Remove the two bolts and remove the starter.
15. Unbolt and remove the plate that covers the lower section of the bell housing.
16. Remove the six bolts attaching the torque converter to the drive plate. You'll have to rotate the engine to gain access to one bolt at a time.
17. Using a wooden block atop a floor jack, raise the engine slightly with pressure on the bottom of the oil pan. Support the transaxle underneath with another floorjack and wooden block. Then, unbolt the left side engine-transmission mount at the body.
18. Remove the transaxle mounting bolts where it attaches to the engine. You'll need a guide pin such as a bolt

smaller than the torque converter bolts with the head cut off. Insert the guide pin through one of the accessible torque converter boltholes. Pry on the outer end of the pin to being forcing the transaxle to disengage from the engine. This will ensure that the converter comes off with the transaxle. Then, lower the left side of the engine and remove the transaxle.

19. To install, first apply multipurpose grease to the center of the converter, where it fits inside the crankshaft. Install the guide pin in one of the holes in the converter. Then, align the pin with the corresponding hole in the drive plate. Align the two knock pins in the block with the corresponding holes in the converter housing.
20. Situate the transmission in its installed position. Install one of the converter-to-guide plate bolts. Then install the transmission converter housing-to-engine bolts. Torque the 12mm bolts to 47 ft. lbs. and the 10mm bolts to 34 ft. lbs.
21. Install the left side engine mount and torque the bolts to 38 ft. lbs.
22. Install the torque converter-to-driveplate bolts by rotating the engine and transmission for access. Torque to 20 ft. lbs. Perform the remaining installation steps in reverse of the removal procedure. Torque the driveshaft attaching nuts/bolts to 27 ft. lbs. Torque the front and rear crossmember and center crossmember mounting bolts to 29 ft. lbs. Make sure to refill the transmission with approved fluid.

CORSICA AND BERETTA

Clutch

A hydralic clutch mechanism is used on all vehicles. This mechanism uses a clutch master cylinder with a remote reservoir and a slave cylinder connected to the master cylinder. Whenever the system is disconnected for repair or replacement, the clutch system must be bleed to insure proper operation.

REMOVAL & INSTALLATION

1. Disconnect the negative battery cable. Disconnect the clutch master cylinder push rod from the clutch pedal.
2. Using the correct procedure, remove the transaxle from the vehicle.
3. With the transaxle removed, matchmark the pressure plate and flywheel assembly to insure proper bal-

ance during reassembly.
4. Loosen the pressure plate retaining bolts until the spring pressure is removed.
5. Support the pressure plate and remove the bolts.
6. Remove the pressure plate and disc assembly. Note which side is the flywheel side of the clutch disc.
7. Inspect the clutch assembly, flywheel, release bearing, clutch fork and pivot shaft for signs of wear. Replace any necessary parts.
8. Clean and inspect the flywheel and pressure plate mounting surfaces.
9. To install, position the clutch disc and pressure plate in the appropriate position and support the assembly with alignment tool J–29074 or J–35822, or equivalent.
10. Make sure that the clutch disc is facing the same side it was in when it was removed.
11. If the same pressure plate is be-

ing reused, align the marks made during removal and install the pressure plate retaining bolts and tighten them gradually and evenly.
12. Remove the alignment tool and torque the pressure plate bolts to 15 ft. lbs.
13. Lightly lubricate the clutch fork ends. Fill the recess ends of the release bearing with grease.
14. Lubricate the input shaft with a light coat of grease.
15. Install the transaxle following the correct procedure.

——————— **CAUTION** ———————
The clutch lever must not be moved towards the flywheel until the transaxle is bolted to the engine. Damage to the transaxle, release bearing and clutch fork could occur if this is not followed.

16. Bleed the clutch system and check the clutch operation when finished.

Clutch Master and Slave Cylinder

REMOVAL & INSTALLATION

The clutch master and slave cylinders are removed as an assembly.

1. Disconnect the negative battery cable. On the 2.8 Liter engine remove the air cleaner, mass air flow sensor and air inlet duct.

2. Remove the left side lower trim panel inside the vehicle.

3. Disconnect the clutch master cylinder push rod from the clutch pedal.

4. Remove the mounting nuts that hold the clutch master cylinder to the body at the front of the dash. Remove the remote reservoir mounting screws.

5. Remove the slave cylinder retaining nuts at the transaxle.

6. Remove the clutch master cylinder and slave cylinder as an assembly. Replace the necessary parts and reassemble the system into an assembly.

7. To install, attach the slave cylinder to the transaxle support bracket by aligning the push rod into the pocket on the clutch fork outer lever.

NOTE: Do not remove the plastic push rod retainer from the slave cylinder. The straps are designed to retain the push rod and break during the first application of the clutch pedal.

8. Evenly tighten the slave cylinder retaining nuts and torque them to 14–22 ft. lbs.

9. Install the master cylinder to the front of the dash.

10. Tighten the retaining nuts evenly and torque the nuts to 15–25 ft. lbs.

11. Install the reservoir and mounting screws.

12. Lubricate the push rod bushing on the clutch pedal and install the push rod.

13. Install the left side lower trim panel inside the vehicle.

14. Press the clutch pedal down several times breaking the slave cylinder pushrod plastic retainer.

15. Using the correct procedure, bleed the clutch system.

ADJUSTMENT

No adjustments are possible on the hydralic clutch system. If the clutch is not engaging correctly, bleed and check the system.

BLEEDING THE CLUTCH SYSTEM

1. Remove any dirt or grease around the reservoir cap so that dirt

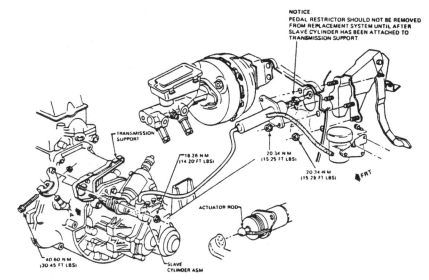

Clutch master and slave cylinder installation

cannot enter the system.

2. Fill the reservoir with an approved DOT 3 brake fluid.

3. Loosen, but do not remove, the bleeder screw on the slave cylinder.

4. Fluid will now flow from the master cylinder to the slave cylinder.

NOTE: It is important that the reservoir remain filled throughout the procedure.

5. Air bubbles should now appear at the bleeder screw.

6. Continue this procedure until a steady stream of fluid without any air bubbles is present.

7. Tighten the bleeder screw. Check the fluid level in the reservoir and fill to the proper mark.

8. The system is now fully bled. Check the clutch operation by starting the engine, pushing the clutch pedal to the floor and placing the transmission in reverse.

9. If any grinding of the gears is noted, repeat the entire procedure.

NOTE: Never under any circumstances reuse fluid that has been in the system. The fluid may be contaminated with dirt and moisture.

Manual Transaxle

REMOVAL & INSTALLATION

NOTE: Engine support fixture J–28467 and adapter J–35953, or equivalent are required for this procedure.

—————— CAUTION ——————

Before performing any maintenance that requires the removal of the slave cylinder, transaxle or clutch housing, the clutch mas-ter cylinder push rod must first be disconnected from the clutch pedal. Failure to disconnect the push rod will result in permanent damage to the slave cylinder if the clutch pedal is depressed with the slave cylinder disconnected.

1. Disconnect the negative battery cable.

2. Install the engine support fixture and adapter. Raise the engine enough to take the engine weight off of the engine mounts.

3. From inside the vehicle, remove the left side sound insulator.

4. Disconnect the clutch master cylinder push rod from the clutch pedal.

5. Remove the air cleaner and duct assembly.

6. Disconnect the clutch slave cylinder from the transaxle support and position it out of the way.

7. Remove the transaxle thru bolt.

8. Raise and safely support the vehicle.

9. Remove the two (2) exhaust crossover bolts at the right side manifold on the 2.8 Liter engine.

10. Lower the vehicle. Remove the left side exhaust manifold on the 2.8 Liter engine.

11. Disconnect the transaxle mounting bracket.

12. Disconnect the shifter cables.

13. Remove the upper transaxle to engine mounting bolts.

14. Raise and safely support the vehicle.

15. Remove the left front wheel and tire. Remove the left side inner splash shield.

16. Remove the transaxle strut and bracket.

17. Drain the transaxle.

18. Remove the clutch housing cover bolts.

19. Disconnect the speedometer wire.

20. Disconnect the stabalizer shaft at the left control arm.

21. Remove the left suspension support mounting bolts and move the support out of the way.

22. Disconnect both halfshafts at the transaxle. Remove the left side shaft from the vehicle.

23. Support the transaxle with a suitable jack.

24. Remove the remaining transaxle to engine mounting bolts.

25. Remove the transaxle from the vehicle by sliding it away from the engine and removing the right side halfshaft while the transaxle is being lowered.

26. Installation is the reverse of the removal. When installing, guide the right side halfshaft into the transaxle while it is being installed in the vehicle. Observe the following torques during installation: Transaxle to engine bolts, 60 ft. lbs.; Transaxle mount to body mounting bolt, 80 ft. lbs.; Transaxle strut bolts 50 ft. lbs.; Slave cylinder to transaxle nuts, 14–20 ft. lbs.; Shifter cable attaching nuts, 90 inch lbs.

——————— CAUTION ———————

During installation, the clutch lever must not be moved towards the flywheel until the transaxle is bolted to the engine. Damage to the transaxle, clutch fork and release bearing could occur if this is not followed.

LINKAGE ADJUSTMENT

No adjustments are possible on the manual transaxle shifting cables or linkage. If the transaxle is not engaging completely, check for stretched cables or broken shifter components or a faulty transaxle.

Automatic Transaxle

REMOVAL & INSTALLATION

An engine support fixture J–28467 and adapter J35953, or equivalents are required for this procedure.

1. Disconnect the negative battery cable. On the 2.0 Liter engine, remove the air cleaner and air intake assembly. On the 2.8 Liter engine, remove the air cleaner, bracket, mass air flow sensor and air tube as an assembly.

2. On the 2.8 Liter engine, disconnect the exhaust crossover at the right side manifold and remove the left side exhaust manifold.

3. Disconnect the T.V. cable at the throttle lever and at the transaxle.

4. Remove the fluid level indicator and the filler tube.

5. Install the engine support fixture with the adapter on the engine.

6. Remove the nut that holds the wiring harness to the transaxle.

7. Disconnect and tag the wires for the speed sensor, TCC connector and the neutral safety/backup light switch.

8. Disconnect the shift linkage from the transaxle.

9. Remove the top two (2) transaxle to engine mounting bolts.

10. Disconnect the rubber hose that runs from the transaxle to the vent pipe.

11. Raise and safely support the vehicle.

12. Remove the front wheels and tires.

13. Disconnect the shift linkage and bracket from the transaxle.

14. Remove the left side splash shield.

15. Using care not to damage the halfshaft boots, disconnect the halfshafts from the transaxle.

16. Remove the transaxle strut. Remove the left side stabalizer link pin bolt.

17. Remove the left frame support bolts and move it out of the way.

18. Disconnect the speedometer wire from the transaxle.

19. Remove the transaxle converter cover and matchmark the converter to the flywheel for assembly.

20. Disconnect and plug the transaxle cooler pipes.

21. Remove the transaxle to engine support.

22. Properly position a jack under the transaxle and remove the remaining transaxle to engine bolts.

23. Make sure that the torque converter does not fall out and remove the transaxle from the vehicle.

NOTE: The transaxle cooler and lines should be flushed any time the transaxle is removed for overhaul, or to replace the pump, case or converter.

24. To install, put a small amount of grease on the pilot hub of the converter and make sure that the converter is properly engaged with the pump.

25. Raise the transaxle to the engine while guiding the right side halfshaft into the transaxle.

26. Install the lower transaxle mounting bolts and remove the jack.

27. Align the converter with the marks made previously on the flywheel and install the bolts hand tight.

28. Torque the converter bolts to 46 ft. lbs. Retorque the first bolt after the others. Torque the transaxle to engine bolts to 55 ft. lbs.

29. The remainder of the installation is the reverse of the removal. Check the fluid level when finished.

LIGHT TRUCKS AND VANS
BLAZER/JIMMY – FULL SIZE, BLAZER/JIMMY – S-SERIES
PICK-UPS – FULL SIZE, PICK-UPS – S-SERIES, SUBURBAN,

Clutch Linkage

ADJUSTMENT

Except S-Series

This adjustment is for the amount of clutch pedal free travel before the throwout bearing contacts the clutch release fingers. It is required periodically to compensate for clutch lining wear. Incorrect adjustment will cause gear grinding and clutch slippage or wear.

NOTE: If you have a problem with grinding when shifting into gear, shorten the pedal stop bumper to $\frac{3}{8}$ in. and readjust the linkage.

1. Disconnect the clutch fork return spring at the fork on the clutch housing.

2. Loosen the outer adjusting nut (A) and back it off approximately $\frac{1}{2}$ in. from the swivel.

3. Hold the clutch fork pushrod against the fork to move the throwout bearing against the clutch fingers. The pushrod will slide through the swivel at the cross-shaft.

4. Adjust the inner adjusting nut (B) to obtain $\frac{1}{4}$ in. clearance between nut (B) and the swivel.

5. Release the pushrod, connect the return spring and tighten the outer nut (A) to lock the swivel against the inner nut (B).

6. Check the free travel at the pedal and readjust as necessary. It should be $1\frac{1}{4}$–$1\frac{1}{2}$ in.

Clutch

REMOVAL & INSTALLATION

Except S-Series

There are two types of clutch pressure plates used, diaphragm and coil spring. In general, the larger heavy duty clutches are usually of the coil spring pressure plate type. Most removal and installation details are similar for both types.

DIAPHRAGM TYPE

1. Remove the transmission.
2. Disconnect the fork pushrod and remove the flywheel housing. Remove the clutch throwout bearing from the fork.
3. Remove the clutch fork by pressing it away from the ball mounting with a screwdriver until the fork snaps loose from the ball or remove the ball stud from the clutch housing.
4. Install a pilot tool (an old mainshaft makes a good pilot tool) to hold the clutch while you are removing it.

NOTE: Before removing the clutch from the flywheel, matchmark the flywheel, the clutch cover and one of the pressure plate lugs. These parts must be reassembled in their original positions as they are a balanced assembly.

5. Loosen the clutch attaching bolts one turn at a time to prevent distortion of the clutch cover until the tension is released.
6. Remove the clutch pilot tool and the clutch from the vehicle. Inspect the flywheel and pressure plate for discoloration, scoring or wear marks. The

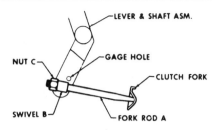

Clutch linkage adjustment

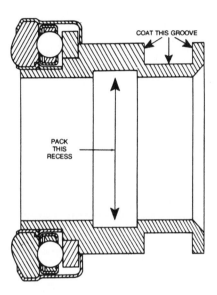

Throwout bearing lube points

flywheel can be refaced if necessary, otherwise replace the parts. Also inspect the clutch fork and throwout bearing for looseness or wear. Replace if either is evident.

7. Install the pressure plate in the cover assembly, aligning the notch in the pressure plate with the notch in the cover flange.
8. Install the pressure plate retracting springs, lockwashers and the drive strap to the pressure plate bolts. Torque to 11 ft. lbs.
9. Turn the flywheel until the X mark is at the bottom.
10. Install the clutch disc, pressure plate and cover using an old mainshaft as an aligning tool.
11. Turn the clutch until the X mark on the clutch cover aligns with the X mark on the flywheel.
12. Install the attaching bolts and tighten them a little at a time in a crisscross pattern until the spring pressure is taken up.
13. Remove the aligning tool.
14. Pack the clutch ball fork seat with a small amount of high temperature grease. Too much grease will cause slippage. Install a new retainer in the groove of the clutch fork, if necessary. Install the retainer with the high side up and the open end on the horizontal.
15. If the clutch fork ball was removed, reinstall it in the clutch housing and snap the clutch fork onto the ball.
16. Lubricate the inside of the throwout bearing collar and the throwout fork groove with a small amount of graphite grease.
17. Install the throwout bearing.
18. Install the flywheel housing and transmission.
19. Further installation is the reverse of removal. Adjust the clutch linkage.

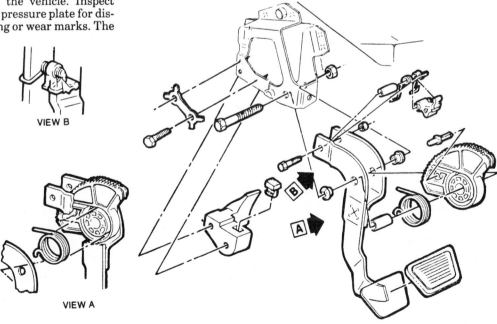

S–Series self-adjusting clutch mechanism

7 DRIVE TRAIN

COIL SPRING TYPE

Basically, the same procedures apply to diaphragm clutch removal as to coil spring clutch removal.

When loosening the clutch holding bolts, loosen them only a turn or two at a time in order to avoid bending the rim of the cover. It will be helpful to place wood or metal spacers, about 3/8 in. thick, between the clutch levers and the cover to hold the levers down as the holding bolts are being removed or when the clutch is being removed from the engine.

S-Series Truck

ADJUSTMENT

1. Lift up on the pedal to allow the self adjuster to adjust the cable length.
2. Depress the pedal several times to set the pawl into mesh with the detent teeth.
3. Check the linkage for lost motion caused by loose or worn swivels, mounting brackets or a damaged cable.

REMOVAL & INSTALLATION

1. Remove the transmission.
2. Remove the flywheel housing.
3. Remove the clutch fork.
4. Insert a clutch alignment tool in the clutch hub and into the crankshaft pilot bearing.
5. Check for an X or other painted mark on the pressure plate and flywheel. If there isn't any mark, mark the assembly for installation purposes.
6. Loosen the pressure plate bolts, evenly and alternately, a little at a time until spring tension is released. Remove the pressure plate and drive plate.
7. Check the flywheel for cracks, wear, scoring or other damage. Check the pilot bearing for wear. Replace it by yanking it out with a slide hammer and driving in a new one with a wood or plastic hammer.
8. Installation is the reverse of removal. Use the alignment tool to aid installation. The raised hub of the driven plate faces the transmission. Align the mating marks and tighten the bolts evenly and alternately to 20 ft. lbs.

Manual Transmission

REMOVAL & INSTALLATION

2WD—Except Vans and S-Series

1. Raise the vehicle and support on jackstands.
2. Drain the transmission.
3. Disconnect the speedometer cable, TCS switch and back-up lamp wire at the transmission.
4. Disconnect the shift control levers or shift control from the transmission. On 4 speeds, remove the gearshift lever by pressing down firmly on the slotted collar plate with a pair of channel lock pliers and rotating counterclockwise. Plug the opening to keep out dirt.
5. Disconnect the parking brake lever and controls (if used).
6. Remove the driveshaft after marking the position of shaft to flange.
7. Position a jack under the transmission to support the weight of the transmission.
8. Remove the crossmember. Visually inspect to see if other equipment, brackets or lines, must be removed to permit removal of transmission.

NOTE: Mark the position of the crossmember when removing to prevent incorrect installation. The tapered surface should face the rear.

9. Remove the flywheel housing underpan.
10. Remove the top two transmission-to-housing bolts and insert two guide pins. The use of guide pins will not only support the transmission but will prevent damage to the clutch disc. Guide pins can be made by taking two bolts, the same as those just removed, only longer, and cutting off the heads. Slot them for a screwdriver. Be sure to support the clutch release bearing and support assembly during removal of the transmission. This will prevent the release bearing from falling out of the flywheel housing.
11. Remove the two remaining bolts and slide transmission straight back from engine. Use care to keep the transmission drive gear straight in line with clutch disc hub. Be sure to support release bearing when removing transmission to avoid having bearing fall into flywheel housing.
12. When the transmission is free from the engine, move from under the vehicle.
13. To install the transmission: Place the transmission on guide pins, slide forward starting the main drive gear into the clutch disc's splines. Place the transmission in gear and rotate transmission flange or output yoke to aid the entry of the main drive gear into the disc's splines. Make sure the clutch release bearing is in position.

CAUTION
Avoid springing the clutch when the transmission is being installed on the engine. Do not force the transmission into the clutch disc hub. Do not let the transmission hang unsupported in the splined portion of the clutch disc.

14. Install the two lower transmission mounting bolts, and flywheel lower pan (if equipped).
15. Remove the guide pins and install upper mounting bolts. Torque to 75 ft. lbs.
16. Install the driveshaft, watch alignment marks. Install the crossmember according to the alignment marks.
17. Connect the parking brake, back-up lamp and TCS switch (if used).
18. Connect the shift levers, or install the shifter, and adjust if needed.
19. Connect the speedometer cable and refill transmission.
20. Lower the vehicle and road test.

Vans—Except Astro

1. Raise and support the van.
2. Drain the transmission. The Tremec top-cover transmission is drained by removing the lower case to extension housing bolt.
3. Disconnect the speedometer cable, back-up light and TCS switch.
4. Remove the shift controls from the transmission.
5. Disconnect the driveshaft and remove it from the vehicle.
6. Support the transmission with a floor jack.
7. Inspect the transmission to be sure that all necessary components have been removed or disconnected.
8. Mark the front of the crossmember to be sure that it is installed correctly.
9. Support the clutch release bearing to prevent it from falling out of the flywheel housing when the transmission is removed.
10. Remove the flywheel housing under pan and transmission mounting bolts.
11. Move the transmission slowly away from the engine, keeping the mainshaft in alignment with the clutch disc hub. Be sure that the transmission is supported.
12. Remove the transmission from under the vehicle.
13. Installation is the reverse of removal. Lightly coat the mainshaft with high temperature grease. Do not use much grease, since, under normal operation, the grease will be thrown onto the clutch, causing it to fail.
14. Tighten the transmission to flywheel housing bolts to 75 ft. lbs. Fill the transmission with lubricant. Road test the vehicle.

Astro

1. Raise and support the vehicle and drain the transmission fluid. Disconnect and remove the driveshaft as described later in this section. Plug the opening at the rear of the transmission with a clean rag.

2. Disconnect the speedometer cable. Mark and then disconnect all electrical connectors at the transmission.

3. Disconnect the shift linkage at the shifter. Then, remove the shifter support attaching bolts the transmission.

4. Remove the transmission mount attaching bolts.

5. Support the transmission in a secure manner from below. Then, remove the crossmember attaching bolts. Remove the crossmember from the vehicle.

6. Finally remove the transmisson attaching bolts and remove the transmission from the vehicle.

7. To install, reverse the removal procedure, noting the following points:

   a. Apply a light coating of high temperature grease fo both the main drive gear bearing retainer and the splined portion of the transmission drive shaft. This is important to ensure free sliding of clutch and transmission parts during assembly.

   b. Observe these torque specifications: Transmission-to-clutch housing bolts 48 ft. lbs.; Crossmember to body bolts 35 ft. lbs.; Mount-to-crossmember bolts 25 ft. lbs.; Mount-to-transmission bolts 45 ft. lbs. Make sure to adjust the shift linkage and refill the transmission to the proper level with approved fluid.

4WD – Except S-Series

3 SPEED

1. Jack up the vehicle and support it safely on stands. Remove the skid plate, if any.

2. Drain the transmission and transfer case. Remove the speedometer cable and the TCS switch from the side of the transmission.

3. Disconnect the driveshafts and secure them out of the way.

4. Remove the shifter lever by removing the pivot bolt to the adapter assembly. You can then push the shifter up out of the way.

5. Remove the bolts attaching the strut to the right side of the transfer case and to the rear of the engine, and remove the strut.

6. While supporting the transfer case securely, remove the attaching bolts to the adapter.

7. Remove the transfer case securing bolts from the frame and lower and remove the transfer case. (The case is attached to the right side of the frame.)

8. Disconnect the shift rods from the transmission.

9. While holding the rear of the engine with a jack, remove the adapter mounting bolts.

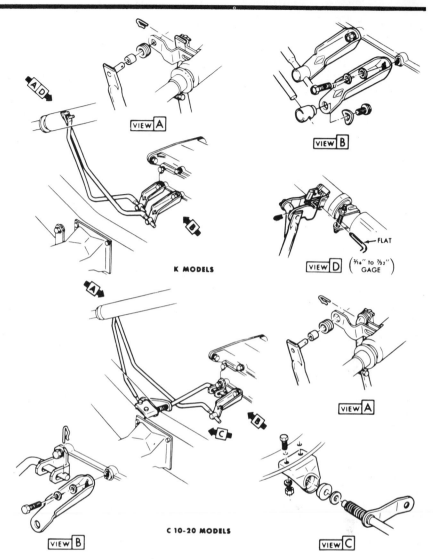

Three speed column shift controls, except vans

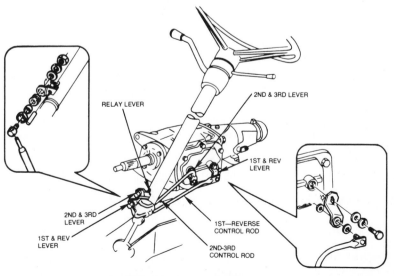

Van 3-speed column shift details

10. Remove the upper transmission bolts and insert two guide pins to keep the assembly aligned. See the two wheel drive procedure (Step 10) for details on making these.

11. Remove the flywheel pan and the lower transmission bolts.

12. Pull the transmission and the adapter straight back on the guide pins until the input shaft is free of the clutch disc.

13. The transmission and the adapter are removed as an assembly. The adapter can be separated once the assembly is out.

14. Installation is the reverse of removal. Place the transmission in gear and turn the output shaft to align the clutch splines. Transmission bolt torque is 75 ft. lbs. See Transfer Case Removal and Installation for adapter bolt torques.

4 SPEED

1. Remove the shifter boots and the floor mat or carpeting from the front passenger compartment.

2. Remove the transmission shift lever. See Step 4 of the two wheel drive procedure for details on removing the lever. It may be necessary to remove the center floor outlet from the heater to complete the next step. Remove the center console, if so equipped.

3. Remove the transmission cover after releasing the attaching screws. It will be necessary to rotate the cover 90° to clear the transfer case shift lever.

4. Disconnect the transfer case shift lever link assembly and the lever from the adapter. Remove the skid plate, if any.

5. Remove the back-up light, the TCS switch, and the speedometer cable from the side of the transmission.

6. Raise and support the truck. Support the engine. Drain the transmission and the transfer case. Detach the transmission and the transfer case. Detach both driveshafts and secure them out of the way.

7. Remove the transmission-to-frame bolts. To do this, it will be necessary to open the locking tabs. Remove the transfer case-to-frame bracket bolts.

8. While supporting the transmission and transfer case, remove the crossmember bolts and the crossmember. It will be necessary to rotate the crossmember to remove it from the frame.

9. Remove the lower clutch housing cover.

NOTE: On V8 engines it is necessary to remove the exhaust crossover pipe.

10. Remove the transmission-to-clutch housing bolts. Remove the upper bolts first and install guide pins. See Step 10 of the two wheel drive procedure for details.

11. Slide the transmission back until the main drive gear clears the clutch assembly and then lower the unit.

12. Install the transfer case on the transmission as an assembly. Attach the assembly to the clutch housing. Put the transmission in gear and turn the output shaft to align the clutch splines. Torque the transmission bolts to 75 ft. lbs.

13. Install the clutch housing cover and, on V8 models, the exhaust pipe.

14. Install the frame crossmember, the retaining adapter, and the transfer case.

15. The front and rear transfer case yoke locknuts must be torqued to 150 ft. lbs.

16. Install the front and rear driveshafts.

17. Connect the speedometer cable, backup lights, and TCS switches.

18. Fill the transmission and the transfer case to the proper level.

19. Position the transfer case shift lever and the shift lever link on the shift rail bar.

20. Install the transmission floor cover and the center heating duct.

21. Install the center console, if so equipped.

22. Install the transmission shift lever.

S-Series Trucks

4 SPEED — 77.5mm

NOTE: On 4WD models, see Transfer Case Removal and Installation

1. Disconnect the battery ground.

2. Remove the upper starter retaining nut.

3. Remove the shift lever boot attaching screws and slide the boot up the shift lever.

4. Disconnect the shift lever at the transmission.

5. Disconnect the electrical connector at the transmission.

6. Raise and support the truck on jackstands.

7. Remove the driveshaft.

8. Disconnect the exhaust pipe at the manifold.

9. Disconnect the exhaust pipe at the manifold.

10. Disconnect the clutch cable at the transmission.

11. Place a floor jack under the transmission to take up its weight.

12. Remove the transmission mount bolts.

13. Remove the catalytic converter hanger.

14. Remove the crossmember.

15. Remove the lower dust cover bolts.

16. Remove the lower starter bolt.

17. Unbolt the transmission from the engine and lower it on the jack.

18. Installation is the reverse of removal. Torque the transmission-to-engine bolts to 25 ft. lbs. on the 4 cylinder and 55 ft. lbs. on the 6 cylinder. Torque the transmission mount-to-transmission bolts to 35 ft. lbs.; the crossmember-to-frame bolts to 25 ft. lbs.; the dust cover bolts to 7 ft. lbs.

4 SPEED — 77mm
5 SPEED — 77mm

NOTE: On 4WD models, see Transfer Case Removal and Installation

1. Disconnect the battery ground.

2. Remove the shift lever boot screws and slide the boot up the lever.

3. Shift the transmission into neutral and remove the shift lever.

4. Raise and support the truck on jackstands.

5. Remove the driveshaft.

6. Disconnect the speedometer cable and wiring at the transmission.

7. Disconnect the clutch cable at the transmission.

8. Place a floor jack under the transmission and take up its weight. Remove the transmission mount bolts.

9. Remove the catalytic converter hanger.

10. Remove the crossmember.

11. Remove the dust cover bolts.

12. Unbolt the transmission from the bell housing and lower the jack. It will be necessary to pull the transmission back a ways to clear the clutch. Installation is the reverse of removal. Lightly grease the input shaft splines with chassis lube. Torque the transmission mount bolts to 35 ft. lbs.; the mount-to-crossmember bolts to 25 ft. lbs.; the crossmember-to-frame bolts to 25 ft. lbs; the transmission-to-bell housing bolts to 55 ft. lbs.

Linkage

ADJUSTMENTS

Except Vans and S-Series
3 SPEED COLUMN SHIFT

1. Place a column lever in the neutral position.

2. Under the truck, loosen the shift rod clamps. These are at the transmission end.

3. Make sure that the two levers on the transmission are in their center, neutral positions.

4. Install a $\frac{3}{16}$–$\frac{7}{32}$ in. pin or drill bit through the alignment holes in the levers at the bottom of the steering col-

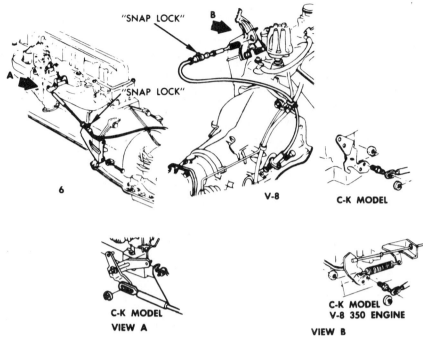

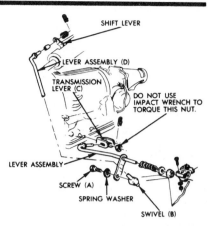

Automatic transmission shift linkage adjustment—except vans

Detent cable adjustment—except diesel

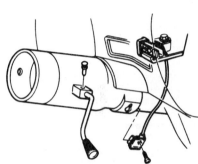

The adjustment point for the transmission shift position indicator is accessible after removing the lower column cover

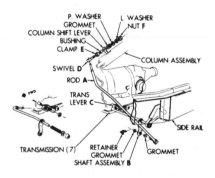

Typical van shift linkage adjustment

umn. This holds these levers in the neutral position.

5. Tighten the shift rod clamps.

6. Remove the pin and check the shifting operation.

Vans

The gearshift linkage should be adjusted each time it is disturbed or removed.

1. Install the control rods to both of the levers and set both shifter levers in the Neutral position.

2. Align both shifter tube levers on the mast jacket in Neutral. Install a $3/16$–$7/16$ in. gauge to hold them in place. The gauge is inserted in the holes of the levers.

3. Connect the control rods to the tube levers, making sure that the clamps and tube levers are properly positioned in Neutral.

4. Remove the gauge and move the gearshift lever through all positions to be sure that the adjustment is correct in all positions.

S-Series Trucks

NOTE: No linkage adjustments are necessary on these vehicles.

Automatic Transmission

ADJUSTMENTS

Shift Linkage
EXCEPT VANS AND S-SERIES

1. The shift tube and lever assembly must be free in the mast jacket.

2. Lift the selector lever toward the steering wheel and allow the selector lever to be positioned in Dive by the detent. Do not use the selector lever pointer as a reference.

3. Release the selector lever. The lever should not be able to go into Low unless the lever is lifted. A properly adjusted linkage will prevent the lever from moving beyond both the Neutral and Drive detents unless the lever is lifted.

6. If adjustment is required, remove the screw (A) and spring washer from the swivel clamp (B).

7. Set the transmission lever (C) in Neutral by moving it to L_1 and then three detents clockwise.

8. Put the transmission selector lever in Neutral as determined by the mechanical stop in the steering column. Do not use the indicator pointer as a reference. The pointer is the last thing to be adjusted.

9. Assemble the swivel spring and washer to the lever (D) and tighten.

10. Readjust the Neutral safety switch if necessary.

11. To adjust the shift position indicator, remove the column cover at the bottom of the instrument panel and loosen the screw to move the pointer.

12. Check the operation. With the switch in RUN, and the transmission in Reverse, be sure that the key cannot be removed and that the steering wheel is locked. With the key in LOCK and the shift lever in PARK, be sure

that the key can be removed, the steering wheel is locked, and that the transmission remains in PARK when the steering column is locked.

VANS

CAUTION

Any inaccuracies in this procedure may lead to premature transmission failure due to operation without the controls in the full detent position. Such operation will result in reduced oil pressure, and therefore only partial engagement of the drive clutches. Partial engagement of the clutches with sufficient pressure to cause apparent normal operation will result in transmission failure after only a few miles of operation.

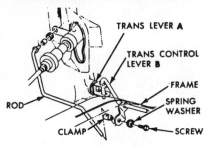

Transmission linkage adjustment

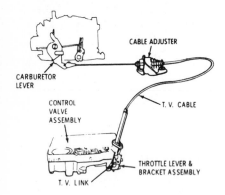

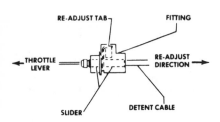

Throttle valve cable adjustment point

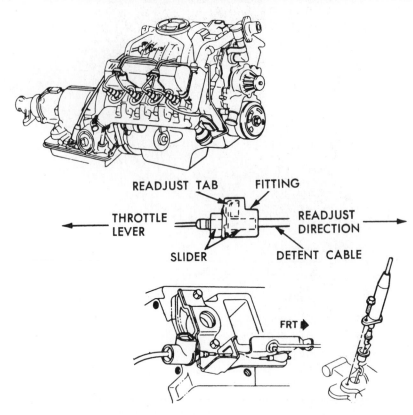

Throttle valve/detent cable adjustment—diesel

1. Remove the nut (F) and slide off the washers, grommet, bushings, and clamp (E). Remove the swivel (D).

2. Remove the retainer, grommets and the transmission lever (C) from the shaft assembly.

3. Set the transmission lever (C) in the Neutral position either by moving the lever (C) counterclockwise to the L_1 position, then clockwise three steps to the Neutral position, or by moving the lever (C) clockwise to the Park position, then counterclockwise two steps to the Neutral position.

4. Set the column shift lever in the Neutral position by rotating the shift lever until it locks into the stop in the column. Do not use the gear select pointer as a reference to position the column shift lever.

5. Attach rod (A) to the shaft assembly (B) as shown.

6. Slide the swivel (D) and the clamp (E) onto rod (A). Align the column shift lever and loosely attach the assembly.

7. Hold the column shift lever against the Neutral stop, on the Park position side.

8. Tighten the nut (F) to 18 ft. lbs.

9. Adjust the indicator needle if necessary. It may also be necessary to adjust the neutral start switch.

Throttle Valve

SIX CYLINDER ENGINES

1. With the accelerator depressed, the bellcrank on the engine must be the wide-open throttle position.

2. The dash lever must be $\frac{1}{64}-\frac{1}{16}$ in. off the lever stop and the transmission lever must be against the transmission internal stop.

V8 ENGINES

1. Remove the air cleaner.

2. Disconnect the accelerator linkage at the carburetor.

3. Disconnect the accelerator return spring and the throttle valve rod return springs.

4. Pull the throttle valve rod forward until the transmission is through the detent. Open the carburetor to the wide-open throttle position. The carburetor must reach the wide-open throttle position at the same time that the ball stud contacts the end of the slot in the upper throttle valve rod.

5. Adjust the swivel on the end of the upper throttle valve rod as per Step 4. The allowable tolerance is approximately $\frac{1}{32}$ in.

6. Connect and adjust the accelerator linkage.

7. Check for freedom of operation. Install the air cleaner.

Neutral Start Switch

This switch prevents the engine from being started unless the transmission is in Neutral or Park. It is located on the shift linkage on the left side of the transmission. The switch is also used for the backup lights.

NOTE: The manual transmission backup light switch is on the rear of the transmission.

1. Loosen the switch mounting screws.

2. Make sure the transmission is in Neutral.

3. Insert a pin through the hole in the switch actuating arm into the switch body to hold the switch in the Neutral position. Adjust as necessary to make the pin fit.

4. Tighten the adjustment. Remove the pin.

5. Check that the engine can be started only in Park and Neutral and that the backup lights go on only in Reverse. Adjust as necessary.

Downshift

TURBO HYDRAMATIC 350

This cable runs from the carburetor linkage to the transmission. It regulates the throttle position at which a downshift occurs. With the snap-lock disengaged from the bracket, position the carburetor at the wide open throttle position. Push the snap-lock downward until the top is flush with the rest of the cable.

TURBO HYDRAMATIC 400 and 700R4

When installing a new downshift switch, press the plunger as far forward as possible. The switch will adjust itself the first time the accelerator oi floorboarded.

S-SERIES

Shift Linkage

With the selector lever in Park, the parking pawl should engage and immobilize the transmission. The pointer on the indicator quadrant should line up properly with the indicated gear position in all ranges. To adjust the linkage, raise an support the truck on jackstands. Place the selector in Park. Loosen the locknut on the linkage arm at the transmission and make sure that the transmission lever is fully in the Park position. Tighten the locknut.

Throttle Valve

1. With the engine off, depress the readjusting tab.
2. Move the slider back through the fitting in the direction away from the throttle body until the slider stops against the fitting. Release the adjusting tab.
3. Open the carburetor throttle plate to the wide open position. This will automatically adjust the cable. Release the throttle plate.

REMOVAL & INSTALLATION

NOTE: It would be best to drain the transmission before starting. It may be necessary to disconnect and remove the exhaust crossover pipe on V8s, and to disconnect the catalytic converter and remove its support bracket, on models so equipped.

2WD

1. Disconnect the battery ground cable. Disconnect the detent cable at the carburetor.
2. Raise and support the truck.
3. Remove the driveshaft, after matchmarking its flanges.
4. Disconnect the speedometer cable, downshift cable, vacuum modulator line, shift linkage, and fluid cooler lines at the transmission. Remove the filler tube. On the Astro only, remove the transmission support brace bolts

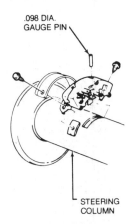

.098 DIA. GAUGE PIN

STEERING COLUMN

Neutral start switch adjustment

at the converter cover; and disconnect the exhaust crossover pipe at the exhaust manifolds.
5. Support the transmission and unbolt the rear mount from the crossmember. On the Astro, raise the transmission very slightly. Remove the crossmember. On the Astro, slide the crossmember rearward and then remove it.
6. Remove the torque converter underpan, matchmark the flywheel and converter, and remove the converter bolts.
7. Support the engine and lower the transmission slightly for access to the upper transmission to engine bolts.
8. Remove the transmission to engine bolts and pull the transmission back. Rig up a strap or keep the front of the transmission up so the converter doesn't fall out.
9. Reverse the procedure for installation. Bolt the transmission to the engine first. Torque to 30 ft. lbs. except on the Astro. On the Astro, torque these bolts to 35 ft. lbs on the V6 and 60 ft. lbs on the inline four., then the converter to the flywheel (35 ft. lbs.). Make sure that the converter attaching lugs are flush and that the converter can turn freely before installing the bolts. Tighten the bolts finger tight, then torque to specification, to ensure proper converter alignment. If the oil filler tube has been removed, install a new seal.

NOTE: Lubricate the internal yoke splines at the transmission end of the driveshaft with lithium base grease. The grease should seep out through the vent hole.

4WD

1. Disconnect the battery ground cable and remove the transmission dipstick. Detach the downshift cable at the carburetor. Remove the transfer case shift lever knob and boot.

2. Raise an support the truck.
3. Remove the skid plate, if any. Remove the flywheel cover.
4. Matchmark the flywheel and torque converter, remove the bolts, and secure the converter so it doesn't fall out of the transmission.
5. Detach the shift linkage, speedometer cable, vacuum modulator line downshift cable, and cooler lines at the transmission. Remove the filler tube.
6. Remove the exhaust crossover pipe to manifold bolts.
7. Unbolt the transfercase adapter from the crossmember. Support the transmission and transfer case. Remove the crossmember.
8. Move the exhaust system aside. Detach the driveshafts after matchmarking their flanges. Disconnect the parking brake cable.
9. Unbolt the transfer case from the frame bracket. Support the engine. Unbolt the transmission from the engine, pull the assembly back and remove.
10. Reverse the procedure for installation. both the transmission to the engine first (30 ft.lbs), then the converter to the flywheel (34 ft. lbs.). Make sure that the converter attaching lugs are flush and that the converter can turn freely before installing the bolts. See Transfer Case Removal and Installation for adapter bolt torques.

Pan & Filter

REMOVAL & INSTALLATION

Except S-Series

1. Jack up your truck and support it with jackstands.
2. Loosen the pan bolts on the transmission.
3. Remove all pan bolts except for 2 or 3 at one corner.
4. Gently tap the pan using a rubber mallet and drain the oil into an appropriate container.
5. Remove the pan and remove the filter. Clean the pan with a lint free rag.
6. Install a new filter and pan gasket.
7. Add new transmission fluid to the proper level. Start your truck and check for leaks.

S-Series Trucks

NOTE: On 4WD models, see Transfer Case Removal and Installation

1. Remove the air cleaner assembly.
2. Disconnect the throttle valve cable at the carburetor.
3. On the 4–119 engine, remove the upper starter bolt.

4. Raise and support the truck on jackstands.

5. Remove the driveshaft.

6. Disconnect the speedometer cable, linkage and wiring at the transmission.

7. Remove any other components attached to the transmission case.

8. Remove the exhaust system from the truck.

9. Remove the torque converter cover and match-mark the converter and flywheel.

10. Remove the converter-to-flywheel bolts.

11. Place a floor jack under the transmission to take up its weight.

12. Unbolt the transmission from its mounts. Unbolt and remove the mounts.

13. Lower the transmission slightly to gain access to the fluid cooler lines. Disconnect and cap these lines.

14. Disconnect the throttle valve cable.

15. Place a jack or jackstands under the engine for support.

16. Unbolt the transmission from the engine.

17. Pull the transmission rearward to disengage it and lower it from the truck.

NOTE: Take care to avoid dropping the converter.

18. Installation is the reverse of removal. Match up the mating marks on the converter. Torque the transmission-to-engine bolts to 25 ft. lbs. on 4 cylinder models and 5 ft. lbs. on the 6 cylinder; torque the converter-to-flywheel bolts to 35 ft. lbs.; torque the transmission-to-mount bolts to 35 ft. lbs.; the mount-to-frame bolts to 25 ft. lbs.

Transfer Case

There are three transfer cases used. The New Process 205 is used in part time systems with all transmissions in 1980. It has a large New Process emblem on the back of the case. The full time New Process 203 is used with automatics through 1979. It can be identified by the H LOC and L LOC positions on the shifter.

The aluminum case New Process 208 was introduced in 1981 on K10 and 20 models. S–Series trucks use the New Process 207. This unit is an aluminum case model with chain drive. Proper fluid for this unit is Dexron© II automatic transmission fluid.

NOTE: Models with a New Process 203 full time four wheel drive transfer case, especially with manual transmissions, may give a front wheel "chatter" or vibra- tion on sharp turns. This is a normal characteristic of this drivetrain combination. If it occurs shortly after shifting out of a LOC position, the transfer case is probably still locked up. This should correct itself after about a mile of driving, or can be alleviated by backing up for a short distance.

CAUTION
Owners of full time four wheel drive trucks (New Process 203 transfer case) often consider either removing the front driveshaft, or installing locking front hubs and operating in a LOC position, as a means of improving gas mileage. This practice will submit the transfer case to stresses beyond its designed limits and will void all warranties. Use of any lubricant additive in the transfer case is also not recommended.

ADJUSTMENT

Shift Linkage
NEW PROCESS 203

1. Place the selector lever in the cab in the Neutral position.

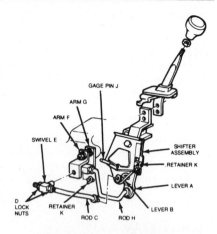

NP 203 linkage adjustment

2. Detach the adjustable rod ends from the transfer case levers.

3. Insert a $^{11}/_{64}$ in. drill bit through the alignment holes in the shifter levers. This will lock the shifter in the neutral position with bolt levers vertical.

4. Place the range shift lever (the outer lever) on the transfer case in the Neutral position.

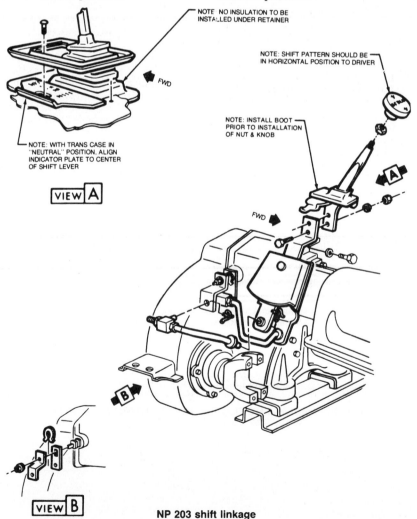

NP 203 shift linkage

5. Place the lockout shift lever (the inner lever) on the transfer case in the unlocked position. Both levers should now be vertical.

6. Adjust the rods so that the linkage fits together. The indicator plate can be moved to align with the correct symbol.

7. Remove the drill bit.

NEW PROCESS 208

1. Put transfer case lever in 4HI detent.

2. Push lower shifter lever forward to 4HI stop.

3. Install rod swivel in shift lever hole.

4. Hang 0.200 thick gauge cover rod behind swivel.

5. Run rear rod nut A against gauge with shifter against 4HI stop.

6. Remove gauge and push swivel rearward against nut A.

7. Run front rod nut B against swivel and tighten.

NEW PROCESS 207

1. Loosen the transfer case switch bolt and the case shift lever pivot bolts.

2. Shift the transfer case to the 4H position.

3. Remove the console and slide the boot up the lever.

4. Install a 5/16 in. drill bit through the shifter and into the switch bracket.

5. Install a bolt at the case lever to lock it in position.

6. Tighten the switch bracket bolt to 30 ft. lbs. and the shifter pivot bolt to 100 ft. lbs.

7. Remove the bolt you installed to lock the lever.

8. Remove the drill bit. Check the drill bit. Check the linkage action.

REMOVAL & INSTALLATION

NP 203 and 205

1. Raise and support the truck.

2. Drain the transfer case.

3. Disconnect the speedometer cable, back-up light switch, and the TCS switch.

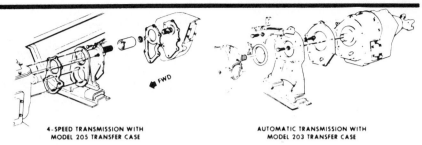

4-SPEED TRANSMISSION WITH MODEL 205 TRANSFER CASE

AUTOMATIC TRANSMISSION WITH MODEL 203 TRANSFER CASE

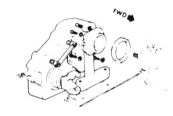

AUTOMATIC TRANSMISSION WITH MODEL 205 TRANSFER CASE

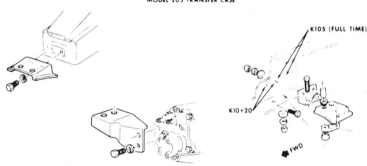

SUPPORT AND BRACKET ASSEMBLY (ALL MODELS)

Typical transfer case installation

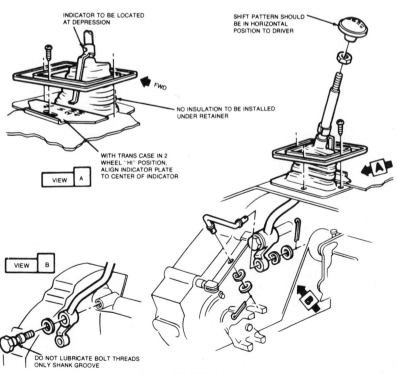

NP 205 linkage

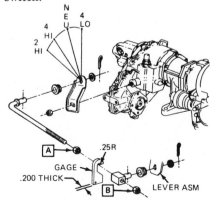

NP 208 linkage adjustment

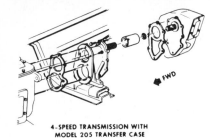

4-SPEED TRANSMISSION WITH
MODEL 205 TRANSFER CASE

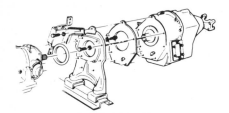

AUTOMATIC TRANSMISSION WITH
MODEL 203 TRANSFER CASE

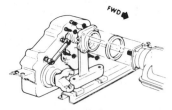

AUTOMATIC TRANSMISSION WITH
MODEL 205 TRANSFER CASE

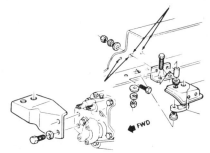

SUPPORT AND BRACKET ASSEMBLY (ALL MODELS)

Transfer case adapters

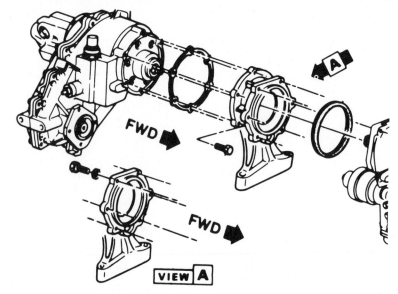

VIEW A

WITH AUTOMATIC TRANSMISSION

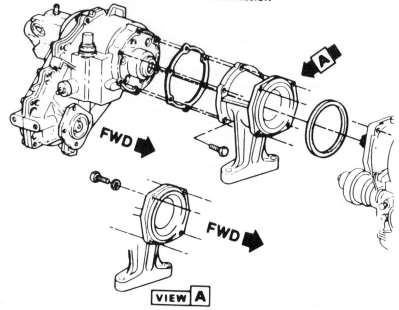

VIEW A

WITH MANUAL TRANSMISSION

NP 208 installation

4. If necessary, remove the skid plate and crossmember support.

5. Disconnect the front and rear driveshafts and support them out of the way. On New Process 205 models, disconnect the shift lever rod from the shift rail link. On New Process 203 models, disconnect the shift levers at the transfer case.

6. Remove the transfer case-to-frame mounting bolts.

7. Support the transfer case and remove the bolts attaching the transfer case to transmission adapter.

8. Move the transfer case to the rear until the input shaft clears the adaptor and lower the transfer case from the truck.

9. To install the transfer case: Lifting the transfer case on a transmission jack, attach the case to the adapter us-

ing through bolts. Torque to specification.

10. Remove the transmission jack and install the transfer case-to-frame rail bolts. Make certain to bend the locking tabs after installation.

11. Connect the shift linkage.

12. Connect the front driveshaft to the front transfer case output shaft and the rear drive shaft to the rear output shaft.

13. Install the crossmember and skid plate, if equipped.

14. Connect the speedometer cable, back-up light, and TCS switches.

15. Fill the transfer case to the proper level with lubricant.

16. Lower the vehicle.

NOTE: Recheck all bolt torques. When attaching the driveshafts, make sure that the flange locknuts are torqued to specifications.

NP 207

1. Shift transfer case into 4 Hi.

2. Disconnect negative cable at battery.

3. Raise vehicle and remove skid plate.

4. Drain lubricant from output shaft yoke and propeller shaft for assembly reference. Disconnect front propeller shaft from transfer case.

5. Mark transfer case front output

Adapter to Transfer Case Bolt Torque

Model	Year	Torque (ft. lbs.)
NP 205	'75–'82	25
NP 203	'75–'79	38

Adapter to Transmission Bolt Torque

Model	Torque (ft. lbs.)
NP 205	22 manual
	35 automatic
NP 203	40

Adapter to Frame Bolt Torque

Model	Torque (ft. lbs.)
NP 205	130
NP 203 (bracket to frame)	50 upper
	65 lower

shaft yoke and propeller shaft for assembly reference. Disconnect the front propeller shaft from transfer case.

6. Mark rear axle yoke and propeller shaft for assembly reference. Remove rear propeller shaft.

7. Disconnect speedometer cable and vacuum harness at transfer case. Remove shift lever from transfer case.

8. Remove catalytic converter hanger bolts at converter.

9. Raise transmission and transfer case and remove transmission mount attaching bolts. Remove mount and catalytic converter hanger and lower transmission and transfer case.

10. Support transfer case and remove transfer case attaching bolts. On vehicles equipped with an automatic transmission, it will be necessary to remove the shift lever bracket mounting bolts from the transfer case adapter in order to remove the upper left transfer case attaching bolt.

11. Separate transfer case from adapter (auto) or extension housing (man.) and remove from vehicle.

12. Position new gasket on the transfer case.

13. Install transfer case, aligning splines of input shaft with transmission and slide transfer case forward until seated against transmission.

14. Install transfer case attaching bolts and torque to specifications. On vehicles equipped with automatic transmission, reinstall shift lever bracket bolts.

15. Raise transmission and transfer case and install mount and hanger bracket. Install attaching bolts and torque to specifications.

16. Install catalytic converter hanger bolts at converter and torque to specification.

17. Attach shift lever at transfer case. Connect speedometer cable and vacuum harness at transfer case.

18. Connect the front and install the rear propeller shaft. Be sure to align reference marks made during removal.

19. Fill transfer case with Dexron II.

20. Install skid plate and lower vehicle.

21. Connect negative cable at battery.

22. Road test vehicle, check to make sure vehicle shifts and operates into all ranges.

NP 208

1. Place the transfer case in 4H.
2. Raise the vehicle.
3. Drain the lubricant from the transfer case.
4. Remove the cotter pin from the shift lever swivel.
5. Mark the transfer case front and rear output shaft yokes and propeller shafts for assembly alignment reference.
6. Disconnect the speedometer cable and indicator switch wires.
7. Disconnect the front propeller shaft at the transfer case yoke.

8. Disconnect the parking brake cable guide from the pivot located on right from rail, if necessary.

9. Remove the engine strut rod from the transfer case on automatic transmission models.

10. Place a support under the transfer case and remove the transfer case-to-transmission adapter bolts.

11. Move the transfer case assembly rearward until free of the transmission output shaft and remove the assembly.

12. Remove all gasket material from the rear of the transmission adapter housing.

13. Install the transmission-to-transfer case gasket on the transmission.

14. Shift the transfer case to 4H position if not done previously.

15. Rotate the transfer case output shaft (by turning yoke) until the transmission output shaft gear engages the transfer case input shaft. Move the transfer case forward until the case seats against the transmission. Be sure the transfer case is flush against the transmission. Severe damage to the transfer case will result if the attaching bolts are tightened while the transfer case is cocked or in a bind.

16. Install the transfer case attaching bolts. Tighten the bolts to 30 ft. lbs.

17. Connect the speedometer driven gear to the transfer case.

18. Connect the front and rear propeller shafts to the transfer case. Be sure to align the shafts-to-yokes using the reference marks made during removal. Tighten the shaft-to-yoke clamp strap nuts to 15 ft. lbs.

19. Remove the support stand from under the transfer case.

20. Connect the parking brake cable if disconnected.

21. Attach the cotter pin to the shift lever swivel.

22. Connect the engine strut to the transfer case on automatic models.

23. Fill the transfer case with Dexron® II.

24. Lower the vehicle.

ft. lbs.; the ball joint stud bolt to 44 ft. lbs. and the axle shaft nut to 144 ft. lbs.

Rear Axle/Axle Shaft

REMOVAL & INSTALLATION

1. Refer to the "Hub and Bearing Removal & Installation" procedures in this section and remove the brake drums.

2. Remove the brake line at the flex hose and the brake line retainers. Plug the brake line and tube to prevent fluid loss.

3. Remove the backing plate nuts and the backing plates.

4. Remove the U-bolt nuts, the U bolts and the jounce stops.

5. Remove the rear axle.

6. To install, align the axle with the pin on top of the spring, tighten the U-bolts (so that the threaded ends are equally exposed) and reverse the removal procedures. Torque the U-bolts to 22–32 ft. lbs. and the backing plate nuts to 13–20 ft. lbs.

NOTE: When installing the backing plate, apply watertight sealant to the joint seam of the backing plate and the axle.

Hub And Bearing

REMOVAL & INSTALLATION

1. Raise and support the rear of the vehicle on jackstands.

2. Remove the wheel assembly.

3. Remove the dust cap, the cotter pin, the castle nut and the washer.

4. Loosen the adjusting nuts of the parking brake cable.

5. Remove the plug from the rear of the backing plate. Insert a screwdriver through the hole, making contact with the shoe hold down spring, then push the spring to release the parking brake shoe lever.

6. Using a slide hammer tool J–2619–01 and a brake drum remover tool J–34866, pull the brake drum from the axle shaft.

7. Using a brass drift and a hammer, drive the rear wheel bearings from the brake drum.

NOTE: When installing the wheel bearings, face the sealed sides (numbered sides) outward. Fill the wheel bearing cavity with bearing grease.

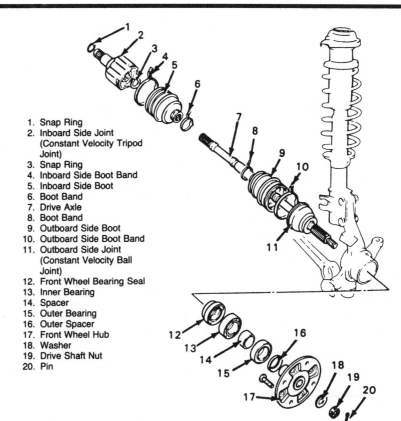

1. Snap Ring
2. Inboard Side Joint (Constant Velocity Tripod Joint)
3. Snap Ring
4. Inboard Side Boot Band
5. Inboard Side Boot
6. Boot Band
7. Drive Axle
8. Boot Band
9. Outboard Side Boot
10. Outboard Side Boot Band
11. Outboard Side Joint (Constant Velocity Ball Joint)
12. Front Wheel Bearing Seal
13. Inner Bearing
14. Spacer
15. Outer Bearing
16. Outer Spacer
17. Front Wheel Hub
18. Washer
19. Drive Shaft Nut
20. Pin

Exploded view of the axle shaft

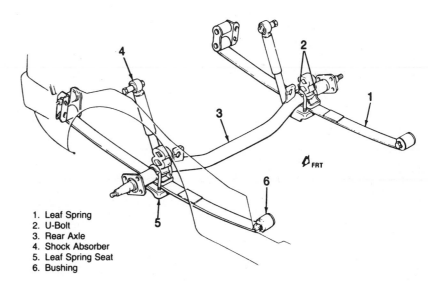

1. Leaf Spring
2. U-Bolt
3. Rear Axle
4. Shock Absorber
5. Leaf Spring Seat
6. Bushing

Rear axle assembly

8. Drive the new bearings into the brake drum with the bearing installation tool J–34482.

9. To install, use a new seal and reverse the removal procedures. Torque the hub castle nut to 58–86 ft. lbs. Bleed the rear brake system. Operate the brakes 3–5 times to obtain the proper drum-to-shoe clearance. Adjust the parking brake cable.

NOVA

Axle Shaft

REMOVAL & INSTALLATION

1. Raise and support the vehicle securely and remove the front wheels. Remove the cotter pin, locknut cap, and bearing locknut.

2. Loosen and remove the six nuts fastening the driveshaft to the flange at the transaxle. Have someone depress the brake pedal to keep the shaft from turning as you loosen the nuts.

3. Remove the bolt and two nuts and disconnect the steering knuckle at the lower control arm.

4. Remove the brake caliper as described later in this section and suspend it with wire without disconnecting the hydraulic line. Remove the disc brake rotor.

5. Cover the outboard CV-joint rubber boot with a cloth to prevent damage. Then, using a two-jawed puller, pull the axle hub from the driveshaft. Remove the driveshaft.

6. To install, first insert the outboard joint into the axle hub; then connect the shaft at the inboard side and install the nuts finger tight.

7. Connect the steering knuckle to the lower arm, torquing nuts/bolt to 47 ft. lbs.

8. Install the brake disc to the axle hub.

9. Install the brake caliper to the steering knuckle, torquing the bolts to 65 ft. lbs.

10. Install the bearing locknut; have someone depress the brake pedal while you torque it to 137 ft. lbs.

11. Torque the six nuts fastening the inboard end of the driveshaft at the transaxle (have someone depress the brake pedal while you do this), torquing to 27 ft. lbs.

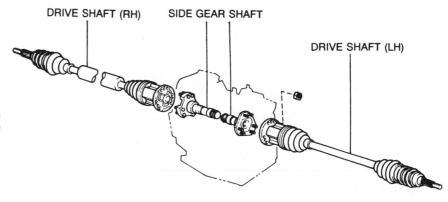

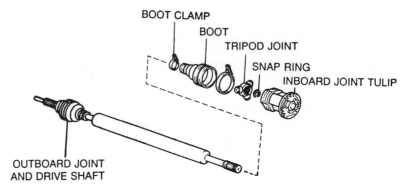

Drive axle assembly

Rear Axle Hub

REMOVAL & INSTALLATION

1. Raise and support the vehicle in a secure manner and remove the rear wheels. Remove the rear brake drum.

2. Disconnect the brake line at the rear of the backing plate and plug the open end of the line.

3. Remove the four bolts holding the axle hub to the axle carrier, using the holes in the axle flange to gain access. Remove the axle hub and rear brake assembly. Remove the O-ring.

4. Install a new O-ring onto the axle carrier.

5. Perform the remaining steps in reverse order. Torque the axle hub and rear brake assembly mounting bolts to 59 ft. lbs. Refill the brake master cylinder with new, approved fluid and bleed the system.

CORSICA AND BERETTA

Halfshaft

REMOVAL & INSTALLATION

The inner joint on the right side halfshaft uses a male spline that lock on the transaxle gears. The left side halfshaft uses a female spline that is installed over the stub shaft on the transaxle.

1. With the weight of the vehicle on the tires, loosen the hub nut.

2. Raise and safely support the vehicle.

3. Remove the hub nut.

4. Install boot protectors on the boots.

5. Remove the brake caliper with the line attached and safely support it out of the way. Do not allow the caliper to hang from the line.

6. Remove the brake rotor and caliper mounting bracket.

7. Remove the strut to steering knuckle bolts. Pull the steering knuckle out of the strut bracket.

8. Using halfshaft removal tool J–33008 and extention J–29794, or equivalent, remove the halfshafts

from the transaxle and support them safely.

9. Using a spindle remover tool J–28733, or equivalent, remove the halfshaft from the hub and bearing.

10. To install, loosely place the halfshaft on the transaxle and in the hub and bearing.

11. Properly position the steering knuckle to the strut bracket and install the bolt. Torque the bolts to 133 ft. lbs.

12. Install the brake rotor, caliper bracket and caliper. Place a holding device in the rotor to prevent it from turning.

13. Install the hub nut and washer. Torque the nut to 71 ft. lbs.

14. Seat the halfshafts into the transaxle using a screwdriver on the groove on the inner retainer.

15. Verify that the shafts are seated by grasping the CV joint and pulling outwards. DO NOT grasp the shaft. If the snap ring is seated, the halfshaft will remain in place.

16. The remainder of the installation is the reverse of the removal.

17. When the vehicle is lowered with the weight on the wheels, apply a final torque of 191 ft. lbs. to hub nut.

Front Wheel Drive Hub, Knuckle and Bearing

REMOVAL & INSTALLATION

The hub and bearing are replaced as an assembly only.

1. With the vehicle weight on the tires, loosen the hub nut.

2. Raise and safely support the ve-

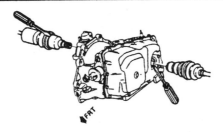

Removing halfshafts from transaxle-automatic shown-manual similar

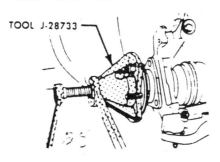

Removing halfshaft from steering knuckle bearing

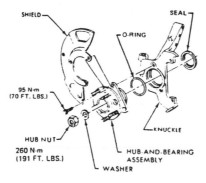

Hub, knuckle and bearing-exploded view

hicle. Remove the wheel and tire.

3. Install a boot cover over the outer CV joint boot.

4. Remove the hub nut. Remove the brake caliper and support it out of the way. DO NOT allow the caliper to hang on the brake line.

5. Remove the three (3) hub and bearing mounting bolts.

6. Remove the brake rotor splash shield.

7. Install hub puller J–28733, or equivalent and pull the hub and bearing off the halfshaft.

8. Disconnect the stabalizer link at the lower control arm.

9. Using a proper tool, separate the ball joint.

10. Remove the halfshaft from the knuckle and support it out of the way.

11. Remove the inner knuckle seal using a brass drift.

12. Clean the steering knuckle bore and the bearing mating surfaces.

13. Install a new O-ring between the bearing and knuckle assembly.

14. Install the hub and bearing assembly and torque the nuts to 90 ft. lbs.

15. Using a seal driver, install a new knuckle seal and lubricate the seal and the area between the seal and the bearing with a high temperature wheel bearing grease.

16. Reconnect the lower ball joint.

17. Install the hub and bearing nut and washer on the halfshaft and torque the nut to 71 ft. lbs.

18. Install the brake rotor and caliper. Install the wheel and tire.

19. Lower the vehicle and torque the hub nut to 191 ft. lbs.

LIGHT TRUCKS AND VANS

Front Driveshaft (4WD Only)

REMOVAL & INSTALLATION

1. Jack the front of the vehicle so that the front wheels are off the ground. Block the rear wheels and safely support the truck on stands.

2. Scribe aligning marks on the driveshaft and the pinion flange to aid in reassembly.

3. Remove the U-bolts or straps at the axle end of the shaft. Compress the shaft slightly and tape the bearings into place to avoid losing them.

4. Remove the U-bolts or straps at

the transfer case end of the shaft. Tape the bearings into place.

5. Remove the driveshaft.

6. Reverse the procedure for installation. Make certain that the marks made earlier line up correctly to prevent possible imbalances. Be sure that the constant velocity joint (the big double one) is at the transfer case end.

Rear Driveshaft

REMOVAL & INSTALLATION

1. Raise and safely support the rear of the truck as necessary. There is less chance of lubricant leakage from the

rear of the transmission on two wheel drive models if the rear is raised. block the front wheels.

2. Scribe alignment marks on the driveshaft and flange of the rear axle., and transfer case or transmission. If the truck is equipped with a two piece driveshaft, be certain to also scribe marks at the center joint near the splined connection. When reinstalling driveshafts, it is necessary to place the shafts into the same position from which they were removed. This is called phasing. Failure to reinstall the driveshaft properly will cause driveline vibrations and reduced component lift.

3. Disconnect the rear universal

joint by removing U-bolts or straps. Tape the bearings into place to avoid losing them.

4. If there are U-bolts or straps at the front end of the shaft, remove them. Tape the bearings into place. For trucks with two piece shafts, remove the bolts retaining the bearing support to the frame crossmember. Compress the shaft slightly and remove it. All four wheel drive trucks are of this type.

5. If there are no fasteners at the front end of the transmission, there will only be a splined fitting. Slide the shaft forward slightly to disengage the axle flange, lower the rear end of the shaft, then pull it back out of the transmission. Most two wheel drive trucks are of this type. For trucks with two piece driveshafts, remove the bolts retaining the bearing support to the from crossmember.

6. Reverse the procedure for installation. It may be tricky to get the scribed alignment marks to match up on trucks with two piece driveshaft.

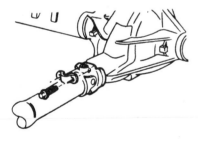

Rear driveshaft U-bolt attachment

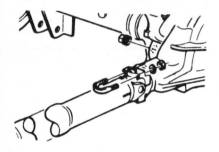

Rear driveshaft strap attachment

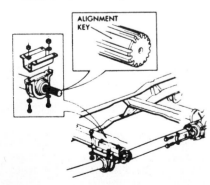

32 splined shaft U-joint alignment keyway

For those models only, the following instructions may be of some help. First, slide the grease cap and gasket onto the rear splines. On 4-wheel drive models with 16 splines, after installing the front shaft to the transmission and bolting the support to the crossmember, arrange the front trunnion vertically and the second trunion horizontally. Most models with 32 splines have an alignment key. The driveshaft cannot be replaced incorrectly. Simply match up the key with the keyway.

7. On 2WD automatic transmission models, lubricate the internal yoke splines at the transmission end of the shaft with lithium base grease. The grease should seep out through the vent hole.

NOTE: A thump in the rear driveshaft sometimes occurs when releasing the brakes after braking to a stop, especially on a downgrade. this is most common with automatic transmission. It is often caused by the driveshaft splines binding and can be cured by removing the driveshaft, inspecting the splines for rough edges, and carefully lubricating. A similar thump may be caused by the clutch plates in Positraction limited slip rear axles binding. If this isn't caused by wear, it can be cured by draining and refilling the rear axle with the special lubricant and adding Positraction additive, both of which are from dealers.

UNIVERSAL JOINT ATTACHMENT TORQUE SPECIFICATIONS

Strap attachments	15 ft. lbs.
U-bolt attachments	20 ft. lbs.

```
BEARING
RETAINER

BEARING CUP

ROUND PLASTIC
WASHER

ROLLER
BEARINGS

SEAL                    FLAT PLASTIC
                        WASHER


CROSS
```

Injection molded retainer U-joint repair kit

DRIVESHAFT ATTACHMENT TORQUE SPECIFICATIONS

To rear axle (strap)	12–17 ft. lbs.
To rear axle (U-bolt)	18–22 ft. lbs.
Bearing support to hanger	20–30 ft. lbs.
Hanger to frame	40–50 ft. lbs.
To transfer case	70–80 ft. lbs.

Locking Hub

REMOVAL & INSTALLATION

NOTE: Locking hubs may not be used with full time four wheel drive. Locking hubs should be run in the lock position for at least 10 miles each month to assure proper differential lubrication. This procedure requires snap-ring pliers and a special hub nut wrench. It isn't very easy without them. You will have to modify this procedure if you have non-factory installed hubs.

1. Set the hub in the Lock position.
2. Remove the outer retaining plate allen head bolts and take off the plate, O-ring, and knob.
3. Take out the large snap-ring inside the hub and remove the outer clutch retaining ring and actuating cam body.
4. Relieve pressure on the axle shaft snap-ring and remove it.
5. Take out the axle shaft sleeve and clutch ring assembly and the inner clutch ring and bushing assembly. Remove the spring and retainer plate.
6. Clean all the hub components in a safe solvent and dry them. Lubricate everything with a high temperature grease.
7. Install the spring retainer plate with the flange side to the bearing and seat it against the outer bearing cup.
8. Install the spring with the large end against the retainer plate.

NOTE: When the spring is properly installed and seated it will extend past the spindle nuts about $7/8$ in.

9. Place the inner clutch ring and bushing assembly into the axle shaft sleeve and clutch ring assembly. Install these components, push in, and install the axle shaft snap-ring. If there are two axle shaft snap ring grooves, use the inner one.

NOTE: You can install a $7/16$ in. bolt in the axle and pull outward on it to aid in seating the snap-ring.

10. Install the actuating cam body with the cams out. Replace the outer

clutch retaining ring and then the internal snap-ring.

11. Install a new O-ring, then install the actuating knob and retaining plate in the lock position. The grooves in the knob must fit into the actuator cam body. Install the cover bolts and seals.

Front Axle Shaft

REMOVAL & INSTALLATION

NOTE: This procedure requires snapring pliers and a special hub nut wrench. It is very difficult without them.

1. Remove the wheel and tire.
2. For K10 or K1500 models and K20 or K2500 models with locking front hubs: Lock the hubs. Remove the outer retaining plate Allen head bolts and take off the plate, O-ring, and knob. Take out the large snap-ring inside the hub and remove the outer clutch retaining ring and actuating cam body. This is a lot easier with snap-ring pliers. Relieve pressure on the axle shaft snap-ring and remove it. Take out the axle shaft sleeve and clutch ring assembly and the inner clutch ring and bushing assembly. Remove the spring and retainer plate.

NOTE: You will have to modify this procedure for either of the models mentioned above if you have non-factory installed locking hubs.

3. If you don't have locking front hubs, remove the hub cap and snapring. Next, remove the drive gear and pressure spring. To prevent the spring from popping out, place a hand over the drive gear and use a screwdriver to pry the gear out. Remove the spring.
4. Remove the wheel bearing outer lock nut, lock ring, and wheel bearing inner adjusting nut. A special wrench is required.
5. Remove the brake disc assembly and outer wheel bearing. Remove the spring retainer plate if you don't have locking hubs. Pull out the axle shaft and universal assembly. When installing the shaft, turn it slowly to mesh with splines.
6. Remove the oil seal and inner bearing cone from the hub using a brass drift and hammer. Discard the oil seal. Use the drift to remove the inner and outer bearing cups.
7. Check the condition of the spindle bearing. If you have drum brakes, remove the grease retainer, gasket, and backing plate after removing the bolts. Unbolt the spindle and tap it with a soft hammer to break it loose. remove the spindle and check the condition of the thrust washer, replacing

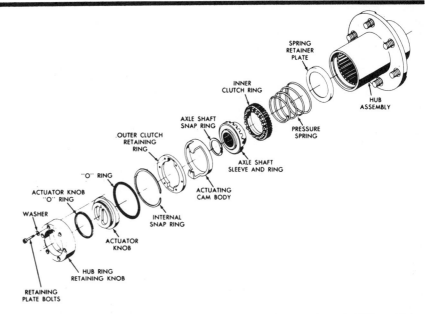

Details of the locking hubs used on all K-10 and 1500 models and 1977 and later K-20 and 2500 models

it if worn. Now you can remove the oil seal and spindle roller bearing.

NOTE: The spindle bearings must be greased each time the wheel bearings are serviced.

8. Clean all parts in solvent, dry, and check for wear or damage.
9. Pack both wheel bearings (and the spindle bearing) using wheel bearing grease. Place a healthy glob of grease in the palm of one hand and force the edge of the bearing into it so that grease fills the bearing. Do this until the whole bearing is packed. Grease packing tools are available to make this job a lot less messy.
10. To reassemble the spindle: drive the repacked bearing into the spindle and install the grease seal onto the slinger with the lip toward the spindle. It would be best to replace the axle shaft slinger when the spindle seal is replaced. If you are using the improve seals, fill the seal end of the spindle with grease. If not, apply grease only to the lip of the seal. Install the thrust washer over the axle shaft. The chamfered side of the thrust washer should be toward the slinger. Replace the spindle and torque the nuts to 33 ft. lbs.
11. to reassemble the wheel bearings: drive the outer bearing cup into the hub, replace the inner bearing cup, and insert the repacked bearing.
12. Install the disc or drum and outer wheel bearing to the spindle.
13. Adjust the bearings by rotating the hub and torquing the inner adjusting nut to 50 ft. lbs. then loosening it and retorquing to 35 ft. lbs. Next back the nut off $\frac{3}{8}$ turn or less. Turn the

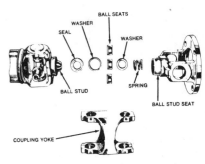

Exploded view of a constant velocity joint

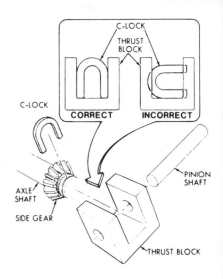

Correct C-lock positioning on locking differentials

nut to the nearest hole in the lockwasher. Install the outer locknut and torque to a minumum of 80 ft. lbs. There should be 0.001–0.010 in. bearing end-play. This can be measured with a dial indictor.

14. Replace the brake components.

15. Lubricate the locking hub components with high temperature grease. Lubrication must be applied to prevent component failure. For K10 or K1500 models, and K20 and K500 models, install the spring retainer plate with the flange side facing the bearing over the spindle nuts and seat it against the bearing outer cup. Install the pressure spring with the large end against the spring retaining plate. The spring is an interference fit; when seated, its end extends past the spindle nuts by approximately $^7/_8$ in. Place the inner clutch ring and bushing assembly into the axle shaft sleeve and clutch ring assembly and install that as an assembly onto the axle shaft. Press in on this assembly and install the axle shaft ring. If there are two axle shaft snap-ring grooves (1979), use the inner one.

NOTE: You can install a $^7/_{16}$ in. bolt in the axle shaft end and pull outward on it to aid in seating the snap-ring.

16. Install the actuating cam body in the cams facing outward, the outer clutch retaining ring, and the internal snap-ring. Install a new O-ring on the retaining plate, and then install the actuating knob in the Lock position. Install the retaining plate. The grooves in the knob must fit into the actuator cam body. Install the seals and six cover bolts and torque them to 30 ft. lbs. Turn the knob to the Free position and check for proper operation.

NOTE: Remove the head from a 5 in. long $^3/_4$ in. bolt and use this to align the hub assembly.

17. Install the headless bolt into one of the hub housing bolt holes. Install a new exterior sleeve extension housing gasket, the housing, and a new hub retainer cap assembly gasket, and the cap assembly. Install the six Allen head bolts and their washers, and torque to 30 ft. lbs. Turn the knob to Lock and check engagement.

18. Without locking hubs, replace the snap-ring and hub cap. If there are two axle shaft snap-ring grooves (1979), use the inner one.

Front Wheel Bearings

REMOVAL, PACKING, INSTALLATION

NOTE: This procedure requires snap ring pliers and a special hub nut wrench. It is very difficult

without them. This procedure does not apply to S-Series trucks.

1. Remove the wheel and tire.

2. For $^1/_2$ and $^3/_4$ ton trucks with locking front hubs, lock the hubs. Remove the outer retaining plate Allen head bolts and take off the plate, O-ring, and knob. Take out the large snap ring inside the hub and remove the outer clutch retaining ring and actuating am body. This is a lot easier with snap ring pliers. Relieve pressure on the axle shaft snap ring and remove it. Take out the axle shaft sleeve and clutch ring assembly and the inner clutch ring and bushing assembly and the inner clutch ring and bushing assembly. Remove the spring and retainer plate.

3. If you don't have locking front hubs, remove the hub cap and snap ring. Next remove the drive gear and pressure spring. To prevent the spring from popping out, place a hand over the drive gear and pry the gear out. Remove the spring.

4. Remove the wheel bearing outer lock nut, lock ring, and wheel bearing inner adjusting nut. A special wrench is required.

5. Remove the brake disc assembly and outer wheel bearing. Remove the spring retainer plate if you don't have locking hubs.

6. Remove the oil seal and inner bearing cone from the hub using a brass drift and hammer. Discard the oil seal. Use the drift to remove the inner and outer bearing cups.

7. Check the condition of the spindle bearing. Unbolt the spindle and tap it with a soft hammer to break it loose. Remove the spindle and check the condition of the thrust washer, replacing it if worn. Now you can remove the oil seal and spindle roller bearing.

NOTE: The spindle bearings must be greased each time the wheel bearings are serviced.

8. Clean all parts in solvent, dry and check for wear or damage.

9. Pack both wheel bearings (and the spindle bearings) using wheel bearing grease. Place a healthy glob of grease in the palm of one hand and force the edge of the bearing into it so that grease fills the bearing. Do this until the wheel bearing is packed. Grease packing tools are available to make this job easier.

10. To reassemble the spindle: drive the repacked bearing into the spindle and install the grease seal onto the slinger with the lip toward he spindle. It would be best to replace the axle shaft slinger when the spindle seal is replaced.

NOTE: If you are using the improved seals, fill the seal end of the spindle with grease. If not, apply grease only to the lip of the seal. Install the thrust washer over the axle shaft. On late 1982-87 models, the chamfered side of the thrust washer should be toward the slinger. Replace the spindle and torque the nuts to, 33 ft. lbs. for 1980: 65 ft. lbs. for 1981-87 models.

11. To reassemble the wheel bearings: drive the outer bearing cup into the hub, replace the inner bearing cup, and insert the repacked bearing.

12. Install the disc or drum and outer wheel bearing to the spindle.

13. Adjust the bearings by rotating the hub and torquing the inner adjusting nut to 50 ft. lbs. Next, back the nut off $^3/_8$ turn or less. Turn the nut to the nearest hole in the lock-washer. Install the outer locknut and torque to minimum of 80 ft. lbs. for 1980: 160–205 ft. lbs. for 1981-87 $^1/_2$ and $^3/_4$ ton and 65 ft. lbs on 1 ton vehicles. There should be 0.001–0.010 in. bearing end play. This can be measured with a dial indicator.

14. Replace the brake components.

15. Lubricate the locking hub components with high temperature grease. Lubrication must be applied to prevent component failure. Install the spring retainer plate with the flange side facing the bearing over the spindle nuts and seat it against the bearing outer cup. Install the pressure spring with the large end against the spring retaining plate. The spring is an interference fit; when seated, its end extends past the spindle nuts by approximately $^7/_8$ in. Place the inner clutch ring and bushing assembly and install that as an assembly onto the axle shaft. Press in on this assembly and install that as an assembly onto the axle shaft. Press in on this assembly and install the axle shaft ring. If there are two axle shafts snap ring grooves (1979), use the inner one.

Tube/Shaft Assembly

REMOVAL & INSTALLATION

S-Series Trucks

1. Disconnect negative battery cable.

2. Disconnect shift cable from vacuum actuator by disengaging locking spring. then push actuator diaphragm in to release cable.

3. Unlock steering wheel at steering column so linkage is free to move.

4. Raise vehicle and place jackstands under the frame.

5. Remove front wheels.

6. Remove engine drive belt shield.

7. Remove front axle skid plate (if equipped).

8. Place support under right hand lower control arm and disconnect right hand upper, ball joint, then remove support so control arm will hang free.

9. Disconnect right hand drive axle shaft from tube assembly by removing six bolts. Keep axle from turning by inserting a drift through opening in top of brake caliper into corresponding vane of brake rotor.

10. Disconnect four wheel drive indicator light electrical connection from switch.

11. Remove three bolts securing cable and switch housing to carrier and pull housing away to gain access to cable locking spring. do not unscrew cable coupling nut unless cable is being replaced.

12. Disconnect cable from shift fork shaft by lifting spring over slot in shift fork.

13. Remove two bolts securing tube bracket to frame.

14. Remove remaining two upper bolts securing tube assembly to carrier.

15. Remove tube assembly by working around drive axle. Be careful not to allow sleeve, thrust washers, connector, and output shaft to fall out of carrier or be damaged when removing tube.

16. Install sleeve, thrust washers, connector and output shaft in carrier. Apply sealer 1052357, Loctite® 514 or equivalent on tube to carrier surface. Be sure to install thrust washer. Apply grease to washer to hold it in place during assembly.

17. Install tube and shaft assembly to carrier and install bolt at one o'clock position but do not torque. Pull assembly down and install cable and switch housing, and remaining four bolts. Torque all bolts to 45–60 ft. lbs.

18. Install two bolts securing tube to frame and torque.

19. Check operation of four wheel drive mechanism using Tool J–33799. Insert tool into shift fork and check for rotation of axle shaft.

20. Remove tool and install shift cable switch housing by pushing cable through into fork shaft hole. Cable will automatically snap in place.

21. Connect four wheel drive indicator light electrical connection to switch.

22. Install support under right hand lower control arm to raise arm and connect upper ball joint.

23. Install right-hand drive axle to axle tube by installing one bolt first, then, rotate axle to install remaining five bolts. Hold axle from turning by inserting a drift through opening in top of brake caliper into corresponding vane of brake rotor. Tighten bolts to 53–63 ft. lbs.

24. Install front axle skid plate, if equipped.

25. Install engine drive belt shield.

26. Install front wheels.

27. Lower vehicle.

28. Connect shift cable to vacuum actuator by pushing cable end into vacuum actuator shaft hole. Cable will snap in place automatically.

29. Connect negative battery cable.

Shift Cable

REMOVAL & INSTALLATION

S-Series Trucks

1. Disengage shift cable from vacuum actuator by disengaging locking spring, then push actuator diaphragm in to release cable. Squeeze the two locking fingers of the cable with pliers, then pull cable out of bracket hole.

2. Raise vehicle and remove three bolts securing cable and switch housing to carrier and pull housing away to gain access to cable locking spring. Disconnect cable from shaft fork shaft by lifting spring over slot in shift fork.

3. Unscrew cable from housing.

4. Remove cable from vehicle.

5. Install cable observing proper routing.

6. Install cable and switch housing to carrier using three attaching bolts. Torque mounting bolts to 30–40 ft. lbs.

7. Guide cable through switch housing into fork shaft hole and push cable in. Cable will automatically snap in place. Start turning coupling nut by hand, to avoid cross threading, then torque nut to 71–106 inch lbs. Do not over torque nut as this will cause thread damage to plastic housing.

8. Lower vehicle.

9. Connect shift cable to vacuum actuator by pressing cable into bracket hole. Cable and housing will snap in place automatically.

10. Check cable operation.

Differential Carrier Right Half Output Shaft and Tube

REMOVAL & INSTALLATION

S-Series Trucks

1. Remove right-hand output shaft from tube by striking inside of flange with a soft face hammer while holding tube.

2. Remove output shaft tub seal by prying out of tube.

3. Remove output shaft tube bearing using J–29369–2.

4. Remove differential shift cable housing seal by driving out with a punch or similar tool.

5. Install output shaft tube bearing using tool J–33844. Tool must be flush with tube when bearing is correctly installed.

6. Install output shaft tube seal using tool J–33893. Flange of seal must be flush with tube outer surface when seal is installed.

7. Install output shaft into tube and seat by striking flange with a soft face hammer.

8. Install differential shift cable housing seal using J–33799.

Axle Shaft U-Joint

REMOVAL & INSTALLATION

S-Series Trucks

1. Remove the axle shaft.

2. Squeeze the ends of the trunnion bearings in a vise to relieve the load on the snap-rings. Remove the snap-rings.

3. Support the yoke in a vise and drive on one end of the trunnion bearing with a brass drift enough to drive the opposite bearing from the yoke.

4. Support the other side of the yoke and drive the other bearing out.

5. Remove the trunnion.

6. Clean and check all parts. You can buy U-joint repair kits to replace all the wearing parts.

7. Lubricate the bearings with wheel bearing grease.

8. Replace the trunnion and press the bearings into the yoke and over the trunnion hubs far enough to install the lock rings.

9. Hold the trunnion in one hand and tap the yoke lightly to seal the bearings against the lock rings.

10. The axle slingers can be pressed off the shafts.

NOTE: Always replace the slingers if the spindle seals are replaced. You can use the spindle to start the slinger on the shaft.

11. Install the shaft.

Ball Joint

REPLACEMENT

The steering knuckle pivot ball joints may need replacement when there is excessive steering play, hard steering, irregular tire wear (especially on the inner edge), or persistent tie rod loosening.

This procedure requires a shop

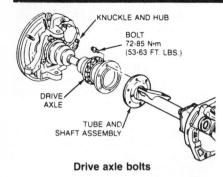

Drive axle bolts

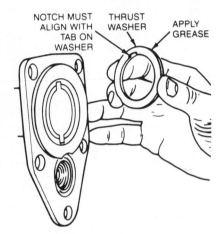

Thrust washer

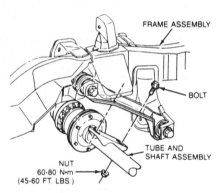

Tube–to–frame attachment

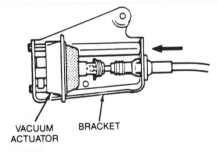

Cable–to–vacuum actuator attachment

press. Your best bet would be to remove the steering knuckle and take it to the machine shop with the new parts.

1. Remove the hub assembly as previously outlined.

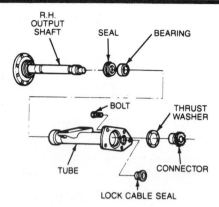

Right side output shaft and tube

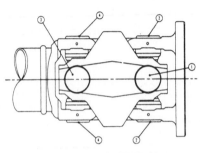

CV joint disassembly sequence

2. Remove the spindle attaching bolts.

3. Tap on the end of the spindle lightly with a wooden mallet (not a metal hammer) to break it loose from the steering knuckle.

4. Remove the spindle and the bronze washer. Replace the washer if it was distorted during removal or if it appears worn.

5. Remove the cotter pin from the tie rod nut.

6. Loosen the tie rod nut and tap on the nut with a wooden mallet in order to break the studs loose from the knuckle arm.

7. Remove the nuts and disconnect the tie rod.

8. Remove the steering arm attaching nuts. Use new, self-locking nuts on installation.

9. Remove the cotter pin from the upper ball joint socket nut.

10. Remove the retaining nuts from the upper and lower ball joint sockets.

11. Remove the knuckle by forcing a wedge between the lower ball stud and the yoke, then between the upper ball stud and the yoke.

NOTE: If you have to loosen the upper ball stud adjusting sleeve to remove the knuckle, don't loosen it more than two turns. The soft threads on the yoke are easily damaged.

12. Remove the lower ball joint snap ring.

13. Remove the lower ball joint as illustrated using special tool J-9519-10 (or a similar C-clamp), J-23454-1 (a solid metal punch), and J-6383-3 (or a piece of $2\frac{1}{2}$ in. outer diameter steel pipe with a $\frac{3}{16}$ in. wall thickness cut to a length of $2\frac{1}{2}$ in.). The lower ball joint must be removed before the upper ball joint can be serviced.

14. Press the new lower ball joint into the knuckle and install the snap-ring. The lower joint doesn't have a cotter pin hole.

15. Press the upper ball joint into the knuckle.

16. Position the knuckle to the yoke. Install new stud nuts finger tight.

17. Push up on the knuckle and tighten the lower nut to 70 ft. lbs.

18. Using a spanner wrench, install and torque the upper ball stud adjusting sleeve to 50 ft. lbs. Torque the upper stud nut to 100 ft. lbs. and install the cotter pin. Don't loosen the nut, but make it tighter to line up the cotter pin hole.

19. Replace the steering arm, using new nuts and torquing to 90 ft. lbs.

20. Attach the tie rod to the steering arm. Tighten the nuts to 45 ft. lbs.

21. Check the knuckle turning torque with a spring scale hooked to the tie rod hole in the steering arm. With the knuckle straight ahead, measure the right angle pull to keep the knuckle turning after initial breakaway, in both directions. The pull should be 25 lbs. or less.

22. Replace the axle shaft and other components. Tighten the steering linkage nuts to 45 ft. lbs.

Pinion Seal

REPLACEMENT

1. Mark the drive shaft and pinion flange so they can be reassembled in the same position.

2. Disconnect the driveshaft from the pinion flange and support shaft up in body tunnel by wiring drive shaft to the exhaust pipe. If joint bearings are not retained by a retainer strap, use a piece of tape to hold bearings on their journals.

3. Mark the position of the pinion flange, pinion shaft and nut so the proper pinion bearing pre-load can be maintained.

4. Remove pinion flange nut and washer.

5. With suitable container in place to hold any fluid that may drain from rear axle, remove pinion flange.

6. Remove oil seal by driving it out of carrier with a blunt chisel. Do not damage carrier.

7. Examine seal surface of pinion flange for tool marks, nicks, or dam-

age, such as a groove worn by the seal. If damaged, replace the flange.

8. Examine carrier bore and remove any burrs that might cause leaks around the O.D. of the seal.

9. Installation is the reverse of removal. Apply Special Seal Lubricant No. 1050169 or equivalent to the O.D. of the pinion flange and sealing lip of new seal.

Rear Axle

Some models are equipped with a locking differential rear axle. If you're not sure which one is in your truck, block the front wheels and jack up the rear of the truck. With the transmission in Neutral, spin one of the rear wheels in a forward motion with your hands. If the other wheel travels in the same direction, it is a locking differential.

Rear Axle Shaft, Bearing and Seal

REMOVAL & INSTALLATION

All Axles Except Floating and Locking Differentials

1. Support the axle on jackstands.
2. Remove the wheels and brake drums.
3. Clean off the differential cover area, loosen the cover to drain the lubricant, and remove the cover.
4. Turn the differential until you can reach the differential pinion shaft lockscrew. Remove the lockscrew and the pinion shaft.
5. Push in on the axle end. Remove the C-lock from the inner (button) end of the shaft.
6. Remove the shaft, being careful of the oil seal.
7. You can pry the oil seal out of the housing by placing the inner end of the axle shaft behind the steel case of the seal, then prying it out carefully.
8. A puller or a slide hammer is required to remove the bearing from the housing.
9. Pack the new or reused bearing with wheel bearing grease and lubricate the cavity between the seal lips with the same grease.
10. The bearing has to be driven into the housing. Don't use a drift, you might cock the bearing in its bore. Use a piece of pipe or a large socket instead. Drive only on the outer bearing race. In a similar manner, drive the seal in flush with the end of the tube.
11. Slide the shaft into place, turning it slowly until the splines are engaged with the differential. Be careful of the oil seal.
12. Install the C-lock on the inner

axle end. Pull the shaft out so that the C-lock seats in the counterbore of the differential side gear.

13. Position the differential pinion shaft through the case and the pinion gears, aligning the lockscrew hole. Install the lockscrew.
14. Install the cover with a new gasket and tighten the bolts evenly in a criss-cross pattern.
15. Fill the axle with lubricant.
16. Replace the brake drum and wheels.

Locking Differential Axles

This axle uses a thrust block on the differential pinion shaft.

1. Follow Steps 1–3 of the preceding procedure.
2. Rotate the differential case so that you can remove the lockscrew and support the pinion shaft so it can't fall into the housing. Remove the differential pinion shaft lockscrew.
3. Carefully pull the pinion shaft partway out and rotate the differential case until the shaft touches the housing at the top.
4. Use a screwdriver to position the C-lock with its open end directly inward. You can't push in the axle shaft until you do this. Do not force the axle shaft in.
5. Push the axle shaft in and remove the C-lock. Remove the axle shaft and repeat Steps 4–5 for the other shaft.
6. Follow Steps 7–11 of the preceding procedure.
7. Keep the pinion shaft partway out of the differential case while installing the C-lock on the axle shaft. Put the C-lock on the axle shaft and carefully pull out on the axle shaft until the C-lock is clear of the thrust block.
8. Follow Steps 13–16 of the previous procedure.

Floating Differentials

Some 20 and 2500 models and all 30 and 3500 models use axles of full floating design. The procedures are the same for locking the non-locking axles. The best way to remove the bearings from the wheel hub is with an arbor press. Use of a press reduces the chances of damaging the bearing races, cocking the bearing in its bore, or scoring the hub walls. A local machine shop is probably equipped with the tools to remove and install bearings and seals. However, if one is not available, the hammer and drift method outlined can be used.

1. Support the axle on jackstands.
2. Remove the wheels.
3. Remove the bolts and lock wash

ers that attach the axle shaft flange to the hub.

4. Rap on the flange with a soft faced hammer to loosen the shaft. Grip the rib on the end of the flange with a pair of locking pliers, and twist to start shaft removal. Remove the shaft from the axle tube.
5. The hub and drum assembly must be removed to remove the bearings and oil seals. You will need a large socket to remove and later adjust the bearing adjustment nut. There are also tools available which resemble the four wheel drive front wheel bearing adjusting tool.
6. Disengage the tang of the locknut retainer from the slot or flat of the locknut, then remove the locknut from the housing tube, using the earlier mentioned tool.
7. Disengage the tang of the retainer from the slot or flat of the adjusting nut and remove the retainer from the housing tube.
8. Remove the adjusting nut from the housing tube with the tool mentioned earlier.
9. Remove the thrust washer from the housing tube.
10. Pull the hub and drum straight off the axle housing.
11. Remove the oil seal and discard.
12. Use a hammer and a long drift to knock the inner bearing cup, and oil seal from the hub assembly.
13. Remove the outer bearing snapring with a pair of pliers. It may be necessary to tap the bearing outer race away from the retaining ring slightly by tapping on the ring to remove the ring.
14. Drive the outer bearing from the hub with a hammer and drift.
15. To reinstall the bearings, place the outer bearing into the hub. The larger outside diameter of the bearing should face the outer end of the hub. Drive the bearing into the hub using a washer that will cover both the inner and outer races of the bearing. Place a socket on the top of this washer, then drive the bearing into place with a series of light taps. If available, an arbor press should be used for this job.
16. Drive the bearing past the snapring groove, and install the snap-ring. Then turning the hub assembly over, drive the bearing back against the snap-ring. Again, protect the bearing by placing a washer on top of it. You can use the thrust washer that fits between the bearing and the adjusting nut for this job.
17. Place the inner bearing into the hub. The thick edge should be toward the shoulder in the hub. Press the bearing into the hub until it seats against the shoulder, using a washer and socket as outlined earlier. Make

certain that the bearing is not cocked and that it is fully seated on the shoulder.

18. Pack the cavity between the oil seal lips with front wheel bearing grease, and position it in the hub bore. Carefully press it into place on top of the inner bearing.

19. Pack the wheel bearings with the grease, and lightly coat the inside diameter of the hub bearing contact surface and the outside diameter of the axle housing tube.

20. Make sure that the inner bearing, oil seal, axle housing oil deflector, and outer bearing are properly positioned. Install the hub and drum assembly on the axle housing, excercising care so as not to damage

the oil seal or dislocate other internal components.

21. Install the thrust washer so that the tang on the inside diameter of the washer is in the keyway on the axle housing.

22. Install the adjusting nut. Tighten to 50 ft. lbs., at the same time rotating the hub to make sure that all the bearing surfaces are in contact. Back off the nut and retighten to 35 ft. lbs., then back off $\frac{1}{4}$ of a turn.

23. Install the tanged retainer against the inner adjusting nut. Align the adjusting nut so that the short tang of the retainer will engage the nearest slot on the adjusting nut.

24. Install the outer locknut and tighten to 65 ft. lbs. Bend the long

tang of the retainer into the slot of the outer nut. This method of adjustment should provide 0.001–0.010 in. of end play.

25. Place a new gasket over the axle shaft and position the axle shaft in the housing so that the shaft splines enter the differential side gear. Position the gasket so that the holes are in alignment, and install the flange-to-hub attaching bolts. Torque to 155 ft. lbs.

NOTE: To prevent lubricant from leaking through the flange holes, apply a non-hardening sealer to the bolt threads. Use the sealer sparingly.

27. Install the wheels.

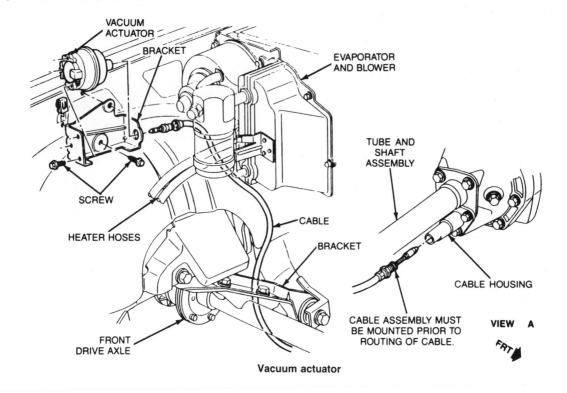

Vacuum actuator

Suspension and Steering 8

INDEX

FRONT SUSPENSION

CORVETTE

Corvette utilizes conventional short-long arm suspension, with coil springs and tube shocks. A stabilizer bar is used between the lower arms to reduce body lean during cornering, thereby keeping more tire surface on the ground. 1984-87 models use a transverse leaf spring on the front suspension, along with forged aluminum components.

Shock Absorber

REMOVAL & INSTALLATION

1. Remove the upper stem nut while holding the stem to keep it from turning.
2. Remove the two bolts holding the shock absorber to the lower control arm and pull the shock through the arm.

NOTE: Pulling the shock through the lower control arm applies only to 1980–82 models.

3. Purge the new shock of air by repeatedly extending it in its normal position and compressing it while invert-

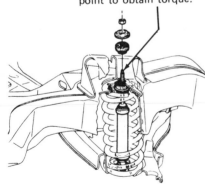

NOTE Hold stud at this point to obtain torque.

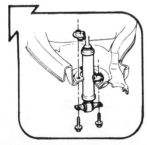

Front shock absorber installation

ed. Extend the shock absorber and insert it up through the lower control arm. Make sure that the upper stem goes through the hole in the upper control arm frame bracket.

4. Install the grommet, retainer cup, and nut to the shock absorber upper stem.
5. Hold the shock absorber stem and tighten the upper nut to 8 ft. lbs. 1980–82, 18 ft. lb. 1984-87 models.
6. Install the lower control arm retaining bolts and tighten to 13 ft. lbs. 1980–82, 22 ft. lbs. 1984 and later models.

DISPOSAL OF PRESSURIZED SHOCK ABSORBERS

1984-87 Models

Due to the high pressure of gas it is advised that, upon scrapping or disposal of these shock absorbers, the pressure be released. This is carried out as follows:

1. Clamp shock in vise with piston rod pointing down.
2. Measure approx. 0.5 in. (10–15mm) from bottom of shock and drill an approx. 5mm hole so the gas can escape.
3. Measure approx. 5.5–6.0 in. (140–150mm) from first hole and drill an approx. 5mm hole to facilitate drainage of oil. Drain all oil from shock absorber.

Spring

REMOVAL & INSTALLATION

1980–82

1. Raise the car on hoist and remove nut, retainer and grommet from the top of the shock absorber. Support car so that the control arms swing free.
2. Disconnect stabilizer bar from lower control arm and remove shock absorber.
3. Bolt a spring remover tool to a suitable jack and place it under the lower control arm bushings so that the bushings seat in the grooves of the tool.

NOTE: This tool is a cradle which, when fastened to a hydraulic jack, allows the lowering of the control arm and slow de-

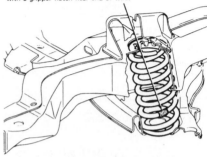

NOTE Spring to be installed with tape at lowest position. Bottom of spring is coiled helical, and the top is coiled flat with a gripper notch near end of wire.

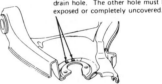

NOTE After assembly, end of spring coil must cover all or part of one inspection drain hole. The other hole must be partly exposed or completely uncovered.

Front spring positioning

compression of the spring. A similar tool can be fabricated in the shop. Always safety chain the spring and control arm when using this method.

4. Remove the cross shaft rear retaining nut and the two front retaining bolts.
5. Slowly release jack, swing control arm forward, then remove spring.
6. Install by reversing procedure above. Torque the retaining nut to 92 ft. lb. Torque the retaining bolts 59–75 ft. lbs.

NOTE: Chevrolet recommends this cradle spring removal tool for all models. Other methods may be used, depending on the availability of tools.

1984-87

1. Raise the vehicle on a hoist.
2. Remove the wheels and tires, left side.
3. Remove the left front caliper bracket and rotor.
4. Remove spring protectors both sides.
5. Install spring compressor J-33432-4 or its equivalent.
6. Disconnect outer tie rod left side.
7. Remove the stabilizer link, left side.

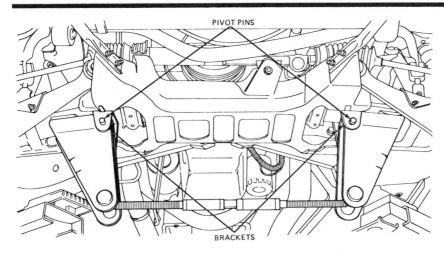

NOTE: PIVOT PINS ARE REMOVED SO THAT THE BRACKET MAY BE PLACED OVER THE TOP OF THE SPRING.

Front spring removal/installation

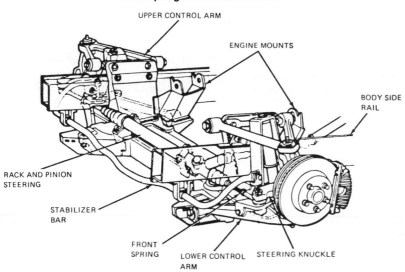

1984 front suspension components

8. Remove the lower shock mount, left side.

9. Compress special tool J-33432-4.

10. Remove the lower ball joint, left side.

11. Remove the spring hold down brackets.

12. Remove the transverse spring from the left side.

13. Installation is the reverse of removal. The following torques are needed during reinstallation: Spring protector to crossmember 18 ft. lbs. Stabilizer link 35 ft. lbs.

BALL JOINT INSPECTION

NOTE: Before performing this inspection, make sure the wheel bearings are adjusted correctly and that the control arm bushings are in good condition.

1. Jack the car up under the front lower control arm at the spring seat.

2. Raise the car until there is 1–2 in. of clearance under the wheel.

3. Insert a bar under the wheel and pry upward. If the wheel raises more then $1/8$ in. the ball joints are worn. Determine if the upper or lower ball joint is worn by visual inspection while prying on the wheel.

NOTE: Due to the distribution of forces in the suspension, the lower ball joint is usually the defective joint.

Upper & Lower Ball Joint

REMOVAL & INSTALLATION

1. Raise the car on a hoist.

2. Remove the tire and wheel assembly.

3. Support the lower control arm with a jack.

4. Loosen the upper ball stud nut.

5. Install a ball joint remover tool and unseat the upper joint from the steering knuckle. Remove the upper stud nut and install a block of wood under the upper control arm.

6. Chisel or grind off the ball joint mounting rivets.

7. Drill out the ball stud attaching holes to accept the service ball joint attaching bolts.

8. Install the ball joint with the nuts and bolts supplied with the new joint.

9. Install the lube fitting in the new joint.

10. Mate the upper control arm to the steering knuckle and install the ball stud through the knuckle boss.

11. Tighten the ball stud nut to 50 ft. lbs. plus whatever is necessary to align the cotter pin holes. Install the cotter pin. Never loosen the nut to align the cotter pin holes.

12. Install the wheel. Lower the car.

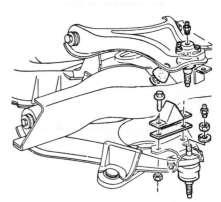

Upper and lower ball joints

Lower Control Arm

REMOVAL & INSTALLATION

1980–82

1. Remove the spring.

2. Remove the ball stud from the steering knuckle as described above.

3. Remove the control arm pivot bolts and remove the control arm. On some Corvettes, the pivot bolt is secured to the frame with two bolts.

4. Installation is the reverse.

1984–87

1. Raise vehicle and remove wheel and tire.

2. Remove spring protector.

3. Using tool J-33432 or its equal compress spring.

343

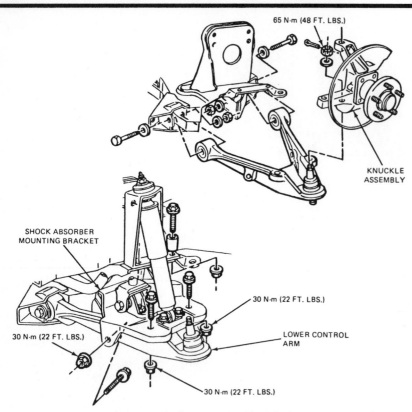

Lower control arm removal/installation

1984-87

1. Raise vehicle and remove wheel and tire.
2. Remove spring protector.
3. Using spring compressor J-33432 or its equivalent, compress and loosen the spring.
4. Use tool J-33436 or its equivalent to disconnect the upper ball joint from the knuckle.
5. Remove the upper control arm.
6. Installation is the reverse of removal. Torque upper control arm bolts to 63 ft. lbs., the ball joint nut to 32 ft. lbs.

Front Wheel Bearing

ADJUSTMENT

1. Jack the car up and support it at the lower arm.
2. Remove the hub dust cover and spindle cotter pin.
3. While spinning the wheel, snug the nut down to seat the bearings. Do not exert over 12 ft. lbs. of force on the nut.
4. Back the nut off ¼–½ a turn. Tighten the nut fingertight (if the roller bearings are preloaded with the wheel off the ground, the inner edges of the bearings will be forced against the bearing cage), then loosen the nut as required to line up the cotter pin hole in the spindle with the hole in the nut.
5. Insert the cotter pin. End-play should be 0.001–0.005 in. If play exceeds this tolerance, the wheel bearings should be replaced.

4. Remove lower shock bracket.
5. Using tool J-33436 or its equal disconnect lower ball joint.
6. Remove lower control arm.
7. Installation is the reverse of removal. Torque the ball joint nut to 48 ft. lbs.

moval. Make sure the shaft to frame bolts are installed in the same position they were in before removal and that the shims are in their original positions. Tighten the shaft to frame bolts to 55 ft. lbs. The control arm shaft nuts are torqued to 60 ft. lbs.

Upper Control Arm

REMOVAL & INSTALLATION

1980–82

1. Raise the vehicle on a hoist.
2. Support the outer end of the lower control arm, with a jack.
3. Remove the wheel.
4. Separate the upper ball joint from the steering knuckle as described above under "Upper Ball Joint Removal & Installation".
5. Remove the control arm shaft to frame nuts.

NOTE: Tape the shims together and identify them so that they can be installed in the positions from which they were removed.

6. Remove the bolts which attach the control arm shaft to the frame and remove the control arm. Note the positions of the bolts.
7. Install in the reverse order of re-

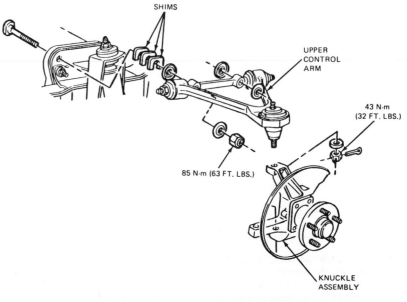

Upper control arm removal/installation

CAPRICE, IMPALA, MALIBU AND MONTE CARLO

NOTE: Many vehicles have been gradually switched over to metric fasteners. Most models use metric prevailing torque nuts to fasten the upper and lower ball joint studs to the steering knuckle. American standard inch calibrated wrenches will not fit metric nuts and bolts.

Coil Spring

REMOVAL & INSTALLATION

1. Raise and support the vehicle on jackstands.
2. Remove shock absorber.
3. Secure tool J-23028 to a jack and position the assembly under the control arm, supporting the inner bushing.
4. Disconnect stabilizer bar at lower control arm.
5. Raise the jack to take the tension off of the control arm pivots. Install a chain around the spring and through the control arm as a safety measure, then remove the inner control arm-to-crossmember pivot bolts.
6. Carefully lower the control arm, allowing the spring to relax.

—————— **CAUTION** ——————

Allow the spring to completely expand before attempting to remove it.

7. Remove the chain and the spring.
8. To install, reverse the removal procedures. Torque the lower control arm pivot nuts to 65 ft. lbs. (Malibu and Monte Carlo) or 90 ft. lbs. (Impala and Caprice) with the weight of the vehicle on the springs.

Shock Absorber

REMOVAL & INSTALLATION

New shock absorbers must be purged of air before installation. This is done by repeatedly extending the shock in its normal mounted position, inverting it and compressing it.

1. Remove the nut, retainer and grommet, which are attached to the upper end of the shock absorber and seat against the frame bracket.

NOTE: It may be necessary to hold the shock absorber shaft to remove the nut. This may be done with a wrench on the end of the shaft.

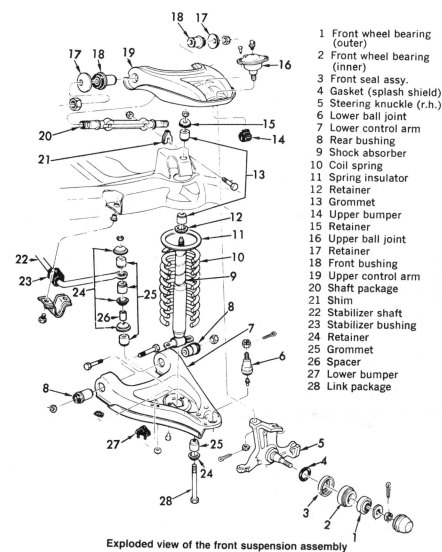

1 Front wheel bearing (outer)
2 Front wheel bearing (inner)
3 Front seal assy.
4 Gasket (splash shield)
5 Steering knuckle (r.h.)
6 Lower ball joint
7 Lower control arm
8 Rear bushing
9 Shock absorber
10 Coil spring
11 Spring insulator
12 Retainer
13 Grommet
14 Upper bumper
15 Retainer
16 Upper ball joint
17 Retainer
18 Front bushing
19 Upper control arm
20 Shaft package
21 Shim
22 Stabilizer shaft
23 Stabilizer bushing
24 Retainer
25 Grommet
26 Spacer
27 Lower bumper
28 Link package

Exploded view of the front suspension assembly

2. Raise and support the vehicle on jackstands to allow the shock to be dropped from the lower control arm.
3. Remove the shock absorber lower attaching screws and lower the shock from the control arm.
4. To install, reverse the removal procedures. Make sure all grommets are in the correct position and tighten the upper nut.

Front Wheel Bearing

ADJUSTMENT

1. Lift the wheel off the ground by jacking under the lower control arm.

2. Remove the dust cap from the hub.
3. Remove the cotter pin and discard it.
4. Snug up the spindle nut while spinning the wheel to seat the bearings (12 ft. lbs.). Then back off the nut $\frac{1}{4}$–$\frac{1}{2}$ turn.
5. Retighten the nut by hand until it is finger tight.
6. Loosen the nut until the nearest hole in the spindle lines up with a slot in the spindle nut, then insert a new cotter pin. When the bearing is properly adjusted, there will be 0.001–0.005 in. end play.
7. Replace the dust cover and lower the vehicle.

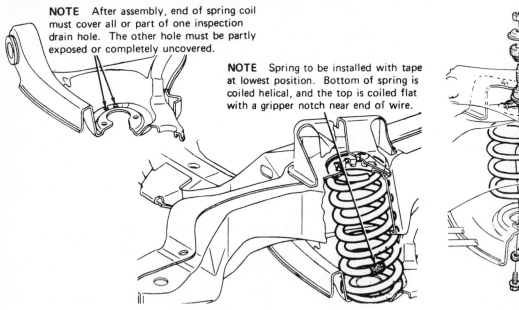

NOTE After assembly, end of spring coil must cover all or part of one inspection drain hole. The other hole must be partly exposed or completely uncovered.

NOTE Spring to be installed with tape at lowest position. Bottom of spring is coiled helical, and the top is coiled flat with a gripper notch near end of wire.

Positioning the coil spring

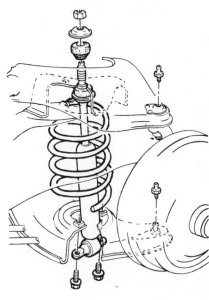

Installing the shock absorbers

Upper Control Arm

NOTE: If the vehicle is equipped with a diesel engine, remove the resonator and the bracket before removing the upper control arm.

REMOVAL & INSTALLATION

1. Raise and support the vehicle on jackstands between the spring seat and the ball joint, at the outer end of lower control arm.
2. Remove wheel and tire assembly.
3. Remove cotter pin and loosen the nut on the upper control arm-to-steering knuckle ball stud.
4. Using tool J-23742, push the ball joint stud from the steering knuckle.
5. Remove the nuts that hold the upper control arm-to-crossmember and the control arm. Count number of shims at each bolt.
6. To install, reverse the removal procedures. Install same number of shims as removed at each bolt. Torque the control arm-to-frame to 48 ft. lbs. (Malibu and Monte Carlo) or 70 ft. lbs. (all others) and the upper ball joint-to-steering knuckle to 52 ft. lbs. Insert cotter pin. Check caster and camber.

Ball Joint

INSPECTION

NOTE: Before performing this inspection, make sure the wheel bearings are adjusted correctly

and that the control arm bushings are in good condition.

1. Raise and support the vehicle on jackstands under the front lower control arm at the spring seat. Raise the vehicle until there is 1–2 in. of clearance under the wheel.
2. Insert a bar under the wheel and pry upward. If the wheel raises more than $1/8$ in., the ball joints are worn. While prying on the wheel, determine by visual inspection whether the upper or lower ball joint is worn.

NOTE: Due to the distribution of forces in the suspension, the

lower ball joint is usually the defective joint.

LOWER BALL JOINT WEAR INDICATORS — ALL MODELS

These vehicles have a visual wear indicator on the lower ball joint. Wear is indicated by the position of the $1/2$ in. nipple into which the grease fitting is screwed. On a new joint, the nipple should project 0.050 in. beyond the ball joint cover surface. If the nipple is flush or inside the cover surface, replace the ball joint.

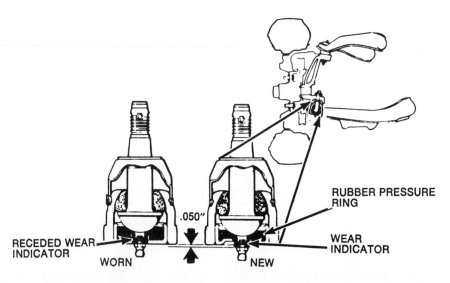

RUBBER PRESSURE RING

WEAR INDICATOR

RECEDED WEAR INDICATOR

.050"

WORN   NEW

Wear indicator arrangement used on the lower ball joint

Upper Ball Joint

REMOVAL & INSTALLATION

1. Refer to the "Upper Control Arm Removal & Installation" procedures in this section and separate the ball joint from the steering knuckle.
2. Using a center punch, punch the center of the 4 rivets.
3. Using an $1/8$ in. drill bit, drill $1/4$ in. deep into the rivets.
4. Using a $1/2$ in. drill bit, drill off the heads of the rivets.
5. Using a drift punch, drive out the remaining parts of the rivets.
6. Install new ball joint against top side of upper control arm. Secure joint to control arm with the special alloy bolts and nuts furnished with the replacement part.
7. Torque these bolts and nuts to 9 ft. lbs. and the ball joint-to-steering knuckle to 52 ft. lbs.

NOTE: The cotter pin must be installed from the rear to the front on the Malibu and the Monte Carlo.

Lower Ball Joint

REMOVAL & INSTALLATION

1. Raise and support the front of the vehicle under the frame with jackstands. Remove the wheel and tire assembly.
2. Support the lower control arm with a floor jack.
3. Remove the cotter pin and loosen the lower ball stud nut.
4. Using tool J-23742, break the ball stud loose from the steering knuckle. Separate the lower control arm from the steering knuckle.

5. Using the ball joint removal tool J-9519-10 and adapter tools J-9519-16 and J-9519-22, press the ball stud from the lower control arm.
6. Install the new ball joint to the lower control arm. Using the installation tool J-9519-10 and adapter tool J9519-9, press the ball joint into the lower control arm until it bottoms on the arm.

NOTE: When installing the new ball joint, position the purge vent in the rubber boot facing inward.

7. To complete the installation, connect the ball joint-to-control arm assembly to the steering knuckle and torque the ball joint nut to 90 ft. lbs., then reverse the removal procedures.

Lower Control Arm

REMOVAL & INSTALLATION

1. Refer to the "Coil Spring Removal & Installation" procedures in this section and remove the spring.
2. Remove the ball stud from the steering knuckle.
3. Remove the control arm through the splash shield opening with a putty knife or a similiar tool.
4. To install, reverse the removal procedures.

Steering Knuckle

REMOVAL & INSTALLATION

1. Siphon some fluid from the brake master cylinder.
2. Raise and support the vehicle on jackstands.
3. Remove the wheel and tire assembly.
4. Remove the caliper from the

steering knuckle and support on a wire.
5. Remove the grease cup, the cotter pin, the castle nut and the hub assembly.
6. Remove the 3 bolts holding the shield to the steering knuckle.
7. Using the ball joint removal tool J-6627, disconnect the tie rod from the steering knuckle.
8. Using ball joint removal tool J-23742, disconnect the ball joints from the steering knuckle.
9. Place a floor jack under the lower control arm (near the spring seat) and disconnect the ball joint from the steering knuckle.
10. Raise the upper control arm and disconnect the ball joint from the steering knuckle.
11. Remove the steering knuckle from the vehicle.
12. To install, reverse the removal procedures. Torque the upper ball joint-to-steering knuckle nut to 65 ft. lbs., the lower ball joint-to-steering knuckle nut to 90 ft. lbs. and the tie rod-to-steering knuckle nut to 40 ft. lbs. Adjust the wheel bearing and refill the master cylinder.

Stabilizer Bar

REMOVAL & INSTALLATION

1. Raise and support the front of the vehicle on jackstands.
2. Disconnect the stabilizer link bolts at the lower control arms.
3. Remove the stabilizer-to-frame clamps.
4. Remove the stabilizer bar.
5. To install, reverse the removal procedures. Torque the stabilizer-to-lower control arm bolts to 13 ft. lbs. and the stabilizer-to-frame bolts to 24 ft. lbs.

CELEBRITY AND CITATION

MacPherson Strut

REMOVAL & INSTALLATION

The MacPherson strut is a combination coil spring and shock absorber (damper) unit. The strut is removed as an assembly from the car. A special strut compressor must be used to disassemble the strut and coil spring.
1. Loosen the wheel nuts, raise the car, and remove the wheel and tire.
2. Remove the brake hose clip-to-strut bolt (if equipped). Do not disconnect the hose from the caliper. Install

a drive axle cover to protect the axle boot.
3. Mark the camber cam eccentric adjuster for assembly.
4. Remove the two lower strut-to-steering knuckle bolts and the three upper strut-to-body nuts. Remove the strut.

Ball Joints

INSPECTION

1. Raise the front of the car with a lift placed under the engine cradle.

The front wheels should be clear of the ground.
2. Grasp the wheel at the top and bottom and shake the wheel in and out.
3. If any movement is seen of the steering knuckle relative to the control arm, the ball joints are defective and must be replaced. Note that movement elsewhere may be due to loose wheel bearings or other troubles; watch the knuckle-to-control arm connection.
4. If the ball stud is disconnected from the steering knuckle and any looseness is noted, often the ball joint

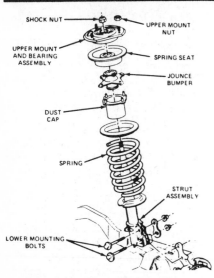

Front suspension components

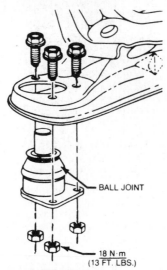

Ball joint installation

stud can be twisted in its socket with your fingers, replace the ball joints.

REMOVAL & INSTALLATION

NOTE: These cars use only a lower ball joint.

1. Loosen the wheel nuts, raise the car, and remove the wheel.
2. Use a $\frac{1}{8}$ in. drill bit to drill a hole approximately $\frac{1}{4}$ in. deep in the center of each of the three ball joint rivets.
3. Use a $\frac{1}{2}$ in. drill bit to drill off the rivet heads. Drill only enough to remove the rivet head.
4. Use a hammer and punch to remove the rivets. Drive them out from the bottom.
5. Loosen the ball joint pinch bolt in the steering knuckle.
6. Remove the ball joint.
7. Install the new ball joint in the control arm. Tighten the bolts supplied with the replacement joint to 13 ft. lbs.
8. Install the ball stud into the steering knuckle pinch bolt fitting. It should go in easily; if not, check the stud alignment. Install the pinch bolt from the rear to the front. Tighten to 45 ft. lbs.
9. Install the wheel and lower the car.

Lower Control Arm

REMOVAL & INSTALLATION

1. Loosen the wheel nuts, raise the car, and remove the wheel.

2. Remove the stabilizer bar from the control arm.
3. Remove the ball joint from the steering knuckle.
4. Remove the control arm pivot bolts and the control arm.

5. To install, insert the control arm into its fittings. Install the pivot bolts from the rear to the front. Tighten the bolts to 48 ft. lbs. on 1980 models and 50 ft. lbs. on 1981–85 models.

6. Insert the ball stud into the pinch bolt fitting. It should go in easily; if not, check the ball joint stud alignment.

7. Install the pinch bolt from the rear to the front. Tighten to 45 ft. lbs. on 1980 models and 40 ft. lbs. on 1981–85 models.

8. Install the stabilizer bar attachment. Tighten to 35 ft. lbs.

9. Install the wheel and lower the car.

Front Wheel Bearing

ADJUSTMENT

These models use a permanently sealed and lubricated front wheel bearing assembly. No adjustments are necessary or possible.

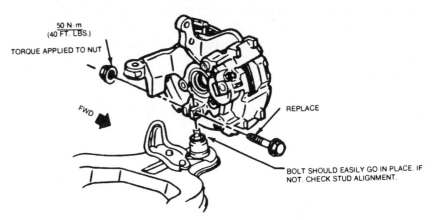

Ball joint stud should go in easily

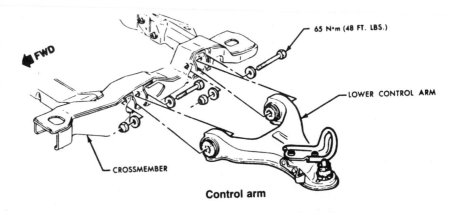

Control arm

CAMARO

Coil Spring

REMOVAL & INSTALLATION

1980-81

1. Remove the shock absorber and disconnect the stabilizer bar.
2. Support the front of the vehicle at the frame so the control arms hang free.
3. Support the inner end of the control arm with a floor jack; dealers have a device that cradles the inner bushings.
4. Raise the jack to take the tension off the lower control arm pivot blots.
5. Chain the spring to the lower control arm, for safety purposes.
6. Remove the rear and then the front pivot bolt.
7. Lower the jack until all the spring tension is released.
8. Note the way in which the spring is installed to the control arm and remove it.
9. To install, position the spring to the control arm and raise it into place, then reverse the removal procedures. Install the pivot bolts and torque the nuts to 90 ft. lbs.

1982-87

1. Raise and support the front of the vehicle on jackstands.
2. Remove the front wheel(s).
3. Disconnect the stabilizer link from the lower control arm.

NOTE: If the steering gear hinders removal procedures, detach the unit and move it aside.

4. Disconnect the tie-rod from the steering knuckle using a ball joint removal tool J-24292A.
5. Using an internal-fit coil spring compressor, compress the coil spring so that it is loose in its seat.

--------- CAUTION ---------

Be sure to follow manufacturer's instructions when using spring compressor. Coil springs in a compressed state contain enormous energy which, if released accidentally, could cause serious injury.

6. To remove the coil spring, disconnect the lower control arm from the crossmember at the pivot bolts. If additional clearance is necessary, disconnect the lower control arm from the steering knuckle at the ball joint.
7. To install, compress the coil spring until spring height is the same as when removed, then position the

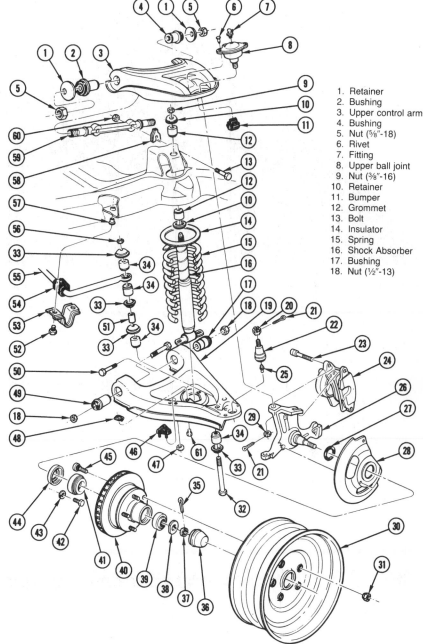

1. Retainer
2. Bushing
3. Upper control arm
4. Bushing
5. Nut (5/8"-18)
6. Rivet
7. Fitting
8. Upper ball joint
9. Nut (3/8"-16)
10. Retainer
11. Bumper
12. Grommet
13. Bolt
14. Insulator
15. Spring
16. Shock Absorber
17. Bushing
18. Nut (1/2"-13)

19. Lower control arm	34. Grommet	
20. Nut	35. Cotter pin (1/4" × 1 1/4")	
21. Cotter pin (1/8" × 1 1/4")	36. Cap	49. Bushing
22. Lower control arm	37. Nut (3/4"-20)	50. Bolt (1/2"-13 × 3 3/4")
23. Bolt	38. Washer	51. Spacer
24. Caliper	39. Bearing	52. Screw
25. Fittings	40. Hub	53. Bracket
26. Steering knuckle	41. Inner front wheel bearing	54. Bushing
27. Gasket	42. Bolt	55. Front stabilizer shaft
28. Shield	43. Washer (9/16")	56. Nut (5/16"-18)
29. Nut	44. Seal	57. Nut (3/8"-16)
30. Wheel	45. Bolt	58. Shim
31. Nut (1/2"-20)	46. Bumper	59. Shaft Kit
32. Stabilizer link kit	47. Nut (3/8"-16)	60. Nut (1/2"-13)
33. Retainer	48. Nut	61. Bolt

Exploded view of the front suspension used on models through 1981

spring on the control arm. Make sure the lower end of the coil spring is properly positioned in the lower control arm and that the upper end fits correctly in its pad.

8. To complete the installation, reverse the removal procedures. Torque the lower control arm-to-steering knuckle to 78 ft. lbs., the pivot bolt nuts to 63 ft. lbs., the tie rod-to-steering knuckle to 35 ft. lbs. and the stabilizer-to-control arm to 13 ft. lbs.

Shock Absorber

REMOVAL & INSTALLATION

1980-81

1. Remove the upper stem nut while holding the stem to keep it from turning.
2. Remove the bolts holding the shock absorber-to-lower control arm and pull the shock through the arm.

3. Extend the new shock absorber and insert it up through the lower control arm. Make sure that the upper stem goes through the hole in the upper control arm frame bracket.

NOTE: Purge new shocks of air by repeatedly compressing them while inverted and extending them in their normal installed position.

4. Install the grommet, retainer cup and nut to the shock absorber upper stem.
5. Hold the shock absorber stem and tighten the upper nut to 8 ft. lbs.
6. Install the lower control arm retaining bolts and tighten to 20 ft. lbs.

Strut

REMOVAL & INSTALLATION

1982-87

1. Place the ignition key in the unlocked position so that the front wheels can be moved.
2. At the front wheelhouse reinforcement, remove the strut-to-upper mount cover and nut.

CAUTION

DO NOT attempt to move the vehicle with the upper strut fastener disconnected.

---

3. Raise and support the front of the vehicle, place jackstands under the lower control arms.
4. Remove the wheel and tire assembly.
5. Remove the brake hose from the strut bracket.
6. Remove the bolts attaching the strut-to-steering knuckle.
7. Lift the strut up from the steering knuckle to compress the rod, then pull down and remove the strut.
8. To install, extend the rod through the upper mount and start the upper fastener, then reverse the removal procedures. Torque the strut-to-wheelhouse nut to 44 ft. lbs., the strut-to-steering knuckle bolts to 202 ft. lbs.

FRONT WHEEL BEARING ADJUSTMENT

1. Raise and support the front of the vehicle on jackstands.
2. Remove the hub dust cover, the cotter pin and loosen the hub nut.
3. Spin the wheel and tighten the nut to seat the bearings. DO NOT exert over 12 ft. lbs. of force on the nut.
4. Back the nut off until it is just loose. Line up the cotter pin hole in the spindle with the hole in the nut.
5. Insert a new cotter pin and bend the ends of the pin.

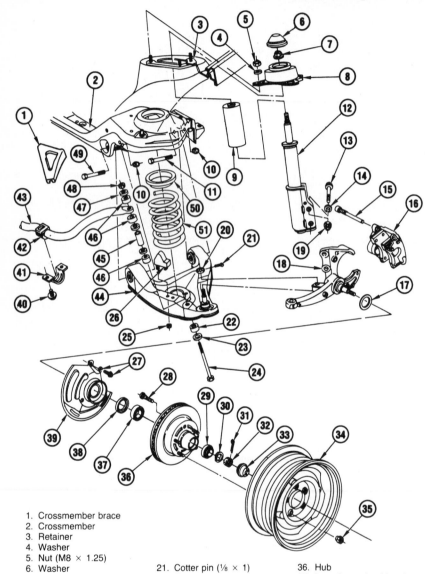

1. Crossmember brace
2. Crossmember
3. Retainer
4. Washer
5. Nut (M8 × 1.25)
6. Washer
7. Nut (M14 × 2)
8. Mount
9. Shield
10. Nut (M12 × 1.75)
11. Bolt (M12 × 1.75 × 95)
12. Absorber w/strut
13. Bolt
14. Washer
15. Bolt
16. Caliper
17. Gasket
18. Knuckle
19. Nut (M16 × 2)
20. Nut (⁹⁄₁₆-18)
21. Cotter pin (⅛ × 1)
22. Grommet
23. Retainer
24. Bolt (⁵⁄₁₆-18 × 7)
25. Nut (⁷⁄₁₆-14)
26. Bumper
27. Bolt
28. Bolt
29. Outer front wheel bearing
30. Washer
31. Cotter pin (M3.2 × 25)
32. Nut
33. Cap
34. Wheel
35. Nut
36. Hub
37. Inner front wheel bearing
38. Seal
39. Shield
40. Bolt (M10 × 1.5 × 30)
41. Bracket
42. Insulator
43. Front stabilizer shaft
44. Lower control arm
45. Spacer
46. Grommet
47. Retainer
48. Nut
49. Bolt (M12 × 1.75 × 115)
50. Insulator

Exploded view of the front suspension used on 1982 and later models

NOTE: The end play should be between 0.001 and 0.005 in. If the play exceeds this tolerance, the wheel bearings should be replaced.

6. To complete the installation, reverse the removal procedures.

Ball Joints

INSPECTION

NOTE: Before performing this inspection, make sure the wheel bearings are adjusted and that the control arm bushings are in good condition.

1. Raise and support the front of the vehicle on jackstands, until there is 1–2 in. of clearance under the wheels.
2. Insert a bar under the wheel and pry upward. If the wheel raises more than $1/8$ in., the ball joints are worn. Determine if the upper or lower ball joint is worn by visual inspection while prying on the wheel.
3. The upper ball joint can be further inspected after partial suspension disassembly. If the stud has any detectable side-to-side movement or if it can be twisted with your fingers, it should be replaced.

NOTE: Due to the distribution of forces in the suspension, the lower ball joint is usually the defective joint. Because of this, most models are equipped with wear indicators on the lower ball joint as long as the indicator extends below the ball stud seat, replacement is unnecessary.

REMOVAL & INSTALLATION

Upper Ball Joint

NOTE: On 1982-87 vehicles, an upper ball joint is not used due to the strut design.

1. Raise and support the vehicle on jackstands.
2. Remove the tire and wheel assembly.
3. Support the lower control arm with a jack.
4. Remove the upper ball stud nut.
5. Using the ball joint removal tool J-23742, press the ball joint from the steering knuckle.
6. Using a $1/8$ in. drill bit, drill heads of the 4 ball joint rivets on the upper control arm to $1/4$ in. deep.
7. Using a $1/2$ in. drill bit, drill the remaining heads flush with the control arm, then use a small punch to drive the rivets out of holes.
8. Install the ball joint with the

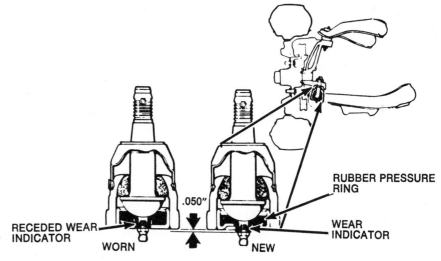

Wear indicator used on the lower ball joints—all models

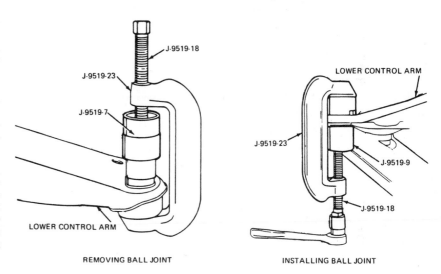

Removing and installing the lower ball joint

nuts and bolts supplied with the new joint (nuts on top). Torque the nuts and bolts to 8 ft. lbs.
9. Install the lube fitting in the new joint.
10. Mate the upper control arm to the steering knuckle and install the ball stud through the knuckle boss. Torque the ball stud to 65 ft. lbs. (1980–81). Install the cotter pin.

———— **CAUTION** ————
DO NOT back off on the nut to align the cotter pin.

11. To complete the installation, reverse the removal procedures.

Lower Ball Joint

1. Raise and support the front of the vehicle under the frame with jackstands. Remove the wheel and tire assembly.

2. Support the lower control arm with a floor jack.
3. Remove the cotter pin and loosen the lower ball stud nut.
4. Using tool J-24292A, break the ball stud loose from the steering knuckle. Separate the lower control arm from the steering knuckle.
5. Using the ball joint removal tool J-9519-10 (1980-81) or J-9519-23 (1982-87) and adapter tool J-9519-7, press the ball stud from the lower control arm.
6. Install the new ball joint to the lower control arm. Using the installation tool J-9510-10 (1980-81) or J-9519-23 (1982-87) and adapter tool J9519-9, press the ball joint into the lower control arm until it bottoms on the arm.

NOTE: When installing the new ball joint, position the purge vent

in the rubber boot facing inward.

7. To complete the installation, connect the ball joint-to-control arm assembly to the steering knuckle and torque the ball joint nut to 83 ft. lbs. (1980-81) or 77 ft. lbs. (1982-87), then reverse the removal procedures.

Lower Control Arm

REMOVAL & INSTALLATION

1. Refer to the "Coil Spring Removal & Installation" procedures in this section and remove the coil spring.
2. Remove the ball stud from the steering knuckle.
3. Remove the pivot bolts and the lower control arm.
4. To install, reverse the removal procedures. Torque the control arm pivot bolts to 90 ft. lbs. (1980-81) or 63 ft. lbs. (1982-87).

Upper Control Arm

REMOVAL & INSTALLATION

1. Refer to the "Upper Ball Joint Removal & Installation" procedures in this section and separate the upper ball joint from the steering knuckle.
2. Remove the upper control arm shaft pivot nuts.

NOTE: Tape the shims together and identify them so that they can be installed in the position from which they were removed.

3. Support the hub assembly to prevent damage to the brake line.
4. Remove the upper control arm from the vehicle.
5. To install, reverse the removal procedures. Make sure the shaft to frame bolts are installed in the same position they were in before removal and that the shims are in their original

positions. Torque the control arm pivot bolt nuts to 85 ft. lbs.

Steering Knuckle

REMOVAL & INSTALLATION

1980-81

1. Siphon some fluid from the brake master cylinder.
2. Raise and support the vehicle on jackstands.
3. Remove the wheel and tire assembly.
4. Remove the caliper from the steering knuckle and support on a wire.
5. Remove the grease cup, the cotter pin, the castle nut and the hub assembly.
6. Remove the three bolts holding the shield to the steering knuckle.
7. Using the ball joint removal tool J-6627, disconnect the tie rod from the steering knuckle.
8. Using ball joint removal tool J-23742, disconnect the ball joints from the steering knuckle.
9. Place a floor jack under the lower control arm (near the spring seat) and disconnect the ball joint from the steering knuckle.
10. Raise the upper control arm and disconnect the ball joint from the steering knuckle.
11. Remove the steering knuckle from the vehicle.
12. To install, reverse the removal procedures. Torque the upper ball joint-to-steering knuckle nut to 65 ft. lbs., the lower ball joint-to-steering knuckle nut to 90 ft. lbs. and the tie rod-to-steering knuckle nut to 40 ft. lbs. Adjust the wheel bearing and refill the master cylinder.

1982-87

1. Siphon some fluid from the brake master cylinder.

2. Raise and support the vehicle on jackstands.
3. Remove the wheel and tire assembly.
4. Remove the brake hose from the strut.
5. Remove the caliper from the steering knuckle and support on a wire.
6. Remove the grease cup, the cotter pin, the castle nut and the hub assembly.
7. Remove the splash shield.
8. Disconnect the tie rod from the steering knuckle.
9. Support the lower control arm on a jackstand. Using ball joint removal tool J-24292A, disconnect the ball joint from the steering knuckle.
10. Remove the strut-to-steering knuckle bolts and remove the steering knuckle.
11. To install, reverse the removal procedures. Torque the strut-to-steering knuckle bolts to 202 ft. lbs., the ball joint-to-steering knuckle nut to 78 ft. lbs. and the tie rod-to-steering knuckle nut to 35 ft. lbs. Adjust the wheel bearing and refill the master cylinder.

Stabilizer Bar

REMOVAL & INSTALLATION

1. Raise and support the front of the vehicle on jackstands.
2. Disconnect the stabilizer link bolts at the lower control arms.
3. Remove the stabilizer-to-frame clamps.
4. Remove the stabilizer bar.
5. To install, reverse the removal procedures. Torque the stabilizer-to-lower control arm bolts to 13 ft. lbs. and the stabilizer-to-frame bolts to 24 ft. lbs. (1980-81) or 37 ft. lbs. (1982-87).

CAVALIER

The J-cars use a MacPherson strut front suspension design. A MacPherson strut combines the functions of a shock absorber and an upper suspension member (upper arm) into one unit. The strut is surrounded by a coil spring, which provides normal front suspension functions.

The strut bolts to the body shell at its upper end, and to the steering knuckle at the lower end. The strut pivots with the steering knuckle by means of a sealed mounting assembly at the upper end which contains a preloaded, non-adjustable bearing.

The steering knuckle is connected to the chassis at the lower end by a conventional lower control arm, and pivots in the arm in a preloaded ball joint stud by means of a castellated nut and cotter pin.

MacPherson Struts

REMOVAL & INSTALLATION

The struts retain the springs under tremendous pressure even when removed from the car. For these reasons,

several expensive special tools and substantial specialized knowledge are required to safely and effectively work on these parts. Do not attempt to service any strut assembly unless these special tools are available.

1. Working under the hood, pry off the shock cover and then unscrew the upper strut-to-body nuts.
2. Loosen the wheel nuts, raise and support the car and then remove the wheel and tire.
3. Install a drive axle protective cover (J28712).
4. Use a two-armed puller and press

the tie rod out of the strut bracket.

5. Remove both strut-to-steering knuckle bolts and carefully lift out the strut.

6. Installation is in the reverse order of removal. Be sure that the flat sides of the strut-to-knuckle bolt heads are horizontal (see illustration).

STRUT MODIFICATION

This modification is made only if a camber adjustment is anticipated.

1. Place the strut in a vise. This step is not absolutely necessary; filing can be accomplished by disconnecting the strut from the steering knuckle.

2. File the holes in the outer flanges so as to enlarge the bottom holes until they match the slots already in the inner flanges.

3. Camber adjustment procedures are detailed later in this chapter.

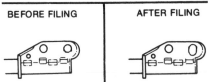

Modifying the strut mounting holes

Coil Springs

REMOVAL & INSTALLATION

────── CAUTION ──────

The coil springs are retained under considerable pressure. They can exert enough force to cause serious injury. Exercise extreme caution when disassembling the strut for coil spring removal.

This procedure requires the use of a spring compressor and several other special tools. It cannot be performed without them. If you do not have access to these tools, DO NOT attempt to disassemble the strut.

1. Remove the strut assembly.

2. Clamp the spring compressor (J26584) in a vise. Position the strut assembly in the bottom adapter of the compressor and install the special tool J26584-86 (see illustration). Be sure that the adapter captures the strut and that the locating pins are engaged.

3. Rotate the strut assembly so that the top mounting assembly lip aligns with the compressor support notch. Insert two top adapters (J26584-88) between the top mounting assembly and the top spring seat. Position the adapters so that the split lines are in the 3 o'clock and 9 o'clock positions.

4. Using a 1 in. socket, turn the screw on top of the compressor clockwise until the top support flange contacts the adapters. Continue turning the screw until the coil spring is compressed approximately $\frac{1}{2}$ in. (4 complete turns). Never bottom the spring or the strut damper rod.

5. Unscrew the nut from the strut damper shaft and then lift off the top mounting assembly.

6. Turn the compressor adjusting screw counterclockwise until the spring tension has been relieved. Remove the adapters and then remove the coil spring.

7. When installing a new spring, NEVER place a hard tool such as pliers or screwdriver against the polished surface of the damper shaft. The shaft can be held up with your fingers or an extension in order to prevent it from receding into the strut assembly while the spring is being compressed.

8. Installation is in the reverse order of removal.

Shock Absorbers

REMOVAL & INSTALLATION

The internal piston rod, cylinder assembly and fluid can be replaced utilizing a service cartridge and nut. Internal threads are located inside the tube immediately below a cut line groove.

1. Remove the strut and the coil springs. Clamp the strut in a vise. Do not overtighten it as this will cause damage to the strut tube.

2. Locate the cut line groove just below the top edge of the strut tube. It is imperative that the groove be accurately located as any mislocation will cause inner thread damage. Using pipe cutters, cut around the groove until the tube is completely cut through.

3. Remove and discard the end cap, the cylinder and the piston rod assembly. Remove the strut assembly from the vise and pour out the old fluid.

4. Reclamp the strut in the vise. A flaring cup tool is included in the replacement cartridge kit to flare and deburr the edge that was cut on the strut tube. Place the flaring cup on the open edge of the tube and strike it with a mallet until its flat outer surface rests on the top edge of the tube. Remove the cup and discard it.

5. Try the new nut to make sure

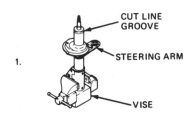

1.

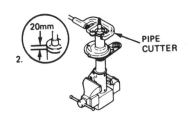

2.

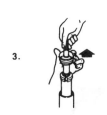

3.

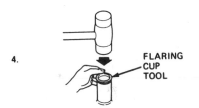

4.

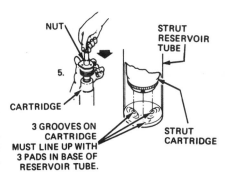

5.

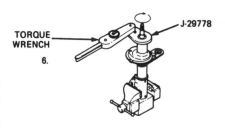

6.

Replacing the strut cartridge

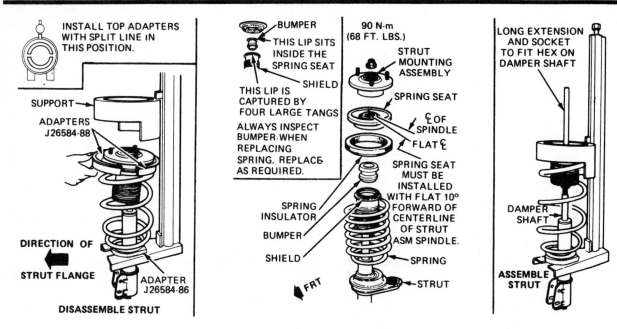

INSTALL TOP ADAPTERS WITH SPLIT LINE IN THIS POSITION.

SUPPORT

ADAPTERS J26584-88

DIRECTION OF

STRUT FLANGE

ADAPTER J26584-86

DISASSEMBLE STRUT

BUMPER

THIS LIP SITS INSIDE THE SPRING SEAT

SHIELD

THIS LIP IS CAPTURED BY FOUR LARGE TANGS

ALWAYS INSPECT BUMPER WHEN REPLACING SPRING. REPLACE AS REQUIRED.

90 N·m (68 FT. LBS.)

STRUT MOUNTING ASSEMBLY

SPRING SEAT

C OF SPINDLE

FLAT C

SPRING SEAT MUST BE INSTALLED WITH FLAT 10° FORWARD OF CENTERLINE OF STRUT ASM SPINDLE.

SPRING INSULATOR

BUMPER

SHIELD

FRT

SPRING

STRUT

LONG EXTENSION AND SOCKET TO FIT HEX ON DAMPER SHAFT

DAMPER SHAFT

ASSEMBLE STRUT

Coil spring removal and installation

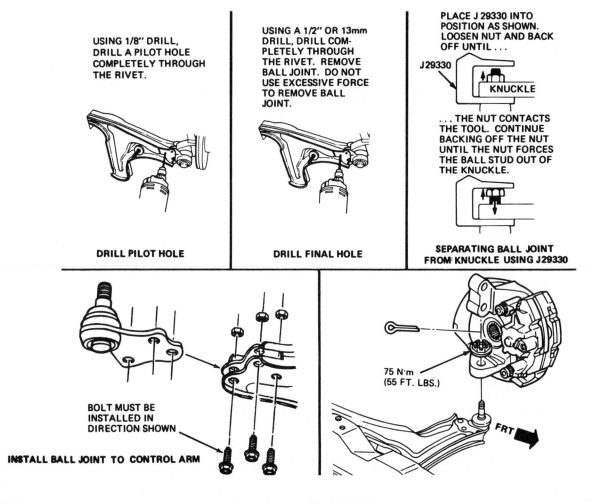

USING 1/8″ DRILL, DRILL A PILOT HOLE COMPLETELY THROUGH THE RIVET.

DRILL PILOT HOLE

USING A 1/2″ OR 13mm DRILL, DRILL COMPLETELY THROUGH THE RIVET. REMOVE BALL JOINT. DO NOT USE EXCESSIVE FORCE TO REMOVE BALL JOINT.

DRILL FINAL HOLE

PLACE J 29330 INTO POSITION AS SHOWN. LOOSEN NUT AND BACK OFF UNTIL . . .

J29330

KNUCKLE

. . . THE NUT CONTACTS THE TOOL. CONTINUE BACKING OFF THE NUT UNTIL THE NUT FORCES THE BALL STUD OUT OF THE KNUCKLE.

SEPARATING BALL JOINT FROM KNUCKLE USING J29330

BOLT MUST BE INSTALLED IN DIRECTION SHOWN

INSTALL BALL JOINT TO CONTROL ARM

75 N·m (55 FT. LBS.)

FRT

Ball joint removal and installation

that it threads properly. If not, use the flaring cup again until it does.

6. Place the new strut cartridge into the tube. Turn the cartridge until it settles into the indentations at the base of the tube. Place the nut over the cartridge.

7. Tighten the nut to 140–170 ft. lbs. Pull the piston rod up and down to check for proper operation.

8. Installation of the remaining components is in the reverse order of removal.

Ball Joints

INSPECTION

1. Raise and support the front of the car and let the suspension hang free.

2. Grasp the wheel at the top and the bottom and shake it in an "in-and-out" motion. Check for any horizontal movement of the steering knuckle relative to the lower control arm. Replace the ball joint if such movement is noted.

3. If the ball stud is disconnected from the steering knuckle and any looseness is detected, or if the ball stud can be twisted in its socket using finger pressure, replace the ball joint.

REMOVAL & INSTALLATION

NOTE: This procedure requires the use of a special tool. Only one ball joint is used in each lower arm. The MacPherson strut design does not use an upper ball joint.

1. Loosen the wheel nuts, raise the car, and remove the wheel.

2. Use a ⅛ in. drill bit to drill a hole through the center of each of the three all joint rivets.

3. Use a ½ in. drill bit to drill completely through the rivet.

4. Use a hammer and punch to remove the rivets. Drive them out from the bottom.

5. Use the special tool J29330 or a ball joint removal tool to separate the ball joint from the steering knuckle (see illustration). Don't forget to remove the cotter pin.

6. Disconnect the stabilizer bar from the lower control arm. Remove the ball joint.

7. Install the new ball joint into the control arm with the three bolts supplied as shown. Installation of the remaining components is in the reverse order of removal. Use a new cotter pin when installing the castellated nut on the ball joint. Check the toe setting and adjust as necessary.

Control Arm

REMOVAL & INSTALLATION

1. Raise and support the front of the car. Remove the wheel.

2. Disconnect the stabilizer bar from the control arm and/or support.

3. Separate the ball joint from the steering knuckle as previously detailed.

4. Remove the two control arm-to-support bolts and remove the control arm.

5. If control arm support bar removal is necessary, unscrew the six mounting bolts and remove the support.

6. Installation is in the reverse order of removal. Tighten the control arm support rail bolts in the sequence shown. Check the toe and adjust as necessary.

Wheel Bearings

The front wheel bearings are sealed, non-adjustable units which require no periodic attention. They are bolted to

the steering knuckle by means of an integral flange.

REPLACEMENT

NOTE: This procedure requires the use of special tools. You will need a special tool to pull the bearing free of the halfshaft, GM tool No. J-28733 or the equivalent. You should also use a halfshaft boot protector, GM tool No. J-28712 or the equivalent to protect the parts from damage.

1. Remove the wheel cover, loosen the hub nut, and raise and support the car. Remove the front wheel.

2. Install the boot cover, GM part No. J-28712 or the equivalent.

3. Remove and discard the hub nut. Be sure to use a new one on assembly, not the old one.

4. Remove the brake caliper and rotor:

    a. Remove the allen head caliper mounting bolts.

    b. Remove the caliper from the knuckle and suspend from a length of wire. Do not allow the caliper to

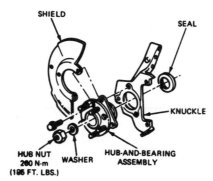

Hub and bearing attachment to the knuckle

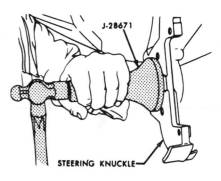

Use a seal driver when installing the new seal into the knuckle

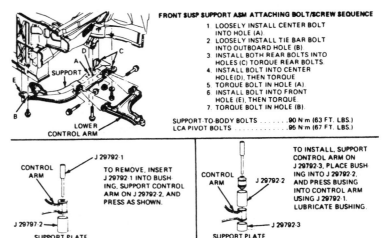

Installing the front suspension (control arm) support rail; be sure to follow the tightening sequence exactly

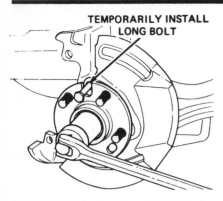

TEMPORARILY INSTALL LONG BOLT

Insert a bolt into the rotor when tightening the hub nut

hang from the brake hose. Pull the rotor from the knuckle.

5. Remove the three hub and bearing attaching bolts. If the old bearing is to be reused, match mark the bolts and holes for installation. The brake rotor splash shield will have to come off, too.

6. Attach a puller, GM part No. J-28733 or the equivalent, and remove the bearing. If corrosion is present, make sure the bearing is loose in the knuckle before using the puller.

7. Clean the mating surfaces of all dirt and corrosion. Check the knuckle bore and knuckle seal for damage. If a new bearing is to be installed, remove the old knuckle seal and install a new one. Grease the lips of the new seal before installation; install with a seal driver made for the purpose, GM tool No. J-28671 or the equivalent.

8. Push the bearing onto the halfshaft. Install a new washer and hub nut.

9. Tighten the new hub nut on the halfshaft until the bearing is seated. If the rotor and hub start to rotate as the hub nut is tightened, insert a long bolt through the cutout in the hub assembly to prevent rotation. Do not apply full torque to the hub nut at this time—just seal the bearing.

10. Install the brake shield and the bearing retaining bolts. Tighten the bolts evenly to 40 ft. lbs.

11. Install the caliper and rotor. Be sure that the caliper hose isn't twisted. Install the caliper bolts and tighten to 21–35 ft. lbs.

12. Install the wheel. Lower the car. Tighten the hub nut to 185 ft. lbs.

CHEVETTE

Shock Absorber

REMOVAL & INSTALLATION

NOTE: Purge new shock absorbers of air by repeatedly extending in the normal position and compressing while inverted.

1. Hold the shock absorber upper stem and remove the nut, upper retainer, and rubber grommet.
2. Raise the car on a hoist.
3. Remove the bolt from the lower end of the shock absorber and remove the shock absorber.
4. With the lower retainer and rubber grommet in position, extend the shock absorber stem and install the stem through the wheelhouse opening.
5. Install and torque the lower bolt to 22 ft. lbs. for 1980 and 35–50 ft. lbs. for 1981-87.

6. Lower the car.
7. Install the upper rubber grommet, retainer, and nut to the shock absorber stem.
8. Hold the shock absorber upper stem and torque the nut to 7 ft. lbs.

Lower Ball Joint

REMOVAL & INSTALLATION

NOTE: The ball joint studs use a special nut which must be discarded whenever loosened and removed. On assembly, use a standard nut to draw the ball joint into position on the knuckle, then remove the standard nut and install a new special nut for final installation.

1. Raise the car on a hoist.
2. Remove the tire and wheel.
3. Support the lower control arm with a hydraulic floor jack.
4. Loosen, but do not remove the lower ball stud nut.
5. Install a ball joint removal tool with the cup end over the upper ball stud nut.
6. Turn the threaded end of the ball joint removal tool until the ball stud is free of the steering knuckle.
7. Remove the ball joint removal tool and remove the nut from the ball stud.
8. Remove the ball joint.

NOTE: Inspect the tapered hole in the steering knuckle. Clean the area. If any out-of-roundness, deformation, or damage is found, the steering knuckle must be replaced.

9. To install the lower ball joint, mate the ball stud through the lower

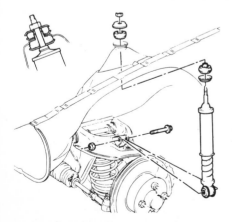

Front shock absorber mounting

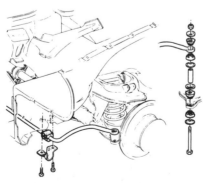

Front suspension stabilizer bar attachment

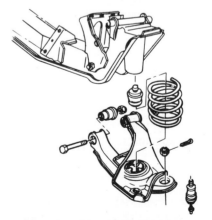

Correct position for front spring installation

control arm and into the steering knuckle.

10. Install and torque the ball stud nut to 41–54 ft. lbs.

11. Install the tire and wheel.

12. Lower the car. ,

Lower Control Arm and Coil Spring

REMOVAL & INSTALLATION

NOTE: **The ball joint studs use a special nut which must be discarded whenever loosened and removed. On assembly, use a standard nut to draw the ball joint into position on the knuckle, then remove the standard nut and install a new special nut for final installation.**

1. Raise the car on a frame contact hoist.

2. Remove the wheel and tire.

3. Disconnect the stabilizer bar from the lower control arm and disconnect the tie-rod from the steering knuckle.

4. Support the lower control arm with a jack.

5. Remove the nut from the lower ball joint, then use a ball joint removal tool to press out the lower ball joint.

6. Swing the knuckle and hub aside and attach them securely with wire.

7. Loosen the lower control arm pivot bolts.

8. As a safety precaution, install a chain through the coil spring.

9. Slowly lower the jack.

10. When the spring is extended as far as possible, use a pry bar to carefully lift the spring over the lower control arm seat. Remove the spring.

11. Remove the pivot bolts and remove the lower control arm.

12. Install the lower control arm and pivot bolts to the underbody brackets. Torque the lower control arm pivot bolts to 49 ft. lbs.

13. Position inspring correctly and install it in the upper pocket. Use tape to hold the insulator onto the spring.

14. Install the lower end of the spring onto the lower control arm. An assistant may be necessary to compress the spring far enough to slide it over the raised area of the lower control arm seat.

15. Use a jack to raise the lower control arm and compress the coil spring.

16. Install the ball joint through the lower control arm and into the steering knuckle. Install the nut on the ball stud and torque to 41–54 ft. lbs.

17. Connect the stabilizer bar to the lower control arm. Connect the tie-rod

to the steering knuckle. Install the wheel and tire.

18. Lower the car.

Upper Ball Joint

REMOVAL & INSTALLATION

NOTE: **The ball joint studs use a special nut which must be discarded whenever loosened and removed. on assembly, use a standard nut to draw the ball joint into position on the knuckle, then remove the standard nut and install a new special nut for the final installation.**

1. Raise the car on a hoist.

2. Remove the tire and wheel.

3. Support the lower control arm with a floor jack.

4. Loosen, but do not remove the upper ball stud nut.

5. Install a ball joint removal tool with the cup end over the lower ball stud nut.

6. Turn the threaded end of the ball joint removal tool until the upper ball stud is free of the steering knuckle.

7. Remove the ball joint removal tool and remove the nut from the ball stud.

8. Remove the two nuts and bolts attaching the ball joint to the upper control arm and remove the ball joint.

NOTE: **Inspect the tapered hole in the steering knuckle. Clean the area. If any out-of-roundness, deformation, or damage is found, the steering knuckle must be replaced.**

9. To install the upper ball joint, install the nuts and bolts attaching the ball joint to the upper control arm. Torque the nuts to 29 ft. lbs. Then mate the upper control arm ball stud to the steering knuckle.

10. Install and torque the ball stud nut to 29–36 ft. lbs.

11. Install the tire and wheel.

12. Lower the car.

Upper Control Arm

REMOVAL & INSTALLATION

NOTE: **The ball joint studs use a special nut which must be discarded whenever loosened and removed. On assembly, use a standard nut to draw the ball joint into position on the knuckle, then remove the standard nut and in-**

stall a new special nut for final installation.

1. Raise the car and support it safely.

2. Remove the tire and wheel.

3. Support the lower control arm with a floor jack.

4. Remove the upper ball joint from the steering knuckle as previously described.

5. Remove the upper control arm pivot bolts and remove the upper control arm.

6. To install the upper control arm, install the upper control arm with its pivot bolts.

NOTE: **The inner pivot bolt must be installed with the bolt head toward the front.**

7. Install the pivot bolt nut.

8. Position the upper control arm in a horizontal plane and torque the nut to 43–50 ft. lbs.

9. Install the ball joint to the upper control arm and to the steering knuckle as previously described. Torque the ball joint-to-upper control arm attaching bolts to 29 ft. lbs. Torque the ball stud nut to 29–36 ft. lbs.

10. Install the tire and wheel.

11. Lower the car.

FRONT WHEEL BEARING ADJUSTMENT

1. Raise the car and support at the front lower control arm.

2. Remove the hub cap or wheel cover from the wheel. Remove the dust cap from the hub.

3. Remove the cotter pin from the spindle and spindle nut.

4. Spin the wheel forward by hand and tighten the spindle nut to 12 ft. lbs. This will fully seat the bearings.

5. Back off the nut to a just loose position.

6. Hand-tighten the spindle nut. Loosen the spindle nut until either hole in the spindle aligns with a slot in the nut, but not more than $\frac{1}{2}$ flat.

7. Install a new cotter pin, bend the ends of the pin against the nut, and cut off any extra length to avoid interference with the dust cap.

8. Proper bearing adjustment should give 0.001–0.005 in. of endplay.

9. Install the dust cap on the hub and the hub cap or wheel cover on the wheel.

10. Lower the car.

11. Adjust the opposite front wheel bearings.

SPECTRUM

Control Arm

REMOVAL & INSTALLATION

1. Raise and support the front of the vehicle.
2. Remove the control arm to tension arm retaining nuts and bolts.
3. Remove the nut/bolt securing the control arm to the body.
4. Remove the control arm and check for cracking or distortion.
5. To install, reverse the removal procedure.

NOTE: Raise the control arm to a distance of 15 in. from the top of the wheel well to the center of the hub. Use 41 ft. lbs. of torque to fasten the control arm to the body and 80 ft. lbs. to secure the control arm to the tension rod. This procedure aligns the bushing arm to the body.

Ball Joint

INSPECTION

Before removing the ball joint for replacement, check it and the boot for excessive wear or damage.

REMOVAL & INSTALLATION

1. Loosen the wheel nuts.
2. Raise the vehicle and support it on jackstands.
3. Remove the wheel and tire assembly.
4. Remove the two nuts retaining the ball joint to the tension rod and control arm assembly.
5. Remove the pinch bolt retaining the ball joint to the steering knuckle.
6. Remove the ball joint.
7. To install, reverse the removal procedure.

Tension Rod

REMOVAL & INSTALLATION

1. Raise and support the vehicle on jackstands.
2. If equipped with a stabilizer bar, remove the nuts, bolts and insulators retaining it to the tension rod.
3. Remove the nut and washer retaining the tension rod to the body.
4. Remove the nuts and bolts retaining the tension rod to the control rod.
5. Remove the tension rod.

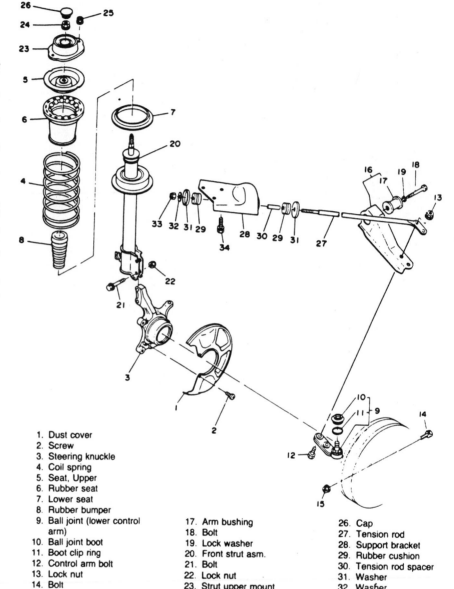

1. Dust cover
2. Screw
3. Steering knuckle
4. Coil spring
5. Seat, Upper
6. Rubber seat
7. Lower seat
8. Rubber bumper
9. Ball joint (lower control arm)
10. Ball joint boot
11. Boot clip ring
12. Control arm bolt
13. Lock nut
14. Bolt
15. Lock nut
16. Lower arm asm.
17. Arm bushing
18. Bolt
19. Lock washer
20. Front strut asm.
21. Bolt
22. Lock nut
23. Strut upper mount
24. Flange nut (strut shaft)
25. Nut
26. Cap
27. Tension rod
28. Support bracket
29. Rubber cushion
30. Tension rod spacer
31. Washer
32. Washer
33. Lock nut
34. Bolt

Exploded view of the front suspension assembly

6. To install, reverse the removal procedure.

Stabilizer Bar

REMOVAL & INSTALLATION

1. Raise and support the vehicle on jack stands.
2. Remove the nuts, bolts and insulators retaining the stabilizer bar to the tension rod.
3. Remove the stabilizer bar.

4. To install, reverse the removal procedure. Align the front side of the insulator edge with the paint mark on the upper rear edge of the tension bar.

MacPherson Strut

REMOVAL & INSTALLATION

1. Open the hood. Remove the nuts retaining the strut to the body.
2. Loosen the wheel nuts. Raise the vehicle and support it on jackstands.

3. Remove the wheel and tire assembly.

4. Remove the brake hose clip at the strut bracket.

5. Disconnect the brake hose at the brake caliper.

6. Tape or cap the brake hose and caliper opening.

7. Pull the brake hose through the opening in the strut bracket.

8. Remove the nuts retaining the strut to the steering knuckle.

9. Remove the strut assembly.

10. To install, reverse the removal procedure and bleed the brake system.

INSPECTION

Check the shock absorber for leaks or defective operation and the coil spring for wear, cracks or distortion.

SPRINT

MacPherson Strut

REMOVAL & INSTALLATION

1. Raise and support the front of the vehicle.

2. Remove the wheel assembly.

3. Remove the brake hose securing ring and the hose from the strut.

4. Remove the upper strut support nuts from the engine compartment.

5. Remove the strut-to-steering knuckle bolts and the strut.

6. To install, reverse the removal procedures. Torque the upper mounting nuts to 13–20 ft. lbs. and the strut-to-steering knuckle bolts to 50–65 ft. lbs.

Stabilizer Bar

REMOVAL & INSTALLATION

1. Raise and support the front of the vehicle on jackstands. Remove the front wheel assemblies.

2. Remove the stabilizer bar-to-body mounting bolts.

3. Remove the cotter pin, the castle nut, the washer, the bushing and the stabilizer bar from the lower control arms.

4. To install, reverse the removal procedures. Torque the stabilizer bar-to-control arm to 29–65 ft. lbs. and the stabilizer bar-to-body bolts to 22–39 ft. lbs.

Ball Joint

The ball joint is part of the control arm and can only be serviced as an assembly. To service the ball joint/control arm assembly, please refer to the "Control Arm Removal & Installation" procedures in this section.

Lower Control Arm

REMOVAL & INSTALLATION

1. Raise and support the front of the vehicle on jackstands. Remove the front wheel assembly.

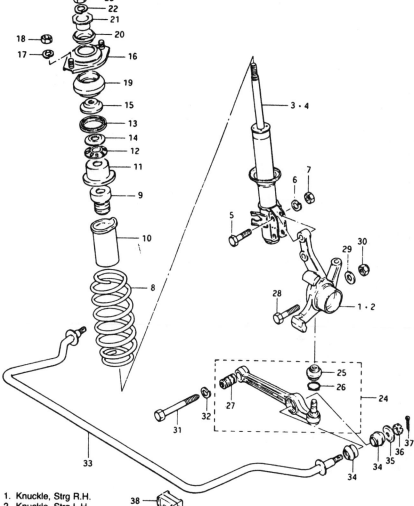

1. Knuckle, Strg R.H.
2. Knuckle, Strg L.H.
3. Absorber, W/Strut R.H.
4. Absorber, W/Strut L.H.
5. Bolt, Strut Brkt
6. Washer, Lk
7. Nut
8. Spring, Frt Coil
9. Stopper, Frt Bpr
10. Seat, Frt Spr
11. Seat, Srt Spr Upr
12. Bearing, Frt Strut
13. Seal, Frt Strut Brg Dust
14. Seat, Frt Strut Brg
15. Seat, Strut Mt
16. Support, Frt Strut
17. Washer (3/8 × 11/16)
18. Nut (M8 × 1.25 × 6)
19. Mount, Frt Strut
20. Stopper, Frt Strut Rebound
21. Support, Frt Strut Inr
22. Washer
23. Nut
24. Arm, Frt Cont
25. Seal, Ball Stud Dust
26. Clip, Dust Seal
27. Bushing, Cont Arm
28. Bolt, Ball Stud
29. Washer, Ball Stud
30. Nut, Ball Stud Lk
31. Bolt, Cont Arm
32. Washer (3/8 × 11/16)
33. Shaft, Frt Stab
34. Bushing, Stab Shf
35. Washer, Stab Shf
36. Nut (M12 × 1.25 × 10)
37. Pin
38. Mount, Stab Shf
39. Bracket, Stab Shf Mt
40. Bolt
41. Washer, Lk

Front suspension

2. Remove the cotter pin, the castle nut, the washer and the bushing from the stabilizer bar.

3. Remove the stabilizer bar-to-body mounting bracket bolts.

4. Remove the ball stud and the control arm bolts.

5. Remove the control arm.

6. To install, reverse the removal procedures. Torque the control arm-to-body bolt to 36–50 ft. lbs.; the ball stud-to-steering knuckle to 36–50 ft. lbs.; the stabilizer bar-to-control arm to 29–65 ft. lbs. and the stabilizer bar-to-body to 22–39 ft. lbs.

Front Hub

REMOVAL & INSTALLATION

1. Raise and support the front of the vehicle on jackstands. Remove the front wheel assembly.

2. Remove the dust cap and the cotter pin from the axle shaft.

3. Loosen the castle nut on the axle shaft.

4. Remove the brake caliper bolts and the brake caliper.

NOTE: When removing the brake caliper, DO NOT remove the brake hose, suspend it on a wire.

5. Remove the castle nut and the washer from the axle shaft.

6. Using a slide hammer tool J–2619–01 and a brake drum remover tool J–34866, pull the hub from the steering knuckle.

7. Remove the spacing ring from the rear of the hub.

8. Remove the bolts and separate the hub from the brake disc.

9. To install, place the spacing ring on the hub (install beveled side first)

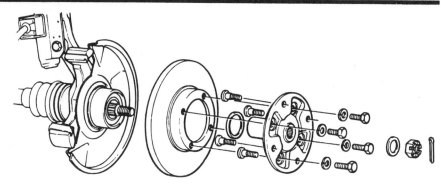

Exploded view of the front wheel hub assembly

and reverse the removal procedures. Torque the hub-to-brake disc bolts to 29–43 ft. lbs., the brake caliper bolts to 17–26 ft. lbs. and the axle shaft nut to 108–195 ft. lbs.

NOTE: When installing the hub to the steering knuckle, tap it with a plastic hammer to align the hub, then, using the installation tool J-34856, drive the hub into the steering knuckle.

Steering Knuckle And Wheel Bearings

REMOVAL & INSTALLATION

1. Refer to the "Front Hub Removal & Installation" procedures in this section and remove the hub from the steering knuckle.

2. Remove the tie rod end cotter pin and nut.

3. Using the ball joint puller tool J-21687-02, remove the ball joint from

the steering knuckle.

4. Remove the ball stud bolt from the steering knuckle.

5. Remove the strut-to-steering knuckle bolts.

6. Remove the steering knuckle and support the axle shaft on a wire.

7. Using a brass drift and a hammer, drive the wheel bearings from the steering knuckle.

8. Remove the spacer and clean the steering knuckle cavity.

9. Lubricate the new bearings and the steering knuckle cavity.

10. Using the installation tool J-34856, drive the new bearings (with the internal seals facing outward) into the steering knuckle.

11. Using the seal installation tool J-34881, drive the new seal into the steering knuckle (grease the seal lip).

12. To complete the installation, reverse the removal procedures. Torque the strut-to-steering knuckle bolts to 50–65 ft. lbs.; the ball joints-to-steering knuckle nuts to 22–40 ft. lbs. and the axle shaft castle nut to 108–195 ft. lbs.

NOVA

MacPherson Strut

REMOVAL & INSTALLATION

1. Remove the hubcap and loosen the lugnuts.

2. Unfasten the three nuts which secure the upper shock absorber mounting plate to the top of the wheel arch. Raise the front of the car and support it securely at approved support points.

3. Remove the lugnuts and the front wheel. Detach the front brake line at the clamp on the strut. Disconnect the brake hose to brake pipe con-

nection at the mount on the body. Catch any fluid that drains in a pan. Pull the brake hose back through the opening the the strut bracket. Tape both open ends of the hydraulic system.

4. Remove the brake caliper and wire it up and out of the way. Support the caliper securely so that the brake hose will not be under any strain (you do not need to disconnect the hose from the caliper.).

5. Mark the adjusting cam so the camber adjustment can be restored when the strut is reassembled. Remove the two bolts attaching the lower end of the shock absorber to the steer-

ing knuckle lower arm. Remove the strut assembly.

6. Remove the camber adjusting cam from the knuckle. Install a cloth over the drive axle boot to protect it while the strut is removed.

7. Install in reverse order. Note the following points:

a. When installing the camber adjusting cam back into the knuckle, make sure to restore the alignment adjustment.

b. Install the strut with the studs at the top passing through the holes in the body. Then, install the strut-to-knuckle attaching bolts and nuts and torque to 105 ft. lbs.

c. When reconnecting the disconnected brake hose, make sure to route it properly (back through the strut bracket) and to torque the fitting to 11 ft. lbs. Bleed the brake system.

d. Install the studs on top of the strut through the body. Then, install the nuts and torque them to 13 ft. lbs. Pack the shaft nut area with grease before installing the dust cover.

e. Lower the vehicle to the ground and torque the wheel lugnuts to 76 ft. lbs.

FRONT WHEEL BEARING ADJUSTMENT

Front wheel bearings on the Nova are not adjusted as a normal maintenance operation. If the hub is disassembled, it is simply pressed back together until fully assembled using special tools.

Ball Joints

INSPECTION

1. Turn the front wheels so they are straight and chock the rear wheels. Raise the vehicle and place a wooden block of 7–8 in. under it. Then, lower the vehicle onto the block until the spring is compressed to only about half its compression when the vehicle is resting on it.

2. Attempt to move the lower arm up and down. There should be no noticeable play.

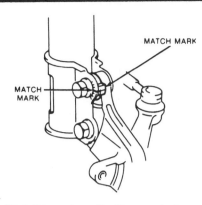

MATCH MARK
MATCH MARK

Mark the camber adjusting cam before removing the knuckle attaching nuts and bolts so camber can be restored without rechecking alignment

3. If the ball joint is off the vehicle you can check the required rotating torque with and inch pound torque wrench. Flip the ball joint all the way back and forth five times. Then, install the nut and turn the stud with a torque wrench at a rate of about one turn in three seconds. At the fifth turn, measure the required torque; it should be 9–30 inch lbs. If outside these specifications, replace the ball joint.

REMOVAL & INSTALLATION

1. Raise and support the vehicle via approved jacking points. Remove the front wheel.

2. Remove the two nuts and one bolt which attach the ball joint to the lower control arm.

3. Remove the nut attaching the ball joint stud to the steering knuckle. Then, press the stud out of the steering knuckle with an appropriate special tool.

— CAUTION —

Use a new self-locking nut in the following step. Failure to do so could create an unsafe front suspension.

4. Install in reverse order. Install a new self-locking nut and torque to 82 ft. lbs. Torque the ball joint-to-lower arm nuts and bolt to 47 ft. lbs.

Lower Control Arm

REMOVAL & INSTALLATION

1. Raise the front of the vehicle and support it with jackstands. Remove the wheel.

2. Remove the two nuts attaching the ball joint to the steering knuckle.

3. Remove the bracket bolts (two each) for the front and rear mounts.

7. Install in reverse order, noting the following points:

a. First install the lower arm-to-body mounting bolts just finger tight.

b. Install and torque the ball joint-to-arm nuts and bolt to 47 ft. lbs.

c. Install the wheel and lower the vehicle. Finally, torque the lower arm bracket bolts to 105 ft. lbs. for the front and 64 ft. lbs. for the rear.

e. Adjust front end alignment.

CORSICA AND BERETTA

MacPherson Strut

REMOVAL & INSTALLATION

1. Inside the engine compartment, remove the upper strut to body mounting bolts.

2. Raise and safely support the vehicle allowing the suspension to hang freely.

3. Remove the wheel and tire.

4. Remove the tie rod nut and disconnect the tie rod from the steering knuckle using tool J-29330, or equivalent.

5. Support the steering knuckle to prevent the brake hose from being torn.

6. Support the strut assembly and remove the strut to steering knuckle mounting bolts.

7. Remove the strut from the vehicle.

8. Installation is the reverse of the removal. Torque the strut to knuckle bolts to 133 ft. lbs. Torque the strut to body nuts and bolt to 18 ft. lbs.

Lower Ball Joints

INSPECTION

1. Raise and safely support the vehicle so the front suspension is hanging freely.

2. Grasp and shake the wheel at the top and bottom to feel if there is any in and out movement.

3. Replace the ball joint if any movement is detected.

4. When the ball joint is disconnected from the knuckle, check for any looseness or if the ball joint can be twisted freely in the socket by hand.

REMOVAL & INSTALLATION

1. Raise and safely support the vehicle. Remove the wheel and tire.

2. Countersink the center of the mounting rivets with a punch.

3. Drill a pilot hole through the rivet with a ⅛ in. drill bit.

4. Use a ½ in. drill bit and drill completely through the rivet.

5. Using ball joint separating tool J-29330, or equivalent, separate the ball joint from the knuckle.

6. Remove the ball joint from the lower control arm. Clean any debris from the ball joint rivet.

7. To install, position the new ball joint on the control arm and install the

three (3) mounting bolts with the nuts on the top. Torque the nuts to 50 ft. lbs.

8. The remainder of the installation is the reverse of the removal. Torque the ball joint stud to 55 ft. lbs.

Lower Control Arm

REMOVAL & INSTALLATION

1. Raise and safely support the vehicle. Remove the wheel and tire.
2. Disconnect the stabalizer bar from the control arm.
3. Separate the ball joint from the knuckle using tool J–29330, or equivalent.
4. Remove the control arm to subframe mounting bolts and remove the control arm.
5. Installation is the reverse of the removal. Torque the control arm mounting bolts to 63 ft. lbs. Torque the ball joint stud to 55 ft. lbs.

Front Wheel Alignment

ADJUSTMENT

Caster and camber are preset at the factory and are not adjustable. Toe can

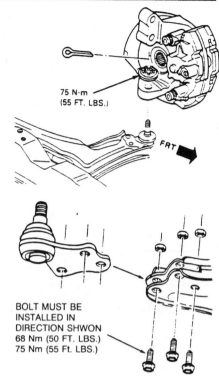

Front strut mounting

be adjusted by loosening the clamps on the outer tie rods and rotating the tie

Lower ball joint installation

rods to obtain the proper specification. Torque the tie rod clamp to 33 ft. lbs.

LIGHT TRUCKS AND VANS
BLAZER/JIMMY — FULL SIZE, BLAZER/JIMMY — S-SERIES PICK-UPS — FULL SIZE, PICK-UPS — S-SERIES, SUBURBAN, VANS — FULL SIZE AND ASTRO

Two wheel drive models use coil spring independent front suspension. A stabilizer (sway) bar is optional to minimize body lean and sway in curves. Four wheel drive models have a non-independent leaf spring front suspension. A stabilizer bar is standard. A steering linkage damper is standard on late models. Heavy duty shock absorbers, springs, and stabilizer bars have been optional for most models. S–Series trucks (2WD) front suspension is similar to standard size pickups. Four wheel drive models use a torsion bar-type front suspension.

Springs

REMOVAL & INSTALLATION

NOTE: Springs, particularly coil springs, are under consider-

able tension. Be very careful when removing and installing them; they can exert enough force to cause very serious injuries.

2WD Models

1. Raise the vehicle and support it under the frame so that the control arms will hang free.
2. Remove the lower shock absorber mounting bolt. Detach the stabilizer bar from the lower control arm.
3. Place a floor jack under the lower control arm crosshaft.

NOTE: As a safety precaution, install a chain through the spring and lower control arm.

4. Raise the jack. This will remove the tension of the lower control arm so that the two U-bolts which secure the cross-shaft can be removed.

5. Lower the control arm slowly by releasing the floor jack to the point where the spring can be removed.
6. Remove the spring.
7. Place the spring on the control arm and then, using a jack, slowly raise the control arm. Use the safety chain as described in Step 3.
8. Place the control arm cross-shaft onto the crossmember and then install

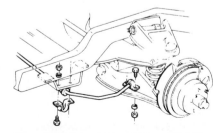

Two wheel drive coil spring and stabilizer

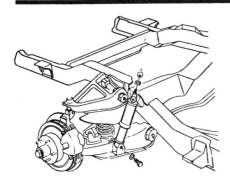

Two wheel drive front shock absorber

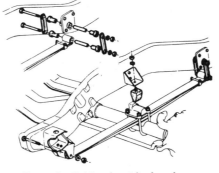

Four wheel drive front leaf spring

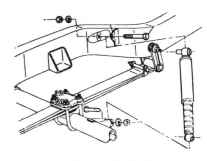

Four wheel drive front shock absorber

the U-bolts and the attaching nuts. Make certain that the indexing hole in the cross-shaft is lined up with the crossmember stud.

9. Torque the U-bolt nuts to 85 ft. lbs. Remove the safety chain.

10. Install the lower part of the shock absorber and the stabilizer bar.

11. Lower the vehicle.

4WD Models

1. Raise and support the truck under the front axle and frame so that the tension on the springs is relieved.

2. Remove the shackle upper retaining bolt and the front spring eye bolt.

3. Remove the spring-to-axle U-bolt nuts. Pull off the spring, the lowerplate, and the spring pads.

4. Remove the shackle-to-spring bolts, bushings and shackle. To replace the bushing, place the spring onto a press or vise and press out the bushing. Press in the new bushing. The new bushing should protrude evenly on both sides of the spring.

5. Install the spring shackle bushings into the spring and then attach the shackle. Do not tighten the bolt.

6. Place the upper spring cushion onto the spring.

7. Place the front of the spring into the frame and install the bolt but do not tighten it.

8. Position the shackle bushing into the frame and attach the rear shackle but do not tighten it.

9. Install the lower spring pad and the spring retainer plate. Tighten the U-bolts to 150 ft. lbs.

10. Torque the rear spring shackle bolts an the rear eye bolts to 50 ft. lbs. and the front eye bolts to 90 ft. lbs.

11. Lower the vehicle.

Torsion Bar (S-Series 4WD)

REMOVAL & INSTALLATION

1. Raise and safely support the vehicle.

2. Remove the torsion bar adjusting screw.

3. Remove support retainer attaching nuts and bolts.

4. Slide torsion bar forward in lower control arm until torsion bar clears support. Pull down on bar and remove from control arm.

5. Count the number of turns when removing the torsion bar for easy reinstallation. Apply lubricant to top of adjusting arm and adjusting bolt for easy reinstallation. Also apply lubricant to hex ends of torsion bar. Installation is the reverse of removal.

Shock Absorbers

The usual procedure for testing shock absorbers is to stand on the bumper at the end nearest the shock being tested and start the vehicle bouncing up and down. Step off; the vehicle should come to rest within one bounce cycle. Another good test is to drive the vehicle over a bumpy road. Bouncing over bumps is normal, but the shock absorbers should stop the bouncing, af-ter the pump is passed, within one or two cycles.

REMOVAL & INSTALLATION

This usual procedure is to replace shock absorbers in axle pairs, to provide equal damping. Heavy duty replacements are available for firmer control.

1. Raise and support the front axle as necessary.

2. Remove the bolt and nut from the lower shock end.

3. On two wheel drive original equipment shocks, remove the upper stud nut from inside the frame. On four wheel drive shocks, remove the upper bolt and nut.

4. Purge the new shock of air by extending it in its normal position and compressing it while inverted. Do this several times. It is normal for there to be more resistance to extension than to compression.

5. Install the shock absorber. Tighten the two wheel drive upper stud nut (inside the frame) to 8 ft. lbs. and the four wheel drive upper bolt to 65 ft. lbs. Tighten the 2WD lower bolt to 60 ft. lbs. Tighten the 4WD lower bolt to 65 ft. lbs.

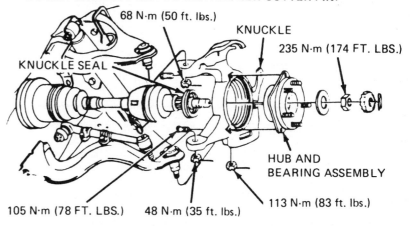

Removal and installation of hub, bearing assembly, knuckle and seal

Steering Knuckle S-Series

REMOVAL & INSTALLATION

1. Raise front of vehicle and support with floor stands under front lift points. Remove the wheel. Spring tension is needed to assist in breaking ball joint studs loose from steering knuckle. Do not place stands under lower control arm.
2. Remove caliper.
3. Remove hub and rotor assembly.
4. Remove the three bolts attaching shield to knuckle.
5. Remove tie-rod end from knuckle using Tool J–6627 or equivalent.
6. Carefully remove knuckle seal if knuckle is to be replaced.
7. Remove ball studs from steering knuckle using tool J–23742 or equivalent.

—————— CAUTION ——————

Floor jack must remain under control arm spring seat during removal and installation to retain spring and control arm in position.

8. Position a floor jack under lower control arm near spring seat and raise jack until it supports lower control arm.
9. Raise upper control arm to disengage ball joint stud from knuckle.
10. Raise knuckle from lower ball joint stud and remove knuckle. Inspect the tapered hole in the steering knuckle. Remove any dirt. If out-of-roundness, deformation, or damage is noted, the knuckle MUST be replaced.
11. Insert upper and lower ball joint studs into knuckle and install nuts.
12. Install shield to knuckle seal and splash shield. Torque attaching bolts to 10 ft. lbs.
13. Install tie rod end into knuckle. Install tool J–29193 or equivalent and torque to 15 ft. lbs. Remove tool and install nut to 40 ft. lbs.
14. Replace wheel bearings. Install hub and disc assembly.
15. Adjust wheel bearings. Install caliper.
16. Install remaining parts in reverse order of removal.

Steering Knuckle 2WD Model

REMOVAL & INSTALLATION

1. Raise vehicle and support lower control arms.
2. Remove wheel.
3. Remove caliper.
4. Remove disc splash shield bolts

securing the shield to the steering knuckle. Remove shield. Disconnect the tie-rod ends
5. Remove upper and lower ball stud cotter pins and loosen ball stud nuts. Free steering knuckle from ball studs by installing Special Tool J–23742 or equivalent. Remove ball stud nuts and withdraw steering knuckle.
6. Place knuckle in position and insert upper and lower ball studs into knuckle bosses. The steering knuckle hole, ball stud and nut should be free of dirt and grease before tightening nut.
7. Install ball stud nuts and tighten nut to 80–100 ft. lbs. If necessary, tighten one more notch to insert cotter pins. Do not loosen nut to insert cotter pin.
8. Reverse remaining removal procedure, and tighten splash shield mounting bolt. Tighten two caliper assembly mounting bolts to 35 ft. lbs. torque.
9. Adjust wheel bearings.
10. Tighten wheel nuts to 75 ft. lbs.

Steering Knuckle 4WD With Ball Joints

REMOVAL & INSTALLATION

1. Remove the automatic locking hub, hub-and-disc assembly, and spindle components.
2. If the steering arm is to be removed, disconnect the tie rod. Remove cotter pin. Loosen tie rod nuts and tap on nut with a soft hammer to break the studs loose from the knuckle arm. Remove nuts and disconnect the tie rod. If it is necessary to remove the steering arm, discard the self-locking nuts and replace with new nuts at assembly.
3. Remove the cotter pin from the upper ball socket nut.
4. Remove the retaining nuts from the upper and lower ball sockets.
5. Remove the knuckle assembly from the yoke by inserting a suitable wedge-shaped tool between the lower ball stud and the yoke and tapping on the tool to release the knuckle assembly. Repeat as required at the upper ball stud location.
6. Do not remove the yoke upper ball stud adjusting sleeve unless new ball studs are being installed, If it is necessary to loosen the sleeve to remove the knuckle, do not loosen it more than two threads. The non-hardened threads in the yoke can be easily damaged by the hardened threads in the adjusting sleeve if caution is not used. Installation is the reverse of removal.
7. Position the knuckle and sockets

to the yoke. Install new nuts finger tight to the upper (the nut with the cotter pin slot) and lower ball socket studs.
8. Push up on the knuckle (to keep the ball socket from turning in the knuckle) while tightening the lower socket retaining nut. PARTIALLY torque lower nut to 30 ft. lbs.
9. Torque the yoke upper ball stud adjusting sleeve to 50 ft. lbs.
10. Torque the upper ball socket nut to 100 ft. lbs. After torquing the nut, do not loosen to install cotter pin, apply additional torque, if necessary, to line up hole in stud with slot in nut.
11. Apply FINAL torque to lower nut, 70 ft. lbs.
12. If the tie rod and steering arm were removed: Assemble the steering arm using the three stud adapters and three new self-locking nuts. Torque the nuts to 90 ft. lbs. Assemble the tie rod to the knuckle arm. Torque the tie rod nuts to 45 ft. lbs. and install cotter pin.

Ball Joints

Service procedures for 4WD models are found under "Steering Knuckle".

INSPECTION

Excessive ball joint wear will usually show up as wear on the inside of the front tires. Don't jump to conclusions; front end misalignment can give the same symptom.

Upper Ball Joint

1. Raise and support the truck; let the control arms hang freely.
2. Measure the distance between the tip of the ball joint stud and the tip of the grease fitting below the ball joint.
3. Move the support to the control arm and allow the wheel and tire to hang free. Measure the distance again. If the vibration between the two measurements exceed $3/32$ in. the ball joint should be replaced.

NOTE: This is the manufacturer's recommended wear limit. Your state inspection regulations may disagree. Follow the state regulations if they are more strict.

REMOVAL & INSTALLATION

NOTE: Observe the Caution under Front Spring Removal and Installation when working with ball joints.

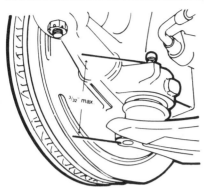

Lower ball joint inspection

Lower Ball Joint

1. Raise and support the truck. Support the lower control arm with a floor jack.

2. Remove the tire and wheel.

3. Remove the lower stud cotter pin and loosen, but do not remove, the stud nut.

4. Loosen the ball joint stud with a ball joint stud removal tool. It may be necessary to remove the brake caliper and wire it to the frame to gain enough clearance. Do not let the caliper hang by the hose.

5. When the stud is loose, remove the tool and ball stud nut.

6. Pull the brake disc and knuckle assembly up and off the ball stud and support the upper arm with a block of wood.

7. Remove the ball joint from the control arm with a ball joint removal tool. It must be pressed out.

8. To install: Start the new ball joint into the control arm. Position the bleed vent in the rubber boot facing inward.

9. Seat the ball joint in the control arm. It must be pressed in.

10. Lower the upper arm and match the steering knuckle to the lower ball stud.

11. Install the brake caliper, if removed.

12. Install the ball stud nut and torque it to 90 ft. lbs. plus the additional torque necessary to align the cotter pin hole. Do not exceed 130 ft. lbs. or back the nut off to align the holes with the pin.

13. Install a new lube fitting and lubricate the new joint.

14. Install the tire and wheel.

15. Lower the truck.

Upper Ball Joint

1. Raise and support the truck.

2. Support the lower control arm with a floor jack.

3. Remove the cotter pin from the upper ball stud and loosen, but do not remove the stud nut.

4. Using a ball joint stud removal tool, loosen the ball stud in the steering knuckle. When the stud is loose, remove the tool and the stud nut. It will be necessary to remove the brake caliper and wire it to the frame to gain clearance. Do not allow the caliper to hang by the hose.

5. Drill out the rivets. Remove the ball joint assembly.

6. Install the service ball joint, using the nuts supplied. Tighten the nuts to 45 ft. lbs.

7. Torque the ball stud nut to 50 ft. lbs. plus the additional torque required to align the cotter pin. Do not exceed 90 ft. lbs. and never back the nut off to align the pin.

8. Install a new cotter pin.

9. Install a new lube fitting and lubricate the new joint.

10. If removed, install the brake caliper.

11. Install the wheel and tire and lower the truck.

Upper Control Arm— Except S-Series

REMOVAL & INSTALLATION

1. Raise and support the truck on jackstands.

2. Support the lower control arm with a floor jack.

3. Remove the wheel and tire.

4. Remove the cotter pin from the upper control arm ball stud and loosen the stud nut one turn.

5. Loosen the upper control arm ball stud in the steering knuckle using a ball joint stud removal tool. Remove the nut from the ball stud and raise the upper arm to clear the steering knuckle. It will be necessary to remove the brake caliper and wire it to the frame to gain clearance.

6. Remove the nuts securing the control arm shaft to the frame and remove the control arm. Tape the shims and spacers together and tag for proper reassembly.

7. Installation is the reverse of removal. Place the control arm in position and install the nuts. Before tightening the nuts to 70 ft. lbs., insert the caster and camber shims in the same order as when removed. Have the front end alignment checked, and as necessary, adjusted.

Lower Control Arm— Except S-Series

REMOVAL & INSTALLATION

1. Raise and support the truck on

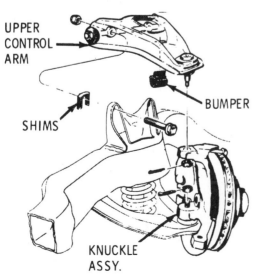

Upper control arm

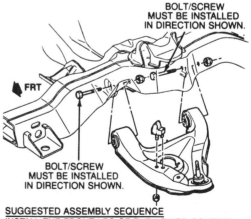

Lower control arm attachment

jackstands.

2. Remove the spring. See Spring Removal and Installation.

3. Support the inboard end of the control arm after spring removal.

4. Remove the cotter pin from the lower ball stud and loosen the nut one turn.

5. Loosen th lower ball stud in the steering knuckle using a ball joint stud removal tool. When the stud is loose, remove the nut from the stud. It will be necessary to remove the brake caliper and wire it to the frame to gain clearance.

6. Remove the lower control arm.

7. Installation is the reverse of removal.

Upper Control Arm— S- Series

REMOVAL & INSTALLATION

1. Note the location of the shims. Alignment shims are to be installed in the same position from which they were removed. Remove nuts and shims. Raise front of vehicle and support lower control arm with floor stands. The floor jack must remain under control arm spring seat during removal and installation to retain spring and control arm in position. Since the weight of the vehicle is used to relieve spring tension on the upper control arm, the floor stands must be posi-

tioned between the spring seats and ball joints of the lower control arms for maximum leverage.

2. Remove wheel, then loosen the upper ball joint from the steering knuckle.

3. Support hub assembly to prevent weight from damaging brake hose.

4. It is necessary to remove the upper control arm attaching bolts to allow clearance to remove upper control arm assembly.

5. Remove upper control arm.

6. Position upper control arm attaching bolts loosely in the frame and install pivot shaft on the attaching bolts. Note that the inner pivot bolts must be installed with the bolt heads to the front (on the front bushing) and to the rear (on the rear bushing).

7. Install alignment shims in their original position between the pivot shaft and frame on their respective bolts. Torque nuts to 45 ft. lbs.

8. Remove the temporary support from the hub assembly, then connect ball joint to steering knuckle.

9. Install wheel, then check wheel alignment, and adjust if necessary.

Lower Control Arm— S- Series

REMOVAL & INSTALLATION

1. Remove coil spring.

2. Remove lower ball joint and stud.

3. After stud breaks loose, hold up on lower control arm. Remove control arm.

4. Guide lower control arm out of opening in splash shield with a putty knife or similar tool.

5. Install lower ball joint stud into knuckle and tighten nut.

6. Install spring.

7. Check front alignment. Reset as required.

Stabilizer Bar— S-Series

REMOVAL & INSTALLATION

1. Raise and support the vehicle.

2. Disconnect each side of stabilizer linkage by removing nut from link bolt, pull bolt from linkage and remove retainers, grommets and spacer.

3. Remove bracket to frame or body bolts and remove stabilizer shaft, rubber bushings and brackets.

4. To replace, reverse sequence of operations, being sure to install with the identification forming on the right side of the vehicle. The rubber bushings should be positioned squarely in the brackets with the slit in the bushings facing the front car. Torque stabilizer link nut to 13 ft. lbs. and the bracket bolts to 24 ft. lbs.

REAR SUSPENSION

CORVETTE

On 1980-82 models, the Corvette uses a three-link, independent suspension with a transverse spring. On 1984-87 models, the rear suspension features a light weight fiberglass transverse spring mounted to the fixed differential carrier cover beam. Light weight aluminum components such as the knuckles, upper and lower control arms, camber control support rods, differential carrier cover beam and the drive line support beam are used throughout the rear suspension. Each wheel is mounted by a five link independent suspension. The five links are identified as the wheel drive shaft, camber control support rod, upper and lower control arms and tie rod.

Shock Absorber

REMOVAL & INSTALLATION

NOTE: Purge new shocks of air by repeatedly extending them in their normal position and compressing them while inverted.

1. Jack the car to a convenient working height.
2. Remove the upper bolt and nut.
3. Remove the lower mounting nut and washers.
4. Pivot the top of the shock absorber out of the frame bracket and pull the bottom off the strut shaft.
5. Slide the upper shock absorber eye into the frame bracket and install the bolt, lockwasher, and nut.
6. Install the rubber grommets on the lower shock eye and place the

shock over the strut shaft. Install the washers and nut.
7. Torque the upper bolt to 50 ft. lbs. and the lower nut to 35 ft. lbs. Lower the car.

NOTE: It may be easier to remove the rear wheels before attempting to remove the shocks. See the note on gas-filled shocks under "Front Suspension."

Transverse Leaf Spring

REMOVAL & INSTALLATION

NOTE: Some 1981 and most 1982 Corvettes have a single leaf fiberglass rear spring. All 1984-87 models use a single leaf rear spring.

1. Raise car and support it by the frame, slightly forward of torque control pivot points. Remove wheel assemblies.
2. Place a floor jack under the spring near the link bolt, and raise the spring until it is nearly flat.
3. Tie the end of the spring to the suspension crossmember to hold this flat attitude, with a $\frac{1}{4}$ in. or $\frac{5}{16}$ in. chain and grab hook wrapped around the spring and crossmember. To prevent chain slipping, use a C-clamp on the spring adjacent to the chain.
4. Remove link bolt and rubber bushings.

5. Support and raise the spring end, as before, and remove chain.
6. Carefully lower jack to completely relax spring.
7. Repeat the procedure on the other side of the car.
8. Remove bolts and washers attaching the springs at the center.
9. Remove the spring by sliding it over the exhaust pipes and out one side of the car.
10. Install by reversing removal procedure. Always use new link bolts and cushions. Torque the rear spring to carrier bolts to 33 ft. lbs. through 1980 and 50 ft. lbs. 1981-87r. Install the nut on the link bolt just far enough to expose the cotter pin hole, then insert the pin.

Strut Rod & Bracket

REMOVAL & INSTALLATION

——— CAUTION ———

The strut rod shaft is often very hard to remove; take care not to distort either the shaft or the spindle support in the removal process.

1. Raise car on a hoist.
2. Disconnect shock absorber lower eye from strut rod shaft.
3. Remove strut rod shaft cotter pin and nut. Withdraw shaft by pulling toward the front of the car.
4. Mark related position of camber adjustment, so that adjustment is maintained upon reassembly.
5. Loosen camber bolt and nut. Re-

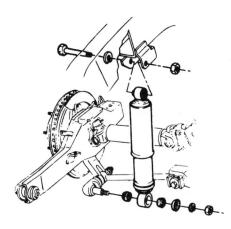

Rear shock absorber mounting

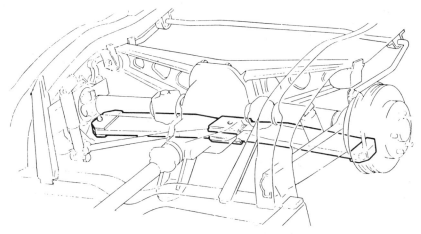

Fiberglass-reinforced plastic (F.R.P.) single leaf rear spring—most 1981 and later models

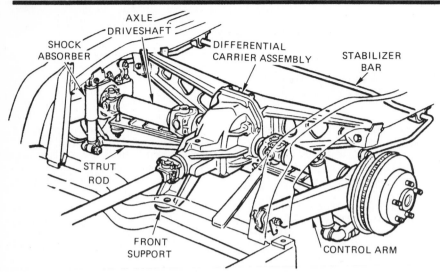

Independent rear suspension—1980 and later

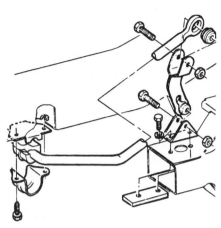

Stabilizer shaft installation, Corvette

move four bolts holding strut rod bracket to carrier and lower the bracket.

6. Remove cam bolt and cam bolt assembly. Pull strut down out of bracket and remove bushing caps.

7. Inspect strut rod bushings for wear and replace where necessary. Replace strut rod if it is bent or damaged in any way.

NOTE: The strut rod shaft has a flat side which should line up with the matching flat in the spindle support.

8. Install by reversing removal procedure. Torque the strut rod-to-spindle support to 75 ft. lbs. plus as needed to align cotter pin hole. Torque the bracket-to-carrier to 35 ft. lbs., 20 ft. lbs. on 1981-87 models.

9. Check rear wheel camber and adjust to specifications.

Spindle Support Rod

REMOVAL & INSTALLATION

1984-87

1. Raise and support vehicle.

2. Scribe mark on cam bolt and mounting bracket so they can be realigned in the same position.

3. Remove cam bolt and separate spindle support rod from the mounting bracket.

4. Remove the spindle support rod bolt at the knuckle and remove rod.

5. Installation is the reverse of removal. Torque the spindle end of support rod 95–188 ft. lbs; differential end 47–62 ft. lbs.

Torque Control Arm

REMOVAL & INSTALLATION

1. Disconnect spring on the side from which the torque arm is to be removed. Follow procedure for "Spring Removal & Installation".

NOTE: If so equipped, disconnect stabilizer rod from torque arm.

2. Remove shock absorber lower eye from strut rod shaft.

3. Disconnect and remove strut rod shaft and swing strut rod down.

4. Remove four bolts holding the

axle driveshaft to spindle flange and disconnect drive shaft.

5. Disconnect the brake line at the caliper and from the torque arm. Disconnect parking brake cable.

6. Remove the torque arm pivot bolt and toe-in shims. Pull the torque arm out of the frame. Tape the shims together to assure proper reassembly.

7. To install, place torque arm in frame opening.

8. Position toe-in shims in original location on both sides of torque arm. Install pivot bolt and lightly tighten at this time.

9. Raise axle driveshaft into position and install to drive flange. Torque bolts to 75 ft. lbs.

10. Raise the strut into position and insert the strut rod shaft so that the flat portion of the shaft lines up with the flat portion on the spindle fork. Install the nut and torque it to 80 ft. lbs.

11. Install shock absorber lower eye and tighten nut to 35 ft. lbs.

12. Connect spring end as outlined under "Leaf Spring Removal & Installation".

NOTE: If car is so equipped, connect stabilizer shaft.

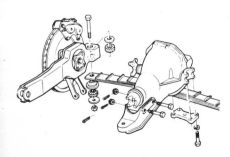

Transverse spring mounting

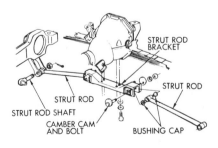

Strut rod mounting

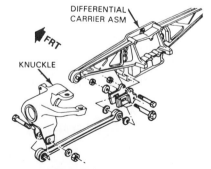

Spindle support rod

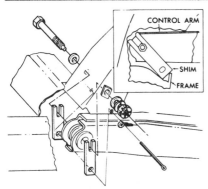

Torque control arm

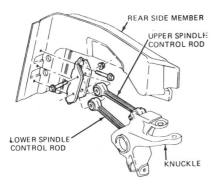

Control arms

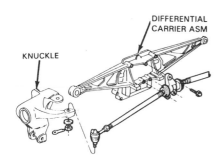

Tie rod assembly

13. Install brake disc and caliper, and wheel. Then lower the car. Tighten torque pivot bolt to 50 ft. lbs.
14. Bleed brakes and check camber and toe-in. Adjust if necessary.

Upper/Lower Control Arms

REMOVAL & INSTALLATION

1984-87

1. Raise and support the vehicle.
2. Remove shock absorber.
3. Remove control arm bolt at the knuckle.
4. Remove control arm bolt at the body bracket and remove the arm.
5. Installation is the reverse of removal. Torque the control arm-to-

body bolts 55–70 ft. lbs; control arm-to-knuckle 125–154 ft. lbs.

Rear Axle Tie Rod and/ or Adjuster Sleeve

REMOVAL & INSTALLATION

1984-87

1. Raise and support your vehicle.
2. Remove cotter pin and retaining nut from tie rod end at knuckle.
3. Loosen jam nut on tie rod end.
4. Using tool J-24319-01, or equivalent, press tie rod end out of the knuckle.
5. Remove tie rod end from the adjusting sleeve. Count the number of turns.
6. Remove adjuster sleeve.
7. Installation is the reverse of removal. Install the same number of turns as removal. Torque tie rod end-to-knuckle: 29–36 ft. lbs; tie rod housing to cover beam: 35–44 ft. lbs. Realign suspension if necessary.

Support Beam

REMOVAL & INSTALLATION

1984-87

1. Raise vehicle and support with jackstands. Allow exhaust system to cool.
2. Remove the complete exhaust system as an assembly by:
   a. Disconnect A.I.R. pipe at the converter.
   b. Disconnect A.I.R. pipe clamps at exhaust pipe.
   c. Disconnect oxygen sensor electrical lead.
   d. Remove the bolts attaching the mufflers to the hangers.
   e. Remove hanger bracket at the converter.
   f. Disconnect the exhaust from the exhaust manifold and remove the exhaust system.
3. Support transmission, using a suitable jack.
4. Remove support beam attaching bolts at the differential carrier and transmission extension housing.
5. Remove the propeller shaft.
6. Remove the support beam by prying transmission to the driver side of vehicle. Remove support beam from the vehicle.
7. Installation is the reverse of removal. Torque the rear support beam bolts: 51–66 ft. lbs; front beam bolts: 47–55 ft. lbs. Apply sealant as illustrated during installation.

Stabilizer Bar

REMOVAL & INSTALLATION

1984-87

1. Raise and support the vehicle on jackstands.
2. Remove spare tire and tire carrier.
3. Disconnect stabilizer bar from knuckles.
4. Remove stabilizer bar bushing retainers, bushings and bar from the vehicle.
5. Installation is the reverse of removal. Torque the stabilizer bar to body bolts and link bracket bolts 14–22 ft. lbs.; Stabilizer link to bracket and bar bolts 25–35 ft. lbs.

Rear Wheel Bearing

REMOVAL & INSTALLATION

1980-82

The Corvette rear wheel spindle is mounted on two tapered roller bearings contained in the spindle support arm, which is bolted to the torque control arm. The flanged end of the spindle is riveted to the brake disc assembly. These rivets are not to be removed for the following service procedures. Bearing end-play is controlled by a solid tubular spacer and a shim.

1. Jack up the vehicle and support it with jackstands.
2. Remove the wheel and tire assembly.
3. Remove the axle drive shaft.
4. Apply the parking brake to prevent the rotors from turning.
5. Remove the cotter pin, nut and flange.

NOTE: It may be necessary to use special tool J08614-01, or its equivalent, to remove the flange.

6. Install tool J-21859-1, or equivalent, over the spindle threads, then remove the drive spindle from its support using tool J-22602 or equivalent. When using this tool make sure the puller plate is positioned vertically in

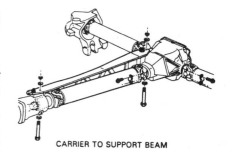

CARRIER TO SUPPORT BEAM

Support beam attachments

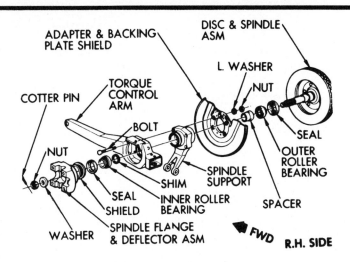

Exploded view of spindle

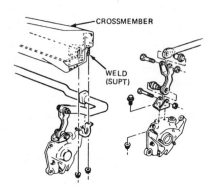

Rear stabilizer bar

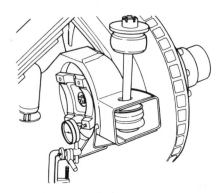

Checking spindle bearing end play

the torque control arm before applying pressure to the puller screw.

7. When the spindle is removed, the outer bearing will remain on the spindle. The inner bearing, tubular spacer, end-play adjustment shim and both outer races will remain in the spindle support.

8. Remove the bearing, spacer and shim. Record the shim thickness for later use.

9. With the spindle assembly on the bench, position tool J24489-1, or equivalent, between the outer bearing and the seal.

10. Using puller J-8433-1, or equivalent, draw the bearing off the spindle.

11. Remove the outer seal from the spindle shaft and inspect it for damage. Replace if necessary.

12. Remove the outer races from the spindle shaft and install new ones, using tool J-7817, or equivalent.

13. Pack the new wheel bearing with grease.

14. Installation is the reverse of removal.

Rear Hub & Bearing

REMOVAL & INSTALLATION

1984-87

1. Remove center cap from wheel.
2. Remove cotter pin, spindle nut and washer.
3. Raise vehicle and support with jack stands.
4. Remove wheel and tire.
5. Remove brake caliper and support.
6. Remove brake rotor.
7. Disconnect tie rod end from the knuckle.
8. Disconnect transverse spring from the knuckle.
9. Scribe mark on cam bolt and mounting bracket so they can be re-aligned in the same position.
10. Remove cam bolt and separate spindle support rod from the mounting bracket.
11. Remove the trunnion straps at the side yoke shaft. Push out on the knuckle and separate axle shaft from the side gear yoke shaft. Remove the axle shaft from the vehicle.
12. Using J-34161 (Torx® No. 45) or its equivalent, remove the hub and bearing mounting bolts.
13. Remove hub and bearing from the vehicle and support the parking brake backing plate.
14. Installation is the reverse of removal. Check suspension alignment and adjust as needed.

WHEEL BEARING END PLAY CHECK

The rear wheel bearings should have end play of 0.001–0.008 inches. When necessary, adjust them using the following procedure.

1. Jack up your vehicle and support it with jackstands.

2. Remove the tire and wheel assembly.

3. Remove the axle driveshaft.

4. Mark the camber cam in relation to the bracket. Loosen and turn the camber bolt until the strut rod forces the torque control arm outward.

5. Mount a dial indicator on the torque control surface and rest the pointer on the flange end.

6. Grasp the rotor and move it in and out. If the bearing movement is with specifications no adjustment is necessary. If the adjustment is not within these limits you must add or subtract shims accordingly.

CAPRICE, IMPALA, MALIBU AND MONTE CARLO

All models use a coil spring rear suspension located by two lower control arms and two diagonally mounted upper control arms. The fore and aft axle movements are controlled by the lower control arms, while the lateral movement is controlled by the upper control arms.

Shock Absorber

REMOVAL & INSTALLATION

New shock absorbers must be purged of air before installation. This is done by repeatedly extending the shock in its normal mounted position, inverting and compressing it.

1. Raise and support the vehicle on jackstands at the axle housing, to prevent stretching the brake hose.

NOTE: If equipped with super lift shock absorbers, disconnect the air line snap on connector at the shock absorber.

2. On some models, it may be necessary to remove the wheel and tire assembly.

3. Remove the nut, the retainer, the grommet and lock washer, which attach the lower end of the shock absorber to its mounting.

NOTE: On some models, it may be necessary to remove the upper shock absorber bracket by reaching between the tire and the frame to remove the mounting nuts.

4. Remove the bolts, nuts and lock washers from the upper end of the shock absorber and the shock absorber.

5. To install, reverse the removal procedures. Torque the lower shock-to-frame bolt to 65 ft. lbs. and the upper shock-to-frame nut to 12 ft. lbs. or bolt to 20 ft. lbs.

NOTE: If equipped with super lift shocks, add 10 psi of air pressure to the shock (to prevent damage) and torque the upper nut to 20 ft. lbs.

Rear Spring

REMOVAL & INSTALLATION

1. Raise and support the rear of vehicle on jackstands at the frame rails.
2. Remove the clip that attaches the

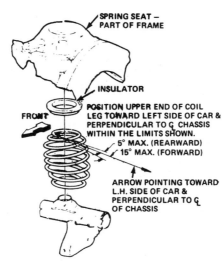

Coil spring positioning

brake hose to the mounting bracket on the frame crossmember.

3. Support the rear axle with a floor jack.

4. Disconnect the upper control arms from the axle housing.

5. If equipped with a stabilizer bar, remove the bar from the control arms.

6. Remove the nut and the lock washer from the shock absorber, then disconnect the shock from the axle. It may be necessary to adjust the height of the jack to disconnect the shock.

7. Carefully lower the jack until the spring is free, then remove the spring.

NOTE: When removing the spring, mark its position so that it may be installed in the same position.

8. To install, reverse the removal procedures. Torque the upper control arm-to-front bushing nut to 92 ft. lbs. (Impala and Caprice) or 70 ft. lbs. (Malibu and Monte Carlo), the upper control arm-to-rear bushing nut to 70 ft. lbs., the upper control arm-to-rear bushing bolt to 80 ft. lbs., the stabilizer bar mounts to 52 ft. lbs. (Impala and Caprice) or 35 ft. lbs. (Malibu and Monte Carlo).

Rear Lower Control Arm

REMOVAL & INSTALLATION

NOTE: Remove and install ONLY one lower control arm at a time. If both arms are removed at the same time, the axle could roll

or slip sideways, making installation of the arms very difficult.

1. Raise and support the rear of the vehicle on jackstands under the rear axle.

NOTE: If equipped the a stabilizer bar, remove it.

2. Remove the control arm attaching fasteners and the control arm.

3. To install, reverse the removal procedures. Torque the control arm-to-frame nut to 92 ft. lbs. (Impala and Caprice) or 70 ft. lbs. (Malibu and Monte Carlo), the control arm-to-axle nut to 92 ft. lbs. (Impala and Caprice) and the control arm-to-axle bolt to 125 ft. lbs. (Impala and Caprice) or 79 ft. lbs. (Malibu and Monte Carlo). If equipped with a stabilizer bar, torque the mounting fasteners to 52 ft. lbs. (Impala and Caprice) or 35 ft. lbs. (Malibu and Monte Carlo).

NOTE: Before torquing the fasteners, the weight of the vehicle must be resting on its wheels.

Rear Upper Control Arm

REMOVAL & INSTALLATION

NOTE: Remove and install ONLY one lower control arm at a time. If both arms are removed at the same time, the axle could roll or slip sideways, making installation of the arms very difficult.

1. Raise and support the rear of vehicle on jackstands under the axle.
2. Remove the upper control arm nut at the axle.

NOTE: To remove the mounting bolt from the axle, it may be necessary to rock the axle. On some models, it may be necessary to remove the lower shock absorber stud to provide clearance for the upper control arm removal.

3. Remove the upper control arm-to-frame nut and bolt, then the control arm.

4. To install, reverse the removal procedures. Torque the upper control arm-to-axle nut to 70 ft. lbs., the upper control arm-to-axle bolt to 79 ft. lbs. and the upper control arm-to-frame bolt to 92 ft. lbs. (Impala and Caprice) or 70 ft. lbs. (Malibu and Monte Carlo).

Stabilizer Bar

REMOVAL & INSTALLATION

1. Raise and support the rear of the vehicle on jackstands under the frame.

2. Support the axle assembly with a floor jack.

3. Remove the stabilizer bar-to-lower control arm bolts and the stabilizer bar.

4. To install, reverse the removal procedures. Torque the stabilizer bar-to-lower control arm to 52 ft. lbs. (Impala and Caprice) or 35 ft. lbs. (Malibu and Monte Carlo).

CELEBRITY AND CITATION

Shock Absorber

REMOVAL & INSTALLATION

1. Open the deck or trunk lid, remove the trim cover, and remove the upper shock nut. Remove and replace one shock at a time when replacing both shocks.

2. Jack the car to a convenient working height. Support the rear axle assembly.

3. Remove the lower attaching bolt and remove the shock absorber. On cars equipped with air shocks, disconnect the air line.

NOTE: Purge new shocks of air by repeatedly compressing them while inverted and extending them in their normal installed position.

4. Install the shock absorber in a reverse of the removal procedure. Torque the lower nuts to 43 ft. lbs.; the upper nut to 13 ft. lbs.

Spring

REMOVAL & INSTALLATION

1. Raise and support the car on a hoist. Do not use twin-post hoist. The swing arc of the axle may cause it to

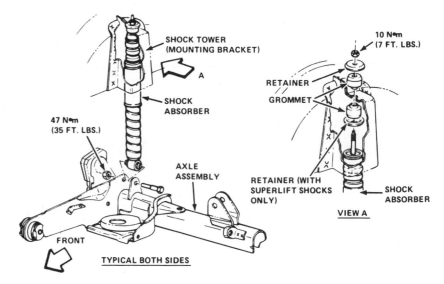

Shock absorber installation

slip from the hoist when the bolts are removed. If a suitable hoist is not available, raise and support the car on jackstands, and use a jack under the axle.

2. Support the axle with a jack that can be raised and lowered.

3. Remove the brake hose attaching brackets (right and left), allowing the hoses to hang freely. Do not disconnect the hoses.

4. Remove the track bar attaching bolts from the rear axle.

5. Remove both shock absorber lower attaching bolts from the axle.

6. Lower the axle. Remove the coil spring and insulator.

NOTE: Do not suspend rear axle by brake hoses.

7. To install, position the spring

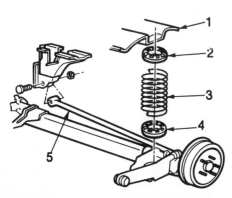

1. Underbody
2. Insulator Upper
3. Spring
4. Lower Insulator on a Series Only
5. Track Bar

A-Body Rear suspension

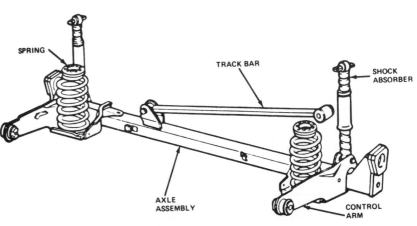

X-Body rear suspension

and insulator on the axle. The leg on the upper coil of the spring must be parallel to the axle, facing the left hand side of the car.

8. Install the shock absorber bolts. Tighten to 43 ft. lbs. Install the track bar, if equipped, tightening to 33 ft. lbs. Install the brake line brackets. Tighten to 8 ft. lbs.

Rear Wheel Hub And Bearing Assembly

REMOVAL & INSTALLATION

1. Raise and support the car on a hoist.
2. Remove the wheel and brake drum.

─────── CAUTION ───────

Do not hammer on the brake drum as damage to the bearing could result.

─────────────────────────

3. Remove the hub and bearing assembly to rear axle attaching bolts and remove the rear axle.

NOTE: The bolts which attach the hub and bearing assembly also support the brake assembly.

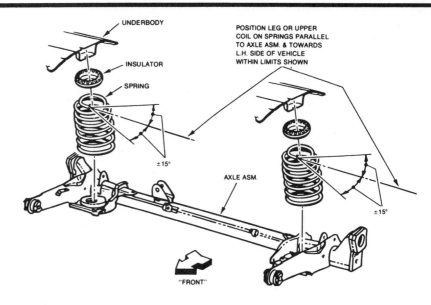

Spring installation

When removing these bolts, support the brake assembly with a wire or other means. Do not let the brake line support the brake assembly.

4. Install the hub and bearing assembly to the rear axle and torque the hub and bearing bolts to 45 ft. lbs.

5. Install the brake drum, tire and wheel assembly and lower the car.

ADJUSTMENT

There is no necessary adjustment to the rear wheel bearing and hub assembly.

CAMARO

1980-81 vehicles use a leaf spring rear suspension; 1982-87 vehicles use a coil spring suspension having a torque arm and a track bar to stabilize the axle assembly. Anti-sway (stabilizer) bars are optional equipment on all models.

Shock Absorber

REMOVAL & INSTALLATION

1. Raise and support the rear of the vehicle on jackstands.
2. If the vehicle is equipped with Superlift shock absorbers, disconnect the air line.
3. On 1980-81 models, remove the lower shock absorber nut, the retainer and the grommet. Remove the upper bolts and the shock.
4. On the 1982-87 models, pull back the carpet, disconnect the upper shock attaching nut, remove the lower shock-to-axle mounting bolt and the shock absorber.
5. To install, reverse the removal procedures. On 1980-81 models, torque the upper fasteners to 18 ft. lbs. and the lower to 7 ft. lbs. On the 1982-

87 models, torque the upper fasteners to 13 ft. lbs. and the lower to 70 ft. lbs.

Springs

REMOVAL & INSTALLATION

1980-81

1. Raise and support the rear of the vehicle by the frame, so that the rear axle can be independently raised and lowered.
2. Support the rear axle with a floor jack.
3. Disconnect the shock absorber lower mount.
4. Loosen the retaining bolt through the front spring eye. Unbolt the front bracket from the body.
5. Lower the axle, then remove the bracket and retaining bolt from the front spring eye.
6. Pry the parking brake cable from the spring mounting plate retainer.
7. Remove the U-bolt nuts, the spring plate, the upper and lower spring pads.
8. Support the spring, then remove

the lower rear shackle bolt and the spring.

9. When installing, install the front bracket to the spring eye, install the rear shackle, bolt the front bracket in place, install the U-bolts and the shock absorber. Torque the bolts with the weight of the vehicle on the springs. Torque the front bracket mounting bolt to 25 ft. lbs., the U-bolts to 40 ft. lbs. and the rear shackle bolts to 50 ft. lbs.

1982-87

1. Raise and support the vehicle with jackstands under the frame, so that the rear axle can be independently raised and lowered.
2. Support the rear axle with a floor jack.
3. If equipped with brake hose attachment brackets, disconnect the brackets allowing the hoses to hang free. DO NOT disconnect the hoses. Perform this step only if the hoses will be unduly stretched when the axle is lowered.
4. Disconnect the track bar from the axle.
5. Remove the lower shock absorber

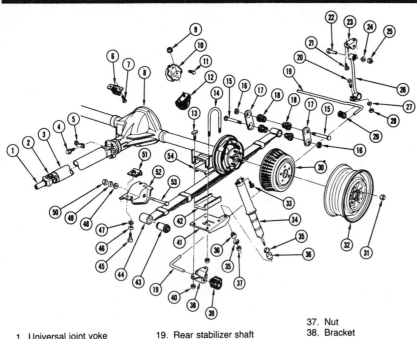

1. Universal joint yoke
2. Universal joint
3. Driveshaft
4. Bolt (5/16"-24 × 1 7/16")
5. Strap
6. Bumper
7. Bolt (5/16"-12 × 3/4")
8. Housing
9. Nut
10. Bracket
11. Screw (3/8"-16 × 1 1/8")
12. Bumper ASM
13. Bolt (7/16"-20 × 1 5/16")
14. Bolt (7/16"-20 U-shape)
15. Pin
16. Nut (7/16"-20)
17. Shackle unit
18. Bushing

19. Rear stabilizer shaft
20. Bolt (5/16"-18 × 3/8")
21. Screw (3/8"-16 × 1 1/8")
22. Bolt (3/8"-16 × 2 1/4")
23. Bracket
24. Washer (1" × 25/64")
25. Nut (3/8"-16)
26. Support
27. Washer (1/4")
28. Nut (5/16"-18)
29. Bushing
30. Brake Drum
31. Nut
32. Wheel
33. Screw (5/16"-18 × 1")
34. Shock Absorber
35. Retainer
36. Grommet

37. Nut
38. Bracket
39. Bushing
40. Nut
41. Plate
42. Cushion
43. Bushing ASM
44. Rear Leaf Spring
45. Bolt
46. Washer (3/8")
47. Washer
48. Washer
49. Washer (1/2")
50. Nut (1/2"-20)
51. Nut (3/8"-16)
52. Bracket
53. Bolt (1/2"-20 × 4 7/8")
54. Cushion

Leaf spring rear suspension used on models through 1981

bolts and lower the axle. Make sure the axle is supported securely on the floor jack and that there is no chance of the axle slipping after the shock absorbers are disconnected.

6. Lower the axle and remove the coil spring. DO NOT lower the axle past the limits of the brake lines or the lines will be damaged.

7. To install, reverse the removal procedures. Make sure the spring is seated in the same position as before removal. Torque the track bar bolt-to-axle to 93 ft. lbs., the track bar-to-body to 58 ft. lbs. and the shock absorber-to-axle bolts to 70 ft. lbs.

Track Bar

REMOVAL & INSTALLATION

1982-87

1. Raise and support the rear of the vehicle on jackstands at the curb height position.

2. Remove the track bar mounting fasteners and the track bar.

3. To install, clean the track bar fasteners and reverse the removal procedures. Torque the track bar-to-axle assembly to 93 ft. lbs. and the track bar-to-body bracket to 58 ft. lbs.

Track Bar Brace

REMOVAL & INSTALLATION

1982-87

1. Raise and support the rear of the vehicle on jackstands under the rear axle.

2. Remove the heat shield screws from the track bar brace.

3. Remove the track bar brace-to-body brace screws.

4. Remove the track bar-to-body bracket fasteners and remove the track bar brace.

5. To install, reverse the removal procedures. Torque the track bar nut-

to-body brace to 58 ft. lbs. and the track bar brace-to-body bracket screws to 34 ft. lbs.

Rear Lower Control Arm

REMOVAL & INSTALLATION

1982-87

NOTE: Remove and install ONLY one lower control arm at a time. If both arms are removed at the same time, the axle could roll or slip sideways, making installation of the arms very difficult.

1. Raise and support the rear of the vehicle on jackstands under the rear axle.

2. Remove the control arm attaching fasteners and the control arm.

3. To install, reverse the removal procedures. Torque the control arm bolts to 68 ft. lbs.

Torque Arm

REMOVAL & INSTALLATION

1982-87

NOTE: The coil springs must be removed BEFORE the torque arm. If the torque arm is removed first, damage will result.

1. Raise and support the rear of the vehicle on jackstands under the frame. Place a floor jack under the rear axle.

2. Remove the track bar mounting bolt at the axle assembly, then loosen the track bar bolt at the body brace.

3. Disconnect the rear brake hose clip at the axle assembly, which will allow additional drop of the axle.

4. Remove the lower attaching nuts from both rear shock absorbers and disconnect the shock absorbers from their lower attaching points.

5. If equipped with a 4 cylinder engine, remove the driveshaft.

6. Carefully lower the rear axle assembly and remove the rear coil springs.

——————— CAUTION ———————
DO NOT over stress the brake hose when lowering the axle—damage will result.
————————————————————

7. Remove the torque arm rear attaching bolts.

8. Remove the front torque arm outer bracket.

9. Remove the torque arm from the vehicle.

10. To install; place the torque arm in position and loosely install the rear torque arm bolts, then reverse the re-

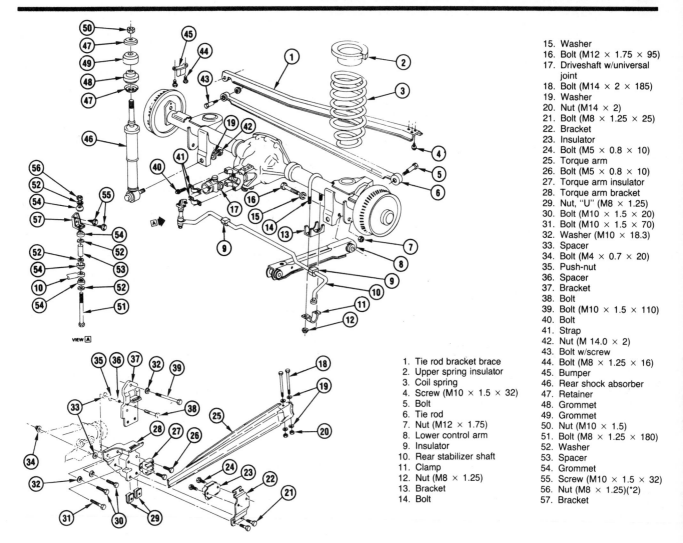

15. Washer
16. Bolt (M12 × 1.75 × 95)
17. Driveshaft w/universal joint
18. Bolt (M14 × 2 × 185)
19. Washer
20. Nut (M14 × 2)
21. Bolt (M8 × 1.25 × 25)
22. Bracket
23. Insulator
24. Bolt (M5 × 0.8 × 10)
25. Torque arm
26. Bolt (M5 × 0.8 × 10)
27. Torque arm insulator
28. Torque arm bracket
29. Nut, "U" (M8 × 1.25)
30. Bolt (M10 × 1.5 × 20)
31. Bolt (M10 × 1.5 × 70)
32. Washer (M10 × 18.3)
33. Spacer
34. Bolt (M4 × 0.7 × 20)
35. Push-nut
36. Spacer
37. Bracket
38. Bolt
39. Bolt (M10 × 1.5 × 110)
40. Bolt
41. Strap
42. Nut (M 14.0 × 2)
43. Bolt w/screw
44. Bolt (M8 × 1.25 × 16)
45. Bumper
46. Rear shock absorber
47. Retainer
48. Grommet
49. Grommet
50. Nut (M10 × 1.5)
51. Bolt (M8 × 1.25 × 180)
52. Washer
53. Spacer
54. Grommet
55. Screw (M10 × 1.5 × 32)
56. Nut (M8 × 1.25)(*2)
57. Bracket

1. Tie rod bracket brace
2. Upper spring insulator
3. Coil spring
4. Screw (M10 × 1.5 × 32)
5. Bolt
6. Tie rod
7. Nut (M12 × 1.75)
8. Lower control arm
9. Insulator
10. Rear stabilizer shaft
11. Clamp
12. Nut (M8 × 1.25)
13. Bracket
14. Bolt

Coil spring rear suspension used on 1982 and later models

moval procedures. Torque the front torque arm bracket nuts to 20 ft. lbs. and the rear torque arm nuts to 100 ft. lbs.

11. Place the rear springs and insulators in position, then raise the rear axle assembly until all of the weight is supported by the spring. Torque the shocks-to-axle nuts to 70 ft. lbs., the track bar-to-axle bolt to 93 ft. lbs. and the track bar-to-bracket nut to 58 ft. lbs.

NOTE: On the 4 cylinder models, reinstall the driveshaft.

CAVALIER

Shock Absorber

REMOVAL & INSTALLATION

1. Open the hatch or trunk lid, remove the trim cover if present, and remove the upper shock absorber nut.

2. Raise and support the car at a convenient working height if you desire. It is not necessary to remove the weight of the car from the shock ab-

sorbers, however, so you can leave the car on the ground if you prefer.

3. Remove the lower attaching bolt and remove the shock.

4. If new shock absorbers are being installed, repeatedly compress them while inverted and extend them in their normal upright position. This will purge them of air.

5. Install the shocks in the reverse order of removal. Tighten the lower mount nut and bolt to 55 ft. lbs. the upper to 13 ft. lbs.

Springs

REMOVAL & INSTALLATION

——— CAUTION ———
The coil springs are under a considerable amount of tension. Be very careful when removing or installing them; they can exert enough force to cause very serious injuries.

1. Raise and support the car on a hoist. Do not use a twin-post hoist.

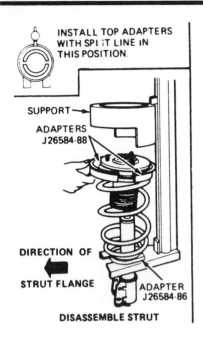

INSTALL TOP ADAPTERS WITH SPLIT LINE IN THIS POSITION.

SUPPORT

ADAPTERS J26584-88

DIRECTION OF

STRUT FLANGE

ADAPTER J26584-86

DISASSEMBLE STRUT

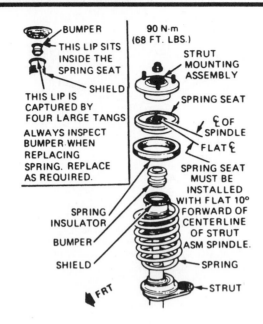

BUMPER

THIS LIP SITS INSIDE THE SPRING SEAT

SHIELD

THIS LIP IS CAPTURED BY FOUR LARGE TANGS

ALWAYS INSPECT BUMPER WHEN REPLACING SPRING. REPLACE AS REQUIRED.

SPRING INSULATOR

BUMPER

SHIELD

90 N·m (68 FT. LBS.)

STRUT MOUNTING ASSEMBLY

SPRING SEAT

₵ OF SPINDLE

FLAT ₵

SPRING SEAT MUST BE INSTALLED WITH FLAT 10° FORWARD OF CENTERLINE OF STRUT ASM SPINDLE.

SPRING

STRUT

FRT

Coil spring removal and installation

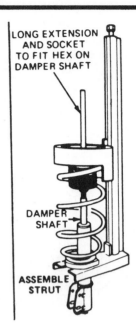

LONG EXTENSION AND SOCKET TO FIT HEX ON DAMPER SHAFT

DAMPER SHAFT

ASSEMBLE STRUT

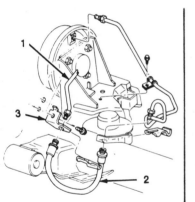

1

3

2

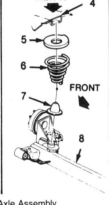

VIEW A

4

5

6

7

8

FRONT

1. Center Brake Pipe
2. Brake Hose
3. Brake Pipe Bracket
4. Underbody

9

10

11

VIEW A (BOTH SPRINGS)

5. Spring Insulator
6. Spring
7. Compression Bumper

8. Axle Assembly
9. .549 Inch (15mm) Max.
10. Spring

11. Spring Stop Part of Spring Seat

Rear spring mounting

The swing arc of the axle may cause it to slip from the hoist when the bolts are removed. If a suitable hoist is not available, raise and support the car on jackstands, and use a jack under the axle.

2. Support the axle with a jack that can be raised and lowered.

3. Remove the brake hose attaching brackets (right and left), allowing the hoses to hang freely. Do not disconnect the hoses.

4. Remove both shock absorber lower attaching bolts from the axle.

5. Lower the axle. Remove the coil spring and insulator.

6. To install, position the spring and insulator on the axle. The leg on the upper coil of the spring must be parallel to the axle, facing the left hand side of the car.

7. Install the shock absorber bolts. Tighten to 41 ft. lbs. Install the brake line brackets. Tighten to 8 ft. lbs.

Rear Hub and Bearing

REMOVAL & INSTALLATION

1. Loosen the wheel lug nuts. Raise and support the car and remove the

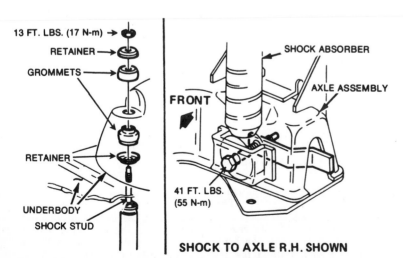

13 FT. LBS. (17 N-m)

RETAINER

GROMMETS

RETAINER

UNDERBODY

SHOCK STUD

SHOCK ABSORBER

AXLE ASSEMBLY

FRONT

41 FT. LBS. (55 N-m)

SHOCK TO AXLE R.H. SHOWN

Shock absorber mounting

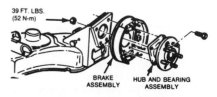

39 FT. LBS. (52 N-m)

BRAKE ASSEMBLY

HUB AND BEARING ASSEMBLY

Rear hub and bearing

wheel.

2. Remove the brake drum.

NOTE: Do not hammer on the brake drum to remove; damage to the bearing will result.

3. Remove the four hub and bearing retaining bolts and remove the assembly from the axle. The top rear attaching bolt will not clear the brake shoe when removing the hub and bearing assembly. Partially remove the hub

and bearing assembly prior to removing this bolt.

4. Installation is in the reverse. Hub and bearing bolt torque is 39 ft. lbs.

CHEVETTE

When using a hoist contacting the rear axle, be sure that the stabilizer links and the track rod are not damaged.

Shock Absorber

REMOVAL & INSTALLATION

NOTE: Purge new shock absorbers of air by repeatedly extending in the normal position and compressing while inverted.

1. Raise the car on a hoist.
2. Support the rear axle.
3. Remove the shock absorber upper attaching nut and lower attaching bolt and nut, and remove the shock absorber.
4. Install the retainer and the rub-

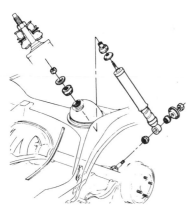

Rear shock absorber mounting

ber grommet onto the shock absorber.

5. Place the shock absorber into its installed position and install and tighten the upper retaining nut to 7 ft. lbs.

6. Install the lower shock absorber nut and bolt and torque to 21 ft. lbs.

7. Remove the rear axle supports and lower the car.

Rear Spring

REMOVAL & INSTALLATION

1. Raise the car on a hoist.
2. Support the rear axle with a floor jack.
3. Disconnect both shock absorbers from their lower brackets.
4. Disconnect the rear axle extension center support bracket from the underbody. Use caution when disconnect the extension and safely support it when disconnected.
5. Lower the rear axle and remove the springs and spring insulators.

─────── **CAUTION** ───────
Do not stretch the rear brake hoses when lowering the rear axle.

6. To install, place the insulators on top and on the bottom of the springs and position the springs between their upper and lower seats.

7. Raise the rear axle. Connect the rear axle extension center support

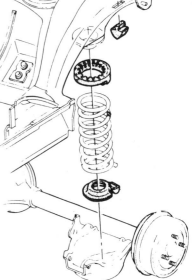

**Rear spring installation—
position both insulators as shown**

bracket to the underbody. Torque the bolts to 37 ft. lbs.

8. Connect the shock absorbers to their lower brackets. Torque the nuts to 21 ft. lbs.

9. Remove the jack from the axle.

10. Lower the car.

Rear Wheel Bearings

Please refer to "Axle, Bearing and Seal" in the Drive Axle Section.

SPECTRUM

Shock Absorber

REMOVAL & INSTALLATION

1. Open the trunk and lift off the trim cover (hatch back models only). Remove the upper shock absorber nut.
2. Remove the lower bolt of the shock absorber.
3. Remove the shock absorber.
4. To install, reverse the removal procedure.

NOTE: When replacing the shock absorber, NEVER reuse the old lower bolt, ALWAYS use a new one.

Axle Assembly

REMOVAL & INSTALLATION

1. Raise the rear end of the vehicle and support it on jack stands.
2. Remove the rear wheels.

3. At the center of the rear axle, remove the brake line, retaining clip and flexible hose.
4. Remove the parking brake tension spring at the rear axle.
5. Disconnect the parking brake cable from the turn buckle and at the cable joint.
6. Support the axle with a jack, then remove the lower shock absorber bolt and disconnect it from the axle.
7. Lower the axle support and remove the coil spring.

8. Remove the bolts retaining the axle to the body and remove the axle assembly.

9. To install, reverse the removal procedure.

10. After installation, bleed the brake system.

NOTE: Raise the axle assembly to a distance of 15.2 in. from the top of the wheel well to the center of the axle hub, then torque the fasteners. ALWAYS replace the lower shock absorber bolt with a new one.

Coil Springs

REMOVAL & INSTALLATION

Refer to the "Axle Assembly Removal and Installation" in this section.

Axle Bushings

REMOVAL & INSTALLATION

1. Refer to the "Axle Assembly Removal and Installation" procedures in this section, then remove the axle assembly.

2. With the axle assembly removed, press the bushings from the housings.

3. To install, press new bushings into the housings and reverse the removal procedure.

Stabilizer Bar

REMOVAL & INSTALLATION

1. Remove the bolts retaining the stabilizer bar to the lower ends of the axle assembly.
2. Remove the stabilizer bar.
3. To install, reverse the removal procedure.

SPRINT

The rear suspension is a rigid axle type. One tapered leaf spring is longitudinally slung under each side of the axle. The front end of the spring is attached to the body bracket through a rubber bushing and shackle assembly. A shock absorber is positioned inboard of the spring and slanted toward the rear of the vehicle.

Shock Absorber

REMOVAL & INSTALLATION

1. Raise and support the rear of the vehicle on jackstands. Remove the wheel assembly.
2. Remove the lower mounting nut, the lock washer and and the outer washer.

3. Remove the upper mounting bolt, the lock washer and nut.
4. Remove the shock absorber.
5. To install, reverse the removal procedures. Torque the upper mounting bolt to 33–50 ft. lbs. and the lower mounting nut to 8–12 ft. lbs.

Spring

REMOVAL & INSTALLATION

1. Raise and support the rear of the vehicle on jackstands. Remove the front wheel assembly.
2. Remove the U-bolt nuts.
3. Remove the shackle and leaf spring front nuts.
4. Remove the front spring bolt.
5. Remove the spring from the vehicle.

NOTE: Apply a thin coat of silicone grease to the springs bushings before installation.

6. To install, align the spring pin with the hole in the axle shaft housing and reverse the removal procedures. Torque the front spring bolt to 33–50 ft. lbs.; the rear spring shackle nuts to 22–40 ft. lbs. and the U-bolt nuts to 22–33 ft. lbs.

Rear Wheel Bearings and Rear Axle

REMOVAL & INSTALLATION

Refer to the rear axle and axle shaft shaft removal and installation procedures in the Drive Train section.

NOVA

MacPherson Strut

REMOVAL & INSTALLATION

1. Working inside the car, remove the rear quarter window garnish molding and back window panel.
2. Raise the rear of the vehicle and support it securely at approved points on jackstands. Remove the rear wheel.
3. Disconnect the flexible hose at

the strut. Plug the openings. Then, remove the flexible hose and clip from the mounting point on the strut. Finally, reconnect the brake line to the flex hose to prevent an excessive amount of brake fluid from draining from the system.
4. Remove the nuts and bolts mounting the strut onto the axle carrier and then disconnect the strut.
5. Remove the three upper strut mounting nuts and carefully remove the strut assembly.

6. Installation is the reverse of the removal procedure. Note the following points:

   a. Torque the upper strut retaining nuts to 17 ft. lbs.

   b. Torque the strut to axle carrier bolts to 105 ft. lbs.

   c. Torque the nut holding the suspension support to the shock absorber to 36 ft. lbs.

   d. Bleed the brakes as described later in this section.

CORSICA AND BERETTA

Shock Absorbers

REMOVAL & INSTALLATION

1. With the deck lid or trunk open, remove the trim cover and remove the upper shock mounting nut.
2. Raise and safely support the vehicle. Support the rear axle.
3. Remove the lower shock absorber mounting nut, lower the rear axle assembly and remove the shock absorber.
4. Installation is the reverse of the removal. Torque the lower nut to 43 ft. lbs. for the Beretta and to 35 ft. lbs for the Corsica. Torque the upper mounting nut to 22 ft. lbs. for both vehicles.

Springs

REMOVAL & INSTALLATION

———— CAUTION ————

Do not use a twin-post type lift when removing the rear springs. This type of lift may cause the rear axle to slip when certain bolts are removed because the rear axle must swing down to remove the springs.

1. Raise and safely support the vehicle on the frame.
2. Remove the wheel and tire. Support the rear axle assembly.
3. Disconnect the right and left brake line brackets from the body and allow the lines to hang freely.

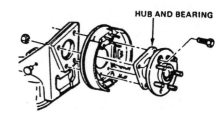

Rear wheel hub and bearing mounting

4. Remove the lower shock absorber mounting bolts.
5. Lower the rear axle and remove the springs.
6. Installation is the reverse of the removal. Torque the lower shock absorber bolts to 43 ft. lbs. for the Beretta and to 35 ft. lbs. for the Corsica.

Rear Wheel Bearings

REMOVAL & INSTALLATION

The rear wheel hub and bearing are replaced as an assembly only.
1. Raise and safely support the vehicle.
2. Remove the wheel and tire. Remove the brake drum.
3. Remove the four (4) bolts attaching the hub and bearing assembly to the rear axle assembly.

NOTE: The top mounting bolt will not clear the brake shoe when removing the hub and bearing. The hub and bearing must be partially removed while the top bolts is being turned out.

4. To install, insert and turn the top bolt in while installing the hub and bearing. Then install the other three bolts.
5. Torque the bolts to 38 ft. lbs.
6. Install the brake drum and wheel and tire.

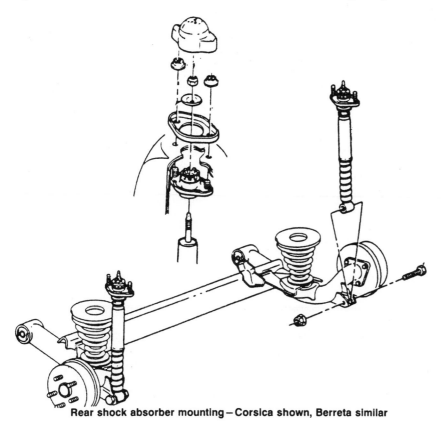

Rear shock absorber mounting—Corsica shown, Berreta similar

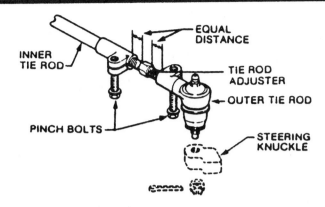

Tie rod end removal and installation

adjuster must be centered between the tie rod and the tie rod end, with an equal number of threads exposed on both sides of the adjuster nut. Tighten the pinch bolts to 20 ft. lbs.

5. Install the tie rod end to the strut assembly and tighten to 50 ft. lbs. If the cotter pin cannot be installed, tighten the nut up to $\frac{1}{16}$ in. further. Never back off the nut to align the holes for the cotter pin.

6. Have the front end alignment adjusted.

CHEVETTE

All models use manual rack and pinion steering which encloses the steering gear and linkage in one unit. Power steering is available as an option in all 1981-87 models with an automatic transmission.

Tie Rod

REMOVAL & INSTALLATION

1. Loosen the jam nut located on the inner tie rod.
2. Remove the outer tie rod cotter pin and nut.
3. Using a tie rod end separating tool, remove the tie rod from the steering knuckle.
4. Remove the outer tie rod from the inner tie rod assembly. Count the number of turns it takes to remove the tie rod end.
5. Install the new outer tie rod end onto the inner tie rod assembly, turning it in the same number of turns as the old tie rod took to remove. Do not

tighten the jam nut.
6. Install the outer tie rod into the steering knuckle and torque the nut to 32 ft. lbs. Install a new cotter pin.
7. Set toe-in adjustment to specification by turning the inner tie rod (an alignment rack is necessary for adjustment). Be sure not to twist the boot when making the adjustment. If an alignment rack is not available, tighten the jam nut and have the front end alignment checked as soon as possible.
8. Torque the jam nut to 50 ft. lbs.

Steering Gear

REMOVAL & INSTALLATION

1. Raise the vehicle and support it with jackstands.
2. Remove the bolts and shield.
3. Remove the outer tie rod cotter pins and nuts on both sides.
4. Using a tie rod separating tool, disconnect the tie rods from the steer-

ing knuckles.
5. On power steering models remove the two hydraulic lines from the steering gear.
6. Remove the flexible coupling pinch bolt to the shaft.
7. Remove the four bolts at the clamps, and remove the assembly from the vehicle.
8. To install, position the assembly to the vehicle with the stub shaft in position with the flexible coupling and install the clamps and four new bolts.
9. Install the flexible coupling pinch bolt to the shaft.
10. Install the tie rods into the steering knuckles and torque the nuts to 30 ft. lbs. Install a new cotter pin.
11. On power steering models install the two hydraulic hoses and bleed the system.
12. Install the bolts and shield. Remove the jackstands and lower the vehicle.

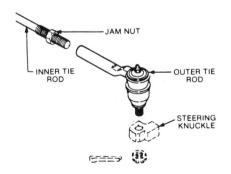

Tie rod end assembly

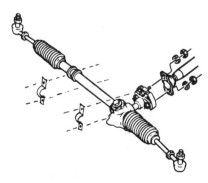

Manual rack and pinion assembly

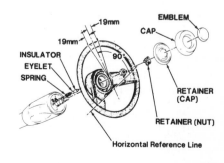

Chevette steering wheel assembly

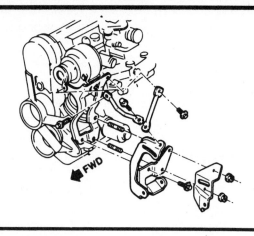

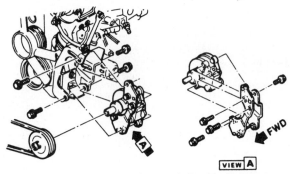

Power steering pump mounting—gasoline engine

Power Steering Pump

REMOVAL & INSTALLATION

1. Remove the upper adjusting bolt.
2. Remove the lower brace bolt-to-pump bracket.
3. Remove the left hand crossmember brace to body.
4. Remove the pressure line and the reservoir line at the pump.
5. Remove the rear pump adjusting bracket.
6. Remove the front pivot bolt at the pump and remove the bolt.
7. Remove the front pump bracket at the bolt-to-engine. Remove the bracket and pump.
8. Installation is the reverse of the removal procedure. In addition, adjust the belt tension, fill the reservoir and bleed the system.

BLEEDING THE POWER STEERING SYSTEM

NOTE: When checking or adjusting the fluid level after service, air must be bled from the system using the following procedure.

1. Install the pump, bracket and all

hoses and lines to specifications, EXCEPT the pressure line at the pump outlet.
2. Add fluid to the reservoir until fluid begins leaving the pump at the pressure fittings.
3. Attach the pressure line to the pump.
4. Continue filling the reservoir until the proper level is reached.
5. Road test the car to make sure the steering system functions normally.
6. Recheck the fluid level and top up as necessary with power steering fluid.

Steering Wheel

REMOVAL & INSTALLATION

1. Disconnect the negative battery cable.
2. Pull up on the horn cap to remove it. Remove the horn ring-to-steering wheel attaching screws and remove the ring.
3. Remove the wheel nut retainer and the wheel nut.

——— **CAUTION** ———
Do not overexpand the retainer.

4. Using a suitable steering wheel puller, thread the puller anchor screws

into the threaded holes in the steering wheel. With the center bolt of the puller butting against the steering shaft, turn the center bolt to remove the steering wheel.
5. To install, place the turn signal lever in the neutral position and install the steering wheel. Torque the steering wheel nut to 30 ft. lbs. and install the nut retainer. Use caution not to overexpand the nut retainer.
6. Connect the negative battery cable.

Turn Signal Switch

REMOVAL & INSTALLATION

1. Remove the steering wheel as previously described.
2. Position a small prybar into one of the three cover slots. Pry up and out (at least two slots) to free the cover.
3. Press down on the lockplate, but do not relieve the full load of the spring because the ring will rotate and make removal difficult. Pry the round wire snap-ring out of the shaft groove and discard it. Lift the lockplate off the end of the shaft.
4. Slide the turn signal canceling cam, upper bearing preload spring, and thrust washer off the end of the shaft.
5. Remove the multi-function lever by rotating it clockwise to its stop (off position), then pull the lever straight out to disengage it.
6. Push the hazard warning knob in and unscrew the knob.
7. Remove the two screws, pivot arm, and spacer.
8. Wrap the upper part of the connector with tape to prevent snagging the wires during switch removal.
9. Remove the three switch mounting screws and pull the switch straight up, guiding the wiring harness through the column housing.

——— **CAUTION** ———
On installation it is extremely important that only the specified screws, bolts, and nuts be used. The use of overlength screws could prevent the steering column from compresssing under impact.

10. Position the switch into the housing.
11. Install the three switch mounting screws. Replace the spacer and pivot arm. Be sure that the spacer protrudes through the hole in the arm. Be sure that the spacer protrudes through the hole in the arm and that the arm finger encloses the turn signal switch frame.
12. Install the hazard warning knob.
13. Make sure that the turn signal switch is in the neutral position and

that the hazard warning knob is out. Slide the thrust washer, upper baring preload spring, and the cancelling cam into the upper end of the shaft.

14. Place the lockplate and a new snapring onto the end of the shaft. Compress the lockplate as far as possible. Slide the new snapring into the shaft groove and remove the lockplate compressor tool.

--- **CAUTION** ---

On assembly, always use a new snapring.

15. Install the multi-function lever, guiding the wire harness through the column housing. Align the lever pin with the switch slot. Push on the end of the lever until it is seated securely.

16. Install the steering wheel as previously described.

Lock Cylinder

REMOVAL & INSTALLATION

The lock cylinder is located on the right side of the steering column and should be removed only in the Run position. Removal in any other position will damage the key buzzer switch. The lock cylinder cannot be disassembled; if replacement is required, a new cylinder coded to the old key must be installed.

1. Remove the steering wheel and turn signal switch as previously described.

2. Do not remove the buzzer switch or damage to the lock cylinder will result.

3. Place the lock cylinder in the RUN position. Remove the securing screw and remove the cylinder.

4. To install the lock cylinder, hold the cylinder sleeve and rotate knob (key in) clockwise to stop. (This retracts the actuator). Insert the cylinder into the housing bore with the key on the cylinder sleeve aligned with the keyway in the housing. Push the cylinder in until it bottoms and install the retaining screw.

5. Install the turn signal switch and the steering wheel as previously described.

Ignition Switch and Dimmer Switch

REMOVAL & INSTALLATION

The ignition switch is mounted on top of the mast jacket near the front of the

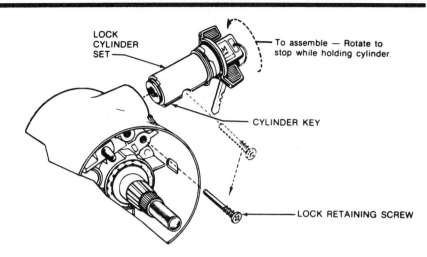

Lock cylinder installation details

instrument panel. The switch is located inside the channel section of the brake pedal support and is completely inaccessible without first lowering the steering column.

1. Disconnect the negative battery cable.

2. Remove the steering wheel as previously described.

3. Move the driver's seat as far back as possible.

4. Remove the floor pan bracket screw.

5. Remove the two column bracket-to-instrument panel nuts and lower the column far enough to disconnect the ignition switch wiring harness.

--- **CAUTION** ---

Be sure that the steering column is properly supported before proceeding.

6. The switch should be in the Lock position before removal. If the lock cylinder has already been removed, the actuating rod to the switch should be pulled up until there is a definite stop, then moved down one detent to the Lock position.

7. Remove the two mounting screws and remove the ignition and dimmer switch.

8. Refer to the lock cylinder installation procedure previously described in "Lock Cylinder Removal & Installation."

9. Turn the cylinder clockwise to stop and then counterclockwise to stop, then counterclockwise again to stop (OFF-UNLOCK) position.

10. Place the ignition switch in the

OFF-UNLOCK position. Move the slider two positions to the right from ACCESSORY to the OFF-UNLOCK position.

11. Fit the actuator rod into the slider hole and install the switch on the column. Be sure to use only the correct screws. Be careful not to move the switch out of its detent.

12. Check the dimmer switch adjustment.

13. Connect the ignition switch wiring harness.

14. Loosely install the column bracket-to-instrument panel nuts.

15. Install the floor pan bracket screw and tighten it to 20 ft. lbs.

16. Tighten the column bracket-to-instrument panel nuts to 22 ft. lbs.

17. Install the steering wheel as previously outlined.

18. Connect the battery negative cable.

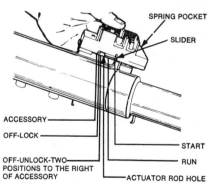

Postioning the ignition switch for installation

SPECTRUM

Tie Rod

REMOVAL & INSTALLATION

1. Raise the vehicle and remove the front wheel.
2. Remove the castle nut from the ball joint. Using a ball joint removal tool, separate the tie rod from the steering knuckle.
3. Disconnect the retaining wire from the inner boot and pull back the boot.
4. Using a chisel, straighten the staked part of the locking washer between the tie rod and the rack.
5. Remove the tie rod from the rack.
6. To install, reverse the removal procedure.

Rack & Pinion

REMOVAL & INSTALLATION

Manual Steering

1. Refer to the "Tie Rod Removal and Installation" procedure in this section. Remove both tie rod ends from the steering knuckles and the left inner tie rod from the rack.
2. Remove the intermediate shaft cover.
3. Loosen the upper pinch bolt and remove the lower pinch bolt at the pinion shaft.
4. Remove the steering gear to body retaining nuts.
5. Remove the rack and pinion assembly.
6. To install, reverse the removal procedure and check the toe-in.

Power Steering

1. Refer to the "Tie Rod Removal and Installation" procedure in this section. Remove both tie rod ends from the steering knuckles and the right inner tie rod from the rack.
2. Place a drain pan under the rack assembly and clean around the pressure lines at the rack valve.
3. Cut the plastic retaining straps at the power steering lines and hose.
4. Remove the power steering pump lines, the rack valve and drain the fluid into the pan.
5. Remove the rack and pinion.
6. To install, reverse the removal procedure, add fluid, bleed the system and check the toe-in.

Power Steering Pump

REMOVAL & INSTALLATION

1. Place a drain pan below the pump.
2. Remove the pressure hose clamp, pressure hose and return hose. Drain the fluid from the pump and reservoir.
3. Remove the adjusting bolt, pivot bolt and drive belt.
4. Remove the pump assembly.
5. To install, reverse the removal procedure, tighten the pressure hose to 20 ft. lbs., adjust the drive belt, fill the reservoir and bleed the system.

BLEEDING

1. Turn the wheels to the extreme left.
2. With the engine stopped, add power steering fluid to the "MIN" mark on the fluid indicator.
3. Start the engine and run it for 15 seconds at fast idle.
4. Stop the engine, recheck the fluid level and refill to the "MIN" mark.
5. Start the engine and turn the wheels from side to side (3 times).
6. Stop the engine check the fluid level.

NOTE: If air bubbles are still present in the fluid, the procedure must be repeated.

Steering Wheel

REMOVAL & INSTALLATION

1. Disconnect the negative battery cable.
2. Using a screwdriver, remove the shroud screws from the rear side of the steering wheel (Type 1) or pry the shroud from the steering wheel (Type 2).
3. Disconnect the horn connector and remove the shroud.
4. Remove the nut/washer retaining the steering wheel to the steering shaft.
5. Using a steering wheel puller, remove the steering wheel.
6. To install, reverse the removal procedure.

NOTE: The steering column is a collision type (designed to collapse upon impact), be careful not to severely jar it at any time.

Steering Column

REMOVAL & INSTALLATION

1. From under the dash, remove the steering column protector nut, clip and protector.
2. Remove the pinch bolt between the intermediate shaft and the steering shaft.
3. Remove the mounting bracket bolts from the lower column.
4. Remove the steering column to instrument panel mounting bolts.
5. Remove the electrical connectors and park lock cable at the ignition switch. If equipped with an automatic transaxle, remove the park lock cable bracket.
6. Remove the steering column assembly.
7. To install, reverse the removal procedure.

Intermediate Shaft

REMOVAL & INSTALLATION

1. Remove the protector nut, clip and protector.
2. Remove the pinch bolts at the pinion shaft and steering shaft.
3. Remove the intermediate shaft.
4. To install, reverse the removal procedure.

Turn Signal/Dimmer Switch

REMOVAL & INSTALLATION

1. Disconnect the negative battery cable.
2. Remove the horn shroud, steering wheel nut/washer and steering wheel assembly.
3. Remove the steering cowl attaching screw and steering cowl.
4. Disconnect the combination/starter switch connector.
5. Remove the turn signal/dimmer switch attaching screw and switch.
6. To install, reverse the removal procedure.

Ignition Switch

REMOVAL & INSTALLATION

1. Refer to the "Turn Signal/Dimmer Switch Removal and Installation" procedure in the this section. Remove the turn signal/dimmer switch.

1. Steering wheel
2. Lower steering whell cover
3. Horn contact ring
4. Screw
5. Screw
6. Steering shaft column
7. Nut
8. Steering shaft column arm
9. Steering shaft
10. Steering column
11. Steering column bush
12. Plate
13. Bolt
14. Washer
15. Bolt
16. Nut
17. Clip
18. Rubber cushion
19. Washer
20. Steering intermediate shaft
21. Bolt
22. Snap ring
23. Washer
24. Cover set
25. Screw
26. Screw
27. Protector
28. Clip
29. Seal
30. Nut
31. Boot
32. Boot clip
33. Boot plate
34. Shroud assm.
35. Screw
36. Steering wheel emblem
37. Steering lock assem.
38. Bolt
39. Ignition starter switch
40. Screw
41. Ignition switch
42. Turn signal switch

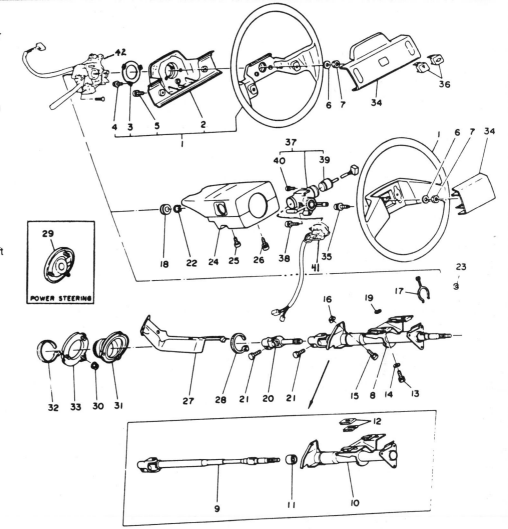

Exploded view of the steering column

2. Insert the key into the ignition and place the key in the ON position (the lock bar must be pulled all the way in).

3. Remove the snap ring and rubber cushion from the steering shaft.

4. Disconnect the switch wires at the connectors.

5. Remove the 2 screws retaining the ignition/starter switch and remove the switch.

6. To install, reverse the removal procedure.

Parking Lock (Auto Trans)

ADJUSTMENT

1. Remove the shift lever knob screws and the shift lever knob.

2. Remove the 4 console screws and console.

3. Place the shift lever in the Park position and the ignition in the Lock position.

4. Loosen the upper and lower ad-

justing nuts of the parking lock cable.

5. Adjust the cable so that the shift lever cannot be moved from the Park position.

6. Tighten the upper nut.

7. Move the key to the OFF position; the shift lever should release from the Park position.

8. Move the shift lever to Drive; the key should not be able to be removed from the ignition assembly.

9. To complete the adjustment, reinstall the items that were removed.

SPRINT

Steering Wheel

REMOVAL & INSTALLATION

1. Disconnect the negative battery cable.

2. Loosen the pad screws and remove the the pad.

3. Remove the steering wheel nut.

4. Scribe a matchmark line on the steering wheel and the shaft.

5. Using the wheel puller tool J-1859-03, pull the steering wheel from the steering shaft.

6. To install, reverse the removal procedures. Torque the steering wheel

nut to 19–29 ft. lbs.

Turn Signal/Dimmer Switch Assembly

REMOVAL & INSTALLATION

1. Refer to the "Steering Wheel Re-

397

moval & Installation" procedures in this section and remove the steering wheel.

2. Remove the upper and lower steering column covers.

3. Disconnect the turn signal/dimmer switch assembly electrical connector.

4. Remove the screws and the turn signal/dimmer switch assembly from the steering column.

5. To install, reverse the removal procedures.

NOTE: When installing, be careful that the lead wires do not get caught by the lower cover.

Steering Column

REMOVAL & INSTALLATION

1. Refer to the "Turn Signal/Dimmer Switch Removal & Installation" procedures in this section and remove

the turn signal/dimmer switch assembly.

2. Remove the bolt and separate the lower steering column shaft from the steering column. Disconnect the electrical connectors from the column.

3. Remove the steering column mounting bolts and the column from the dash.

4. To install, reverse the removal procedures. Torque the lower bracket bolts to 8–12 ft. lbs., the upper bracket bolts to 10 ft. lbs. and the steering shaft bolt to 15–22 ft. lbs.

Ignition Switch And Key Lock Assembly

REMOVAL & INSTALLATION

1. Refer to the "Steering Column Removal & Installation" procedures in this section and remove the steering column.

2. Place the column on a bench.

3. Using a sharp point center punch and a hammer, remove the steering lock mounting bolts.

4. Turn the ignition key to ACC or ON positions and remove the lock assembly from the steering column.

5. To install, reverse the removal procedures. After installing the lock, turn the key to LOCK position and pull out the key. Turn the steering shaft to make sure the shaft is locked. Install new mounting bolts to the lock housing, tighten until the bolt heads break off. Torque the lower bracket bolts to 8–12 ft. lbs.; the upper bracket bolts to 10 ft. lbs. and the steering shaft bolt to 15–22 ft. lbs.

Steering Gear

REMOVAL & INSTALLATION

1. Refer to the "Tie Rod Removal &

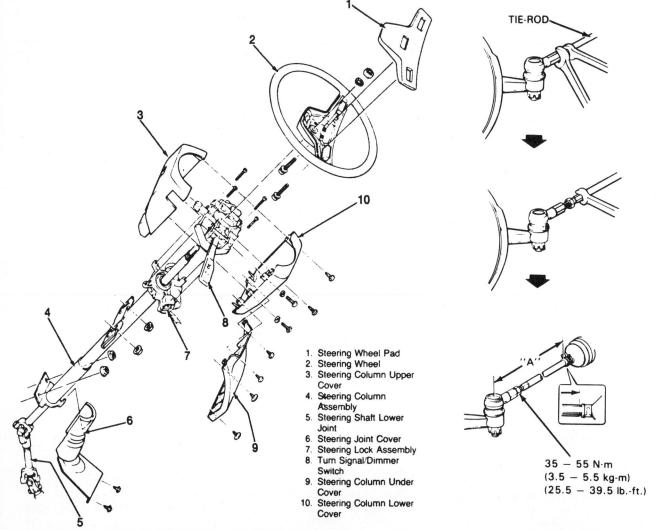

1. Steering Wheel Pad
2. Steering Wheel
3. Steering Column Upper Cover
4. Steering Column Assembly
5. Steering Shaft Lower Joint
6. Steering Joint Cover
7. Steering Lock Assembly
8. Turn Signal/Dimmer Switch
9. Steering Column Under Cover
10. Steering Column Lower Cover

TIE-ROD

"A"

35 — 55 N·m
(3.5 — 5.5 kg-m)
(25.5 — 39.5 lb.-ft.)

Exploded view of the steering column assembly

Toe adjustment

Installation" procedures in this section and remove the tie rod ends from the steering knuckles.

2. Under the dash, remove the steering joint cover.

3. Remove the lower steering shaft-to-steering gear clinch bolt and separate the steering shaft from the steering gear.

4. Remove the steering gear mounting bolts, the brackets and the steering gear case from the vehicle.

5. To install, reverse the removal procedures. Torque the steering gear case bolts to 14–22 ft. lbs.; the steering gear-to-steering shaft bolt to 14–22 ft. lbs. and the tie rod end-to-steering knuckle nut to 22–40 ft. lbs.

Tie Rod

REMOVAL & INSTALLATION

1. Raise and support the front of the vehicle on jackstands. Remove the front wheel assembly.

2. Remove the cotter pin and the castle nut from the tie rod end.

3. Using the ball joint remover tool J-21687-02, remove the tie rod end ball joint from the steering knuckle.

4. Loosen the lock nut on the tie rod end.

5. Unscrew the the tie rod end from the tie rod, count the number of revolutions necessary to remove the tie rod end, for installation purposes.

6. At the steering gear, remove the boot clamps and pull the boot back over the tie rod.

7. Using a pair of pliers, bend the lock washer back from the tie rod joint.

8. Using two wrenches, hold the steering gear and unscrew the tie rod end.

9. Remove the tie rod and slide the boot from the tie rod.

10. To install, reverse the removal procedures. Torque the tie rod-to-steering gear to 51–72 ft. lbs.; the tie rod end lock nut to 26–40 ft. lbs. and the tie rod end-to-steering knuckle to 22–40 ft. lbs. With the tie rod secured to the steering gear, bend the lock washer over the flat spot on the tie rod ball end.

TOE ADJUSTMENT

Toe is adjusted by changing the tie rod length. Loosen the right and left tie rod end lock nuts first and then turn left and right tie rods by the same

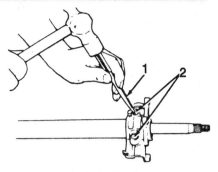

1. Center Punch (With Sharp Point)
2. Steering Lock Mounting Bolts

Removing the ignition switch/key lock assembly

amount to align toe to specification. In this adjustment right and left tie rods should be equal in length. Toe adjustment should be (0 ± 0.157 in.).

NOTE: Before turning the tie rods, apply grease between tie rods and rack boots so that the boots won't be twisted. After adjustment, tighten lock nuts to specified torque and make sure that the rack boots are not twisted.

NOVA

Tie Rod

REMOVAL & INSTALLATION

1. Remove the cotter pin and nut holding the knuckle arm to the tie rod end. Then, use a tool designed for this purpose to press the stud up and out of the steering knuckle.

2. Loosen the tie rod-to-steering rack-end nut. Matchmark the position of the tie rod on the rack-end so you can restore toe-in.

3. Install in reverse order, making sure you align the matchmarks. Torque the tie rod-to-rack-end locknut to 35 ft. lbs. Torque the tie-rod end-to-steering knuckle nut to 36 ft. lbs. and then install a new cotter pin.

Manual Steering Gear

REMOVAL & INSTALLATION

1. Remove the clamp bolts at top and bottom of the universal joint linking the steering box and steering shaft. Then, remove the U-joint.

2. Remove the cotter pin and nut holding the knuckle arm to the tie rod end. Then, use a tool designed for this purpose to press the stud up and out of the steering knuckle.

3. Remove the two bolts and two nuts and remove the steering gear housing and brackets.

4. Install the housing in reverse order. Make sure the clamps are installed squarely over the rubber insulators so they will not be damaged when the nuts and bolts are torqued. Torque the attaching nuts and bolts to 43 ft. lbs. Torque the tie rod end nuts attaching the studs to the knuckle arms to 36 ft. lbs. Torque the U-joint clamp bolts to 26 ft. lbs. If new parts have been installed, have the toe-in and steering wheel center point checked and adjusted.

Power Steering Gear

REMOVAL & INSTALLATION

1. Remove the intermediate steering shaft protector. Loosen the upper shaft pinch bolt and remove the lower one.

2. Open the hood and place a drain pan under the steering gear assembly. Clean the area around the inlet and return lines at the steering gear valve.

3. Loosen the wheel lugnuts, and then raise and securely support the vehicle. Remove both front wheels and tires.

4. Remove the cotter pins and nuts and press both tie rod ends out of the knuckles.

5. Support the transaxle with a jack. Remove the rear center engine mounting member-to-body mounting bolts.

6. Remove the rear engine mount-to-mount bracket attaching nut and bolt.

7. Disconnect the pressure and return lines at the steering gear. Remove the four steering gear-to-body attaching nuts and bolts, raising and lowering the rear of the transaxle as necessary to gain access to the steering gear-to-body attaching bolts and nuts.

8. Remove the steering gear through the access hole.

9. Installation is the reverse of removal. Add fluid to the pump reservoir and bleed the system.

Power Steering Pump

REMOVAL & INSTALLATION

1. Remove the air cleaner. Loosen the nut at the center of the pump pulley while the belt is still attached.

2. Loosen the pump mounting and adjusting bolts, move the pump so as to reduce belt tension and then remove the belt.

3. Remove the nut, pulley, and key from the pump shaft.

4. Place a drain pan under the pump. Remove the return hose clamp. Disconnect the hoses at the pump reservoir and then tie them up high so fluid will not drain out. In the case of the return line, pull it well back from the fitting, and pull the hose off the pump with a twisting motion.

5. Remove the adjusting bolt. Remove the pivot bolt and disconnect the drive belt. Remove the pump assembly. Remove the pump bracket.

6. Installation is the reverse of removal. If you are replacing the pump, switch the pulley and the mounting nut to the new pump. Be careful not to lose the woodruff key. The nut is tightened after the pump is installed and tension is put on the belt. Torque the pressure hose fitting to 34 ft. lbs. Tension the belt so deflection is .31–.39 in. with moderate thumb pressure (about 20 lbs.) applied in the center of the span. Fill the reservoir with Dexron II automatic transmission fluid and bleed the system as described below. Check for leaks and correct if necessary.

BLEEDING THE POWER STEERING SYSTEM

1. Raise the front of the car and support it securely on jackstands (this will minimize steering effort). Fill the power steering pump reservoir with Dexron® II.

2. With the engine OFF, keep the reservoir full as someone turns the steering wheel from lock to lock several times. Stop with the steering system at one lock.

3. Pull the high tension lead out of the coil. Continue to keep the reservoir full as someone cranks the engine for 30 seconds at a time (with a one minute rest in between) until fluid level remains constant.

4. Turn the steering wheel to the opposite lock and repeat Step 3.

5. Reconnect the high tension lead, start the engine and allow it to idle. Turn the wheel from lock to lock several times. Note the level of the fluid.

6. Lower the car to the ground. Note the fluid level. Repeat Step 5,

stopping with the wheel at the centered position.

7. The fluid level should not have risen more than .2 in. If it has, repeat Step 6 until the level does not rise appreciably.

Steering Wheel

REMOVAL & INSTALLATION

1. Remove the screw from the bottom of the steering wheel pad and pull the pad upward and off the wheel.

2. Remove the steering wheel attaching nut from the end of the column. Matchmark the relationship between the end of the column and the wheel.

3. Screw the attaching bolts of a steering wheel puller into the threads on either side of the column and turn the center bolt of the puller to remove the wheel.

4. Install the wheel in reverse order. Once the wheel is started onto the splines (with the matchmarks lined up), the nut can be installed and torqued to force it onto the column. Torque the nut to 25 ft. lbs.

Combination Switch

REMOVAL & INSTALLATION

1. Disconnect the negative battery cable. Remove the instrument lower finish panel, air duct, and column lower cover.

2. Disconnect the ignition and turn signal switch wiring from the connector.

3. Remove the combination switch

with the column upper cover.

4. Installation is the reverse of removal.

Ignition Lock and Switch

REMOVAL & INSTALLATION

1. Disconnect the negative battery cable. Unscrew the two retaining bolts and remove the steering column garnish.

2. Remove the upper and lower steering column covers.

3. Turn the key to the "ACC" position.

4. Push in the lock cylinder stop, located near the inner end of the cylinder, with a cotter pin or center punch. Then, pull out the key and lock cylinder. If you have trouble gaining access, it may help to remove the steering wheel and combination switch as described above.

5. Remove the mounting screw and withdraw the ignition switch from the lock housing.

6. To install, first line up the notch on the top of the switch with the projection inside the housing and turn the slot in the switch shaft so it will engage the projection on the steering lock shaft. Then position the switch inside the lock and install the retaining screw.

7. Make sure that both the lock cylinder and the column lock are in "ACC" position. Slide the cylinder into the lock housing until the stop tab engages the hole in the lock.

8. The rest of the installation procedure is the reverse of removal.

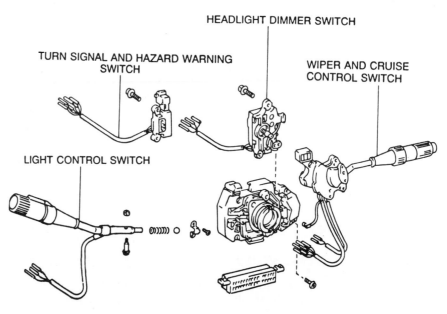

Exploded view of the combination switch

CORSICA AND BERETTA

Steering Wheel

REMOVAL & INSTALLATION

1. Disconnect the negative battery cable.

2. Remove the horn cover by pulling the cover outwards.

3. Remove the steering wheel attaching nut and washer and install a steering wheel puller.

4. Remove the steering wheel.

5. Installation is the reverse of the removal. Torque the steering wheel nut to 30 ft. lbs.

Turn Signal Switch

REMOVAL & INSTALLATION

NOTE: Tool J–35689–A, or equivalent is required to remove the terminals from the connector on the turn signal switch.

1. Disconnect the negative battery cable.

2. Using the correct procedure, remove the steering wheel.

3. Pull the turn signal cancelling cam off of the steering shaft.

4. Remove the screw retaining the hazard knob and remove the knob.

5. Remove the turn signal switch housing retaining ring and washer. Remove the turn signal switch housing cover.

6. Remove the screws retaining the dimmer switch accuator and remove the dimmer switch and turn signal lever. One screw is in the front and one is in the rear. Disconnect the wires on the turn signal lever if the vehicle is equipped with cruise control.

7. Using tool J–35689–A, or equivalent, disconnect and tag the wires on the connector at the buzzer switch assembly from the turn signal switch connector.

8. Remove the turn signal switch retaining screws and remove the switch.

9. Installation is the reverse of the removal. Torque the turn signal switch mounting screws to 35 inch lbs. Torque the dimmer switch actuator screws to 18 inch lbs. Torque the steering wheel nut to 30 ft. lbs.

Ignition Lock/Switch

REMOVAL & INSTALLATION

The manufacture recommends that on steering columns with a Park Lock, the steering column must be removed from the vehicle prior to ignition lock removal and installation.

1. Disconnect the negative battery cable. Remove the left side lower trim panel.

2. Remove the two (2) steering column to support mounting screws and lower the steering column.

3. Disconnect the dimmer switch and turn signal switch connectors.

4. Remove the nuts holding the wiring harness to the firewall and steering column.

5. Remove the two (2) lower steering column to steering gear mounting bolts and remove the steering column from the vehicle.

NOTE: On steering columns without a Park Lock, lower the column onto the seat and continue the procedure without removing the steering column from the vehicle.

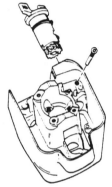

Ignition lock cylinder removal

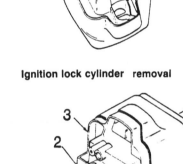

1. Retaining ring
2. Thrust washer
3. Turn signal switch housing
4. Steering shaft assembly

Removing turn signal switch housing

Steering column mounting

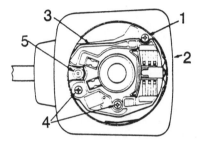

1. Screw
2. Housing cover
3. Turn signal switch
4. Screw
5. Self tapping screw

Turn signal switch mounting

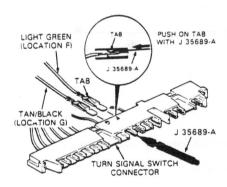

Removing terminals from turn signal switch connector

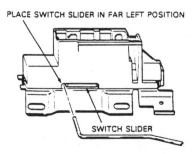

Ignition switch installation position

6. Using the correct procedure, remove the steering wheel and turn signal switch.

7. Place the lock cylinder in the RUN position.

8. Remove the steering shaft and turn signal switch housing as an assembly.

9. Using a suitable tool, remove the wiring for the buzzer switch lifting the tab and pulling gently on the wires.

10. Place the lock cylinder in the RUN position and remove the buzzer switch.

11. Place the lock cylinder in the ACCESSORY position.

12. Remove the lock cylinder retaining screw and remove the lock cylinder.

13. Remove the dimmer switch nut and bolt and remove the dimmer switch and actuator rod.

14. Remove the dimmer switch mounting stud that the mounting nut was mounted to.

15. Remove the ignition switch mounting screws and remove the ignition switch.

16. Remove the lock bolt retaining screws and remove the lock bolt.

17. Remove the switch actuator rack and ignition switch.

18. Remove the steering shaft lock and spring.

19. Observe the following torques during installation: Steering Lock retaining screw 27 inch lbs.; Dimmer Switch mounting stud, 35 inch lbs.; Turn Signal Switch housing screws, 88 inch lbs.; Turn Signal Switch screws, 35 inch lbs.; Steering Wheel lock nut, 30 ft. lbs.

20. To install, lubricate the lock bolt with lithium grease and install the lock bolt, spring and retaining plate.

21. Lubricate the teeth on the switch actuator rack and install the rack and the ignition switch through the opening in the steering bolt until it rests on the retaining plate.

22. Install the steering column lock cylinder set by holding the barrel of the lock cylinder, inserting the key and turning the key to the ACCESSORY position.

23. Install the lock set in the steering column while holding the rack against the lock plate.

24. Install the lock retaining screw. Insert the key in the lock cylinder and turn the lock cylinder to the START position and the rack will extend.

25. Center the slotted holes on the ignition switch mounting plate and install the ignition switch mounting screw and nut.

26. Install the dimmer switch and actuator rod into the center slot on the switch mounting plate.

27. Install the buzzer switch and turn the lock cylinder to the RUN position. Push the switch in until it is bottomed out with the plastic tab that covers the lock retaining screw.

28. Install the steering shaft and turn signal housing as an assembly.

29. Install the turn signal switch.

30. The remainder of the installation is the reverse of the removal.

Power Steering Gear

REMOVAL & INSTALLATION

1. Remove the left side lower sound insulator inside the vehicle.

2. Remove the upper pinch bolt on the steering shaft to steering rack coupling.

3. Place a drain pan under the steering gear and disconnect the steering fluid lines at the steering gear.

4. Raise and safely support the vehicle.

5. Remove both front wheels and tires.

6. Disconnect the tie rod ends from the steering knuckles using J–24319–01, or equivalent.

7. Lower the vehicle.

8. Remove both steering gear mounting clamps.

9. Slide the steering gear forward and remove the lower pinch bolt on the steering shaft to steering rack coupling.

10. Disconnect the coupling and seal from the steering gear at the firewall.

11. Raise and safely support the vehicle.

12. Remove the steering gear, with the tie rods, through the left wheel opening.

13. Installation is the reverse of the removal.

14. Bleed the power steering system after installation.

15. Observe the following torques during installation: Torque the mounting clamp bolts to 28 ft. lbs.; torque the tie rod nut to 44 ft. lbs.; torque the fluid lines to 18 ft. lbs.

ADJUSTMENT

No adjustments are possible on the steering gear.

Power Steering Pump

REMOVAL & INSTALLATION

2.0 & 2.8 Liter Engines

1. Disconnect the negative battery cable.

2. Remove the pressure and return hoses from the pump and drain the system into a suitable container.

3. Cap the fittings at the pump.

4. Remove the serpentine belt.

5. Locate the pump attaching bolts through the pulley and remove the bolts.

6. Remove the pump assembly.

7. Installation is the reverse of the removal. Torque the mounting bolts to 20 ft. lbs.

8. Fill and bleed the system when finished.

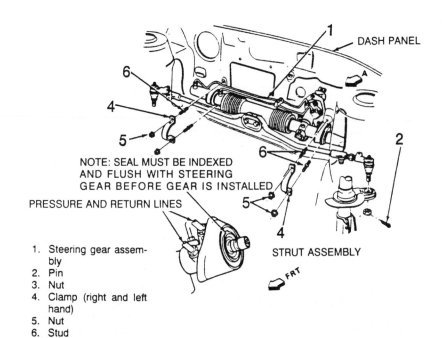

NOTE: SEAL MUST BE INDEXED AND FLUSH WITH STEERING GEAR BEFORE GEAR IS INSTALLED

PRESSURE AND RETURN LINES

DASH PANEL

STRUT ASSEMBLY

FRT

1. Steering gear assembly
2. Pin
3. Nut
4. Clamp (right and left hand)
5. Nut
6. Stud

Power steering gear mounting

SYSTEM BLEEDING

─────── CAUTION ───────

Automatic transmission fluid IS NOT compatible with the seals and hoses of the power steering system. Under no circumstances should automatic transmission be used in place of power steering fluid in this system.

1. With the engine off, turn the wheels all the way to the left.
2. Fill the reservoir with power steering fluid until the level is at the COLD mark on the reservoir.
3. Start and run the engine at fast idle for 15 seconds. Turn the engine off.
4. Recheck the fluid level and fill it to the COLD mark.
5. Start the engine and bleed the system by turning the wheels in both directions slowly to the stops.
6. Stop the engine and check the fluid. Fluid that still has air in it will be a light tan color.
7. Repete this procedure until all of the air is removed from the system.

Tie Rod Ends

REMOVAL & INSTALLATION

Outer

1. Raise and safely support the vehicle. Remove the wheel and tire.
2. Remove the cotter pin and nut from the outer tie rod end.
3. Loosen the outer tie rod pinch bolts.
4. Separate the tie rod from the steering knuckle using tool J–24319–01, or equivalent.
5. Remove the outer tie rod from the adjuster by counting the exact number of turns required to remove it. This will allow proper installation without having to reset the toe in.
6. Install the new tie rod end by turning it in the same amount of turns as during the removal.
7. Connect the tie rod to the steering knuckle. Torque the nut to 35–50 ft. lbs.
8. Torque the pinch bolts to 35 ft. lbs.

Inner

1. Remove the inner tie rod end lock plate bolt. If both inner tie rods are being replaced, discard the used lock plate.
2. Slide the inner tie rod out from between the plate and the steering rack.
3. Reinstall the lock plate bolt to insure proper tie rod to steering gear realignment.
4. Remove the cotter pin and nut from the outer tie rod end.
5. Disconnect the outer tie rod end from the knuckle using tool J–24319–01, or equivalent.
6. Remove the inner and outer tie rod assembly from the vehicle.
7. Note the position of the inner and outer tie rods in relation to each other. Place the assembly in a vise and loosen the pinch bolts on the adjuster.
8. Remove the outer tie rod from the adjuster by counting the exact number of turns required to remove it. This will allow proper installation without having to reset the toe in.
9. Place the new inner tie rod in the vise and install the outer tie rod end and adjuster the same amount of turns as when removing it.

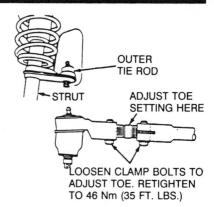

Outer tie rod mounting

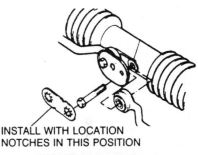

INSTALL WITH LOCATION NOTCHES IN THIS POSITION

Inner tie rod mounting

10. Check to make sure that the alignment between the inner and outer tie rods is the same as during removal.
11. Installation is the reverse of the removal. Use a new lock plate when installing both inner tie rods.
12. Torque the inner tie rod to lock plate bolts to 65 ft. lbs. Torque the pinch bolts to 35 ft. lbs. Torque the outer tie rod nut to 35–50 ft. lbs.

LIGHT TRUCKS AND VANS
BLAZER/JIMMY – FULL SIZE, BLAZER/JIMMY – S-SERIES
PICK-UPS – FULL SIZE, PICK-UPS – S-SERIES, SUBURBAN,
VANS – FULL SIZE AND ASTRO

A common cause of excessive steering play on these trucks is the steering gear box coming loose from the frame. The torque for these bolts is 65 ft. lbs.

Steering Wheel

REMOVAL & INSTALLATION

Except S-Series

1. Disconnect the battery ground cable.
2. Remove the horn button. Remove the receiving cup, bellville washer, and bushing (if equipped).
3. Mark the steering wheel-to-steering shaft relationship.
4. Remove the snap-ring from the steering shaft.
5. Remove the nut and washer from the steering shaft.
6. Remove the steering wheel with a puller.

─────── CAUTION ───────

Don't hammer on the steering shaft.

7. Installation is the reverse of removal. The turn signal control assembly must be in the neutral position to prevent damaging the cancelling cam and control assembly. Tighten the nut to 30 ft. lbs.

S-Series

1. Disconnect battery ground cable.
2. Remove steering wheel shroud screws on underside of steering wheel.
3. Lift steering wheel shroud and

horn contact lead assembly from the steering wheel.

4. Remove snap ring.

5. Remove steering wheel nut.

6. Using Tool J–2927, thread puller anchor screws into threaded holes provided in steering wheel. Turn center bolt of tool clockwise (butting against the steering shaft) to remove the steering wheel.

NOTE: Do not hammer on puller while turning. The tool centering adapters need not be installed.

7. Installation is the reverse of removal. Torque steering wheel nut 30 ft. lbs. Do not over-torque shaft nut or steering wheel rub may result.

Turn Signal Switch

REPLACEMENT

Except S-Series

1. Remove the steering wheel

2. Remove the column to instrument panel trim cover. Loosen the three cover screws and lift the cover off the shaft or place a screwdriver in the cover slot and pry out to free the cover, depending on year and model.

3. The round lockplate must be pushed down to remove the wire snapring from the shaft. A special tool is available to do this. The tool is an inverted U-shape with a hole for the shaft. The shaft nut is used to force it down. Pry the wire snap-ring out of the shaft groove.

4. Remove the tool and lift the lockplate off the shaft.

5. Slip the canceling cam, upper bearing preload spring, and thrust washer off the shaft.

6. Remove the turn signal lever screw and the lever. Push the flasher knob in and unscrew it.

7. Pull the switch connector out of the mast jacket and tape the upper part to facilitate switch removal. On tilt wheels, place the turn signal and shifter housing in the low position and remove the harness cover.

8. Remove the three switch mounting screws. Remove the switch by pulling it straight up while guiding the wiring harness cover through the column.

9. Install the replacement switch by working the connector and cover down through the housing and under the bracket. On tilt models, the connector is worked down through the housing, under the bracket, and then cover is installed on the harness.

10. Install the switch mounting screw and the connector on the mast

jacket bracket. Install the column to instrument panel trim plate.

11. Install the flasher knob and the turn signal lever.

12. With the turn signal lever in neutral and the flasher knob out, slide the thrust washer, upper bearing pre-load spring, and canceling cam onto the shaft.

13. Position the lockplate on the shaft and press it down until a new snap-ring can be inserted in the shaft groove.

14. Install the cover and the steering wheel.

S-Series

1. Remove the steering wheel.

2. Pry out the steering shaft lock cover.

3. Remove the retaining ring and shaft lock.

4. Remove the canceling cam and spring.

5. Remove the switch actuator arm, unscrew and remove the switch and unplug the wire connector.

6. Installation is the reverse of removal.

Ignition Switch and Lock Cylinder

REMOVAL & INSTALLATION

Except S-Series

1. Remove the steering wheel and the turn signal switch as previously outlined. It is not necessary to completely remove the turn signal switch. Just pull the switch out far enough so it can hang out of the steering column shift. Do not disconnect the wiring harness.

2. With the lock cylinder in the Run position, remove the lock cylinder attaching screw and the cylinder.

3. To install, align the cylinder key with the keyway in the housing and rotate the key all the way clockwise while holding the cylinder body.

4. Insert the cylinder into the housing and install the attaching screw.

5. Install the turn signal switch and the steering wheel as previously outlined.

S-Series Trucks

1. Disconnect the battery ground.

2. Turn the lock to the RUN position.

3. Remove the turn signal switch.

4. Remove the cylinder retaining screw.

5. Pull out the cylinder.

6. Installation is the reverse of removal. Turn the cylinder to the STOP position while installing.

Ignition Switch

REMOVAL & INSTALLATION

Except S-Series

1. The switch is on the steering column, behind the instrument panel. Lower the steering column, making sure that it is supported. Extreme care is necessary to prevent damage to the collapsible column.

2. Make sure the switch is in the Lock position. If the lock cylinder is out, pull the switch rod up to the stop, then go down one detent.

3. Remove the two screws and the switch.

4. Before installation, make sure the switch is in the lock position. The switch can be moved to the Lock position using a screwdriver inserted into the locking rod slot.

5. Install the switch using the original screws. Use of screws that are too long could prevent the column from collapsing on impact.

6. Reinstall the column.

S-Series

1. Remove the steering wheel, lock cylinder, turn signal switch, shift lever, shift lever bowl, shift bowl shroud and bowl lower bearing.

2. Unbolt and remove the ignition switch and dimmer switch from the column.

3. For installation, on all columns except key release type, move the switch slider to the extreme left position, then two detents right. this is the OFF-LOCK position. On key release columns, leave the slider in the extreme left position. This is ACCESSORIES. To adjust the dimmer switch, depress the switch slightly to allow insertion of a $3/32$ in. drill bit into the hole above the actuator rod. Force the switch upward to take up any lash, then tighten the screw. On tilt columns, the ACC position on the ignition switch is the extreme right position. On these columns, move the slider two detents left to the OFF-LOCK position.

Power Steering Pump

REMOVAL & INSTALLATION

1. Disconnect the hoses at the pump. When the hoses are disconnected, secure the ends in a raised position to prevent leakage. Cap the ends of the hoses to prevent the entrance of dirt.

2. Cap the pump fittings.

3. Loosen the bracket-to-pump mounting nuts.

4. Remove the pump drive belt.

5. Remove the bracket-to-pump bolts and remove the pump from the truck.

6. Installation is the reverse of removal. Fill the reservoir and bleed the pump by turning the pulley counterclockwise (as viewed from the front) until bubble stop forming. Bleed the system. Adjust the belt tension.

System Bleeding

1. Fill the reservoir to the proper level and let the fluid remain undisturbed for at least 2 minutes.

2. Start the engine and run it for only about 2 seconds.

3. Add fluid as necessary.

4. Repeat Steps 1–3 until the level remains constant.

5. Raise the front of the vehicle so that the front wheels are off the ground. Set the parking brake and block both rear wheels front and rear. Manual transmission should be in Neutral; automatic transmission should be in Park.

6. Start the engine and run it at approximately 1,500 rpm.

7. Turn the wheels (off the ground) to the right and left, lightly contacting the stops.

8. Add fluid as necessary.

9. Lower the vehicle and turn the wheels right and left on the ground.

10. Check the level and refill as necessary.

11. If the fluid is extremely foamy, let the truck stand for a few minutes with the engine off and repeat the above procedure. Check the belt tension and check for a bent or loose pulley. The pulley should not wobble with the engine running.

12. Check that no hoses are contacting any parts of the truck, particularly sheet metal.

13. Check the level and refill as necessary. This step and the next are very important. When filling, follow Steps 1–10.

14. Check for air in the fluid. Aerated fluid appears milky. If air is present, repeat the above operations. If it is obvious that the pump will not respond to bleeding after several attempts, a pressure test may be required.

Power Steering Gear

REMOVAL & INSTALLATION

1. Disconnect hoses at gear. When hoses are disconnected, secure ends in raised position to prevent drainage of oil Cap or tape the ends of the hoses to prevent entrance of dirt.

2. Install two plugs in gear fittings to prevent entrance of dirt.

3. Remove the flexible coupling to steering shaft flange bolts. Mark the relationship of the universal yoke to the stub shaft.

4. Mark the relationship of the Pitman arm to the Pitman shaft. Remove the Pitman shaft nut or Pitman arm from the Pitman shaft using puller J-6632.

5. Remove the steering gear to frame bolts and remove the gear assembly.

6. On G, C, and K models, remove the flexible coupling pinch bolt and remove the coupling from the steering gear stub shaft.

7. Install the flexible coupling onto the steering gear stub shaft, aligning the flat in the coupling with the flat on the shaft. Push the coupling onto the shaft until the stub shaft bottoms on the coupling reinforcement. Install the pinch bolt.

NOTE: The coupling bolt must pass through the shaft undercut, or damage to the components could occur.

8. Place the steering gear in position, guiding the coupling bolt into the steering shaft flange.

9. Install the steering gear to frame bolts.

10. If flexible coupling alignment pin plastic spacers were used, make sure they are buttoned on the pins, tighten the flange bolt nuts and then remove the plastic spacers.

11. If flexible coupling alignment pin plastic spacers were not used, center the pins in the slots in the steering shaft flange and then install and torque the flange bolt nuts.

12. Install the Pitman arm onto the Pitman shaft, lining up the marks made at removal. Install the Pitman shaft nut.

13. Remove the plugs and caps from the steering gear and hoses and connect the hoses to the gear. Tighten the hose fittings.

Manual Steering Gear

REMOVAL & INSTALLATION

1. Set the front wheels in straight ahead position by driving vehicle a short distance on a flat surface.

2. Remove the flexible coupling to steering shaft flange bolts. Mark the relationship of the universal yoke to the wormshaft.

3. Mark the relationship of the Pitman arm to the Pitman shaft. Remove the Pitman shaft nut or Pitman arm pinch bolt and then remove the Pitman arm from the Pitman shaft, using puller J-6632.

4. Remove the steering gear to frame bolts and remove the gear assembly.

5. Remove the flexible coupling pinch bolt and remove the coupling from the steering gear wormshaft.

6. Install the flexible coupling onto the steering gear wormshaft, aligning the flat in the coupling with the flat on the shaft. Push the coupling onto the shaft until the wormshaft bottoms on the coupling reinforcement. Install the pinch bolt and torque to 24 ft. lbs. The coupling bolt must pass through the shaft undercut.

7. Place the steering gear in position, guiding the coupling bolt into the steering shaft flange.

8. Install the steering gear to frame bolts and torque to 70 ft. lbs. or 55 ft. lbs. for S-Series trucks.

9. If flexible coupling alignment pin plastic spacers were used, make sure they are bottomed on the pins, torque the flange bolt nuts to 25 ft. lbs., and then remove the plastic spacers.

10. If flexible coupling alignment pin plastic spacers were not used, center the pins in the slots in the steering shaft flange and then install and torque the flange bolt nuts to 25 ft. lbs.

11. Install the Pitman arm onto the Pitman shaft, lining up the marks made at removal. Install the Pitman shaft nut torque to 185 ft. lbs.

Tie Rod Ends

REMOVAL & INSTALLATION

1. Raise the front of the truck and support it safely on jackstands.

2. Remove the tie rod end stud cotter pin and nut.

3. Use a tie rod end ball joint removal to loosen the stud.

4. Remove the inner stud in the same way.

5. Loosen the tie rod adjuster sleeve clamp nuts.

6. Unscrew the tie rod end from the threaded sleeve. The threads may be left or right hand threads. Count the number of turns required to remove it.

7. To install, grease the threads and turn the new tie rod end in as many turns as were needed to remove it. This will give approximately correct toe-in. tighten the clamp bolts.

8. Tighten the stud nuts to 45 ft. lbs. and install new cotter pins. You may tighten the nut to align the cotter pin, but don't loosen it.

9. Adjust the toe-in.

Relay Rod

REMOVAL & INSTALLATION

1. Raise and safely support the

8 SUSPENSION AND STEERING

vehicle.

2. Disconnect the inner ends of tie rods from relay rod.

3. Remove the nut from relay and rod ball stud attachment at Pitman arm.

4. Detach relay rod from pitman arm by using tool such as J–24319–01. Shift steering linkage as required to free pitman arm from relay rod.

5. Remove nut from idler arm and remove relay rod from idler arm.

6. Installation is the reverse of removal. Torque the nuts to 40 ft. lbs. Adjust toe-in if necessary.

Idler Arm

REMOVAL & INSTALLATION

1. Raise and safely support the vehicle.

2. Remove idler arm to frame nuts, washers, and bolts.

3. Remove nut from idler arm to relay rod ball stud.

4. Disconnect relay rod from idler arm by using J–24319–01 or similar puller.

5. Remove idler arm.

6. Installation is the reverse of removal. Torque nuts to 30 ft. lbs.

Brakes 9

INDEX

BRAKE SERVICE

Hydraulic Brake Component Service

BASIC OPERATING PRINCIPLES

The hydraulic brake system transports the power required to force the frictional surfaces of the braking system together from the pedal to the individual brake units at each wheel. A hydraulic system is used for two reasons. First, fluid under pressure can be carried to all parts of an automobile by small hoses (some of which are flexible) without taking up a significant amount of room or posing routing problems. Second, a great mechanical advantage can be given to the brake pedal end of the system and the foot pressure required to actuate the brakes can be reduced by making the surface area of the master cylinder pistons smaller than that of any of the pistons in the wheel cylinders or calipers.

The master cylinder consists of a double reservoir and piston assembly as well as other springs, fittings, etc. Double (dual) master cylinders are designed to separate two wheels from the others. The standard approach has been have separate circuits for the front and rear wheels. Newer models may have a diagonally split system; i.e. one front wheel and the opposite side rear wheel are in a separate circuit from the other front and rear wheel.

Steel lines carry the brake fluid to a point on the vehicles frame near each wheel. A flexible hose usually carries the fluid to the disc caliper or wheel cylinder. The flexible line allows for suspension and steering movement.

The rear wheel cylinders contain two pistons each, one at either end, which push outward in opposite directions. The brake calipers usually contain one piston, however in some cases they contain four.

All pistons employ some type of seal, usually made of rubber, to minimize fluid leakage. A rubber dust boot seals the outer end of the cylinder against dust and dirt. The boot fits around the outer end of the piston on disc brake calipers and around the brake actuating rod on the wheel cylinders.

The hydraulic system operates as follows: When at rest, the entire system, from the piston(s) in the master cylinder to those in the wheel cylinders or calipers, is full of brake fluid. Upon application of the brake pedal, fluid trapped in front of the master cylinder piston(s) is forced through the lines to the wheel cylinders and calipers. Here, it forces the pistons outward, in the case of drum brakes and inward toward the disc, in the case of disc brakes. The motion of the pistons is opposed by return springs mounted outside the cylinders in drum brakes and by internal springs or spring seals, in disc brakes.

Upon release of the brake pedal, a spring located inside the master cylinder immediately returns the master cylinder pistons to the normal position. The pistons contain check valves and the master cylinder has compensating ports drilled in it. These are uncovered as the pistons reach their normal position. The piston check valves allow fluid to flow toward the wheel cylinders or calipers as the pistons withdraw. Then, as the rubber boot/seal or return springs force the brake pads or shoes into the released position, the excess fluid returns to the reservoir through the compensating ports.

The dual master cylinder has two pistons, located one behind the other. The primary piston is actuated directly by mechanical linkage from the brake pedal. The secondary piston is actuated by fluid trapped between the two pistons. If a leak develops in front of the secondary piston, it moves forward until it bottoms against the front of the master cylinder. The fluid trapped between the pistons will operate one side of the split system. If the other side of the system develops a leak, the primary piston will move forward until direct contact with the secondary piston takes place and it will force the secondary piston to actuate the other side of the split system. In either case the brake pedal drops closer to the floor board and less braking power is available.

The brake system uses a switch to warn the driver when only half of the brake system is operational. This switch is usually located in a valve body which is mounted on the firewall or the frame below the master cylinder. A hydraulic piston receives pressure from both circuits, each circuit's pressure being applied to one end of the piston. When the pressures are in balance, the piston remains stationary. When one circuit has a leak, however, the greater pressure in that circuit during brake application will push the piston to one side, closing the switch and activating the brake warning light.

In disc brake systems, this valve body contains a metering valve and, in some cases, a proportioning valve or valves. The metering valve keeps pressure from traveling to the disc brakes on the front wheels until the brake shoes on the rear wheels have contacted the drums, ensuring that the front brakes will never be used alone. The proportioning valve controls the pressure to the rear brakes to avoid rear wheel lock-up during very hard braking.

Warning lights may be tested by depressing the brake pedal and holding it

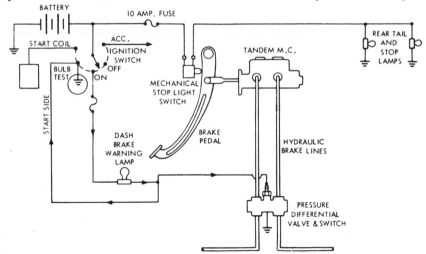

Typical dual brake system

while opening one of the wheel cylinder bleeder screws. If this does not cause the light to turn On, substitute a new lamp, make continuity checks, and, finally, replace the switch as necessary.

The hydraulic system may be checked for leaks by applying pressure to the pedal gradually and steadily. If the pedal sinks very slowly to the floor, the system has a leak. This is not to be confused with a springy or spongy feel due to the compression of air within the lines. If the system leaks, there will be a gradual change in the position of the pedal when a constant pressure is applied.

Check for leaks along all lines and at wheel cylinders or calipers. If no external leaks are apparent, the problem is inside the master cylinder.

DISC BRAKES

Disc brake systems utilize a disc (rotor) with brake pads positioned on either side of it. Braking effect is achieved in a manner similar to the way you would squeeze a spinning phonograph record between your fingers. The disc (rotor) is a casting which may be equipped with cooling fins between the two braking surfaces. The fins (if equipped) enable air to circulate between the braking surfaces making them less sensitive to heat buildup and more resistant to fade. Dirt and water do not affect braking action since contaminants are thrown off by the centrifugal action of the rotor or scraped off by the pads. Also, the equal clamping action of the two brake pads tends to ensure uniform, straightline stops. Disc brakes are inherently self-adjusting.

DRUM BRAKES (REAR)

Drum brakes employ two brake shoes mounted on a stationary backing plate. These shoes are positioned inside a circular drum which rotates with the wheel assembly. The shoes are held in place by springs, this allows them to slide toward the drums (when they are applied) while keeping the linings and drums in alignment. The shoes are actuated by a wheel cylinder which is mounted at the top of the backing plate. When the brakes are applied, hydraulic pressure forces the wheel cylinder's actuating links outward. Since these links bear directly against the top of the brake shoes, the tops of the shoes are then forced against the inner side of the drum. This action forces the bottoms of the two shoes to contact the brake drum by rotating the entire assembly slightly (known as servo action). When pres-

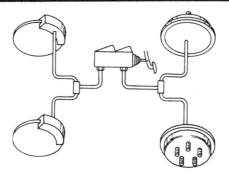

Typical front/rear split hydraulic brake system

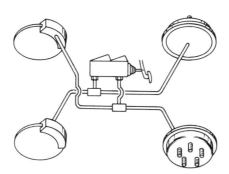

Typical diagonally split hydraulic brake system

sure within the wheel cylinder is relaxed, return springs pull the shoes back away from the drum.

Rear drum brakes are (in most cases) designed to self-adjust themselves during application. Motion causes both shoes to rotate very slightly with the drum, rocking an adjusting lever, thereby causing rotation of the adjusting screw or lever.

POWER BRAKE SYSTEM

Power brakes operate just as standard brake systems except in the actuation of the master cylinder pistons. A vacuum diaphragm is located on the front of the master cylinder and assists the driver in applying the brakes, reducing both the effort and travel he must put into moving the brake pedal.

The vacuum diaphragm housing is connected to the intake manifold by a vacuum hose. A check valve is placed at the point where the hose enters the diaphragm housing, so that during periods of low manifold vacuum brake assist vacuum will not be lost.

Depressing the brake pedal closes off the vacuum source and allows atmospheric pressure to enter on one side of the diaphragm. This causes the master cylinder pistons to move and apply the brakes. When the brake pedal is released, vacuum is applied to both sides of the diaphragm, and the

return springs return the diaphragm and the master cylinder pistons to the released position. If the vacuum fails, the brake pedal rod will butt against the end of the master cylinder actuating rod and direct mechanical application will occur as the pedal is depressed.

HYDRAULIC CYLINDERS AND VALVES

Master Cylinders

——————— CAUTION ———————

The master cylinder unit is a highly calibrated unit specifically designed for the vehicle it is on. Although cylinders may look alike there are many differences in calibration. If replacement is necessary, make sure the replacement unit is the one specified for the vehicle.

NOTE: Some 1981-87 vehicles are equipped with "Quick Take-Up" master cylinders which provide a large volume of fluid to the brakes at low pressure when the brake pedal is initially applied. This large volume of fluid is needed because self retracting piston seals are used on the caliper pistons. The piston seals pull the pistons into the calipers after the brakes are released, thereby preventing the brake pads from causing a drag on the rotors.

The "Quick Take-Up" master cylinder has a hydraulically operated brake warning light switch incorporated in the master cylinder body. The piston is accessible by removing the large plug at the front of the master cylinder body. Only remove the plug when overhauling the cylinder, as brake fluid will escape.

Overhaul procedures on these master cylinders are basically the same as those on conventional master cylinders.

SERVICING MASTER CYLINDERS

NOTE: Plastic reservoirs need to be removed only for the following reasons: Reservoir is damaged or the rubber grommet(s) between the reservoir and bore is leaking. Service "Quick Take-up" valve on GM quick take-up master cylinders. The reservoir should be removed by first clamping the cylinder flange in a vice. GM reservoirs must be removed by prying between the reservoir and casting with a pry bar. Grommets can be reused if they are in good condi-

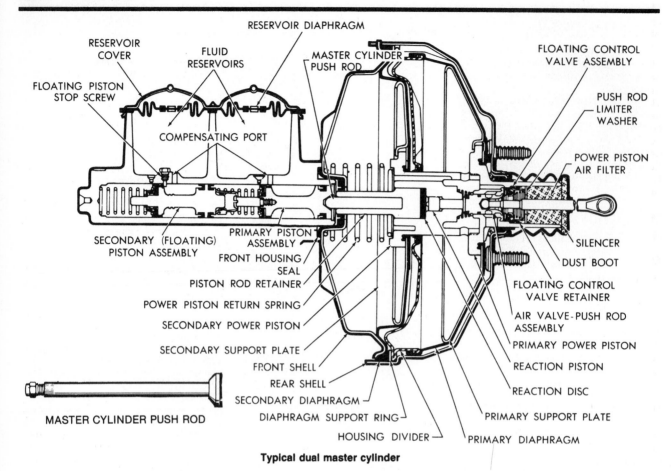

RESERVOIR DIAPHRAGM

RESERVOIR COVER

FLUID RESERVOIRS

MASTER CYLINDER PUSH ROD

FLOATING CONTROL VALVE ASSEMBLY

FLOATING PISTON STOP SCREW

PUSH ROD LIMITER WASHER

COMPENSATING PORT

POWER PISTON AIR FILTER

SECONDARY (FLOATING) PISTON ASSEMBLY

PRIMARY PISTON ASSEMBLY

SILENCER

FRONT HOUSING SEAL

DUST BOOT

PISTON ROD RETAINER

FLOATING CONTROL VALVE RETAINER

POWER PISTON RETURN SPRING

AIR VALVE-PUSH ROD ASSEMBLY

SECONDARY POWER PISTON

PRIMARY POWER PISTON

SECONDARY SUPPORT PLATE

REACTION PISTON

FRONT SHELL

REACTION DISC

REAR SHELL

SECONDARY DIAPHRAGM

DIAPHRAGM SUPPORT RING

PRIMARY SUPPORT PLATE

HOUSING DIVIDER

PRIMARY DIAPHRAGM

MASTER CYLINDER PUSH ROD

Typical dual master cylinder

tion. **Whether or not the reservoir is removed, it and the cover or caps should be thoroughly cleaned.**

1. Remove the cylinder from the vehicle and drain the brake fluid.

2. Mount the cylinder in a vise so that the outlets are up and remove the rubber boot seal from the hub.

3. Remove the stop pin or screw from the bottom of the front reservoir, if present.

4. Remove the snapring from the front of the bore and the primary piston assembly.

5. Remove the secondary piston assembly using compressed air or a piece of wire.

6. Clean the metal parts in brake fluid and discard the rubber parts.

7. Inspect the bore for damage or wear, then check the pistons for damage and proper clearance in the bore.

——— **CAUTION** ———

Aluminum cylinder bores cannot be honed. The cylinder must be replaced if the bore is pitted or scored.

8. If the bore is only slightly scored or pitted it may be honed. (See CAUTION). Always use hones that are in good condition and completely clean the cylinder with brake fluid when the

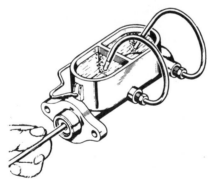

Pre-bleeding master cylinder

honing is completed. If any sign of wear or corrosion is apparent on "Quick Take-Up" master cylinder bores, the master cylinder must be replaced; it cannot be honed. If any evidence of contamination exists in the master cylinder the entire hydraulic system should be flushed and refilled with clean brake fluid. Blow out the passages with compressed air.

NOTE: Most rebuilding kits provide a primary and secondary piston assembly. If the kit you are using only provides seals, see Steps 9–13.

9. Install new secondary seals in the two grooves in the flat end of the front

piston. The lips of the seals will be facing away from each other.

10. Install a new primary seal and the seal protector on opposite end of the front piston with the lips of the seal facing outward.

11. Coat the seals with brake fluid. Install the spring on the front piston with the spring retainer in the primary seal.

12. Insert the piston assembly, spring end first, into the bore and use a wooden rod to seat it.

13. Coat the rear piston seals with brake fluid and install them into the piston grooves with the lips facing the spring end.

14. Assemble the spring onto the piston and install the assembly into the bore spring first. Install the snapring.

15. Hold the piston at the bottom of the bore and install the stop screw.

16. On GM models with the hydraulic brake warning light switch ("Quick Take-Up" units), remove the Allen head plug and the switch assembly with needle nose pliers. Remove the O-rings and retainers from the piston. Install new O-rings and retainers, fit the piston back into the master cylinder after lubricating with brake fluid.

NOTE: If any corrosion is present in the switch piston bore

the master cylinder must be replaced: do not attempt to hone the bore.

17. Fit a new O-ring on the Allen head plug, then install the plug and tighten.

18. On all master cylinders, install a new seal in the hub (if equipped), then either bench bleed or bleed the cylinder on the vehicle. Some master cylinders have bleed screws on the outlet flanges and may be bled without disturbing the wheel cylinders or calipers.

MASTER CYLINDER PUSH ROD ADJUSTMENT

Models Equipped with Adjustable Push Rod

After assembly of the master cylinder to the power section, the piston cup in the hydraulic cylinder should just clear the compensating port hole when the brake pedal is full released. If the push rod is too long, it will hold the piston over the port. A push rod that is too short, will give too much loose travel (excessive pedal play). Apply the brakes and release the pedal all the way observing the brake fluid flow back into the master cylinder. A full flow indicates the piston is coming back far enough to release the fluid. A slow return of the fluid indicates the piston is not coming back far enough to clear the ports. The push rod adjustment is too tight and should be shortened.

Disc Brake Calipers

NOTE: Caliper disc brakes can be divided into three types: the four-piston, fixed-caliper type; the single-piston, floating-caliper type and the single-piston sliding-caliper type. Refer to the Brake Specifications Chart for applications.

In the four piston type (two in each side of the caliper), the braking effect is achieved by hydraulically pushing both shoes against the disc sides.

With the single piston floating-caliper type the inboard shoe is pushed hydraulically into contact with the disc, while the reaction force thus generated is used to pull the outboard shoe into frictional contact (made possible by letting the caliper move slightly along the axle centerline).

In the sliding caliper (single piston) type, the caliper assembly slides along the machined surfaces of the anchor plate. A steel key located between the machined surfaces of the caliper and the machines surfaces of the anchor

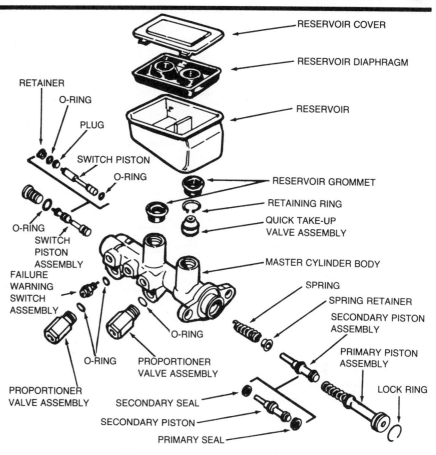

GM "Quick Take Up" master cylinder

plate is held in place with either a retaining screw or two cotter pins. The caliper is held in place against the anchor plate with one or two support springs.

SERVICING THE CALIPER ASSEMBLY

NOTE: The following is a general caliper service procedure. Before proceeding, check under the individual disc brake section for your vehicle (Delco Moraine, Girlock, etc.) for any special servicing procedures.

1. Raise and support the front of the vehicle on jackstands, then remove the front wheels.

2. Working on one side at a time only, disconnect the hydraulic inlet line from the caliper and plug the end. Remove the caliper mounting bolts or pins and the shims (if used), then slide the caliper off the disc.

3. Remove the disc pads from the caliper or mounting adapter. If the old ones are to be reused, make them so that they can be reinstalled in their original positions.

4. Open the caliper bleed screw and drain the fluid. Clean the outside of the caliper and mount it in a vise with padded jaws.

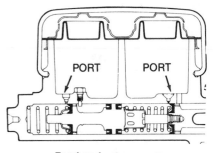

Feed and return ports

——— CAUTION ———

When cleaning any brake components, use only brake fluid or denatured (Isopropyl) alcohol. Never use a mineral-based solvent, such as gasoline or paint thinner, since it will swell and quickly deteriorate the rubber parts.

5. Remove the bridge bolts (fixed type), separate the caliper halves and remove the two O-ring seals from the transfer holes.

6. Pry the lip on (each) piston dust boot from its groove, then remove the piston assemblies and spring(s) from the bore(s). If necessary, air pressure may be used to force the pistons(s) out of the bore(s), using care to prevent the piston from popping out of control.

7. Remove the boot(s) and seal(s)

9 BRANES

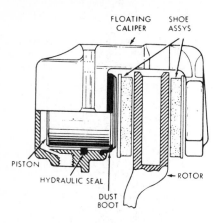

Floating caliper disc brake

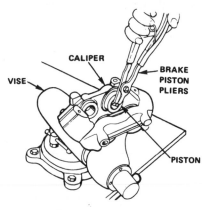

Removing piston pneumatically

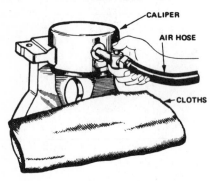

Removing pistons

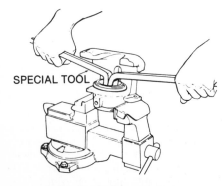

Removing hollow end piston

from the piston(s), then clean the piston(s) in brake fluid. Blow out the caliper passages with an air hose.

8. Inspect the cylinder bore(s) for scoring, pitting or corrosion. Corrosion is a pitted or rough condition not to be confused with staining. Light rough spots may be removed by rotating crocus cloth, using finger pressure, in the bores. DO NOT polish with an in and out motion or use any other abrasive.

9. If the piston(s) are pitted, scored or worn, they must be replaced. A corroded or deeply scored caliper should also be replaced.

10. Check the clearance of the piston(s) in the bores using a feeler gauge. Clearance should be 0.002–0.006 in. If there is excessive clearance the caliper must be replaced.

11. Replace all rubber parts and lubricate with brake fluid. Install the seals (or square cut rings) and boots in the grooves in each piston. The seal should be installed in the groove closest to the closed end of the piston with the seal lips facing the closed end. The lip on the boot should be facing the seal.

12. Lubricate the piston and bore with brake fluid. Position the piston return spring (if equipped), large coil first, in the piston bore.

13. Install the piston in the bore, taking great care to avoid damaging the seal lip as it passes the edge of the cylinder bore.

14. Compress the lip on the dust boot into the groove in the caliper. Be sure the boot is full seated in the groove, as poor sealing will allow contaminants to ruin the bore.

15. On fixed calipers: Position the O-rings in the cavities around the caliper transfer holes, and fit the caliper halves together. Install the bridge bolts (lubricated with brake fluid) and be sure to torque to specification.

16. Install the disc pads in the caliper or adapter and remount the caliper on the hub (see "Disc Pad Replacement"). Connect the brake line to the caliper and bleed the brakes (see "Brake Bleeding"). Replace the wheels. Recheck the brake fluid level, check the brake pedal travel and road test the vehicle.

OVERHAUL TIPS

Field reports indicate that two factors determine whether to replace or rebuild calipers: Can the piston or pistons be removed? Will the bleed screw break off when removal is attempted? (Rebuilders will not accept a caliper with a broken bleed screw.) Since there is no way to predict how a bleed

screw will react, follow this procedure to attempt removal.

1. Insert a drill shank into the bleed screw hole (snug fit).
2. Tap the screw on all sides.
3. Using a six-point wrench, apply pressure gently while working the drill up and down slightly.
4. If the drill starts to bind, the screw is beginning to collapse and cannot be removed intact.
5. Heating the caliper is another successful, but time consuming, bleed screw removal technique. Remove the caliper from the vehicle. Heat the caliper. Shrink the bleed screw by applying dry ice and attempt to remove.

DISC BRAKE BLEEDER SCREW REPLACEMENT

1. Using the existing hole in bleed screw for a pilot, drill a $\frac{1}{4}$ in. hole completely through existing bleeder.
2. Increase the hole size to $\frac{7}{16}$ in.
3. Tap the hole using a $\frac{1}{4}$ in. (18-national pipe thread) $\frac{1}{2}$ in. deep (full thread).
4. Install the bleeder repair kit.
5. Test for leaks and full brake pedal pressure.

FROZEN PISTONS

Sliding or Floating Caliper

1. Hydraulic removal:
  a. Remove the caliper assembly from the rotor.
  b. Remove brake pads and dust seal.
  c. With the brake flexible line connected and bleed screw closed apply enough pedal pressure to move the piston most of the way out of the bore (brake fluid will begin to ooze past the piston inner seal).
2. Pneumatic removal:
  a. Remove the caliper from the vehicle.
  b. With the bleed screw closed, apply air pressure to force the piston out.

NOTE: Hydraulic and pneumatic methods of piston removal should be done carefully to prevent personal injury or piston damage.

Fixed Caliper

NOTE: The hydraulic or pneumatic methods which apply to the single piston type caliper will not work on the multiple piston type brake caliper.

1. Remove the caliper from the vehicle with the two halves separated.
2. Mount in a vise and use a piston

puller (many types available) to remove the pistons.

CALIPER CLEANING

NOTE: Castings may be cleaned with any type cleaning fluid after all the rubber seals have been removed.

It is important that all traces of cleaning fluid be completely removed from the caliper casting. Rubber components are compatible with alcohol and/or brake fluid. Use a lint free wiping cloth to clean the caliper and parts. Black stains on the pistons or walls, caused by the seals, will not do harm; however, extreme cleanliness is essential. Blow out the passages with compressed air. A fine grade of crocus cloth may be used to correct minor imperfections in the cylinder bore. Slide crocus cloth with finger pressure in a circular rather than a lengthwise motion. DO NOT use any form of abrasive on a plated piston. Discard a piston which is pitted or has signs of plating wear.

REBUILDING CALIPERS

NOTE: If a fine stone honing of a caliper bore is necessary it should be done with skill and caution. Some vehicles can develop 800 psi hydraulic pressure on severe application so the honing must never exceed 0.003 in. Also the dust seal groove must be free of rust or nicks so that a perfect mating surface is possible on the piston and casting.

Installing Stroking Type Seals and Boots

Stretch the boot and seal over the piston and seat them. The seal lip on the Bendix and Delco styles, faces toward hydraulic pressure; boot lips face toward the brake shoe. Locate the return spring (if used) in the cylinder and carefully start the piston into the cylinder to avoid nicking the seal. Alignment tools are available for inserting the lip cup seals. Fully depress the piston into the bore in order to fasten the boot lip to the caliper housing. On the Delco types, use a wooden drift or a special seating tool to seat the boot ring in the caliper counterbore. It must be flush or below the caliper machined surface.

Installing Fixed Position (Rectangular Ring) Seals and Boots

Insert a rectangular ring seal into bore and at any location, push the ring into

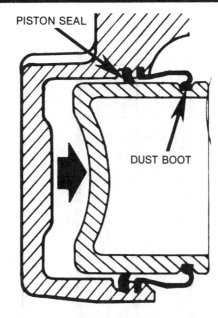

Brake applied

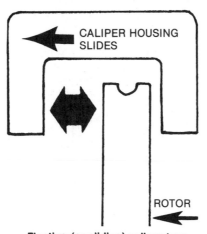

Floating (or sliding) caliper type

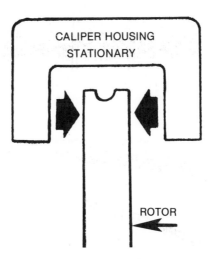

Fixed caliper type

the seal groove. From this area, with a finger, gently work around the bore until the ring is seated in this channel. Be sure the ring does not twist or roll in the groove. When the boot lip is retained inside the cylinder bore, insert the boot in the same manner. Then work the inside of the boot over the pressure end of the piston, stretching the boot with a small plastic tool and pressing the piston through the seal, straight in, until it bottoms. The inside of the boot should slide on the piston and come to rest in the boot groove. If the boot lip is retained outside of the cylinder bore, first stretch boot over the piston and seat it in its groove, then press the piston through the seal. Fully depress the piston to 50–100 lbs. in order to fasten the boot lip in place. On the Delco-Moraine types, use a wooden drift or a special seating tool to seat the metal boot ring in the caliper counterbore below the face of the caliper.

Installing Fixed-Caliper Bridge Bolts

If the caliper contains internal fluid crossover passages, be sure to install new O-ring seals at the joints. Mate the caliper halves and install high tensile strength bridge bolts. Never replace the bridge bolts with ordinary standard hardware bolts.

Wheel Cylinders

Wheel cylinders contain a pair of opposed pistons fitted with rubber cups, compression spring and sometimes expander washers to keep the cups tight against the pistons.

SERVICING

1. Raise and support the vehicle on jackstands. Remove the wheel and drum assemblies from the side to be serviced.
2. Remove the brake shoes, then clean the backing plate and the wheel cylinder. Rebuilding can be done on the vehicle, depending on the design of the brake backing plate. If the backing plate is recessed to the point that it is impossible to get a hone into the cylinder, the cylinder has to be removed.
3. To remove the cylinder; disconnect the brake line from the rear of the cylinder, remove the mounting bolts or retainers and the cylinders.

NOTE: On some models, the wheel cylinder is contained by a retaining ring. In order to remove the rear wheel cylinders, remove the wheel cylinder retainer. Insert two pin punches or equivalent tools into the access slots and

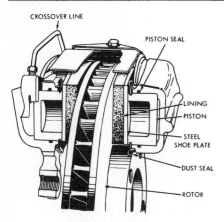

Fixed caliper disc brake

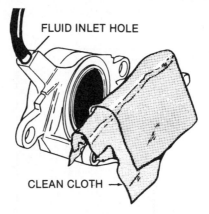

Removing piston hydraulically

Bleed screw

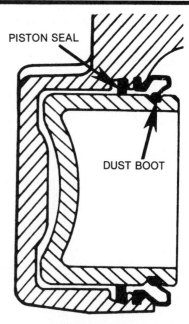

Brake released

Replacing disc brake bleeder screw

bend both tabs at the same time thereby releasing the cylinder. Use a new retainer when reinstalling the wheel cylinder. The new retainer can be driven on using a $1\frac{1}{8}$ in. socket with an extension bar.

4. Remove the rubber boots (dust covers) from the ends of the cylinder. Remove the pistons, the piston cups (expanders, if equipped) and the spring from the inside of the cylinder. Remove the bleeder screw and make sure it is not clogged.

5. Discard all of the parts that the rebuilding kit will replace.

6. Examine the inside of the cylinder. If it is severely rusted, pitted or scratched install a new or rebuilt cylinder.

7. If the condition of the cylinder indicates that it can be rebuilt, hone the bore. Light honing will provide a new surface on the inside of the cylinder which promotes better cup sealing.

8. Wash out the cylinder with brake fluid after honing. Reassemble the cylinder using the new parts provided in the kit. When assembling the cylinder dip all parts in brake fluid.

9. Install the cylinder on the vehicle. Reinstall the brakes, drum/wheel and bleed the brake system.

Hydraulic Control Valves

PRESSURE DIFFERENTIAL VALVE

The pressure differential valve activates a dash panel warning light if pressure loss in the brake system occurs. If pressure loss occurs in $\frac{1}{2}$ of the split system the other system's normal pressure causes the piston in the switch to compress a spring until it touches an electrical contact. This turns the warning lamp on the dash panel to light, thus warning the driver of possible brake failure.

On some vehicles, the spring balance piston automatically resets as the brake pedal is released warning the driver only upon brake application. On other vehicles, the light remains on until manually cancelled.

Valves may be located separately, as part of a combination valve, or incorporated into the master cylinder.

Resetting Valves

On some vehicles, the valve piston(s) remain off center after failure until necessary repairs are made. The valve will automatically reset itself (after repairs) when pressure is equal on both sides of the system.

If the light does not go out, bleed the brake system that is opposite the failed system. If front brakes failed,

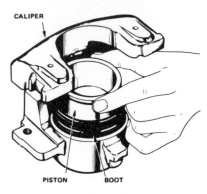

Installing piston

bleed the rear brakes, this should force the light control piston toward center.

If this fails, remove the terminal switch. If brake fluid is present in the electrical area, the seals are gone, replace the complete valve assembly.

METERING VALVE

The metering valve's function is to improve braking balance between the front disc and rear drum brakes, especially during light brake application.

The metering valve prevents the application of the front disc brakes until the rear brakes overcome the return spring pressure. Thus, when the front disc pads contact the rotor, the rear shoes will contact the brake drum at the same time.

Inspect the metering valve each time the brakes are serviced. A slight amount of moisture inside the boot does not indicate a defective valve, however, fluid leakage indicates a damaged or worn valve. If fluid leakage is present the valve must be replaced.

The metering valve can be checked very simply. With the vehicle stopped, gently apply the brakes. At about an inch of travel a very small change in pedal effort (like a small bump) will be felt if the valve is operating properly. Metering valves are not serviceable and must be replaced (if defective).

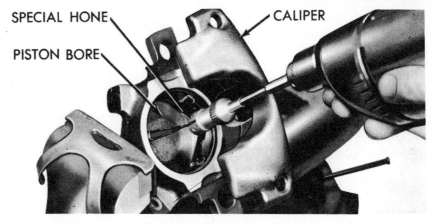

Honing cylinder bore

PROPORTIONING VALVE

The proportioning (pressure control) valve is used, on some vehicles, to reduce the hydraulic pressure to the rear wheels to prevent skidding during heavy brake application and to provide better brake balance. It is usually mounted in line to the rear wheels.

When the brakes are serviced the valve should be inspected for leakage. Premature rear brake application during lighting braking can mean a bad proportioning valve. Repair is by replacement of the valve. Make sure the valve port marked "R" is connected toward the rear wheels.

On "Quick Take-Up" master cylinders, the proportioning valve(s) is (are) screwed into the master cylinder. Since these vehicles have a diagonally split brake system, two valves are required. One rear brake line screws into each valve. The early type valves (front wheel drive) were steel and silver colored, an occasional "clunking" noise was encountered on some early models, but does not affect brake efficiency. Replacement valves are now made of aluminum. Never mix an aluminum valve with a steel valve, always use two aluminum valves.

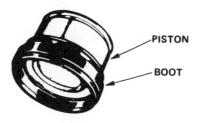

Assembling boot on piston

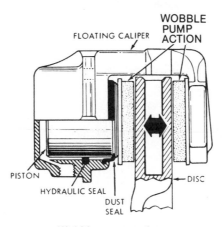

Wobble pump action

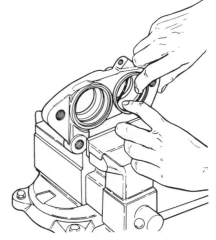

Installing fixed position rectangular ring seal (seal lip toward pressure side)

COMBINATION VALVE

The combination valve may perform two or three functions. They are: metering, proportioning and brake failure warning.

Variations of the two-way combination valve are: proportioning and brake failure warning or metering and brake failure warning.

A three-way combination valve directs the brake fluid to the appropriate wheel, performs necessary valving and contains a brake failure warning.

The combination valve is usually mounted under the hood close to the master cylinder, where the brake lines can easily be connected and routed to the front or rear wheels.

The combination valve is non-serviceable and must be replaced if malfunctioning.

Brake Bleeding

The hydraulic brake system must be free of air to operate properly. Air can enter the system when hydraulic parts are disconnected for servicing or replacement, or when the fluid level in the master cylinder reservoirs is very low. Air in the system will give the brake pedal a spongy feeling upon application.

The quickest and easiest of the two

ways for system bleeding is the pressure method but special equipment is needed to externally pressurize the hydraulic system. The other, more commonly used method of brake bleeding is done manually.

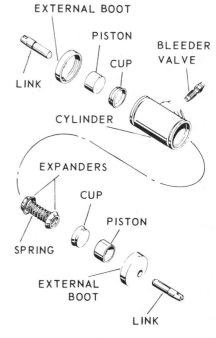

Wheel cylinder components

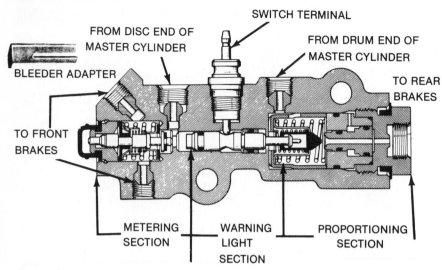

Push valve in when pressure bleeding-not necessary when using pedal bleed method

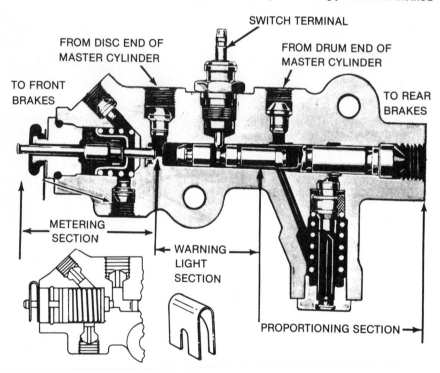

Hold valve out .060 in pressure bleed only-not necessary when using pedal bleed method

BLEEDING SEQUENCE

Bleeding may be required at only one or two wheels or at the master cylinder, depending upon what point the system was opened to air. If after bleeding the cylinder caliper that was rebuilt or replaced and the pedal still has a spongy feeling upon application, it will be necessary to bleed the entire system. Bleed the system in the following order:

1. Master cylinder: If the cylinder is not equipped with bleeder screws, open the brake line(s) to the wheels slightly while pressure is applied to the brake pedal. Be sure to tighten the line before the brake pedal is released. The procedure for bench bleeding the master cylinder is in the following section.

2. Power Brake Booster: If the unit is equipped with bleeder screws, it should be bled after the master cylinder. The vehicle's engine should be off and the brake pedal applied several times to exhaust any vacuum in the booster. If the unit is equipped with two bleeder screws, always bleed the higher one first.

3. Combination Valve: If equipped with a bleeder screw.

4. Front/Back Split Systems: Start with the wheel farthest away from the master cylinder, usually the right-rear wheel. Bleed the other rear wheel then the right-front and left-front.

NOTE: If you are unsuccessful in bleeding the front wheels, it me be necessary to deactivate the metering valve. This is accomplished by either pushing in, or pulling out a button or stem on the valve. The valve may be held by hand, with a special tool or taped, it should remain deactivated while the front brakes are bled.

5. Diagonally Split System: Start with the right-rear then the left-front. The left-rear then the right-front (refer to the following "Quick Take-Up Master Cylinder" section).

6. Rear Disc Brakes: If the vehicle is equipped with rear disc brakes and the calipers have two bleeder screws, bleed the inner first then the outer.

——— CAUTION ———

DO NOT allow brake fluid to spill on the vehicles finish, it will remove the paint. Flush the area with water.

MANUAL BLEEDING

1. Clean the bleed screw at each wheel.

2. Start with the wheel farthest from the master cylinder (right-rear).

3. Attach a small rubber hose to the bleed screw and place the end in a clear container of brake fluid.

4. Fill the master cylinder with brake fluid. (Check often during bleeding). Have an assistant slowly pump up the brake pedal and hold pressure.

5. Open the bleed screw about one-quarter turn, press the brake pedal to the floor, close the bleed screw and slowly release the pedal. Continue until no more air bubbles are forced from the cylinder on application of the brake pedal.

6. Repeat procedure on remaining wheel cylinders and calipers, still working from cylinder/caliper farthest from the master cylinder.

NOTE: Master cylinders equipped with bleed screws may be bled independently. When bleeding the Bendix-type dual master cylinder it is necessary to solidly cap one reservoir section while bleeding the other to prevent pressure loss through the cap vent hole.

——— CAUTION ———

The bleeder valve at the wheel cylinder must be closed at the end of each stroke, and be-

fore the brake pedal is released, to insure that no air can enter the system. It is also important that the brake pedal be returned to the full up position so the piston in the master cylinder moves back enough to clear the bypass outlets.

PRESSURE BLEEDING DISC BRAKES

Pressure bleeding disc brakes will close the metering valve and the front brakes will not bleed. For this reason it is necessary to manually hold the metering valve open during pressure bleeding. Never use a block or clamp to hold the valve open and never force the valve stem beyond its normal position. Two different types of valves are used. The most common type requires the valve stem to be held in while bleeding the brakes, while the second type requires the valve stem to be held out (0.060 in. minimum travel). Determine the type of visual inspection.

——————— CAUTION ———————

Special adapters are required when pressure bleeding cylinders with plastic reservoirs. Pressure bleeding equipment should be diaphragm type; placing a diaphragm between the pressurized air supply and the brake fluid. This prevents moisture and other contaminants from entering the hydraulic system.

NOTE: Front disc/rear drum equipped vehicles use a metering valve which closes off pressure to the front brakes under certain conditions. These systems contain manual release actuators, which must be engaged to pressure bleed the front brakes.

1. Connect the tank hydraulic hose and adapter to the master cylinder.
2. Close the hydraulic valve on the bleeder equipment.
3. Apply air pressure to the bleeder equipment following the equipment manufacturer's recommendations for correct air pressure.
4. Open the valve to bleed air out of the pressure hose to the master cylinder. Never bleed this system using the secondary piston stopscrew on the bottom of many master cylinders.
5. Open the hydraulic valve and bleed each wheel cylinder or caliper. Bleed the rear brake system first when bleeding both front and rear systems.

FLUSHING HYDRAULIC BRAKE SYSTEMS

Hydraulic brake systems must be totally flushed if the fluid becomes contaminated with water, dirt or other corrosive chemicals. To flush, simply bleed the entire system until all of the fluid has been replaced with the correct type of new fluid.

BENCH BLEEDING MASTER CYLINDER

Bench bleeding the master cylinder before installing it on the vehicle reduces the possibility of getting air into the lines.

1. Connect two short pieces of brake line to the outlet fittings, bend them until the free end is below the fluid level in the master cylinder reservoirs.
2. Fill the reservoirs with fresh brake fluid. Pump the piston until no more air bubbles appear in the reservoir(s).
3. Disconnect the two short lines, refill the master cylinder and securely install the cylinder cap(s).
4. Install the master cylinder on the vehicle. Attach the lines but do not completely tighten them. Force any air that might have been trapped in the connection by slowly depressing the brake pedal. Tighten the lines before releasing the brake pedal.

QUICK TAKE-UP SYSTEM BLEEDING

Bleed the master cylinder as follows: disconnect the left-front brake line from the master cylinder. Fill the cylinder with fluid until it flows from the opened port. Connect the line and tighten the fitting. Apply the brake pedal slowly one time and keep it applied. Loosen the same brake line fitting to allow any air to escape. Retighten the fitting and release the brake pedal slowly. Wait 15 seconds and repeat the procedure until all of the air is expelled. Bleed the right-front connection in the same manner. Bleed the cylinders and calipers after you are sure all the air is out of the master cylinder.

——————— CAUTION ———————

Rapid pumping will move the secondary piston down the bore and make it difficult to bleed the system. Always apply slow pedal pressure.

Power Brakes

Vacuum Operated Booster

Power brakes operate just as standard brake systems except in the actuation of the master cylinder pistons. A vacuum diaphragm is located on the front of the master cylinder and assist the drive in applying the brakes, reducing both the effort and travel he must put into moving the brake pedal.

The vacuum diaphragm housing is connected to the intake manifold by a vacuum hose. A check valve is placed at the point where the hose enters the diaphragm housing, so that during periods of low manifold vacuum brake assist vacuum will not be lost. Depressing the brake pedal closes off the vacuum source and allows atmospheric pressure to enter on one side of the diaphragm. This causes the master cylinder pistons to move and apply the brakes. When the brake pedal is released, vacuum is applied to both sides of the diaphragm, the return springs return the diaphragm and master cylinder pistons to the released position. If the vacuum fails, the brake pedal rod will butt against the end of the master cylinder actuating rod and direct mechanical application will occur as the pedal is depressed.

The hydraulic and mechanical problems that apply to conventional brake systems also apply to power brakes should be checked if the tests and chart below do not reveal the problem. Tests for a system vacuum leak as described below:

1. Operate the engine at idle with the transmission in Neutral without touching the brake pedal for at least one minute.
2. Turn Off the engine and wait one minute.
3. Test for the presence of assist vacuum by depressing the brake pedal and releasing it several times. Light application will produce less and less pedal travel, if vacuum was present. If there is no vacuum, air is leaking into the system somewhere.
4. Test the system operation as follows:
   a. Pump the brake pedal (with engine off) until the supply vacuum is entirely gone.
   b. Put light, steady pressure on the pedal. Start the engine and operate it at idle with the transmission in Neutral.
   c. If the system is operating, the brake pedal should fall toward the floor when constant pressure is maintained on the pedal.

NOTE: Power brake systems may be tested for hydraulic leaks just as ordinary systems are tested, except that the engine should be idling with the transmission in Neutral throughout the test.

POWER BRAKE BOOSTER TROUBLESHOOTING

NOTE: The following items are in addition to those listed in the "General Troubleshooting" section. Check those items first.

Hard Pedal

1. Faulty vacuum check valve.
2. Vacuum hose kinked, collapsed, plugged leaky or improperly connected.
3. Internal leak in unit.
4. Damaged vacuum cylinder.
5. Damaged valve plunger.
6. Broken or faulty springs.
7. Broken plunger stem.

Grabbing Brakes

1. Damaged vacuum cylinder.
2. Faulty vacuum check valve.
3. Vacuum hose leaky or improperly connected.
4. Broken plunger stem.

Pedal Goes to Floor

Generally, when this problem occurs, it is not caused by the power brake booster. In rare cases, a broken plunger stem may be at fault.

Overhaul

Most power brake boosters are serviced by replacement only. In many cases, repair parts are not available. A good many special tools are required for rebuilding these units. For these reasons, it would be most practical to replace a failed booster with a new or remanufactured unit.

Hydro-Boost, Hydro-Boost II

Hydro-Boost differs from conventional power brake systems, in that it operates from the power steering pump fluid pressure rather than intake manifold vacuum.

The Hydro-Boost unit contains a spool valve with an open center which controls the strength of pump pressure when braking occurs. A lever assembly controls the valve's position. A boost piston provides the force necessary to operate the conventional master cylinder on the front of the booster.

A reserve of at least two assisted brake applications is supplied by an accumulator which is spring loaded on earlier and pneumatic on later models. The accumulator is an integral part of the Hydro-Boost II unit. The brakes can be applied manually if the reserve system is depleted.

All system checks, tests and troubleshooting procedure are the same for the two systems.

HYDRO-BOOST SYSTEM CHECKS

1. A defective Hydro-Boost cannot cause any of the following conditions:

Noisy brakes, fading pedal or pulling brakes. If any of these occur, check elsewhere in the brake system.

2. Check the fluid level in the master cylinder. It should be within $\frac{1}{4}$ in. of the top; if not, add only DOT-3 or DOT-4 brake fluid until the correct level is reached.

3. Check the fluid level in the power steering pump. The engines should be at normal running temperature and stopped. The level should register on the pump dipstick. Add power steering fluid to bring the reservoir level up to the correct level. Low fluid level will result in both poor steering and stopping ability.

——————— CAUTION ———————

The brake hydraulic system uses brake fluid only, while the power steering and Hydro-Boost systems use power steering fluid only. Don't mix the two.

4. Check the power steering pump belt tension and inspect all of the power steering/Hydro-Boost hoses for kinks or leaks.
5. Check and adjust the engine idle speed, as necessary.
6. Check the power steering pump fluid for bubbles. If air bubbles are present in the fluid, bleed the system. Fill the power steering pump reservoir to specifications with the engine at normal operating temperature. With the engine running, rotate the steering wheel through its normal travel 3–4 times, without holding the wheel against the stops. Check the fluid level again.
7. If the problem still exists, go on to the Hydro-Boost test sections and troubleshooting chart.

HYDRO-BOOST TESTS

Functional Test

1. Check the brake system for leaks or low fluid level. Correct as necessary.
2. Place the transmission in Neutral and stop the engine. Apply the brakes 4–5 times to empty the accumulator.
3. Keep the pedal depressed with moderate (25–40 lbs.) pressure and start the engine.
4. The brake pedal should fall slightly and then push back up against your foot. If no movement is felt, the Hydro-Boost system is not working.

Accumulator Leak Test

1. Run the engine at normal idle. Turn the steering wheel against one of the stops; hold it there for no longer than 5 seconds. Center the steering wheel and stop the engine.

2. Keep applying the brakes until a "hard" pedal is obtained. There should be a minimum of 2 power (1 on Hydro-Boost II) assisted brake applications when pedal pressure of 20–25 lbs. is applied.
3. Start the engine and allow it to idle. Rotate the steering wheel against the stop. Listen for a light "hissing" sound; this is the accumulator being charged. Center the steering wheel and stop the engine.
4. Wait one hour and apply the brakes without starting the engine. As in Step 2, there should be at least 2 (1 on Hydro-Boost II) stops with power assist. If not, the accumulator is defective and must be replaced.

Hydro-Boost System Bleeding

NOTE: The system should be bled whenever the booster is removed and installed.

1. Fill the power steering pump until the fluid level is at the base of the pump reservoir neck. Disconnect the battery lead from the distributor.

NOTE: On diesel engines remove the electrical lead to the fuel solenoid terminal on the injection pump before cranking the engine.

2. Raise the front of the vehicle, turn the wheels all the way to the left and crank the engine for a few seconds.

3. Check the steering pump fluid level. If necessary, add fluid to the "Add" mark on the dipstick.
4. Lower the vehicle, connect the battery lead and start the engine. Check the fluid level and add fluid to the "Add" mark if necessary. With the engine running, turn the wheels from side-to-side to bleed air from the system. Make sure that the fluid level stays above the internal pump casting.

5. The Hydro-Boost system should now be fully bled. If the fluid is foaming after bleeding, stop the engine, let the system set for one hour, then repeat the 2nd part of Step 4.

6. The preceding procedures should be effective in removing excess air from the system, however, sometimes air may still remain trapped. When this happens the booster may make a "gulping" noise when the brake is applied. Lightly pumping the brake pedal with the engine running should cause this noise to disappear. After the noise stops, check the pump fluid level and add as necessary.

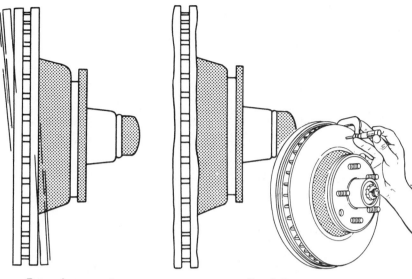

Excessive runout　　　　**Parallelism**

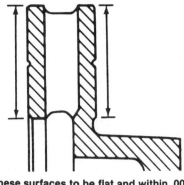

These surfaces to be flat and within .002 in.

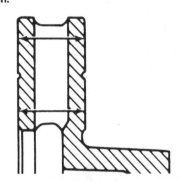

Taper variation not to exceed .003 in.

HYDRO-BOOST TROUBLESHOOTING

High Pedal and Steering Effort (Idle)

1. Loose/broken power steering pump belt
2. Low power steering fluid level
3. Leaking hoses or fittings
4. Low idle speed
5. Hose restriction
6. Defective power steering pump

High Pedal Effort (Idle)

1. Binding pedal/linkage
2. Fluid contamination
3. Defective Hydro-Boost unit

Poor Pedal Return

1. Binding pedal linkage
2. Restricted booster return line
3. Internal return system restriction

Pedal Chatter/Pulsation

1. Power steering/pump drivebelt slipping
2. Low power steering fluid level
3. Defective power steering pump
4. Defective Hydro-Boost unit

Brakes Oversensitive

1. Binding pedal/linkage
2. Defective Hydro-Boost unit

Noise

1. Low power steering fluid level
2. Air in the power steering fluid
3. Loose power steering pump drivebelt
4. Hose restrictions

OVERHAUL

Hydro-Boost units may be overhauled by qualified mechanics.

———— **CAUTION** ————
DO NOT attempt to interchange the parts between the Hydro-Boost units of different makes of vehicles, because of pressure differentials and differences of the tolerances of the internal parts. Pressure could exceed the normal accumulator release pressure of 1400 psi and injury or damage could result.

Disc Brake Rotors

RUNOUT

Manufacturers differ widely on permissible runout but too much can sometimes be felt as a pulsation at the brake pedal. A wobble pump effect is created when a rotor is not perfectly smooth and the pad hits the high spots forcing fluid back into the master cylinder. This alternating pressure causes a pulsating feeling which can be felt at the pedal when the brakes are applied.

To check the actual runout of the rotor, perform the following procedures:

1. Tighten the wheel spindle nut to a snug bearing adjustment, end-play removed.

2. Fasten a dial indicator on the suspension at a convenient place so

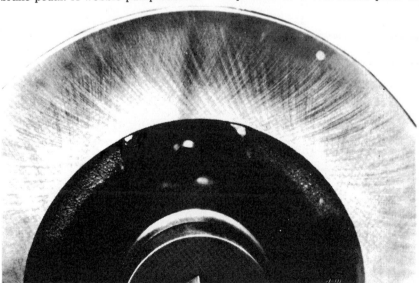

Ideal rotor surface condition

and a 16 oz. brass hammer, position the ball-peen hammer on the outboard pad tabs, then strike the ball-peen hammer with the brass hammer to bend the pad tabs at 45° to the caliper; this clinches the outboard pad to the caliper. Bleed the brake system, if necessary.

DRUM BRAKES

DRUM BRAKE SPECIFICATIONS

(Note: State and local inspection regulation will take precedence over manufacturer's minimum lining and drum specifications.)

Manufacturer	Vehicle Year, Make and Model	Brake Shoe Minimum Lining Thickness	Brake Drum Diameter		Wheel Lugs or Nuts Torque (ft. lbs.)
			Standard Size	Machine To	
	'82–'87 Celebrity, Cavalier	①	7.880	7.899	100
	'82–'87 Camaro w/rear drum brakes	①	9.500	9.560	80†
	w/rear disc brakes	—	—	—	80†
	'86–'87 Sprint	.110	7.090	29–50	
	'86–'87 Spectrum	.039	7.090	65	
	'85–'87 Nova	.039	7.913	76	
	'82–'87 Malibu, '82–'83 Monte Carlo	①	9.500	9.560	80†
	'80–'85 Ciitation	①	7.880	7.899	103
	'80–'87 Impala, '80–'85 Caprice w/9 1/2" rear brakes	①	9.500	9.560	80
	w/11" rear brakes	①	11.000	11.060	100
	'80–'87 Chevette	①	7.874	7.899	70
	'80–'87 Corvette front	—	—	—	70④
	rear	—	—	—	70④
	'80–'81 Malibu, Camaro, Monte Carlo	①	9.500	9.560	80④
	'80 Monza	①	9.500	9.560	80④

① .030" over rivet head, if bonded lining use .062"
④ Aluminum whls; Corvette 80, Camaro 105, others 90.

Brake Drums

BRAKE DRUM TYPES

The FULL-CAST drum has a cast iron web (back) of 3/16–1/4 in. thickness (passenger vehicle sizes) whereas the COMPOSITE drum has a steel web approximately 1/8 in. thick. These two types of drums, with few exceptions are not interchangeable.

BRAKE DRUM DEPTH

Rest a straight edge across the drum diameter on the open side. The actual drum depth then is the measurement at a right angle from the straight edge to that part of the web which mates against the hub mounting flange.

ALUMINUM DRUMS

When replaced by other types, aluminum drums must be replaced in pairs.

METALLIC BRAKES

Drums designed for use with standard brake linings should not be used with metallic brakes.

REMOVING TIGHT DRUMS

Difficulty removing a brake drum can be caused by shoes which are expanded beyond the drum's inner diameter or shoes which have cut into and ridged the drum. In either case back off the adjuster to obtain sufficient clearance for removal.

BRAKE DRUM INSPECTION

The condition of the brake drum surface is just as important as the surface to the brake lining. All drum surfaces should be clean, smooth, free from hard spots, heat checks, score marks and foreign matter imbedded in the drum surface. They should not be out of round, bell-mouthed or barrel shaped. It is recommended that all drums be first checked with a drum micrometer to see if they are within oversize limits. If the drum is within safe limits, even though the surface appears smooth, it should be turned not only to assure a true drum surface but also to remove any possible contamination in the surface from previous brake linings, road dusts, etc. Too much metal removed from a drum is unsafe and may result in:

1. Brake fade due to the thin drum being unable to absorb the heat generated.

Hard or Chill Spots

LOOK HERE FOR TURNED DRUM TOOL MARK RIDGE

0.60"

Oversize drum

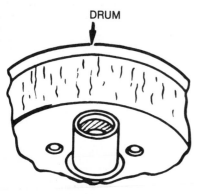

DRUM

Heat checks

Sanding brake drums

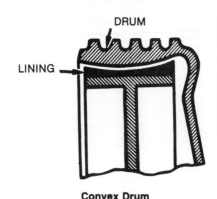

DRUM

LINING

Scored drum surface

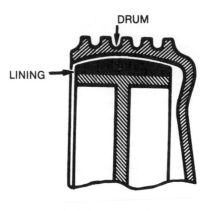

DRUM

LINING

Convex Drum

DRUM

LINING

Concave Drum

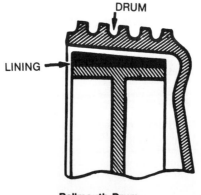

DRUM

LINING

Bellmouth Drum

2. Poor and erratic brake due to distortion of drums.

3. Noise due to possible vibration caused by thin drums.

4. A cracked or broken drum on a severe or very hard brake application.

NOTE: Brake drum run-out should not exceed 0.005 in. Drums turned to more than 0.060 in. oversize are unsafe and should be replaced with new drums, except for some heavy ribbed drums which have an 0.080 in. limit. It is recommended that the diameters of the left and right drums on any one axle be within 0.010 in. of each other. In order to avoid erratic brake action when replacing drums, it is always good to replace the drums on both wheels at the same time. If the drums are true, smooth up any slight scores by polishing with fine emery cloth. If deep scores or grooves are present, which cannot be removed by this method, then the drum must be turned.

Duo-Servo Brake

Refer to the Drum Brake Application Chart for adjuster applications. In the Duo-Servo design, the force which the wheel cylinder applies to the shoes is supplemented by the tendency of the shoes to wrap or twist into the drum during braking. Thus two braking forces are applied at each drum every time the brakes are activated.

ADJUSTMENT

The duo-servo brake, with star and screw type self-adjusters, is used on most late model American vehicles. The same basic brake unit has been used on all vehicles. General Motors vehicles use a rod-operated lever to turn the star-wheel. This is the only difference, other than size, among units used on different models. The drum brakes, used on today's vehicles, are usually self-adjusting. They require manual adjustment only when the shoes have been replaced or when the star and screw adjuster has been disturbed.

NOTE: The drum brakes on most vehicles can be initially adjusted by removing the brake drum, measuring its internal diameter, then adjusting the shoes to that measurement and installing the drum. Use a vernier gauge to make the measurements. This method can be used on all models and may be preferable to punching out the covering over the ac-

cess hole in the backing plate or brake drum edge.

1. Remove the access slot plug from the backing plate or front of drum. On some vehicles no access slot in the backing plate or in the front of the drums is provided. Some have been filled in and must be punched out to gain access to the adjuster. Complete the adjustment and cover the hole with a plug to prevent entrance of dirt and water.

2. Using a brake adjusting spoon or screwdriver, pry downward on the end of the tool (starwheel teeth moving up) to tighten the brakes or upward on the end of the tool (starwheel teeth moving down) to loosen the brakes.

NOTE: It will be necessary to use a small rod or suitable tool to hold the adjusting lever away from the starwheel. Be careful not to bend the adjusting lever.

3. When the brakes are tight almost to the point of being locked, back off the starwheel until the wheel is able to rotate freely. The starwheel on each set of brakes (front or rear) must be backed off the same number of turns to prevent brake pull from side-to-side.

4. After adjustment, check brake pedal travel and then make several stops, while backing the vehicle up, to equalize both wheel systems.

TESTING ADJUSTER

1. Raise and support the vehicle on jackstands. Have a helper handy to apply the brakes.

2. On models with access plugs in the backing plate, loosen the brakes by holding the adjuster lever away from the starwheel and backing off the starwheel approximately 30 notches. On models without access plugs in the backing plate, remove wheel and drum, loosen the adjuster, then reinstall the drum and wheel.

3. Spin the wheel and brake drum

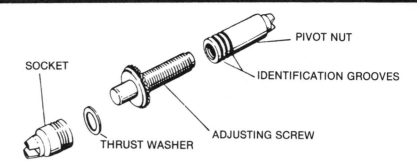

Adjusting screw assembly

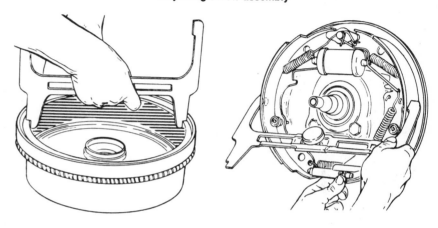

Brake drum guage

in reverse and apply the brakes. The movement of the secondary shoe should pull the adjuster lever up and when the brakes are released the lever should snap down and turn the starwheel.

4. If the automatic adjuster doesn't work, the drum must be removed and the adjuster components inspected carefully for breakage, wear or improper installation.

BRAKE SHOE REMOVAL

NOTE: If you are not thoroughly familiar with the procedures involved in brake replacement, disassemble and assemble one side at a time, leaving the other wheel intact, as a reference.

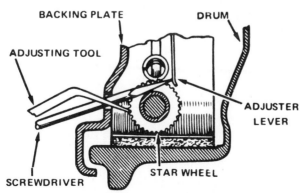

All cars except "H" body (Chevette)

1. Remove the brake drum.

2. Place the hollow end of a brake spring service tool on the brake shoe anchor pin and twist it to disengage one of the brake shoe return springs. Repeat this operation to remove the other return spring.

--- **CAUTION** ---

Be careful that the springs do not slip off the tool during removal, as the spring could break loose and cause personal injury.

3. Reach behind the brake backing plate and place a finger on the end of one of the brake hold-down mounting pins. Using a pair of pliers or special brake pin retainer tool, grasp the washer on the top of the hold-down spring that corresponds to the pin that you are holding. Push down on the pliers and turn them 90° to align the slot in the washer with the head on the spring mounting pin. Remove the spring and washer, then repeat this operation on the hold-down spring of the other brake shoe.

5. Remove the automatic adjuster link. Remove the automatic adjuster lever, the pivot and the override spring from the secondary spring as an assembly. Move the top of each brake shoe outward to clear the wheel cylinder pins and the parking brake link. Lift the brakes from the backing plate and remove the adjusting screw.

6. Grasp the end of the brake cable

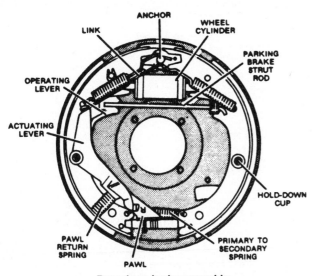

Rear drum brake assembly

spring with a pair of pliers and, using the brake lever as a fulcrum, pull the end of the spring away from the lever. Disengage the cable from the brake lever.

BRAKE SHOE INSTALLATION

1. The brake cable must be connected to the secondary brake shoe before the shoe is installed on the backing plate. To do this, transfer the parking brake lever from the old secondary shoe to the new one. This is accomplished by spreading the bottom of the horseshoe clip and disengaging the lever. Position the lever on the new secondary shoe, then install the spring washer and the horseshoe clip. Close the bottom of the clip after installing it. Grasp the metal tip of the parking brake cable with a pair of pliers. Position a pair of side cutters on the end of the cable coil spring and using the pliers as a fulcrum, pull the coil spring back with the side cutters. Position the cable in the parking brake lever.

2. Apply a light coating of high temperature grease to the brake shoe contact points on the backing plate. Position the primary brake shoe on the front of the backing plate, then install the hold-down spring and washer over the mounting pin. Install the secondary shoe on the rear of the backing plate.

3. If working on rear brakes, install the parking brake link between the primary brake shoe and the secondary brake shoe.

4. Step 4 varies according to the manufacturer.

5. Assemble the automatic adjuster lever, the pivot and the override spring, then install to the secondary springs as an assembly.

——— CAUTION ———

Be careful to make sure that the spring does not slip off the tool during installation, as the spring could break loose and cause personal injury.

6. Install the automatic adjuster cable guide in the secondary brake shoe, making sure that the flared hole in the

cable guide is inside the hole in the brake shoe. Fit the cable into the groove in the top of the cable guide.

7. Install the secondary shoe return return spring through the hole in the cable guide and the brake shoe. Using the brake spring tool, slide the top of the spring onto the anchor pin.

8. Clean the threads on the adjusting screw and apply a light coating of high-temperature grease to the threads. Screw the adjuster closed, then open it ½ turn.

9. Install the adjusting screw between the brake shoes with the star wheel nearest to the secondary shoe. Make sure that the star wheel is in a position that is accessible from the adjusting slot in the backing plate.

10. Install the short, hooked end of the automatic adjuster spring in the proper hole in the primary brake shoe.

11. Connect the hooked end of the automatic adjuster cable and the free end of the automatic adjuster spring in the slot in the top of the automatic adjuster lever.

12. Pull the automatic adjuster lever (the lever will pull the cable and spring with it) downward and to the left, and engage the pivot hook of the lever in the hole in the secondary brake shoe.

13. Check the entire brake assembly to make sure everything is installed properly. Make sure that the shoes engage the wheel cylinder properly and are flush on the anchor pin. Make sure that the automatic adjuster cable is flush on the anchor pin and in the slot on the block of cable guide. Make sure that the adjusting lever rests on the adjusting screw star wheel. Pull upward on the adjusting cable until the adjusting lever is free of the star wheel, then release the cable. The adjusting lever should snap back into place on the adjusting screw star wheel and turn the wheel one tooth.

14. Expand the brake adjusting screw until the brake drum will just fit over the brake shoes. Install the wheel and drum and adjust the brakes.

BRAKE COMPONENT SERVICE

CORVETTE

--------- **CAUTION** ---------

When servicing wheel brake parts, do not create dust by grinding or sanding brake linings or by cleaning wheel brake parts with a dry brush or with compressed air (a water dampened cloth should be used). Many wheel brake parts contain asbestos fibers which can become airborne if dust is created during servicing. Breathing dust containing asbestos fibers may cause serious bodily harm.

Brake adjustments, lining replacement, bleeding procedure, master and wheel cylinder and caliper overhaul can be found in the previous section. A dual hydraulic brake system is employed. The front and rear brakes are each separate systems with a common tandem master cylinder. In the event of a failure in either of the systems, the other will remain operable.

NOTE: Caliper bore corrosion is a relatively common problem with Corvettes. If the corrosion is too severe to be removed with a hone, it may be best to replace the calipers with stainless steel-sleeved units available from the aftermarket. If new original calipers are used, the corrosion problem will return over a period of time.

Parking Brake

ADJUSTMENT

1980-82

1. Raise the vehicle and support it with jack stands. Remove the rear wheels. Loosen the brake cables at the equalizer nuts, until the parking brake levers move freely to the Off position with slack in the cables.
2. Rotate the disc until the adjusting screw can be seen through the hole in the disc.
3. Insert an appropriate tool in this hole and adjust with an up-and-down motion.
4. Tighten the adjuster until the disc cannot move, then back off 6–8 notches.
5. Install the rear wheels.
6. Apply the parking brake to the 13th notch.
7. Tighten the check nuts until an 80 lb. pull is obtained while pulling into the 14th notch.
8. Torque the check nuts to 70 inch lbs.

9. Release the parking brake and check for a no drag condition.

1984-87

1. Raise the vehicle and remove the rear wheels, place two wheel lug nuts opposite of each other to insure correct disc/drum position.
2. Back the caliper piston into its bore.
3. Loosen the park brake cable so that there is no tension on the park brake shoes.
4. Rotate the disc so that the hole in the disc/drum face will align with the star adjuster.
5. To make the adjustment, insert a brake adjusting spoon through the hole in the disc face. For the driver's side, move the handle of the tool towards the ceiling to adjust the shoes out and towards the floor to adjust the shoes in. For the passenger side, move the handle of the tool towards the floor to adjust the shoes out and towards the ceiling to adjust them in.
6. Adjust one side at a time until there is no rotation of the disc/drum, then back the star adjuster off 5–7 notches. Then go to the opposite side and do the same procedure.
7. Apply the park brake lever two notches.
8. Adjust the cable at the equalizer so that the wheel has a drag.
9. Release the park brake lever and check the wheel for free rotation.
10. Correct adjustment will result in no drag on the wheel.

Power Brake Unit

REMOVAL & INSTALLATION

1. Remove the vacuum hose from the brake booster.
2. Disconnect the hydraulic brake lines from the master cylinder.

NOTE: Do not spill brake fluid on painted surfaces.

3. Remove the master cylinder from the brake booster.
4. Disconnect the push rod at the brake pedal.
5. Remove the nuts and lockwashers that secure the unit to the firewall.
6. Installation is the reverse of removal. Torque the mounting bolts to 24 ft. lbs. Remember to bleed the brake system.

Master Cylinder

REMOVAL & INSTALLATION

1. Disconnect the brake lines at the master cylinder.
2. Remove the two mounting nuts and lift off the cylinder.
3. Installation is the reverse of removal. Torque the nuts to 24 ft. lbs. and bleed the system.

--------- **CAUTION** ---------

The use of silicone brake fluid such as Delco Supreme No. 24 can damage the seals and rubber components in the brake system. Use brake fluid that meets or exceeds DOT 3 specifications, such as Delco Supreme No. 11 or equivalent.

REMOVAL & INSTALLATION

1980-82

1. Disconnect and plug the hydraulic lines at the combination valve.
2. Disconnect the warning switch wiring harness from the valve switch terminal.
3. Remove the combination valve.
4. Installation is the reverse of removal. Make sure to bleed the entire brake system and that a firm brake pedal is obtained before moving the vehicle.

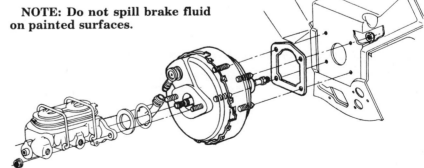

Power brake booster installation

CAPRICE, IMPALA, MALIBU AND MONTE CARLO

Master Cylinder

NOTE: Vehicles with disc brakes do not have a check valve in the front outlet port of the master cylinder. If one is installed, the front discs will quickly wear out due to residual hydraulic pressure holding the pads against the rotor.

REMOVAL & INSTALLATION

1. Disconnect the hydraulic lines from master cylinder.
2. Remove the retaining nuts and the lockwashers holding the cylinder to the cowl or the brake booster.

NOTE: If equipped with non-power brakes, disconnect the pushrod at brake pedal.

3. Remove the master cylinder, the gasket and the rubber boot.
4. To install, reverse the removal procedures. Torque the master cylinder mounting nuts to 22 ft. lbs. and the hydraulic lines to 18 ft. lbs. Refill the master cylinder, bleed the brake system and check the brake pedal free-play.

NOTE: On non-powered brakes, position the master cylinder on the cowl, making sure that the pushrod goes through the rubber boot into the piston. Reconnect the pushrod clevis to the brake pedal. If equipped with power brakes, install the master cylinder on the power booster.

Power Brake Booster

REMOVAL & INSTALLATION

1. Disconnect the vacuum hose from the vacuum check valve.
2. Unbolt the master cylinder and carefully move it aside without disconnecting the hydraulic lines.

NOTE: If sufficient booster clearance cannot be obtained, it will be necessary to disconnect the hydraulic lines from the master cylinder, then remove the master cylinder.

3. Disconnect the pushrod at the brake pedal assembly.

NOTE: Some brake boosters may be held on with sealant; this can be easily removed with tar remover.

4. Remove the booster-to-cowl nuts and lockwashers and the booster from engine compartment.
5. To install, reverse the removal procedures. Torque the booster-to-cowl and the master cylinder-to-booster mounting nuts to 28 ft. lbs.

NOTE: Make sure to check the operation of the stop lights. Allow the engine vacuum to build before applying the brakes. Bleed the hydraulic system if the lines were disconnected from the master cylinder.

Hydro-Boost Brake Booster

REMOVAL & INSTALLATION

For an explanation, troubleshooting and bleeding of the Hydro-Boost brake system, please refer to the previous section.

1. Turn the engine off and pump the brake pedal 4 or 5 times to deplete the accumulator.
2. Remove the nuts from the master cylinder, then move the master cylinder away from the booster, with brake lines still attached.
3. Remove the hydraulic lines from the booster.
4. Remove the retainer and washer at the brake pedal.
5. Remove the attaching nuts retaining the booster fastened to the cowl and the booster.
6. To install, reverse the removal procedures. Torque the booster-to-cowl nuts to 15 ft. lbs. and the master cylinder-to-booster nuts to 20 ft. lbs. Bleed the power steering and hydro booster system.

Powermaster Power Brake Assembly

The unit is a complete, integral power brake system. The assembly consists of an Electro-Hydraulic (E-H) pump, a fluid accumulator, a pressure switch, a fluid reservoir and a hydraulic booster with a dual master cylinder.

For further information on the Powermaster system, please refer to the previous section.

REMOVAL & INSTALLATION

— CAUTION —
Before performing any service to the brake

system, depressurize the powermaster assembly.

1. Turn the ignition OFF, then depress the brake pedal 10 times using at least 50 lbs. of force.

NOTE: Before removing the master cylinder form the cowl, remove some of the brake fluid from the reservoir.

2. Remove the electrical connectors from the pressure switch and the E-H pump.
3. Disconnect and plug the brake lines at the master cylinder.
4. Remove the master cylinder-to-cowl mounting nuts.
5. Disconnect the master cylinder push rod from the brake pedal.
6. Remove the powermaster unit from the vehicle.
7. To install, reverse the removal procedures. Torque the master cylinder-to-cowl nuts to 22–30 ft. lbs. Refill the master cylinder and bleed the brake system.

BLEEDING POWERMASTER UNIT

1. Fill the reservoir to the full marks.
2. Remove the brake lines at the outlet ports of the master cylinder and allow the cylinder to bleed until the fluid runs out, the reconnect the brake lines. ONLY tighten the line closest to the cowl.
3. Have an assistant depress the brake pedal slowly (exerting 50 lbs. of pressure) until the full pedal travel is accomplished, then tighten the forward brake line. WAIT for 5 seconds.
4. Reapply the brake pedal and hold it, then open the forward connector $1/2$ turn to release the air and retighten the connector. Repeat the procedure until the air is bled from the master cylinder.
5. Refill the master cylinder.

Combination Valve

REMOVAL & INSTALLATION

NOTE: The combination valve is not repairable and must be replaced if found to be defective. On some models hoisting might be necessary.

1. Disconnect the electrical connector at the pressure differential switch.

It is recommended , that with the aid of pliers, you squeeze the eliptical shaped plastic locking ring and then pull up. This will move the locking tangs away from the switch.

2. Disconnect and plug the hydraulic lines at the combination valve then remove the valve.

3. Installation is the reverse of removal.

4. Bleed the entire brake system.

——————— CAUTION ———————

Do not move the car until a firm brake pedal is obtained.

Wheel Cylinder

REMOVAL & INSTALLATION

Impala and Caprice

1. Raise and safely support the car.
2. Mark the relationship of the wheel to the axle flange.
3. Remove the wheel, drum and brake shoes.

4. Clean all dirt around around the wheel cylinder at the brake line and disconnect the brake line.
5. Remove the wheel cylinder from the backing plate.
6. Installation is the reverse of removal. Torque the rear wheel brake pipe to wheel cylinder to 12 ft. lbs.

7. Bleed the system.

Malibu and Monte Carlo

1. Insert awls or pins, $1/8$ in. diameter or less, into the access slots between the wheel cylinder pilot and retainer locking tabs.

2. Bend both tabs away simultanously until they spring over the abutment shoulder releasing the wheel cylinder. Discard the old retaining clip.

3. For ease of installation hold the wheel cylinder against the backing plate by inserting a block betwen the wheel cylinder and the axle shaft flange.

4. Position the wheel cylinder retainer clip so the tabs will be away from and in a horizontal position with the backing plate when installing.

5. Press the new retaining clip over the wheel cylinder abutment and into position using a $1 1/8$ in. 12 point socket. Make sure the retainer tabs are properly snapped under the abutment shoulder.

6. Install the brake shoes, drum and wheel.

7. Flush and bleed the hydraulic system.

Parking Brake

ADJUSTMENT

The automatic self-adjusting feature incorporated in the rear brake mechanism normally maintains proper parking brake adjustment. For this reason, the rear brake adjustment must be checked before any adjustment of the parking brake cables is made. Check the parking brake mechanism and cables for free movement and lubricate all working surfaces before proceeding.

——————— CAUTION ———————

It is very important that the parking brake cables not be too tight. If the cables are too tight, they create a drag and position the secondary shoes so that the self-adjusters continue to operate to compensate for drag wear. The result is rapidly worn rear brake linings.

1. Raise and support the rear of the vehicle on jackstands.
2. Set the parking brake at 2 clicks.
3. Loosen the equalizer locknut. Tighten the adjusting nut until the left wheel can be turned backward with two hands, but is locked in the forward rotation.
4. Tighten the locknut.
5. Fully release the parking brake and rotate the rear wheels; no drag should be felt in either direction.

CELEBRITY AND CITATION

Master Cylinder

REMOVAL & INSTALLATION

1. Disconnect hydraulic lines at master cylinder.
2. Remove the retaining nuts and lockwashers that hold cylinder to firewall or the brake booster. Disconnect pushrod at brake pedal (non-power brakes only).
3. Remove the master cylinder, gasket and rubber boot.

4. On non-power brakes, position master cylinder on firewall, making sure pushrod goes through the rubber boot into the piston. Reconnect pushrod clevis to brake pedal. With power brakes, install the cylinder on the booster. Torque the attaching nuts to 25 ft. lbs.

5. Install nuts and lockwashers.
6. Install hydraulic lines then check brake pedal free play.
7. Bleed brakes.

NOTE: Cars having disc brakes do not have a check valve in the front outlet port of the master cylinder. If one is installed, front discs will quickly wear out due to residual pressure holding pads against rotor.

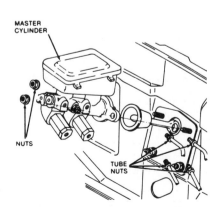

Typical master cylinder installation

Proportioning Valve and Failure Warning Switch

REMOVAL & INSTALLATION

These parts are installed in the master cylinder body. No seperate proportion-

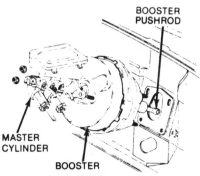

Power booster removal

ing or metering valve is used. Replacement of these parts requires disassembly of the master cylinder.

For master cylinder disassembly and overhaul procedures please refer to the previous section.

Power Brake Booster

REMOVAL & INSTALLATION

1. Disconnect vacuum hose from vacuum check valve.
2. Unbolt the master cylinder and carefully move it aside without disconnecting the hydraulic lines.
3. Disconnect pushrod at brake pedal assembly.
4. Remove nuts and lockwashers that secure booster to firewall and remove booster from engine compartment.
5. Install by reversing removal procedure. Torque the mounting nuts to 25 ft. lbs. Make sure to check operation of stop lights. Allow engine vacuum to build before applying brakes.

Wheel Cylinder

REMOVAL & INSTALLATION

1. Loosen the wheel lug nuts, raise and support the vehicle properly, and remove the wheel. Remove the drum and brake shoes. Leave the hub and wheel bearing assembly in place.
2. Remove any dirt from around the brake line fitting. Disconnect the brake line.
3. Remove the wheel cylinder retainer by using two awls or punches with a tip diameter of $\frac{1}{8}$ in. or less. Insert the awls or punches into the access slots between the wheel cylinder pilot and retainer locking tabs. Bend both tabs away simultaneously. Remove the wheel cylinder from the backing plate.
4. To install, position the wheel cylinder against the backing plate and holt it in place with a wooden block between the wheel cylinder and the hub and bearing assembly.
5. Install a new retainer over the wheel cylinder abutment on the rear of

the backing plate by pressing it into place with a $1\frac{1}{8}$ in. 12 point socket and an extension.
6. Install a new bleeder screw into the wheel cylinder. Install the brake line and tighten to 10–15 ft. lbs.
7. The rest of installation is the reverse of the removal procedure. After installing the brake drum, bleed the system.

Parking Brake

ADJUSTMENT

1. Raise the rear of the car and support it safely with jackstands, with both rear wheels off the ground.
2. Apply parking brake two ratchet clicks (1980-81), or three ratchet clicks (1982-87) from fully released position.
3. Loosen the equalizer locknut, then tighten the adjusting nut until a light to moderate drag is felt when the rear wheels are rotated.
4. Tighten the locknut.
5. Fully release parking brake and rotate rear wheels—no drag should be felt.

CAMARO

Master Cylinder

REMOVAL & INSTALLATION

1. Disconnect the brake tubes from the master cylinder. If NOT equipped with a power brake booster, disconnect the brake pedal from the master cylinder push rod.
2. Remove the nuts securing the master cylinder to the cowl or the power brake booster.
3. Remove the master cylinder from the vehicle.

—————— CAUTION ——————
Be careful not to spill brake fluid on the painted surfaces. It will lift the paint.

4. To install, reverse the removal procedures. Torque the master cylinder mounting nuts to 20–30 ft. lbs. Bleed the brake system.

Power Brake Booster

REMOVAL & INSTALLATION

1. Refer to the "Master Cylinder Removal & Installation" procedures in this section and remove the master cylinder.
2. Disconnect the push rod from the brake pedal. Remove the vacuum hose from the power brake booster.

3. From under the dash, remove the 4 mounting nuts from the power brake booster unit.
4. Remove the power brake booster unit.
5. To install, reverse the removal procedures. Torque the power brake booster-to-cowl and the master cylinder-to-booster mounting nuts to 22–30 ft. lbs.

Combination Valve

REMOVAL & INSTALLATION

NOTE: The combination valve is not repairable and must be replaced if found to be defective. On some models hoisting might be necessary.

1. Disconnect the electrical connector at the pressure differential switch. It is recommended , that with the aid of pliers, you squeeze the eliptical shaped plastic locking ring and then pull up. This will move the locking tangs away from the switch.
2. Disconnect and plug the hydraulic lines at the combination valve then remove the valve.
3. Installation is the reverse of removal.
4. Bleed the entire brake system.

—————— CAUTION ——————
Do not move the car until a firm brake pedal is obtained.

Wheel Cylinder

REMOVAL & INSTALLATION

1980-81

1. Raise and safely support the car.
2. Mark the relationship of the wheel to the axle flange.
3. Remove the wheel, drum and brake shoes.
4. Clean all dirt around around the wheel cylinder at the brake line and disconnect the brake line.
5. Remove the wheel cylinder from the backing plate.
6. Installation is the reverse of removal. Torque the rear wheel brake pipe to wheel cylinder to 12 ft. lbs.
7. Bleed the system.

1982-87

1. Insert awls or pins, $\frac{1}{8}$ in. diameter or less, into the access slots between the wheel cylinder pilot and retainer locking tabs.
2. Bend both tabs away simultanously until they spring over the abutment shoulder releasing the

wheel cylinder. Discard the old retaining clip.

3. For ease of installation hold the wheel cylinder against the backing plate by inserting a block betwen the wheel cylinder and the axle shaft flange.

4. Position the wheel cylinder retainer clip so the tabs will be away from and in a horizontal position with the backing plate when installing.

5. Press the new retaining clip over the wheel cylinder abutment and into position using a $1\frac{1}{8}$ in. 12 point socket. Make sure the retainer tabs are properly snapped under the abutment shoulder.

6. Install the brake shoes, drum and wheel.
7. Flush and bleed the hydraulic system.

Parking Brake

ADJUSTMENT

Rear Drum Brakes

1. Depress the parking brake pedal exactly two ratchet clicks.
2. Raise and support the rear of the vehicle on jackstands.
3. Tighten the brake cable adjusting nut until the left rear wheel can be turned rearward with both hands, but locks when forward rotation is attempted.
4. Release the parking brake pedal; both rear wheels must turn freely in either direction without brake drag.

Rear Disc Brakes

1. Check for free movement of the parking brake cables and lubricate the

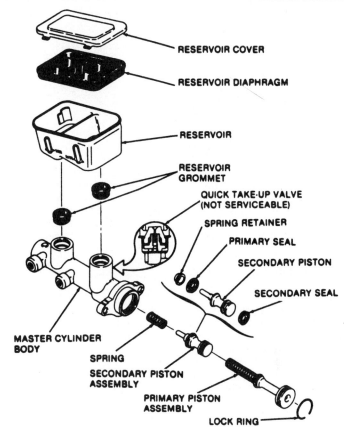

RESERVOIR COVER
RESERVOIR DIAPHRAGM
RESERVOIR
RESERVOIR GROMMET
QUICK TAKE-UP VALVE (NOT SERVICEABLE)
SPRING RETAINER
PRIMARY SEAL
SECONDARY PISTON
SECONDARY SEAL
MASTER CYLINDER BODY
SPRING
SECONDARY PISTON ASSEMBLY
PRIMARY PISTON ASSEMBLY
LOCK RING

Exploded view of the master cylinder

underbody rub points of the cables. Also lubricate the equalizer hooks.
2. Release the parking brake pedal completely.
3. Raise and support the rear of the vehicle on jackstands.
4. Hold the brake cable stud from turning, then tighten the adjusting nut until all cable slack is taken up.

NOTE: Make sure that the parking brake levers on the rear

calipers are against the stops on the caliper housing. If the levers are not contacting the stops, loosen the cable adjusting nut until the levers just contact the stops.

5. Operate the parking brake cable several times. Parking brake pedal travel should be $5\frac{1}{4}$–$6\frac{3}{4}$ in. (1980-81) or 14 clicks (1982-87) with approximately 130–150 lbs. of force applied to the pedal.

CAVALIER

Master Cylinder

REMOVAL & INSTALLATION

1. Unplug the electrical connector from the master cylinder.
2. Place a number of cloths or a container under the master cylinder to catch the brake fluid. Disconnect the brake tubes from the master cylinder; use a flare nut wrench if one is available. Tape over open ends of the tubes.

NOTE: Brake fluid eats paint. Wipe up any spilled fluid immedi-

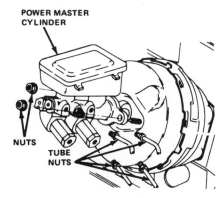

POWER MASTER CYLINDER
NUTS
TUBE NUTS

Master cylinder mounting on cars with power brakes

ately, then flush the area with clear water.

3. Remove the two nuts attaching the master cylinder to the booster or firewall.

4. Remove the master cylinder.

5. To install, attach the master cylinder to the booster with the nuts. Torque to 22–30 ft. lbs.

6. Remove the tape from the lines and connect to the master cylinder. Torque to 10–15 ft. lbs. Connect the electrical lead.

7. Bleed the brakes.

Proportioning Valve

REMOVAL & INSTALLATION

There is a front and a rear proportioning valve located at the lower left side of the master cylinder. To remove the proportioning valves, disconnect the brake lines from the valves, then disconnect the valves from the master cylinder and remove the O-rings. Replace the old O-rings and proportioning valves with new ones and reinstall into the master cylinder. Torque the proportioning valves to 18–30 ft. lbs.

Vacuum Booster

REMOVAL & INSTALLATION

1. Remove the master cylinder from the booster. It is not necessary to disconnect the lines from the master cylinder. Just move the cylinder aside.
2. Disconnect the vacuum booster pushrod from the brake pedal inside the car. It is retained by a bolt. A spring washer is under the bolt head, and a flat washer goes on the other side of the pushrod eye, next to the pedal arm.
3. Remove the four attaching nuts from inside the car. Remove the booster.
4. Install the booster on the firewall. Tighten the mounting nuts to 22–33 ft. lbs.
5. Connect the pushrod to the brake pedal.
6. Install the master cylinder. Mounting torque is 22–33 ft. lbs.

Wheel Cylinder

REMOVAL & INSTALLATION

1. Raise the rear of the vehicle and support it safely.
2. Remove the rear wheel and brake drum assembly.
3. Disconnect the inlet tube nut and line from the wheel cylinder.

4. Remove the wheel cylinder retainer using two awls or pins $1/8$ inch diameter or less.
   a. Insert the awls or pins into the access slots between the wheel cylinder pilot and the retainer locking tabs.
   b. Bend both tabs away simultaneously.
5. Remove the wheel cylinder.

To install:

1. Position the wheel cylinder and hold it in place using a wooden block placed between the the wheel cylinder and the axle flange.
2. Install a new wheel cylinder retainer over the wheel cylinder abutment using a $1\,1/8$ inch 12 point socket and extension.
3. Reconnect the inlet tube nut and torque to 12 ft. lbs.
4. Reinstall the brake drum and bleed the brake system.
5. Install the wheels, lower the vehicle and check for leaks.

Parking Brake

ADJUSTMENT

1. Raise and support the car with both rear wheels off the ground.
2. Pull the parking brake lever exactly two ratchet clicks.

NOTE: To prevent damage to the threaded adjusting rod, thoroughly clean and lubricate the threads before turning the adjusting nut.

3. Loosen the equalizer locknut, then tighten the adjusting nut until the left rear wheel can just be turned backward using two hands, but is locked in forward rotation.
4. Tighten the locknut.
5. Release the parking brake. Rotate the rear wheels – there should be no drag.
6. Lower the car.

CABLE REMOVAL & INSTALLATION

Front Cable

1. Place the gear selector in Neutral and apply the parking brake.
2. Remove the center console.
3. Disconnect the parking brake cable from the lever.
4. Remove the cable retaining nut and the bracket securing the front cable to the floor panel.
5. Raise the car and loosen the equalizer nut.
6. Loosen the catalytic converter shield and then remove the parking brake cable from the body.
7. Disconnect the cable from the equalizer and then remove the cable from the guide and the underbody clips.
8. Reverse the procedure and adjust the cable.

Right and Left Rear Cables

1. Raise and support the rear of the car.
2. Back off the equalizer nut until the cable tension is eliminated.
3. Remove the tires, wheels and brake drums.
4. Insert a screwdriver between the brake shoe and the top part of the brake adjuster bracket. Push the bracket to the front and then release the top brake adjuster rod.
5. Remove the rear hold down spring. Remove the actuator lever and the lever return spring.
6. Remove the adjuster screw spring.
7. Remove the top rear brake shoe return spring.
8. Unhook the parking brake cable from the parking brake lever.
9. Depress the conduit fitting retaining tangs and then remove the conduit fitting from the backing plate.
10. Remove the cable end button from the connector.
11. Depress the conduit fitting retaining tangs and remove the conduit fitting from the axle bracket.
12. Reverse the procedure to install and adjust the cable.

CHEVETTE

Combination Valve

REMOVAL & INSTALLATION

NOTE: If the combination valve is found defective it must be replaced.

1. Disconnect the negitive battery cable.
2. Clean all the dirt from the switch and connections.
3. Disconnect he electrical lead from the switch connection.
4. Disconnect the hydraulic lines

from the connections at the switch. It may be necessary to loosen the line connections at the master cylinder to loosen lines. Cover the open ends with a clean, lint-free material.

5. Remove the mounting screw and remove the combination valve.

6. Installation is the reverse of removal. Bleed the brake system.

Wheel Cylinder

REMOVAL

1. Clean the area around the inlet tube line and disconnect the tube line.
2. Remove the wheel cylinder retainer by inserting two awls into the access slots between the wheel cylinder pilot and the retainer locking tabs. Bend both tabs away simutaneously.

INSTALLATION

1. Place the wheel cylinder into position and hold in place using a wooden block between the cylinder and axle flange.
2. Use a $1\frac{1}{8}$ inch, 12 point socket and socket extension to aid in installing a new retainer over the wheel cylinder abutment.
3. Connect the inlet tube and torque the nut to 120–180 inch lbs.

Master Cylinder

REMOVAL & INSTALLATION

1. Disconnect the master cylinder pushrod from the brake pedal.
2. Remove the pushrod boot.
3. Remove the air cleaner.
4. Thoroughly clean all dirt from the master cylinder and the brake lines. Disconnect the brake lines from the master cylinder and plug them to prevent the entry of dirt.
5. Remove the master cylinder securing nuts and remove the master cylinder.
6. Install the master cylinder with its spacer. Tighten the securing nuts.
7. Connect the brake lines to their ports.
8. Place the pushrod boot over the end of the pushrod. Secure the pushrod to the brake pedal with the pin and clip.
9. Fill the master cylinder and bleed the entire hydraulic system. After bleeding, fill the master cylinder to within $\frac{1}{4}$ in. from the top of the reservoir. Check for leaks.
10. Install the air cleaner.
11. Check brake operation before moving the car.

PARKING BRAKE ADJUSTMENT

1. Raise the car on a hoist.
2. Apply the parking brake three notches from the fully released position.
3. Tighten the parking brake cable equalizer adjusting nut under the car until a light drag is felt when the rear wheels are rotated forward.
4. Fully release the parking brake and rotate the rear wheels. There should be no drag.
5. Lower the car.

Power Brake Booster

REMOVAL & INSTALLATION

1. Remove the air cleaner.
2. Disconnect the vacuum hose from the check valve.
3. Remove the master cylinder brace.
4. Remove the master cylinder-to-power cylinder nut, and pull forward on the master cylinder until it clears the power cylinder mounting studs. Move the master cylinder aside and support it, being careful of the brake lines.
5. Remove the nuts securing the power cylinder to the firewall.
6. Remove the pushrod-to-pedal retainer and slip the pushrod off the pedal pin. Remove the power cylinder.
7. Installation is the reverse of removal.

SPECTRUM

Master Cylinder

REMOVAL & INSTALLATION

1. Remove some brake fluid from the master cylinder with a syringe.
2. Disconnect and cap or tape the openings of the brake tube.
3. Disconnect the brake fluid level warning switch connector.
4. Remove the 2 nuts securing the master cylinder to the power brake booster.
5. Remove the master cylinder from the power brake booster.
6. To install, reverse the removal procedure, add fluid to the reservoir and bleed the brake system.

Power Brake Booster

REMOVAL & INSTALLATION

1. Refer to the "Master Cylinder Removal and Installation" procedure in this section and remove the master cylinder.
2. Remove the vacuum hose from

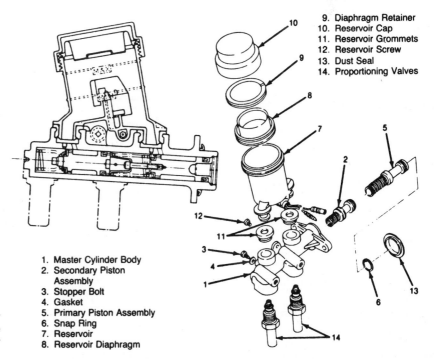

9. Diaphragm Retainer
10. Reservoir Cap
11. Reservoir Grommets
12. Reservoir Screw
13. Dust Seal
14. Proportioning Valves

1. Master Cylinder Body
2. Secondary Piston Assembly
3. Stopper Bolt
4. Gasket
5. Primary Piston Assembly
6. Snap Ring
7. Reservoir
8. Reservoir Diaphragm

Exploded view of the master assembly

the vacuum servo.

3. Remove the clevis pin from the brake pedal.

4. Remove the 4 nuts from the brake assembly under the dash and remove the power booster from the engine compartment.

5. To install, reverse the removal procedure.

Proportioning Valves

Removal & Installation

1. Clean the area around the reservoir and brake pipe connections.

2. Remove the brake fluid from the master cylinder reservoir with a syringe.

3. Disconnect the brake pipes from the proportioning valves. Cap or tape all openings.

4. While holding the master cylinder, Use a box wrench and remove the proportioning valves from the master cylinder.

5. Installation is the reverse of removal. Fill the reservoir and bleed the system.

Wheel Cylinder

Removal & Installation

1. Remove the bnrake shoe and components toi gain access to the wheel cylinder.

2. Clean the area around the brake pipe and disconnect it from the wheel cylinder. Cap or tape all openings.

3. Remove the two bolts and remove the wheel cylinder.

4. Installation is the reverse of removal. Torque the mounting nuts to 7 ft. lbs.

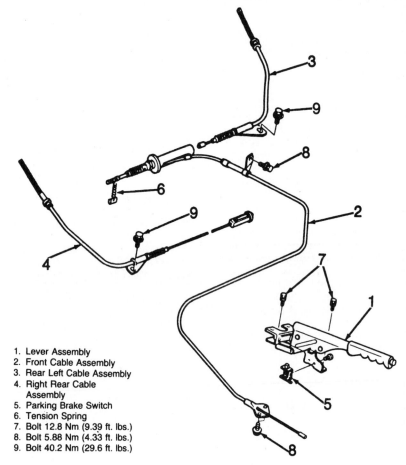

1. Lever Assembly
2. Front Cable Assembly
3. Rear Left Cable Assembly
4. Right Rear Cable Assembly
5. Parking Brake Switch
6. Tension Spring
7. Bolt 12.8 Nm (9.39 ft. lbs.)
8. Bolt 5.88 Nm (4.33 ft. lbs.)
9. Bolt 40.2 Nm (29.6 ft. lbs.)

Exploded view of the parking brake assembly

Parking Brake

ADJUSTMENT

The parking brake adjustment is nor-mal when the lever moves 7–9 notches at 66 lbs. of force. If it is not within limits, adjust the rear brakes. If this adjustment does not affect the specifications, adjust the parking brake turnbuckle.

SPRINT

Master Cylinder

REMOVAL & INSTALLATION

1. Clean around the reservoir cap and take some of the fluid out with a syringe.

2. Disconnect and plug the brake tubes from the master cylinder.

3. Remove the mounting nuts and washers.

4. Remove the master cylinder.

5. To install, reverse the removal procedures. Torque the mounting bolts to 8–12 ft. lbs. Bleed the brake system.

Power Brake Booster

REMOVAL & INSTALLATION

1. Refer to the "Master Cylinder Removal & Installation" procedures in this section and remove the master cylinder.

2. Disconnect the push rod clevis pin from the brake pedal arm.

3. Disconnect the vacuum hose from the brake booster.

4. Remove the mounting nuts from under the dash and the booster.

5. To install, reverse the removal procedures. Torque the booster-to-cowl nuts to 14–20 ft. lbs. Bleed the brake system, if necessary.

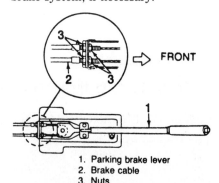

1. Parking brake lever
2. Brake cable
3. Nuts

Adjusting the parking brakes

PARKING BRAKE ADJUSTMENT

1. Remove both door seal plates and the seat belt buckle bolts at the floor.
2. Disconnect the shoulder harness bolts at the floor and the interior, bottom trim panels.
3. Raise the rear seat cushion.
4. Pull up the carpet to gain access to the parking brake lever.
5. Loosen the parking brake cable adjusting nuts.
6. Adjust the parking brake cables, so that they work evenly.
7. Adjust the cable, so that when the parking brake handle is pulled, its travel is between 5–8 notches, with 44 lbs. of force.
8. After adjustment, reverse the removal procedures.

NOVA

Master Cylinder

REMOVAL & INSTALLATION

——————— CAUTION ———————

Be careful not to spill brake fluid on the painted surfaces of the vehicle; it will damage the finish.

1. Disconnect the hydraulic lines from the master cylinder and plug the openings. Drain brake fluid from the reservoir with a syringe.
2. Disconnect the hydraulic fluid pressure differential switch wiring connector.
3. If you're planning to disassemble the master cylinder, loosen the master cylinder reservoir mounting (or set) bolts.
4. Remove the nuts and remove the master cylinder from the power brake booster.
5. Install the master cylinder by first cleaning out the groove on the lower installation surface. Confirm that the "UP" mark on the master cylinder boot is in the correct position (at the top).
6. Adjust the booster pushrod as described below under "Power Brake Booster Removal & Installation."
7. Install the master cylinder to the power brake booster with a new gasket. Torque the attaching nuts to 9 ft. lbs.
8. Connect the brake lines and torque them to 11 ft. lbs. Connect the level warning switch connector.
9. Fill the fluid reservoir and bleed the brake system. Check for fluid leakage and tighten or replace fittings as necessary.

Power Brake Booster

REMOVAL & INSTALLATION

NOTE: To perform this procedure, you will need a booster push rod gauge GM part No. J–34873–A or equivalent to set the booster push rod length.

1. Remove the master cylinder as described above. Disconnect the hydraulic lines at the three-way union and plug all openings. Diusconnect the union from its mount.
3. Pull back the clamp and disconnect the booster vacuum line at the booster.
4. Remove the instrument panel lower finish panel and the air duct. Remove the pedal return spring. Locate the clevis rod where it attaches to the brake pedal underneath the dash. Pull out the clip and then remove the clevis pin.
5. Remove the four attaching nuts and then remove the booster, bracket and gasket.
6. Adjust the booster push rod as follows:
   a. Set the booster push rod gauge in position with the gasket in place. The outer portion of the gauge rests on the gasket that seals the mounting surface and the pin at the center rests against the master cylinder pushrod. The head of the pin, of course, sticks upward. Lower the pin until its tip touches the master cylinder piston lightly. Lock it in place with the nuts on the special tool.
   b. Now, turn the tool over and rest its housing against the power booster so the head of the pin sits near the end of the booster push rod. Check the gap between the head of the tool's pin and the pushrod. It should be zero. If necessary, adjust the pushrod by turning it until the push rod just touches the pin.
7. Install in reverse order, torquing the mounting nuts to 9 ft. lbs. Make sure to bleed the brake system thoroughly and check for leaks in the system.

8. Adjust the pedal as follows:
   a. Check pedal height from the asphalt sheet on the floor. It should be 5.79–6.18 in. If necessary, adjust it by turning the pedal pushrod. You must remove the instrument lower finish panel and air duct to reach the pushrod. Make sure to then adjust the stop lamp switch until it just touches the pedal stop.
   b. Check the pedal freeplay by first removing all vacuum from the system by repeatedly pressing the brake pedal downward with full force. Push in the pedal until resistance is just felt, and then measure the distance from its untouched position to the point where it begins to resist, using an assistant. It must be 0.12–0.24 in. If necessary, adjust the pedal freeplay with the pedal pushrod.
   c. Start the engine and confirm that freeplay still exists. Install the air duct and finish panel.

PARKING BRAKE ADJUSTMENT

1. Release the parking brake all the way and release the button. Then, pull the lever upward slowly as you count the clicks. Count two clicks as one notch.

2. The lever should move upward 4–7 notches before it is snugly applied. If the number of clicks is incorrect, loosen the cable nut cap, located at the rear of the brake lever. Hold the cap in this position with an open-end wrench.

3. Use another open-end wrench to rotate the adjusting nut; turn it counterclockwise if the number of notches is too low and clockwise if the number of notches is too great.

4. Hold the position of the adjusting nut as you tighten the adjusting cap. Check the adjustment and repeat Steps 2 and 3 if necessary. Tighten the adjusting nut securely and ensure that the adjustment is correct.

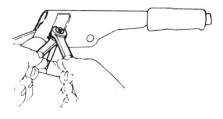

Parking brake adjustment

BERETTA AND CORSICA

Master Cylinder

REMOVAL & INSTALLATION

1. Disconnect the electrical connector from the fluid level sensor.
2. Disconnect and cap the four (4) brake lines on the master cylinder.
3. Remove the master cylinder to power booster mounting nuts.
4. Remove the master cylinder with the reservoir attached.
5. Install the reservoir on the new master cylinder and using the correct procedure, bench bleed the new master cylinder before installation.
6. Install the new master cylinder with the reservoir on the booster and connect the brake lines.
7. Torque the master cylinder mounting nuts to 20 ft. lbs. Torque the brake lines to 13 ft. lbs.
8. Connect the fluid level electrical sensor wires.
9. Fill the reservoir with an approved DOT 3 brake fluid and using the correct procedure, bleed the brake system.

Proportioning Valve

REMOVAL & INSTALLATION

NOTE: It may be necessary to remove the reservoir in order to remove the proportioning valve. If the reservoir is removed, bleed the brake system when finished.

1. Remove the proportioning valve cap on the master cylinder.
2. Remove and save the O-rings.
3. Remove the springs.
4. Remove the proportioning valve pistons.
5. Remove the seals from the valves.
6. Inspect the valves for corrosion or abnormal wear. Replace if necessary.
7. Clean all parts in denatured alcohol and dry them with air before reassembling.
8. Lubricate the O-rings, seals and stem of the valves with silicone grease before installation.
9. Install the new seals on the pistons with the lip facing the cap.
10. Install the pistons and seals in the master cylinder body.
11. Install the springs.
12. Install the new O-rings in the grooves of the valve caps.
13. Install and tighten the caps to 20 ft. lbs.

14. Install the reservoir if removed.
15. If the reservoir was removed, use the correct procedure and bleed the brake system.

Power Brake Booster

REMOVAL & INSTALLATION

1. Remove the master cylinder mounting nuts.
2. Disconnect and plug the brake lines at the master cylinder.
3. Disconnect the fluid level sensor and remove the master cylinder from the booster. Place the master cylinder in an upright position to prevent fluid loss.
4. Remove the left lower trim panel inside the vehicle and disconnect the brake pedal to booster push rod at the brake pedal.
5. Disconnect the vacuum line at the booster.
6. Remove the brake booster mounting nuts and remove the booster.
7. Installation is the reverse of the removal.
8. Torque the master cylinder and booster mounting nuts to 20 ft. lbs. Bleed the brake system when finished.

Wheel Cylinder

REMOVAL & INSTALLATION

1. Raise and safely support the vehicle. Remove the wheel, tire and brake drum. Remove the brake shoes and attaching hardware.
2. Clean any dirt from around the wheel cylinder.
3. Disconnect and plug the brake line at the wheel cylinder.
4. Remove the wheel cylinder mounting bolt and lockwasher.
5. Remove the wheel cylinder.
6. To install, apply a liquid gasket to the shoulder of the wheel cylinder that faces the backing plate.
7. Position the wheel cylinder correctly and install the mounting bolt and lock washer.
8. Torque the bolt to 106 inch lbs.
9. Reconnect the brake line and torque the line to 13 ft. lbs.
10. Install the brake shoes and attaching hardware.
11. Bleed the wheel cylinder. Install the brake drum, wheel and tire. Check the brake operation.

Parking Brake Cable

ADJUSTMENT

1. Apply the parking brake four (4) clicks on the handle.
2. Raise and safely support the vehicle.
3. Locate the access hole in the backing plate and adjust the parking brake cable until a 1/8 in. drill bit can be inserted between the the brake shoe webbing and the parking brake lever.
4. Check to make sure that a 1/4 in. drill bit will NOT fit in the same position.
5. Release the parking brake and check to see if both wheels turn freely by hand.

REMOVAL & INSTALLATION

Front

1. Raise and safely support the vehicle.
2. Loosen, but do not remove, the equalizer nut to remove the cable.
3. Disconnect the cable from the equalizer and right side cable.
4. Remove the hand grip from the parking brake lever inside the vehicle.
5. Remove the console.
6. Disconnect the cable from the parking brake lever.
7. Remove the nut holding the cable to the floor.
8. Remove the exhaust hanger bracket mounting nuts.
9. Remove the catalytic converter shield.
10. Remove the cable.
11. Installation is the reverse of the removal. Adjust the parking brake when finished.

Rear

1. Raise and safely support the vehicle.
2. Loosen the equalizer nut until the cable tension is released.
3. Disconnect the right side cable button from the connector.
4. Disconnect the conduit end of the cable from the bracket on the axle.
5. Remove the wheel, tire and brake drum.
6. Disconnect the cable from the parking brake lever attached to the brake shoes.
7. Remove the conduit end from the brake shoe backing plate.
8. Installation is the reverse of the removal. Adjust the parking brake when finished.

LIGHT TRUCKS AND VANS
BLAZER/JIMMY — FULL SIZE, BLAZER/JIMMY — S-SERIES PICK-UPS — FULL SIZE, PICK-UPS — S-SERIES, SUBURBAN, VANS — FULL SIZE AND ASTRO

ADJUSTMENT

Rear Drum Brakes

These brakes equipped with self-adjusters and no manual adjustment should be necessary, except when brake linings are replaced.

Front Disc Brakes

These brakes are inherently self-adjusting and no adjustment is ever necessary or possible.

Master Cylinder

REMOVAL & INSTALLATION

NOTE: Clean any master cylinder parts in alcohol or brake fluid. Never use mineral based cleaning solvents such as gasoline, kerosene, carbon-tetrachloride, acetone, or paint thinner as these will destroy rubber parts.

1. Using a clean cloth, wipe the master cylinder an its lines to remove excess dirt and then place cloths under the unit to absorb spilled fluid.
2. Remove the hydraulic lines from the master cylinder and plug the outlets to prevent the entrance of foreign material.
3. Disconnect the brake pushrod from the brake pedal on non-powered brakes.
4. Remove the attaching bolts and remove the master cylinder from the firewall or the brake booster.
5. To install: Connect the pushrod to the brake pedal with the pin and retainer.
6. Connect the brake lines and fill the master cylinder reservoirs to the proper levels.
7. Bleed the brake system as outlined in the Unit Repair Section.

Brake Light Switch

ADJUSTMENT

With pedal in fully released position, the stop light switch plunger should be fully depressed against the pedal shank. Adjust switch by moving in or out as necessary.

1. Make certain that the tubular clip is in brake pedal mounting bracket.
2. With brake pedal depressed, insert switch into tubular clip until switch body seats on clip. Audible clicks can be heard as the threaded portion of the switch is pushed through the clip toward the brake pedal.
3. Pull brake pedal fully rearward against pedal stop until audible clicking sounds can no longer be heard. Switch will be moved in tubular clip providing adjustment.
4. Release brake pedal and then repeat Step 3 to assure that no audible clicking sounds remain.

Parking Brakes

ADJUSTMENT

Before attempting parking brake adjustment, make sure that the rear brakes are fully adjusted by making several stops in reverse.

Except S-Series

1. Raise and support the rear axle. Release the parking brake.
2. Apply the pedal four clicks.
3. Adjust the cable equalizer nut under the truck until a moderate drag can be felt when the rear wheels are turned forward.
4. Release the parking brake and check that there is no drag when the wheels are turned forward.

NOTE: If the parking brake cable is replaced, prestretch it by applying the parking brake hard about three times before attempting adjustment.

S-Series

Adjustment of parking brake system is necessary whenever the parking brake cables have been disconnected.
1. Set parking brake pedal at specified number of clicks: 2WD pickups — 8 clicks. 4WD pickups — 10 clicks. All Blazers — 10 clicks
2. Raise and suitably support vehicle.
3. Place a properly calibrated cable tension gauge on the designated rear

cable as close to the equalizer as practical. LH cable on 2WD pickups. RH cable on 4WD pickups. RH cable on all Blazers
4. Drive the adjusting nut until specified tension is indicated on gauge. 200–220 lbs. for 2WD pickups. 140–150 lbs. for 4WD pickups and 140–150 lbs. on Blazers
5. Cables are not to be adjusted too tightly, as this will result in brake drag.
6. Remove support and lower vehicle.

CABLE REPLACEMENT

Except S-Series

FRONT CABLE

1. Raise and safely support the vehicle.
2. Remove adusting nut from equalizer.
3. Remove retainer clip from rear portion of front cable at frame and from lever arm.
4. Disconnect front brake cable from parking brake pedal or lever assemblies. Remove front brake cable. On some models, it may assist installation of new cable if a heavy cord is tied to the other end of cable in order to guide new cable through proper routing.
5. Install cable by reversing removal procedure.
6. Adjust parking brake.

CENTER CABLE

1. Raise and safely support the vehicle.
2. Remove adjusting nut from equalizer.
3. Unbolt connector at each end and disengage hooks and guides.
4. Install new cable by reversing removal procedure.
5. Adjust parking brake.
6. Apply parking brake 3 times with heavy pressure and repeat adjustment.

REAR CABLE

1. Raise and safely support the vehicle.
2. Remove rear wheel and brake drum.

3. Loosen adjusting nut at equalizer.

4. Disengage rear cable at connector.

5. Bend retainer fingers.

6. Disengage cable at brake shoe operating lever.

7. Install new cable by reversing removal procedure.

S–Series

FRONT CABLE

1. Raise and suitably support the vehicle.

2. Loosen adjuster nut and disconnect front cable from connector. Compress retainer fingers and loosen at frame.

3. Remove support and lower vehicle.

4. Remove windshield washer bottle.

5. Disconnect cable from parking brake pedal assembly, compress retainer fingers and remove cable.

6. Install cable by reversing procedure.

7. Adjust parking brake.

CENTER CABLE

1. Raise and suitably support the vehicle.

2. Remove adjuster nut at equalizer and pull cable from equalizer.

3. Disconnect cable at retainers.

4. Install cable by reversing procedure and adjust parking brake.

LEFT/RIGHT REAR

1. Raise and suitably support the vehicle.

2. Mark relationship of tire and wheel assembly to axle flange and remove.

3. Remove brake drum.

4. Loosen equalizer and disconnect cable at center retainer.

5. Compress plastic retainer fingers and remove retainer from frame bracket.

6. Remove rear brake shoe and disconnect cable.

7. Remove rear brake shoe and disconnect cable.

8. Install cable by reversing procedure. Make sure cable is routed properly and securely retained.

9. Adjust parking brake cable and lower vehicle.

Manual Transmission/ Transaxle Overhaul 10

INDEX

MANUAL TRANSMISSION/TRANSAXLE OVERHAUL

HOW TO IDENTIFY A TRANSMISSION

Refer to the Basic Manual Transmission Application chart to determine if more than one type of transmission could have been used in your vehicle. If only one type is applicable, refer to the page index of the Manual Transmission Identification and Page Index chart, which will tell you where the overhaul procedures for your transmission are located. Several special tools may be required for disassembly or assembly of various transmission components; whenever necessary, these special tools are identified by their OEM part number. By using the OEM part number, an equivalent special tool can be cross-referenced to various aftermarked tool suppliers.

Should more than one type of transmission be listed under the same basic description (e.g. two different 4 speeds), then refer to the Manual Transmission Identification and Page Index chart. This chart contains identifying characteristics of each transmission which will enable you to make a positive identification. In many cases, it will be necessary to view the transmission from beneath the vehicle to correctly identify a particular model.

CAUTION

Care must be exercised during the disassembly and assembly of the manual transmission due to the usage of metric nuts and bolts. Proper wrenches and sockets should be used to avoid damage to the transmission and fasteners. DO NOT attempt to interchange metric threaded fasteners with U.S. Fine or Standard fasteners as damage can result.

MANUAL TRANSMISSION IDENTIFICATION

Chilton Type	Transmission Designation	Identifying Characteristics
1	Saginaw	A, F, H
2	76mm	C, F, I, N
3	70mm	E, I, M
4	MTX	G, K
5	Warner-10	B, F, I, R
6	83mm	J
7	C51	G, K
8	76mm	G, K, O
9	76mm	G, I, O
10	77mm	D, E, L, P
11	69.5mm	E, L, Q
12	Muncie	C, F, I, O, S

A Side cover
B 6 bolt side cover
C 7 bolt side cover
D Top cover
E Internal shift linkage
F External linkage shift
G Transaxle
H Three-speed
I Four-speed
J Four-speed overdrive
K Five-speed
L Five-speed overdrive
M The belkhousing is bolted to the transmission case from INSIDE the bellhousing—bolts not exposed while installed
N Cast iron case
O Aluminum case
P Reverse is positioned at the right rear portion of the gearshaft pattern
Q No cover on transmission case: bellhousing integral with transmission case
R Side cover has curved bottom
S Side cover has straight bottom

BASIC MANUAL TRANSMISSION APPLICATIONS

Manufacturer	Model	Year	Transmission Type		
			3 Speed	4 Speed	5 Speed
Chevrolet	Rear Wheel Drive	1980–81	1	—	—
	except	1980–84	—	2, 12	—
	Corvette,	1982–86	—	—	10
	Chevette (84–87)	1980–83	—	5	—
	Corvette	1984–87	—	6	—
	Chevette	1980–81	—	3	—
		1982–87 ①	—	3	10
		1982–87 ②	—	—	11
	Front Wheel Drive except Nova, Sprint	1980–87	—	9	8
	Nova	1985–87	—	—	7
	Sprint	1985–87	—	—	4

① Gasoline engines only
② Diesel engines only

CHILTON TYPE 1

Transmission Case

DISASSEMBLY

1. Remove the side cover assembly and the shift forks.
2. Remove the clutch gear bearing retainer.
3. Remove the clutch gear bearing-to-gear stem snap ring. Pull the clutch gear outward until a screwdriver can be inserted between the bearing and the case. Remove the clutch gear bearing.
4. Remove the speedometer driven gear and the extension bolts.
5. Remove the Reverse idler shaft snap ring.
6. Remove the mainshaft and the extension assembly through the rear of the case.
7. Remove the clutch gear and the 3rd speed blocking ring from inside the case. Remove the 14 roller bearings from the clutch gear.
8. Expand the snap ring which retains the mainshaft rear bearing and remove the extension.
9. Using a dummy shaft, drive the countershaft and the key out through the rear of the case. Remove the gear, the two tanged thrust washers and the dummy shaft. Remove the bearing washer and the 27 roller bearings from each end of the countergear.
10. Using a long drift, drive the Reverse idler shaft and key through the rear of the case.

11. Remove the Reverse idler gear and the tanged steel thrust washer.

ASSEMBLY

1. Using a dummy shaft, grease and load a row of 27 roller bearings and a thrust washer at each end of countergear.
2. Place the countergear assembly into the case from the rear. Place a tanged thrust washer (tang away from the gear) at each end. Install the countershaft and the key, making sure that the tangs align with the notches in the case.
3. Install the Reverse idler gear thrust washer, the gear and the shaft with a key from the rear of the case.

NOTE: Be sure the thrust washer is between the gear and the rear of the case with the tang toward the notch in the case.

4. Expand the snap ring in the extension housing. Assemble the extension over the rear of the mainshaft and onto the rear bearing. Seat the snap ring in the rear bearing groove.
5. Install the 14 mainshaft pilot bearings into the clutch gear cavity. Assemble the 3rd speed blocking ring onto the clutch gear clutching surface with the teeth toward the gear.
6. Place the clutch gear, the pilot bearings and the 3rd speed blocking ring assembly over the front of the mainshaft assembly; be sure the blocking rings align with the keys in the 2nd–3rd synchronizer assembly.
7. Stick the extension gasket to the case with grease. Install the clutch gear, the mainshaft and the extension together; be sure the clutch gear engages the teeth of the countergear anti lash plate. Torque the extension bolts to 45 ft. lbs.
8. Place the bearing over the stem of the clutch gear and into the front case bore. Install the front bearing to the clutch gear snap ring.
9. Install the clutch gear bearing retainer and the gasket. The retainer oil return hole must be at the bottom. Torque the retainer bolts to 10 ft. lbs.
10. Install the Reverse idler gear shaft E-ring.
11. Shift the synchronizer sleeves to the Neutral positions. Install the cover, the gasket and the forks; aligning the forks with the synchronizer sleeve grooves. Torque the side cover bolts to 10 ft. lbs.
12. Install the speedometer driven gear.

Mainshaft

DISASSEMBLY

1. Remove the 2nd–3rd speed sliding clutch hub snap ring from the mainshaft. Remove the clutch assembly, the 2nd speed blocking ring and the 2nd gear from front of the mainshaft.
2. Depress the speedometer drive gear retaining clip and remove the gear. Some units have a metal speedometer driver gear which must be pulled off.
3. Remove the rear bearing snap ring.
4. Support the Reverse gear and

1 Synchronizer retainer ring
2 Synchronizer blocking ring
3 Synchronizer assembly
4 Second speed gear
5 Main shaft
6 Synchronizer assembly
7 Gear assembly
8 Thrust washer
9 Retainer clip

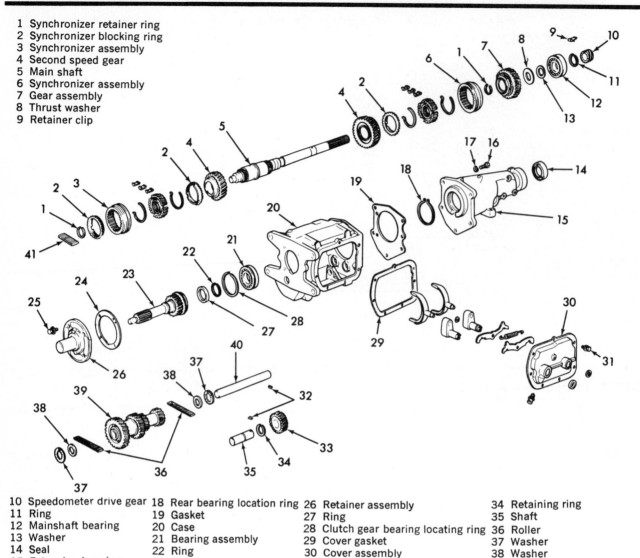

10 Speedometer drive gear	18 Rear bearing location ring	26 Retainer assembly	34 Retaining ring
11 Ring	19 Gasket	27 Ring	35 Shaft
12 Mainshaft bearing	20 Case	28 Clutch gear bearing locating ring	36 Roller
13 Washer	21 Bearing assembly	29 Cover gasket	37 Washer
14 Seal	22 Ring	30 Cover assembly	38 Washer
15 Extension housing	23 Clutch gear	31 Bolt and lockwasher	39 Gear assembly
16 Bolt	24 Gasket	32 Woodruff keys	40 Counter gear shaft
17 Washer	25 Bolt and lockwasher	33 Gear assembly	41 Mainshaft bearing roller

Exploded view of the Saginaw 3 speed transmission—Type One

press on the rear of the mainshaft. Remove the Reverse gear, the thrust washer, the spring washer, the rear bearing and the snap ring.

NOTE: When pressing off the rear bearing, be careful not to cock the bearing on the shaft.

5. Remove the 1st and Reverse sliding clutch hub snap ring. Remove the clutch assembly, 1st speed blocking ring and the 1st gear; sometimes the synchronizer hub and gear must be pressed off.

ASSEMBLY

1. Turn the front of the mainshaft up.
2. Install the 2nd gear with the clutching teeth up; the rear face of the gear butts against the flange on the mainshaft.
3. Install a blocking ring with the clutching teeth down. The three blocking rings are the same.
4. Install the 2nd–3rd speed synchronizer assembly with the fork slot down; press it onto the mainshaft splines.

NOTE: Both synchronizer assemblies are the same. Be sure that the blocking ring notches align with the synchronizer assembly keys.

5. Install the synchronizer snap ring; both synchronizer snap rings are the same.
6. Turn the rear of the shaft up, then install the 1st gear with the clutching teeth up; the front face of the gear butts against the flange on the mainshaft.
7. Install a blocking ring with the clutching teeth down.
8. Install the 1st–Reverse synchronizer assembly with the fork slot down, then press it onto the mainshaft splines; be sure the blocking ring notches align with the synchronizer assembly keys.
9. Install the snap ring.
10. Install the Reverse gear with the clutching teeth down.
11. Install the steel Reverse gear thrust washer and the spring washer.
12. Press the rear ball bearing onto the shaft with the snap ring slot down.
13. Install the snap ring.

14. Install the speedometer drive gear and the retaining clip; press on the metal speedometer drive gear.

Clutch Keys and Springs

REPLACEMENT

The keys and the springs may be replaced if worn or broken, but the hubs and sleeves are matched pairs, they must be kept together.

1. Mark the hub and sleeve for reassembly.
2. Push the hub from the sleeve, then remove the keys and the springs.
3. Place the three keys and the two springs (one on each side of hub) in position, so the three keys are engaged by both springs; the tanged ends of the springs should not be installed into the same key.
4. Slide the sleeve onto the hub by aligning the marks.

NOTE: A groove around the outside of the synchronizer hub marks the end that must be opposite the fork slot in the sleeve when assembled.

Extension Oil Seal and Bushing

REPLACEMENT

1. Remove the seal.
2. Using the bushing removal and installation tool, drive the bushing into the extension housing.
3. Drive the new bushing in from the rear. Lubricate the inside of the bushing and the seal. Install a new oil seal with the extension seal installation tool or other suitable tool.

Clutch Bearing Retainer Oil Seal

REPLACEMENT

1. Pry the old seal out.
2. Install the new seal using the seal installer. Seat the seal in the bore.

CHILTON TYPE 2

Transmission Case

DISASSEMBLY

1. Drain the lubricant. Remove the side cover and the shift forks.
2. Remove the clutch gear bearing retainer. Remove the bearing-to-gear stem snap ring and pull out on the clutch gear until a small pry bar can be inserted between the bearing, the large snap ring and case to pry the bearing off.

NOTE: The clutch gear bearing is a slip fit on the gear and in the case. Removal of the bearing will provide clearance for the clutch gear and the mainshaft removal.

3. Remove the extension housing bolts, then remove the clutch gear, the mainshaft and the extension as an assembly.
4. Spread the snap ring which holds the mainshaft rear bearing and remove the extension case.
5. Using a dummy shaft, drive the countershaft and its woodruff key out through the rear of the case. Remove the countergear assembly and the bearings.
6. Using a long drift, drive the Reverse idler shaft and the woodruff key through the rear of the case.
7. Expand and remove the 3rd–4th speed sliding clutch hub snap ring from the mainshaft. Remove the clutch assembly, the 3rd gear blocking ring and the 3rd speed gear from the front of the mainshaft.
8. Press in the speedometer gear retaining clip and slide the gear off the mainshaft. Remove the rear bearing snap ring from the mainshaft.
9. Using an arbor press, support the 1st gear on press plates, then press the 1st gear, the thrust washer, the spring washer, the rear bearing and snap ring from the rear of the mainshaft.

—————— **CAUTION** ——————
Be sure to center the gear, the washers, the bearings and the snap ring when pressing the rear bearing.

10. Expand and remove the 1st–2nd sliding clutch hub snap ring from the mainshaft, then remove the clutch assembly, the 2nd speed blocking ring and the 2nd speed gear from the rear of the mainshaft.

NOTE: After thoroughly cleaning the parts and the transmission case, inspect and replace the damaged or worn parts. When checking the bearings, do not spin them at high speeds. Clean and rotate the bearings by hand to detect the roughness or unevenness. Spinning can damage the balls and the races.

ASSEMBLY

1. Grease both inside ends of the countergear. Install a dummy shaft into the countergear, then load a row of roller bearings (27) and thrust washers at each end of the countergear.
2. Position the countergear assembly into the case through the rear opening. Place a tanged thrust washer at each end of the countergear.
3. Install the countergear shaft and woodruff key from the rear of the case.

NOTE: Make sure that the shaft engages both thrust washers and that the tangs align with their notches in the case.

4. Install the Reverse idler gear, the shaft and the woodruff key. Install the extension-to-rear bearing snap ring. Assemble the extension housing over the rear of the mainshaft and onto the rear bearing.
5. Install the 14 mainshaft pilot bearings into the clutch opening and the 4th speed blocking ring onto the clutching surface of the clutch gear (with the clutching teeth facing the gear).
6. Assemble the clutch gear, the pilot bearings and the 4th speed blocking ring unit over the front of the mainshaft. Do not assemble the bearing to the gear at this point.

—————— **CAUTION** ——————
Be sure that the blocking ring notches align with the 3rd–4th synchronizer assembly keys.

7. Install the extension-to-case gasket and secure it with grease. Install the clutch gear, the mainshaft and the extension housing as an assembly. Install the extension-to-case bolts (apply sealer to the bottom bolt) and torque to 45 ft. lbs.
8. Install the outer snap ring on the front bearing and place the bearing over the stem of the clutch gear and into the case bore.
9. Install the snap ring to the clutch gear stem. Install the clutch gear bearing retainer and the gasket, with the retainer oil return hole at the bottom.
10. Place the synchronizer sleeves into the Neutral positions and install the cover, the gasket and the fork assemblies to the case; be sure the forks align with the synchronizer sleeve grooves. Torque the cover bolts to 22 ft. lbs.

Mainshaft

ASSEMBLY

Install the following parts with the front of the mainshaft facing up:

1. Install the 3rd speed gear with the clutching teeth up; the rear face of

1 Clip
2 Speedometer drive gear
3 Snap ring
4 Mainshaft rear bearing
5 Washer (wavy)
6 Washer (wavy)
7 First speed gear
8 Blocking ring
9 Retaining ring
10 Synchronizer assembly

11 Spring
12 Synchronizer key
13 Synchronizer hub
15 Second speed gear
16 Main shaft
17 Third speed gear
18 Synchronizer assembly
19 Mainshaft bearing rollers
20 Extension housing oil seal
21 Extension housing

22 Bolt
23 Washer
24 Rear bearing ring
25 Gasket
26 Case assembly
27 Drain plug

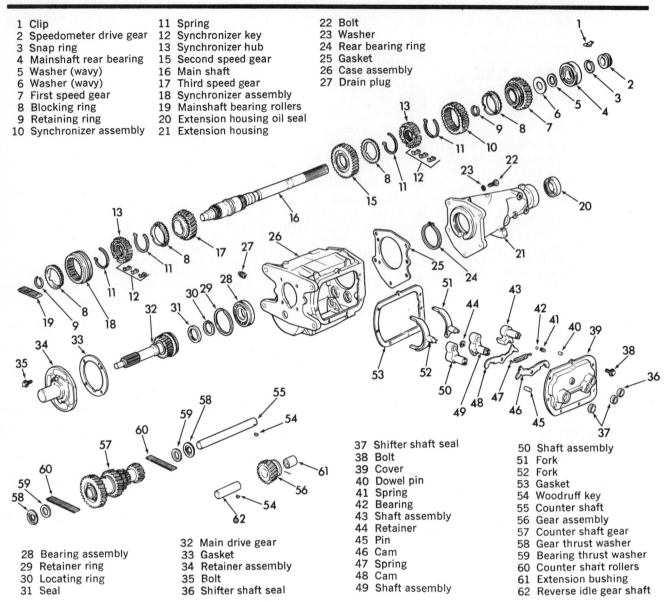

28 Bearing assembly
29 Retainer ring
30 Locating ring
31 Seal

32 Main drive gear
33 Gasket
34 Retainer assembly
35 Bolt
36 Shifter shaft seal

37 Shifter shaft seal
38 Bolt
39 Cover
40 Dowel pin
41 Spring
42 Bearing
43 Shaft assembly
44 Retainer
45 Pin
46 Cam
47 Spring
48 Cam
49 Shaft assembly

50 Shaft assembly
51 Fork
52 Fork
53 Gasket
54 Woodruff key
55 Counter shaft
56 Gear assembly
57 Counter shaft gear
58 Gear thrust washer
59 Bearing thrust washer
60 Counter shaft rollers
61 Extension bushing
62 Reverse idle gear shaft

Exploded view of the Saginaw 4 speed transmission—Type Two

the gear will abut with the mainshaft flange.

2. Install a blocking ring (with the clutching teeth down) over the 3rd speed gear synchronizing surface.

NOTE: The four blocking rings are the same.

3. Press the 3rd–4th synchronizer assembly (with the fork slot down) onto the mainshaft splines until it bottoms.

—————— **CAUTION** ——————
The blocking ring notches must align with the synchronizer assembly keys.

4. Install the synchronizer hub-to-mainshaft snap ring; both synchronizer snap rings are the same.
Install the following parts with the

rear of the mainshaft facing up:

5. Install the 2nd speed gear with the clutching teeth up; the front face of the gear will abut with the flange on the mainshaft.

6. Install a blocking ring (with the clutching teeth down) over the 2nd speed gear synchronizing surface.

7. Press the 1st–2nd synchronizer assembly (with the fork slot down) onto the mainshaft.

—————— **CAUTION** ——————
The blocking ring notches must align with the synchronizer assembly keys.

8. Install the synchronizer hub-to-mainshaft snap ring.

9. Install a blocking ring with the notches down so they align with the 1st–2nd synchronizer assembly keys.

10. Install the 1st gear with the clutching teeth down. Install the 1st gear thrust washer and the spring washer.

11. Press the rear ball bearing (with the slot down) onto the mainshaft. Install the snap ring. Install the speedometer gear and clip.

CHILTON TYPE 3

Transmission Case

DISASSEMBLY

1. Place the transmission so that it

is resting on the bell housing.

2. Drive the spring pin from the shifter shaft arm assembly and the shifter shaft, then remove the shifter shaft arm assembly.

3. Remove the five extension housing-to-case bolts and the extension housing.

4. Press down on the speedometer gear retainer, then remove the gear and the retainer from the mainshaft.

5. Remove the snap rings from the shifter shaft, then the Reverse shifter shaft cover, the shifter shaft detent cap, the spring, the ball and the interlock lock pin.

6. Pull the Reverse lever shaft outward to disengage the Reverse idler, then remove the idler shaft with the gear attached.

7. Remove the Reverse gear snap ring, the Reverse countershaft gear and the gears.

8. Turn the case on its side and remove the clutch gear bearing retainer bolts, the retainer and the gasket.

9. Remove the clutch gear ball bearing-to-bell housing snap ring, then the bell housing-to-case bolts.

10. Turn the case so that it rests on the bell housing, then expand the mainshaft bearing snap ring and re-

move the case by lifting it off the mainshaft.

NOTE: Make sure that the mainshaft assembly, the countergear and shifter shaft assembly stay with the bell housing.

11. Lift the entire mainshaft assembly complete with shifter forks and countergear from the bell housing.

ASSEMBLY

1. Using a press, install the shielded ball bearing to the clutch gear shaft with the snap ring groove up.

1 Bolt	6 Wire assembly
2 Bearing retainer	7 Switch assembly (TCS)
3 Seal assembly	8 Gasket assembly
4 Gasket	9 Case assembly
5 Clutch housing	10 Spring

11 Cap	16 Back-up light switch
12 Ball	17 Plug
13 Gasket	18 Cap
14 Cap	19 Bolt
15 Retainer	20 Retaining ring

21 Locating ring
22 Bearing assembly
23 Bearing assembly
24 Bolt
25 Main drive gear
26 Bearing rollers
27 Shift fork
28 Pin
29 Bushing
30 Detent lever
31 Shift fork
32 Shift shaft
33 Pin
34 Lock ring
35 Extension assembly
36 Gasket
37 Arm assembly
38 Pin
39 Bushing
40 Seal
41 Reverse shaft and lever
42 Lock ring
43 Clip
44 Retaining ring
45 Synchronizer assembly
46 Mainshaft
47 Second speed gear
48 Synchronizer assembly
49 Synchronizer blocking ring
50 Synchronizer spring
51 Synchronizer key
52 Third speed gear
53 First speed gear
54 Locating ring
55 Mainshaft rear bearing
56 Reverse gear
57 Retaining ring
58 Speedometer drive gear
59 Retainer ring
60 Thrust washer
61 Countershaft gear
62 Locating ring
63 Bearing race
64 Bearing assembly
65 Countershaft reverse gear
66 Reverse idler shaft
67 Retainer ring
68 Thrust washer
69 Reverse idler gear

Exploded view of the GM 70mm transmission—Type Three

2. Install the snap ring on the clutch gear shaft. Place the pilot bearings into the clutch gear cavity, using heavy grease to hold them in place.

3. Assemble the clutch gear to the mainshaft and the detent lever to the shift shaft with the roll pin.

4. Position the 1st–2nd gear shifter so that it engages the detent lever.

5. Assemble the 3rd–4th gear shifter fork to the detent bushing and slide the assembly on the shift shaft to place it below the 1st–2nd shifter fork arm.

6. Install the shifter assembly to the synchronizer sleeve grooves on the mainshaft.

7. With the front of the bell housing resting on wooden blocks, place a thrust washer over the hole for the countergear shaft. The thrust washer must be placed in the holes in the bellhousing.

8. Mesh the countershaft gears to the mainshaft gears and install this assembly into the bellhousing.

9. Turn the bellhousing on its side, then install the snap ring to the ball bearing on the clutch gear and the bearing retainer to the bell housing. Use sealant on the four retaining bolts.

10. Turn the bell housing (so that it is resting on the blocks) and install the Reverse lever to the case using grease to hold it in place. When installing the Reverse lever, the screwdriver slot should be parallel to the front of the case.

11. Install the Reverse lever snap ring and the roller bearing-to-countergear opening with the snap ring groove inside of the case.

12. Using rubber cement, install the gasket on the bell housing. Before installing the case, make sure the synchronizers are in the Neutral position, the detent bushing slot is facing outward and the Reverse lever is flush with the inside wall of the case.

13. Expand the snap ring in the mainshaft case opening and let it slide over the bearing.

14. Install the interlock lock pin with locking compound to hold the shifter shaft in place and the idler shaft so it engages with the Reverse lever inside the shaft.

15. Install the cover over the screwdriver arm to hold the Reverse lever in place.

16. Install the detent ball, the spring and the cap in the case, then the Reverse gear (with the chamfer on the gear teeth facing up). Push the Reverse gear onto the splines and secure with a snap ring.

17. Install the smaller Reverse gear on the countergear shaft (with the shoulder resting against the countergear bearing) and secure with a snap ring.

18. Install the snap ring, the thrust washer and the Reverse idler gear (with the gear teeth chamfer facing down) to the idler shaft, then secure with the thrust washer and the snap ring.

19. Install the shifter shaft snap rings and engage the speedometer gear retainer in the hole in the mainshaft (with the retainer loop toward the front), then slide the speedometer gear over the mainshaft and into position.

NOTE: Before installation, heat the gear to 175°F; use an oven or heat lamp, not a torch.

20. Place the extension housing and the gasket on the case, then loosely install the two pilot bolts (one in the top right hand corner and the other in the bottom left hand corner) and the other three bolts. The pilot bolts must be installed in the right holes to prevent splitting the case.

21. Assemble the shifter shaft arm over the shifter shaft, align with the drilled hole near the end of the shaft, then drive the spring pin into the shifter shaft arm and shaft.

22. Turn the case on its side and loosely install the two pilot bolts through the bell housing and then the four retaining bolts.

Mainshaft

DISASSEMBLY

1. Separate the shift shaft assembly and countergear from the mainshaft.

2. Remove the clutch gear and the blocking ring from the mainshaft; make sure you don't lose any of the clutch gear roller bearings.

3. Remove the 3rd–4th gear synchronizer hub snap ring and the hub, using an arbor press (if necessary).

4. Remove the blocking ring and the 3rd speed gear. Using an arbor press and press plates, remove the ball bearing from the rear of the mainshaft. Remove the remaining parts from the mainshaft keeping them in order for later reassembly.

ASSEMBLY

1. With the rear of the mainshaft turned up, install the 2nd speed gear with the clutching teeth facing upward; the rear face of the gear will butt against the flange of the mainshaft.

2. Install a blocking ring (with the clutching teeth down) over the 2nd speed gear.

3. Install the 1st–2nd synchronizer assembly (with the fork slot down), then press it onto the splines on the mainshaft until it bottoms.

NOTE: Make sure the notches of the blocking ring align with the keys of the synchronizer assembly.

4. Install the synchronizer hub-to-mainshaft snap ring, then install a blocking ring (with the notches facing down) so they align with the keys of the 1st–2nd gear synchronizer assembly.

5. Install the 1st speed gear (with the clutching teeth down), then the rear ball bearing (with the snap ring groove down) and press it into place on the mainshaft.

6. Turn the mainshaft up and install the 3rd speed gear (with the clutching teeth facing up); the front face of the gear will butt against the flange on the mainshaft.

7. Install a blocking ring (with the clutching teeth facing down) over the synchronizer surface of the 3rd speed gear.

8. Install the 3rd–4th gear synchronizer assembly (with the fork slot facing down); make sure the notches of the blocking ring align with the keys of the synchronizer assembly.

9. Install the synchronizer hub-to-mainshaft snap ring and a blocking ring (with the notches facing down) so that they align with the keys of the 3rd–4th gear synchronizer assembly.

Synchronizer Keys And Springs

REPLACEMENT

1. The synchronizer hubs and the sliding sleeves are an assembly which should be kept together as an assembly; the keys and the springs can be replaced.

2. Mark the position of the hub and the sleeve for reassembly.

3. Push the hub from the sliding sleeve; the keys will fall out and the springs can be easily removed.

4. Place the new springs in position (with one on each side of the hub) so that the three keys are engaged by both springs.

5. Place and hold the keys in position, then slide the sleeve into the hub aligning the marks made during disassembly.

Extension Oil Seal

REPLACEMENT

1. Pry the oil seal and drive the bushing from rear of the extension housing.

2. Coat the inside diameter of the

seal and bushing with transmission fluid and install them.

Drive Gear Bearing Oil Seal

REPLACEMENT

Pry out the old seal and install a new one making sure that it bottoms properly in its bore.

CHILTON TYPE 4

Transaxle Case

DISASSEMBLY

1. Remove the backup light switch, then the 7 side case bolts and the case from the transaxle.

2. Remove the snap ring and the hub plate from the input shaft, then the shift fork screw and the 5th gear shift fork guide ball. Place the 5th gear in the Neutral position and remove the roll pin from the 5th gear shift fork.

3. Push the gear shift shaft In, to place the transaxle in gear, then slide the 5th gear synchronizer to engage the 5th gear; the transaxle should now be locked in two gears. Remove the 5th gear lock nut staked mark, then the nut.

4. Remove the 5th gear shift fork, the sleeve, the hub, the synchronizer ring, the spring and the keys as an assembly.

5. Remove the 5th drive gear, the bearing, the spacer and the washer from the input shaft, then the 5th driven gear from the countershaft.

6. Remove the bearing/shim plate-to-left case bolts and the plate.

NOTE: Mark or tag the input shaft and the countershaft shims for reassembly reference.

7. Remove the three left case cap bolts and the cap, then the gear shift yoke-to-gear shift/selector shaft roll pin.

NOTE: Using a drift punch, install it into the gear shift/selector shaft roll pin hole, then raise the shaft to remove the yoke and the roll pin.

8. Remove the Reverse spring and the detent ball bolt, the spring and the ball from the case. Remove the gear shift/selector shaft locating bolt, the gear shift guide-to-case bolts, the gear shift/selector shaft assembly and the

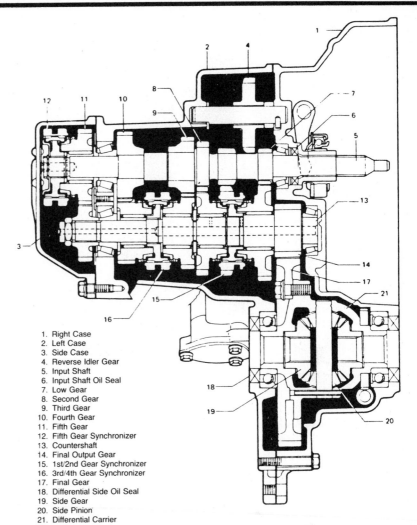

1. Right Case
2. Left Case
3. Side Case
4. Reverse Idler Gear
5. Input Shaft
6. Input Shaft Oil Seal
7. Low Gear
8. Second Gear
9. Third Gear
10. Fourth Gear
11. Fifth Gear
12. Fifth Gear Synchronizer
13. Countershaft
14. Final Output Gear
15. 1st/2nd Gear Synchronizer
16. 3rd/4th Gear Synchronizer
17. Final Gear
18. Differential Side Oil Seal
19. Side Gear
20. Side Pinion
21. Differential Carrier

Cut-away view of the 5 speed transaxle—Type Four

low speed selector spring from the case.

9. Remove the three bolts holding the detent balls and springs of the shift fork shafts. Remove the 13 case bolts, then insert a small pry bar between the case halves and separate the cases.

10. Remove the left case; the the input shaft, the countershaft, the differential and other parts should remain on the right case.

11. Raise the 5th and the Reverse shift shafts. Remove the Reverse idler shift lever-to-case bolts and the lever, then the 5th and the Reverse gear shift shafts (together) as an assembly.

12. Remove the input shaft, the countershaft, the 1st–2nd and the 3rd–4th shift shafts (together) as an assembly.

NOTE: To remove the components in Step 12, it may be necessary to raise the differential assembly.

13. Remove the differential assembly from the right case. Using tool No. J-29369-2 and a slide hammer, pull the input shaft and the countershaft bearing cups from the right case.

14. Using tool No. J-23907, remove the input shaft seal from the right case. Remove the differential side oil seals from both cases.

15. Position the gear shift arm above the square recess in the right case (by moving the shift shaft). Using a drift punch, remove the gear shift arm roll pin.

16. Remove the shifter shaft retaining bolt, the detent ball and the spring. Slide the shifter shaft out, then remove the arm, the roll pin and the shaft from the case.

17. Remove the shifter shaft boot from the oil seal flange. Using a pair of pliers, remove the shifter shaft seal from the case.

18. Remove the input shaft and the countershaft bearing cups from the left case.

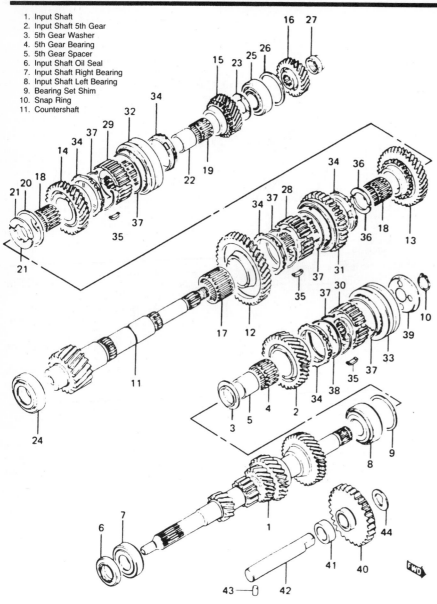

1. Input Shaft
2. Input Shaft 5th Gear
3. 5th Gear Washer
4. 5th Gear Bearing
5. 5th Gear Spacer
6. Input Shaft Oil Seal
7. Input Shaft Right Bearing
8. Input Shaft Left Bearing
9. Bearing Set Shim
10. Snap Ring
11. Countershaft

12. Countershaft Low Gear	23. 4th Gear Thrust Washer	34. Synchronizer Ring
13. Countershaft 2nd Gear	24. Countershaft Right Bearing	35. Synchronizer Shifting Key
14. Countershaft 3rd Gear	25. Countershaft Left Bearing	36. 1st/2nd Gear Sync. Hub Ring
15. Countershaft 4th Gear	26. Bearing Set Shim	37. Synchronizer Spring
16. Countershaft 5th Gear	27. Countershaft Nut	38. Sync. Ring 5th Spring
17. 1st Gear Bearing	28. 1st/2nd Gear Sync. Hub	39. Fifth Gear Sync. Hub Plate
18. 2nd/3rd Gear Bearing	29. 3rd/4th Gear	40. Reverse Idle Gear
19. 4th Gear Bearing	30. Over Top Sync. Hub	41. Idle Gear Spacer
20. 2nd/3rd Gear Ring Washer	31. 1st/2nd Gear	42. Reverse Gear Shaft
21. 2nd/3rd Gear Ring	32. 3rd/4th Gear Sync. Sleeve	34. Pin
22. 4th Gear Spacer	33. Fifth Gear Sync. Sleeve	44. Washer

Exploded view of the 5 speed gear assembly—Type Four

ASSEMBLY

NOTE: Before installing the oil seals, apply a coat of grease to the seal lips.

1. Using tools No. J-34855 and J-7079-2, install the input shaft seal to the right case. Using tools No. J-34849 and J-7079-2, install the input shaft and the countershaft bearing cups to the right case.

2. Using tools No. J-29130 and J-8092, install the differential oil seals to both cases.

3. Apply locking cement to the bolt threads and install the Reverse gear shift lever, then torque the bolts to 14–20 ft. lbs.

4. Using tool No. J-34857, drive the new gear shift shaft seal into the case, then install the gear shift lever and the boot.

5. Install the detent ball, the spring, the gasket and the bolt to the shift shaft, then the gear shift arm and the roll pin to the gear shift shaft.

6. Install the differential assembly, then the 5th and the Reverse gear shift shafts into the right case. Install the input shaft, the countershaft, the 1st–2nd and the 3rd–4th gear shift shafts into the right case.

7. Install the idler gear, the shaft, the pin, the spacer, the washer and the magnet into the right case.

8. Apply Loctite® 518 to the left case mounting surface, then install the left case to the right case and torque the bolts to 14–20 ft. lbs.

NOTE: After installing the cases, check the input shaft and the countershaft for smooth turning (turn by hand).

9. Install the three shift fork shaft detent balls, the springs, the gaskets and the bolts, then torque the bolts to 8–11 ft. lbs.

10. Install the gear shift yoke onto the gear shift arm. Install the gear shift/selector shaft assembly, by guiding the shaft into the gear shift yoke hole. Align the yoke hole with the shaft hole and install a new roll pin.

11. Install the gear shift locating bolt and washer, then torque the bolt to 30–43 ft. lbs. Install the gear shift guide case and torque the bolts to 6–7 ft. lbs.

12. Install the Reverse check ball, the spring, the washer and the bolt. Install the case cap with a new O-ring to the left case.

13. Using tool No. J-34858, measure and determine the bearing shim size for the input shaft and the countershaft as follows:

  a. Install the left bearing cups for the input shaft and the countershaft. Using finger pressure, push the countershaft's left bearing cup against the bearing rollers. Rotate the countershaft 3–4 times to seat the bearings. Install the nut (from tool No. J-34858) onto the shaft, followed by the countershaft nut, then torque the nut to 44–58 ft. lbs.

  b. Install the Dial Gauge tool No. J-29763 on the Shim Selector tool No. J-34858, then place the tools on a flat surface and zero the gauge. Place the tools on the countershaft and the left case, then press down on the selector tool and read the dial indicator.

NOTE: The reading on the dial indicator will indicate the size of the shim to be used. The shim

stock has 12 selective thicknesses, the size is stamped on one side; select the correct size and install it on the back side of the left hand countershaft bearing cup.

c. For the input shaft, repeat the above procedures; select the correct size and install it on the back side of the left hand input shaft bearing cup.

14. Install the case plate by fitting the plate's protrusion into the groove of the gear shift guide shaft. Apply locking cement to the screw threads and torque to 5 ft. lbs.

15. Install tool No. J-34852 onto the input shaft and connect a spring balance to the wire of the tool. Place the transaxle in the Neutral and the 4th gear positions, then pull the spring balance to check the preload.

NOTE: If the preload is not to specifications, change the shims of the input shaft and the countershaft.

16. With the transaxle in the 4th gear, install the 5th gear onto the input shaft and the countershaft, then engage the synchronizer so the transaxle will be locked in two gears. Install and stake the countershaft nut after torquing it to 44–57 ft. lbs.

17. Disengage the 5th gear synchronizer and shift the transaxle in the Neutral position.

18. Install the shift guide ball and the shift fork screw to the shifting fork; after torquing the screw to 6–8 ft. lbs., stake the screw.

19. Using a drift punch and a hammer, drive a new roll pin into the 5th and the Reverse gear shift shaft. Install the synchronizer hub plate and a new snap ring.

20. Apply Loctite® 518 to the side case mounting surface and the install the side case. Fit the side case oil receiver cup into the input shaft hole, then install the bolts and torque to 14–20 ft. lbs.

21. Install the backup light switch.

Input Shaft

DISASSEMBLY

NOTE: The 3rd and the 4th gears should not be removed from the input shaft. If the gears are damaged, replace the input shaft.

Using tool No. J-34843 and an arbor press, press the right bearing (small) and the left bearing (large) from the input shaft.

ASSEMBLY

Using tool No. J-34844 and an arbor press, press the right and the left bearings onto the input shaft.

CHILTON TYPE 5

Transmisson Case

DISASSEMBLY

1. Drain the lubricant and shift into the 2nd gear position. Remove the side cover and the shift controls.

2. Remove the four front bearing retainer bolts, the retainer and the gasket.

3. If equipped with an output companion flange, remove it.

4. At the Reverse shifter lever boss, drive the lock pin up, then pull the shift shaft out about $\frac{1}{8}$ in. to disengage the shifter fork from the Reverse gear.

5. Remove the five extension housing bolts and tap the extension (with soft hammer) rearward. When the idler gear shaft is out (as far as it will go), move the extension housing to the left so that the Reverse fork clears the Reverse gear, then remove extension housing and the gasket.

6. Remove the speedometer gear outer snap ring, then tap or slide the speedometer from the mainshaft.

7. Remove the 2nd snap ring.

8. Remove the Reverse gear from the mainshaft and the rear part of the Reverse idler gear from the case.

9. Remove the front bearing snap ring and the spacer washer.

10. Pull the front bearing from the case.

11. Remove the rear retainer lock bolt.

12. Shift the 1st–2nd and the 3rd–4th clutch sliding sleeves forward for clearance.

13. Remove the mainshaft and the rear bearing retainer assembly from the case.

14. Remove the front Reverse idler gear and the thrust washer from the case (the gear teeth must face forward).

15. Using a dummy shaft, drive the countergear shaft out through the rear of the case. Remove the countergear and the tanged thrust washers.

ASSEMBLY

1. Place the case on its side and install the countergear tanged washers with the tangs in the thrust face notches, secure them with grease.

2. Install the countergear (with a dummy shaft) in the case. Drive the countergear shaft through the rear of the case, forcing the dummy shaft out through the front. Install the shaft key and tap the shaft in until it is flush with the rear face of the case.

3. Install the front Reverse idler gear with the teeth forward, using grease to secure the thrust washer in place.

4. Use heavy grease to secure the 16 roller bearings and the washer in the main drive gear, mate the main drive gear with the mainshaft. Hold them together by moving the 3rd–4th clutch sliding sleeve forward.

5. Place a new gasket on the rear of the case. Install the mainshaft and drive gear assembly into the case.

6. Align the rear bearing retainer with the case, then install the locating pin and the locking bolt.

7. Install the bearing snap ring on the front main bearing. Tap the bearing into the case, then install the spacer washer and the thickest snap ring that can be fitted.

8. Install the front bearing retainer and the gasket, using sealer on the bolts.

9. Install the rear Reverse idler gear, engaging the splines with the portion of the gear in the case.

10. Slide the Reverse gear onto the shaft. Install the speedometer gear and the two thickest snap rings that can be fitted.

11. Install the idler shaft into the extension housing until the hole in the shaft aligns with the lockpin hole, then drive the lockpin and a sealant coated plug into place.

12. Place the Reverse shifter shaft and the detent into the extension housing, using grease to hold the Reverse shift fork in position. Install the shaft O-ring, after the shaft is in place.

13. Put the tanged thrust washer on the Reverse idler shaft; the tang must be in the notch of the extension housing thrust face.

14. Place the 1st–2nd and the 3rd–4th clutch sliding sleeves in the Neutral positions. Pull the Reverse shift shaft part way out and push the Reverse shift fork in as far as possible. Start the extension housing onto the mainshaft and push in on the shifter shaft to engage the shift fork with the Reverse gear collar. When the fork engages, turn the shifter shaft to let the Reverse gear go to the rear and the extension housing to fit in place.

15. Install the Reverse shift shaft lockpin.

16. Install the extension housing bolts.

NOTE: Use sealant on the upper left side bolt.

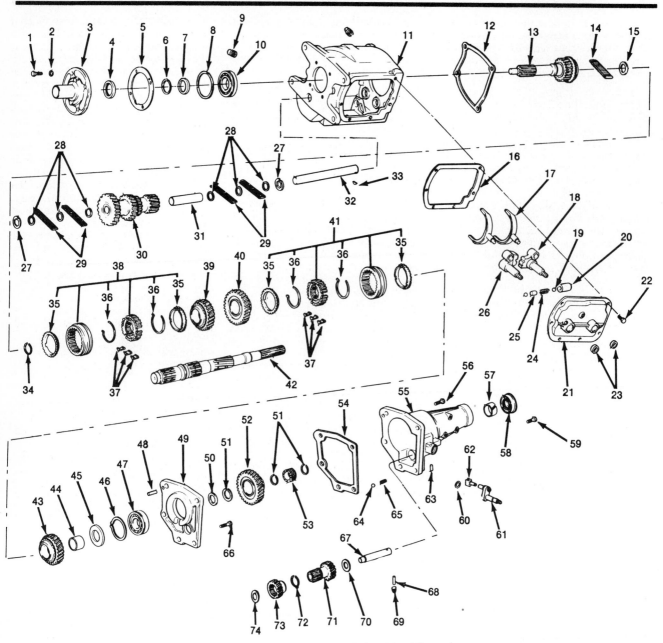

1. Bolt	20. Interlock sleeve	39. 3rd speed gear	57. Extension bushing
2. Lock washer	21. Transmission cover	40. 2nd speed gear	58. Extension seal
3. Bearing retainer	22. Bolt	41. 1st and 2nd synchronizer	59. Bolt
4. Seal	23. Shifter shaft seal	42. Transmission main shaft	60. Shifter shaft oil seal
5. Gasket	24. Rev. lever poppet spring	43. 1st speed gear	61. Reverse shifter shaft
6. Snap ring	25. Interlock pin	44. 1st speed sleeve	62. Reverse fork
7. Ring	26. 3rd and 4th shaft assy.	45. 1st speed thrust washer	63. Lock pin
8. Snap ring	27. Washer	46. Snap ring	64. Lever poppet spring
9. Drain plug	28. Countershaft bearing washer	47. Main shaft rear bearing	65. Ball
10. Bearing	29. Roller	48. Pin	66. Bolt
11. Transmission case	30. Countershaft gear	49. Retainer assy.	67. Shaft
12. Front gasket	31. Spacer	50. Ring	68. Pin
13. Clutch gear	32. Counter shaft	51. Retainer ring	69. Plug
14. Roller	33. Key (1/8" × 5/8")	52. Reverse gear	70. Rev. idler gear washer
15. Spacer	34. Clutch hub retainer ring	53. Speedometer drive gear	71. Reverse idler gear
16. Side gasket	35. Blocking ring	54. Gasket	72. Front ring
17. 1st, 2nd, 3rd and 4th fork	36. Synchronizer spring	55. Extension assy.	73. Rev. idler gear (front)
18. 1st and 2nd shaft assy.	37. Shifting key	56. Bolt	74. Washer
19. Balls	38. 3rd and 4th synchronizer		

Exploded view of the Borg Warner 4 speed transmission—Type Five

17. Position the 1st–2nd clutch sliding sleeve into 2nd gear and the 3rd–4th clutch sliding sleeve into Neutral positions. Position the forward shift forks into the sliding sleeves.

18. Place the 1st–2nd shifter shaft and the detent plate into the 2nd gear position and install the side cover gasket, with sealant.

Mainshaft

DISASSEMBLY

1. Using snap ring pliers, remove the 3rd–4th clutch assembly retaining ring from the front of the mainshaft. Remove the washer, the syncrhonizer/clutch assembly, the synchronizer ring and the 3rd gear.

2. Spread the rear bearing retainer snap ring and slide the retainer off. Remove the rear bearing-to-mainshaft snap ring.

3. Support the 2nd gear and press the mainshaft out; remove the rear bearing, the 1st gear, the sleeve, the 1st–2nd clutch/synchronizer assembly and the 2nd gear.

ASSEMBLY

1. At the rear of the shaft, install the 2nd gear with the hub facing the rear.

2. Install the 1st–2nd synchronizer clutch assembly with the sliding clutch sleeve taper facing the rear and the hub to the front. Put a synchronizer ring on both sides of the clutch assemblies.

3. Place the 1st gear sleeve on the shaft. Press the sleeve on until the 2nd gear, the clutch assembly and sleeve bottom against the shoulder of the mainshaft.

4. Install the 1st gear with the hub facing the front and the inner race. Press the rear bearing on with the snap ring groove to the front.

5. Install the spacer and select the thickest snap ring that can be fitted into the mainshaft behind the rear bearing.

6. Install the 3rd gear with the hub to the front and the 3rd gear synchronizing ring with the notches to the front.

7. Install the 3rd–4th gear clutch assembly with the taper facing the front.

NOTE: Make sure that the keys in the hub match the notches in the 3rd gear synchronizing ring.

8. Install the thickest snap ring that will fit in the mainshaft groove in front of the 3rd–4th clutch assembly.

9. Place the rear bearing retainer over the end of the shaft and the snap ring in the groove of the rear bearing.

10. Install the Reverse gear with the shift collar to the rear.

11. Install a snap ring, the speedometer drive gear and a snap ring.

Countergear

ASSEMBLY

1. Install a dummy shaft and a tubular roller bearing spacer into the countergear.

2. Using heavy grease to hold the rollers, install 20 bearing rollers in either end of the countergear, the two spacers, the 20 more rollers, then a spacer. Install the same combination of rollers and spacers in the other end of the countergear.

3. Set the countergear assembly in the bottom of the case, be sure the tanged thrust washers are in their proper position.

CHILTON TYPE 6

Transmission Case

DISASSEMBLY

1. Thoroughly clean the exterior of the case.

2. Remove the 7 Overdrive unit-to-Reverse housing bolts and separate the two units.

3. Remove the drain plug from the lower right side of the case and drain the lubricant.

4. Shift the transmission into 2nd gear, then remove the shift cover bolts, the cover, the gasket and both shift forks.

5. Remove the backup switch from the Reverse housing.

6. Rotate the Reverse shifter shaft, then remove the shift fork and gear from the mainshaft.

7. Remove the lock pin from the Reverse shift lever boss and pull the shaft from the housing.

8. Remove the drive gear bearing retainer bolts, the retainer and the gasket from the front of the case.

9. Remove the front bearing snap ring, the selective fit snap ring and the spacer washer.

10. Using tool No. J-6654-01 and J-8433-1, pull the drive gear bearing from the case.

11. Remove the six Reverse housing-to-case bolts. Using a small drift and a hammer, tap the reverse housing locating pin into the case.

12. Rotate the Reverse housing on the mainshaft until the Reverse idler gear shaft hole in the housing aligns with the countergear shaft.

13. Using tool No. J-24658 or a dummy shaft, drive the countergear shaft rearward out of the gear and through the Reverse housing. The countergear will drop to the bottom of the case allowing clearance for the removal of the mainshaft.

14. Remove the mainshaft with the Reverse housing and the drive gear from the case.

15. Remove the front Reverse idler gear and thrust washer from the case.

16. Remove the countergear and the two tanged thrust washers from the case. Check the bottom of the case for loose pilot bearings. Remove the Reverse housing locating pin and any other loose components.

ASSEMBLY

1. Place the transmission case on its side with the shift cover opening toward the assembler. Position the countergear tanged washers in place, using a heavy grease to retain them.

NOTE: Be sure the tangs are in the notches of the thrust face.

2. Position the countergear assembly in the bottom of the case.

3. Install the front Reverse idler gear (teeth facing forward) and the thrust washer in the case; use a heavy grease to the hold thrust washer in position.

4. Using heavy grease, install the 16 roller bearings and the washer into the main drive gear. Mate the main drive gear with the mainshaft assembly. Position the 3rd–4th synchronizer sliding sleeve forward.

NOTE: This will provide clearance for installation as well as hold the assembly together.

5. Position a new Reverse housing to the case gasket on the rear of the case.

6. Install the mainshaft and drive gear assembly into the case.

7. Place the bearing snap ring on the front main bearing. Using tool No. J-5590 or a hollow tube, position the front main bearing into the case opening and tap into place. Install the spacer washer and the snap ring to secure the main drive bearing.

8. Raise the countergear in the case, aligning the holes in the case with the center of the gear. With the thrust washers in place, slide the countershaft through the rear of the case. Install the woodruff key and tap the shaft into the case, until it is flush with the rear face of the case.

9. Align the Reverse housing and

the gasket to the case. Install the locating pin for the Reverse housing and tap the pin in until it is flush with the housing.

10. Install the 6 Reverse housing-to-case bolts.

11. Install the Reverse shift shaft and the O-ring into the housing, then the retaining pin.

12. Install the Reverse gear and the shift fork. Slide the gear and the fork forward on the mainshaft until the shift fork and the shifter shaft can be indexed into position.

13. Position the drive gear bearing retainer and the gasket to the front of the case. Apply sealant to the bolts.

14. Install the rear Reverse idler gear. Align the splines on the rear gear with the front gear and slide together.

15. Assemble the overdrive unit to the Reverse housing. Guide the idler shaft on the O/D unit into the idler gears and align the splines on the mainshaft with the splines in the input sun gear. Slide the units together and install the retaining bolts.

16. Slide the 1–2 synchronizer forward into the 2nd gear. Install the shift forks into the grooves of the synchronizers. Place the side cover with a gasket on the transmission. Guide the shift forks into the cover and install the bolts.

17. Check the operation of the transmission by manually shifting the transmission into all gears.

Mainshaft

DISASSEMBLY

1. Using snap ring pliers, remove the 3–4 synchronizer assembly retaining ring from front of the mainshaft, then slide the washer, the synchronizer assembly and the synchronizer ring 3rd speed gear from the mainshaft.

2. Spread the rear bearing retainer snap ring and slide the retainer from the mainshaft.

3. Remove the rear bearing-to-mainshaft snap ring.

4. Support the mainshaft under the 2nd gear and press the mainshaft from the rear bearing, the 1st gear and sleeve, the 1–2 synchronizer assembly and the 2nd gear.

ASSEMBLY

1. At the rear of mainshaft, assemble the 2nd speed gear with the hub of the gear facing the rear of the shaft.

2. Install the 1st–2nd synchronizer assembly (sliding the synchronizer sleeve taper toward the rear, the hub to the front) on the mainshaft together with a synchronizer ring on both sides of the synchronizer assemblies.

3. Position the 1st gear sleeve on the shaft and press the sleeve onto the mainshaft until the 2nd gear, the synchronizer assembly and the sleeve bottom against the shoulder of the mainshaft.

4. Install the 1st speed gear (with the hub facing the front) and support the inner race, then press the rear bearing onto the mainshaft with the snap ring groove toward the front of the case.

5. Install the spacer and the new snap ring (thickest one that will fit) in the mainshaft behind the rear bearing.

6. Install the 3rd speed gear (the hub to the front of the case) and the 3rd speed gear synchronizing ring (with the notches to the front of the case).

7. Install the 3rd–4th speed gear synchronizer assembly (hub and sliding sleeve) with the taper facing the front.

NOTE: Make sure that the keys in hub correspond to the notches in the 3rd speed gear synchronizing ring.

8. Install the new snap ring (the thickest that will fit) in the groove of the mainshaft in front of the 3rd–4th speed synchronizer assembly.

9. Install the rear bearing retainer (Reverse housing) over the end of the mainshaft. Spread the snap ring to drop around the rear bearing, then release the snap ring when it aligns with the groove in the rear bearing.

Countergear

DISASSEMBLY

1. Remove the dummy shaft or the

1. Overdrive Valve Body GASKET
2. Overdrive Valve Body Spacer PLATE
3. Overdrive Valve BODY ASSEMBLY
4. Steel BALL
5. Overdrive Oil Screen TUBE

6. Overdrive Oil Screen Tube "O" RING
7. Overdrive Throt. Valve Lvr. CAM
8. Overdrive Throt. Valve LEVER
9. Overdrive Throt. Valve Lvr. STOP
10. Overdrive Throt. Valve Lvr. BOLT
11. Overdrive Throt. Valve Cable CLIP
12. Overdrive Throt. Valve Lvr. Stop WASHER
13. Overdrive Valve Body BOLT
14. Hex BOLT
15. Hex BOLT
    Hex BOLT
16. Overdrive Valve Body Throt. Valve CABLE
17. End PLUG
18. Overdrive Oil Pump "O" RING
19. Modulator SPOOL
20. Modulator SPRING
21. Piston BUSHING
22. Modulator PISTON
23. Shift SPRING
24. Shift SPOOL
25. Overdrive Valve Body SOLENOID

26. Overdrive Valve Body Solenoid Bolt WASHER
27. Overdrive Valve Body Solenoid BOLT
28. PIN
29. Relief SPOOL
30. Inner Relief SPRING
31. Outer Relief SPRING
32. Press Overdrive Valve Body SWITCH
33. Overdrive Piston Exh. Chk. Valve Ball SPRING
34. Overdrive Oil Cooler By-Pass CONNECTOR
35. Overdrive Oil Cooler Valve Conn. "O" RING
36. Overdrive Oil Cooler Chk. Valve SPRING
37. Cooler Valve SPOOL
38. Overdrive Oil Cooler VALVE
39. Overdrive Oil Cooler Valve "O" RING
40. Oil Cooler FITTING
41. Overdrive Oil Cooler TUBE
42. Overdrive Oil Cooler Valve Bolt Lk. WASHER
43. Overdrive Oil Cooler Valve BOLT

Exploded view of the valve body—Type Six

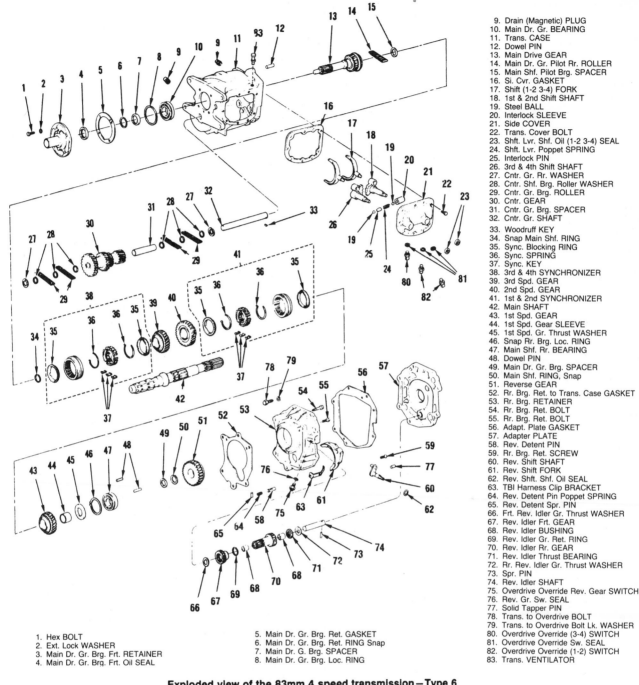

9. Drain (Magnetic) PLUG
10. Main Dr. Gr. BEARING
11. Trans. CASE
12. Dowel PIN
13. Main Drive GEAR
14. Main Dr. Gr. Pilot Rr. ROLLER
15. Main Shf. Pilot Brg. SPACER
16. Si. Cvr. GASKET
17. Shift (1-2 3-4) FORK
18. 1st & 2nd Shift SHAFT
19. Steel BALL
20. Interlock SLEEVE
21. Side COVER
22. Trans. Cover BOLT
23. Shft. Lvr. Shf. Oil (1-2 3-4) SEAL
24. Shft. Lvr. Poppet SPRING
25. Interlock PIN
26. 3rd & 4th Shift SHAFT
27. Cntr. Gr. Rr. WASHER
28. Cntr. Shf. Brg. Roller WASHER
29. Cntr. Gr. Brg. ROLLER
30. Cntr. GEAR
31. Cntr. Gr. Brg. SPACER
32. Cntr. Gr. SHAFT
33. Woodruff KEY
34. Snap Main Shf. RING
35. Sync. Blocking RING
36. Sync. SPRING
37. Sync. KEY
38. 3rd & 4th SYNCHRONIZER
39. 3rd Spd. GEAR
40. 2nd Spd. GEAR
41. 1st & 2nd SYNCHRONIZER
42. Main SHAFT
43. 1st Spd. GEAR
44. 1st Spd. Gear SLEEVE
45. 1st Spd. Gr. Thrust WASHER
46. Snap Rr. Brg. Loc. RING
47. Main Shf. Rr. BEARING
48. Dowel PIN
49. Main Dr. Gr. Brg. SPACER
50. Main Shf. RING, Snap
51. Reverse GEAR
52. Rr. Brg. Ret. to Trans. Case GASKET
53. Rr. Brg. RETAINER
54. Rr. Brg. Ret. BOLT
55. Rr. Brg. Ret. BOLT
56. Adapt. Plate GASKET
57. Adapter PLATE
58. Rev. Detent PIN
59. Rr. Brg. Ret. SCREW
60. Rev. Shift SHAFT
61. Rev. Shift FORK
62. Rev. Shft. Shf. Oil SEAL
63. TBI Harness Clip BRACKET
64. Rev. Detent Pin Poppet SPRING
65. Rev. Detent Spr. PIN
66. Frt. Rev. Idler Gr. Thrust WASHER
67. Rev. Idler Frt. GEAR
68. Rev. Idler BUSHING
69. Rev. Idler Gr. Ret. RING
70. Rev. Idler Rr. GEAR
71. Rev. Idler Thrust BEARING
72. Rr. Rev. Idler Gr. Thrust WASHER
73. Spr. PIN
74. Rev. Idler SHAFT
75. Overdrive Override Rev. Gear SWITCH
76. Rev. Gr. Sw. SEAL
77. Solid Tapper PIN
78. Trans. to Overdrive BOLT
79. Trans. to Overdrive Bolt Lk. WASHER
80. Overdrive Override (3-4) SWITCH
81. Overdrive Override Sw. SEAL
82. Overdrive Override (1-2) SWITCH
83. Trans. VENTILATOR

1. Hex BOLT
2. Ext. Lock WASHER
3. Main Dr. Gr. Brg. Frt. RETAINER
4. Main Dr. Gr. Brg. Frt. Oil SEAL

5. Main Dr. Gr. Brg. Ret. GASKET
6. Main Dr. Gr. Brg. Ret. RING Snap
7. Main Dr. G. Brg. SPACER
8. Main Dr. Gr. Brg. Loc. RING

Exploded view of the 83mm 4 speed transmission – Type 6

tool No. J-24658 from the countergear.

2. Tip the countergear on end and let the six spacers, the 112 rollers and the roller sleeve slide out of the gear.

ASSEMBLY

1. Install the roller spacer in the countergear (if removed).

2. Insert a dummy shaft or the loading tool No. J-24658 into the countergear.

3. Using heavy grease to retain the

rollers, install the spacer, the 28 rollers, a spacer, the 28 rollers and a spacer in either end of the countergear. Repeat the procedure in the other end of the countergear.

CHECKING COUNTERGEAR END PLAY

1. Rest the transmission case on its side with the side cover opening toward the assembler. Put the countergear tanged thrust washers in

place, retaining them with heavy grease.

NOTE: Make sure the tangs are resting in the notches of the case.

2. Set the countergear in place in the bottom of the case.

3. Position the case to rest on its front face.

4. Lubricate and insert the countershaft (pushing the loading tool No. J-24658 out through the front of the case) until woodruff key slot is in its

installed position (do not install key).

5. Attach a dial indicator and check end play of the countergear. If the end play is greater than 0.025 in., a new thrust washer must be installed.

Synchronizer Keys And Springs

REPLACEMENT

The synchronizer hubs and the sliding sleeves are a selected assembly and should be kept together as originally assembled, but the keys and the two springs may be replaced if worn or broken.

1. If the relation of the hub and the sleeve are not already marked, mark for assembly purposes.

2. Push the hub from the sliding sleeve, the keys will fall free and the springs may be easily removed.

3. Place the springs in position (one on each side of hub) so the keys are engaged by both springs.

NOTE: Place the keys in position and while holding them in place, slide the sleeve onto the hub, aligning the marks made before disassembly.

Drive Gear Bearing Retainer Oil Seal

REPLACEMENT

1. Pry out the old seal.

2. Using a new seal, drive it into the retainer using tool No. J-23096 until it bottoms in bore. Lubricate the I.D. of the seal with transmission lubricant.

Reverse Shifter Shaft And/Or Seal

REPLACEMENT

1. With the Reverse housing removed from case, the Reverse shifter shaft lock pin will already be removed.

2. Carefully drive shifter shaft into the Reverse housing allowing the ball detent to drop into the case. Remove the shaft and the ball detent spring. Remove the O-ring seal from the shaft.

3. Place the ball detent spring into the detent spring hole and start the Reverse shifter shaft into the hole in the boss.

4. Place the detent ball on the spring and while holding the ball down, push the shifter shaft into place and turn until the ball drops into place

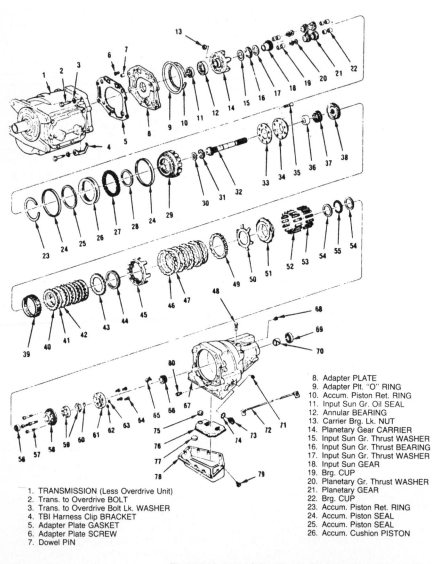

27. Accum. Piston SPRING
28. Accum. Piston SEAL
29. Accum. PISTON
30. Otpt. Shf. Thrust WASHER
31. Otpt. Shf. Thrust BEARING
32. Otpt. SHAFT
33. Planetary Gear Thrust PLATE
34. Clu. Drum PLATE
35. Clu. Drum BOLT
36. Inner RACE
37. Dir. Clu. SPRAG
38. Dir. Clu. HUB
39. Dir. Clu. DRUM
40. Dir. Clu. Inr. Driven PLATE
41. Dir. Clu. PLATE
42. Dir. Clu. Driven PLATE
43. Dir. Clu. Press PLATE
44. Dir. Clu. BEARING
45. Overdrive Clu. PISTON
46. Overdrive Clu. Driven PLATE
47. Overdrive Clu. PLATE
48. Overdrive Vent TUBE
49. Overdrive Clu. Press PLATE
50. Dir. Clu. Thrust WASHER
51. Overdrive Dir. Clu. PISTON
52. Overdrive Dir. Clu. Otr. SPRING
53. Overdrive Dir. Clu. Inr. SPRING
54. Overdrive Dir. Clu. Hub Thrust WASHER
55. Overdrive Dir. Clu. Hub Thrust BEARING
56. Pump Brg. CUP
57. Overdrive Pump & Otpt. Shf. SCREW
58. W/Brg. Overdrive Pump (Gerotor) HOUSING
59. Overdrive Oil (Gerotor) PUMP
60. Oil Pump Drive PIN
61. Pump (Gerotor) SPOOL
62. Overdrive Oil Pump "O" RING
63. Overdrive Oil Pump "O" RING
64. Overdrive Pump Spool (Gerotor) SCREW
65. Speedo Drive Gr. CLIP
66. Speedo Drive GEAR
67. Overdrive CASE
68. Headless Slotted PLUG
69. Overdrive Otpt. Shf. Oil SEAL
70. Case BUSHING
71. Overdrive Vlv. Body Press Sw. WIRE
72. Sq. Hd. Filler PLUG
73. Overdrive Sol. Elec. CONNECTOR
74. Overdrive Sol. Elec. Conn. "O" RING
75. Overdrive Oil Screen Tube GROMMET
76. Overdrive Oil SCREEN
77. Overdrive Oil Pan MAGNET
78. Overdrive Oil PAN
79. Overdrive Oil Pan BOLT
80. Oil Cooler FITTING

8. Adapter PLATE
9. Adapter Plt. "O" RING
10. Accum. Piston Ret. RING
11. Input Sun Gr. Oil SEAL
12. Annular BEARING
13. Carrier Brg. Lk. NUT
14. Planetary Gear CARRIER
15. Input Sun Gr. Thrust WASHER
16. Input Sun Gr. Thrust BEARING
17. Input Sun Gr. Thrust WASHER
18. Input Sun GEAR
19. Brg. CUP
20. Planetary Gr. Thrust WASHER
21. Planetary GEAR
22. Brg. CUP
23. Accum. Piston Ret. RING
24. Accum. Piston SEAL
25. Accum. Piston SEAL
26. Accum. Cushion PISTON

1. TRANSMISSION (Less Overdrive Unit)
2. Trans. to Overdrive BOLT
3. Trans. to Overdrive Bolt Lk. WASHER
4. TBI Harness Clip BRACKET
5. Adapter Plate GASKET
6. Adapter Plate SCREW
7. Dowel PIN

Exploded view of the 83mm 4 speed overdrive unit – Type Six

in the detent on the shaft detent plate.

5. Install the O-ring seal on the shaft.

6. Install the shift fork. Do not drive the shifter shaft lock pin into place until the Reverse housing has been installed on the case.

Reverse Idler Shaft

REPLACEMENT

1. Place a small punch into the front cover hole of the overdrive unit and drive the pin into the shaft until the shaft can be pulled from front cover.

2. Insert a new idler shaft into cover until the hole in the shaft aligns with the hole in the boss.

3. Insert the roll pin into the boss opening and drive the pin into the cover until the shaft is securely locked in place.

Side Cover

ASSEMBLY

Although the service of the side cover is covered here, the transmission does not have to be removed to perform these operations. To remove the side cover in the vehicle, simply drain the transmission, disconnect the electrical leads at the side cover switches, disconnect the 1st–2nd and the 3rd–4th linkage, then remove the attaching bolts.

1. Remove the outer shifter lever nuts and the lockwasher, then pull the levers from the shafts.

2. Carefully push the shifter shafts into the cover, allowing the detent balls to fall free, then remove both shifter shafts.

3. Remove the interlock sleeve, the interlock pin and the poppet spring.

4. Replace the necessary parts and the assembly by reversing the Steps 1–3.

Overdrive Unit

DISASSEMBLY

Cleanliness is an important factor in the overhaul procedures. Before attempting any disassembly operation, the exterior of the transmission should be thoroughly cleaned to prevent the possibility of dirt entering the internal mechanism. During the inspection and the reassembly, the parts should be thoroughly cleaned with cleaning fluid and then air dried. Wiping cloths or rags should not be used to dry parts. Do not use solvents on neoprene seals, composition faced clutch plates or thrust washers. All oil passages should be blown out and checked to make sure that they are not obstructed. The small passages should be checked with a tag wire.

1. Remove the fill plug and drain the oil from the case.

2. Remove the retaining bolt and the bracket from the speedometer sensor and the driven gear. Remove the sensor and the gear.

3. Remove the three $1/8$ in. pipe plugs from the rear of the unit.

4. Using tool No. J-34681, install the pressure plate bolts until they are flush with the case. Turn the bolts two additional turns, by rotating each bolt one turn at a time.

NOTE: This sequence must be followed in order to prevent the pressure plate from cocking and causing damage to the unit.

5. Remove the 4 adapter plate-to-case Allen head bolts.

6. Using a plastic hammer and a small pry bar, remove the adapter plate. Tap the adapter plate to separate it from the case.

NOTE: Do not pry between the case and the adapter plate, damage to the sealing surfaces could occur.

7. Bolt the overdrive unit to tool No. J-34162. Mount the holding fixture to the base plate tool No. J-3389-20.

8. Remove the large snap ring from the O/D unit forward of the accumulator piston.

--------- CAUTION ---------

If pressure is felt at the snap ring, do not remove it. Check to insure that the pressure plate bolts are installed. If the bolts are installed, tighten each bolt (one additional turn) until the pressure is relieved. The pressure plate is under a 1200 lb. spring load. If the bolts are not installed, personal injury could occur.

9. Remove the piston/accumulator assembly. Using an Allen wrench, pry the assembly up evenly by lifting under the flange. Do not pry at or near the seal surface.

10. Remove the carrier and the bearing assembly (includes the input sun and pinion gears) as an assembly.

11. Remove the finger pressure plate.

12. Remove the overdrive clutches, (4) composition, (4) steel and (1) clutch stop plate.

13. Remove the direct clutch plates, (5) composition, (5) steel and (1) steel bearing plate. Measure each selective clutch plate in the direct clutch pack and record the readings.

NOTE: The selective clutch plates are used to control the clutch pack clearance. When replacing the clutch plates, replace each selective clutch plate with one of the same size.

14. Inspect the overdrive and the direct clutch plates as follows:

   a. Compositioned Plates – Dry the plates and inspect for pitting, flaking wear, glazing, cracking, charring and chips or metal particles imbedded in lining. If a plate shows any of the above conditions, replacement is required.

   b. Steel Plates – Wipe the plates dry and check for discoloration. If the surface is smooth and even color, reuse the plate. If severe heat spot discoloration or surface scuffing is indicated, the plate must be replaced.

15. Remove the thrust washer and the bearing from the output sun gear; the thrust washer may stick to the input sun gear hub.

16. Remove pump housing Allen head bolts by rotating the hub to gain access to the bolts.

17. Remove the output shaft assembly (the output sun gear, the sprag clutch, the clutch hub, the gerotor pump and the speedometer drive gear).

18. Remove the pressure plate and the springs by positioning tool No. J-21420-2 on the pressure plate (with the bolt from tool No. J-23327) through the center of the plate. Next position tool No. J-23327 on the rear of the case and install the retaining nut. Remove the three retaining bolts and the tool No. J-34681, from the rear of the case. Loosen the retaining nut on the tool No. J-23327 bolt to relieve the spring pressure.

19. Remove the cooler valve assembly by loosening the nuts on the tube and then the valve-to-case bolts.

20. Remove the 12 oil pan bolts and then pry the pan from the case.

21. Remove the oil filter and the tube from the valve body.

22. Disconnect the T.V. cable from the lever, then remove the cable retaining bolt and the cable assembly.

23. Remove the T.V. lever bolt and the lever from the valve body.

24. Remove the remaining valve body bolts and the valve body with the spacer plate.

NOTE: There are two check balls, one on each side of the spacer plate. One ball is located in the case and the other is spring loaded in the valve body.

ASSEMBLY

1. Install the pressure plate springs into the transmission case pockets.

2. Place the pressure plate on top of the springs and seat the springs into the pockets of pressure plate.

3. Position the plate tool No. J-21420-2 on top of the pressure plate with the bolt from tool No. J-23327 through the center of the plate. Next, position tool No. J-23327 on the rear of the case and install the retaining nut. Tighten the nut until the pressure plate is drawn approximately $\frac{1}{8}$ in. below the step for the overdrive clutch plates. Install the three pressure plate bolts (J-34681). Remove the tools No. J-21420-2 and J-23327 from the case.

4. Install the output shaft assembly into the case. Install the pump bolts and torque.

NOTE: Be sure the O-rings are positioned properly on pump cover before installing the output shaft assembly.

5. Install the thrust bearing on the output sun gear.

6. Install the tanged direct clutch thrust washer with the tabs facing pressure plate.

7. Install the direct clutch thrust bearing and the thrust washer.

NOTE: The thrust washer will have a tooth missing from its outer edge. The side of the thrust washer with the circular grind pattern must face the thrust bearing. The side with the grind pattern can be identified by the notch ground into the tooth.

8. Install one composition clutch disc and then a selective clutch plate.

NOTE: The selective clutch plates come in five sizes (0.080–0.120 in.) and is used to control the clutch pack clearance; a 0.050–0.070 in. clearance must be maintained in the direct clutch pack. Excessive or insufficient amount of clutch travel will cause failure to the clutch plates and discs.

9. Alternate the remaining clutch discs and plates until all five plates and discs are installed.

10. Install the lower half of the carrier assembly onto the direct clutch pack; index the carrier until all of the clutch plates are engaged.

11. Install the steel overdrive stop clutch plate and then alternate with a disc and a plate until the four plates and disc are installed.

12. Install the finger pressure plate.

13. Install the carrier thrust plate with tabs facing the sprag clutch.

14. Install the two pinion gears with the index mark on the gears facing inward or towards each other. Install the other two pinion gears with the index mark 90° from the first two gears.

15. Install the output sun thrust washer into the rear of the input sun gear; use petrolatum to retain the thrust washer to the input sun gear.

16. Install the input sun gear.

NOTE: If the input sun gear spreads the pinion gears when installing, the pinion gears are not indexed properly.

17. Install the selective thrust washer with the washer oil grooves facing the input sun gear.

18. Install the thrust bearing on the input sun gear.

19. Install the carrier thrust washer to the cover; use petrolatum to retain the thrust washer to the cover.

20. Install the four pinion gear thrust washers onto the carrier cover; use petrolatum to retain washers to the cover.

21. Install the carrier cover, the four new nuts and torque.

NOTE: If the pinion gears are not indexed properly, the four cover bolt holes will not align with the lower half of the carrier bolts.

22. Measure the end play for the overdrive unit as follows:

a. Place the straight edge tool No. J-34673 across the face of the overdrive unit. Using the Depth Micrometer tool No. J-34672, measure the distance from the bearing to the top of the bar. Next, using tool No. J-34673 and a 0–1 micrometer, measure the thickness of the bar and subtract this from the reading of the depth micrometer tool No. J-34672 and record this reading.

b. Place the straight edge tool No. J-34673 across the rear of the adapter plate. Using the Depth Micrometer tool No. J-34672, measure the distance from the top of the bar to the adapter plate mounting surface and record the reading.

c. Next, measure the distance from the top of the bar to the bearing seat in the adapter plate and record the reading.

d. Subtract the reading of Step (c) from Step (b) and record the difference.

e. Next, subtract the difference of step (d) from step (a). The difference will be the end play, it should be − 0.003–0.003 in.

NOTE: If the results of your measurements are not within the

specifications, it will be necessary to remove the carrier cover and change the input sun selective thrust washer. The selective thrust washers are available in eight sizes, in 0.005 in. increments, ranging from 0.123–0.158 in.

23. Install the accumulator and the piston assembly; coat the lips of the seals with clean Dexron® II automatic transmission fluid before installing.

24. Install the large snap ring at the front of the overdrive unit.

25. Place the a new seal on the tool No. J-34523 and install it at the front side of the adapter plate.

26. Place seal protector tool No. J-34621 on the input sun gear and install the adapter plate. Apply a light coating of RTV Sealant No. 1052366 around the heads of the adapter plate bolts. Install the adapter plate bolts and torque.

27. Remove the seal protector.

28. Remove the first $\frac{1}{8}$ in. pipe plug from the left side of the overdrive unit. Install the air line fitting tool No. J-34742 into the plug hole and torque.

29. Measure the clutch pack clearance as follows:

a. Loosen the pressure plate bolts (J-34681) evenly until the spring pressure is released.

b. Assemble the Dial Indicator tool No. J-8001 to the rear of the overdrive unit.

c. Apply a minimum of 100 psi to the air line fitting tool No. J-34742 and read the dial indicator, it should be between 0.050–0.070 in.

NOTE: If the reading does not fall within the specification, it will be necessary to disassemble the overdrive unit to change the direct clutch selective clutch plates. The selective clutch plates are available in five sizes, they are in 0.010 in. increments ranging from 0.080–0.120 in. If the clutch pack clearance is within specification, remove the clutch pack retaining bolts (J-34681).

30. Coat the three $\frac{1}{8}$ in. pipe plugs with anti-sieze compound, then install and torque the plugs.

31. Remove the air line adapter tool No. J-34742. Coat the plug with anti seize compound, then install and torque the plug.

32. Install the speedometer gear and the sensor.

33. Using tool No. J-21426, install a new output seal; coat the lip of the seal with Dexron® II transmission fluid.

34. Install the valve body as follows:

a. Install the check ball into the case.

b. Position the gaskets, one on

each side of the separator plate and position the separator plate on the valve body.

c. Position the valve to the case, then install and torque the bolts.

d. Install the T.V. cable, the retaining clip and the bolt, then torque bolt.

e. Install the T.V. lever and torque bolt, then connect T.V. cable to the lever.

f. Install the Throttle Setting Gage tool No. J-34671-1 into the T.V. cable bore on the side of the case. Set the T.V. cable hook onto the high step of the gauge. Place the valve body cam stop as close to the lever as possible, then install and torque the bolt.

g. Set the T.V. cable hook onto the lower step of the gauge. Place the tool No. J-34671-2 between the piston and the solenoid bracket, then adjust the T.V. lever screw/bolt until the bolt makes contact with the cam stop.

35. Install the pickup tube and the oil filter on the valve body.

36. Apply a bead of RTV Sealant No. 1052366 or equivalent to the oil pan flange and assemble it wet. Install the magnet in the oil pan. The bead of RTV should be applied around the inside of the bolt holes. Install the pan bolts and torque.

37. Assemble the Overdrive unit to the Reverse housing. Guide the idler shaft on the adapter plate into the idler gears and align the mainshaft splines with the input sun gear splines. Slide the units together, then install the bolts and torque the bolts.

Valve Body

DISASSEMBLY

NOTE: In the following procedures, use tool No. J-34529 to relieve the valve pressures.

1. Relieve the shift valve pressure, then remove the pin, the spring and the valve.

2. Relieve the pressure relief valve pressure, then remove the pin, the spring and the valve.

3. Relieve the accumulator valve pressure, then remove the pin, the spring, the valve, the plug, the sleeve and the plunger.

4. Disconnect the solenoid electrical lead at the pressure switch, then remove the solenoid bolts, the solenoid and the check ball.

5. Disconnect the other electrical lead at the pressure switch, then remove the switch from the valve body.

6. To assemble, reverse the removal procedures. Coat the components with

clean Dexron® II automatic transmission fluid before assembling.

Output Shaft

DISASSEMBLY

1. Remove the speedometer gear retaining clip and the gear.

2. Remove the pump cover-to-pump housing Allen head bolts and the cover.

3. Mark the pump gears with a grease pencil; the gears must be installed in same direction as removed.

4. Position the output shaft with the splines down, then rotate the pump housing until gears slide out.

5. Remove the drive pin from the output shaft.

6. Remove the pump housing from the output shaft and the thrust washer from the pump housing.

7. Remove the thrust bearing and the washer from the clutch hub and the clutch hub from the output shaft.

NOTE: Record the direction of the hub on the shaft. The oil grooves face the sprag clutch or forward on shaft.

8. Remove the sprag clutch from the output shaft.

NOTE: Record the direction of the sprag clutch; the lip on the sprag clutch cage faces the oil grooves on the clutch hub.

ASSEMBLY

NOTE: Before installation, coat the parts with clean Dexron® II automatic transmission fluid.

1. Install the sprag clutch on the output shaft; the lip on the sprag clutch cage faces rearward or towards the oil grooves on the clutch hub.

2. Install the clutch hub on the output shaft; the oil grooves on the hub face the sprag clutch or forward on the shaft.

3. Install the thrust washer and the thrust bearing on the clutch hub.

4. Install the thrust washer on the pump housing; use petrolatum to retain the thrust washer to the housing.

5. Install the pump housing and the pin to the output shaft.

6. Install the pump gears in the housing; the gears must be installed in same direction as removed.

7. Place the pump cover on the housing, then install the cover-to-pump housing bolts and torque.

8. Install the speedometer gear and the retaining clip on the output shaft.

9. Install new O-rings on the pump; use petrolatum to retain the O-rings to the cover.

Carrier Assembly

DISASSEMBLY

1. Remove the four carrier cover nuts and the cover.

2. Remove the thrust washer, the thrust bearing, the selective washer and the input sun gear.

3. Remove the four pinion gears.

4. Remove the steel thrust plate from the carrier.

5. Clean and inspect the parts, then replace any parts that are cracked, chipped or show excessive wear. The carrier assembly must be reassembled in the transmission case.

Piston/Accumulator Assembly

DISASSEMBLY

1. Remove the accumulator-to-piston snap-ring, the accumulator and the 24 springs from the piston.

2. Remove the two accumulator and the two piston O-rings.

3. To assemble, reverse the removal procedures. Coat the O-rings with clean Dexron® II automatic transmission fluid before installing.

CHILTON TYPE 7

Transaxle case

DISASSEMBLY

1. Remove the speedometer drive gear and the front bearing retainer, then the case cover.

2. Remove the selecting bellcrank assembly bolts, the set bolt, the shift and the selector lever assembly.

3. Move the shift levers into the Lock position, then remove the output shaft lock nut and return the transaxle to the Neutral position.

4. Remove the No. 3 shifting fork bolt and the lock washer. Using two small pry bars and a hammer, tap out the input shaft snap ring.

5. Using tool No. 09602-10010, remove the No. 3 hub sleeve assembly and the shifting fork.

6. Using tool No. 09950-20015, remove the 5th driven gear, then the synchronizer ring, the needle roller bearing and the spacer.

7. Remove the rear bearing retainer and the Reverse idler shaft lock bolt. Using snapring pliers, remove the two

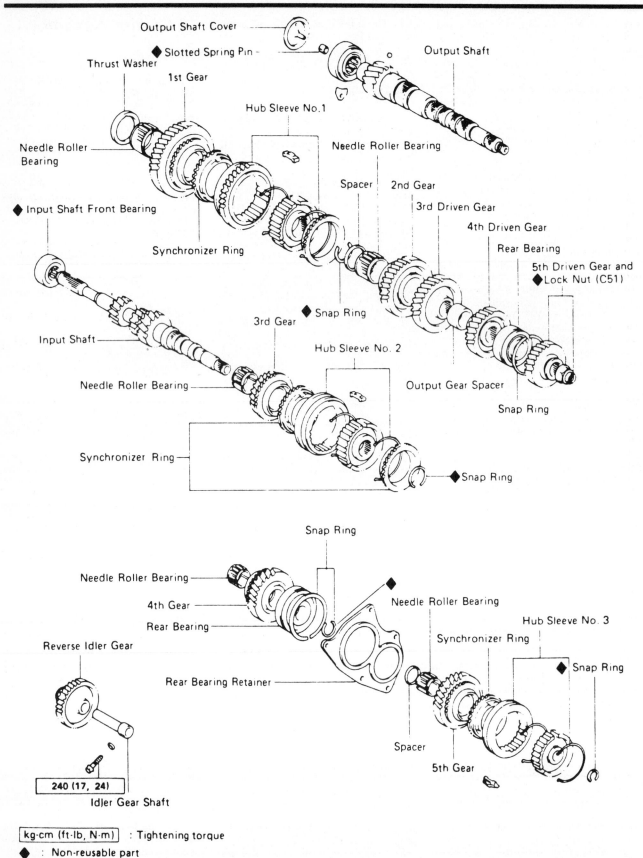

Output Shaft Cover

◆ Slotted Spring Pin

Thrust Washer

1st Gear

Hub Sleeve No.1

Output Shaft

Needle Roller Bearing

Needle Roller Bearing

Spacer

2nd Gear

3rd Driven Gear

4th Driven Gear

Rear Bearing

5th Driven Gear and
◆ Lock Nut (C51)

◆ Input Shaft Front Bearing

Synchronizer Ring

◆ Snap Ring

3rd Gear

Input Shaft

Hub Sleeve No. 2

Needle Roller Bearing

Output Gear Spacer

Snap Ring

Synchronizer Ring

◆ Snap Ring

Snap Ring

Needle Roller Bearing

4th Gear

Rear Bearing

◆ Needle Roller Bearing

Hub Sleeve No. 3

Synchronizer Ring

Reverse Idler Gear

◆ Snap Ring

Rear Bearing Retainer

Spacer

5th Gear

240 (17, 24)

Idler Gear Shaft

kg·cm (ft·lb, N·m) : Tightening torque

◆ : Non-reusable part

Exploded view of the C51 5 speed gear assembly—Type Seven

snap rings.

8. Using two small pry bars and a hammer, tap out the No. 2 shifting fork snap ring.

9. Using tool No. 09313-30021, remove the three plugs and the lock ball assembly. Using a magnet, remove the four seats, the springs and the balls.

10. Remove the 16 case-to-housing bolts and separate the case from the housing, using a plastic hammer.

11. Remove the two Reverse shift arm bracket bolts and the bracket, then pull out the Reverse idler gear and the shaft.

12. Using two small pry bars and a hammer, tap out the 3 snap rings. Remove the shifting fork set bolts, then the No. 2 shifting fork shaft and the head. Using a magnet, remove the two balls.

13. Remove the No. 3 shifting fork shaft and the reverse shifting fork. Remove the No. 1 shifting shaft, then the No. 1 and the No. 2 shifting forks.

14. Remove the input and the output shafts (together), the differential assembly, the magnet and the oil receiver.

15. Using two small pry bars and a hammer, tap the snap ring from the input shaft.

16. Using an arbor press, press the radial ball bearing and the 4th speed gear from the input shaft, then remove the needle roller bearing and the synchronizer ring.

17. Using snap ring pliers, remove the snap ring. Using an arbor press, press the No. 2 hub sleeve, the 3rd gear, the synchronizer ring and the needle roller bearings as an assembly.

18. Using an arbor press, remove the radial ball bearing and the 4th driven gear from the output shaft, then the spacer.

19. Shift the No. 1 hub sleeve into the 1st gear position. Using an arbor press, press the 3rd driven and the 2nd gears from the output shaft, then remove the needle roller bearing, the spacer and the synchronizer ring.

20. Using two small pry bars and a hammer, tap the snap ring from the output shaft.

21. Using an arbor press, press the No. 1 hub sleeve, the 1st gear and the synchronizer ring from the output shaft, then remove the needle roller bearing, the thrust washer and the locking ball.

ASSEMBLY

NOTE: Before installing the roller bearings and other moving parts, coat with a multipurpose grease.

1. Install the clutch hub and the keys onto the No. 2 hub sleeve, then the springs under the keys.

—— **CAUTION** ——

The springs must be positioned so that the end gaps are not aligned with each other.

2. Install the needle roller bearings onto the input shaft and the synchronizer ring onto the No. 2 hub sleeve assembly (align the ring slots with the keys).

3. Using a arbor press, press the 3rd gear and the No. 2 hub sleeve assembly onto the input shaft, then secure with a snap ring (select one which will allow the minimum axial play).

NOTE: Using a feeler gauge, check the 3rd gear thrust clearance; it should be 0.004–0.014 in.

4. Install the synchronizer ring onto the No. 2 hub sleeve assembly (align the ring slots with the keys), then the 4th gear and the needle roller bearing onto the input shaft.

5. Using tool No. 09608-20011 and an arbor press, press the radial ball bearing onto the input shaft, then secure with a snap ring (select one which will allow the minimum axial play).

NOTE: Using a feeler gauge, check the 4th gear thrust clearance; it should be 0.004–0.022 in. If the output shaft was replaced, drive the slotted spring 0.236 in. into the new shaft.

6. Install the clutch hub and the keys onto the No. 1 hub sleeve, then the springs under the keys.

—— **CAUTION** ——

The springs must be positioned so that the end gaps are not aligned with each other.

7. On the output shaft, install the locking ball and fit the thrust washer securely over it. Using an arbor press, press the 1st gear, the synchronizer ring, the hub and the sleeve assembly onto the output shaft, then install the snap ring (select one which will allow the minimum axial play).

NOTE: Using a feeler gauge, check the 1st gear thrust clearance; it should be 0.004–0.016 in.

8. Install the spacer, the synchronizer ring, the needle roller bearing and the 2nd gear. Using an arbor press, press the 3rd driven gear onto the output shaft.

NOTE: Using a feeler gauge, check the 2nd gear thrust clearance; it should be 0.004–0.018 in.

9. Install the spacer. Using an arbor press and the tool No. 09608-12010, press the 4th driven gear and the radial ball bearing onto the output shaft.

10. Install the magnet and the oil receiver (using two bolts).

11. Install the thinnest side bearing shim into the case. Using tool No. 09608-20011, drive the outer side bearing race into the case.

12. Install the differential and the case, then torque the case bolts to 22 ft. lbs. Using tool No. 09564-32011 and a torque meter, measure the bearing preload; it should be 6.9–13.9 inch lbs. (new) or 4.3–8.7 inch lbs. (used).

NOTE: When adjusting the shim thickness, the preload will change 2.6–3.5 inch lbs. with each new shim thickness.

13. Remove the case and install the input and the output shafts at the same time.

  a. Install the No. 1 and No. 2 shift forks into the No. 1 and the No. 2 hub sleeve grooves.

  b. Install the No. 1 fork shaft into the No. 1 shift fork hole.

  c. Install the 2 interlock balls into the Reverse shift fork hole.

  d. Install the No. 3 and the Reverse fork shaft.

  e. Install the No. 2 fork shaft and the shift head.

  f. Install the 3 set bolts and torque to 13 ft. lbs., then install the snap rings.

14. Install the Reverse shift fork pivot into the Reverse shift arm, the Reverse shift arm to the case, the case and torque the bolts to 17 ft. lbs.

15. Install the Reverse idler gear and the shaft.

16. Apply new Three Bond® TB1281 packing material to the case mounting surface, then install the case and torque the 16 bolts to 22 ft. lbs.

NOTE: Apply sealant to the lock balls and the plugs.

17. Install the balls, the springs and the seats into their holes. Using tool No. 09313-30021, torque the three plugs and the lock ball assembly to 18 ft. lbs.

18. Install the Reverse idler gear shaft lock bolt and torque the bolt to 29 ft. lbs. Install the bearing snap rings and the No. 2 fork shaft snap ring. Install the rear bearing retainer and torque the bolts to 14 ft. lbs.

19. Install the spacer, the 5th gear with the needle roller bearing and the synchronizer ring.

20. Install the No. 3 clutch hub into the sleeve, then the keys and the springs. Install the No. 3 hub sleeve assembly with the shift fork.

21. Support the input shaft tip with a spacer (to raise the transaxle assembly). Using tool No. 09612-22011, drive the No. 3 hub sleeve assembly

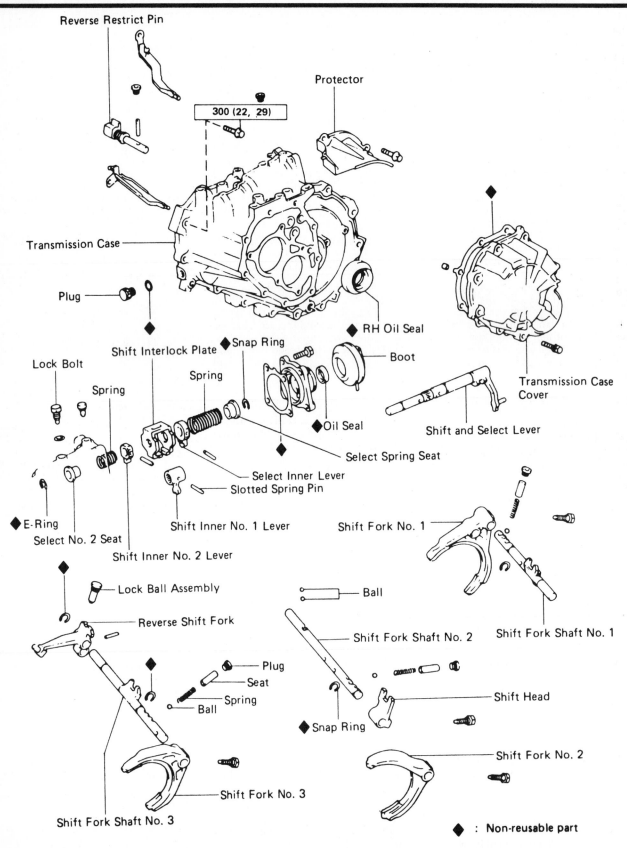

Reverse Restrict Pin

Protector

300 (22, 29)

Transmission Case

Plug

RH Oil Seal

Shift Interlock Plate ◆ Snap Ring

Boot

Lock Bolt

Spring

Spring

Oil Seal

Transmission Case Cover

Shift and Select Lever

Select Spring Seat

Select Inner Lever

Slotted Spring Pin

Shift Inner No. 1 Lever

Shift Fork No. 1

◆ E-Ring

Select No. 2 Seat

Shift Inner No. 2 Lever

Ball

Shift Fork Shaft No. 2

Shift Fork Shaft No. 1

Lock Ball Assembly

Reverse Shift Fork

Plug

Seat

Shift Head

Spring

Ball

◆ Snap Ring

Shift Fork No. 2

Shift Fork No. 3

Shift Fork Shaft No. 3

◆ : Non-reusable part

kg·cm (ft-lb, N·m) : Tightening torque

Exploded view of the C51 5 speed transaxle case—Type Seven

Carburetor Overhaul

11

INDEX

CARBURETOR OVERHAUL
CARS—ALL MODELS

FUNCTIONS

Gasoline is the source of fuel for power in the automobile engine and the carburetor is the mechanism which automatically mixes liquid fuel with air in the correct proportions to provide the desired power output from the engine. The carburetor performs this function by metering, atomizing, and mixing fuel with air flowing through the engine. A carburetor also regulates the volume of air-to-fuel mixture which enters the engine. It is the carburetor's regulation of the mixture flow which gives the operator control of the engine speed.

Metering

The automotive internal combustion engine operates efficiently within a relatively small range of air-to-fuel ratios. It is the function of the carburetor to meter the fuel in exact proportions to the air flowing into the engine, so that the optimum ratio of air-to-fuel is maintained under all operating conditions. Regulations governing exhaust gas emissions have made the proper metering of fuel by the carburetor an increasingly important factor. Too rich a mixture will result in poor economy and increased emissions, while too lean a mixture will result in loss of power and generally poor performance. Carburetors are matched to engines so that metering can be accomplished by using carefully calibrated metering jets which allow fuel to enter the engine at a rate proportional to the engine's ability to draw air.

Atomization

The liquid fuel must be broken up into small particles so that it will more readily mix with air and vaporize. The more contact the fuel has with the air, the better the vaporization. Atomization can be accomplished in two ways; air may be drawn into a stream of fuel which will cause a turbulence and break the solid stream of fuel into smaller particles; or a nozzle can be positioned at the point of highest air velocity in the carburetor and the fuel will be torn into a fine spray as it enters the air stream.

Distribution

The carburetor is the primary device involved in the distribution of fuel to the engine. The more efficiently fuel and air are combined in the carburetor, the smoother the flow of vaporized mixture through the intake manifold to each combustion chamber. Hence, the importance of the carburetor in fuel distribution.

PRINCIPLES

Vacuum

All carburetors operate on the basic principle of pressure difference. Any pressure less than atmospheric pressure is considered vacuum or a low pressure area. In the engine, as the piston moves down on the intake stroke with the intake valve open, a partial vacuum is created in the intake manifold. The farther the piston travels downward, the greater the vacuum created in the manifold. As vacuum increases in the manifold, a difference in pressure occurs between the carburetor and cylinder. The carburetor is positioned in such a way that the high pressure above it, and the vacuum or low pressure above it, and the vacuum or low pressure beneath it, causes air to be drawn through it. Fuel and air always move from high to low pressure areas.

Venturi Principle

To obtain greater pressure drop at the tip of the fuel nozzle so that fuel will flow, the principle of increasing the air velocity to create a low pressure area is used. The device used to increase the velocity of the air flowing through the carburetor is called a venturi. A venturi is a specially designed restriction placed in the air flow. In order for the air to pass through the restriction, it must accelerate causing a pressure drop or vacuum as it passes.

CARBURETOR CIRCUITS

Float Circuit

The float circuit includes the float, float bowl, and a needle valve and seat. This circuit controls the amount of gas allowed to flow into the carburetor. As the fuel level rises, it causes the float to rise which pushes the needle valve into its seat. As soon as the valve and seat make contact, the flow of gas is cut off from the fuel inlet.

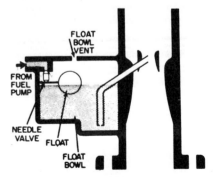

Float circuit

When the level of fuel drops, the float sinks and releases the needle valve from its seat which allows the gas to flow in. In actual operation, the fuel is maintained at practically a constant level. The float tend to hold the needle valve partly closed so that the incoming fuel just balances the fuel being withdrawn.

Idle and Low Speed Circuit

When the throttle is closed or only slightly opened, the air speed is low and practically no vacuum develops in the venturi. This means that the fuel nozzle will not feed. Thus, the carburetor must have another circuit to supply fuel during operation with a closed or slightly opened throttle. This circuit is called the idle and low speed circuit. It consists of passages in which air and gas can flow beneath the throttle plate. With the throttle plate closed, there is high vacuum from the intake manifold. Atmospheric pressure pushes the air/fuel mixture through the passages of the idle and low speed circuit and past the tapered point of the idle adjustment screw, which regulates engine idle mixture volume.

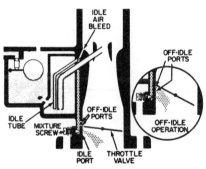

Idle and low speed circuit

High Speed Partial Load Circuit

When the throttle plate is opened sufficiently, there is little difference in vacuum between the upper and lower part of the air horn. Thus, little air/fuel mixture will discharge from the low speed and idle circuit. However, under this condition enough air is moving through the air horn to produce vacuum in the venturi to cause the main nozzle or high speed nozzle to discharge fuel. The circuit from the float bowl to the main nozzle is called the high speed partial load circuit. A

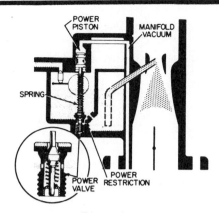

Power circuit

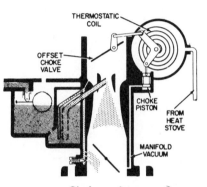

Choke system

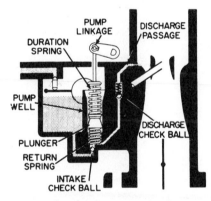

Accelerator pump circuit

nearly constant air/fuel ratio is maintained by this circuit from part to full-throttle.

High Speed Full Power Circuit

For high-speed, full-power, wide open throttle operation, the air/fuel mixture must be enriched; this is done either mechanically or by intake manifold vacuum.

Full Power Circuit (Mechanical)

This circuit includes a metering rod jet and a metering rod. The rod has two steps of different diameters and is attached to the throttle linkage. When the throttle is wide open, the metering rod is lifted bringing the smaller diameter of the rod into the jet. When the throttle is partly closed, the larger diameter of the metering rod is in the jet. This restricts fuel flow to the main nozzle but adequate amounts of fuel do flow for part-throttle operation.

Full Power Circuit (Vacuum)

This circuit is operated by intake manifold vacuum. It includes a vacuum diaphragm or piston linked to a valve. When the throttle is opened so that intake manifold vacuum is reduced, the spring raises the diaphragm or piston. This allows more fuel to flow in, either by lifting a metering rod or by opening a power valve.

Accelerator Pump Circuit

For acceleration, the carburetor must deliver additional fuel. A sudden inrush of air is caused by rapid acceleration or applying full throttle. When the throttle is opened, the pump lever pushes the plunger down and this forces fuel to flow through the accelerator pump circuit and out the pump jet. This fuel enters the air passage through the carburetor to supply additional fuel demands.

Choke

When starting an engine, it is necessary to increase the amount of fuel delivered to the intake manifold. This increase is controlled by the choke. The choke consists of a valve in the top of the air horn controlled mechanically by an automatic device. When the choke valve is closed, only a small amount of air can get past it.

When the engine is cranked, a fairly high vacuum develops in the air horn. This vacuum causes the main nozzle to discharge a heavy stream of fuel. The quantity delivered is sufficient to produce the correct air/fuel mixture needed for starting the engine. The choke is released either manually or by heat from the engine.

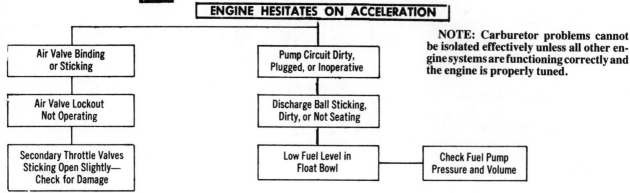

TROUBLE SHOOTING

ENGINE HESITATES ON ACCELERATION

NOTE: Carburetor problems cannot be isolated effectively unless all other engine systems are functioning correctly and the engine is properly tuned.

```
Air Valve Binding
or Sticking
       |
Air Valve Lockout
Not Operating
       |
Secondary Throttle Valves
Sticking Open Slightly—
Check for Damage


Pump Circuit Dirty,
Plugged, or Inoperative
       |
Discharge Ball Sticking,
Dirty, or Not Seating
       |
Low Fuel Level in  ———  Check Fuel Pump
Float Bowl               Pressure and Volume
```

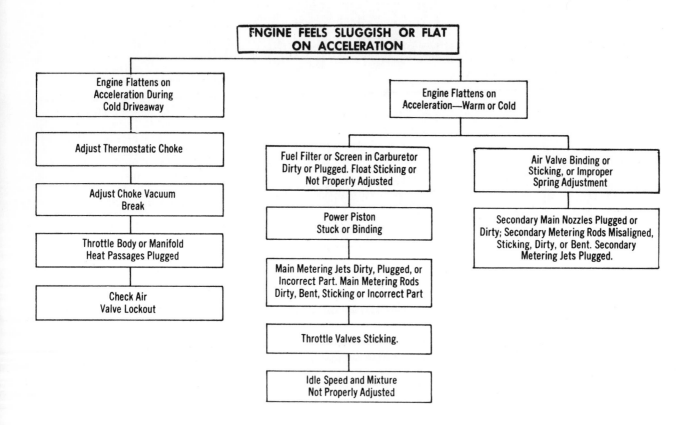

ENGINE FEELS SLUGGISH OR FLAT ON ACCELERATION

```
Engine Flattens on
Acceleration During
Cold Driveaway
       |
Adjust Thermostatic Choke
       |
Adjust Choke Vacuum
Break
       |
Throttle Body or Manifold
Heat Passages Plugged
       |
Check Air
Valve Lockout


Engine Flattens on
Acceleration—Warm or Cold
       |
Fuel Filter or Screen in Carburetor        Air Valve Binding or
Dirty or Plugged. Float Sticking or        Sticking, or Improper
Not Properly Adjusted                      Spring Adjustment
       |                                          |
Power Piston                              Secondary Main Nozzles Plugged or
Stuck or Binding                          Dirty; Secondary Metering Rods Misaligned,
       |                                  Sticking, Dirty, or Bent. Secondary
Main Metering Jets Dirty, Plugged, or     Metering Jets Plugged.
Incorrect Part. Main Metering Rods
Dirty, Bent, Sticking or Incorrect Part
       |
Throttle Valves Sticking.
       |
Idle Speed and Mixture
Not Properly Adjusted
```

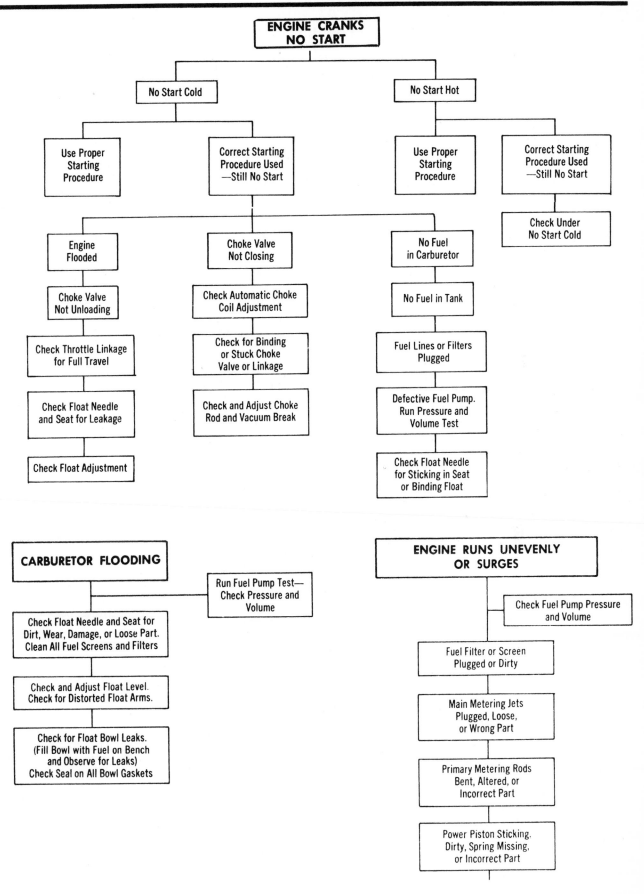

ENGINE CRANKS
NO START

No Start Cold

No Start Hot

Use Proper
Starting
Procedure

Correct Starting
Procedure Used
—Still No Start

Use Proper
Starting
Procedure

Correct Starting
Procedure Used
—Still No Start

Check Under
No Start Cold

Engine
Flooded

Choke Valve
Not Closing

No Fuel
in Carburetor

Choke Valve
Not Unloading

Check Automatic Choke
Coil Adjustment

No Fuel in Tank

Check Throttle Linkage
for Full Travel

Check for Binding
or Stuck Choke
Valve or Linkage

Fuel Lines or Filters
Plugged

Check Float Needle
and Seat for Leakage

Check and Adjust Choke
Rod and Vacuum Break

Defective Fuel Pump.
Run Pressure and
Volume Test

Check Float Adjustment

Check Float Needle
for Sticking in Seat
or Binding Float

CARBURETOR FLOODING

Run Fuel Pump Test—
Check Pressure and
Volume

Check Float Needle and Seat for
Dirt, Wear, Damage, or Loose Part.
Clean All Fuel Screens and Filters

Check and Adjust Float Level.
Check for Distorted Float Arms.

Check for Float Bowl Leaks.
(Fill Bowl with Fuel on Bench
and Observe for Leaks)
Check Seal on All Bowl Gaskets

ENGINE RUNS UNEVENLY
OR SURGES

Check Fuel Pump Pressure
and Volume

Fuel Filter or Screen
Plugged or Dirty

Main Metering Jets
Plugged, Loose,
or Wrong Part

Primary Metering Rods
Bent, Altered, or
Incorrect Part

Power Piston Sticking,
Dirty, Spring Missing,
or Incorrect Part

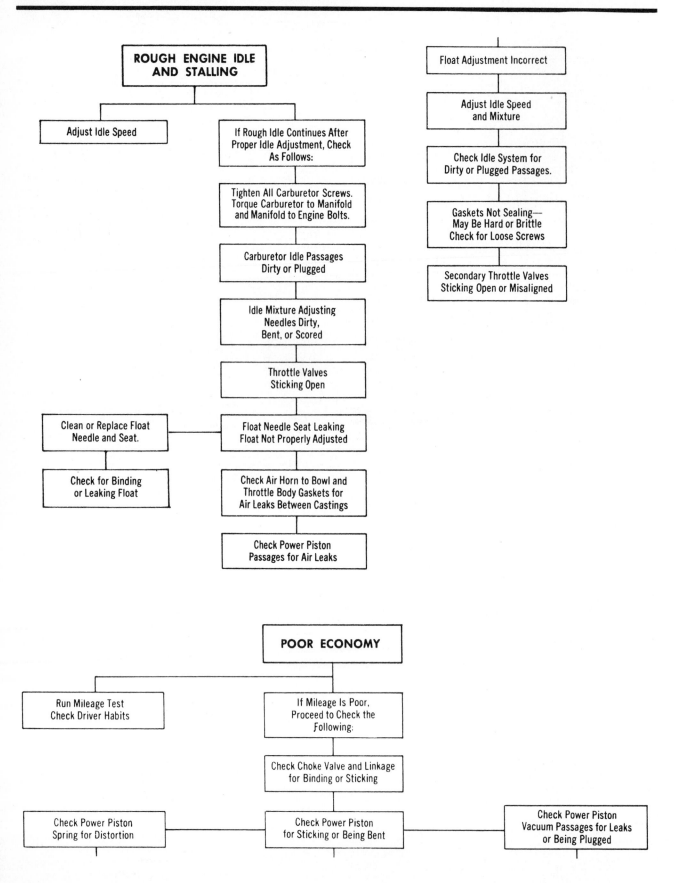

ROUGH ENGINE IDLE AND STALLING

Adjust Idle Speed

If Rough Idle Continues After Proper Idle Adjustment, Check As Follows:

Tighten All Carburetor Screws. Torque Carburetor to Manifold and Manifold to Engine Bolts.

Carburetor Idle Passages Dirty or Plugged

Idle Mixture Adjusting Needles Dirty, Bent, or Scored

Throttle Valves Sticking Open

Clean or Replace Float Needle and Seat.

Float Needle Seat Leaking Float Not Properly Adjusted

Check for Binding or Leaking Float

Check Air Horn to Bowl and Throttle Body Gaskets for Air Leaks Between Castings

Check Power Piston Passages for Air Leaks

Float Adjustment Incorrect

Adjust Idle Speed and Mixture

Check Idle System for Dirty or Plugged Passages.

Gaskets Not Sealing— May Be Hard or Brittle Check for Loose Screws

Secondary Throttle Valves Sticking Open or Misaligned

POOR ECONOMY

Run Mileage Test Check Driver Habits

If Mileage Is Poor, Proceed to Check the Following:

Check Choke Valve and Linkage for Binding or Sticking

Check Power Piston Spring for Distortion

Check Power Piston for Sticking or Being Bent

Check Power Piston Vacuum Passages for Leaks or Being Plugged

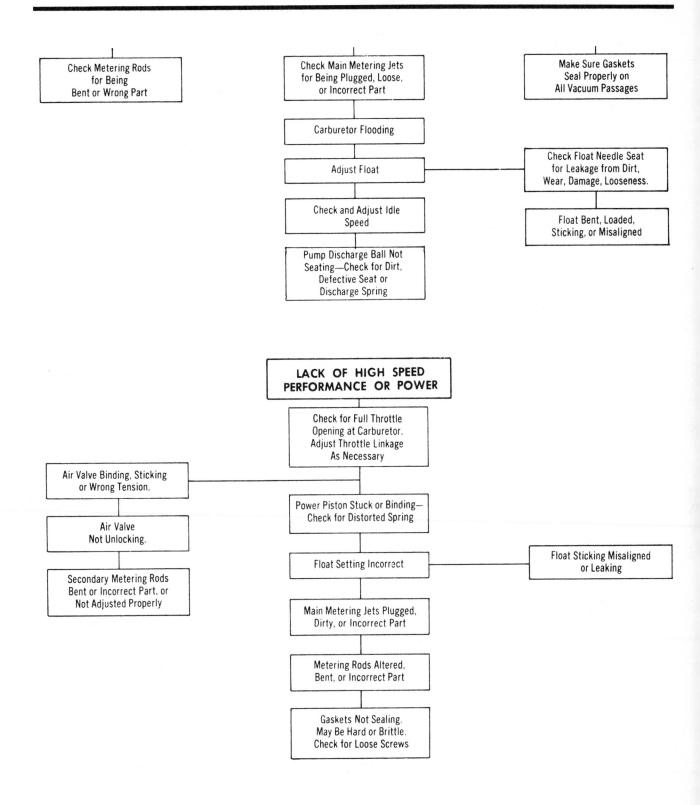

Check Metering Rods
for Being
Bent or Wrong Part

Check Main Metering Jets
for Being Plugged, Loose,
or Incorrect Part

Make Sure Gaskets
Seal Properly on
All Vacuum Passages

Carburetor Flooding

Adjust Float

Check Float Needle Seat
for Leakage from Dirt,
Wear, Damage, Looseness.

Check and Adjust Idle
Speed

Float Bent, Loaded,
Sticking, or Misaligned

Pump Discharge Ball Not
Seating—Check for Dirt,
Defective Seat or
Discharge Spring

**LACK OF HIGH SPEED
PERFORMANCE OR POWER**

Check for Full Throttle
Opening at Carburetor.
Adjust Throttle Linkage
As Necessary

Air Valve Binding, Sticking
or Wrong Tension.

Power Piston Stuck or Binding—
Check for Distorted Spring

Air Valve
Not Unlocking.

Float Setting Incorrect

Float Sticking Misaligned
or Leaking

Secondary Metering Rods
Bent or Incorrect Part, or
Not Adjusted Properly

Main Metering Jets Plugged,
Dirty, or Incorrect Part

Metering Rods Altered,
Bent, or Incorrect Part

Gaskets Not Sealing.
May Be Hard or Brittle.
Check for Loose Screws

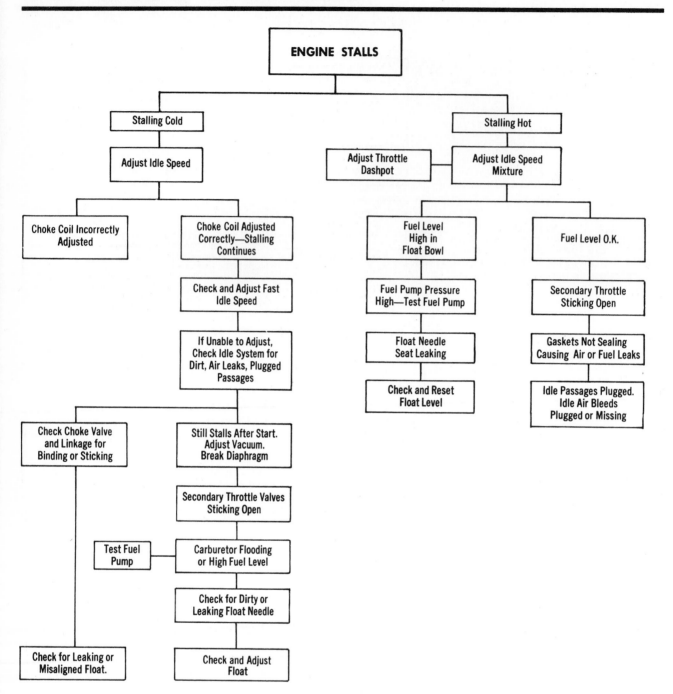

ENGINE STALLS

Stalling Cold

Adjust Idle Speed

Choke Coil Incorrectly Adjusted

Choke Coil Adjusted Correctly—Stalling Continues

Check and Adjust Fast Idle Speed

If Unable to Adjust, Check Idle System for Dirt, Air Leaks, Plugged Passages

Check Choke Valve and Linkage for Binding or Sticking

Still Stalls After Start. Adjust Vacuum. Break Diaphragm

Secondary Throttle Valves Sticking Open

Test Fuel Pump

Carburetor Flooding or High Fuel Level

Check for Dirty or Leaking Float Needle

Check for Leaking or Misaligned Float.

Check and Adjust Float

Stalling Hot

Adjust Throttle Dashpot

Adjust Idle Speed Mixture

Fuel Level High in Float Bowl

Fuel Level O.K.

Fuel Pump Pressure High—Test Fuel Pump

Secondary Throttle Sticking Open

Float Needle Seat Leaking

Gaskets Not Sealing Causing Air or Fuel Leaks

Check and Reset Float Level

Idle Passages Plugged. Idle Air Bleeds Plugged or Missing

Model 5210-C

The Holley 5210-C is a progressive two barrel carburetor with an automatic choke system which is activated by a water heated thermostatic coil. An electrically heated choke is used on most later models. It also has an exhaust gas recirculation system with the valve located in the intake manifold. It is used on 1980 Chevettes (USA). 1980–86 Chevettes (Canada).

FLOAT LEVEL

1. With the carburetor air horn inverted, and the float tang resting lightly on the inlet needle, insert the specified gauge between the air horn and the float.
2. Bend the float tang if an adjustment is needed.

FAST IDLE CAM ADJUSTMENT

1. Place the fast idle screw on the second step of the fast idle cam and against the shoulder of the high step.
2. Place the specified drill or gauge on the down side of the choke plate.
3. To adjust, bend the choke lever tang.

CHOKE PLATE PULLDOWN (VACUUM BREAK) ADJUSTMENT

1980–86 Models

1. Attach a hand vacuum pump to the vacuum break diaphragm; apply vacuum and seat the diaphragm.
2. Push the fast idle cam lever down to close the choke plate.
3. Take any slack out of the linkage in the open choke position.
4. Insert the specified gauge between the lower edge of the choke plate and the air horn wall.
5. If the clearance is incorrect, turn the vacuum break adjusting screw, located in the break housing, to adjust.

CHOKE UNLOADER ADJUSTMENT

1. Position the throttle lever at the wide open position.
2. Insert a gauge of the size specified in the chart between the lower edge of the choke valve and the air horn wall.
3. Bend the unloader tang for adjustment.

FAST IDLE SPEED ADJUSTMENT

1. The engine must be at normal operating temperature with the air cleaner off.
2. With the engine running, position the fast idle screw on the high step of the cam for GM cars, or on the second step against the shoulder of the high step for AMC cars. Plug the EGR Port on the carburetor.
3. Adjust the speed by turning the fast idle screw.

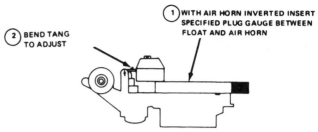

2 BEND TANG TO ADJUST

1 WITH AIR HORN INVERTED INSERT SPECIFIED PLUG GAUGE BETWEEN FLOAT AND AIR HORN

5210-C Float level adjustment

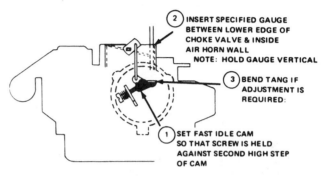

2 INSERT SPECIFIED GAUGE BETWEEN LOWER EDGE OF CHOKE VALVE & INSIDE AIR HORN WALL NOTE: HOLD GAUGE VERTICAL

3 BEND TANG IF ADJUSTMENT IS REQUIRED:

1 SET FAST IDLE CAM SO THAT SCREW IS HELD AGAINST SECOND HIGH STEP OF CAM

5210-C Fast idle cam adjustment

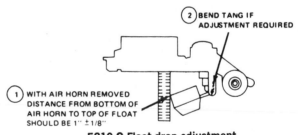

2 BEND TANG IF ADJUSTMENT REQUIRED

1 WITH AIR HORN REMOVED DISTANCE FROM BOTTOM OF AIR HORN TO TOP OF FLOAT SHOULD BE 1″ ±1/8″

5210-C Float drop adjustment

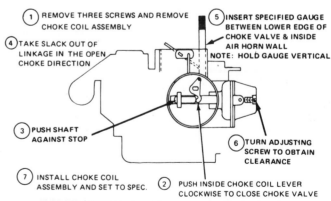

1 REMOVE THREE SCREWS AND REMOVE CHOKE COIL ASSEMBLY

4 TAKE SLACK OUT OF LINKAGE IN THE OPEN CHOKE DIRECTION

5 INSERT SPECIFIED GAUGE BETWEEN LOWER EDGE OF CHOKE VALVE & INSIDE AIR HORN WALL NOTE: HOLD GAUGE VERTICAL

3 PUSH SHAFT AGAINST STOP

6 TURN ADJUSTING SCREW TO OBTAIN CLEARANCE

7 INSTALL CHOKE COIL ASSEMBLY AND SET TO SPEC.

2 PUSH INSIDE CHOKE COIL LEVER CLOCKWISE TO CLOSE CHOKE VALVE

5210-C Vacuum break (choke plate pulldown) adjustment

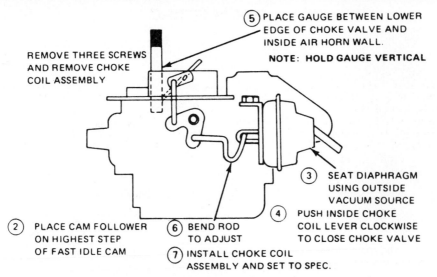

⑤ PLACE GAUGE BETWEEN LOWER EDGE OF CHOKE VALVE AND INSIDE AIR HORN WALL.

NOTE: HOLD GAUGE VERTICAL

REMOVE THREE SCREWS AND REMOVE CHOKE COIL ASSEMBLY

③ SEAT DIAPHRAGM USING OUTSIDE VACUUM SOURCE

② PLACE CAM FOLLOWER ON HIGHEST STEP OF FAST IDLE CAM

⑥ BEND ROD TO ADJUST

④ PUSH INSIDE CHOKE COIL LEVER CLOCKWISE TO CLOSE CHOKE VALVE

⑦ INSTALL CHOKE COIL ASSEMBLY AND SET TO SPEC.

5210-C Secondary vacuum break adjustment

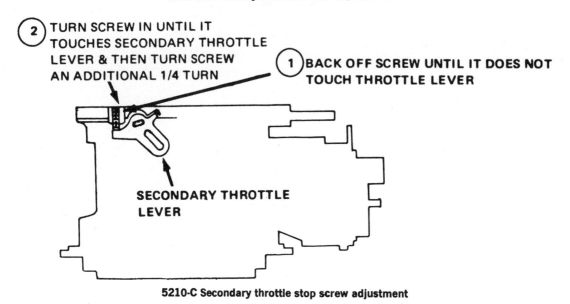

② TURN SCREW IN UNTIL IT TOUCHES SECONDARY THROTTLE LEVER & THEN TURN SCREW AN ADDITIONAL 1/4 TURN

① BACK OFF SCREW UNTIL IT DOES NOT TOUCH THROTTLE LEVER

SECONDARY THROTTLE LEVER

5210-C Secondary throttle stop screw adjustment

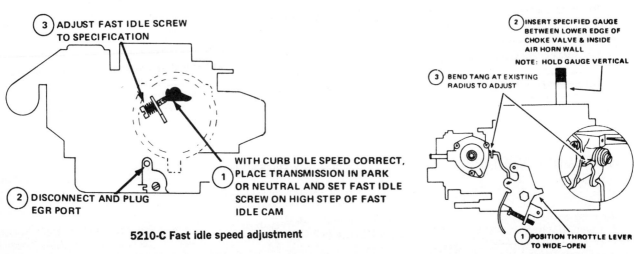

③ ADJUST FAST IDLE SCREW TO SPECIFICATION

② DISCONNECT AND PLUG EGR PORT

① WITH CURB IDLE SPEED CORRECT, PLACE TRANSMISSION IN PARK OR NEUTRAL AND SET FAST IDLE SCREW ON HIGH STEP OF FAST IDLE CAM

5210-C Fast idle speed adjustment

② INSERT SPECIFIED GAUGE BETWEEN LOWER EDGE OF CHOKE VALVE & INSIDE AIR HORN WALL

NOTE: HOLD GAUGE VERTICAL

③ BEND TANG AT EXISTING RADIUS TO ADJUST

① POSITION THROTTLE LEVER TO WIDE-OPEN

5210-C Choke unloader adjustment

MODEL 5210-C
Chevrolet Chevette

Year	Carb. Part No. ① ②	Float Level (Dry) (in.)	Fast Idle Cam (in.)	Secondary Vacuum Break (in.)	Fast Idle Setting (rpm)	Choke Unloader (in.)	Choke Setting
'80	All	0.50	0.110	0.120	2500	0.350	Fixed
'81	14032301	0.50	0.110	0.120	2500	0.350	Fixed
	14032302	0.50	0.110	0.120	2500	0.275	Fixed
'82	14043392	0.50	0.110	0.120	2500	0.275	Fixed
	14043393	0.50	0.110	0.120	2500	0.350	Fixed
'83 (Canada)	All	0.50	0.090	③	④	0.275	Fixed
'84-'85 (Canada)	14076317	0.50	0.110	⑤	④	0.350	Fixed
	14076318	0.50	0.110	⑤	④	0.300	Fixed
	14076319	0.50	0.120	⑥	④	0.350	Fixed
'86 (Canada)	14076393	0.50	0.100	⑤	④	0.325	Fixed
	14076394	0.50	0.090	⑤	④	0.275	Fixed

① Located on tag attached to the carburetor, or on the casting or choke plate
② GM identification numbers are used in place of the Holley numbers
③ Hot: 0.280
   Cold: 0.100
④ See underhood sticker
⑤ Hot: 0.250
   Cold: 0.100
⑥ Hot: 0.290
   Cold: 0.110

Model 6500 and 6510-C

The 6500 is a Holley-Weber Unit used on 1980 and later Pinto and Bobcat California models with the 2.3L engine. It is also used on all 1981–82 models with the 2.3L engine equipped with the Feedback Electronic Engine Control System. With the exception of an externally variable fuel metering system in place of the fuel enrichment valve, it is identical to the model Motorcraft 5200. For all adjustments, refer to this listing in the Motorcraft section of Carburetor Unit Repair.

The 6510-C is used on the Chevette and T-1000. This is a staged, two barrel unit which incorporates a feedback air/fuel metering system.

For further information on feedback carburetors, please refer to *Chilton's Guide To Fuel Injection And Feedback Carburetors.*

VACUUM BREAK ADJUSTMENT

1980–83 Models

1. Attach a hand vacuum pump to

3 TAKE SLACK OUT OF LINKAGE IN THE OPEN CHOKE DIRECTION

4 INSERT SPECIFIED GAGE BETWEEN LOWER EDGE OF CHOKE VALVE & INSIDE AIR HORN WALL (HOLD GAGE VERTICAL)

2 PUSH FAST IDLE CAM LEVER DOWN (CLOCKWISE) TO CLOSE CHOKE VALVE

5 TURN ADJUSTING SCREW TO OBTAIN CLEARANCE

1 APPLY EXTERNAL VACUUM SOURCE AND SEAT VACUUM BREAK DIAPHRAGM

Vacuum break adjustment, 1980 and later—Holley 6510C

the vacuum break diaphragm. Apply vacuum until the diaphragm is seated.

2. Push the fast idle cam lever down to close the choke plate.

3. Take the slack out of the linkage in the open choke position.

4. Insert the specified gauge between the lower edge of the choke plate and the air horn wall.

5. If the clearance is incorrect, turn

the screw in the end of the diaphragm to adjust.

FAST IDLE CAM ADJUSTMENT

1. Set the fast idle cam so that the screw is on the second highest step of the fast idle cam.

2. Insert the specified gauge between the lower edge of the choke valve and the air horn wall.

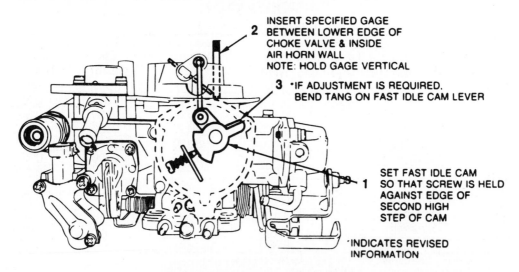

2 INSERT SPECIFIED GAGE BETWEEN LOWER EDGE OF CHOKE VALVE & INSIDE AIR HORN WALL
NOTE: HOLD GAGE VERTICAL

3 *IF ADJUSTMENT IS REQUIRED, BEND TANG ON FAST IDLE CAM LEVER

1 SET FAST IDLE CAM SO THAT SCREW IS HELD AGAINST EDGE OF SECOND HIGH STEP OF CAM

*INDICATES REVISED INFORMATION

Fast idle cam adjustment—Holley 6510C

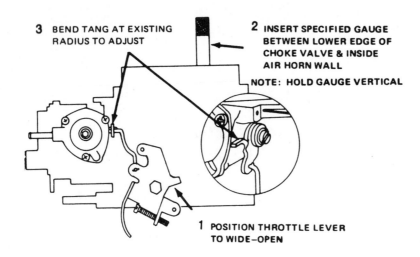

3 BEND TANG AT EXISTING RADIUS TO ADJUST

2 INSERT SPECIFIED GAUGE BETWEEN LOWER EDGE OF CHOKE VALVE & INSIDE AIR HORN WALL

NOTE: HOLD GAUGE VERTICAL

1 POSITION THROTTLE LEVER TO WIDE—OPEN

Choke unloader adjustment

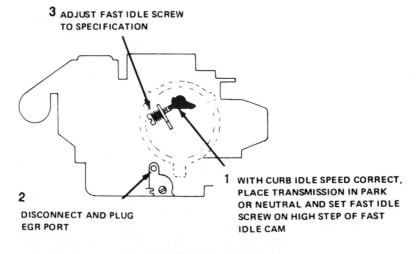

3 ADJUST FAST IDLE SCREW TO SPECIFICATION

2 DISCONNECT AND PLUG EGR PORT

1 WITH CURB IDLE SPEED CORRECT, PLACE TRANSMISSION IN PARK OR NEUTRAL AND SET FAST IDLE SCREW ON HIGH STEP OF FAST IDLE CAM

Fast idle speed adjustment

MODEL 6510-C
General Motors Corporation

Year	Part Number	Vacuum Break Adjustment (in.)	Fast Idle Cam Adjustment (in.)	Unloader Adjustment (in.)	Fast Idle Adjustment (rpm)	Float Level Adjustment (in.)	Choke Setting
'81	14004768	.300	.130	.350	①	.500	Fixed
	14004769	.300	.130	.350	①	.500	Fixed
	14004770	.300	.130	.350	①	.500	Fixed
	14004771	.300	.130	.350	①	.500	Fixed
	14004777	.300	.130	.350	①	.500	Fixed
'82	14032364	.270	.080	.350	①	.500	Fixed
	14032365	.270	.080	.350	①	.500	Fixed
	14032366	.270	.080	.350	①	.500	Fixed
	14032367	.270	.080	.350	①	.500	Fixed
	14032368	.270	.080	.350	①	.500	Fixed
	14032369	.270	.080	.350	①	.500	Fixed
	14032370	.270	.080	.350	①	.500	Fixed
	14032371	.270	.080	.350	①	.500	Fixed
	14033392	.270	.080	.350	①	.500	Fixed
	14033393	.270	.080	.350	①	.500	Fixed
	14047072	.270	.080	.350	①	.500	Fixed
'83	14048827	.270	.080	.350	①	.500	Fixed
	14048828	.300	.080	.350	①	.500	Fixed
	14048829	.270	.080	.350	①	.500	Fixed
'84–'86	14068690	.270	.080	.350	①	.500	Fixed
	14068691	.270	.080	.350	①	.500	Fixed
	14068692	.300	.080	.350	①	.500	Fixed
	14076363	.300	.080	.350	①	.500	Fixed

① See underhood decal

ROCHESTER CARBURETORS

Angle Degree Tool

An angle degree tool is recommended by Rochester Products Division, for use to confirm adjustments to the choke valve and related linkages on their late model two and four barrel carburetors, in place of the plug type gauges. Decimal and degree conversion charts are provided for use by technicians who have access to an angle gauge and not plug gauges. It must be remembered that the relationship between the decimal and the angle readings are not exact, due to manufacturers tolerances.

To use the angle gauge, rotate the degree scale until zero (0) is opposite the pointer. With the choke valve completely closed, place the gauge magnet squarely on top of the choke valve and rotate the bubble until it is centered. Make the necessary adjustments to have the choke valve at the specified degree angle opening as read from the degree angle tool.

NOTE: The carburetor may be off the engine for adjustments. Be sure the carburetor is held firmly during the use of the angle gauge.

Model Identification

General Motors Rochester carburetors are identified by their model number. The first number indicates the number of barrels, while one of the last letters indicates the type of choke used. These are V for the manifold mounted choke coil, C for the choke coil mounted on the carburetor, and E for electric choke, also mounted on the carburetor. Model numbers ending in A indicate an altitude-compensating carburetor.

Models 2SE and E2SE

The Rochester 2SE and E2SE Varajet II carburetors are two barrel, two stage downdraft units. Most carburetor components are aluminum, although a zinc choke housing is used on four cylinder engines installed in 1980 models. The E2SE is used both in conventional installations and in the Computer Controlled Catalytic Converter System. In that installation the E2SE is equipped with an electrically operated mixture control solenoid, controlled by the Electronic Control Module. The 2SE and E2SE are also used on the AMC four cylinder in 1980–83.

For further information on feedback carburetors, please refer to *Chilton's Guide To Fuel Injection And Feedback Carburetors.*

FLOAT ADJUSTMENT

1. Remove the air horn from the throttle body.
2. Use your fingers to hold the retainer in place, and to push the float down into light contact with the needle.
3. Measure the distance from the toe of the float (furtherest from the hinge) to the top of the carburetor (gasket removed).

ANGLE DEGREE TO DECIMAL CONVERSION
Model 4MV Carburetor

Angle Degrees	Decimal Equiv. Top of Valve	Angle Degrees	Decimal Equiv. Top of Valve
5	.019	33	.158
6	.022	34	.164
7	.026	35	.171
8	.030	36	.178
9	.034	37	.184
10	.038	38	.190
11	.042	39	.197
12	.047	40	.204
13	.051	41	.211
14	.056	42	.217
15	.060	43	.225
16	.065	44	.231
17	.070	45	.239
18	.075	46	.246
19	.080	47	.253
20	.085	48	.260
21	.090	49	.268
22	.095	50	.275
23	.101	51	.283
24	.106	52	.291
25	.112	53	.299
26	.117	54	.306
27	.123	55	.314
28	.128	56	.322
29	.134	57	.329
30	.140	58	.337
31	.146	59	.345
32	.152	60	.353

PLUGGING AIR BLEED HOLES

PUMP CUP OR VALVE STEM SEAL

TAPE HOLE IN TUBE

TAPE END OF COVER

Vacuum break information—E2SE

4. To adjust, remove the float and gently bend the arm to specification. After adjustment, check the float alignment in the chamber.

NOTE: Some models have a float stabilizer spring. If used, remove the spring with float. Use care when removing.

PUMP ADJUSTMENT

1. With the throttle closed and the fast idle screw off the steps of the fast idle cam, measure the distance from the air horn casting to the top of the pump stem.

2. To adjust, remove the retaining screw and washer and remove the pump lever. Bend the end of the lever to correct the stem height. Do not twist the lever or bend it sideways.

3. Install the lever, washer and screw and check the adjustment. When correct, open and close the throttle a few times to check the linkage movement and alignment.

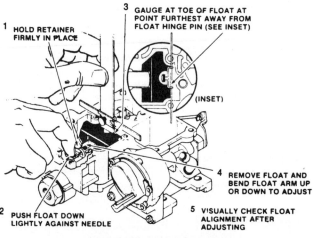

1 HOLD RETAINER FIRMLY IN PLACE

3 GAUGE AT TOE OF FLOAT AT POINT FURTHEST AWAY FROM FLOAT HINGE PIN (SEE INSET)

(INSET)

2 PUSH FLOAT DOWN LIGHTLY AGAINST NEEDLE

4 REMOVE FLOAT AND BEND FLOAT ARM UP OR DOWN TO ADJUST

5 VISUALLY CHECK FLOAT ALIGNMENT AFTER ADJUSTING

2SE, E2SE float adjustment

NOTE: No pump adjustment is required on 1981 and later models.

ANGLE DEGREE TO DECIMAL CONVERSION
Model M2MC, M2ME and M4MC Carburetor

Angle Degrees	Decimal Equiv. Top of Valve	Angle Degrees	Decimal Equiv. Top of Valve
5	.023	33	.203
6	.028	34	.211
7	.033	35	.220
8	.038	36	.227
9	.043	37	.234
10	.049	38	.243
11	.054	39	.251
12	.060	40	.260
13	.066	41	.269
14	.071	42	.277
15	.077	43	.287
16	.083	44	.295
17	.090	45	.304
18	.096	46	.314
19	.103	47	.322
20	.110	48	.332
21	.117	49	.341
22	.123	50	.350
23	.129	51	.360
24	.136	52	.370
25	.142	53	.379
26	.149	54	.388
27	.157	55	.400
28	.164	56	.408
29	.171	57	.418
30	.179	58	.428
31	.187	59	.439
32	.195	60	.449

NOTE: ON MODELS USING A CLIP TO RETAIN PUMP ROD IN PUMP LEVER, NO PUMP ADJUSTMENT IS REQUIRED. ON MODELS USING THE "CLIPLESS" PUMP ROD, THE PUMP ADJUSTMENT SHOULD NOT BE CHANGED FROM ORIGINAL FACTORY SETTING UNLESS GAUGING SHOWS OUT OF SPECIFICATION. THE PUMP LEVER IS MADE FROM HEAVY DUTY, HARDENED STEEL MAKING BENDING DIFFICULT. DO NOT REMOVE PUMP LEVER FOR BENDING UNLESS ABSOLUTELY NECESSARY.

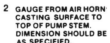

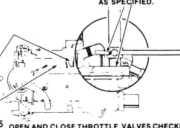

1 THROTTLE VALVES COMPLETELY CLOSED. MAKE SURE FAST IDLE SCREW IS OFF STEPS OF FAST IDLE CAM.

2 GAUGE FROM AIR HORN CASTING SURFACE TO TOP OF PUMP STEM. DIMENSION SHOULD BE AS SPECIFIED.

3 IF NECESSARY TO ADJUST, REMOVE PUMP LEVER RETAINING SCREW AND WASHER AND REMOVE PUMP LEVER BY ROTATING LEVER TO REMOVE FROM PUMP ROD. PLACE LEVER IN A VISE, PROTECTING LEVER FROM DAMAGE, AND BEND END OF LEVER (NEAREST NECKED DOWN SECTION).

NOTE: DO NOT BEND LEVER IN A SIDEWAYS OR TWISTING MOTION.

5 OPEN AND CLOSE THROTTLE VALVES CHECKING LINKAGE FOR FREEDOM OF MOVEMENT AND OBSERVING PUMP LEVER ALIGNMENT.

4 REINSTALL PUMP LEVER, WASHER AND RETAINING SCREW. RECHECK PUMP ADJUSTMENT ① AND ②. TIGHTEN RETAINING SCREW SECURELY AFTER THE PUMP ADJUSTMENT IS CORRECT.

2SE, E2SE pump adjustment

FAST IDLE ADJUSTMENT

1. Set the ignition timing and curb idle speed, and disconnect and plug hoses as directed on the emission control decal.
2. Place the fast idle screw on the highest step of the cam.
3. Start the engine and adjust the engine speed to specification with the fast idle screw.

NOTE: On models using a clip to retain pump rod in pump lever, no pump adjustment is required. On models using the "CLIPLESS" pump rod, the pump rod adjustment should not be changed from the origional factory setting unless gauging shows out of specification. The pump lever is made from heavy duty, hardened steel making bending difficult. Do not remove pump lever for bendsing unless absolutely necessary.

CHOKE COIL LEVER ADJUSTMENT

1. Remove the three retaining screws and remove the choke cover and coil. On models with a riveted choke cover, drill out the three rivets and remove the cover and choke coil.

NOTE: A choke stat cover retainer kit is required for reassembly.

2. Place the fast idle screw on the high step of the cam.
3. Close the choke by pushing in on the intermediate choke lever. On front wheel drive models, the intermediate choke lever is behind the choke vacuum diaphragm.
4. Insert a drill or gauge of the specified size into the hole in the choke housing. The choke lever in the housing should be up against the side of the gauge.
5. If the lever does not just touch the gauge, bend the intermediate choke rod to adjust.

FAST IDLE CAM (CHOKE ROD) ADJUSTMENT

1980–82 Models

NOTE: A special angle gauge should be used.

1. Adjust the choke coil lever and fast idle first.
2. Rotate the degree scale until it is zeroed.
3. Close the choke and install the

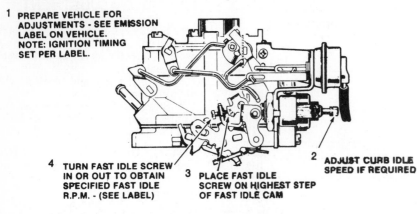

1 PREPARE VEHICLE FOR ADJUSTMENTS - SEE EMISSION LABEL ON VEHICLE. NOTE: IGNITION TIMING SET PER LABEL.

4 TURN FAST IDLE SCREW IN OR OUT TO OBTAIN SPECIFIED FAST IDLE R.P.M. - (SEE LABEL)

3 PLACE FAST IDLE SCREW ON HIGHEST STEP OF FAST IDLE CAM

2 ADJUST CURB IDLE SPEED IF REQUIRED

2SE, E2SE fast idle adjustment

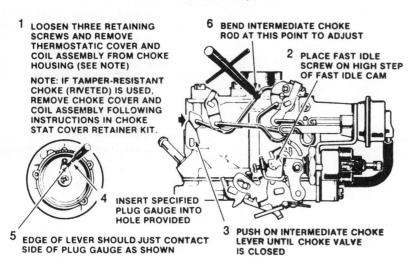

1 LOOSEN THREE RETAINING SCREWS AND REMOVE THERMOSTATIC COVER AND COIL ASSEMBLY FROM CHOKE HOUSING (SEE NOTE)

NOTE: IF TAMPER-RESISTANT CHOKE (RIVETED) IS USED, REMOVE CHOKE COVER AND COIL ASSEMBLY FOLLOWING INSTRUCTIONS IN CHOKE STAT COVER RETAINER KIT.

4 INSERT SPECIFIED PLUG GAUGE INTO HOLE PROVIDED

5 EDGE OF LEVER SHOULD JUST CONTACT SIDE OF PLUG GAUGE AS SHOWN

6 BEND INTERMEDIATE CHOKE ROD AT THIS POINT TO ADJUST

2 PLACE FAST IDLE SCREW ON HIGH STEP OF FAST IDLE CAM

3 PUSH ON INTERMEDIATE CHOKE LEVER UNTIL CHOKE VALVE IS CLOSED

2SE, E2SE choke coil lever adjustment

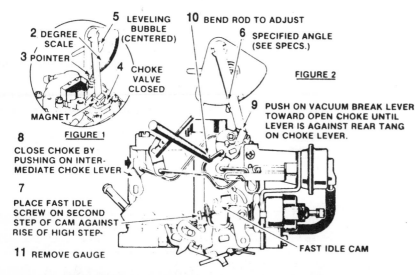

5 LEVELING BUBBLE (CENTERED)

2 DEGREE SCALE

3 POINTER

4 CHOKE VALVE CLOSED

MAGNET

8 FIGURE 1

CLOSE CHOKE BY PUSHING ON INTER-MEDIATE CHOKE LEVER

7 PLACE FAST IDLE SCREW ON SECOND STEP OF CAM AGAINST RISE OF HIGH STEP.

11 REMOVE GAUGE

10 BEND ROD TO ADJUST

6 SPECIFIED ANGLE (SEE SPECS.)

FIGURE 2

9 PUSH ON VACUUM BREAK LEVER TOWARD OPEN CHOKE UNTIL LEVER IS AGAINST REAR TANG ON CHOKE LEVER.

FAST IDLE CAM

2SE, E2SE fast idle cam adjustment—models through 1982

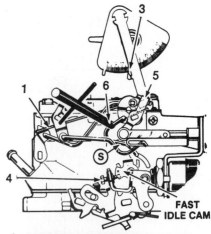

1 ATTACH RUBBER BAND TO INTER-MEDIATE CHOKE LEVER.

2 OPEN THROTTLE TO ALLOW CHOKE VALVE TO CLOSE.

3 SET UP ANGLE GAGE AND SET ANGLE TO SPECIFICATIONS.

4 PLACE FAST IDLE SCREW ON SECOND STEP OF CAM AGAINST RISE OF HIGH STEP.

5 PUSH ON CHOKE SHAFT LEVER TO OPEN CHOKE VALVE AND TO MAKE CONTACT WITH BLACK CLOSING TANG.

6 SUPPORT AT "S" AND ADJUST BY BENDING FAST IDLE CAM ROD UNTIL BUBBLE IS CENTERED.

FAST IDLE CAM

E2SE fast idle cam (choke rod) adjustment—1983 and later

in the direction of opening choke until the lever is against the rear tang on the choke lever.

7. Bend the fast idle cam rod at the U to adjust angle to specifications.

1983–84 Models

Refer to the illustration for adjustment procedure on these models.

AIR VALVE ROD ADJUSTMENT

1980 Models

1. Seat the vacuum diaphragm with an outside vacuum source. Tape over the purge bleed hole if present.
2. Close the air valve.
3. Insert the specified gauge between the rod and the end of the slot in the plunger on fours, or between the rod and the end of the slot in the air valve on V6s.
4. Bend the rod to adjust the clearance.

1981–82 Models

1. Align the zero degree mark with the pointer on an angle gauge.

degree scale onto the choke plate. Center the leveling bubble.

4. Rotate the scale so that the specified degree is opposite the scale pointer.

5. Place the fast idle screw on the second step of the cam (against the high step). Close the choke by pushing in the intermediate lever.

6. Push on the vacuum break lever

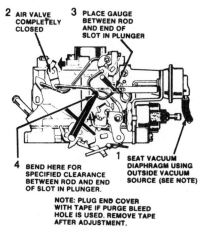

2SE and E2SE air valve rod adjustment—1980

2. Close the air valve and place a magnet on top of it.
3. Rotate the bubble until it is centered.
4. Rotate the degree scale until the specified degree mark is aligned with the pointer.
5. Seat the vacuum diaphragm using an external vacuum source.
6. On four cylinder models plug the end cover. Unplug after adjustment.
7. Apply light pressure to the air valve shaft in the direction to open the air valve until all the slack is removed between the air link and plunger slot. 8.Bend the air valve link until the bubble is centered.

1983–84 Models

Refer to the illustration for the adjustment procedure on these models.

PRIMARY SIDE VACUUM BREAK ADJUSTMENT

1980

1. Follow Steps 1–4 of the "Fast Idle Cam Adjustment" procedure.
2. Seat the choke vacuum diaphragm with an outside vacuum source.
3. Push in on the intermediate choke lever to close the choke valve, and hold closed during adjustment.
4. Adjust by bending the vacuum break rod until the bubble is centered.

1981–82

NOTE: Prior to adjustment, remove the vacuum break from the carburetor. Place the bracket in a vise and using the proper safety precautions, grind off the adjustment screw cap then reinstall the vacuum break.

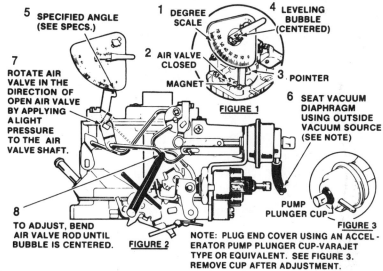

E2SE air valve adjustment—1981–82 4 cyl. except G.M. "J" series

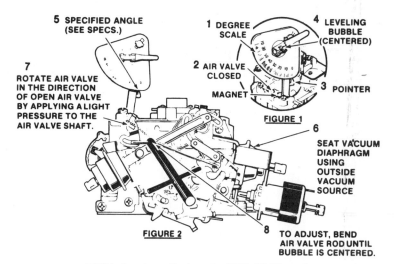

E2SE air valve adjustment—1981–82 V6 engine

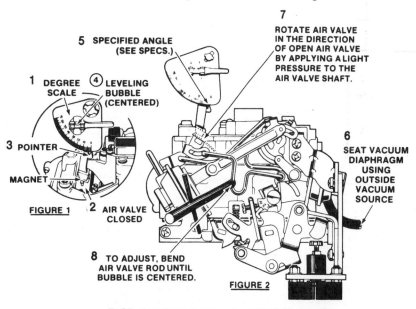

E2SE air valve adjustment—1982 G.M. J series

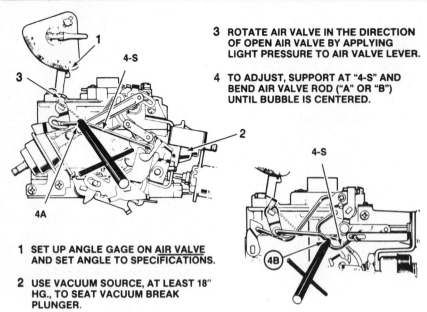

3 ROTATE AIR VALVE IN THE DIRECTION OF OPEN AIR VALVE BY APPLYING LIGHT PRESSURE TO AIR VALVE LEVER.

4 TO ADJUST, SUPPORT AT "4-S" AND BEND AIR VALVE ROD ("A" OR "B") UNTIL BUBBLE IS CENTERED.

1 SET UP ANGLE GAGE ON AIR VALVE AND SET ANGLE TO SPECIFICATIONS.

2 USE VACUUM SOURCE, AT LEAST 18" HG., TO SEAT VACUUM BREAK PLUNGER.

E2SE air valve rod adjustment—1983 and later

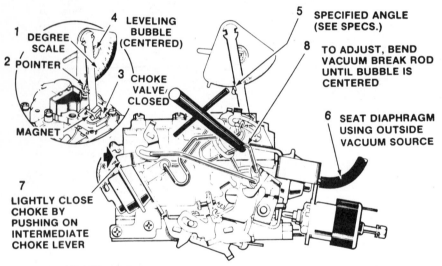

1 DEGREE SCALE
2 POINTER
3 CHOKE VALVE CLOSED
4 LEVELING BUBBLE (CENTERED)
5 SPECIFIED ANGLE (SEE SPECS.)
8 TO ADJUST, BEND VACUUM BREAK ROD UNTIL BUBBLE IS CENTERED
6 SEAT DIAPHRAGM USING OUTSIDE VACUUM SOURCE
7 LIGHTLY CLOSE CHOKE BY PUSHING ON INTERMEDIATE CHOKE LEVER
MAGNET

V6 2SE and E2SE primary vacuum break adjustment—1980

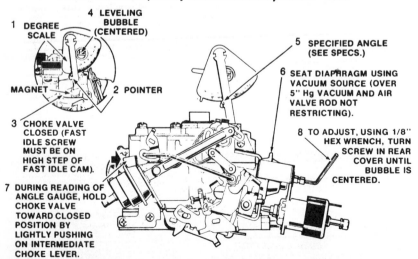

1 DEGREE SCALE
2 POINTER
3 CHOKE VALVE CLOSED (FAST IDLE SCREW MUST BE ON HIGH STEP OF FAST IDLE CAM).
4 LEVELING BUBBLE (CENTERED)
5 SPECIFIED ANGLE (SEE SPECS.)
6 SEAT DIAPHRAGM USING VACUUM SOURCE (OVER 5" Hg VACUUM AND AIR VALVE ROD NOT RESTRICTING).
7 DURING READING OF ANGLE GAUGE, HOLD CHOKE VALVE TOWARD CLOSED POSITION BY LIGHTLY PUSHING ON INTERMEDIATE CHOKE LEVER.
8 TO ADJUST, USING 1/8" HEX WRENCH, TURN SCREW IN REAR COVER UNTIL BUBBLE IS CENTERED.
MAGNET

E2SE primary vacuum break adjustment—1981–82 G.M. "A" and "X" series with V6 engine

1. Rotate the degree scale on the measuring gauge until the zero is opposite the pointer.

2. Seat the choke vacuum diaphragm by applying an external vacuum source of over 5 in. Hg vacuum to the vacuum brake.

NOTE: If the air valve rod is restricting the vacuum diaphragm from seating it may be necessary to bend the air valve rod slightly to gain clearance. Make an air valve rod adjustment after the vacuum break adjustment.

3. Read the angle gauge while lightly pushing on the intermediate choke lever so that the choke valve is toward the close position.

4. Use a $\frac{1}{8}$ in. hex wrench and turn the screw in the rear cover until the bubble is centered. Apply a silicone sealant over the screw head to seal the setting.

1983–84

Refer to the illustration for the adjustment procedure on these models.

ELECTRIC CHOKE SETTING

This procedure is only for those carburetors with choke covers retained by screws. Riveted choke covers are preset and nonadjustable.

1. Loosen the three retaining screws.

2. Place the fast idle screw on the high step of the cam.

3. Rotate the choke cover to align the cover mark with the specified housing mark.

NOTE: The specification "index" which appears in the specification table refers to the mark between "1 notch lean" and "1 notch rich".

SECONDARY VACUUM BREAK ADJUSTMENT

1980

This procedure is for V6 installations in front wheel drive models only.

1. Follow Steps 1–4 of the "Fast Idle Cam Adjustment" procedure.

2. Seat the choke vacuum diaphragm with an outside vacuum source.

3. Push in on the intermediate choke lever to close the choke valve, and hold closed during adjustment. Make sure the plunger spring is compressed and seated, if present.

4. Bend the vacuum break rod at the U next to the diaphragm until the bubble is centered.

NOTE: Prior to adjustment, remove the vacuum break from the carburetor. Place the bracket in the vise and using the proper safety precautions, grind off the adjustment screw cap then reinstall the vacuum break.

1981-82

NOTE: Plug the end cover using an accelerator pump plunger cup or equivalent. Remove the cup after the adjustment (A and X series only).

1. Rotate the degree scale on the measuring gauge until the zero is opposite the pointer.

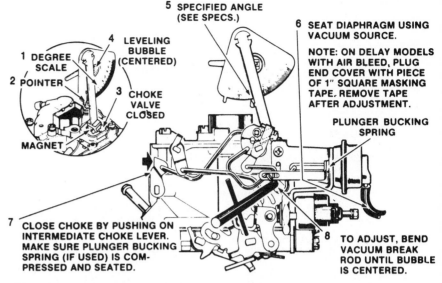

5 SPECIFIED ANGLE (SEE SPECS.)

1 DEGREE SCALE
2 POINTER
3 CHOKE VALVE CLOSED
4 LEVELING BUBBLE (CENTERED)
MAGNET

6 SEAT DIAPHRAGM USING VACUUM SOURCE.

NOTE: ON DELAY MODELS WITH AIR BLEED, PLUG END COVER WITH PIECE OF 1" SQUARE MASKING TAPE. REMOVE TAPE AFTER ADJUSTMENT.

PLUNGER BUCKING SPRING

7 CLOSE CHOKE BY PUSHING ON INTERMEDIATE CHOKE LEVER. MAKE SURE PLUNGER BUCKING SPRING (IF USED) IS COMPRESSED AND SEATED.

8 TO ADJUST, BEND VACUUM BREAK ROD UNTIL BUBBLE IS CENTERED.

2SE, E2SE primary vacuum break adjustment—1980

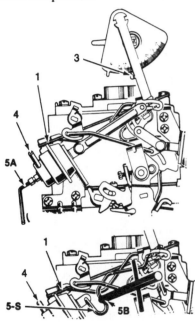

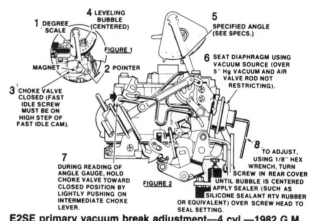

4 LEVELING BUBBLE (CENTERED)
1 DEGREE SCALE
FIGURE 1
MAGNET
2 POINTER

3 CHOKE VALVE CLOSED (FAST IDLE SCREW MUST BE ON HIGH STEP OF FAST IDLE CAM).

5 SPECIFIED ANGLE (SEE SPECS.)

6 SEAT DIAPHRAGM USING VACUUM SOURCE (OVER 5" Hg VACUUM AND AIR VALVE ROD NOT RESTRICTING).

7 DURING READING OF ANGLE GAUGE, HOLD CHOKE VALVE TOWARD CLOSED POSITION BY LIGHTLY PUSHING ON INTERMEDIATE CHOKE LEVER.

FIGURE 2

8 TO ADJUST, USING 1/8" HEX WRENCH, TURN SCREW IN REAR COVER UNTIL BUBBLE IS CENTERED APPLY SEALER (SUCH AS SILICONE SEALANT RTV RUBBER OR EQUIVALENT) OVER SCREW HEAD TO SEAL SETTING.

E2SE primary vacuum break adjustment—4 cyl.—1982 G.M. J series

1 **ATTACH RUBBER BAND TO INTERMEDIATE CHOKE LEVER.**

2 **OPEN THROTTLE TO ALLOW CHOKE VALVE TO CLOSE.**

3 **SET UP ANGLE GAGE AND SET ANGLE TO SPECIFICATION.**

4 **RETRACT VACUUM BREAK PLUNGER USING VACUUM SOURCE, AT LEAST 18" HG. PLUG AIR BLEED HOLES WHERE APPLICABLE.**

WHERE APPLICABLE, PLUNGER STEM MUST BE EXTENDED FULLY TO COMPRESS PLUNGER BUCKING SPRING.

5 **TO CENTER BUBBLE, EITHER:**

   A. **ADJUST WITH 1/8" (3.175 mm) HEX WRENCH (VACUUM STILL APPLIED)**

   -OR

   B. **SUPPORT AT "5-S", BEND WIRE-FORM VACUUM BREAK ROD (VACUUM STILL APPLIED)**

E2SE secondary vacuum break adjustment—1983 and later

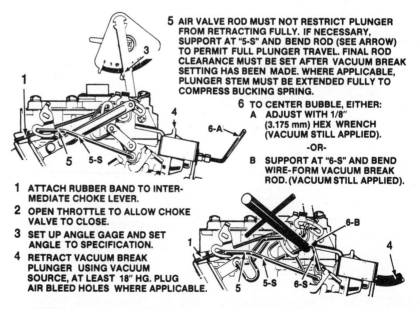

5 AIR VALVE ROD MUST NOT RESTRICT PLUNGER FROM RETRACTING FULLY. IF NECESSARY, SUPPORT AT "5-S" AND BEND ROD (SEE ARROW) TO PERMIT FULL PLUNGER TRAVEL. FINAL ROD CLEARANCE MUST BE SET AFTER VACUUM BREAK SETTING HAS BEEN MADE. WHERE APPLICABLE, PLUNGER STEM MUST BE EXTENDED FULLY TO COMPRESS BUCKING SPRING.

6 TO CENTER BUBBLE, EITHER:
   A ADJUST WITH 1/8" (3.175 mm) HEX WRENCH (VACUUM STILL APPLIED).
   -OR-
   B SUPPORT AT "6-S" AND BEND WIRE-FORM VACUUM BREAK ROD. (VACUUM STILL APPLIED).

1 **ATTACH RUBBER BAND TO INTERMEDIATE CHOKE LEVER.**

2 **OPEN THROTTLE TO ALLOW CHOKE VALVE TO CLOSE.**

3 **SET UP ANGLE GAGE AND SET ANGLE TO SPECIFICATION.**

4 **RETRACT VACUUM BREAK PLUNGER USING VACUUM SOURCE, AT LEAST 18" HG. PLUG AIR BLEED HOLES WHERE APPLICABLE.**

E2SE primary vacuum break adjustment—1983 and later

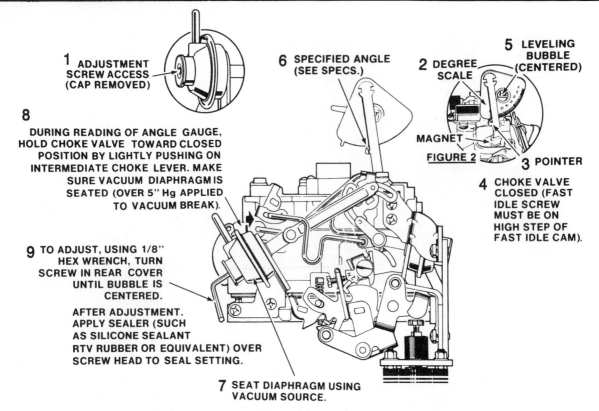

1 ADJUSTMENT SCREW ACCESS (CAP REMOVED)

6 SPECIFIED ANGLE (SEE SPECS.)

5 LEVELING BUBBLE (CENTERED)

2 DEGREE SCALE

MAGNET

FIGURE 2

3 POINTER

4 CHOKE VALVE CLOSED (FAST IDLE SCREW MUST BE ON HIGH STEP OF FAST IDLE CAM).

8 DURING READING OF ANGLE GAUGE, HOLD CHOKE VALVE TOWARD CLOSED POSITION BY LIGHTLY PUSHING ON INTERMEDIATE CHOKE LEVER. MAKE SURE VACUUM DIAPHRAGM IS SEATED (OVER 5" Hg APPLIED TO VACUUM BREAK).

9 TO ADJUST, USING 1/8" HEX WRENCH, TURN SCREW IN REAR COVER UNTIL BUBBLE IS CENTERED.

AFTER ADJUSTMENT. APPLY SEALER (SUCH AS SILICONE SEALANT RTV RUBBER OR EQUIVALENT) OVER SCREW HEAD TO SEAL SETTING.

7 SEAT DIAPHRAGM USING VACUUM SOURCE.

E2SE secondary vacuum break adjustment—1982 G.M. J series

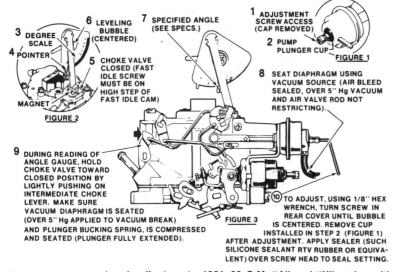

3 DEGREE SCALE

4 POINTER

6 LEVELING BUBBLE (CENTERED)

5 CHOKE VALVE CLOSED (FAST IDLE SCREW MUST BE ON HIGH STEP OF FAST IDLE CAM)

MAGNET

FIGURE 2

7 SPECIFIED ANGLE (SEE SPECS.)

1 ADJUSTMENT SCREW ACCESS (CAP REMOVED)

2 PUMP PLUNGER CUP

FIGURE 1

8 SEAT DIAPHRAGM USING VACUUM SOURCE (AIR BLEED SEALED, OVER 5" Hg VACUUM AND AIR VALVE ROD NOT RESTRICTING).

9 DURING READING OF ANGLE GAUGE, HOLD CHOKE VALVE TOWARD CLOSED POSITION BY LIGHTLY PUSHING ON INTERMEDIATE CHOKE LEVER. MAKE SURE VACUUM DIAPHRAGM IS SEATED (OVER 5" Hg APPLIED TO VACUUM BREAK) AND PLUNGER BUCKING SPRING, IS COMPRESSED AND SEATED (PLUNGER FULLY EXTENDED).

FIGURE 3

10 TO ADJUST, USING 1/8" HEX WRENCH, TURN SCREW IN REAR COVER UNTIL BUBBLE IS CENTERED. REMOVE CUP INSTALLED IN STEP 2 (FIGURE 1) AFTER ADJUSTMENT. APPLY SEALER (SUCH SILICONE SEALANT RTV RUBBER OR EQUIVALENT) OVER SCREW HEAD TO SEAL SETTING.

E2SE primary vacuum break adjustment—1981–82 G.M. "A" and "X" series with 4 cyl engine

2. Seat the choke vacuum diaphragm by applying an external vacuum source of over 5 in. vacuum to the vacuum break.

NOTE: If the air valve rod is restricting the vacuum diaphragm from seating it may be necessary to bend the air valve rod slightly to gain clearance. Make an air valve rod adjustment after the vacuum break adjustment.

3. Read the angle gauge while lightly pushing on the intermediate choke lever so that the choke valve is toward the close position.

4. Use a 1/8 in. hex wrench and turn the screw in the rear cover until the bubble is centered. Apply a silicone sealant over the screw head to seal the setting.

1983–84

Refer to the illustration for the adjustment procedure on these models.

CHOKE UNLOADER ADJUSTMENT

Through 1982

1. Follow Steps 1–4 of the "Fast Idle Cam Adjustment" procedure.

2. Install the choke cover and coil, if removed, aligning the marks on the housing and cover as specified.

3. Hold the primary throttle wide open.

4. If the engine is warm, close the choke valve by pushing in on the intermediate choke lever.

5. Bend the unloader tang until the bubble is centered.

1983–84 Models

Refer to the illustration for the adjustment procedure on these models.

SECONDARY LOCKOUT ADJUSTMENT

1. Pull the choke wide open by pushing out on the intermediate choke lever.

2. Open the throttle until the end of the secondary actuating lever is opposite the toe of the lockout lever.

3. Gauge clearance between the lockout lever and secondary lever should be as specified.◊

4. To adjust, bend the lockout lever where it contacts the fast idle cam.

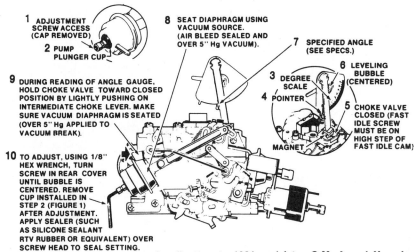

1 ADJUSTMENT SCREW ACCESS (CAP REMOVED)

2 PUMP PLUNGER CUP

8 SEAT DIAPHRAGM USING VACUUM SOURCE. (AIR BLEED SEALED AND OVER 5" Hg VACUUM).

7 SPECIFIED ANGLE (SEE SPECS.)

6 LEVELING BUBBLE (CENTERED)

3 DEGREE SCALE

4 POINTER

5 CHOKE VALVE CLOSED (FAST IDLE SCREW MUST BE ON HIGH STEP OF FAST IDLE CAM)

MAGNET

9 DURING READING OF ANGLE GAUGE, HOLD CHOKE VALVE TOWARD CLOSED POSITION BY LIGHTLY PUSHING ON INTERMEDIATE CHOKE LEVER. MAKE SURE VACUUM DIAPHRAGM IS SEATED (OVER 5" Hg APPLIED TO VACUUM BREAK).

10 TO ADJUST, USING 1/8" HEX WRENCH, TURN SCREW IN REAR COVER UNTIL BUBBLE IS CENTERED. REMOVE CUP INSTALLED IN STEP 2 (FIGURE 1) AFTER ADJUSTMENT. APPLY SEALER (SUCH AS SILICONE SEALANT RTV RUBBER OR EQUIVALENT) OVER SCREW HEAD TO SEAL SETTING.

E2SE secondary vacuum break adjustment—1981 and later G.M. A and X series

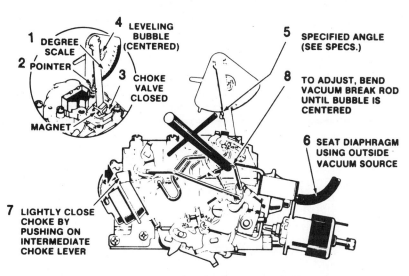

1 DEGREE SCALE

2 POINTER

4 LEVELING BUBBLE (CENTERED)

3 CHOKE VALVE CLOSED

MAGNET

5 SPECIFIED ANGLE (SEE SPECS.)

8 TO ADJUST, BEND VACUUM BREAK ROD UNTIL BUBBLE IS CENTERED

6 SEAT DIAPHRAGM USING OUTSIDE VACUUM SOURCE

7 LIGHTLY CLOSE CHOKE BY PUSHING ON INTERMEDIATE CHOKE LEVER

E2SE secondary vacuum break adjustment—1980 models

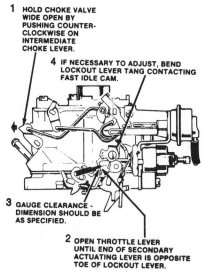

1 HOLD CHOKE VALVE WIDE OPEN BY PUSHING COUNTER-CLOCKWISE ON INTERMEDIATE CHOKE LEVER.

4 IF NECESSARY TO ADJUST, BEND LOCKOUT LEVER TANG CONTACTING FAST IDLE CAM.

3 GAUGE CLEARANCE - DIMENSION SHOULD BE AS SPECIFIED.

2 OPEN THROTTLE LEVER UNTIL END OF SECONDARY ACTUATING LEVER IS OPPOSITE TOE OF LOCKOUT LEVER.

2SE and E2SE secondary lockout adjust-ment—typical

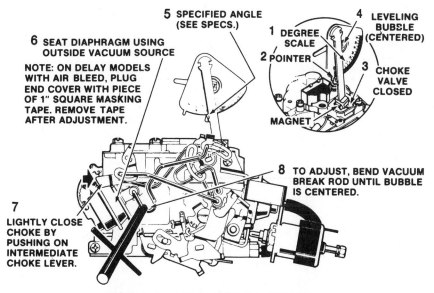

6 SEAT DIAPHRAGM USING OUTSIDE VACUUM SOURCE

NOTE: ON DELAY MODELS WITH AIR BLEED, PLUG END COVER WITH PIECE OF 1" SQUARE MASKING TAPE. REMOVE TAPE AFTER ADJUSTMENT.

5 SPECIFIED ANGLE (SEE SPECS.)

1 DEGREE SCALE

2 POINTER

4 LEVELING BUBBLE (CENTERED)

3 CHOKE VALVE CLOSED

MAGNET

8 TO ADJUST, BEND VACUUM BREAK ROD UNTIL BUBBLE IS CENTERED.

7 LIGHTLY CLOSE CHOKE BY PUSHING ON INTERMEDIATE CHOKE LEVER.

E2SE choke unloader adjuster—typical

1. ATTACH RUBBER BAND TO INTER-MEDIATE CHOKE LEVER.

2. OPEN THROTTLE TO ALLOW CHOKE VALVE TO CLOSE.

3. SET UP ANGLE GAGE AND SET ANGLE TO SPECIFICATIONS.

4. HOLD THROTTLE LEVER IN WIDE OPEN POSITION.

5. PUSH ON CHOKE SHAFT LEVER TO OPEN CHOKE VALVE AND TO MAKE CONTACT WITH BLACK CLOSING TANG.

6. ADJUST BY BENDING TANG UNTIL BUBBLE IS CENTERED.

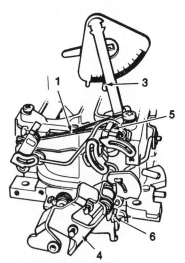

E2SE choke unloader adjustment—1983 and later

2SE, E2SE CARBURETOR SPECIFICATIONS
General Motors—U.S.A.

Year	Carburetor Identification	Float Lever (in.)	Pump Rod (in.)	Fast Idle (rpm)	Choke Coil Lever (in.)	Fast Idle Cam (deg./in.)	Air Valve Rod (in.)	Primary Vacuum Break (deg./in.)	Choke Setting (notches)	Secondary Vacuum Break (deg./in.)	Choke Unloader (deg./in.)	Secondary Lockout (in.)
'80	17059614	3/16	1/2	2600	.085	18/.096	.025	17/.090	Fixed	—	36/.227	.120
	17059615	3/16	5/32	2600	.085	18/.096	.025	19/.103	Fixed	—	36/.227	.120
	17059616	3/16	1/2	2600	.085	18/.096	.025	17/.090	Fixed	—	36/.227	.120
	17059617	3/16	5/32	2600	.085	18/.096	.025	19/.103	Fixed	—	36/.227	.120
	17059618	3/16	1/2	2600	.085	18/.096	.025	17/.090	Fixed	—	36/.227	.120
	17059619	3/16	5/32	2600	.085	18/.096	.025	19/.103	Fixed	—	36/.227	.120
	17059620	3/16	1/2	2600	.085	18/.096	.025	17/.090	Fixed	—	36/.227	.120
	17059621	3/16	5/32	2600	.085	18/.096	.025	19/.103	Fixed	—	36/.227	.120
	17059650	3/16	3/32	2600	.085	27/.157	.025	30/.179	Fixed	38/.243	30/.179	.120
	17059651	3/16	3/32	1900	.085	27/.157	.025	22/.123	Fixed	23/.120	30/.179	.120
	17059652	3/16	3/32	2000	.085	27/.157	.025	30/.179	Fixed	38/.243	30/.179	.120
	17059653	3/16	3/32	1900	.085	27/.157	.025	22/.123	Fixed	23/.120	30/.179	.120
	17059714	11/16	5/32	2600	.085	18/.096	.025	23/.129	Fixed	—	32/.195	.120
	17059715	11/16	3/32	2200	.085	18/.096	.025	25/.142	Fixed	—	32/.195	.120
	17059716	11/16	5/32	2600	.085	18/.096	.025	23/.129	Fixed	—	32/.195	.120
	17059717	11/16	3/32	2200	.085	18/.096	.025	25/.142	Fixed	—	32/.195	.120
	17059760	1/8	5/64	2000	.085	17.5/.093	.025	20/.110	Fixed	33/.203	35/.220	.120
	17059762	1/8	5/64	2000	.085	17.5/.093	.025	20/.110	Fixed	33/.203	35/.220	.120
	17059763	1/8	5/64	2000	.085	17.5/.093	.025	20/.110	Fixed	33/.203	35/.220	.120
	17059774	5/32	1/2	①	.085	18/0.096	.018	19/.103	Fixed	—	32/.195	.012
	17059775	5/32	17/32	①	.085	18/0.096	.018	21/.117	Fixed	—	32/.195	.012
	17059776	5/32	1/2	①	.085	18/0.096	.018	19/.103	Fixed	—	32/.195	.012
	17059777	5/32	17/32	①	.085	18/0.096	.018	21/.117	Fixed	—	32/.195	.012
	17080674	3/16	1/2	①	.085	18/0.096	.018	19/.103	Fixed	—	32/.195	.012
	17080675	3/16	1/2	①	.085	18/0.096	.018	21/.117	Fixed	—	32/.195	.012
	17080676	3/16	1/2	①	.085	18/0.096	.018	19/.103	Fixed	—	32/.195	.012
	17080677	3/16	1/2	①	.085	18/0.096	.018	21/.117	Fixed	—	32/.195	.012
'81	17081650	1/4	Fixed	2600	.085	17/.090	1 ②	25/.142	Fixed	34/.211	35/.220	.012
	17081651	1/4	Fixed	2400	.085	17/.090	1 ②	29/.171	Fixed	35/.220	35/.220	.012
	17081652	1/4	Fixed	2600	.085	17/.090	1 ②	25/.142	Fixed	34/.211	35/.220	.012
	17081653	1/4	Fixed	2600	.085	17/.090	1 ②	29/.171	Fixed	35/.220	35/.220	.012
	17081670	5/32	Fixed	2600	.085	18/.096	1 ②	19/.103	Fixed	—	32/.195	.012
	17081671	5/32	Fixed	2600	.085	33.5/.207	1 ②	21/.117	Fixed	—	32/.195	.012

2SE, E2SE CARBURETOR SPECIFICATIONS
General Motors—U.S.A.

Year	Carburetor Identification	Float Lever (in.)	Pump Rod (in.)	Fast Idle (rpm)	Choke Coil Lever (in.)	Fast Idle Cam (deg./in.)	Air Valve Rod (in.)	Primary Vacuum Break (deg./in.)	Choke Setting (notches)	Secondary Vacuum Break (deg./in.)	Choke Unloader (deg./in.)	Secondary Lockout (in.)
'81	17081672	$5/32$	Fixed	2600	.085	18/.096	1 ②	19/.103	Fixed	—	32/.195	.012
	17081673	$5/32$	Fixed	2600	.085	33.4/.207	1 ②	21/.117	Fixed	—	32/.195	.012
	17081740	$1/4$	Fixed	2400	.085	17/.090	1 ②	25/.142	Fixed	35/.220	35/.220	.012
	17081742	$1/4$	Fixed	2400	.085	17/.090	1 ②	25/.142	Fixed	35/.220	35/.220	.012
'82	17081600	$5/16$	Fixed	①	③	24/.136	1 ②	20/.110	Fixed	27/.157	35/.220	③
	17081601	$5/16$	Fixed	①	③	24/1.36	1 ②	20/.110	Fixed	27/.157	35/.220	③
	17081607	$5/16$	Fixed	①	③	24/.136	1 ②	20/.110	Fixed	27/.157	35/.220	③
	17081700	$5/16$	Fixed	①	③	24/.136	1 ②	20/.110	Fixed	27/.157	35/.220	③
	17081701	$5/16$	Fixed	①	③	24/.136	1 ②	20/.110	Fixed	27/.157	35/.220	③
	17082196	$5/16$	Fixed	①	.085	18/.096	1 ②	21/.117	Fixed	19/.103	27/.157	③
	17082316	$1/4$	Fixed	2600	.085	17/.090	1 ②	30/.179	Fixed	34/.211	45/.304	③
	17082317	$1/4$	Fixed	2600	.085	17/.090	1 ②	30/.179	Fixed	35/.220	45/.304	③
	17082320	$1/4$	Fixed	2800	.085	25/.142	1 ②	30/.179	Fixed	35/.220	45/.304	③
	17082321	$1/4$	Fixed	2600	.085	25/.142	1 ②	30/.179	Fixed	35/.220	45/.304	③
	17082390	$13/32$	Fixed	2500	.085	17/.090	1 ②	26/.149	Fixed	34/.211	35/.220	.011–.040
	17082391	$13/32$	Fixed	2600	.085	25/.142	1 ②	29/.171	Fixed	35/.220	35/.220	.011–.040
	17082490	$13/32$	Fixed	2500	.085	17/.090	1 ②	26/.149	Fixed	34/.211	35/.220	.011–.040
	17082491	$13/32$	Fixed	2600	.085	25/.142	1 ②	29/.171	Fixed	35/.220	35/.220	.011–.040
	17082640	$1/4$	Fixed	2600	.085	17/.090	1 ②	30/.179	Fixed	34/.211	45/.304	③
	17082641	$1/4$	Fixed	2400	.085	17/.090	1 ②	30/.179	Fixed	35/.220	45/.304	③
	17082642	$1/4$	Fixed	2800	.085	25/.142	1 ②	30/.179	Fixed	35/.220	45/.304	③
'83	17083356	$13/32$	Fixed	①	.085	22/.123	1 ②	25/.142	Fixed	35/.220	30/.179	.025
	17083357	$13/32$	Fixed	①	.085	22/.123	1 ②	25/.142	Fixed	35/.220	30/.179	.025
	17083358	$13/32$	Fixed	①	.085	22/.123	1 ②	25/.142	Fixed	35/.220	30/.179	.025
	17083359	$13/32$	Fixed	①	.085	22/.123	1 ②	25/.142	Fixed	35/.220	30/.179	.025
	17083368	$13/32$	Fixed	①	.085	22/.123	1 ②	25/.142	Fixed	35/.220	30/.179	.025
	17083369	$13/32$	Fixed	①	.085	22/.123	1 ②	25/.142	Fixed	35/.220	30/.179	.025
	17083370	$13/32$	Fixed	①	.085	22/.123	1 ②	25/.142	Fixed	35/.220	30/.179	.025
	17083391	$13/32$	Fixed	①	.085	28/.164	1 ②	30/.179	Fixed	35/.220	38/.243	.025
	17083392	$13/32$	Fixed	①	.085	28/.164	1 ②	30/.179	Fixed	35/.220	38/.243	.025
	17083393	$13/32$	Fixed	①	.085	28/.164	1 ②	30/.179	Fixed	35/.220	38/.243	.025
	17083394	$13/32$	Fixed	①	.085	28/.164	1 ②	30/.179	Fixed	35/.220	38/.243	.025
	17083395	$13/32$	Fixed	①	.085	28/.164	1 ②	30/.179	Fixed	35/.220	38/.243	.025
	17083396	$13/32$	Fixed	①	.085	28/.164	1 ②	30/.179	Fixed	35/.220	38/.243	.025
	17083397	$13/32$	Fixed	①	.085	28/.164	1 ②	30/.179	Fixed	35/.220	38/.243	.025
	17083450	$1/4$	Fixed	①	.085	28/.164	1 ②	27/.157	Fixed	35/.220	45/.304	.025
	17083451	$1/4$	Fixed	①	.085	28/.164	1 ②	27/.157	Fixed	35/.220	45/.304	.025
	17083452	$1/4$	Fixed	①	.085	28/.164	1 ②	27/.157	Fixed	35/.220	45/.304	.025
	17083453	$1/4$	Fixed	①	.085	28/.164	1 ②	27/.157	Fixed	35/.220	45/.304	.025
	17083454	$1/4$	Fixed	①	.085	28/.164	1 ②	27/.157	Fixed	35/.220	45/.304	.025
	17083455	$1/4$	Fixed	①	.085	28/.164	1 ②	27/.157	Fixed	35/.220	45/.304	.025
	17083456	$1/4$	Fixed	①	.085	28/.164	1 ②	27/.157	Fixed	35/.220	45/.304	.025
	17083630	$1/4$	Fixed	①	.085	28/.164	1 ②	27/.157	Fixed	35/.220	45/.304	.025
	17083631	$1/4$	Fixed	①	.085	28/.164	1 ②	27/.157	Fixed	35/.220	45/.304	.025
	17083632	$1/4$	Fixed	①	.085	28/.164	1 ②	27/.157	Fixed	35/.220	45/.304	.025
	17083633	$1/4$	Fixed	①	.085	28/.164	1 ②	27/.157	Fixed	35/.220	45/.304	.025
	17083634	$1/4$	Fixed	①	.085	28/.164	1 ②	27/.157	Fixed	35/.220	45/.304	.025
	17083635	$1/4$	Fixed	①	.085	28/.164	1 ②	27/.157	Fixed	35/.220	45/.304	.025
	17083636	$1/4$	Fixed	①	.085	28/.164	1 ②	27/.157	Fixed	35/.220	45/.304	.025
'84	17072683	$9/32$	Fixed	①	.085	28/.164	1 ②	25/.142	Fixed	35/.220	45/.304	.025
	17074812	$9/32$	Fixed	①	.085	28/.164	1 ②	25/.142	Fixed	35/.220	45/.304	.025
	17084356	$9/32$	Fixed	①	.085	22/.123	1 ②	25/.142	Fixed	30/.179	30/.179	.025
	17084357	$9/32$	Fixed	①	.085	22/.123	1 ②	25/.142	Fixed	30/.179	30/.179	.025
	17084358	$9/32$	Fixed	①	.085	22/.123	1 ②	25/.142	Fixed	30/.179	30/.179	.025

2SE, E2SE CARBURETOR SPECIFICATIONS
General Motors—U.S.A.

Year	Carburetor Identification	Float Lever (in.)	Pump Rod (in.)	Fast Idle (rpm)	Choke Coil Lever (in.)	Fast Idle Cam (deg./in.)	Air Valve Rod (in.)	Primary Vacuum Break (deg./in.)	Choke Setting (notches)	Secondary Vacuum Break (deg./in.)	Choke Unloader (deg./in.)	Secondary Lockout (in.)
'84	17084359	9/32	Fixed	①	.085	22/.123	1 ②	25/.142	Fixed	30/.179	30/.179	.025
	17084368	1/8	Fixed	①	.085	22/.123	1 ②	25/.142	Fixed	30/.179	30/.179	.025
	17084370	1/8	Fixed	①	.085	22/.123	1 ②	25/.142	Fixed	30/.179	30/.179	.025
	17084430	11/32	Fixed	①	.085	15/.077	1 ②	26/.149	Fixed	30/.179	30/.179	.025
	17084431	11/32	Fixed	①	.085	15/.077	1 ②	26/.149	Fixed	38/.243	42/.277	.025
	17084434	11/32	Fixed	①	.085	15/.077	1 ②	26/.149	Fixed	38/.243	42/.277	.025
	17084435	11/32	Fixed	①	.085	15/.077	1 ②	26/.149	Fixed	38/.243	42/.277	.025
	17084452	5/32	Fixed	①	.085	28/.164	1 ②	25/.142	Fixed	38/.243	42/.377	.025
	17084453	5/32	Fixed	①	.085	28/.164	1 ②	25/.142	Fixed	35/.220	45/.304	.025
	17084455	5/32	Fixed	①	.085	28/.164	1 ②	25/.142	Fixed	35/.220	45/.304	.025
	17084456	5/32	Fixed	①	.085	28/.164	1 ②	25/.142	Fixed	35/.220	45/.304	.025
	17084458	5/32	Fixed	①	.085	28/.164	1 ②	25/.142	Fixed	35/.220	45/.304	.025
	17084532	5/32	Fixed	①	.085	28/.164	1 ②	25/.142	Fixed	35/.220	45/.304	.025
	17084534	5/32	Fixed	①	.085	28/.164	1 ②	25/.142	Fixed	35/.220	45/.304	.025
	17084535	5/32	Fixed	①	.085	28/.164	1 ②	25/.142	Fixed	35/.220	45/.304	.025
	17084537	5/32	Fixed	①	.085	28/.164	1 ②	25/.142	Fixed	35/.220	45/.304	.025
	17084538	5/32	Fixed	①	.085	28/.164	1 ②	25/.142	Fixed	35/.220	45/.304	.025
	17084540	5/32	Fixed	①	.085	28/.164	1 ②	25/.142	Fixed	35/.220	45/.304	.025
	17084542	1/8	Fixed	①	.085	28/.164	1 ②	25/.142	Fixed	35/.220	45/.304	.025
	17084632	9/32	Fixed	①	.085	28/.164	1 ②	25/.142	Fixed	35/.220	45/.304	.025
	17084633	9/32	Fixed	①	.085	28/.164	1 ②	25/.142	Fixed	35/.220	45/.304	.025
	17084635	9/32	Fixed	①	.085	28/.164	1 ②	25/.142	Fixed	35/.220	45/.304	.025
	17084636	9/32	Fixed	①	.085	28/.164	1 ②	25/.142	Fixed	35/.220	45/.304	.025
'85	17084534	5/32	Fixed	①	.085	28/.164	1 ②	25/.142	Fixed	35/.220	45/.304	—
	17084535	5/32	Fixed	①	.085	28/.164	1 ②	25/.142	Fixed	35/.220	45/.304	—
	17084540	5/32	Fixed	①	.085	28/.164	1 ②	25/.142	Fixed	35/.220	45/.304	—
	17084542	4/32	Fixed	①	.085	28/.164	1 ②	25/.142	Fixed	35/.220	45/.304	—
	17085356	9/32	Fixed	①	.085	22/.123	1 ②	25/.142	Fixed	30/.179	30/.179	—
	17085357	9/32	Fixed	①	.085	22/.123	1 ②	25/.142	Fixed	30/.179	30/.179	—
	17085358	9/32	Fixed	①	.085	22/.123	1 ②	25/.142	Fixed	30/.179	30/.179	—
	17085359	9/32	Fixed	①	.085	22/.123	1 ②	25/.142	Fixed	30/.179	30/.179	—
	17085368	4/32	Fixed	①	.085	22/.123	1 ②	25/.142	Fixed	30/.179	30/.179	—
	17085369	9/32	Fixed	①	.085	22/.123	1 ②	25/.142	Fixed	30/.179	30/.179	—
	17085370	4/32	Fixed	①	.085	22/.123	1 ②	25/.142	Fixed	30/.179	30/.179	—
	17085371	9/32	Fixed	①	.085	22/.123	1 ②	25/.142	Fixed	30/.179	30/.179	—
	17085452	5/32	Fixed	①	.085	28/.164	1 ②	25/.142	Fixed	35/.220	45/.304	—
	17085453	5/32	Fixed	①	.085	28/.164	1 ②	25/.142	Fixed	35/.220	45/.304	—
	17085458	5/32	Fixed	①	.085	28/.164	1 ②	25/.142	Fixed	35/.220	45/.304	—
'86	17084534	5/32	Fixed	①	.085	28/.164	1 ②	25/.142	Fixed	35/.220	45/.304	—
	17084535	5/32	Fixed	①	.085	28/.164	1 ②	25/.142	Fixed	35/.220	45/.304	—
	17084540	5/32	Fixed	①	.085	28/.164	1 ②	25/.142	Fixed	35/.220	45/.304	—
	17084542	5/32	Fixed	①	.085	28/.164	1 ②	25/.142	Fixed	35/.220	45/.304	—

① See underhood decal
② Measurement in degrees
③ Not available

2SE, E2SE CARBURETOR SPECIFICATIONS
General Motors—Canada

Year	Carburetor Identification	Float Lever (in.)	Pump Rod (in.)	Fast Idle (rpm)	Choke Coil Lever (in.)	Fast Idle Cam (deg./in.)	Air Valve Rod (in.)	Primary Vacuum Break (deg./in.)	Choke Setting (notches)	Secondary Vacuum Break (deg./in.)	Choke Unloader (deg./in.)	Secondary Lockout (in.)
'81	17059660	1/4	17/32	①	.085	24/.136	1	30/.179	Fixed	32/.195	30/.179	②
	17059662	1/4	17/32	①	.085	24/.136	1	30/.179	Fixed	37/.195	30/.179	②
	17059651	1/4	17/32	①	.085	24/.136	1	30/.179	Fixed	32/.195	30/.179	②
	17059666	1/4	17/32	①	.085	24/.136	1	26/.149	Fixed	32/.195	30/.179	②
	17059667	1/4	17/32	①	.085	24/.136	1	26/.149	Fixed	32/.195	30/.179	②
	17059622	5/32	17/32	①	.085	18/.096	1	17/.090	Fixed	—	36/.227	②
	17059623	5/32	17/32	①	.085	18/.096	1	19/.103	Fixed	—	36/.227	②
	17059624	5/32	17/32	①	.085	18/.096	1	17/.090	Fixed	—	36/.227	②
'82	17082440	1/4	19/32	①	.085	24/.136	1	30/.179	Fixed	32/.195	45/.304	②
	17082441	1/4	19/32	①	.085	24/.136	1	30/.179	Fixed	32/.195	45/.304	②
	17082443	1/4	19/32	①	.085	24/.136	1	30/.179	Fixed	32/.195	45/.304	②
	17082460	1/4	19/32	①	.085	18/.096	1	21/.117	Fixed	—	36/.227	②
	17082461	1/4	19/32	①	.085	18/.096	1	21/.117	Fixed	—	36/.227	②
	17082462	1/4	19/32	①	.085	18/.096	1	21/.117	Fixed	—	36/.227	②
	17082464	1/8	19/32	①	.085	18/.096	1	21/.117	Fixed	—	36/.227	②
	17082465	1/8	19/32	①	.085	18/.096	1	21/.117	Fixed	—	36/.227	②
	17082466	1/8	19/32	①	.085	18/.096	1	21/.117	Fixed	—	36/.227	②
	17082620	7/16	19/32	①	.085	24/.136	1	30/.179	Fixed	32/.195	45/.304	②
	17082621	7/16	19/32	①	.085	24/.136	1	30/.179	Fixed	32/.195	45/.304	②
	17082622	7/16	19/32	①	.085	24/.136	1	30/.179	Fixed	32/.195	45/.304	②
	17082623	7/16	19/32	①	.085	24/.136	1	30/.179	Fixed	32/.195	45/.304	②
'83	17083311	5/16	Fixed	①	.085	24/.136	1	18/.096	Fixed	20/.110	35/.220	.025
	17083314	5/16	Fixed	①	.085	24/.136	1	16/.083	Fixed	20/.110	35/.220	.025
	17083401	5/16	Fixed	①	.085	24/.136	1	18/.096	Fixed	20/.110	35/.220•	.025
	17083440	1/4	19/32	①	.085	24/.136	1	28/.164	Fixed	32/.195	40/.260	.025
	17083441	1/4	19/32	①	.085	24/.136	1	28/.164	Fixed	32/.195	40/.260	.025
	17083442	1/4	19/32	①	.085	24/.136	1	28/.164	Fixed	32/.195	40/.260	.025
	17083443	1/4	19/32	①	.085	24/.136	1	28/.164	Fixed	32/.195	40/.260	.025
	17083444	1/4	19/32	①	.085	24/.136	1	28/.164	Fixed	32/.195	40/.260	.025
	17083445	1/4	19/32	①	.085	24/.136	1	28/.164	Fixed	32/.195	40/.260	.025
	17083460	1/4	19/32	①	.085	18/.096	1	19/.103	Fixed	—	36/.227	.025
	17083461	1/4	19/32	①	.085	18/.096	1	18/.096	Fixed	—	36/.227	.025
	17083462	1/4	19/32	①	.085	18/.096	1	19/.103	Fixed	—	36/.227	.025
	17083464	1/8	19/32	①	.085	18/.096	1	19/.103	Fixed	—	36/.227	.025
	17083465	1/8	19/32	①	.085	18/.096	1	20/.110	Fixed	—	36/.227	.025
	17083466	1/8	19/32	①	.085	18/.096	1	19/.103	Fixed	—	36/.227	.025
	17083620	7/16	19/32	①	.085	24/.136	1	28/.164	Fixed	32/.195	40/.260	.025
	17083621	7/16	19/32	①	.085	24/.136	1	28/.164	Fixed	32/.195	40/.260	.025
	17083622	7/16	19/32	①	.085	24/.136	1	28/.164	Fixed	34/.195	40/.260	.025
	17083623	7/16	19/32	①	.085	24/.136	1	28/.164	Fixed	32/.195	40/.260	.025
'84	17084312	5/16	Fixed	①	.085	24/.136	1	18/.096	Fixed	20/.110	35/.220	.025
	17084314	5/16	Fixed	①	.085	29/.171	1	16/.083	Fixed	20/.110	30/.179	.025
	17084480	1/4	Fixed	①	.085	24/.136	1	28/.164	Fixed	32/.195	45/.304	.025
	17084481	1/4	Fixed	①	.085	24/.136	1	28/.164	Fixed	32/.195	45/.304	.025
	17084482	1/4	Fixed	①	.085	24/.136	1	28/.164	Fixed	32/.195	45/.304	.025
	17084483	1/4	Fixed	①	.085	24/.136	1	28/.164	Fixed	32/.195	45/.304	.025
	17084484	1/4	Fixed	①	.085	24/.136	1	28/.164	Fixed	32/.195	45/.304	.025
	17084485	1/4	Fixed	①	.085	24/.136	1	28/.164	Fixed	32/.195	45/.304	.025
	17084486	1/4	Fixed	①	.085	24/.136	1	28/.164	Fixed	32/.195	45/.304	.025
	17084487	1/4	Fixed	①	.085	24/.136	1	28/.164	Fixed	32/.195	45/.304	.025
	17084620	7/16	Fixed	①	.085	24/.136	1	26/.149	Fixed	32/.195	45/.304	.025
	17084621	7/16	Fixed	①	.085	24/.136	1	26/.149	Fixed	32/.195	45/.304	.025
	17084622	7/16	Fixed	①	.085	24/.136	1	26/.149	Fixed	32/.195	45/.304	.025
	17084623	7/16	Fixed	①	.085	24/.136	1	26/.149	Fixed	32/.195	45/.304	.025

2SE, E2SE CARBURETOR SPECIFICATIONS
General Motors—Canada

Year	Carburetor Identification	Float Lever (in.)	Pump Rod (in.)	Fast Idle (rpm)	Choke Coil Lever (in.)	Fast Idle Cam (deg./in.)	Air Valve Rod (in.)	Primary Vacuum Break (deg./in.)	Choke Setting (notches)	Secondary Vacuum Break (deg./in.)	Choke Unloader (deg./in.)	Secondary Lockout (in.)
'85	17084312	5/16	Fixed	①	.085	—	1	18/.096	Fixed	20/.110	35/.220	—
	17084314	5/16	Fixed	①	.085	—	1	16/.083	Fixed	20/.110	30/.179	—
	17085484	12/32	Fixed	①	.085	—	1	28/.164	Fixed	32/.195	45/.304	—
	17085485	12/32	Fixed	①	.085	—	1	28/.164	Fixed	32/.195	45/.304	—
	17085482	12/32	Fixed	①	.085	—	1	28/.164	Fixed	32/.195	45/.304	—
	17085483	12/32	Fixed	①	.085	—	1	28/.164	Fixed	32/.195	45/.304	—
	17085484	12/32	Fixed	①	.085	—	1	28/.164	Fixed	32/.195	45/.304	—
	17085485	12/32	Fixed	①	.085	—	1	28/.164	Fixed	32/.195	45/.304	—
	17085486	12/32	Fixed	①	.085	—	1	28/.164	Fixed	32/.195	45/.304	—
	17085487	12/32	Fixed	①	.085	—	1	28/.164	Fixed	32/.195	45/.304	—
'86	17086484	12/32	Fixed	①	.085	—	1	28/.164	Fixed	32/.195	45/.304	—
	17086485	12/32	Fixed	①	.085	—	1	28/.164	Fixed	32/.195	45/.304	—
	17086486	4/32	Fixed	①	.085	—	1	28/.164	Fixed	32/.195	45/.304	—
	17086487	4/32	Fixed	①	.085	—	1	28/.164	Fixed	32/.195	45/.304	—

① See underhood decal
② Not available

Models 2MC, M2MC, M2ME and E2ME

The Rochester model 2MC carburetor is a two-barrel single stage carburetor which incorporates the design features of the primary side of the Rochester Quadrajet four-barrel carburetor. It is used on small displacement V8s. The M2MC version with front and rear vacuum brake diaphragms, was introduced on the 301 V8.

The Dualjet E2ME Model 210 is a variation of the M2ME, modified for use with the Electronic Fuel Control System (also called the Computer Controlled Catalytic Converter, or C-4, System). An electrically operated mixture control solenoid is mounted in the float bowl. Mixture is thus controlled by the Electronic Control Module, in response to signals from the oxygen sensor mounted in the exhaust system upstream of the catalytic converter.

For further information on feedback carburetors, please refer to *Chilton's Guide To Fuel Injection And Feedback Carburetors.*

FLOAT LEVEL ADJUSTMENT

See the illustration for float level adjustment for all carburetors. The E2ME procedure is the same except for adjustment (step 4 in the figure). For the E2ME only, if the float level is too high, hold the retainer firmly in place and push down on the center of the float to adjust.

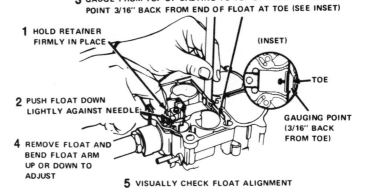

3 GAUGE FROM TOP OF CASTING TO TOP OF FLOAT – GAUGING POINT 3/16" BACK FROM END OF FLOAT AT TOE (SEE INSET)

1 HOLD RETAINER FIRMLY IN PLACE

(INSET)

2 PUSH FLOAT DOWN LIGHTLY AGAINST NEEDLE

4 REMOVE FLOAT AND BEND FLOAT ARM UP OR DOWN TO ADJUST

5 VISUALLY CHECK FLOAT ALIGNMENT AFTER ADJUSTING

TOE

GAUGING POINT (3/16" BACK FROM TOE)

2MC, M2MC, M2ME, E2ME float level adjustment—typical

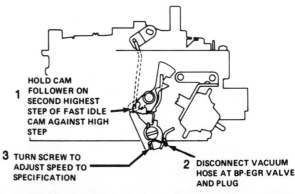

1 HOLD CAM FOLLOWER ON SECOND HIGHEST STEP OF FAST IDLE CAM AGAINST HIGH STEP

3 TURN SCREW TO ADJUST SPEED TO SPECIFICATION

2 DISCONNECT VACUUM HOSE AT BP-EGR VALVE AND PLUG

M2MC and E2ME fast idle speed adjustment—typical

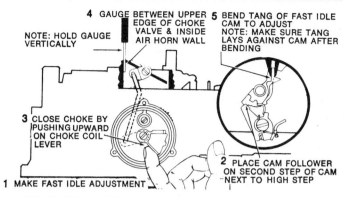

2MC, M2MC, M2ME, E2ME fast idle cam adjustment—typical

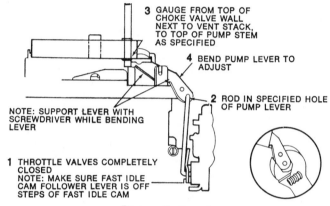

Pump adjustment

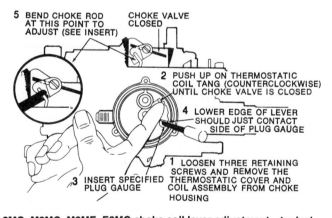

2MC, M2MC, M2ME, E2MC choke coil lever adjustment—typical

FAST IDLE CAM (CHOKE ROD) ADJUSTMENT

1. Adjust the fast idle speed.
2. Place the cam follower lever on the second step of the fast idle cam, holding it firmly against the rise of the high step.
3. Close the choke valve by pushing upward on the choke coil lever inside the choke housing, or by pushing up on the vacuum break lever tang.
4. Gauge between the upper edge of the choke valve and the inside of the air horn wall.
5. Bend the tang on the fast idle cam to adjust.

PUMP ADJUSTMENT

This adjustment is not required on E2ME carburetors used in conjunction with the computer controlled systems.

1. With the fast idle cam follower off the steps of the fast idle cam, back out the idle speed screw until the throttle valves are completely closed.
2. Place the pump rod in the proper hole of the lever.
3. Measure from the top of the choke valve wall, next to the vent stack, to the top of the pump stem.
4. Bend the pump lever to adjust.

CHOKE COIL LEVER ADJUSTMENT

1. Remove the choke cover and thermostatic coil from the choke housing. On models with a fixed choke cover, drill out the rivets and remove the cover. A stat cover kit will be required for assembly.
2. Push up on the coil tang (counterclockwise) until the choke valve is closed. The top of the choke rod should be at the bottom of the slot in the choke valve lever. Place the fast idle cam follower on the high step of the cam.
3. Insert a 0.120 in. plug gauge in the hole in the choke housing.
4. The lower edge of the choke coil lever should just contact the side of the plug gauge.
5. Bend the choke rod to adjust.

2MC LEAN/RICH VACUUM BRAKE ADJUSTMENT

1. Place the cam follower on the highest step of the fast idle cam.
2. Seat the vacuum break diaphragm by using an outside vacuum source. Tape over the bleed hole, if any, under the rubber cover on the diaphragm.
3. Remove the choke cover and

If the float level is too low on the E2ME, lift out the metering rods. Remove the solenoid connector screws. Turn the lean mixture solenoid screw in clockwise, counting the exact number of turns until the screw is lightly bottomed in the bowl. Then turn the screw out counterclockwise and remove it. Lift out the solenoid and connector. Remove the float and bend the arm up to adjust. Install the parts, installing the mixture solenoid screw in until it is lightly bottomed, then turn-ing it out the exact number of turns counted earlier.

FAST IDLE SPEED

1. Place the fast idle lever on the high step of the fast idle cam.
2. Turn the fast idle screw out until the throttle valves are closed.
3. Turn the screw in to contact the lever, then turn it in the number of turns listed in the specifications. Check this preliminary setting against the sticker figure.

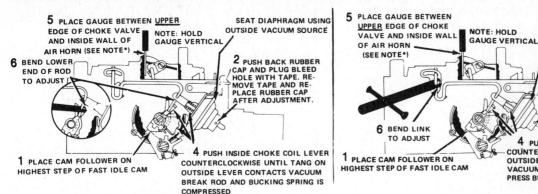

5 PLACE GAUGE BETWEEN UPPER EDGE OF CHOKE VALVE AND INSIDE WALL OF AIR HORN (SEE NOTE*)

NOTE: HOLD GAUGE VERTICAL

6 BEND LOWER END OF ROD TO ADJUST

SEAT DIAPHRAGM USING OUTSIDE VACUUM SOURCE

2 PUSH BACK RUBBER CAP AND PLUG BLEED HOLE WITH TAPE. REMOVE TAPE AND REPLACE RUBBER CAP AFTER ADJUSTMENT.

1 PLACE CAM FOLLOWER ON HIGHEST STEP OF FAST IDLE CAM

4 PUSH INSIDE CHOKE COIL LEVER COUNTERCLOCKWISE UNTIL TANG ON OUTSIDE LEVER CONTACTS VACUUM BREAK ROD AND BUCKING SPRING IS COMPRESSED

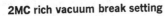

2MC rich vacuum break setting

5 PLACE GAUGE BETWEEN UPPER EDGE OF CHOKE VALVE AND INSIDE WALL OF AIR HORN (SEE NOTE*)

NOTE: HOLD GAUGE VERTICAL

3 SEAT DIAPHRAGM USING OUTSIDE VACUUM SOURCE

2 PUSH BACK RUBBER CAP AND PLUG BLEED HOLE WITH TAPE. REMOVE TAPE AND REPLACE RUBBER CAP AFTER ADJUSTMENT.

6 BEND LINK TO ADJUST

1 PLACE CAM FOLLOWER ON HIGHEST STEP OF FAST IDLE CAM

4 PUSH INSIDE CHOKE COIL LEVER COUNTERCLOCKWISE UNTIL TANG ON OUTSIDE LEVER JUST CONTACTS VACUUM BREAK ROD (DO NOT COMPRESS BUCKING SPRING)

2MC lean vacuum break setting

thermostatic coil and push up on the coil lever inside the choke housing until the tang on the vacuum break lever contacts the tang on the vacuum break plunger stem. Do not compress the bucking spring for lean adjustment. Compress the bucking spring for rich adjustment.

4. With the choke rod in the bottom of the slot in the choke lever, gauge between the upper edge of the choke valve and the inside wall of the air horn.

5. Bend the link rod at the vacuum break plunger stem to adjust the rich setting. Bend the link rod at the opposite end from the diaphragm to adjust the lean setting.

FRONT/REAR VACUUM BRAKE ADJUSTMENT
M2MC, M2ME and E2ME (1980)

1. Sat the front diaphragm, using an outside vacuum source. If there is an air bleed hole on the diaphragm, tape it over.

2. Remove the choke cover and coil. Rotate the inside coil lever counterclockwise. On models with a fixed choke cover (riveted), push up on the vacuum break lever tang and hold it in position with a rubber band.

3. Check that the specified gap is present between the top of the choke valve and the air horn wall.

4. Turn the front vacuum break adjusting screw to adjust.

5. To adjust the rear vacuum break diaphragm, perform Steps 1–3 on the rear diaphragm, but make sure that the plunger bucking spring is compressed and seated in Step 2. Adjust by bending the link at the bend nearest the diaphragm.

1981–84 Models

On these models a choke valve measuring gauge J-26701 or equivalent is used to measure angle (degrees instead of inches). See illustration for procedure.

1 REMOVE VACUUM BREAK FROM CARBURETOR. PLACE BRACKET IN A VISE AND, USING SAFETY PRECAUTIONS, GRIND OFF ADJUSTMENT SCREW CAP. REINSTALL VACUUM BREAK.

9 TO ADJUST, USING 1/8" HEX WRENCH TURN SCREW IN REAR COVER UNTIL BUBBLE IS CENTERED. APPLY SEALER (SUCH AS SILICONE SEALANT RTV RUBBER OR EQUIVALENT) OVER SCREW HEAD TO SEAL SETTING.

RUBBER BAND

PLUNGER BUCKING SPRING

7 SEAT DIAPHRAGM USING VACUUM SOURCE (SEE NOTE 2)

FIGURE 2

6 SPECIFIED ANGLE (SEE SPECS.)

5 LEVELING BUBBLE (CENTERED)

2 DEGREE SCALE
3 POINTER MAGNET

4 CHOKE VALVE CLOSED

FIGURE 1

PUMP PLUNGER CUP   FIGURE 3

8 LIGHTLY CLOSE CHOKE BY PUSHING UPWARD ON CHOKE COIL LEVER OR VACUUM BREAK LEVER TANG (HOLD IN POSITION WITH RUBBER BAND). MAKE SURE PLUNGER BUCKING SPRING (IF USED) IS COMPRESSED AND SEATED.

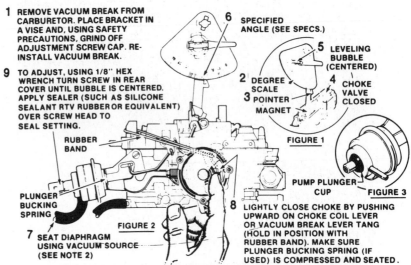

NOTE 2: ON DELAY MODELS, PLUG END COVER USING AN ACCELERATOR PUMP PLUNGER CUP - 2G TYPE (FIGURE 3) OR EQUIVALENT. SEAT VACUUM DIAPHRAGM MAKING SURE VACUUM IS ABOVE 5" Hg WHEN READING GAUGE (STEP 9). REMOVE CUP AFTER ADJUSTMENT.

NOTE 1: MAKE CHOKE COIL LEVER ADJUSTMENT AND FAST IDLE ADJUSTMENT. DO NOT REMOVE RIVETS AND CHOKE COVER TO PERFORM THIS ADJUSTMENT. USE RUBBER BAND ON VACUUM BREAK LEVER TANG TO HOLD CHOKE VALVE CLOSED (STEP 8).

E2ME rear vacuum break adjustment—1981–82

NOTE 2: LEAF BUCKING SPRING MUST BE SEATED AGAINST LEVER (WHERE USED)

RUBBER BAND

8 LIGHTLY CLOSE CHOKE BY PUSHING UPWARD ON CHOKE COIL LEVER OR VACUUM BREAK LEVER TANG (HOLD IN POSITION WITH RUBBER BAND).

6 SPECIFIED ANGLE (SEE SPECS.)

5 LEVELING BUBBLE (CENTERED)

2 DEGREE SCALE
3 POINTER MAGNET

4 CHOKE VALVE CLOSED

9 TURN SCREW TO ADJUST UNTIL BUBBLE IS CENTERED

FIGURE 1

7 SEAT DIAPHRAGM USING VACUUM SOURCE

NOTE: ON DELAY MODELS WITH AIR BLEED, REMOVE RUBBER COVER OVER FILTER ELEMENT AND PLUG SMALL BLEED HOLE IN VACUUM TUBE WITH TAPE. REMOVE TAPE AFTER ADJUSTMENT.

FIGURE 2

1 REMOVE VACUUM BREAK FROM CARBURETOR. PLACE BRACKET IN A VISE AND, USING SAFETY PRECAUTIONS, GRIND OFF WELD HOLDING ADJUSTMENT SCREW COVER. REMOVE COVER AND REINSTALL VACUUM BREAK.

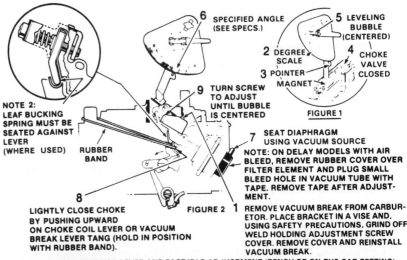

NOTE 1: MAKE CHOKE COIL LEVER AND FAST IDLE ADJUSTMENT (BENCH OR ON-THE-CAR SETTING). DO NOT REMOVE RIVETS AND CHOKE COVER TO PERFORM THIS ADJUSTMENT. USE RUBBER BAND ON VACUUM BREAK LEVER TANG TO HOLD CHOKE VALVE CLOSED (STEP 8).

E2ME front vacuum break adjustment—1981–82

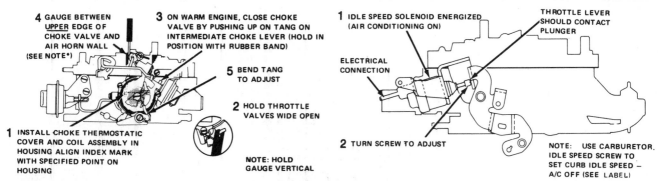

4 GAUGE BETWEEN <u>UPPER</u> EDGE OF CHOKE VALVE AND AIR HORN WALL (SEE NOTE*)

3 ON WARM ENGINE, CLOSE CHOKE VALVE BY PUSHING UP ON TANG ON INTERMEDIATE CHOKE LEVER (HOLD IN POSITION WITH RUBBER BAND)

5 BEND TANG TO ADJUST

2 HOLD THROTTLE VALVES WIDE OPEN

1 INSTALL CHOKE THERMOSTATIC COVER AND COIL ASSEMBLY IN HOUSING ALIGN INDEX MARK WITH SPECIFIED POINT ON HOUSING

NOTE: HOLD GAUGE VERTICAL

2MC, M2MC, M2ME, E2ME unloader adjustment—typical

1 IDLE SPEED SOLENOID ENERGIZED (AIR CONDITIONING ON)

THROTTLE LEVER SHOULD CONTACT PLUNGER

ELECTRICAL CONNECTION

2 TURN SCREW TO ADJUST

NOTE: USE CARBURETOR IDLE SPEED SCREW TO SET CURB IDLE SPEED — A/C OFF (SEE LABEL)

2MC, M2MC air conditioning idle speed-up solenoid adjustment

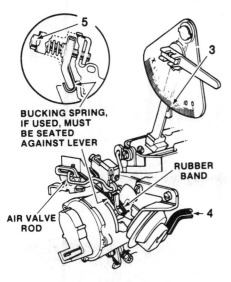

5

BUCKING SPRING, IF USED, MUST BE SEATED AGAINST LEVER

RUBBER BAND

AIR VALVE ROD

4

1 ATTACH RUBBER BAND TO GREEN TANG OF INTERMEDIATE CHOKE SHAFT

2 OPEN THROTTLE TO ALLOW CHOKE VALVE TO CLOSE

3 SET UP ANGLE GAGE AND SET TO SPECIFICATION

4 RETRACT VACUUM BREAK PLUNGER USING VACUUM SOURCE, AT LEAST 18" HG. PLUG AIR BLEED HOLES WHERE APPLICABLE ON QUADRAJETS, AIR VALVE ROD MUST NOT RESTRICT PLUNGER FROM RETRACTING FULLY. IF NECESSARY, BEND ROD (SEE ARROW) TO PERMIT FULL PLUNGER TRAVEL. FINAL ROD CLEARANCE MUST BE SET AFTER VACUUM BREAK SETTING HAS BEEN MADE.

5 WITH AT LEAST 18" HG STILL APPLIED, ADJUST SCREW TO CENTER BUBBLE

E2ME front vacuum break adjstment—1983 and later

1 ATTACH RUBBER BAND TO GREEN TANG OF INTERMEDIATE CHOKE SHAFT.

2 OPEN THROTTLE TO ALLOW CHOKE VALVE TO CLOSE.

3 SET UP ANGLE GAGE AND SET ANGLE TO SPECIFICATION.

4 RETRACT VACUUM BREAK PLUNGER, USING VACUUM SOURCE, AT LEAST 18" HG. PLUG AIR BLEED HOLES WHERE APPLICABLE.

4A ON QUADRAJETS, AIR VALVE ROD MUST NOT RESTRICT PLUNGER FROM RETRACTING FULLY. IF NECESSARY. BEND ROD HERE TO PERMIT FULL PLUNGER TRAVEL. WHERE APPLICABLE, PLUNGER STEM MUST BE EXTENDED FULLY TO COMPRESS PLUNGER BUCKING SPRING.

5 TO CENTER BUBBLE, EITHER:
A. ADJUST WITH 1/8" HEX WRENCH (VACUUM STILL APPLIED)

-OR-

B. SUPPORT AT "S" AND BEND VACUUM BREAK ROD (VACUUM STILL APPLIED)

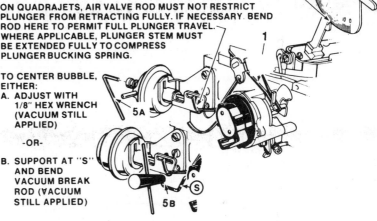

E2ME rear vacuum break adjustment— 1983 and later

UNLOADER ADJUSTMENT

1. With the choke valve completely closed, hold the throttle valves wide open.

2. Measure between the upper edge of the choke valve and air horn wall.

3. Bend the tang on the fast idle lever to obtain the proper measurement.

AIR CONDITIONING IDLE SPEED-UP SOLENOID ADJUSTMENT

1. With the engine at normal operating temperature and the air conditioning turned on but the compressor clutch lead disconnected, the solenoid should be electrically energized (plunger stem extended). Open the throttle slightly to allow the solenoid plunger to fully extend.

2. Adjust the plunger screw to obtain the specified idle speed.

3. Turn off the air conditioner. The solenoid plunger should move away from the tang on the throttle lever.

4. Adjust the curb idle speed with the idle speed screw, if necessary.

NOTE: Do not adjust if carburetor is computer controlled.

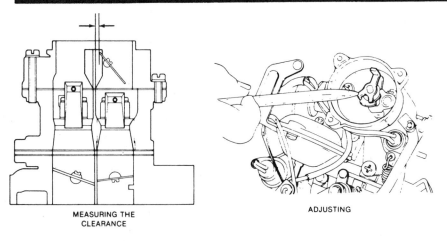

MEASURING THE
CLEARANCE

ADJUSTING

Choke valve adjustment (third stage) — Spectrum

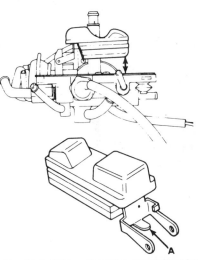

Throttle position sensor adjustment — Spectrum

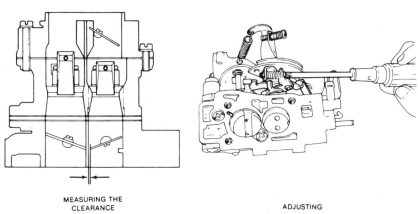

MEASURING THE
CLEARANCE

ADJUSTING

Primary throttle valve opening (second stage) — Spectrum

Bend tab (A) to adjust the upper float level — Spectrum

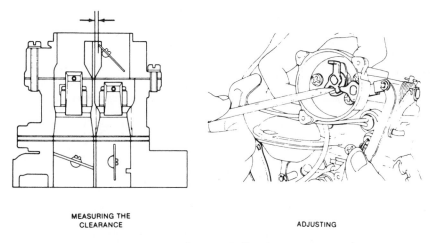

MEASURING THE
CLEARANCE

ADJUSTING

Unloader adjustment — Spectrum

THROTTLE POSITION SENSOR (TPS) TEST AND ADJUSTMENT

NOTE: After the connection of the ohmmeter is made to the TPS, this test should be performed in as short of time as possible.

1. Check that the TPS bracket screws are tight.
2. Check that there is no play in the TPS arm and primary throttle valve arm.
3. Connect an ohmmeter to the green and black leads of the TPS.
4. Open the throttle lever about one-third (no continuity in this case) and then gradually close the lever and check that there is continuity when the primary slot valve reaches the the prescribed clearance of .015(A/T), .011(M/T).
5. Adjust by loosening the TPS screws. After adjustment check the clearance as in step 4.

SECONDARY TOUCH ANGLE

1. Measure the primary throttle

the housing. Reinstall the choke lever by riveting.

CHOKE BREAKER ADJUSTMENT

1. Apply a vacuum of about 400mm

Hg to the choke breaker diaphragm unit.

2. Lightly push the choke valve to the closing side. The clearance should be 1985: 0.053 in., 1986: 0.057 in.

3. Adjust by bending the choke lever.

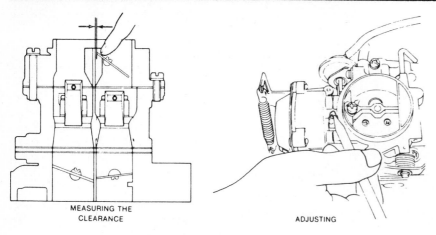

MEASURING THE CLEARANCE

ADJUSTING

Choke breaker adjustment – Spectrum

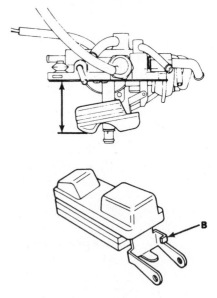

B

Bend tab (B) to adjust the lower float level – Spectrum

valve opening at the same time the secondary throttle valve starts to open.

2. The clearance should be 0.023 in. Adjust by bending the throttle adjusting arm.

FLOAT LEVEL ADJUSTMENT

1. Measure the clearance between

the float top and gasket when the float is in the raised position. The clearance should be 0.059 in.

2. Bend tab (A) to adjust.

NOTE: Care should be taken not to damage the needle valve when adjusting the float level.

3. Measure the clearance between the float bottom and gasket at the

lowered position of the float. the clearance should be 1.7 in. Adjust by bending (B) shown in the illustration.

Sprint Two Barrel Carburetor (MRO8)

FLOAT LEVEL ADJUSTMENT

The fuel level in the float chamber should be within the round mark at the center of the level gauge. If it is not check and adjust the float level as follows:

1. Remove and invert the air horn.
2. Measure the distance between the float and the gasketed surface of the choke chamber. The measured distance is the float level and it should be 0.21–0.24 in. The measurement should be made without the gasket on the air horn.
3. Adjustment is made by bending the tounge up and down.

IDLE-UP ADJUSTMENT

The idle-up actuator operates even when the cooling fan is running. Therefore the idle-up adjustment must be performed when the cooling fan is not running.

M/T Models

1. Warm up the engine to normal operating temperature.

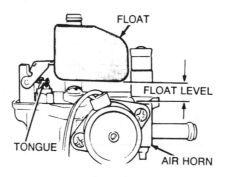

FLOAT

FLOAT LEVEL

TONGUE

AIR HORN

Float level adjustment – Sprint

2. After warming up, run the engine at idle speed.

3. Check to make sure that the idle-up adjusting screw moves down (indicating that the idle-up is at work) when the lights are turned ON.

4. With the lights turned ON, check the engine rpm (idle-up speed). Be sure that the heater fan, rear defogger (if equipped), engine cooling fan, and air conditioner (if equipped) are all turned OFF. The idle-up speed should be 750–850 rpm. Adjust by turning the adjusting screw.

5. After making the idle-up adjust-

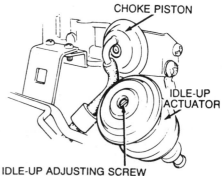

CHOKE PISTON

IDLE-UP ACTUATOR

IDLE-UP ADJUSTING SCREW

Idle-up adjusting screw – Sprint

ment, make sure the idle-up adjusting screw moves as in Step 3 when only the heater fan is operated and then only the rear defogger or engine cooling fan is operated (lights should be off).

A/T Models

1. Warm up the engine to normal operating temperature.
2. After warming up, run the engine at idle speed.
3. Apply the parking brake and

block the drive wheels.

4. Turn all accessories OFF.

5. With the brake pedal depressed, shift the selector lever to "D" (Drive) range. Check to make sure that the idle-up adjusting screw moves down (indicating that the idle-up is at work).

6. Check the idle-up speed (do not depress the accelerator pedal). The Idle-up speed should be between 700–800 rpm. Adjustment is made by turning the adjusting screw.

CHOKE ADJUSTMENT

Perform the following check and adjustments with the air cleaner top removed and the engine cold.

Choke Valve

1. Check the choke valve for smooth movement by pushing it with a finger.

2. Make sure that the choke valve is closed almost completely when ambient temperature is below 77°F and the engine is cold.

3. Check to see that the choke valve to carburetor bore clearance is within specifications when the ambient temperature is above 77°F and the engine is cool.

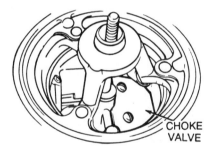

Choke valve – Sprint

4. If clearance is found excessively large or small in the above check, remove the air cleaner case and check the strangler spring, choke piston and each link in the choke system for smooth operation. Lubricate the choke valve shaft and each link with a spray lubricant if necessary. Do not remove the rivetted choke lever guide.

5. If after lubrication the clearance is still out of specification, remove the carburetor from the intake manifold and remove the idle-up actuator from the carburetor. Turn the fast idle cam counterclockwise and insert an available pin into the holes on the cam and bracket to lock the cam. In this state, bend the choke lever up or down with pliers. Bending up causes the choke valve to close, and vice versa.

Ambient temperature	Clearance
25°C (77°F)	0.1—0.5 mm 0.004—0.019 in
35°C (95°F)	0.7—1.7 mm 0.03—0.06 in

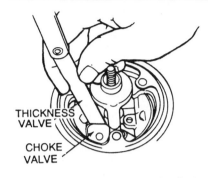

Choke valve to bore clearance – Sprint

Choke Piston

1. Disconnect the choke piston hose at the throttle chamber.

2. While lightly pushing down on the choke valve to the closing position with your finger, apply vacuum to the choke piston hose, and check to make sure that the choke valve to the carburetor bore clearance is 0.09–0.10 in.

3. With vacum applied as in step 2, move the choke piston rod with a small tool and check to see that the choke valve to carburetor bore clearance is within 0.16–0.18 1n.

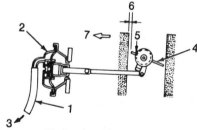

1. Choke piston hose
2. Choke piston
3. Vacuum
4. Choke valve
5. Push here lightly
6. Choke valve to bore clearance
7. Forward

Checking choke piston – Sprint

FAST IDLE CAM ADJUSTMENT

NOTE: Ambient temperature must be between 72–82°F before performing this check.

1. Drain the cooling system when the engine is cold, and remove the carburetor from the intake manifold.

2. Leave the carburetor in a place

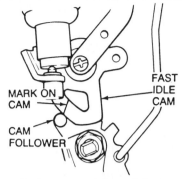

Mark on cam and cam follower

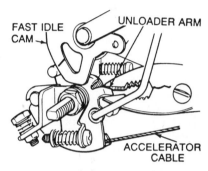

Unloader level arm – Sprint

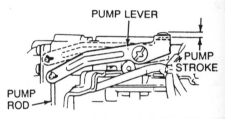

Pump stroke – Sprint

where the ambient temperature is between 72–82°F for an hour.

3. After an hour, make sure that the mark on the cam and the center of the cam follower are in alignment.

UNLOADER ADJUSTMENT

NOTE: Perform this check and adjustment when the engine is cool.

1. Remove the air cleaner cover.

2. Make sure that the choke valve is closed.

3. Fully open the throttle valve and check the choke valve to carburetor bore clearance is within 0.10–0.12 in.

4. If the clearance is out of specification adjust by bending the unloader arm.

PUMP STROKE ADJUSTMENT

1. Warm up the engine to normal operating temperature.

2. Stop the engine and remove the air cleaner.

3. Depress the accelerator pedal all the way from idle position to wide open throttle and take the measurement of the pump stroke. The pump stroke should be 0.16–0.18 in. If out of specification check the pump lever and pump rod for smooth movement.

Nova Two Barrel Carburetor

FLOAT ADJUSTMENT

1. Allow the float the hang down by its own weight. Check the clearance between the float tip and air horn. The float level should be 0.075 in.

NOTE: This measurement should be made without a gasket on the air horn.

2. Adjust by bending a portion of the float lip.

3. Lift up the float and check the clearance between the needle valve plunger and the float lip. The float level in the lowered position should be 0.0657–0.0783 in.

4. Adjust by bending a portion of the float lip.

THROTTLE VALVE OPENING

1. Check the full opening angle of the primary throttle valve, with a T scale. The standard angle should be 90° from the horizontal plane.

2. Adjust by bending the 1st throttle lever stopper.

3. Check the full opening clearance between the secondary throttle valve and the body. The standard clearance should be 0.500 in.

4. Adjust by bending the secondary throttle lever stopper.

KICK-UP ADJUSTMENT

1. With the primary throttle valve fully opened, check the clearance between the secondary throttle valve and the body. The clearance should be 0.006 in.

2. Adjust by bending the secondary throttle lever.

SECONDARY TOUCH ADJUSTMENT

1. Check the primary throttle valve opening clearance at the same time the 1st kick lever just touches the 2nd kick lever. The clearance should be 1985: 0.170 in., 1986: 0.230 in.

2. Adjust by bending the 1st kick lever.

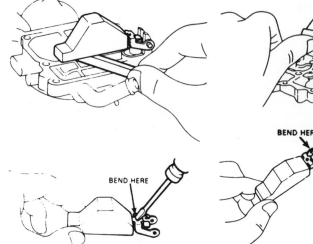

BEND HERE

BEND HERE

Checking the float level in the upper position—Nova

Checking the float level in the lower position—Nova

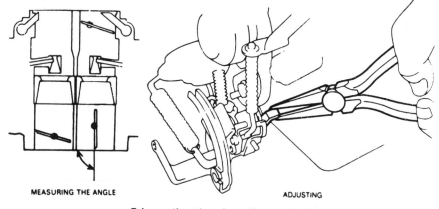

MEASURING THE ANGLE

ADJUSTING

Primary throttle valve adjustment—Nova

UNLOADER ADJUSTMENT

1. With the primary throttle valve fully opened, check that the choke valve clearance is 0.120 in.

2. Adjust by bending the fast idle lever.

CHOKE BREAKER ADJUSTMENT

1. Set the idle cam. While holding the throttle slightly open, push the choke valve closed, and hold it closed as you release the throttle valve.

2. Apply vacuum to the choke breaker 1st diaphragm.

3. Check the choke valve clearance. It should be 0.095 in.

4. Adjust by bending the relief lever.

5. Apply vacuum to choke diaphragms 1st and 2nd.

6. Check the choke valve clearance. It should be 0.245 in.

7. Adjust by turning the diaphragm adjusting screw.

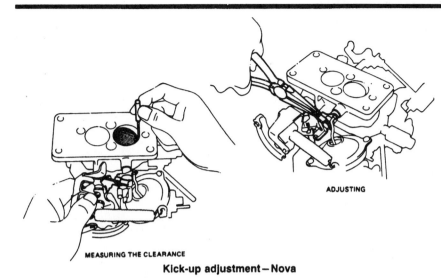

ADJUSTING

Kick-up adjustment – Nova

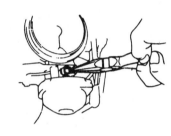

1ST DIAPHRAGM·

MEASURING THE CLEARANCE

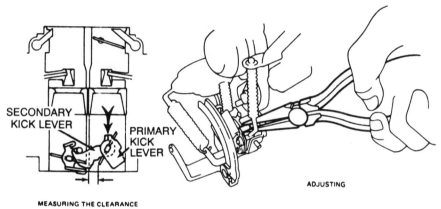

SECONDARY KICK LEVER

PRIMARY KICK LEVER

MEASURING THE CLEARANCE

ADJUSTING

Secondary touch adjustment – Nova

ADJUSTING

Choke breaker 1st diaphragm adjustment – Nova

2ND DIAPHRAGM

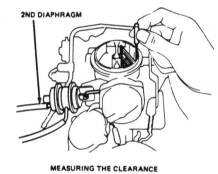

MEASURING THE CLEARANCE

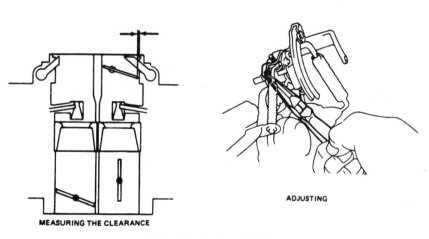

MEASURING THE CLEARANCE

Unloader adjustment – Nova

ADJUSTING

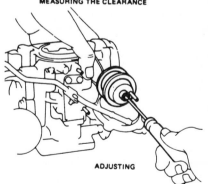

ADJUSTING

Choke breaker lst and 2nd diaphragm adjustment – Nova

PUMP STROKE ADJUSTMENT

1. With the choke fully opened, measure the length of the stroke. 1985: 0.157 in., 1986: 0.079 in.

2. Adjust the pump stroke by bending the connecting link.

LIGHT TRUCKS & VANS—ALL MODELS

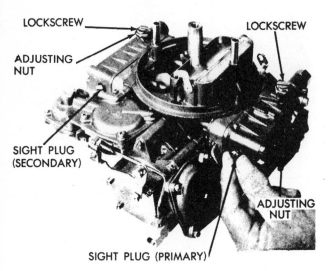

LOCKSCREW

ADJUSTING NUT

SIGHT PLUG (SECONDARY)

LOCKSCREW

ADJUSTING NUT

SIGHT PLUG (PRIMARY)

Fuel level sight plug location—Holley 4150 typical

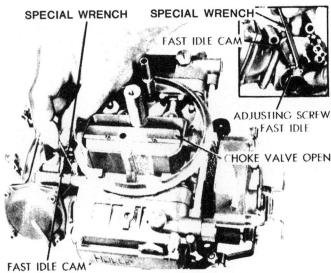

SPECIAL WRENCH

SPECIAL WRENCH

FAST IDLE CAM

ADJUSTING SCREW FAST IDLE

CHOKE VALVE OPEN

FAST IDLE CAM

Fast idle speed adjustment—Holley 4150 typical

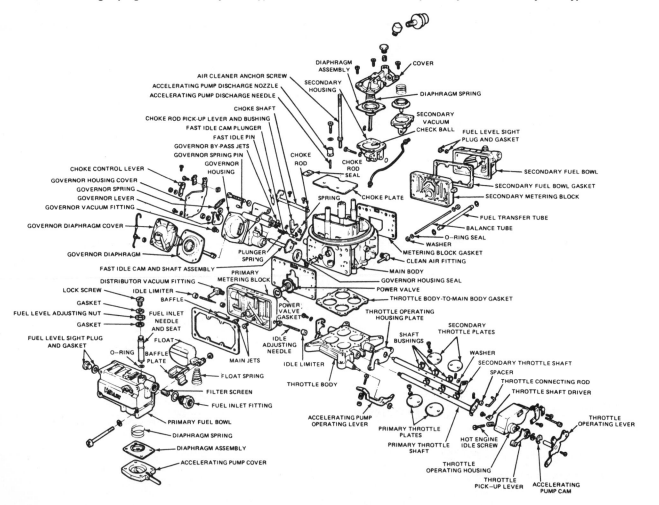

DIAPHRAGM ASSEMBLY

COVER

AIR CLEANER ANCHOR SCREW

ACCELERATING PUMP DISCHARGE NOZZLE

ACCELERATING PUMP DISCHARGE NEEDLE

SECONDARY HOUSING

DIAPHRAGM SPRING

CHOKE SHAFT

CHOKE ROD PICK-UP LEVER AND BUSHING

FAST IDLE CAM PLUNGER

FAST IDLE PIN

GOVERNOR BY-PASS JETS

GOVERNOR SPRING PIN

GOVERNOR HOUSING

CHOKE ROD

SECONDARY VACUUM CHECK BALL

FUEL LEVEL SIGHT PLUG AND GASKET

CHOKE CONTROL LEVER

GOVERNOR HOUSING COVER

GOVERNOR SPRING

GOVERNOR LEVER

GOVERNOR VACUUM FITTING

GOVERNOR DIAPHRAGM COVER

GOVERNOR DIAPHRAGM

FAST IDLE CAM AND SHAFT ASSEMBLY

DISTRIBUTOR VACUUM FITTING

LOCK SCREW

GASKET

FUEL LEVEL ADJUSTING NUT

GASKET

FUEL LEVEL SIGHT PLUG AND GASKET

O-RING

IDLE LIMITER

BAFFLE

PLUNGER SPRING

PRIMARY METERING BLOCK

POWER VALVE GASKET

FUEL INLET NEEDLE AND SEAT

FLOAT

BAFFLE PLATE

MAIN JETS

FLOAT SPRING

FILTER SCREEN

FUEL INLET FITTING

PRIMARY FUEL BOWL

DIAPHRAGM SPRING

DIAPHRAGM ASSEMBLY

ACCELERATING PUMP COVER

CHOKE ROD SEAL

SPRING

CHOKE PLATE

IDLE ADJUSTING NEEDLE

IDLE LIMITER

THROTTLE BODY

ACCELERATING PUMP OPERATING LEVER

PRIMARY THROTTLE PLATES

PRIMARY THROTTLE SHAFT

SECONDARY FUEL BOWL

SECONDARY FUEL BOWL GASKET

SECONDARY METERING BLOCK

FUEL TRANSFER TUBE

BALANCE TUBE

O-RING SEAL

WASHER

METERING BLOCK GASKET

CLEAN AIR FITTING

MAIN BODY

GOVERNOR HOUSING SEAL

POWER VALVE

THROTTLE BODY-TO-MAIN BODY GASKET

THROTTLE OPERATING HOUSING PLATE

SECONDARY THROTTLE PLATES

SHAFT BUSHINGS

WASHER

SECONDARY THROTTLE SHAFT

SPACER

THROTTLE CONNECTING ROD

THROTTLE SHAFT DRIVER

HOT ENGINE IDLE SCREW

THROTTLE OPERATING HOUSING

THROTTLE PICK-UP LEVER

ACCELERATING PUMP CAM

THROTTLE OPERATING LEVER

Holley four barrel—typical

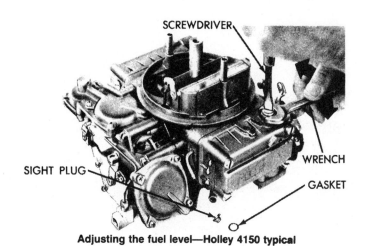

SCREWDRIVER

SIGHT PLUG

WRENCH

GASKET

Adjusting the fuel level—Holley 4150 typical

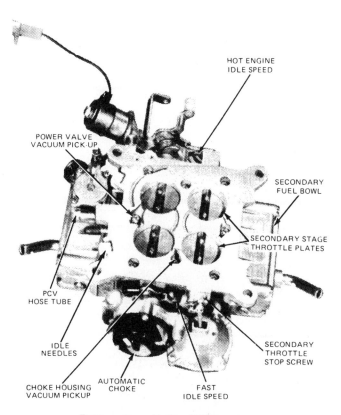

HOT ENGINE
IDLE SPEED

POWER VALVE
VACUUM PICK-UP

SECONDARY
FUEL BOWL

SECONDARY STAGE
THROTTLE PLATES

PCV
HOSE TUBE

IDLE
NEEDLES

CHOKE HOUSING
VACUUM PICKUP

AUTOMATIC
CHOKE

FAST
IDLE SPEED

SECONDARY
THROTTLE
STOP SCREW

Bottom view—Holley 4180C carburetor

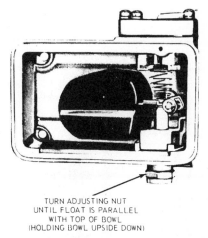

TURN ADJUSTING NUT
UNTIL FLOAT IS PARALLEL
WITH TOP OF BOWL
(HOLDING BOWL UPSIDE DOWN)

**Adjusting the float level (dry)—Holley 4150
typical**

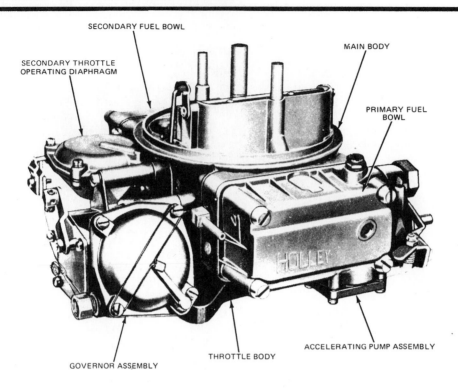

SECONDARY FUEL BOWL

SECONDARY THROTTLE
OPERATING DIAPHRAGM

MAIN BODY

PRIMARY FUEL
BOWL

ACCELERATING PUMP ASSEMBLY

GOVERNOR ASSEMBLY

THROTTLE BODY

Holley 4150 carburetor—typical

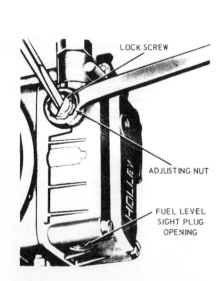

LOCK SCREW

ADJUSTING NUT

FUEL LEVEL
SIGHT PLUG
OPENING

**Adjusting the fuel level (wet)—Holley 4150
typical**

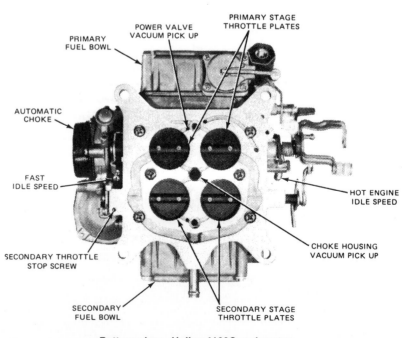

PRIMARY
FUEL BOWL

POWER VALVE
VACUUM PICK UP

PRIMARY STAGE
THROTTLE PLATES

AUTOMATIC
CHOKE

FAST
IDLE SPEED

HOT ENGINE
IDLE SPEED

SECONDARY THROTTLE
STOP SCREW

CHOKE HOUSING
VACUUM PICK UP

SECONDARY
FUEL BOWL

SECONDARY STAGE
THROTTLE PLATES

Bottom view—Holley 4160C carburetor

MODEL 4150EG
Chevrolet/GMC
(All measurements in inches)

Year	Carburetor Number	Float Level (Dry)	Accelerator Pump (Min.)	Fast Idle (rpm)	Air Vent Clearance	Fast Idle Mechanical Clearance
'79	R8278A	②	.015	2200	.045–.075	.031
	R8280A	②	.015	2200	.045–.075	.031
	R8282A	②	.015	2200	.045–.075	.031
	R8283A	②	.015	2200	.045–.075	.031
	R8444A	②	.015	2200	.045–.075	.031
	R8279A	②	.015	2200	.045–.075	.031
	R8281A	②	.015	2200	.045–.075	.031
'80–'84	R8848A	②	.015	2200	.045–.075	.031
	R8849A	②	.015	2200	.045–.075	.031
	R8852A	②	.015	2200	.045–.075	.031
	R8853A	②	.015	2200	.045–.075	.031
	R8856A	②	.015	2200	.045–.075	.031
	R8850A	②	.015	2200	—	.031
	R8851A	②	.015	2200	—	.031
	R8854A	②	.015	2200	—	.031
	R8855A	②	.015	2200	—	.031
	R8857A	②	.015	2200	—	.031
'85	All Numbers (Federal and Canadian)	②	#1	③	.045–.075	.031
	All Numbers (California)	②	#1	③	—	.031

Note: Secondary set screw should be ½ turn open
③ See underhood specifications sticker
① Primary bowl—.197
  Secondary bowl—.166
② Primary bowl—.194
  Secondary bowl—.213

MODEL 4152EG
Chevrolet/GMC
(All measurements in inches)

Year	Carburetor Number	Dry Float Level		Secondary Set Screw	Fast Idle	Pump Cam Position
		Primary	Secondary			
'85	All	.194	.213	½ turn open	.031 ①	#1 hole

① Mechanical setting

ROCHESTER CARBURETORS

IDLE MIXTURE ADJUSTMENT

Model 1ME Carburetor
LEAN IDLE DROP PROCEDURE

1. Set the parking brake and block the drive wheels of the vehicle.

2. Remove the air cleaner for access to the carburetor, but leave all vacuum hoses connected.

3. Disconnect and plug any vacuum hoses as directed on the underhood emission control sticker.

4. Place the transmission in Park (A/T) or Neutral (M/T).

5. Start the engine and allow it to reach normal operating temperature. The choke should be fully open and all accessories switched off.

6. Connect an accurate tachometer to the engine according to the manufacturer's instructions.

7. Disconnect the vacuum advance and plug the hose. Check the ignition timing and, if necessary, adjust to the specifications listed on the underhood sticker. Reconnect the vacuum advance.

8. Carefully remove the cap from the idle mixture screw. Exercise caution so as not to bend the screw. Lightly seat the screw, then back it out just enough so the engine will run.

9. Back the screw out ⅛ turn at a time until maximum idle speed is obtained, then set the idle speed to the higher value shown on the underhood specifications sticker. Repeat the step to make sure you have maximum idle speed.

10. Turn the mixture screw in ⅛ turn at a time until the idle speed reaches the lower value shown on the underhood specifications sticker.

11. Reset the idle speed to specification shown on the underhood sticker, then check and adjust the fast idle as described on the sticker. Reconnect all vacuum hoses.

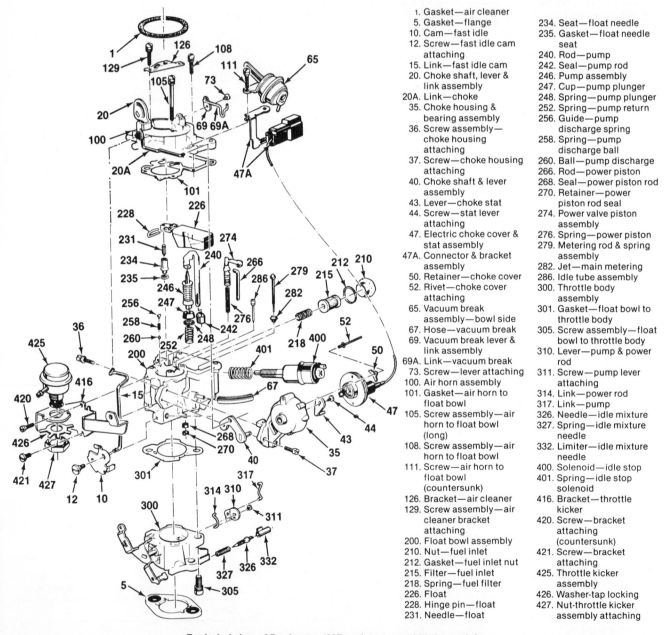

1. Gasket—air cleaner
5. Gasket—flange
10. Cam—fast idle
12. Screw—fast idle cam attaching
15. Link—fast idle cam
20. Choke shaft, lever & link assembly
20A. Link—choke
35. Choke housing & bearing assembly
36. Screw assembly—choke housing attaching
37. Screw—choke housing attaching
40. Choke shaft & lever assembly
43. Lever—choke stat
44. Screw—stat lever attaching
47. Electric choke cover & stat assembly
47A. Connector & bracket assembly
50. Retainer—choke cover
52. Rivet—choke cover attaching
65. Vacuum break assembly—bowl side
67. Hose—vacuum break
69. Vacuum break lever & link assembly
69A. Link—vacuum break
73. Screw—lever attaching
100. Air horn assembly
101. Gasket—air horn to float bowl
105. Screw assembly—air horn to float bowl (long)
108. Screw assembly—air horn to float bowl
111. Screw—air horn to float bowl (countersunk)
126. Bracket—air cleaner
129. Screw assembly—air cleaner bracket attaching
200. Float bowl assembly
210. Nut—fuel inlet
212. Gasket—fuel inlet nut
215. Filter—fuel inlet
218. Spring—fuel filter
226. Float
228. Hinge pin—float
231. Needle—float
234. Seat—float needle
235. Gasket—float needle seat
240. Rod—pump
242. Seal—pump rod
246. Pump assembly
247. Cup—pump plunger
248. Spring—pump plunger
252. Spring—pump return
256. Guide—pump discharge spring
258. Spring—pump discharge ball
260. Ball—pump discharge
266. Rod—power piston
268. Seal—power piston rod
270. Retainer—power piston rod seal
274. Power valve piston assembly
276. Spring—power piston
279. Metering rod & spring assembly
282. Jet—main metering
286. Idle tube assembly
300. Throttle body assembly
301. Gasket—float bowl to throttle body
305. Screw assembly—float bowl to throttle body
310. Lever—pump & power rod
311. Screw—pump lever attaching
314. Link—power rod
317. Link—pump
326. Needle—idle mixture
327. Spring—idle mixture needle
332. Limiter—idle mixture needle
400. Solenoid—idle stop
401. Spring—idle stop solenoid
416. Bracket—throttle kicker
420. Screw—bracket attaching (countersunk)
421. Screw—bracket attaching
425. Throttle kicker assembly
426. Washer-tap locking
427. Nut-throttle kicker assembly attaching

Exploded view of Rochester 1ME carburetor—1981-84 models

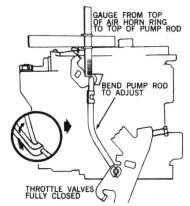

Accelerator pump rod adjustment—Rochester model 2G

IDLE MIXTURE ADJUSTMENT

Model 2SE Carburetor

PROPANE ENRICHMENT PROCEDURE

NOTE: The idle mixture screws have been adjusted at the time of manufacture and are sealed. Only after major carburetor overhaul, throttle body replacement or if high emissions are occurring, should any attempt be made to adjust the mixture screws. Mixture adjustment requires artificial enrichment by adding propane through the air cleaner assembly using suitable propane equipment and adapters. Refer to the underhood emission control sticker for instructions and propane enrichment rpm specifications before attempting adjustment.

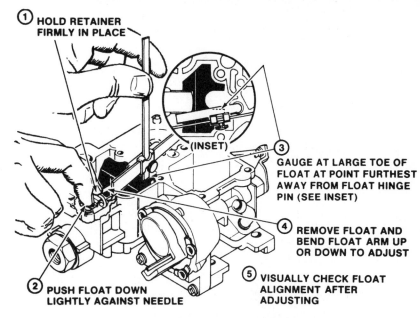

Setting float level—model 2SE carburetor

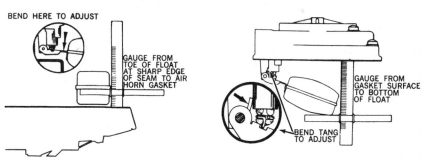

Float level adjustment—Rochester model 2G

Float drop adjustment—Rochester model 2G

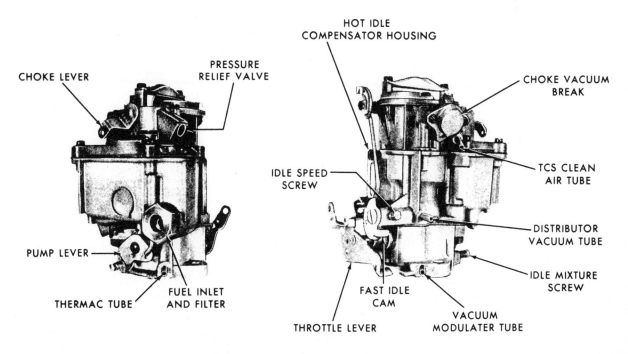

Rochester Monojet® carburetor—typical

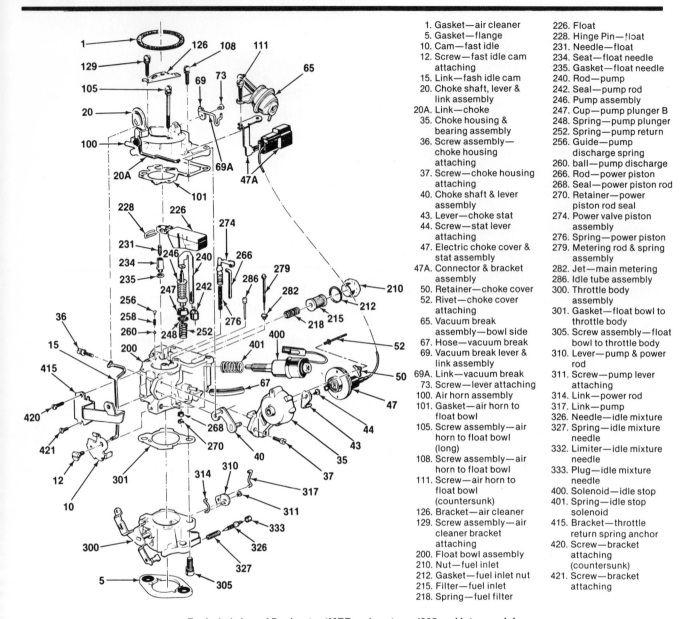

1. Gasket—air cleaner
5. Gasket—flange
10. Cam—fast idle
12. Screw—fast idle cam attaching
15. Link—fash idle cam
20. Choke shaft, lever & link assembly
20A. Link—choke
35. Choke housing & bearing assembly
36. Screw assembly—choke housing attaching
37. Screw—choke housing attaching
40. Choke shaft & lever assembly
43. Lever—choke stat
44. Screw—stat lever attaching
47. Electric choke cover & stat assembly
47A. Connector & bracket assembly
50. Retainer—choke cover
52. Rivet—choke cover attaching
65. Vacuum break assembly—bowl side
67. Hose—vacuum break
69. Vacuum break lever & link assembly
69A. Link—vacuum break
73. Screw—lever attaching
100. Air horn assembly
101. Gasket—air horn to float bowl
105. Screw assembly—air horn to float bowl (long)
108. Screw assembly—air horn to float bowl
111. Screw—air horn to float bowl (countersunk)
126. Bracket—air cleaner
129. Screw assembly—air cleaner bracket attaching
200. Float bowl assembly
210. Nut—fuel inlet
212. Gasket—fuel inlet nut
215. Filter—fuel inlet
218. Spring—fuel filter

226. Float
228. Hinge Pin—float
231. Needle—float
234. Seat—float needle
235. Gasket—float needle
240. Rod—pump
242. Seal—pump rod
246. Pump assembly
247. Cup—pump plunger B
248. Spring—pump plunger
252. Spring—pump return
256. Guide—pump discharge spring
260. ball—pump discharge
266. Rod—power piston
268. Seal—power piston rod
270. Retainer—power piston rod seal
274. Power valve piston assembly
276. Spring—power piston
279. Metering rod & spring assembly
282. Jet—main metering
286. Idle tube assembly
300. Throttle body assembly
301. Gasket—float bowl to throttle body
305. Screw assembly—float bowl to throttle body
310. Lever—pump & power rod
311. Screw—pump lever attaching
314. Link—power rod
317. Link—pump
326. Needle—idle mixture
327. Spring—idle mixture needle
332. Limiter—idle mixture needle
333. Plug—idle mixture needle
400. Solenoid—idle stop
401. Spring—idle stop solenoid
415. Bracket—throttle return spring anchor
420. Screw—bracket attaching (countersunk)
421. Screw—bracket attaching

Exploded view of Rochester 1MEF carburetor—1985 and later models

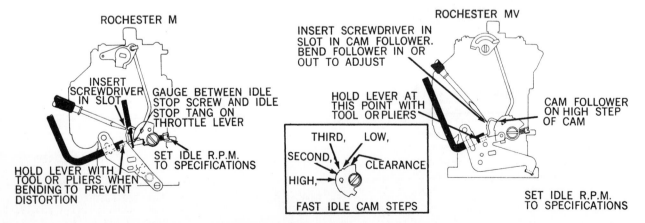

Fast idle adjustment—Monojet" carburetor

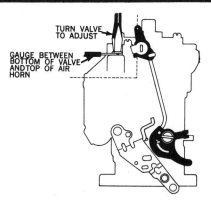

TURN VALVE TO ADJUST

GAUGE BETWEEN BOTTOM OF VALVE AND TOP OF AIR HORN

Idle vent adjustment—Monojet® carburetor

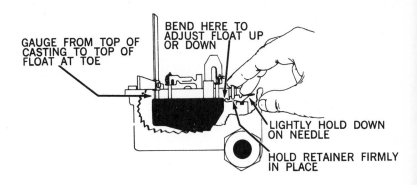

BEND HERE TO ADJUST FLOAT UP OR DOWN

GAUGE FROM TOP OF CASTING TO TOP OF FLOAT AT TOE

LIGHTLY HOLD DOWN ON NEEDLE

HOLD RETAINER FIRMLY IN PLACE

Float level adjustment—Monojet® carburetor

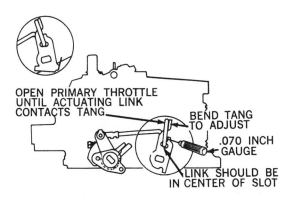

OPEN PRIMARY THROTTLE UNTIL ACTUATING LINK CONTACTS TANG

BEND TANG TO ADJUST

.070 INCH GAUGE

LINK SHOULD BE IN CENTER OF SLOT

Secondary opening adjustment—typical Quadrajet® carburetor

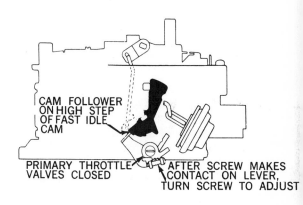

CAM FOLLOWER ON HIGH STEP OF FAST IDLE CAM

PRIMARY THROTTLE VALVES CLOSED

AFTER SCREW MAKES CONTACT ON LEVER, TURN SCREW TO ADJUST

Fast idle adjustment—typical Quadrajet® carburetor

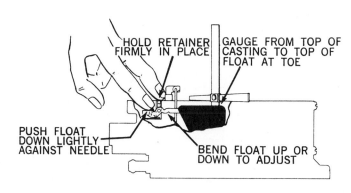

HOLD RETAINER FIRMLY IN PLACE

GAUGE FROM TOP OF CASTING TO TOP OF FLOAT AT TOE

PUSH FLOAT DOWN LIGHTLY AGAINST NEEDLE

BEND FLOAT UP OR DOWN TO ADJUST

Float level adjustment—typical Quadrajet® carburetor

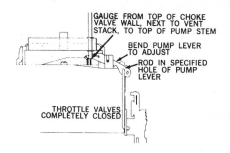

GAUGE FROM TOP OF CHOKE VALVE WALL, NEXT TO VENT STACK, TO TOP OF PUMP STEM

BEND PUMP LEVER TO ADJUST

ROD IN SPECIFIED HOLE OF PUMP LEVER

THROTTLE VALVES COMPLETELY CLOSED

Pump rod adjustment—typical Quadrajet® carburetor

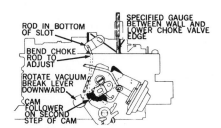

ROD IN BOTTOM OF SLOT

SPECIFIED GAUGE BETWEEN WALL AND LOWER CHOKE VALVE EDGE

BEND CHOKE ROD TO ADJUST

ROTATE VACUUM BREAK LEVER DOWNWARD

CAM FOLLOWER ON SECOND STEP OF CAM

Choke rod adjustment—typical Quadrajet® carburetor

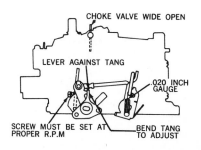

CHOKE VALVE WIDE OPEN

LEVER AGAINST TANG

.020 INCH GAUGE

SCREW MUST BE SET AT PROPER R.P.M

BEND TANG TO ADJUST

Secondary closing adjustment—typical Quadrajet® carburetor

FLOAT LEVEL ADJUSTMENT

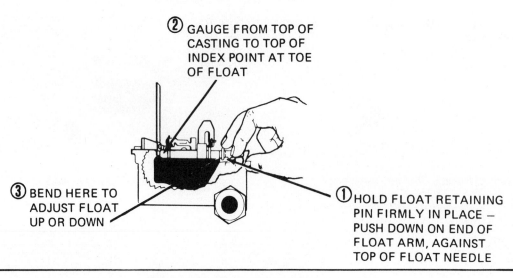

② GAUGE FROM TOP OF CASTING TO TOP OF INDEX POINT AT TOE OF FLOAT

③ BEND HERE TO ADJUST FLOAT UP OR DOWN

① HOLD FLOAT RETAINING PIN FIRMLY IN PLACE — PUSH DOWN ON END OF FLOAT ARM, AGAINST TOP OF FLOAT NEEDLE

METERING ROD ADJUSTMENT

③ HOLD POWER PISTON DOWN AND SWING METERING ROD HOLDER OVER FLAT SURFACE (GASKET REMOVED) OF BOWL CASTING NEXT TO CARBURETOR BORE

① REMOVE METERING ROD BY HOLDING THROTTLE VALVE WIDE OPEN. PUSH DOWNWARD ON METERING ROD AGAINST SPRING TENSION, THEN SLIDE METERING ROD OUT OF SLOT IN HOLDER AND REMOVE FROM MAIN METERING JET.

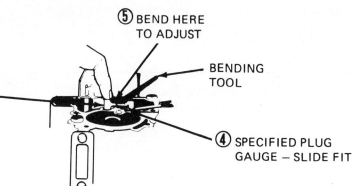
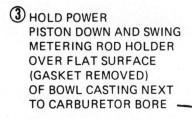

⑤ BEND HERE TO ADJUST

BENDING TOOL

④ SPECIFIED PLUG GAUGE — SLIDE FIT

② BACK OUT IDLE STOP SOLENOID — HOLD THROTTLE VALVE COMPLETELY CLOSED

CHOKE COIL LEVER ADJUSTMENT — 1ME

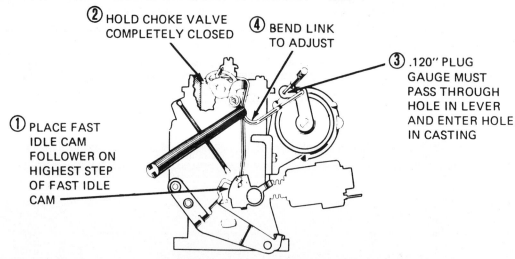

② HOLD CHOKE VALVE COMPLETELY CLOSED

④ BEND LINK TO ADJUST

③ .120" PLUG GAUGE MUST PASS THROUGH HOLE IN LEVER AND ENTER HOLE IN CASTING

① PLACE FAST IDLE CAM FOLLOWER ON HIGHEST STEP OF FAST IDLE CAM

Carburetor adjustments—1ME, 1MEF models

CHOKE ROD (FAST IDLE CAM) ADJUSTMENT (2ND STEP)

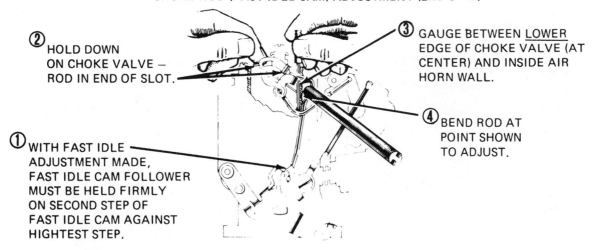

② HOLD DOWN
ON CHOKE VALVE —
ROD IN END OF SLOT.

③ GAUGE BETWEEN LOWER
EDGE OF CHOKE VALVE (AT
CENTER) AND INSIDE AIR
HORN WALL.

④ BEND ROD AT
POINT SHOWN
TO ADJUST.

① WITH FAST IDLE
ADJUSTMENT MADE,
FAST IDLE CAM FOLLOWER
MUST BE HELD FIRMLY
ON SECOND STEP OF
FAST IDLE CAM AGAINST
HIGHTEST STEP.

VACUUM BREAK ADJUSTMENT — 1ME (BOWL SIDE)

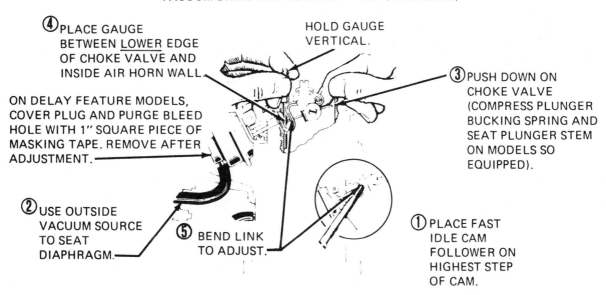

④ PLACE GAUGE
BETWEEN LOWER EDGE
OF CHOKE VALVE AND
INSIDE AIR HORN WALL.

HOLD GAUGE
VERTICAL.

③ PUSH DOWN ON
CHOKE VALVE
(COMPRESS PLUNGER
BUCKING SPRING AND
SEAT PLUNGER STEM
ON MODELS SO
EQUIPPED).

ON DELAY FEATURE MODELS,
COVER PLUG AND PURGE BLEED
HOLE WITH 1" SQUARE PIECE OF
MASKING TAPE. REMOVE AFTER
ADJUSTMENT.

② USE OUTSIDE
VACUUM SOURCE
TO SEAT
DIAPHRAGM.

⑤ BEND LINK
TO ADJUST.

① PLACE FAST
IDLE CAM
FOLLOWER ON
HIGHEST STEP
OF CAM.

UNLOADER ADJUSTMENT — 1ME (WIDE OPEN KICK)

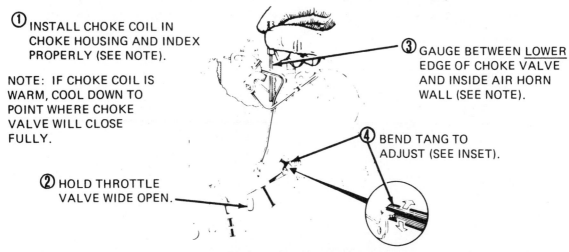

① INSTALL CHOKE COIL IN
CHOKE HOUSING AND INDEX
PROPERLY (SEE NOTE).

NOTE: IF CHOKE COIL IS
WARM, COOL DOWN TO
POINT WHERE CHOKE
VALVE WILL CLOSE
FULLY.

③ GAUGE BETWEEN LOWER
EDGE OF CHOKE VALVE
AND INSIDE AIR HORN
WALL (SEE NOTE).

④ BEND TANG TO
ADJUST (SEE INSET).

② HOLD THROTTLE
VALVE WIDE OPEN.

Carburetor adjustments—1ME, 1MEF models

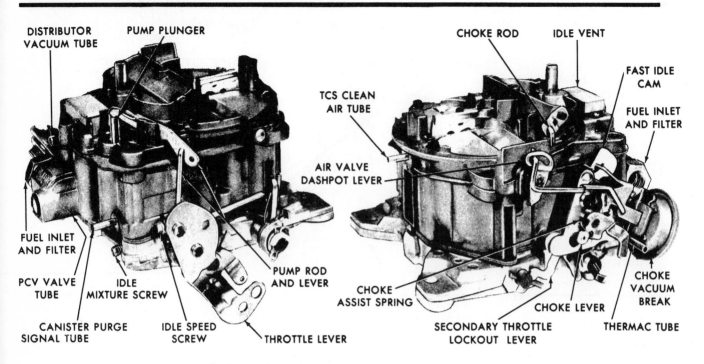

DISTRIBUTOR VACUUM TUBE

PUMP PLUNGER

CHOKE ROD

IDLE VENT

FAST IDLE CAM

FUEL INLET AND FILTER

TCS CLEAN AIR TUBE

AIR VALVE DASHPOT LEVER

FUEL INLET AND FILTER

PCV VALVE TUBE

IDLE MIXTURE SCREW

PUMP ROD AND LEVER

CHOKE VACUUM BREAK

CANISTER PURGE SIGNAL TUBE

IDLE SPEED SCREW

THROTTLE LEVER

CHOKE ASSIST SPRING

SECONDARY THROTTLE LOCKOUT LEVER

CHOKE LEVER

THERMAC TUBE

Rochester Quadrajet® carburetor (4MV shown)—typical

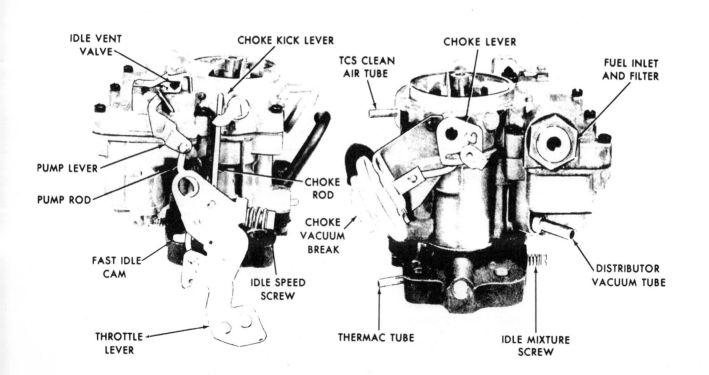

IDLE VENT VALVE

CHOKE KICK LEVER

CHOKE LEVER

FUEL INLET AND FILTER

TCS CLEAN AIR TUBE

PUMP LEVER

PUMP ROD

CHOKE ROD

CHOKE VACUUM BREAK

FAST IDLE CAM

IDLE SPEED SCREW

DISTRIBUTOR VACUUM TUBE

THROTTLE LEVER

THERMAC TUBE

IDLE MIXTURE SCREW

Rochester model 2GV—typical

1. Gasket—air cleaner
5. Gasket—flange
10. Cam—fast idle
12. Screw—fast idle cam attaching
15. Link—choke
18. Choke lever & swivel assembly
19. Screw—choke rod swivel
30. Choke control bracket assembly
100. Air horn assembly
101. Gasket—air horn to float bowl
105. Screw assembly—air horn to float bowl
107. Screw assembly—air horn to float bowl (long)
120. Nut—fuel inlet
122. Gasket—fuel inlet nut
125. Filter—fuel inlet
128. Spring—fuel filter
130. Link—pump
131. Retainer—pump link
134. Pump shaft & outside lever assembly
136. Washer—pump shaft
138. Seal—pump shaft
140. Lever—pump, inside
141. Screw—pump lever attaching
149. Pump assembly
150. Cup—pump plunger
151. Spring—pump plunger
152. Retainer—pump assembly
160. Float
162. Baffle—fuel inlet
165. Pin—float lever hinge
170. Needle—float
175. Seat—float needle
176. Gasket—float needle seat
180. Power valve piston assembly
200. Float bowl assembly
210. Spring—pump return
211. Ball—pump inlet check
230. Venturi cluster assembly
231. Gasket—venturi cluster to float bowl
235. Screw—venturi cluster—bowl attaching
236. Lockwasher—venturi cluster—bowl screw
238. Screw—venturi cluster—bowl attaching (center)
239. Gasket—venturi cluster to bowl pump discharge screw
245. Guide—pump discharge spring
247. Spring—pump discharge ball
248. Ball—pump discharge check
253. Jet—main metering
258. Power valve assembly—vacuum
259. Gasket—power valve assembly
262. power valve assembly (pump plunger-actuated)

263. Gasket—power valve assembly
300. Throttle body assembly
301. Gasket—float bowl to throttle body
305. Screw—float bowl to throttle body
306. Lockwasher—float bowl to throttle body screw
310. Needle—idle mixture
311. Spring—idle mixture needle
315. Limiter—idle mixture needle
318. Screw—(throttle stop)

319. Spring—(throttle stop screw)
400. Bracket—idle speed device
401. Screw—solenoid bracket assembly attaching
405. Bracket—idle speed device
406. Rivet—bracket attaching
420. Throttle kicker assembly
421. Washer—tab locking
422. Nut—throttle kicker assembly attaching
425. Solenoid—idle stop
427. Nut—solenoid attaching

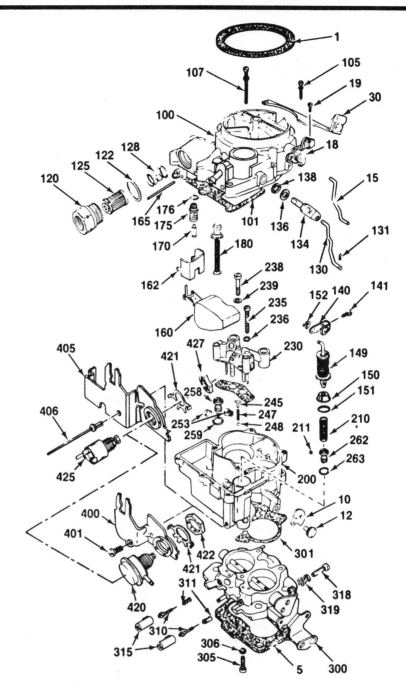

Exploded view of Rochester 2G, 2GF carburetor

1. Screw—air horn (long) (2)
2. Screw—air horn (large)
3. Screw—air horn (short) (3)
4. Screw—air horn (medium)
5. Vent stack assembly
6. Screw—hot idle compensator (2)
7. Hot idle compensator
8. Gasket—hot idle compensator
9. Air horn assembly
10. Gasket—air horn
11. Retainer—pump link
12. Seal—pump stem
13. Retainer—stem seal
14. Vacuum break and bracket assembly—primary
15. Screw—vacuum break attaching
16. Bushing—air valve—link
17. Retainer—air valve link
18. Hose—vacuum break—primary
19. Link—air valve
20. Link—fast idle cam
21. Intermediate choke shaft/lever/link assembly
22. Bushing—intermediate choke shaft link
23. Retainer—intermediate choke shaft link
24. Vacuum break and bracket assembly—secondary
25. Choke cover and coil assembly
26. Screw—choke lever
27. Choke lever and contact assembly
28. Choke housing
29. Screw—choke housing (2)
30. Stat cover retainer kit
31. Screw—vacuum break attaching (2)

32. Float bowl assembly
33. Nut—fuel inlet
34. Gasket—fuel inlet nut
35. Filter—fuel inlet
36. Spring—fuel filter
37. Float assembly
38. Hinge pin—float
39. Insert—float bowl
40. Needle and seat assembly
41. Spring—pump return
42. Pump—assembly
43. Jet—main metering
44. Rod—main metering assembly
45. Ball—pump discharge
46. Spring—pump discharge

47. Retainer—pump discharge spring
48. Power piston assembly
49. Spring—power piston
50. Gasket—throttle body
51. Throttle body assembly
52. Pump rod
53. Clip—cam screw
54. Screw—cam
55. Spring—throttle stop screw
56. Screw—throttle stop
57. Idle needle and spring
58. Screw—throttle body attaching (4)
59. Nut—idle solenoid
60. Retainer—idle solenoid
61. Idle solenoid

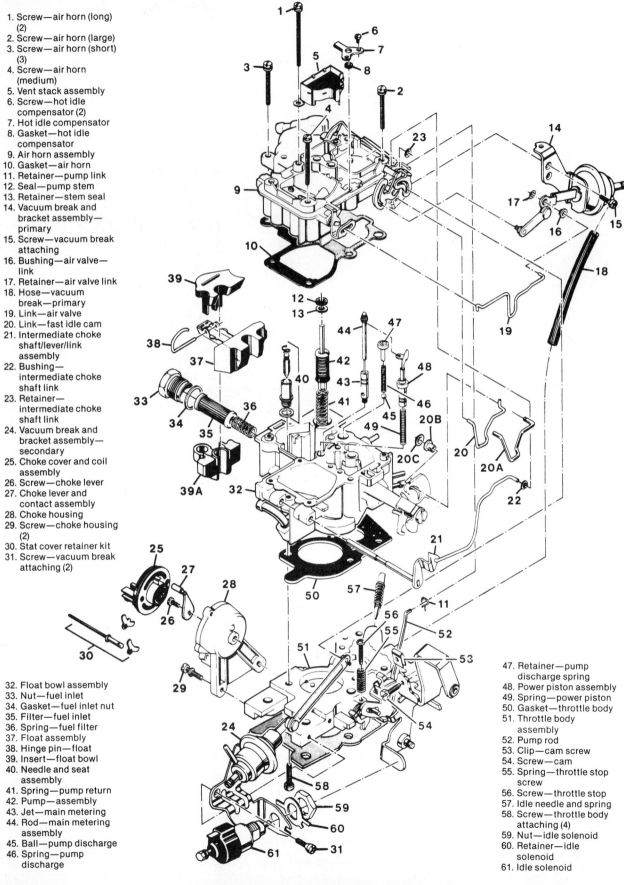

Exploded view of Rochester 2SE carburetor

1. Set the parking brake and block the wheels. Attach a calibrated tachometer to the engine.

2. Disconnect and plug the canister purge line to the carburetor.

3. Disconnect the vacuum advance hose and plug it. Adjust the ignition, timing, if necessary.

4. Adjust the carburetor idle speed to specifications. Disconnect the crankcase ventilation hose from the air cleaner.

5. Insert the hose with the rubber stopper from the propane valve and special adapter tool, into the air cleaner crankcase ventilation hose hole.

NOTE: The propane cylinder must be vertical during the adjustment procedure.

6. With the engine at normal operating temperature and running, the A/T equipped vehicles in the DRIVE position and the M/T equipped vehicles in the NEUTRAL po-

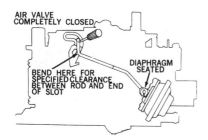

Air valve dashpot adjustment—typical Quadrajet® carburetor

sition, slowly open the propane cylinder control valve to allow propane to enter the carburetor.

7. Continue to add propane until the idle speed increases to the maximum enriched idle rpm and then, because of over richness, will drop. Note the maximum enriched idle rpm.

NOTE: If a rich rpm cannot be obtained, check for an empty propane cylinder or propane system leaks.

8. The propane enrichment is the difference between curb idle speed and the maximum enrichment idle rpm.

9. The maximum enrichment idle rpm is the curb idle rpm plus the propane enrichment rpm.

10. If the maximum enrichment idle rpm is within the specifications, the idle mixture is correct. If so, remove the propane tube and install the crankcase ventilation tube in the air cleaner assembly.

11. If the maximum enriched idle rpm is not within the specifications, remove the carburetor from the engine to gain access to the tamper resistant plugs covering the idle mixture screw.

NOTE: A portion of the throttle base must be cut and the plugs crushed in order to expose the idle mixture adjusting screws.

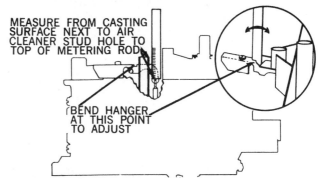

Secondary metering adjustment—typical Quadrajet® carburetor

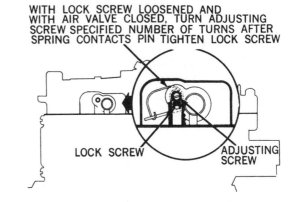

Air valve spring adjustment—typical Quadrajet® carburetor

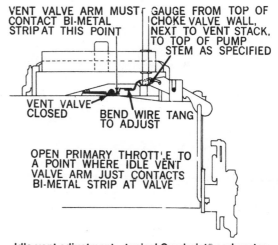

Idle vent adjustment—typical Quadrajet® carburetor

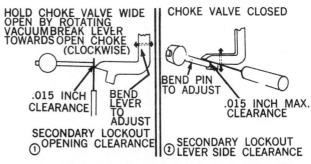

Secondary lockout adjustment—typical Quadrajet® carburetor

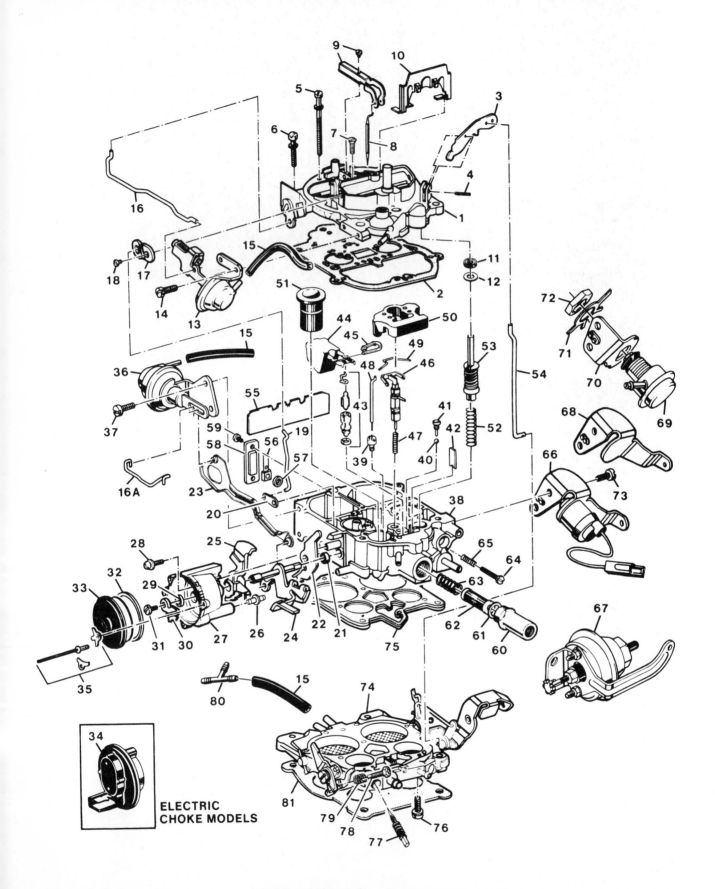

M4MC/M4ME carburetor exploded view

ELECTRIC CHOKE MODELS

1. Air Horn Assy.
2. Gasket—Air Horn
3. Lever—Pump Actuating
4. Roll Pin—Pump Lever Hinge
5. Screw—Air Horn Long (2)
6. Screw—Air Horn Short ( )
7. Screw — Air Horn Countersunk (2)
8. Metering Rod—Secondary (2)
9. Holder and Screw—Secondary Metering Rod
10. Baffle—Secondary Air
11. Seal—Pump Plunger
12. Retainer—Pump Seal
13. Vac. Break Control & Bracket—Front
14. Screw—Control Attaching (2)
15. Hose—Vacuum
16. Rod—Air Valve
16A. Rod—Air Valve (Truck)
17. Lever—Choke Rod (Upper)
18. Screw—Choke Lever
19. Rod—Choke
20. Lever—Choke Rod (Lower)

21. Seal—Intermediate Choke Shaft
22. Lever—Secondary Lockout
23. Link—Rear Vacuum Break
24. Int. Choke Shaft & Lever
25. Cam—Fast Idle
26. Seal—Choke Housing to Bowl (Hot Air Choke)
27. Kit—Choke Housing
28. Screw—Choke Housing to Bowl
29. Seal—Intermediate Choke Shaft (Hot Air Choke)
30. Lever—Choke Coil
31. Screw—Choke Coil Lever
32. Gasket—Stat Cover (Hot Air Choke)
33. Stat Cover & Coil Assy. (Hot Air Choke)
34. Stat Cover & Coil Assy. (Electric Choke)
35. Kit — Stat Cover Attaching
36. Rear Vacuum Break Assembly
37. Screw—Vacuum Break Attaching (2)
40. Ball—Pump Discharge

41. Retainer—Pump Discharge Ball
42. Baffle—Pump Well
43. Needle & Seat Assembly
44. Float Assembly
45. Hinge Pin — Float Assembly
46. Power Piston Assembly
47. Spring—Power Piston
48. Rod—Primary Metering (2)
49. Spring—Metering Rod Retainer
50. Insert—Float Bowl
51. Insert—Bowl Cavity
52. Spring—Pump Return
53. Pump Assembly
54. Rod—Pump
55. Baffle—Secondary Bores
56. Idle Compensator Assembly
57. Seal—Idle Compensator
58. Cover—Idle Compensator
59. Screw—Idle Compensator Cover (2)
60. Filter Nut—Fuel Inlet
61. Gasket—Filter Nut
62. Filter—Fuel Inlet
63. Spring—Fuel Filter

64. Screw—Idle Stop
65. Spring — Idle Stop Screw
66. Idle Speed Solenoid & Bracket Assembly
67. Idle Load Compensator & Bracket Assembly
68. Bracket—Throttle Return Spring
69. Actuator—Throttle Lever (Truck Only)
70. Bracket—Throttle Lever Actuator (Truck Only)
71. Washer—Actuator Nut (Truck Only)
72. Nut—Actuator Attaching (Truck Only)
73. Screw—Bracket Attaching (2)
74. Throttle Body Assembly
75. Gasket—Throttle Body
76. Screw—Throttle Body (3)
77. Idle Mixture Needle & Spring Assy. (2)
78. Screw — Fast Idle Adjusting
79. Spring — Fast Idle Screw
80. Tee—Vacuum Hose
81. Gasket—Flange

(1) IF NECESSARY, REMOVE INTERMEDIATE CHOKE ROD, TO GAIN ACCESS TO LOCK SCREW.

(2) LOOSEN LOCK SCREW USING 3/32″ (2.381mm) HEX WRENCH.

(3) TURN TENSION-ADJUSTING SCREW CLOCKWISE UNTIL AIR VALVE OPENS SLIGHTLY.

TURN ADJUSTING SCREW COUNTER-CLOCKWISE UNTIL AIR VALVE JUST CLOSES. CONTINUE COUNTER-CLOCKWISE SPECIFIED NUMBER OF TURNS.

(4) TIGHTEN LOCK SCREW.

(5) APPLY LITHIUM BASE GREASE TO LUBRICATE PIN AND SPRING CONTACT AREA.

Air valve spring adjustment—2SE carburetor

① IF RIVETED, DRILL OUT AND REMOVE RIVETS. REMOVE CHOKE COVER AND COIL ASSEMBLY.

② PLACE FAST IDLE SCREW ON HIGH STEP OF FAST IDLE CAM.

③ PUSH ON INTERMEDIATE CHOKE LEVER UNTIL CHOKE VALVE IS CLOSED.

④ INSERT .085″ (2.18mm) PLUG GAGE IN HOLE.

⑤ EDGE OF LEVER SHOULD JUST CONTACT SIDE OF GAGE.

⑥ SUPPORT AT "S" AND BEND INTERMEDIATE CHOKE ROD TO ADJUST.

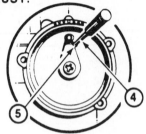
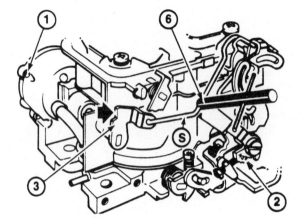

Choke coil lever adjustment—2SE carburetor

12. Remove the screws; a special tool (Kent Moore J–29030–B or equivalent) is used to attach to the heads of the screws to gain access for movement of the screws. Re-install the carburetor on the engine and connect all components.

NOTE: Modify special Kent Moore tool J–29030–B by grinding ⅛ inch off the rear and ¼ inch off the front of the tool.

13. Install the propane cylinder kit to the air cleaner assembly. Snug the idle mixture screw to its seat and back it out three (3) turns.

14. Start the engine, bring to normal operating temperature, set the parking brake, chock the wheels and place the transmission in the Drive (automatic) or the Neutral (manual) position.

15. Back the idle mixture screws out (richer, ⅛ turn at a time) until the maximum idle speed is obtained. The adjust the idle speed to the maximum enriched idle rpm.

16. Turn the mixture screws in clockwise (⅛ turn at a time) until the idle speed attains the specified curb idle speed.

17. Check the maximum enriched rpm with the propane too. If not within specifications, refer to Step 5 and repeat the procedure.

18. When the mixture and idle speed have been properly adjusted, stop the engine, remove the propane cylinder and hose from the air cleaner.

19. Remove the carburetor, remove the special tool (K/M J–29030–B or equivalent), seal the idle mixture screw access hole with RTV sealant and re-install the carburetor.

20. Install the air cleaner, connect the crankcase ventilation hose and any vacuum hoses that were previously removed. Adjust the idle speed as required.

LEAN IDLE DROP PROCEDURE

1. The carburetor must be removed from the vehicle and the tamper resistant plugs removed from the throttle body as noted under the idle mixture adjustment with propane outline.

2. Connect a tachometer to the ignition system, have the engine at normal operating temperature, apply the parking brakes securely, chock the wheels and position the A/T gear selector in DRIVE and the M/T in NEUTRAL.

3. Adjust the idle speed to specifications.

4. Turn the idle mixture adjusting screw clockwise (lean) until a perceptible loss of rpm is noted.

5. Turn the idle mixture adjusting screw counterclockwise (rich) until the highest engine rpm is attained, Do not turn the screw any further than the point at which the highest engine rpm is first attained. This is referred to as LEAN BEST IDLE.

NOTE: The engine speed will increase above curb idle speed an amount that corresponds approximately to the lean drop specifications of 20 rpm.

6. As a final adjustment, turn the idle mixture screw clockwise in increments until the specified drop (20 rpm) is attained.

NOTE: If the final rpm differs more than ± 30 rpm from the original set curb idle speed, adjust the curb idle speed to the specified engine rpm and repeat the above steps.

7. Remove the air cleaner, remove the carburetor and the modified special tool or its equivalent. Install RTV sealer in the idle mixture screw access hole.

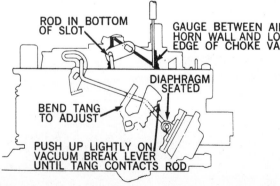

ROD IN BOTTOM OF SLOT

GAUGE BETWEEN AIR HORN WALL AND LOWER EDGE OF CHOKE VALVE

DIAPHRAGM SEATED

BEND TANG TO ADJUST

PUSH UP LIGHTLY ON VACUUM BREAK LEVER UNTIL TANG CONTACTS ROD

Vacuum break adjustment—typical Quadrajet® carburetor

8. Install the carburetor and air cleaner assembly. Adjust the engine idle speed to specifications as required.

IDLE MIXTURE ADJUSTMENT

Model E2SE Carburetor (Feedback Type)

NOTE: Each carburetor has been calibrated at the factory and should not normally need adjustment in the field. However, should a diagnosis indicate the need for adjustment due to emission failure or replacement of critical components, the idle mixture can be adjusted using the following procedure.

1. Remove the carburetor from the engine and remove the tamper resistant plug in order to gain access to the idle mixture adjusting screw.

2. Modify special Kent Moore tool J–29030–B or its equivalent, by grinding $\frac{1}{8}$ inch off the rear and $\frac{1}{4}$ inch off the front of the tool. Place the modified tool onto the idle mixture adjusting screw.

3. Turn the idle mixture screw in until it is lightly seated and back out four (4) turns.

NOTE: If the seal in the air horn concealing the idle air bleed has been removed, replace the air horn. If the seal is still in place, do not remove the seal.

4. Remove the vent stack screen assembly to gain access to the lean mixture screw.

5. Turn the lean mixture screw in until lightly bottomed and then back out 2½ turns.

NOTE: Some resistance should be felt. If not, remove the screw and inspect for the presence of the spring.

6. Install the carburetor on the engine with the modified tool installed on the mixture adjusting screw. Do not install the air cleaner and gasket.

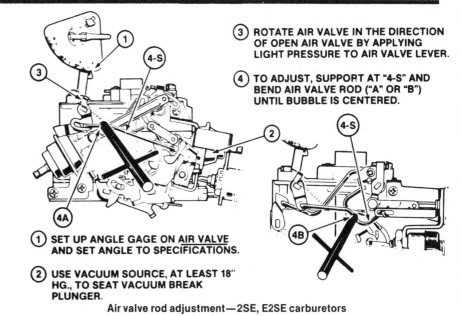

① SET UP ANGLE GAGE ON AIR VALVE AND SET ANGLE TO SPECIFICATIONS.

② USE VACUUM SOURCE, AT LEAST 18″ HG., TO SEAT VACUUM BREAK PLUNGER.

③ ROTATE AIR VALVE IN THE DIRECTION OF OPEN AIR VALVE BY APPLYING LIGHT PRESSURE TO AIR VALVE LEVER.

④ TO ADJUST, SUPPORT AT "4-S" AND BEND AIR VALVE ROD ("A" OR "B") UNTIL BUBBLE IS CENTERED.

Air valve rod adjustment—2SE, E2SE carburetors

① ATTACH RUBBER BAND TO INTERMEDIATE CHOKE LEVER.

② OPEN THROTTLE TO ALLOW CHOKE VALVE TO CLOSE.

③ SET UP ANGLE GAGE AND SET ANGLE TO SPECIFICATIONS.

④ PLACE FAST IDLE SCREW ON SECOND STEP OF CAM AGAINST RISE OF HIGH STEP.

⑤ PUSH ON CHOKE SHAFT LEVER TO OPEN CHOKE VALVE AND TO MAKE CONTACT WITH BLACK CLOSING TANG.

⑥ SUPPORT AT "S" AND ADJUST BY BENDING FAST IDLE CAM ROD UNTIL BUBBLE IS CENTERED.

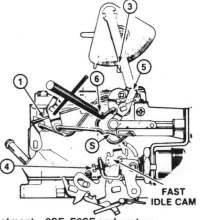

Choke rod and fast idle cam adjustment—2SE, E2SE carburetors

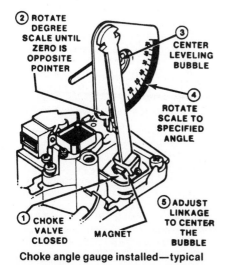

② ROTATE DEGREE SCALE UNTIL ZERO IS OPPOSITE POINTER

③ CENTER LEVELING BUBBLE

④ ROTATE SCALE TO SPECIFIED ANGLE

① CHOKE VALVE CLOSED

MAGNET

⑤ ADJUST LINKAGE TO CENTER THE BUBBLE

Choke angle gauge installed—typical

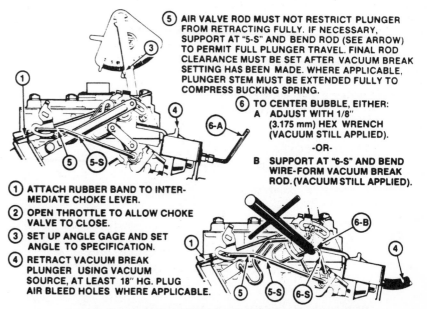

⑤ AIR VALVE ROD MUST NOT RESTRICT PLUNGER FROM RETRACTING FULLY. IF NECESSARY, SUPPORT AT "5-S" AND BEND ROD (SEE ARROW) TO PERMIT FULL PLUNGER TRAVEL. FINAL ROD CLEARANCE MUST BE SET AFTER VACUUM BREAK SETTING HAS BEEN MADE. WHERE APPLICABLE, PLUNGER STEM MUST BE EXTENDED FULLY TO COMPRESS BUCKING SPRING.

⑥ TO CENTER BUBBLE, EITHER:
A ADJUST WITH 1/8″ (3.175 mm) HEX WRENCH (VACUUM STILL APPLIED).
-OR-
B SUPPORT AT "6-S" AND BEND WIRE-FORM VACUUM BREAK ROD. (VACUUM STILL APPLIED).

① ATTACH RUBBER BAND TO INTERMEDIATE CHOKE LEVER.

② OPEN THROTTLE TO ALLOW CHOKE VALVE TO CLOSE.

③ SET UP ANGLE GAGE AND SET ANGLE TO SPECIFICATION.

④ RETRACT VACUUM BREAK PLUNGER USING VACUUM SOURCE, AT LEAST 18″ HG. PLUG AIR BLEED HOLES WHERE APPLICABLE.

Primary vacuum break adjustment—2SE, E2SE carburetors

① ATTACH RUBBER BAND TO INTER-MEDIATE CHOKE LEVER.

② OPEN THROTTLE TO ALLOW CHOKE VALVE TO CLOSE.

③ SET UP ANGLE GAGE AND SET ANGLE TO SPECIFICATION.

④ RETRACT VACUUM BREAK PLUNGER USING VACUUM SOURCE, AT LEAST 18" HG. PLUG AIR BLEED HOLES WHERE APPLICABLE.

WHERE APPLICABLE, PLUNGER STEM MUST BE EXTENDED FULLY TO COMPRESS PLUNGER BUCKING SPRING.

⑤ TO CENTER BUBBLE, EITHER:

A. ADJUST WITH 1/8" (3.175 mm) HEX WRENCH (VACUUM STILL APPLIED)
-OR-

B. SUPPORT AT "5-S", BEND WIRE-FORM VACUUM BREAK ROD (VACUUM STILL APPLIED)

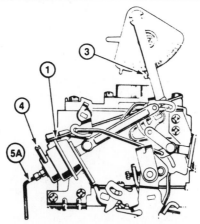

Secondary vacuum break adjustment—2SE, E2SE carburetors

① ATTACH RUBBER BAND TO INTER-MEDIATE CHOKE LEVER.

② OPEN THROTTLE TO ALLOW CHOKE VALVE TO CLOSE.

③ SET UP ANGLE GAGE AND SET ANGLE TO SPECIFICATIONS.

④ HOLD THROTTLE LEVER IN WIDE OPEN POSITION.

⑤ PUSH ON CHOKE SHAFT LEVER TO OPEN CHOKE VALVE AND TO MAKE CONTACT WITH BLACK CLOSING TANG.

⑥ ADJUST BY BENDING TANG UNTIL BUBBLE IS CENTERED.

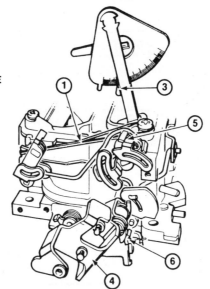

Choke unloader adjustment—2SE, E2SE carburetors

① HOLD CHOKE VALVE WIDE OPEN BY PUSHING DOWN ON INTERMEDIATE CHOKE LEVER.

② OPEN THROTTLE LEVER UNTIL END OF SECONDARY ACTUATING LEVER IS OPPOSITE TOE OF LOCKOUT LEVER.

③ GAGE CLEARANCE - DIMENSION SHOULD BE .025".

④ IF NECESSARY TO ADJUST, BEND LOCKOUT LEVER TANG CONTACTING FAST IDLE CAM.

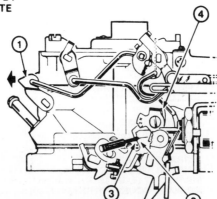

Secondary lockout adjustment—2SE, E2SE carburetors

7. Disconnect the bowl vent line at the carburetor, disconnect the EGR valve hose and the canister purge hose at the carburetor. Cap the carburetor ports.

8. Refer to the Vehicle Emission Control Information label diagram, located under the vehicle hood, and locate the hose from port 'D' on the carburetor to the temperature sensor and the secondary vacuum break thermal vacuum switch.

9. Disconnect the hose at the temperature sensor on the air cleaner and plug the hose.

10. Connect a dwell meter positive probe to the mixture control solenoid dwell test wire with a green connection.

11. Connect the negative probe to ground and set the meter at the 6 cylinder scale position.

12. Connect a tachometer to the ignition system, set the parking brake and chock the wheels.

13. Place the transmission in Park (automatic) or Neutral (manual).

14. Start and operate the engine until normal operating temperature is reached and the Electronic Engine Control System is in the closed loop mode of operation.

15. Operate the engine at 3000 rpm and adjust the lean mixture screw slowly in small increments, allowing time for the dwell to stabilize after turning the screw to obtain an average dwell of 35 degrees.

16. If the dwell is too low, back the screw out and if too high, turn the screw in. If unable to adjust to specifications, inspect the main metering system for leaks, restriction, etc.

17. Return the engine to idle speed. Allow the engine to stabilize before the dwell is recorded.

NOTE: The mixture control (MC) solenoid dwell is an indication of the ratio of ON to OFF time. The dwell of the MC solenoid is used to determine the calibration and is sensitive to changes in the fuel mixture caused by heat, air leaks, etc. While the engine is idling, it is normal for the dwell to increase and decrease fairly constant over a relativity narrow range, such as 5 degrees. However, it may occasionally vary as much as 10–15 degrees momentarily because of temporary mixture changes. The dwell specified is the average of the most consistant variations. The engine must be allowed to stabilize its self for a few minutes after returning the engine to idle in order to obtain a correct average.

18. Adjust the idle mixture screw with the modified tool J–29030–A or its equivalent, to obtain an average dwell of 25 degrees. If the dwell is too high, turn the screw in and if the dwell is too low, back the screw out. Allow time for the dwell to stabilize after each adjustment, because the adjustment is very sensitive. If unable to adjust to specifications, check for idle system air or vacuum leaks and restrictions.

19. Disconnect the mixture control so-

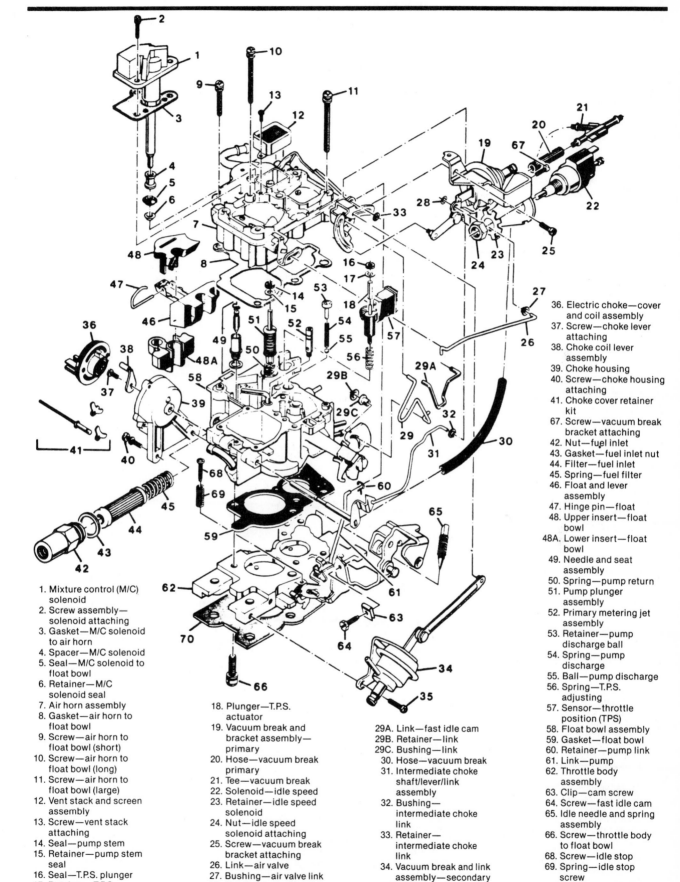

1. Mixture control (M/C) solenoid
2. Screw assembly—solenoid attaching
3. Gasket—M/C solenoid to air horn
4. Spacer—M/C solenoid
5. Seal—M/C solenoid to float bowl
6. Retainer—M/C solenoid seal
7. Air horn assembly
8. Gasket—air horn to float bowl
9. Screw—air horn to float bowl (short)
10. Screw—air horn to float bowl (long)
11. Screw—air horn to float bowl (large)
12. Vent stack and screen assembly
13. Screw—vent stack attaching
14. Seal—pump stem
15. Retainer—pump stem seal
16. Seal—T.P.S. plunger
17. Retainer—T.P.S. plunger seal

18. Plunger—T.P.S. actuator
19. Vacuum break and bracket assembly—primary
20. Hose—vacuum break primary
21. Tee—vacuum break
22. Solenoid—idle speed
23. Retainer—idle speed solenoid
24. Nut—idle speed solenoid attaching
25. Screw—vacuum break bracket attaching
26. Link—air valve
27. Bushing—air valve link
28. Retainer—air valve link
29. Link—fast idle cam

29A. Link—fast idle cam
29B. Retainer—link
29C. Bushing—link
30. Hose—vacuum break
31. Intermediate choke shaft/lever/link assembly
32. Bushing—intermediate choke link
33. Retainer—intermediate choke link
34. Vacuum break and link assembly—secondary
35. Screw—vacuum break attaching

36. Electric choke—cover and coil assembly
37. Screw—choke lever attaching
38. Choke coil lever assembly
39. Choke housing
40. Screw—choke housing attaching
41. Choke cover retainer kit
67. Screw—vacuum break bracket attaching
42. Nut—fuel inlet
43. Gasket—fuel inlet nut
44. Filter—fuel inlet
45. Spring—fuel filter
46. Float and lever assembly
47. Hinge pin—float
48. Upper insert—float bowl
48A. Lower insert—float bowl
49. Needle and seat assembly
50. Spring—pump return
51. Pump plunger assembly
52. Primary metering jet assembly
53. Retainer—pump discharge ball
54. Spring—pump discharge
55. Ball—pump discharge
56. Spring—T.P.S. adjusting
57. Sensor—throttle position (TPS)
58. Float bowl assembly
59. Gasket—float bowl
60. Retainer—pump link
61. Link—pump
62. Throttle body assembly
63. Clip—cam screw
64. Screw—fast idle cam
65. Idle needle and spring assembly
66. Screw—throttle body to float bowl
68. Screw—idle stop
69. Spring—idle stop screw
70. Gasket—insulator flange

Exploded view of Rochester E2SE carburetor

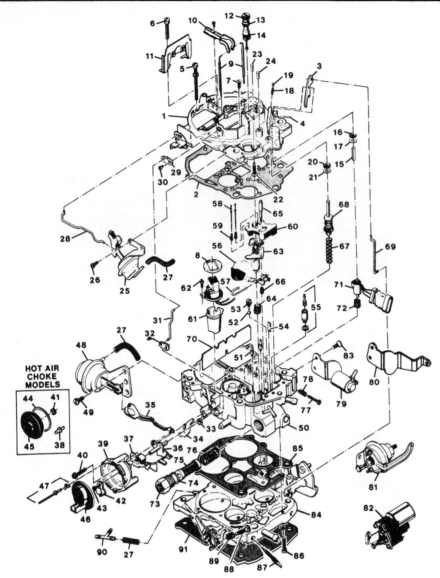

Exploded view of Rochester E4ME carburetor

49. Screw—vacuum break attaching (2)
50. Float Bowl Assembly
51. Jet—primary metering (2)
52. Ball—pump discharge
53. Retainer—pump discharge ball
54. Baffle—pump well
55. Needle & seat assembly
56. Float assembly
57. Hinge pin—float assembly
58. Rod—primary metering (2)
59. Spring—primary metering rod (2)
60. Insert—float bowl
61. Insert—bowl cavity
62. Screw—connector attaching
63. Mixture control (M/C) solenoid & plunger assembly
64. Spring—solenoid tension
65. Screw—solenoid adjusting (lean mixture)
66. Spring—solenoid adjusting screw
67. Spring—pump return
68. Pump assembly
69. Link—pump
70. Baffle—secondary bores
71. Throttle position sensor (TPS)
72. Spring—TPS Tension
73. Filter nut—fuel inlet
74. Gasket—filter nut
75. Filter—fuel inlet
76. Spring—fuel filter
77. Screw—idle stop
78. Spring—idle stop screw
79. Idle speed solenoid & bracket assembly
80. Bracket—throttle return spring
81. Idle load compensator & bracket assembly
82. Idle speed control & bracket assembly
83. Screw—bracket attaching
84. Throttle body assembly
85. Gasket—throttle body
86. Screw—throttle body
87. Idle needle & spring assembly (2)
88. Screw—fast idle adjusting
89. Spring fast idle screw
90. Tee—vacuum hose
91. Gasket—flange

1. Air horn assembly
2. Gasket—air horn
3. Lever—pump actuating
4. Roll pin—pump lever hinge
5. Screw—air horn, long (2)
6. Screw—air horn, short
7. Screw—air horn, countersunk (2)
8. Gasket—solenoid connector to air horn
9. Metering rod—secondary (2)
10. Holder & screw—secondary metering rod
11. Baffle—secondary air
12. Valve—idle air bleed
13. "O" ring (thick)—idle air bleed valve
14. "O" ring (thin)—idle air bleed valve
15. Plunger—TPS actuator
16. Seal—TPS plunger
17. Retainer—TPS seal
18. Screw—TPS adjusting

19. Plug—TPS screw
20. Seal—pump plunger
21. Retainer—pump seal
22. Screw—solenoid plunger stop (rich mixture stop)
23. Plug—plunger stop screw (rich mixture stop)
24. Plug—solenoid adjusting screw (lean mixture)
25. Vacuum break & bracket—front
26. Screw—vacuum break attaching (2)
27. Hose—vacuum
28. Rod—air valve
29. Lever—choke rod (upper)
30. Screw—choke lever
31. Rod—choke
32. Lever—choke rod (lower)
33. Seal—intermediate choke shaft
34. Lever—secondary lockout

35. Link—rear vacuum break
36. Intermediate choke shaft & lever
37. Cam—fast idle
38. Seal—choke housing to bowl (hot air choke)
39. Choke housing
40. Screw—choke housing to bowl
41. Seal—intermediate choke shaft (hot air choke)
42. Lever—choke coil
43. Screw—choke coil lever
44. Gasket—Stat cover (hot air choke)
45. Stat cover & coil assembly (hot air choke)
46. Stat cover & coil assembly (electric choke)
47. Kit—stat cover attaching
48. Vacuum break assembly—rear

lenoid and check for and engine speed change of at least 50 rpm. If the rpm does not change enough, inspect the idle air bleed circuit for restrictions, leaks, etc.

20. Increase the engine speed to 3000 rpm and operate for a few minutes. Note the dwell which should be varying with an average indications of 35 degrees.

21. If the average dwell is not at 25 degrees, adjust the lean mixture screw.

22. After adjusting the lean mixture screw, adjust the idle mixture screw to obtain 25 degrees dwell.

23. If at an average dwell of 25 degrees, remove the carburetor from the engine, remove the modified tool J–29030–A or equivalent from the idle mixture screw and seal the access hole with RTV sealant.

24. Install the carburetor, connect all disconnected components and install the vent screen. Verify the idle speed is within specifications.

THROTTLE POSITION SWITCH (TPS) ADJUSTMENT

1. Drill a 5/64 in. hole in the TPS adjustment screw plug and remove the plug with a small slide hammer. Be careful when drilling so as not to damage the adjustment screw head.

2. Disconnect the TPS connector and jumper all three terminals.

3. Connect a digital voltmeter from TPS center terminal (B) to bottom terminal (C).

4. With the ignition ON (engine off), turn the TPS adjustment screw to obtain the specified voltage at curb idle position with the A/C off and the ISC fully retracted. See the TPS Adjustment Chart for voltage specifications.

5. After adjustment, install a new adjustment screw plug into the air horn.

IDLE SPEED AND MIXTURE ADJUSTMENT

Model E4ME, M4ME, M4MC Carburetors

1. Set the parking brake and block the drive wheels. Disconnect and plug the hoses as directed on the underhood emission control sticker. Connect a dwell meter to the mixture control solenoid dwell terminal and a tachometer to the engine.

2. Start the engine and allow it to reach normal operating temperature; a varying dwell should be noted on the dwell meter.

3. Check the engine idle speed and adjust to specifications listed on the underhood sticker if necessary.

4. With the engine idling in Drive (Neutral for manual transmissions), check the dwell readings on the six cylinder scale. If varying within the 10–50° range, mixture is correct. If not, continue with adjustment procedure.

5. Remove the idle air bleed valve cover by drilling out the rivets with a No. 35 drill bit. Use care when drilling to prevent damage to the air horn casting. Cover the carburetor intake ports with masking tape to prevent metal filings from falling into the engine. With the cover removed, look for the presence or absence of an identification letter on top of the idle air bleed valve. If the valve doesn't have an identification letter, use Procedure A below. If the valve does have an identification letter, use Procedure B to continue adjustment.

PROCEDURE A (WITHOUT ID LETTER)

1. Install idle air bleed valve gauging tool J–33815–2, BT–8253–B, or equivalent in throttle side D-shaped vent hole in the air horn casting. The upper end of the tool should be positioned over the open cavity next to the idle air bleed valve.

2. While holding the gauging tool down lightly so that the solenoid plunger is against the solenoid stop, adjust the idle air bleed valve so tha the gauging tool will pivot over and just contact the top of the valve. This presets the valve for on-vehicle adjustment. Remove the gauging tool.

3. Start the engine and allow it to reach normal operating temperature.

4. While idling in Drive (Neutral for manual transmission), use a screwdriver to slowly turn the idle air bleed valve until the dwell varies within the 25–35° range, attempting to get as close to 30° as possible. Perform this step carefully, as the bleed valve is very sensitive and should be turned in 1/8 turn increments only. If the dwell cannot be set within the range, it will be necessary to remove the plugs and adjust the idle mixture needles.

5. Remove the carburetor and place on a suitable holding fixture with the manifold side up. Be careful not to damage any linkage, tubes or parts protruding from the air horn. Make two parallel cuts in the throttle body with a hacksaw, one on each side of the locator points beneath the idle mixture needle plug. The cuts should reach down

to the steel plugs, but should not extend more than 1/8 in. beyond the locator points.

6. Place a flat punch near the ends of the saw marks, hold the punch at a 45° angle, then drive it into the throttle body until the casting breaks away, exposing the steel plug. Remove the plug.

7. Using tool J–29030–B, BT–7610–B, or equivalent, turn both mixture screws in until lightly seated, then out the number of turns listed in the Specifications Chart.

8. Install the carburetor on the engine using a new flange mounting gasket.

9. Readjust the idle air bleed valve as described above. If the dwell is still below 25°, turn both mixture screws counterclockwise an additional turn and try again. If above 35°, turn both mixture screws clockwise an additional turn.

10. After adjustments are complete, seal the mixture screw openings with silicone sealer to discourage further adjustment and prevent a possible fuel vapor leak. On vehicles without an ISC, adjust curb idle speed if necessary. Check and adjust the fast idle speed as described on the underhood emission sticker.

PROCEDURE B (WITH ID LETTER)

1. Install air bleed valve gauging tool J–33815–2, BT–8253–B, or equivalent in throttle side D-shaped vent hole in the upper air horn casting. The upper end of the tool should be positioned over the open cavity next to the idle air bleed valve.

2. While holding the gauging tool down lightly so that the solenoid plunger is against the solenoid stop, adjust the idle air bleed valve so that the gauging tool will pivot over and just contact the top of the valve. The valve is now set properly and no further adjustment is necessary.

3. If the dwell readings are still incorrect, remove the idle mixture plugs as described in Steps 5–8, above.

4. While idling in Drive (Neutral on manual transmission), adjust both mixture screws equally in 1/8 turn increments until the dwell reading varies within the 25–35° range, attempting to get as close to 30° as possible. If the reading is too low, turn the mixture screws counterclockwise and vice-versa. Allow time for dwell readings to stabilize after each adjustment.

5. Once all adjustments are complete, seal the idle mixture screws with silicone sealant to discourage further adjustment and prevent a fuel vapor leak. On vehicles without ISC, adjust the curb idle speed if necessary and adjust the fast idle speed as described on the underhood sticker.

11 CARBURETOR OVERHAUL

MODEL 1ME/1M/1MEF
Chevrolet/GMC
(All measurements in inches)

Year	Carburetor Number	Float Level	Choke Unloader Setting	Choke Setting	Fast Idle Speed (rpm)	Metering Rod Setting	Fast Idle Cam 2nd Step	Choke Vacuum Break
'79	17058009	¼	—	Index	2400	.065	—	—
	17058011	¼	—	Index	2400	.065	—	—
	17059009	5⁄16	.520	2 Rich	2400	.065 ①	.275	.400
	17059309	5⁄16	.521	2 Rich	2400	.065	.275	.400
	17059359	5⁄16	.521	2 Rich	2400	.065	.275	.400
'80	17080009	11⁄32	.520	②	2400	.090	.275	.400
	17080309	11⁄32	.520	②	2400	.090	.275	.400
	17080359	11⁄32	.520	②	2400	.090	.275	.400
'81–'83	17081009	11⁄32	.520	②	③	.090	.275	.400
	17081309	11⁄32	.520	②	③	.090	.275	.400
	17081329	11⁄32	.520	②	③	.090	.275	.400
'84–'86	17081009	11⁄32	.520	②	③	.090	.275	.400
	17084329	11⁄32	.520	②	③	.090	.275	.400
	17085009	11⁄32	.520	②	③	.090	.275	.400
	17085036	11⁄32	.520	②	③	.090	.275	.400
	17085044	11⁄32	.520	②	③	.090	.275	.400
	17085045	11⁄32	.520	②	③	.090	.275	.400
	17086096	11⁄32	.520	②	③	.090	.275	.400
	17086101	11⁄32	.520	②	③	.090	.275	.400
	17086102	11⁄32	.520	②	③	.090	.275	.400

① .090 inches on medium duty truck applications
② Not adjustable
③ See emission label under hood
④ Lower edge of choke valve

MODEL 2G/2GV/2GC/2GE/2GF
Chevrolet/GMC
(All measurements in inches)

Year	Carburetor Number	Float Level	Float Drop	Choke Setting	Pump Rod Location	Fast Idle Speed (rpm)	Choke Vacuum Break
'79	7044133	19⁄32	19⁄32	Index	19⁄16	①	—
	7044134	19⁄32	19⁄32	Index	17⁄16	①	—
	17059126	5⁄8	19⁄32	Index	115⁄32	①	—
	17059127	17⁄32	19⁄32	Index	115⁄32	①	—

MODEL 2G/2GV/2GC/2GE/2GF
Chevrolet/GMC
(All measurements in inches)

Year	Carburetor Number	Float Level	Float Drop	Choke Setting	Pump Rod Location	Fast Idle Speed (rpm)	Choke Vacuum Break
'79	17059423	5/8	1 9/32	Index	1 21/32	①	—
	17059424	17/32	1 9/32	Index	1 15/32	①	—
	17059420	17/32	1 9/32	Index	1 15/32	①	—
'80–'86	7044133	11/16	1 9/32	Manual	1 9/16	①	—
	7044134	11/16	1 9/32	Manual	1 7/16	①	—
	17058120	11/16	1 9/32	Manual	1 21/32	①	—
	17080120	5/8	1 9/32	Manual	1 21/32	①	—
	17080126	5/8	1 9/32	Manual	1 21/32	①	—
	17080127	5/8	1 9/32	Manual	1 21/32	①	—
	17080129	5/8	1 9/32	Index	1 21/32	①	.130
	17080420	5/8	1 9/32	Manual	1 21/32	①	—
	17080423	5/8	1 9/32	Manual	1 21/32	①	—
	17080424	5/8	1 9/32	Manual	1 21/32	①	—
	17082129	5/8	1 9/32	Manual	1 21/32	①	—
	17082420	5/8	1 9/32	Manual	1 15/32	①	—
	17084432	5/8	1 9/32	Manual	1 15/32	①	—
	17084433	5/8	1 9/32	Manual	1 21/32	①	—
	17085120	5/8	1 9/32	Manual	1 15/32	①	—
	17085126	5/8	1 9/32	Manual	1 15/32	①	—
	17085464	5/8	1 9/32	Manual	1 15/32	①	—
	17085465	5/8	1 9/32	Manual	1 21/32	①	—

① See Tune-Up Specifications or underhood sticker

MODEL 2SE
Chevrolet/GMC
(All measurements in inches)

Year	Carburetor Number	Float Level	Choke Unloader ①	Choke Setting	Pump Rod Adj. ③	Fast Idle (rpm)	Fast Idle Cam 2nd step ①	Choke Vacuum Break ①
'79	17059640	1/8	49°	②	9/16	2000	—	20°
	17059641	1/8	49°	②	9/16	1800	—	23.5°
	17059643	1/8	49°	②	9/16	1800	—	23.5°
	17059740	1/8	49°	②	9/16	2000	—	20°
	17059741	1/8	49°	②	9/16	2100	—	20°
	17059764	1/8	49°	②	9/16	2100	—	20°
	17059765	1/8	49°	②	9/16	2100	—	23.5°
	17059767	1/8	49°	②	9/16	2100	—	23.5°

MODEL 2SE
Chevrolet/GMC
(All measurements in inches)

Year	Carburetor Number	Float Level	Choke Unloader①	Choke Setting	Pump Rod Adj.③	Fast Idle (rpm)	Fast Idle Cam 2nd step①	Choke Vacuum Break①
'80	17080621	⅛	41°	⑤	9/16	④	17°	22°
	17080622	⅛	41°	⑤	9/16	④	17°	22°
	17080623	⅛	41°	⑤	9/16	④	17°	22°
	17080626	⅛	41°	⑤	9/16	④	17°	22°
	17080720	⅛	41°	⑤	9/16	④	17°	22°
	17080721	⅛	41°	⑤	9/16	④	17°	23.5°
	17080722	⅛	41°	⑤	9/16	④	17°	20°
	17080723	⅛	41°	⑤	9/16	④	17°	23.5°
'81	17081621	3/16	38°	⑤	⅝	④	15°	38°
	17081622	3/16	38°	⑤	⅝	④	15°	38°
	17081623	3/16	38°	⑤	⅝	④	15°	38°
	17081624	3/16	38°	⑤	⅝	④	15°	38°
	17081625	3/16	38°	⑤	⅝	④	15°	38°
	17081626	3/16	38°	⑤	⅝	④	15°	38°
	17081627	3/16	38°	⑤	⅝	④	15°	38°
	17081629	3/16	41°	⑤	⅝	④	15°	38°
	17081630	3/16	38°	⑤	⅝	④	15°	38°
	17081633	3/16	38°	⑤	⅝	④	15°	38°
	17081720	3/16	41°	⑤	⅝	④	15°	38°
	17081721	3/16	41°	⑤	⅝	④	15°	38°
	17081725	3/16	41°	⑤	⅝	④	15°	38°
	17081726	3/16	41°	⑤	⅝	④	15°	38°
	17081727	3/16	41°	⑤	⅝	④	15°	38°

①Use angle degree tool or change over to decimal equivalent on the conversion chart at the end of this section
②1 notch counterclockwise
③Measure distance from air horn casting
④See emissions label underhood for exact rpm specification
⑤Riveted choke cap is not adjustable under normal circumstances

MODEL 2SE
Chevrolet/GMC
(All measurements in inches or degrees)

Year	Carburetor Number	Float Level	Choke Coil Lever	Choke Rod①	Primary Vacuum Break	Secondary Vacuum Break	Air Valve Rod	Choke Unloader
'82	17082334	³⁄₁₆	.085	15°	26°	38°	1°	42°
	17082335	³⁄₁₆	.085	15°	26°	38°	1°	42°
	17082336	³⁄₁₆	.085	15°	26°	38°	1°	42°
	17082337	³⁄₁₆	.085	15°	26°	38°	1°	42°
	17082338	³⁄₁₆	.085	15°	26°	38°	1°	42°
	17082339	³⁄₁₆	.085	15°	26°	38°	1°	42°
	17082341	³⁄₁₆	.085	15°	30°	37°	1°	42°
	17082342	³⁄₁₆	.085	15°	30°	37°	1°	42°
	17082344	³⁄₁₆	.085	15°	30°	37°	1°	42°
	17082345	³⁄₁₆	.085	15°	30°	37°	1°	42°
	17082431	³⁄₁₆	.085	15°	24°	38°	1°	42°
	17082433	³⁄₁₆	.085	15°	24°	38°	1°	42°
	17082480	³⁄₁₆	.085	15°	26°	38°	1°	42°
	17082481	³⁄₁₆	.085	15°	26°	38°	1°	42°
	17082482	³⁄₁₆	.085	15°	23°	38°	1°	42°
	17082483	³⁄₁₆	.085	15°	26°	38°	1°	42°
	17082484	³⁄₁₆	.085	15°	26°	38°	1°	42°
	17082485	³⁄₁₆	.085	15°	26°	38°	1°	42°
	17082486	³⁄₁₆	.085	15°	28°	38°	1°	42°
	17082487	³⁄₁₆	.085	15°	28°	38°	1°	42°
	17082488	³⁄₁₆	.085	15°	28°	38°	1°	42°
	17082489	³⁄₁₆	.085	15°	28°	38°	1°	42°
	17082348	⁷⁄₁₆	.085	22°	26°	32°	1°	40°
	17082349	⁷⁄₁₆	.085	22°	28°	32°	1°	40°
	17082350	⁷⁄₁₆	.085	22°	26°	32°	1°	40°
	17082351	⁷⁄₁₆	.085	22°	28°	32°	1°	40°
	17082353	⁷⁄₁₆	.085	22°	28°	35°	1°	30°
	17082355	⁷⁄₁₆	.085	22°	28°	35°	1°	30°
'83	17083410	³⁄₁₆	.085	15°	23°	38°	1°	42°
	17083411	³⁄₁₆	.085	15°	26°	38°	1°	42°
	17083412	³⁄₁₆	.085	15°	23°	38°	1°	42°
	17083413	³⁄₁₆	.085	15°	26°	38°	1°	42°
	17083414	³⁄₁₆	.085	15°	23°	38°	1°	42°
	17083415	³⁄₁₆	.085	15°	26°	38°	1°	42°
	17083416	³⁄₁₆	.085	15°	23°	38°	1°	42°
	17083417	³⁄₁₆	.085	15°	26°	38°	1°	42°
	17083419	³⁄₁₆	.085	15°	28°	38°	1°	42°

MODEL 2SE
Chevrolet/GMC
(All measurements in inches or degrees)

Year	Carburetor Number	Float Level	Choke Coil Lever	Choke Rod①	Primary Vacuum Break	Secondary Vacuum Break	Air Valve Rod	Choke Unloader
'83	17083421	3/16	.085	15°	26°	38°	1°	42°
	17083423	3/16	.085	15°	28°	38°	1°	42°
	17083425	3/16	.085	15°	26°	38°	1°	42°
	17083427	3/16	.085	15°	26°	38°	1°	42°
	17083429	3/16	.085	15°	28°	38°	1°	42°
	17083560	3/16	.085	15°	28°	38°	1°	42°
	17083562	3/16	.085	15°	28°	38°	1°	42°
	17083565	3/16	.085	15°	28°	38°	1°	42°
	17083569	3/16	.085	15°	28°	38°	1°	42°
	17083348	7/16	.085	22°	30°	32°	1°	40°
	17083349	7/16	.085	22°	30°	32°	1°	40°
	17083350	7/16	.085	22°	30°	32°	1°	40°
	17083351	7/16	.085	22°	30°	32°	1°	40°
	17083352	7/16	.085	22°	30°	35°	1°	40°
	17083353	7/16	.085	22°	30°	35°	1°	40°
	17083354	7/16	.085	22°	30°	35°	1°	40°
	17083355	7/16	.085	22°	30°	35°	1°	40°
	17083360	7/16	.085	22°	30°	32°	1°	40°
	17083361	7/16	.085	22°	28°	32°	1°	40°
	17083362	7/16	.085	22°	30°	32°	1°	40°
	17083363	7/16	.085	22°	28°	32°	1°	40°
	17083364	7/16	.085	22°	30°	35°	1°	40°
	17083365	7/16	.085	22°	30°	35°	1°	40°
	17083366	7/16	.085	22°	30°	35°	1°	40°
	17083367	7/16	.085	22°	30°	35°	1°	40°
	17083390	13/32	.085	28°	30°	35°	1°	38°
	17083391	13/32	.085	28°	30°	35°	1°	38°
	17083392	13/32	.085	28°	30°	35°	1°	38°
	17083393	13/32	.085	28°	30°	35°	1°	38°
	17083394	13/32	.085	28°	30°	35°	1°	38°
	17083395	13/32	.085	28°	30°	35°	1°	38°
	17083396	13/32	.085	28°	30°	35°	1°	38°
	17083397	13/32	.085	28°	30°	35°	1°	38°
'84	17084348	11/32	.085	22°	30°	32°	1°	40°
	17084349	11/32	.085	22°	30°	32°	1°	40°
	17084350	11/32	.085	22°	30°	32°	1°	40°
	17084351	11/32	.085	22°	30°	32°	1°	40°

MODEL 2SE
Chevrolet/GMC

(All measurements in inches or degrees)

Year	Carburetor Number	Float Level	Choke Coil Lever	Choke Rod ①	Primary Vacuum Break	Secondary Vacuum Break	Air Valve Rod	Choke Unloader
'84	17084352	11/32	.085	22°	30°	35°	1°	40°
	17084353	11/32	.085	22°	30°	35°	1°	40°
	17084354	11/32	.085	22°	30°	35°	1°	40°
	17084355	11/32	.085	22°	30°	35°	1°	40°
	17084360	5/32	.085	22°	30°	32°	1°	40°
	17084362	5/32	.085	22°	30°	32°	1°	40°
	17084364	5/32	.085	22°	30°	35°	1°	40°
	17084366	5/32	.085	22°	30°	35°	1°	40°
	17084390	7/16	.085	28°	30°	38°	1°	38°
	17084391	7/16	.085	28°	30°	38°	1°	38°
	17084392	7/16	.085	28°	30°	38°	1°	38°
	17084393	7/16	.085	28°	30°	38°	1°	38°
	17084394	7/16	.085	28°	30°	40°	1°	38°
	17084395	7/16	.085	28°	30°	40°	1°	38°
	17084396	7/16	.085	28°	30°	40°	1°	38°
	17084397	7/16	.085	28°	30°	40°	1°	38°
	17084410	11/32	.085	15°	23°	38°	1°	42°
	17084412	11/32	.085	15°	23°	38°	1°	42°
	17084425	11/32	.085	15°	26°	36°	1°	40°
	17084427	11/32	.085	15°	26°	36°	1°	40°
	17084560	11/32	.085	15°	24°	34°	1°	38°
	17084562	11/32	.085	15°	24°	34°	1°	38°
	17084569	11/32	.085	15°	24°	34°	1°	38°
'85	17085348	5/32	.085	22°	32°	36°	1°	40°
	17085350	5/32	.085	22°	32°	36°	1°	40°
	17085351	11/32	.085	22°	32°	36°	1°	40°
	17085352	5/32	.085	22°	30°	34°	1°	40°
	17085354	5/32	.085	22°	30°	34°	1°	40°
	17085355	11/32	.085	22°	30°	34°	1°	40°
	17085360	5/32	.085	22°	32°	36°	1°	40°
	17085362	5/32	.085	22°	32°	36°	1°	40°
	17085363	11/32	.085	22°	32°	36°	1°	40°
	17085364	5/32	.085	22°	30°	34°	1°	40°
	17085366	5/32	.085	22°	30°	34°	1°	40°
	17085367	11/32	.085	22°	30°	34°	1°	40°
	17085372	5/32	.085	22°	32°	36°	1°	40°
	17085374	5/32	.085	22°	32°	36°	1°	40°

Note: Specified angle for use with angle degree tool.
① Adjust with fast idle cam on 2nd step.

MODEL E2SE
Chevrolet/GMC
(All measurements in inches or degrees)

Year	Carburetor Number	Float Level	Choke Coil Lever	Choke Rod①	Primary Vacuum Break	Secondary Vacuum Break	Air Valve Rod	Choke Unloader
'83	17083356	13/32	.085	22°	25°	35°	1°	30°
	17083357	13/32	.085	22°	25°	35°	1°	30°
	17083358	13/32	.085	22°	25°	35°	1°	30°
	17083359	13/32	.085	22°	25°	35°	1°	30°
	17083368	1/8	.085	22°	25°	35°	1°	30°
	17083370	1/8	.085	22°	25°	35°	1°	30°
	17083450	1/8	.085	28°	27°	35°	1°	45°
	17083451	1/4	.085	28°	27°	35°	1°	45°
	17083452	1/8	.085	28°	27°	35°	1°	45°
	17083453	1/4	.085	28°	27°	35°	1°	45°
	17083454	1/8	.085	28°	27°	35°	1°	45°
	17083455	1/4	.085	28°	27°	35°	1°	45°
	17083456	1/8	.085	28°	27°	35°	1°	45°
	17083630	1/4	.085	28°	27°	35°	1°	45°
	17083631	1/4	.085	28°	27°	35°	1°	45°
	17083632	1/4	.085	28°	27°	35°	1°	45°
	17083633	1/4	.085	28°	27°	35°	1°	45°
	17083634	1/4	.085	28°	27°	35°	1°	45°
	17083635	1/4	.085	28°	27°	35°	1°	45°
	17083636	1/4	.085	28°	27°	35°	1°	45°
	17083650	1/8	.085	28°	27°	35°	1°	45°
	17083430	11/32	.085	15°	26°	38°	1°	42°
	17083431	11/32	.085	15°	26°	38°	1°	42°
	17083434	11/32	.085	15°	26°	38°	1°	42°
	17083435	11/32	.085	15°	26°	38°	1°	42°
'84	17072683	9/32	.085	28°	25°	35°	1°	45°
	17074812	9/32	.085	28°①	25°	35°	1°	45°
	17084356	9/32	.085	22°	25°	30°	1°	30°
	17084357	9/32	.085	22°	25°	30°	1°	30°
	17084358	9/32	.085	22°	25°	30°	1°	30°
	17084359	9/32	.085	22°	25°	30°	1°	30°
	17084368	1/8	.085	22°	25°	30°	1°	30°

MODEL E2SE
Chevrolet/GMC
(All measurements in inches or degrees)

Year	Carburetor Number	Float Level	Choke Coil Lever	Choke Rod①	Primary Vacuum Break	Secondary Vacuum Break	Air Valve Rod	Choke Unloader
'84	17084370	⅛	.085	22°	25°	30°	1°	30°
	17084430	11⁄32	.085	15°	26°	38°	1°	42°
	17084431	11⁄32	.085	15°	26°	38°	1°	42°
	17084434	11⁄32	.085	15°	26°	38°	1°	42°
	17084435	11⁄32	.085	15°	26°	38°	1°	42°
	17084452	5⁄32	.085	28°	25°	35°	1°	45°
	17084453	5⁄32	.085	28°	25°	35°	1°	45°
	17084455	5⁄32	.085	28°	25°	35°	1°	45°
	17084456	5⁄32	.085	28°	25°	35°	1°	45°
	17084458	5⁄32	.085	28°	25°	35°	1°	45°
	17084532	5⁄32	.085	28°	25°	35°	1°	45°
	17084534	5⁄32	.085	28°	25°	35°	1°	45°
	17084535	5⁄32	.085	28°	25°	35°	1°	45°
	17084537	5⁄32	.085	28°	25°	35°	1°	45°
	17084538	5⁄32	.085	28°	25°	35°	1°	45°
	17084540	5⁄32	.085	28°	25°	35°	1°	45°
	17084542	⅛	.085	28°	25°	35°	1°	45°
	17084632	9⁄32	.085	28°	25°	35°	1°	45°
	17084633	9⁄32	.085	28°	25°	35°	1°	45°
	17084635	9⁄32	.085	28°	25°	35°	1°	45°
	17084636	9⁄32	.085	28°	25°	35°	1°	45°
'85	17085356	4⁄32	.085	22°	25°	30°	1°	30°
	17085357	9⁄32	.085	22°	25°	30°	1°	30°
	17085358	4⁄32	.085	22°	25°	30°	1°	30°
	17085359	9⁄32	.085	22°	25°	30°	1°	30°
	17085368	4⁄32	.085	22°	25°	30°	1°	30°
	17085369	9⁄32	.085	22°	25°	30°	1°	30°
	17085370	4⁄32	.085	22°	25°	30°	1°	30°
	17085371	9⁄32	.085	22°	25°	30°	1°	30°
	17085452	5⁄32	.085	28°	25°	35°	1°	45°
	17085453	5⁄32	.085	28°	25°	35°	1°	45°
	17085458	5⁄32	.085	28°	25°	35°	1°	45°

Note: Specified angle for use with angle
degree tool
① All models: Lean mixture screw–2½ turns
Idle mixture screw–4 turns

MODEL M2MC/M2ME
Chevrolet/GMC
(All measurements in inches ro degrees)

Year	Carburetor Number	Float Level	Choke Unloader	Choke Setting	Pump① Rod Adj.	Fast② Idle (rpm)	Fast Idle Cam Setting	Choke Vacuum Break
'79	17059100	$^{15}/_{32}$	—	1 Lean	$^{13}/_{32}$	1600	38°	29°
	17059101	$^{15}/_{32}$	—	1 Lean	$^{13}/_{32}$	1600	38°	29°
	17059102	$^{15}/_{32}$	—	1 Lean	$^{13}/_{32}$	1600	38°	29°
	17059103	$^{15}/_{32}$	—	1 Lean	$^{13}/_{32}$	1600	38°	29°
	17059142	$^{15}/_{32}$	—	1 Lean	$^{13}/_{32}$	1600	38°	29°
	17059143	$^{15}/_{32}$	—	1 Lean	$^{13}/_{32}$	1600	38°	29°
	17059144	$^{15}/_{32}$	—	1 Lean	$^{13}/_{32}$	1600	38°	29°
	17059145	$^{15}/_{32}$	—	1 Lean	$^{13}/_{32}$	1600	38°	29°
'80	17080100	$^{7}/_{16}$	38°	—	$^{9}/_{32}$	③	38°	29°
	17080102	$^{7}/_{16}$	38°	—	$^{9}/_{32}$	③	38°	29°
	17080142	$^{7}/_{16}$	38°	—	$^{9}/_{32}$	③	38°	29°
	17080143	$^{7}/_{16}$	38°	—	$^{9}/_{32}$	③	38°	29°
	17080145	$^{7}/_{16}$	38°	—	$^{9}/_{32}$	③	38°	29°
'81	17081101	$^{13}/_{32}$	38°	—	$^{5}/_{16}$	③	38°	29°
	17081103	$^{13}/_{32}$	38°	—	$^{5}/_{16}$	③	38°	29°
	17081142	$^{13}/_{32}$	38°	—	$^{5}/_{16}$	③	38°	29°
	17081143	$^{13}/_{32}$	38°	—	$^{5}/_{16}$	③	38°	29°
	17081144	$^{13}/_{32}$	38°	—	$^{5}/_{16}$	③	38°	29°
	17081145	$^{13}/_{32}$	38°	—	$^{5}/_{16}$	③	38°	29°

Note: Specified angle for use with angle degree tool
① Rod installed in the inner hole of the pump lever (nearest the carburetor)
② Manual transmission—1300 rpm in neutral
③ See underhood emissions label for idle speed specifications

MODEL E4ME
Chevrolet/GMC
(All measurements in inches or degrees)

Year	Carburetor Number	Float Level	Rich Mixture Screw	Idle Mixture Needle Turns	Air Valve Spring Turns	Choke Rod	Front Vacuum Break	Rear Vacuum Break	Air Valve Rod	Choke Unloader	Idle Air Bleed Valve
'83	17083202	11/32	—	3⅜	⅞	20°	—	27°	—	38°	①
	17083203	11/32	—	3⅜	⅞	38°	—	27°	—	38°	①
	17083204	11/32	—	3⅜	⅞	20°	—	27°	—	38°	①
	17083207	11/32	—	3⅜	⅞	38°	—	27°	—	38°	①
	17083216	11/32	—	3⅜	⅞	20°	—	27°	—	38°	①
	17083218	11/32	—	3⅜	⅞	20°	—	27°	—	38°	①
	17083236	11/32	—	②	⅞	20°	—	27°	—	38°	1.756
	17083506	7/16	—	②	⅞	20°	27	36°	—	36°	1.756
	17083508	7/16	—	②	⅞	20°	27	36°	—	36°	1.756
	17083524	7/16	—	②	⅞	20°	25	36°	—	36°	1.756
	17083526	7/16	—	②	⅞	20°	25	36°	—	36°	1.756
'84	17084201	11/32	4/32	3⅜	⅞	20°	27°	—	.025	38°	①
	17084205	11/32	4/32	3⅜	⅞	38°	27°	—	.025	38°	①
	17084208	11/32	4/32	3⅜	⅞	20°	27°	—	.025	38°	①
	17084209	11/32	4/32	3⅜	⅞	38°	27°	—	.025	38°	①
	17084210	11/32	4/32	3⅜	⅞	20°	27°	—	.025	38°	①
	17084507	7/16	4/32	②	1	20°	27°	36°	.025	36°	①
	17084509	7/16	4/32	②	1	20°	27°	36°	.025	36°	①
	17084525	7/16	4/32	②	1	20°	25°	36°	.025	36°	①
	17084527	7/16	4/32	②	1	20°	25°	36°	.025	36°	①
'85	17085202	11/32	4/32	3⅜	⅞	20°	27°	—	.025	38°	①
	17085203	11/32	4/32	3⅜	⅞	20°	27°	—	.025	38°	①
	17085204	11/32	4/32	3⅜	⅞	20°	27°	—	.025	38°	①
	17085207	11/32	4/32	3⅜	⅞	38°	27°	—	.025	38°	①
	17085218	11/32	4/32	3⅜	⅞	20°	27°	—	.025	38°	①
	17085502	7/16	—	②	⅞	20°	26°	36°	.025	39°	①
	17085503	7/16	—	②	⅞	20°	26°	36°	.025	39°	①
	17085506	7/16	—	②	1	20°	27°	36°	.025	36°	①
	17085508	7/16	—	②	1	20°	27°	36°	.025	36°	①
	17085524	7/16	—	②	1	20°	25°	36°	.025	36°	①
	17085526	7/16	—	②	1	20°	25°	36°	.025	36°	①

Note: Specified angle for use with angle
degree tool
Lean mixture screw-1.304 gauge
Choke stat lever-.120 gauge
① Preset with 1.756 gauge, final adjustment
on vehicle
② Preset 3 turns, final adjustment on vehicle

MODEL M4MC/4MV QUADRAJET
Chevrolet/GMC
(All measurements in inches)

Year	Carburetor Number	Float Level	Air Valve Dashpot	Pump Rod Adj.	Pump Rod Hole	Initial Choke Valve Opening	Vacuum Break	Choke Unloader	Air Valve Spring Turns
'79	17059212	7/16	.015	9/32	Inner	.314	.136	.260	3/4
	17059512	13/32	.015	9/32	Inner	.314	.136	.260	3/4
	17059061	15/32	.015	13/32	Inner	.314	.129	.277	7/8
	17059201	15/32	.015	13/32	Inner	.314	.129	.277	7/8
	17059065	15/32	.015	13/32	Inner	.314	.129	.277	7/8
	17059205	15/32	.015	13/32	Inner	.314	.129	.277	7/8
	17059066	15/32	.015	13/32	Inner	.314	.129	.277	7/8
	17059206	15/32	.015	13/32	Inner	.314	.129	.277	7/8
	17059068	15/32	.015	13/32	Inner	.314	.129	.277	7/8
	17059208	15/32	.015	13/32	Inner	.314	.129	.277	7/8
	17059069	15/32	.015	13/32	Inner	.314	.129	.277	7/8
	17059209	15/32	.015	13/32	Inner	.314	.129	.277	7/8
	17059076	15/32	.015	13/32	Inner	.314	.129	.277	7/8
	17059226	15/32	.015	13/32	Inner	.314	.129	.277	7/8
	17059077	15/32	.015	13/32	Inner	.314	.129	.277	7/8
	17059227	15/32	.015	13/32	Inner	.314	.129	.277	7/8
	17059213	15/32	.015	9/32	Inner	.234	.129	.260	1
	17059215	15/32	.015	9/32	Inner	.234	.129	.260	1
	17059363	15/32	.015	13/32	Inner	.314	.149	.277	7/8
	17059503	15/32	.015	13/32	Inner	.314	.149	.277	7/8
	17059506	15/32	.015	13/32	Inner	.314	.149	.277	7/8
	17059368	15/32	.015	13/32	Inner	.314	.149	.277	7/8
	17059508	15/32	.015	13/32	Inner	.314	.149	.277	7/8
	17059377	15/32	.015	9/32	Outer	.314	.149	.277	7/8
	17059527	15/32	.015	9/32	Outer	.314	.149	.277	7/8
	17059378	15/32	.015	9/32	Outer	.314	.149	.277	7/8
	17059528	15/32	.015	9/32	Outer	.314	.149	.277	7/8
	17059509	15/32	.015	13/32	Inner	.314	.179	.277	3/4
	17059515	15/32	.015	9/32	Inner	.234	.129	.260	1
	17059510	15/32	.015	13/32	Inner	.314	.179	.277	7/8
	17059529	15/32	.015	9/32	Inner	.234	.129	.260	1
	17059513	15/32	.015	9/32	Inner	.234	.129	.260	1
	17059586	15/32	.015	13/32	Inner	.314	.179	.277	7/8
	17059588	15/32	.015	13/32	Inner	.314	.179	.277	7/8
	17059229	15/32	.015	9/32	Inner	.234	.129	.260	1
	17059520	3/8	.015	9/32	Inner	.324	.164	.277	7/8
	17059521	3/8	.015	9/32	Inner	.314	.164	.277	7/8

MODEL M4MC/4MV QUADRAJET
Chevrolet/GMC
(All measurements in inches)

Year	Carburetor Number	Float Level	Choke Unloader	Choke Setting	Pump① Rod Adj.	Fast Idle Cam 2nd Step	Choke Vacuum Break
'80	17080201	$^{15}/_{32}$	42°	②	$^9/_{32}$	46°	23°
	17080205	$^{15}/_{32}$	42°	②	$^9/_{32}$	46°	23°
	17080206	$^{15}/_{32}$	42°	②	$^9/_{32}$	46°	23°
	17080224	$^{15}/_{32}$	42°	②	$^9/_{32}$	46°	23°
	17080290	$^{15}/_{32}$	42°	②	$^9/_{32}$	46°	26°
	17080291	$^{15}/_{32}$	42°	②	$^9/_{32}$	46°	26°
	17080292	$^{15}/_{32}$	42°	②	$^9/_{32}$	46°	26°
	17080295	$^{15}/_{32}$	42°	②	$^9/_{32}$	46°	23°
	17080297	$^{15}/_{32}$	42°	②	$^9/_{32}$	46°	23°
	17080503	$^{15}/_{32}$	42°	②	$^9/_{32}$	46°	26°
	17080506	$^{15}/_{32}$	42°	②	$^9/_{32}$	46°	26°
	17080508	$^{15}/_{32}$	42°	②	$^9/_{32}$	46°	26°
	17080523	$^{15}/_{32}$	42°	②	$^9/_{32}$	26°	23°
	17080524	$^{15}/_{32}$	42°	②	$^9/_{32}$	46°	23°
	17080525	$^{15}/_{32}$	42°	②	$^9/_{32}$	46°	23°
	17080526	$^{15}/_{32}$	42°	②	$^9/_{32}$	46°	23°
	17080226	$^{15}/_{32}$	42°	②	$^9/_{32}$	46°	23°
	17080227	$^{15}/_{32}$	42°	②	$^9/_{32}$	46°	23°
	17080527	$^{15}/_{32}$	42°	②	$^9/_{32}$	46°	23°
	17080528	$^{15}/_{32}$	42°	②	$^9/_{32}$	46°	23°
	17080213	$^3/_8$	40°	②	$^9/_{32}$	37°	30°
	17080215	$^3/_8$	40°	②	$^9/_{32}$	37°	30°
	17080513	$^3/_8$	40°	②	$^9/_{32}$	37°	30°
	17080515	$^3/_8$	40°	②	$^9/_{32}$	37°	30°
	17080229	$^3/_8$	40°	②	$^9/_{32}$	37°	30°
	17080529	$^3/_8$	40°	②	$^9/_{32}$	37°	30°
	17080225	$^{15}/_{32}$	42°	②	$^9/_{32}$	46°	23°
	17080212	$^3/_8$	40°	②	$^9/_{32}$	30°	24°
	17080512	$^3/_8$	40°	②	$^9/_{32}$	30°	24°
'81	17080212	$^3/_8$	40°	②	$^9/_{32}$	30°	24°
	17080213	$^3/_8$	40°	②	$^9/_{32}$	30°	23°
	17080215	$^3/_8$	40°	②	$^9/_{32}$	30°	23°
	17080298	$^3/_8$	40°	②	$^9/_{32}$	30°	23°
	17080507	$^3/_8$	40°	②	$^9/_{32}$	30°	23°
	17080512	$^3/_8$	40°	②	$^9/_{32}$	30°	24°
	17080513	$^3/_8$	40°	②	$^9/_{32}$	30°	23°
	17081200	$^{15}/_{32}$	42°	②	$^9/_{32}$	23°	24°

MODEL M4MC/4MV QUADRAJET
Chevrolet/GMC
(All measurements in inches)

Year	Carburetor Number	Float Level	Choke Unloader	Choke Setting	Pump① Rod Adj.	Fast Idle Cam 2nd Step	Choke Vacuum Break
'81	17081201	15/32	42°	②	9/32	23°	23°
	17081205	15/32	42°	②	9/32	23°	23°
	17081206	15/32	42°	②	9/32	23°	23°
	17081220	15/32	42°	②	9/32	23°	23°
	17081226	15/32	42°	②	9/32	23°	24°
	17081227	15/32	42°	②	9/32	—	24°
	17081290	13/32	42°	②	9/32	24°	23°
	17081291	13/32	42°	②	9/32	24°	23°
	17081292	13/32	42°	②	9/32	24°	23°
	17081506	13/32	36°	②	9/32	36°	23°
	17081508	13/32	36°	②	9/32	36°	23°
	17081524	13/32	36°	②	5/16③	36°	25°
	17081526	13/32	36°	②	5/16③	36°	25°

Note: Specified angle for use with angle degree tool
① Place the pump arm linkage in the inner hole of the arm, except on carburetors with a 5/16 pump rod height (see ③)
② 1980 and 1981 choke cover are riveted in position and are not adjustable under normal conditions
③ On carburetors with 5/16 pump rod height, place the pump arm linkage in the outer hole of the arm

MODEL M4MC/M4ME QUADRAJET
Chevrolet/GMC
(All measurements in inches or degrees)

Year	Carburetor Number	Float Level	Pump Rod Hole	Pump Rod Setting	Choke Rod① Setting	Air Valve Rod	Vacuum Break Front	Vacuum Break Rear	Air Valve Turns	Choke Unloader	Propane Enrichment (rpm)
'82	17080212	3/8	inner	9/32	46°	.025	24°	30°	3/4	40°	②
	17080213	3/8	inner	9/32	37°	.025	23°	30°	1	40°	②
	17080215	3/8	inner	9/32	37°	.025	23°	30°	1	40°	②
	17080298	3/8	inner	9/32	37°	.025	23°	30°	1	40°	②
	17080507	3/8	inner	9/32	37°	.025	23°	30°	1	40°	②
	17080512	3/8	inner	9/32	46°	.025	24°	30°	3/4	40°	②
	17080513	3/8	inner	9/32	37°	.025	23°	30°	3/4	40°	②
	17082213	3/8	inner	9/32	37°	.025	23°	30°	1	40°	②

MODEL M4MC/M4ME QUADRAJET
Chevrolet/GMC
(All measurements in inches or degrees)

Year	Carburetor Number	Float Level	Pump Rod Hole	Pump Rod Setting	Choke Rod① Setting	Air Valve Rod	Vacuum Break Front	Vacuum Break Rear	Air Valve Turns	Choke Unloader	Propane Enrichment (rpm)
'82	17082220	13/32	inner	9/32	46°	.025	24°	34°	7/8	39°	②
	17082221	13/32	inner	9/32	46°	.025	24°	34°	7/8	39°	150
	17082222	13/32	inner	9/32	46°	.025	24°	34°	7/8	39°	50
	17082223	13/32	inner	9/32	46°	.025	24°	34°	7/8	39°	100
	17082224	13/32	inner	9/32	46°	.025	24°	34°	7/8	39°	50
	17082225	13/32	inner	9/32	46°	.025	24°	34°	7/8	39°	150
	17082226	13/32	inner	9/32	46°	.025	24°	34°	7/8	39°	50
	17082227	13/32	inner	9/32	46°	.025	24°	34°	7/8	39°	50
	17082230	13/32	inner	9/32	46°	.025	26°	36°	7/8	39°	②
	17082231	13/32	inner	9/32	46°	.025	26°	36°	7/8	39°	②
	17082234	13/32	inner	9/32	46°	.025	26°	36°	7/8	39°	②
	17082235	13/32	inner	9/32	46°	.025	26°	36°	7/8	39°	②
	17082290	13/32	inner	9/32	46°	.025	24°	34°	7/8	39°	②
	17082291	13/32	inner	9/32	46°	.025	24°	34°	7/8	39°	②
	17082292	13/32	inner	9/32	46°	.025	24°	34°	7/8	39°	②
	17082293	13/32	inner	9/32	46°	.025	24°	34°	7/8	39°	100
	17082506	13/32	inner	9/32	46°	.025	23°	36°	7/8	39°	50
	17082508	3/8	inner	9/32	46°	.025	23°	36°	7/8	39°	50
	17082513	13/32	inner	9/32	46°	.025	23°	30°	3/4	40°	②
	17082524	13/32	outer	5/16	46°	.025	25°	36°	7/8	39°	20
	17082526	13/32	outer	5/16	46°	.025	25°	36°	7/8	39°	20
'83	17080201	15/32	inner	9/32	46°	.025	—	23°	7/8	42°	②
	17080205	15/32	inner	9/32	46°	.025	—	23°	7/8	42°	②
	17080206	15/32	inner	9/32	46°	.025	—	23°	7/8	42°	②
	17080213	3/8	inner	9/32	37°	.025	23°	30°	1	40°	②
	17080290	15/32	inner	9/32	46°	.025	—	26°	7/8	42°	②
	17080291	15/32	inner	9/32	46°	.025	—	26°	7/8	42°	②
	17080292	15/32	inner	9/32	46°	.025	—	26°	7/8	42°	②
	17080298	3/8	inner	9/32	37°	.025	23°	30°	1	40°	②
	17080507	3/8	inner	9/32	37°	.025	23°	30°	1	40°	②
	17080513	3/8	inner	9/32	37°	.025	23°	30°	1	40°	②
	17082213	9/32	inner	9/32	37°	.025	23°	30°	1	40°	②
	17083234	13/32	inner	9/32	46°	.025	—	26°	7/8	39°	20
	17083235	13/32	inner	9/32	46°	.025		26°	7/8	39°	100
	17083290	13/32	inner	9/32	46°	.025	—	24°	7/8	39°	40
	17083291	13/32	inner	9/32	46°	.025	—	24°	7/8	39°	100
	17083292	13/32	inner	9/32	46°	.025	—	24°	7/8	39°	40

MODEL M4MC/M4ME QUADRAJET
Chevrolet GMC
(All measurements in inches or degrees)

Year	Carburetor Number	Float Level	Pump Rod Hole	Pump Rod Setting	Choke Rod① Setting	Air Valve Rod	Vacuum Break Front	Vacuum Break Rear	Air Valve Turns	Choke Unloader	Propane Enrichment (rpm)
'83	17083293	$^{13}/_{32}$	inner	$^{9}/_{32}$	46°	.025	—	24°	$^{7}/_{8}$	39°	100
	17083298	$^{3}/_{8}$	inner	$^{9}/_{32}$	37°	.025	23°	30°	1	40°	②
	17083507	$^{3}/_{8}$	inner	$^{9}/_{32}$	37°	.025	23°	30°	1	40°	②
	17080212	$^{3}/_{8}$	inner	$^{9}/_{32}$	46°	.025	24°	30°	$^{3}/_{4}$	40°	②
	17080512	$^{3}/_{8}$	inner	$^{9}/_{32}$	46°	.025	24°	30°	$^{3}/_{4}$	40°	②
	17083220	$^{13}/_{32}$	inner	$^{9}/_{32}$	46°	.025	—	24°	$^{7}/_{8}$	39°	150
	17083221	$^{13}/_{32}$	inner	$^{9}/_{32}$	46°	.025	—	24°	$^{7}/_{8}$	39°	150
	17083222	$^{13}/_{32}$	inner	$^{9}/_{32}$	46°	.025	—	24°	$^{7}/_{8}$	39°	50
	17083223	$^{13}/_{32}$	inner	$^{9}/_{32}$	46°	.025	—	24°	$^{7}/_{8}$	39°	150
	17083224	$^{13}/_{32}$	inner	$^{9}/_{32}$	46°	.025	—	24°	$^{7}/_{8}$	39°	50
	17083225	$^{13}/_{32}$	inner	$^{9}/_{32}$	46°	.025	—	24°	$^{7}/_{8}$	39°	150
	17083226	$^{13}/_{32}$	inner	$^{9}/_{32}$	46°	.025	—	24°	$^{7}/_{8}$	39°	50
	17083227	$^{13}/_{32}$	inner	$^{9}/_{32}$	46°	.025	—	24°	$^{7}/_{8}$	39°	50
	17083230	$^{13}/_{32}$	inner	$^{9}/_{32}$	46°	.025	—	26°	$^{7}/_{8}$	39°	20
	17083231	$^{13}/_{32}$	inner	$^{9}/_{32}$	46°	.025	—	26°	$^{7}/_{8}$	39°	100
'84	17084200	$^{13}/_{32}$	inner	$^{9}/_{32}$	46°	.025	—	26°	$^{7}/_{8}$	39°	②
	17084206	$^{13}/_{32}$	inner	$^{9}/_{32}$	46°	.025	—	26°	$^{7}/_{8}$	39°	20
	17084211	$^{13}/_{32}$	inner	$^{9}/_{32}$	46°	.025	—	26°	$^{7}/_{8}$	39°	②
	17084220	$^{13}/_{32}$	inner	$^{9}/_{32}$	46°	.025	—	26°	$^{7}/_{8}$	39°	80
	17084221	$^{13}/_{32}$	inner	$^{9}/_{32}$	46°	.025	—	26°	$^{7}/_{8}$	39°	80
	17084226	$^{13}/_{32}$	inner	$^{9}/_{32}$	46°	.025	—	24°	$^{7}/_{8}$	39°	30
	17084227	$^{13}/_{32}$	inner	$^{9}/_{32}$	46°	.025	—	24°	$^{7}/_{8}$	39°	30
	17084228	$^{13}/_{32}$	inner	$^{9}/_{32}$	46°	.025	—	26°	$^{7}/_{8}$	39°	80
	17084229	$^{13}/_{32}$	inner	$^{9}/_{32}$	46°	.025	—	26°	$^{7}/_{8}$	39°	80
	17084230	$^{13}/_{32}$	inner	$^{9}/_{32}$	46°	.025	—	26°	$^{7}/_{8}$	39°	20
	17084231	$^{13}/_{32}$	inner	$^{9}/_{32}$	46°	.025	—	26°	$^{7}/_{8}$	39°	40
	17084234	$^{13}/_{32}$	inner	$^{9}/_{32}$	46°	.025	—	26°	$^{7}/_{8}$	39°	20
	17084235	$^{13}/_{32}$	inner	$^{9}/_{32}$	46°	.025	—	26°	$^{7}/_{8}$	39°	80
	17084290	$^{13}/_{32}$	inner	$^{9}/_{32}$	46°	.025	—	24°	$^{7}/_{8}$	39°	30
	17084291	$^{13}/_{32}$	inner	$^{9}/_{32}$	46°	.025	—	26°	$^{7}/_{8}$	39°	100
	17084292	$^{13}/_{32}$	inner	$^{9}/_{32}$	46°	.025	—	24°	$^{7}/_{8}$	39°	30
	17084293	$^{13}/_{32}$	inner	$^{9}/_{32}$	46°	.025	—	26°	$^{7}/_{8}$	39°	100
	17084294	$^{13}/_{32}$	inner	$^{9}/_{32}$	46°	.025	—	26°	$^{7}/_{8}$	39°	30
	17084298	$^{13}/_{32}$	inner	$^{9}/_{32}$	46°	.025	—	26°	$^{7}/_{8}$	39°	30

MODEL M4MC/M4ME QUADRAJET
Chevrolet/GMC
(All measurements in inches or degrees)

Year	Carburetor Number	Float Level	Pump Rod Hole	Pump Rod Setting	Choke Rod① Setting	Air Valve Rod	Vacuum Break Front	Vacuum Break Rear	Air Valve Turns	Choke Unloader	Propane Enrichment (rpm)
'85	17084500	12/32	inner	9/32	37°	.025	23°	30°	1	40°	②
	17084501	12/32	inner	9/32	37°	.025	23°	30°	1	40°	②
	17084502	12/32	inner	9/32	46°	.025	24°	30°	7/8	40°	②
	17085000	12/32	inner	9/32	46°	.025	24°	30°	7/8	40°	②
	17085001	12/32	inner	9/32	46°	.025	23°	30°	1	40°	②
	17085003	12/32	inner	9/32	46°	.025	23°	—	7/8	35°	②
	17085004	13/32	inner	9/32	46°	.025	23°	—	7/8	35°	②
	17085205	13/32	inner	9/32	20°	.025	26°	38°	7/8	39°	②
	17085206	13/32	inner	9/32	46°	.025	—	26°	7/8	39°	20
	17085208	13/32	inner	9/32	20°	.025	26°	38°	7/8	39°	10
	17085209	13/32	outer	3/8	20°	.025	26°	36°	7/8	39°	50
	17085210	13/32	inner	9/32	20°	.025	26°	38°	7/8	39°	10
	17085211	13/32	outer	3/8	20°	0.25	26°	36°	7/8	39°	50
	17085212	13/32	inner	9/32	46°	.025	23°	—	7/8	35°	②
	17085213	13/32	inner	9/32	46°	.025	23°	—	7/8	35°	②
	17085215	13/32	inner	9/32	46°	.025	—	26°	7/8	32°	②
	17085216	13/32	inner	9/32	20°	.025	26°	38°	7/8	39°	②
	17085217	13/32	inner	9/32	20°	.025	26°	36°	1/2	39°	②
	17085219	13/32	inner	9/32	20°	.025	26°	36°	1/2	39°	②
	17085220	13/32	outer	3/8	20°	.025	—	26°	7/8	32°	75
	17085221	13/32	outer	3/8	20°	.025	—	26°	7/8	32°	75
	17085222	13/32	inner	9/32	20°	.025	26°	36°	1/2	39°	20
	17085223	13/32	outer	3/8	20°	.025	26°	36°	1/2	39°	50
	17085224	13/32	inner	9/32	20°	.025	26°	36°	1/2	39°	20
	17085225	13/32	outer	3/8	20°	.025	26°	36°	1/2	39°	50
	17085226	13/32	inner	9/32	20°	.025	—	24°	7/8	32°	20
	17085227	13/32	inner	9/32	20°	.025	—	24°	7/8	32°	20
	17085228	13/32	inner	9/32	46°	.025	—	24°	7/8	39°	30
	17085229	13/32	inner	9/32	46°	.025	—	24°	7/8	39°	30
	17085230	13/32	inner	9/32	20°	.025	—	26°	7/8	32°	20
	17085231	13/32	inner	9/32	20°	.025	—	26°	7/8	32°	40
	17085235	13/32	inner	9/32	46°	.025	—	26°	7/8	39°	80
	17085238	13/32	outer	3/8	20°	.025	—	26°	7/8	32°	75
	17085239	13/32	outer	3/8	20°	.025	—	26°	7/8	32°	75
	17085290	13/32	inner	9/32	46°	.025	—	24°	7/8	39°	30
	17085291	13/32	outer	3/8	46°	.025	—	26°	7/8	39°	100
	17085292	13/32	inner	9/32	46°	.025	—	24°	7/8	39°	30

MODEL M4MC/M4ME QUADRAJET
Chevrolet/GMC
(All measurements in inches or degrees)

Year	Carburetor Number	Float Level	Pump Rod Hole	Pump Rod Setting	Choke Rod① Setting	Air Valve Rod	Vacuum Break Front	Vacuum Break Rear	Air Valve Turns	Choke Unloader	Propane Enrichment (rpm)
'85	17085293	¹³⁄₃₂	outer	³⁄₈	46°	.025	—	26°	⅞	39°	100
	17085294	¹³⁄₃₂	inner	⁹⁄₃₂	46°	.025	—	26°	⅞	39°	②
	17085298	¹³⁄₃₂	inner	⁹⁄₃₂	46°	.025	—	26°	⅞	39°	②

Note: Specified angle for use with angle
    degree tool. Choke coil lever setting is
    .120 in. for all carburetors.
① Second step of fast idle cam
② See Underhood Specifications sticker

ANGLE DEGREE TO DECIMAL CONVERSION
Model M2MC, M2ME and M4MC Carburetor

Angle Degrees	Decimal Equiv. Top of Valve	Angle Degrees	Decimal Equiv. Top of Valve
5	.023	33	.203
6	.028	34	.211
7	.033	35	.220
8	.038	36	.227
9	.043	37	.234
10	.049	38	.243
11	.054	39	.251
12	.060	40	.260
13	.066	41	.269
14	.071	42	.277
15	.077	43	.287
16	.083	44	.295
17	.090	45	.304
18	.096	46	.314
19	.103	47	.322

ANGLE DEGREE TO DECIMAL CONVERSION
Model M2MC, M2ME and M4MC Carburetor

Angle Degrees	Decimal Equiv. Top of Valve	Angle Degrees	Decimal Equiv. Top of Valve
20	.110	48	.332
21	.117	49	.341
22	.123	50	.350
23	.129	51	.360
24	.136	52	.370
25	.142	53	.379
26	.149	54	.388
27	.157	55	.400
28	.164	56	.408
29	.171	57	.418
30	.179	58	.428
31	.187	59	.439
32	.195	60	.449

ANGLE DEGREE TO DECIMAL CONVERSION
Model 4MV Carburetor

Angle Degrees	Decimal Equiv. Top of Valve	Angle Degrees	Decimal Equiv. Top of Valve
5	.019	33	.158
6	.022	34	.164
7	.026	35	.171
8	.030	36	.178
9	.034	37	.184
10	.038	38	.190
11	.042	39	.197
12	.047	40	.204
13	.051	41	.211
14	.056	42	.217
15	.060	43	.225
16	.065	44	.231
17	.070	45	.239
18	.075	46	.246
19	.080	47	.253
20	.085	48	.260
21	.090	49	.268
22	.095	50	.275
23	.101	51	.283
24	.106	52	.291
25	.112	53	.299
26	.117	54	.306
27	.123	55	.314
28	.128	56	.322
29	.134	57	.329
30	.140	58	.337
31	.146	59	.345
32	.152	60	.353

TPS ADJUSTMENT SPECIFICATIONS
Chevrolet/GMC Models

Year	Engine Code	TPS Voltage
'83	H	.51
	G	.51
	F	.40
	L	.40
'84	B	.255
	X	.31
	Z	.255
	G	.48
	H	.48
	G	.48
	F	.41
	L	.41
'85	G	.48
	H	.48
	G	.48
	F	.41
	L	.41
	N	.25

Note: Measure voltage with throttle at curb
idle position, ignition ON, engine and A/
C OFF. All values ± 0.1 volt.

STROMBERG CARBURETORS

IDLE SPEED AND MIXTURE ADJUSTMENT

1979–80 Models

1. Start the engine and run it until it reaches operating temperature.

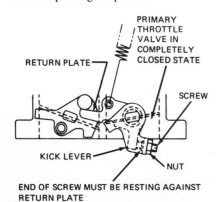

Kick lever adjustment—DCH340

2. If it hasn't already been done, check and adjust the ignition timing. After you have set the timing, turn off the engine.

3. Attach tachometer to the engine.

4. Remove the air cleaner.

5. Start the engine and, with transmission in Neutral, check the idle speed on the tachometer. If the reading is correct, turn off the engine and remove the tachometer. If it is not correct, proceed to the following steps.

6. Turn the idle adjusting screw with a screwdriver clockwise to increase idle speed and counterclockwise to decrease it.

7. If the vehicle is equipped with air conditioning:

a. Turn on the A/C to maximum cold and high blower. Disconnect the vacuum line to the air cleaner housing air compensator and plug the intake manifold.

b. Open the throttle approximately ⅓ and allow the throttle to close. This will allow the speed-up solenoid to reach full travel.

c. Adjust the fast idle screw to set the idle speed to 900 rpm.

d. Open the throttle about ⅓ and allow it to close. Read the idle rpm. Repeat Step C until the correct reading is obtained. Shut off the engine.

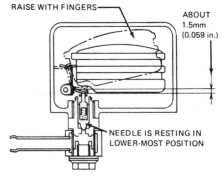

DCH340 needle valve stroke adjustment

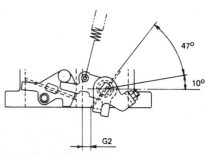

Secondary throttle opening point clearance—DCH340

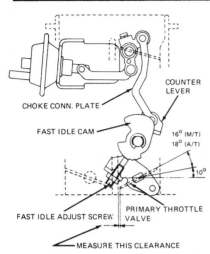

Primary throttle valve adjustment—DCH340

8. Turn the mixture adjusting screw all the way in. Seat the needle tip lightly to avoid damaging the tip. Back the screw out $3\frac{1}{2}$ turns.

9. Start the engine. Turn the mixture screw until the maximum engine rpm is achieved.

10. Reset the engine idle speed.

11. Turn the idle mixture screw clockwise (lean) until the engine speed drops 50 rpm.

12. Reset the idle mixture screw $\frac{1}{2}$ turn counterclockwise (rich) from Step 11 position.

13. Reset the throttle adjusting screw to required idle speed.

14. Unplug and reconnect any vacuum lines that may have been disconnected.

1981 and Later Models

The idle mixture adjustment is the same as previously described with the following exceptions:

1. Make the idle speed adjustment with the engine at normal operating temperature. Be sure the choke is fully opened, air conditioning off and the air cleaner installed.

2. Disconnect and plug the distributor vacuum, the canister purge and EGR vacuum lines. Shut off the vacuum to the idle compensator by bending the rubber hose.

3. Adjust to required idle speed with throttle adjusting screw.

4. If equipped with air conditioning, turn AC to max cold and high blower.

5. Open throttle to approx. $\frac{1}{3}$ and allow throttle to close, the speed up solenoid should activate. Adjust speed up solenoid screw until 900 rpm is reached.

6. In order to adjust the idle mixture you must first remove the plug that covers the mixture screw. To remove the plug, first remove the carburetor and turn it upside down.

7. Knock out the plug carefully with a hammer and screwdriver (see illustration).

8. Reinstall the carburetor.

9. Turn the mixture screw all the way in (seated lightly) and then back it out 2 turns for Federal models and 1 turn for California models. Readjust the idle if necessary.

THROTTLE LINKAGE ADJUSTMENT

When the primary throttle valve is opened to an angle of 50° from its closed position, the adjust plate which is interlocked with the primary throttle valve is brought into contact with the return plate. When the primary throttle valve is opened farther, the return plate is pulled apart from the stopper allowing the secondary throtttle valve to open. To adjust the linkage:

1. Measure the clearance between the primary throttle valve and the wall of the throttle chamber at the center of the throttle valve when the adjust plate is brought into contact with the return plate. Standard clearance is 0.26–0.32 in.

2. If necessary, make the adjustment by bending the tab of the return plate.

FLOAT LEVEL ADJUSTMENT

The fuel level is normal if it is within the lines on the window glass of the float chamber when the vehicle is resting on level ground and the engine is off. If the fuel level is outside the lines, remove the float housing cover. Have an absorbent cloth under the cover to catch the fuel from the fuel bowl. Adjust the float level by bending the needle seat on the float. The needle valve

should have an effective stroke of about 0.059 in. When necessary, the needle valve stroke can be adjusted by bending the float stopper.

NOTE: Be careful not to bend the needle valve rod when installing the float and baffle plate, if removed.

KICK LEVER ADJUSTMENT

1. Bring the primary side throttle valve into the complete closed position, by turning the throttle adjustment screw.

2. On manual transmission models, with the throttle valve completely closed, loosen the lock nut on the kick lever screw and turn the screw until it is in contact with the return plate and tighten the lock nut.

3. On automatic transmission models with the throttle valve completely closed, bend the end of the kick lever until it is in contact with the return plate.

ELECTRIC AUTOMATIC CHOKE

1. Install the thermostat cover by fitting the end of the choke lever into the bimetal hook.

2. Align the thermostat housing line (thickest one) with the line on the thermostat cover.

3. Measure the clearance between the choke valve edge and the choke chamber wall when the choke is fully closed. The standard clearance should be 0.11–0.29 in. This clearance is equal to a bimetal lever angle of 30°.

4. If the measured value is not correct, adjust it by bending the bimetal lever as necessary.

ELECTRIC CHOKE ADJUSTMENT

Align the thickest line on the thermostat housing with the line on the thermostat cover. Measure clearance between the cover side stopper and the bimetal level side stopper when the diaphragm is fully stroked with negative pressure or finger pressure. If the measured value deviates from the standard clearance of 0.28–0.29 in. or the equivalent bimetal lever angle of 20°, adjust with the adjusting screw.

11 CARBURETOR OVERHAUL

MODEL DCH340
Chevrolet S-10
(All measurements in inches)

Float Needle Valve Stroke	Primary Throttle Valve Adjustment	Secondary Throttle Opening Point	Kick Lever Adjustment
.059	.050–.059①	.24–.30	②

① Applies to manual trans. automatic trans-
.059–.069
② Zero clearance between kick lever screw
and return plate—throttle fully closed.

Engine Rebuilding  12

This section describes, in detail, the procedures involved in rebuilding a typical engine. The procedures are basically identical to those used in rebuilding engines of nearly all design and configurations.

The section is divided into two parts. The first, Cylinder Head Reconditioning, assumes that the cylinder head is removed from the engine, all manifolds are removed, and the cylinder head is on a workbench. The camshaft should be removed from overhead cam cylinder heads. The second section, Cylinder Block Reconditioning, covers the block, pistons, connecting rods and crankshaft. It is assumed that the engine is mounted on a work stand, and the cylinder head and all accessories are removed.

Procedures are identified as follows:

Unmarked—Basic procedures that must be performed in order to successfully complete the rebuilding process.

Starred (*)—Procedures that should be performed to ensure maximum performance and engine life.

Double starred (**)—Procedures that may be performed to increase engine performance and reliability.

In many cases, a choice of methods is also provided. Methods are identified in the same manner as procedures. The choice of method for a procedure is at the discretion of the user.

The tools required for the basic rebuilding procedure should, with minor exceptions, be those included in a mechanic's tool kit. An accurate torque wrench, and a dial indicator (reading in thousandths) mounted on a universal base should be available. Special tools, where required, are all readily available from the major tool suppliers. The services of a competent automotive machine shop must also be readily available.

When assembling the engine, any parts that will be in frictional contact must be prelubricated, to provide protection on initial start-up. Any product specifically formulated for this purpose may be used. NOTE: *Do not use engine oil.* Where semi-permanent (locked but removable) installation of bolts or nuts is desired, threads should be cleaned and coated with Loctite® or a similar product (non-hardening).

Aluminum has become increasingly popular for use in engines, due to its low weight and excellent heat transfer characteristics. The following precautions must be observed when handling aluminum engine parts:

—Never hot-tank aluminum parts.

—Remove all aluminum parts (identification tags, etc.) from engine parts before hot-tanking (otherwise they will be removed during the process).

—Always coat threads lightly with engine oil or anti-seize compounds before installation, to prevent seizure.

—Never over-torque bolts or spark plugs in aluminum threads. Should stripping occur, threads can be restored using any of a number of thread repair kits available (see next section).

Magnaflux and Zyglo are inspection techniques used to locate material flaws, such as stress cracks. Magnafluxing coats the part with fine magnetic particles, and subjects the part to a magnetic field. Cracks cause breaks in the magnetic field, which are outlined by the particles. Since Magnaflux is a magnetic process, it is applicable only to ferrous materials. The Zyglo process coats the material with a fluorescent dye penetrant, and then subjects it to blacklight inspection, under which cracks glow brightly. Parts made of any material may be tested using Zyglo. While Magnaflux and Zyglo are excellent for general inspection, and locating hidden defects, specific checks of suspected cracks may be made at lower cost and more readily using spot check dye. The dye is sprayed onto the suspected area, wiped off, and the area is then sprayed with a developer. Cracks then will show up brightly. Spot check dyes will only indicate surface cracks; therefore, structural cracks below the surface may escape detection. When questionable, the part should be tested using Magnaflux or Zyglo.

REPAIRING DAMAGED THREADS

Several methods of repairing damaged threads are available. Heli-Coil® (shown here), Keenserts® and Microdot® are among the most widely used. All involve basically the same principle—drilling out stripped threads, tapping the hole and installing a prewound insert— making welding, plugging and oversize fasteners unnecessary.

Two types of thread repair inserts are usually supplied—a standard type for most Inch Coarse, Inch Fine, Metric Coarse and Metric Fine thread sizes and a spark plug type to fit most spark plug port sizes. Consult the individual manufacturer's catalog to determine exact applications. Typical thread repair kits will contain a selection of prewound threaded inserts, a tap (corresponding to the outside diameter threads of the insert) and an installation tool. Most manufacturers also supply blister-packed thread repair inserts separately and a master kit with a variety of taps and inserts plus installation tools.

Before effecting a repair to a threaded hole, remove any snapped, broken or damaged bolts or studs. Penetrating oil can be used to free frozen threads; the offending item can be removed with locking pliers or with a screw or stud extractor. After the hole is clear, the thread can be repaired as follows.

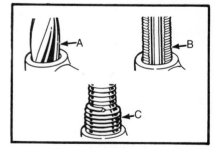

A. Drill out the damaged threads with the specified drill. Drill completely through the hole or to the bottom of a blind hole.

B. With the tap supplied tap the hole to receive the threaded insert. Keep the tap well oiled and back it out frequently to avoid clogging the threads.

C. Screw the threaded insert onto the installation tool until the tang engages the slot. Screw the insert into the tapped hole until it is ¼–½ turn below the top surface. After installation, break the tang off with a hammer and punch.

STANDARD TORQUE SPECIFICATIONS AND CAPSCREW MARKINGS

Newton-Meter has been designated as the world standard for measuring torque and will gradually replace the foot-pound and kilogram-meter torque measuring standard. Torquing tools are still being manufactured with foot-pounds and kilogram-meter scales, along with the new Newton-Meter standard. To assist the repairman, foot-pounds, kilogram-meter and Newton-Meter are listed in the following charts, and should be followed as applicable.

U.S. BOLTS

SAE Grade Number	1 or 2			5			6 or 7			8		
Capscrew Head Markings Manufacturer's marks may vary. Three-line markings on heads below indicate SAE Grade 5.												
Usage	Used Frequently			Used Frequently			Used at Times			Used at Times		
Quality of Material	Indeterminate			Minimum Commercial			Medium Commercial			Best Commercial		
Capacity Body Size	**Torque**			**Torque**			**Torque**			**Torque**		
(inches)–(thread)	Ft-Lb	kgm	Nm	Ft-Lb	kgm	Nm	Ft-Lb	kgm	Nm	Ft-Lb	kgm	Nm
1/4–20	5	0.6915	6.7791	8	1.1064	10.8465	10	1.3630	13.5582	12	1.6596	16.2698
–28	6	0.8298	8.1349	10	1.3830	13.5582				14	1.9362	18.9815
5/16–18	11	1.5213	14.9140	17	2.3511	23.0489	19	2.6277	25.7605	24	3.3192	32.5396
–24	13	1.7979	17.6256	19	2.6277	25.7605				27	3.7341	36.6071
3/8–16	18	2.4894	24.4047	31	4.2873	42.0304	34	4.7022	46.0978	44	6.0852	59.6560
–24	20	2.7660	27.1164	35	4.8405	47.4536				49	6.7767	66.4351
7/16–14	28	3.8132	37.9629	49	6.7767	66.4351	55	7.6065	74.5700	70	9.6810	94.9073
–20	30	4.1490	40.6745	55	7.6065	74.5700				78	10.7874	105.7538
1/2–13	39	5.3937	52.8769	75	10.3725	101.6863	85	11.7555	115.2445	105	14.5215	142.3609
–20	41	5.6703	55.5885	85	11.7555	115.2445				120	16.5860	162.6960
9/16–12	51	7.0533	69.1467	110	15.2130	149.1380	120	16.5960	162.6960	155	21.4365	210.1490
–18	55	7.6065	74.5700	120	16.5960	162.6960				170	23.5110	230.4860
5/8–11	83	11.4789	112.5329	150	20.7450	203.3700	167	23.0961	226.4186	210	29.0430	284.7180
–18	95	13.1385	128.8027	170	23.5110	230.4860				240	33.1920	325.3920
3/4–10	105	14.5215	142.3609	270	37.3410	366.0660	280	38.7240	379.6240	375	51.8625	508.4250
–16	115	15.9045	155.9170	295	40.7985	399.9610				420	58.0860	568.4360
7/8–9	160	22.1280	216.9280	395	54.6285	535.5410	440	60.8520	596.5520	605	83.6715	820.2590
–14	175	24.2025	237.2650	435	60.1605	589.7730				675	93.3525	915.1650
1–8	236	32.5005	318.6130	590	81.5970	799.9220	660	91.2780	894.8280	910	125.8530	1233.7780
–14	250	34.5750	338.9500	660	91.2780	849.8280				990	136.9170	1342.2420

METRIC BOLTS

Description	Torque ft-lbs. (Nm)			
Thread for general purposes (size x pitch (mm))	**Head Mark 4**		**Head Mark 7**	
6 x 1.0	2.2 to 2.9	(3.0 to 3.9)	3.6 to 5.8	(4.9 to 7.8)
8 x 1.25	5.8 to 8.7	(7.9 to 12)	9.4 to 14	(13 to 19)
10 x 1.25	12 to 17	(16 to 23)	20 to 29	(27 to 39)
12 x 1.25	21 to 32	(29 to 43)	35 to 53	(47 to 72)
14 x 1.5	35 to 52	(48 to 70)	57 to 85	(77 to 110)
16 x 1.5	51 to 77	(67 to 100)	90 to 120	(130 to 160)
18 x 1.5	74 to 110	(100 to 150)	130 to 170	(180 to 230)
20 x 1.5	110 to 140	(150 to 190)	190 to 240	(160 to 320)
22 x 1.5	150 to 190	(200 to 260)	250 to 320	(340 to 430)
24 x 1.5	190 to 240	(260 to 320)	310 to 410	(420 to 550)

CAUTION: Bolts threaded into aluminum require much less torque

NOTE: This engine rebuilding section is a guide to accepted rebuilding procedures. Typical examples of standard rebuilding procedures are illustrated.

CYLINDER HEAD RECONDITIONING

Procedure	Method
Identify the valves:	Invert the cylinder head, and number the valve faces front to rear, using a permanent felt-tip marker.
Remove the rocker arms (OHV engines only):	Remove the rocker arms with shaft(s) or balls and nuts. Wire the sets of rockers, balls and nuts together, and identify according to the corresponding valve.
Remove the camshaft (OHC engines only):	See the engine service procedures earlier in this book for details concerning specific engines.
Remove the valves and springs:	Using an appropriate valve spring compressor (depending on the configuration of the cylinder head), compress the valve springs. Lift out the keepers with needlenose pliers, release the compressor, and remove the valve, spring, and spring retainer.
Remove glow plugs and fuel injectors (Diesel engines only):	Label and remove all fuel injectors and glow plugs from the head. Glow plugs unscrew. See the appropriate car section for injector removal. Inspect glow plugs for bulges, cracks or signs of melting. Clean injector tips with a steel brush, then inspect for evidence of melting.
**Remove pre-combustion chamber inserts (Diesel engines only): 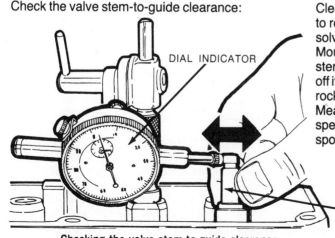 Removing pre-combustion chamber with a drift (© G.M. Corp.)	**Remove the pre-combustion chambers using a hammer and a thin, blunt brass drift, inserted through the injector hole (or glow plug hole, whichever is more convenient). If chamber is to be reused, carefully remove all carbon from it. NOTE: *Remove chamber only if being replaced, if a glow plug tip has broken off and must be removed, or if chamber is obviously damaged or loose.*
Check the valve stem-to-guide clearance:	Clean the valve stem with lacquer thinner or a similar solvent to remove all gum and varnish. Clean the valve guides using solvent and an expanding wire-type valve guide cleaner. Mount a dial indicator so that the stem is at 90° to the valve stem, as close to the valve guide as possible. Move the valve off its seat, and measure the valve guide-to-stem clearance by rocking the stem back and forth to actuate the dial indicator. Measure the valve stems using a micrometer, and compare to specifications, to determine whether stem or guide wear is responsible for excessive clearance.

Checking the valve stem-to-guide clearance

CYLINDER HEAD RECONDITIONING

Procedure	Method

De-carbon the cylinder head and valves:

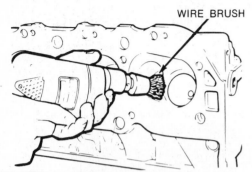

WIRE BRUSH

Removing carbon from the cylinder head

Chip carbon away from the valve heads, combustion chambers, and ports, using a chisel made of hardwood. Remove the remaining deposits with a stiff wire brush.
NOTE: *Ensure that the deposits are actually removed, rather than burnished.*

Hot-tank the cylinder head (cast iron heads only):
CAUTION: *Do not hot-tank aluminum parts.*

Have the cylinder head hot-tanked to remove grease, corrosion, and scale from the water passages.
NOTE: *In the case of overhead cam cylinder heads, consult the operator to determine whether the camshaft bearings will be damaged by the caustic solution.*

Degrease the remaining cylinder head parts:

Using solvent (i.e., Gunk), clean the rockers, rocker shaft(s) (where applicable), rocker balls and nuts, springs, spring retainers, and keepers. Do not remove the protective coating from the springs.

Check the cylinder head for warpage:

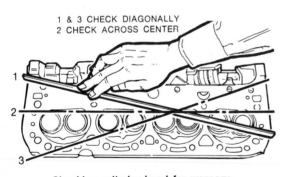

1 & 3 CHECK DIAGONALLY
2 CHECK ACROSS CENTER

Checking cylinder head for warpage

Place a straight-edge across the gasket surface of the cylinder head. Using feeler gauges, determine the clearance at the center of the straight-edge. Measure across both diagonals, along the longitudinal centerline, and across the cylinder head at several points. If warpage exceeds .003′ in a 6′ span, or .006′ over the total length, the cylinder head must be resurfaced.
NOTE: *If warpage exceeds the manufacturer's maximum tolerance for material removal, the cylinder head must be replaced.*
When milling the cylinder heads of V-type engines, the intake manifold mounting position is altered, and must be corrected by milling the manifold flange a proportionate amount.

**Porting and gasket matching:

**Coat the manifold flanges of the cylinder head with Prussian blue dye. Glue intake and exhaust gaskets to the cylinder head in their installed position using rubber cement and scribe the outline of the ports on the manifold flanges. Remove the gaskets. Using a small cutter in a hand-held power tool gradually taper the walls of the port out to the scribed outline of the gasket. Further enlargement of the ports should include the removal of sharp edges and radiusing of sharp corners. Do not alter the valve guides.
NOTE: *The most efficient port configuration is determined only by extensive testing. Therefore, it is best to consult someone experienced with the head in question to determine the optimum alterations.*

CYLINDER HEAD RECONDITIONING

Procedure	Method

*Knurling the valve guides:

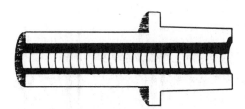

Cut-away view of a knurled valve guide

*Valve guides which are not excessively worn or distorted may, in some cases, be knurled rather than replaced. Knurling is a process in which metal is displaced and raised, thereby reducing clearance. Knurling also provides excellent oil control. The possibility of knurling rather than replacing valve guides should be discussed with a machinist.

Replacing the valve guides:
NOTE: *Valve guides should only be replaced if damaged or if an oversize valve stem is not available.*

A—VALVE GUIDE I.D.   B—LARGER THAN THE VALVE GUIDE O.D.

Valve guide removal tool

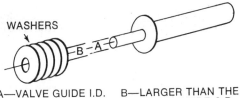

WASHERS

A—VALVE GUIDE I.D.   B—LARGER THAN THE VALVE GUIDE O.D.

Valve guide installation tool (with washers used for installation)

Depending on the type of cylinder head, valve guides may be pressed, hammered, or shrunk in. In cases where the guides are shrunk into the head, replacement should be left to an equipped machine shop. In other cases, the guides are replaced as follows: Press or tap the valve guides out of the head using a stepped drift (see illustration). Determine the height above the boss that the guide must extend, and obtain a stack of washers, their I.D. similar to the guide's O.D., of that height. Place the stack of washers on the guide, and insert the guide into the boss.
NOTE: *Valve guides are often tapered or beveled for installation.*
Using the stepped installation tool (see illustration), press or tap the guides into position. Ream the guides according to the size of the valve stem.

Replacing valve seat inserts:

Replacement of valve seat inserts which are worn beyond resurfacing or broken, if feasible, must be done by a machine shop.

Resurfacing the valve seats using reamers:

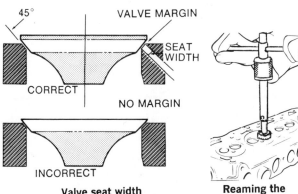

45°
VALVE MARGIN
SEAT WIDTH
CORRECT
NO MARGIN
INCORRECT

Valve seat width and centering

Reaming the valve seat

Select a reamer of the correct seat angle, slightly larger than the diameter of the valve seat, and assemble it with a pilot of the correct size. Install the pilot into the valve guide, and using steady pressure, turn the reamer clockwise.
CAUTION: *Do not turn the reamer counterclockwise.*
Remove only as much material as necessary to clean the seat. Check the concentricity of the seat (see below). If the dye method is not used, coat the valve face with Prussian blue dye, install and rotate it on the valve seat. Using the dye marked area as a centering guide, center and narrow the valve seat to specifications with correction cutters.
NOTE: *When no specifications are available, minimum seat width for exhaust valves should be 5/64", intake valves 1/16".*
After making correction cuts, check the position of the valve seat on the valve face using Prussian blue dye.
NOTE: *Do not cut induction hardened seats; they must be ground.*

CYLINDER HEAD RECONDITIONING

Procedure	Method

*Resurfacing the valve seats using a grinder:

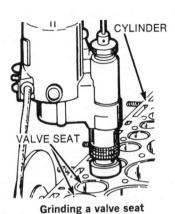

Grinding a valve seat

*Select a pilot of the correct size, and a coarse stone of the correct seat angle. Lubricate the pilot if necessary, and install the tool in the valve guide. Move the stone on and off the seat at approximately two cycles per second, until all flaws are removed from the seat. Install a fine stone, and finish the seat. Center and narrow the seat using correction stones, as described above.

Resurfacing (grinding) the valve face:

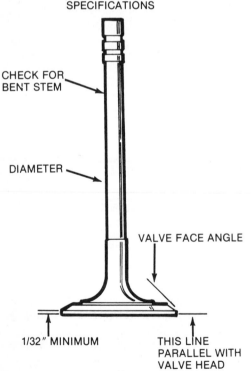

FOR DIMENSIONS, REFER TO SPECIFICATIONS

CHECK FOR BENT STEM

DIAMETER

VALVE FACE ANGLE

1/32" MINIMUM

THIS LINE PARALLEL WITH VALVE HEAD

Critical valve dimensions

Using a valve grinder, resurface the valves according to specifications.
CAUTION: *Valve face angle is not always identical to valve seat angle.*
A minimum margin of 1/32" should remain after grinding the valve. The valve stem top should also be squared and resurfaced, by placing the stem in the V-block of the grinder, and turning it while pressing lightly against the grinding wheel.
NOTE: *Do not grind sodium filled exhaust valves on a machine. These should be hand lapped.*

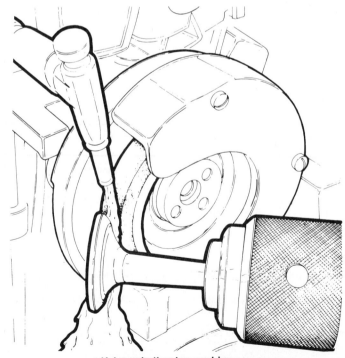

Valve grinding by machine

CYLINDER HEAD RECONDITIONING

Procedure	Method

Checking the valve seat concentricity:

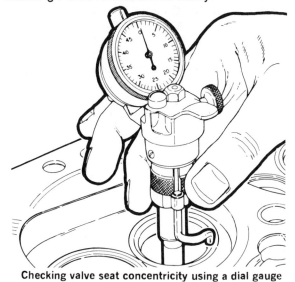

Checking valve seat concentricity using a dial gauge

Coat the valve face with Prussian blue dye, install the valve, and rotate it on the valve seat. If the entire seat becomes coated, and the valve is known to be concentric, the seat is concentric.
*Install the dial gauge pilot into the guide, and rest the arm on the valve seat. Zero the gauge, and rotate the arm around the seat. Run-out should not exceed .002″.

---

*Lapping the valves:
NOTE: *Valve lapping is done to ensure efficient sealing of resurfaced valves and seats.*

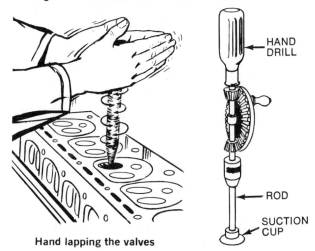

HAND DRILL

ROD

SUCTION CUP

Hand lapping the valves

Home made mechanical valve lapping tool

*Invert the cylinder head, lightly lubricate the valve stems, and install the valves in the head as numbered. Coat valve seats with fine grinding compound, and attach the lapping tool suction cup to a valve head.
NOTE: *Moisten the suction cup.*
Rotate the tool between the palms, changing position and lifting the tool often to prevent grooving. Lap the valve until a smooth, polished seat is evident. Remove the valve and tool, and rinse away all traces of grinding compound.
**Fasten a suction cup to a piece of drill rod, and mount the rod in a hand drill. Proceed as above, using the hand drill as a lapping tool.
CAUTION: *Due to the higher speeds involved when using the hand drill, care must be exercised to avoid grooving the seat.* Lift the tool and change direction of rotation often.

Check the valve springs:

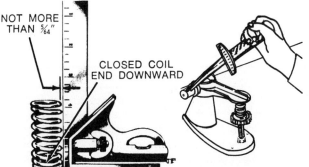

NOT MORE THAN 5/64″

CLOSED COIL END DOWNWARD

Checking valve spring free length and squareness

Measuring valve spring test pressure

Place the spring on a flat surface next to a square. Measure the height of the spring, and rotate it against the edge of the square to measure distortion. If spring height varies (by comparison) by more than 1/16″ or if distortion exceeds 1/16″, replace the spring.
**In addition to evaluating the spring as above, test the spring pressure at the installed and compressed (installed height minus valve lift) height using a valve spring tester. Springs used on small displacement engines (up to 3 liters) should be ∓ 1 lb. of all other springs in either position. A tolerance of ∓ 5 lbs. is permissible on larger engines.

CYLINDER HEAD RECONDITIONING

Procedure	Method

Install pre-combustion chambers (Diesel engines only)

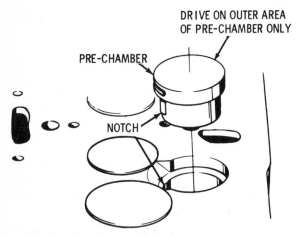

Align the notches to install the pre-combustion chamber (© G.M. Corp.)

Pre-combustion chambers are press-fit into the head. The chambers will fit only one way: on G.M. V8, align the notches in the chamber and head; on 1.8L 4 cyl., install lock ball into groove in chamber, then align lock ball in chamber with groove in cylinder head. Press the chamber into the head. Fit a piece of metal against the chamber face for protection. On 1.8L, after installation, grind the face of the chamber flush with the face of the cylinder head. On G.M. V8, use a 1¼ in. socket to install the chamber (the chamber should be flush ± .003 in. to the face of the head).

Install fuel injectors and glow plugs (Diesel engines)

Before installing glow plugs, check for continuity across plug terminals and body. If no continuity exists, the heater wire is broken and the plug should be replaced.

---

*Install valve stem seals:

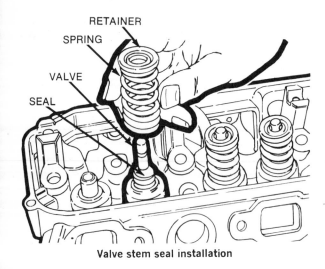

Valve stem seal installation

*Due to the pressure differential that exists at the ends of the intake valve guides (atmospheric pressure above, manifold vacuum below), oil is drawn through the valve guides into the intake port. This has been alleviated somewhat since the addition of positive crankcase ventilation, which lowers the pressure above the guides. Several types of valve stem seals are available to reduce blow-by. Certain seals simply slip over the stem and guide boss, while others require that the boss be machined. Recently, Teflon guide seals have become popular. Consult a parts supplier or machinist concerning availability and suggested usages.

NOTE: *When installing seals, ensure that a small amount of oil is able to pass the seal to lubricate the valve guides; otherwise, excessive wear may result.*

Install the valves:

Lubricate the valve stems, and install the valves in the cylinder head as numbered. Lubricate and position the seals (if used, see above) and the valve springs. Install the spring retainers, compress the springs, and insert the keys using needlenose pliers or a tool designed for this purpose.

NOTE: *Retain the keys with wheel bearing grease during installation.*

CYLINDER HEAD RECONDITIONING

Procedure	Method

Check valve spring installed height:

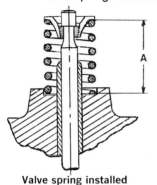

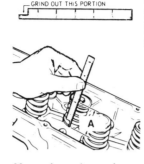

GRIND OUT THIS PORTION

A

Valve spring installed height dimension

Measuring valve spring installed height

Measure the distance between the spring pad and the lower edge of the spring retainer, and compare to specifications. If the installed height is incorrect, add shim washers between the spring pad and the spring.
CAUTION: *Use only washers designed for this purpose.*

Install the camshaft (OHC engines only) and check end play:

See the engine service procedures earlier in this book for details concerning specific engines.

Inspect the rocker arms, balls, studs, and nuts (OHV engines only):

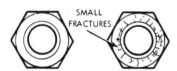

SMALL FRACTURES

Stress cracks in the rocker nuts

Visually inspect the rocker arms, balls, studs, and nuts for cracks, galling, burning, scoring or wear. If all parts are intact, liberally lubricate the rocker arms and balls, and install them on the cylinder head. If wear is noted on a rocker arm at the point of valve contact, grind it smooth and square, removing as little material as possible. Replace the rocker arm if excessively worn. If a rocker stud shows signs of wear, it must be replaced (see below). If a rocker nut shows stress cracks, replace it. If an exhaust ball is galled or burned, substitute the intake ball from the same cylinder (if it is intact), and install a new intake ball.
NOTE: *Avoid using new rocker balls on exhaust valves.*

Replacing rocker studs (OHV engines only):

AS STUB BEGINS TO PULL UP, IT WILL BE NECESSARY TO REMOVE THE NUT AND ADD MORE WASHERS

⅜" NUT

FLAT WASHERS

Extracting a pressed-in rocker stud

In order to remove a threaded stud, lock two nuts on the stud, and unscrew the stud using the lower nut. Coat the lower threads of the new stud with Loctite®, and install.
Two alternative methods are available for replacing pressed in studs. Remove the damaged stud using a stack of washers and a nut (see illustration). In the first, the boss is reamed .005–.006" oversize, and an oversize stud pressed in. Control the stud extension over the boss using washers, in the same manner as valve guides. Before installing the stud, coat it with white lead and grease. To retain the stud more positively drill a hole through the stud and boss, and install a roll pin. In the second method, the boss is tapped, and a threaded stud installed. Retain the stud using Loctite® Stud and Bearing Mount.

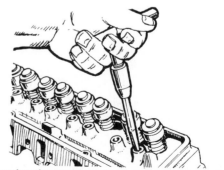

Reaming the stud bore for oversize rocker studs

CYLINDER HEAD RECONDITIONING

Procedure	Method

Inspect the rocker shaft(s) and rocker arms (OHV engines only):

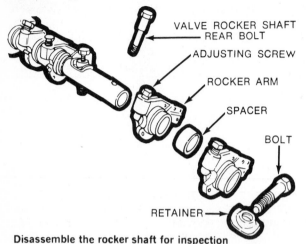

Disassemble the rocker shaft for inspection

Remove rocker arms, springs and washers from rocker shaft. NOTE: *Lay out parts in the order as they are removed.*
Inspect rocker arms for pitting or wear on the valve contact point, or excessive bushing wear. Bushings need only be replaced if wear is excessive, because the rocker arm normally contacts the shaft at one point only. Grind the valve contact point of rocker arm smooth if necessary, removing as little material as possible. If excessive material must be removed to smooth and square the arm, it should be replaced. Clean out all oil holes and passages in rocker shaft. If shaft is grooved or worn, replace it. Lubricate and assemble the rocker shaft.

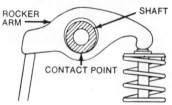

Rocker arm-to-rocker shaft contact area

Inspect the camshaft bushings and the camshaft (OHC engines):

See next section.

Inspect the pushrods (OHV engines only):

Remove the pushrods, and, if hollow, clean out the oil passages using fine wire. Roll each pushrod over a piece of clean glass. If a distinct clicking sound is heard as the pushrod rolls, the rod is bent, and must be replaced.

*The length of all pushrods must be equal. Measure the length of the pushrods, compare to specifications, and replace as necessary.

Inspect the valve lifters (OHV engines only):

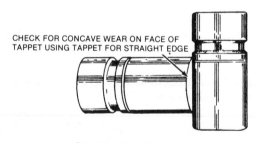

Checking the lifter face

Remove lifters from their bores, and remove gum and varnish, using solvent. Clean walls of lifter bores. Check lifters for concave wear as illustrated. If face is worn concave, replace lifter, and carefully inspect the camshaft. Lightly lubricate lifter and insert it into its bore. If play is excessive, an oversize lifter must be installed (where possible). Consult a machinist concerning feasibility. If play is satisfactory, remove, lubricate, and reinstall the lifter.
NOTE: *1981 and later G.M. diesel V8 valve lifters have roller cam followers. Check these for smooth operation and wear. The roller should rotate freely, but without excessive play. Check the rollers for missing or broken needle bearings. If the roller is pitted or rough, check the camshaft lobe for wear.*

---

*Testing hydraulic lifter leak down (OHV gasoline engines only):

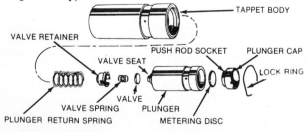

Typical exploded view of hydraulic valve lifter

Submerge lifter in a container of kerosene. Chuck a used pushrod or its equivalent into a drill press. Position container of kerosene so pushrod acts on the lifter plunger. Pump lifter with the drill press, until resistance increases. Pump several more times to bleed any air out of lifter. Apply very firm, constant pressure to the lifter, and observe rate at which fluid bleeds out of lifter. If the fluid bleeds very quickly (less than 15 seconds), lifter is defective. If the time exceeds 60 seconds, lifter is sticking. In either case, recondition or replace lifter. If lifter is operating properly (leak down time 15–60 seconds), lubricate and install it.

CYLINDER HEAD RECONDITIONING

Procedure	Method
Bleed the hydraulic lifters (diesel engines only):	After the cylinder heads are installed on G.M. V8 diesels, the valve lifters must be bled down before the crankshaft is turned. Failure to bleed down the lifters will cause damage to the valve train. See diesel engine rocker arm replacement procedure in Oldsmobile 88, 98, etc. car section for procedures. NOTE: *When installing new lifters, prime by working the lifter plunger while submerged in clean kerosene or diesel fuel.*

CYLINDER BLOCK RECONDITIONING

Procedure	Method
Checking the main bearing clearance: 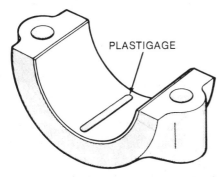 Plastigage® installed on the lower bearing shell 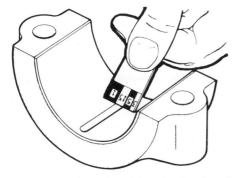 Measuring Plastigage® to determine bearing clearance	Invert engine, and remove cap from the bearing to be checked. Using a clean, dry rag, thoroughly clean all oil from crankshaft journal and bearing insert. NOTE: *Plastigage is soluble in oil; therefore, oil on the journal or bearing could result in erroneous readings.* Place a piece of Plastigage along the full length of journal, reinstall cap, and torque to specifications. Remove bearing cap, and determine bearing clearance by comparing width of Plastigage to the scale on Plastigage envelope. Journal taper is determined by comparing width of the Plastigage strip near its ends. Rotate crankshaft 90° and retest, to determine journal eccentricity. NOTE: *Do not rotate crankshaft with Plastigage installed.* If bearing insert and journal appear intact, and are within tolerances, no further main bearing service is required. If bearing or journal appear defective, cause of failure should be determined before replacement. *Remove crankshaft from block (see below). Measure the main bearing journals at each end twice (90° apart) using a micrometer, to determine diameter, journal taper and eccentricity. If journals are within tolerances, reinstall bearing caps at their specified torque. Using a telescope gauge and micrometer, measure bearing I.D. parallel to piston axis and at 30° on each side of piston axis. Subtract journal O.D. from bearing I.D. to determine oil clearance. If crankshaft journals appear defective, or do no meet tolerances, there is no need to measure bearings; for the crankshaft will require grinding and/or undersize bearings will be required. If bearing appears defective, cause for failure should be determined prior to replacement.
Checking the connecting rod bearing clearance:	Connecting rod bearing clearance is checked in the same manner as main bearing clearance, using Plastigage. Before removing the crankshaft, connecting rod side clearance also should be measured and recorded. *Checking connecting rod bearing clearance, using a micrometer, is identical to checking main bearing clearance. If no other service is required, the piston and rod assemblies need not be removed.

CYLINDER BLOCK RECONDITIONING

Procedure	Method

Removing the crankshaft:

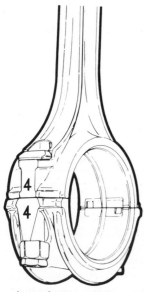

Connecting rod matched to cylinder with a number stamp

Using a punch, mark the corresponding main bearing caps and saddles according to position (i.e., one punch on the front main cap and saddle, two on the second, three on the third, etc.). Using number stamps, identify the corresponding connecting rods and caps, according to cylinder (if no numbers are present). Remove the main and connecting rod caps, and place sleeves of plastic tubing over the connecting rod bolts, to protect the journals as the crankshaft is removed. Lift the crankshaft out of the block.

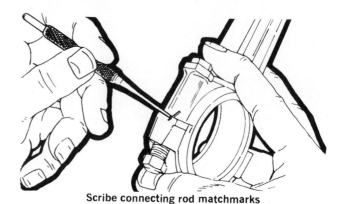

Scribe connecting rod matchmarks

Remove the ridge from the top of the cylinder:

RIDGE CAUSED BY CYLINDER WEAR

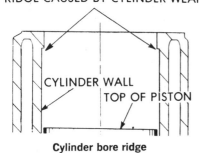

CYLINDER WALL
TOP OF PISTON

Cylinder bore ridge

In order to facilitate removal of the piston and connecting rod, the ridge at the top of the cylinder (unworn area; see illustration) must be removed. Place the piston at the bottom of the bore, and cover it with a rag. Cut the ridge away using a ridge reamer, exercising extreme care to avoid cutting to deeply. Remove the rag, and remove cuttings that remain on the piston.

CAUTION: *If the ridge is not removed, and new rings are installed, damage to rings will result.*

Removing the piston and connecting rod:

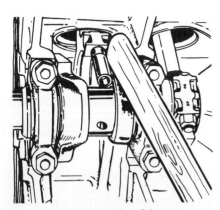

Removing the piston

Invert the engine, and push the pistons and connecting rods out of the cylinders. If necessary, tap the connecting rod boss with a wooden hammer handle, to force the piston out.

CAUTION: *Do not attempt to force the piston past the cylinder ridge (see above).*

CYLINDER BLOCK RECONDITIONING

Procedure	Method
Service the crankshaft:	Ensure that all oil holes and passages in the crankshaft are open and free of sludge. If necessary, have the crankshaft ground to the largest possible undersize. **Have the crankshaft Magnafluxed, to locate stress cracks. Consult a machinist concerning additional service procedures, such as surface hardening (e.g., nitriding, Tuftriding) to improve wear characteristics, cross drilling and chamfering the oil holes to improve lubrication, and balancing.
Removing freeze plugs:	Drill a small hole in the middle of the freeze plugs. Thread a large sheet metal screw into the hole and remove the plug with a slide hammer.
Remove the oil gallery plugs:	Threaded plugs should be removed using an appropriate (usually square) wrench. To remove soft, pressed in plugs, drill a hole in the plug, and thread in a sheet metal screw. Pull the plug out by the screw using pliers.
Hot-tank the block: NOTE: *Do not hot-tank aluminum parts.*	Have the block hot-tanked to remove grease, corrosion, and scale from the water jackets. NOTE: *Consult the operator to determine whether the camshaft bearings will be damaged during the hot-tank process.*

Check the block for cracks:	Visually inspect the block for cracks or chips. The most common locations are as follows:
	    Adjacent to freeze plugs.
	    Between the cylinders and water jackets.
	    Adjacent to the main bearing saddles.
	    At the extreme bottom of the cylinders.
	Check only suspected cracks using spot check dye (see introduction). If a crack is located, consult a machinist concerning possible repairs.
	
	**Magnaflux the block to locate hidden cracks. If cracks are located, consult a machinist about feasibility of repair.

Install the oil gallery plugs and freeze plugs:	Coat freeze plugs with sealer and tap into position using a piece of pipe, slightly smaller than the plug, as a driver. To ensure retention, stake the edges of the plugs. Coat threaded oil gallery plugs with sealer and install. Drive replacement soft plugs into block using a large drift as a driver. *Rather than reinstalling lead plugs, drill and tap the holes, and install threaded plugs.
*Check the deck height:	*The deck height is the distance from the crankshaft centerline to the block deck. To measure, invert the engine, and install the crankshaft, retaining it with the center main cap. Measure the distance from the crankshaft journal to the block deck, parallel to the cylinder centerline. Measure the diameter of the end (front and rear) main journals, parallel to the centerline of the cylinders, divide the diameter in half, and subtract it from the previous measurement. The results of the front and rear measurements should be identical. If the difference exceeds .005″, the deck height should be corrected. NOTE: *Block deck height and warpage should be corrected at the same time.*

CYLINDER BLOCK RECONDITIONING

Procedure	Method
Check the block deck for warpage:	Using a straightedge and feeler gauges, check the block deck for warpage in the same manner that the cylinder head is checked (see Cylinder Head Reconditioning). If warpage exceeds specifications, have the deck resurfaced. NOTE: *In certain cases a specification for total material removal (Cylinder head and block deck) is provided. This specification must not be exceeded.*
Check the bore diameter and surface: 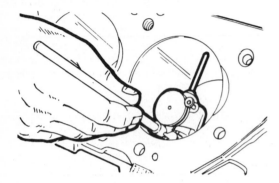 Measuring the cylinder bore with a dial gauge	Visually inspect the cylinder bores for roughness, scoring, or scuffing. If evident, the cylinder bore must be bored or honed oversize to eliminate imperfections, and the smallest possible oversize piston used. The new pistons should be given to the machinist with the block, so that the cylinders can be bored or honed exactly to the piston size (plus clearance). If no flaws are evident, measure the bore diameter using a telescope gauge and micrometer, or dial guage, parallel and perpendicular to the engine centerline, at the top (below the ridge) and bottom of the bore. Subtract the bottom measurements from the top to determine taper, and the parallel to the centerline measurements from the perpendicular measurements to determine eccentricity. If the measurements are not within specifications, the cylinder must be bored or honed, and an oversize piston installed. If the measurements are within specifications the cylinder may be used as is, with only finish honing (see below). NOTE: *Prior to boring, check the block deck warpage, height and bearing alignment.* CAUTION: *The 4 cyl. 140 G.M. engine cylinder walls are impregnated with silicone. Boring or honing can be done only by a shop with the proper equipment.*

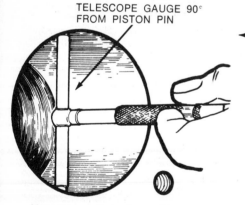

TELESCOPE GAUGE 90°
FROM PISTON PIN

Measuring cylinder bore with a
telescope gauge

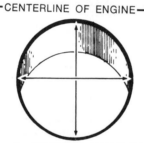

← CENTERLINE OF ENGINE →

A—AT RIGHT ANGLE TO
CENTERLINE OF ENGINE
B—PARALLEL TO
CENTERLINE OF ENGINE
Cylinder bore measuring points

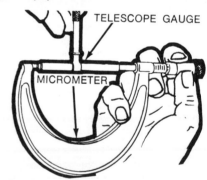

TELESCOPE GAUGE

MICROMETER

Determining cylinder bore by measuring
telescope gauge with a micrometer

Check the cylinder block bearing alignment: 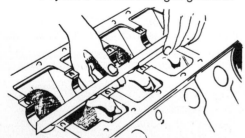 Checking main bearing saddle alignment	Remove the upper bearing inserts. Place a straightedge in the bearing saddles along the centerline of the crankshaft. If clearance exists between the straightedge and the center saddle, the block must be alignbored.

CYLINDER BLOCK RECONDITIONING

Procedure	Method

Clean and inspect the pistons and connecting rods:

Using a ring expander, remove the rings from the piston. Remove the retaining rings (if so equipped) and remove piston pin.

NOTE: *If the piston pin must be pressed out, determine the proper method and use the proper tools; otherwise the piston will distort.*

Clean the ring grooves using an appropriate tool, exercising care to avoid cutting too deeply. Thoroughly clean all carbon and varnish from the piston with solvent.

CAUTION: *Do not use a wire brush or caustic solvent on pistons.*

Inspect the pistons for scuffing, scoring, cracks, pitting, or excessive ring groove wear. If wear is evident, the piston must be replaced. Check the connecting rod length by measuring the rod from the inside of the large end to the inside of the small end using calipers (see illustration). All connecting rods should be equal length. Replace any rod that differs from the others in the engine.

*Have the connecting rod alignment checked in an alignment fixture by a machinist. Replace any twisted or bent rods.

*Magnaflux the connecting rods to locate stress cracks. If cracks are found, replace the connecting rod.

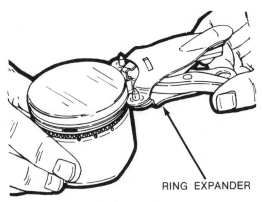

RING EXPANDER

Removing the piston rings

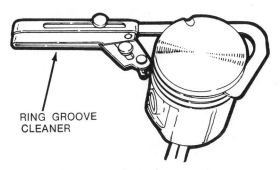

RING GROOVE CLEANER

Cleaning the piston ring grooves

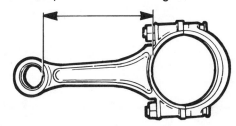

Check the connecting rod length (arrow)

Fit the pistons to the cylinders:

Using a telescope gauge and micrometer, or a dial gauge, measure the cylinder bore diameter perpendicular to the piston pin, 2½° below the deck. Measure the piston perpendicular to its pin on the skirt. The difference between the two measurements is the piston clearance. If the clearance is within specifications or slightly below (after boring or honing), finish honing is all that is required. If the clearance is excessive, try to obtain a slightly larger piston to bring clearance within specifications. Where this is not possible, obtain the first oversize piston, and hone (or if necessary, bore) the cylinder to size.

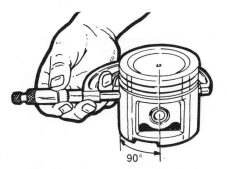

90°

Measuring the piston prior to fitting

Assemble the pistons and connecting rods:

Inspect piston pin, connecting rod small end bushing, and piston bore for galling, scoring, or excessive wear. If evident, replace defective part(s). Measure the I.D. of the piston boss and connecting rod small end, and the O.D. of the piston pin. If within specifications, assemble piston pin and rod.

CAUTION: *If piston pin must be pressed in, determine the proper method and use the proper tools; otherwise the piston will distort.*

CYLINDER BLOCK RECONDITIONING

Procedure	Method

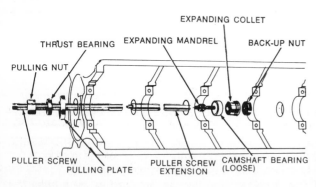

Installing piston pin lock rings

Install the lock rings; ensure that they seat properly. If the parts are not within specifications, determine the service method for the type of engine. In some cases, piston and pin are serviced as an assembly when either is defective. Others specify reaming the piston and connecting rods for an oversize pin. If the connecting rod bushing is worn, it may in many cases be replaced. Reaming the piston and replacing the rod bushing are machine shop operations.

Clean and inspect the camshaft:

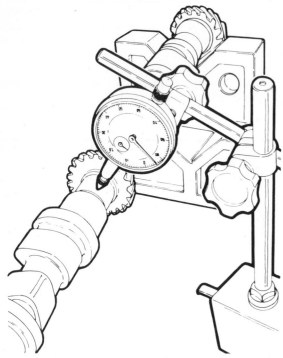

Checking the camshaft for straightness

Degrease the camshaft, using solvent, and clean out all oil holes. Visually inspect cam lobes and bearing journals for excessive wear. If a lobe is questionable, check all lobes as indicated below. If a journal or lobe is worn, the camshaft must be reground or replaced.

NOTE: *If a journal is worn, there is a good chance that the bushings are worn.*

If lobes and journals appear intact, place the front and rear journals in V-blocks, and rest a dial indicator on the center journal. Rotate the camshaft to check straightness. If deviation exceeds .001°, replace the camshaft.

*Check the camshaft lobes with a micrometer, by measuring the lobes from the nose to base and again at 90° (see illustration). The lift is determined by subtracting the second measurement from the first. If all exhaust lobes and all intake lobes are not identical, the camshaft must be reground or replaced.

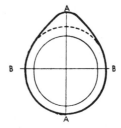

Camshaft lobe measurement

Replace the camshaft bearings (OHV engines only):

THRUST BEARING EXPANDING MANDREL EXPANDING COLLET BACK-UP NUT

PULLING NUT

PULLER SCREW PULLING PLATE PULLER SCREW EXTENSION CAMSHAFT BEARING (LOOSE)

Camshaft removal and installation tool (typical)

If excessive wear is indicated, or if the engine is being completely rebuilt, camshaft bearings should be replaced as follows: Drive the camshaft rear plug from the block. Assemble the removal puller with its shoulder on the bearing to be removed. Gradually tighten the puller nut until bearing is removed. Remove remaining bearings, leaving the front and rear for last. To remove front and rear bearings, reverse position of the tool, so as to pull the bearings in toward the center of the block. Leave the tool in this position, pilot the new front and rear bearings on the installer, and pull them into position: Return the tool to its original position and pull remaining bearings into postion.

NOTE: *Ensure that oil holes align when installing bearings.*

Replace camshaft rear plug, and stake it into position to aid retention.

CYLINDER BLOCK RECONDITIONING

Procedure	Method

Finish hone the cylinders:

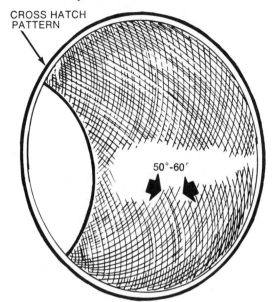

CROSS HATCH PATTERN

50°-60°

Chuck a flexible drive hone into a power drill, and insert it into the cylinder. Start the hone, and move it up and down the cylinder at a rate which will produce approximately a 60° cross-hatch pattern (see illustration).
NOTE: *Do not extend the hone below the cylinder bore.*
After developing the pattern, remove the hone and recheck piston fit. Wash the cylinders with a detergent and water solution to remove abrasive dust, dry, and wipe several times with a rag soaked in engine oil.

Check piston ring end-gap:

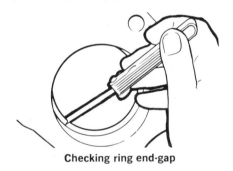

Checking ring end-gap

Compress the piston rings to be used in a cylinder, one at a time, into that cylinder, and press them approximately 1" below the deck with an inverted piston. Using feeler gauges, measure the ring end-gap, and compare to specifications. Pull the ring out of the cylinder and file the ends with a fine file to obtain proper clearance.
CAUTION: *If inadequate ring end-gap is utilized, ring breakage will result.*

Install the piston rings:

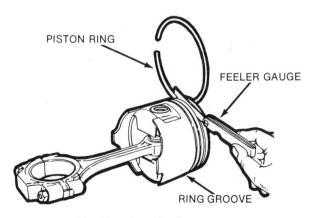

PISTON RING

FEELER GAUGE

RING GROOVE

Checking ring side clearance

Inspect the ring grooves in the piston for excessive wear or taper. If necessary, recut the groove(s) for use with an over-width ring or a standard ring and spacer. If the groove is worn uniformly, overwidth rings, or standard rings and spacers may be installed without recutting. Roll the outside of the ring around the groove to check for burrs or deposits. If any are found, remove with a fine file. Hold the ring in the groove, and measure side clearance. If necessary, correct as indicated above.
NOTE: *Always install any additional spacers above the piston ring.*
The ring groove must be deep enough to allow the ring to seat below the lands (see illustration). In many cases, a "go-no-go" depth gauge will be provided with the piston rings. Shallow grooves may be corrected by recutting, while deep grooves require some type of filler or expander behind the piston. Consult the piston ring supplier concerning the suggested method. Install the rings on the piston, lowest ring first, using a ring expander.
NOTE: *Position the ring markings as specified by the manufacturer (see car section).*

CYLINDER BLOCK RECONDITIONING

Procedure	Method
Install the camshaft (OHV engines only):	Liberally lubricate the camshaft lobes and journals, and install the camshaft. CAUTION: *Exercise extreme care to avoid damaging the bearings when inserting the camshaft.* Install and tighten the camshaft thrust plate retaining bolts. See the appropriate procedures for each individual engine.
Check camshaft end-play (OHV engines only): 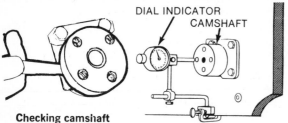 **Checking camshaft end-play with a feeler gauge** **Checking camshaft end-play with a dial indicator**	Using feeler gauges, determine whether the clearance between the camshaft boss (or gear) and backing plate is within specifications. Install shims behind the thrust plate, or reposition the camshaft gear and retest end-play. In some cases, adjustment is by replacing the thrust plate. *Mount a dial indicator stand so that the stem of the dial indicator rests on the nose of the camshaft, parallel to the camshaft axis. Push the camshaft as far in as possible and zero the gauge. Move the camshaft outward to determine the amount of camshaft endplay. If the endplay is not within tolerance, install shims behind the thrust plate, or reposition the camshaft gear and retest.
Install the rear main seal (where applicable):	See the appropriate procedures for each individual engine.
Install the crankshaft: 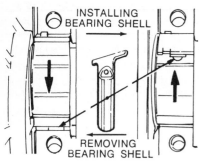 **Removal and installation of upper bearing insert using a roll-out pin** 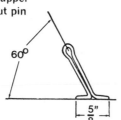 **Home-made bearing roll-out pin**	Thoroughly clean the main bearing saddles and caps. Place the upper halves of the bearing inserts on the saddles and press into position. NOTE: *Ensure that the oil holes align.* Press the corresponding bearing inserts into the main bearing caps. Lubricate the upper main bearings, and lay the crankshaft in position. Place a strip of Plastigage on each of the crankshaft journals, install the main caps, and torque to specifications. Remove the main caps, and compare the Plastigage to the scale on the Plastigage envelope. If clearances are within tolerances, remove the Plastigage, turn the crankshaft 90°, wipe off all oil and retest. If all clearances are correct, remove all Plastigage, thoroughly lubricate the main caps and bearing journals, and install the main caps. If clearances are not within tolerance, the upper bearing inserts may be removed, without removing the crankshaft, using a bearing roll out pin (see illustration). Roll in a bearing that will provide proper clearance, and retest. Torque all main caps, excluding the thrust bearing cap, to specifications. Tighten the thrust bearing cap finger tight. To properly align the thrust bearing, pry the crankshaft the extent of its axial travel several times, the last movement held toward the front of the engine, and torque the thrust bearing cap to specifications. Determine the crankshaft end-play (see below), and bring within tolerance with thrust washers.

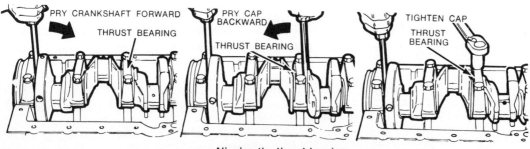

Aligning the thrust bearing

CYLINDER BLOCK RECONDITIONING

Procedure	Method

Measure crankshaft end-play:

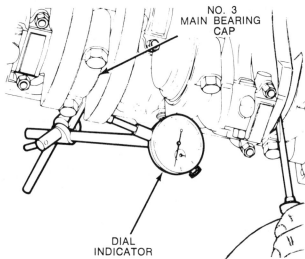

NO. 3
MAIN BEARING
CAP

DIAL
INDICATOR

Checking crankshaft end-play with a dial indicator

Mount a dial indicator stand on the front of the block, with the dial indicator stem resting on the nose of the crankshaft, parallel to the crankshaft axis. Pry the crankshaft the extent of its travel rearward, and zero the indicator. Pry the crankshaft forward and record crankshaft end-play.

NOTE: *Crankshaft end-play also may be measured at the thrust bearing, using feeler gauges* (see illustration).

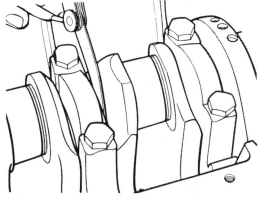

Checking crankshaft end-play with a feeler gauge

Install the pistons:

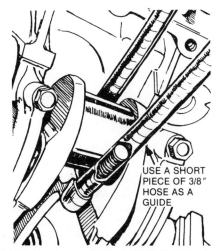

USE A SHORT
PIECE OF 3/8″
HOSE AS A
GUIDE

Tubing used to protect crankshaft journals and cylinder walls during piston installation

Press the upper connecting rod bearing halves into the connecting rods, and the lower halves into the connecting rod caps. Position the piston ring gaps according to specifications (see car section), and lubricate the pistons. Install a ring compressor on a piston, and press two long (8″) pieces of plastic tubing over the rod bolts. Using the tubes as a guide, press the pistons into the bores and onto the crankshaft with a wooden hammer handle. After seating the rod on the crankshaft journal, remove the tubes and install the cap finger tight. Install the remaining pistons in the same manner. Invert the engine and check the bearing clearance at two points (90° apart) on each journal with Plastigage.

NOTE: *Do not turn the crankshaft with Plastigage installed.*
If clearance is within tolerances, remove *all* Plastigage, thoroughly lubricate the journals, and torque the rod caps to specifications. If clearance is not within specifications, install different thickness bearing inserts and recheck.

CAUTION: *Never shim or file the connecting rods or caps.*
Always install plastic tube sleeves over the rod bolts when the caps are not installed, to protect the crankshaft journals.

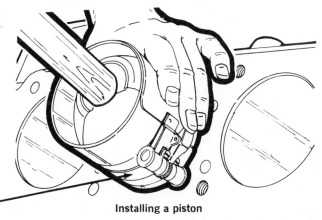

RING COMPRESSOR

Installing a piston

CYLINDER BLOCK RECONDITIONING

Procedure	Method
Check connecting rod side clearance: 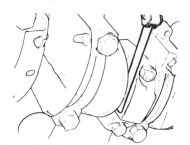 Checking connecting rod side clearance	Determine the clearance between the sides of the connecting rods and the crankshaft, using feeler gauges. If clearance is below the minimum tolerance, the rod may be machined to provide adequate clearance. If clearance is excessive, substitute an unworn rod, and recheck. If clearance is still outside specifications, the crankshaft must be welded and reground, or replaced.
Inspect the timing chain (or belt):	Visually inspect the timing chain for broken or loose links, and replace the chain if any are found. If the chain will flex sideways, it must be replaced. Install the timing chain as specified. Be sure the timing belt is not stretched, frayed or broken. NOTE: *If the original timing chain is to be reused, install it in its original position.*
Check timing gear backlash and runout (OHV engines): 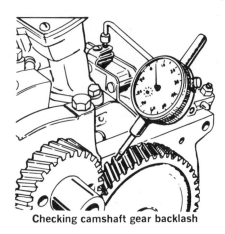 Checking camshaft gear backlash	Mount a dial indicator with its stem resting on a tooth of the camshaft gear (as illustrated). Rotate the gear until all slack is removed, and zero the indicator. Rotate the gear in the opposite direction until slack is removed, and record gear backlash. Mount the indicator with its stem resting on the edge of the camshaft gear, parallel to the axis of the camshaft. Zero the indicator, and turn the camshaft gear one full turn, recording the runout. If either backlash or runout exceed specifications, replace the worn gear(s). 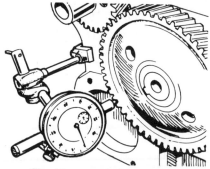 Checking camshaft gear runout

Completing the Rebuilding Process

Following the above procedures, complete the rebuilding process as follows:

Fill the oil pump with oil, to prevent cavitating (sucking air) on initial engine start up. Install the oil pump and the pickup tube on the engine. Coat the oil pan gasket as necessary, and install the gasket and the oil pan. Mount the flywheel and the crankshaft vibration damper or pulley on the crankshaft. NOTE: *Always use new bolts when installing the flywheel.*

Inspect the clutch shaft pilot bushing in the crankshaft. If the bushing is excessively worn, remove it with an expanding puller and a slide hammer, and tap a new bushing into place.

Position the engine, cylinder head side up. Lubricate the lifters, and install them into their bores. Install the cylinder head, and torque it as specified. Insert the pushrods (where applicable), and install the rocker shaft(s) (if so equipped) or position the rocker arms on the pushrods. Adjust the valves.

Install the intake and exhaust manifolds, the carburetor(s), the distributor and spark plugs. Adjust the point gap and the static ignition timing. Mount all accessories and install the engine in the car. Fill the radiator with coolant, and the crankcase with high quality engine oil.

Break-in Procedure

Start the engine, and allow it to run at low speed for a few minutes, while checking for leaks. Stop the engine, check the oil level, and fill as necessary. Restart the engine, and fill the cooling system to capacity. Check the point dwell angle and adjust the ignition timing and the valves. Run the engine at low to medium speed (800–2500 rpm) for approximately ½ hour, and retorque the cylinder head bolts. Road test the car, and check again for leaks.

Follow the manufacturer's recommended engine break-in procedure and maintenance schedule for new engines.

Troubleshooting 13

ENGINE

Gasoline Engine Troubleshooting

See applicable Car or Unit Repair section for specific service procedures

INDEX TO PROBLEMS

Problem Symptom	Begin at Specific Diagnosis, Number
Engine Won't Start	
Starter doesn't turn	1.1, 2.1
Starter turns, engine doesn't	2.1
Starter turns engine very slowly	1.1, 2.4
Starter turns engine normally	3.1, 4.1
Starter turns engine very quickly	6.1
Engine fires intermittently	4.1
Engine fires consistently	5.1, 6.1
Engine Runs Poorly	
Hard starting	3.1, 4.1, 5.1, 8.1
Rough idle	4.1, 5.1, 8.1
Stalling	3.1, 4.1, 5.1, 8.1
Engine dies at high speeds	4.1, 5.1
Hesitation (on acceleration from standing stop)	5.1, 8.1
Poor pickup	4.1, 5.1, 8.1
Lack of power	3.1, 4.1, 5.1, 8.1
Backfire through the carburetor	4.1, 8.1, 9.1
Backfire through the exhaust	4.1, 8.1, 9.1
Blue exhaust gases	6.1, 7.1
Black exhaust gases	5.1
Running on (after the ignition is shut off)	3.1, 8.1
Susceptible to moisture	4.1
Engine misfires under load	4.1, 7.1, 8.4, 9.1
Engine misfires at speed	4.1, 8.4
Engine misfires at idle	3.1, 4.1, 5.1, 7.1, 8.4

SAMPLE SECTION

Test and Procedure	Results and Indications	Proceed to
4.1 Check for spark: Hold each spark plug wire approximately ¼″ from ground with gloves or a heavy, dry rag. Crank the engine and observe the spark.	If no spark is evident	4.2
	If spark is good in some cases	4.3
	If spark is good in all cases	4.6

SPECIFIC DIAGNOSIS

This section is arranged so that following each test, instructions are given to proceed to another, until a problem is diagnosed.

SECTION 1—BATTERY

Test and Procedure	Results and Indications	Proceed to
1.1 Inspect the battery visually for case condition (corrosion, cracks) and water level.	If case is cracked, replace battery.	1.4
	If the case is intact, remove corrosion with a solution of baking soda and water. **(CAUTION: Do not get the solution into the battery).** Fill with water.	1.2

DIRT ON TOP OF BATTERY   PLUGGED VENT
CORROSION
LOOSE CABLE
OR
POSTS
CRACKS
LOW WATER LEVEL

Inspect the battery case

Test and Procedure	Results and Indications	Proceed to
1.2 Check the battery cable connections: Insert a screwdriver between the battery post and the cable clamp. Turn the headlights on high beam, and observe them as the screwdriver is gently twisted to ensure good metal to metal contact.	If the lights brighten, remove and clean the clamp and post; coat the post with petroleum jelly, install and tighten the clamp.	1.4
	If no improvement is noted	1.3

TESTING BATTERY
CABLE CONNECTIONS
USING A SCREWDRIVER

Test and Procedure	Results and Indications	Proceed to
1.3 Test the state of charge of the battery using an individual cell tester or hydrometer.	If indicated, charge the battery. **NOTE: If no obvious reason exists for the low state of charge (i.e., battery age, prolonged storage), proceed to:**	1.4

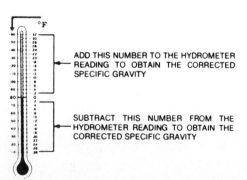

°F

ADD THIS NUMBER TO THE HYDROMETER READING TO OBTAIN THE CORRECTED SPECIFIC GRAVITY

SUBTRACT THIS NUMBER FROM THE HYDROMETER READING TO OBTAIN THE CORRECTED SPECIFIC GRAVITY

Specific Gravity (@ 80° F.)

Minimum	Battery Charge
1.260	100% Charged
1.230	75% Charged
1.200	50% Charged
1.170	25% Charged
1.140	Very Little Power Left
1.110	Completely Discharged

The effects of temperature on battery specific gravity (left) and amount of battery charge in relation to specific gravity (right)

Test and Procedure	Results and Indications	Proceed To
1.4 Visually inspect battery cables for cracking, bad connection to ground, or bad connection to starter.	If necessary, tighten connections or replace the cables.	**2.1**

SECTION 2—STARTING SYSTEM

Test and Procedure	Results and Indications	Proceed to
Note: Tests in Group 2 are performed with coil high tension lead disconnected to prevent accidental starting.		
2.1 Test the starter motor and solenoid: Connect a jumper from the battery post of the solenoid (or relay) to the starter post of the solenoid (or relay).	If starter turns the engine normally	**2.2**
	If the starter buzzes, or turns the engine very slowly	**2.4**
	If no response, replace the solenoid (or relay).	**3.1**
	If the starter turns, but the engine doesn't, ensure that the flywheel ring gear is intact. If the gear is undamaged, replace the starter drive.	**3.1**
2.2 Determine whether ignition override switches are functioning properly (clutch start switch, neutral safety switch), by connecting a jumper across the switch(es), and turning the ignition switch to "start".	If starter operates, adjust or replace switch.	**3.1**
	If the starter doesn't operate	**2.3**
2.3 Check the ignition switch "start" position: Connect a 12V test lamp or voltmeter between the starter post of the solenoid (or relay) and ground. Turn the ignition switch to the "start" position, and jiggle the key.	If the lamp doesn't light or the meter needle doesn't move when the switch is turned, check the ignition switch for loose connections, cracked insulation, or broken wires. Repair or replace as necessary.	**3.1**
	If the lamp flickers or needle moves when the key is jiggled, replace the ignition switch.	**3.3**

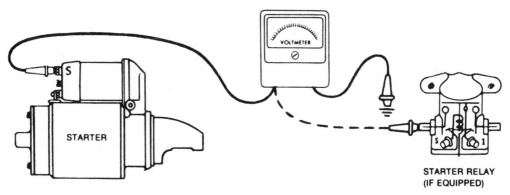

Checking the ignition switch "start" position

2.4 Remove and bench test the starter, according to specifications in the car section.	If the starter does not meet specifications, repair or replace as needed	**3.1**
	If the starter is operating properly	**2.5**

Test and Procedure	Results and Indications	Proceed To
2.5 Determine whether the engine can turn freely: Remove the spark plugs, and check for water in the cylinders. Check for water on the dipstick, or oil in the radiator. Attempt to turn the engine using an 18″ flex drive and socket on the crankshaft pulley nut or bolt.	If the engine will turn freely only with the spark plugs out, and hydrostatic lock (water in the cylinders) is ruled out, check valve timing.	9.2
	If engine will not turn freely, and it is known that the clutch and transmission are free, the engine must be disassembled for further evaluation.	See Car Section

SECTION 3—PRIMARY ELECTRICAL SYSTEM

Test and Procedure	Results and Indications	Proceed to
3.1 Check the ignition switch "on" position: Connect a jumper wire between the distributor side of the coil and ground, and a 12V test lamp between the switch side of the coil and ground. Remove the high tension lead from the coil. Turn the ignition switch on and jiggle the key.	If the lamp lights	3.2
	If the lamp flickers when the key is jiggled, replace the ignition switch.	3.3
	If the lamp doesn't light, check for loose or open connections. If none are found, remove the ignition switch and check for continuity. If the switch is faulty, replace it.	3.3

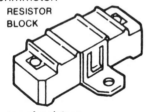

Checking the ignition switch "on" position

3.2 Check the ballast resistor or resistance wire for an open circuit, using an ohmmeter.  RESISTOR BLOCK CALIBRATED RESISTANCE LEAD **Two types of resistors**	Replace the resistor or resistance wire if the resistance is zero. **NOTE: Some ignition systems have no ballast resistor.**	3.3
3.3 On point-type ignition systems, visually inspect the breaker points for burning, pitting or excessive wear. Gray coloring of the point contact surfaces is normal. Rotate the crankshaft until the contact heel rests on a high point of the distributor cam and adjust the point gap to specifications. On electronic ignition models, remove the distributor cap and visually inspect the armature. Ensure that the armature pin is in place, and that the armature is on tight and rotates when the engine is cranked. Make sure there are no cracks, chips or rounded edges on the armature.	If the breaker points are intact, clean the contact surfaces with fine emery cloth, and adjust the point gap to specifications. If the points are worn, replace them. On electronic systems, replace any parts which appear defective. If condition persists	3.4

Test and Procedure	Results and Indications	Proceed To
3.4 On point-type ignition systems, connect a dwell-meter between the distributor primary lead and ground. Crank the engine and observe the point dwell angle. On electronic ignition systems, conduct a stator (magnetic pickup assembly) test. See Electronic Ignition Unit Repair Section.	On point-type systems, adjust the dwell angle if necessary. **NOTE: Increasing the point gap decreases the dwell angle and vice-versa.** If the dwell meter shows little or no reading On electronic ignition systems, if the stator is bad, replace the stator. If the stator is good, proceed to the other tests in The Electronic Ignition Unit Repair Section.	**3.6** **3.5**

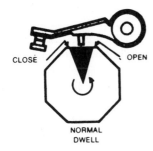
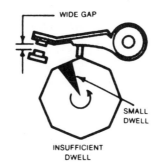
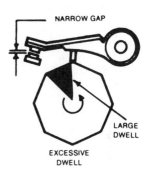

Dwell is a function of point gap

Test and Procedure	Results and Indications	Proceed To
3.5 On the point-type ignition systems, check the condenser for short: connect an ohmeter across the condenser body and the pigtail lead.	If any reading other than infinite is noted, replace the condenser	**3.6**

Checking the condenser for short

Test and Procedure	Results and Indications	Proceed To
3.6 Test the coil primary resistance: On point-type ignition systems, connect an ohmmeter across the coil primary terminals, and read the resistance on the low scale. Note whether an external ballast resistor or resistance wire is used. On electronic ignition systems, test the coil primary resistance.	Point-type ignition coils utilizing ballast resistors or resistance wires should have approximately 1.0 ohms resistance. Coils with internal resistors should have approximately 4.0 ohms resistance. If values far from the above are noted, replace the coil.	**4.1**

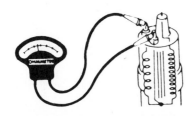

Checking the coil primary resistance

SECTION 4—SECONDARY ELECTRICAL SYSTEM

Test and Procedure	Results and Indications	Proceed to
4.1 Check for spark: Hold each spark plug wire approximately ¼" from ground with gloves or heavy, dry rag. Crank the engine, and observe the spark.	If no spark is evident	4.2
	If spark is good in some cylinders	4.3
	If spark is good in all cylinders	4.6

Check for spark at the plugs

4.2 Check for spark at the coil high tension lead: Remove the coil high tension lead from the distributor and position it approximately ¼" from ground. Crank the engine and observe spark. **CAUTION: This test should not be performed on engines equipped with electronic ignition.**	If the spark is good and consistent	4.3
	If the spark is good but intermittent, test the primary electrical system starting at 3.3.	3.3
	If the spark is weak or non-existent, replace the coil high tension lead, clean and tighten all connections and retest. If no improvement is noted	4.4

4.3 Visually inspect the distributor cap and rotor for burned or corroded contacts, cracks, carbon tracks, or moisture. Also check the fit of the rotor on the distributor shaft (where applicable).	If moisture is present, dry thoroughly, and retest per 4.1.	4.1
	If burned or excessively corroded contacts, cracks, or carbon tracks are noted, replace the defective part(s) and retest per 4.1.	4.1
	If the rotor and cap appear intact, or are only slightly corroded, clean the contacts thoroughly (including the cap towers and spark plug wire ends) and retest per 4.1.	
	If the spark is good in all cases	4.6
	If the spark is poor in all cases	4.5

CORRODED OR LOOSE WIRE

HIGH RESISTANCE CARBON

EXCESSIVE WEAR OF BUTTON

ROTOR TIP BURNED AWAY

Inspect the distributor cap and rotor

4.4 Check the coil secondary resistance: On point-type systems connect an ohmmeter across the distributor side of the coil and the coil tower. Read the resistance on the high scale of the ohmmeter. On electronic ignition systems, see The Electronic Ignition Unit Repair Section for specific tests.	The resistance of a satisfactory coil should be between 4,000 and 10,000 ohms. If resistance is considerably higher (i.e., 40,000 ohms) replace the coil and retest per 4.1. **NOTE: This does not apply to high performance coils.**

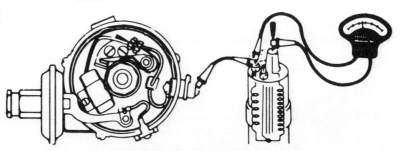

Testing the coil secondary resistance

Spark Plug Analysis

Normal

APPEARANCE

This plug is typical of one operating normally. The insulator nose varies from a light tan to grayish color with slight electrode wear. The presence of slight deposits is normal on used plugs and will have no adverse effect on engine performance. The spark plug heat range is correct for the engine and the engine is running normally.

CAUSE

Properly running engine

RECOMMENDATION

Before reinstalling this plug, the electrodes should be cleaned and filed square. Set the gap to specifications. If the plug has been in service for more than 10–12,000 miles, the entire set should probably be replaced with a fresh set of the same heat range.

Incorrect Heat Range

APPEARANCE

The effects of high temperature on a spark plug are indicated by clean white, often blistered insulator. This can also be accompanied by excessive wear of the electrode, and the absence of deposits.

CAUSE

Check for the correct spark plug heat range. A plug which is too hot for the engine can result in overheating. A car operated mostly at high speeds may require a colder plug. Also check ignition timing, cooling system level, fuel mixture and leaking intake manifold.

RECOMMENDATION

If all ignition and engine adjustments are known to be correct, and no other malfunction exists, install spark plugs one heat range colder.

Oil Deposits

APPEARANCE

The firing end of the plug is covered with a wet, oily coating.

CAUSE

The problem is poor oil control. On high mileage engines, oil is leaking past the rings or valve guides into the combustion chamber. A common cause is also a plugged PCV valve, and a ruptured fuel pump diaphragm can also cause this condition. Oil fouled plugs such as these are often found in new or recently overhauled engines, before normal oil control is achieved, and can be cleaned and reinstalled.

RECOMMENDATION

A hotter spark plug may temporarily relieve the problem, but the engine is probably in need of engine work.

Carbon Deposits

APPEARANCE

Carbon fouling is easily identified by the presence of dry, soft, black, sooty deposits.

CAUSE

Changing the heat range can often lead to carbon fouling, as can prolonged slow, stop-and-start driving. If the heat range is correct, carbon fouling can be attributed to a rich fuel mixture, sticking choke, clogged air cleaner, worn breaker points, retarded timing or low compression. If only one or two plugs are carbon fouled, check for corroded or cracked wires on the affected plugs. Also look for cracks in the distributor cap between the towers of affected cylinders.

RECOMMENDATION

After the problem is corrected, these plugs can be cleaned and reinstalled if not worn severely.

Ash Deposits

APPEARANCE

Ash deposits are characterized by light brown or white colored deposits crusted on the side or center electrodes. In some cases it may give the plug a rusty appearance.

CAUSE

Ash deposits are normally derived from oil or fuel additives burned during normal combustion. Normally they are harmless, though excessive amounts can cause misfiring. If deposits are excessive in short mileage, the valve guides may be worn. Reddish or rusty deposits are caused by manganese, an anti-knock compound replacing lead in unleaded gas. No engine malfunction is indicated.

RECOMMENDATION

Ash-fouled plugs can be cleaned, gapped and reinstalled.

Splash Deposits

APPEARANCE

Splash deposits occur in varying degrees as spotty deposits on the insulator.

CAUSE

These usually occur after a long delayed tune-up. By-products of combustion have accumulated on pistons and valves because of a delayed tune-up. Following tune-up or during hard acceleration, the deposits loosen and are thrown against the hot surface of the plug. If the deposits accumulate sufficiently, misfiring can occur.

RECOMMENDATION

These plugs can be cleaned, gapped and reinstalled.

High Speed Glazing

APPEARANCE

Glazing appears as shiny coating on the plug, either yellow or tan in color.

CAUSE

During hard, fast acceleration, plug temperatures rise suddenly. Deposits from normal combustion have no chance to fluff-off; instead, they melt on the insulator forming an electrically conductive coating which causes misfiring.

RECOMMENDATION

Glazed plugs are not easily cleaned. They should be replaced with a fresh set of plugs of the correct heat range. If the condition recurs, using plugs with a heat range one step colder may cure the problem.

Detonation

APPEARANCE

Detonation is usually characterized by a broken plug insulator.

CAUSE

A portion of the fuel charge will begin to burn spontaneously, from the increased heat following ignition. The explosion that results applies extreme pressure to engine components, frequently damaging spark plugs and pistons.

Detonation can result by over-advanced ignition timing, inferior gasoline (low octane) lean air fuel mixture, poor carburetion, engine lugging or an increase in compression ratio due to combustion chamber deposits or engine modification.

RECOMMENDATION

Replace the plugs after correcting the problem.

Test and Procedure	Results and Indications	Proceed To

4.5 Visually inspect the spark plug wires for cracking or brittleness. Ensure that no two wires are positioned so as to cause induction firing (adjacent and parallel). Remove each wire, one by one, and check resistance with an ohmmeter.

Replace any cracked or brittle wires. If any of the wires are defective, replace the entire set. Replace any wires with excessive resistance (over 8000 Ω per foot for suppression wire), and separate any wires that might cause induction firing.

4.6

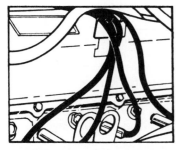

Misfiring can be the result of spark plug leads to adjacent, consecutively firing cylinders running parallel and too close together

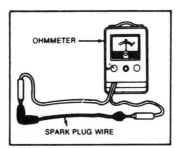

On point-type ignition systems, check the spark plug wires as shown. On electronic ignitions, do not remove the wire from the distributor cap terminal; instead, test through the cap

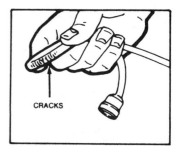

Spark plugs wires can be checked visually by bending them in a loop over your finger. This will reveal any cracks, burned or broken insulation. Any wire with cracked insulation should be replaced

4.6 Remove the spark plugs, noting the cylinders from which they were removed, and evaluate according to the chart in this section.

See chart.

See Chart

4.7 Reinstall the spark plugs.
NOTE: Modern electronic ignition systems generate extremely high voltages and high heats. The spark plug boots can soften and actually fuse to the ceramic insulator of the spark plugs after long exposures to high temperature and voltage. If this happens, the boot (and possibly the wire) must be replaced.

To help alleviate this condition, many manufacturers are recommending new silicone compounds to slow the deterioration. The compounds are generally nonconductive, protective lubricants that will not dry out, harden, or melt away. They form a weather-tight seal between rubber or plastic and metal and are found in several typical locations: Inside the insulating boots of spark plug wires, inside primary ignition circuit cable connectors, on distributor and rotor cap electrodes, and under the GM HEI control module.

4.8

Application Point	Silicone Compound
GENERAL MOTORS: Under HEI module	Supplied with new module, or use GE-642 or DC-340
FORD MOTOR COMPANY: Inside spark plug boots, on end of cable when installing new boot, and on rotor and cap electrodes	Ford part number D7AZ-19A331-A or use GE-627 or DC-111
CHRYSLER CORPORATION: ¼" deep within spark control computer connector cavity coating rotor electrode	Use Mopar part number 2932524 or NLGI Grade 2 EP (not a silicone) supplied with new rotor, or use GE-628 or DC-111
AMERICAN MOTORS (Prestolite system): Distributor primary connector—coat male terminal, fill female ¼ full	AMC part number 8127445 or GE-623

GE: General Electric
DC: Dow Corning

13 TROUBLESHOOTING AND DIAGNOSIS

Test and Procedure	Results and Indications	Proceed To

4.8 Examine the location of all the plugs.

The following diagrams illustrate some of the conditions that the location of plugs will reveal.

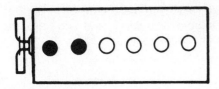

Two adjacent plugs are fouled in a 6-cylinder engine, 4-cylinder engine or either bank of a V-8. This is probably due to a blown head gasket between the two cylinders.

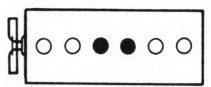

The two center plugs in a 6-cylinder engine are fouled. Raw fuel may be "boiled" out of the carburetor into the intake manifold after the engine is shut-off. Stop-start driving can also foul the center plugs, due to overly rich mixture. Proper float level, a new float needle and seat or use of an insulating spacer may help this problem.

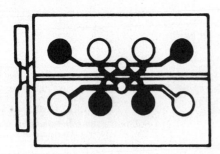

An unbalanced carburetor is indicated. Following the fuel flow on this particular design shows that the cylinders fed by the right-hand barrel are fouled from overly rich mixture, while the cylinders fed by the left-hand barrel are normal.

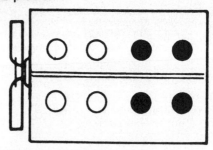

If the four rear plugs are overheated, a cooling system problem is suggested. A thorough cleaning of the cooling system may restore coolant circulation and cure the problem.

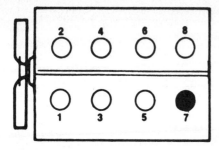

Finding one plug overheated may indicate an intake manifold leak near the affected cylinder. If the overheated plug is the second of two adjacent, consecutively firing plugs, it could be the result of ignition cross-firing. Separating the leads to these two plugs will eliminate cross-fire.

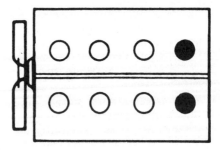

Occasionally, the two rear plugs in large, lightly used V-8's will become oil fouled. High oil consumption and smoky exhaust may also be noticed. It is probably due to plugged oil drain holes in the rear of the cylinder head, causing oil to be sucked in around the valve stems. This usually occurs in the rear cylinders first, because the engine slants that way.

Test and Procedure		Results and Indications	Proceed To
4.9	Determine the static ignition timing. Using the crankshaft pulley timing marks as a guide, locate top dead center on the compression stroke of the number one cylinder.	The rotor should be pointing toward the No. 1 tower in the distributor cap, and, on electronic ignitions, the armature spoke for that cylinder should be lined up with the stator.	4.10
4.10	Check coil polarity: Connect a voltmeter negative lead to the coil high tension lead, and the positive lead to ground. **NOTE: Reverse the hook-up for positive ground systems.** Crank the engine momentarily.	If the voltmeter reads up-scale, the polarity is correct.	5.1
		If the voltmeter reads down-scale, reverse the coil polarity (switch the primary leads).	5.1

Checking coil polarity

SECTION 5—FUEL SYSTEM

Test and Procedure		Results and Indications	Proceed to
5.1	Determine that the air filter is functioning efficiently: Hold paper elements up to a strong light, and attempt to see light through the filter.	Clean permanent air filters in solvent (or manufacturer's recommendation), and allow to dry. Replace paper elements through which light cannot be seen.	5.2
5.2	Determine whether a flooding condition exists: Flooding is identified by a strong gasoline odor, and excessive gasoline present in the throttle bore(s) of the carburetor.	If flooding is not evident	5.3
		If flooding is evident, permit the gasoline to dry for a few moments and restart.	
		If flooding doesn't recur	5.7
		If flooding is persistent	5.5

If the engine floods repeatedly, check the choke butterfly flap

5.3	Check that fuel is reaching the carburetor: Detach the fuel line at the carburetor inlet. Hold the end of the line in a cup (not styrofoam), and crank the engine.	If fuel flows smoothly	5.7
		If fuel doesn't flow	5.4
		If fuel flows erratically. **NOTE: Make sure that there is fuel in the tank**	

Check the fuel pump by disconnecting the output line (fuel pump-to-carburetor) at the carburetor and operating the starter briefly

Test and Procedure	Results and Indications	Proceed To
5.4 Test the fuel pump: Disconnect all fuel lines from the fuel pump. Hold a finger over the input fitting, crank the engine (with electric pump, turn the ignition or pump on); and feel for suction.	If suction is evident, blow out the fuel line to the tank with low pressure compressed air until bubbling is heard from the fuel filler neck. Also blow out the carburetor fuel line (both ends disconnected).	5.7
	If no suction is evident, replace or repair the fuel pump. **NOTE: Repeated oil fouling of the spark plugs, or a no-start condition, could be the result of a ruptured vacuum booster pump diaphragm, through which oil or gasoline is being drawn into the intake manifold (where applicable).**	5.7
5.5 Occasionally, small specks of dirt will clog the small jets and orifices in the carburetor. With the engine cold, hold a flat piece of wood or similar material over the carburetor, where possible, and crank the engine.	If the engine starts, but runs roughly the engine is probably not run enough. If the engine won't start.	5.9
5.6 Check the needle and seat: Tap the carburetor in the area of the needle and seat.	If flooding stops, a gasoline additive (e.g., Gumout) will often cure the problem.	5.7
	If flooding continues, check the fuel pump for excessive pressure at the carburetor (according to specifications). If the pressure is normal, the needle and seat must be removed and checked, and/or the float level adjusted.	5.7
5.7 Test the accelerator pump by looking into the throttle bores while operating the throttle.	If the accelerator pump appears to be operating normally	5.8
	If the accelerator pump is not operating, the pump must be reconditioned. Where possible, service the pump with the carburetor(s) installed on the engine. If necessary, remove the carburetor. Prior to removal	5.8

Check for gas at the carburetor by looking down the carburetor throat while someone moves the accelerator

5.8 Determine whether the carburetor main fuel system is functioning: Spray a commercial starting fluid into the carburetor while attempting to start the engine.	If the engine starts, runs for a few seconds, and dies	5.9
	If the engine doesn't start	6.1
5.9 Uncommon fuel system malfunctions: See below:	If the problem is solved	6.1
	If the problem remains, remove and recondition the carburetor.	

Condition	Indication	Test	Prevailing Weather Conditions	Remedy
Vapor lock	Engine will not re-start shortly after running.	Cool the components of the fuel system until the engine starts. Vapor lock can be cured faster by draping a wet cloth over a mechanical fuel pump.	Hot to very hot	Ensure that the exhaust manifold heat control valve is operating. Check with the vehicle manufacturer for the recommended solution to vapor lock on the model in question.
Carburetor icing	Engine will not idle, stalls at low speeds.	Visually inspect the throttle plate area of the throttle bores for frost.	High humidity, 32–40° F.	Ensure that the exhaust manifold heat control valve is operating, and that the intake manifold heat riser is not blocked.
Water in the fuel	Engine sputters and stalls; may not start.	Pump a small amount of fuel into a glass jar. Allow to stand, and inspect for droplets of a layer of water.	High humidity, extreme temperature changes.	For droplets, use one or two cans of commercial gas line anti-freeze. For a layer of water, the tank must be drained, and the fuel lines blown out with compressed air.

SECTION 6—ENGINE COMPRESSION

Test and Procedure	Results and Indications	Proceed to
6.1 Test engine compression: Remove all spark plugs. Block the throttle wide open. Insert a compression gauge into a spark plug port, crank the engine to obtain the maximum reading, and record.	If compression is within limits on all cylinders	7.1
	If gauge reading is extremely low on all cylinders	6.2
	If gauge reading is low on one or two cylinders: (If gauge readings are identical and low on two or more adjacent cylinders, the head gasket must be replaced.)	6.2

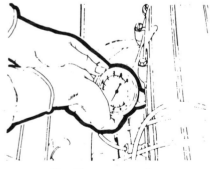

Checking compression

6.2 Test engine compression (wet): Squirt approximately 30 cc. of engine oil into each cylinder, and retest per 6.1.	If the readings improve, worn or cracked rings or broken pistons are indicated:	See Car Section
	If the readings do not improve, burned or excessively carboned valves or a jumped timing chain are indicated. **NOTE: A jumped timing chain is often indicated by difficult cranking.**	7.1

SECTION 7—ENGINE VACUUM

Test and Procedure	Results and Indications	Proceed to
7.1 Attach a vacuum gauge to the intake manifold beyond the throttle plate. Start the engine, and observe the action of the needle over the range of engine speeds.	See below.	**See below**

   INDICATION: Normal engine in good condition

Proceed to: 8.1

Normal engine

Gauge reading: Steady, from 17–22 in./Hg.

   INDICATION: Sticking valves or ignition miss

Proceed to: 9.1, 8.3

Sticking valves

Gauge reading: Intermittent fluctuation at idle

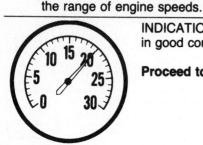   INDICATION: Late ignition or valve timing, low compression, stuck throttle valve, leaking carburetor or manifold gasket

Proceed to: 6.1

Incorrect valve timing

Gauge reading: Low (10–15 in./Hg) but steady

   INDICATION: Improper carburetor adjustment or minor intake leak.

Proceed to: 7.2

Carburetor requires adjustment

Gauge reading: Drifting needle

   INDICATION: Ignition miss, blown cylinder head gasket, leaking valve or weak valve spring

Proceed to: 8.3, 6.1

Blown head gasket

Gauge reading: Needle fluctuates as engine speed increases

   INDICATION: Burnt valve or faulty valve clearance: Needle will fall when defective valve operates

Proceed to: 9.1

Burnt or leaking valves

Gauge reading: Steady needle, but drops regularly

   INDICATION: Choked muffler, excessive back pressure in system

Proceed to: 10.1

Clogged exhaust system

Gauge reading: Gradual drop in reading at idle

   INDICATION: Worn valve guides

Proceed to: 9.1

Worn valve guides

Gauge reading: Needle vibrates excessively at idle, but steadies as engine speed increases

---

White pointer = steady gauge hand

Black pointer = fluctuating gauge hand

Test and Procedure	Results and Indications	Proceed To
7.2 Attach a vacuum gauge per 7.1, and test for an intake manifold leak. Squirt a small amount of oil around the intake manifold gaskets, carburetor gaskets, plugs and fittings. Observe the action of the vacuum gauge.	If the reading improves, replace the indicated gasket, or seal the indicated fitting or plug: If the reading remains low:	8.1 7.3
7.3 Test all vacuum hoses and accessories for leaks as described in 7.2. Also check the carburetor body (dashpots, automatic choke mechanism, throttle shafts) for leaks in the same manner.	If the reading improves, service or replace the offending part(s): If the reading remains low:	8.1 6.1

SECTION 8—SECONDARY ELECTRICAL SYSTEM

Test and Procedure	Results and Indications	Proceed to
8.1 Remove the distributor cap and check to make sure that the rotor turns when the engine is cranked. Visually inspect the distributor components.	Clean, tighten or replace any components which appear defective.	8.2
8.2 Connect a timing light (per manufacturer's recommendation) and check the dynamic ignition timing. Disconnect and plug the vacuum hose(s) to the distributor if specified, start the engine, and observe the timing marks at the specified engine speed.	If the timing is not correct, adjust to specifications by rotating the distributor in the engine: (Advance timing by rotating distributor opposite normal direction of rotor rotation, retard timing by rotating distributor in same direction as rotor rotation.)	8.3
8.3 Check the operation of the distributor advance mechanism(s): To test the mechanical advance, disconnect the vacuum lines from the distributor advance unit and observe the timing marks with a timing light as the engine speed is increased from idle. If the mark moves smoothly, without hesitation, it may be assumed that the mechanical advance is functioning properly. To test vacuum advance and or retard systems, alternately crimp and release the vacuum line, and observe the timing mark for movement. If movement is noted, the system is operating.	If the systems are functioning If the systems are not functioning, remove the distributor, and test on a distributor tester.	8.4 8.4
8.4 Locate an ignition miss: With the engine running, remove each spark plug wire, one at a time, until one is found that doesn't cause the engine to roughen and slow down. **CAUTION: Do not pull on the wire to remove the boot from the plug. Be sure your hand is insulated from the wire.**	When the missing cylinder is identified	4.1

SECTION 9—VALVE TRAIN

Test and Procedure	Results and Indications	Proceed to
9.1 Evaluate the valve train: Remove the valve cover, and ensure that the valves are adjusted to specifications. A mechanic's stethoscope may be used to aid in the diagnosis of the valve train. By pushing the probe on or near push rods or rockers, valve noise often can be isolated. A timing light also may be used to diagnose valve problems. Connect the light according to manufacturer's recommendations, and start the engine. Vary the firing moment of the light by increasing the engine speed (and therefore the ignition advance), and moving the trigger from cylinder to cylinder. Observe the movement of each valve.	Sticking valves or erratic valve train motion can be observed with the timing light. The cylinder head must be disassembled for repairs.	See Car Section
9.2 Check the valve timing: Locate top dead center of the No. 1 piston, and install a degree wheel or tape on the crankshaft pulley or damper with zero corresponding to an index mark on the engine. Rotate the crankshaft in its direction of rotation, and observe the opening of the No. 1 cylinder intake valve. The opening should correspond with the correct mark on the degree wheel according to specifications.	If the timing is not correct, the timing cover must be removed for further investigation.	See Car Section

SECTION 10—EXHAUST SYSTEM

Test and Procedure	Results and Indications	Proceed to
10.1 Determine whether the exhaust manifold heat control valve is operating: Operate the valve by hand to determine whether it is free to move. If the valve is free, run the engine to operating temperature and observe the action of the valve, to ensure that it is opening.	If the valve sticks, spray it with a suitable solvent, open and close the valve to free it, and retest. If the valve functions properly	10.2
	If the valve does not free, or does not operate, replace the valve.	10.2
10.2 Ensure that there are no exhaust restrictions: Visually inspect the exhaust system for kinks, dents, or crushing. Also note that gases are flowing freely from the tailpipe at all engine speeds, indicating no restriction in the muffler or resonator.	Replace any damaged portion of the system.	11.1

SECTION 11—COOLING SYSTEM

Test and Procedure	Results and Indications	Proceed to
11.1 Visually inspect the fan belt for glazing, cracks, and fraying, and replace if necessary. Tighten the belt so that the longest span has approximately ½″ play at its midpoint under thumb pressure (see Maintenance Section).	Replace or tighten the fan belt as necessary.	**11.2**

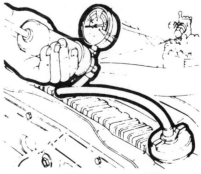

Checking belt tension

Test and Procedure	Results and Indications	Proceed to
11.2 Check the fluid level of the cooling system.	If full or slightly low, fill as necessary.	**11.5**
	If extremely low	**11.3**
11.3 Visually inspect the external portions of the cooling system (radiator, radiator hoses, thermostat elbow, water pump seals, heater hoses, etc.) for leaks. If none are found, pressurize the cooling system to 14–15 psi.	If cooling system holds the pressure	**11.5**
	If cooling system loses pressure rapidly, reinspect external parts of the system for leaks under pressure. If none are found, check dipstick for coolant in crankcase. If no coolant is present, but pressure loss continues	**11.4**
	If coolant is evident in crankcase, remove cylinder head(s), and check gasket(s). If gaskets are intact, block and cylinder head(s) should be checked for cracks or holes.	
	If the gasket(s) is blown, replace, and purge the crankcase of coolant.	**12.6**
	NOTE: Occasionally, due to atmospheric and driving conditions, condensation of water can occur in the crankcase. This causes the oil to appear milky white. To remedy, run the engine until hot, and change the oil and oil filter.	
11.4 Check for combustion leaks into the cooling system: Pressurize the cooling system as above. Start the engine, and observe the pressure gauge. If the needle fluctuates, remove each spark plug wire, one at a time, noting which cylinder(s) reduce or eliminate the fluctuation.	Cylinders which reduce or eliminate the fluctuation, when the spark plug wire is removed, are leaking into the cooling system. Replace the head gasket on the affected cylinder bank(s).	**See Car Section**

Pressurizing the cooling system

Test and Procedure	Results and Indications	Proceed To
11.5 Check the radiator pressure cap: Attach a radiator pressure tester to the radiator cap (wet the seal prior to installation). Quickly pump up the pressure, noting the point at which the cap releases.	If the cap releases within ± 1 psi of the specified rating, it is operating properly.	**11.6**
	If the cap releases at more than ± 1 psi of the specified rating, it should be replaced.	**11.6**

Checking radiator pressure cap

Test and Procedure	Results and Indications	Proceed To
11.6 Test the thermostat: Start the engine cold, remove the radiator cap, and insert a thermometer into the radiator. Allow the engine to idle. After a short while, there will be a sudden, rapid increase in coolant temperature. The temperature at which this sharp rise stops is the thermostat opening temperature.	If the thermostat opens at or about the specified temperature	**11.7**
	If the temperature doesn't increase (If the temperature increases slowly and gradually, replace the thermostat.)	**11.7**
11.7 Check the water pump: Remove the thermostat elbow and the thermostat, disconnect the coil high tension lead (to prevent starting), and crank the engine momentarily.	If coolant flows, replace the thermostat and retest per 11.6.	**11.6**
	If coolant doesn't flow, reverse flush the cooling system to alleviate any blockage that might exist. If system is not blocked, and coolant will not flow, replace the water pump.	**See Car Section**

SECTION 12—LUBRICATION

Test and Procedure	Results and Indications	Proceed to
12.1 Check the oil pressure gauge or warning light: If the gauge shows low pressure, or the light is on for no obvious reason, remove the oil pressure sender. Install an accurate oil pressure gauge and run the engine momentarily.	If oil pressure builds normally, run engine for a few moments to determine that it is functioning normally, and replace the sender.	—
	If the pressure remains low	12.2
	If the pressure surges	12.3
	If the oil pressure is zero	12.3
12.2 Visually inspect the oil: If the oil is watery or very thin, milky, or foamy, replace the oil and oil filter.	If the oil is normal	12.3
	If after replacing oil the pressure remains low	12.3
	If after replacing oil the pressure becomes normal	—
12.3 Inspect the oil pressure relief valve and spring, to ensure that it is not sticking or stuck. Remove and thoroughly clean the valve, spring, and the valve body.	If the oil pressure improves	—
	If no improvement is noted	12.4

Test and Procedure	Results and Indications	Proceed To
12.4 Check to ensure that the oil pump is not cavitating (sucking air instead of oil): See that the crankcase is neither over nor underfull, and that the pickup in the sump is in the proper position and free from sludge.	Fill or drain the crankcase to the proper capacity, and clean the pickup screen in solvent if necessary. If no improvement is noted	**12.5**
12.5 Inspect the oil pump drive and the oil pump:	If the pump drive or the oil pump appear to be defective, service as necessary and retest per 12.1. If the pump drive and pump appear to be operating normally, the engine should be disassembled to determine where blockage exists.	**12.1**
12.6 Purge the engine of ethylene glycol coolant: Competely drain the crankcase and the oil filter. Obtain a commercial butyl cellosolve base solvent, designated for this purpose, and follow the instructions precisely. Following this, install a new oil filter and refill the crankcase with the proper weight oil. The next oil and filter change should follow shortly thereafter (1000 miles).		

13 TROUBLESHOOTING AND DIAGNOSIS

Diesel Engine Troubleshooting

NOTE: The following troubleshooting procedures cover problems usually associated with diesel engines. Those problems common to both gasoline and diesel engines are covered in the gasoline engine troubleshooting procedures.

INDEX TO PROBLEMS

Problem/Symptom	Begin at Specific Diagnosis, Number
Fuel System	Section 1
Engine Starting Difficulty:	
Feed pump does not feed fuel	1.1
Injection pump does not feed fuel	1.2
Incorrect injection timing	1.3
Defective injection nozzles	1.4
Engine Operating Instability:	
Engine shuts off immediately after starting	1.5
Uneven idling	1.6
Engine will not reach maximum rated speed	1.7
Engine exceeds maximum rated speed	1.8
Loss of power	1.9
Engine Knock:	
Associated with exhaust gas problems	1.10
Not associated with exhaust gas problems	1.11
Engine Mechanical	Section 2
Engine Starting Difficulty	2.1
Unusual Noises	2.2
Engine Operating Instability	2.3
Loss of Power	2.4
Exhaust gas Problem	2.5
Engine Shut-Off	2.6
Loss of Oil Pressure	2.7
Oil Leakage	2.8
Compression Pressure Leakage	2.9

SECTION 1—Fuel System

Test and Procedure		Results and Indication	Proceed To
1.1a	Check for pressure at the outlet of the feed pump	If pressure exists, there is a clog in the supply line. Clean or replace it. If there is little or no pressure at the outlet, the filter is clogged. Clean or replace the filter. If the filter is clear, the feed pump piston is inoperative. Relace it.	1.1b
1.1b	Check the feed pump valves	If the inlet and outlet valves do not operate, the check valve or spring is broken. Replace it.	1.2a
1.2a	Check for fuel leakage at the overflow or return line	A clogged filter can result in high pressure causing leakage. Replace the filter.	1.2b
1.2b	Check for fuel in the filter leaking at the overflow valve	If leakage is found, the overflow valve is damaged. Replace it.	1.2c
1.2c	Check for leakage at the injection pump overflow valve	If leakage is found, it is caused by: damaged overflow valve, sticking plunger, or sticking delivery valve. Replace the defective part(s).	1.2d
1.2d	Check the injection pump plunger feed pressures.	If pressure at the plungers is low, replace the plunger(s).	1.2e

Test and Procedure		Results and Indication	Proceed To
1.2e	Check to make sure the injection pump is operating	An inoperative pump is caused by: a damaged or missing shaft key, or a damaged drive gear train.	1.3a
1.3a	Check that the pump timing marks are correctly aligned in the gear train	Incorrect timing marks alignment must be corrected.	1.3b
1.3b	Check that the injection pump is properly mounted	Remove and install the pump correctly	1.4a
1.4a	Install an injection nozzle on a tester and make sure that fuel is continuously ejected	A broken or intermittent stream is caused by a damaged spring or a sticking nozzle needle	1.4b
1.4b	With the nozzle on the tester as in 1.4a, check that shutoff is clean with no dribble or afterdrip	Dribble is caused by a defective nozzle valve seat. Replace the nozzle.	1.4c
1.4c	Using a tester, check injection pressure	Low pressure is a result of a weak spring. Replace the spring or adjust the initial injection pressure.	1.5a
1.5a	See 1.2a	Proceed as in 1.2a	1.5b
1.5b	Check for water in the fuel	Drain and clean the tank	1.5c
1.5c	Check for air in the fuel lines	Air can be introduced through a damaged fuel inlet line, a loose inlet line connector or a damaged gasket	1.5d
1.5d	Check for insufficient fuel feed	Insufficient fuel feed is caused by: a damaged feed pump, a clogged tank vent, or a clogged filter. Replace or repair as necessary.	1.6a
1.6a	Check the control rack action for smooth operation	Uneven control rack operation is caused by: a sticking plunger, improper meshing of the rack and pinion, poor seating of the plunger spring, insufficient clearance between the plunger and lower spring seat, or an overly tight delivery valve holder. Replace or adjust as necessary.	1.6b
1.6b	Check that the injection pump discharge is uniform	If the output is uneven, adjust as necessary	1.6c
1.6c	Check that the injection pump discharge volume is adequate	An inadequate discharge volume is caused by a worn plunger or a broken spring	1.6d
1.6d	Check for even low speed engine performance	If the engine performs unevenly or erratically at low speed only, a worn feed pump piston or defective feed pump valve is the cause.	1.6e
1.6e	Check for smooth engine operation throughout the operating range	This problem is usually caused by mechanical governor defects such as: a defective low speed spring, defective damper spring, or excessive friction among moving parts. Replace the defective parts.	1.6f
1.6f	Check the injectors on a tester	Improper nozzle operation should be corrected accordingly	1.7a
1.7a	Check the operating governor	A broken or weak spring in the governor will prevent full speed operation.	1.7b
1.7b	Check the injectors on a tester for a drop in injector output	A drop in output is caused by a sticking needle or a dirty nozzle. Replace or clean as necessary.	1.8a

13 TROUBLESHOOTING AND DIAGNOSIS

Test and Procedure		Results and Indications	Proceed To
1.8a	Check the injection pump for proper rack and pinion action	A catching or dirty rack and pinion will cause overspeeding.	1.8b
1.8b	Check the governor adjustment	An improperly adjusted governor will cause overspeeding. Adjust.	1.9a
1.9a	Check the injection pump output	Low output can be caused by: Incorrect adjustment—Adjust Loose delivery valve—Tighten Broken delivery valve seal—Replace Poor valve seat contact—Replace Broken/weak delivery valve spring—Replace	1.9b
1.9b	Check for unusual noise at the injection pump	A noisy pump is an indication of a broken plunger spring	1.9c
1.9c	Check plunger operation	A sticking injection pump plunger will cause power loss. Replace.	1.9d
1.9d	Check the injection timer	A lag in injection timing is caused by large clearances in the timer due to wear. Replace.	1.9e
1.9e	Check for air or water in the fuel	Bleed the air or drain the fuel and clean the tank and lines	1.9f
1.9f	Check the injection timing	Readjust timing if necessary	1.10a
1.10a	Check the initial injection timing	Adjust if necessary	1.10b
1.10b	Check the injection pressure	High pressure will cause knock. Adjust as necessary	1.10c
1.10c	Check the injector nozzle	A clogged nozzle causes knock. Clean or replace the nozzle.	1.11a
1.11a	Check the injection pump output and timing	Excessive output, coupled with incorrect timing causes knock. Adjust as necessary	1.11b
1.11b	Check the delivery valve seat	Replace a defective seat	1.11c
1.11c	Check the pump plungers	Replace badly worn plungers	1.11d
1.11d	Check injector opening pressure on a tester	Adjust as necessary	1.11e
1.11e	Check the injector	Replace a broken nozzle spring or sticking needle.	

SECTION 2—ENGINE MECHANICAL

Test and Procedure		Results and Indications	Proceed To
2.1a	Check for piston seizing	Seized pistons are caused by low oil pressure, oil breakdown, or overheating. Replace the pistons and liners.	2.1b
2.1b	Check for a damaged flywheel ring gear	A damaged ring gear will cause poor meshing with the starter. Replace the ring gear.	2.1c
2.1c	Make a compression check	Low compression can be caused by: sticking rings, worn rings, worn liners. Replace the rings or liners.	2.2a
2.2a	A knocking noise at idle or during acceleration can be caused by a variety of wear problems.	Use a stethoscope or similar listening device to try to pinpoint the source of the noise. Among other reasons for knocking are: piston pins, rod bearings, loose rod caps, crankshaft journals and/or bearings, crankshaft thrust washer. Replace any worn parts.	2.2b
2.2b	An infrequently encountered noise is a continuous growl during acceleration	This problem is usually caused by problems in the engine timing gears. Poor contact, excessive backlash or loose gears are usually at fault.	2.2c
2.2c	Intermittent noises are the hardest to find. They are usually caused by broken moving parts.	Check the gear train for a chipped or cracked gear; the oil pan for broken parts or foreign objects or the cylinder head for a broken valve or valve spring.	2.3
2.3	Check for oil in the combustion chambers	Oil entering the combustion chambers will cause the engine to overspeed if the amount of oil is too great, or run unevenly. Check for broken or sticking rings, bad head gasket(s) or worn valve guides.	2.4
2.4	Check the compression	Low compression is the main cause of power loss. The main causes for low compression are: worn rings or liners, cracked valves, warped head or block, and bad head gasket.	2.5
2.5	A large amount of black exhaust is caused by low compression	See 2.4 above	2.6
2.6	If the engine stops suddenly during operation, the cause is usually sudden damage	Check the pistons, main bearings or rod bearings for lack of lubrication. A seized camshaft is also a result of low or no lubrication. Check the timing gears for damage.	2.7
2.7	Check for excessive clearance between the bearings and journals on both the mains and rod bearings. Check the oil pressure.	Replace as necessary. Replace the pump as necessary.	2.8
2.8	Aside from the usual leaking gasket problems, check the condition of the combustion chamber O-rings.	Replace as necessary	2.9
2.9	Compression leakage is usually caused by a seal defect between the head and the block	Check the head gasket; check for loose head bolts; check for head or block warpage. Replace or repair as necessary.	

Engine Overheating Troubleshooting

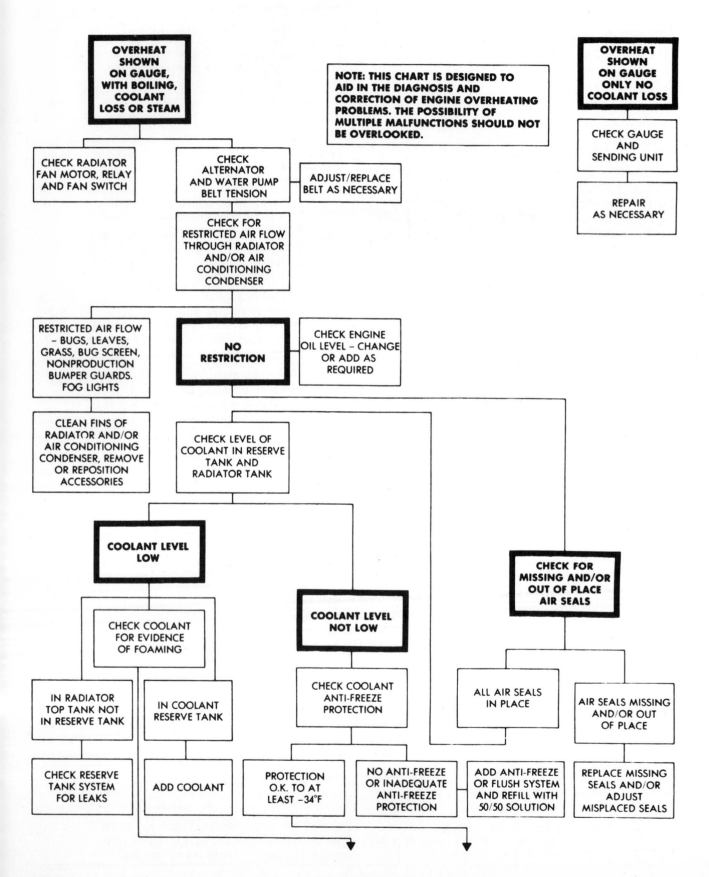

OVERHEAT SHOWN ON GAUGE, WITH BOILING, COOLANT LOSS OR STEAM

NOTE: THIS CHART IS DESIGNED TO AID IN THE DIAGNOSIS AND CORRECTION OF ENGINE OVERHEATING PROBLEMS. THE POSSIBILITY OF MULTIPLE MALFUNCTIONS SHOULD NOT BE OVERLOOKED.

OVERHEAT SHOWN ON GAUGE ONLY NO COOLANT LOSS

CHECK RADIATOR FAN MOTOR, RELAY AND FAN SWITCH

CHECK ALTERNATOR AND WATER PUMP BELT TENSION

ADJUST/REPLACE BELT AS NECESSARY

CHECK GAUGE AND SENDING UNIT

REPAIR AS NECESSARY

CHECK FOR RESTRICTED AIR FLOW THROUGH RADIATOR AND/OR AIR CONDITIONING CONDENSER

RESTRICTED AIR FLOW – BUGS, LEAVES, GRASS, BUG SCREEN, NONPRODUCTION BUMPER GUARDS. FOG LIGHTS

NO RESTRICTION

CHECK ENGINE OIL LEVEL – CHANGE OR ADD AS REQUIRED

CLEAN FINS OF RADIATOR AND/OR AIR CONDITIONING CONDENSER, REMOVE OR REPOSITION ACCESSORIES

CHECK LEVEL OF COOLANT IN RESERVE TANK AND RADIATOR TANK

COOLANT LEVEL LOW

CHECK FOR MISSING AND/OR OUT OF PLACE AIR SEALS

CHECK COOLANT FOR EVIDENCE OF FOAMING

COOLANT LEVEL NOT LOW

IN RADIATOR TOP TANK NOT IN RESERVE TANK

IN COOLANT RESERVE TANK

CHECK COOLANT ANTI-FREEZE PROTECTION

ALL AIR SEALS IN PLACE

AIR SEALS MISSING AND/OR OUT OF PLACE

CHECK RESERVE TANK SYSTEM FOR LEAKS

ADD COOLANT

PROTECTION O.K. TO AT LEAST –34°F

NO ANTI-FREEZE OR INADEQUATE ANTI-FREEZE PROTECTION

ADD ANTI-FREEZE OR FLUSH SYSTEM AND REFILL WITH 50/50 SOLUTION

REPLACE MISSING SEALS AND/OR ADJUST MISPLACED SEALS

Engine Overheating Troubleshooting

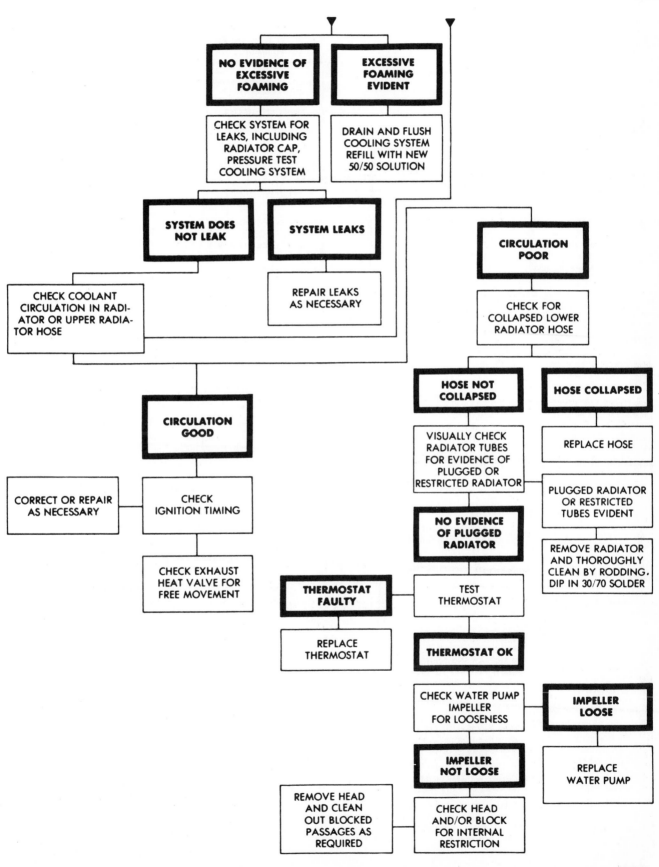

Low Engine Temperature Troubleshooting

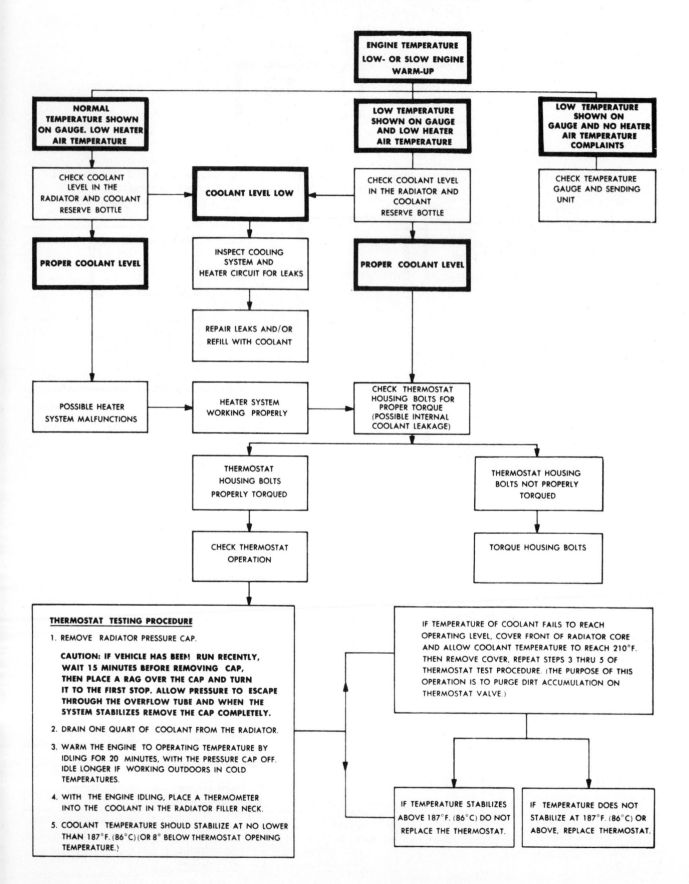

DRIVELINE
Clutch System Troubleshooting

Condition	Possible Cause	Corrective Action
Clutch chatter	1. Grease on driven plate (disc) facing. 2. Binding clutch linkage. 3. Loose, damaged facings on driven plate (disc). 4. Engine mounts loose. 5. Incorrect height adjustment of pressure plate release levers. 6. Clutch housing or housing to transmission adapter misalignment. 7. Loose driven plate hub.	1. Replace plate. 2. Check for worn, bent, broken parts. Replace as required. Lube linkage. 3. Replace driven plate. 4. Tighten mounts. Replace if damaged. 5. Adjust release lever height. 6. Check bore and face run out. Correct as required. 7. Replace driven plate.
Clutch grabbing	1. Oil, grease on driven plate (disc) facing. 2. Broken pressure plate. 3. Warped or binding driven plate. Driven plate binding on clutch shaft.	1. Replace driven plate. 2. Replace pressure plate. 3. Replace warped driven plate. Replace clutch shaft if defective, scored, worn.
Clutch slips	1. Lack of lubrication in clutch linkage (linkage binds, causes incomplete engagement. 2. Incorrect pedal, or linkage adjustment. 3. Broken pressure plate springs. 4. Weak pressure plate springs. 5. Grease on driven plate facings (disc).	1. Lubricate linkage. 2. Adjust as required. 3. Replace pressure plate. 4. Replace pressure plate. 5. Replace driven plate.
Incomplete clutch release	1. Incorrect pedal or linkage adjustment or linkage binding. 2. Incorrect height adjustment on pressure plate release levers. 3. Loose, broken facings on driven plate (disc). 4. Bent, dished, warped driven plate caused by overheating.	1. Adjust as required. Lubricate linkage. 2. Adjust release lever height. 3. Replace driven plate. 4. Replace driven plate.
Grinding, whirring grating noise when pedal is depressed	1. Worn or defective throwout bearing. 2. Starter drive teeth contacting flywheel ring gear teeth.	1. Replace throwout bearing. 2. Look for milled or polished teeth on ring gear. Align clutch housing, replace starter drive or drive spring as required.
Squeal, howl, trumpeting noise when pedal is being released (occurs during first inch to inch and one-half of pedal travel)	1. Pilot bushing worn or lack of lubricant.	1. Replace worn bushing. If bushing appears OK, polish bushing with emery, soak lube wick in oil, lube bushing with oil, apply film of chassis grease to clutch shaft pilot hub, reassemble. **NOTE:** Bushing wear may be due to misalignment of clutch housing or housing to transmission adapter.
Vibration or clutch pedal pulsation with clutch disengaged (pedal fully depressed)	1. Worn or defective engine transmission mounts. 2. Flywheel run out, or damaged or defective clutch components.	1. Inspect and replace as required. 2. Replace components as required. (Flywheel run out at face not to exceed 0.005").

Manual Transmission Troubleshooting

Condition	Probable Cause
Jumping out of high gear	1. Misalignment of transmission case or clutch housing. 2. Worn pilot bearing in crankshaft. 3. Bent transmission shaft. 4. Worn high speed sliding gear. 5. Worn teeth in clutch shaft. 6. Insufficient spring tension on shifter rail plunger. 7. Bent or loose shifter fork. 8. End-play in clutch shaft. 9. Gears not engaging completely. 10. Loose or worn bearings on clutch shaft or mainshaft.
Sticking in high gear	1. Clutch not releasing fully. 2. Burred or battered teeth on clutch shaft. 3. Burred or battered transmission mainshaft. 4. Frozen synchronizing clutch. 5. Stuck shifter rail plunger. 6. Gearshift lever twisting and binding shifter rail. 7. Battered teeth on high speed sliding gear or on sleeve. 8. Lack of lubrication. 9. Improper lubrication. 10. Corroded transmission parts. 11. Defective mainshaft pilot bearing.
Jumping out of second gear	1. Insufficient spring tension on shifter rail plunger. 2. Bent or loose shifter fork. 3. Gears not engaging completely. 4. End-play in transmission mainshaft. 5. Loose transmission gear bearing. 6. Defective mainshaft pilot bearing. 7. Bent transmission shaft. 8. Worn teeth on second speed sliding gear or sleeve. 9. Loose or worn bearings on transmission mainshaft. 10. End-play in countershaft.
Sticking in second gear	1. Clutch not releasing fully. 2. Burred or battered teeth on sliding sleeve. 3. Burred or battered transmission mainshaft. 4. Frozen synchronizing clutch. 5. Stuck shifter rail plunger. 6. Gearshift lever twisting and binding shifter rail. 7. Lack of lubrication. 8. Second speed transmission gear bearings locked will give same effect as gears stuck in second. 9. Improper lubrication. 10. Corroded transmission parts.
Jumping out of low gear	1. Gears not engaging completely. 2. Bent or loose shifter fork. 3. End-play in transmission mainshaft. 4. End-play in countershaft. 5. Loose or worn bearings on transmission mainshaft. 6. Loose or worn bearings in countershaft. 7. Defective mainshaft pilot bearing.
Sticking in low gear	1. Clutch not releasing fully. 2. Burred or battered transmission mainshaft. 3. Stuck shifter rail plunger. 4. Gearshift lever twisting and binding shifter rail. 5. Lack of lubrication. 6. Improper lubrication. 7. Corroded transmission parts.

Condition	Probable Cause
Jumping out of reverse gear	1. Insufficient spring tension on shifter rail plunger. 2. Bent or loose shifter fork. 3. Badly worn gear teeth. 4. Gears not engaging completely. 5. End-play in transmission mainshaft. 6. Idler gear bushings loose or worn. 7. Loose or worn bearings on transmission mainshaft. 8. Defective mainshaft pilot bearing.
Sticking in reverse gear	1. Clutch not releasing fully. 2. Burred or battered transmission mainshaft. 3. Stuck shifter rail plunger. 4. Gearshift lever twisting and binding shifter rail. 5. Lack of lubrication. 6. Improper lubrication. 7. Corroded transmission parts.
Failure of gears to synchronize	1. Binding pilot bearing on mainshaft, will synchronize in high gear only. 2. Clutch not releasing fully. 3. Detent spring weak or broken. 4. Weak or broken springs under balls in sliding gear sleeve. 5. Binding bearing on clutch shaft. 6. Binding countershaft. 7. Binding pilot bearing in crankshaft. 8. Badly worn gear teeth. 9. Scored or worn cones. 10. Improper lubrication. 11. Constant mesh gear not turning freely on transmission mainshaft. Will synchronize in that gear only.
Gears spinning when shifting into gear from neutral	1. Clutch not releasing fully. 2. In some cases an extremely light lubricant in transmission will cause gears to continue to spin for a short time after clutch is released. 3. Binding pilot bearing in crankshaft.
Noisy in all gears	1. Insufficient lubricant. 2. Worn countergear bearings. 3. Worn or damaged main drive gear or countergear. 4. Damaged main drive gear or mainshaft bearings. 5. Worn or damaged countergear anti-lash plate.
Noisy in high gear	1. Damaged main drive gear bearing. 2. Damaged mainshaft bearing. 3. Damaged high speed gear synchronizer.
Noisy in neutral	1. Damaged main drive gear bearing. 2. Damaged or loose mainshaft pilot bearing. 3. Worn or damaged countergear anti-lash plate. 4. Worn countergear bearings.
Noisy in all reduction gears	1. Insufficient lubricant. 2. Worn or damaged drive gear or countergear.
Noisy in second only	1. Damaged or worn second gear constant mesh gears. 2. Worn or damaged countergear rear bearings. 3. Damaged or worn second gear synchronizer.
Noisy in second only	1. Damaged or worn second gear constant mesh gears. 2. Worn or damaged countergear rear bearings. 3. Damaged or worn second gear synchronizer.
Noisy in third only (four speed)	1. Damaged or worn third gear constant mesh gears. 2. Worn or damaged countergear bearings.

Condition	Probable Cause
Noisy in reverse only	1. Worn or damaged reverse idler gear or idler bushing. 2. Worn or damaged mainshaft reverse gear. 3. Worn or damaged reverse countergear. 4. Damaged shift mechanism.
Excessive backlash in all reduction gears	1. Worn countergear bearings. 2. Excessive end–play in countergear.

Automatic Transmission Troubleshooting

Keeping alert to changes in the operating characteristics of the transmission (changing shift points, noises, etc.) can prevent small problems from becoming large ones. If the problem cannot be traced to loose bolts, fluid level, misadjusted linkage, clogged filters or similar problems, you should probably seek professional service.

TRANSMISSION FLUID INDICATIONS

The appearance and odor of the transmission fluid can give valuable clues to the overall condition of the transmission. Always note the appearance of the fluid when you check the fluid level or change the fluid. Rub a small amount of fluid between your fingers to feel for grit and smell the fluid on the dipstick.

If The Fluid Appears	It Indicates
Clear and red colored	Normal operation
Discolored (extremely dark red or brownish) or smells burned	Band or clutch pack failure, usually caused by an overheated transmission. Hauling very heavy loads with insufficient power or failure to change the fluid often results in overheating. Do not confuse this appearance with newer fluids that have a darker red color and a strong odor (though not a burned odor).
Foamy or aerated (light in color and full of bubbles)	The level is too high (gear train is churning oil) An internal air leak (air is mixing with the fluid). Have the transmission checked professionally.
Solid residue in the fluid	Defective bands, clutch pack or bearings. Bits of band material or metal abrasives are clinging to the dipstick. Have the transmission checked professionally.
Varnish coating on the dipstick	The transmission fluid is overheating

Problem	Possible Cause	Correction
Slow initial engagement	1. Improper fluid level. 2. Damaged or improperly adjusted linkage. 3. Contaminated fluid. 4. Faulty clutch and band application, or oil control pressure system.	1. Add fluid as required. 2. Repair or adjust linkage. 3. Perform fluid level check. 4. Perform control pressure test.
Rough initial engagement in either forward or reverse	1. Improper fluid level. 2. High engine idle. 3. Looseness in the driveshaft, U-joints or engine mounts. 4. Incorrect linkage adjustment. 5. Faulty clutch or band application, or oil control pressure system. 6. Sticking or dirty valve body.	1. Perform fluid level check. 2. Adjust idle to specifications. 3. Repair as required. 4. Repair or adjust linkage. 5. Perform control pressure test. 6. Clean, repair or replace valve body.

Problem	Possible Cause	Correction
No drive, slips or chatters in first gear in D. All other gears normal.	1. Faulty one-way clutch.	1. Repair or replace one-way clutch.
No drive, slips or chatters in second gear.	1. Improper fluid level. 2. Damaged or improperly adjusted linkage. 3. Intermediate band out of adjustment. 4. Faulty band or clutch application, or oil pressure control system. 5. Faulty servo and/or internal leaks. 6. Dirty or sticking valve body. 7. Polished, glazed intermediate band or drum.	1. Perform fluid level check. 2. Repair or adjust linkage. 3. Adjust intermediate band. 4. Perform control pressure test. 5. Perform air pressure test. 6. Clean, repair or replace valve body. 7. Replace or repair as required.
No drive in any gear.	1. Improper fluid level. 2. Damaged or improperly adjusted linkage. 3. Faulty clutch or band application, or oil control pressure system. 4. Internal leakage. 5. Valve body loose. 6. Faulty clutches. 7. Sticking or dirty valve body.	1. Perform fluid level check. 2. Repair or adjust linkage. 3. Perform control pressure test. 4. Check and repair as required. 5. Tighten to specification. 6. Perform air pressure test. 7. Clean, repair or replace valve body.
No drive forward—reverse OK.	1. Improper fluid level 2. Damaged or improperly adjusted linkage. 3. Faulty clutch or band application, or oil pressure control system. 4. Faulty forward clutch or governor. 5. Valve body loose 6. Dirty or sticking valve body.	1. Perform fluid level check. 2. Repair or adjust linkage. 3. Perform control pressure test. 4. Perform air pressure test. 5. Tighten to specification. 6. Clean, repair or replace valve body.
No drive, slips or chatters in reverse—forward OK.	1. Improper fluid level 2. Damaged or improperly adjusted linkage. 3. Looseness in the drivehsaft, U-joints or engine mounts. 4. Bands or clutches out of adjustment. 5. Faulty oil pressure control system. 6. Faulty reverse clutch or servo. 7. Valve body loose. 8. Dirty or sticking valve body.	1. Perform fluid level check. 2. Repair or adjust linkage. 3. Repair as required. 4. Adjust as necessary. 5. Perform control pressure test. 6. Perform air pressure test. 7. Tighten to specifications. 8. Clean, repair or replace valve body.
Starts in high—in D drag or lockup at 1–2 shift point or in 2 or 1.	1. Improper fluid level. 2. Damaged or improperly adjusted linkage. 3. Faulty governor. 4. Faulty clutches and/or internal leaks. 5. Valve body loose. 6. Dirty, sticking valve body. 7. Poor mating of valve body to case mounting surfaces.	1. Perform fluid level check. 2. Repair or adjust linkage. 3. Repair or replace governor, clean screen. 4. Perform air pressure test. 5. Tighten to specifications. 6. Clean, repair or replace valve body. 7. Replace valve body or case.

Problem	Possible Cause	Correction
Starts up in 2nd or 3rd but no lockup at 1-2 shift points.	1. Improper fluid level. 2. Damaged or improperly adjusted linkage. 3. Improper band and/or clutch application, or oil pressure control system. 4. Faulty governor. 5. Valve body loose. 6. Dirty or sticking valve body. 7. Cross leaks between valve body and case mating surface.	1. Perform fluid level check. 2. Repair or adjust linkage. 3. Perform control pressure test. 4. Perform governor check. Replace or repair governor, clean screen. 5. Tighten to specification. 6. Clean, repair or replace valve body. 7. Replace valve body and/or case as required.
Shift points incorrect.	1. Improper fluid level. 2. Improper vacuum hose routing or leaks. 3. Improper operation of EGR system. 4. Linkage out of adjustment. 5. Improper speedometer gear installed. 6. Improper clutch or band application, or oil pressure control system. 7. Faulty governor. 8. Dirty or sticking valve body.	1. Perform fluid level check. 2. Correct hose routing. 3. Repair or replace as required. 4. Repair or adjust linkage. 5. Replace gear. 6. Perform shift test and control pressure test. 7. Repair or replace governor—clean screen. 8. Clean, repair or replace valve body.
No upshift at any speed in D.	1. Improper fluid level. 2. Vacuum leak to diaphragm unit. 3. Linkage out of adjustment. 4. Improper band or clutch application, or oil pressure control system. 5. Faulty governor. 6. Dirty or sticking valve bdy.	1. Perform fluid level check. 2. Repair vacuum line or hose. 3. Repair or adjust linkage. 4. Perform control pressure test. 5. Repair or replace governor, clean screen. 6. Clean, repair or replace valve body.
Shifts 1-3 in D.	1. Improper fluid level. 2. Intermediate band out of adjustment. 3. Faulty front servo and/or internal leaks. 4. Polished, glazed band or drum. 5. Improper band or clutch application, or oil pressure control system. 6. Dirty or sticking valve body.	1. Perform fluid level check. 2. Adjust band. 3. Perform air pressure test. Repair front servo and/or internal leaks. 4. Repair or replace band or drum. 5. Perform control pressure test. 6. Clean, repair or replace valve body.
Engine over-speeds on 2-3 shift.	1. Improper fluid level. 2. Linkage out of adjustment. 3. Improper band or clutch application, or oil pressure control system. 4. Faulty high clutch and/or intermediate servo. 5. Dirty or sticking valve body.	1. Perform fluid level check. 2. Repair or adjust linkage. 3. Perform control pressure test. 4. Perform air pressure test. Repair as required. 5. Clean repair or replace valve body.
Mushy 1-2 shift.	1. Improper fluid level 2. Incorrect engine idle and/or performance. 3. Improper linkage adjustment. 4. Intermediate band out of adjustment.	1. Perform fluid level check. 2. Tune, adjust engine idle as required. 3. Repair or adjust linkage. 4. Adjust intermediate band. 5. Perform control pressure test.

Problem	Possible Cause	Correction
Mushy 1-2 shift.	5. Improper band or clutch application, or oil pressure control system. 6. Faulty high clutch and/or intermediate servo release. 7. Polished, glazed band or drum. 8. Dirty or sticking valve body.	6. Perform air pressure test. Repair as required. 7. Repair or replace as required. 8. Clean, repair or replace valve body.
Rough 1-2 shift.	1. Improper fluid level. 2. Incorrect engine idle or performance. 3. Intermediate band out of adjustment. 4. Improper band or clutch application, or oil pressure control system. 5. Faulty intermediate servo. 6. Dirty or sticking valve body.	1. Perform fluid level check. 2. Tune, and adjust engine idle. 3. Adjust intermediate band. 4. Perform control pressure test. 5. Air pressure check intermediate servo. 6. Clean, repair or replace valve body.
Rough 2-3 shift	1. Improper fluid level. 2. Incorrect engine idle or performance. 3. Improper band or clutch application, or oil control pressure system. 4. Faulty intermediate servo apply and release and high clutch piston check ball. 5. Dirty or sticking valve body.	1. Perform fluid level check. 2. Tune and adjust engine idle. 3. Perform control pressure test. 4. Air pressure test the intermediate servo apply and release and the high clutch piston check ball. Repair as required. 5. Clean, repair or replace valve body.
Rough 3-1 shift at closed throttle in D.	1. Improper fluid level. 2. Incorrect engine idle or performance. 3. Improper linkage adjustment. 4. Improper clutch or band application or oil pressure control system. 5. Faulty governor operation. 6. Dirty or sticking valve body.	1. Perform fluid level check. 2. Tune, and adjust engine idle. 3. Repair or adjust linkage. 4. Perform control pressure test. 5. Perform governor test. Repair as required. 6. Clean, repair or replace valve body.
No forced downshifts.	1. Improper fluid level. 2. Linkage out of adjustment. 3. Improper clutch or band application, or oil pressure control system. 4. Faulty internal kickdown linkage. 5. Dirty or sticking valve body.	1. Perform fluid level check. 2. Repair or adjust linkage. 3. Perform control pressure test. 4. Repair internal kickdown linkage. 5. Clean, repair or replace valve body.
No 3-1 shift in D.	1. Improper fluid level. 2. Incorrect engine idle, or performance. 3. Faulty governor. 4. Dirty or sticking valve body.	1. Perform fluid level check. 2. Tune, and adjust engine idle. 3. Perform govenor check. Repair as required. 4. Clean, repair or replace valve body.
Runaway engine on 3-2 downshift.	1. Improper fluid level. 2. Linkage out of adjustment. 3. Intermediate band out of adjustment. 4. Improper band or clutch application, or oil pressure control system.	1. Perform fluid level check. 2. Repair or adjust linkage. 3. Adjust intermediate band. 4. Perform control pressure test. 5. Air pressure test check the intermediate servo. Repair servo and/or seals.

Problem	Possible Cause	Correction
Runaway engine on 3-2 downshift.	5. Faulty intermediate servo. 6. Polished, glazed band or drum. 7. Dirty or sticking valve body.	6. Repair or replace as required. 7. Clean, repair or replace valve body.
No engine braking in manual first gear.	1. Improper fluid level. 2. Linkage out of adjustment. 3. Bands or clutches out of adjustment. 4. Faulty oil pressure control system. 5. Faulty reverse servo. 6. Polished, glazed band or drum.	1. Perform fluid level check. 2. Repair or adjust linkage. 3. Adjust as necessary. 4. Perform control pressure test. 5. Perform air pressure test of reverse servo. Repair reverse clutch or rear servo as required. 6. Repair or replace as required.
No engine braking in manual second gear.	1. Improper fluid level. 2. Linkage out of adjustment. 3. Intermediate band out of adjustment. 4. Improper band or clutch application, or oil pressure control system. 5. Intermediate servo leaking. 6. Polished or glazed band or drum.	1. Perform fluid level check. 2. Repair or adjust linkage. 3. Adjust intermediate band. 4. Perform control pressure test. 5. Perform air pressure test of intermediate servo for leakage. Repair as required. 6. Repair or replace as required.
Transmission noisy—valve resonance.	1. Improper fluid level. 2. Linkage out of adjustment. 3. Improper band or clutch application, or oil pressure control system. 4. Cooler lines grounding. 5. Dirty sticking valve body. 6. Internal leakage or pump cavitation.	1. Perform fluid level check. 2. Repair or adjust linkage. 3. Perform control pressure test. 4. Free up cooler lines. 5. Clean, repair or replace valve body. 6. Repair as required.
Transmission overheats.	1. Improper fluid level. 2. Incorrect engine idle, or performance. 3. Improper clutch or band application, or oil pressure control system. 4. Restriction in cooler or lines. 5. Seized one-way clutch. 6. Dirty or sticking valve body.	1. Perform fluid level check. 2. Tune, or adjust engine idle. 3. Perform control pressure test. 4. Repair restriction. 5. Replace one-way clutch. 6. Clean, repair or replace valve body.
Transmission fluid leaks.	1. Improper fluid level. 2. Leakage at gasket, seals, etc. 3. Vacuum diaphragm unit leaking.	1. Perform fluid level check. 2. Remove all traces of lube on exposed surfaces of transmission. Check the vent for free breathing. Operate transmission at normal temperatures and inspect for leakage. Repair as required. 3. Replace diaphragm.

Automatic Transmission Troubleshooting

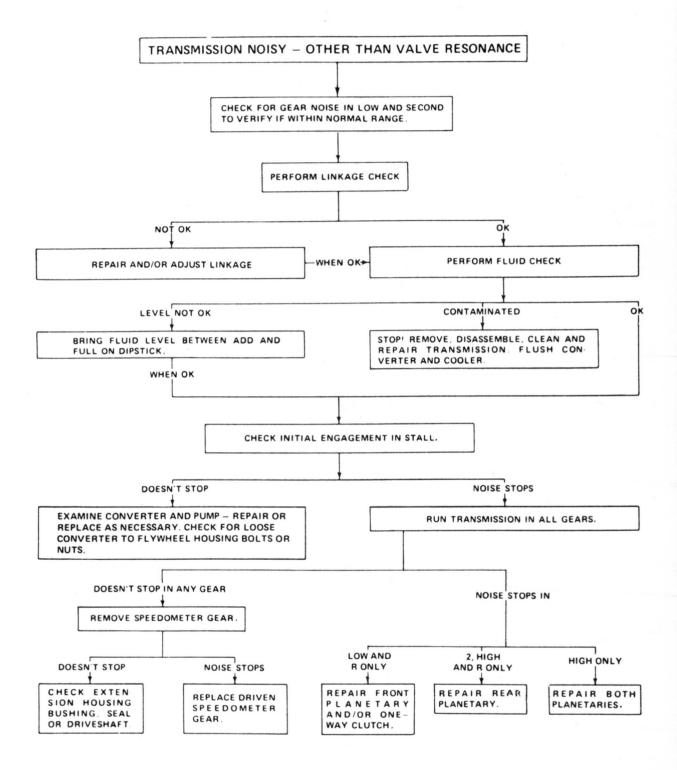

| TRANSMISSION NOISY — OTHER THAN VALVE RESONANCE |

CHECK FOR GEAR NOISE IN LOW AND SECOND TO VERIFY IF WITHIN NORMAL RANGE.

PERFORM LINKAGE CHECK

NOT OK — REPAIR AND/OR ADJUST LINKAGE — WHEN OK →

OK — PERFORM FLUID CHECK

LEVEL NOT OK — BRING FLUID LEVEL BETWEEN ADD AND FULL ON DIPSTICK. — WHEN OK

CONTAMINATED — STOP! REMOVE, DISASSEMBLE, CLEAN AND REPAIR TRANSMISSION. FLUSH CONVERTER AND COOLER.

OK

CHECK INITIAL ENGAGEMENT IN STALL.

DOESN'T STOP — EXAMINE CONVERTER AND PUMP — REPAIR OR REPLACE AS NECESSARY. CHECK FOR LOOSE CONVERTER TO FLYWHEEL HOUSING BOLTS OR NUTS.

NOISE STOPS — RUN TRANSMISSION IN ALL GEARS.

DOESN'T STOP IN ANY GEAR — REMOVE SPEEDOMETER GEAR.

DOESN'T STOP — CHECK EXTENSION HOUSING BUSHING, SEAL OR DRIVESHAFT.

NOISE STOPS — REPLACE DRIVEN SPEEDOMETER GEAR.

NOISE STOPS IN

LOW AND R ONLY — REPAIR FRONT PLANETARY AND/OR ONE-WAY CLUTCH.

2, HIGH AND R ONLY — REPAIR REAR PLANETARY.

HIGH ONLY — REPAIR BOTH PLANETARIES.

Driveshaft Troubleshooting
Vibration, Roughness, Rumble and/or Boom

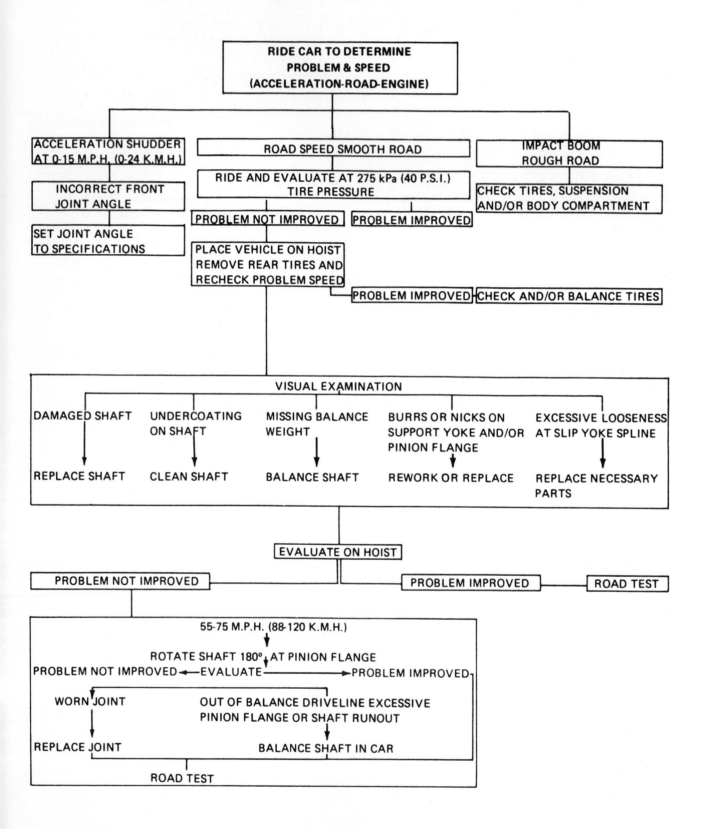

Universal Joint Troubleshooting

Problem	Possible Cause	Correction
Leak at front slip yoke. **NOTE:** An occasional drop of lubricant leaking from splined yoke is normal and requires no attention.	1. Rough outside surface on splined yoke. 2. Defective transmission rear oil seal.	1. Replace seal if cut by burrs on yoke. Minor burrs can be smoothed by careful use of crocus cloth or honing with a fine stone. Replace yoke if outside surface is rough or burred badly. 2. Replace transmission rear oil seal. 3. Bring transmission oil up to proper level after correction.
Knock in drive line, clunking noise when car is operated under floating condition at 10 mph in high gear or neutral.	1. Worn or damaged universal joints. 2. Side gear hub counterbore in differential worn oversize.	1. Disassemble universal joints, inspect and replace worn or damaged parts. 2. Replace differential case and/or side gears as required.
Ping, snap or click in drive line. **NOTE:** Usually occurs on initial load application after transmission has been put into gear, either forward or reverse.	1. Loose upper or lower control arm bushing bolts. 2. Loose companion flange.	1. Tighten bolts to specified torque. 2. Remove companion flange, turn 180° from its original position, apply white lead to splines and reinstall. Tighten pinion nut to specified torque.

Front Wheel Drive Halfshaft Troubleshooting

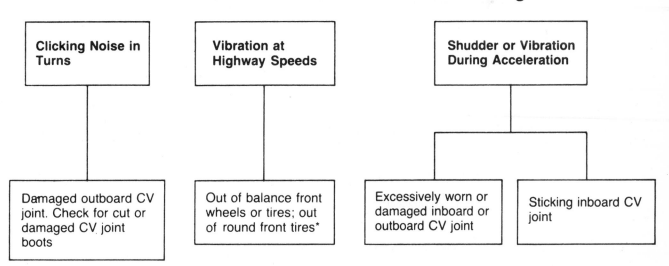

*Halfshafts do not usually contribute to rotational vibrations.

Drive Axle Troubleshooting

Condition	Possible Cause	Correction
Rear wheel noise	1. Loose wheel. 2. Spalled wheel bearing cup or cone. 3. Defective or brinelled wheel bearing. 4. Excessive axle shaft endplay. 5. Bent or sprng axle shaft flange.	1. Tighten loose wheel nuts. 2. Check rear wheel bearings. If spalled or worn, replace. 3. Defective or brinelled bearings must be replaced. Check rear axle shaft end play. 4. Readjust axle shaft end play. 5. Replace bent or sprung axle shaft.
Scoring of differential gears and pinions	1. Insufficient lubrication. 2. Improper grade of lubricant. 3. Excessive spinning of one wheel.	1. Replace scored gears. Scoring marks on the pressure face of gear teeth or in the bore are caused by instantaneous fusing of the mating surfaces. Scored gears should be replaced. Fill rear axle to required capacity with proper lubricant. 2. Replace scored gears. Inspect all gears and bearings for possible damage. Clean and refill axle to required capacity with proper lubricant. 3. Replace scored gears. Inspect all gears, pinion bores and shaft for scoring, or bearings for possible damage.
Tooth breakage (ring gear and pinion)	1. Overloading. 2. Erratic clutch operation. 3. Ice-spotted pavements. 4. Improper adjustments.	1. Replace gear. Examine other gears and bearings for possible damage. Avoid future overloading. 2. Replace gear, and examine remaining parts for possible damage. Avoid erratic clutch operation. 3. Replace gears. Examine remaining parts for possible damage. Replace parts as required. 4. Replace gears. Examine other parts for possible damage. Be sure ring gear and pinion backlash is correct.
Rear axle noise	1. Insufficient lubricant. 2. Improper ring gear and pinion adjustment. 3. Unmatched ring gear and pinion. 4. Worn teeth on ring gear or pinion. 5. End-play in drive pinion bearings. 6. Side play in differential bearings. 7. Incorrect drive gearlash. 8. Limited-slip differential—moan and chatter.	1. Refill rear axle with correct amount of the proper lubricant. Also check for leaks and correct as necessary. 2. Check ring gear and pinion tooth contact. 3. Remove unmatched ring gear and pinion. Replace with a new matched gear and pinion set. 4. Check teeth on ring gear and pinion for contact. If necessary, replace with new matched set. 5. Adjust drive pinion bearing preload.

Problem	Possible Cause	Correction
Rear axle noise		6. Adjust differential bearing preload. 7. Correct drive gear lash. 8. Drain and flush lubricant. Refill with proper lubricant.
Loss of lubricant	1. Lubricant level too high. 2. Worn axle shaft oil seals. 3. Cracked rear axle housing. 4. Worn drive pinion oil seal. 5. Scored and worn companion flange. 6. Clogged vent. 7. Loose carrier housing bolts or housing cover screws.	1. Drain excess lubricant. 2. Replace worn oil seals with new ones. Prepare new seals before replacement. 3. Repair or replace housing as required. 4. Replace worn drive pinion oil seal with a new one. 5. Replace worn or scored companion flange and oil seal. 6. Remove obstructions. 7. Tighten bolts or cover screws to specifications and fill to correct level with proper lubricant.
Overheating of unit	1. Lubricant level too low. 2. Incorrect grade of lubricant. 3. Bearing adjusted too tightly. 4. Excessive wear in gears. 5. Insufficient ring gear-to-pinion clearance.	1. Refill rear axle. 2. Drain, flush and refill rear axle with correct amount of the proper lubricant. 3. Readjust bearings. 4. Check gears for excessive wear or scoring. Replace as necessary. 5. Readjust ring gear and pinion backlash and check gears for possible scoring.

CHASSIS

Shock Absorber and Rear Spring Troubleshooting

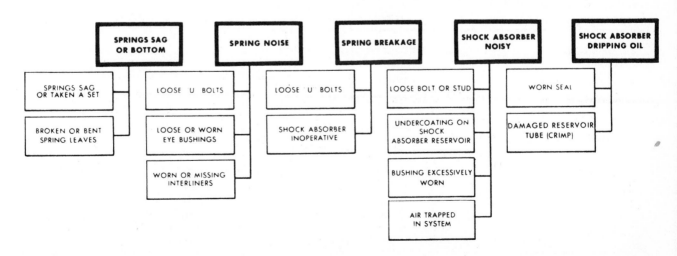

Front Suspension and Steering Linkage
Troubleshooting—Rear Wheel Drive

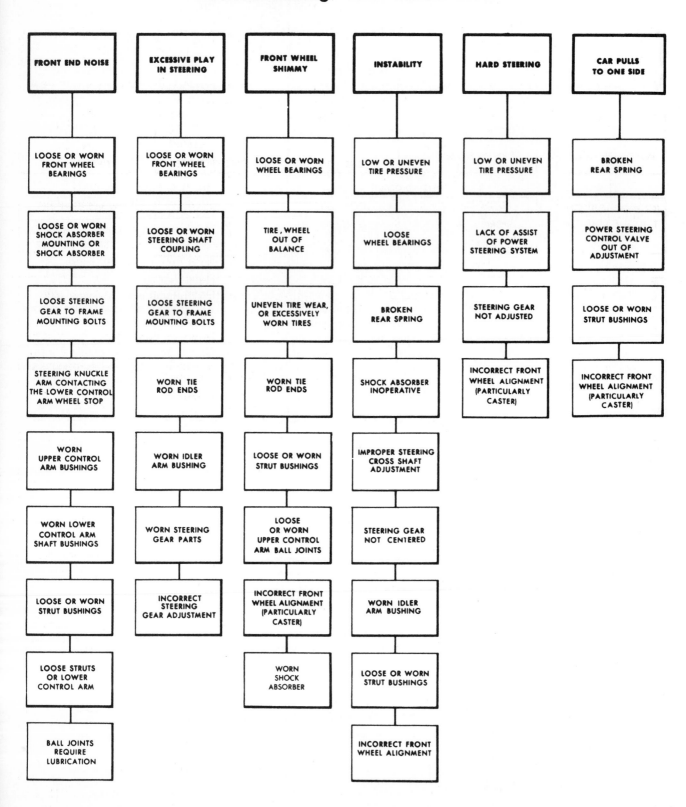

FRONT END NOISE	EXCESSIVE PLAY IN STEERING	FRONT WHEEL SHIMMY	INSTABILITY	HARD STEERING	CAR PULLS TO ONE SIDE
LOOSE OR WORN FRONT WHEEL BEARINGS	LOOSE OR WORN FRONT WHEEL BEARINGS	LOOSE OR WORN WHEEL BEARINGS	LOW OR UNEVEN TIRE PRESSURE	LOW OR UNEVEN TIRE PRESSURE	BROKEN REAR SPRING
LOOSE OR WORN SHOCK ABSORBER MOUNTING OR SHOCK ABSORBER	LOOSE OR WORN STEERING SHAFT COUPLING	TIRE, WHEEL OUT OF BALANCE	LOOSE WHEEL BEARINGS	LACK OF ASSIST OF POWER STEERING SYSTEM	POWER STEERING CONTROL VALVE OUT OF ADJUSTMENT
LOOSE STEERING GEAR TO FRAME MOUNTING BOLTS	LOOSE STEERING GEAR TO FRAME MOUNTING BOLTS	UNEVEN TIRE WEAR, OR EXCESSIVELY WORN TIRES	BROKEN REAR SPRING	STEERING GEAR NOT ADJUSTED	LOOSE OR WORN STRUT BUSHINGS
STEERING KNUCKLE ARM CONTACTING THE LOWER CONTROL ARM WHEEL STOP	WORN TIE ROD ENDS	WORN TIE ROD ENDS	SHOCK ABSORBER INOPERATIVE	INCORRECT FRONT WHEEL ALIGNMENT (PARTICULARLY CASTER)	INCORRECT FRONT WHEEL ALIGNMENT (PARTICULARLY CASTER)
WORN UPPER CONTROL ARM BUSHINGS	WORN IDLER ARM BUSHING	LOOSE OR WORN STRUT BUSHINGS	IMPROPER STEERING CROSS SHAFT ADJUSTMENT		
WORN LOWER CONTROL ARM SHAFT BUSHINGS	WORN STEERING GEAR PARTS	LOOSE OR WORN UPPER CONTROL ARM BALL JOINTS	STEERING GEAR NOT CENTERED		
LOOSE OR WORN STRUT BUSHINGS	INCORRECT STEERING GEAR ADJUSTMENT	INCORRECT FRONT WHEEL ALIGNMENT (PARTICULARLY CASTER)	WORN IDLER ARM BUSHING		
LOOSE STRUTS OR LOWER CONTROL ARM		WORN SHOCK ABSORBER	LOOSE OR WORN STRUT BUSHINGS		
BALL JOINTS REQUIRE LUBRICATION			INCORRECT FRONT WHEEL ALIGNMENT		

Suspension and Steering Linkage
Troubleshooting— Front Wheel Drive

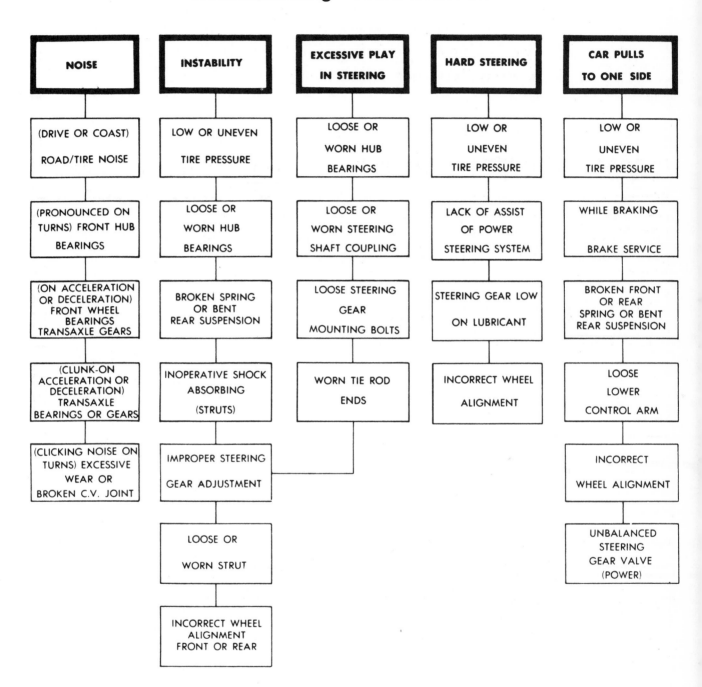

NOISE	INSTABILITY	EXCESSIVE PLAY IN STEERING	HARD STEERING	CAR PULLS TO ONE SIDE
(DRIVE OR COAST) ROAD/TIRE NOISE	LOW OR UNEVEN TIRE PRESSURE	LOOSE OR WORN HUB BEARINGS	LOW OR UNEVEN TIRE PRESSURE	LOW OR UNEVEN TIRE PRESSURE
(PRONOUNCED ON TURNS) FRONT HUB BEARINGS	LOOSE OR WORN HUB BEARINGS	LOOSE OR WORN STEERING SHAFT COUPLING	LACK OF ASSIST OF POWER STEERING SYSTEM	WHILE BRAKING BRAKE SERVICE
(ON ACCELERATION OR DECELERATION) FRONT WHEEL BEARINGS TRANSAXLE GEARS	BROKEN SPRING OR BENT REAR SUSPENSION	LOOSE STEERING GEAR MOUNTING BOLTS	STEERING GEAR LOW ON LUBRICANT	BROKEN FRONT OR REAR SPRING OR BENT REAR SUSPENSION
(CLUNK-ON ACCELERATION OR DECELERATION) TRANSAXLE BEARINGS OR GEARS	INOPERATIVE SHOCK ABSORBING (STRUTS)	WORN TIE ROD ENDS	INCORRECT WHEEL ALIGNMENT	LOOSE LOWER CONTROL ARM
(CLICKING NOISE ON TURNS) EXCESSIVE WEAR OR BROKEN C.V. JOINT	IMPROPER STEERING GEAR ADJUSTMENT			INCORRECT WHEEL ALIGNMENT
	LOOSE OR WORN STRUT			UNBALANCED STEERING GEAR VALVE (POWER)
	INCORRECT WHEEL ALIGNMENT FRONT OR REAR			

Tapered Wheel Bearing Troubleshooting

CONSIDER THE FOLLOWING FACTORS WHEN DIAGNOSING BEARING CONDITION:

1. GENERAL CONDITION OF ALL PARTS DURING DISASSEMBLY AND INSPECTION.

2. CLASSIFY THE FAILURE WITH THE AID OF THE ILLUSTRATIONS.

3. DETERMINE THE CAUSE.

4. MAKE ALL REPAIRS FOLLOWING RECOMMENDED PROCEDURES.

GOOD BEARING

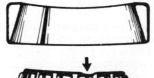

BENT CAGE

CAGE DAMAGE DUE TO IMPROPER HANDLING OR TOOL USAGE.

REPLACE BEARING.

BENT CAGE

CAGE DAMAGE DUE TO IMPROPER HANDLING OR TOOL USAGE.

REPLACE BEARING.

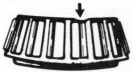

GALLING

METAL SMEARS ON ROLLER ENDS DUE TO OVERHEAT, LUBRICANT FAILURE OR OVERLOAD.

REPLACE BEARING — CHECK SEALS AND CHECK FOR PROPER LUBRICATION.

ABRASIVE STEP WEAR

PATTERN ON ROLLER ENDS CAUSED BY FINE ABRASIVES.

CLEAN ALL PARTS AND HOUSINGS, CHECK SEALS AND BEARINGS AND REPLACE IF LEAKING, ROUGH OR NOISY.

ETCHING

BEARING SURFACES APPEAR GRAY OR GRAYISH BLACK IN COLOR WITH RELATED ETCHING AWAY OF MATERIAL USUALLY AT ROLLER SPACING.

REPLACE BEARINGS — CHECK SEALS AND CHECK FOR PROPER LUBRICATION.

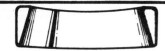

MISALIGNMENT

OUTER RACE MISALIGNMENT DUE TO FOREIGN OBJECT.

CLEAN RELATED PARTS AND REPLACE BEARING. MAKE SURE RACES ARE PROPERLY SEATED.

INDENTATIONS

SURFACE DEPRESSIONS ON RACE AND ROLLERS CAUSED BY HARD PARTICLES OF FOREIGN MATERIAL.

CLEAN ALL PARTS AND HOUSINGS, CHECK SEALS AND REPLACE BEARINGS IF ROUGH OR NOISY.

FATIGUE SPALLING

FLAKING OF SURFACE METAL RESULTING FROM FATIGUE.

REPLACE BEARING — CLEAN ALL RELATED PARTS.

Tapered Wheel Bearing Troubleshooting

BRINELLING

SURFACE INDENTATIONS IN RACEWAY CAUSED BY ROLLERS EITHER UNDER IMPACT LOADING OR VIBRATION WHILE THE BEARING IS NOT ROTATING.

REPLACE BEARING IF ROUGH OR NOISY.

CAGE WEAR

WEAR AROUND OUTSIDE DIAMETER OF CAGE AND ROLLER POCKETS CAUSED BY ABRASIVE MATERIAL AND INEFFICIENT LUBRICATION. CHECK SEALS AND REPLACE BEARINGS.

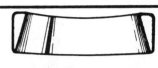

ABRASIVE ROLLER WEAR

PATTERN ON RACES AND ROLLERS CAUSED BY FINE ABRASIVES.

CLEAN ALL PARTS AND HOUSINGS, CHECK SEALS AND BEARINGS AND REPLACE IF LEAKING, ROUGH OR NOISY.

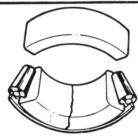

CRACKED INNER RACE

RACE CRACKED DUE TO IMPROPER FIT, COCKING, OR POOR BEARING SEATS.

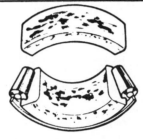

SMEARS

SMEARING OF METAL DUE TO SLIPPAGE, SLIPPAGE CAN BE CAUSED BY POOR FITS, LUBRICATION, OVERHEATING, OVERLOADS OR HANDLING DAMAGE.

REPLACE BEARINGS, CLEAN RELATED PARTS AND CHECK FOR PROPER FIT AND LUBRICATION.

REPLACE SHAFT IF DAMAGED.

FRETTAGE

CORROSION SET UP BY SMALL RELATIVE MOVEMENT OF PARTS WITH NO LUBRICATION.

REPLACE BEARING. CLEAN RELATED PARTS. CHECK SEALS AND CHECK FOR PROPER LUBRICATION.

HEAT DISCOLORATION

HEAT DISCOLORATION CAN RANGE FROM FAINT YELLOW TO DARK BLUE RESULTING FROM OVERLOAD OR INCORRECT LUBRICANT.

EXCESSIVE HEAT CAN CAUSE SOFTENING OF RACES OR ROLLERS.

TO CHECK FOR LOSS OF TEMPER ON RACES OR ROLLERS A SIMPLE FILE TEST MAY BE MADE. A FILE DRAWN OVER A TEMPERED PART WILL GRAB AND CUT META, WHEREAS, A FILE DRAWN OVER A HARD PART WILL GLIDE READILY WITH NO METAL CUTTING.

REPLACE BEARINGS IF OVER HEATING DAMAGE IS INDICATED. CHECK SEALS AND OTHER PARTS.

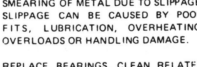

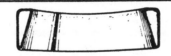

STAIN DISCOLORATION

DISCOLORATION CAN RANGE FROM LIGHT BROWN TO BLACK CAUSED BY INCORRECT LUBRICANT OR MOISTURE.

RE-USE BEARINGS IF STAINS CAN BE REMOVED BY LIGHT POLISHING OR IF NO EVIDENCE OF OVERHEATING IS OBSERVED.

CHECK SEALS AND RELATED PARTS FOR DAMAGE.

How To Read Tire Wear

The way your tires wear is a good indicator of other parts of the suspension. Abnormal wear patterns are often caused by the need for simple tire maintenance, or for front end alignment.

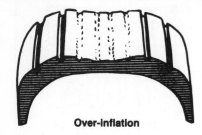

Over-inflation

Excessive wear at the center of the tread indicates that the air pressure in the tire is consistently too high. The tire is riding on the center of the tread and wearing it prematurely. Occasionally, this wear pattern can result from outrageously wide tires on narrow rims. The cure for this is to replace either the tires or the wheels.

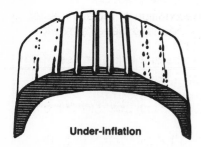

Under-inflation

This type of wear usually results from consistent under-inflation. When a tire is under-inflated, there is too much contact with the road by the outer treads, which wear prematurely. When this type of wear occurs, and the tire pressure is known to be consistently correct, a bent or worn steering component or the need for wheel alignment could be indicated.

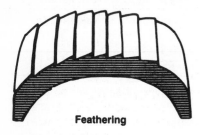

Feathering

Feathering is a condition when the edge of each tread rib develops a slightly rounded edge on one side and a sharp edge on the other. By running your hand over the tire, you can usually feel the sharper edges before you'll be able to see them. The most common causes of feathering are incorrect toe-in setting or deteriorated bushings in the front suspension.

One side wear

When an inner or outer rib wears faster than the rest of the tire, the need for wheel alignment is indicated. There is excessive camber in the front suspension, causing the wheel to lean too much putting excessive load on one side of the tire. Misalignment could also be due to sagging springs, worn ball joints, or worn control arm bushings. Be sure the vehicle is loaded the way it's normally driven when you have the wheels aligned.

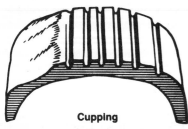

Cupping

Cups or scalloped dips appearing around the edge of the tread almost always indicate worn (sometimes bent) suspension parts. Adjustment of wheel alignment alone will seldom cure the problem. Any worn component that connects the wheel to the suspension can cause this type of wear. Occasionally, wheels that are out of balance will wear like this, but wheel imbalance usually shows up as bald spots between the outside edges and center of the tread.

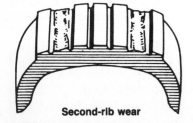

Second-rib wear

Second-rib wear is usually found only in radial tires, and appears where the steel belts end in relation to the tread. It can be kept to a minimum by paying careful attention to tire pressure and frequently rotating the tires. This is often considered normal wear but excessive amounts indicate that the tires are too wide for the wheels.

Drum Brake Troubleshooting

Condition	Possible Cause	Correction Action
Pedal goes to floor	1. Fluid low in reservoir. 2. Air in hydraulic brake system. 3. Improperly adjusted brake. 4. Leaking wheel cylinders. 5. Loose or broken brake lines. 6. Leaking or worn master cylinder. 7. Excessively worn brake lining.	1. Fill and bleed master cylinder. 2. Fill and bleed hydraulic brake system. 3. Repair or replace self-adjuster as required. 4. Recondition or replace wheel cylinder and replace both brake shoes. 5. Tighten all brake fittings or replace brake line. 6. Recondition or replace master cylinder and bleed hydraulic system. 7. Reline and adjust brakes.
Spongy brake pedal	1. Air in hydraulic system. 2. Improper brake fluid (low boiling point). 3. Excessively worn or cracked brake drums. 4. Broken pedal pivot bushing.	1. Fill master cylinder and bleed hydraulic system. 2. Drain, flush and refill with brake fluid. 3. Replace all faulty brake drums. 4. Replace nylon pivot bushing.
Brakes pulling	1. Contaminated lining. 2. Front end out of alignment. 3. Incorrect brake adjustment. 4. Unmatched brake lining. 5. Brake drums out of round. 6. Brake shoes distorted. 7. Restricted brake hose or line. 8. Broken rear spring.	1. Replace contaminated brake lining. 2. Align front end. 3. Adjust brakes and check fluid. 4. Match primary, secondary with same type of lining on all wheels. 5. Grind or replace brake drums. 6. Replace faulty brake shoes. 7. Replace plugged hose or brake line. 8. Replace broken spring.
Squealing brakes	1. Glazed brake lining. 2. Saturated brake lining. 3. Weak or broken brake shoe retaining spring. 4. Broken or weak brake shoe return spring. 5. Incorrect brake lining. 6. Distorted brake shoes. 7. Bent support plate. 8. Dust in brakes or scored brake drums.	1. Cam grind or replace brake lining. 2. Replace saturated lining. 3. Replace retaining spring. 4. Replace return spring. 5. Install matched brake lining. 6. Replace brake shoes. 7. Replace support plate. 8. Blow out brake assembly with compressed air and grind brake drums.
Chirping brakes	1. Out of round drum or eccentric axle flange pilot.	1. Repair as necessary, and lubricate support plate contact areas (6 places).
Dragging brakes	1. Incorrect wheel or parking brake adjustment. 2. Parking brakes engaged. 3. Weak or broken brake shoe return spring. 4. Brake pedal binding. 5. Master cylinder cup sticking. 6. Obstructed master cylinder relief port. 7. Saturated brake lining. 8. Bent or out of round brake drum.	1. Adjust brake and check fluid. 2. Release parking brakes. 3. Replace brake shoe return spring. 4. Free up and lubricate brake pedal and linkage. 5. Recondition master cylinder. 6. Use compressed air and blow out relief port. 7. Replace brake lining. 8. Grind or replace faulty brake drum.

Condition	Possible Cause	Corrective Action
Hard pedal	1. Brake booster inoperative. 2. Incorrect brake lining. 3. Restricted brake line or hose. 4. Frozen brake pedal linkage.	1. Replace brake booster. 2. Install matched brake lining. 3. Clean out or replace brake line or hose. 4. Free up and lubricate brake linkage.
Wheel locks	1. Contaminated brake lining. 2. Loose or torn brake lining. 3. Wheel cylinder cups sticking. 4. Incorrect wheel bearing adjustment.	1. Reline both front or rear of all four brakes. 2. Replace brake lining. 3. Recondition or replace wheel cylinder. 4. Clean, pack and adjust wheel bearings.
Brakes fade (high speed)	1. Incorrect lining. 2. Overheated brake drums. 3. Incorrect brake fluid (low boiling temperature) 4. Saturated brake lining.	1. Replace lining. 2. Inspect for dragging brakes. 3. Drain, flush, refill and bleed hydraulic brake system. 4. Reline both front or rear or all four brakes.
Pedal pulsates	1. Bent or out of round brake drum.	1. Grind or replace brake drums.
Brake chatter and shoe knock	1. Out of round brake drum. 2. Loose support plate. 3. Bent support plate. 4. Distorted brake shoes. 5. Machine grooves in contact face of brake drum. (Shoe Knock). 6. Contaminated brake lining.	1. Grind or replace brake drums. 2. Tighten support plate bolts to proper specifications. 3. Replace support plate. 4. Replace brake shoes. 5. Grind or replace brake drum. 6. Replace either front or rear or all four linings.
Brakes do not self adjust	1. Adjuster screw frozen in thread. 2. Adjuster screw corroded at thrust washer. 3. Adjuster level does not engage star wheel. 4. Adjuster installed on wrong wheel.	1. Clean and free-up all thread areas. 2. Clean threads and replace thrust washer if necessary. 3. Repair, free up or replace adjusters as required. 4. Install correct adjuster parts.

Disc Brake Troubleshooting

Condition	Possible Cause	Correction Action
Noise—Groan—Brake noise emanating when slowly releasing brakes (creep-groan).	1. Not detrimental to function of disc brakes—no corrective action required. (Indicate to operator this noise may be eliminated by slightly increasing or decreasing brake pedal efforts.)	
Rattle—Brake noise or rattle emanating at low speeds on rough roads, (front wheels only).	1. Shoe anti-rattle spring missing or not properly positioned. 2. Excessive clearance between shoe and caliper.	1. Install new anti-rattle spring or position properly. 2. Install new shoe and lining assemblies.

Condition	Possible Cause	Corrective Action
Scraping	1. Mounting bolts too long. 2. Loose wheel bearings.	1. Install mounting bolts of correct length. 2. Readjust wheel bearings to correct specifications.
Front brakes heat up during driving and fail to release	1. Operator riding brake pedal. 2. Stop light switch improperly adjusted. 3. Sticking pedal linkage. 4. Frozen or seized piston. 5. Residual pressure valve in master cylinder. 6. Power brake malfunction.	1. Instruct owner how to drive with disc brakes. 2. Adjust stop light to allow full return of pedal. 3. Free up sticking pedal linkage. 4. Disassemble caliper and free up piston. 5. Remove valve. 6. Replace.
Leaky wheel cylinder	1. Damaged or worn caliper piston seal. 2. Scores or corrosion on surface of cylinder bore.	1. Disassemble caliper and install new seal. 2. Disassemble caliper and hone cylinder bore. Install new seal.
Grabbing or uneven brake action	1. Causes listed under "Pull." 2. Power brake malfunction.	1. Corrections listed under "Pull". 2. Replace.
Brake pedal can be depressed without braking effect	1. Air in hydraulic system or improper bleeding procedure. 2. Leak past primary cup in master cylinder. 3. Leak in system. 4. Rear brakes out of adjustment. 5. Bleeder screw open.	1. Bleed system. 2. Recondition master cylinder. 3. Check for leak and repair as required. 4. Adjust rear brakes. 5. Close bleeder screw and bleed entire system.
Excessive pedal travel	1. Air, leak, or insufficient fluid in system or caliper. 2. Warped or excessively tapered shoe and lining assembly. 3. Excessive disc runout. 4. Rear brake adjustment required. 5. Loose wheel bearing adjustment. 6. Damaged caliper piston seal. 7. Improper brake fluid (boil). 8. Power brake malfunction.	1. Check system for leaks and bleed. 2. Install new shoe and linings. 3. Check disc for runout with dial indicator. Install new or refinished disc. 4. Check and adjust rear brakes. 5. Readjust wheel bearing to specified torque. 6. Install new piston seal. 7. Drain and install correct fluid. 8. Replace.
Brake roughness or chatter (pedal pumping)	1. Excessive thickness variation of braking disc. 2. Excessive lateral runout of braking disc. 3. Rear brake drums out-of-round. 4. Excessive front bearing clearance.	1. Check disc for thickness variation using a micrometer. 2. Check disc for lateral runout with dial indicator. Install new or refinished disc. 3. Reface rear drums and check for out-of-round. 4. Readjust wheel bearings to specified torque.
Excessive pedal effort	1. Brake fluid, oil or grease on linings. 2. Incorrect lining. 3. Frozen or seized pistons. 4. Power brake malfunction.	1. Install new shoe linings as required. 2. Remove lining and install correct lining. 3. Disassemble caliper and free up pistons. 4. Replace.

Condition	Possible Cause	Corrective Action
Pull	1. Brake fluid, oil or grease on linings. 2. Unmatched linings. 3. Distorted brake shoes. 4. Frozen or seized pistons. 5. Incorrect tire pressure. 6. Front end out of alignment. 7. Broken rear spring. 8. Rear brake pistons sticking. 9. Restricted hose or line. 10. Caliper not in proper alignment to braking disc.	1. Install new shoe and linings. 2. Install correct lining. 3. Install new brake shoes. 4. Disassemble caliper and free up pistons. 5. Inflate tires to recommended pressures. 6. Align front end and check. 7. Install new rear spring. 8. Free up rear brake pistons. 9. Check hoses and lines and correct as necessary. 10. Remove caliper and reinstall. Check alignment.